MW00490741

YOUR

personal guide to the content-rich, free online resources for

HORNGREN/HARRISON/BAMBER ACCOUNTING *Edition*

Featuring one-click access to all of the new resources created by our award-winning team of educators, myPHLIP provides a PERSONALIZED VIEW of the great new resources available:

MyPHLIP pages — Your personal access page unites all your Prentice Hall myPHLIP texts.

Notes — Add personal notes to our resources for personal reminders and references.

Messages — Instructors can send messages to individual students, or all students linked to any given course.

Student Resources — Instructors can add premium PHLIP resources for students to view and download (such as PowerPoints and spreadsheets).

Syllabus — Improved new online syllabus tools help instructors add personal syllabi to our text site in minutes.

Business Headlines — Provide links to articles in today's business news!

Search — Search all PHLIP resources for relevant articles and exercises.

Instructor's Manual — MyPHLIP Instructor's Manual provides tips and suggestions from our PHLIP faculty for integrating PHLIP resources into a course.

COMBINED WITH THE RESOURCES YOU HAVE TRUSTED THROUGHOUT THE YEARS TO PROVIDE YOU WITH THE BEST BUSINESS RESOURCES AVAILABLE:

◎ **In the News**—New current events articles are added throughout the year. Each article is summarized by our teams of experts, and fully supported by exercises, activities, and instructor materials.

◎ **Online Study Guide**—Three quizzes are linked to each text chapter and include "hints" for each question. Each quiz is graded immediately upon submission, provides immediate feedback on each given answer, and enables students to e-mail results to the instructor.

◎ **Research Area**—Your own personal resource library includes tutorials, descriptive links to virtual libraries, and a wealth of search engines and resources.

◎ **Internet Resources**—provide discipline-specific sites, including preview information that allows you to review site information before you view the site, ensuring you visit the best available business resources found by our learning community.

www.prenhall.com/horngren

For the professor

◎ **Teaching Resources** provide material contributed by professors throughout the world–including teaching tips, techniques, academic papers, and sample syllabi–and **Talk to the Team**, a moderated faculty chat room.
◎ **Online Faculty** Support includes downloadable supplements, additional cases, articles, links, and suggested answers to Current Events Activities.
◎ **What's New** gives you one-click access to all newly posted PHLIP resources.

For the student

◎ **Talk to the Tutor** schedules virtual office hours that allow students to post questions from any supported discipline and receive responses from the dedicated PHLIP/CW faculty team.
◎ **Writing Resource Center** provides an online writing center that supplies links to online directories, thesauruses, writing tutors, style and grammar guides, and additional tools.
◎ **Career Center** helps students access career information, view sample résumés, even apply for jobs online.
◎ **Study Tips** provides an area where students can learn to develop better study skills.

ONLINE LEARNING SOLUTIONS IN BLACKBOARD, WEBCT, AND PEARSON COURSECOMPASS
NOW AVAILABLE IN **TWO** LEVELS OF CONTENT!

STANDARD COURSES

(Free with New Text Purchase) Standard courses include traditional online course features:

- Online Testing
- Course Management and Page Tracking
- Gradebook
- Course Information
- Multiple-Section Chat Rooms
- Bulletin Board Conferencing
- Syllabus and Calendar Functions
- E-mail Capability

PREMIUM COURSES

(Available at a nominal charge with New Text Purchase)
The Premium course for Accounting, 5th ed., provides these additional enhancements:

- **Rich, Prentice Hall Custom-Created** course and lecture materials ready for immediate use.

- **Custom-Created PowerPoint slides with audio** (by an accounting faculty member) to assist students in understanding key concepts.

- **Unique video "wraps"** for each text chapter feature an accounting faculty member experienced in conducting on-line courses. The insights he or she shares with students help them (1) better prepare to read the chapter and (2) review the key concepts and takeaway lessons prior to taking an exam.

ACCOUNTING

ACCOUNTING

CHAPTERS 1-13

ACCOUNTING

FIFTH EDITION

Charles T. Horngren
Stanford University

Walter T. Harrison Jr.
Baylor University

Linda Smith Bamber
University of Georgia

 Upper Saddle River, New Jersey 07458

Library of Congress Cataloging-in-Publication Data

Horngren, Charles T.
    Accounting / Charles T. Horngren, Walter T. Harrison, Linda Smith Bamber;
annotations by Betsy Willis, Becky Jones. — 5th ed.

        p. cm.
    Includes index.
    ISBN 0-13-090699-9
    1. Accounting.   I. Harrison, Walter T.   II. Bamber, Linda S. (Linda Smith),   III.
Willis, Betsy.   IV. Jones, Becky.   V. Title.

HF5635.H8 2001
657—dc21   2001016424

Executive Editor:	Deborah Hoffman
Developmental Editor:	Jeannine Ciliotta
Assistant Editor:	Kasey Sheehan
Director of Development:	Steve Deitmer
Editor-in-Chief:	P.J. Boardman
Senior Editorial Assistant:	Jane Avery
Media Project Manager:	Nancy Welcher
Executive Marketing Manager:	Beth Toland
Senior Production Editor:	Anne Graydon
Managing Editor (Production):	Sondra Greenfield
Production Manager:	Arnold Vila
Associate Director, Manufacturing:	Vincent Scelta
Text Permissions Coordinator:	Suzanne Grappi
Design Manager:	Pat Smythe
Interior Design:	Blair Brown, Christine Cantera
Cover Design and Illustration:	Blair Brown
Infographic Illustrations:	Kenneth Batelman
Manager, Multimedia Production:	Christy Mahon
Photo Researcher:	Abby Reip
Photo Permissions Coordinator:	Michelina Viscusi
Composition:	Progressive Information Technologies
Full-Service Project Management:	Progressive Publishing Alternatives
Printer/Binder:	R.R. Donnelley, Willard

Credits and acknowledgments of images borrowed from other sources and reproduced, with permission:

page 4 Harry Cabluck/AP/Wide World Photos; **page 8** Todd Cross/Washington Post © 1999; **pages 38 & 50** Hisham F. Ibrahim/PhotoDisc, Inc.; **page 82** It's Just Lunch! Inc.; **page 98** The Image Bank; **page 126** NetGenesis; **page 143** Corbis; **page 166** Target; **page 187** PhotoDisc, Inc. **page 226** Price & Associates, PLLC; **page 231** TADOnline; **page 266** Stone; **page 269** Corbis; **page 310** AP/Wide World Photos; **page 320** Index Stock Imagery, Inc.; **page 346** Corbis; **page 352** Richard Neville/Check Six/George Hall Photography LLC; **page 386** PhotoEdit; **page 407** Corbis; **page 424** AP/Wide World Photos; **page 429** PhotoEdit; **page 464** Stone; **page 469** Ed Kashi/Corbis; **page 500** The Image Works; **page 509** Photo-Edit.

Microsoft Excel, Solver, and Windows are registered trademarks of Microsoft Corporation in the U.S.A. and other countries. Screen shots and icons reprinted with permission from the Microsoft Corporation. This book is not sponsored or endorsed by or affiliated with Microsoft Corporation.

Copyright © 2002, 1999, 1996, 1993, 1992 by Prentice-Hall, Inc., Upper Saddle River, New Jersey, 07458. All rights reserved. Printed in the United States of America. This publication is protected by copyright and permission should be obtained from the publisher prior to any prohibited reproduction, storage in a retrieval system, or transmission in any form or by any means, electronic, mechanical, photocopying, recording, or likewise. For information regarding permission(s), write to: Rights and Permissions Department.

10 9 8 7 6 5 4 3

ISBN 0-13-090698-0

To Betsy Willis and Becky Jones for their wisdom on learning and teaching over a 10-year period and to Michael Bamber for his insight on business practices and ethical issues in management accounting.

About the Authors

Charles T. Horngren is the Edmund W. Littlefield Professor of Accounting, Emeritus, at Stanford University. A graduate of Marquette University, he received his MBA from Harvard University and his Ph.D. from the University of Chicago. He is also the recipient of honorary doctorates from Marquette University and DePaul University.

A Certified Public Accountant, Horngren served on the Accounting Principles Board for six years, the Financial Accounting Standards Board Advisory Council for five years, and the Council of the American Institute of Certified Public Accountants for three years. For six years, he served as a trustee of the Financial Accounting Foundation, which oversees the Financial Accounting Standards Board and the Government Accounting Standards Board.

Horngren is a member of the Accounting Hall of Fame.

A member of the American Accounting Association, Horngren has been its President and its Director of Research. He received its first annual Outstanding Accounting Educator Award.

The California Certified Public Accountants Foundation gave Horngren its Faculty Excellence Award and its Distinguished Professor Award. He is the first person to have received both awards.

The American Institute of Certified Public Accountants presented its first Outstanding Educator Award to Horngren.

Horngren was named Accountant of the Year, Education, by the national professional accounting fraternity, Beta Alpha Psi.

Professor Horngren is also a member of the Institute of Management Accountants, where he has received its Distinguished Service Award. He was a member of the Institute's Board of Regents, which administers the Certified Management Accountant examinations.

Horngren is the author of other accounting books published by Prentice-Hall: *Cost Accounting: A Managerial Emphasis*, Tenth Edition, 2000 (with George Foster and Srikant Datar); *Introduction to Management Accounting*, Twelfth Edition (with Gary L. Sundem and William Stratton); *Introduction to Financial Accounting*, Eighth Edition, 2002 (with Gary L. Sundem and John A. Elliott); and *Financial Accounting*, Fourth Edition, 2001 (with Walter T. Harrison, Jr.).

Horngren is the Consulting Editor for the Charles T. Horngren Series in Accounting.

Walter T. Harrison, Jr. is Professor of Accounting at the Hankamer School of Business, Baylor University. He received his B.B.A. degree from Baylor University, his M.S. from Oklahoma State University, and his Ph.D. from Michigan State University.

Professor Harrison, recipient of numerous teaching awards from student groups as well as from university administrators, has also taught at Cleveland State Community College, Michigan State University, the University of Texas, and Stanford University.

A member of the American Accounting Association and the American Institute of Certified Public Accountants, Professor Harrison has served as Chairman of the Financial Accounting Standards Committee of the American Accounting Association, on the Teaching/Curriculum Development Award Committee, on the Program Advisory Committee for Accounting Education and Teaching, and on the Notable Contributions to Accounting Literature Committee.

Professor Harrison has lectured in several foreign countries and published articles in numerous journals, including *The Accounting Review, Journal of Accounting Research, Journal of Accountancy, Journal of Accounting and Public Policy, Economic Consequences of*

Financial Accounting Standards, Accounting Horizons, Issues in Accounting Education, and *Journal of Law and Commerce.* He is coauthor of *Financial Accounting,* Fourth Edition, 2001 (with Charles T. Horngren and *Accounting, Fifth Edition,* 2002 (with Charles T. Horngren and Linda S. Bamber) published by Prentice Hall. Professor Harrison has received scholarships, fellowships, research grants or awards from PriceWaterhouseCoopers, Deloitte & Touche, the Ernst & Young Foundation, and the KPMG Foundation.

Linda Smith Bamber is Professor of Accounting at the J.M. Tull School of Accounting at the University of Georgia. She graduated summa cum laude from Wake Forest University, where she was a member of Phi Beta Kappa. She is a certified public accountant. For her performance on the CPA examination, Professor Bamber received the Elijah Watt Sells Award in addition to the North Carolina Bronze Medal. Before returning to graduate school, she worked in cost accounting at RJR Foods. She then earned an MBA from Arizona State University, and a Ph.D. from The Ohio State University.

Professor Bamber has received numerous teaching awards from The Ohio State University, the University of Florida, and the University of Georgia, including selection as Teacher of the Year at the University of Florida's Fisher School of Accounting.

She has lectured in Canada and Australia in addition to the U.S., and her research has appeared in numerous journals, including *The Accounting Review, Journal of Accounting Research, Journal of Accounting and Economics, Journal of Finance, Contemporary Accounting Research, Auditing: A Journal of Practice and Theory, Accounting Horizons, Issues in Accounting Education,* and *CPA Journal.* She provided the annotations for the *Annotated Instructor's Edition* of Horngren, Foster, and Datar's *Cost Accounting: A Managerial Emphasis,* Seventh, Eighth, and Ninth Editions.

A member of the Institute of Management Accounting, the American Accounting Association (AAA), and the AAA's Management Accounting Section and Financial Accounting and Reporting Section, Professor Bamber has chaired the AAA New Faculty Consortium Committee, served on the AAA Council, the AAA Research Advisory Committee, the AAA Corporate Accounting Policy Seminar Committee, the AAA Wildman Medal Award Committee, the AAA Nominations Committee, and has chaired the Management Accounting Section's Membership Outreach Committee. She served as Associate Editor of *Accounting Horizons,* and is serving as editor of *The Accounting Review* from 1999 to 2002.

> *This is what I especially like about this textbook. There are always ways of checking yourself to make sure you are understanding what you are reading. I am really impressed with the book. It is so well put together that all the subjects seem to flow together and offer a complete knowledge of the accounting world.*
>
> **—Lisa Cronauer, student, Saint Leo University**
>
> *[This textbook is] easy to understand and made me feel that accounting could possibly be my major. . . . This textbook [is] a valuable learning tool that will aid me in the future.*
>
> **—Carrie Hupp, student, Middle Tennessee State University**

Teaching accounting today means helping students navigate a changing business world. It means helping them succeed in the classroom and in their careers. Whether this is the first or only accounting course students take, learning the fundamentals of accounting can help them make better decisions, evaluate real-world situations, and understand the value of "crunching the numbers."

In *Accounting, fifth ed.*, publisher, authors, faculty, and students target a common goal: improving student success and understanding of accounting concepts. This edition provides:

- The most motivational text and writing style
- The best assessment and reinforcement tools
- The widest assortment of technology resources
- The best free student resources
- The best service and support for faculty

We believe *Accounting, fifth ed.,* offers the best possible system for student success, and we invite you to learn more about it. We welcome your comments and suggestions.

CHARLES T. HORNGREN ◉ **WALTER T. HARRISON, JR.** ◉ **LINDA SMITH BAMBER**
STANFORD UNIVERSITY **BAYLOR UNIVERSITY** **UNIVERSITY OF GEORGIA**

TARGET STUDENT SUCCESS: MOTIVATE LEARNING

Chapter Opening Vignettes and On Location! Videos

The chapter-opening vignettes thrust students into the real world of accounting—where business decisions affect the future of actual organizations. Vignettes provide the real business context for chapter topics. Companies include Target, NetGenesis, Lucent and MCI WorldCom, McDonald's, AOL Time Warner, and more.

Many of the chapter-opening vignettes are linked to our unique, custom-created *On Location! Videos*. Each 5- to 10-minute video provides a "plant tour" introducing students to the business professionals who are using accounting information to enhance the success of their organizations. *NEW* **segments** include Cisco, Nantucket Nectars, Teva Sandals, Oracle, and others.

You probably recognize the bulls'-eye logo. You may even do your shopping at a **Target, Mervyn, Marshall Field, Dayton,** or **Hudson** store. All these companies are part of the retail empire known as **Target Corporation**. It is a pacesetter in retailing: Target stores are currently the place to find the latest fashions at the best prices. Target is also a pacesetter in philanthropy and community relations. Through its Five Percent Club, the company donates 5% of its taxable income to support charities in the communities where it operates. In 2000, Target gave more than $1 million every week to local communities. The company, which employs about 189,000 people nationwide, is considered a good employer. *Working Mother* magazine has recognized Target as a "Top Work Place for Women." Target sells its merchandise through nearly 900 stores in 44 states, and through its Web site on the Internet. It is one of the largest mass-merchandise retailers in the United States, ringing up sales of over $33 billion in the year ended January 31, 2000.

NEW Featured Company: Target

The fifth edition includes the **Target Annual Report** both as an appendix within the text and as a separate booklet shrinkwrapped with each copy. We also highlight Target in Chapter 5 and in financial statement cases throughout the book.

Varsitybooks.com: A Textbook Case on the Fulfillment Cost Conundrum

Order the fifth edition of *Accounting* from Varsitybooks.com and the company arranges for Baker & Taylor—book distributors—to ship it to you immediately. Varsitybooks doesn't have a warehouse or any inventory, but it does have to pay Baker & Taylor for this convenient arrangement. How does the fledgling dot.com account for these costs?

As you know from personal experience, e-commerce has revolutionized business. It has bent certain accounting rules in the process. One such rule is that the cost of goods sold to customers is usually considered the "cost of goods sold." Yet, on-line powerhouses like Amazon.com and eToys, Inc. count some of this cost as "sales and marketing expenses" because they never own the inventory." By listing these "fulfillment costs" as marketing expense, new-age companies don't have to subtract the costs from their gross profit. This seemed like a good idea to Varsitybooks, and its managers announced to their auditor, KPMG, that they wanted to do the same.

After all, Varsitybooks argued, mail-order companies have always done this. And the practice would allow the new agers to keep from reporting razor-thin profit margins. For instance, if the SEC tightens the rules and makes Amazon.com account for fulfillment cost as "cost of sales," gross profit margins for the last quarter of 1999 would go from 15% to −3%. The company's sales and net profit or net loss amounts would remain the same, but analysts looked at the gross profit figure to see how well a company can make money from basic business operations.

Small wonder that this approach is controversial! Varsitybooks.com fired KPMG when the auditors objected to it. They hired PricewaterhouseCoopers instead, but in the end Varsitybooks had to follow the traditional accounting procedures anyway. The auditors knew best after all.

Source: Based on Shannon Henry, "An E-Tail Identity Crisis," *The Washington Post*, May 4, 2000, p. E01. Anonymous, "Web Retailers' 'Gross Profit' Questioned; E-commerce; The SEC may make some firms account ! distribution costs, possibly turning their profits into losses," *The Los Angeles Times*, February 19, 2000, p. 2.

NEW e-Accounting Boxes

Nothing has changed business more in recent years than the Internet. Horngren/Harrison/Bamber's new e-Accounting boxes focus on the accounting issues affecting companies doing business on the World Wide Web, such as CDNow, Priceline.com, and DHL.

Exhibits 5-10 and 5-11 tell an interesting s...
at a low gro...

Work It Out Boxes

These exercises allow students to work out problems related to text concepts. Answers are provided for immediate
reinforcement.

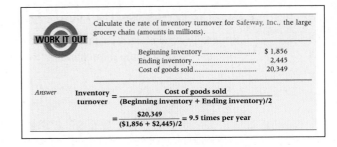

Think It Over Boxes

These exercises ask students to reflect on and apply concepts they've just learned. Again, answers are provided for
immediate reinforcement.

Decision Guidelines with *NEW* Excel Application Problems

Why should English or engineering majors care about accounting? Easy! **Decision Guidelines** are designed to
show *when, why, and how* all managers—not just accountants—use accounting information to make good business decisions. Many of the Decision Guidelines now include **optional Excel Application Problems** for a
hands-on approach. Excel is the single piece of applications software every business professional must master.
These problems give students a step-by-step guide to creating Excel templates to solve accounting and financial
dilemmas.

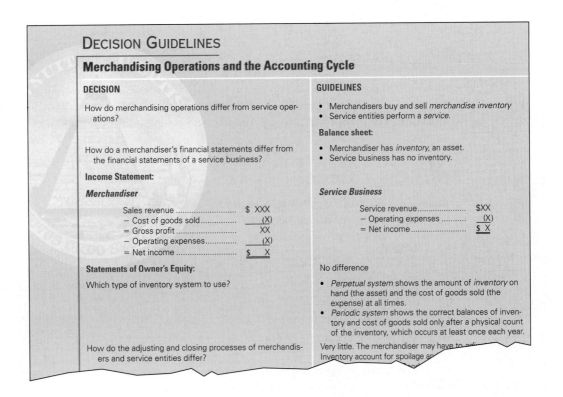

NEW "Lessons Learned"

At the end of each chapter, this feature gives students the key "takeaway" lessons from the chapter that they should retain in preparation for testing.

LESSONS LEARNED

1. **Use sales and gross profit to evaluate a company.** The major revenue of a merchandising business is *sales revenue*, or *sales*. The major expense is *cost of goods sold*. Net sales minus cost of goods sold is *gross profit*, or *gross margin*. This amount measures the business's success or failure in selling its products at a higher price than it paid for them.

2. **Account for the purchase and sale of inventory.** The merchandiser's major asset is inventory. In a merchandising entity, the accounting cycle is from cash to inventory as the inventory is purchased for resale, and back to cash as the inventory is sold. The *invoice* is the business document generated by a purchase or sale transaction. Most merchandising entities allow customers to *return* unsuitable merchandise and to offer dis....

4. **Prepare a merchandise** income statement may ap *step format.* A single-step i sections—one for revenue and a single income amou income statement has income from operations.

5. **Use the gross profit percen ratio to evaluate a busine** merchandiser are the *gross sales revenue) and the r goods sold/average inven sures usually

UNIQUE Concept Links

To keep previously covered material fresh in students' minds, concept links appear in the margins of the text. They explain how earlier topics are relevant to the new material being introduced. For students who need to go back and review, the margin links include a page cross reference.

Running Glossary

Is terminology important to student success? You bet! All key terms are boldface within the text at introduction, with a definition in the margin.

MORE Internet Exercises

Internet Exercises now appear in every chapter, and include such companies as eBay, Intuit Inc., Southwest Airlines, General Motors, FedEx, and Amazon.com. To do these exercises, students go first to the book Web site, and then use hotlinks to the company sites to complete the work.

NEW CyberCoach

www.prenhall.com/horngren

At three points in each chapter, the CyberCoach icon directs the student to exercises on the text Web site at **www.prenhall.com/horngren**

- At the beginning of each chapter, to see if they have mastered concepts covered in the previous chapter. *(Readiness Assessment)*
- At mid-chapter, to see if they have learned chapter topics up to this point. *(Mid-Chapter Assessment)*
- At the end of each chapter, to see if they have mastered the chapter as a whole. *(End-of-Chapter Assessment)*

With CyberCoach, students can check their answers and monitor their progress as they learn. Now they're better prepared for class, for homework assignments, and for examinations.

TARGET STUDENT SUCCESS: REINFORCEMENT

In addition to CyberCoach, the fifth edition offers other unique, targeted student self-evaluation materials, plus a full program of assignment exercises, problems, and cases for each chapter.

Daily Exercises

These unique, single-concept exercises appear in the end-of-chapter assignment material. Daily Exercises serve as warm-ups or confidence builders. Each is linked to the text material so that students may refer back for additional assistance. Each is also cited in the margin at the appropriate point in the text.

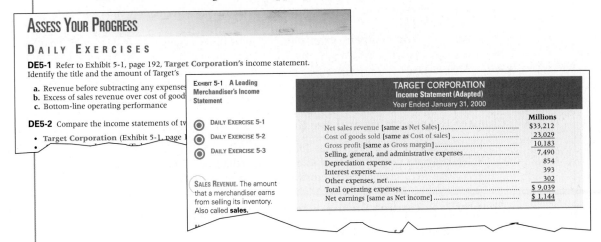

ASSESS YOUR PROGRESS

DAILY EXERCISES

DE5-1 Refer to Exhibit 5-1, page 192, **Target Corporation**'s income statement. Identify the title and the amount of Target's

  a. Revenue before subtracting any expenses
  b. Excess of sales revenue over cost of goods
  c. Bottom-line operating performance

DE5-2 Compare the income statements of tw

  • **Target Corporation** (Exhibit 5-1, page 1

DAILY EXERCISE 5-1
DAILY EXERCISE 5-2
DAILY EXERCISE 5-3

EXHIBIT 5-1 A Leading Merchandiser's Income Statement

SALES REVENUE. The amount that a merchandiser earns from selling its inventory. Also called **sales.**

TARGET CORPORATION
Income Statement (Adapted)
Year Ended January 31, 2000

	Millions
Net sales revenue [same as Net Sales]	$33,212
Cost of goods sold [same as Cost of sales]	23,029
Gross profit [same as Gross margin]	10,183
Selling, general, and administrative expenses	7,490
Depreciation expense	854
Interest expense	393
Other expenses, net	302
Total operating expenses	$ 9,039
Net earnings [same as Net income]	$ 1,144

Enhanced PH ReEnforcer Tutorial Software*

This Windows-based tutorial software enables students to test their understanding of key concepts through a variety of exercises, with immediate feedback. A "Quick Tour" tutorial provides an overview of the program. New and enhanced exercise types include:

  • *Multiple Choice Questions*
  • *Financial Statement Analysis Questions* (Students manipulate a financial statement by entering transactions.)
  • *T-account Problems* (Students complete journal entries, then select the T-accounts, and then enter numbers.)
  • *General Problems* (Students integrate accounting terms into their vocabulary by writing journal entries, using terms from the text.)

Enhanced PHAS General Ledger Tutorial*

This Windows-based software reinforces accounting procedures through hands-on activity. Problem templates allow students to enter their own problems and complete the entire accounting cycle: journalize, post, print multiple reports, and close. A "Quick Tour" overviews the program and offers online help.

The software is free to students when downloaded from the text Web site. Students may also purchase a CD-ROM containing the software packaged to their book.

TARGET STUDENT SUCCESS: WHAT'S NEW IN THIS EDITION

Every topic, every sentence, every word in every chapter has been carefully reviewed to

- **Streamline the exposition** to make text clearer and more direct.
- **Enhance readability** to make the text as accessible as possible to students taking accounting for the first time.
- **Place exhibits** as close to the introductory text reference as possible to make them easier for students to use and learn from.
- **Integrate e-commerce, Internet, and technology** information and examples wherever possible.
- **Add new real-company examples,** including hi-tech companies like Lucent Technologies and Cisco Systems, MCI WorldCom, Dell Computer, and dot.coms like Priceline.com, and Amazon.com.

Here are the major chapter changes:

Chapter 1: Accounting and the Business Environment

- *NEW* Chapter vignette: Texas Tobacco Lawyers
- *NEW* Continuing example of sole proprietorship: Gay Gillen eTravel
- *NEW* e-Accounting box: Microstrategy: A Cautionary Tale for the New Economy

Chapter 2: Recording Business Transactions

- *NEW* Chapter vignette: e-Retailers
- *NEW* e-Accounting box: The Seven Trillion Dollar Mistake (the Pentagon's accounting problems)

Chapter 3: Measuring Business Income: The Adjusting Process

- *NEW* e-Accounting box: Grossing up the Revenue: Priceline.com and Ventro
- *NEW* Decision Guidelines Excel exercise

Chapter 4: Completing the Accounting Cycle

- *NEW* Vignette: NetGenesis
- *NEW* e-Accounting box: A Forced Debt Ratio for South Korea's Companies
- *NEW* Decision Guidelines Excel exercise

Chapter 5: Merchandising Operations and the Accounting Cycle

- *NEW* Vignette: Target (annual report company), also used throughout chapter
- *NEW* e-Accounting box: Varsitybooks.com: A Textbook Case on the Fulfillment Cost Conundrum
- *NEW* Comparison of service entities vs. merchandisers for ease of understanding

Chapter 6: Accounting Information Systems

- *NEW* e-Accounting box: Accounting Pioneers on the Virtual Frontier (virtual/online accountants)

Chapter 7: Internal Control, Managing Cash, and Making Ethical Judgments

- *NEW* e-Accounting box: The Barings Bank Debacle
- *NEW* section on Internal Controls for e-Commerce

Chapter 8: Accounts and Notes Receivable

- *NEW* Vignette: NYJets/Oracle
- *NEW* e-Accounting box: Merchant Beware: Credit Cards Boom with Online Sales . . . But So Does Fraud

Chapter 9: Merchandise Inventory

- *NEW* Vignette: Deckers Outdoor (Teva)
- *NEW* e-Accounting box: It's a Bird . . . It's a Plane . . . It's a Warehouse! DHL Worldwide Express
- *NEW* Decision Guidelines Excel exercise

Chapter 10: Plant Assets and Intangible Assets

- *NEW* e-Accounting box: Singapore International Airlines: Ratcheting Up the Value of Tangibles and Intangibles
- Intangibles: expanded and updated section to reflect fact that intangibles are sometimes now more important than tangibles.

Chapter 11: Current Liabilities and Payroll

- *NEW* e-Accounting box: A Taxing Dilemma: Sales Tax Liability and the Internet
- Simplified and revised section on Contingent Liabilities with new and current example of Sun Microsystems and Microsoft lawsuit

Chapter 12: Partnerships

- *NEW* Vignette: Arthur Andersen
- *NEW* e-Accounting box: The Limited But Lively Life of a Dot.Com Partnership
- Updated and expanded section on S Corporations

Chapter 13: Corporations: Paid-in Capital and the Balance Sheet

- *NEW* e-Accounting box: UPS Delivers the Dough at Record-breaking IPO
- *NEW* Work It Out boxes using IHOP

Chapter 14: Retained Earnings, Treasury Stock, and the Income Statement

- *NEW* Vignette: America OnLine and TimeWarner
- *NEW* e-Accounting box: Stock Buybacks Catch On in Europe
- Streamlined and revised: Recording Stock Dividends, Stock Splits, Treasury Stock

Chapter 15: Long-Term Liabilities

- *NEW* Vignette on Internet startups and online information
- *NEW* e-Accounting box: Borrowers OnLine: Click Here to Lend Us $6 Billion
- Extensive example material using Amazon.com and eBay throughout chapter
- Internet startups like Vista.com

Chapter 16: Investments and International Operations

- *NEW* Vignette: McDonald's
- *NEW* e-Accounting box: Avon Products Inc.: Staying Up When the Currency Goes Down
- Streamlined coverage of Accounting for International Operations, with new examples such as Infosys and Nokia

Chapter 17: The Statement of Cash Flows

- *NEW* Vignette: drkoop.com's and MotherNature.com's cash flow problems
- *NEW* e-Accounting box: Cash Crunch Turns CDNow into CDThen

Chapter 18: Financial Statement Analysis

- *NEW* Vignette: Lucent and MCI WorldCom
- *NEW* e-Accounting box: Peer Performance: Benchmarking on the Web
- *NEW* Decision Guidelines Excel exercise

Chapter 19: Introduction to Management Accounting

- *NEW* e-Accounting box: Refining Dining with Data Mining
- *NEW* section on Time-Based Competition including updated e-commerce and JIT discussion
- *NEW* Decision Guidelines Excel exercise

Chapter 20: Job Costing

- *NEW* e-Accounting box: Radio-frequency Identification System: Smart Tags for Tracking Parts and Products
- *NEW* Think It Over exercises on how managers can use job costing information
- *NEW* section: "How Technology Has Affected Job Costing"

Chapter 21: Process Costing

- *NEW* e-Accounting box: Using Overseas Labor to Cut Process Costs
- Step-by-step explanation of conversion costs and equivalent units in "Building Blocks of Process Costing," with detailed example

Chapter 22: Cost-Volume-Profit Analysis

- *NEW* e-Accounting box: Kozmo.com and Urbanfetch.com: Can They Continue to Deliver the Goods for Free?
- *NEW* continuing CVP example: e-retailer
- *NEW* discussion of ERP and CVP analysis
- *NEW* Financial Statement Case, using Target
- *NEW* Decision Guidelines Excel exercise

Chapter 23: The Master Budget and Responsibility Accounting

- *NEW* Vignette: Habitat for Humanity
- *NEW* section: Budgeting, Sensitivity Analysis, and Information Technology
- Responsibility Accounting revised to highlight role of budget in performance evaluation
- *NEW* Financial Statement case linked to Target annual report

Chapter 24: Flexible Budgets and Standard Costs

- Setting Standards: Completely revised, with new discussion of effects of e-commerce on price standards
- *NEW* Think It Over with user emphasis
- *NEW* examples of how real companies use variance information

Chapter 25: Activity-Based Costing and Other Cost Management Tools

- *NEW* e-Accounting box: Point, Click, Buy, Sell: Businesses Cut Costs by Buying and Selling Online
- Heavily revised to provide more and better coverage of ABC, including numerical examples and more user focus, plus more and better coverage of JIT
- More real-world examples and survey evidence
- *NEW* Discussion of supply chain management and JIT

Chapter 26: Special Business Decisions and Capital Budgeting

- *NEW* e-Accounting box: We Brand It, You Make It: The Outsourcing Trend
- Expanded discussion of outsourcing, including Web's role in outsourcing decisions
- *NEW* Decision Guidelines Excel exercise

TARGET STUDENT SUCCESS: THE TEACHING AND LEARNING PACKAGE

ACCOUNTING, FIFTH ED., OFFERS A COMPLETE TEACHING AND LEARNING PACKAGE TO PROVIDE STUDENTS AND INSTRUCTORS WITH THE BEST AIDS TO SUCCESS. AND DEPENDING ON HOW YOU TEACH YOUR COURSE, WE OFFER ACCOUNTING, FIFTH ED., IN SEVERAL VERSIONS: HARD COVER CHAPTERS 1–26; PAPERBACKS CHAPTERS 1–13 AND CHAPTERS 12–26; AND A NEW! HARDCOVER CHAPTERS 1–18, THE FINANCIAL ACCOUNTING CHAPTERS.

TEXT ICONS

www.prenhall.com/horngren
CyberCoach

WRITING ASSIGNMENT

EXCEL SPREADSHEET TEMPLATES

STUDENT RESOURCE CD
INSTRUCTOR COURSE ORGANIZER CD

Instructor Resources

- Annotated Instructor's Edition
- Instructor's Manual and Video Guide
- Solutions Manual with Transparencies
- Four-Color Teaching Transparencies
- Test Item File
- Prentice Hall Test Manager
- *NEW Free* Instructor's CD-ROM (contains all print and technology resources on CD-ROM)
- Accounting and Taxation Services Hotline (call your PH representative for hotline number and e-mail address)
- Prentice Hall Accounting Faculty Directory (call your PH representative for information)

Student Resources

- *NEW Free* Target Annual Report
- *NEW* Student CD-ROM (contains all PowerPoint slides, tutorial, and general ledger software)
- *NEW Free e-BIZ: The Prentice Hall Guide to e-Business and e-Commerce in Accounting*
- *Free How to Study Accounting* Guidebook
- *NEW The Wall Street Journal* discount subscription offer
- *NEW* MoviesDoorToDoor.com by Mark Beasley and Frank Buckless
- Working Papers
- Study Guides
- Practice Sets

Technology Resources

- *NEW Free* Standard Online Distance Learning Course (WebCT, Blackboard, Pearson CourseCompass)
- *NEW* Premium Online Distance Learning Course (WebCT, Blackboard, Pearson CourseCompass)
- *NEW Free* myPHLIP companion Web site available at www.prenhall.com/horngren
- *Enhanced Free* ReEnforcer Tutorial Software*
- *Free* General Ledger Software*
- *Enhanced Free* Excel Spreadsheet Templates with Excel Tutorial
- *Free* Powerpoint Slides/Ready Notes*
- *NEW Free* "Getting Started with Peachtree" Guidebook
- *NEW Free* "Getting Started with QuickBooks" Guidebook
- *NEW Free* "Getting Started with Simply Accounting" Guidebook
- *NEW* Peachtree Software
- *NEW* Mastering Accounting CD-ROM
- *On Location!* Videos with *NEW segments on* Cisco, Nantucket Nectars (The Juice Guys!), Teva Sandals, Oracle, Amy's Ice Cream, and more
- PHACTS Tutorial Videos
- Accounting Made Easy CD-ROM (available in two CDs)

All may be downloaded at no charge from the text Web site by adopters. These items are also available on our Student CD-ROM, at a nominal price, with text purchase.

TARGET STUDENT SUCCESS: ONLINE AND INTEGRATED COURSE SOLUTIONS

Online Courses

Are you interested in offering a complete and fully functional online course? Would you like to take advantage of existing technology to better communicate with your students, post supplementary course materials, or conduct online testing and grading?

As the leading college textbook publisher, Prentice Hall has formed close alliances with each of the leading online platform providers—Blackboard, WebCT, and our own Pearson CourseCompass.

Two Levels of Content

We offer two levels of content for most of our online principles of accounting courses:

Standard Courses

(Free with New Text Purchase)
Standard Courses include traditional online course features: online testing, course management and page tracking, communication (i.e., bulletin board, chat rooms, and e-mail), course information, calendar, Powerpoints, Gradebook, etc. Test questions for faculty use, along with sample quizzes and tests for students, are **pre-loaded** for ease of use. Both may be edited by an instructor.

Premium Courses

(Available at a Nominal Price with New Text Purchase)
Prentice Hall offers many distinctive features for our textbook adopters—**including the highest possible service** from our platform partners. For several of our online courses, including Horngren/Harrison/Bamber *Accounting*, fifth ed., the Premium course provides:

- **Rich, Prentice Hall custom-created** course and lecture materials
- **Custom-created PowerPoint slides with audio** to assist students in understanding key concepts
- **Unique video segments** for each text chapter feature an accounting faculty member experienced in conducting online courses, who shares insights with students that help them (1) better prepare to read the chapter and then (2) review the key concepts and takeaway lessons prior to taking an exam.

Each of these features is designed to personalize the course and enhance student understanding of the material.

myPHLIP

Welcome to myPHLIP— your personal guide to the FREE online resources for your book.

Featuring one-click access to all the new materials created by our award-winning team of educators, myPHLIP provides a personalized view of the great new resources available:

- **myPHLIP pages**—your personal access page unites all your myPHLIP texts.
- **Notes**—add personal notes to our resources.
- **Messages**—send messages to individual students, or all students linked to your course.
- **Student Resources**—such as our PowerPoints, videos, and spreadsheets
- **Business Headlines**—provide links to articles in today's business news!
- **Search**—search all PHLIP resources for relevant articles and exercises.
- **Instructor Manual**—tips and suggestions for integrating PHLIP resources into your course.

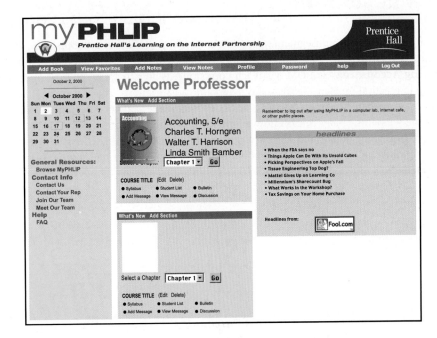

And of course you and your students will still have access to the original PHLIP resources you have trusted throughout the years to provide the best business education support available:

For Instructors

- In the News current events articles
- Teaching Resources
- Online faculty support
- Research Area
- Internet Resources
- What's New on your myPHLIP Web site

For the Student

1. In the News current events articles
2. Research Area
3. Internet Resources
4. Online Study Guide
5. Talk to the Tutor virtual office hours
6. Writing Resource Center
7. Career Center

MoviesDoorToDoor.com: How Accounting Helped Make the Difference

Mark Beasley and Frank Buckless, both of North Carolina State University

MoviesDoorToDoor.com is the fictional story of three college friends who sense a unique business opportunity. Although none of them majored in accounting, the book shows how accounting information is a key component of the major business decisions they make for their start-up business—one that enables customers to select and order videotape rentals via the Internet, which are then delivered direct to the customer's home. The book can be a supplementary reading assignment or a team project.

 The Mastering Business Series

Mastering Business is a multisegment, multimedia CD-ROM series that uses video and interactive exercises. The series covers all the core business disciplines. Through dramatic situations and rigorous exercises, the **Mastering Accounting** CD-ROM will teach your students how to apply the fundamental concepts of accounting to practical problems facing today's dynamic organizations. The Mastering Business series has been developed around an e-business startup, CanGo. By seeing the same people handle a variety of situations in each of the segments, students learn how all the areas of a business are affected by decisions such as making a new product, going public, and starting a new marketing campaign. The Mastering Accounting CD-ROM may be shrinkwrapped to this text for a nominal fee. Go to www.prenhall.com/accountingconnection for more details.

ACKNOWLEDGMENTS

Special thanks to

Student reviewers who provided us with quotable assessments of the book:
Patricia Colarusso, Luzerne County Community College
Lisa Cronauer, Saint Leo University
Carla Hillhouse, Middle Tennessee State University
Carrie Hupp, Middle Tennessee State University
JoAnne Jones, Macomb Community College
Pam Walsh, Oakland Community College

Professor Michael Bamber of the University of Georgia for help and support in preparing text and assignments

Professor Lynn Mazzola of Nassau Community College for her help in checking assignment material and reading the text of Chapters 19–26

Students Chaundolyn Johnson and Grant Rumsey, at the University of Georgia, for their help in checking assignments for Chapters 19–26

Professor Jean Hawkes of William Jewell College for revising the instructor's edition annotations

Writer Nancy Brandwein for the new e-Accounting boxes

Reviewers of ACCOUNTING, Fifth Ed.

Hicks E. Anderson Jr., Montreat College
Thomas Badley, Baker College
David S. Baglia, Grove City College
Robert C. Brush, Cecil Community College
David T. Collins, Bellarmine College
Joan E. Cook, Milwaukee Area Technical College
Kenneth P. Couvillion, San Joaquin Delta College
Ann S. DeCapite, Coastal Carolina College
Anthony J. Dellarte, Luzerne Community College
Joan Demko, Wor-Wic Community College
Mari Suzanne duToit, Okaloosa-Walton Community College
James J. Formosa, Nashville State Technical College
Sally W. Gilfillan, Longwood College
Shirley Glass, Macomb Community College
Janet L. Grange, Chicago State University
Susan S. Hamlen, State University of New York at Buffalo
Ken Harmon, Middle Tennessee State University
Steven Jackson, University of Southern Maine
Fred R. Jex, Macomb Community College
Peg Johnson, Metropolitan Community College

Thomas K. Y. Kam, Hawaii Pacific University
John E. Karayan, California State Polytechnic University, Pomona
Lynn R. Krausse, Bakersfield College
Steven P. Landry, University of Hawaii at Hilo
Suzanne Lowensohn, Barry University
Angelo Luciano, Columbia College-Chicago
Susan Murphy, Monroe Community College
Michael Palma, Gwinnett Technical Institute
William D. Parrish, Delgado Community College
James E. Racic, Lakeland Community College
Rodney R. Ridenour, Montana State University-Bozeman
E. Thomas Robinson, University of Alaska-Fairbanks
Barbara E. Roper, Chicago State University
Gerald W. Rosson, Lynchburg College
Robin D. Turner, Dabney S. Lancaster Community College
Scott Wallace, Blue Mountain Community College
Idalene Williams, Metropolitan Community College
Kitty Williams, Georgia Southern University
Lori S. Zulauf, Slippery Rock University

Focus Group Participants

Richard Ahrens, Los Angeles Pierce College
Charles Alvis, Winthrop University
Juanita Ardevany, Los Angeles Valley College
Patricia Ayres, Arapahoe Community College
David S. Baglia, Grove City College
Carl Ballard, Central Piedmont Community College
Maria Barillas, Phoenix College
James F. Benedum, Milwaukee Area Technical College
Dorcus Berg, Wingate College
Angela Blackwood, Belmont Abbey College
Gary R. Bower, Community College of Rhode Island
Jack Brown, Los Angeles Valley College
Virginia Brunell, Diablo Valley College
James Carriger, Ventura College
Stan Carroll, New York City Technical College
Janet Cassagio, Nassau Community College
Lester Chadwick, University of Delaware
Stanley Chu, Borough of Manhattan Community College
Kerry Colton, Aims Community College
Shaun Crayton, New York City Technical College
Susan Crosson, Santa Fe Community College
Donald Daggett, Mankato State University
Joneal W. Daw, Los Angeles Valley College
Lyle E. Dehning, Metropolitan State College
Wanda DeLeo, Winthrop University
Jim Donnelly, Bergen Community College
Bruce England, Massasoit Community College
Dave Fellows, Red Rocks Community College
Mike Foland, Southwestern Illinois College
Roger Gee, San Diego Mesa College
Martin Ginsberg, Rockland Community College
Earl Godfrey, Gardner Webb University
Edward S. Goodhart, Shippensburg University
Janet L. Grange, Chicago State University
Jean Gutmann, University of Southern Maine
Ralph W. Hernandez, New York City Technical College
Carl High, New York City Technical College
Mary Hill, University of North Carolina - Charlotte
Jean Insinga, Middlesex Community College
Fred R. Jex, Macomb Community College
Bernard Johnson, Santa Monica College
Diane G. Kanis, Bergen Community College

John Keelan, Massachusetts Bay Community College
Mary Thomas Keim, California State University - Bakersfield
Shirly A. Kleiner, Johnson County Community College
Cynthia Kreisner, Austin Community College
Raymond L. Larson, Appalachian State University
Cathy Larson, Middlesex Community College
Linda Lessing, SUNY College of Technology - Farmingdale
Angela Letourneau, Winthrop University
Frank Lordi, Widener University
Audra Lowray, New York City Technical College
Grace Lyons, Bergen Community College
Edward Malmgren, University of North Carolina - Charlotte
Paola Marocchi, New York City Technical College
Larry McCarthy, Slippery Rock University
Linda Spotts Michael, Maple Woods Community College
Greg Mostyn, Mission College
Kitty Nessmith, Georgia Southern University
Lee Nicholas, University of Northern Iowa
Terry Nunnelly, University of North Carolina - Charlotte
Alfonso R. Oddo, Niagara University
Margie Sinclair-Parish, Lewis & Clark Community College
Al Partington, Los Angeles Pierce College
Lynn Mazzola Paluska, Nassau Community College
Juan Perez, New York City Technical College
Ronald Pierno, University of Missouri
Geraldine Powers, Northern Essex Community College
Harry Purcell, Ulster County Community College
John Ribezzo, Community College of Rhode Island
Rosemarie Ruiz, York University
Stephen Schaefer, Contra Costa College
Parmar Sejal, Bergen Community College
Lynn Shoaf, Belmont Abbey College
Walter J. Silva, Roxbury Community College
Leon Singleton, Santa Monica College
David Skougstad, Metropolitan State College
Donna Sum, Prairie State College
Paul Sunko, Olive-Harvey College
Mary Ann Swindlehurst, Carroll Community College
Chandra Taylor, New York City Technical College
Phillip Thornton, Metropolitan State College
John L. Vaccaro, Bunker Hill Community College

Supplement Authors/Reviewers

Instructor's Manual and Video Guides

Betsy Willis, Baylor University
Becky Jones, Baylor University

Video Guides by Beverly Amer, Northern Arizona University

Study Guide

Stephen C. Schaefer, Contra Costa Community College

Allan D. Campbell, Saint Leo University

Mastering Accounting CD

Active Learning Technologies

Working Papers

Ellen Sweatt, Georgia Perimeter College

Anthony Dellarte, Luzerne County Community College

Solutions Manual and Solutions Transparencies

Charles T. Horngren, Stanford University
Walter T. Harrison, Baylor University

Linda Smith Bamber, University of Georgia

Technical Reviewers:

Robert Bauman, Allan Hancock College
Becky Jones, Baylor University
Betsy Willis, Baylor University
Thomas Hoar, Houston Community College

Lynn Mazzola, Nassau Community College
Blake Willis
Chaundolyn Johnson
Grant Rumsey

Test Item File

Alice B. Sineath, Forsyth Technical Community College

Sharie L. Dow, Saint Leo University Center for Online Learning

WIN PH Custom Test Manager

Alice B. Sineath and Engineering Software Associates

Student Resource CD-ROM
Instructor's Resource CD-ROM

PowerPoint Presentations by Olga Quintana, University of Miami
PHAS General Ledger by Lanny Nelms and Jean Insinga

PH ReEnforcer by Albert Oddo, Niagra Univeristy
Spreadsheet Templates by Albert Fisher, Community College of Southern Nevada

On Location Videos

Beverly Amer, Northern Arizona University

Companion Website PHLIP/COMPANION WEBSITE

Randy Kidd, Penn Valley Community College

OnLine Courses (WebCT, Blackboard, Pearson Course Compass)

Michele Bevan, Anthony Fortini, and Maryann Pionegro Carol, with special thanks to Nancy Welcher at Prentice Hall Business Publishing for her technical assistance.

Brief Contents

Contents

Chapter 13
Corporations: Paid-in Capital and the Balance Sheet 500

ACCOUNTING

Prologue: Careers in Accounting

Every organization uses accounting. The corner store keeps accounting records to measure its success selling groceries. The largest corporations need accounting to keep track of their locations, employees, and transactions. And all the dot.coms must account for their transactions. Why is accounting so important? Because it helps an organization the same way a model helps an architect construct a building. Accounting helps the manager understand the organization without drowning in its details.

Accounting offers exciting career opportunities. Accounting careers are usually divided into two areas: private accounting and public accounting.

PRIVATE ACCOUNTING

Private accountants work for a single business, such as a local department store, the **McDonald's** restaurant chain, or **Eastman Kodak Company.** Charitable organizations, educational institutions, and government agencies also employ private accountants. The chief accounting officer usually carries the title of controller, treasurer, or chief financial officer (CFO). This person often has the status of a vice president. Accountants who have met certain professional requirements in the area of management accounting are designated as *certified management accountants (CMAs).*

Private accountants perform a wide variety of services:

- *Budgeting* sets sales and profit goals and develops detailed plans (called *budgets*) for achieving those goals. Some of the most successful companies in the United States have been pioneers in the field of budgeting—**Procter & Gamble** and **General Electric,** for example.
- *Information systems design* identifies the organization's information needs, both internal and external. Systems designers develop and implement information systems to meet those needs.
- *Cost accounting* analyzes a business's costs to help managers control expenses. Cost accounting records guide managers in pricing their products and services to achieve greater profits. Also, cost accounting information shows when a product is not profitable and should be dropped.
- *Internal auditing* is performed by a business's own accountants. Large organizations—**Motorola, Bank of America,** and **3M** among them—maintain a staff of internal auditors. These accountants evaluate the firm's accounting and management systems to improve operating efficiency and to ensure that employees follow company policies.

PUBLIC ACCOUNTING

Public accountants serve the general public and collect professional fees for their work, much as doctors and lawyers do. Public accountants are a small fraction (about 10%) of all accountants. Accountants who have met certain professional requirements in law, auditing, and accounting are designated as *certified public accountants (CPAs).*

Like private accountants, public accountants provide valuable services:

- *Consulting* describes the wide scope of advice CPAs provide to help managers run a business. As accountants look deep into an organization, they find many ways to improve the business's operations. Accountants help their clients recruit executives, reorganize the business, and plan mergers with other companies.
- *Assurance* is the service of providing a professional statement that certain information is accurate. CPAs *audit,* or examine, the financial statements of companies and attest to the accuracy and completeness of the data in the statements. Auditors also examine companies' Web sites and provide statements that the information is accurate.
- *Tax accounting* has two aims: complying with the tax laws and minimizing the company's tax bill. Reducing the company's tax bill is an important management consideration. CPAs advise companies and individuals on what type of investments to make and how to structure transactions.

Some public accountants pool their talents and work together within a single firm. Most of their professional employees are CPAs. CPA firms vary greatly in size. Most are small businesses, but many are large partnerships. Exhibit P-1 gives data on the largest U.S. accounting firms.

Exhibit P-2 shows the accounting positions within public accounting firms and other organizations. Note the upward movement of accounting personnel, as indicated by the arrows. In particular, note how accountants may move from positions in public accounting firms to similar or higher positions in industry and government. This is a frequently traveled career path. Because accounting deals with all facets of an organization—such as purchasing, manufacturing, marketing, and distribution—it provides an excellent opportunity for gaining broad business experience.

During this term, you will learn how to use accounting to make business decisions. Consider a career in accounting as you work through this first course.

Rank (2000)	Firm Location	Net Revenue (in millions)	Partners	Number of Offices	Revenue per Partner (in millions)
1	Andersen Worldwide* New York	$7,824	2,117	92	$3.7
2	PricewaterhouseCoopers New York	$6,750	2,938	189	$2.3
3	Ernst & Young New York	$6,375	2,546	87	$2.5
4	Deloitte & Touche Wilton, Connecticut	$5,300	1,913	101	$2.8
5	KPMG New York	$4,656	1,800	136	$2.6
6	H&R Block Tax Services Kansas City, Missouri	$1,267	3,361	8,923	$0.4
7	Century Business Services** Cleveland, Ohio	$460	N/A	798	N/A
8	RSM McGladrey Bloomington, Minnesota	$381	369	65	$1.1
9	Grant Thornton Chicago	$375	274	48	$1.5
10	BDO Seidman Chicago	$298	335	42	$0.9

* During 2000, Andersen Worldwide separated into two firms: Arthur Andersen and Accenture.
** Unlike the other firms, Century Business Services is not a partnership.
Source: Adapted from *Accounting Today* (March 13–April 2, 2000), Special Supplement.

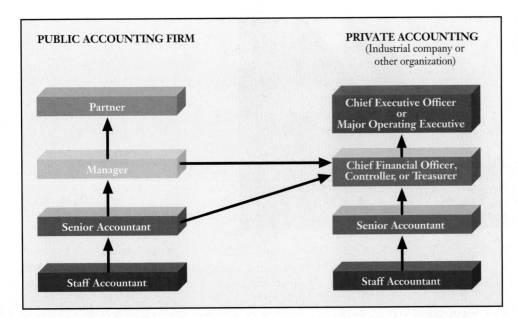

Accounting and the Business Environment

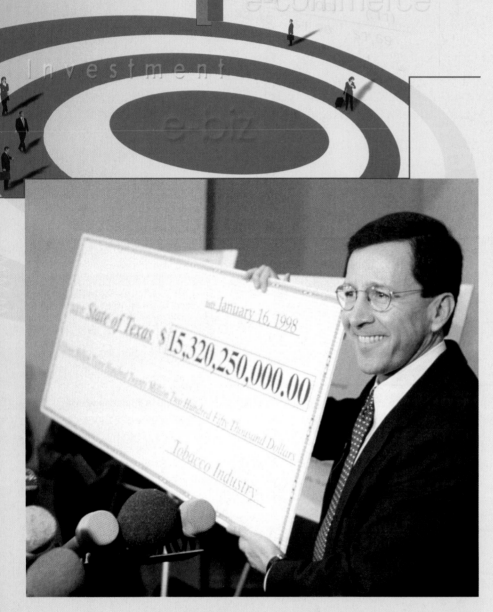

LEARNING OBJECTIVES

After studying this chapter, you should be able to

1. Use accounting vocabulary

2. Apply accounting concepts and principles to business situations

3. Use the accounting equation to describe an organization's financial position

4. Use the accounting equation to analyze business transactions

5. Prepare and use the financial statements

6. Evaluate the performance of a business

www.prenhall.com/horngren

Readiness Assessment

Every three months, five Texas lawyers receive $25 million for their work in a lawsuit against the large tobacco companies. These attorneys proved in court that the tobacco companies withheld information that could have helped people make better decisions about whether to smoke. So far the attorneys have collected more than $400 million from the cigarette makers. With this new-found income, they are helping build a new law center for Baylor University, their college alma mater. How do the attorneys account for this legal income? How do they account for the donations to Baylor? The legal agreements require the tobacco companies to pay billions to the states and to their attorneys. How do the cigarette makers, such as **Philip Morris** and **American Brands,** account for these payments?

As you work through this book, you will learn how to account for the attorneys' earnings and for the tobacco companies' expenses. In this chapter, you'll see how one of the attorneys, Harold Nix, uses accounting to manage his practice. We begin the study of accounting with a small single-person business, known as a proprietorship. Many attorneys practice law alone as a proprietorship. Others, such as the "Texas tobacco lawyers," work in partnerships with other attorneys. The large tobacco companies are corporations, the most complex form of business organization. As you study accounting principles, you will also learn to account for the affairs of partnerships and corporations.

Let's begin our study by learning exactly what accounting is.

ACCOUNTING: THE BASIS FOR BUSINESS DECISIONS

Objective 1
Use accounting vocabulary

Accounting is the information system that measures business activities, processes that information into reports, and communicates the results to decision makers. Accounting is not the same as bookkeeping. *Bookkeeping* is a procedure in accounting, just as arithmetic is a procedure in mathematics. Accounting is often called "the language of business." The better you understand this language, the better your business decisions will be, and the better you can manage the financial aspects of living. Personal financial planning, education expenses, loans, car payments, income taxes, and investments are based on the information system that we call accounting.

ACCOUNTING. The information system that measures business activities, processes that information into reports, and communicates the results to decision makers.

A key product of an accounting system is a set of financial statements. **Financial statements** report on a business in monetary terms. Is my business making a profit? Should I hire assistants? Am I earning enough money to pay my rent? Answers to business questions like these are based on accounting information.

FINANCIAL STATEMENTS. Documents that report on a business in monetary amounts, providing information to help people make informed business decisions.

Today people use computers to do detailed bookkeeping—in households, businesses, and organizations of all types. Exhibit 1-1 illustrates the role of accounting in business. The process starts and ends with people making decisions.

Decision Makers: The Users of Accounting Information

Decision makers need information. The more important the decision, the greater the need for information. Virtually all businesses and most individuals keep accounting records to aid in making decisions.

INDIVIDUALS   People such as you use accounting information to manage bank accounts, evaluate job prospects, make investments, and decide whether to rent or buy a house. Harold Nix, one of the Texas tobacco lawyers, uses accounting information to manage his law office.

BUSINESSES   Business managers use accounting information to set goals for their organizations, to evaluate progress toward those goals, and to take corrective action if necessary. Decisions based on accounting information may include which building to purchase, how much merchandise to keep on hand, and how much cash to borrow.

Exhibit 1-1   The Accounting System: The Flow of Information

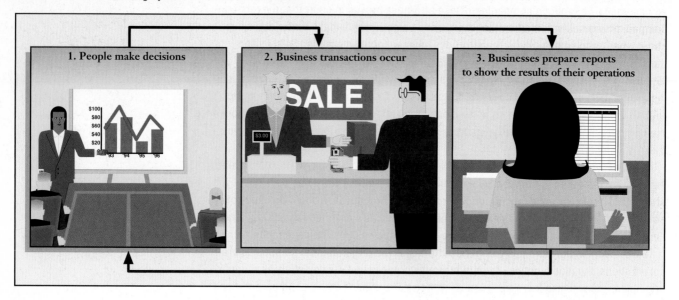

1. People make decisions

2. Business transactions occur

3. Businesses prepare reports to show the results of their operations

INVESTORS   Investors provide the money a business needs to begin operations. To decide whether to invest in a company, potential investors evaluate what income they can expect from their investment. This means analyzing the financial statements of the business and keeping up with developments in the business press—for example, *The Wall Street Journal* and *Business Week.*

CREDITORS   Before making a loan, creditors (lenders) such as banks determine the borrower's ability to meet scheduled payments. This evaluation includes a report on the borrower's financial position and a prediction of future operations, both of which are based on accounting information. To borrow from a bank before striking it rich, Harold Nix probably had to document his income and financial position.

GOVERNMENT REGULATORY AGENCIES   Most organizations face government regulation. For example, the *Securities and Exchange Commission (SEC),* a federal agency, requires businesses to disclose certain financial information to the investing public.

TAXING AUTHORITIES   Local, state, and federal governments levy taxes on individuals and businesses. Income tax is figured using accounting information. Businesses determine the sales tax they owe from accounting records that show how much they have sold.

NONPROFIT ORGANIZATIONS   Nonprofit organizations—such as churches, hospitals, government agencies, and colleges—use accounting information in much the same way that profit-oriented businesses do.

OTHER USERS   Employees and labor unions make wage demands based on employers' reported income. Consumer groups and the general public are also interested in the amount of income businesses earn. Newspapers report "improved profit pictures" for companies as the nation emerges from economic downturns. Such news, based on accounting information, has an effect on our standard of living.

Financial Accounting and Management Accounting

Users of accounting information may be categorized as *external users or internal users.* This distinction allows us to classify accounting into two fields—financial accounting and management accounting.

FINANCIAL ACCOUNTING. The branch of accounting that focuses on information for people outside the firm.

Financial accounting focuses on information for people outside the firm. Creditors and outside investors, for example, are not part of the day-to-day management of the company. Government agencies and the general public are external users of a firm's accounting information. Chapters 2–18 of this book deal primarily with financial accounting.

Management accounting focuses on information for internal decision makers, such as top executives, department heads, college deans, and hospital administrators. Chapters 19–26 cover management accounting.

THE AUTHORITY UNDERLYING ACCOUNTING

In the United States, a private organization called the **Financial Accounting Standards Board (FASB)** determines how accounting is practiced. The FASB works with a governmental agency, the Securities and Exchange Commission (SEC), the American Institute of Certified Public Accountants (AICPA), and the Institute of Management Accountants (IMA), two large professional organizations of accountants. **Certified public accountants,** or **CPAs,** are accountants who are licensed to serve the general public rather than one particular company. **Certified management accountants,** or **CMAs,** are licensed accountants who work for a single company. The rules that govern public accounting information are called generally accepted accounting principles (GAAP). Exhibit 1-2 diagrams the relationships among the various accounting organizations.

MANAGEMENT ACCOUNTING. The branch of accounting that focuses on information for internal decision makers of a business.

FINANCIAL ACCOUNTING STANDARDS BOARD (FASB). The private organization that determines how accounting is practiced in the United States.

CERTIFIED PUBLIC ACCOUNTANT (CPA). A licensed accountant who serves the general public rather than one particular company.

CERTIFIED MANAGEMENT ACCOUNTANT (CMA). A licensed accountant who works for a single company.

EXHIBIT 1-2   Key Accounting Organizations

PUBLIC SECTOR
The Securities and Exchange Commission (SEC), a government agency, regulates securities markets in the United States.

PRIVATE SECTOR
Accountants apply generally accepted accounting principles.

PRIVATE SECTOR
The Financial Accounting Standards Board (FASB) determines generally accepted accounting principles.

Generally accepted accounting principles (GAAP)

Ethics in Accounting and Business

Ethical considerations pervade all areas of accounting and business. Consider a current situation: Tobacco companies are defendants in a large number of lawsuits. The managers of **Philip Morris, RJR Nabisco,** and **American Brands** have reason to downplay these lawsuits for fear investors will stop buying their stock and banks will stop lending them money. Should Philip Morris, RJR Nabisco, and American Brands disclose this sensitive information? Accounting guidelines require companies to describe such lawsuits in their financial statements. And each company's auditor is required to state whether the information each company reports to the public is adequate.

By what criteria do accountants address such ethical questions? The AICPA, other professional accounting organizations, and most large companies have codes of ethics that bind members and employees to high standards of ethical conduct.

Standards of Professional Conduct

The AICPA's Code of Professional Conduct for Accountants was adopted by its members to provide guidance to CPAs in their work. Ethical standards in accounting are designed to produce accurate information for decision making. The preamble to the Code states: "[A] certified public accountant assumes an obligation of self-discipline above and beyond the requirements of laws and regulations . . . [and] an unswerving commitment to honorable behavior. . . ."

The opening paragraph of the Standards of Ethical Conduct of the Institute of Management Accountants (IMA) states: "Management accountants have an

MicroStrategy: A Cautionary Tale for the New Economy

MicroStrategy illustrates both the tremendous rise of e-commerce and the accounting temptations that go with it. MicroStrategy was founded ten years ago as a data-mining software company, and the Internet helped its revenues soar. The company became a darling of Wall Street. In 12 months, the stock rose from $7.34 to $333 and turned its CEO, 35-year-old Michael Saylor, into one of the nation's youngest billionaires. Then boom: On March 20, 2000, MicroStrategy announced a change in accounting practices and the stock lost 60% of its value in one day. Suddenly 1999's profit of $12.6 million turned into a loss of around $40 million. Seems that MicroStrategy had been booking revenue for software contracts even though the revenue would be earned over a multi-year period.

In the frenzy accompanying the rise of e-commerce—estimated to reach $4 trillion by 2003—there is tremendous pressure to project optimism and push up stock prices. Fledgling companies are spending tremendous amounts of investors' money to launch, promote, and maintain their Web sites, and many are losing money. Hence, the new wizards of e-commerce face the temptation to make the financials look better than the actual results. The SEC has formed a new team to investigate and get tough on issues such as the overstatement of revenues. "Think about a bottle of fine wine," says SEC chairman Arthur Levitt: "You wouldn't pop the cork on that bottle before it was ready. But some companies are doing this—recognizing revenues before a sale is complete, before the product is delivered, or [while] the customer still [can] void . . . the sale." MicroStrategy popped the cork prematurely, and in so doing, alerted its dot.com cousins to some real-world consequences.

Sources: Based on Adam Zagorin, "The E-numbers game," *Time,* April 3, 2000, p. 66. Sandra Sugawara, "SEC Unit Targets Accounting Tricks; New Team to Focus on Cooked Books," *The Washington Post,* May 26, 2000, p. E5. James Lardner, "A tech highflier's day of reckoning: How Michael Saylor went from 'boy visionary' to poster boy for dot-com shenanigans," *U.S. News & World Report,* April 10, 2000, pp. 42–43. Robert J. Samuelson, "A high-tech accounting?" *Newsweek,* April 3, 2000, p. 37.

obligation to the organizations they serve, their profession, the public, and themselves to maintain the highest standards of ethical conduct." The requirements are similar to those in the AICPA code.

Most corporations also set standards of ethical conduct for their employees. For example, **The Boeing Company,** a leading manufacturer of aircraft, has a highly developed set of business conduct guidelines. In the introduction to those guidelines, the chairperson of the board and the chief executive officer state: "We owe our success as much to our reputation for integrity as we do to the quality and dependability of our products and services. This reputation is fragile and can easily be lost."

TYPES OF BUSINESS ORGANIZATIONS

A business takes one of three forms of organization. In some cases, accounting procedures depend on which form the organization takes. You should understand the differences among the three: proprietorships, partnerships, and corporations.

PROPRIETORSHIPS   A **proprietorship** has a single owner, called the proprietor, who is generally also the manager. Suppose the law office of Harold Nix started out as a proprietorship. Proprietorships tend to be small retail establishments or individual professional businesses, such as those of physicians, attorneys, and accountants. From the accounting viewpoint, each proprietorship is distinct from its proprietor: The accounting records of the proprietorship do *not* include the proprietor's personal financial records.

PROPRIETORSHIP. A business with a single owner.

PARTNERSHIPS A **partnership** joins two or more individuals together as co-owners. Each owner is a partner. Mr. Nix's law firm will become a partnership if Nix takes on a partner. Many retail establishments, as well as some professional organizations of physicians, attorneys, and accountants, are partnerships. Most partnerships are small or medium-sized, but some are gigantic, exceeding 2,000 partners. Accounting treats the partnership as a separate organization, distinct from the personal affairs of each partner.

PARTNERSHIP. A business with two or more owners.

CORPORATIONS A **corporation** is a business owned by **stockholders,** or shareholders, people who own stock (shares of ownership) in the business. A business becomes a corporation when the state approves its articles of incorporation. A corporation is a legal entity, an "artificial person" that conducts its business in its own name. Like the proprietorship and the partnership, the corporation is an organization with an existence separate from its owners.

CORPORATION. A business owned by stockholders; it begins when the state approves its articles of incorporation. A corporation is a legal entity, an "artificial person," in the eyes of the law.

Corporations differ significantly from proprietorships and partnerships in one very important way. If a proprietorship or a partnership cannot pay its debts, lenders can take the owners' personal assets—cash and belongings—to satisfy the business's obligations. But if a corporation goes bankrupt, lenders cannot take the personal assets of the stockholders. This *limited personal liability* of stockholders for corporate debts partly explains why corporations are the dominant form of business organization: People can invest in corporations with limited personal risk.

STOCKHOLDER. A person who owns stock in a corporation. Also called a **shareholder.**

Another factor in corporate growth is the division of ownership into individual shares. **The Coca-Cola Company,** for example, has 3.5 billion shares of stock owned by many stockholders. An investor with no personal relationship either to the corporation or to any other stockholder can become a co-owner by buying 30, 100, 5,000, or any number of shares of its stock.

Exhibit 1-3 summarizes the differences among the three types of business organization.

EXHIBIT 1-3 **Comparison of the Three Forms of Business Organization**

	Proprietorship	Partnership	Corporation
1. Owner(s)	Proprietor—there is only one owner	Partners—there are two or more owners	Stockholders—there are generally many owners
2. Life of the organization	Limited by the owner's choice, or death	Limited by the owners' choices, or death	Indefinite
3. Personal liability of the owner(s) for the business's debts	Proprietor is personally liable	Partners are personally liable	Stockholders are not personally liable
4. Accounting status of the organization	The proprietorship is separate from the proprietor	The partnership is separate from the partners	The corporation is separate from the stockholders

ACCOUNTING CONCEPTS AND PRINCIPLES

Accounting follows certain guidelines. The rules that govern how accountants measure, process, and communicate financial information fall under the heading **GAAP,** which stands for **generally accepted accounting principles.** GAAP is the "law" of accounting—rules for conducting behavior in a way acceptable to the majority of people.

Objective 2
Apply accounting concepts and principles to business situations

GAAP rests on a conceptual framework written by the FASB: *The primary objective of financial reporting is to provide information useful for making investment and lending decisions.* To be useful, information must be relevant, reliable, and comparable. We begin the discussion of GAAP by introducing basic accounting concepts and principles.

GENERALLY ACCEPTED ACCOUNTING PRINCIPLES (GAAP). Accounting guidelines, formulated by the Financial Accounting Standards Board, that govern how accountants measure, process, and communicate financial information.

The Entity Concept

The most basic concept in accounting is that of the **entity.** An accounting entity is an organization or a section of an organization that stands apart as a separate

ENTITY. An organization or a section of an organization that, for accounting purposes, stands apart from other organizations and individuals as a separate economic unit.

economic unit. In accounting, boundaries are drawn around each entity so as not to confuse its affairs with those of other entities.

Consider Harold Nix, one of the Texas lawyers. Think back to when Nix was starting out as a young lawyer, fresh out of law school. Suppose he began his law practice with $5,000 obtained from a bank loan. Following the entity concept, Nix would account for the $5,000 separately from his personal assets, such as his clothing, house, and automobile. To mix the $5,000 of business cash with his personal assets would make it difficult to measure the financial position of Nix's business.

Consider **Toyota,** a huge organization with several divisions. Toyota management evaluates each division as a separate accounting entity. If sales in the Lexus division are dropping, Toyota can find out why. If sales figures from all divisions of the company are combined, management will not know that Lexus sales are going down. Thus, the entity concept also applies to the parts of a large organization—in fact, *to any economic unit that needs to be evaluated separately.*

The Reliability (Objectivity) Principle

Accounting records and statements are based on the most reliable data available so that they will be accurate and useful. This guideline is the *reliability principle,* also called the *objectivity principle.* Reliable data are verifiable. They may be confirmed by any independent observer. For example, Harold Nix's $5,000 bank loan is supported by a promissory note. This is objective evidence of the loan. Ideally, accounting records are based on information that flows from activities documented by objective evidence. Without the reliability principle, accounting data might be based on whims and opinions.

Suppose you want to open a stereo shop. For a store location, you transfer a small building to the business. You believe the building is worth $155,000. To confirm its cost to the business, you hire two real estate appraisers, who value the building at $147,000. Which is the more reliable estimate of the building's value, your estimate of $155,000 or the $147,000 professional appraisal? The appraisal of $147,000 is more reliable because it is supported by an independent, objective observation. The business should record the building cost as $147,000.

The Cost Principle

The *cost principle* states that acquired assets and services should be recorded at their actual cost (also called *historical cost*). Even though the purchaser may believe the price is a bargain, the item is recorded at the price paid in the transaction and not at the "expected" cost. Suppose your stereo shop purchases equipment from a supplier who is going out of business. Assume that you get a good deal and pay only $2,000 for equipment that would have cost you $3,000 elsewhere. The cost principle requires you to record the equipment at its actual cost of $2,000, not the $3,000 that you believe the equipment is worth.

The cost principle also holds that the accounting records should maintain the historical cost of an asset for as long as the business holds the asset. Why? Because cost is a reliable measure. Suppose your store holds the stereo equipment for six months. During that time, stereo prices rise, and the equipment can be sold for $3,500. Should its accounting value—the figure "on the books"—be the actual cost of $2,000 or the current market value of $3,500? According to the cost principle, the accounting value of the equipment remains at actual cost, $2,000.

The Going-Concern Concept

Another reason for measuring assets at historical cost is the *going-concern concept,* which holds that the entity will remain in operation for the foreseeable future. Most firm resources—such as supplies, land, buildings, and equipment—are acquired to use rather than to sell. Under the going-concern concept, accountants assume that the business will remain in operation long enough to use existing resources for their intended purpose.

To understand the going-concern concept better, consider the alternative, which is to go out of business. A store that is holding a Going-Out-of-Business Sale is trying to sell all its holdings. In that case, instead of historical cost, the relevant measure is current market value. Going out of business, however, is the exception rather than the rule.

The Stable-Monetary-Unit Concept

In the United States, we record transactions in dollars because the dollar is the medium of exchange. British accountants record transactions in pounds sterling, and the Japanese record transactions in yen. The value of a dollar or a Mexican peso changes over time. A rise in the price level is called *inflation*. During inflation, a dollar will purchase less milk, less toothpaste, and less of other goods. When prices are stable—when there is little inflation—a dollar's purchasing power is also stable.

Accountants assume that the dollar's purchasing power is stable. The *stable-monetary-unit concept* is the basis for ignoring the effect of inflation in accounting. It allows us to add and subtract dollar amounts as though each dollar has the same purchasing power as any other dollar at any other time.

 DAILY EXERCISE 1-1

 You are considering the purchase of land for future expansion. The seller is asking $50,000 for land that cost her $35,000. An appraisal shows a value of $47,000. You first offer $44,000. The seller counter-offers with $48,000, and you agree on a price of $46,000. What dollar value for this land is reported on your financial statements? Which accounting concept or principle guides your answer?

Answer: According to the *cost principle,* assets and services should be recorded at their actual cost. You paid $46,000 for the land. Therefore, $46,000 is the cost to report on your financial statements.

Objective 3
Use the accounting equation to describe an organization's financial position

ACCOUNTING EQUATION. The basic tool of accounting, presenting the resources of the business and the claims to those resources: Assets = Liabilities + Owner's Equity.

ASSET. An economic resource that is expected to be of benefit in the future.

LIABILITY. An economic obligation (a debt) payable to an individual or an organization outside the business.

THE ACCOUNTING EQUATION

Financial statements tell how a business is performing and where it stands. They are the final product of the accounting process. But how do we produce the financial statements? The basic tool of accounting is the **accounting equation.** It presents the resources of the business and the claims to those resources.

Assets and Liabilities

Assets are the economic resources of a business that are expected to be of benefit in the future. Cash, office supplies, merchandise, furniture, land, and buildings are assets.

Claims to those assets come from two sources. **Liabilities** are *outsider* claims, which are economic obligations—debts—payable to outsiders. These outside parties are called *creditors.* For example, a creditor who has loaned money to a business has a claim—a legal right—to a part of the assets until the business pays the debt. *Insider* claims to the business's assets are called **owner's equity,** or **capital.** These are the claims held by the owners of the business. Owners have a claim to the entity's assets because they have invested in the business.

The accounting equation shows the relationship among assets, liabilities, and owner's equity. Assets appear on the left-hand side of the equation. The legal and economic claims against the assets—the liabilities and owner's equity—appear on the right-hand side of the equation. As Exhibit 1-4 shows, the two sides must be equal:

OWNER'S EQUITY. The claim of a business owner to the assets of the business. Also called **capital.**

EXHIBIT 1-4
The Accounting Equation

(Economic Resources)	*(Claims to Economic Resources)*
ASSETS	= **LIABILITIES + OWNER'S EQUITY**

Let's take a closer look at the elements that make up the accounting equation. Suppose you run Top Cut Meats, which supplies beef to **McDonald's** and other restaurants. Some customers pay you in cash when you deliver the meat. Cash is an asset. Other customers buy on credit and promise to pay you within a certain time after delivery. This promise is also an asset because it is an economic resource that will benefit you in the future, when you receive the cash. To Top Cut Meats, this

ACCOUNT RECEIVABLE. A promise to receive cash from customers to whom the business has sold goods or for whom the business has performed services.

NOTE RECEIVABLE. A written promise for future collection of cash.

ACCOUNT PAYABLE. A liability backed by the general reputation and credit standing of the debtor.

NOTE PAYABLE. A written promise of future payment.

REVENUE. Amounts earned by delivering goods or services to customers. Revenues increase owner's equity.

EXHIBIT 1-5
Transactions That Increase or Decrease Owner's Equity

 DAILY EXERCISE 1-2

OWNER WITHDRAWALS. Amounts removed from the business by an owner.

EXPENSE. Decrease in owner's equity that occurs from using assets or increasing liabilities in the course of delivering goods or services to customers.

 DAILY EXERCISE 1-3

 DAILY EXERCISE 1-4

promise is an **account receivable.** A *written* promise for future collection is called a **note receivable.** McDonald's promise to pay you for the meat it purchases on credit creates a debt for McDonald's. This liability is an **account payable** of McDonald's—the debt is not written. Instead, it is backed by the reputation and the credit standing of McDonald's. A written promise of future payment is called a **note payable.** All receivables are assets. All payables are liabilities.

Owner's Equity

Owner's equity is the amount of an entity's assets that remain after the liabilities are subtracted.

ASSETS − LIABILITIES = OWNER'S EQUITY

The purpose of business is to increase owner's equity through **revenues,** which are increases in owner's equity earned by delivering goods or services to customers. Revenues increase owner's equity because they increase the business's assets or decrease its liabilities. As a result, the owner's share of business assets increases. Exhibit 1-5 shows that owner investments and revenues increase the owner's equity of the business.

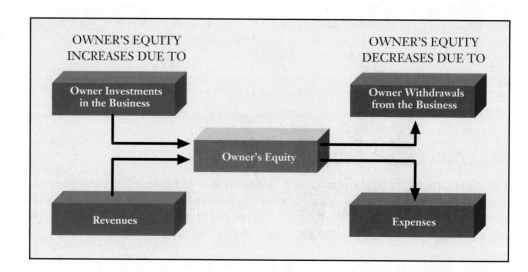

Exhibit 1-5 also indicates the types of transactions that decrease owner's equity. **Owner withdrawals** are amounts removed from the business by the owner. Withdrawals are the opposite of owner investments. **Expenses** are decreases in owner's equity that occur from using assets or increasing liabilities in the course of delivering goods and services to customers. Expenses are the cost of doing business and are the opposite of revenues. Expenses include

- office rent
- salaries of employees
- newspaper advertisements
- utility payments
- interest on loans
- insurance
- property taxes

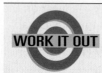 **WORK IT OUT**

1. If the assets of a business are $174,300 and the liabilities total $82,000, how much is the owner's equity?
2. If the owner's equity in a business is $22,000 and the liabilities are $36,000, how much are the assets?

Answers: To answer both questions, use the accounting equation:

1.

ASSETS	−	LIABILITIES	=	OWNER'S EQUITY
$174,300	−	$82,000	=	$92,300

2.

ASSETS	=	LIABILITIES	+	OWNER'S EQUITY
$58,000	=	$36,000	+	$22,000

ACCOUNTING FOR BUSINESS TRANSACTIONS

In accounting terms, a **transaction** is any event that *both* affects the financial position of the business entity *and* can be recorded reliably. Many events can affect a company, including (1) elections, (2) economic booms and downturns, (3) purchases and sales of merchandise inventory, (4) payment of rent, and (5) collection of cash from customers. But an accountant records only those events with effects that can be measured reliably. Which of these events would an accountant record? The answer is events (3), (4), and (5), because their dollar amounts can be measured reliably. The accountant would not record events (1) and (2) because the dollar effects of elections and economic trends cannot be measured reliably.

TRANSACTION. An event that affects the financial position of a particular entity and can be recorded reliably.

To illustrate accounting for a business, let's use Gay Gillen eTravel. Gillen operates a travel agency that offers service in two ways. Some customers phone or e-mail Gay Gillen eTravel. Other customers do business with the travel agency strictly on-line. On-line customers plan and pay for their trips through the Gillen Web site. The Web site is linked to airlines, hotels, and cruise lines, so clients can obtain the latest information 24 hours a day, 7 days a week. Gillen's Web site allows the agency to transact more business than would be possible through phone calls, fax, or e-mail. As a result, Gillen is able to operate with fewer employees, and this saves on operating expenses. She passes along the cost savings to clients by charging them lower commissions. It is a win/win situation for both parties. Gillen provides more service and generates a nice profit. Customers save on travel costs.

Now let's analyze Gillen eTravel's transactions.

TRANSACTION 1: STARTING THE BUSINESS   Gay Gillen invests $30,000 of her own money to begin the business. Specifically, she deposits $30,000 in a bank account entitled Gay Gillen eTravel. The effect of this transaction on the accounting equation of the Gay Gillen eTravel business entity is

Objective 4
Use the accounting equation to analyze business transactions

Assets	=	Liabilities	+	Owner's Equity	Type of Owner's Equity Transaction
Cash				Gay Gillen, Capital	
(1) +30,000				+30,000	*Owner investment*

For every transaction, the amount on the left side of the equation must equal the amount on the right side. The first transaction increases both the assets (in this case, Cash) and the owner's equity of the business (Gay Gillen, Capital). To the right of the transaction, we write "Owner investment" to keep track of the reason for the effect on the owner's equity.

TRANSACTION 2: PURCHASE OF LAND   Gillen purchases land for an office location, paying cash of $20,000. The effect of this transaction on the accounting equation is

Assets			=	Liabilities	+	Owner's Equity	Type of Owner's Equity Transaction
Cash	+	Land				Gay Gillen, Capital	
(1) 30,000						30,000	*Owner investment*
(2) −20,000	+	20,000					
Bal. 10,000		20,000				30,000	
	30,000					30,000	

 DAILY EXERCISE 1-5

  DAILY EXERCISE 1-6

The cash purchase of land increases one asset, Land, and decreases another asset, Cash, by the same amount. After the transaction is completed, Gillen's business has cash of $10,000, land of $20,000, no liabilities, and owner's equity of $30,000. Note that the sums of the balances (abbreviated Bal.) on both sides of the equation must always be equal.

TRANSACTION 3: PURCHASE OF OFFICE SUPPLIES Gillen buys stationery and other office supplies, agreeing to pay $500 within 30 days. This transaction increases both the assets and the liabilities of the business. Its effect on the accounting equation is

	Assets					Liabilities +	Owner's Equity
	Cash	+	Office Supplies	+	Land	Accounts Payable	Gay Gillen, Capital
Bal.	10,000				20,000		30,000
(3)			+500			+500	
Bal.	10,000		500		20,000	500	30,000
		30,500					30,500

Office Supplies is an asset, not an expense, because the supplies can be used in the future. The liability created by this transaction is an account payable. Recall that a *payable* is a liability.

TRANSACTION 4: EARNING OF SERVICE REVENUE Gay Gillen eTravel earns service revenue by providing travel services for clients. She earns $5,500 revenue and collects this amount in cash. The effect on the accounting equation is an increase in the asset Cash and an increase in Gay Gillen, Capital, as follows:

	Assets			Liabilities +	Owner's Equity	Type of Owner's Equity Transaction
	Cash +	Office Supplies +	Land	Accounts Payable +	Gay Gillen, Capital	
Bal.	10,000	500	20,000	500	30,000	
(4)	+5,500				+5,500	*Service revenue*
Bal.	15,500	500	20,000	500	35,500	
		36,000			36,000	

DAILY EXERCISE 1-7

This revenue transaction caused the business to grow, as shown by the increases in total assets and in the sum of total liabilities plus owner's equity. A company that sells goods to customers is a merchandising business. Its revenue is called *sales revenue*. By contrast, Gay Gillen and Harold Nix, the attorney, perform services for clients; their revenue is called *service revenue*.

WORK IT OUT

Gillen's travel business has now completed four business transactions. Answer these questions about the business:

1. How much in total assets does Gillen's business have to work with?
2. How much of the total assets of the business does Gillen actually own? How much does the business owe outsiders?

Answers

1. Look at the balances under the Assets heading for transaction 4. Gillen's business owns three assets: Cash ($15,500), Office Supplies ($500), and Land ($20,000). By adding these amounts, we see that the business has $36,000 in total assets.
2. Recall that *owner's equity* represents the owner's claim to the assets of the business. Gillen's owner's equity is $35,500.
   Liabilities are the amounts that a business owes to outsiders. After transaction 4, the company owes $500 in liabilities.

TRANSACTION 5: EARNING OF SERVICE REVENUE ON ACCOUNT Gillen performs services for clients who do not pay immediately. In return for her travel services, Gillen receives clients' promises to pay $3,000 within one month. This promise is an asset to Gillen, an account receivable because she expects to collect the cash in the future. In accounting, we say that Gillen performed this service *on account*. When the business performs service for a client, the business earns revenue whether it receives cash now or expects to collect the cash later. This $3,000 of service revenue increases the wealth of Gillen's business just like the $5,500 of revenue that she collected immediately in transaction 4. Gillen records an increase in the asset Accounts Receivable and an increase in owner's equity as follows:

		Assets					Liabilities +	Owner's Equity	Type of Owner's Equity Transaction
	Cash +	Accounts Receivable +	Office Supplies +	Land	=		Accounts Payable +	Gay Gillen, Capital	
Bal.	15,500		500	20,000			500	35,500	
(5)		+3,000						+3,000	Service revenue
Bal.	15,500	3,000	500	20,000			500	38,500	
		39,000						39,000	

TRANSACTION 6: PAYMENT OF EXPENSES During the month, Gillen pays $3,100 in cash expenses: lease expense on a computer, $400; office rent, $1,100; employee salary, $1,200 (part-time assistant); and utilities, $400. The effects on the accounting equation are:

		Assets					Liabilities +	Owner's Equity	Type of Owner's Equity Transaction
	Cash +	Accounts Receivable +	Office Supplies +	Land	=		Accounts Payable +	Gay Gillen, Capital	
Bal.	15,500	3,000	500	20,000			500	38,500	
	− 400							− 400	Lease expense, computer
(6)	− 1,100							− 1,100	Rent expense, office
	− 1,200							− 1,200	Salary expense
	− 400							− 400	Utilities expense
Bal.	12,400	3,000	500	20,000			500	35,400	
		35,900						35,900	

Because expenses have the opposite effect of revenues, they cause the business to shrink, as shown by the smaller balances of total assets and owner's equity.

Each expense should be recorded in a separate transaction. They are listed together here for simplicity. We could record the cash payment in a single amount for the sum of the four expenses, $3,100 ($400 + $1,100 + $1,200 + $400). In all cases, the "balance" of the equation holds, as we know it must.

Businesspeople, Gay Gillen included, run their businesses to have more revenues than expenses. An excess of total revenues over total expenses is called **net income, net earnings,** or **net profit.** If total expenses exceed total revenues, the result is a **net loss.**

TRANSACTION 7: PAYMENT ON ACCOUNT Gillen pays $300 to the store from which she purchased $500 worth of office supplies in transaction 3. In accounting, we say that she pays $300 *on account*. The effect on the accounting equation is a decrease in the asset Cash and a decrease in the liability Accounts Payable as shown at the top of page 16.

NET INCOME. Excess of total revenues over total expenses. Also called **net earnings** or **net profit.**

NET LOSS. Excess of total expenses over total revenues.

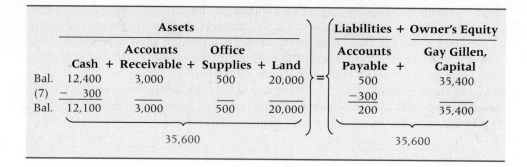

		Assets				Liabilities +	Owner's Equity
	Cash +	Accounts Receivable +	Office Supplies +	Land	=	Accounts Payable +	Gay Gillen, Capital
Bal.	12,400	3,000	500	20,000		500	35,400
(7)	− 300					−300	
Bal.	12,100	3,000	500	20,000		200	35,400
		35,600				35,600	

The payment of cash on account has no effect on the asset Office Supplies because the payment does not increase or decrease the supplies available to the business.

TRANSACTION 8: PERSONAL TRANSACTION   Gillen remodels her home at a cost of $15,000, paying cash from personal funds. This event is *not* a transaction of Gay Gillen eTravel. It has no effect on the travel agency and therefore is not recorded by the business. It is a transaction of the Gay Gillen *personal* entity, not Gay Gillen eTravel. This transaction illustrates the *entity concept.*

TRANSACTION 9: COLLECTION ON ACCOUNT   In transaction 5, Gillen performed services for a client on account. The business now collects $1,000 from the client. We say that Gillen collects the cash *on account.* Gillen will record an increase in the asset Cash. Should she also record an increase in service revenue? No, because she already recorded the revenue when she earned it in transaction 5. The phrase "collect cash on account" means to record an increase in Cash and a decrease in the asset Accounts Receivable. The effect on the accounting equation of Gay Gillen eTravel is:

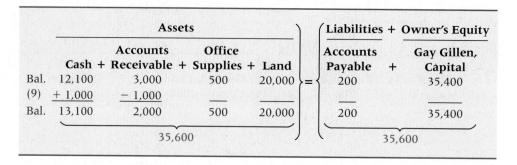

		Assets				Liabilities +	Owner's Equity
	Cash +	Accounts Receivable +	Office Supplies +	Land	=	Accounts Payable +	Gay Gillen, Capital
Bal.	12,100	3,000	500	20,000		200	35,400
(9)	+ 1,000	− 1,000					
Bal.	13,100	2,000	500	20,000		200	35,400
		35,600				35,600	

DAILY EXERCISE 1-8

Total assets are unchanged from the preceding transaction's total. Why? Because Gillen merely exchanged one asset for another. Also, total liabilities and owner's equity are unchanged.

TRANSACTION 10: SALE OF LAND   An individual approaches Gillen about selling land owned by the travel agency. Gillen and the other person agree to a sale price of $9,000, which is equal to Gillen's cost of the land. Gillen's business sells the land and receives $9,000 cash. The effect on the accounting equation of the travel agency is as follows:

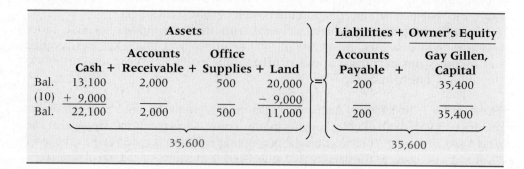

		Assets				Liabilities +	Owner's Equity
	Cash +	Accounts Receivable +	Office Supplies +	Land	=	Accounts Payable +	Gay Gillen, Capital
Bal.	13,100	2,000	500	20,000		200	35,400
(10)	+ 9,000			− 9,000			
Bal.	22,100	2,000	500	11,000		200	35,400
		35,600				35,600	

TRANSACTION 11: WITHDRAWING OF CASH   Gillen withdraws $2,100 cash from the business for personal use. The effect on the accounting equation is

		Assets						Liabilities	+	Owner's Equity	Type of Owner's Equity Transaction
	Cash	+	Accounts Receivable	+	Office Supplies	+	Land	Accounts Payable	+	Gay Gillen, Capital	
Bal.	22,100		2,000		500		11,000	200		35,400	
(11)	− 2,100									− 2,100	Owner withdrawal
Bal.	20,000		2,000		500		11,000	200		33,300	
				33,500						33,500	

Gillen's withdrawal of $2,100 cash decreases the asset Cash and also the owner's equity of the business. *The withdrawal does not represent a business expense because the cash is used for personal affairs.* We record this decrease in owner's equity as Withdrawals or as Drawings. The double underlines below each column indicate a final total.

EVALUATING BUSINESS TRANSACTIONS

Exhibit 1-6 on page 18 summarizes the 11 preceding transactions. Panel A lists the details of the transactions, and Panel B presents the analysis. As you study the exhibit, note that every transaction maintains the equality

$$\text{ASSETS} = \text{LIABILITIES} + \text{OWNER'S EQUITY}$$

THE FINANCIAL STATEMENTS

After analyzing transactions, we need a way to present the results. We look now at the *financial statements,* the formal reports of an entity's financial information. The primary financial statements are the

- income statement
- statement of owner's equity
- balance sheet
- statement of cash flows

INCOME STATEMENT   The **income statement** presents a summary of an entity's revenues and expenses for a specific period of time, such as a month or a year. The income statement, also called the **statement of earnings** or **statement of operations,** is like a video—it presents a moving financial picture of business operations during the period. The income statement holds one of the most important pieces of information about a business—its *net income,* or revenues minus expenses. If expenses exceed revenues, there is a net loss for the period.

STATEMENT OF OWNER'S EQUITY   The **statement of owner's equity** presents a summary of the changes that occurred in the entity's *owner's equity* during a specific time period, such as a month or a year. Increases in owner's equity arise from investments by the owner and from net income earned during the period. Decreases result from owner withdrawals and from a net loss for the period. Net income or net loss come directly from the income statement. Owner investments and withdrawals are capital transactions between the business and its owner, so they do not affect the income statement.

BALANCE SHEET   The **balance sheet** lists all the entity's assets, liabilities, and owner's equity as of a specific date, usually the end of a month or a year. The balance sheet is like a snapshot of the entity. For this reason, it is also called the **statement of financial position.**

STATEMENT OF CASH FLOWS   The **statement of cash flows** reports the amount of cash coming in (cash receipts) and the amount of cash going out (*cash payments* or

Objective 5
Prepare and use the financial statements

INCOME STATEMENT. Summary of an entity's revenues, expenses, and net income or net loss for a specific period. Also called the **statement of earnings** or the **statement of operations.**

STATEMENT OF OWNER'S EQUITY. Summary of the changes in an entity's owner's equity during a specific period.

BALANCE SHEET. List of an entity's assets, liabilities, and owner's equity as of a specific date. Also called the **statement of financial position.**

STATEMENT OF CASH FLOWS. Reports cash receipts and cash payments during a period.

Exhibit 1-6 Analysis of Transactions, Gay Gillen eTravel

PANEL A—Details of Transactions

(1) Gillen invested $30,000 cash in the business.
(2) Paid $20,000 cash for land.
(3) Bought $500 of office supplies on account.
(4) Received $5,500 cash from clients for service revenue earned.
(5) Performed travel service for clients on account, $3,000.
(6) Paid cash expenses: computer lease, $400; office rent, $1,100; employee salary, $1,200; utilities, $400.
(7) Paid $300 on the account payable created in transaction 3.
(8) Remodeled Gillen's personal residence. This is *not* a transaction of the business.
(9) Collected $1,000 on the account receivable created in transaction 5.
(10) Sold land for cash at its cost of $9,000.
(11) Withdrew $2,100 cash for personal expenses.

PANEL B—Analysis of Transactions

	Cash	+ Accounts Receivable	+ Office Supplies	+ Land	=	Accounts Payable	+ Gay Gillen, Capital	Type of Owner's Equity Transaction
(1)	+30,000						+30,000	Owner investment
Bal.	30,000						30,000	
(2)	−20,000			+20,000				
Bal.	10,000			20,000			30,000	
(3)			+500			+500		
Bal.	10,000		500	20,000		500	30,000	
(4)	+ 5,500						+ 5,500	Service revenue
Bal.	15,500		500	20,000		500	35,500	
(5)		+3,000					+ 3,000	Service revenue
Bal.	15,500	3,000	500	20,000		500	38,500	
	− 400						− 400	Lease expense, computer
(6)	− 1,100						− 1,100	Rent expense, office
	− 1,200						− 1,200	Salary expense
	− 400						− 400	Utilities expense
Bal.	12,400	3,000	500	20,000		500	35,400	
(7)	− 300					−300		
Bal.	12,100	3,000	500	20,000		200	35,400	
(8)	Not a transaction of the business							
(9)	+ 1,000	−1,000						
Bal.	13,100	2,000	500	20,000		200	35,400	
(10)	+ 9,000			− 9,000				
Bal.	22,100	2,000	500	11,000		200	35,400	
(11)	− 2,100						− 2,100	Owner withdrawal
Bal.	20,000	2,000	500	11,000		200	33,300	

33,500   =   33,500

disbursements) during a period. Business activities result in a net cash inflow (receipts greater than payments) or a net cash outflow (payments greater than receipts). The statement of cash flows shows the net increase or net decrease in cash during the period and the cash balance at the end of the period. (We cover the statement of cash flows in greater depth in Chapter 17.)

Financial Statement Headings

Each financial statement has a heading giving the name of the business (in our discussion, Gay Gillen eTravel), the name of the particular statement, and the date or time period covered by the statement. A balance sheet taken at the end of year 20X1 would be dated December 31, 20X1. A balance sheet prepared at the end of March 20X3 is dated March 31, 20X3.

An income statement or a statement of owner's equity that covers an annual period ended in December 20X5 is dated "Year Ended December 31, 20X5." A monthly income statement or statement of owner's equity for September 20X4 has in its heading "Month Ended September 30, 20X4," "For the Month Ended September 30, 20X4," or "For the Month of September 20X4." Income is meaningless unless identified with a particular time period.

Software programs such as Quick Books and Peachtree have streamlined the preparation of the financial statements. These statements can now be produced instantaneously after the financial records are entered into the computer. Of course, any errors in the financial records will show up in the financial statements. So the person who analyzes the data controls the accuracy of the financial statements.

Relationships Among the Financial Statements

Objective 6
Evaluate the performance of a business

Exhibit 1-7 illustrates all four financial statements. Their data come from the transaction analysis in Exhibit 1-6, which covers the month of April 20X1. Study the exhibit carefully. Specifically, observe the following in Exhibit 1-7:

1. The *income statement* for the month ended April 30, 20X1
   a. Reports all revenues and all expenses during the period. Expenses are listed in decreasing order of amount, with the largest expense first.
   b. Reports *net income* of the period if total revenues exceed total expenses, as in the case of Gay Gillen eTravel's operations for April. If total expenses exceed total revenues, a *net loss* is reported instead.
2. The *statement of owner's equity* for the month ended April 30, 20X1
   a. Opens with the owner's capital balance at the beginning of the period.
   b. Adds *investments by the owner* and adds net income (or subtracts net loss, as the case may be). Net income or net loss come directly from the income statement (see arrow ① in Exhibit 1–7).
   c. Subtracts withdrawals by the owner. Parentheses indicate a subtraction.
   d. Ends with the owner's capital balance at the end of the period.
3. The *balance sheet* at April 30, 20X1
   a. Reports all assets, all liabilities, and owner's equity at the end of the period.
   b. Reports that total assets equal the sum of total liabilities plus total owner's equity.
   c. Reports the owner's ending capital balance, taken directly from the statement of owner's equity (see arrow ②).
4. The *statement of cash flows* for the month ended April 30, 20X1
   a. Reports cash flows from three types of business activities (*operating, investing,* and *financing activities*) during the month.
      • *Operating activities* are cash receipts from revenues and cash payments of expenses.
      • *Investing activities* are the results of purchasing and selling the long-term assets that the business uses for operations.
      • *Financing activities* are the cash receipts from people who finance the organization (the owner and the lenders), and also payments back to those people.
      Each category of cash-flow activities includes both cash receipts, which are positive amounts, and cash payments, which are negative amounts (denoted by parentheses). Each category results in a net cash inflow or a net cash outflow for the period. We discuss these categories in detail in later chapters.
   b. Reports a net increase in cash during the month and ends with the cash balance at April 30, 20X1. This is the amount of cash to report on the balance sheet (see arrow ③).

EXHIBIT 1-7
**Financial Statements of
Gay Gillen eTravel**

GAY GILLEN ETRAVEL
Income Statement
Month Ended April 30, 20X1

Revenue		
Service revenue		$8,500
Expenses:		
Salary expense	$1,200	
Rent expense, office	1,100	
Lease expense, computer	400	
Utilities expense	400	
Total expenses		3,100
Net income		$5,400

①

GAY GILLEN ETRAVEL
Statement of Owner's Equity
Month Ended April 30, 20X1

Gay Gillen, capital, April 1, 20X1	$ 0	
Add: Investments by owner	30,000	
Net income for the month	5,400	
	35,400	
Less: Withdrawals by owner	(2,100)	
Gay Gillen, capital, April 30, 20X1	$33,300	

②

GAY GILLEN ETRAVEL
Balance Sheet
April 30, 20X1

Assets		Liabilities	
Cash	$20,000	Accounts payable	$ 200
Accounts receivable	2,000		
Office supplies	500	**Owner's Equity**	
Land	11,000	Gay Gillen, capital	33,300
		Total liabilities and	
Total assets	$33,500	owner's equity	$33,500

GAY GILLEN ETRAVEL
Statement of Cash Flows*
Month Ended April 30, 20X1

Cash flows from **operating** activities:		
Receipts:		
Collections from customers ($5,500 + $1,000)		$ 6,500
Payments:		
To suppliers ($1,100 + $400 + $400 + $300)	$ (2,200)	
To employees	(1,200)	(3,400)
Net cash inflow from operating activities		3,100
Cash flows from **investing** activities:		
Acquisition of land	$(20,000)	
Sale of land	9,000	
Net cash outflow from investing activities		(11,000)
Cash flows from **financing** activities:		
Investment by owner	$ 30,000	
Withdrawal by owner	(2,100)	
Net cash inflow from financing activities		27,900
Net increase in cash		20,000
Cash balance, April 1, 20X1		0
Cash balance, April 30, 20X1		$20,000

③

*Chapter 17 explains how to prepare this statement.

DAILY EXERCISE 1-9

DAILY EXERCISE 1-10

DAILY EXERCISE 1-11

DAILY EXERCISE 1-12

DAILY EXERCISE 1-13

DAILY EXERCISE 1-14

DAILY EXERCISE 1-15

DAILY EXERCISE 1-16

DAILY EXERCISE 1-17

DAILY EXERCISE 1-18

The Decision Guidelines feature summarizes the chapter in terms of decisions businesspeople must make. Decision Guidelines appear in each chapter of this book. They serve as useful summaries of the decision-making process in business.

DECISION GUIDELINES

Major Business Decisions

DECISION	GUIDELINES
How to organize the business?	If a single owner—a *proprietorship*. If two or more owners, but not incorporated—a *partnership*. If the business issues stock to stockholders—a *corporation*.
What to account for?	Account for the business, a separate entity apart from its owner *(entity concept)*. Account for transactions and events that affect the business and can be measured objectively *(reliability principle)*.
How much to record for assets and liabilities?	Actual historical amount *(cost principle)*.
How to organize the various effects of a transaction?	The accounting equation: Assets = Liabilities + Owner's Equity
How to measure profits and losses?	Income statement: Revenues − Expenses = Net Income (or Net Loss)
Did owner's equity increase or decrease?	Statement of owner's equity: Beginning capital + Owner investments + Net income (or − Net loss) − Owner withdrawals = Ending capital
Where does the business stand financially?	Balance sheet (accounting equation): Assets = Liabilities + Owner's Equity
Where did the business's cash come from? Where did cash go?	Statement of cash flows *Operating activities* Net cash inflow (or outflow) + *Investing activities* Net cash inflow (or outflow) + *Financing activities* Net cash inflow (or outflow) = Net increase (decrease) in cash

REVIEW ACCOUNTING AND THE BUSINESS ENVIRONMENT

SUMMARY PROBLEM

Jill Smith opens an apartment-location business near a college campus. She is the sole owner of the proprietorship, which she names Campus Apartment Locators. During the first month of operations, July 20X1, she engages in the following transactions:
a. Smith invests $35,000 of personal funds to start the business.
b. She purchases on account office supplies costing $350.
c. Smith pays cash of $30,000 to acquire a lot next to the campus. She intends to use the land as a future building site for her business office.
d. Smith locates apartments for clients and receives cash of $1,900.
e. She pays $100 on the account payable she created in transaction (b).
f. She pays $2,000 of personal funds for a vacation.
g. She pays cash expenses for office rent, $400, and utilities, $100.
h. The business sells office supplies to another business for its cost of $150.
i. Smith withdraws cash of $1,200 for personal use.

www.prenhall.com/horngren

End-of-Chapter Assessment

1. Analyze the preceding transactions in terms of their effects on the accounting equation of Campus Apartment Locators. Use Exhibit 1-6 as a guide, but show balances only after the last transaction.
2. Prepare the income statement, statement of owner's equity, and balance sheet of the business after recording the transactions. Use Exhibit 1-7 as a guide.

Solution

Requirement 1

PANEL A—Details of transactions

(a) Smith invested $35,000 cash to start the business.
(b) Purchased $350 of office supplies on account.
(c) Paid $30,000 to acquire land as a future building site.
(d) Earned service revenue and received cash of $1,900.
(e) Paid $100 on account.
(f) Paid for a personal vacation, which is not a transaction of the business.
(g) Paid cash expenses for rent, $400, and utilities, $100.
(h) Sold office supplies for cost of $150.
(i) Withdrew $1,200 cash for personal use.

PANEL B—Analysis of transactions:

	Cash	+	Office Supplies	+	Land	=	Accounts Payable	+	Jill Smith, Capital	Type of Owner's Equity Transaction
(a)	+35,000								+35,000	Owner investment
(b)			+350				+350			
(c)	−30,000				+30,000					
(d)	+ 1,900								+ 1,900	Service revenue
(e)	− 100						−100			
(f)	Not a transaction of the business									
(g)	− 400								− 400	Rent expense
	− 100								− 100	Utilities expense
(h)	+ 150		−150							
(i)	− 1,200								− 1,200	Owner withdrawal
Bal.	5,250		200		30,000		250		35,200	

Assets = 35,450   Liabilities + Owner's Equity = 35,450

Requirement 2   **Financial Statements of Campus Apartment Locators**

CAMPUS APARTMENT LOCATORS
Income Statement
Month Ended July 31, 20X1

Revenue:		
Service revenue...............		$1,900
Expenses:		
Rent expense...................	$400	
Utilities expense	100	
Total expenses		500
Net income..........................		$1,400

CAMPUS APARTMENT LOCATORS
Statement of Owner's Equity
Month Ended July 31, 20X1

Jill Smith, capital, July 1, 20X1	$	0
Add: Investment by owner		35,000
Net income for the month		1,400
		36,400
Less: Withdrawals by owner		(1,200)
Jill Smith, capital, July 31, 20X1		$35,200

CAMPUS APARTMENT LOCATORS
Balance Sheet
July 31, 20X1

Assets		Liabilities	
Cash	$ 5,250	Accounts payable	$ 250
Office supplies	200		
Land	30,000	**Owner's Equity**	
		Jill Smith, capital	35,200
		Total liabilities and	
Total assets	$35,450	owner's equity	$35,450

LESSONS LEARNED

1. **Use accounting vocabulary.** Accounting is an information system for measuring, processing, and communicating financial information. As the "language of business," accounting helps a wide range of decision makers.

2. **Apply accounting concepts and principles to analyze business situations.** *Generally accepted accounting principles (GAAP)* guide accountants in their work. Accountants use the entity concept to keep the business's records separate from other economic units. Other important guidelines are the *reliability principle,* the *cost principle,* the *going-concern concept,* and the *stable-monetary-unit concept.*

3. **Use the accounting equation to describe an organization's financial position.** In its most common form, the accounting equation is

    Assets = Liabilities + Owner's Equity

4. **Use the accounting equation to analyze business transactions.** A transaction is any event that both affects the financial position of a business entity and can be reliably recorded. Transactions affect a business's assets, liabilities, and owner's equity.

5. **Prepare and use the financial statements.** The *financial statements* communicate information for decision making by an entity's managers, owners, and creditors and by government agencies. The *income statement* summarizes the entity's operations in terms of revenues earned and expenses incurred during a specific period. The *statement of owner's equity* reports the changes in owner's equity during the period. The *balance sheet* lists the entity's assets, liabilities, and owner's equity at a specific time. The *statement of cash flows* reports the cash receipts and the cash payments during the period.

6. **Evaluate the performance of a business.** High net income indicates success in business; net loss indicates a bad business year.

ACCOUNTING VOCABULARY

Accounting has a special vocabulary and it is important that you understand the following terms. They are explained in the chapter and also in the glossary at the end of the book.

account payable (p. 12)
account receivable (p. 12)
accounting (p. 5)
accounting equation (p. 11)
asset (p. 11)
balance sheet (p. 17)
capital (p. 11)
certified management accountant (CMA) (p. 7)
certified public accountant (CPA) (p. 7)
corporation (p. 9)

entity (p. 10)
expense (p. 12)
financial accounting (p. 6)
Financial Accounting Standards Board (FASB) (p. 7)
financial statements (p. 5)
generally accepted accounting principles (GAAP) (p. 9)
income statement (p. 17)
liability (p. 11)
management accounting (p. 7)
net earnings (p. 15)

net income (p. 15)
net loss (p. 15)
net profit (p. 15)
note payable (p. 12)
note receivable (p. 12)
owner's equity (p. 11)
owner withdrawals (p. 12)
partnership (p. 9)
proprietorship (p. 8)
revenue (p. 12)
shareholder (p. 9)
statement of cash flows (p. 17)

statement of earnings (p. 17) statement of operations (p. 17) stockholder (p. 9)
statement of financial position statement of owner's equity transaction (p. 13)
    (p. 17)   (p. 17)

QUESTIONS

1. Distinguish between accounting and bookkeeping.
2. Identify five users of accounting information, and explain how they use it.
3. What organization formulates generally accepted accounting principles? Is this organization a government agency?
4. Why are ethical standards important in accounting? Which organization directs its standards toward independent auditors? Which organization directs its standards more toward management accountants?
5. Why is the entity concept so important to accounting?
6. Briefly describe the reliability principle.
7. What role does the cost principle play in accounting?
8. If *assets = liabilities + owner's equity*, then how can liabilities be expressed?
9. Explain the difference between an account receivable and an account payable.

10. Give a more descriptive title for the balance sheet. What feature of the balance sheet gives this financial statement its name?
11. Give another title for the income statement. Which financial statement is like a snapshot of the entity at a specific time? Which financial statement is like a video of the entity's operations during a period of time?
12. What information does the statement of owner's equity report?
13. Give a synonym for the owner's equity of a proprietorship.
14. What piece of information flows from the income statement to the statement of owner's equity? What information flows from the statement of owner's equity to the balance sheet? What balance sheet item is explained by the statement of cash flows?

ASSESS YOUR PROGRESS

DAILY EXERCISES

Applying accounting concepts and principles
(Obj. 2)

DE1-1 Suppose you are starting a business, Montvale Delivery Service, that will provide delivery services for law firms in your city. In organizing the business and setting up its accounting records, consider the following:

1. In keeping the books of the business, you must decide the amount to record for assets purchased and liabilities incurred. At what amount should you record assets and liabilities? Which accounting concept or principle provides guidance?
2. Should you account for your personal assets and personal liabilities along with the assets and the liabilities of the business, or should you keep the two sets of records separate? Why? Which accounting concept or principle provides guidance?

Explaining assets, liabilities, owner's equity
(Obj. 1)

DE1-2 Shortly after starting Gifts for You, you realize the need for a bank loan in order to purchase office equipment. In evaluating your loan request, the banker asks about the assets and liabilities of your business. In particular, he wants to know the amount of your owner's equity. In your own words, explain the differences among *assets, liabilities,* and *owner's equity.* Give the mathematical relationship among assets, liabilities, and owner's equity.

Explaining revenues, expenses
(Obj. 1)

DE1-3 Gay Gillen eTravel has been open for one year, and Gillen wants to know the amount of the business's profit (net income) or net loss for the year. First, she must identify the revenues earned and the expenses incurred during the year. What are *revenues* and *expenses?* How do revenues and expenses enter into the determination of net income or net loss? Review the definitions on page 12 and Exhibit 1-7 on page 20.

Using the accounting equation
(Obj. 3)

DE1-4 You begin Montvale Delivery Service by investing $2,000 of your own money in a business bank account. Before starting operations, you borrow $8,000 cash by signing a note payable to Summit Bank. Write the business's accounting equation (page 12) after completing these transactions.

Using the accounting equation
(Obj. 3)

DE1-5 Brenda Trujillo owns Town East Travel, near the campus of Birmingham College. The business has cash of $5,000 and furniture that cost $12,000. Debts include accounts payable of $1,000 and a $6,000 note payable. How much equity does Trujillo have in the business? Using Trujillo's figures, write the accounting equation (page 11) of the travel agency.

Analyzing transactions
(Obj. 4)

DE1-6 Review transaction 2 of Gay Gillen eTravel, on page 13. In that transaction, Gillen's business purchased land for $20,000. To buy the land, Gillen was obligated to pay for it. Why, then, did she record no liability in this transaction?

Analyzing transactions
(Obj. 4)

DE1-7 Study Gay Gillen's transaction 4 on page 14. Gillen recorded revenues she earned from providing travel planning services for clients. Suppose the amount of revenue earned in transaction 4 was $3,500 instead of $5,500. How much are the business's cash and total assets after the transaction? How much is Gay Gillen, Capital?

DE1-8 Review transaction 9 of Gay Gillen eTravel, on page 16. Gillen collected cash from a client for whom she had provided travel services earlier. Why did the travel agency not record any revenue in transaction 9?

Analyzing transactions
(Obj. 4)

DE1-9 Return to Gay Gillen's first business transaction on page 13. Gillen deposited $30,000 in a business bank account to start her company (assume Gillen started on April 2, 20X1). Prepare the travel agency's balance sheet on April 2, 20X1, immediately after the first transaction. The figures are given on page 13, and Exhibit 1-7 (page 20), shows the format of the balance sheet.

Preparing a balance sheet
(Obj. 5)

Note: This exercise shows that financial statements can be prepared at any time. Usually, however, they are prepared at the end of the accounting period.

DE1-10 Examine Exhibit 1-6 on page 18. The exhibit summarizes the transactions of Gay Gillen eTravel for the month of April 20X1. Suppose Gillen has completed only the first seven transactions and needs a bank loan on April 21, 20X1. The vice president of the bank requires financial statements to support all loan requests.

Preparing the financial statements
(Obj. 5)

Prepare the income statement, statement of owner's equity, and balance sheet that Gay Gillen would present to the banker after completing the first seven transactions on April 21, 20X1. Exhibit 1-7, page 20, shows the format of these financial statements.

DE1-11 Gay Gillen wishes to know how well her business performed during April. The income statement in Exhibit 1-7, page 20, helps answer this question. Write the formula for the income statement as an equation: $X - Y = Z$. What are X, Y, and Z?

Format of the income statement
(Obj. 5)

DE1-12 Examine Exhibit 1-7 on page 20. The exhibit gives the financial statements of Gay Gillen eTravel at the end of the company's first month of operations. Focus on the arrows that show the flow of information from statement to statement, and then answer these questions:

Using the financial statements
(Obj. 5)

1. Which statement measures net income or net loss? Into which other statement does net income flow? That is, where is net income's final resting place in the financial statements?
2. Which statement lists the assets, liabilities, and owner's equity of the business? Which of these elements is most directly affected by net income?

DE1-13 Return to Exhibit 1-7 on page 20, which gives the financial statements of Gay Gillen eTravel, at April 30, 20X1. Suppose Gay Gillen's travel agency paid Salary Expense of $2,500 for April instead of the actual amount of $1,200.

Evaluating performance
(Obj. 6)

1. What would be the amount of the business's net income or net loss for April?
2. What would be the amount of Gay Gillen's capital at April 30?
3. What would be the ending amount of cash at April 30?

DE1-14 Exhibit 1-7, page 20, gives the statement of cash flows of Gay Gillen eTravel for the month of April. Study the exhibit and answer these questions to solidify your understanding of the accounting process and the financial statements:

Using the statement of cash flows
(Obj. 5)

1. The statement of cash flows is organized in terms of three categories of *activities*. What are the three main categories of cash-flow activities?
2. Why do you think collections from customers is an operating activity? Why is the acquisition of land an investing activity? Why is the business's receipt of cash from the investment by the owner a financing activity? Answer in your own words.
3. How does the statement of cash flows relate to the balance sheet?

DE1-15 Montvale Delivery Service has just completed operations for the year ended December 31, 20X3. This is the third year of operations for the company. As the proprietor, you want to know how well the business performed during the year. You also wonder where the business stands financially at the end of the year. To address these questions, you have assembled the following data:

Preparing the income statement
(Obj. 5)

Salary expense............	$32,000	Insurance expense............	$ 4,000
Accounts payable...........	8,000	Service revenue............	101,000
Owner, capital,		Accounts receivable...........	17,000
December 31, 20X2	13,000	Supplies expense............	1,000
Supplies	2,000	Cash........................	16,000
Withdrawals by owner	36,000	Fuel expense..............	6,000
Rent expense.............	8,000		

Prepare the income statement of Montvale Delivery Service for the year ended December 31, 20X3. Follow the format shown in Exhibit 1-7, page 20.

DE1-16 Use the data in Daily Exercise 1-15 to prepare the statement of owner's equity of Montvale Delivery Service for the year ended December 31, 20X3. Follow the format in Exhibit 1-7. Compute net income from the data in Daily Exercise 1-15.

Preparing the statement of owner's equity
(Obj. 5)

DE1-17 Use the data in Daily Exercise 1-15 to prepare the balance sheet of Montvale Delivery Service at December 31, 20X3. The year-end balance sheet will show where the business stands financially at the end of the year. Follow the format in Exhibit 1-7. Owner's equity (Owner, capital) at December 31, 20X3, is $27,000.

Preparing the balance sheet
(Obj. 5)

Note: Daily Exercise 1-18 should be used in conjunction with Daily Exercises 1-15, 1-16, and 1-17.

Evaluating performance
(Obj. 6)

DE1-18 Review the Montvale Delivery Service financial statements that you prepared for Daily Exercises 1-15, 1-16, and 1-17. Use the statements to evaluate the business's performance by answering these questions:

1. The income statement gives the results of operations. Did the business earn a profit or suffer a loss? The owner had hoped to earn at least $40,000. Will he be pleased or disappointed?
2. The statement of owner's equity reveals whether the owner's capital increased or decreased during the year—and why. Did Montvale Delivery Service's equity increase or decrease? Is this a good sign or a bad sign about the company? State your reason.
3. The balance sheet reports the financial position of the business. Which are greater, total assets or total liabilities? By how much? What is the name of the difference between assets and liabilities? Is the financial position of Montvale Delivery Service strong or weak? Give your reason.

EXERCISES

Explaining the income statement and the balance sheet
(Obj. 1)

E1-1 Lisa Malesovas publishes a travel magazine. In need of cash, she asks Community Bank & Trust for a loan. The bank's procedures require borrowers to submit financial statements to show likely results of operations for the first year and likely financial position at the end of the first year. With little knowledge of accounting, Malesovas doesn't know how to proceed. Explain to her the information provided by the balance sheet and the income statement. Indicate why a lender would require this information.

Business transactions
(Obj. 2)

E1-2 For each of the following items, give an example of a business transaction that has the described effect on the accounting equation:

a. Increase an asset and increase a liability.
b. Increase one asset and decrease another asset.
c. Decrease an asset and decrease owner's equity.
d. Decrease an asset and decrease a liability.
e. Increase an asset and increase owner's equity.

Transaction analysis
(Obj. 2)

E1-3 Sterling Design, a proprietorship (Eric Sterling, owner), experienced the following events. State whether each event (1) increased, (2) decreased, or (3) had no effect on the total assets of the business. Identify any specific asset affected.

a. Sterling Design received a cash investment from the owner.
b. Cash purchase of land for a building site.
c. Paid cash on accounts payable.
d. Purchased machinery and equipment for a manufacturing plant; signed a promissory note in payment.
e. Performed service for a customer on account.
f. Sterling withdrew cash from the business for personal use.
g. Received cash from a customer on account receivable.
h. Sterling used personal funds to purchase a swimming pool for his home.
i. Sold land for a price equal to the cost of the land; received cash.
j. Borrowed money from the bank.

Accounting equation
(Obj. 3)

E1-4 Compute the missing amount in the accounting equation for each entity:

	Assets	Liabilities	Owner's Equity
Company A	$?	$61,800	$34,400
Company B	65,900	?	34,000
Company C	81,700	79,800	?

Accounting equation
(Obj. 4, 5)

E1-5 **Oracle Corporation** started 19X9 with total assets of $5,819 million and total liabilities of $2,861 million. At the end of 19X9, Oracle's total assets stood at $7,260 million, and total liabilities were $3,565 million.

Required

1. Did the owners' equity of Oracle Corporation increase or decrease during 19X9? By how much?
2. Identify two possible reasons for the change in owners' equity of Oracle during the year.

E1-6 Telemarketing Associates' balance sheet data at May 31, 20X2, and June 30, 20X2, follow:

Accounting equation (Obj. 4, 5)

	May 31, 20X2	June 30, 20X2
Total assets	$150,000	$195,000
Total liabilities	109,000	131,000

Required

Following are three assumptions about investments and withdrawals by the owner of the business during June. For each assumption, compute the amount of net income or net loss of the business during June 20X2.

1. The owner invested $5,000 in the business and made no withdrawals.
2. The owner made no additional investments in the business but withdrew $11,000 for personal use.
3. The owner invested $41,000 in the business and withdrew $6,000 for personal use.

E1-7 Indicate the effects of the following business transactions on the accounting equation. Transaction (a) is answered as a guide.

Transaction analysis (Obj. 4)

a. Received cash of $18,000 from the owner, who was investing in the business.
   Answer: Increase asset (Cash)
              Increase owner's equity (Capital)
b. Paid $700 cash to purchase office supplies.
c. Performed legal service for a client on account, $3,000.
d. Purchased on account office furniture at a cost of $500.
e. Received cash on account, $900.
f. Paid cash on account, $250.
g. Sold land for $12,000, which was our cost of the land.
h. Performed legal service for a client and received cash of $680.
i. Paid monthly office rent of $500.

E1-8 Lance Huber opens a medical practice. During the first month of operation, May, the business, entitled Lance Huber, M.D., experienced the following events.

Transaction analysis; accounting equation (Obj. 2, 4)

May 6	Huber invested $90,000 in the business by opening a bank account in the name of Lance Huber, M.D.
9	Huber paid $55,000 cash for land. He plans to build an office building on the land.
12	He purchased medical supplies for $2,000 on account.
15	Huber officially opened for business.
15–31	During the rest of the month, he treated patients and earned service revenue of $7,000, receiving cash.
15–31	He paid cash expenses: employees' salaries, $1,400; office rent, $1,000; utilities, $300.
28	He sold supplies to another physician for the cost of those supplies, $500.
31	He paid $1,500 on account.

Required

Analyze the effects of these events on the accounting equation of the medical practice of Lance Huber, M.D. Use a format similar to that of Exhibit 1-6, with headings for Cash; Medical Supplies; Land; Accounts Payable; and Lance Huber, Capital.

E1-9 The analysis of the transactions that Sinclair Leasing completed during its first month of operations follows. The company buys equipment that it leases out to earn revenue. The owner of the business made only one investment to start the business and no withdrawals.

Business organization, transactions, and net income (Obj. 1, 2, 3, 4)

	Cash	+	Accounts Receivable	+	Lease Equipment	=	Accounts Payable	+	Owner Capital
(a)	+50,000								+50,000
(b)	− 750				+ 750				
(c)					+100,000		+100,000		
(d)			+800						+ 800
(e)	− 2,000								− 2,000
(f)	+ 6,600								+ 6,600
(g)	−10,000						− 10,000		
(h)	+ 150		−150						

Required

1. Describe each transaction of Sinclair Leasing.
2. If these transactions fully describe the operations of Sinclair Leasing during the month, what was the amount of net income or net loss?

Business organization, balance sheet

(Obj. 1, 2, 5)

E1-10 The balances of the assets and liabilities of TELETAX as of September 30, 20X2, follow. Also included are the revenue and expense figures of this tax-preparation business for September.

Delivery service revenue	$9,100	Office equipment	$15,500
Accounts receivable	6,900	Supplies	600
Accounts payable	1,750	Note payable	8,000
M. Dalton, capital	?	Rent expense	500
Salary expense	2,000	Cash	950

Required

1. What type of business organization is TELETAX? How can you tell?
2. Prepare the balance sheet of TELETAX as of September 30, 20X2.
3. What does the balance sheet report—financial position or operating results? Which financial statement reports the other information?

Income statement

(Obj. 2, 5)

E1-11 The assets, liabilities, owner's equity, revenues, and expenses of Venecor Import Service at December 31, 20X3, the end of its first year of business, have the following balances. During the year, T. Venecor, the owner, invested $15,000 in the business.

Office furniture	$ 45,000	Note payable	$30,000
Utilities expense	6,800	Rent expense	24,000
Accounts payable	3,300	Cash	3,600
T. Venecor, capital	27,100	Office supplies	4,800
Service revenue	161,200	Salary expense	49,000
Accounts receivable	9,000	Salaries payable	2,000
Supplies expense	4,000	Property tax expense	1,200

Required

1. Prepare the income statement of Venecor Import Service for the year ended December 31, 20X3. What is the result of Venecor's operations for 20X3?
2. What was the amount of the proprietor's withdrawals during the year?

Evaluating the performance of a real company

(Obj. 6)

E1-12 In this exercise you will practice using the actual data of a well-known company. The 19X9 annual report of **Toys "Я" Us** reported net sales revenue of $11,170 million. Total expenses for the year were $11,302 million. Toys "Я" Us ended the year with total assets of $7,899 million, and the company owed debts totaling $4,275 million at year end.

During the preceding year, 19X8, Toys "Я" Us earned net income of $490 million. At year-end 19X8, Toys "Я" Us reported total assets of $7,963 million and total liabilities of $3,535 million.

Required

1. Compute Toys "Я" Us's net income for 19X9. Did net income increase or decrease from 19X8 to 19X9, and by how much?
2. Did Toys "Я" Us's owners' equity increase or decrease during 19X9? By how much?
3. Toys "Я" Us management strives for a steady increase in net income and owners' equity. How would you rate Toys "Я" Us's performance for 19X9—excellent, fair, or poor? Give your reason.

Preparing a statement of cash flows

(Obj. 5)

E1-13 During 19X8, **Lands' End, Inc.**, the catalog merchant located in Dodgeville, Wisconsin, experienced the following cash flows (adapted):

	Millions
Collections from customers	$1,257
Payments to suppliers and employees	1,284
Purchases of assets	35
Dividend payments to owners (same as withdrawals by owner)	10
Cash balance, beginning of year	93

Required

Prepare the statement of cash flows of Lands' End, Inc., for the year. Follow the format of the statement of cash flows in Exhibit 1-7, page 20.

CHALLENGE EXERCISE

E1-14 Compute the missing amounts for each of the following companies. For each company, you will need to prepare a statement of owner's equity.

Using the financial statements (Obj. 5)

	Circle Co.	Triangle Co.	Square Co.
Beginning:			
Assets	$105,000	$ 50,000	$110,000
Liabilities	50,000	20,000	60,000
Ending:			
Assets	$160,000	$ 70,000	$?
Liabilities	70,000	35,000	80,000
Owner's Equity:			
Investments by owner...............	$?	$ 0	$ 10,000
Withdrawals by owner.............	100,000	40,000	70,000
Income Statement:			
Revenues....................................	$430,000	$230,000	$400,000
Expenses	320,000	?	300,000

PROBLEMS

(Group A)

P1-1A Blake Dubis practiced law with a partnership for five years after graduating from law school. Recently he resigned his position to open his own law office, which he operates as a proprietorship. The name of the new entity is Blake Dubis, Attorney. Dubis experienced the following events during the organizing phase of his new business and its first month of operations. Some of the events were personal and did not affect his law practice. Others were business transactions and should be accounted for by the business.

Entity concept, transaction analysis, accounting equation (Obj. 2, 4)

Feb.	4	Dubis received $90,000 cash from his former law-firm partners.
	5	Dubis deposited $80,000 cash in a new business bank account entitled Blake Dubis, Attorney.
	6	Dubis paid $300 cash for letterhead stationery for his new law office.
	7	Dubis purchased office furniture for his law office. He agreed to pay the account payable, $7,000, within six months.
	10	Dubis sold 500 shares of IBM stock, which he and his wife had owned for several years, receiving $75,000 cash from his stockbroker.
	11	Dubis deposited the $75,000 cash from sale of the IBM stock in his personal bank account.
	12	A representative of a large company telephoned Dubis and told him of the company's intention to transfer its legal business to the new entity of Blake Dubis, Attorney.
	18	Dubis finished court hearings on behalf of a client and submitted his bill for legal services, $5,000. Dubis expected to collect from this client within two weeks.
	25	Dubis paid office rent, $1,000.
	28	Dubis withdrew $1,000 cash from the business for personal living expenses.

Required

1. Classify each of these events as one of the following:
   a. A business transaction to be accounted for by the proprietorship of Blake Dubis, Attorney.
   b. A business-related event but not a transaction to be accounted for by the proprietorship of Blake Dubis, Attorney.
   c. A personal transaction not to be accounted for by the proprietorship of Blake Dubis, Attorney.
2. Analyze the effects of the above events on the accounting equation of the proprietorship of Blake Dubis, Attorney. Use a format similar to that in Exhibit 1-6.

P1-2A The bookkeeper of Trésoro Publishing Co. prepared the company's balance sheet while the accountant was ill. The balance sheet contains numerous errors. In particular, the bookkeeper knew that the balance sheet should balance, so he plugged in the owner's equity amount needed to achieve this balance. The owner's equity amount, however, is not correct. All other amounts are accurate, but some are out of place.

Balance sheet (Obj. 2, 5)

TRÉSORO PUBLISHING CO.
Balance Sheet
Month Ended July 31, 20X3

Assets		Liabilities	
Cash..................................	$12,000	Accounts receivable	$ 3,000
Office supplies	1,000	Service revenue	68,000
Land	44,000	Property tax expense	800
Salary expense.................	2,500	Accounts payable	9,000
Office furniture...............	8,000		
Note payable..................	16,000	**Owner's Equity**	
Rent expense.................	4,000	Owner's equity.........................	6,700
Total assets.....................	$87,500	Total liabilities	$87,500

Required

1. Prepare the correct balance sheet, and date it correctly. Compute total assets, total liabilities, and owner's equity.
2. Identify the accounts that should *not* be presented on the balance sheet and state why you excluded them from the correct balance sheet you prepared for requirement 1.

Balance sheet, entity concept
(Obj. 2, 3, 5)

P1-3A Olivia Casinelli is a realtor. She buys and sells properties on her own, and she also earns commissions as a real estate agent for buyers and sellers. She organized her business as a proprietorship on November 24, 20X4. Consider the following facts as of November 30, 20X4.

a. Casinelli owed $55,000 on a note payable for some undeveloped land that had been acquired by her business for a total price of $100,000.
b. Casinelli's business had spent $20,000 for a Century 21 real estate franchise, which entitled her to represent herself as a Century 21 agent. Century 21 is a national affiliation of independent real estate agents. This franchise is a business asset.
c. Casinelli owed $60,000 on a personal mortgage on her personal residence, which she acquired in 20X1 for a total price of $150,000.
d. Casinelli had $8,000 in her personal bank account and $22,000 in her business bank account.
e. Casinelli owed $1,800 on a personal charge account with the Neiman-Marcus store.
f. Casinelli acquired business furniture for $17,000 on November 25. Of this amount, her business owed $6,000 on open account at November 30.
g. Office supplies on hand at the real estate office totaled $1,000.
   (1) Prepare the balance sheet of the real estate business of Olivia Casinelli, Realtor, at November 30, 20X4.
   (2) Identify the personal items that would not be reported on the balance sheet of the business.

Business transactions and analysis
(Obj. 4)

P1-4A Mandarin Enterprises was recently formed. The balance of each item in the company's accounting equation is shown for October 10 and for each of the nine following business days.

	Cash	Accounts Receivable	Supplies	Land	Accounts Payable	Owner's Equity
Oct. 10	$ 4,000	$4,000	$1,000	$ 8,000	$4,000	$13,000
11	13,000	4,000	1,000	8,000	4,000	22,000
12	6,000	4,000	1,000	15,000	4,000	22,000
15	6,000	4,000	3,000	15,000	6,000	22,000
16	5,000	4,000	3,000	15,000	5,000	22,000
17	7,000	2,000	3,000	15,000	5,000	22,000
18	15,000	2,000	3,000	15,000	5,000	30,000
19	12,000	2,000	3,000	15,000	2,000	30,000
22	11,000	2,000	4,000	15,000	2,000	30,000
23	3,000	2,000	4,000	15,000	2,000	22,000

Required

Assuming that a single transaction took place on each day, briefly describe the transaction that most likely occurred on each day, beginning with October 11. Indicate which accounts were increased or decreased and by what amount. No revenue or expense transactions occurred on these dates.

Income statement, statement of owner's equity, balance sheet (Obj. 5)

P1-5A Presented below are (a) the assets and liabilities of Starmate Talent Search as of December 31, and (b) the revenues and expenses of the company for the year ended on that date. The items are listed in alphabetical order.

Accounts payable	$ 19,000	Land	$ 60,000
Accounts receivable	12,000	Note payable	85,000
Advertising expense	13,000	Property tax expense	4,000
Building	170,000	Rent expense	23,000
Cash	14,000	Salary expense	63,000
Equipment	20,000	Salary payable	1,000
Insurance expense	2,000	Service revenue	178,000
Interest expense	9,000	Supplies	3,000

The owner's beginning balance, Brian Sartor, Capital, was $150,000, and during the year Sartor withdrew $40,000 for personal use.

Required

1. Prepare Starmate's income statement for the year ended December 31 of the current year.
2. Prepare the company's statement of owner's equity for the year ended December 31.
3. Prepare the company's balance sheet at December 31.
4. Answer these questions about the company:
   a. Was the result of operations for the year a profit or a loss? How much?
   b. Did Sartor drain off all the earnings for the year, or did he build the company's capital during the period? How will his actions affect the company's ability to borrow in the future?
   c. How much in total economic resources does the company have as it moves into the new year? How much does the company owe? What is the dollar amount of Sartor's equity interest in the business at the end of the year?

Transaction analysis, accounting equation, financial statements (Obj. 4, 5)

P1-6A Helen Ingersoll owns and operates an interior design studio called Ingersoll Interiors. The following amounts summarize the financial position of her business on August 31, 20X2:

	Assets			=	Liabilities	+	Owner's Equity
		Accounts			Accounts		Helen Ingersoll,
	Cash +	Receivable +	Supplies + Land =		Payable +		Capital
Bal.	2,250	1,500	12,000		8,000		7,750

During September 20X2, the following events occurred.

a. Ingersoll inherited $20,000 and deposited the cash in the business bank account.
b. Performed services for a client and received cash of $700.
c. Paid off the beginning balance of accounts payable.
d. Purchased supplies on account, $1,000.
e. Collected cash from a customer on account, $1,000.
f. Invested personal cash of $1,000 in the business.
g. Consulted on the interior design of a major office building and billed the client for services rendered, $2,400.
h. Recorded the following business expenses for the month:
   (1) Paid office rent, $900.
   (2) Paid advertising, $100.
i. Sold supplies to another business for $150 cash, which was the cost of the supplies.
j. Withdrew cash of $1,100 for personal use.

Required

1. Analyze the effects of the preceding transactions on the accounting equation of Ingersoll Interiors. Adapt the format of Exhibit 1-6.
2. Prepare the income statement of Ingersoll Interiors for the month ended September 30, 20X2. List expenses in decreasing order by amount.
3. Prepare the entity's statement of owner's equity for the month ended September 30, 20X2.
4. Prepare the balance sheet of Ingersoll Interiors at September 30, 20X2.

Entity concept, transaction
analysis, accounting equation
(Obj. 2, 4)

P1-1B Sharon Marsh practiced law with a partnership for ten years after graduating from law school. Recently she resigned her position to open her own law office, which she operates as a proprietorship. The name of the new entity is Sharon Marsh, Attorney. Marsh experienced the following events during the organizing phase of her new business and its first month of operation. Some of the events were personal and did not affect the law practice. Others were business transactions and should be accounted for by the business.

July 1	Marsh sold 1,000 shares of Eastman Kodak stock, which she had owned for several years, receiving $68,000 cash from her stockbroker.
2	Marsh deposited the $68,000 cash from sale of the Eastman Kodak stock in her personal bank account.
3	Marsh received $170,000 cash from her former law-firm partners.
5	Marsh deposited $100,000 cash in a new business bank account entitled Sharon Marsh, Attorney.
6	A representative of a large company telephoned Marsh and told her of the company's intention to transfer its legal business to the new entity of Sharon Marsh, Attorney.
7	Marsh paid $450 cash for letterhead stationery for her new law office.
9	Marsh purchased office furniture for the law office, agreeing to pay the account payable, $9,500, within three months.
23	Marsh finished court hearings on behalf of a client and submitted her bill for legal services, $3,000. She expected to collect from this client within one month.
30	Marsh paid office rent, $1,900.
31	Marsh withdrew $5,500 cash from the business for personal living expenses.

Required

1. Classify each of these events as one of the following:
   a. A business transaction to be accounted for by the proprietorship of Sharon Marsh, Attorney.
   b. A business-related event but not a transaction to be accounted for by the proprietorship of Sharon Marsh, Attorney.
   c. A personal transaction not to be accounted for by the proprietorship of Sharon Marsh, Attorney.

2. Analyze the effects of the preceding events on the accounting equation of the proprietorship of Sharon Marsh, Attorney. Use a format similar to Exhibit 1-6.

P1-2B The bookkeeper of Haynes Editorial Service prepared the balance sheet of the company while the accountant was ill. The balance sheet contains numerous errors. In particular, the bookkeeper knew that the balance sheet should balance, so he plugged in the owner's equity amount to achieve this balance. The owner's equity amount, however, is not correct. All other amounts are accurate, but some are out of place.

HAYNES EDITORIAL SERVICE
Balance Sheet
Month Ended October 31, 20X7

Assets		Liabilities	
Cash	$ 5,400	Notes receivable	$14,000
Insurance expense	300	Interest expense	2,000
Land	31,500	Office supplies	800
Salary expense	3,300	Accounts receivable	2,600
Office furniture	6,700	Note payable	21,000
Accounts payable	3,000		
Utilities expense	2,100	**Owner's Equity**	
		Owner's equity	11,900
Total assets	$52,300	Total liabilities	$52,300

Required

1. Prepare the correct balance sheet, and date it correctly. Compute total assets, total liabilities, and owner's equity.
2. Identify the accounts that should *not* be presented on the balance sheet and state why you excluded them from the correct balance sheet you prepared for requirement 1.

P1-3B Nik Tahari is a realtor. He buys and sells properties on his own, and he also earns commission as a real estate agent for buyers and sellers. He organized his business as a proprietorship on March 10, 20X2. Consider the following facts as of March 31, 20X2:

a. Tahari had $15,000 in his personal bank account and $7,000 in his business bank account.

b. Office supplies on hand at the real estate office totaled $1,000.

c. Tahari's business had spent $15,000 for an Electronic Realty Associates (ERA) franchise, which entitled Tahari to represent himself as an ERA agent. ERA is a national affiliation of independent real estate agents. This franchise is a business asset.

d. Tahari owed $34,000 on a note payable for some undeveloped land that had been acquired by his business for a total price of $60,000.

e. Tahari owed $65,000 on a personal mortgage on his personal residence, which he acquired in 20X1 for a total price of $90,000.

f. Tahari owed $950 on a personal charge account with Sears.

g. Tahari had acquired business furniture for $12,000 on March 26. Of this amount, Tahari's business owed $6,000 on open account at March 31.

Required

1. Prepare the balance sheet of the real estate business of Nik Tahari, Realtor, at March 31, 20X2.
2. Identify the personal items that would not be reported on the balance sheet of the business.

P1-4B Royal Gulf Oil Company was recently formed. The balance of each item in the company's accounting equation follows for April 4 and for each of the nine business days given:

Business transactions and analysis
(Obj. 4)

	Cash	Accounts Receivable	Supplies	Land	Accounts Payable	Owner's Equity
Apr. 4	$2,000	$7,000	$ 800	$11,000	$3,800	$17,000
9	6,000	3,000	800	11,000	3,800	17,000
14	4,000	3,000	800	11,000	1,800	17,000
17	4,000	3,000	1,100	11,000	2,100	17,000
19	5,000	3,000	1,100	11,000	2,100	18,000
20	3,900	3,000	1,100	11,000	1,000	18,000
22	9,900	3,000	1,100	5,000	1,000	18,000
25	9,900	3,700	400	5,000	1,000	18,000
26	9,300	3,700	1,000	5,000	1,000	18,000
28	4,200	3,700	1,000	5,000	1,000	12,900

Required

Assuming that a single transaction took place on each day, describe briefly the transaction that most likely occurred on each day, beginning with April 9. Indicate which accounts were increased or decreased and by what amount. No revenue or expense transactions occurred on these dates.

P1-5B The amounts of (a) the assets and liabilities of Aspen Supply Co. as of December 31, 20X4, and (b) the revenues and expenses of the company for the year ended on that date follow. The items are listed in alphabetical order.

Income statement, statement of owner's equity, balance sheet
(Obj. 5)

L Accounts payable....................	$12,000	L Note payable...........................	$ 31,000
A Accounts receivable................	3,000	E Property tax expense..............	2,000
A Building..................................	56,000	E Rent expense.........................	14,000
A Cash......................................	7,000	E Salary expense.......................	38,000
A Equipment.............................	21,000	R Service revenue......................	108,000
E Interest expense......................	4,000	A Supplies	7,000
L Interest payable	1,000	E Utilities expense	3,000
A Land......................................	8,000		

The owner's beginning balance, Linda Elkins, Capital, was $43,000, and during the year Elkins withdrew $32,000 for personal use.

Required

1. Prepare the income statement of Aspen Supply Co. for the year ended December 31, 20X4.
2. Prepare the company's statement of owner's equity for the year ended December 31, 20X4.
3. Prepare the company's balance sheet at December 31, 20X4.
4. Answer these questions about the company.
    a. Was the result of operations for the year a profit or a loss? How much?
    b. Did Elkins drain off all the earnings for the year, or did she build the company's capital during the period? How would her actions affect the company's ability to borrow in the future?

c. How much in total economic resources does the company have as it moves into the new year? How much does the company owe? What is the dollar amount of Elkins's equity interest in the business at the end of the year?

Transaction analysis, accounting equation, financial statements (Obj. 4, 5)

P1-6B Joel Clark owns and operates an interior design studio called Clark Design Studio. The following amounts summarize the financial position of his business on April 30, 20X5:

	Assets				= Liabilities	+ Owner's Equity
	Cash +	**Accounts** Receivable +	Supplies +	Land =	**Accounts** Payable +	**Joel Clark,** Capital
Bal.	1,720	3,240		24,100	5,400	23,660

During May 20X5, the following events occurred.

a. Clark received $12,000 as a gift and deposited the cash in the business bank account.
b. Paid off the beginning balance of accounts payable.
c. Performed services for a client and received cash of $1,100.
d. Collected cash from a customer on account, $750.
e. Purchased supplies on account, $720.
f. Consulted on the interior design of a major office building and billed the client for services rendered, $5,000.
g. Invested personal cash of $1,700 in the business.
h. Recorded the following business expenses for the month:
  (1) Paid office rent, $1,200.
  (2) Paid advertising, $660.
i. Sold supplies to another interior designer for $80 cash, which was the cost of the supplies.
j. Withdrew cash of $1,400 for personal use.

Required

1. Analyze the effects of the preceding transactions on the accounting equation of Clark Design Studio. Adapt the format of Exhibit 1-6.
2. Prepare the income statement of Clark Design Studio for the month ended May 31, 20X5. List expenses in decreasing order by amount.
3. Prepare the statement of owner's equity of Clark Design Studio for the month ended May 31, 20X5.
4. Prepare the balance sheet of Clark Design Studio at May 31, 20X5.

APPLY YOUR KNOWLEDGE

DECISION CASES

Using financial statements to evaluate a request for a loan (Obj. 1, 2, 6)

Case 1. The proprietors of two businesses, L. L. Sams Company and Melinda Garcia Career Services, have sought business loans from you. To decide whether to make the loans, you have requested their balance sheets.

L. L. SAMS COMPANY
Balance Sheet
August 31, 20X4

Assets		Liabilities	
Cash...	$ 9,000	Accounts payable....................	$ 12,000
Accounts receivable................	14,000	Note payable...........................	18,000
Merchandise inventory..........	85,000	Total liabilities........................	30,000
Store supplies	500		
Furniture and fixtures............	9,000	**Owner's Equity**	
Building..................................	80,000	L. L. Sams, capital...................	181,500
Land..	14,000	Total liabilities	
Total assets............................	$211,500	and owner's equity	$211,500

MELINDA GARCIA CAREER SERVICES
Balance Sheet
August 31, 20X4

Assets		Liabilities	
Cash..	$ 11,000	Accounts payable	$ 6,000
Accounts receivable................	7,000	Note payable.............................	168,000
Office supplies	1,000	Total liabilities..........................	174,000
Office furniture.......................	56,000		
Land	169,000	**Owner's Equity**	
		Melinda Garcia, capital...........	70,000
		Total liabilities and	
Total assets..............................	$244,000	owner's equity	$244,000

Required

1. Solely on the basis of these balance sheets, to which entity would you be more comfortable lending money? Explain fully, citing specific items and amounts from the balance sheets.
2. In addition to the balance sheet data, what other information would you require? Be specific.

Case 2. Camp Trinity conducts summer camps for children with disabilities. Samuel and Margaret Shields operate the camp near Leander, Texas. Because of the nature of its business, the camp experiences many unusual transactions. Evaluate each of the following transactions in terms of its effect on Camp Trinity's income statement and balance sheet.

Transaction analysis, effects on the financial statements (Obj. 4)

1. A camper suffered an injury that was not covered by insurance. Camp Trinity paid $900 for the child's medical care. How does this transaction affect the camp's income statement and balance sheet?
2. Camp Trinity sold land adjacent to the camp for $190,000, receiving cash of $70,000 and a note receivable for $120,000. When purchased five years earlier, the land cost Camp Trinity $100,000. How should the camp account for the sale of the land?
3. One camper's father is a physician. Camp Trinity allows this child to attend camp in return for the father's serving part-time in the camp infirmary for the two-week term. The standard fee for a camp term is $1,000. The physician's salary for this part-time work would be $1,000. How should Camp Trinity account for this arrangement?
4. A tornado damaged the camp dining hall. The cost to repair the damage will be $12,000 over and above what the insurance company will pay.

ETHICAL ISSUES

Ethical Issue 1. The chapter-opening story relates to the billions of dollars the tobacco companies have paid because of smoking-related illnesses. In particular, **Philip Morris**, a leading cigarette manufacturer, paid over $3 billion in 1998.

Required

1. Suppose you are the chief financial officer (CFO) responsible for the financial statements of Philip Morris. What ethical issue would you face as you consider what to report in your company's annual report about the cash payments? What is the ethical course of action for you to take in this situation?
2. What are some of the negative consequences to Philip Morris for not telling the truth? What are some of the negative consequences to Philip Morris for telling the truth?

Ethical Issue 2. The board of directors of Silvertron Corporation is meeting to discuss the past year's results before releasing financial statements to the public. The discussion includes this exchange: Amanda Blume, company president: "Well, this has not been a good year! Revenue is down and expenses are up—way up. If we don't do some fancy stepping, we'll report a loss for the third year in a row. I can temporarily transfer some land that I own into the company's name, and that will beef up our balance sheet. Kent, can you shave $500,000 from expenses? Then we can probably get the bank loan that we need."

Kent Kohler, company chief accountant: "Amanda, you are asking too much. Generally accepted accounting principles are designed to keep this sort of thing from happening."

Required

1. What is the fundamental ethical issue in this situation?
2. Discuss how Amanda Blume's proposals violate generally accepted accounting principles. Identify the specific concept or principle involved.

FINANCIAL STATEMENT CASE

Identifying items from a company's financial statements (Obj. 4)

This and similar cases in later chapters focus on the financial statements of a real company—**Target Corporation,** the upscale discount chain. As you work each problem, you will build your confidence in understanding and using the financial statements of real companies.

Refer to Target Corporation's financial statements in Appendix A at the end of the book.

Required

1. How much in cash (including cash equivalents) did Target Corporation have on January 29, 2000?
2. What were the company's total assets at January 29, 2000? At January 30, 1999?
3. Write the company's accounting equation at January 29, 2000, by filling in the dollar amounts:

ASSETS = LIABILITIES + STOCKHOLDERS' EQUITY

4. Identify total revenue for the year ended January 29, 2000 (fiscal year 1999). How much did total revenue increase or decrease in fiscal year 1999?
5. How much net income or net loss did Target experience for fiscal year 1999 and for fiscal year 1998? Was fiscal year 1999 a good year or a bad year compared to 1998? State your reasons.

TEAM PROJECTS

Project 1. You are opening a pet kennel. Your purpose is to earn a profit, so you will need to establish the business. Assume you organize as a proprietorship.

1. Make a detailed list of ten factors you must consider to establish the business.
2. Identify ten or more transactions that your business will undertake to open and operate the kennel.
3. Prepare the kennel's income statement, statement of owner's equity, and balance sheet at the end of the first month of operations before you have had time to pay all the business's bills. Use made-up figures and include a complete heading for each financial statement. Date the balance sheet as of August 31, 20XX.
4. Discuss how you will evaluate the success of your business and how you will decide whether to continue its operation.

Project 2. You are promoting a rock concert in your area. Your purpose is to earn a profit, so you will need to establish the business. Assume you organize as a proprietorship.

Required

1. Make a detailed list of ten factors you must consider to establish the business.
2. Describe ten of the items your business must arrange in order to promote and stage the rock concert.
3. Prepare your business's income statement, statement of owner's equity, and balance sheet on August 31, 20XX, immediately after the rock concert and before you have had time to pay all the business's bills and to collect all receivables. Use made-up amounts, and include a complete heading for each financial statement. For the income statement and the statement of owner's equity, assume the period is the three months ended August 31, 20XX.
4. Assume that you will continue to promote rock concerts if the venture is successful. If it is unsuccessful, you will terminate the business within three months after the concert. Discuss how you will evaluate the success of your venture and how you will decide whether to continue in business.

INTERNET EXERCISE

eBay

Hoover's Online, The Business Network offers information about companies, industries, people, and products. For researching a company, this site is a good place to start gathering basic information.

1. Go to **http://www.hoovers.com** and then use the "Search" scroll bar to select *Company*. In the next box type eBay and then click on *Go*. For **eBay Inc.** click on *Capsule*.
   a. Read the written description of the company and briefly summarize its contents.
   b. Review the other site information and comment on one item of interest.
2. Go to the top of the page and click on the *Financials* tab. Under "Free Financial Information" click on *Annual Financials*.

a. For the three most recent years, list the amounts reported for "Revenue" and "Total Net Income." Is eBay growing and expanding? Is eBay a profitable company?

b. For the most recent year, list amounts reported for "Total Assets," "Total Liabilities," and "Total (Owner's) Equity." Does the accounting equation hold true? Are assets primarily financed by debt or owner's equity?

3. Go to the top of the page and click on the *Company Capsule* tab. Click on the URL for eBay (www.ebay.com) and then click on *Browse* to explore the world's largest online marketplace. Comment on one item you found of interest.

Recording Business Transactions

LEARNING OBJECTIVES

*After studying this chapter,
you should be able to*

1. Define and use key accounting terms

2. Apply the rules of debit and credit

3. Record transactions in the journal

4. Post from the journal to the ledger

5. Prepare and use a trial balance

6. Set up a chart of accounts for a business

7. Analyze transactions without a journal

Forget about e-retailers putting **Wal-Mart** out of business. Their task now is simply to stay alive. Time is running out because many e-retailers have yet to turn a profit. They are spending so much on advertising they may soon run out of cash. In fact, during the fourth quarter of 1999, only four e-retailers—**priceline.com, Drugstore.com, Value America,** and **eBay**—increased their gross profit margins.

How do these companies monitor their financial progress, or lack of it? Managers don't roll dice to decide whether to launch a new product or whether the business is profitable. They keep accounting records like those we illustrate in this chapter. Accounting helps to measure profits and losses.

Chapter 1 introduced transaction analysis and the financial statements but did not show how the financial statements are prepared. Chapters 2, 3, and 4 cover the accounting process that results in the financial statements.

Chapter 2 discusses the processing of accounting information as it is done in practice. Throughout this and the next two chapters, we continue to illustrate accounting procedures with service businesses, such as Gay Gillen eTravel, a CPA, a law practice, or a sports franchise like the **Atlanta Braves.** In Chapter 5, we move into merchandising businesses such as **Macy's** and **Wal-Mart.** All these businesses use the basic accounting system we illustrate in this book.

THE ACCOUNT

The basic summary device of accounting is the **account,** the detailed record of the changes that have occurred in a particular asset, liability, or owner's equity during a period of time. For convenient access to the information, accounts are grouped in a record called the **ledger.** This is what we mean when we say "keeping the books" and "auditing the books." A ledger usually takes the form of a computer listing.

Accounts are grouped in three broad categories, according to the accounting equation ➡ :

ASSETS = LIABILITIES + OWNER'S EQUITY

Suppose you bought a $20,000 Pontiac Grand Am and had to borrow $12,000 to pay for it. Can you write your personal accounting equation for this transaction?

Answer

Assets	**=**	**Liabilities**	**+**	**Owner's Equity**
$20,000	=	$12,000	+	$8,000

Objective 1
Define and use key accounting terms

ACCOUNT. The detailed record of the changes that have occurred in a particular asset, liability, or owner's equity during a period. The basic summary device of accounting.

LEDGER. The book of accounts.

◄ In Chapter 1, p. 11, we learned that the accounting equation is the basic tool in all of accounting. It measures the assets of the business and the claims to those assets.

Assets

Assets are economic resources that benefit the business and will continue to do so in the future. Most firms use the following asset accounts.

CASH   The Cash account is a record of the cash effects of a business's transactions. Cash includes money and any medium of exchange that a bank accepts at face value, such as bank account balances, paper currency, coins, certificates of deposit, and checks. Successful companies such as **Wal-Mart** have plenty of cash. Many e-retailers may go bankrupt due to a shortage of cash.

NOTES RECEIVABLE   A business may sell its goods or services in exchange for a *promissory note,* which is a written pledge that the customer will pay a fixed amount of money by a certain date. The Notes Receivable account is a record of the promissory notes the business expects to collect in cash. A note receivable offers more security for collection than an account receivable.

ACCOUNTS RECEIVABLE   A business may sell its goods or services in exchange for an oral or implied promise of future cash receipt. Such sales are made on credit ("on account"). The Accounts Receivable account contains these amounts. Most sales in the United States and in other developed countries are made on account receivable.

PREPAID EXPENSES A business often pays certain expenses, such as rent and insurance, in advance. A *prepaid expense* is an asset because the prepayment provides a future benefit for the business. The ledger has a separate asset account for each prepaid expense. Prepaid Rent, Prepaid Insurance, and Office Supplies are prepaid expense accounts.

LAND The Land account is a record of the cost of land a business owns and uses in its operations. Land held for sale is accounted for separately—in an investment account.

BUILDING The cost of a business's buildings—office, warehouse, store, and the like—appear in the Buildings account. The e-retailers need little in the way of buildings because of the electronic nature of their business. Wal-Mart, on the other hand, owns buildings in many locations. Buildings held for sale are separate assets accounted for as investments.

EQUIPMENT, FURNITURE, AND FIXTURES A business has a separate asset account for each type of equipment—Computer Equipment, Office Equipment, and Store Equipment, for example. The Furniture and Fixtures account shows the cost of this asset. Computers and the related software are the most important assets of e-retailers.

Liabilities

Recall that a *liability* is a debt. A business generally has fewer liability accounts than asset accounts because a business's liabilities are summarized in a few accounts.

NOTES PAYABLE The Notes Payable account is the opposite of the Notes Receivable account. Notes Payable represents amounts the business must pay because it signed promissory notes to borrow money or to purchase goods or services.

ACCOUNTS PAYABLE The Accounts Payable account is the opposite of Accounts Receivable. The oral or implied promise to pay off debts arising from credit purchases appears in the Accounts Payable account. Such a purchase is said to be made on account. All companies, including **CBS, Coca-Cola,** and **eBay** have accounts payable.

ACCRUED LIABILITIES An *accrued liability* is a liability for an expense that has not been paid. Accrued liability accounts are added as needed. Taxes Payable, Interest Payable, and Salary Payable are liability accounts of most companies.

Owner's Equity

The owner's claim to the assets of the business is called *owner's equity*. In a proprietorship or a partnership, owner's equity is split into separate accounts for the owner's capital balance and the owner's withdrawals.

CAPITAL The Capital account shows the owner's claim to the assets of the business. Consider Gay Gillen eTravel. After the travel agency's total liabilities are subtracted from its total assets, the remainder is the owner's capital. The Capital balance equals the owner's investments in the business plus the business's net income and minus any net losses and owner withdrawals. ◄

➥ See the statement of owner's equity in Chapter 1, Exhibit 1-7.

WITHDRAWALS When Gay Gillen withdraws cash or other assets from the business for her personal use, the travel agency's assets and owner's equity decrease. The amounts taken out of the business appear in a separate account entitled Gay Gillen, Withdrawals, or Gay Gillen, Drawing. If withdrawals were recorded directly in the Capital account, the amount of owner withdrawals would not be highlighted and decision making would be more difficult. The Withdrawals account *decreases* owner's equity.

REVENUES The increase in owner's equity created by delivering goods or services to customers or clients is called *revenue*. The ledger contains as many revenue accounts as needed. Gay Gillen eTravel needs a Service Revenue account for amounts earned by providing travel services for clients. If a business lends money to an outsider, it needs an Interest Revenue account for the interest earned on the loan. If the business rents a building to a tenant, it needs a Rent Revenue account.

EXPENSES Expenses use up assets or create liabilities in the course of operating a business. Expenses have the opposite effect of revenues; they *decrease* owner's equity. A business needs a separate account for each type of expense, such as Salary Expense, Rent Expense, Advertising Expense, and Utilities Expense. Businesses of all sizes strive to minimize their expenses in order to maximize net income—whether it's **General Electric** or Gay Gillen eTravel.

Exhibit 2-1 shows how asset, liability, and owner's equity accounts can be grouped in the ledger.

 DAILY EXERCISE 2-1

EXHIBIT 2-1
The Ledger (Asset, Liability, and Owner's Equity Accounts)

DOUBLE-ENTRY ACCOUNTING

Accounting is based on a *double-entry system*, which means that we record the *dual effects* of a business transaction. *Each transaction affects at least two accounts.* For example, Gay Gillen's $30,000 cash investment in her travel agency increased both the Cash account and the Capital account of the business. It would be incomplete to record only the increase in the entity's cash without recording the increase in its owner's equity.

Consider a cash purchase of supplies. What are the dual effects of this transaction? The purchase (1) decreases cash and (2) increases supplies. A purchase of supplies on credit (1) increases supplies and (2) increases accounts payable. All transactions have at least two effects on the entity.

The T-Account

The most widely used account format is called the *T-account* because it takes the form of the capital letter "T." The vertical line in the T-account divides the account into its left and right sides. The account title rests on the horizontal line. For example, the Cash account of a business appears in the following T-account format:

CASH

(Left side) | (Right side)
Debit | *Credit*

DEBIT. The left side of an account.

CREDIT. The right side of an account.

The left side of the account is called the **debit** side, and the right side is called the **credit** side. The words *debit* and *credit* can be confusing because they are new. To become comfortable using them, remember that

Debit = Left side   Credit = Right side

Even though *left side* and *right side* are more descriptive, the terms *debit* and *credit* are deeply entrenched in business.[1] Debit and credit are abbreviated as follows:

- Dr = Debit   • Cr = Credit

Increases and Decreases in the Accounts

The account category determines how increases and decreases in it are recorded. For any given account, all increases are recorded on one side, and all decreases are recorded on the other side.

Objective 2
Apply the rules of debit and credit

- Increases in *assets* are recorded on the left (*debit*) side of the account.
- Decreases in assets are recorded on the right (credit) side.

Conversely,

- Increases in *liabilities* and *owner's equity* are recorded by *credits*.
- Decreases in liabilities and owner's equity are recorded by debits.

These are the *rules of debit and credit.*

In your study of accounting, forget the general usage of credit and debit. Remember that *debit means left side* and *credit means right side*. Whether an account is increased or decreased by a debit or a credit depends on the type of account. In a computerized accounting system, the computer interprets debits and credits as increases or decreases by account category. For example, a computer reads a debit to Cash as an increase to that account and an increase to Accounts Payable as a credit.

This pattern of recording debits and credits is based on the accounting equation:

⊙ DAILY EXERCISE 2-2

Assets = Liabilities + Owner's Equity
Debits = Credits

Assets are on the opposite side of the equation from liabilities and owner's equity. Therefore, increases and decreases in assets are recorded in the opposite manner from those in liabilities and owner's equity. And liabilities and owner's equity, which are on the same side of the equal sign, are treated in the same way. Exhibit 2-2 shows the relationship between the accounting equation and the rules of debit and credit.

EXHIBIT 2-2
The Accounting Equation and the Rules of Debit and Credit

To illustrate the ideas diagrammed in Exhibit 2-2, reconsider the first transaction from Chapter 1. Gay Gillen invested $30,000 in cash to begin her travel agency. The business received $30,000 cash from Gillen and gave her the owner's equity in the business. We are accounting for the business entity, Gay Gillen eTravel. Which accounts of the business are affected? By what amounts? On what side (debit or credit)? The answer: The business's Assets and Capital would increase by $30,000, as the following T-accounts show.

ASSETS	=	LIABILITIES	+	OWNER'S EQUITY
CASH				GAY GILLEN, CAPITAL
Debit for Increase, 30,000				Credit for Increase, 30,000

---

[1] The words *debit* and *credit* have a Latin origin (*debitum* and *creditum*). Luca Pacioli, the Italian monk who wrote about accounting in the 15th century, popularized these terms.

The amount remaining in an account is called its *balance*. The first transaction gives Cash a $30,000 debit balance and Gay Gillen, Capital a $30,000 credit balance.

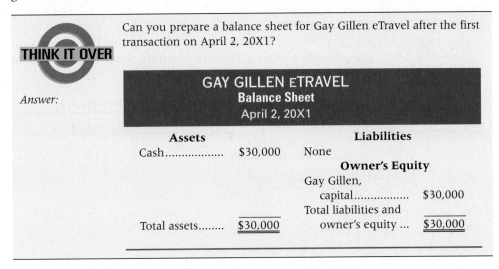

THINK IT OVER

Can you prepare a balance sheet for Gay Gillen eTravel after the first transaction on April 2, 20X1?

Answer:

GAY GILLEN eTRAVEL
Balance Sheet
April 2, 20X1

Assets		Liabilities	
Cash..................	$30,000	None	
		Owner's Equity	
		Gay Gillen,	
		capital.................	$30,000
		Total liabilities and	
Total assets........	$30,000	owner's equity ...	$30,000

Notice that Assets = Liabilities + Owner's Equity *and* that total debit amounts = total credit amounts. Exhibit 2-3 illustrates the accounting equation and Gay Gillen eTravel's first three transactions.

EXHIBIT 2-3   The Accounting Equation and the First Three Transactions of the Business Entity, Gay Gillen eTravel

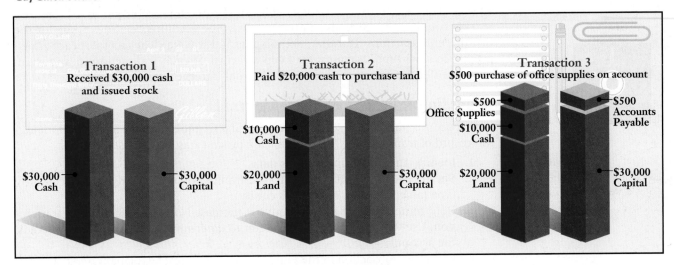

The second transaction is a $20,000 cash purchase of land. This transaction affects two assets: Cash and Land. It decreases (credits) Cash and increases (debits) Land, as shown in the T-accounts:

ASSETS	=	LIABILITIES	+	OWNER'S EQUITY

CASH			GAY GILLEN, CAPITAL	
Balance 30,000	**Credit for Decrease, 20,000**			Balance 30,000
Balance 10,000				

LAND	
Debit for Increase, 20,000	
Balance 20,000	

After this transaction, Cash has a $10,000 debit balance ($30,000 debit amount minus $20,000 credit amount), Land has a debit balance of $20,000, and Gay Gillen, Capital has a $30,000 credit balance, as shown here and in the middle section of Exhibit 2-3 (labeled transaction 2).

Transaction 3 is a $500 purchase of office supplies on account. This transaction increases the asset Office Supplies and the liability Accounts Payable, as shown in the following accounts and in the right side of Exhibit 2-3 (labeled transaction 3):

We create accounts as needed. The process of creating a new T-account in preparation for recording a transaction is called *opening the account.* For transaction 1, we opened the Cash account and the Gay Gillen, Capital account. For transaction 2, we opened the Land account and for transaction 3, Office Supplies and Accounts Payable. For each transaction, total debits must equal total credits.

We could record all transactions directly in the accounts, as shown here for the first three transactions. But that method does not leave a clear record of each transaction. To save time, accountants keep a record of each transaction in a journal. They transfer the information from the journal into the accounts.

Recording Transactions in the Journal

Objective 3
Record transactions in the journal

JOURNAL. The chronological accounting record of an entity's transactions.

In practice, accountants record transactions first in a **journal,** which is a chronological record of transactions. The journalizing process has four steps:

1. Identify the transaction and its data.
2. Specify each account affected by the transaction and classify each account by type (asset, liability, or owner's equity).
3. Determine whether each account is increased or decreased by the transaction. Use the rules of debit and credit to determine whether to debit or credit the account.
4. Enter the transaction in the journal, including a brief explanation for the journal entry. The debit side of the entry is entered first and the credit side last.

Step 4, "Enter the transaction in the journal," means to record the transaction in the journal. This step is also called "making the journal entry" or "journalizing the transaction."

These four steps are the same in a computerized accounting system or in a manual system. In step 4, however, the journal entry is generally entered into the computer by account number, and the account name is then listed automatically.

Let's apply the four steps to journalize the first transaction of Gay Gillen eTravel–the receipt of Gillen's $30,000 cash investment in the business.

Step 1. The data appear on Gillen's bank deposit slip and on her $30,000 check, which she deposits in the business bank account. See Exhibit 2-3.

Step 2. The accounts affected by the transaction are *Cash* and *Gay Gillen, Capital.* Cash is an asset account. Gay Gillen, Capital is an owner's equity account.

Step 3. Both accounts increase by $30,000. Therefore, we debit Cash, the asset account, and we credit Gay Gillen, Capital, the owner's equity account.

Step 4. The journal entry is

Journal				Page 1
Date	Accounts and Explanation		Debit	Credit
Apr. 2[a]	Cash[b]		30,000[d]	
	Gay Gillen, Capital[c]...........................			30,000[e]
	Received initial investment from owner.[f]			

The journal entry includes (a) the date of the transaction; (b) the title of the account debited (placed flush left); (c) the title of the account credited (indented); the dollar amounts of the (d) debit (left) and (e) credit (right), and (f) a short explanation of the transaction. Note that dollar signs are omitted in the money columns. It is understood that the debit and credit amounts are in dollars.

To journalize a transaction, first pinpoint the obvious effects on the accounts. For example, cash effects are easy to identify. Did cash increase or decrease? Then find the transaction's effects on other accounts.

The journal holds information that the ledger accounts do not provide. Each journal entry shows the complete effect of a business transaction. Consider Gay Gillen's initial investment. The Cash account shows a single figure, the $30,000 debit. We know that every transaction must also have a credit, so in what account will we find the corresponding $30,000 credit? In this illustration, we know that the Capital account holds this figure. But imagine the difficulty of linking debits and credits for hundreds of transactions without a separate record of each transaction. The journal solves this problem and presents the full story for each transaction. Exhibit 2-4 shows how Journal page 1 looks after Gillen has recorded the first transaction.

EXHIBIT 2-4 The Journal

Journal				Page 1
Date	Accounts and Explanation		Debit	Credit
Apr. 2	Cash		30,000	
	Gay Gillen, Capital...........................			30,000
	Received initial investment from owner.			

WORK IT OUT

Prepare the journal entry to record a $1,600 payment on account.
1. Identify the accounts.
2. Are these accounts increased or decreased? Should they be debited or credited?
3. Make the journal entry, with an explanation.

Answers
1. The company paid $1,600 on account. The accounts affected are Cash and Accounts Payable.
2. Cash (an asset) decreases by $1,600. Accounts Payable (a liability) decreases by $1,600. To account for a decrease in an asset, we record a credit. For a decrease in a liability, we use a debit. Review Exhibit 2-2.
3. The journal entry is   Accounts Payable 1,600
                                        Cash..   1,600
                            Made payment on account.

Objective 4
Post from the journal to the ledger

Copying Information (Posting) from the Journal to the Ledger

Posting means copying the amounts from the journal to the accounts in the ledger. Debits in the journal are posted as debits in the ledger, and credits in the journal are credits in the ledger. The initial investment transaction of Gay Gillen eTravel is posted to the ledger in Exhibit 2-5. Here we ignore the date of the transaction to focus on the accounts and their dollar amounts.

POSTING. Copying amounts from the journal to the ledger.

EXHIBIT 2-5
Journal Entry and Posting to
the Ledger

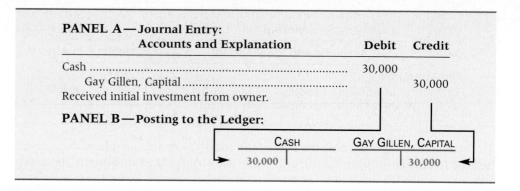

PANEL A—Journal Entry:

Accounts and Explanation	Debit	Credit
Cash	30,000	
Gay Gillen, Capital...		30,000
Received initial investment from owner.		

PANEL B—Posting to the Ledger:

CASH	GAY GILLEN, CAPITAL
30,000	30,000

THE FLOW OF ACCOUNTING DATA

Exhibit 2-6 summarizes the flow of accounting data from a business transaction through the accounting system to the ledger. In the pages that follow, we account for six of Gay Gillen eTravel's early transactions. Keep in mind that we are accounting for the travel agency. We are *not* accounting for Gay Gillen's *personal* transactions.

EXHIBIT 2-6   Flow of Accounting Data from the Journal to the Ledger

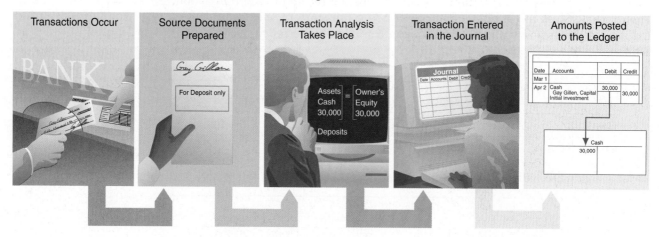

Transaction Analysis, Journalizing, and Posting to the Accounts

1. *Transaction Analysis*   The business received $30,000 cash that Gay Gillen invested to begin her travel agency. The business increased its asset cash, so we debit Cash. The business also increased its owner's equity; to record this increase, credit Gay Gillen, Capital.

Accounting Equation

ASSETS	=	LIABILITIES	+	OWNER'S EQUITY
Cash				Gay Gillen, Capital
+50,000	=	0	+	+30,000

Journal Entry

Cash	30,000	
Gay Gillen, Capital..............		30,000
Received investment from owner.		

The journal entry records the same information that you learned by using the accounting equation in Chapter 1. Both accounts—Cash and Gay Gillen, Capital—increased because the business received $30,000 cash and gave Gillen $30,000 of capital (owner's equity) in the business.

Ledger Accounts

CASH	GAY GILLEN, CAPITAL
(1) 30,000	(1) 30,000

2. Transaction
Analysis

Gillen paid $20,000 cash for land to be used as an office location. The purchase decreased the business's cash; therefore, credit Cash. The entity's asset, land, increased, so we debit the Land account.

Accounting
Equation

ASSETS		=	LIABILITIES	+	OWNER'S EQUITY
Cash	Land				
−20,000	+20,000 =		0	+	0

Journal
Entry

Land	20,000	
Cash		20,000
Paid cash for land.		

This transaction increased one asset, land, and decreased another asset, cash. The *net* effect on total assets was zero, and there was no effect on liabilities or owner's equity. (The term *net* in business means an amount after a subtraction.)

Ledger
Accounts

CASH			LAND	
(1) 30,000	(2)	20,000	(2) 20,000	

● DAILY EXERCISE 2-3

3. Transaction
Analysis

Gillen purchased $500 in office supplies on account payable. The asset office supplies increased, so we debit Office Supplies. The purchase also increased the liability accounts payable; to record this increase, credit Accounts Payable.

Accounting
Equation

ASSETS	=	LIABILITIES	+	OWNER'S EQUITY
Office Supplies		Accounts Payable		
+500	=	+500	+	0

Journal
Entry

Office Supplies	500	
Accounts Payable		500
Purchased office supplies on account.		

Ledger
Accounts

OFFICE SUPPLIES		ACCOUNTS PAYABLE	
(3) 500			(3) 500

4. Transaction
Analysis

Gillen paid $300 on the account payable created in transaction 3. The payment decreased the asset cash; therefore, credit Cash. The payment also decreased the liability accounts payable, so we debit Accounts Payable.

Accounting
Equation

ASSETS	=	LIABILITIES	+	OWNER'S EQUITY
Cash		Accounts Payable		
−300	=	−300	+	0

Journal
Entry

Accounts Payable	300	
Cash		300
Paid cash on account.		

Ledger
Accounts

CASH				ACCOUNTS PAYABLE		
(1) 30,000	(2)	20,000	(4)	300	(3)	500
	(4)	300				

5. Transaction
Analysis

Gay Gillen remodeled her home with personal funds and a loan from Nations Bank. This is not a transaction of the travel agency, so we make no journal entry on its books.

6. Transaction
Analysis

Gillen withdrew $2,100 cash for personal living expenses. The withdrawal decreased the entity's cash; therefore, credit Cash. The transaction also decreased owner's equity. Decreases in a proprietorship's owner's equity that result from owner withdrawals are debited to a separate account, Withdrawals. Therefore, debit Gay Gillen, Withdrawals.

	ASSETS	=	LIABILITIES	+	OWNER'S EQUITY
Accounting *Equation*	Cash −2,100	= =	0		Gay Gillen, Withdrawals −2,100

Journal
Entry

Gay Gillen, Withdrawals 2,100
     Cash 2,100
Withdrawal of cash by owner.

Ledger
Accounts

	CASH				GAY GILLEN, WITHDRAWALS	
(1)	30,000	(2)	20,000	(6)	2,100	
		(4)	300			
		(6)	2,100			

Each journal entry posted to the ledger is keyed by date or by transaction number. In this way, any transaction can be traced from the journal to the ledger and back to the journal. This linking allows you to locate any information you may need for decision making.

Accounts After Posting

We next show how the accounts look when the preceding transactions have been posted. The accounts are grouped under their headings.

    Each account has a balance, denoted *Bal.* An account balance is the difference between the account's total debits and its total credits. For example, the balance in the Cash account is the difference between the total debits, $30,000, and the total amount of the credits, $22,400 ($20,000 + $300 + $2,100). Thus, the cash balance is $7,600. The balances are residual amounts left over after the journal entries have been posted to the accounts. We set an account balance apart from the transaction amounts by a horizontal line. The final figure in an account, below the horizontal line, is the balance after the transactions have been posted.

	ASSETS		=		LIABILITIES		+		OWNER'S EQUITY	
	CASH				ACCOUNTS PAYABLE				GAY GILLEN, CAPITAL	
(1)	30,000	(2)	20,000	(4)	300	(3)	500		(1)	30,000
		(4)	300			Bal.	200		Bal.	30,000
		(6)	2,100							
Bal.	7,600									

	OFFICE SUPPLIES			GAY GILLEN, WITHDRAWALS	
(3)	500		(6)	2,100	
Bal.	500		Bal.	2,100	

	LAND	
(2)	20,000	
Bal.	20,000	

    If the sum of an account's debits is greater than the sum of its credits, that account has a debit balance, as the Cash account does. If the sum of its credits is greater, that account has a credit balance, as for Accounts Payable.

Objective 5
Prepare and use a trial balance

TRIAL BALANCE. A list of all the accounts with their balances.

The Trial Balance

A **trial balance** is a list of all the accounts with their balances—assets first, followed by liabilities and then owner's equity—taken from the ledger. Before computers, the trial balance provided a check on accuracy by showing whether total debits equal total credits. The trial balance is now a useful summary of all the accounts and their balances. A trial balance may be taken whenever the postings are up to date. The most common time is at the end of the accounting period. Exhibit 2-7 is the trial balance of Gay Gillen eTravel after the first six transactions.

EXHIBIT 2-7
Trial Balance

DAILY EXERCISE 2-4

GAY GILLEN ETRAVEL
Trial Balance
April 30, 20X1

Account Title	Debit	Credit
	Balance	
Cash	$ 7,600	
Office supplies.............................	500	
Land	20,000	
Accounts payable		$ 200
Gay Gillen, capital.......................		30,000
Gay Gillen, withdrawals	2,100	
Total	$30,200	$30,200

Correcting Trial Balance Errors

In a trial balance, total debits and total credits should be equal. If they are not, there must be an accounting error. Computerized accounting systems eliminate most errors because the journal amounts are posted precisely as they have been journalized. But computers cannot *eliminate* all errors because humans sometimes input the wrong data.

Out-of-balance conditions are detected by computing the difference between total debits and total credits on the trial balance. Then perform one or more of the following actions:

1. Search the trial balance for a missing account. For example, suppose the accountant omitted Gay Gillen, Withdrawals, from the trial balance in Exhibit 2-7. The total amount of the debits would be $28,100 ($30,200 − $2,100). Trace each account from the ledger to the trial balance, and you will locate the missing account.

2. Divide the difference between total debits and total credits by 2. A debit treated as a credit, or vice versa, doubles the amount of error. Suppose Gay Gillen's accountant posted a $300 credit as a debit. Total debits contain the $300, and total credits omit the $300. The out-of-balance amount is $600. Dividing the difference by 2 identifies the $300 amount of the transaction. Then search the journal for a $300 transaction and trace to the account affected.

3. Divide the out-of-balance amount by 9. If the result is evenly divisible by 9, the error may be a *slide* (example: writing $300 as $30) or a *transposition* (example: treating $61 as $16). Suppose Gillen printed her $2,100 Withdrawal as $21,000 on the trial balance—a slide-type error. Total debits would differ from total credits by $18,900 ($21,000 − $2,100 = $18,900). Dividing $18,900 by 9 yields $2,100, the correct amount of withdrawals. Trace this amount through the ledger until you reach the Gay Gillen, Withdrawals account with a balance of $2,100. Computer-based systems avoid such errors.

A warning: Do not confuse the trial balance with the balance sheet. A trial balance is an internal document seen only by the company's owners, managers, and accountants. The company reports its balance sheet, a formal financial statement, to the public.

The Seven Trillion Dollar Mistake

"If we can send missiles to a bull's-eye at a . . . training camp in Afghanistan, we ought to be able to set up an accounting system at the Defense Department. . . ." This is what Senator Charles Grassley (R-Iowa) said in 1998 after embezzlements at U.S. military installations were allowed to occur because of weaknesses in the Pentagon's accounting system.

A year later, precision was still lacking at the Department of Defense. Pentagon money managers required almost $7 trillion of accounting adjustments to make their books balance. Each adjustment represents an accountant's correction of a discrepancy. The lesson of the $7 trillion mistake is this: Computers don't keep books; people do.

These bookkeeping errors affect all our pocketbooks. Without sound costing data, military managers simply can't make good decisions—like whether to close a base or keep it open. The public never knows the real cost of defense programs such as the missile defense shield or the cost of health care for military retirees. With more reliable accounting data, we would know how to vote on these issues.

Sources: Based on: Julia Malone, "Auditors cite failings in 11 of 24 agencies," *The Atlanta Constitution,* March 31, 2000, p. A; 20. John M. Donnelly, "Pentagon's Finances Just Don't Add Up; Audit: Hundreds of computer systems fail to keep running totals of income and outgo. Last year, the Defense Department's bookkeeping errors totaled more than the entire federal budget," *The Los Angeles Times,* March 5, 2000, p. 8. Ralph Vartabedian, "Thefts Reveal Flawed Pentagon Contract System," *The Los Angeles Times,* September 28, 1998, p. 1.

MID-CHAPTER

SUMMARY PROBLEM

www.prenhall.com/horngren

Mid-Chapter Assessment

On August 1, 20X5, Liz Shea opens Shea's Research Service. She is the owner of the proprietorship. During the entity's first ten days of operations, the business completes these transactions:
a. To begin operations, Shea deposits $40,000 of personal funds in a bank account entitled Shea's Research Service. The business receives the cash and gives Shea capital (owner's equity).
b. Shea pays $30,000 cash for a small building to be used as an office for the business.
c. Shea purchases office supplies for $500 on account.
d. Shea pays cash of $6,000 for office furniture.
e. Shea pays $150 on the account payable she created in transaction (c).
f. Shea withdraws $1,000 cash for personal use.

Required

1. Give the accounting equation for each transaction. Then journalize these transactions and post to the accounts. Key the journal entries by letter.
2. Show all the T-accounts after posting.
3. Prepare the trial balance of Shea's Research Service at August 10, 20X5.

Solution

Requirement 1

a. *Accounting Equation*

ASSETS	=	LIABILITIES	+	OWNER'S EQUITY
Cash				Liz Shea, Capital
+40,000	=	0	+	$40,000

Journal Entry

Cash 40,000
    Liz Shea, Capital   40,000
Received investment from owner.

Ledger Accounts

CASH		LIZ SHEA, CAPITAL	
(a) 40,000			(a) 40,000

b. *Accounting Equation*

ASSETS		=	LIABILITIES	+	OWNER'S EQUITY
Cash	Building				
−30,000	+30,000	=	0	+	0

Journal Entry

Building 30,000
    Cash   30,000
Purchased building.

Ledger Accounts

CASH		BUILDING	
(a) 40,000	(b) 30,000	(b) 30,000	

c. *Accounting Equation*

ASSETS	=	LIABILITIES	+	OWNER'S EQUITY
Office Supplies		Accounts Payable		
+500	=	+500	+	0

Journal Entry

Office Supplies 500
    Accounts Payable   500
Purchased office supplies on account.

Ledger Accounts

OFFICE SUPPLIES		ACCOUNTS PAYABLE	
(c) 500			(c) 500

d. *Accounting Equation*

ASSETS		=	LIABILITIES	+	OWNER'S EQUITY
	Office				
Cash	Furniture				
−6,000	+6,000	=	0	+	0

Journal Entry

Office Furniture 6,000
    Cash   6,000
Purchased office furniture.

Ledger Accounts

CASH		OFFICE FURNITURE	
(a) 40,000	(b) 30,000	(d) 6,000	
	(d) 6,000		

e. *Accounting Equation*

ASSETS	=	LIABILITIES	+	OWNER'S EQUITY
Cash		Accounts Payable		
−150	=	−150	+	0

Journal Entry

Accounts Payable 150
    Cash   150
Paid cash on account.

Ledger Accounts

CASH		ACCOUNTS PAYABLE	
(a) 40,000	(b) 30,000	(e) 150	(c) 500
	(d) 6,000		
	(e) 150		

f. *Accounting Equation*

ASSETS	=	LIABILITIES	+	OWNER'S EQUITY
Cash				Liz Shea, Withdrawals
−1,000	=	0		−1,000

Journal Entry

Liz Shea, Withdrawals 1,000
    Cash 1,000

Ledger Accounts

CASH				LIZ SHEA, WITHDRAWALS	
(a) 40,000	(b)	30,000		(f) 1,000	
	(d)	6,000			
	(e)	150			
	(f)	1,000			

Requirement 2

ASSETS

CASH		
(a) 40,000	(b)	30,000
	(d)	6,000
	(e)	150
	(f)	1,000
Bal. 2,850		

OFFICE FURNITURE	
(d) 6,000	
Bal. 6,000	

OFFICE SUPPLIES	
(c) 500	
Bal. 500	

BUILDING	
(b) 30,000	
Bal. 30,000	

LIABILITIES

ACCOUNTS PAYABLE		
(e) 150	(c)	500
	Bal.	350

OWNER'S EQUITY

LIZ SHEA, CAPITAL		
	(a)	40,000
	Bal.	40,000

LIZ SHEA, WITHDRAWALS	
(f) 1,000	
Bal. 1,000	

Requirement 3

SHEA'S RESEARCH SERVICE
Trial Balance
August 10, 20X5

	Balance	
Account Title	**Debit**	**Credit**
Cash..	$ 2,850	
Office supplies	500	
Office furniture	6,000	
Building......................................	30,000	
Accounts payable		$ 350
Liz Shea, capital.........................		40,000
Liz Shea, withdrawals	1,000	
Total...	$40,350	$40,350

DETAILS OF JOURNALS AND LEDGERS

To focus on the main points of journalizing and posting, we purposely omitted certain essential data. In practice, the journal and the ledger provide additional details that create a "trail" through the accounting records. For example, a supplier may bill us twice for the same item that we purchased on account. To prove we paid the bill, we would search the accounts payable records to find our payment. To see how this process works, let's take a closer look at the journal and the ledger.

DETAILS IN THE JOURNAL Exhibit 2-8, Panel B, presents the journal. The journal page number appears in the upper right corner, and the journal displays the following information:

1. The *date* when the transaction occurred, April 2, 20X1, for the first transaction.
2. The *account title* and explanation of the transaction.

EXHIBIT 2-8 **Journalizing and Posting**

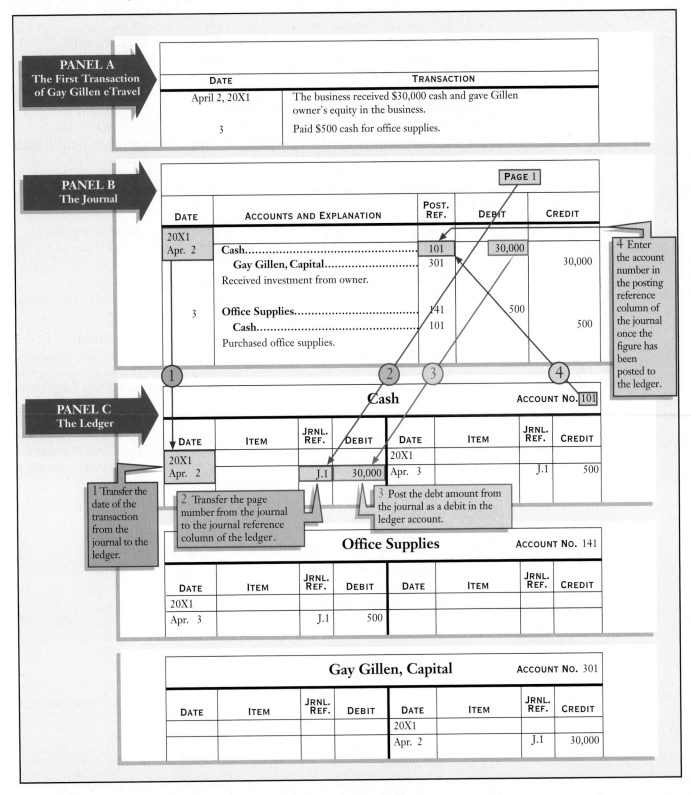

PANEL A
The First Transaction
of Gay Gillen eTravel

DATE	TRANSACTION
April 2, 20X1	The business received $30,000 cash and gave Gillen owner's equity in the business.
3	Paid $500 cash for office supplies.

PANEL B
The Journal

PAGE 1

DATE	ACCOUNTS AND EXPLANATION	POST. REF.	DEBIT	CREDIT
20X1 Apr. 2	Cash..	101	30,000	
	Gay Gillen, Capital.............................	301		30,000
	Received investment from owner.			
3	Office Supplies.................................	141	500	
	Cash..	101		500
	Purchased office supplies.			

4 Enter the account number in the posting reference column of the journal once the figure has been posted to the ledger.

PANEL C
The Ledger

Cash   ACCOUNT NO. 101

DATE	ITEM	JRNL. REF.	DEBIT	DATE	ITEM	JRNL. REF.	CREDIT
20X1 Apr. 2		J.1	30,000	20X1 Apr. 3		J.1	500

1 Transfer the date of the transaction from the journal to the ledger.

2 Transfer the page number from the journal to the journal reference column of the ledger.

3 Post the debt amount from the journal as a debit in the ledger account.

Office Supplies   ACCOUNT NO. 141

DATE	ITEM	JRNL. REF.	DEBIT	DATE	ITEM	JRNL. REF.	CREDIT
20X1 Apr. 3		J.1	500				

Gay Gillen, Capital   ACCOUNT NO. 301

DATE	ITEM	JRNL. REF.	DEBIT	DATE	ITEM	JRNL. REF.	CREDIT
				20X1			
				Apr. 2		J.1	30,000

3. The *posting reference,* abbreviated Post. Ref. Use of this column will become clear when we discuss the details of posting.
4. The *debit* column, which shows the dollar amount debited.
5. The *credit* column, which shows the dollar amount credited.

DETAILS IN THE LEDGER Exhibit 2-8, Panel C, presents the T-accounts affected by the first transaction: Cash and Gay Gillen's Capital account. The account number appears at the upper right corner of each account. Each account has a separate column for

1. The date.
2. The item column, which can be used for any special notation.
3. The journal reference column, abbreviated Jrnl. Ref. The importance of this column will become clear when we discuss the mechanics of posting.
4. The debit column, with the amount debited.
5. The credit column, with the amount credited.

Posting from the Journal to the Ledger

We know that posting means copying information from the journal to the ledger accounts. But how do we handle the additional details that we have just seen? Exhibit 2-8 illustrates the steps in full detail. Panel A lists the first transaction of the business entity, Gay Gillen eTravel; Panel B presents the journal; and Panel C shows the ledger.

The posting process includes four steps. After recording the transaction in the journal:

Arrow ①—Copy (post) the transaction **date** from the journal to the ledger.
Arrow ②—Copy (post) the journal page number from the journal to the ledger. We use several abbreviations:

Jrnl. Ref. means Journal Reference. **J.1** refers to Journal page 1.
This step indicates where the information in the ledger came from: Journal page 1.

Arrow ③—Copy (post) the dollar amount of the debit (**$30,000**) from the journal as a debit to the same account (Cash) in the ledger. Likewise, post the dollar amount of the credit (also **$30,000**) from the journal to the appropriate account in the ledger. Now the ledger accounts have their correct amounts.
Arrow ④—Copy (post) the account number (**101**) from the ledger back to the journal. This step indicates that the $30,000 debit to Cash has been posted to the Cash account in the ledger. Also, copy the account number (**301**) for Gay Gillen, Capital, back to the journal to show that the $30,000 amount of the credit has been posted to the ledger.

Post. Ref. is the abbreviation for Posting Reference. After posting, you can prepare the trial balance.

The Four-Column Account Format: An Alternative to the T-Account Format

The ledger accounts illustrated in Exhibit 2-8 appear in the T-account format, with the debit on the left and the credit on the right. The T-account clearly separates debits from credits and is used for teaching purposes in situations that do not have much detail. Another standard format has four amount columns, as illustrated for the Cash account in Exhibit 2-9.

EXHIBIT 2-9
Account in Four-Column Format

Account Cash					Account No. 101	
		Jrnl.			Balance	
Date	Item	Ref.	Debit	Credit	Debit	Credit
20X1						
Apr. 2		J.1	30,000		30,000	
3		J.1		500	29,500	

The first pair of amount columns are for the debit and credit amounts posted from individual entries, as just discussed. The second pair of amount columns are for the account balance. This four-column format keeps a running balance in the account. For this reason, it is used more often in practice than the two-column format. In Exhibit 2-9, Cash has a debit balance of $30,000 after the first transaction and a debit balance of $29,500 after the second transaction.

Chart of Accounts in the Ledger

As you know, the ledger contains the business's accounts grouped under these headings:

- Balance sheet accounts: Assets, Liabilities, and Owner's Equity
- Income statement accounts: Revenues and Expenses

Organizations use a **chart of accounts** to list all the accounts they use along with their account numbers. These account numbers are used as posting references, illustrated by arrow 4 in Exhibit 2-8.

Accounts are identified by account numbers with two or more digits. Assets are often numbered beginning with 1, liabilities with 2, owner's equity with 3, revenues with 4, and expenses with 5. The second, third, and higher digits in an account number indicate the position of each account within the category. For example, Cash may be account number 101, which is the first asset account. Accounts Receivable may be account number 111, the second asset account. Accounts Payable may be number 201, the first liability account. All accounts are numbered by this system. Organizations with many accounts use lengthy account numbers.

The chart of accounts for Gay Gillen eTravel, appears in Exhibit 2-10. Notice the gap in account numbers between 111 and 141. Gillen realizes that at some later dates she may need to add another category of receivables—for example, Notes Receivable, which she might number 121.

Objective 6
Set up a chart of accounts for a business

CHART OF ACCOUNTS. List of all the accounts and their account numbers in the ledger.

BALANCE SHEET ACCOUNTS:

Assets	Liabilities	Owner's Equity
101 Cash	201 Accounts Payable	301 Gay Gillen, Capital
111 Accounts Receivable	231 Notes Payable	311 Gay Gillen, Withdrawals
141 Office Supplies		
151 Office Furniture		
191 Land		

INCOME STATEMENT ACCOUNTS (PART OF OWNER'S EQUITY):

Revenues	Expenses
401 Service Revenue	501 Rent Expense
	502 Salary Expense
	503 Utilities Expense

EXHIBIT 2-10
Chart of Accounts— Gay Gillen eTravel

Appendix B gives two expanded charts of accounts that you will find helpful as you work through this course. The first chart lists the typical accounts of a large *service* proprietorship, such as Gay Gillen eTravel after a period of growth. The second chart is for a *merchandising* corporation, one that sells a product rather than a service. The third chart gives some accounts that a *manufacturing* company uses. You will use these accounts in Chapters 19–26. Study the service proprietorship now, and refer to the other charts of accounts as needed later.

The Normal Balance of an Account

An account's **normal balance** appears on the side of the account—debit or credit—where we record *increases*. That is, the normal balance is on the side that is positive. For example, Cash and other assets usually have a debit balance (the debit side is positive and the credit side negative), so the normal balance of assets is on the debit side. Assets are called *debit-balance accounts*. Conversely, liabilities and owner's equity usually have a credit balance, so their normal balances are on the credit side. They are called *credit-balance accounts*. Exhibit 2-11 illustrates the normal balances of assets, liabilities, and owner's equity.

An account that normally has a debit balance may occasionally have a credit balance. That indicates a negative amount of the item. For example, Cash will have a temporary credit balance if the entity overdraws its bank account. Similarly, the

 DAILY EXERCISE 2-5

NORMAL BALANCE. The account balance that appears on the side of the account—debit or credit—where we record increases.

EXHIBIT 2-11
Normal Balances of the Balance
Sheet Accounts

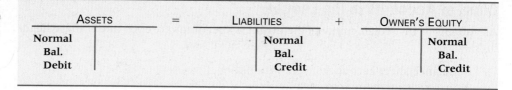

liability Accounts Payable—normally a credit-balance account—will have a debit balance if the entity overpays its account. In other instances, an odd balance may indicate an accounting error. For example, a credit balance in Office Supplies, Office Furniture, or Buildings indicates an error because negative amounts of these assets cannot exist.

As we saw earlier, owner's equity contains the Capital account and the Withdrawals account. In total, these accounts show a normal credit balance. An individual owner's equity account with a normal credit balance, such as Gay Gillen, Capital, represents an *increase* in owner's equity. An owner's equity account that has a normal debit balance, such as Gay Gillen, Withdrawals, represents a *decrease* in owner's equity.

EXPANDING THE ACCOUNTING EQUATION TO ACCOUNT FOR REVENUES AND EXPENSES

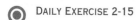
DAILY EXERCISE 2-15

Owner's equity also includes Revenues and Expenses because revenues and expenses make up net income or net loss, which flows into owner's equity. As we have noted, *revenues* are increases in owner's equity that result from delivering goods or services to customers in the course of operating the business. *Expenses* are decreases in owner's equity that occur from using assets or increasing liabilities in the course of operations. Therefore, the accounting equation may be expanded as shown in Exhibit 2-12. Revenues and expenses appear in parentheses to highlight the fact that their net effect—revenues minus expenses—equals net income, which increases owner's equity. If expenses are greater than revenues, the net effect of operations is a net loss, which decreases owner's equity.

EXHIBIT 2-12
Expansion of the Accounting
Equation to Include Revenues
and Expenses

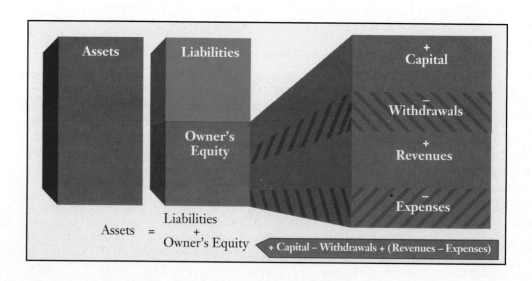

We can now express the rules of debit and credit in final form, as shown in Exhibit 2-13, Panel A. Panel B shows the *normal* balances of the five types of accounts: *Assets; Liabilities;* and *Owner's Equity* and its subparts, *Revenues and Expenses*. All of accounting is based on these five types of accounts.

You should not proceed until you have learned the rules of debit and credit and the normal balances of the five types of accounts.

PANEL A—Rules of Debit and Credit:

ASSETS			LIABILITIES			CAPITAL	
Debit for Increase	Credit for Decrease	=	Debit for Decrease	Credit for Increase	+	Debit for Decrease	Credit for Increase

PANEL B—Normal Balances:

Assets .... Debit
Liabilities... Credit
Owner's equity—overall .... Credit
  Capital .... Credit
  Withdrawals.................................. Debit
  Revenues....................................... Credit
  Expenses .... Debit

WITHDRAWALS

Debit for Increase	Credit for Decrease

REVENUES

Debit for Decrease	Credit for Increase

EXPENSES

Debit for Increase	Credit for Decrease

WORK IT OUT

Compute the missing amounts in each of the following T-accounts.

1. CASH

Bal. 10,000	
20,000	13,000
Bal. ?	

2. ACCOUNTS RECEIVABLE

Bal. 12,800	
45,600	?
Bal. 23,500	

3. ANNIE TODD, CAPITAL

	Bal. ?
22,000	56,000
	15,000
	Bal. 73,000

Answers

1. The ending balance (X) for Cash is:

$$X = \$10,000 + \$20,000 - \$13,000$$
$$X = \$17,000$$

2. We are given the beginning and ending balances. We can compute the credit entry (X) as follows for Accounts Receivable:

$$\$12,800 + \$45,600 - X = \$23,500$$
$$\$58,400 - \$23,500 = X$$
$$X = \$34,900$$

3. The Capital account has an ending credit balance of $73,000. We can figure the beginning credit balance (X), as follows:

$$X + \$56,000 + \$15,000 - \$22,000 = \$73,000$$
$$X = \$73,000 - \$56,000 - \$15,000 + \$22,000$$
$$X = \$24,000$$

EXPANDED PROBLEM INCLUDING REVENUES AND EXPENSES

Let's account for the revenues and expenses of the law practice of Jeff Hatton, Attorney, for the month of July 20X1. We follow the same steps illustrated earlier in this chapter: Analyze the transaction, journalize, post to the ledger, and prepare the trial balance.

Transaction Analysis, Journalizing, and Posting

1. *Transaction Analysis* Jeff Hatton invested $10,000 cash in a business bank account to open his law practice. The business received the cash and gave Hatton owner's equity. The business's asset cash is increased; therefore, debit Cash. The owner's equity of the business increased, so credit Jeff Hatton, Capital.

Accounting Equation	**ASSETS**	**=**	**LIABILITIES**	**+**	**OWNER'S EQUITY**
	Cash				Jeff Hatton,
	+10,000	=	0	+	Capital 10,000

Journal Entry

Cash.. 10,000
    Jeff Hatton, Capital   10,000
Received investment from owner.

Ledger Accounts

CASH		JEFF HATTON, CAPITAL	
(1) 10,000			(1) 10,000

2. *Transaction Analysis*

Hatton performed service for a client and collected $3,000 cash. The asset cash is increased, so debit Cash. The revenue account Service Revenue is increased; credit Service Revenue.

Accounting Equation	**ASSETS**	**=**	**LIABILITIES**	**+**	**OWNER'S EQUITY**	**+**	**REVENUES**
							Service
	Cash						Revenue
	+3,000	=	0			+	3,000

Journal Entry

Cash.. 3,000
    Service Revenue   3,000
Performed service and received cash.

Ledger Accounts

CASH		SERVICE REVENUE	
(1) 10,000			(2) 3,000
(2) 3,000			

3. *Transaction Analysis*

Hatton performed service for a client and billed the client for $500 on account receivable. This means the client owes the business $500, and Hatton expects to collect the $500 later. The asset accounts receivable is increased; therefore, debit Accounts Receivable. Service revenue is increased; credit Service Revenue. Remember that revenues are credit-balance accounts.

Accounting Equation	**ASSETS**	**=**	**LIABILITIES**	**+**	**OWNER'S EQUITY**	**+**	**REVENUES**
	Accounts						Service
	Receivable						Revenue
	+500	=	0			+	500

Journal Entry

Accounts Receivable 500
    Service Revenue   500
Performed service on account.

Ledger Accounts

ACCOUNTS RECEIVABLE		SERVICE REVENUE	
(3) 500			(2) 3,000
			(3) 500

4. *Transaction Analysis*

Hatton earned $700 service revenue by performing legal service for a client. The client paid Hatton $300 cash immediately. Hatton billed the remaining $400 to the client on account receivable. The assets cash and accounts receivable are increased; therefore, debit both of these asset accounts. Service revenue is increased; credit Service Revenue for the sum of the two debit amounts.

Accounting Equation	**ASSETS**		**=**	**LIABILITIES**	**+**	**OWNER'S EQUITY**	**+**	**REVENUES**
		Accounts						Service
	Cash	Receivable						Revenue
	+300	+400	=	0			+	700

Journal Entry	Cash..	300	
	Accounts Receivable..	400	
	Service Revenue		700

Performed service for cash and on account.

Note: Because this transaction affects more than two accounts at the same time, the entry is called a *compound entry*. **No matter how many accounts a compound entry affects—there may be any number—total debits must equal total credits.**

⬤ DAILY EXERCISE 2-7

Ledger Accounts

CASH		ACCOUNTS RECEIVABLE		SERVICE REVENUE	
(1) 10,000		(3) 500		(2) 3,000	
(2) 3,000		(4) 400		(3) 500	
(4) 300				(4) 700	

5. *Transaction Analysis* Hatton paid the following cash expenses: office rent, $900; employee salary, $1,500; and utilities, $500. The asset cash is decreased; therefore, credit Cash for the sum of the three expense amounts. The following expenses are increased: Rent Expense, Salary Expense, and Utilities Expense. Each expense account should be debited separately. Remember that expenses are debit-balance accounts, the opposite of revenues.

Accounting Equation

ASSETS	=	LIABILITIES	+	OWNER'S EQUITY	−	EXPENSES		
						Rent Expense	Salary Expense	Utilities Expense
Cash −2,900	=	0				−900	−1,500	−500

Journal Entry

Rent Expense	900	
Salary Expense	1,500	
Utilities Expense...	500	
Cash		2,900

Paid cash expenses.

Note: In practice, the business would record these three transactions separately. To save space, we can record them together in a compound journal entry.

Ledger Accounts

CASH			RENT EXPENSE	
(1) 10,000	(5) 2,900		(5) 900	
(2) 3,000				
(4) 300				

SALARY EXPENSE			UTILITIES EXPENSE	
(5) 1,500			(5) 500	

6. *Transaction Analysis* Hatton received a telephone bill for $120 and will pay this expense next week. There is no cash payment now. Utilities expense is increased, so debit this expense. The liability accounts payable is increased, so credit Accounts Payable.

Accounting Equation

ASSETS	=	LIABILITIES	+	OWNER'S EQUITY	−	EXPENSES
		Accounts Payable				Utilities Expense
0	=	+120			−	120

Journal Entry

Utilities Expense...	120	
Accounts Payable		120

Received utility bill.

Ledger Accounts

ACCOUNTS PAYABLE			UTILITIES EXPENSE	
	(6) 120		(5) 500	
			(6) 120	

7. *Transaction*
   Analysis   Hatton collected $200 cash from the client established in transaction 3. The asset cash is increased, so debit Cash. The asset accounts receivable is decreased; credit Accounts Receivable.

Accounting
Equation

ASSETS		=	LIABILITIES	+	OWNER'S EQUITY
Cash	Accounts Receivable				
+200	−200	=	0	+	0

Journal   Cash 200
Entry   Accounts Receivable 200
   Received cash on account.

Note: This transaction has no effect on revenue; the related revenue was accounted for in transaction 3.

Ledger
Accounts

CASH				ACCOUNTS RECEIVABLE			
(1)	10,000	(5)	2,900	(3)	500	(7)	200
(2)	3,000			(4)	400		
(4)	300						
(7)	200						

8. *Transaction*
   Analysis   Hatton paid the telephone bill that was received and recorded in transaction 6. The asset cash is decreased; credit Cash. The liability accounts payable is decreased; therefore, debit Accounts Payable.

Accounting
Equation

ASSETS	=	LIABILITIES	+	OWNER'S EQUITY
Cash		Accounts Payable		
−120	=	−120	+	0

Journal   Accounts Payable 120
Entry   Cash 120
   Paid cash on account.

Note: This transaction has no effect on expense because the related expense was recorded in transaction 6.

Ledger
Accounts

CASH				ACCOUNTS PAYABLE			
(1)	10,000	(5)	2,900	(8)	120	(6)	120
(2)	3,000	(8)	120				
(4)	300						
(7)	200						

9. *Transaction*
   Analysis   Hatton withdrew $1,100 cash for personal use. The asset cash decreased; credit Cash. The withdrawal decreased owner's equity; therefore, debit Jeff Hatton, Withdrawals.

Accounting
Equation

ASSETS	=	LIABILITIES	+	OWNER'S EQUITY
Cash				Jeff Hatton, Withdrawals
−1,100	=	0		−1,100

Journal   Jeff Hatton, Withdrawals 1,100
Entry   Cash 1,100
   Withdrew cash for personal use.

Ledger
Accounts

CASH				JEFF HATTON, WITHDRAWALS	
(1)	10,000	(5)	2,900	(9)	1,100
(2)	3,000	(8)	120		
(4)	300	(9)	1,100		
(7)	200				

◉ DAILY EXERCISE 2-8

◉ DAILY EXERCISE 2-9

◉ DAILY EXERCISE 2-10

◉ DAILY EXERCISE 2-11

Ledger Accounts After Posting

ASSETS	LIABILITIES	OWNER'S EQUITY	REVENUE	EXPENSES

ASSETS

CASH

(1)	10,000	(5)	2,900
(2)	3,000	(8)	120
(4)	300	(9)	1,100
(7)	200		
Bal.	9,380		

ACCOUNTS RECEIVABLE

(3)	500	(7)	200
(4)	400		
Bal.	700		

LIABILITIES

ACCOUNTS PAYABLE

(8)	120	(6)	120
		Bal.	0

OWNER'S EQUITY

JEFF HATTON, CAPITAL

		(1)	10,000
		Bal.	10,000

JEFF HATTON, WITHDRAWALS

(9)	1,100		
Bal.	1,100		

REVENUE

SERVICE REVENUE

		(2)	3,000
		(3)	500
		(4)	700
		Bal.	4,200

EXPENSES

RENT EXPENSE

(5)	900		
Bal.	900		

SALARY EXPENSE

(5)	1,500		
Bal.	1,500		

UTILITIES EXPENSE

(5)	500		
(6)	120		
Bal.	620		

Trial Balance

The trial balance lists the balance of each account.

JEFF HATTON, ATTORNEY
Trial Balance
July 31, 20X1

	Balance	
Account Title	**Debit**	**Credit**
Cash	$ 9,380	
Accounts receivable	700	
Accounts payable		$ 0
Jeff Hatton, capital		10,000
Jeff Hatton, withdrawals..............	1,100	
Service revenue		4,200
Rent expense	900	
Salary expense	1,500	
Utilities expense...........................	620	
Total	$14,200	$14,200

○ DAILY EXERCISE 2-12

○ DAILY EXERCISE 2-13

○ DAILY EXERCISE 2-14

Now you have seen how to record business transactions, post to the ledger accounts, and prepare a trial balance. Solidify your understanding of the accounting process by reviewing the Decision Guidelines below.

DECISION GUIDELINES

Analyzing and Recording Transactions

DECISION	GUIDELINES
• Has a transaction occurred?	If the event affects the entity's financial position and can be reliably recorded—*Yes* If either condition is absent—*No*
• Where to record the transaction?	In the *journal*, the chronological record of transactions
• What to record for each transaction?	Increases and/or decreases in all the accounts affected by the transaction
• How to record an increase/decrease in a (an)	Rules of debit and credit:

	Increase	Decrease
Asset	Debit	Credit
Liability	Credit	Debit
Owner's Equity...	Credit	Debit
Revenue	Credit	Debit
Expense	Debit	Credit

DECISION	GUIDELINES
• Where to store all the information for each account?	In the *ledger*, the book of accounts and their balances
• Where to list all the accounts and their balances?	In the *trial balance*
• Where to report the results of operations?	In the income statement (Revenues − Expenses = Net income or Net loss)
• Where to report financial position?	In the balance sheet (Assets = Liabilities + Owner's equity)

USING ACCOUNTING INFORMATION FOR QUICK DECISION MAKING

Objective 7
Analyze transactions without a journal

Often businesspeople make decisions without taking the time to follow all the steps in an accounting system. For example, suppose Drugstore.com needs more warehouse space to meet customer demand. The company can purchase a warehouse building for $700,000, or it can rent a building at an overall cost of $100,000. Whether to buy or rent the building will depend on the decision's financial and other effects on the company.

 DAILY EXERCISE 2-16

The Drugstore.com vice president does not need to record in the journal all the transactions that would be affected by his decision. After all, the company has not completed a transaction yet. But the vice president does need to know how the decision will affect Drugstore.com. If he knows accounting, he can visualize how the ledger accounts would be affected. The following accounts summarize the immediate effects of renting or purchasing the warehouse building.

RENT THE BUILDING			BUY THE BUILDING	
CASH	RENT EXPENSE		CASH	BUILDING
100,000	100,000		700,000	700,000

Immediately the Drugstore.com vice president can see that buying the building will require more cash. But he can also see that he will obtain the building as an asset. This may motivate him to borrow cash and buy the building. A low cash balance may lead to renting.

Companies do not actually keep their records in this short-cut fashion. But a decision maker who needs information immediately can quickly analyze the effect of a set of transactions on the company's financial statements.

REVIEW THE RECORDING OF BUSINESS TRANSACTIONS

SUMMARY PROBLEM

www.prenhall.com/horngren
End-of-Chapter Assessment

The trial balance of Tomassini Computer Service Center on March 1, 20X2, lists the entity's assets, liabilities, and owner's equity on that date.

Account Title	Balance Debit	Balance Credit
Cash	$26,000	
Accounts receivable	4,500	
Accounts payable		$ 2,000
Larry Tomassini, capital...............		28,500
Total...	$30,500	$30,500

During March, the business engaged in the following transactions:

a. Borrowed $45,000 from the bank and signed a note payable in the name of the business.

b. Paid cash of $40,000 to a real estate company to acquire land.

c. Performed service for a customer and received cash of $5,000.

d. Purchased supplies on credit, $300.

e. Performed customer service and earned revenue on account, $2,600.

f. Paid $1,200 on account.

g. Paid the following cash expenses: salaries, $3,000; rent, $1,500; and interest, $400.

h. Received $3,100 on account.

i. Received a $200 utility bill that will be paid next week.

j. Withdrew $1,800 for personal use.

Required

1. Open the following accounts, with the balances indicated, in the ledger of Tomassini Computer Service Center. Use the T-account format.
- Assets—Cash, $26,000; Accounts Receivable, $4,500; Supplies, no balance; Land, no balance
- Liabilities—Accounts Payable, $2,000; Note Payable, no balance
- Owner's Equity—Larry Tomassini, Capital, $28,500; Larry Tomassini, Withdrawals, no balance
- Revenues—Service Revenue, no balance
- Expenses—(none have balances) Salary Expense, Rent Expense, Utilities Expense, Interest Expense

2. For each transaction, give the accounting equation. Then journalize the transaction. Key journal entries by transaction letter.

3. Post to the ledger.

4. Prepare the trial balance of Tomassini Computer Service Center at March 31, 20X2.

Solution

Requirement 1

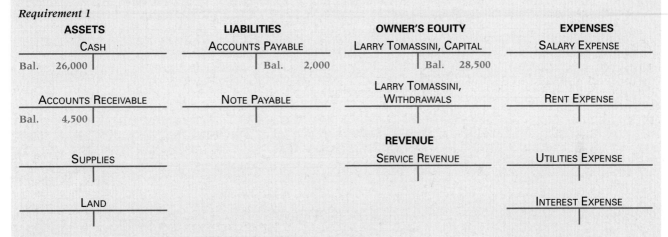

ASSETS	LIABILITIES	OWNER'S EQUITY	EXPENSES
CASH	ACCOUNTS PAYABLE	LARRY TOMASSINI, CAPITAL	SALARY EXPENSE
Bal. 26,000	Bal. 2,000	Bal. 28,500	
ACCOUNTS RECEIVABLE	NOTE PAYABLE	LARRY TOMASSINI, WITHDRAWALS	RENT EXPENSE
Bal. 4,500			
		REVENUE	
SUPPLIES		SERVICE REVENUE	UTILITIES EXPENSE
LAND			INTEREST EXPENSE

Requirement 2

a. *Accounting Equation*

ASSETS	=	LIABILITIES	+	OWNER'S EQUITY
Cash		Note Payable		
+45,000	=	+45,000	+	0

Journal Entry

```
Cash .................................................  45,000
     Note Payable...................................          45,000
Borrowed cash on note payable.
```

b. *Accounting Equation*

ASSETS		=	LIABILITIES	+	OWNER'S EQUITY
Cash	Land				
−40,000	+40,000	=	0	+	0

Journal Entry

```
Land ..................................................  40,000
     Cash .............................................          40,000
Purchased land.
```

63

c. *Accounting Equation*

ASSETS	=	LIABILITIES	+	OWNER'S EQUITY	+	REVENUES
Cash						Service Revenue
+5,000	=	0			+	5,000

Journal Entry

Cash	5,000	
Service Revenue		5,000

Performed service and received cash.

d. *Accounting Equation*

ASSETS	=	LIABILITIES	+	OWNER'S EQUITY
Supplies		Accounts Payable		
+300	=	+300	+	0

Journal Entry

Supplies	300	
Accounts Payable..................................		300

Purchased supplies on account.

e. *Accounting Equation*

ASSETS	=	LIABILITIES	+	OWNER'S EQUITY	+	REVENUES
Accounts Receivable						Service Revenue
+2,600	=	0			+	2,600

Journal Entry

Accounts Receivable	2,600	
Service Revenue		2,600

Performed service on account.

f. *Accounting Equation*

ASSETS	=	LIABILITIES	+	OWNER'S EQUITY
Cash		Accounts Payable		
−1,200	=	−1,200	+	0

Journal Entry

Accounts Payable..	1,200	
Cash		1,200

Paid on account.

g. *Accounting Equation*

ASSETS	=	LIABILITIES	+	OWNER'S EQUITY	−	EXPENSES		
						Salary Expense	Rent Expense	Interest Expense
Cash								
−4,900	=	0				−3,000	−1,500	−400

Journal Entry

Salary Expense	3,000	
Rent Expense..	1,500	
Interest Expense	400	
Cash		4,900

Paid expenses.

h. *Accounting Equation*

ASSETS		=	LIABILITIES	+	OWNER'S EQUITY
Cash	Accounts Receivable				
+3,100	−3,100	=	0	+	0

Journal Entry

Cash	3,100	
Accounts Receivable		3,100

Received cash on account.

i. *Accounting Equation*

ASSETS	=	LIABILITIES	+	OWNER'S EQUITY	−	EXPENSES
		Accounts Payable				Utilities Expense
0	=	+200			−	200

Journal Entry	Utilities Expense..	200	
	Accounts Payable		200
	Received utility bill.		

j. *Accounting Equation*

ASSETS	=	LIABILITIES	+	OWNER'S EQUITY
				Larry Tomassini,
Cash				Withdrawals
−1,800	=	0		−1,800

Journal Entry	Larry Tomassini, Withdrawals.................	1,800	
	Cash		1,800
	Owner withdrawal.		

Requirement 3

ASSETS

CASH

Bal.	26,000	(b)	40,000
(a)	45,000	(f)	1,200
(c)	5,000	(g)	4,900
(h)	3,100	(j)	1,800
Bal.	31,200		

ACCOUNTS RECEIVABLE

Bal.	4,500	(h)	3,100
(e)	2,600		
Bal.	4,000		

SUPPLIES

(d)	300		
Bal.	300		

LAND

(b)	40,000		
Bal.	40,000		

LIABILITIES

ACCOUNTS PAYABLE

(f)	1,200	Bal.	2,000
		(d)	300
		(i)	200
		Bal.	1,300

NOTE PAYABLE

		(a)	45,000
		Bal.	45,000

OWNER'S EQUITY

LARRY TOMASSINI, CAPITAL

		Bal.	28,500

LARRY TOMASSINI, WITHDRAWALS

(j)	1,800		
Bal.	1,800		

REVENUE

SERVICE REVENUE

		(c)	5,000
		(e)	2,600
		Bal.	7,600

EXPENSES

SALARY EXPENSE

(g)	3,000		
Bal.	3,000		

RENT EXPENSE

(g)	1,500		
Bal.	1,500		

INTEREST EXPENSE

(g)	400		
Bal.	400		

UTILITIES EXPENSE

(i)	200		
Bal.	200		

Requirement 4

TOMASSINI COMPUTER SERVICE CENTER
Trial Balance
March 31, 20X2

	Balance	
Account Title	**Debit**	**Credit**
Cash..	$31,200	
Accounts receivable.............................	4,000	
Supplies	300	
Land..	40,000	
Accounts payable		$ 1,300
Note payable...		45,000
Larry Tomassini, capital........................		28,500
Larry Tomassini, withdrawals...............	1,800	
Service revenue		7,600
Salary expense.......................................	3,000	
Rent expense	1,500	
Interest expense	400	
Utilities expense	200	
Total..	$82,400	$82,400

LESSONS LEARNED

1. **Define and use key accounting terms.** Accounts can be viewed in the form of the letter "T." The left side of each T-account is its *debit* side. The right side is its *credit* side. The *ledger*, which contains a record for each account, groups and numbers accounts by category in the following order: assets, liabilities, and owner's equity (and its subparts, revenues and expenses).

2. **Apply the rules of debit and credit.** *Assets* and *expenses* are increased by debits and decreased by credits. *Liabilities, owner's equity,* and *revenues* are increased by credits and decreased by debits. An account's *normal balance* is the side of the account—debit or credit—in which increases are recorded. Thus, the normal balance of assets and expenses is a debit, and the normal balance of liabilities, owner's equity, and revenues is a credit. The Withdrawals account, which decreases owner's equity, normally has a debit balance. Revenues, which are increases in owner's equity, have a normal credit balance. Expenses, which are decreases in owner's equity, have a normal debit balance.

3. **Record transactions in the journal.** The recording process begins by entering each transaction in the *journal,* a chronological list of all the entity's transactions.

4. **Post from the journal to the ledger.** *Posting* means copying the amounts from the journal to the *ledger* accounts. Posting references are used to trace amounts back and forth between journal and ledger.

5. **Prepare and use a trial balance.** *The trial balance* is a summary of all the account balances in the ledger. When *double-entry accounting* is done correctly, the total debits and the total credits in the trial balance are equal.

6. **Set up a chart of accounts for a business.** A chart of accounts lists all the accounts in the ledger and their account numbers.

7. **Analyze transactions without a journal.** Decision makers must often make decisions without a complete accounting system. They can analyze the transactions without a journal.

ACCOUNTING VOCABULARY

account (p. 39)
chart of accounts (p. 55)
credit (p. 42)

debit (p. 42)
journal (p. 44)
ledger (p. 39)

normal balance (p. 55)
posting (p. 45)
trial balance (p. 48)

QUESTIONS

1. Name the basic summary device of accounting. What letter of the alphabet does it resemble? Name its two sides.
2. Is the following statement true or false? Debit means decrease and credit means increase. Explain your answer.
3. What are the three *basic* types of accounts? Name two additional types of accounts. Which of the three basic types are these two additional types of accounts most closely related to?
4. Briefly describe the flow of accounting information.
5. Indicate the normal balance of the five types of accounts.

Account Type	Normal Balance
Assets	
Liabilities	
Capital	
Revenues	
Expenses	

6. What does posting accomplish? Why is it important? Does it come before or after journalizing?
7. Label each of the following transactions as increasing owner's equity (+), decreasing owner's equity (−), or as having no effect on owner's equity (0). Write the appropriate symbol in the space provided.

_____a. Investment by owner
_____b. Revenue transaction
_____c. Purchase of supplies on credit
_____d. Expense transaction
_____e. Cash payment on account
_____f. Withdrawal by owner
_____g. Borrowing money on a note payable
_____h. Sale of service on account

8. Rearrange the following accounts in their logical sequence in the ledger:

Notes Payable   Cash
Accounts Receivable   Jane East, Capital
Sales Revenue   Salary Expense

9. What is the meaning of this statement? Accounts Payable has a credit balance of $1,700.
10. Why do accountants prepare a trial balance?
11. What is a compound journal entry?
12. The accountant for Bower Construction Company mistakenly recorded a $500 purchase of supplies on account as a $5,000 purchase. He debited Supplies and credited Accounts Payable for $5,000. Does this error cause the trial balance to be out of balance? Explain your answer.
13. What is the effect on total assets of collecting cash on account from customers?
14. What is the advantage of analyzing transactions without the use of a journal? Describe how this analysis works.

ASSESS YOUR PROGRESS

DAILY EXERCISES

DE2-1 There are three broad categories of accounts: assets, liabilities, and owner's equity.

Using key terms (Obj. 1)

1. Owner's equity is more complex than assets and liabilities. What is the definition of *owner's equity?* Suppose your assets total $8,000 and your liabilities are $5,000. How much is your owner's equity?
2. Identify two categories of transactions that *increase* owner's equity. Name two categories of transactions that *decrease* owner's equity. This concept is discussed beginning on page 40.
3. Give a short (one- or two-word) synonym for an *asset* and a *liability.* Then list several individual assets and several specific liabilities.

DE2-2 Review basic accounting definitions by completing the following crossword puzzle.

Using key terms (Obj. 1)

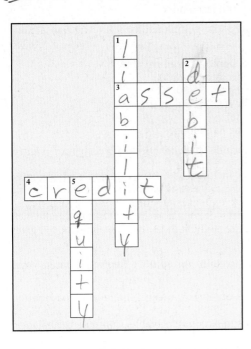

Across:
3. Economic resource of an entity.
4. Records an increase in a liability or owner's equity.

Down:
1. A debt.
2. Records an increase in an asset or an expense.
5. Assets − Liabilities = Owner's _____.

DE2-3 Rolfe Schmidt opened an architectural firm and immediately paid $60,000 for equipment to be used in the business. Was Schmidt's payment an expense of the business? If not, what did he acquire? Explain your reasoning after reviewing the definitions of *assets* on page 39 and *expenses* on page 41.

Explaining an asset versus an expense (Obj. 1)

DE2-4 Understanding basic concepts is essential for success in accounting. Tighten your grip on the accounting process by filling in the blanks to review the definitions of key terms.

Using key terms (Obj. 1)

Erika Darby, an introductory accounting student, is describing the accounting process for a friend who is a philosophy major. Erika states, "The basic summary device in accounting is the **account,** which can be represented by the letter ___T___. The left side of an account is called the _debit_ side, and the right side is called the _credit_ side.

"We record transactions first in a _journal_. Then we post (copy the data) to the accounts in the _ledger_. It is helpful to list all the accounts with their balances on a _trial balance_

DE2-5 Accounting has its own vocabulary and basic relationships. Match the accounting terms at left with the corresponding definition at right.

Using accounting terms (Obj. 1)

1. Ledger	A. Record of transactions
2. Posting	B. Always an asset
3. Normal balance	C. Left side of an account
4. Payable	D. Side of an account where increases are recorded
5. Journal	E. Copying data from the journal to the ledger
6. Receivable	F. Using up assets in the course of operating a business
7. Capital	G. Always a liability
8. Debit	H. Revenues − Expenses
9. Expense	I. Grouping of accounts
10. Net income	J. Owner's equity in the business

DE2-6 Josh Birbary, a recent graduate, is tutoring Trevor Grant, who is taking introductory accounting. Josh explains to Trevor that *debits* are used to record increases in accounts and *credits* record decreases. Trevor is confused and seeks your advice.

• When are credits increases? When are credits decreases?
• When are debits increases? When are debits decreases?

Exhibit 2-13, page 57, gives the rules of debit and credit.

DE2-7 Lee Jackson opened a medical practice in Cincinnati, Ohio. Record the following transactions in the journal of Lee Jackson, M.D. Include an explanation with each journal entry.

June 1   Jackson invested $25,000 cash in a business bank account to start his medical practice. The business received the cash and gave Jackson owner's equity in the business.
2   Purchased medical supplies on account, $10,000.
2   Paid monthly office rent of $4,000.
3   Recorded $5,000 revenue for service rendered to patients. Received cash of $1,000 and sent bills to patients for the remainder.

DE2-8 After operating for a month, Lee Jackson, M.D., completed the following transactions during the latter part of July:

July 15   Borrowed $20,000 from the bank, signing a note payable.
22   Performed service for patients on account, $2,800.
30   Received cash on account from patients, $1,000.
31   Received a utility bill, $200, which will be paid during August.
31   Paid monthly salary to nurse, $3,000.
31   Paid interest expense of $200 on the bank loan.

Journalize the transactions of Lee Jackson, M.D. Include an explanation with each journal entry.

DE2-9 The accounting records of all businesses include three basic categories of accounts: assets, liabilities, and owner's equity. In turn, owner's equity is divided into the following categories: capital, withdrawals, revenues, and expenses. Identify which categories of accounts—including the subparts of owner's equity—have a normal debit balance and which categories of accounts have a normal credit balance. Exhibit 2-13, Panel B, on page 57, gives the normal balance in each category of account.

DE2-10 Marianne Vogel purchased supplies on account for $3,000. Two weeks later, Vogel paid half on account.

1. Journalize the two transactions on the books of Marianne Vogel. Include an explanation for each transaction.
2. Open the Accounts Payable account and post to Accounts Payable. Compute the balance, and denote it as *Bal.*
3. How much does Vogel owe after both transactions? In which account does this amount appear?

DE2-11 Peter Nguyen performed legal service for a client who could not pay immediately. Nguyen expected to collect the $5,000 the following month. Later, Nguyen received $2,700 cash from the client.

1. Record the two transactions on the books of Peter Nguyen, Attorney. Include an explanation for each transaction.
2. Open these accounts: Cash; Accounts Receivable; Service Revenue. Post to all three accounts. Compute each account's balance, and denote as *Bal.*
3. Answer these questions based on your analysis:
   a. How much did Nguyen earn? Which account shows this amount?
   b. How much in total assets did Nguyen acquire as a result of the two transactions? Show the amount of each asset.

Note: Daily Exercise 2-12 should be used in connection with Daily Exercise 2-7.

DE2-12 Use the June transaction data for Lee Jackson, M.D., given in Daily Exercise 2-7.

1. Open the following T-accounts of Lee Jackson, M.D.: Cash; Accounts Receivable; Medical Supplies; Accounts Payable; Lee Jackson, Capital; Service Revenue; Rent Expense.
2. After making the journal entries in Daily Exercise 2-7, post from the journal to the ledger. No dates or posting references are required. Compute the balance of each account, and denote it as *Bal.*
3. Prepare the trial balance, complete with a proper heading, at June 3, 20X8. Use the trial balance on page 52 as a guide.

DE2-13 **Intel Corporation,** famous for the Pentium© processor, reported the following summarized data at December 31, 19X9. Accounts appear in no particular order; dollar amounts are in billions.

Revenues............................	$29	Other liabilities................	$11	
Other assets.........................	40	Cash.................................	4	
Accounts payable................	1	Expenses............................	22	
Capital..................................	25			

Prepare the trial balance of Intel Corporation at December 31, 19X9. List the accounts in their proper order, as on page 52.

DE2-14 Jeff Hatton, Attorney, prepared the business's trial balance on page 61. Suppose Hatton made two errors in preparing the trial balance, as follows:

Correcting a trial balance (Obj. 5)

> **Error 1**—Hatton erroneously listed his capital balance of $10,000 as a debit rather than as a credit.
>
> **Error 2**—Hatton erroneously listed Service Revenue as a credit balance of $42,000 rather than the correct amount of $4,200.

Consider each error separately.

1. For each error, compute the incorrect trial balance totals for total debits and total credits.
2. Refer to the discussion of correcting trial balance errors on page 49 and show how to correct each error.

DE2-15 Metrolink Apartment Finder Service helps college students locate apartments because Dundalk Community College has no student housing on campus. Wayne Gibbs, the owner of Metrolink, is setting up the business's chart of accounts after making an initial investment of cash in the business.

Setting up a chart of accounts (Obj. 6)

Gibbs will perform apartment locator services for clients on account. His office will need some supplies, a computer (equipment), and furniture. Gibbs has borrowed money by signing a note payable to the bank. The business will also purchase on account some of the things it needs.

Expenses of the business will include rent, utilities, and advertising.

Prepare the chart of accounts for Metrolink Apartment Finder Service, including three-digit account numbers. Use Exhibit 2-10, page 55, as a guide.

DE2-16 Marta Fraser established Bodyfit, a health club, with an initial cash investment of $100,000. The business immediately purchased equipment on account for $45,000. Marta needs to know her account balances immediately and doesn't have time to journalize the transactions.

Analyzing transactions without a journal (Obj. 7)

1. Open the following T-accounts on the books of Bodyfit. Cash; Equipment; Accounts Payable; Marta Fraser, Capital.
2. Record the first two transactions of Bodyfit directly in the T-accounts without using a journal.
3. Compute the balance in each account and show that total debits equal total credits.

EXERCISES

E2-1 Your employer, Digitech Enterprises, has just hired an office manager who does not understand accounting. Digitech's trial balance lists Cash of $43,000. Write a short memo to the office manager, explaining the accounting process that produced this listing on the trial balance. Mention *debits, credits, journal, ledger, posting,* and *trial balance.*

Using accounting vocabulary (Obj. 1)

E2-2 ◄ *Link Back to Chapter 1 (Accounting Equation).* **The Coca-Cola Company** is famous worldwide for its soft drinks. At the end of 1999, Coca-Cola had total assets of $22 billion and liabilities totaling $12 billion.

Using debits and credits with the accounting equation (Obj. 1, 2)

Required

1. Write the company's accounting equation, and label each element as a debit amount or a credit amount.
2. Coca-Cola's total revenues for 1999 were $20 billion, and total expenses for the year were $18 billion. How much was Coca-Cola's net income (or net loss) for 1999? Write the equation to compute Coca-Cola's net income, and indicate which element is a debit amount and which element is a credit amount. Does net income represent a net debit or a net credit? Does net loss represent a net debit or a net credit? Review Exhibit 1-7, page 20, if needed.
3. During 1999, the owners of Coca-Cola withdrew $1 billion in the form of dividends (same as owner Withdrawals). Did the dividends represent a debit amount or a credit amount?

RECORDING BUSINESS TRANSACTIONS 69

4. Considering both Coca-Cola's net income (or net loss) and dividends for 1999, by how much did the company's owners' equity increase or decrease during 1999? Was the increase in owners' equity a debit amount or a credit amount?

Analyzing and journalizing transactions
(Obj. 2, 3)

E2-3 Analyze the following transactions in the manner shown for the December 1 transaction of Miramar Electronics. Also record each transaction in the journal. Explanations are not required.

Dec. 1 Paid utilities expense of $700. (*Analysis:* The expense, Utilities Expense, is increased; therefore, debit Utilities Expense. The asset, Cash, is decreased; therefore, credit Cash.)

    1 Utilities Expense 700
             Cash........................... 700

    5 Purchased office furniture on account, $800.
  10 Performed service on account for a customer, $1,600.
  12 Borrowed $7,000 cash, signing a note payable.
  19 Sold for $29,000 land that had cost this same amount.
  24 Purchased building for $140,000; signed a note payable.
  27 Paid the liability created on December 5.

Applying the rules of debit and credit
(Obj. 2)

E2-4 Refer to Exercise 2-3 for the transactions of Miramar Electronics.

Required

1. Open the following T-accounts with their December 1 balances: Cash, debit balance $6,000; Land, debit balance $29,000; Martha Cross, Capital, credit balance $35,000.
2. Record the transactions of Exercise 2-3 directly in the T-accounts affected. Use the dates as posting references. Journal entries are not required.
3. Compute the December 31 balance for each account, and prove that total debits equal total credits.

Journalizing transactions
(Obj. 3)

E2-5 New Balance Spa engaged in the following transactions during March 20X3, its first month of operations:

Mar. 1 Joy Liebermann invested $55,000 of cash to start the business.
    2 Purchased office supplies of $200 on account.
    4 Paid $40,000 cash for a building to use as an office in the very near future.
    6 Performed service for customers and received cash, $3,000.
    9 Paid $100 on accounts payable.
  17 Performed service for customers on account, $1,600.
  23 Received $1,200 cash from a customer on account.
  31 Paid the following expenses: salary, $1,200; rent, $500.

Required

Record the preceding transactions in the journal of New Balance Spa. Key transactions by date and include an explanation for each entry, as illustrated in the chapter. Use the following accounts: Cash; Accounts Receivable; Office Supplies; Building; Accounts Payable; Joy Liebermann, Capital; Service Revenue; Salary Expense; Rent Expense.

Posting to the ledger and preparing a trial balance
(Obj. 4, 5)

E2-6 Refer to Exercise 2-5 for the transactions of New Balance Spa.

Required

1. After journalizing the transactions of Exercise 2-5, post the entries to the ledger, using T-account format. Key transactions by date. Date the ending balance of each account Mar. 31.
2. Prepare the trial balance of New Balance Spa at March 31, 20X3.

Describing transactions and posting
(Obj. 2, 3)

E2-7 The journal of Freebin & Associates includes the following transaction entries for May 20X6.

Required

1. Describe each transaction.
2. Post the transactions to the ledger using the following account numbers: Cash, 110; Accounts Receivable, 120; Supplies, 130; Accounts Payable, 210; Note Payable, 230; Leonard Freebin, Capital, 310; Service Revenue, 410; Rent Expense, 510; Advertising Expense, 520; Utilities Expense, 530. Use dates, journal references, and posting references as illustrated in Exhibit 2-8. You may write the account numbers as posting references directly in your book unless directed otherwise by your instructor.
3. Compute the balance in each account after posting. Prepare Freebin & Associates' trial balance at May 31, 20X6.

Journal

Date	Accounts and Explanation	Post. Ref.	Debit	Credit
May 2	Cash..		20,000	
	Leonard Freebin, Capital...............			20,000
5	Cash..		15,000	
	Note Payable			15,000
9	Supplies		270	
	Accounts Payable			270
11	Accounts Receivable......................		2,630	
	Service Revenue			2,630
14	Rent Expense................................		3,200	
	Cash			3,200
22	Accounts Payable...........................		270	
	Cash			270
25	Advertising Expense.......................		350	
	Cash			350
27	Cash..		1,400	
	Accounts Receivable			1,400
31	Utilities Expense		220	
	Accounts Payable..........................			220

E2-8 The first five transactions of Flores Security Company have been posted to the company's accounts as follows:

Journalizing transactions (Obj. 3)

CASH				SUPPLIES		EQUIPMENT		LAND	
(1)	62,000	(3)	56,000	(2)	400	(5)	6,000	(3)	56,000
(4)	7,000	(5)	6,000						

ACCOUNTS PAYABLE		NOTE PAYABLE		TONY FLORES, CAPITAL	
(2)	400	(4)	7,000	(1)	62,000

Required

Prepare the journal entries that served as the sources for the five transactions. Include an explanation for each entry as illustrated in the chapter.

E2-9 Prepare the trial balance of Flores Security Company at April 30, 20X4, using the account data from Exercise 2-8.

Preparing a trial balance (Obj. 5)

E2-10 The accounts of Beaulieu Company follow with their normal balances at December 31, 20X4. The accounts are listed in no particular order.

Preparing a trial balance (Obj. 5)

Account	Balance
Pierre Beaulieu, capital........................	$48,800
Advertising expense............................	650
Accounts payable...............................	4,300
Sales commission revenue.................	26,000
Land..	29,000
Supplies expense	300
Cash..	5,000
Salary expense	6,000
Building	65,000
Rent expense	2,000
Pierre Beaulieu, withdrawals..............	6,000
Utilities expense................................	400
Accounts receivable	9,500
Note payable	45,000
Supplies	250

Required

Prepare the company's trial balance at December 31, 20X4, listing accounts in proper sequence, as illustrated in the chapter. For example, Supplies comes before Building and Land. List the expense with the largest balance first, the expense with the next largest balance second, and so on.

E2-11 The trial balance of Atlantis Enterprises at March 31, 20X9, does not balance:

Cash	$ 4,500	
Accounts receivable	2,000	
Supplies	600	
Land	66,000	
Accounts payable		$23,000
Paige Dylan, capital		41,600
Service revenue		9,700
Salary expense	1,700	
Rent expense	800	
Utilities expense	300	
Total	$75,900	$74,300

Investigation of the accounting records reveals that the bookkeeper

a. Recorded a $400 cash revenue transaction by debiting Accounts Receivable. The credit entry was correct.
b. Posted a $1,000 credit to Accounts Payable as $100.
c. Did not record utilities expense or the related account payable in the amount of $200.
d. Understated Paige Dylan, Capital, by $700.

Required

Prepare the correct trial balance at March 31, complete with a heading; journal entries are not required.

E2-12 Open the following T-accounts of Cole Gates, CPA: Cash; Accounts Receivable; Office Supplies; Office Furniture; Accounts Payable; Cole Gates, Capital; Cole Gates, Withdrawals; Service Revenue; Salary Expense; Rent Expense.

Record the following transactions directly in the T-accounts without using a journal. Use the letters to identify the transactions. Compute the balance of each account.

a. Gates opened an accounting firm by investing $12,400 cash and office furniture valued at $5,400.
b. Paid monthly rent of $1,500.
c. Purchased office supplies on account, $700.
d. Paid employee's salary, $1,800.
e. Paid $400 of the account payable created in transaction (c).
f. Performed accounting service on account, $1,600.
g. Withdrew $7,000 for personal use.

E2-13 After recording the transactions in Exercise 2-12, prepare the trial balance of Cole Gates, CPA, at May 31, 20X7.

E2-14 Moseley Supply began when Lynette Moseley invested $75,000 cash in a business bank account. During the first week, the business purchased supplies on credit for $8,000 and paid $12,000 cash for equipment. Moseley later paid $5,000 on account.

Required

1. Open the following T-accounts: Cash; Supplies; Equipment; Accounts Payable; Lynette Moseley, Capital.
2. Record the four transactions described above directly in the T-accounts without using a journal.
3. Compute the balance in each account, and show that total debit balances equal total credit balances after you have recorded all the transactions. The T-accounts on page 48 provide a guide for your answer.

Continuing Exercise Exercise 2-15 is the first exercise in a sequence that begins an accounting cycle. The cycle is completed in Chapter 5.

E2-15 Amos Faraday completed these transactions during the first half of December:

Dec.	2	Invested $14,000 to start a consulting practice, Amos Faraday, Consultant.
	2	Paid monthly office rent, $500.
	3	Paid cash for a Dell computer, $2,000. The computer is expected to remain in service for five years.
	4	Purchased office furniture on account, $3,600. The furniture should last for five years.
	5	Purchased supplies on account, $300.
	9	Performed consulting service for a client on account, $1,700.
	12	Paid utility expenses, $200.
	18	Performed service for a client and received cash for the full amount of $800.

Required

1. Open T-accounts in the ledger: Cash; Accounts Receivable; Supplies; Equipment; Furniture; Accounts Payable; Amos Faraday, Capital; Amos Faraday, Withdrawals; Service Revenue; Rent Expense; Utilities Expense; and Salary Expense.
2. Journalize the transactions. Explanations are not required.
3. Post to the T-accounts. Key all items by date, and denote an account balance as *Bal.* Formal posting references are not required.
4. Prepare a trial balance at December 18. In the Continuing Exercise of Chapter 3, we will add transactions for the remainder of December and prepare a trial balance at December 31.

Challenge Exercises

E2-16 The owner of Midwest Catering Services needs to compute the following summary information from the accounting records:

Computing financial statement amounts without a journal (Obj. 7)

a. Net income for the month of March.
b. Total cash paid during March.
c. Cash collections from customers during March.
d. Cash paid on a note payable during March.

The quickest way to compute these amounts is to analyze the following accounts:

Account	Balance Feb. 28	Balance Mar. 31	Additional Information for the Month of March
a. Owner, Capital....................	$ 9,000	$15,000	Withdrawals, $7,000
b. Cash	7,000	2,000	Cash receipts, $61,000
c. Accounts Receivable	24,000	26,000	Revenues on account, $76,000
d. Note Payable	11,000	16,000	New-borrowing on a note payable, $7,500

The net income for March can be computed as follows:

	OWNER, CAPITAL		
	Feb. 28 Bal.	9,000	
March Withdrawals 7,000	March Net Income	X = $13,000	
	March 31 Bal.	15,000	

Use a similar approach to compute the other three items.

E2-17 Tara Hale has trouble keeping her debits and credits equal. During a recent month, she made the following errors:

Analyzing accounting errors (Obj. 2, 3, 4, 5)

a. In journalizing a receipt of cash for service revenue, Hale debited Cash for $1,800 instead of the correct amount of $800. Hale credited Service Revenue for $1,800, the incorrect amount.
b. Hale recorded a $120 purchase of supplies on account by debiting Supplies and crediting Accounts Payable for $210.
c. In preparing the trial balance, Hale omitted a $40,000 note payable.
d. Hale posted a $700 utility expense as $70. The credit posting to Cash was correct.
e. In recording a $400 payment on account, Hale debited Supplies and credited Accounts Payable.

Required

1. For each of these errors, state whether the total debits equal total credits on the trial balance.
2. Identify any accounts with misstated balances, and indicate the amount and direction of the error (such as account balance too high or too low).

PROBLEMS

(Group A)

P2-1A ← *Link Back to Chapter 1 (Balance Sheet, Income Statement).* The owner of Cantor Polling Service is selling the business. She offers the trial balance shown here to prospective buyers. Your best friend is considering buying Cantor Polling Service. He seeks your advice in interpreting this information. Specifically, he asks whether this trial balance is the same as a balance sheet and an income statement. He also wonders whether Cantor is a sound business. After all, the company's accounts are in balance.

Analyzing a trial balance (Obj. 1)

CANTOR POLLING SERVICE
Trial Balance
December 31, 20X8

Cash	$ 12,000	
Accounts receivable	27,000	
Prepaid expenses	4,000	
Land	63,000	
Accounts payable		$ 35,000
Note payable		32,000
Kendra Cantor, capital		30,000
Kendra Cantor, withdrawals	48,000	
Service revenue		116,000
Rent expense	26,000	
Advertising expense	3,000	
Wage expense	23,000	
Supplies expense	7,000	
Total	$213,000	$213,000

Required

Write a short note to answer your friend's questions. To aid his decision, state how he can use the information on the trial balance to compute Cantor's net income or net loss for the current period. State the amount of net income or net loss in your note. Refer to Exhibit 1-7, page 20, if needed.

Analyzing and journalizing transactions
(Obj. 2, 3)

P2-2A Silverstar Cinemas owns movie theaters in the shopping centers of a major metropolitan area. Its owner, Joseph Reese, engaged in the following business transactions:

April 1	Reese invested $500,000 personal cash in the business by depositing that amount in a bank account entitled Silverstar Cinemas. The business gave Reese owner's equity in the company.
2	Paid $400,000 cash to purchase a theater building.
5	Borrowed $220,000 from the bank. Reese signed a note payable to the bank in the name of Silverstar Cinemas.
10	Purchased theater supplies on account, $1,700.
15	Paid $800 on account.
15	Paid property tax expense on theater building, $1,200.
16	Paid employee salaries, $2,800, and rent on equipment, $1,800.
17	Withdrew $6,000 from the business for personal use.
30	Received $20,000 cash from ticket sales and deposited that amount in the bank. (Label the revenue as Sales Revenue.)

Silverstar uses the following accounts: Cash; Supplies; Building; Accounts Payable; Notes Payable; Joseph Reese, Capital; Joseph Reese, Withdrawals; Sales Revenue; Salary Expense; Rent Expense; Property Tax Expense.

Required

1. Analyze each business transaction of Silverstar Cinemas, as shown for the April 1 transaction:

   Apr. 1   The asset Cash is increased. Increases in assets are recorded by debits; therefore, debit Cash. The owner's equity of the entity is increased. Increases in owner's equity are recorded by credits; therefore, credit Joseph Reese, Capital.

2. Journalize each transaction. Explanations are not required.

Journalizing transactions, posting to T-accounts, and preparing a trial balance
(Obj. 2, 3, 4, 5)

P2-3A Terence Larkin opened a law office on September 3 of the current year. During the first month of operations, the business completed the following transactions:

Sep. 3	Larkin transferred $43,000 cash from his personal bank account to a business account entitled Terence Larkin, Attorney. The business gave Larkin owner's equity in the business.
4	Purchased supplies, $200, and furniture, $1,800, on account.
6	Performed legal services for a client and received $4,000 cash.
7	Paid $15,000 cash to acquire land for a future office site.
10	Defended a client in court, billed the client, and received her promise to pay the $800 within one week.
14	Paid for the furniture purchased September 4 on account.
15	Paid secretary's salary, $600.
17	Received partial collection from client on account, $500.

Sep. 20   Prepared legal documents for a client on account, $800.
    28   Received $1,500 cash for helping a client sell real estate.
    30   Paid secretary's salary, $600.
    30   Paid rent expense, $500.
    30   Withdrew $2,900 for personal use.

Required

Open the following T-accounts: Cash; Accounts Receivable; Supplies; Furniture; Land; Accounts Payable; Terence Larkin, Capital; Terence Larkin, Withdrawals; Service Revenue; Salary Expense; Rent Expense.

1. Record each transaction in the journal, using the account titles given. Key each transaction by date. Explanations are not required.
2. Post the transactions to the ledger, using transaction dates as posting references in the ledger. Label the balance of each account *Bal.*, as shown in the chapter.
3. Prepare the trial balance of Terence Larkin, Attorney, at September 30 of the current year.

P2-4A The trial balance of the accounting practice of Jill Case, CPA, is dated February 14, 20X3:

Journalizing transactions, posting to accounts in four-column format, and preparing a trial balance (Obj. 2, 3, 4, 5)

JILL CASE, CPA
Trial Balance
February 14, 20X3

Account Number	Account	Debit	Credit
11	Cash..	$ 2,000	
12	Accounts receivable................	9,500	
13	Supplies	800	
14	Land..	18,600	
21	Accounts payable.....................		$ 3,000
31	Jill Case, capital		26,500
32	Jill Case, withdrawals..............	1,200	
41	Service revenue.......................		7,200
51	Salary expense.........................	3,600	
52	Rent expense	1,000	
	Total...	$36,700	$36,700

During the remainder of February, Case completed the following transactions:

Feb. 15   Case collected $3,500 cash from a client on account.
    16   Performed tax services for a client on account, $700.
    20   Paid on account, $1,000.
    21   Purchased supplies on account, $100.
    21   Withdrew $1,200 for personal use.
    21   Paid for a wooden deck for private residence, using personal funds, $9,000.
    22   Received cash of $5,100 for consulting work just completed.
    28   Paid rent, $800.
    28   Paid employees' salaries, $1,800.

Required

1. Record the transactions that occurred during February 15–28 in page 3 of the journal. Include an explanation for each entry.
2. Open the ledger accounts listed in the trial balance, together with their balances at February 14. Use the four-column account format illustrated in the chapter (Exhibit 2-9). Enter *Bal.* (for previous balance) in the Item column, and place a check mark (✓) in the journal reference column for the February 14 balance in each account. Post the transactions to the ledger using dates, account numbers, journal references, and posting references.
3. Prepare the trial balance of Jill Case, CPA, at February 28, 20X3.

P2-5A ← *Link Back to Chapter 1 (Income Statement).* The trial balance for Chapel Lawn Service at the top of the next page does not balance.
    The following errors were detected:

Correcting errors in a trial balance (Obj. 2, 5)

a. The cash balance is understated by $700.
b. The cost of the land was $43,000, not $46,000.
c. A $200 purchase of supplies on account was neither journalized nor posted.
d. The balance of Utilities Expense is overstated by $70.
e. Rent expense of $200 was erroneously posted as a credit rather than a debit.

CHAPEL LAWN SERVICE
Trial Balance
June 30, 20X2

Cash.....................................	$ 3,000	
Accounts receivable........................	10,000	
Supplies...............................	900	
Equipment..........................	5,100	
Land	46,000	
Accounts payable		$ 5,000
Note payable		22,000
Rob Rylander, capital		31,600
Rob Rylander, withdrawals..............	2,000	
Service revenue.............................		6,500
Salary expense............................	2,100	
Rent expense..............................	1,000	
Advertising expense	500	
Utilities expense	400	
Total...	$71,000	$65,100

f. The balance of Advertising Expense is $600, but it was listed as $500 on the trial balance.

g. A $300 debit to Accounts Receivable was posted as $30.

h. A $4,300 credit to Service Revenue was not posted.

i. A $900 debit to the Withdrawals account was posted as a debit to Rob Rylander, Capital.

Required

1. Prepare the correct trial balance at June 30. Journal entries are not required.
2. Prepare the company's income statement for the month ended June 30, 20X2, in order to determine Chapel Lawn Service's net income or net loss for the month. Refer to Exhibit 1-7, page 20, if needed.

Recording transactions directly in T-accounts; preparing a trial balance (Obj. 2, 5, 7)

P2-6A Allen Musser started a consulting service and during the first month of operations (June 20X3) completed the following selected transactions:

a. Musser began the business with an investment of $5,000 cash and a building valued at $60,000. The business gave Musser owner's equity in the business.

b. Borrowed $30,000 from the bank; signed a note payable.

c. Purchased office supplies on account, $2,100.

d. Paid $18,000 for office furniture.

e. Paid employee's salary, $2,200.

f. Performed consulting service on account for client, $5,100.

g. Paid $800 of the account payable created in transaction (c).

h. Received a $600 bill for advertising expense that will be paid in the near future.

i. Performed consulting service for customers and received cash, $1,600.

j. Received cash on account, $1,200.

k. Paid the following cash expenses:
   (1) Rent on land, $700.   (2) Utilities, $400.

l. Withdrew $7,500 for personal use.

Required

1. Open the following T-accounts: Cash; Accounts Receivable; Office Supplies; Office Furniture; Building; Accounts Payable; Note Payable; Allen Musser, Capital; Allen Musser, Withdrawals; Service Revenue; Salary Expense; Advertising Expense; Rent Expense; Utilities Expense.
2. Record each transaction directly in the T-accounts without using a journal. Use the letters to identify the transactions.
3. Prepare the trial balance of Musser Consulting Service at June 30, 20X3.

Note: Problem 2-7A should be used in conjunction with Problem 2-6A.

Preparing the financial statements (Obj. 5)

P2-7A ◄═ *Link Back to Chapter 1 (Income Statement, Statement of Owner's Equity, Balance Sheet).* Refer to Problem 2-6A. After completing the trial balance in Problem 2-6A, prepare the following financial statements for Musser Consulting Service:

1. Income statement for the month ended June 30, 20X3.
2. Statement of owner's equity for the month ended June 30, 20X3.
3. Balance sheet at June 30, 20X3.

Draw arrows to link the statements. If needed, use Exhibit 1-7, page 20, as a guide for preparing the financial statements.

PROBLEMS

(Group B)

P2-1B ← *Link Back to Chapter 1 (Balance Sheet, Income Statement).* The owner of Biokinetic Engineering is selling the business. He offers the following trial balance to prospective buyers. Your best friend is considering buying Biokinetic. She seeks your advice in interpreting this information. Specifically, she asks whether this trial balance is the same as a balance sheet and an income statement. She also wonders whether Biokinetic is a sound business. After all, the company's accounts are in balance.

Analyzing a trial balance
(Obj. 1)

BIOKINETIC ENGINEERING
Trial Balance
December 31, 20X4

Cash	$ 7,000	
Accounts receivable	6,000	
Prepaid expenses	4,000	
Land	51,000	
Accounts payable		$ 31,000
Note payable		20,000
Avery Patella, capital		33,000
Avery Patella, withdrawals	21,000	
Service revenue		72,000
Wage expense	28,000	
Rent expense	14,000	
Advertising expense	18,000	
Supplies expense	7,000	
Total	$156,000	$156,000

Required

Write a short note to answer your friend's questions. To aid her decision, state how she can use the information on the trial balance to compute Biokinetic's net income or net loss for the current period. State the amount of net income or net loss in your note. Refer to Exhibit 1-7, page 20, if needed.

P2-2B Deborah Fedro practices medicine under the business title Deborah Fedro, M.D. During June, her medical practice engaged in the following transactions:

Analyzing and journalizing transactions
(Obj. 2, 3)

June 1	Fedro deposited $55,000 cash in the business bank account. The business gave Fedro owner's equity in the business.
5	Paid monthly rent on medical equipment, $700.
9	Paid $22,000 cash to purchase land for an office site.
10	Purchased supplies on account, $1,200.
19	Borrowed $20,000 from the bank for business use. Fedro signed a note payable to the bank in the name of the business.
22	Paid $1,000 on account.
30	Revenues earned during the month included $6,000 cash and $5,000 on account.
30	Paid employees' salaries ($2,400), office rent ($1,500), and utilities ($400).
30	Withdrew $10,000 from the business for personal use.

Fedro's business uses the following accounts: Cash; Accounts Receivable; Supplies; Land; Accounts Payable; Notes Payable; Deborah Fedro, Capital; Deborah Fedro, Withdrawals; Service Revenue; Salary Expense; Rent Expense; Utilities Expense.

Required

1. Analyze each transaction of Deborah Fedro, M.D., as shown for the June 1 transaction:

    June 1   The asset Cash is increased. Increases in assets are recorded by debits; therefore, debit Cash. The owner's equity is increased. Increases in owner's equity are recorded by credits; therefore, credit Deborah Fedro, Capital.

2. Journalize each transaction. Explanations are not required.

P2-3B Rodney Troon opened a law office on December 2 of the current year. During the first month of operations, the business completed the following transactions:

Dec. 2	Troon deposited $50,000 cash in the business bank account Rodney Troon, Attorney.
3	Purchased supplies, $500, and furniture, $2,600, on account.
4	Performed legal service for a client and received cash, $1,500.
7	Paid cash to acquire land for a future office site, $22,000.
11	Prepared legal documents for a client on account, $900.
15	Paid secretary's salary, $570.
16	Paid for the furniture purchased December 3 on account.
18	Received $1,800 cash for helping a client sell real estate.
19	Defended a client in court and billed the client for $800.
29	Received partial collection from client on account, $400.
31	Paid secretary's salary, $570.
31	Paid rent expense, $700.
31	Withdrew $2,200 for personal use.

Required

Open the following T-accounts: Cash; Accounts Receivable; Supplies; Furniture; Land; Accounts Payable; Rodney Troon, Capital; Rodney Troon, Withdrawals; Service Revenue; Salary Expense; Rent Expense.

1. Record each transaction in the journal, using the account titles given. Key each transaction by date. Explanations are not required.
2. Post the transactions to the ledger, using transaction dates as posting references in the ledger. Label the balance of each account *Bal.,* as shown in the chapter.
3. Prepare the trial balance of Rodney Troon, Attorney, at December 31 of the current year.

P2-4B The trial balance of the law practice of Brent Busch, Attorney, at November 15, 20X3, follows.

BRENT BUSCH, ATTORNEY
Trial Balance
November 15, 20X3

Account Number	Account	Debit	Credit
11	Cash	$ 3,000	
12	Accounts receivable	8,000	
13	Supplies	600	
14	Land	35,000	
21	Accounts payable		$ 4,600
31	Brent Busch, capital		40,000
32	Brent Busch, withdrawals	2,300	
41	Service revenue		7,100
51	Salary expense	1,800	
52	Rent expense	1,000	
	Total	$51,700	$51,700

During the remainder of November, Busch completed the following transactions:

Nov. 16	Collected $6,000 cash from a client on account.
17	Performed tax service for a client on account, $1,700.
21	Used personal funds to pay for the renovation of private residence, $55,000.
22	Purchased supplies on account, $800.
23	Withdrew $2,100 for personal use.
23	Paid on account, $2,600.
24	Received $1,900 cash for legal work just completed.
30	Paid rent, $700.
30	Paid employees' salaries, $2,100.

Required

1. Record the transactions that occurred during November 16–30 on page 6 of the journal. Include an explanation for each entry.
2. Post the transactions to the ledger, using dates, account numbers, journal references, and posting references. Open the ledger accounts listed in the trial balance together with their balances at November 15. Use the four-column account format illustrated in the chapter

(Exhibit 2-9). Enter *Bal.* (for previous balance) in the Item column, and place a check mark (✓) in the journal reference column for the November 15 balance of each account.

3. Prepare the trial balance of Brent Busch, Attorney, at November 30, 20X3.

P2-5B ◄= *Link Back to Chapter 1 (Income Statement).* The trial balance for Ballard Financial Services does not balance. The following errors were detected:

Correcting errors in a trial balance (Obj. 2, 5)

a. The cash balance is understated by $400.
b. Rent expense of $350 was erroneously posted as a credit rather than a debit.
c. An $8,300 credit to Service Revenue was not posted.
d. A $600 debit to Accounts Receivable was posted as $60.
e. The balance of Utilities Expense is understated by $60.
f. A $1,300 debit to the Withdrawal account was posted as a debit to Meredith Ballard, Capital.
g. A $100 purchase of supplies on account was neither journalized nor posted.
h. The balance of Advertising Expense is $300, but it is listed as $400 on the trial balance.
i. Office furniture should be listed in the amount of $1,300.

BALLARD FINANCIAL SERVICES
Trial Balance
March 31, 20X1

Cash	$ 6,200	
Accounts receivable	2,000	
Supplies	500	
Office furniture	2,300	
Land	46,000	
Accounts payable		$ 2,700
Note payable		18,300
Meredith Ballard, capital		29,500
Meredith Ballard, withdrawals	3,700	
Service revenue		4,900
Salary expense	1,300	
Rent expense	500	
Advertising expense	400	
Utilities expense	200	
Total	$63,100	$55,400

Required

1. Prepare the correct trial balance at March 31. Journal entries are not required.
2. Prepare Ballard Financial Services' income statement for the month ended March 31, 20X1, to determine whether the business had a net income or a net loss for the month. Refer to Exhibit 1-7, page 20, if needed.

P2-6B Vince Serrano started Serrano Catering Service, and during the first month of operations (January 20X7), he completed the following selected transactions:

Recording transactions directly in T-accounts; preparing a trial balance (Obj. 2, 5, 7)

a. Serrano began the business with an investment of $23,000 cash and a van (automobile) valued at $13,000. The business gave Serrano owner's equity in the business.
b. Borrowed $25,000 from the bank; signed a note payable.
c. Paid $32,000 for food-service equipment.
d. Purchased supplies on account, $400.
e. Paid employee's salary, $1,300.
f. Received $800 for a catering job performed for customers.
g. Received an $800 bill for advertising expense that will be paid in the near future.
h. Paid $100 of the account payable created in transaction (d).
i. Performed service at a wedding on account, $3,300.
j. Received cash on account, $1,100.
k. Paid the following cash expenses:
   (1) Rent, $1,000.   (2) Insurance, $600.
l. Withdrew $2,600 for personal use.

Required

1. Open the following T-accounts: Cash; Accounts Receivable; Supplies; Food-Service Equipment; Automobile; Accounts Payable; Note Payable; Vince Serrano, Capital; Vince Serrano, Withdrawals; Service Revenue; Salary Expense; Rent Expense; Advertising Expense; Insurance Expense.
2. Record the transactions directly in the T-accounts without using a journal. Use the letters to identify the transactions.
3. Prepare the trial balance of Serrano Catering Service at January 31, 20X7.

Note: Problem 2-7B should be used in conjunction with Problem 2-6B.

P2-7B ← *Link Back to Chapter 1 (Income Statement, Statement of Owner's Equity, Balance Sheet).* Refer to Problem 2-6B. After completing the trial balance in Problem 2-6B, prepare the following financial statements for Serrano Catering Service:

1. Income statement for the month ended January 31, 20X7.
2. Statement of owner's equity for the month ended January 31, 20X7.
3. Balance sheet at January 31, 20X7.

Draw arrows to link the statements. If needed, use Exhibit 1-7, page 20, as a guide for preparing the financial statements.

APPLY YOUR KNOWLEDGE

DECISION CASES

Case 1. Answer the following questions. Consider each question separately.

1. Explain the advantages of double-entry bookkeeping over single-entry bookkeeping to a friend who is opening a used book store.
2. When you deposit money in your bank account, the bank credits your account. Is the bank misusing the word *credit* in this context? Why does the bank use the term *credit* to refer to your deposit, and not *debit*?
3. Your friend asks, "When revenues increase assets and expenses decrease assets, why are revenues credits and expenses debits and not the other way around?" Explain to your friend why revenues are credits and expenses are debits.

Case 2. You have been requested by a friend named Belinda Nathews to give advice on the effects that certain transactions will have on her business. Time is short, so you cannot journalize the transactions. Instead, you must analyze the transactions without the use of a journal. Nathews will continue the business only if she can expect to earn monthly net income of $5,000. The following transactions have occurred during March:

a. Nathews deposited $8,000 cash in a business bank account to start the company.
b. Borrowed $6,000 cash from the bank and signed a note payable due within one year.
c. Paid $300 cash for supplies.
d. Paid cash for advertising in the local newspaper, $700.
e. Paid the following cash expenses for one month: secretary's salary, $1,400; office rent, $800; utilities, $300; interest, $50.
f. Earned service revenue on account, $5,300.
g. Earned service revenue and received $3,500 cash.
h. Collected cash from customers on account, $1,200.

Required

1. Open the following T-accounts: Cash; Accounts Receivable; Supplies; Notes Payable; Belinda Nathews, Capital; Service Revenue; Salary Expense; Rent Expense; Advertising Expense; Utilities Expense; Interest Expense.
2. Record the transactions directly in the accounts without using a journal. Key each transaction by letter.
3. Prepare a trial balance at March 31, 20X9. List expenses with the largest amount first, the next largest amount second, and so on. The business name is Nathews Apartment Locators.
4. Compute the amount of net income or net loss for this first month of operations. Would you recommend that Nathews continue in business?

ETHICAL ISSUE

Brave Hearts, a charitable organization in Panama City, Florida, has a standing agreement with De Leon State Bank. The agreement allows Brave Hearts to overdraw its cash balance at the bank when donations are running low. In the past, Brave Hearts managed funds wisely and rarely used this privilege. Jacob Henson has recently become the president of Brave Hearts. To expand operations, Henson acquired office equipment and spent large amounts on fundraising. During Henson's presidency, Brave Hearts has maintained a negative bank balance of approximately $6,000.

Required

What is the ethical issue in this situation? State why you approve or disapprove of Henson's management of Brave Hearts' funds.

FINANCIAL STATEMENT CASE

Journalizing transactions for a company
(Obj. 2, 3)

This problem helps you develop skill in recording transactions by using a company's actual account titles. Refer to the **Target Corporation** financial statements in Appendix A. Assume that Target completed the following selected transactions during October 2001:

Oct. 5 Earned sales revenue on account, $110,000.
9 Borrowed $500,000 by signing a note payable (long-term debt).
12 Purchased equipment and paid cash, $50,000.
17 Paid $100,000, a current maturity of a long-term debt, plus interest expense of $8,000.
19 Earned sales revenue and immediately received cash of $86,000.
22 Collected half the cash on account that was earned on October 5.
28 Received a home-office electricity bill for $3,000, which will be paid in November (this is an administrative expense).

Required

Journalize these transactions, using the following account titles taken from the Target financial statements: Cash; Retained Securitized Receivables (same as Accounts Receivable), Equipment; Accounts Payable; Current Portion of Long-Term Debt; Long-Term Debt; Sales (Revenue), Selling, General and Administrative Expense; Interest Expense. Explanations are not required.

TEAM PROJECT

Contact a local business and arrange with the owner to learn what accounts the business uses.

Required

1. Obtain a copy of the business's chart of accounts.
2. Prepare the company's financial statements for the most recent month, quarter, or year. You may use either made-up account balances or balances supplied by the owner.

If the business has a large number of accounts within a category, combine related accounts and report a single amount on the financial statements. For example, the company may have several cash accounts. Combine all cash amounts and report a single Cash amount on the balance sheet.

You will probably encounter numerous accounts that you have not yet learned. Deal with these as best you can. The chart of accounts given in Appendix B at the end of the book will be helpful.

Keep in mind that the financial statements report the balances of the accounts listed in the company's chart of accounts. Therefore, the financial statements must be consistent with the chart of accounts.

INTERNET EXERCISE

The accounting process illustrated in this chapter may be simplified with the aid of financial software. **Intuit Inc.** is a leader in e-finance and develops and supports Quicken®, the leading personal finance software; Turbo Tax®, the best-selling tax preparation software; and QuickBooks®, the most popular small business accounting software.

Intuit Inc.

1. Go to **http://www.quicken.com** and read the "Top News" headlines. In the "Get Quotes & Research" section type <u>INTU</u>, the stock symbol of Intuit Inc., and then click on *Go*. Review the information provided and comment on one item of interest.
2. In the left-hand column, click on *Financial Statements*. Amounts are reported in thousands.
   a. For the three most recent fiscal years, list the amounts reported for "Total Revenues" and "Net Incomes." For each of these amounts, comment on the results from 1997 to 1999. Is the trend favorable or unfavorable? In 1999, Intuit started to promote its Internet financial support services. Has this marketing strategy been profitable for Intuit?
   b. For the three most recent years, list the amounts reported for "Property and Equipment, Net" and "Total Assets." What percentage of total assets does property and equipment comprise? Would you expect this for an e-finance company?
   c. For property and equipment, what is the normal balance? Is the amount reported from before or after posting to the ledger?
3. It is important to understand the accounting process even though financial software is available. Explain why this is true.
4. Select one other feature of this Web site to explore. Comment on what you found and whether you consider this feature useful.

3

Measuring Business Income: The Adjusting Process

LEARNING OBJECTIVES

*After studying this chapter,
you should be able to*

1. Distinguish accrual-basis accounting from cash-basis accounting

2. Apply the revenue and matching principles

3. Make adjusting entries at the end of the accounting period

4. Prepare an adjusted trial balance

5. Prepare the financial statements from the adjusted trial balance

Disappointed by blind dates and personal ads, Andrea McGinty started her own dating service. She also found a lucrative career. When McGinty's fiancé walked out on her five weeks before the wedding, it was back to the singles scene. Wouldn't it be nice if a dating service could arrange prescreened lunch dates for busy professionals like herself? "Lunch is over in an hour, and you don't have to kiss goodnight," she dreamed.

McGinty made her dream a reality. Her company, **It's Just Lunch**, now has thousands of customers. McGinty charges $1,000 to arrange 12 dates. "These are people who work long hours in fast-track careers. They need help with their social lives," says McGinty.

The business is a money-making machine, netting over $2 million of profit in a recent year.

Source: Adapted from Suzanne Oliver, "Yuppie Yenta," *Forbes* (March 25, 1996), pp. 102–103.

What do we mean when we say that **It's Just Lunch** *nets* over $2 million per year? The business earns net income, or profit, of more than $2 million, as reported on its income statement. The business's revenues consist of service-revenue fees earned by arranging lunch dates for clients. What are its expenses? Advertising, computer data searches, mailings to clients, and office expenses (such as employee salaries, rent, and supplies). It's Just Lunch operates in much the same way as **Gay Gillen eTravel**, the business studied in Chapters 1 and 2.

Whether the business is **It's Just Lunch**, Gillen's travel agency, or **IBM**, the profit motive increases the owner's drive to carry on the business. In this chapter, we'll consider how important net income is to a business.

FINANCIAL STATEMENTS AND ADJUSTING ENTRIES

How does a business know whether it is profitable? At the end of each accounting period, the entity prepares its financial statements. The period may be a month, three months, or a full year. **It's Just Lunch** is typical. The company reports on a quarterly basis every three months—with annual financial statements at the end of each year.

Whatever the length of the period, the main product of the accounting system is the financial statements. And the most important single amount in these statements is net income or net loss—the profit or loss—for the period. Net income captures much information: total revenues minus total expenses for the period.

An important step in financial statement preparation is the trial balance that we covered in Chapter 2. To measure its income, a business must bring the records up to date at the end of the period. This process is called *adjusting the books*, and it consists of making special journal entries called *adjusting entries*. This chapter focuses on these adjusting entries to show how to measure business income.

The accounting profession has concepts and principles to guide the measurement of business income. Chief among these are accrual-basis accounting, the accounting period, the revenue principle, and the matching principle. In this chapter, we apply these (and other) concepts and principles to measure income and prepare the financial statements of Gay Gillen eTravel for the month of April.

Accrual-Basis Accounting Versus Cash-Basis Accounting

There are two ways to do accounting:

- **Accrual-basis accounting** records the effect of every business transaction as it occurs. Most businesses use the accrual basis, and that is the method covered in this book.
- **Cash-basis accounting** records only cash receipts and cash payments. It ignores receivables, payables, and depreciation. Only very small businesses use cash-basis accounting.

Objective 1
Distinguish accrual-basis accounting from cash-basis accounting

ACCRUAL-BASIS ACCOUNTING.
Accounting that records the impact of a business event as it occurs, regardless of whether the transaction affected cash.

CASH-BASIS ACCOUNTING.
Accounting that records transactions only when cash is received or paid.

Suppose **Drugstore.com** purchased $2,000 of supplies on account from **Johnson & Johnson,** the health-care products company. On the accrual basis, Drugstore.com records the asset Supplies and the liability Accounts Payable as follows:

Supplies	2,000
Accounts Payable	2,000
Purchased supplies on account.	

Under the accrual basis, Drugstore.com's balance sheet reports the asset Supplies and the liability Accounts Payable.

In contrast, cash-basis accounting ignores this transaction because Drugstore.com paid no cash. The cash basis records only cash receipts and cash payments. *Cash receipts are treated as revenues, and cash payments are handled as expenses.* Therefore, under the cash basis, Drugstore.com would record a $2,000 cash payment as an expense rather than as an asset. This is faulty accounting: Drugstore.com acquired supplies, which are assets because they provide future benefit to the company.

Now let's see how differently the accrual basis and the cash basis account for a revenue. Suppose Drugstore.com sold goods on account. Under the accrual basis, Drugstore.com records a $10,000 sale as follows:

Accounts Receivable..................	10,000
Sales Revenue..................	10,000
Sold goods on account.	

The balance sheet then reports the asset Accounts Receivable, and the income statement reports Sales Revenue. We have a complete picture of the transaction.

Under the cash basis, Drugstore.com would not even bother to record a sale *on account* because there is no cash receipt. Instead, it would wait until cash is received and then record the cash as revenue. As a result, cash-basis accounting never reports accounts receivable from customers. It shows the revenue in the wrong accounting period, when cash is received. Revenue should be recorded when it is earned, and that is how the accrual basis operates.

Exhibit 3-1 illustrates the difference between the accrual basis and the cash basis. Keep in mind that the accrual basis is the correct way to do accounting. Panel A of the exhibit illustrates a revenue, and Panel B covers an expense.

EXHIBIT 3-1
Accrual-Basis Accounting Versus Cash-Basis Accounting

⊙ DAILY EXERCISE 3-1

⊙ DAILY EXERCISE 3-2

PANEL A (a revenue)—Collect $3,000 cash on January 1. The $3,000 of revenue is to be earned evenly during January, February, and March.

		Jan.	Feb.	Mar.
Accrual-basis accounting:	Service revenue...................	$1,000	$1,000	$1,000
Cash-basis accounting:	Service revenue...................	$3,000		

PANEL B (an expense)—Prepay $6,000 for TV advertising to be run during October, November, and December.

		Oct.	Nov.	Dec.
Accrual-basis accounting:	Advertising expense.............	$2,000	$2,000	$2,000
Cash-basis accounting:	Advertising expense.............	$6,000		

The Accounting Period

The only way to know for certain how successfully a business has operated is to close its doors, sell all its assets, pay the liabilities, and return any leftover cash to the owners. This process, called *liquidation,* is the same as going out of business. It is not practical to measure business income in this manner. Instead, businesses need periodic reports on their situation. Accountants slice time into small segments and prepare financial statements for specific periods.

The basic accounting period is one year, and virtually all businesses prepare annual financial statements. For about 60% of large companies in a recent survey, the annual accounting period runs the calendar year from January 1 through December 31. Other companies use a *fiscal year,* which can end on any date other than December 31. The year-end date is usually the low point in business activity for the year. Retailers are a notable example. For instance, **J.C. Penney Company** uses a fiscal year ending on January 31 because the low point in Penney's business activity falls after the Christmas sales. J.C. Penney does more than 30% of its yearly sales during November and December, but only 5% in January.

Managers and investors cannot wait until the end of the year to gauge a company's progress. Companies therefore prepare financial statements for *interim* periods. Managers want financial information often, so monthly statements are common. A series of monthly statements can be combined for quarterly and semiannual periods. Most of the discussions in this book are based on an annual accounting period, but the procedures and statements can be applied to interim periods as well.

The Revenue Principle

The **revenue principle** tells accountants (1) *when* to record revenue by making a journal entry, and (2) the *amount* of revenue to record. ➡ When we speak of "recording" something in accounting, we mean "make an entry in the journal." That is where the accounting process starts.

The general principle guiding *when* to record revenue says to record revenue once it has been earned—but not before. In most cases, revenue is earned when the business has delivered a completed good or service to the customer. The business has done everything required by the sale agreement, including transferring the item to the customer. Exhibit 3-2 shows two situations that provide guidance on when to record revenue. The first situation illustrates when *not* to record revenue—because the client merely states her plans. Situation 2 illustrates when revenue should be recorded—after Gay Gillen has performed a service for the client.

Objective 2
Apply the revenue and matching principles

REVENUE PRINCIPLE. The basis for recording revenues; tells accountants when to record revenue and the amount of revenue to record.

◄ Revenue, defined in Chapter 1, p. 12, is the increase in owner's equity from delivering goods and services to customers in the course of operating a business.

Exhibit 3-2 Recording Revenue: The Revenue Principle

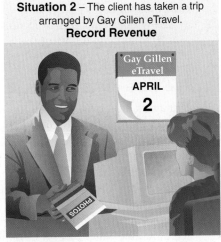

◉ DAILY EXERCISE 3-3

The general principle guiding the *amount* of revenue says to record revenue equal to the cash value of the goods or the service transferred to the customer. Suppose that in order to obtain a new client, Gillen Travel performs accounting service for the price of $500. Ordinarily, Gillen would have charged $600 for this service. How much revenue should Gillen record? The answer is $500, because that was the cash value of the transaction. Gillen will not receive the full value of $600, so that is not the amount of revenue to record. She will receive only $500 cash, so that is the amount of revenue she has earned.

The Matching Principle

MATCHING PRINCIPLE. The basis for recording expenses. Directs accountants to identify all expenses incurred during the period, to measure the expenses, and to match them against the revenues earned during that same span of time.

The **matching principle** is the basis for recording expenses. ← Recall that expenses—such as rent, utilities, and advertising—are the costs of operating a business. Expenses are the costs of assets that are used up and liabilities that are increased in the earning of revenue. The matching principle directs accountants to (1) identify all expenses incurred during the accounting period, (2) measure the expenses, and (3) match the expenses against the revenues earned during that same span of time. To match expenses against revenues means to subtract expenses from revenues in order to compute net income or net loss. Exhibit 3-3 illustrates the matching principle.

EXHIBIT 3-3
Recording Expenses:
The Matching Principle

➡ An expense, defined in Chapter 1, p. 12, is a decrease in owner's equity that occurs from using assets or increasing liabilities in the course of operating a business.

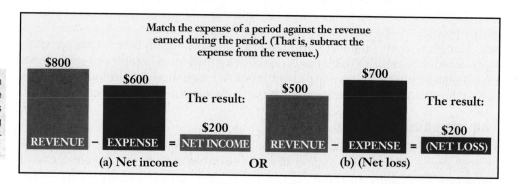

◉ DAILY EXERCISE 3-4
◉ DAILY EXERCISE 3-5

There is a natural link between revenues and some types of expenses. Accountants first identify a period's revenues and the expenses that can be linked to particular revenues. For example, a business that pays sales commissions to its sales personnel will have commission expense only if the employees make sales. *Cost of goods sold* is another example. If there are no sales of Ford automobiles, **Ford Motor Company** has no cost of goods sold.

Other expenses are not so easy to link with particular sales. For example, monthly rent expense occurs regardless of the revenues earned during the period. The matching principle directs accountants to identify those expenses with a particular time period, such as a month or a year. If Gay Gillen eTravel employs a secretary at a monthly salary of $1,900, the business will record salary expense of $1,900 for each month.

How does Gay Gillen account for a transaction that begins in April but ends in May? How does she bring the accounts up to date for preparing the financial statements? To answer these questions, accountants use the time-period concept.

The Time-Period Concept

TIME-PERIOD CONCEPT. Ensures that accounting information is reported at regular intervals.

Managers, investors, and creditors make decisions daily and need periodic readings on the state of the business. The **time-period concept** ensures that accounting information is reported at regular intervals. It interacts with the revenue principle and the matching principle. To measure income accurately, companies update the revenue and expense accounts immediately before the end of the period. **US Airways** provides an example of an expense accrual. At December 31, 1999, US Airways recorded employee compensation of $341 million that the company owed its workers for unpaid services performed before year end. The company's accrual entry, adapted and in millions of dollars, was

1999			
Dec. 31	Salary Expense............................	341	
	Salary Payable		341
	Accrued salary expense.		

◉ DAILY EXERCISE 3-6

This entry serves two purposes. First, it assigns the expense to the proper period. Without the accrual entry at December 31, total expenses of 1999 would be understated, and as a result, net income would be overstated. The expense would incorrectly fall in 2000 when US Airways pays the next payroll. Second, the accrual entry records the liability for the balance sheet at December 31, 1999. Without the accrual entry, total liabilities would be understated.

At the end of an accounting period, companies also accrue revenues that have been earned but not collected. The remainder of the chapter discusses how to make the adjusting entries to show these transactions and bring the accounts up to date.

ADJUSTING THE ACCOUNTS

Objective 3
Make adjusting entries at the end of the accounting period

At the end of the period, the accountant prepares the financial statements. The end-of-period process begins with the trial balance, which lists the accounts and their balances after the period's transactions have been recorded in the journal and posted to the accounts. We saw how to prepare the trial balance in Chapter 2.

Exhibit 3-4 is the trial balance of Gay Gillen eTravel at April 30, 20X1. This *unadjusted trial balance* includes some new accounts that we will explain in this section. It lists most of the revenues and expenses of the travel agency for the month of April. These trial balance amounts are incomplete because they omit certain revenue and expense transactions that affect more than one accounting period. That is why the trial balance is *unadjusted*. In most cases, however, we refer to it simply as the trial balance, without the label "unadjusted."

EXHIBIT 3-4
Unadjusted Trial Balance

GAY GILLEN eTRAVEL Unadjusted Trial Balance April 30, 20X1		
Cash...	$24,800	
Accounts receivable........................	2,250	
Supplies.......................................	700	
Prepaid rent..................................	3,000	
Furniture......................................	16,500	
Accounts payable...........................		$13,100
Unearned service revenue...............		450
Gay Gillen, capital.........................		31,250
Gay Gillen, withdrawals..................	3,200	
Service revenue..............................		7,000
Salary expense...............................	950	
Utilities expense............................	400	
Total...	$51,800	$51,800

Under cash-basis accounting, there is no need for adjustments to the accounts because all April cash transactions have already been recorded. However, the accrual basis requires adjusting entries at the end of the period in order to produce correct balances for the financial statements. To see why, consider the Supplies account in Exhibit 3-4.

Gay Gillen eTravel uses supplies in providing travel services for clients during the month. This reduces the quantity of supplies on hand and thus constitutes an expense, just like salary or rent. It is not worth the effort to record supplies expense more than once a month. It takes time to make daily or weekly journal entries. So how does Gillen account for supplies expense?

By the end of the month, the Supplies balance of $700 on the unadjusted trial balance (Exhibit 3-4) is not correct. The unadjusted balance represents the amount of supplies on hand at the start of the month plus any supplies purchased during the month. This balance fails to take into account the supplies used (*supplies expense*) during the accounting period. It is necessary, then, to subtract the month's expenses from the amount of supplies listed on the trial balance. The resulting new adjusted balance will measure the cost of supplies that are still on hand at April 30, say $400. This is the correct amount of Supplies to report on the balance sheet—$400. The adjusting entry will bring the supplies account up to date.

Adjusting entries assign revenues to the period in which they are earned and expenses to the period in which they are incurred. Adjusting entries also update the asset and liability accounts. They are needed to (1) properly measure the period's

ADJUSTING ENTRY. Entry made at the end of the period to assign revenues to the period in which they are earned and expenses to the period in which they are incurred. Adjusting entries help measure the period's income and bring the related asset and liability accounts to correct balances for the financial statements.

income on the income statement, and (2) bring related asset and liability accounts to correct balances for the balance sheet. Adjusting entries, which are the key to accrual-basis accounting, are made before the financial statements are prepared. The end-of-period process of updating the accounts is called *adjusting the accounts, making the adjusting entries,* or *adjusting the books.*

A large company uses accounting software to print out a trial balance. For example, **Occidental Petroleum (OXY),** a large oil company, has accounting software that prints a monthly trial balance. The accountants then analyze the amounts on the trial balance. This analysis results in the adjusting entries that OXY makes. The trial balance has now become the *adjusted* trial balance. This chapter shows the adjusting process as it moves from the trial balance to the adjusted trial balance. Two basic types of adjustments are *prepaids* and *accruals.*

PREPAIDS (DEFERRALS) AND ACCRUALS

In a *prepaid* adjustment, the cash transaction occurs before the related expense or revenue is recorded. Prepaids are also called *deferrals* because the recording of the expense or the revenue is deferred until after cash is paid or received. *Accrual*-type adjustments are the opposite of prepaids. For accruals, we record the expense or revenue before the related cash settlement.

Adjusting entries can be further divided into five categories:

1. Prepaid expenses
2. Depreciation of plant assets
3. Accrued expenses
4. Accrued revenues
5. Unearned revenues

The core of this chapter is the discussion of these five types of adjusting entries on pages 88–96. Study this material carefully because it is the most challenging topic in all of introductory accounting.

Prepaid Expenses

PREPAID EXPENSE. Advance payments of expenses. A category of current assets that typically expire or are used up in the near future. Examples include prepaid rent, prepaid insurance, and supplies.

Prepaid expenses are advance payments of expenses. The category includes prepayments that typically expire or that will be used up in the near future. Prepaid rent and prepaid insurance are examples. They are called "prepaid" expenses because they are paid in advance. Salary expense and utilities expense, among others, are typically *not* prepaid because they are not paid in advance. All companies, large and small, must make adjustments regarding prepaid expenses. For example, **McDonald's Corporation,** the restaurant chain, must contend with such prepayments as rents, packaging supplies, and insurance. Keep in mind that prepaid expenses are assets, not expenses.

PREPAID RENT   Landlords usually require tenants to pay rent in advance. This prepayment creates an asset for the renter, who has purchased the future benefit of using the rented item. Suppose Gay Gillen eTravel prepays three months' office rent on April 1, 20X1. If the lease specifies monthly rental amounts of $1,000, the entry to record the payment for three months is a debit to the asset account, Prepaid Rent, as follows:

Apr. 1	Prepaid Rent ($1,000 × 3)	3,000	
	Cash		3,000
	Paid three months' rent in advance.		

After posting, Prepaid Rent appears as follows:

ASSETS

PREPAID RENT
Apr. 1 3,000	

The trial balance at April 30, 20X1, lists Prepaid Rent as an asset with a debit balance of $3,000. Throughout April, the Prepaid Rent account maintains this beginning balance, as shown in Exhibit 3-4. But $3,000 is *not* the amount to report for Prepaid Rent on the travel agency's balance sheet at April 30. Why?

At April 30, Prepaid Rent should be adjusted to remove from its balance the amount of the asset that has been used up, which is one month's worth of the prepayment. By definition, the amount of an asset that has expired is *expense*. The adjusting entry transfers one-third, or $1,000 ($3,000 $\times$ 1/3), of the debit balance from Prepaid Rent to Rent Expense. The debit side of the entry records an increase in Rent Expense, and the credit records a decrease in the asset Prepaid Rent:

Apr. 30	Rent Expense ($3,000 $\times$ 1/3)...............	1,000	
	Prepaid Rent		1,000
	To record rent expense.		

After posting, Prepaid Rent and Rent Expense appear as follows:

ASSETS				EXPENSES		
PREPAID RENT			→	**RENT EXPENSE**		
Apr. 1	3,000	Apr. 30 1,000		Apr. 30	1,000	
Bal.	2,000			Bal.	1,000	

Correct asset amount: **$2,000** → Total accounted for: **$3,000** ← Correct expense amount: **$1,000**

The full $3,000 has been accounted for: Two-thirds measures the asset, and one-third measures the expense. Recording this expense illustrates the matching principle.

The same analysis applies to prepayment of three months of insurance premiums. The only difference is in the account titles, which would be Prepaid Insurance and Insurance Expense instead of Prepaid Rent and Rent Expense. In a computerized system, the adjusting entry crediting the prepaid account and debiting the expense account could be established to recur automatically in each accounting period until the prepaid account has a zero balance.

The chapter appendix shows an alternative treatment of prepaid expenses. The end result on the financial statements is the same as illustrated here.

SUPPLIES Supplies are accounted for in the same way as prepaid expenses. On April 2, Gay Gillen paid cash of $700 for office supplies:

Apr. 2	Supplies	700	
	Cash		700
	Paid cash for supplies.		

Assume that Gillen purchased no additional supplies during April. The April 30 trial balance, therefore, lists Supplies with a $700 debit balance, as shown in Exhibit 3-4. But Gillen's April 30 balance sheet should *not* report supplies of $700. Why?

During April, Gillen used supplies in performing services for clients. The cost of the supplies used is the measure of *supplies expense* for the month. To measure supplies expense during April, Gillen counts the supplies on hand at the end of the month. This is the amount of the asset (the economic resource) still available to the business. Assume the count at April 30 indicates that supplies costing $400 remain. Subtracting the $400 of supplies on hand at the end of April from the cost of supplies available during April ($700) measures supplies expense during the month ($300).

Cost of asset available during the period	−	Cost of asset on hand at the end of the period	=	Cost of asset used (expense) during the period
$700	−	$400	=	$300

The April 30 adjusting entry to update the Supplies account and to record the supplies expense for the month debits the expense and credits the asset, as follows:

Apr. 30	Supplies Expense ($700 − $400)	300	
	Supplies		300
	To record supplies expense.		

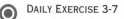

After posting, the Supplies and Supplies Expense accounts appear as follows:

ASSETS				**EXPENSES**		
SUPPLIES				SUPPLIES EXPENSE		
Apr. 2	700	Apr. 30	300	Apr. 30	300	
Bal.	400			Bal.	300	

Correct asset amount: $400	→	Total accounted for: $700	←	Correct expense amount: $300

The Supplies account then enters the month of May with a $400 balance, and the adjustment process is repeated at the end of May.

 WORK IT OUT

At the beginning of the month, Supplies were $5,000. During the month, the company purchased $7,800 of supplies. At month's end, $3,600 of supplies were still on hand.

1. What was the cost of supplies used during the month?
2. What is the ending balance of Supplies? Where is this item reported?
3. Make the adjusting entry to update the Supplies account at the end of the month.

Answers

1.

Beginning balance	$ 5,000
+Purchases	7,800
=Supplies available	12,800
−Ending balance	(3,600)
=Expense (supplies used during the period).........	$ 9,200

2. The ending balance of Supplies is $3,600. This is the amount that should be reported on the *balance sheet*.

3.

Supplies Expense	9,200	
Supplies		9,200

Depreciation of Plant Assets

PLANT ASSET. Long-lived tangible assets—such as land, buildings, and equipment—used in the operations of a business.

The logic of the accrual basis is probably best illustrated by how businesses account for plant assets. **Plant assets** are long-lived tangible assets—such as land, buildings, furniture, machinery, and equipment—used in the operations of the business. As one accountant said, "All assets but land are on a march to the junkyard." That is, all plant assets except land decline in usefulness as they age. This decline is an expense to the business. Accountants systematically spread the cost of each plant asset, except land, over the years of its useful life. This allocation of a plant asset's cost to expense over its useful life is called **depreciation.**

DEPRECIATION. The allocation of a plant asset's cost to expense over its useful life.

SIMILARITY TO PREPAID EXPENSES   The concept underlying accounting for plant assets is the same as for prepaid expenses. In a sense, plant assets are merely prepaid expenses that expire over a number of periods. With both prepaid expenses and plant assets, the business purchases an asset that wears out. As the asset is used, its cost is transferred from the asset account to the expense account. The major difference between prepaid expenses and plant assets is the length of time it takes for the asset to expire. Prepaid expenses usually expire within a year, while most plant assets remain useful for a number of years.

Consider Gay Gillen eTravel. Suppose that on April 3 Gillen purchased furniture on account for $16,500 and made this journal entry:

Apr. 3	Furniture..	16,500	
	Accounts Payable		16,500
	Purchased office furniture on account.		

After posting, the Furniture account appears as follows:

ASSETS

FURNITURE

Apr. 3 16,500	

Gillen believes the furniture will remain useful for five years and will be worth-less at the end of its life. One way to compute the amount of depreciation for each year is to divide the cost of the asset ($16,500 in our example) by its expected useful life (five years). This procedure—called the straight-line method—computes annual depreciation of $3,300 ($16,500/5 years = $3,300 per year). Depreciation for the month of April is $275 ($3,300/12 months = $275 per month).

THE ACCUMULATED DEPRECIATION ACCOUNT Depreciation expense for April is recorded by the following entry:

Apr. 30	Depreciation Expense—Furniture............................	275	
	Accumulated Depreciation—Furniture		275
	To record depreciation on furniture.		

Accumulated Depreciation is credited instead of Furniture because the original cost of a plant asset (the furniture) should remain in the asset account as long as the business uses the asset. Accountants and managers can then refer to the Furniture account to see how much the asset cost. This information may be useful in a deci-sion about whether to replace the furniture and how much to pay.

The amount of depreciation is an estimate. The Accumulated Depreciation account holds the cumulative sum of all depreciation expense recorded for the asset. The balance of the Accumulated Depreciation account increases over the life of the asset.

Accumulated Depreciation is a contra asset account, which means an asset account with a normal credit balance. A **contra account** has two distinguishing char-acteristics:

- A contra account has a companion account.
- A contra account's normal balance (debit or credit) is opposite that of the companion account.

In this case, Accumulated Depreciation is the contra account that accompanies Furniture. It appears in the ledger directly after Furniture. Furniture has a debit bal-ance, and therefore Accumulated Depreciation, a contra asset, has a credit balance. *All contra asset accounts have credit balances.*

A business carries an accumulated depreciation account for each depreciable asset. If a business has a building and a machine, for example, it will carry the accounts Accumulated Depreciation—Building and Accumulated Depreciation—Machine.

After the depreciation entry has been posted, the Furniture, Accumulated Depreciation, and Depreciation Expense accounts of Gay Gillen eTravel, appear as follows:

ASSETS		**CONTRA ASSET**		**EXPENSES**	
FURNITURE		ACCUMULATED DEPRECIATION—FURNITURE		DEPRECIATION EXPENSE—FURNITURE	
Apr. 3 16,500			Apr. 30 275	Apr. 30 275	
Bal. 16,500			Bal. 275	Bal. 275	

BOOK VALUE The balance sheet shows the relationship between Furniture and Accumulated Depreciation. The balance of Accumulated Depreciation is subtracted from the balance of Furniture. The resulting net amount of a plant asset (cost minus accumulated depreciation) is called its **book value,** or *net book value,* as shown at top of next page for Furniture:

ACCUMULATED DEPRECIATION. The cumulative sum of all depreciation expense recorded for an asset.

CONTRA ACCOUNT. An account that always has a companion account and whose normal balance is opposite that of the companion account.

BOOK VALUE (OF A PLANT ASSET). The asset's cost minus accumulated depreciation.

Plant Assets:	
Furniture..	$16,500
Less: Accumulated depreciation..............	(275)
Book value	$16,225

Suppose Gillen eTravel also owns a building that cost $48,000 and on which annual depreciation is $2,400 ($48,000/20 years). The amount of depreciation for one month would be $200 ($2,400/12), and the following entry records depreciation for April:

DAILY EXERCISE 3-8

Apr. 30	Depreciation Expense—Building............................	200	
	Accumulated Depreciation—Building............		200
	To record depreciation on building.		

The balance sheet at April 30 reports Gillen's plant assets as shown in Exhibit 3-5.

EXHIBIT 3-5
Plant Assets on the Balance Sheet of Gay Gillen eTravel (April 30)

Plant Assets:		
Furniture..	$16,500	
Less: Accumulated depreciation..............	(275)	$16,225
Building	48,000	
Less: Accumulated depreciation..............	(200)	47,800
Book value of plant assets..........................		$64,025

Exhibit 3-6 shows how **Johnson & Johnson**—maker of Band-Aids, Tylenol, and other health-care products—displayed Property, Plant, and Equipment in its annual report. Johnson & Johnson has real-estate holdings around the world; they are reported in line 1 of Exhibit 3-6. Line 2 includes the cost of buildings and the related equipment (air conditioners and elevators) in those buildings. The company's manufacturing machinery, office equipment, and furniture are given in line 3, and line 4 reports the cost of assets that are under construction.

EXHIBIT 3-6
Johnson & Johnson's Reporting of Property, Plant, and Equipment

	Millions
(1) Land and land improvements	$ 344
(2) Buildings and building equipment..............	2,611
(3) Machinery and equipment..........................	4,217
(4) Construction in progress	1,003
	8,175
Less: Accumulated depreciation........................	(2,979)
	$5,196

Johnson & Johnson's cost of plant assets was $8,175 million (cost principle). Of the total cost, Johnson & Johnson has depreciated a total of $2,979 million (matching principle). The book value of J&J's plant assets is therefore $8,175 − $2,979 = $5,196 million.

Now let's return to Gay Gillen eTravel.

Accrued Expenses

ACCRUED EXPENSE. An expense that the business has incurred but not yet paid.

Businesses often incur expenses before they pay for them. Consider an employee's salary. The employer's salary expense and salary payable grow as the employee works, so the liability is said to *accrue*. Another example is interest expense on a note payable. Interest accrues as the clock ticks. The term **accrued expense** refers to an expense the business has incurred but has not yet paid. Accrued expenses can be viewed as the opposite of prepaid expenses.

It is time-consuming to make weekly journal entries to accrue expenses. Consequently, the accountant waits until the end of the period. Then an adjusting entry brings each expense (and related liability) up to date just before the financial statements are prepared.

Remember the key difference between a prepaid expense and an accrued expense: A prepaid expense is paid first and expensed later. An accrued expense is expensed first and paid later. Prepaids and accruals are opposites.

SALARY EXPENSE   Most companies pay their employees at set times. Suppose Gay Gillen pays her employee a monthly salary of $1,900, half on the 15th and half on the last day of the month. Here is a calendar for April with the two paydays circled:

APRIL						
S	M	T	W	T	F	S
					1	2
3	4	5	6	7	8	9
10	11	12	13	14	(15)	16
17	18	19	20	21	22	23
24	25	26	27	28	29	(30)

Assume that if either payday falls on the weekend, Gillen pays the employee on the following Monday. During April, Gillen paid her employee's first half-month salary of $950 on Friday, April 15, and recorded the following entry:

Apr. 15	Salary Expense	950	
	Cash		950
	To pay salary.		

After posting, the Salary Expense account is

EXPENSES

SALARY EXPENSE

Apr. 15	950	

The trial balance at April 30 (Exhibit 3-4) includes Salary Expense, with its debit balance of $950. This unadjusted balance of $950 is Gillen's salary expense for only the first half of April. Because April 30, the second payday of the month, falls on a Saturday, the second half-month amount of $950 will be paid on Monday, May 2. However, Gillen must record salary expense for the second half of April. Because of the need to accrue salary expense at April 30, Gillen makes an adjusting entry for additional Salary Expense and Salary Payable of $950 as follows:

Apr. 30	Salary Expense	950	
	Salary Payable		950
	To accrue salary expense.		

This is the accrual basis of accounting in action. After posting, the Salary Expense and Salary Payable accounts are updated to April 30:

EXPENSES

SALARY EXPENSE

Apr. 15	950	
Apr. 30	950	
Bal.	1,900	

LIABILITIES

SALARY PAYABLE

	Apr. 30	950
	Bal.	950

The accounts at April 30 now contain complete salary information for the month of April. The expense account has a full month's salary, and the liability account shows the portion that the business still owes at April 30. Gillen will record the payment of this liability on Monday, May 2.

Weekly salaries for a five-day workweek total $3,500, payable on a Friday. This month, November 30 falls on a Tuesday.

1. Which accounts require adjustment at November 30?
2. Make the adjusting entry.

Answers

1. Salary Expense and Salary Payable.
2.   Salary Expense ($3,500 × 2/5) 1,400
               Salary Payable   1,400
        To accrue salary expense.

Accrued Revenues

ACCRUED REVENUE. A revenue that has been earned but not yet collected in cash.

Some expenses occur before the cash payment, and we must record an accrued expense. Likewise, businesses may also earn revenue before they receive the cash. This calls for an **accrued revenue,** which is a revenue that has been earned but not yet collected in cash.

Assume that Gay Gillen eTravel is hired on April 15 by **Procter & Gamble** to perform travel services on a continuing basis. Under this agreement, Gillen will receive $500 monthly, with the first cash receipt on May 15. During April, she will earn half a month's fee, $250, for work performed April 15 through April 30. On April 30, she makes the following adjusting entry to accrue the revenue earned during April 15–30:

     Apr. 30   Accounts Receivable ($500 × 1/2) 250
                    Service Revenue................................   250
               To accrue service revenue...........................

We see from the unadjusted trial balance in Exhibit 3-4 that Accounts Receivable has an unadjusted balance of $2,250. Service Revenue's unadjusted balance is $7,000. Posting the April 30 adjusting entry has the following effects on these two accounts:

ASSETS		REVENUES	
ACCOUNTS RECEIVABLE		SERVICE REVENUE	
	2,250		7,000
Apr. 30	250	Apr. 30	250
Bal.	2,500	Bal.	7,250

This adjusting entry illustrates the revenue principle. Without the adjustment, Gillen's financial statements would be incomplete and misleading—they would understate Accounts Receivable and Service Revenue by $250 each. All accrued revenues are accounted for similarly—by debiting a receivable and crediting a revenue.

Now we turn to a different category of adjusting entries.

Unearned Revenues

UNEARNED REVENUE. A liability created when a business collects cash from customers in advance of doing work. The obligation is to provide a product or a service in the future. Also called **deferred revenue.**

Some businesses collect cash from customers in advance of doing work for them. Receiving cash in advance creates a liability called **unearned revenue** or **deferred revenue.** This liability arises from receiving cash in advance of providing a product or a service. Only when the job is completed will the business have *earned* the revenue.

Suppose **Baldwin Piano Company** engages Gillen to provide travel services, agreeing to pay her $450 monthly, beginning immediately. Baldwin makes the first payment on April 20. Gillen records the cash receipt and the related increase in liabilities as follows:

     Apr. 20   Cash.. 450
                    Unearned Service Revenue...............   450
               Collected revenue in advance.

After posting, the liability account Unearned Service Revenue appears as follows:

LIABILITIES

UNEARNED SERVICE REVENUE

	Apr. 20	450

Unearned Service Revenue is a liability account because it represents Gillen's obligation to perform service for the client. The April 30 unadjusted trial balance (Exhibit 3-4) lists Unearned Service Revenue with a $450 credit balance prior to the adjusting entries. During the last ten days of the month—April 21 through April 30—Gillen will have *earned* one-third (10 days divided by April's total 30 days) of the $450, or $150. Therefore, Gillen makes the following adjustment to decrease the liability, Unearned Service Revenue, and to record an increase in Service Revenue, as follows:

Apr. 30	Unearned Service Revenue ($450 × 1/3)	150	
	Service Revenue		150
	To record service revenue that was collected in advance.		

This adjusting entry shifts $150 of the total amount of unearned service revenue from the liability account to the revenue account. After posting, the balance of Service Revenue is increased by $150, and the balance of Unearned Service Revenue is reduced by $150, to $300. Now, both accounts have the correct balances at April 30:

LIABILITIES

UNEARNED SERVICE REVENUE

Apr. 30	150	Apr. 20	450
		Bal.	300

REVENUES

SERVICE REVENUE

			7,000
		Apr. 30	250
		Apr. 30	150
		Bal.	7,400

Correct liability amount: $300 → **Total accounted for: $450** ← **Correct revenue amount: $150**

All types of revenues collected in advance are accounted for in the same way.

 DAILY EXERCISE 3-11

An unearned revenue to one company is a prepaid expense to the company that made the payment. For example, suppose that **Xerox Corporation** paid **American Airlines** $1,800 two months in advance for the air travel expenses of Xerox executives. To Xerox, the payment is Prepaid Travel Expense. To American Airlines, the receipt of cash creates Unearned Service Revenue. After the executives take the trip, American Airlines records the revenue and Xerox records travel expense.

Remember: An unearned revenue is a liability, not a revenue.

 WORK IT OUT Consider the tuition you pay your college or university. Assume that one semester's tuition costs $500 and that you make a single payment at the start of the term. Can you make the journal entries to record the tuition transactions on your own books and on the books of your college or university?

Answer

	Your Books			**Your College's Books**		
Start of Semester	Prepaid Tuition	500		Cash...........................	500	
	Cash		500	Unearned Tuition		
	Paid semester tuition.			Revenue...............		500
				Collected revenue in advance.		
End of Semester	Tuition Expense	500		Unearned Tuition		
	Prepaid Tuition..............		500	Revenue	500	
	To record tuition expense.			Tuition Revenue ...		500
				To record tuition revenue that was collected in advance.		

Exhibit 3-7 summarizes the timing of prepaid- and accrual-type adjusting entries. The chapter appendix shows an alternative treatment for unearned revenues.

EXHIBIT 3-7   Prepaid- and Accrual-Type Adjustments

PREPAIDS—The cash transaction occurs initially.

	Initially			Later	

Prepaid Expenses	Pay cash and record an asset:
	Prepaid Expense XXX
	    Cash ....
			XXX	Record an expense and decrease the asset:
				Expense...................................... XXX
				    Prepaid Expense ....
						XXX

Unearned Revenues	Receive cash and record unearned revenue:
	Cash.. XXX
	    Unearned Revenue ....
			XXX	Record a revenue and decrease unearned revenue:
				Unearned Revenue XXX
				    Revenue ....
						XXX

ACCRUALS—The cash transaction occurs later.

	Initially			Later	

Accrued Expenses	Accrue an expense and the related payable:
	Expense XXX
	    Payable......................................
			XXX	Pay cash and decrease the payable:
				Payable..................................... XXX
				    Cash..
						XXX

Accrued Revenues	Accrue a revenue and the related receivable:
	Receivable.............................. XXX
	    Revenue ....
			XXX	Receive cash and decrease the receivable:
				Cash XXX
				    Receivable ....
						XXX

Source: The authors thank Darrel Davis and Alfonso Oddo for suggesting this exhibit.

www.prenhall.com/horngren
Mid-Chapter Assessment

EXHIBIT 3-8
Summary of Adjusting Entries

Summary of the Adjusting Process

The adjusting process has two purposes:

1. Measure net income or net loss on the *income statement*. Every adjusting entry affects either a *Revenue* or an *Expense*.
2. Update the *balance sheet*. Every adjusting entry affects either an *Asset* or a *Liability*.

No adjusting entry debits or credits Cash because the cash transactions are recorded before the end of the period. Exhibit 3-8 summarizes the adjusting entries.

	Type of Account	
Category of Adjusting Entry	**Debited**	**Credited**
Prepaid expense	Expense	Asset
Depreciation	Expense	Contra asset
Accrued expense	Expense	Liability
Accrued revenue	Asset	Revenue
Unearned revenue	Liability	Revenue

Source: Adapted from material provided by Beverly Terry.

Exhibit 3-9 summarizes the adjusting entries of Gay Gillen eTravel at April 30. Panel A briefly describes the data for each adjustment, Panel B gives the adjusting entries, and Panel C shows the accounts after they have been posted. The adjustments are keyed by letter.

Objective 4
Prepare an adjusted trial balance

THE ADJUSTED TRIAL BALANCE

This chapter began with the trial balance before any adjusting entries—the unadjusted trial balance (Exhibit 3-4). After the adjustments are journalized and posted, the accounts appear as shown in Exhibit 3-9, Panel C. A useful step in preparing the

PANEL A—Information for Adjustments at April 30, 20X1

(a) Prepaid rent expired, $1,000.
(b) Supplies on hand, $400.
(c) Depreciation on furniture, $275.
(d) Accrued salary expense, $950.

(e) Accrued service revenue, $250
(f) Service revenue earned that was collected in advance, $150.

PANEL B—Adjusting Entries

(a)	Rent Expense	1,000	
	Prepaid Rent		1,000
	To record rent expense.		
(b)	Supplies Expense	300	
	Supplies...		300
	To record supplies used.		
(c)	Depreciation Expense—Furniture	275	
	Accumulated Depreciation—Furniture..............		275
	To record depreciation on furniture.		
(d)	Salary Expense..	950	
	Salary Payable		950
	To accrue salary expense.		
(e)	Accounts Receivable	250	
	Service Revenue		250
	To accrue service revenue.		
(f)	Unearned Service Revenue...	150	
	Service Revenue		150
	To record revenue that was collected in advance.		

PANEL C—Ledger Accounts

ASSETS		LIABILITIES	OWNER'S EQUITY	EXPENSES

CASH

Bal. 24,800		

PREPAID RENT

3,000	(a)	1,000	
Bal. 2,000			

ACCOUNTS PAYABLE

	Bal. 13,100

GAY GILLEN, CAPITAL

	Bal. 31,250

RENT EXPENSE

(a)	1,000	
Bal.	1,000	

ACCOUNTS RECEIVABLE

	2,250	
(e)	250	
Bal.	2,500	

FURNITURE

Bal. 16,500	

SALARY PAYABLE

	(d)	950
	Bal.	950

GAY GILLEN, WITHDRAWALS

Bal. 3,200	

SALARY EXPENSE

	950	
(d)	950	
Bal.	1,000	

SUPPLIES

700	(b)	300
Bal. 400		

ACCUMULATED DEPRECIATION— FURNITURE

	(c)	275
	Bal.	275

UNEARNED SERVICE REVENUE

(f)	150	450
	Bal.	300

REVENUE

SERVICE REVENUE

	7,000
(e)	250
(f)	150
Bal.	7,400

SUPPLIES EXPENSE

(b)	300	
Bal.	300	

DEPRECIATION EXPENSE— FURNITURE

(c)	275	
Bal.	275	

UTILITIES EXPENSE

Bal. 400	

financial statements is to list the accounts, along with their adjusted balances, on an **adjusted trial balance.** This document has the advantage of listing all the accounts and their adjusted balances in a single place. Exhibit 3-10 shows the preparation of the adjusted trial balance.

Exhibit 3-10 is a *work sheet*. We will discuss the work sheet in detail in Chapter 4. For now, simply note how clearly this format presents the data. The information in

ADJUSTED TRIAL BALANCE. A list of all the accounts with their adjusted balances.

Grossing up the Revenue: Priceline.com and Ventro

Suppose you're going to Australia. You want a cheap air ticket, and **Priceline.com** lets you "name your price" for airline tickets and hotel rooms. Your bid of $975 is accepted, and Priceline pockets the spread between your price and the amount that Priceline pays the airline company. What should Priceline claim as revenue—the fee Priceline earns or the full price of your ticket?

Priceline.com and other Internet service companies are claiming the entire value of the products sold through their sites. The SEC and the FASB call this practice "grossing up" revenue. Dot.com companies do it to show a profit when they're actually operating at a loss. The practice draws investors and pushes up stock prices. Grossing up may be legal, but the SEC and the FASB are considering placing restrictions on it.

Ventro, which handles the sale of specialty medical products over the Internet, is one company that would be adversely affected by such a restriction. Ventro's $29 million in grossed-up revenue for 1999 was expected to more than quadruple to $140 million in 2000. The company argues that its accounting method is sound since the company assumes various revenue risks: shelling out money if a product is returned, bearing credit risk if the customer won't pay, and taking title to the products sold. Yet Ventro never takes actual products into its own inventory and only takes title to the products during the time it takes to ship them. Ventro's suppliers are happy to absorb refund costs and Ventro's blue-chip customers rarely pose credit problems. If the accounting rulemakers decide that grossing up is okay, expect to see the value of business-to-business sites like Ventro soar.

Sources: Based on: Elizabeth McDonald, "Plump from Web Sales, Some Dot.Coms Face Crash Diet of Restriction on Booking Revenue," *Wall Street Journal,* February 28, 2000, p. C4. Jeremy Kahn, "Presto chango! Sales are huge!" *Fortune,* March 20, 2000, pp. 90–96.

---

the Account Title column and in the Trial Balance columns is copied directly from the trial balance. The two Adjustments columns list the debit and credit adjustments directly across from the appropriate account title. Each adjusting debit is identified by a letter that refers to the adjusting entry. For example, the debit labeled (a) on the work sheet refers to the debit adjusting entry of $1,000 to Rent Expense in Panel B of Exhibit 3-9. For adjusting credits, the corresponding credit—labeled (a)—refers to the $1,000 credit to Prepaid Rent.

○ DAILY EXERCISE 3-12

○ DAILY EXERCISE 3-13

○ DAILY EXERCISE 3-14

○ DAILY EXERCISE 3-15

○ DAILY EXERCISE 3-16

The Adjusted Trial Balance columns give the adjusted account balances. Each amount in these columns is computed by combining the amounts from the unadjusted trial balance plus or minus the adjustments. For example, Accounts Receivable starts with a debit balance of $2,250. Adding the $250 debit amount from adjusting entry (e) gives Accounts Receivable an adjusted debit balance of $2,500. Supplies begins with a debit balance of $700. After the $300 credit adjustment, its adjusted balance is $400. More than one entry may affect a single account, as is the case for Service Revenue. If an account is unaffected by the adjustments, it will show the same amount on both the unadjusted and the adjusted trial balances. In this example, the balances of Cash, Furniture, Accounts Payable, Capital, and Withdrawals do not change.

EXHIBIT 3-10 Preparation of Adjusted Trial Balance

GAY GILLEN eTRAVEL
Preparation of Adjusted Trial Balance
April 30, 20X1

Account Title	Trial Balance Debit	Trial Balance Credit	Adjustments Debit	Adjustments Credit	Adjusted Trial Balance Debit	Adjusted Trial Balance Credit
Cash	24,800				24,800	
Accounts receivable	2,250		(e) 250		2,500	
Supplies	700			(b) 300	400	
Prepaid rent	3,000			(a) 1,000	2,000	
Furniture	16,500				16,500	
Accumulated depreciation				(c) 275		275
Accounts payable		13,100				13,100
Salary payable				(d) 950		950
Unearned service revenue		450	(f) 150			300
Gay Gillen, capital		31,250				31,250
Gay Gillen, withdrawals	3,200				3,200	
Service revenue		7,000		(e) 250		7,400
				(f) 150		
Rent expense			(a) 1,000		1,000	
Salary expense	950		(d) 950		1,900	
Supplies expense			(b) 300		300	
Depreciation expense			(c) 275		275	
Utilities expense	400				400	
	51,800	51,800	2,925	2,925	53,275	53,275

EXHIBIT 3-11 Preparing the Financial Statements of Gay Gillen eTravel from the Adjusted Trial Balance

Account Title	Adjusted Trial Balance Debit	Adjusted Trial Balance Credit	
Cash	24,800		
Accounts receivable	2,500		
Supplies	400		
Prepaid rent	2,000		**Balance Sheet** (Exhibit 3-14)
Furniture	16,500		
Accumulated depreciation		275	
Accounts payable		13,100	
Salary payable		950	
Unearned service revenue		300	
Gay Gillen, capital		31,250	**Statement of Owner's Equity** (Exhibit 3-13)
Gay Gillen, withdrawals	3,200		
Service revenue		7,400	
Rent expense	1,000		
Salary expense	1,900		**Income Statement** (Exhibit 3-12)
Supplies expense	300		
Depreciation expense	275		
Utilities expense	400		
	53,275	53,275	

PREPARING THE FINANCIAL STATEMENTS

The April financial statements of Gay Gillen eTravel can be prepared from the adjusted trial balance. Exhibit 3-11 shows how the accounts are distributed from the adjusted trial balance to three of the four main financial statements. As we have seen in Chapters 1–3, the income statement (Exhibit 3-12) comes from the revenue and expense accounts. The statement of owner's equity (Exhibit 3-13) shows why the owner's capital changed during the period. The balance sheet (Exhibit 3-14) reports the assets, liabilities, and owner's equity.

The financial statements are best prepared in the order shown: the income statement first, followed by the statement of owner's equity, and then the balance sheet.

EXHIBIT 3-12
Income Statement

GAY GILLEN eTRAVEL
Income Statement
Month Ended April 30, 20X1

Revenue:		
Service revenue		$7,400
Expenses:		
Salary expense	$1,900	
Rent expense.....................	1,000	
Utilities expense	400	
Supplies expense................	300	
Depreciation expense.........	275	
Total expenses		3,875
Net income		$3,525

EXHIBIT 3-13
Statement of Owner's Equity

GAY GILLEN eTRAVEL
Statement of Owner's Equity
Month Ended April 30, 20X1

Gay Gillen, capital, April 1, 20X1................	$31,250
Add: Net income	3,525
	34,775
Less: Withdrawals..	(3,200)
Gay Gillen, capital, April 30, 20X1	$31,575

EXHIBIT 3-14
Balance Sheet

GAY GILLEN eTRAVEL
Balance Sheet
April 30, 20X1

Assets			Liabilities		
Cash		$24,800	Accounts payable		$13,100
Accounts			Salary payable		950
receivable		2,500	Unearned service		
Supplies		400	revenue		300
Prepaid rent		2,000	Total liabilities		14,350
Furniture	$16,500				
Less:					
Accumulated					
depreciation	(275)	16,225	**Owner's Equity**		
			Gay Gillen, capital...............		31,575
			Total liabilities and		
Total assets		$45,925	owner's equity.................		$45,925

The essential features of all financial statements are these:

> Heading
>
> - Name of the entity
> - Title of the statement
> - Date, or period, covered by the statement
>
> Body of the statement

It is customary to list expenses in descending order by amount on the income statement, as shown in Exhibit 3-12. However, Miscellaneous Expense, a catchall account for expenses that do not fit another category, is usually reported last.

RELATIONSHIPS AMONG THE THREE FINANCIAL STATEMENTS

The arrows in Exhibits 3-12, 3-13, and 3-14 illustrate the relationships among the income statement, the statement of owner's equity, and the balance sheet. ➤ Consider why the income statement is prepared first and the balance sheet last.

◄ The relationships among the financial statements were introduced in Chapter 1, p. 20.

1. The income statement reports net income or net loss (revenues minus expenses). Because revenues and expenses are owner's equity accounts, their net amount is transferred to the statement of owner's equity. Note that net income in Exhibit 3-12, $3,525, increases owner's equity in Exhibit 3-13. A net loss would decrease owner's equity.
2. Capital is a balance sheet account, so the ending balance in the statement of owner's equity is transferred to the balance sheet. This amount is the final balancing element of the balance sheet. To solidify your understanding of this relationship, trace the $31,575 figure from Exhibit 3-13 to Exhibit 3-14.

You may be wondering why the total assets on the balance sheet ($45,925 in Exhibit 3-14) do not equal the total debits on the adjusted trial balance ($53,275 in Exhibit 3-11). Likewise, the total liabilities and owner's equity ($45,925 in Exhibit 3-14) do not equal the total credits on the adjusted trial balance ($53,275 in Exhibit 3-11). The reason for these differences is that Accumulated Depreciation and Owner's Withdrawals are contra accounts. Recall that contra accounts are *subtracted* from their companion accounts on the balance sheet. But on the adjusted trial balance, contra accounts are *added* as a debit or a credit in their respective columns.

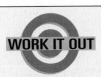 **WORK IT OUT**

Examine Gillen eTravel's adjusted trial balance in Exhibit 3-10. Suppose Gillen forgot to record the $950 accrual of salary expense at April 30. What net income would the travel agency then report for April? What total assets, total liabilities, and total owner's equity would the balance sheet report at April 30?

Answer: Omitting the salary accrual would produce these effects:

1. Net income (Exhibit 3-12) would have been $4,475 ($3,525 + $950).
2. Total assets would have been unaffected by the error—$45,925 (Exhibit 3-14).
3. Total liabilities (Exhibit 3-14) would have been $13,400 ($14,350 − $950).
4. Owner's equity (Gay Gillen, capital) would have been $32,525 ($31,575 + $950) (Exhibit 3-14).

ETHICAL ISSUES IN ACCRUAL ACCOUNTING

Like other aspects of business, accounting poses ethical challenges. At the most fundamental level, accountants must be honest in their work. Only with honest and complete information, including accounting data, can people expect to make wise decisions. An example will illustrate.

It's Just Lunch has done well as a business. Andrea McGinty is an excellent businesswoman. The company has opened offices in most major cities in the United States. Suppose It's Just Lunch wishes to open an office in Nashville, Tennessee, and needs to borrow $100,000 for prepaid rent, office equipment, and so on. Assume It's Just Lunch understated expenses in order to inflate net income as reported on the company's income statement. A banker could be tricked into lending the company money. Then if It's Just Lunch could not repay the loan, the bank would lose money—all because the banker relied on incorrect accounting information.

Accrual accounting provides several opportunities for unethical accounting. It would be easy for a dishonest businessperson to overlook an accrued expense or depreciation expense at the end of the period. Failing to make these adjustments would overstate net income and paint an overly favorable picture of the company's financial situation.

The cash basis of accounting poses fewer ethical challenges because either the company has the cash, or it does not. Therefore, the amount of cash a company reports is rarely disputed. By contrast, adjusting entries for accrued expenses, accrued revenues, and depreciation often must be estimated. Whenever there is an estimate, the accountant must deal with the temptation to make the company look different from its true condition. Fortunately, accounting has a good reputation for honesty.

The Decision Guidelines feature provides a map of the adjusting process that leads to the financial statements.

DECISION GUIDELINES

Measuring Business Income: The Adjusting Process

DECISION	GUIDELINES
Which basis of accounting better measures business income (revenues − expenses)?	*Accrual basis*, because it provides more complete reports of operating performance and financial position
How to measure revenues?	Revenue principle
How to measure expenses?	Matching principle
Where to start with the measurement of income at the end of the period?	Unadjusted trial balance, usually referred to simply as the *trial balance*
How to update the accounts for preparation of the financial statements?	*Adjusting entries* at the end of the accounting period
What are the categories of adjusting entries?	Prepaid expenses Accrued revenues Depreciation of plant assets Unearned revenues Accrued expenses

How do the adjusting entries differ from other journal entries?	1. Adjusting entries are usually made only at the end of the accounting period.
	2. Adjusting entries never affect cash.
	3. All adjusting entries debit or credit.
	    • At least one *income statement* account (a revenue or an expense), and
	    • At least one *balance sheet* account (an asset or a liability)

Where are the accounts with their adjusted balances summarized?	*Adjusted trial balance*, which becomes the basis for preparing the financial statements

EXCEL APPLICATION PROBLEM

Goal: Create an Excel spreadsheet that contains an income statement, statement of owner's equity, and balance sheet, complete with the formula relationships among all three statements.

Scenario: The three financial statements are related. The relationships show up when net income changes. Using Exhibits 3-12, 3-13, and 3-14, replicate the Income Statement, Statement of Owner's Equity, and Balance sheet for Gay Gillen eTravel. When you are finished, you will change just two related variables, but see the effect ripple through all the statements you have created.

1. Change service revenue from $7,400 to $10,900 and cash from $24,800 to $28,300. (Remember, every transaction requires at least one debit entry and one credit entry.) What is the new net income figure?
2. What is the new balance for Gay Gillen, Capital, April 30, 20X1?
3. Did any other amounts change? If so, which ones?

Step-by-step:

1. Open a new Excel spreadsheet.
2. Create a boldfaced heading for your spreadsheet that contains the following:

   a. Chapter 3 Decision Guidelines
   b. Gay Gillen eTravel

3. Refer to Exhibit 3-12. Prepare the Income Statement as it appears in the text near the top of your spreadsheet, formatting and using formulas as appropriate. When finished, put a border around the Income Statement.
4. Refer to Exhibit 3-13. In your spreadsheet, prepare the Statement of Owner's Equity as it appears in the text to the right of the Income Statement. Be sure "Net Income" is a cell reference to your Income Statement's Net Income. Format and use formulas as appropriate. When finished, put a border around the Statement of Owner's Equity.
5. Refer to Exhibit 3-14. Prepare the Balance Sheet as it appears in the text below the income statement in your spreadsheet. Be sure "Gay Gillen, Capital" is a cell reference to the ending capital balance in your Statement of Owner's Equity. When finished, put a border around the Balance Sheet.
6. Make the two changes in scenario question 1. Save your file to disk and print a copy for comparison against Exhibits 3-12, 3-13, and 3-14 in the textbook.

REVIEW THE ADJUSTING PROCESS

SUMMARY PROBLEM

The trial balance of State Service Company pertains to December 31, 20X3, which is the end of its year-long accounting period. Data needed for the adjusting entries include

a. Supplies on hand at year end, $2,000.
b. Depreciation on furniture and fixtures, $20,000.
c. Depreciation on building, $10,000.
d. Salaries owed but not yet paid, $5,000.
e. Accrued service revenue, $12,000.
f. Of the $45,000 balance of unearned service revenue, $32,000 was earned during the year.

www.prenhall.com/horngren
End-of-Chapter Assessment

Required

1. Open the ledger accounts with their unadjusted balances. Show dollar amounts in thousands as done for Accounts Receivable:

Accounts Receivable
370

2. Journalize State Service Company's adjusting entries at December 31, 20X3. Key entries by letter, as in Exhibit 3-9.
3. Post the adjusting entries.
4. Write the trial balance on a work sheet, enter the adjusting entries, and prepare an adjusted trial balance, as shown in Exhibit 3-10.
5. Prepare the income statement, the statement of owner's equity, and the balance sheet. Draw arrows linking these three financial statements.

STATE SERVICE COMPANY
Trial Balance
December 31, 20X3

Cash	$ 198,000	
Accounts receivable	370,000	
Supplies	6,000	
Furniture and fixtures	100,000	
Accumulated depreciation—furniture and fixtures		$ 40,000
Building	250,000	
Accumulated depreciation—building		130,000
Accounts payable		380,000
Salary payable		
Unearned service revenue		45,000
Owner's capital		293,000
Owner's withdrawals	65,000	
Service revenue		286,000
Salary expense	172,000	
Supplies expense		
Depreciation expense—furniture and fixtures		
Depreciation expense—building		
Miscellaneous expense	13,000	
Total	$1,174,000	$1,174,000

Solution

Requirements 2 and 3 (amounts in thousands)

ASSETS

CASH

Bal.	198	

ACCOUNTS RECEIVABLE

	370	
(e)	12	
Bal.	382	

SUPPLIES

	6	(a)	4
Bal.	2		

FURNITURE AND FIXTURES

Bal.	100	

ACCUMULATED DEPRECIATION—FURNITURE AND FIXTURES

			40
		(b)	20
		Bal.	60

BUILDING

Bal.	250	

ACCUMULATED DEPRECIATION—BUILDING

			130
		(c)	10
		Bal.	140

LIABILITIES

ACCOUNTS PAYABLE

		Bal.	380

SALARY PAYABLE

		(d)	5
		Bal.	5

UNEARNED SERVICE REVENUE

(f)	32		45
		Bal.	13

REVENUE

SERVICE REVENUE

			286
		(e)	12
		(f)	32
		Bal.	330

OWNER'S EQUITY

OWNER'S CAPITAL

		Bal.	293

OWNER'S WITHDRAWALS

Bal.	65	

EXPENSES

SALARY EXPENSE

	172	
(d)	5	
Bal.	177	

SUPPLIES EXPENSE

(a)	4	
Bal.	4	

DEPRECIATION EXPENSE—FURNITURE AND FIXTURES

(b)	20	
Bal.	20	

DEPRECIATION EXPENSE—BUILDING

(c)	10	
Bal.	10	

MISCELLANEOUS EXPENSE

Bal.	13	

Requirement 2

20X3

a.	Dec. 31	Supplies Expense ($6,000 − $2,000)................................	4,000	
		Supplies...		4,000
		To record supplies used.		
b.	31	Depreciation Expense—Furniture and Fixtures.................	20,000	
		Accumulated Depreciation—Furniture and Fixtures		20,000
		To record depreciation expense on furniture and fixtures.		
c.	31	Depreciation Expense—Building	10,000	
		Accumulated Depreciation—Building		10,000
		To record depreciation expense on building.		
d.	31	Salary Expense...	5,000	
		Salary Payable..		5,000
		To accrue salary expense.		
e.	31	Accounts Receivable	12,000	
		Service Revenue		12,000
		To accrue service revenue.		
f.	31	Unearned Service Revenue..	32,000	
		Service Revenue		32,000
		To record service revenue that was collected in advance.		

Requirement 4

STATE SERVICE COMPANY
Preparation of Adjusted Trial Balance
December 31, 20X3
(amounts in thousands)

Account Title	Trial Balance Debit	Trial Balance Credit	Adjustments Debit	Adjustments Credit	Adjusted Trial Balance Debit	Adjusted Trial Balance Credit
Cash..	198				198	
Accounts receivable	370		(e) 12		382	
Supplies..	6			(a) 4	2	
Furniture and fixtures.............................	100				100	
Accumulated depreciation— furniture and fixtures		40		(b) 20		60
Building...	250				250	
Accumulated depreciation—building......		130		(c) 10		140
Accounts payable		380				380
Salary payable				(d) 5		5
Unearned service revenue		45	(f) 32			13
Owner's capital.......................................		293				293
Owner's withdrawals	65				65	
Service revenue......................................		286		(e) 12		330
				(f) 32		
Salary expense	172		(d) 5		177	
Supplies expense			(a) 4		4	
Depreciation expense— furniture and fixtures			(b) 20		20	
Depreciation expense—building			(c) 10		10	
Miscellaneous expense............................	13				13	
	1,174	1,174	83	83	1,221	1,221

STATE SERVICE COMPANY
Income Statement
Year Ended December 31, 20X3
(amounts in thousands)

Revenue:		
Service revenue		$330
Expenses:		
Salary expense..	$177	
Depreciation expense—furniture and fixtures	20	
Depreciation expense—building................................	10	
Supplies expense	4	
Miscellaneous expense	13	
Total expenses...		224
Net income		$106

STATE SERVICE COMPANY
Statement of Owner's Equity
Year Ended December 31, 20X3
(amounts in thousands)

Capital, January 1, 20X3............................	$293
Add: Net income	106
	399
Less: Withdrawals	(65)
Capital, December 31, 20X3	$334

STATE SERVICE COMPANY
Balance Sheet
December 31, 20X3
(amounts in thousands)

Assets			Liabilities	
Cash...................................		$198	Accounts payable	$380
Accounts receivable.........		382	Salary payable	5
Supplies		2	Unearned service revenue ..	13
Furniture and fixtures	$100		Total liabilities	398
Less: Accumulated				
depreciation..............	(60)	40		
			Owner's Equity	
Building...........................	$250			
Less: Accumulated			Owner's capital....................	334
depreciation..............	(140)	110	Total liabilities and	
Total assets......................		$732	owner's equity.................	$732

LESSONS LEARNED

1. **Distinguish accrual-basis accounting from cash-basis accounting.** In *accrual-basis accounting*, business events are recorded as they occur. In *cash-basis accounting*, only those events that affect cash are recorded. Some small organizations use cash-basis accounting, but the generally accepted method is the accrual basis.

2. **Apply the revenue and matching principles.** Businesses divide time into definite periods—such as a month, a quarter, or a year—to report the entity's financial statements. The year is the basic *accounting period*, but companies prepare financial statements as often as they need the information. The *revenue principle* helps accountants determine when to record revenue and the amount of revenue to record. Revenue is recorded after it has been earned, and not before. The *matching principle* directs accountants to match expenses against revenues earned during a particular period of time.

3. **Make adjusting entries at the end of the accounting period.** Adjusting entries are a result of the accrual basis of accounting. Made at the end of the period, these entries update the accounts for preparation of the financial statements. Adjusting entries are divided into five categories: *prepaid expenses, depreciation, accrued expenses, accrued revenues,* and *unearned revenues.*

4. **Prepare an adjusted trial balance.** To prepare the *adjusted trial balance*, accountants enter the adjusting entries next to the *unadjusted trial balance* and compute each account's balance.

5. **Prepare the financial statements from the adjusted trial balance.** The adjusted trial balance can be used to prepare the financial statements. Income, shown on the *income statement*, increases the owner's capital, which also appears on the *statement of owner's equity*. The ending balance of capital is the last amount reported on the *balance sheet*.

ACCOUNTING VOCABULARY

accrual-basis accounting (p. 83)
accrued expense (p. 92)
accrued revenue (p. 94)
Accumulated Depreciation (p. 91)
adjusted trial balance (p. 97)
adjusting entry (p. 87)

book value (of a plant asset) (p. 91)
cash-basis accounting (p. 83)
contra account (p. 91)
deferred revenue (p. 94)
depreciation (p. 90)
matching principle (p. 86)

plant asset (p. 90)
prepaid expense (p. 88)
revenue principle (p. 85)
time-period concept (p. 86)
unearned revenue (p. 94)

QUESTIONS

1. Distinguish accrual-basis accounting from cash-basis accounting.
2. How long is the basic accounting period? What is a fiscal year? What is an interim period?
3. What two questions does the revenue principle help answer?
4. Briefly explain the matching principle.
5. What is the purpose of making adjusting entries?
6. Why are adjusting entries made at the end of the accounting period?
7. Name five categories of adjusting entries, and give an example of each.
8. Do all adjusting entries affect the net income or net loss of the period? Include the definition of an adjusting entry.
9. Why must the balance of Supplies be adjusted at the end of the period?
10. On January 1, ABC Company pays $1,800 for an insurance policy that covers three years. At the end of the first year, the balance of its Prepaid Insurance account contains two elements. What are the two elements, and what is the correct amount of each?
11. The title Prepaid Expense suggests that this account is an expense. If it is, explain why. If it is not, what type of account is it?
12. What is a contra account? Identify the contra account introduced in this chapter, along with the account's normal balance.
13. The balance sheet reports plant assets at book value of $135,000 and accumulated depreciation of $65,000. What does *book value* of a plant asset mean? What was the cost of the plant assets?
14. Why is an unearned revenue a liability? Give an example.
15. What purposes does the adjusted trial balance serve?
16. Explain the relationship among the income statement, the statement of owner's equity, and the balance sheet.

ASSESS YOUR PROGRESS

DAILY EXERCISES

DE3-1 Study Exhibit 3-1, and the related discussion on pages 83 and 84. Suppose **Drugstore.com** is preparing its income statement. Identify the amount of revenue Drugstore.com would report on its January income statement under (a) cash-basis accounting and (b) accrual-basis accounting. How much advertising expense would Drugstore.com report for December under the (a) cash basis and (b) accrual basis?

Accrual accounting versus cash-basis accounting for revenues (Obj. 1)

DE3-2 It's Just Lunch, the business featured at the beginning of this chapter, uses computer databases to help its clients meet each other. Suppose It's Just Lunch paid $2,900 for a Dell computer. Review pages 00 and 00, and then describe how It's Just Lunch would account for the $2,900 expenditure under (a) the cash basis and (b) the accrual basis. State in your own words why the accrual basis is more realistic for this situation.

DE3-3 Intel Corporation produces the Pentium© processor that is featured in many computers. Demand for Pentium© processors is very strong. Suppose Intel has completed production of 2,000 processor units that it expects to sell to IBM. Assume that Intel's cost to manufacture each processor is $140 and that Intel sells each processor for $375.

Apply the revenue principle to determine (1) when Intel should record revenue for this situation, and (2) the amount of revenue Intel should record for the sale of 2,000 Pentium© processors.

DE3-4 Return to the Intel Corporation situation described in Daily Exercise 3-3. Suppose that Intel has sold 2,000 Pentium© processors to IBM. What will Intel record in order to apply the matching principle? Give the name of the expense that Intel will record, and specify its amount.

DE3-5 Storage USA operates approximately 475 miniwarehouses across the United States. The company's headquarters are in Memphis, Tennessee. During 1998, Storage USA earned rental revenue of $217 million and collected cash of $223 million from customers. Total expenses for 1998 were $162 million, of which Storage USA paid $153 million.

1. Using the data supplied here, apply the revenue principle and the matching principle to compute Storage USA's net income for 1998.
2. Identify the information that you did not use to compute Storage USA's net income. Give the reason for not using the information.

DE3-6 At December 31, 1999, US Airways recorded Salary Expense and Salary Payable of $341 million, as shown on page 86. Suppose US Airways paid $350 million to its employees on January 3, 2000, the company's next payday after the end of the 1999 year.

1. Consider the salary expense that US Airways accrued at December 31, 1999, and the related payment on January 3, 2000. Assuming no other expenses in this category, how much Salary Expense would US Airways report on its 1999 income statement? How much Salary Expense would the company report on its year 2000 income statement?
2. Journalize US Airways' entry for payment of the payroll on January 3, 2000. Include the date and an explanation for the entry.

DE3-7 Answer the following questions.

1. Prepaid expenses are discussed beginning on page 88. Focus on the accounting for prepaid rent. Assume that Gay Gillen's initial $3,000 prepayment of rent on April 1 (page 88) was for 12 months rather than three. Give Gay Gillen's adjusting entry to record rent expense at April 30. Include the date of the entry and an explanation. Then post to the two accounts involved, and show their balances at April 30.
2. Refer to the supplies example on pages 88–90. Assume that Gillen's travel agency has $200 of supplies on hand (rather than $400) at April 30. Give the adjusting entry, complete with date and explanation, at April 30. Post to the accounts and show their balances at April 30.

DE3-8 ←← Link Back to Chapters 1 and 2 (Income Statement and Balance Sheet). It's Just Lunch uses computers for data searches. Suppose that on May 1 the company paid cash of $36,000 for Gateway computers that are expected to remain useful for two years. At the end of two years, the value of the computers is expected to be zero.

1. Make journal entries to record (a) purchase of the computers on May 1 and (b) depreciation on May 31. Include dates and explanations, and use the following accounts: Computer Equipment; Accumulated Depreciation—Computer Equipment; and Depreciation Expense—Computer Equipment.
2. Post to the accounts listed in requirement 1, and show their balances at May 31.
3. What is the equipment's book value at May 31?
4. Which account(s) listed in requirement 1 will It's Just Lunch report on the income statement for the month of May? Which account(s) will appear on the balance sheet at May 31? Show the amount to report for each account.

DE3-9 Suppose Gay Gillen borrowed $20,000 on October 1 by signing a note payable to Community One Bank. Gillen's interest expense for each month is $100. The loan agreement requires Gillen to pay October interest at the end of December, along with the interest that will accrue for November and December.

1. Make the same adjusting entry to record interest expense and interest payable at October 31, at November 30, and at December 31. Date each entry and include its explanation.
2. Post all three entries to the Interest Payable account. You need not take the balance of the account at the end of each month.

3. On which financial statement and under what category will Gillen report the interest payable? How much interest payable will Gillen report at October 31 and at November 30?

DE3-10 Return to the situation of Daily Exercise 3-9. Suppose you are accounting for the same transactions on the books of Community One Bank, which lent the money to Gay Gillen eTravel. Perform all three requirements of Daily Exercise 3-9 for Community One Bank using its own accounts: Interest Receivable and Interest Revenue. (For requirements 2 and 3, use the Interest Receivable account.)

Accruing and receiving cash from interest revenue
(Obj. 3)

DE3-11 Write a paragraph to explain why unearned revenues are liabilities rather than revenues. In your explanation, use the following actual example: **Southern Living Magazine** collects cash from subscribers in advance and later mails the magazines to subscribers over a one-year period. Explain what happens to the unearned subscription revenue over the course of a year as Southern Living mails the magazines to subscribers. Where (into what account) does the unearned subscription revenue go as Southern Living mails magazines to subscribers? Give the adjusting entry that Southern Living makes to record the earning of $20,000 of Subscription Revenue. Include an explanation for the entry, as illustrated in the chapter.

Explaining unearned revenues
(Obj. 3)

DE3-12 Study the T-accounts in Exhibit 3-9, Panel C, on page 97. Focus on the Prepaid Rent account. Which amount in the Prepaid Rent account appeared on the *unadjusted* trial balance (Exhibit 3-10, page 99)? Which amount in the Prepaid Rent account will appear on the *adjusted* trial balance? Which amount will be reported on the balance sheet at April 30? Why will the balance sheet report this amount? Under what balance sheet category will Prepaid Rent appear?

Contrasting the unadjusted and the adjusted trial balances
(Obj. 4)

DE3-13 In the Adjustments columns of Exhibit 3-10, page 99, two adjustments affected Service Revenue.

Using the adjusted trial balance
(Obj. 4)

1. Make journal entries for the two adjustments. Date each entry and include an explanation.
2. The journal entries you just made affected three accounts: Accounts Receivable; Unearned Service Revenue; and Service Revenue. Show how Gay Gillen eTravel will report all three accounts in its financial statements at April 30. For each account, identify its (a) financial statement, (b) category on the financial statement, and (c) balance.

DE3-14 Write a business memorandum to your supervisor explaining the difference between the unadjusted amounts and the adjusted amounts in Exhibit 3-10, page 99. Use Accounts Receivable in your explanation. If necessary, refer to the discussion of Accrued Revenues that begins on page 94.

Explaining the adjusted trial balance
(Obj. 4)

Business memos are formatted as follows:

Date:	_____
To:	_____
From:	_____
Subject:	Difference between the *unadjusted* and the *adjusted* amounts on an adjusted trial balance

DE3-15 Refer to the adjusted trial balance in Exhibit 3-10, page 99.

Preparing the balance sheet
(Obj. 5)

1. Focus first on the *unadjusted* amounts. Compute the amount of **total assets** that Gay Gillen would have reported on the balance sheet at April 30 if she had *not* made the adjusting entries at the end of the period. Also compute unadjusted **total liabilities.**
2. Now focus on the *adjusted* figures. Compute Gillen's total assets and total liabilities at April 30. Compare your totals to the balance sheet in Exhibit 3-14, page 100. Are they the same?
3. Why does a business need to make adjusting entries at the end of the period?

DE3-16 Refer to the adjusted trial balance in Exhibit 3-10 page 99.

Preparing the income statement
(Obj. 5)

1. Focus first on the *unadjusted* amounts. Compute the amount of **total revenues** that Gay Gillen eTravel would have reported on the income statement for the month of April if she had *not* made the adjusting entries at the end of the period. Also compute unadjusted **total expenses.** Finally, determine the amount of **net income** Gillen would have reported if she had not adjusted the accounts.
2. Now focus on the *adjusted* figures. Compute Gillen's total revenues, total expenses, and net income for April. Compare your totals to the income statement in Exhibit 3-12, page 100. Are they the same?
3. Why does a business need to make adjusting entries at the end of the period?

Cash basis versus accrual basis
(Obj. 1)

E3-1 Homewood Suites had the following selected transactions during January:

Jan. 1 Prepaid rent for three months, $2,700.
    5 Paid electricity expenses, $400.
    9 Received cash for the day's room rentals, $1,400.
   14 Paid cash for six television sets, $3,000.
   23 Served a banquet, receiving a note receivable, $1,600.
   31 Made the adjusting entry for rent (from Jan. 1).
   31 Accrued salary expense, $900.

Show how each transaction would be handled using the accrual basis. Give the amount of revenue or expense for January. Journal entries are not required. Use the following format for your answer, and show your computations:

Amount of Revenue (Expense) for January		
Date	Revenue or (Expense)	Accrual-Basis Amount

Applying accounting concepts and principles
(Obj. 2)

E3-2 Identify the accounting concept or principle (there may be more than one) that gives the most direction on how to account for each of the following situations:

a. The owner of a business desires monthly financial statements to measure the progress of the entity on an ongoing basis.
b. Expenses of the period total $6,700. This amount should be subtracted from revenue to compute the period's income.
c. Expenses of $1,200 must be accrued at the end of the period to measure income properly.
d. A customer states her intention to switch health clubs. Should the new health club record revenue based on this intention? Give the reason for your answer.

Applying accounting concepts
(Obj. 2)

E3-3 Write a memo to your supervisor explaining in your own words the need for adjusting entries at the end of the period. Cite two accounts that need to be adjusted. Adapt the format for a business memo that is given with Daily Exercise 3-14.

Allocating prepaid expense to the asset and the expense
(Obj. 2, 3)

E3-4 Compute the amounts indicated by question marks for each of the following situations for Prepaid Insurance. For situations A and B, journalize the needed entry. Consider each situation separately.

	Situation			
	A	B	C	D
Beginning Prepaid Insurance.........	$ 450	$500	$ 900	$ 600
Payments for Prepaid Insurance during the year	1,400	_800_	1,100	_?00_
Total amount to account for	_1850_	_1300_	2,000	1,500
Ending Prepaid Insurance.............	250	400	_800_	700
Insurance Expense.......................	_1600_	$900	$1,200	$ 800

Journalizing adjusting entries
(Obj. 3)

E3-5 Journalize the entries for the following adjustments at January 31, the end of the accounting period.

a. Employee salaries owed for Monday and Tuesday of a five-day workweek; weekly payroll, $15,000.
b. Unearned service revenue earned, $800.
c. Depreciation, $3,200.
d. Prepaid insurance expired, $300.
e. Interest revenue accrued, $4,400.

Analyzing the effects of adjustments on net income
(Obj. 3)

E3-6 Suppose the adjustments required in Exercise 3-5 were not made. Compute the overall overstatement or understatement of net income as a result of the omission of these adjustments.

Journalizing adjusting entries
(Obj. 3)

E3-7 Journalize the adjusting entry needed at December 31 for each of the following independent situations.

a. On July 1, when we collected $10,000 rent in advance, we debited Cash and credited Unearned Rent Revenue. The tenant was paying for one year's rent in advance.

b. The business owes interest expense of $400, which it will pay early in the next period.

c. Interest revenue of $700 has been earned but not yet received. The business holds a $20,000 note receivable.

d. Salary expense is $1,500 per day—Monday through Friday—and the business pays employees each Friday. This year December 31 falls on a Wednesday.

e. The unadjusted balance of the Supplies account is $3,100. The cost of supplies on hand is $1,200.

f. Equipment was purchased last year at a cost of $10,000. The equipment's useful life is four years. Record the year's depreciation.

g. On September 1, when we prepaid $1,200 for a two-year insurance policy, we debited Prepaid Insurance and credited Cash.

E3-8 The accounting records of Lane Ginsburg, Architect, include the following unadjusted balances at March 31: Accounts Receivable, $1,000; Supplies, $600; Salary Payable, $0; Unearned Service Revenue, $400; Service Revenue, $4,700; Salary Expense, $1,200; Supplies Expense, $0. Ginsburg's accountant develops the following data for the March 31 adjusting entries:

Recording adjustments in T-accounts
(Obj. 3)

a. Service revenue accrued, $650.

b. Unearned service revenue that has been earned, $200.

c. Supplies on hand, $100.

d. Salary owed to employee, $600.

Open T-accounts for each and record the adjustments directly in the accounts, keying each adjustment amount by letter. Show each account's adjusted balance. Journal entries are not required.

E3-9 The adjusted trial balance of Signet Repair Company is incomplete. Enter the adjustment amounts directly in the adjustment columns of the text. Service Revenue is the only account affected by more than one adjustment.

Adjusting the accounts
(Obj. 3, 4)

	SIGNET REPAIR COMPANY Preparation of Adjusted Trial Balance May 31, 20X2						
	Trial Balance		**Adjustments**		**Adjusted Trial Balance**		
Account Title	**Debit**	**Credit**	**Debit**	**Credit**	**Debit**	**Credit**
Cash	3,000				3,000	
Accounts receivable	4,500				7,400	
Supplies.......................	1,040				800	
Office furniture	32,300				32,300	
Accumulated depreciation		14,040				14,400
Salary payable.......................						900
Unearned service revenue		900				690
Capital.........................		26,360				26,360
Owner's withdrawals	6,000				6,000	
Service revenue		9,630				12,740
Salary expense	2,690				3,590	
Rent expense	1,400				1,400	
Depreciation expense......................					360	
Supplies expense..........................					240	
	50,930	50,930			55,090	55,090

E3-10 Make journal entries for the adjustments that would complete the preparation of the adjusted trial balance in Exercise 3-9. Date the entries and include explanations.

Journalizing adjustments
(Obj. 3, 4)

E3-11 Refer to the adjusted trial balance in Exercise 3-9. Prepare Signet Repair Company's income statement and statement of owner's equity for the month ended May 31, 20X2, and its balance sheet on that date. Draw arrows linking the three statements.

Preparing the financial statements
(Obj. 5)

E3-12 The accountant for Kay Fuston, Publisher, has posted adjusting entries (a)–(e) to the accounts at December 31, 20X2. Selected balance sheet accounts and all the revenues and expenses of the entity follow in T-account form.

Preparing the financial statements
(Obj. 5)

ACCOUNTS RECEIVABLE

23,000	
(e) 7,000	

SUPPLIES

4,000	(a) 1,000

ACCUMULATED DEPRECIATION— EQUIPMENT

	5,000
	(b) 2,000

ACCUMULATED DEPRECIATION—BUILDING

	33,000
	(c) 5,000

SALARY PAYABLE

	(d) 1,500

SERVICE REVENUE

	105,000
	(e) 7,000

SALARY EXPENSE

28,000	
(d) 1,500	

SUPPLIES EXPENSE

(a) 1,000	

DEPRECIATION EXPENSE— EQUIPMENT

(b) 2,000	

DEPRECIATION EXPENSE— BUILDING

(c) 5,000	

Required

1. Prepare the income statement of Kay Fuston, Publisher, for the year ended December 31, 20X2. List expenses in order from the largest to the smallest.
2. Were 20X2 operations successful? Give the reason for your answer.

Preparing the statement of owner's equity (Obj. 5)

E3-13 Quikwash Laundromat began the year with capital of $155,000. On July 12, Kent Carmichael (the owner) invested $12,000 cash in the business. On September 26, he transferred to the company land valued at $70,000. The income statement for the year ended December 31, 20X5, reported a net loss of $28,000. During this fiscal year, Carmichael withdrew $1,500 monthly for personal use.

Required

1. Prepare the laundromat's statement of owner's equity for the year ended December 31, 20X5.
2. Did the owner's equity of the business increase or decrease during the year? What caused this change?

Continuing Exercise. *Exercise 3-14 continues the Amos Faraday, Consultant, situation begun in Exercise 2-15 of Chapter 2.*

Adjusting the accounts, preparing an adjusted trial balance, and preparing the financial statements (Obj. 3, 4, 5)

E3-14 Refer to Exercise 2-15 of Chapter 2. Start from the trial balance and the posted T-accounts that Amos Faraday, Consultant, prepared for his business at December 18, as follows:

AMOS FARADAY, CONSULTANT
Trial Balance
December 18, 20XX

Account	Debit	Credit
Cash	$12,100	
Accounts receivable	1,700	
Supplies	300	
Equipment	2,000	
Furniture	3,600	
Accounts payable		$ 3,900
Amos Faraday, capital		14,000
Amos Faraday, withdrawals	—	
Service revenue		2,500
Rent expense	500	
Utilities expense	200	
Salary expense		
Total	$20,400	$20,400

Later in December, the business completed these transactions, as follows:

Dec. 21   Received $900 in advance for client service to be performed evenly over the next 30 days.

21   Hired a secretary to be paid $1,500 on the 20th day of each month. The secretary begins work immediately.

26   Paid $300 on account.

28   Collected $600 on account.

30   Withdrew $1,600 for personal use.

Required

1. Open these additional T-accounts: Accumulated Depreciation—Equipment; Accumulated Depreciation—Furniture; Salary Payable; Unearned Service Revenue; Depreciation Expense—Equipment; Depreciation Expense—Furniture; Supplies Expense.
2. Journalize the transactions of December 21–30.
3. Post to the T-accounts, keying all items by date.
4. Prepare a trial balance at December 31. Also set up columns for the adjustments and for the adjusted trial balance, as illustrated in Exhibit 3-10.
5. At December 31, Faraday gathers the following information for the adjusting entries:
   a. Accrued service revenue, $400.
   b. Earned a portion of the service revenue collected in advance on December 21.
   c. Supplies on hand, $100.
   d. Depreciation expense—equipment, $50; furniture, $60.
   e. Accrued expense for secretary's salary—10 days worked.

   Make these adjustments directly in the adjustments columns, and complete the adjusted trial balance at December 31. Throughout the book, to avoid rounding errors, we base adjusting entries on 30-day months and 360-day years.

6. Journalize and post the adjusting entries. Denote each adjusting amount as *Adj.* and an account balance as *Bal.*
7. Prepare the income statement and the statement of owner's equity of Amos Faraday, Consultant, for the month ended December 31, and prepare the balance sheet at that date.

Challenge Exercises

E3-15 Morris Chang Enterprises aids Chinese students upon their arrival in the United States. Paid by the Chinese government, Morris Chang collects some service revenue in advance. In other cases, he receives cash after performing relocation services. At the end of August—a particularly busy period—Morris Chang's books show the following:

Computing the amount of revenue (Obj. 3)

	July 31	August 31
Accounts receivable.......................	$1,900	$2,500
Unearned service revenue.............	1,200	300

During August, Morris Chang Enterprises received cash of $7,000 from the Chinese government. How much service revenue did the business earn during August? Show your work.

E3-16 For the situation of Exercise 3-15, assume the service revenue of Morris Chang Enterprises was $5,900 during August. How much cash did the business collect from the Chinese government that month? Show your work.

Computing cash amounts (Obj. 3)

PROBLEMS

(Group A)

P3-1A Normandy Psychiatric Group had the following selected transactions during January:

Cash basis versus accrual basis (Obj. 1, 2)

Jan. 1   Prepaid insurance for January through March, $600.
     4   Performed medical service on account, $1,000.
     5   Purchased office furniture on account, $150.
     8   Paid advertising expense, $450.
     11   Purchased office equipment for cash, $800.
     19   Performed medical service and received cash, $700.
     24   Collected $400 on account for January 4 service.
     26   Paid account payable from January 5.
     29   Paid salary expense, $900.
     31   Recorded adjusting entry for January insurance expense (see Jan. 1).
     31   Debited unearned revenue and credited revenue to adjust the accounts, $600.

Required

1. Show how each transaction would be handled using the accrual basis of accounting. Give the amount of revenue or expense for January. Journal entries are not required. Use the following format for your answer, and show your computations:

Amount of Revenue (Expense) for January

Date	Revenue (Expense)	Accrual-Basis Amount

2. Compute January net income or net loss under the accrual basis of accounting.

3. State why the accrual basis of accounting is preferable to the cash basis.

*Applying accounting principles
(Obj. 1, 2)*

P3-2A As the controller of Lake Cypress Lumber Company, you have hired a new bookkeeper, whom you must train. He objects to making an adjusting entry for accrued salaries at the end of the period. He reasons, "We will pay the salaries soon. Why not wait until payment to record the expense? In the end, the result will be the same." Write a business memo to explain to the bookkeeper why the adjusting entry for accrued salary expense is needed. The format of a business memo follows.

Date:	_____
To:	New Bookkeeper
From:	(Student Name)
Subject:	Why the adjusting entry for salary expense is needed

*Journalizing adjusting entries
(Obj. 3)*

P3-3A Journalize the adjusting entry needed on December 31, end of the current accounting period, for each of the following independent cases affecting Arvin Marketing Associates.

a. Each Friday, Arvin pays its employees for the current week's work. The amount of the payroll is $6,000 for a five-day workweek. The current accounting period ends on Thursday.

b. Arvin has received notes receivable from some clients for professional services. During the current year, Arvin has earned accrued interest revenue of $170, which will be collected next year.

c. The beginning balance of Supplies was $3,800. During the year, the entity purchased supplies costing $5,530, and at December 31, the inventory of supplies on hand is $2,970.

d. Arvin designed a marketing campaign, and the client paid Arvin $36,000 at the start of the project. Arvin recorded this amount as Unearned Service Revenue. The campaign will run for several months. Arvin estimates that the company has earned three-fourths of the total fee during the current year.

e. Depreciation for the current year includes: Office Furniture, $5,500; Building, $3,790. Make a compound entry, as illustrated in Chapter 2.

f. Details of Prepaid Insurance are shown in the account:

PREPAID INSURANCE			
Jan. 1	Bal.	900	
April 30		2,700	

Arvin pays insurance each year on April 30. At December 31, part of the last payment is still in force.

*Analyzing and journalizing
adjustments
(Obj. 3)*

P3-4A Platt Investment Brokers' unadjusted and adjusted trial balances at December 31, 20X7, follow at the top of page 115.

Required

Journalize the adjusting entries that account for the differences between the two trial balances.

*Journalizing and posting adjustments to T-accounts; preparing the adjusted trial balance
(Obj. 3, 4)*

P3-5A The trial balance of Liberty Duplicating Services at August 31, 20X6, year and the data needed for the month-end adjustments follow at the bottom of page 115.

Adjustment data:

a. Unearned service revenue still unearned at August 31, $1,670. *Subtract*
b. Prepaid rent still in force at August 31, $620. *Subtract*
c. Supplies used during the month, $700. *USE it*
d. Depreciation for the month, $400.
e. Accrued advertising expense at August 31, $610. (Credit Accounts Payable.)
f. Accrued salary expense at August 31, $550.

Required

1. Open T-accounts for the accounts listed in the trial balance, inserting their August 31 unadjusted balances.

2. Journalize the adjusting entries and post them to the T-accounts. Key the journal entries and the posted amounts by letter.

3. Prepare the adjusted trial balance.

4. How will the company use the adjusted trial balance?

PLATT INVESTMENT BROKERS
Adjusted Trial Balance
December 31, 20X7

Account Title	Trial Balance		Adjusted Trial Balance	
	Debit	Credit	Debit	Credit
Cash	4,120		4,120	
Accounts receivable	5,260		14,090	
Supplies	1,200		280	
Prepaid insurance	2,600		2,330	
Office furniture	21,630		21,630	
Accumulated depreciation		8,220		10,500
Accounts payable		6,420		6,420
Salary payable				960
Interest payable				480
Note payable		12,000		12,000
Unearned commission revenue		1,840		1,160
Claire Platt, capital		13,510		13,510
Claire Platt, withdrawals	29,370		29,370	
Commission revenue used twice		66,890		76,400
Depreciation expense			2,280	
Supplies expense			920	
Utilities expense	4,960		4,960	
Salary expense	26,660		27,620	
Rent expense	12,200		12,200	
Interest expense	880		1,360	
Insurance expense			270	
	108,880	108,880	121,430	121,430

LIBERTY DUPLICATING SERVICES
Trial Balance
August 31, 20X6

Account	Debit	Credit
Cash	$ 7,100	
Accounts receivable	19,780	
Prepaid rent	2,420	
Supplies	1,180	
Furniture	19,740	
Accumulated depreciation		$ 3,630
Accounts payable		3,310
Salary payable		
Unearned service revenue		2,790
Milton Hupp, capital		35,510
Milton Hupp, withdrawals	5,350	
Service revenue		15,700
Salary expense	3,800	
Rent expense		
Depreciation expense		
Advertising expense	1,570	
Supplies expense		
Total	$60,940	$60,940

Preparing an adjusted trial
balance and the financial
statements
(Obj. 3, 4, 5)

P3-6A The adjusted trial balance of Mastercraft Marble Cutters at December 31, 20X8, follows.

MASTERCRAFT MARBLE CUTTERS
Adjusted Trial Balance
December 31, 20X8

Cash	$ 2,340	
Accounts receivable	50,490	
Prepaid rent	1,350	
Supplies	970	
Equipment	75,690	
Accumulated depreciation—equipment		$ 22,240
Office furniture	24,100	
Accumulated depreciation—office furniture		3,670
Accounts payable		13,600
Unearned service revenue		4,520
Interest payable		2,130
Salary payable		930
Note payable		45,000
B. Masters, capital		32,380
B. Masters, withdrawals	48,000	
Service revenue		204,790
Depreciation expense—equipment	11,300	
Depreciation expense—office furniture	2,410	
Salary expense	87,800	
Rent expense	12,000	
Interest expense	4,200	
Utilities expense	3,770	
Insurance expense	3,150	
Supplies expense	1,690	
Total	$329,260	$329,260

Required

1. Prepare Mastercraft's 20X8 income statement and statement of owner's equity and year-end balance sheet. List expenses in decreasing order on the income statement and show total liabilities on the balance sheet. Draw arrows linking the three financial statements.
2. **a.** Which financial statement reports Mastercraft's results of operations? Were 20X8 operations successful? Cite specifics from the financial statements to support your evaluation.
   b. Which statement reports the company's financial position? Does Mastercraft's financial position look strong or weak? Give the reason for your evaluation.

Preparing an adjusted trial
balance and the financial
statements
(Obj. 3, 4, 5)

P3-7A Consider the unadjusted trial balance of ReliaMark Insurers at October 31, 20X2, and the related month-end adjustment data.

RELIAMARK INSURERS
Trial Balance
October 31, 20X2

Cash	$ 6,300	
Accounts receivable	8,000	
Prepaid rent	6,000	
Supplies	600	
Equipment	27,000	
Accumulated depreciation		$ 3,000
Accounts payable		2,800
Salary payable		
Karen Cabot, capital		38,000
Karen Cabot, withdrawals	3,600	
Service revenue		9,400
Salary expense	1,400	
Rent expense		
Utilities expense	300	
Depreciation expense		
Supplies expense		
Total	$53,200	$53,200

Adjustment data:

a. Accrued service revenue at October 31, $2,000.
b. Prepaid rent expired during the month. The unadjusted prepaid balance of $6,000 relates to the period October 20X2 through January 20X3.
c. Supplies on hand October 31, $200.
d. Depreciation on equipment for the month. The equipment's expected useful life is five years.
e. Accrued salary expense at October 31 for one day only. The five-day weekly payroll is $2,000.

Required

1. Write the trial balance on a work sheet, using Exhibit 3-10 as an example, and prepare the adjusted trial balance of ReliaMark Insurers at October 31, 20X2. Key each adjusting entry by letter.
2. Prepare the income statement and the statement of owner's equity for the month ended October 31, 20X2, and the balance sheet at that date. Draw arrows linking the three financial statements.

PROBLEMS

(Group B)

P3-1B Valleydale Bone and Joint Clinic completed the following selected transactions during May:

Cash basis versus accrual basis (Obj. 1, 2)

May	2	Prepaid insurance for May through July, $800.
	4	Paid gas bill, $550.
	5	Performed services on account, $1,000.
	9	Purchased office equipment for cash, $1,400.
	12	Received cash for services performed, $900.
	14	Purchased office equipment on account, $300.
	28	Collected $500 on account from May 5.
	29	Paid salary expense, $1,100.
	30	Paid account payable from May 14.
	31	Recorded adjusting entry for May insurance expense (see May 2).
	31	Debited unearned revenue and credited revenue in an adjusting entry, $700.

Required

1. Show how each transaction would be handled using the accrual basis of accounting. Give the amount of revenue or expense for May. Journal entries are not required. Use the following format for your answer, and show your computations:

Amount of Revenue (Expense) for May

Date	Revenue (Expense)	Accrual-Basis Amount

2. Compute May net income or net loss under the accrual basis of accounting.
3. Why is the accrual basis of accounting preferable to the cash basis?

P3-2B Write a business memo to a new bookkeeper to explain the difference between the cash basis of accounting and the accrual basis. Mention the roles of the revenue principle and the matching principle in accrual-basis accounting. The format of a business memo follows.

Applying accounting principles (Obj. 1, 2)

Date:	_____
To:	New Bookkeeper
From:	(Student Name)
Subject:	Difference between the cash basis and the accrual basis

P3-3B Journalize the adjusting entry needed on December 31, end of the current accounting period, for each of the following independent cases affecting Coronado Heating and Cooling.

Journalizing adjusting entries (Obj. 3)

a. Details of Prepaid Rent are shown in the account:

PREPAID RENT

| Jan. 1 | Bal. | 600 |
| Mar. 31 | | 2,400 |

Coronado pays office rent annually on March 31. At December 31, part of the last payment is still an asset.

b. Coronado pays its employees each Friday. The amount of the weekly payroll is $2,000 for a five-day workweek, and the daily salary amounts are equal. The current accounting period ends on Monday.

c. Coronado has loaned out money, receiving notes receivable. During the current year, the entity has earned accrued interest revenue of $737, which it will collect next year.

d. The beginning balance of Supplies was $2,680. During the year, the entity purchased supplies costing $6,180, and at December 31, the cost of supplies on hand is $2,150.

e. Coronado is servicing the air-conditioning system in a large building, and the owner of the building paid Coronado $12,900 as the annual service fee. Coronado recorded this amount as Unearned Service Revenue. Enrique Coronado, the owner, estimates that the company has earned one-fourth the total fee during the current year.

f. Depreciation for the current year includes Equipment, $3,850; Trucks, $10,320. Make a compound entry, as illustrated in Chapter 2.

Analyzing and journalizing adjustments
(Obj. 3)

P3-4B Olen Chemical Servicing's unadjusted and adjusted trial balances at April 30, 20X1, follow.

		OLEN CHEMICAL SERVICING Adjusted Trial Balance April 30, 20X1		
	Trial Balance		**Adjusted Trial Balance**	
Account Title	**Debit**	**Credit**	**Debit**	**Credit**
Cash	6,180		6,180	
Accounts receivable	5,990		6,700	
Interest receivable.......................			300	
Note receivable	4,100		4,100	
Supplies..	980		290	
Prepaid rent	2,480		720	
Building	66,450		66,450	
Accumulated depreciation		16,010		17,290
Accounts payable		6,920		6,920
Wages payable				320
Unearned service revenue		670		110
Paul Olen, capital........................		58,790		58,790
Paul Olen, withdrawals...............	3,600		3,600	
Service revenue		9,570		10,840
Interest revenue..........................				300
Wage expense	1,600		1,920	
Rent expense			1,760	
Depreciation expense..................			1,280	
Insurance expense	370		370	
Supplies expense.........................			690	
Utilities expense..........................	210		210	
	91,960	91,960	94,570	94,570

Required

Journalize the adjusting entries that account for the differences between the two trial balances.

Journalizing and posting adjustments to T-accounts; preparing the adjusted trial balance
(Obj. 3, 4)

P3-5B The trial balance of Great Lakes Investments at December 31, 20X2, and the data needed for the month-end adjustments follow at the top of the next page.

Adjustment data:

a. Prepaid rent still in force at December 31, $600.
b. Supplies used during the month, $640.
c. Depreciation for the month, $900.
d. Accrued advertising expense at December 31, $320. (Credit Accounts Payable.)
e. Accrued salary expense at December 31, $180.
f. Unearned commission revenue still unearned at December 31, $1,150.

GREAT LAKES INVESTMENTS
Trial Balance
December 31, 20X2

Cash	$ 2,200	
Accounts receivable	14,100	
Prepaid rent	3,100	
Supplies	780	
Furniture	22,710	
Accumulated depreciation		$11,640
Account payable		1,940
Salary payable		
Unearned commission revenue		2,290
Gina Pulver, capital		25,060
Gina Pulver, withdrawals	2,900	
Commission revenue		7,750
Salary expense	2,160	
Rent expense		
Depreciation expense		
Advertising expense	730	
Supplies expense		
Total	$48,680	$48,680

710

Required

1. Open T-accounts for the accounts listed in the trial balance, inserting their December 31 unadjusted balances.
2. Journalize the adjusting entries and post them to the T-accounts. Key the journal entries and the posted amounts by letter.
3. Prepare the adjusted trial balance.
4. How will the company use the adjusted trial balance?

P3-6B The adjusted trial balance of Marineland Travel Designers at December 31, 20X6, follows.

Preparing the financial statements from an adjusted trial balance (Obj. 5)

MARINELAND TRAVEL DESIGNERS
Adjusted Trial Balance
December 31, 20X6

9,570
710
10,280
560
0.840

Cash	$ 1,320	
Accounts receivable	4,920	
Supplies	2,300	
Prepaid rent	1,600	
Office equipment	20,180	
Accumulated depreciation—office equipment		$ 4,350
Office furniture	37,710	
Accumulated depreciation—office furniture		4,870
Accounts payable		4,740
Interest payable		830
Unearned service revenue		620
Note payable		13,500
Ken Sorley, capital		26,090
Ken Sorley, withdrawals	29,000	
Service revenue		120,910
Depreciation expense—office equipment	6,680	
Depreciation expense—office furniture	2,370	
Salary expense	39,900	
Rent expense	17,400	
Interest expense	3,100	
Utilities expense	2,670	
Insurance expense	3,810	
Supplies expense	2,950	
Total	$175,910	$175,910

Required

1. Prepare Marineland's 20X6 income statement and statement of owner's equity and year-end balance sheet. List expenses in decreasing order on the income statement and show total liabilities on the balance sheet. Draw arrows linking the three financial statements.
2. **a.** Which financial statement reports Marineland's results of operations? Were operations successful during 20X6? Cite specifics from the financial statements to support your evaluation.
   b. Which statement reports the company's financial position? Does Marineland's financial position look strong or weak? Give the reason for your evaluation.

Preparing an adjusted trial balance and the financial statements
(Obj. 3, 4, 5)

P3-7B The unadjusted trial balance of Christine Salomon, at July 31, 20X2, and the related month-end adjustment data follow.

CHRISTINE SALOMON, CPA **Trial Balance** July 31, 20X2		
Cash	$ 5,600	
Accounts receivable	11,600	
Prepaid rent	4,000	
Supplies	800	
Furniture	28,800	
Accumulated depreciation		$ 3,500
Accounts payable		3,450
Salary payable		
Christine Salomon, capital		39,050
Christine Salomon, withdrawals	4,000	
Accounting service revenue		11,750
Salary expense	2,400	
Rent expense		
Utilities expense	550	
Depreciation expense		
Supplies expense		
Total	$57,750	$57,750

Adjustment data:

a. Accrued accounting service revenue at July 31, $900.
b. Prepaid rent expired during the month. The unadjusted prepaid balance of $4,000 relates to the period July through October.
c. Supplies on hand at July 31, $400.
d. Depreciation on furniture for the month. The estimated useful life of the furniture is four years.
e. Accrued salary expense at July 31 for one day only. The five-day weekly payroll is $1,000.

Required

1. Using Exhibit 3-10 as an example, write the trial balance on a work sheet and prepare the adjusted trial balance of Christine Salomon, CPA, at July 31, 20X2. Key each adjusting entry by letter.
2. Prepare the income statement and the statement of owner's equity for the month ended July 31, 20X2, and the balance sheet at that date. Draw arrows linking the three financial statements.

APPLY YOUR KNOWLEDGE

DECISION CASES

Valuing a business on the basis of its net income
(Obj. 4, 5)

Case 1. Benjamin O'Henry has owned and operated O'Henry's Data Services since its beginning ten years ago. From all appearances, the business has prospered. In the past few years, you have become friends with O'Henry and his wife through your church. Recently, O'Henry mentioned that he has lost his zest for the business and would consider selling it for the right price. You are interested in buying this business and obtain its most recent monthly unadjusted trial balance, which follows.

O'HENRY'S DATA SERVICES
Unadjusted Trial Balance
November 30, 20XX

Cash	$ 9,700	
Accounts receivable	7,900	
Prepaid expenses	2,600	
Furniture, fixtures, and equipment	151,300	
Accumulated depreciation		$ 15,600
Accounts payable		3,800
Salary payable		
Unearned service revenue		6,700
Benjamin O'Henry, capital		137,400
Benjamin O'Henry, withdrawals	2,000	
Service revenue		14,300
Rent expense		
Salary expense	3,400	
Utilities expense	900	
Depreciation expense		
Supplies expense		
Total	$177,800	$177,800

Revenues and expenses vary little from month to month, and November is a typical month. Your investigation reveals that the unadjusted trial balance does not include the effects of monthly revenues of $2,100 and monthly expenses totaling $2,750. If you were to buy O'Henry's Data Services, you would hire a manager who would require a monthly salary of $3,000.

Required

1. The most you would pay for the business is 20 times the monthly net income *you could expect to earn* from it. Compute this possible price.
2. The least O'Henry will take for the business is his ending capital. Compute this amount.
3. Under these conditions, how much should you offer O'Henry? Give your reason.

Case 2. Suppose a new management team is in charge of Sunpool, Inc., an appliance manufacturer. Assume Sunpool's new top managers rose through the ranks in the sales and marketing departments and have little appreciation for the details of accounting. Consider the following conversation between these two managers:

Explaining why adjusting entries are needed
(Obj. 3)

Morgan Gummelt, President:	"I want to avoid the hassle of adjusting the books every time we need financial statements. Sooner or later we receive cash for all our revenues, and we pay cash for all our expenses. I can understand cash transactions, but all these accruals confuse me. If I cannot understand *our own accounting*, I'm fairly certain the average person who invests in our company cannot understand it either. Let's start recording only our cash transactions. I bet it won't make any difference to anyone."
Sarah Mead, Chief Financial Officer:	"Sounds good to me. This will save me lots of headaches. I'll implement the new policy immediately."

Write a business memo to the company president giving your response to the new policy. Identify at least five individual items (such as specific accounts) in the financial statements that will be reported incorrectly. Will outside investors care? Adapt the format of a business memo given with Daily Exercise 3-14.

ETHICAL ISSUE

The net income of Simon & Hobbs, a department store, decreased sharply during 2000. Carol Simon, owner of the store, anticipates the need for a bank loan in 2001. Late in 2000, Simon instructs the store's accountant to record a $10,000 sale of furniture to the Simon family, even though the goods will not be shipped from the manufacturer until January 2001. Simon also tells the accountant *not* to make the following December 31, 2000, adjusting entries:

Salaries owed to employees..........................	$900
Prepaid insurance that has expired..............	400

Required

1. Compute the overall effects of these transactions on the store's reported income for 2000.
2. Why is Simon taking this action? Is her action ethical? Give your reason, identifying the parties helped and the parties harmed by Simon's action.
3. As a personal friend, what advice would you give the accountant?

FINANCIAL STATEMENT CASE

Journalizing and posting transactions and tracing account balances to the financial statements (Obj. 3, 5)

Target Corporation—like all other businesses—makes adjusting entries prior to year end in order to measure assets, liabilities, revenues, and expenses properly. Examine Target's balance sheet, and pay particular attention to Other Current Assets (which includes Prepaid Expenses) and Accrued Liabilities (which includes Salary Payable and Interest Payable).

1. Open T-accounts for Other Current Assets (Prepaid Expenses), Accrued Liabilities, and Accumulated Depreciation. Insert Target's balances (in millions) at January 30, 1999. (Example: Other Current Assets (Prepaid Expenses), $619)
2. Journalize the following transactions for the current year, ended January 29, 2000. Key entries by letter. Explanations are not required.
   Cash transactions (amounts in millions):
   a. Paid prepaid expenses, $2,113.
   b. Paid the January 30, 1999, accrued liabilities.
   Adjustments at January 29, 2000 (amounts in millions):
   c. Prepaid expenses expired, $2,104. (Debit Administrative Expense)
   d. Accrued liabilities, $1,520. (Debit Selling Expense.)
   e. Depreciation expense, $157.
3. Post to the Other Current Assets (Prepaid Expenses) account the Accrued Liabilities account and the Accumulated Depreciation account. Then these accounts should agree with the corresponding amounts reported in the January 29, 2000, balance sheet. Check to make sure they do agree with Target's actual balances.

TEAM PROJECT

Return to the chapter-opening story, which describes Andrea McGinty's business, **It's Just Lunch.** Suppose your group is opening an It's Just Lunch office in your area. You must make some important decisions—where to locate, how to advertise, and so on—and you must also make some accounting decisions. For example, what will be the end of your business's accounting year? How often will you need financial statements to evaluate operating performance and financial position? Will you use the cash basis or the accrual basis? When will you account for the revenue that the business earns? How will you account for the expenses?

Required

Write a report (or prepare an oral presentation, as directed by your professor) to address the following considerations:

1. Will you use the cash basis or the accrual basis of accounting? Give a complete explanation of your reasoning.
2. How often do you want financial statements? Why? Discuss how you will use each financial statement.
3. What kind of revenue will you earn? When will you record it as revenue? How will you decide when to record the revenue?
4. Prepare a made-up income statement for It's Just Lunch for the Year ended December 31, 1998. List all the business's expenses, starting with the most important (largest dollar amount) and working through the least important (smallest dollar amount). Try to come as close as you can to the actual figures, as follows: Net revenues, $20,175,920; Net income, $2,018,516.
5. Using made-up dollar amounts, prepare all the adjusting entries your business will need at the end of the year. Identify the date of your adjustments.

INTERNET EXERCISE

1. **It's Just Lunch** customers may meet their dates at one of the many **Darden** restaurants. Go to **http://www.darden.com** and list at least three of the Darden restaurant chains.
2. In the left-hand column click on *The Numbers* followed by *Annual Report and Financials*. Select the HTML version of the *most recent annual report*. Click on *next* to reach the table of contents. Use the Consolidated Balance Sheets to answer the following questions.
   a. Does the Darden Restaurants company use cash-basis or accrual-basis accounting? How can you tell?
   b. For the two most recent years list the amounts reported for "Cash and cash equivalents" and for "Land, Buildings and Equipment." For each of these accounts, identify whether it requires an adjustment at the end of the accounting period.
3. Use the Consolidated Statements of Earnings to answer the following questions.
   a. For the three most recent fiscal years list the amounts reported for "Sales." Comment on whether the three-year trend of sales is favorable or unfavorable. Sales is what type of an account? Which principle of accounting is relevant for recording these amounts?
   b. For the three most recent fiscal years list the amounts reported for "Total Cost of Sales." Total Cost of Sales is what type of account? Were all of these amounts paid in cash? Which principle of accounting is relevant for recording these amounts?
   c. For the three most recent fiscal years list the amounts reported for "Net Earnings (Loss)." Is the three-year trend of net income favorable or unfavorable? What title does the text use to refer to net earnings?

Darden Corporation

Go to the "Deferrals (Unearned Revenues and Prepaid Expenses)" episode on the *Mastering Accounting* CD-ROM for an interactive, video-enhanced exercise explaining the principles of income statements and timing of recorded transactions to CanGo managers to help them interpret financial reports.

APPENDIX TO CHAPTER 3

ALTERNATIVE TREATMENT OF PREPAID EXPENSES AND UNEARNED REVENUES

Chapters 1–3 illustrate the most popular way to account for prepaid expenses and unearned revenues. This appendix illustrates an alternative—and equally appropriate—approach.

Prepaid Expenses

Prepaid expenses are advance payments of expenses. Prepaid Insurance, Prepaid Rent, Prepaid Advertising, and Prepaid Legal Cost are prepaid expenses. Supplies that will be used up in the current period or within one year are also accounted for as prepaid expenses.

When a business prepays an expense—rent, for example—it can debit an *asset* account (Prepaid Rent), as illustrated on page 88:

Aug. 1	Prepaid Rent	XXX	
	Cash		XXX

Alternatively, it can debit an *expense* account to record this cash payment:

Aug. 1	Rent Expense	XXX	
	Cash		XXX

Regardless of the account debited at the time of the prepayment, the business must adjust the accounts at the end of the period to report the correct amounts of the expense and the asset.

Prepaid Expense Recorded Initially as an Expense

Prepaying an expense creates an asset, as explained on page 88. However, the asset may be so short-lived that it will expire in the current accounting period—within one year or less. Thus, the accountant may decide to debit the prepayment to an expense account at the time of payment. A $6,000 cash payment for rent (one year, in advance) on August 1 may be debited to Rent Expense:

20X6			
Aug. 1	Rent Expense..............	6,000	
	Cash		6,000

At December 31, only five months' prepayment has expired (for August through December), leaving seven months' rent still prepaid. In this case, the accountant must transfer 7/12 of the original prepayment of $6,000, or $3,500, to the asset account Prepaid Rent. At December 31, 20X6, the business still has the benefit of the prepayment for January through July of 20X7. The adjusting entry at December 31 is

---

Adjusting Entries

20X6

Dec. 31   Prepaid Rent ($6,000 × 7/12)................ 3,500

             Rent Expense................................   3,500

After posting, the two accounts appear as follows (where CP = cash payment entry; Adj = adjusting entry):

PREPAID RENT			RENT EXPENSE		
20X6			20X6		20X6
Dec. 31 Adj.	3,500		Aug. 1 CP	6,000	Dec. 31 Adj. 3,500
Dec. 31 Bal.	3,500		Dec. 31 Bal.	2,500	

The balance sheet at the end of 20X6 reports Prepaid Rent of $3,500, and the income statement for 20X6 reports Rent Expense of $2,500, regardless of whether the business initially debits the prepayment to an asset account or to an expense account.

Unearned (Deferred) Revenues

Unearned (deferred) revenues arise when a business collects cash before earning the revenue. Unearned revenues are liabilities because the business that receives cash owes the other party goods or services to be delivered later.

Unearned (Deferred) Revenue Recorded Initially as a Revenue

Receipt of cash in advance creates a liability, as recorded on page 000. Another way to account for the receipt of cash is to credit a *revenue account*. If the business has earned all the revenue within the same period, no adjusting entry is needed at the end of the period. However, if the business earns only part of the revenue at the end of the period, it must make an adjusting entry.

Suppose on October 1, 20X2, a law firm records as revenue the receipt of cash for a nine-month fee of $7,200 received in advance. The cash receipt entry is

20X2

Oct. 1   Cash.. 7,200

           Legal Revenue   7,200

At December 31, the attorney has earned only 3/9 of the $7,200, or $2,400, for the months of October, November, and December. Accordingly, the firm makes an adjusting entry to transfer the unearned portion (6/9 of $7,200, or $4,800) from the revenue account to a liability account, as follows:

Adjusting Entries

20X2

Dec. 31   Legal Revenue ($7,200 × 6/9)............... 4,800

            Unearned Legal Revenue..............   4,800

The adjusting entry transfers the unearned portion (6/9, or $4,800) of the original amount to the liability account because the law firm still owes legal service to the client during January through June of 20X3. After posting, the total amount ($7,200) is properly divided between the liability account ($4,800) and the revenue account ($2,400), as follows (where CR = Cash receipt entry and Adj. = Adjusting entry).

UNEARNED LEGAL REVENUE			LEGAL REVENUE			
	20X2		20X2		20X2	
	Dec. 31 Adj. 4,800		Dec. 31 Adj	4,800	Oct. 1 CR	7,200
	Dec. 31 Bal. 4,800				Dec. 31 Bal.	2,400

The attorney's 20X2 income statement reports legal revenue of $2,400, and the balance sheet at December 31, 20X2, reports the unearned legal revenue of $4,800 as a liability, regardless of whether the business initially credits a liability account or a revenue account.

ASSESS YOUR PROGRESS

APPENDIX EXERCISES

E3A-1 At the beginning of the year, supplies of $1,190 were on hand. During the year, Laser Printing Company paid $5,400 cash for supplies. At the end of the year, the count of supplies indicates the ending balance is $860.

Recording supplies transactions two ways
(Obj. A1)

Required

1. Assume that Laser Printing records supplies by initially debiting an *asset* account. Therefore, place the beginning balance in the Supplies T-account, and record the preceding entries directly in the accounts without using a journal.
2. Assume that Laser Printing records supplies by initially debiting an *expense* account. Therefore, place the beginning balance in the Supplies Expense T-account, and record the preceding entries directly in the accounts without using a journal.
3. Compare the ending account balances under both approaches. Are they the same?

E3A-2 At the beginning of the year, Laser Printing Company owed customers $2,750 for unearned service collected in advance. During the year, Laser Printing received advance cash receipts of $7,000. At year end, the liability for unearned revenue is $3,700.

Recording unearned revenues two ways
(Obj. A2)

Required

1. Assume that Laser Printing records unearned revenues by initially crediting a *liability* account. Open T-accounts for Unearned Service Revenue and Service Revenue, and place the beginning balance in Unearned Service Revenue. Journalize the cash collection and adjusting entries, and post their dollar amounts. As references in the T-accounts, denote a balance by *Bal.*, a cash receipt by *CR*, and an adjustment by *Adj.*
2. Assume that Laser Printing records unearned revenues by initially crediting a *revenue* account. Open T-accounts for Unearned Service Revenue and Service Revenue, and place the beginning balance in Service Revenue. Journalize the cash collection and adjusting entries, and post their dollar amounts. As references in the T-accounts, denote a balance by *Bal.*, a cash receipt by *CR*, and an adjustment by *Adj.*
3. Compare the ending balances in the two accounts.

APPENDIX PROBLEM

P3A-1 Diebolt Sales and Service completed the following transactions during 20X4:

Recording prepaid rent and rent revenue collected in advance two ways
(Obj. A1, A2)

Oct. 1 Paid $4,500 store rent covering the six-month period ending March 31, 20X5.
Dec. 1 Collected $3,200 cash in advance from customers. The service revenue will be earned $800 monthly over the period ending March 31, 20X5.

Required

1. Journalize these entries by debiting an asset account for Prepaid Rent and by crediting a liability account for Unearned Service Revenue. Explanations are unnecessary.
2. Journalize the related adjustments at December 31, 20X4.
3. Post the entries to the ledger accounts, and show their balances at December 31, 20X4. Posting references are unnecessary.
4. Repeat requirements 1–3. This time, debit Rent Expense for the rent payment and credit Service Revenue for the collection of revenue in advance.
5. Compare the account balances in requirements 3 and 4. They should be equal.

4 Completing the Accounting Cycle

LEARNING OBJECTIVES

After studying this chapter, you should be able to

1. Prepare an accounting work sheet

2. Use the work sheet to complete the accounting cycle

3. Close the revenue, expense, and withdrawal accounts

4. Classify assets and liabilities as current or long-term

5. Use the current and debt ratios to evaluate a business's ability to pay its debts

www.prenhall.com/horngren

Readiness Assessment

Matt Cutler is 27 years old and the co-founder of **NetGenesis,** which sells software to help other companies understand their customers better. He started NetGenesis in 1994 and in February 2000 he took the company public. That means Cutler and his co-founder sold some shares of NetGenesis stock (the ownership in the company) to the public. By May 2000, NetGenesis was worth about $350 million. When asked how a business downturn would affect NetGenesis, Matt replied: "Any organization successful in dealing with rapid change in an upswing will be able to deal with a downswing." The key is to be able to deal with rapid change.

The way for Matt to convince people that NetGenesis is a sound company is the same way that **Procter and Gamble, Xerox Corporation,** and **Sony** do it. Earn a profit year after year, and build up more assets than liabilities. In this chapter, we complete the accounting cycle that produces the financial statements investors use for their decision making.

Source: *Wall Street Journal,* May 22, 2000, p. R18.

I n Chapter 3, we prepared the financial statements of Gay Gillen eTravel from an adjusted trial balance. That approach works well for quick decision making, but organizations of all sizes take the accounting process a step further. At the end of each period, after making the adjusting entries, they close their books. Whether the company is **NetGenesis, Xerox,** or Gay Gillen eTravel, the closing process follows the same basic pattern. Closing the books marks the end of the *accounting cycle* for a given period.

Accountants often use a document known as the *work sheet.* There are many different types of work sheets in business—as many, in fact, as there are needs for summary data. Work sheets are valuable because they summarize lots of data.

THE ACCOUNTING CYCLE

The **accounting cycle** is the process by which companies produce their financial statements for a specific period of time. For a new business, the cycle begins with setting up (opening) the ledger accounts. **NetGenesis** opened its doors in January 1994, and the first step in the accounting cycle was to open the accounts. After a business has operated for one period, the account balances carry over from period to period. Therefore, the accounting cycle starts with the beginning account balances. Exhibit 4-1 outlines the complete accounting cycle of NetGenesis, Gillen eTravel, and every other business. The boldface items in Panel A indicate the new concepts we introduce in this chapter.

Accounting Cycle. Process by which companies produce an entity's financial statements for a specific period.

The accounting cycle includes work performed at two different times:

- During the period—Journalizing transactions
  - Posting to the ledger
- End of the period—Adjusting the accounts, including journalizing and posting the adjusting entries
  - Closing the accounts, including journalizing and posting the closing entries
  - Preparing the financial statements (income statement, statement of owner's equity, and balance sheet)

The end-of-period work also readies the accounts for the next period. In Chapters 3 and 4, we cover the end-of-period accounting for a service business such as Gay Gillen eTravel. Chapter 5 shows how a merchandising entity adjusts and closes its books.

Companies prepare financial statements on a monthly or a quarterly basis. Steps 1–6a in Exhibit 4-1 are adequate for statement preparation. Steps 6b–7 can be performed monthly or quarterly, but are necessary only at the end of the year.

EXHIBIT 4-1   The Accounting Cycle

PANEL A

During the Period	End of the Period

1. Start with the account balances in the ledger at the beginning of the period.
 2. Analyze and journalize transactions as they occur.
 3. Post journal entries to the ledger accounts.
	4. Compute the unadjusted balance in each account at the end of the period.
	 5. Enter the trial balance on the work sheet, and complete the work sheet (optional).
	 6. Using the adjusted trial balance or the full work sheet as a guide,
	     a. Prepare the financial statements.
	     b. Journalize and post the adjusting entries.
	     c. Journalize and post the closing entries.
	 7. Prepare the **postclosing trial balance.** This trial balance becomes step 1 for the next period.

PANEL B

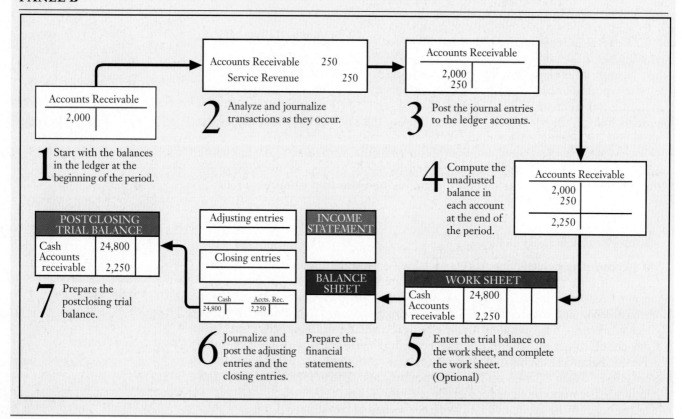

THE WORK SHEET

Objective 1

Prepare an accounting work sheet.

WORK SHEET. A columnar document designed to help move data from the trial balance to the financial statements.

Accountants often use a **work sheet**—a document with several columns—to help summarize and move data from the trial balance to the financial statements. The work sheet is not part of the ledger or the journal, and it is not a financial statement. It is merely a summary device that aids the accounting process. Listing all the accounts and their unadjusted balances helps identify accounts that need adjustment.

Exhibits 4-2 through 4-6 illustrate the development of a typical work sheet for the business of Gay Gillen eTravel. The heading at the top names the business, identifies the document, and states the accounting period.

A step-by-step description of its preparation follows.

Steps introduced in Chapter 3 to prepare the adjusted trial balance:

    1. Enter the account titles and their unadjusted ending balances in the Trial Balance columns of the work sheet, and total the amounts (Exhibit 4-2).

2. Enter the adjustments in the Adjustments columns, and total the amounts (Exhibit 4-3). Total debits must equal total credits.

3. Compute each account's adjusted balance by combining the trial balance and adjustment figures. Enter the adjusted amounts in the Adjusted Trial Balance columns (Exhibit 4-4). Then compute the total for each column. Total debits should equal total credits.

Steps introduced in this chapter:

4. Extend the asset, liability, and owner's equity amounts from the Adjusted Trial Balance to the Balance Sheet columns. Extend the revenue and expense amounts to the Income Statement columns. Total the statement columns (Exhibit 4-5). For a change, total debits will not equal total credits.

5. Compute net income or net loss as the difference between total revenues and total expenses on the income statement. Enter net income or net loss as a balancing amount on the income statement and on the balance sheet, and compute the final column totals (Exhibit 4-6). Now all pairs of debit and credit columns should hold equal totals.

Let's examine these steps in greater detail.

1. *Enter the account titles and their unadjusted balances in the Trial Balance columns of the work sheet, and total the amounts.* Total debits must equal total credits, as shown in Exhibit 4-2. The account titles and unadjusted balances come directly from the ledger accounts before the adjusting entries are prepared. Accounts are grouped on the work sheet by category (assets, liabilities, owner's equity, revenues, and expenses) and are usually listed in the order they appear in the ledger (Cash first, Accounts Receivable second, and so on).

Accounts may have zero balances (for example, Depreciation Expense). All accounts are listed on the trial balance because they appear in the ledger.

2. *Enter the adjusting entries in the Adjustments columns, and total the amounts.* Exhibit 4-3 includes the April adjusting entries. These are the same adjustments that we used in Chapter 3 to prepare the adjusted trial balance.

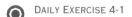

DAILY EXERCISE 4-1

We can identify the accounts that need to be adjusted by scanning the trial balance. Cash needs no adjustment because all cash transactions are recorded as they occur during the period. Consequently, Cash's balance is up to date.

Accounts Receivable is listed next. Has Gay Gillen earned revenue she has not yet recorded? The answer is yes. At April 30, Gillen has earned $250 that she has not yet recorded because the cash will be received during May. Gillen debits Accounts Receivable and credits Service Revenue on the work sheet in Exhibit 4-3. A letter is used to link the debit and the credit of each adjusting entry.

By moving down the trial balance, Gillen identifies the remaining accounts that need adjustment. Supplies is next. The business has used supplies during April, so Gillen debits Supplies Expense and credits Supplies. The other adjustments are analyzed and entered on the work sheet as in Chapter 3.

Listing the accounts in proper sequence aids the process of identifying accounts that need to be adjusted. But suppose some accounts are omitted from the trial balance. An account title can always be written below the first column totals—51,800. Assume that Supplies Expense was accidentally omitted and thus did not appear on the trial balance. The accountant can write Supplies Expense beneath the amount totals and enter the debit adjustment—$300—on the Supplies Expense line. After the adjustments are entered on the work sheet, the amount columns are totaled.

3. *Compute each account's adjusted balance by combining the trial balance and adjustment figures. Enter the adjusted amounts in the Adjusted Trial Balance columns.* Exhibit 4-4 shows the work sheet with the adjusted trial balance columns completed. For example, the Cash balance is up to date, so it receives no adjustment. Accounts Receivable's adjusted balance of $2,500 is computed by adding the trial balance amount of $2,250 to the $250 debit adjustment. Supplies' adjusted balance is determined by subtracting the $300 credit adjustment from the unadjusted debit balance of $700. An account may receive more than one adjustment, as Service Revenue does. The column totals must maintain the equality of debits and credits.

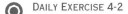

DAILY EXERCISE 4-2

EXHIBIT 4-2 Trial Balance

GAY GILLEN ETRAVEL
Accounting Work Sheet
For the Month Ended April 30, 20X1

Account Title	Trial Balance Dr.	Trial Balance Cr.	Adjustments Dr.	Adjustments Cr.	Adjusted Trial Balance Dr.	Adjusted Trial Balance Cr.	Income Statement Dr.	Income Statement Cr.	Balance Sheet Dr.	Balance Sheet Cr.
Cash	24,800									
Accounts receivable	2,250									
Supplies	700									
Prepaid rent	3,000									
Furniture	16,500									
Accumulated depreciation										
Accounts payable		13,100								
Salary payable										
Unearned service revenue		450								
Gay Gillen, capital		31,250								
Gay Gillen, withdrawals	3,200									
Service revenue		7,000								
Rent expense										
Salary expense	950									
Supplies expense										
Depreciation expense										
Utilities expense	400									
	51,800	51,800								
Net income										

Write the account titles and their unadjusted ending balances in the Trial Balance columns of the work sheet, and total the amounts.

4. *Extend (that is, copy) the asset, liability, and owner's equity amounts from the Adjusted Trial Balance to the Balance Sheet columns. Copy the revenue and expense amounts to the Income Statement columns. Total the statement columns.* Every account is either a balance sheet account or an income statement account. The asset, liability, and owner's equity accounts go to the balance sheet, and the revenues and expenses go to the income statement. Debits on the adjusted trial balance remain debits in the statement columns, and credits remain credits. Each account's balance should appear in only one statement column, as shown in Exhibit 4-5.

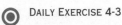 DAILY EXERCISE 4-3

First, total the *income statement columns,* as follows:

INCOME STATEMENT

- Debits (Dr.) Total expenses = $3,875 ⎫ Difference = $3,525, a net income
- Credits (Cr.) Total revenues = $7,400 ⎭ because revenues exceed expenses

Then total the *balance sheet* columns:

BALANCE SHEET

- Debits (Dr.) Total assets and withdrawals = $49,400 ⎫ Difference = $3,525,
- Credits (Cr.) Total liabilities, owner's equity, = $45,875 ⎬ a net income because
  and accumulated depreciation ⎭ total assets are greater

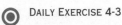 DAILY EXERCISE 4-4

5. *Compute net income or net loss as the difference between total revenues and total expenses on the income statement. Enter net income as the balancing amount on the income statement and as the balancing amount on the balance sheet. Then compute the adjusted column totals.* Exhibit 4-6 presents the completed accounting work sheet, which shows net income of $3,525, computed as follows:

Revenue (total credits on the income statement)	$7,400
Less: Expenses (total debits on the income statement)	(3,875)
Net income	$3,525

Net income of $3,525 is entered in the debit column of the income statement to balance with the credit column of the income statement, which totals $7,400. The net income amount is then extended to the credit column of the balance sheet, because an excess of revenues over expenses increases capital, and increases in capital are recorded by a credit. In the closing process, net income will find its way into the Capital account.

If expenses exceed revenues, the result is a net loss. In that event, Net Loss is printed on the work sheet. The loss amount should be entered in the *credit* column of the income statement (to balance out) and in the *debit* column of the balance sheet (to balance out). After completion, total debits equal total credits in the Income Statement columns and in the Balance Sheet columns. The balance sheet columns are totaled at $49,400.

SUMMARY PROBLEM

www.prenhall.com/horngren

Mid-Chapter Assessment

The trial balance of State Service Company at December 31, 20X1, the end of its fiscal year, is as follows.

STATE SERVICE COMPANY Trial Balance December 31, 20X1		
Cash	$ 198,000	
Accounts receivable	370,000	
Supplies	6,000	
Furniture and fixtures	100,000	
Accumulated depreciation—furniture and fixtures		$ 40,000
Building	250,000	
Accumulated depreciation—building		130,000
Accounts payable		380,000
Salary payable		
Unearned service revenue		45,000
Capital		293,000
Withdrawals	65,000	
Service revenues		286,000
Salary expense	172,000	
Supplies expense		
Depreciation expense—furniture and fixtures		
Depreciation expense—building		
Miscellaneous expense	13,000	
Total	$1,174,000	$1,174,000

Data needed for the adjusting entries include:
a. Supplies on hand at year end, $2,000.
b. Depreciation on furniture and fixtures, $20,000.
c. Depreciation on building, $10,000.
d. Salaries owed but not yet paid, $5,000.
e. Accrued service revenue, $12,000.
f. Of the $45,000 balance of Unearned Service Revenue, $32,000 was earned during 20X1.

Required

Prepare the accounting work sheet of State Service Company for the year ended December 31, 20X1. Key each adjusting entry by the letter corresponding to the data given.

Solution

STATE SERVICE COMPANY
Work Sheet
Year Ended December 31, 20X1

Account Title	Trial Balance Dr.	Trial Balance Cr.	Adjustments Dr.	Adjustments Cr.	Adjusted Trial Balance Dr.	Adjusted Trial Balance Cr.	Income Statement Dr.	Income Statement Cr.	Balance Sheet Dr.	Balance Sheet Cr.
Cash..............................	198,000				198,000				198,000	
Accounts receivable........	370,000		(e) 12,000		382,000				382,000	
Supplies	6,000			(a) 4,000	2,000				2,000	
Furniture and fixtures....	100,000				100,000				100,000	
Accumulated depreciation— furniture and fixtures........................		40,000		(b) 20,000		60,000				60,000
Building........................	250,000				250,000				250,000	
Accumulated depreciation— building........................		130,000		(c) 10,000		140,000				140,000
Accounts payable............		380,000				380,000				380,000
Salary payable				(d) 5,000		5,000				5,000
Unearned service revenue......................		45,000	(f) 32,000			13,000				13,000
Capital		293,000				293,000				293,000
Withdrawals	65,000				65,000				65,000	
Service revenue..............		286,000		(e) 12,000 (f) 32,000		330,000		330,000		
Salary expense................	172,000		(d) 5,000		177,000		177,000			
Supplies expense			(a) 4,000		4,000		4,000			
Depreciation expense— furniture and fixtures........................			(b) 20,000		20,000		20,000			
Depreciation expense— building........................			(c) 10,000		10,000		10,000			
Miscellaneous expense ...	13,000				13,000		13,000			
	1,174,000	1,174,000	83,000	83,000	1,221,000	1,221,000	224,000	330,000	997,000	891,000
Net income							106,000			106,000
							330,000	330,000	997,000	997,000

COMPLETING THE ACCOUNTING CYCLE

Objective 2
Use the work sheet to complete the accounting cycle

The work sheet helps organize the data for the computation of the net income or net loss for the period. The work sheet aids in preparing the financial statements, recording the adjusting entries, and closing the accounts.

Preparing the Financial Statements

The work sheet shows the amount of net income or net loss for the period, but we still must prepare the financial statements. ➤ The sorting of accounts to the balance sheet and the income statement eases the preparation of the statements. The work sheet also provides the data for the statement of owner's equity. Exhibit 4-7 presents the April financial statements for Gay Gillen eTravel (based on data from the work sheet in Exhibit 4-6). Most accountants prepare the financial statements immediately after completing the work sheet.

◀ The financial statements can be prepared directly from the adjusted trial balance; see p. 99. This is why completion of the work sheet is optional.

Recording the Adjusting Entries

The actual adjustment of the accounts requires journal entries and posting to the ledger accounts. Panel A of Exhibit 4-8 gives the adjusting entries of Gay Gillen eTravel at April 30. Panel B shows the postings to the accounts; *Adj.* denotes an amount posted from an adjusting entry. The adjusting entries can be recorded in the journal when they are entered on the work sheet. Only the revenue and expense accounts are presented in the exhibit in order to focus on the closing process.

EXHIBIT 4-7
**April Financial Statements of
Gay Gillen eTravel**

GAY GILLEN ETRAVEL
Income Statement
Month Ended April 30, 20X1

Revenue:		
Service revenue		$7,400
Expenses:		
Salary expense	$1,900	
Rent expense	1,000	
Utilities expense..	400	
Supplies expense	300	
Depreciation expense—furniture..............	275	
Total expenses...		3,875
Net income		$3,525

GAY GILLEN ETRAVEL
Statement of Owner's Equity
Month Ended April 30, 20X1

Gay Gillen, capital, April 1, 20X1................	$31,250
Add: Net income	3,525
	34,775
Less: Withdrawals	(3,200)
Gay Gillen, capital, April 30, 20X1..............	$31,575

GAY GILLEN ETRAVEL
Balance Sheet
April 30, 20X1

Assets			**Liabilities**		
Cash.......................................		$24,800	Accounts payable...................		$13,100
Accounts receivable...............		2,500	Salary payable		950
Supplies		400	Unearned service		
Prepaid rent		2,000	revenue		300
Furniture..............	$16,500		Total liabilities.......................		14,350
Less:					
Accumulated			**Owner's Equity**		
depreciation......	(275)	16,225	Gay Gillen, capital		31,575
			Total liabilities and		
Total assets.............................		$45,925	owner's equity		$45,925

CLOSING THE ACCOUNTS. Step in
the accounting cycle at the
end of the period. Closing the
accounts consists of journalizing and posting the closing
entries to set the balances of
the revenue, expense, and
withdrawal accounts to zero
for the next period.

Many companies journalize and post the adjusting entries (as in Exhibit 4-8)
only once annually—at the end of the year. Accountants can use the work sheet to
prepare monthly or quarterly statements without journalizing and posting the
adjusting entries.

Closing the Accounts

Closing the accounts is the end-of-period process that prepares the accounts for
the next period. Closing the accounts consists of journalizing and posting the closing
entries. Closing zeroes out the balances of the revenue and expense accounts in
order to clearly measure the net income of each period separately from all other
periods.

Recall that the income statement reports only one period's net income. For
example, net income for **NetGenesis Corp.** for 2001 relates exclusively to 2001. At
December 31, 2001, the NetGenesis accountants close the company's revenue and
expense accounts for that year. Because the revenue and expense account balances

EXHIBIT 4-8 Journalizing and Posting the Adjusting Entries

PANEL A—Journalizing: Page 4

Adjusting Entries

Apr. 30	Accounts Receivable..................................	250	
	Service Revenue		250
30	Supplies Expense.....................................	300	
	Supplies...		300
30	Rent Expense...	1,000	
	Prepaid Rent		1,000
30	Depreciation Expense................................	275	
	Accumulated Depreciation		275
30	Salary Expense	950	
	Salary Payable..................................		950
30	Unearned Service Revenue	150	
	Service Revenue		150

PANEL B—Posting the Adjustments to the Revenue and Expense Accounts:

REVENUE				EXPENSES		

SERVICE REVENUE			RENT EXPENSE			SALARY EXPENSE			SUPPLIES EXPENSE	
	7,000		Adj.	1,000			950		Adj.	300
Adj.	250		Bal.	1,000		Adj.	950		Bal.	300
Adj.	150					Bal.	1,900			
Bal.	7,400									

DEPRECIATION EXPENSE			UTILITIES EXPENSE	
Adj.	275			400
Bal.	275		Bal.	400

Adj. = Amount posted from an adjusting entry   Bal. = Balance

---

relate to a particular accounting period and are therefore closed at the end of the period (December 31, 2001), the revenue and expense accounts are called **temporary (nominal) accounts.** For example, Gay Gillen's balance of Service Revenue at April 30, 20X1, is $7,400. This balance relates exclusively to the month of April and must be zeroed out before Gillen records revenue for May.

The owner's Withdrawal account—although not a revenue or an expense—is also a temporary account because it measures withdrawals for only one period. The Withdrawals account is also closed.

To better understand the closing process, contrast the nature of the temporary accounts with the nature of the **permanent (real) accounts**—the asset, liability, and capital accounts. The asset, liability, and owner's capital accounts are *not* closed at the end of the period because their balances are not used to measure income. Consider Cash, Accounts Receivable, Accounts Payable, and Gay Gillen, Capital. These accounts do not represent business *activity* for a single period and thus are not closed at the end of the period. Their balances carry over to become the beginning balances of the next period. For example, the Cash balance at December 31, 20X1, becomes the beginning balance for 20X2.

Closing entries transfer the revenue, expense, and owner withdrawal balances from their respective accounts to the capital account. As you know,

Posting the closing entries causes the Capital account to absorb the balances in all temporary accounts.

TEMPORARY ACCOUNTS. The revenue and expense accounts that relate to a particular accounting period and are closed at the end of the period. For a proprietorship, the owner withdrawal account is also temporary. Also called **nominal accounts.**

PERMANENT ACCOUNTS. Accounts that are *not* closed at the end of the period— asset, liability, and capital accounts. Also called **real accounts.**

CLOSING ENTRIES. Entries that transfer the revenue, expense, and owner withdrawal balances from these respective accounts to the capital account.

EXHIBIT 4-9 **Journalizing and Posting the Closing Entries**

PANEL A—Journalizing   **Page 5**

Closing Entries

①	Apr. 30	Service Revenue...	7,400	
②		Income Summary		7,400
	30	Income Summary..	3,875	
		Rent Expense..		1,000
		Salary Expense		1,900
		Supplies Expense		300
		Depreciation Expense.........................		275
		Utilities Expense		400
③	30	Income Summary ($7,400 − $3,875)	3,525	
		Gay Gillen, Capital..............................		3,525
④	30	Gay Gillen, Capital	3,200	
		Gay Gillen, Withdrawals......................		3,200

PANEL B—Posting

RENT EXPENSE	
Adj. 1,000	
Bal. 1,000	**Clo.** 1,000

SALARY EXPENSE	
950	
Adj. 950	
Bal. 1,900	**Clo.** 1,900

SUPPLIES EXPENSE	
Adj. 300	
Bal. 300	**Clo.** 300

DEPRECIATION EXPENSE	
Adj. 275	
Bal. 275	**Clo.** 275

UTILITIES EXPENSE	
400	
Bal. 400	**Clo.** 400

② | INCOME SUMMARY | | ①

INCOME SUMMARY	
Clo. 3,875	**Clo.** 7,400
Clo. 3,525	**Bal.** 3,525

③

SERVICE REVENUE	
	7,000
	Adj. 250
	Adj. 150
Clo. 7,400	**Bal.** 7,400

GAY GILLEN, WITHDRAWALS	
Bal. 3,200	**Clo.** 3,200

④

GAY GILLEN, CAPITAL	
Clo. 3,200	31,250
	Clo. 3,525
	Bal. 31,575

Adj. = Amount posted from an adjusting entry   Clo. = Amount posted from a closing entry   Bal. = Balance

INCOME SUMMARY. A temporary "holding tank" account into which revenues and expenses are transferred prior to their final transfer to the capital account.

As an intermediate step, the revenues and the expenses are transferred first to an account entitled **Income Summary,** which collects the total debit for the sum of all expenses and the total credit for the sum of all revenues of the period. The Income Summary account is like a "holding tank." The balance of Income Summary is then transferred to capital.

The steps in closing the accounts of a proprietorship such as Gay Gillen eTravel are as follows (the circled numbers are keyed to Exhibit 4-9).

① Debit each *revenue* account for the amount of its credit balance. Credit Income Summary for the total of the revenues. This entry transfers total revenues to the *credit* side of Income Summary.

② Credit each *expense* account for the amount of its debit balance. Debit Income Summary for the total of the expenses. This entry transfers total expenses to the *debit* side of Income Summary. It is not necessary to make a separate closing entry for each expense. In one closing entry, record one debit to Income Summary and a separate credit to each expense account.

③ To close net income, debit Income Summary for the amount of its *credit balance* (if there is a *net income*), and credit the Capital account. If there is a *net loss*, Income Summary has a *debit balance*. In that case, credit Income Summary for the amount of the loss, and debit Capital. This closing entry transfers net income or net loss from Income Summary to the Capital account.

④ Credit the *Withdrawals* account for the amount of its debit balance. Debit the Capital account of the proprietor. This entry transfers the amount of owner withdrawals during the period to the *debit* side of the Capital account. *Withdrawals do not affect net income or net loss because withdrawals are not an expense.*

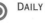 DAILY EXERCISE 4-5

These steps are best illustrated with an example. Suppose Gay Gillen closes the books at the end of April. Exhibit 4-9 presents the complete closing process for Gillen's travel agency. Panel A gives the closing journal entries, and Panel B shows the accounts after the closing entries have been posted.

Each expense account holds its adjusted balance. For example, Rent Expense has a $1,000 debit balance. Service Revenue has a credit balance of $7,400 before closing. These amounts come directly from the adjusted balances in Exhibit 4-8, Panel B.

- Closing entry ① in Exhibit 4-9 transfers Service Revenue's balance to the Income Summary account. This entry zeroes out Service Revenue for April and transfers total revenue to the credit side of Income Summary.
- Closing entry ② zeroes out the expenses and moves their total ($3,875) to the debit side of Income Summary. At this point, Income Summary contains all of April's revenues and expenses. Income Summary's credit balance shows the month's net income ($3,525).
- Closing entry ③ closes the Income Summary account by transferring net income ($3,525) to the credit side of Gay Gillen, Capital.[1]
- The last closing entry, entry ④, moves the owner withdrawals to the debit side of Gay Gillen, Capital, leaving a zero balance in Withdrawals.

The closing entries set all the revenues, the expenses, and the Withdrawals account back to zero. Now the owner's Capital account includes the full effects of April's revenues, expenses, and withdrawals, plus the beginning Capital balance. The Gay Gillen, Capital account has an ending balance of $31,575. Trace this ending Capital balance to the statement of owner's equity and also to the balance sheet in Exhibit 4-7.

DAILY EXERCISE 4-6

DAILY EXERCISE 4-7

DAILY EXERCISE 4-8

DAILY EXERCISE 4-9

CLOSING A NET LOSS   What would the closing entries be if Gillen's travel agency had suffered a net *loss* during April? Suppose expenses totaled $7,700 and all other factors were unchanged (revenues were $7,400, so Gillen's business suffered a net loss of $300 for April). Only closing entries ② and ③ would change. Closing entry ② would transfer expenses of $7,700 to the debit side of Income Summary, as follows:

INCOME SUMMARY			
Clo.	7,700	Clo.	7,400
Bal.	300		

Closing entry ③ would then credit Income Summary to close this account and to transfer the net loss to Gay Gillen, Capital:

③ Apr. 30   Gay Gillen, Capital 300
                       Income Summary   300

After posting, these two accounts would appear as follows:

INCOME SUMMARY					GAY GILLEN, CAPITAL		
Clo.	7,700	Clo.	7,400	Clo.	300		31,250
Bal.	300	Clo.	300				

---

[1]The Income Summary account is a convenience for combining the effects of the revenues and expenses before transferring their income effect to Capital. It is not necessary to use the Income Summary account in the closing process. In an alternative procedure, revenues and expenses are closed directly to Capital.

POSTCLOSING TRIAL BALANCE.
List of the accounts and their balances at the end of the period after journalizing and posting the closing entries. The last step of the accounting cycle, the postclosing trial balance ensures that the ledger is in balance to start the next accounting period.

EXHIBIT 4-10
Postclosing Trial Balance

⊙ DAILY EXERCISE 4-10

Finally, the Withdrawals balance would be closed to Capital, as before. The double underline in an account means that the account has a zero balance; nothing more will be posted to it in the current period.

The closing process is fundamentally mechanical and is completely automated in a computerized system. Accounts are identified as either temporary or permanent. The temporary accounts are closed automatically by selecting that option from the software menu. Posting also occurs automatically.

Postclosing Trial Balance

The accounting cycle ends with the **postclosing trial balance** (Exhibit 4-10). It lists the accounts and their adjusted balances after closing. This step shows where the business stands as it moves into the next accounting period. The postclosing trial balance is dated as of the end of the period.

GAY GILLEN ETRAVEL Postclosing Trial Balance April 30, 20X1		
Cash	$24,800	
Accounts receivable	2,500	
Supplies	400	
Prepaid Rent	2,000	
Furniture	16,500	
Accumulated depreciation		$ 275
Accounts payable		13,100
Salary Payable		950
Unearned service revenue		300
Gay Gillen, capital		31,575
Total	$46,200	$46,200

The postclosing trial balance resembles the balance sheet. It contains the ending balances of the permanent accounts—the balance sheet accounts: the assets, liabilities, and capital. No temporary accounts—revenues, expenses, or withdrawal accounts—are included because their balances have been closed. The ledger is up to date and ready for the next period's transactions.

Reversing entries are special journal entries that ease the burden of accounting for transactions that key off the adjustments at the end of the period. Reversing entries are optional, and for that reason, we cover them in the appendix at the end of this chapter.

REVERSING ENTRIES. Special journal entries that ease the burden of accounting for transactions that key off adjustments at the end of the period.

Objective 4
Classify assets and liabilities as current or long-term

LIQUIDITY. Measure of how quickly an item can be converted to cash.

CURRENT ASSET. An asset that is expected to be converted to cash, sold, or consumed during the next 12 months, or within the business's normal operating cycle.

CLASSIFYING ASSETS AND LIABILITIES

Assets and liabilities are classified as either *current* or *long-term* to indicate their relative liquidity. **Liquidity** measures how quickly an item can be converted to cash. Cash is the most liquid asset. Accounts receivable is relatively liquid because the business expects to collect the money in the near future. Supplies are less liquid than receivables, and furniture and buildings are even less liquid.

Managers and owners are interested in liquidity because business difficulties often arise from a shortage of cash. How quickly can the business convert an asset to cash and pay a debt? How soon must a liability be paid? These are questions of liquidity. A classified balance sheet helps to answer questions such as these.

Assets

CURRENT ASSETS **Current assets** are assets that are expected to be converted to cash, sold, or consumed during the next 12 months or within the business's normal operating cycle. The **operating cycle** is the time span during which (1) cash is used to acquire goods and services, (2) these goods and services are sold to customers, and (3) the business collects cash. For most businesses, the operating cycle is a few months. A few types of businesses have operating cycles longer than a year. Cash, Accounts Receivable, Notes Receivable due within a year or less, and Prepaid Expenses are current assets. Merchandising entities such as **Intel, Sears,** and **IBM** have an additional current asset, Inventory. This account shows the cost of the goods the business is holding for sale to customers.

LONG-TERM ASSETS   **Long-term assets** are all assets other than current assets. One category of long-term assets is **plant** (or **fixed**) **assets,** another name for Property, Plant, and Equipment. Land, Buildings, Furniture and Fixtures, and Equipment are fixed assets. Of these, Gay Gillen eTravel has only Furniture.

Other categories of long-term assets include Long-Term Investments in Stock, and Other Assets (a catchall category). We discuss these categories in later chapters.

Liabilities

Managers and owners are interested in the due dates of an entity's liabilities. Liabilities that must be paid the quickest create the greatest strain on cash. Therefore, the balance sheet lists liabilities in the order in which they are due to be paid. Knowing how much of a business's liabilities is current and how much is long-term helps creditors assess the likelihood of collecting cash from the entity. Balance sheets have two liability classifications, *current liabilities* and *long-term liabilities.*

CURRENT LIABILITIES   **Current liabilities** are debts that must be paid with cash or with goods and services within one year or within the entity's operating cycle if the cycle is longer than a year. Accounts Payable, Notes Payable due within one year, Salary Payable, Unearned Revenue, and Interest Payable owed on notes payable are current liabilities.

LONG-TERM LIABILITIES   All liabilities that are not current are classified as **long-term liabilities.** Many notes payable are long-term—payable after one year or the entity's operating cycle. Some notes payable are paid in installments, with the first installment due within one year, the second installment due the second year, and so on. In that case, the first installment is a current liability, and the remaining installments long-term liabilities. For example, a $100,000 note payable to be paid $10,000 per year over ten years would include a current liability of $10,000 for next year's payment and a long-term liability of $90,000.

Thus far we have presented the *unclassified* balance sheet of Gay Gillen eTravel. Our purpose was to focus on the main points of assets, liabilities, and owner's equity without the details of *current* assets, *current* liabilities, and so on. Exhibit 4-11 presents Gillen's classified balance sheet.

OPERATING CYCLE. Time span during which cash is paid for goods and services, which are then sold to customers from whom the business collects cash.

LONG-TERM ASSET. An asset other than a current asset.

PLANT OR FIXED ASSET. Another name for property, plant, and equipment.

CURRENT LIABILITY. A debt due to be paid with cash or with goods and services within one year or within the entity's operating cycle if the cycle is longer than a year.

LONG-TERM LIABILITY. A liability other than a current liability.

◉ DAILY EXERCISE 4-11

EXHIBIT 4-11 Classified Balance Sheet of Gay Gillen eTravel

GAY GILLEN ETRAVEL
Balance Sheet
April 30, 20X1

Assets			Liabilities		
Current assets:			Current liabilities:		
Cash		$24,800	Accounts payable		$13,100
Accounts receivable		2,500	Salary payable		950
Supplies		400	Unearned service revenue		300
Prepaid rent		2,000	Total current liabilities		14,350
Total current assets		29,700	Long-term liabilities (None)		0
Fixed assets:			Total liabilities		14,350
Furniture	$16,500				
Less: Accumulated			**Owner's Equity**		
depreciation	(275)	16,225	Gay Gillen, capital		31,575
			Total liabilities and		
Total assets		$45,925	owner's equity		$45,925

Gillen classifies each asset and each liability as current or long-term. She could have labeled fixed assets as *long-term assets.*

Compare Gillen's *classified* balance sheet in Exhibit 4-11 with the *unclassified* balance sheet in Exhibit 4-7. The classified balance sheet reports more information—totals for current assets and current liabilities, which do not appear on the unclassified balance sheet. Gillen has no long-term liabilities, so there are none to report on either balance sheet.

 THINK IT OVER Why is the classified balance sheet in Exhibit 4-11 more useful than an unclassified balance sheet (Exhibit 4-7) to (a) Gay Gillen and (b) a banker considering whether to lend $10,000 to Gillen?

Answer: A classified balance sheet indicates to (a) Gillen and (b) a banker

- Which of Gillen's liabilities, and the dollar amounts, Gillen must pay within the next year
- Which of Gillen's assets are the most liquid and thus available to pay the liabilities
- Which assets and liabilities (and amounts) are long-term

A Real Classified Balance Sheet

Exhibit 4-12 is an actual classified balance sheet of **PepsiCo, Inc.** Dollar amounts are reported in millions to avoid clutter. You should be familiar with all but a few of PepsiCo's account titles. Among the Current Assets are Short-term investments, which are investments that PepsiCo expects to sell within one year. These assets are very liquid, which explains why they are reported before the receivables.

EXHIBIT 4-12
PepsiCo's Classified Balance
Sheet

PEPSICO, INC. Balance Sheet (Adapted) December 31,1999	
ASSETS	*(In millions)*
Current Assets	
Cash and cash equivalents...	$ 964
Short-term investments, at cost	92
	1,056
Accounts and notes receivable, net	1,704
Inventories..	899
Prepaid expenses and other current assets...................	514
Total Current Assets.......................................	4,173
Property, plant and equipment, net of Accumulated depreciation of $3,550	5,266
Intangible assets, net	4,735
Investments in other companies	2,846
Other assets	531
Total Assets..	$17,551
LIABILITIES AND SHAREHOLDERS' EQUITY	
Current Liabilities	
Short-term borrowings..	$ 233
Accounts payable and other current liabilities.............	3,399
Income taxes payable	156
Total Current Liabilities................................	3,788
Long-term debt...	2,812
Other liabilities	4,070
Shareholders' equity..	6,881
Total Liabilities and Shareholders' Equity.................	$17,551

 DAILY EXERCISE 4-12

PepsiCo reports Property, Plant, and Equipment, *net,* of $5,266 million. *Net* means the amount of the assets after subtracting Accumulated Depreciation. At

December 31, 1999, Accumulated Depreciation of PepsiCo's property, plant, and equipment totaled $3,550 million. Another way for PepsiCo to report property, plant, and equipment would be (in millions)

Property, Plant, and Equipment, at cost	$8,816
Less: Accumulated Depreciation.........................	(3,550)
Property, Plant and Equipment, net	$5,266

PepsiCo also reports **Intangible Assets.** Intangibles are assets, such as patents, trademarks, and goodwill, which have no physical form. Intangibles are valuable because of the rights they provide the owner. PepsiCo's trademarks (Pepsi and Tropicana drinks, Lay's chips, and Aquafina) are worth a lot.

INTANGIBLE ASSETS. Assets, such as patents, trademarks, and goodwill, which have no physical form.

All of PepsiCo's liabilities should be familiar to you. We can compute total liabilities two ways, as follows (in millions):

- Add: Total Current liabilities, Long-Term Debt, and Other Liabilities
  ($3,788 + $2,812 + $4,070) $10,670
- Total Liabilities = Total Assets − Shareholders' (Owners') Equity
  ($17,551 − $6,881) $10,670

Both computations are valid. When all the liability amounts are available, as on PepsiCo's balance sheet, you can add them up. When some data are missing, you can still compute total liabilities by using the accounting equation: Assets = Liabilities + Shareholders' Equity (same as Owners' Equity).

BALANCE SHEET FORMATS

The balance sheet of PepsiCo in Exhibit 4-12 lists the assets at the top and the liabilities and owners' equity below. This arrangement is known as the *report format.* The balance sheet of Gay Gillen eTravel presented in Exhibit 4-7 lists the assets at the left and the liabilities and the owner's equity at the right. That arrangement is known as the *account format.*

Either format is acceptable. A recent survey of 600 companies indicated that 73% (436 companies) use the report format and only 27% (164 companies) use the account format.

ACCOUNTING RATIOS

The purpose of accounting is to provide information for decision making. Chief users of accounting information are managers, business owners, and creditors. A creditor considering lending money must predict whether the borrower can repay the loan. If the borrower already has a lot of debt, the probability of repayment is lower than if the borrower doesn't owe much money. To assess a company's financial position, decision makers use ratios computed from the company's financial statements.

Objective 5
Use the current and debt ratios to evaluate a business's ability to pay its debts

Current Ratio

One of the most widely used financial ratios is the **current ratio,** which compares an entity's current assets to its current liabilities:

$$\text{Current ratio} = \frac{\textbf{Total current assets}}{\textbf{Total current liabilities}}$$

CURRENT RATIO. Current assets divided by current liabilities. Measures the company's ability to pay current liabilities from current assets.

The current ratio measures the ability to pay current liabilities with current assets. A company prefers to have a high current ratio, which means that the business has plenty of current assets to pay current liabilities. An increasing current ratio from period to period indicates improvement in the ability to pay current debts.

A rule of thumb: A very strong current ratio is 2.00, which indicates that the company has $2.00 in current assets for every $1.00 in current liabilities. A company with a current ratio of 2.00 would probably have little trouble paying its current liabilities. Most successful businesses operate with current ratios between 1.50 and 2.00. A current ratio of 1.00 is considered low.

WORK IT OUT Compute PepsiCo's current ratio at December 31, 1999. Use the company's balance sheet in Exhibit 4-12 and show dollar amounts in millions.

Answer: $$\text{Current} = \frac{\text{Total current assets}}{\text{Total current liabilities}} = \frac{\$4,173}{\$3,788} = 1.10$$

How much in current assets does PepsiCo have for every dollar the company owes in current liabilities?

Answer: $1.10

Is PepsiCo's current ratio high or low? Is this ratio value risky?

Answer: PepsiCo's current ratio is low, which makes it look risky. However, PepsiCo operates successfully with a low current ratio because the company sells food products that people buy in both good times and hard times. Thus far, PepsiCo has had no trouble paying its debts.

Debt Ratio

DEBT RATIO. Ratio of total liabilities to total assets. Tells the proportion of a company's assets that it has financed with debt.

A second aid to decision making is the **debt ratio,** which is the ratio of total liabilities to total assets:

$$\text{Debt ratio} = \frac{\text{Total liabilities}}{\text{Total assets}}$$

The debt ratio indicates the proportion of a company's assets that are financed with debt. This ratio measures a business's overall ability to pay both current and long-term debts—total liabilities. The debt ratio measures debt-paying ability differently than the current ratio.

A low debt ratio is safer than a high debt ratio. Why? Because a company with a small amount of liabilities has low required payments. Such a company is unlikely to get into financial difficulty. By contrast, a business with a high debt ratio may have trouble paying its liabilities, especially when sales are low and cash is scarce. When a company fails to pay its debts, the creditors can take the business away from its owner. The largest retail bankcruptcy in history, **Federated Department Stores,** the parent company of Bloomingdale's, was due largely to high debt during an economic recession in the retail industry. Federated was unable to weather the downturn and had to declare bankcruptcy.

A rule of thumb: A debt ratio below 0.60, or 60%, is considered safe for most businesses. A debt ratio above 0.80, or 80%, borders on high risk. Most companies have debt ratios in the range of 0.60–0.80.

THINK IT OVER We saw that PepsiCo has a low current ratio, but PepsiCo nevertheless operates successfully (profits are high, cash is plentiful, and the company grows steadily). Now compute PepsiCo's debt ratio from the company's balance sheet in Exhibit 4-12. Show dollar amounts in millions.

Answer: $$\text{Debt ratio} = \frac{\text{Total liabilities}}{\text{Total assets}} = \frac{\$10,670^*}{\$17,551} = 0.61, \text{ or } 61\%$$

For each dollar of its total assets, how much does PepsiCo owe in total liabilities?

Answer: $0.61

What percentage of PepsiCo's total assets is financial with debt?

Answer: 0.61, or 61%

If you owed $0.61 for every dollar of your total assets, would you worry about your ability to pay your debts?

Answer: You would probably be worried if your cash flow (excess of cash receipts over cash payments) was weak. But if your cash flow is strong—as PepsiCo's cash flow is—you shouldn't worry about a debt ratio of 0.61, or 61%. Many companies operate successfully with higher (more risky) debt ratios.

---
*$3,788 + $2,812 + $4,070 = $10,670

Managing Both the Current Ratio and the Debt Ratio

● DAILY EXERCISE 4-13
● DAILY EXERCISE 4-14

In general, a *high* current ratio is preferable to a low current ratio. *Increases* in the current ratio indicate improving financial position. By contrast, a low debt ratio is preferable to a high debt ratio. Improvement is indicated by a *decrease* in the debt ratio.

Financial ratios aid decision making. It is unwise, however, to place too much confidence in a single ratio. A company may have a high current ratio, which indicates financial strength. It may also have a high debt ratio, which suggests weakness. Which ratio gives the more reliable signal? Experienced lenders and investors examine a large number of ratios over several years to spot trends and turning points. They also consider other factors, such as the company's cash flow and its trend of net income.

As you progress through your study of accounting, we will introduce key ratios used for decision making. Chapter 18 summarizes all the ratios discussed in this book and provides an overview of the more common ratios used in decision making.

e-Accounting

A Forced Debt Ratio for South Korea's Companies

Samsung. Daewoo. Hyundai. Just five years ago these companies were the economic engines driving South Korea's economy. Now they are mired in debt. When the Asian currency crisis hit South Korea in 1997, investors fled and companies had to borrow money. The bigger the company, the more debt they had to take on. According to the **Bank of Korea**, the average debt ratio of Korea's manufacturing companies was 71% in 1999.

According to the government of President Kim Dae Jung, the only way for the giant family-run companies to move toward financial stability is to meet a hard and fast debt ratio target of 67%. Carmaking giant Daewoo was struggling to meet payments on $47 billion in debt—equivalent to the entire national debt of Poland or Malaysia. The Korean government strong-armed Daewoo into selling off the pieces of the company. President Kim's reform plan may save some companies from going bust, but it may hurt others.

Source: Based on Howard W. French, "Dismantling of yesterday's economic engines," *New York Times*, September 3, 1999, p. C1. Jane L. Lee, "Korea moves anew to reform top 5 chaebols; this time, control by families could diminish," *Wall Street Journal*, August 26, 1999, p. A13. Anonymous, "Government under fire for strict debt ratio target," *Business Korea*, December 1999, pp. 18–19.

Now study the Decision Guidelines feature, which summarizes what you have learned in this chapter.

DECISION GUIDELINES

Completing the Accounting Cycle

DECISION	GUIDELINES
How (where) to summarize the effects of all the entity's transactions and adjustments throughout the period?	Accountant's *work sheet* with columns for • Trial balance • Income statement • Adjustments • Balance sheet • Adjusted trial balance
What is the last *major* step in the accounting cycle?	*Closing entries* for the *temporary accounts:* • Revenues ⎱ Income statement accounts • Expenses ⎰ • Owner's withdrawals
Why close out revenues, expenses, and owner withdrawals?	Because these *temporary accounts* have balances that relate only to one accounting period and do *not* carry over to the next period.
Which accounts do not get closed out?	*Permanent (balance sheet) accounts:* • Assets • Owner's capital • Liabilities The balances of these accounts *do* carry over to the next period.
How do businesses classify their assets and liabilities for reporting on the balance sheet?	*Current* (within one year or the entity's operating cycle if longer than a year) *Long-term* (not current)
How do decision makers evaluate a company?	There are many ways, such as the company's net income or net loss on the income statement. Another way to evaluate a company is based on the company's *financial ratios*. Two key ratios:

$$\text{Current ratio} = \frac{\text{Total current assets}}{\text{Total current liabilities}}$$

The *current ratio* measures the entity's ability to pay its current liabilities with its current assets.

$$\text{Debt ratio} = \frac{\text{Total liabilities}}{\text{Total assets}}$$

The *debt ratio* shows the proportion of the entity's assets that are financed with debt. The debt ratio measures the entity's overall ability to pay its liabilities.

EXCEL APPLICATION PROBLEM

Goal: Create an Excel spreadsheet to calculate the current ratio and debt ratio for Target and use the results to answer questions about the company.

Scenario: You are deciding whether to buy the stock in **Target.** You know that the current ratio and the debt ratio measure whether a company has the assets to cover its liabilities.

Your task is to create a simple spreadsheet to calculate the current ratio and the debt ratio for the company. Data may be found in Target's annual report (Web site: www.target-corp.com). When done, answer these questions:
1. Does the company have an acceptable current ratio? How can you tell?
2. Does the company have an acceptable debt ratio? How can you tell?

3. What is the trend (up or down) for the ratios? Is the trend positive or negative? Why?

Step-by-step:

1. Locate the following current and prior years' information for Target (found on the "Consolidated Statements of Financial Position"):
   a. Current Assets
   b. Total Assets
   c. Current Liabilities
   d. Long-Term Liabilities (computed on the spreadsheet)
   e. Total Liabilities (computed on the spreadsheet)
   f. Total Shareholders' Investment (Owners' Equity)
   g. Total Liabilities and Shareholders' Investment
2. Open a new Excel spreadsheet.

EXCEL APPLICATION PROBLEM (CONT.)

Step-by-step (cont.)

3. Create a boldfaced heading for your spreadsheet that contains the following:
   a. Chapter 4 Decision Guideline
   b. The Current Ratio and the Debt ratio
   c. Target
   d. Today's date
4. Two rows down from your worksheet heading, create a column heading titled "TARGET (in millions)." Make it bold and underline the heading.
5. One row down from Target's column heading, create a row with the following bold, underlined column titles:
   a. Account
   b. FYxx (xx = the most recent fiscal year, for example, 00)
   c. FYyy (yy = the prior fiscal year, for example, 99)

6. Starting with the "Account" column heading, enter the data found in 1, above. You should have seven rows of data, with row descriptions (for example, "Current Assets"). Format the columns as necessary.
7. Skip a row at the end of your data, and then create a row titled "Current Ratio" and another row titled "Debt Ratio."
8. Enter the formula for each ratio in the "Fyxx" and "FYyy" columns. You should have four formulas. Make both rows bold.
9. Save your work to disk, and print a copy for your files.

REVIEW THE ACCOUNTING CYCLE

SUMMARY PROBLEM

Refer to the data in the Mid-Chapter Summary Problem (State Service Company, page 132–133).

Required

1. Journalize and post the adjusting entries. (Before posting to the accounts, enter into each account its balance as shown in the trial balance. For example, enter the $370,000 balance in the Accounts Receivable account before posting its adjusting entry.) Key adjusting entries by *letter*, as shown in the work sheet solution to the Mid-Chapter Summary Problem. You can take the adjusting entries straight from the work sheet on page 133.
2. Journalize and post the closing entries. (Each account should carry its balance as shown in the adjusted trial balance.) To distinguish closing entries from adjusting entries, key the closing entries by *number*. Draw arrows to illustrate the flow of data, as shown in Exhibit 4-9. Indicate the balance of the Capital account after the closing entries are posted.
3. Prepare the income statement for the year ended December 31, 20X1. List Miscellaneous Expense last among the expenses, a common practice.
4. Prepare the statement of owner's equity for the year ended December 31, 20X1. Draw an arrow linking the income statement to the statement of owner's equity.
5. Prepare the classified balance sheet at December 31, 20X1. Use the report form. All liabilities are current. Draw an arrow linking the statement of owner's equity to the balance sheet.

www.prenhall.com/horngren
End-of-Chapter Assessment

Solution

Requirement 1

Adjusting Entries

a. Dec. 31	Supplies Expense	4,000	
	Supplies		4,000
b.	31	Depreciation Expense—Furniture and Fixtures	20,000	
		Accumulated Depreciation—Furniture and Fixtures		20,000
c.	31	Depreciation Expense—Building	10,000	
		Accumulated Depreciation—Building		10,000
d.	31	Salary Expense	5,000	
		Salary Payable		5,000
e.	31	Accounts Receivable	12,000	
		Service Revenue		12,000
f.	31	Unearned Service Revenue	32,000	
		Service Revenue		32,000

T-Accounts (top section)

ACCOUNTS RECEIVABLE
370,000	
(e) 12,000	

SUPPLIES
6,000	(a) 4,000

ACCUMULATED DEPRECIATION— FURNITURE AND FIXTURES
	40,000
	(b) 20,000

ACCUMULATED DEPRECIATION — BUILDING
	130,000
	(c) 10,000

SALARY PAYABLE
	(d) 5,000

UNEARNED SERVICE REVENUE
(f) 32,000	45,000

SERVICE REVENUE
	286,000
	(e) 12,000
	(f) 32,000
	Bal. 330,000

SALARY EXPENSE
172,000	
(d) 5,000	
Bal. 177,000	

SUPPLIES EXPENSE
(a) 4,000	
Bal. 4,000	

DEPRECIATION EXPENSE— FURNITURE AND FIXTURES
(b) 20,000	
Bal. 20,000	

DEPRECIATION EXPENSE— BUILDING
(c) 10,000	
Bal. 10,000	

Requirement 2

Closing Entries

1. Dec. 31	Service Revenue		330,000	
	Income Summary			330,000
2. 31	Income Summary		224,000	
	Salary Expense			177,000
	Supplies Expense			4,000
	Depreciation Expense—Furniture and Fixtures			20,000
	Depreciation Expense—Building			10,000
	Miscellaneous Expense			13,000
3. 31	Income Summary ($330,000 − $224,000)		106,000	
	Capital			106,000
4. 31	Capital		65,000	
	Withdrawals			65,000

T-Accounts (bottom section)

SALARY EXPENSE
172,000	
(d) 5,000	
Bal. 177,000	(2) 177,000

SUPPLIES EXPENSE
(a) 4,000	
Bal. 4,000	(2) 4,000

DEPRECIATION EXPENSE— FURNITURE & FIXTURES
(b) 20,000	
Bal. 20,000	(2) 20,000

DEPRECIATION EXPENSE — BUILDING
(c) 10,000	
Bal. 10,000	(2) 10,000

MISCELLANEOUS EXPENSE
13,000	
Bal. 13,000	(2) 13,000

INCOME SUMMARY
(2) 224,000	(1) 330,000
(3) 106,000	Bal. 106,000

SALARY EXPENSE
	286,000
	(e) 12,000
	(f) 32,000
(1) 330,000	Bal. 330,000

WITHDRAWALS
Bal. 65,000	(4) 65,000

CAPITAL
(4) 65,000	293,000
	(3) 106,000
	Bal. 334,000

Requirement 3

STATE SERVICE COMPANY
Income Statement
Year Ended December 31, 20X1

Revenue:		
Service revenue		$330,000
Expenses:		
Salary expense...	$177,000	
Depreciation expense—furniture and fixtures		20,000
Depreciation expense—building....................	10,000	
Supplies expense...	4,000	
Miscellaneous expense	13,000	
Total expenses...		224,000
Net income		$106,000

Requirement 4

STATE SERVICE COMPANY
Statement of Owner's Equity
Year Ended December 31, 20X1

Capital, January 1, 20X1	$293,000
Add: Net income	106,000
	399,000
Less: Withdrawals	(65,000)
Capital, December 31, 20X1	$334,000

Requirement 5

STATE SERVICE COMPANY
Balance Sheet
December 31, 20X1

Assets

Current assets:		
Cash..		$198,000
Accounts receivable		382,000
Supplies		2,000
Total current assets		582,000
Long-term assets:		
Furniture and fixtures	$100,000	
Less: Accumulated depreciation.	(60,000)	40,000
Building	$250,000	
Less: Accumulated depreciation.	(140,000)	110,000
Total assets		$732,000

Liabilities

Current liabilities:		
Accounts payable............................		$380,000
Salary payable.................................		5,000
Unearned service revenue		13,000
Total current liabilities		398,000

Owner's Equity

Capital		334,000
Total liabilities and owner's equity....		$732,000

LESSONS LEARNED

1. **Prepare an accounting work sheet.** The *accounting cycle* is the process by which accountants produce the financial statements for a specific period of time. The cycle starts with the beginning account balances. During the period, the business journalizes transactions and posts them to the ledger accounts. At the end of the period, the trial balance is prepared, and the accounts are adjusted in order to measure the period's net income or net loss. A *work sheet* summarizes the effects of all the period's activity.

2. Use the work sheet to complete the accounting cycle. The work sheet is a convenient device for completing the accounting cycle. It has columns for the trial balance, the adjustments, the adjusted trial balance, the income statement, and the balance sheet. It aids the adjusting process, and it is the place where the period's net income or net loss is first computed. The work sheet also provides the data for the financial statements and the *closing entries*. However, the accounting cycle can also be completed from the less elaborate adjusted trial balance.

3. Close the revenue, expense, and withdrawal accounts. Revenues, expenses, and withdrawals represent increases and decreases in owner's equity for a specific period. At the end of the period, their balances are closed out to zero. For this reason, they are called *temporary accounts*. Assets, liabil-

ities, and capital are not closed because they are the *permanent accounts*. Their balances at the end of one period become the beginning balances of the next period. The final accuracy check of the period is the *postclosing trial balance*.

4. Classify assets and liabilities as current or long-term. The balance sheet reports *current* and *long-term assets* and *current* and *long-term liabilities*. It can be presented in *report format* or *account format*.

5. Use the current and debt ratios to evaluate a business's ability to pay its debts. Two decision-making aids are the *current ratio* (total current assets divided by total current liabilities) and the *debt ratio* (total liabilities divided by total assets).

ACCOUNTING VOCABULARY

accounting cycle (p. 127)
closing the accounts (p. 134)
closing entries (p. 135)
current asset (p. 138)
current liability (p. 139)
current ratio (p. 141)
debt ratio (p. 142)
fixed asset (p. 139)

Income Summary (p. 136)
intangible assets (p. 141)
liquidity (p. 138)
long-term asset (p. 139)
long-term liability (p. 139)
nominal account (p. 135)
operating cycle (p. 139)

permanent account (p. 135)
plant asset (p. 139)
postclosing trial balance (p. 138)
real account (p. 135)
reversing entry (p. 138)
temporary account (p. 135)
work sheet (p. 128)

QUESTIONS

1. Identify the steps in the accounting cycle. Distinguish those that occur during the period from those that are performed at the end.
2. Why is the work sheet a valuable accounting tool?
3. Why must the adjusting entries be journalized and posted if they have already been entered on the work sheet?
4. Which types of accounts are closed?
5. What purpose is served by closing the accounts?
6. Distinguish between permanent accounts and temporary accounts; indicate which type is closed at the end of the period. Give five examples of each type of account.
7. Is Income Summary a permanent account or a temporary account? When and how is it used?
8. Give the closing entries for the following accounts (balances in parentheses): Service Revenue ($5,900); Salary Expense ($1,100); Income Summary (credit balance of $2,000); Asa Warner, Withdrawals ($2,300).
9. Why are assets classified as current or long-term? On what basis are they classified? Where do the classified amounts appear?

10. Indicate which of the following accounts are current assets and which are long-term assets: Prepaid Rent, Building, Furniture, Accounts Receivable, Merchandise Inventory, Cash, Note Receivable (due within one year), Note Receivable (due after one year).
11. In what order are assets and liabilities listed on the balance sheet?
12. Identify an outside party that would be interested in whether a liability is current or long-term. Why would this party be interested in this information?
13. A friend tells you that the difference between a current liability and a long-term liability is that the two types are payable to different types of creditors. Is your friend correct? Define these two categories of liabilities.
14. Show how to compute the current ratio and the debt ratio. Indicate what ability each ratio measures, and state whether a high value or a low value is safer for each.

ASSESS YOUR PROGRESS

DAILY EXERCISES

Explaining items on the work sheet
(Obj. 1)

DE4-1 ◄ *Link Back to Chapter 3 (Adjusting Entries).* Return to the trial balance in Exhibit 4-2, on the acetate between pages 130 and 131. In your own words, explain why at April 30 the following accounts must be adjusted:

a. Supplies
b. Prepaid rent
c. Accumulated depreciation

d. Salary payable
e. Unearned service revenue

Explain why these accounts do *not* need to be adjusted at April 30:

f. Cash

g. Furniture

Explaining items on the work sheet (Obj. 1, 2)

DE4-2 ◄ *Link Back to Chapters 1, 2, and 3 (Definitions of Accounts).* Examine the Adjusted Trial Balance columns of Exhibit 4-4, on the acetate between pages 130 and 131. Explain what the following items mean at April 30:

a. Accounts receivable
b. Supplies
c. Prepaid rent
d. Furniture
e. Accumulated depreciation

f. Accounts payable
g. Unearned service revenue
h. Service revenue
i. Rent expense

DE4-3 Study the completed work sheet (Exhibit 4-6) on the acetates between pages 130 and 131. How is the work sheet in Exhibit 4-2 similar to the adjusted trial balance in Chapter 3? How does the work sheet differ from the adjusted trial balance of Chapter 3 (Exhibit 3-10, page 99)?

Comparing the work sheet and the adjusted trial balance (Obj. 1, 2)

DE4-4 Consider the Income Statement columns and the Balance Sheet columns of the work sheet in Exhibit 4-6, on the acetates between pages 130 and 131. Answer the following questions:

Using the work sheet and closing entries (Obj. 2, 3)

1. What balance does the Owner's Capital account have—debit or credit?
2. Which Income Statement account has the same type of balance as the Capital account?
3. Which Income Statement accounts have the opposite type of balance?
4. What do we call the difference between the total dollar amounts in the debit and credit columns of the Income Statement? Into what account is the difference figure closed?

DE4-5 Examine Exhibits 4-2 and 4-4 on the acetates between pages 130 and 131. Answer this question about closing entries:

Identifying accounts that need to be closed (Obj. 3)

Exhibit 4-2, the (unadjusted) Trial Balance, lists all the accounts of the business entity Gay Gillen eTravel. Draw a horizontal line to separate the accounts that do *not* get closed out at the end of the period from those accounts that *do* get closed out. Identify the categories of accounts that do and do *not* get closed (assets, liabilities, and so on).

DE4-6 Study Exhibit 4-5 on the acetates between pages 130 and 131.

Making closing entries (Obj. 3)

1. Journalize the closing entries for
   a. Owner's withdrawals
   b. Service revenue
   c. All the expenses (make a single closing entry for all the expenses)
   d. Income Summary
2. Set up all the T-accounts affected by requirement 1 and insert their adjusted balances (denote as *Bal.*) at April 30. Also set up a T-account for Income Summary. Post the closing entries to the accounts, denoting posted amounts as *Clo.*
3. What is the ending balance of
   a. Gay Gillen, Capital?
   b. All the other accounts for which you set up T-accounts?

DE4-7 This exercise should be used in conjunction with Daily Exercise 4-6.

Analyzing the overall effect of the closing entries on the owner's capital account (Obj. 3)

1. Return to Exhibit 4-5 on the acetates between pages 130 and 131. Without making any closing entries or using any T-accounts, compute the ending balance of Gay Gillen, Capital.
2. Trace Gay Gillen's ending capital balance to its two appropriate places in Exhibit 4-7 (page 134). In which financial statements do you find Gay Gillen, Capital? Where on each statement?

DE4-8 **Oracle Corporation,** the world's second largest software company, reported the following items adapted from its financial statements at May 31, 1999 (amounts in millions):

Making closing entries (Obj. 3)

Cash...	$1,786	Sales and marketing expense.....	$2,622
Service revenue......................	5,139	Other assets................................	477
Accounts payable	284	Interest expense	21
Accounts receivable................	2,238	Long-term liabilities	382

Make Oracle's closing entries, as needed, for these accounts.

DE4-9 This exercise should be used in conjunction with Daily Exercise 4-8. Use the data in Daily Exercise 4-8 to set up T-accounts for those accounts that **Oracle Corporation** closed out at May 31, 1999. Insert these account balances prior to closing, post the closing entries to these accounts, and show each account's final balance after closing. Denote a balance as *Bal.* and a closing entry amount as *Clo.* For posting to the T-accounts, you may ignore the Income Summary account.

Posting closing entries (Obj. 3)

DE4-10 After closing its accounts at May 31, 1999, **Oracle Corporation** had the following account balances (adapted) with amounts given in millions:

Preparing a postclosing trial balance (Obj. 3)

Property.............................	$ 988	Long-term liabilities	$ 518	
Cash.................................	1,786	Other assets	825	
Service revenue.....................	0	Accounts receivable	2,479	
Owners' equity......................	3,695	Total expenses	0	
Other current assets	1,182	Accounts payable	284	
Short-term notes payable........	4	Other current liabilities.............	2,759	

Prepare Oracle's postclosing trial balance at May 31, 1999. List accounts in proper order, as shown in Exhibit 4-10, page 138.

Classifying assets and liabilities as current or long-term (Obj. 4)

DE4-11 **Lands' End** had sales of $1,320 million during the year ended January 31, 2000, and total assets of $456 million at January 31, 2000, the end of the company's fiscal year. The financial statements of Lands' End reported the following (amounts in millions):

Land and buildings..................	$ 103	Sales revenue	$1,320
Accounts payable	75	Inventory	162
Total expenses	1,073	Receivables..............................	18
Accumulated depreciation.......	117	Interest expense	2
Accrued liabilities (such as		Equipment	176
Salary payable)	44	Prepaid expenses.......................	22

1. Identify the assets (including contra assets) and liabilities.
2. Classify each asset and each liability as current or long-term.

Classifying assets and liabilities as current or long-term (Obj. 4)

DE4-12 ◄ *Link Back to Chapter 3 (Book Value).* Examine **PepsiCo's** balance sheet in Exhibit 4-12 on page 140. Identify or compute the following amounts for PepsiCo at December 31, 1999.

a. Total current assets   **d.** Total long-term assets
b. Total current liabilities   **e.** Total long-term liabilities
c. Book value of Property, Plant, and Equipment

Computing and using the current ratio and the debt ratio (Obj. 5)

DE4-13 This exercise should be used in conjunction with Daily Exercise 4-10. Use the postclosing trial balance that you prepared for Daily Exercise 4-10 to compute **Oracle Corporation's** current ratio and debt ratio.

1. How much in *current* assets does Oracle have for every dollar of *current* liabilities that it owes?
2. What percentage of Oracle's total assets are financed with debt?
3. What percentage of Oracle's total assets do the owners of the company actually own free and clear of debt?

Computing and evaluating the current ratio and the debt ratio (Obj. 5)

DE4-14 Use Gay Gillen eTravel's classified balance sheet in Exhibit 4-11, page 139, to compute the current ratio and the debt ratio of Gillen's business at April 30.

1. How do Gillen's ratios compare to those of **PepsiCo,** which are presented in the Work It Out feature on page 142 and the Think It Over feature on pages 142–143? Based solely on these ratios, which business looks stronger? Why?
2. Do these two ratios tell the complete story of a company's financial position? What other factors should a lender consider in evaluating a business's ability to pay its debts?

EXERCISES

Preparing a work sheet (Obj. 1)

E4-1 The trial balance of Pfeiffer Pack-n-Mail Service follows at the top of the next page.

Additional information at September 30, 20X6:

a. Accrued service revenue, $600.   **d.** Prepaid rent expired, $800.
b. Depreciation, $40.   **e.** Supplies used, $1,650
c. Accrued salary expense, $500.

Required

Complete Pfeiffer's work sheet for September 20X6. How much was net income for September?

Journalizing adjusting and closing entries (Obj. 2, 3)

E4-2 Journalize the adjusting and closing entries in Exercise 4-1.

Posting adjusting and closing entries (Obj. 2, 3)

E4-3 Set up T-accounts for those accounts affected by the adjusting and closing entries in Exercise 4-1. Post the adjusting and closing entries to the accounts; denote adjustment amounts by *Adj.,* closing amounts by *Clo.,* and balances by *Bal.* Double underline the accounts with zero balances after you close them, and show the ending balance in each account.

PFEIFFER PACK-N-MAIL SERVICE
Trial Balance
September 30, 20X6

Cash	$ 3,560	
Accounts receivable	3,440	
Prepaid rent	1,200	
Supplies	3,390	
Equipment	32,600	
Accumulated depreciation		$ 1,840
Accounts payable		3,600
Salary payable		
Gail Pfeiffer, capital		36,030
Gail Pfeiffer, withdrawals	2,000	
Service revenue		7,300
Depreciation expense		
Salary expense	1,800	
Rent expense		
Utilities expense	780	
Supplies expense		
Total	$48,770	$48,770

Beggining capital
+
net income *x*
withdrawal

Preparing a postclosing trial balance (Obj. 2, 3)

E4-4 After completing Exercises 4-1, 4-2, and 4-3, prepare the postclosing trial balance in Exercise 4-1.

E4-5 ◄ *Link Back to Chapter 2 (Adjusting Entries).* TelSurf accounting records include the following account balances:

*Adjusting and closing the accounts
(Obj. 2, 3)*

	December 31,	
	20X1	**20X2**
Prepaid insurance	$1,400	$1,600
Unearned service revenue	4,100	3,700

During 20X2, TelSurf recorded these transactions and adjusting entries:

a. Collected $17,000 cash in advance for service revenue to be earned later.
b. Made the year-end adjustment to record the earning of $17,400 service revenue that had been collected in advance.
c. Paid the annual insurance premium of $4,400.
d. Made the year-end adjustment to record insurance expense for the year. You must compute this amount.

Required

1. Set up T-accounts for Prepaid Insurance, Insurance Expense, Unearned Service Revenue, and Service Revenue. Insert beginning and ending balances for Prepaid Insurance and Unearned Service Revenue.
2. Journalize entries a–d above, and post to the T-accounts. Explanations are not required. Ensure that the ending balances for Prepaid Insurance and Unearned Service Revenue agree with the December 31, 20X2, balances given here for those accounts.
3. Make the closing entries for the above accounts, as needed. Post to the accounts to bring their balances to zero. You need not post to the Income Summary account.

E4-6 From the following selected accounts of Hyundai Energy at June 30, 20X4, prepare the entity's closing entries:

*Identifying and journalizing entries
(Obj. 3)*

Liu Hyundai, capital	$ 21,600		Interest expense	$ 2,200
Service revenue	101,100		Accounts receivable	14,000
Unearned revenues	1,350		Salary payable	850
Salary expense	12,500		Depreciation expense	10,200
Accumulated depreciation	35,000		Rent expense	5,900
Supplies expense	1,700		Liu Hyundai, withdrawals	40,000
Interest revenue	700		Supplies	1,400

What is Hyundai's ending capital balance at June 30, 20X4? 50,900

Identifying and journalizing closing entries (Obj. 3)

E4-7 The accountant for MissouriOne.com has posted adjusting entries (a) through (e) to the following selected accounts at December 31, 20X8. All the revenue, expense, and owner's equity accounts—plus a few of the assets and liabilities—of the entity are listed here in T-account form.

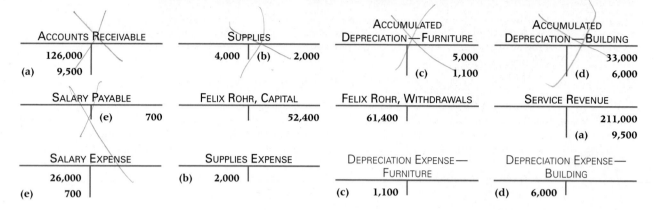

ACCOUNTS RECEIVABLE			
126,000			
(a) 9,500			

SUPPLIES			
4,000	(b) 2,000		

ACCUMULATED DEPRECIATION—FURNITURE		
	5,000	
	(c) 1,100	

ACCUMULATED DEPRECIATION—BUILDING		
	33,000	
	(d) 6,000	

SALARY PAYABLE	
	(e) 700

FELIX ROHR, CAPITAL	
	52,400

FELIX ROHR, WITHDRAWALS	
61,400	

SERVICE REVENUE	
	211,000
	(a) 9,500

SALARY EXPENSE	
26,000	
(e) 700	

SUPPLIES EXPENSE	
(b) 2,000	

DEPRECIATION EXPENSE—FURNITURE	
(c) 1,100	

DEPRECIATION EXPENSE—BUILDING	
(d) 6,000	

Required

1. Journalize MissouriOne.com's closing entries at December 31, 20X8.
2. Determine Felix Rohr's ending capital balance at December 31, 20X8.

Preparing a statement of owner's equity (Obj. 3)

E4-8 From the following accounts of Lubricon Chemical Company, prepare the entity's statement of owner's equity for the year ended December 31, 20X2.

MATTHEW KNOWLES, CAPITAL		
Dec. 31 142,000	Jan. 1	436,000
	Mar. 9	28,000
	Dec. 31	143,000

MATTHEW KNOWLES, WITHDRAWALS	
Mar. 31 39,000	Dec. 31 142,000
Jun. 30 27,000	
Sep. 30 39,000	
Dec. 31 37,000	

INCOME SUMMARY	
Dec. 31 285,000	Dec. 31 428,000
Dec. 31 143,000	

net income

Identifying and recording adjusting and closing entries (Obj. 2, 3)

E4-9 The trial balance and income statement amounts from the April work sheet of H.B. Fuller Polling Company follow:

Account Title	Unadjusted Trial Balance		Income Statement	
Cash	$ 5,200			
Supplies	2,400			
Prepaid rent	1,100			
Computer equipment	51,100			
Accumulated depreciation		$ 6,200		
Accounts payable		4,600		
Salary payable				
Unearned service revenue		4,400		
Long-term note payable		10,000		
H.B. Fuller, capital		25,800		
H.B. Fuller, withdrawals	1,000			
Service revenue		14,800		$19,100
Salary expense	3,000		$ 3,800	
Rent expense	1,200		1,400	
Depreciation expense			300	
Supplies expense			400	
Utilities expense	800		800	
	$65,800	$65,800	6,700	19,100
Net income or net loss			?	
			$19,100	$19,100

Required

1. Journalize the adjusting and closing entries of H.B. Fuller Polling Company at April 30.
2. How much net income or net loss did Fuller have for April? How can you tell?

E4-10 Refer to Exercise 4-9.

Preparing a classified balance sheet
(Obj. 4, 5)

Required

1. After solving Exercise 4-9, use the data in that exercise to prepare the classified balance sheet of H.B. Fuller Polling Company at April 30 of the current year. Use the report format.
2. Compute Fuller Polling's current ratio and debt ratio at April 30. One year ago, the current ratio was 1.20 and the debt ratio was 0.30. Indicate whether Fuller's ability to pay its debts has improved or deteriorated or hasn't changed much during the current year.

Continuing Exercise. *This exercise continues the Amos Faraday, Consultant, situation begun in Exercise 2-15 of Chapter 2 and continued in Exercise 3-14 of Chapter 3.*

E4-11 Refer to Exercise 3-14 of Chapter 3. Start from the posted T-accounts and the adjusted trial balance that Amos Faraday, Consultant, prepared for his business at December 31:

Closing the books, preparing a classified balance sheet, and evaluating a business
(Obj. 3, 4, 5)

AMOS FARADAY, CONSULTANT
Adjusted Trial Balance
December 31, 20XX

Account	Adjusted Trial Balance Debit	Credit
Cash	$11,700	
Accounts receivable	1,500	
Supplies	100	
Equipment	2,000	
Accumulated depr.—equipment		$ 50
Furniture	3,600	
Accumulated depr.—furniture		60
Accounts payable		3,600
Salary payable		500
Unearned service revenue		600
Amos Faraday, capital		14,000
Amos Faraday, withdrawals	1,600	
Service revenue		3,200
Rent expense	500	
Utilities expense	200	
Salary expense	500	
Depreciation expense—equipment	50	
Depreciation expense—furniture	60	
Supplies expense	200	
Total	$22,010	$22,010

Required

1. Journalize and post the closing entries at December 31. Denote each closing amount as *Clo.* and an account balance as *Bal.*
2. Prepare a classified balance sheet at December 31.
3. If your instructor assigns it, complete the accounting work sheet at December 31.

Challenge Exercise

E4-12 Data for the unadjusted trial balance of Links Resorts at December 31, 20X2, follow:

Computing financial statement amounts
(Obj. 2, 4)

Cash	$ 3,000	Horst Schulz, capital	$49,100
Other current assets	9,400	Horst Schulz, withdrawals	51,800
Property, plant,		Service revenue	93,600
and equipment	66,200	Salary expense	42,700
Accumulated depreciation	21,800	Depreciation expense	
Accounts payable	6,100	Supplies expense	
Salary payable		Insurance expense	
Unearned service revenue	5,300	Utilities expense	2,800

Adjusting data at the end of the year include the following:

a. Unearned service revenue that has been earned, $3,600.

b. Accrued service revenue, $8,100

c. Supplies used in operations, $600.

d. Accrued salary expense, $1,400.

e. Insurance expense, $1,800.

f. Depreciation expense, $2,900.

Horst Schulz, the owner, has received an offer to sell the company. He needs to know the following information within one hour: Net income for the year covered by these data.

Required

Without opening any accounts, making any journal entries, or using a work sheet, provide Schulz with the requested information. Prepare an income statement, and show all computations.

(Group A) PROBLEMS

Preparing a work sheet
(Obj. 1)

P4-1A The trial balance of Cohen Construction Co. at June 30, 20X3, follows.

COHEN CONSTRUCTION CO. Trial Balance June 30, 20X3		
Cash	$ 21,200	
Accounts receivable	37,820	
Supplies	17,660	
Prepaid insurance	2,300	
Equipment	32,690	
Accumulated depreciation—equipment		$ 26,240
Building	42,890	
Accumulated depreciation—building		10,500
Land	28,300	
Accounts payable		22,690
Interest payable		
Wages payable		
Unearned service revenue		10,560
Note payable, long-term		22,400
Lynn Cohen, capital		79,130
Lynn Cohen, withdrawals	4,200	
Service revenue		20,190
Depreciation expense—equipment		
Depreciation expense—building		
Wage expense	3,200	
Insurance expense		
Interest expense		
Utilities expense	1,110	
Advertising expense	340	
Supplies expense		
Total	$191,710	$191,710

Additional data at June 30, 20X3:

a. Depreciation: equipment, $630; building, $370.

b. Accrued wage expense, $240.

c. Supplies on hand, $14,370

d. Prepaid insurance expired during June, $500.

e. Accrued interest expense, $180.

f. Unearned service revenue earned during June, $4,970.

g. Accrued advertising expense, $100 (credit Accounts Payable).

h. Accrued service revenue, $1,100.

Required

Complete Cohen Construction's work sheet for June. Key adjusting entries by letter.

P4-2A The *adjusted* trial balance of Gallo Shipping & Handling at June 30, 20X9, after all adjustments, follows.

Preparing financial statements
from an adjusted trial balance;
journalizing the adjusting and
closing entries
(Obj. 2, 3, 5)

GALLO SHIPPING & HANDLING
Adjusted Trial Balance
June 30, 20X9

Cash	$ 12,350	
Accounts receivable	26,470	
Supplies	31,290	
Prepaid insurance	3,200	
Equipment	135,800	
Accumulated depreciation—equipment		$ 16,480
Building	34,900	
Accumulated depreciation—building		16,850
Land	30,000	
Accounts payable		38,400
Interest payable		1,490
Wages payable		770
Unearned service revenue		2,300
Note payable, long-term		97,000
Linda Gallo, capital		58,390
Linda Gallo, withdrawals	45,300	
Service revenue		139,860
Depreciation expense—equipment	7,300	
Depreciation expense—building	3,970	
Wage expense	21,470	
Insurance expense	3,100	
Interest expense	8,510	
Utilities expense	4,300	
Supplies expense	3,580	
Total	$371,540	$371,540

Adjusting data at June 30, 20X9, which have all been incorporated into the *adjusted* trial balance figures:

a. Prepaid insurance expired during the year, $2,200.
b. Accrued interest expense, $540.
c. Accrued service revenue, $940.
d. Unearned service revenue earned during the year, $7,790.
e. Accrued wage expense, $770.
f. Depreciation for the year: equipment, $7,300; building, $3,970.
g. Supplies used during the year, $3,580.

Required

1. Journalize the adjusting entries that would lead to the adjusted trial balance shown here. Also journalize the closing entries.
2. Prepare Gallo's income statement and statement of owner's equity for the year ended June 30, 20X9, and the classified balance sheet on that date. Use the account format for the balance sheet.
3. Compute Gallo's current ratio and debt ratio at June 30, 20X9. One year ago, the current ratio stood at 1.41 and the debt ratio was 0.71. Did Gallo's ability to pay debts improve or deteriorate during fiscal year 20X9?

P4-3A The unadjusted T-accounts of Fidelity Sound Studio, at December 31, 20X2, and the related year-end adjustment data follow at the top of the next page.

Taking the accounting cycle
through the closing entries
(Obj. 2, 3)

Adjustment data at December 31, 20X2:

a. Unearned service revenue earned during the year, $5,000.
b. Supplies on hand, $1,000.
c. Depreciation for the year, $9,000.
d. Accrued salary expense, $1,000.
e. Accrued service revenue, $2,000.

Required

1. Enter the trial balance on a work sheet, and complete the work sheet. Key each adjusting entry by the letter corresponding to the data given. List all the accounts, including those with zero balances. Leave a blank line under Service Revenue.
2. Prepare the income statement, the statement of owner's equity, and the classified balance sheet in account format.
3. Journalize the adjusting and closing entries.
4. Did Fidelity Sound Studio have a good or a bad year during 20X2? Give the reason for your answer.

CASH		ACCOUNTS RECEIVABLE		SUPPLIES		EQUIPMENT	
Bal. 15,000		Bal. 36,000		Bal. 9,000		Bal. 99,000	

ACCUMULATED DEPRECIATION		ACCOUNTS PAYABLE		SALARY PAYABLE		UNEARNED SERVICE REVENUE	
	Bal. 13,000		Bal. 6,000				Bal. 5,000

NOTE PAYABLE, LONG-TERM				BETSY WILLIS, CAPITAL		BETSY WILLIS, WITHDRAWALS	
	Bal. 60,000				Bal. 36,000	Bal. 62,000	

SERVICE REVENUE				SALARY EXPENSE		SUPPLIES EXPENSE	
	Bal. 182,000			Bal. 53,000			

DEPRECIATION EXPENSE		INTEREST EXPENSE		RENT EXPENSE		INSURANCE EXPENSE	
		Bal. 6,000		Bal. 15,000		Bal. 7,000	

Completing the accounting cycle (Obj. 2, 3)

P4-4A This problem should be used in conjunction with Problem 4-3A. It completes the accounting cycle by posting to T-accounts and preparing the postclosing trial balance.

Required

1. Using the Problem 4-3A data, post the adjusting and closing entries to the T-accounts, denoting adjusting amounts by *Adj.*, closing amounts by *Clo.*, and account balances by *Bal.*, as shown in Exhibit 4-9. You must set up a T-account for Income Summary. Double underline all accounts with a zero ending balance.
2. Prepare the postclosing trial balance.

Completing the accounting cycle (Obj. 2, 3, 4)

P4-5A The trial balance of Allianz Publishing at August 31, 20X9, and the data needed for the month-end adjustments follow:

ALLIANZ PUBLISHING
Trial Balance
August 31, 20X9

Account Number	Account Title	Debit	Credit
11	Cash	$ 23,800	
12	Accounts receivable	15,560	
13	Prepaid rent	1,290	
14	Supplies	900	
15	Equipment	15,350	
16	Accumulated depreciation—equipment		$ 12,800
17	Building	89,900	
18	Accumulated depreciation—building		28,600
21	Accounts payable		4,240
22	Salary payable		
23	Unearned service revenue		8,900
31	Lou Kraft, capital		71,920
32	Lou Kraft, withdrawals	4,800	
41	Service revenue		27,300
51	Salary expense	1,100	
52	Rent expense		
53	Utilities expense	410	
54	Depreciation expense—equipment		
55	Depreciation expense—building		
56	Advertising expense	650	
57	Supplies expense		
	Total	$153,760	$153,760

Adjustment data:

a. Unearned commission revenue still unearned at August 31, $6,500.
b. Prepaid rent still in force at August 31, $1,050.
c. Supplies used during the month, $340.
d. Depreciation on equipment for the month, $370.
e. Depreciation on building for the month, $130.
f. Accrued salary expense at August 31, $460.

Required

1. Open the accounts listed in the trial balance and insert their August 31 unadjusted balances. Also open the Income Summary account, number 33. Use four-column accounts. Date the balances of the following accounts as of August 1: Prepaid Rent, Supplies, Equipment, Accumulated Depreciation—Equipment, Building, Accumulated Depreciation—Building, Unearned Service Revenue, and Lou Kraft, Capital.
2. Enter the trial balance on a work sheet and complete the work sheet of Allianz Publishing for the month ended August 31, 20X9. See the trial balance on page 156.
3. Prepare the income statement, the statement of owner's equity, and the classified balance sheet in report format.
4. Using the work sheet data that you prepare, journalize and post the adjusting and closing entries. Use dates and posting references. Use 7 as the number of the journal page.
5. Prepare a postclosing trial balance.

P4-6A The accounts of Martinez Political Consulting at December 31, 20X6, follow:

Preparing a classified balance sheet in report format
(Obj. 4, 5)

Accounts payable	$ 5,100	Angel Martinez, capital,	
Accounts receivable	6,600	December 31, 20X5	$59,800
Accumulated depreciation—		Angel Martinez, withdrawals	50,400
building	37,800	Note payable, long-term	27,800
Accumulated depreciation—		Other assets	3,600
computers	11,600	Other current liabilities	4,700
Advertising expense	2,200	Prepaid insurance	1,100
Building	104,400	Prepaid rent	6,600
Cash	16,500	Salary expense	24,600
Service revenue	93,500	Salary payable	3,900
Computers	22,700	Supplies	2,500
Depreciation expense	1,300	Supplies expense	5,700
Insurance expense	800	Unearned service	
Interest payable	600	revenue	5,400
Interest expense	1,200		

Required

1. All adjustments have been journalized and posted, but the closing entries have not yet been made. Prepare the company's classified balance sheet in report format at December 31, 20X6. Show totals for total assets, total liabilities, and total liabilities and owner's equity.
2. Compute Martinez's current ratio and debt ratio at December 31, 20X6. At December 31, 20X5, the current ratio was 1.52 and the debt ratio was 0.39. Did Martinez's ability to pay debts improve or deteriorate during 20X6?

P4-7A ↞ *Link Back to Chapter 2 (Accounting Errors).* The accountant for Liberty Landscaping encountered the following situations while adjusting and closing the books at December 31. Consider each situation independently.

Analyzing errors and journalizing adjusting and closing entries
(Obj. 3)

a. A $500 credit to Accounts Receivable was posted as a debit.
   (1) At what stage of the accounting cycle will this error be detected?
   (2) Describe the technique for identifying the amount of the error.

b. The $16,000 balance of Equipment was entered as $1,600 on the trial balance.
   (1) What is the name of this type of error?
   (2) Assume that this is the only error in the trial balance. Which will be greater, the total debits or the total credits, and by how much?
   (3) How can this type of error be identified?

c. The accountant failed to make the following adjusting entries at December 31:
   (1) Accrued property tax expense, $200.
   (2) Supplies expense, $1,090.
   (3) Accrued interest revenue on a $50,000 note receivable, $1,650.
   (4) Depreciation of equipment, $400.
   (5) Earned service revenue that had been collected in advance, $1,100.
   Compute the overall net income effect of these omissions.

d. Record each of the adjusting entries identified in item c.

PROBLEMS

(Group B)

P4-1B The trial balance of Reneé Greenspan Productions at May 31, 20X2, follows at the top of the next page.

Preparing a work sheet
(Obj. 1)

RENEÉ GREENSPAN PRODUCTIONS
Trial Balance
May 31, 20X2

Cash	$ 4,370	
Notes receivable	10,340	
Interest receivable		
Supplies	560	
Prepaid insurance	1,790	
Furniture	27,410	
Accumulated depreciation—furniture		$ 1,480
Building	53,900	
Accumulated depreciation—building		34,560
Land	18,700	
Accounts payable		14,730
Interest payable		
Salary payable		
Unearned service revenue		8,800
Note payable, long-term		18,700
Reneé Greenspan, capital		29,990
Reneé Greenspan, withdrawals	3,800	
Service revenue		16,970
Interest revenue		
Depreciation expense—furniture		
Depreciation expense—building		
Salary expense	2,170	
Insurance expense		
Interest expense		
Utilities expense	1,130	
Advertising expense	1,060	
Supplies expense		
Total	$125,230	$125,230

Additional data at May 31, 20X2:

a. Depreciation: furniture, $480; building, $460.
b. Accrued salary expense, $420.
c. Supplies on hand, $410.
d. Prepaid insurance expired during May, $390.
e. Accrued interest expense, $220.
f. Unearned service revenue earned during May, $4,400.
g. Accrued advertising expense, $60 (credit Accounts Payable).
h. Accrued interest revenue, $170.

Required

Complete Greenspan's work sheet for May. Key adjusting entries by letter.

Preparing financial statements from an adjusted trial balance; journalizing the adjusting and closing entries
(Obj. 2, 3, 5)

P4-2B The *adjusted* trial balance of Chase Webmaster Service at April 30, 20X2, after all adjustments, follows at the top of the next page. Adjusting data at April 30, 20X2, which have all been incorporated into the *adjusted* trial balance figures above, consist of

a. Accrued service revenue, $2,200.
b. Depreciation for the year: equipment, $6,900; building, $3,710.
c. Accrued wage expense, $830.
d. Unearned service revenue earned during the year, $4,180.
e. Supplies used during the year, $5,880.
f. Prepaid insurance expired during the year, $5,110.
g. Accrued interest expense, $1,280.

Required

1. Journalize the adjusting entries that would lead to the adjusted trial balance shown here. Also journalize the closing entries.
2. Prepare Chase's income statement and statement of owner's equity for the year ended April 30, 20X2, and the classified balance sheet on that date. Use the account format for the balance sheet.
3. Compute Chase's current ratio and debt ratio at April 30, 20X2. One year ago, the current ratio stood at 1.61 and the debt ratio was 0.72. Did Chase's ability to pay debts improve or deteriorate during fiscal year 20X2?

CHASE WEBMASTER SERVICE
Adjusted Trial Balance
April 30, 20X2

Cash	$ 14,570	
Accounts receivable	43,740	
Supplies	3,690	
Prepaid insurance	2,290	
Equipment	63,930	
Accumulated depreciation—equipment		$ 28,430
Building	74,330	
Accumulated depreciation—building		18,260
Land	20,000	
Accounts payable		19,550
Interest payable		2,280
Wages payable		830
Unearned service revenue		3,660
Note payable, long-term		69,900
Monica Chase, capital		77,140
Monica Chase, withdrawals	27,500	
Service revenue		98,550
Depreciation expense—equipment	6,900	
Depreciation expense—building	3,710	
Wage expense	32,810	
Insurance expense	5,110	
Interest expense	8,170	
Utilities expense	4,970	
Supplies expense	6,880	
Total	$318,600	$318,600

P4-3B The unadjusted T-accounts of Lisa Tenney, M.D., at December 31, 20X2, and the related year-end adjustment data follow.

Taking the accounting cycle through the closing entries (Obj. 2, 3)

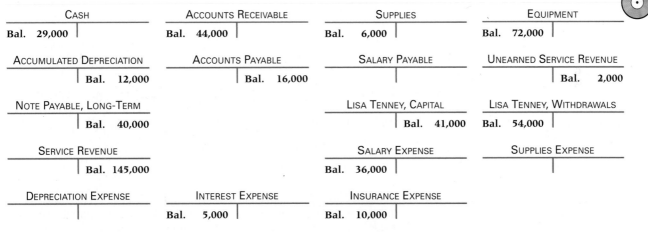

Adjustment data at December 31, 20X2:

a. Depreciation for the year, $5,000.
b. Supplies on hand, $2,000.
c. Accrued service revenue, $4,000.

d. Unearned service revenue earned during the year, $2,000.
e. Accrued salary expense, $4,000.

Required

1. Enter the trial balance on a work sheet, and complete the work sheet. Key each adjusting entry by the letter corresponding to the data given. List all the accounts, including those with zero balances. Leave a blank line under Service Revenue.
2. Prepare the income statement, the statement of owner's equity, and the classified balance sheet in account format.
3. Journalize the adjusting and closing entries.
4. Did Tenney have a good or a bad year during 20X2? Give the reason for your answer.

P4-4B This problem should be used in conjunction with Problem 4-3B. It completes the accounting cycle by posting to T-accounts and preparing the postclosing trial balance.

Completing the accounting cycle (Obj. 2, 3)

1. Using the Problem 4-3B data, post the adjusting and closing entries to the T-accounts, denoting adjusting amounts by *Adj.*, closing amounts by *Clo.*, and account balances by *Bal.*, as shown in Exhibit 4-9. You must set up a T-account for Income Summary. Double underline all accounts with a zero ending balance.
2. Prepare the postclosing trial balance.

Completing the accounting cycle (Obj. 2, 3, 4)

P4-5B The trial balance of Uniworld Language Services at October 31, 20X0, follows. The data needed for the month-end adjustments also follow.

	UNIWORLD LANGUAGE SERVICES Trial Balance October 31, 20X0			
Account Number	**Account Title**	**Debit**	**Credit**	
11	Cash	$ 4,900		
12	Accounts receivable	15,310		
13	Prepaid rent	2,200		
14	Supplies	840		
15	Equipment	26,830		
16	Accumulated depreciation—equipment		$ 3,400	
17	Building	68,300		
18	Accumulated depreciation—building		12,100	
21	Accounts payable		7,290	
22	Salary payable			
23	Unearned service revenue		5,300	
31	Chris Stott, capital		84,490	
32	Chris Stott, withdrawals	3,900		
41	Service revenue		12,560	
51	Salary expense	1,840		
52	Rent expense			
53	Utilities expense	1,020		
54	Depreciation expense—equipment			
55	Depreciation expense—building			
56	Supplies expense			
	Total	$125,140	$125,140	

Adjusting data:

a. Unearned service revenue still unearned at October 31, $800.
b. Prepaid rent still in force at October 31, $2,000.
c. Supplies used during the month, $770.

d. Depreciation on equipment for the month, $250.
e. Depreciation on building for the month, $580.
f. Accrued salary expense at October 31, $310.

Required

1. Open the accounts listed in the trial balance, inserting their October 31 unadjusted balances. Also open the Income Summary account, number 33. Use four-column accounts. Date the balances of the following accounts October 1: Prepaid Rent, Supplies, Equipment, Accumulated Depreciation—Equipment, Building, Accumulated Depreciation—Building, Unearned Service Revenue, and Chris Stott, Capital.
2. Enter the trial balance on a work sheet and complete the work sheet of Uniworld Language Services for the month ended October 31, 20X0.
3. Prepare the income statement, the statement of owner's equity, and the classified balance sheet in report format.
4. Using the work sheet data that you prepare, journalize and post the adjusting and closing entries. Use dates and posting references. Use 12 as the number of the journal page.
5. Prepare a postclosing trial balance.

Preparing a classified balance sheet in report format (Obj. 4, 5)

P4-6B The accounts of Justin Leonard, Architect, at December 31, 20X3, are listed on the following page:

Required

1. All adjustments have been journalized and posted, but the closing entries have not yet been made. Prepare the company's classified balance sheet in report format at December 31, 20X3. Show totals for total assets, total liabilities, and total liabilities and owner's equity.

Accounts payable	$34,700	Insurance expense	$ 600
Accounts receivable	41,500	Interest payable	300
Accumulated depreciation—		Interest receivable	900
building	47,300	Note payable, long-term	3,200
Accumulated depreciation—		Note receivable, long-term	6,900
equipment	7,700	Other assets	2,300
Advertising expense	900	Other current liabilities	1,100
Building	55,900	Prepaid insurance	600
Cash	3,400	Prepaid rent	4,700
Depreciation expense	1,900	Salary expense	17,800
Justin Leonard, capital,		Salary payable	2,400
December 31, 20X2	50,700	Service revenue	71,100
Justin Leonard,		Supplies	3,800
withdrawals	31,200	Supplies expense	4,600
Equipment	43,200	Unearned service revenue	1,700

2. Compute Leonard's current ratio and debt ratio at December 31, 20X3. At December 31, 20X2, the current ratio was 1.28 and debt ratio was 0.42. Did Leonard's ability to pay debts improve, deteriorate, or change very little during 20X3?

P4-7B ← *Link Back to Chapter 2 (Accounting Errors).* The accountant of Iowa Packing Company encountered the following situations while adjusting and closing the books at February 28. Consider each situation independently.

Analyzing errors and journalizing adjusting and closing entries (Obj. 3)

a. A $1,400 debit to Supplies was posted as $4,100.
  (1) At what stage of the accounting cycle will this error be detected?
  (2) What is the name of this type of error? Explain how to identify the error.
b. The $1,300 balance of Computer Software was entered as $13,000 on the trial balance.
  (1) What is the name of this type of error?
  (2) Assume that this is the only error in the trial balance. Which will be greater, the total debits or the total credits, and by how much?
  (3) How can this type of error be identified?
c. The accountant failed to make the following adjusting entries at February 28:
  (1) Depreciation of equipment, $700.
  (2) Earned service revenue that had been collected in advance, $2,700.
  (3) Accrued service revenue, $1,400.
  (4) Insurance expense, $360.
  (5) Accrued interest expense on a note payable, $520.
  Compute the overall net income effect of these omissions.
d. Record each of the adjusting entries identified in item c.

APPLY YOUR KNOWLEDGE

DECISION CASES

Case 1. One year ago, Alex Fleming founded Jack-of-All-Trades Job Search, and the business has prospered. Fleming comes to you for advice. He wishes to know how much net income his business earned during the past year. He also wants to know what the entity's total assets, liabilities, and capital are. The accounting records consist of the T-accounts in the ledger, which were prepared by an accountant who has moved. The ledger at December 31 appears at the top of the next page.

Completing the accounting cycle to develop the information for a bank loan (Obj. 3, 4)

Fleming indicates that at year end customers owe him $1,600 accrued service revenue, which he expects to collect early next year. These revenues have not been recorded. During the year, he collected $4,130 service revenue in advance from customers, but the business has earned only $2,500 of that amount. Rent expense for the year was $2,400, and he used up $2,100 of the supplies. Fleming estimates that depreciation on equipment was $5,900 for the year. At December 31, he owes his employee $1,200 accrued salary.

Fleming expresses concern that his withdrawals during the year might have exceeded the business's net income. To get a loan to expand the business, Fleming must show the bank that his capital account has grown from its original $25,000 balance. Has it? You and Fleming agree that you will meet again in one week.

Required

Prepare the work sheet and the financial statements to answer Fleming's questions.

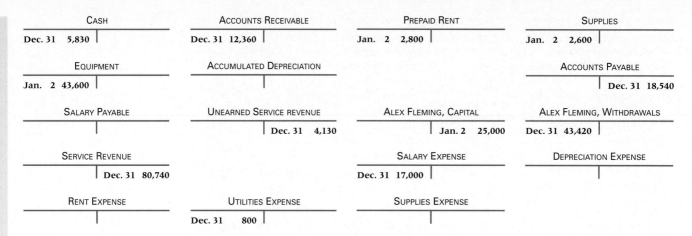

CASH		ACCOUNTS RECEIVABLE		PREPAID RENT		SUPPLIES	
Dec. 31 5,830		Dec. 31 12,360		Jan. 2 2,800		Jan. 2 2,600	

EQUIPMENT		ACCUMULATED DEPRECIATION			ACCOUNTS PAYABLE	
Jan. 2 43,600						Dec. 31 18,540

SALARY PAYABLE		UNEARNED SERVICE REVENUE		ALEX FLEMING, CAPITAL		ALEX FLEMING, WITHDRAWALS	
			Dec. 31 4,130		Jan. 2 25,000	Dec. 31 43,420	

SERVICE REVENUE			SALARY EXPENSE		DEPRECIATION EXPENSE	
	Dec. 31 80,740		Dec. 31 17,000			

RENT EXPENSE		UTILITIES EXPENSE		SUPPLIES EXPENSE	
		Dec. 31 800			

Finding an error in the work sheet
(Obj. 1)

Case 2. You are preparing the financial statements for the year ended October 31, 20X5, for Zadell Software Company.

- You began with the trial balance of the ledger, which balanced, and then made the required adjusting entries.
- To save time, you omitted preparing an adjusted trial balance.
- After making the adjustments on the work sheet, you extended the balances from the trial balance, adjusted for the adjusting entries, and computed amounts for the income statement and the balance sheet columns.

Required

a. When you added the total debits and the total credits on the income statement, you found that the credits exceeded the debits by $45,000. Did the business have a profit or a loss?

b. You took the balancing amount from the income statement columns to the debit column of the balance sheet and found that the total debits exceeded the total credits in the balance sheet. The difference between the total debits and the total credits on the balance sheet is $90,000. What is the cause of this difference? (Except for these errors, everything else is correct.)

ETHICAL ISSUE

◄◄ *Link Back to Chapter 3 (Revenue Principle).* Forbes Painting Company wishes to expand and has borrowed $2 million. As a condition for making this loan, the bank requires that Forbes maintain a current ratio of at least 1.50.

Business has been good but not great. Expansion costs have brought the current ratio down to 1.40 at December 15. Jacob Forbes, owner of the company, is considering what might happen if the business reports a current ratio of 1.40 to the bank. One course of action for Forbes is to record in December some revenue that the business will earn in January of next year. The contract for this job has been signed.

Required

1. Journalize the revenue transaction, and indicate how recording this revenue in December would affect the current ratio.

2. State whether it is ethical to record the revenue transaction in December. Identify the accounting principle relevant to this situation.

3. Propose a course of action that is ethical for Forbes.

FINANCIAL STATEMENT CASE

Using a balance sheet
(Obj. 4, 5)

This problem, based on the balance sheet of **Target Corporation** in Appendix A, will familiarize you with some of the assets and liabilities of that company. Use the Target balance sheet to answer the following questions.

Required

1. Which balance sheet format does Target Corporation use?

2. Name the company's largest current asset and largest current liability at January 29, 2000.

3. Compute Target's current ratios and debt ratios at January 30, 1999, and at January 29, 2000. Target treats Convertible Preferred Stock as a liability. Did the ratio values improve, worsen, or hold steady during the fiscal year ended January 29, 2000? Refer to the income statement to explain your evaluation of the ratio values.

4. Under what category does Target report land, buildings, fixtures, and equipment?

5. What was the cost of the company's plant assets at January 29, 2000? What was the amount of accumulated depreciation? What was the book value of the plant assets?

TEAM PROJECT

Doug Maltbee formed a lawn service business as a summer job. To start the business on May 1, he deposited $1,000 in a new bank account in the name of the proprietorship. The $1,000 consisted of a $600 loan from his father and $400 of his own money. Doug rented lawn equipment, purchased supplies, and hired fellow students to mow and trim his customer's lawns.

At the end of each month, Doug mailed bills to his customers. On August 31, he was ready to dissolve the business and return to Louisiana State University for the fall semester. Because he was so busy, he kept few records other than his checkbook and a list of amounts owed to him by customers.

At August 31, Doug's checkbook shows a balance of $690, and his customers still owe him $500. During the summer, he collected $4,250 from customers. His checkbook lists payments for supplies totaling $400, and he still has gasoline, weedeater cord, and other supplies that cost a total of $50. He paid his employees $1,900, and he still owes them $200 for the final week of the summer.

Doug rented some equipment from Scholes Machine Shop. On May 1, he signed a six-month lease on mowers and paid $600 for the full lease period. Scholes will refund the unused portion of the prepayment if the equipment is in good shape. In order to get the refund, Doug has kept the mowers in excellent condition. In fact, he had to pay $300 to repair a mower.

To transport employees and equipment to jobs, Doug used a trailer that he bought for $300. He figures that the summer's work used up one-third of the trailer's service potential. The business checkbook lists a payment of $460 for cash withdrawals by Doug during the summer. Doug paid his father back during August.

Required

1. Prepare the income statement of Maltbee Lawn Service for the four months May through August.
2. Prepare the classified balance sheet of Maltbee Lawn Service at August 31.
3. Was Maltbee's summer work successful? Give the reason for your answer.

INTERNET EXERCISE

Southwest Airlines Company started in 1971 with three planes and now has more than 300 planes that fly into 55 different cities. In years when many other airlines reported net losses, Southwest Airlines' low-cost, no-frills flights resulted in profits.

1. Go to **http://www.Southwest.com,** click on *About SWA,* and read "A Brief History of Southwest Airlines." Who is the CEO of Southwest Airlines? Why can Southwest Airlines offer lower fares than other airlines?
2. In the left-hand column click on *History* and read the information provided. What is the Triple Crown? How often has Southwest Airlines won this award? Comment on one other item that you found of interest.
3. Go to **http://www.Forbes.com** to get the latest financial information. In the "Stock" section type LUV, the stock symbol of Southwest Airlines Co., and then click on *Go.* In the left-hand column, click on "Company Info" and read the information provided. Comment on one item that makes Southwest Airlines different from other airlines.
4. In the left-hand column, click on "Financials." Menu selections are presented in the left-hand column.
   a. For the most recent year, list the amount reported for "Passenger revenue." Is this account closed at the end of the accounting period?
   b. For the two most recent years, list the amounts reported for "Cash/Equivalents," "Total current assets," "Total assets," "Total current liabilities," and "Total liabilities."
   c. Is the balance sheet presented in a classified format? How can you tell?
   d. Is Cash/Equivalents closed at the end of the accounting period? Why or why not?
   e. For the two most recent years, calculate Southwest's current ratio and debt ratio. Do these values look strong or weak?

APPENDIX TO CHAPTER 4

REVERSING ENTRIES: AN OPTIONAL STEP

Reversing entries are special types of entries that ease the burden of accounting for transactions that key off the adjustments at the end of the period. Reversing entries are used most often in conjunction with accrual-type adjustments such as accrued salary expense and accrued service revenue. *Generally accepted accounting principles do not require reversing entries. They are used only for convenience and to save time.*

ACCOUNTING FOR ACCRUED EXPENSES

To see how reversing entries work, return to Gay Gillen's unadjusted trial balance at April 30 (Exhibit 4-2, page 130). Salary Expense has a debit balance of $950 for salaries paid during April. At April 30, the business still owes its employee an additional $950 for the last half of the month, so Gillen makes this adjusting entry:

Adjusting Entries

Apr. 30	Salary Expense	950
	Salary Payable	950

After posting, the accounts are updated at April 30.[2]

SALARY PAYABLE		SALARY EXPENSE	
	Apr. 30 Adj. 950	Paid during April CP 950	
	Apr. 30 Bal. 950	Apr. 30 Adj. 950	
		Apr. 30 Bal. 1,900	

After the adjusting entry,

- The April income statement reports salary expense of $1,900.
- The April 30 balance sheet reports salary payable of $950.

The $1,900 debit balance of Salary Expense is closed at April 30, 20X1, with this closing entry:

Closing Entries

Apr. 30	Income Summary	1,900
	Salary Expense	1,900

After posting, Salary Expense has a zero balance as follows:

SALARY EXPENSE			
Paid during April CP	950		
Apr. 30 Adj.	950		
Apr. 30 Bal.	1,900	Apr. 30 Clo.	1,900

Zero balance

Assume for this illustration that on May 5, the next payday, Gillen will pay the $950 of accrued salary left over from April 30 plus $100 of salary for the first few days of May. Gillen's next payroll payment will be $1,050 ($950 + $100).

ACCOUNTING WITHOUT A REVERSING ENTRY

On May 5, the next payday, Gillen pays the payroll of $1,050 and makes this journal entry:

May 5	Salary Payable	950	
	Salary Expense	100	
	Cash		1,050

This method of recording the cash payment is correct. However, it wastes time because Gillen must refer to the adjusting entries of April 30. Otherwise, she does not know the amount of the debit to Salary Payable (in this example, $950). Searching the preceding period's adjusting entries takes time and, in business, time is money. To save time, accountants use reversing entries.

---

[2]Entry explanations used throughout this discussion are

Adj. = entry	CP = Cash payment entry—a credit to Cash
Bal. = Balance	CR = Cash receipt entry—a debit to Cash
Clo. = Closing entry	Rev. = Reversing entry

MAKING A REVERSING ENTRY

A **reversing entry** switches the debit and the credit of a previous adjusting entry. *A reversing entry, then, is the exact opposite of a prior adjusting entry.* The reversing entry is dated the first day of the period that follows the adjusting entry.

To illustrate reversing entries, recall that on April 30, Gillen made the following adjusting entry to accrue Salary Payable:

REVERSING ENTRY. An entry that switches the debit and the credit of a previous adjusting entry. The reversing entry is dated the first day of the period after the adjusting entry.

Adjusting Entries

Apr. 30 Salary Expense	950	
Salary Payable......................		950

The reversing entry simply reverses the debit and the credit of the adjustment:

Reversing Entries

May 1 Salary Payable	950	
Salary Expense.....................		950

Observe that the reversing entry is dated the first day of the new period. It is the exact opposite of the April 30 adjusting entry. Ordinarily, the accountant who makes the adjusting entry also prepares the reversing entry at the same time. Gillen dates the reversing entry as of the first day of the next period, however, so that it affects only the new period. Note how the accounts appear after Gillen posts the reversing entry:

SALARY PAYABLE				SALARY EXPENSE			
May 1 Rev. 950	Apr. 30 Bal. 950			Apr. 30 Bal. 1,900	Apr. 30 Clo. 1,900		
Zero balance				Zero balance			
					May 1 Rev. 950		

The arrow shows the transfer of the $950 credit balance from Salary Payable to Salary Expense. This credit balance in Salary Expense does not mean that the entity has negative salary expense, as you might think. Instead, the odd credit balance in the Salary Expense account is merely a temporary result of the reversing entry. The credit balance is eliminated on May 5, when Gillen pays the payroll and debits Salary Expense in the customary manner:

May 5 Salary Expense	1,050	
Cash		1,050

Then this cash payment entry is posted as follows:

SALARY EXPENSE		
May 5 CP 1,050	May 1 Rev. 950	
May 5 Bal. 100		

Now Salary Expense has its correct debit balance of $100, which is the amount of salary expense incurred thus far in May. The $1,050 cash disbursement also pays the liability for Salary Payable so that Salary Payable has a zero balance, which is correct.

ASSESS YOUR PROGRESS

APPENDIX PROBLEM

P4A-1 Refer to the data in Problem 4-5A, page 156.

Using reversing entries

Required

1. Open accounts for Salary Payable and Salary Expense. Insert their unadjusted balances at August 31, 20X9.
2. Journalize adjusting entry (f) and the closing entry for Salary Expense at August 31. Post to the accounts.
3. On September 5, Allianz Publishing paid the next payroll amount of $580. Journalize this cash payment, and post to the accounts. Show the balance in each account.
4. Using a reversing entry, repeat requirements 1–3. Compare the balances of Salary Payable and Salary Expense computed using a reversing entry with those balances computed without the reversing entry (as they appear in your answer to requirement 3).

5

Merchandising Operations and the Accounting Cycle

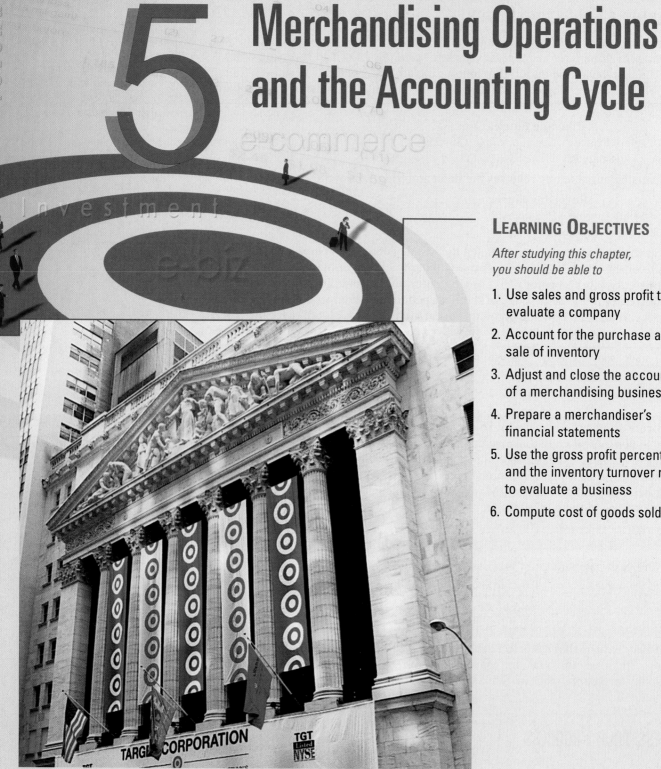

LEARNING OBJECTIVES

After studying this chapter, you should be able to

1. Use sales and gross profit to evaluate a company

2. Account for the purchase and sale of inventory

3. Adjust and close the accounts of a merchandising business

4. Prepare a merchandiser's financial statements

5. Use the gross profit percentage and the inventory turnover ratio to evaluate a business

6. Compute cost of goods sold

www.prenhall.com/horngren
Readiness Assessment

You probably recognize the bulls'-eye logo. You may even do your shopping at a **Target, Mervyn, Marshall Field, Dayton,** or **Hudson** store. All these companies are part of the retail empire known as **Target Corporation.** It is a pacesetter in retailing: Target stores are currently the place to find the latest fashions at the best prices. Target is also a pacesetter in philanthropy and community relations. Through its Five Percent Club, the company donates 5% of its taxable income to support charities in the communities where it operates. In 2000, Target gave more than $1 million every week to local communities. The company, which employs about 189,000 people nationwide, is considered a good employer. *Working Mother* magazine has recognized Target as a "Top Work Place for Women." Target sells its merchandise through nearly 900 stores in 44 states, and through its Web site on the Internet. It is one of the largest mass-merchandise retailers in the United States, ringing up sales of over $33 billion in the year ended January 31, 2000.

Chapter 5 marks a new direction for this book. In Chapters 1–4, we studied accounting through the lens of Gay Gillen eTravel, which earns revenue by providing travel services for clients. **Yahoo!, Sprint,** physicians, and lawyers are other examples of service entities.

We now shift gears and focus on merchandising operations like **Target** stores, **Drugstore.com,** and **Best Buy** electronics centers. They earn their revenues by selling products rather than services. These companies are identified by the goods they sell—their *merchandise inventory,* or simply *inventory.*

This chapter demonstrates the central role of inventory in a business that sells merchandise. **Inventory** includes all goods that the company owns and expects to sell in the normal course of operations. We illustrate accounting for the purchase and sale of inventory, and we also illustrate how to adjust and close the books of a merchandiser. The chapter covers two ratios investors and creditors use to evaluate companies. Before launching into merchandising, let's compare service entities, with which you are familiar, to merchandising companies.

INVENTORY. All the goods that the company owns and expects to sell in the normal course of operations.

Chapters 1–4 have used both service entities and merchandisers to illustrate key accounting concepts. Chapter 5 jumps into the world of merchandising with both feet. As you make this transition, the following summarized financial statements will show how the two types of companies are similar and different. Observe that Merchandising Co.'s income statement reports Sales Revenue, Cost of Goods Sold, and Gross Profit. Merchandising Co.'s balance sheet reports Inventory. Service Co. reports none of these items. All the new merchandising items are italicized for easy reference.

SERVICE CO.* Income Statement Year Ended June 30, 20XX		MERCHANDISING CO.** Income Statement Year Ended June 30, 20XX	
Service revenue	$XXX →	*Sales* revenue......................	$XXX
Expenses:		*Cost of goods sold*	X
Salary expense	X	*Gross profit*	XX
Depreciation expense	X	Operating *expenses:*	
Income tax expense	X	Salary expense	X
Net income.......................	$ X	Depreciation expense...	X
		Income tax expense	$ X
		Net income......................	$ X
*Such as Gay Gillen eTravel		**Such as Target Corporation	

SERVICE CO. Balance Sheet June 30, 20XX		MERCHANDISING CO. Balance Sheet June 30, 20XX	
Assets		**Assets**	
Current assets:		Current assets:	
Cash..................................	$X	Cash	$X
Short-term investments	X	Short-term investments	X
Accounts receivable, net	X	Accounts receivable, net	X
Prepaid expenses................	X	*Inventory*	X
		Prepaid expenses................	X

WHAT ARE MERCHANDISING OPERATIONS?

Objective 1
Use sales and gross profit to evaluate a company

EXHIBIT 5-1
A Leading Merchandiser's Income Statement

 DAILY EXERCISE 5-1

DAILY EXERCISE 5-2

DAILY EXERCISE 5-3

Exhibit 5-1 shows the income statement of **Target Corporation**. The six highlighted items are unique to merchandisers.

TARGET CORPORATION Income Statement (Adapted) Year Ended January 31, 2000	
	Millions
Net sales revenue [same as Net sales]	$33,212
Cost of goods sold [same as Cost of sales]	23,029
Gross profit [same as Gross margin]...	10,183
Selling, general, and administrative expenses............................	7,490
Depreciation expense	854
Interest expense...	393
Other expenses, net..	302
Total operating expenses	$ 9,039
Net earnings [same as Net income]	$ 1,144

Sales Revenue, Cost of Goods Sold, and Gross Profit

The amount that a business earns from selling merchandise inventory is called **sales revenue,** often abbreviated as **sales.** (**Net sales** equals sales revenue minus any returns and discounts.) The major revenue of a merchandising entity is sales revenue, which results from delivering inventory to customers. The major expense of a merchandiser is **cost of goods sold,** also called **cost of sales.** It represents the entity's cost of the goods (the inventory) sold to customers.

While the inventory is held by a business, the inventory is an asset. When the inventory is sold, the inventory's cost becomes an expense to the seller. When Target sells you a shirt, the shirt's cost is expensed as cost of goods sold on Target's books.

SALES REVENUE. The amount that a merchandiser earns from selling its inventory. Also called **sales.**

NET SALES. Sales revenue less sales discounts and sales returns and allowances.

COST OF GOODS SOLD. The cost of the inventory that the business has sold to customers. Also called **cost of sales.**

Net sales revenue minus cost of goods sold is called **gross profit** or **gross margin**.

GROSS PROFIT. Excess of net sales revenue over cost of goods sold. Also called **gross margin**.

Net sales revenue (abbreviated as Sales)	−	Cost of goods sold (same as Cost of sales)	=	Gross profit (same as Gross margin)

or, more simply,

Sales − Cost of sales = Gross profit

Gross profit is a measure of business success. A sufficiently high gross profit is vital to a merchandiser. Target's operations were quite successful during the year ended January 31, 2000. Target's gross profit was over $10 billion.

The following example will clarify the nature of gross profit. Suppose Target's cost to purchase a man's shirt is $30 and Target sells the shirt for $50. Target's gross profit per shirt is $20, computed as follows:

Sales revenue earned by selling one shirt........	$50
Less: Cost of goods sold for the shirt	
(what the shirt cost Target)	(30)
Gross profit on the sale of one shirt.................	$20

The gross profit reported on Target Corporation's income statement, $10,183 million, is the sum of the gross profits on all the shirts and other products the company sold during its fiscal year.

The Operating Cycle of a Merchandising Business

A merchandising entity buys inventory, sells the goods to customers, and uses the cash to purchase more inventory and repeat the cycle. Exhibit 5-2 diagrams the operating cycle for *cash sales* and for *sales on account*.

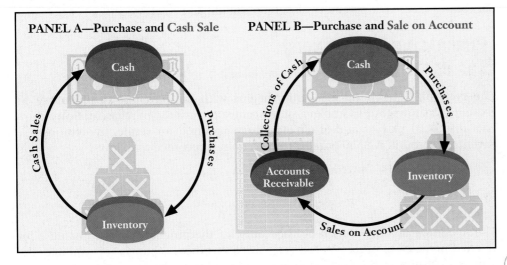

EXHIBIT 5-2
Operating Cycle of a Merchandiser

For a cash sale—Panel A—the cycle is from cash to inventory, and back to cash. For a sale on account—Panel B—the cycle is from cash to inventory to accounts receivabfle and back to cash. In all lines of business, managers try to shorten the cycle in order to keep assets active. The faster the sale of inventory and the collection of cash, the higher the profits.

Inventory Systems: Perpetual and Periodic

There are two main types of inventory accounting systems:

- the periodic system
- the perpetual system

The **periodic inventory system** is used by businesses that sell relatively inexpensive goods. A grocery store without optical-scanning cash registers does not keep a

PERIODIC INVENTORY SYSTEM. An inventory accounting system in which the business does not keep a continuous record of the inventory on hand. Instead, at the end of the period the business makes a physical count of the on-hand inventory and uses this information to prepare the financial statements.

daily running record of every loaf of bread and every can of pineapple that it sells. The cost of recordkeeping would be overwhelming. Instead, grocers count their inventory periodically—at least once a year—to determine the quantities on hand. The inventory amounts are used to prepare the annual financial statements. Businesses such as restaurants and small retail stores also use the periodic inventory system. The end-of-chapter appendix covers this system, which is becoming less popular as more businesses keep their inventory records by computer.

PERPETUAL INVENTORY SYSTEM. The accounting inventory system in which the business keeps a running record of inventory and cost of goods sold.

Under the **perpetual inventory system,** the business maintains a running record of inventory and cost of goods sold. This system achieves control over expensive goods such as automobiles, jewelry, and furniture. The loss of one item would be significant, and this justifies the cost of a perpetual system. Computers increase a company's ability to control its merchandise. But even under a perpetual system, the business counts inventory on hand at least once a year. The physical count establishes the correct amount of ending inventory and serves as a check on the perpetual records.

The following chart compares the periodic and perpetual systems:

PERPETUAL INVENTORY SYSTEM
- Keeps a running record of all goods bought and sold.
- Inventory counted at least once a year.
- Used for all types of goods.

PERIODIC INVENTORY SYSTEM
- Does *not* keep a running record of all goods bought and sold.
- Inventory counted at least once a year.
- Used for *inexpensive* goods.

Computerized Inventory Systems

A computerized inventory system can keep accurate, up-to-date records of the number of units purchased, the number of units sold, and the quantities on hand. Inventory systems are often integrated with accounts receivable and sales. For example, Target's computers keep up-to-the-minute records, so managers can call up current inventory information at any time. In a perpetual system, the "cash register" at a Target store is a computer terminal that records the sale and also updates inventory records. Bar codes are scanned by a laser as part of the perpetual inventory system. The lines of the bar coding represent coded data that keep track of each item. Because most businesses use bar codes, we base our inventory discussions on the perpetual system.[1]

PURCHASING MERCHANDISE: THE PERPETUAL INVENTORY SYSTEM

Objective 2
Account for the purchase and sale of inventory

The cycle of a merchandising entity begins with the purchase of inventory, as Exhibit 5-2 shows. For example, a stereo center records the purchase of **Sony** compact disc (CD) players and other inventory acquired for resale, by debiting the Inventory account. A $500 purchase on account is recorded as follows:

June 14	Inventory...	500	
	Accounts Payable		500
	Purchased inventory on account.		

The Inventory account should be used only for the purchases of merchandise for resale. Purchases of other assets are recorded in other accounts. For example, the purchase of supplies is debited to Supplies, not to Inventory.

The Purchase Invoice: A Basic Business Document

Business documents give tangible evidence of transactions. In this section, we trace the steps that **Austin Sound Center,** in Austin, Texas, takes to order, receive, and pay for inventory. Many companies buy and sell their goods electronically—with no invoices, no checks, and so on. Here we use actual documents to illustrate what takes place behind the scenes.

---

[1]For instructors who prefer to concentrate on the periodic inventory system, an overview starts on page 188 and a comprehensive treatment of that system begins on page 211. Follow Appendix Objectives A2–A5 instead of Chapter Objectives 2 through 4.

1. Suppose Austin Sound wants to stock **JVC** brand CD players and speakers. Austin Sound prepares a *purchase order* and faxes it to JVC.
2. On receipt of the purchase order, JVC's computer scans its warehouse for the inventory that Austin Sound ordered. JVC ships the equipment and sends the invoice to Austin the same day. The **invoice** is the seller's request for cash from the purchaser. It is also called the *bill*.
3. Often the purchaser receives the invoice before the inventory arrives. Austin Sound does not pay immediately. Instead, Austin waits until the inventory arrives in order to ensure that it is the correct type and quantity ordered, and in good condition. After the inventory is inspected and approved, Austin Sound pays JVC the invoice amount.

> **INVOICE.** A seller's request for cash from the purchaser.

Exhibit 5-3 is an updated copy of an actual invoice from JVC to Austin Sound Center.

- From Austin Sound's perspective, this document is a *purchase invoice*.
- To JVC, it is a *sales invoice*.

EXHIBIT 5-3 An Invoice

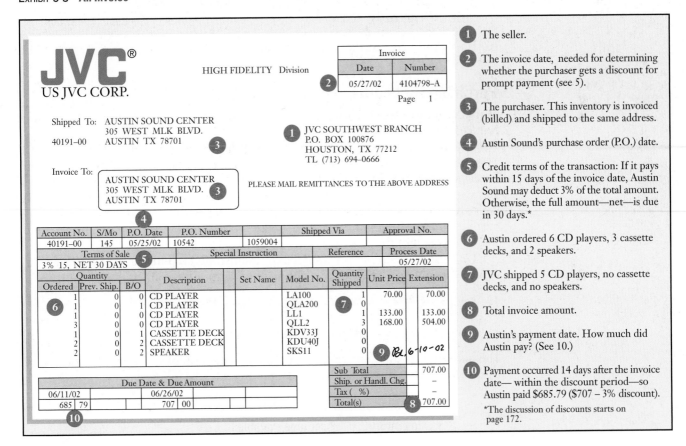

Purchase Returns and Allowances

Most businesses allow their customers to *return* merchandise that is defective, damaged in shipment, or otherwise unsuitable. But if the buyer chooses to keep the damaged goods, the seller may deduct an *allowance* from the amount the buyer owes. Both purchase returns and purchase allowances decrease the amount that the buyer must pay the seller.

Suppose the $70 CD player purchased by Austin Sound (top line of section 6 in Exhibit 5-3) was not the CD player Austin ordered. Austin returns the merchandise to the seller and records the purchase return as follows:

June 3	Accounts Payable	70.00	
	Inventory		70.00
	Returned inventory to seller.		

Now assume that one of the CD players was damaged in shipment to Austin Sound. The damage is minor, and Austin decides to keep the CD player in exchange for a $10 allowance from JVC. To record this purchase allowance, Austin Sound makes this entry:

June 4	Accounts Payable...........................	10.00	
	Inventory		10.00
	Received a purchase allowance.		

The return and the allowance have two effects:

1. They decrease Austin Sound's liability, which is why we debit Accounts Payable.
2. They decrease Austin Sound's net cost of the goods, so we credit Inventory.

Assume that Austin Sound has not yet paid its debt to JVC. After the return ($70) and the allowance ($10) transactions are posted, Austin Sound's accounts will show these balances:

<table>
<tr><td colspan="2">INVENTORY</td><td colspan="2"></td><td colspan="2">ACCOUNTS PAYABLE</td><td colspan="2"></td></tr>
<tr><td>May 27</td><td>707.00</td><td>June 3</td><td>70.00</td><td>June 3</td><td>70.00</td><td>May 27</td><td>707.00</td></tr>
<tr><td></td><td></td><td>June 4</td><td>10.00</td><td>June 4</td><td>10.00</td><td></td><td></td></tr>
<tr><td>Bal.</td><td>627.00</td><td></td><td></td><td></td><td></td><td>Bal.</td><td>627.00</td></tr>
</table>

Austin Sound's cost of the *inventory* is $627, and Austin Sound owes JVC $627 on *account payable*.

Purchase Discounts

Many businesses also offer their customers purchase discounts. A purchase discount reduces the cost of inventory.

JVC's credit terms of 3% 15, NET 30 DAYS can also be expressed as 3/15 n/30. This means that Austin Sound may deduct 3% of the total debt if Austin pays within 15 days of the invoice date. Otherwise, the full amount—NET—is due in 30 days. Terms of simply n/30 mean that no discount is offered and that payment is due 30 days after the invoice date. Terms of *eom* mean that payment is due at the end of the current month. But a purchase after the 25th of the month can be paid at the end of the following month.

Let's use the Exhibit 5-3 transaction to illustrate accounting for a purchase discount. Austin Sound records this purchase on account as follows:

May 27	Inventory...	707.00	
	Accounts Payable		707.00
	Purchased inventory on account.		

The accounting equation shows that a credit purchase of inventory increases both assets (Inventory) and liabilities (Accounts Payable), as follows:

ASSETS	=	LIABILITIES	+	OWNER'S EQUITY
Inventory	=	Accounts Payable		
$707	=	$707	+	0

Austin Sound paid within the discount period, so its cash payment entry is

June 10	Accounts Payable...........................	707.00	
	Cash ($707.00 × 0.97)..........		685.79
	Inventory ($707.00 × 0.03)..		21.21
	Paid within discount period.		

After paying the account, Austin Sound's assets and liabilities both decrease, as follows:

	ASSETS			=	LIABILITIES	+	OWNER'S EQUITY
	Cash	+	Inventory	=	Accounts Payable		
	−$685.29		−$21.21	=	−$707	+	0
		−$707					

Side margin notes:

DAILY EXERCISE 5-4

DAILY EXERCISE 5-5

DAILY EXERCISE 5-6

DAILY EXERCISE 5-7

Note the credit to Inventory. After Austin Sound has taken its discount, this inventory costs Austin Sound $685.79 ($707.00 – Purchase discount of $21.21), as shown in the Inventory account:

INVENTORY			
May 27	707.00	June 10	21.21
Bal.	685.79		

But if Austin Sound pays this invoice after the discount period, it must pay the full amount of $707. In that case, the payment entry is

June 29   Accounts Payable 707.00
                  Cash 707.00
          Paid after discount period.

INVENTORY		
May 27	707 .00	

WORK IT OUT

On September 15, Austin Sound purchases $1,000 of merchandise on account, with terms 2/10, n/30. Austin returns $100 of merchandise for credit on September 20, then makes payment in full on September 25. Journalize these transactions.

Answer: Three separate journal entries are needed here. The initial purchase entry is

Purchase: Sep. 15   Inventory 1,000
                              Accounts Payable   1,000

The second entry records the return of inventory, as follows:

Return: Sep. 20   Accounts Payable 100
                            Inventory   100

The third entry records the payment of $882, as follows: Original amount, $1,000, minus the $100 return equals the net payable of $900. Now subtract the 2% discount ($900 × 0.02 = $18) to arrive at the final payment of $882.

Payment: Sep. 25   Accounts Payable 900
                              Cash   882
                              Inventory   18

Transportation Cost: Who Pays?

The transportation cost of moving inventory from seller to buyer can be significant. The purchase agreement specifies FOB terms to indicate who pays the shipping charges. *FOB* means *free on board*. FOB governs (1) when legal title to the goods passes from seller to buyer, and (2) who pays the freight.

- Under FOB *shipping point* terms, title passes when the inventory leaves the seller's place of businesss—the shipping point. The buyer owns the goods while they are in transit and therefore the buyer pays the transportation cost.
- Under FOB *destination* terms, title passes when the goods reach the destination, so the seller pays the transportation cost.

Exhibit 5-4 summarizes FOB terms.

EXHIBIT 5-4
FOB Terms

Factors to Consider	FOB Shipping Point	FOB Destination
When does the title to the goods pass to the buyer?	At the shipping point	At the destination
Who pays the transportation cost?	Buyer	Seller

FREIGHT IN FOB shipping point terms are most common, so the buyer generally pays the freight. A freight cost that the buyer pays on an inventory purchase is called *freight in.* In accounting, the cost of an asset includes all costs incurred to bring the asset to its intended use. For inventory, cost therefore includes the

- *Net cost* after all discounts and returns have been subtracted, plus
- *Freight* (transportation, or shipping) costs to be paid

To record the payment for freight in, the buyer debits Inventory and credits Cash or Accounts Payable for the amount. Suppose Austin Sound receives a $60 shipping bill directly from the freight company. Austin Sound's entry to record payment of the freight charge is

June 1	Inventory..	60	
	Cash		60
	Paid a freight bill.		

The freight charge increases the final cost of the inventory to $687, as follows:

INVENTORY					
May 27	Purchase	707.00	**June 3**	Return	70.00
June 1	Freight	60.00	**June 4**	Allowance	10.00
Bal.	Net cost	687.00			

Any discounts would be computed only on the account payable to the seller, not on the transportation costs, because the freight company offers no discount.

Under FOB shipping point terms, the seller sometimes prepays the transportation cost as a convenience and lists this cost on the invoice. The buyer debits Inventory for the combined cost of the inventory and the shipping cost because both costs apply to the merchandise. A $5,000 purchase of goods, coupled with a related freight charge of $400, would be recorded as follows:

March 12	Inventory..	5,400	
	Accounts Payable		5,400
	Purchased on account including freight.		

If the buyer pays within the discount period, the discount will be computed on the $5,000 merchandise cost, not on the $5,400. For example, a 2% discount would be $100 ($5,000 × 0.02).

FREIGHT OUT The cost of freight charges paid to ship goods sold to customers is called *freight out.* Freight out is delivery expense paid by the seller. Delivery expense is an operating expense for the seller. It is debited to the Delivery Expense account.

WORK IT OUT This Work It Out example is exactly like the preceding one, but with freight in added to illustrate the accounting for shipping cost. On September 15, Austin Sound purchased $1,000 of merchandise, with *$80 freight added,* for an invoice total of $1,080. Austin returns $100 of the goods for credit on September 20 and pays the account payable in full on September 25. Journalize these transactions.

Answer

Purchase:	Sept. 15	Inventory ($1,000 + $80).....................................	1,080	
		Accounts Payable		1,080
Return:	Sept. 20	Accounts Payable	100	
		Inventory		100
Payment:	Sept. 25	Accounts Payable ($1,080 − $100).....................	980	
		Inventory [($1,000 − $100) × 0.02]..........		18
		Cash ($1,000 + $80 − $100 − $18)...........		962

The buyer does *not* get a discount on the cost of freight in.

Detailed Accounting for Purchase Returns and Allowances, Discounts, and Transportation Costs

Some businesses keep detailed records of purchase returns and allowances, discounts, and transportation costs. For example, Austin Sound receives defective CD players from an off-brand manufacturer. In recording purchase returns, Austin Sound can credit a special account, Purchase Returns and Allowances, which serves as a running record of defective merchandise.

The Purchase Returns and Allowances account carries a credit balance and is a contra account to Inventory. Freight In can be debited for transportation costs. Then, for reporting on the financial statements, these accounts can be combined with the Inventory account to determine the total cost of inventory (amounts assumed):

Inventory		$35,000
Less: Purchase discounts	$(700)	
Purchase returns and allowances	(800)	(1,500)
Net purchases of inventory		33,500
Freight in		2,100
Total cost of inventory		$35,600

SELLING INVENTORY AND RECORDING COST OF GOODS SOLD

After a company buys inventory, the next step in the operating cycle is to sell the goods. We shift now to the selling side and follow **Austin Sound Center** through a sequence of selling transactions. A sale earns a reward, Sales Revenue. A sale also requires a sacrifice in the form of an expense, Cost of Goods Sold, as the seller gives up the asset Inventory.

After making a sale on account, Austin Sound may experience any of the following:

- A sales return: The customer may return goods to Austin Sound.
- A sales allowance: Austin Sound may grant a sales allowance to reduce the amount of cash collected from the customer.
- A sales discount: If the customer pays within the discount period—under terms such as 2/10 n/30—Austin Sound collects the discounted amount.
- Freight out: Austin Sound may have to pay delivery expense to transport the goods to the buyer's location.

Let's begin with a cash sale.

Cash Sale

Sales of retailers, such as grocery stores and restaurants, are often for cash. Cash sales of $3,000 would be recorded by debiting Cash and crediting Sales Revenue as follows:

Jan. 9	Cash	3,000	
	Sales Revenue		3,000
	Cash sale.		

To update the inventory records, the business also must decrease the Inventory balance. Suppose these goods cost the seller $1,900. An accompanying entry is needed to transfer the $1,900 cost of the goods—not their selling price of $3,000—from the Inventory account to Cost of Goods Sold as follows:

Jan. 9	Cost of Goods Sold	1,900	
	Inventory		1,900
	Recorded the cost of goods sold.		

← The recording of cost of goods sold along with sales revenue is an example of the matching principle (Chapter 3, p. 86).

Cost of goods sold (also called cost of sales) is the largest single expense of most merchandisers. ➡ The Cost of Goods Sold account keeps a current balance throughout the period as transactions are journalized and posted.

After posting, the Cost of Goods Sold account holds the cost of the merchandise sold ($1,900 in this case):

INVENTORY		COST OF GOODS SOLD	
Purchases 50,000 (amount assumed)	Jan. 9 1,900	Jan. 9	1,900

The computer automatically records the cost of goods sold entry when the cashier keys in the code number of the inventory that is sold. Optical scanners perform this task in most stores.

Sale on Account

Most sales in the United States are made on account (on credit). A $5,000 sale on account is recorded by a debit to Accounts Receivable and a credit to Sales Revenue, as follows:

Jan. 11	Accounts Receivable............................	5,000	
	Sales Revenue............................		5,000
	Sale on account.		

If we assume that these goods cost the seller $2,900, the accompanying cost of goods sold entry is

Jan. 11	Cost of Goods Sold..............................	2,900	
	Inventory		2,900
	Recorded the cost of goods sold.		

When the cash comes in, the seller records the related cash receipt on account as follows:

Jan. 19	Cash...	5,000	
	Accounts Receivable		5,000
	Collection on account.		

Offering Sales Discounts and Sales Returns and Allowances

We just saw that purchase purchase returns and allowances and purchase discounts decrease the cost of inventory purchases. In the same way, **sales returns and allowances** and **sales discounts,** which are contra accounts to Sales Revenue, decrease the net amount of revenue earned on sales.

SALES RETURNS AND ALLOWANCES. Decreases in the seller's receivable from a customer's return of merchandise or from granting the customer an allowance from the amount owed to the seller. A contra account to Sales Revenue.

SALES DISCOUNT. Reduction in the amount receivable from a customer, offered by the seller as an incentive for the customer to pay promptly. A contra account to Sales Revenue.

Credit-balance account		Debit-balance accounts			Credit subtotal (*not* a separate account)
Sales Revenue	−	Sales Returns and Allowances	−	Sales Discounts =	Net sales revenue[2]

This equation calculates net sales. Note that sales discounts can be given on both goods and services.

Companies keep close watch on their customers' paying habits and on their own sales of defective and unsuitable merchandise. They maintain separate accounts for Sales Discounts and Sales Returns and Allowances. Now let's examine a sequence of JVC sale transactions. Assume **JVC** is selling to Austin Sound.

On July 7, JVC sells stereo components for $7,200 on credit terms of 2/10 n/30. These goods cost JVC $4,700. JVC's entries to record this credit sale and the related cost of the goods sold are

July 7	Accounts Receivable.................................	7,200	
	Sales Revenue.................................		7,200
	Sale on account.		
July 7	Cost of Goods Sold	4,700	
	Inventory		4,700
	Recorded the cost of goods sold.		

[2]Often abbreviated as Net sales.

Assume that the buyer returns goods that sold for $600. JVC records the sales return and the related decrease in Accounts Receivable as follows:

July 12	Sales Returns and Allowances	600	
	Accounts Receivable		600
	Received returned goods.		

JVC receives the returned merchandise and updates the inventory records. JVC must also decrease Cost of Goods Sold as follows (these goods cost JVC $400):

July 12	Inventory	400	
	Cost of Goods Sold..............................		400
	Placed goods back in inventory.		

Suppose JVC grants a $100 sales allowance for damaged goods. Austin Sound then subtracts $100 from the amount it will pay JVC. JVC journalizes this transaction by debiting Sales Returns and Allowances and crediting Accounts Receivable as follows:

July 15	Sales Returns and Allowances	100	
	Accounts Receivable		100
	Granted a sales allowance for damaged goods.		

No inventory entry is needed for a sales allowance transaction because the seller receives no returned goods from the customer. Instead, JVC will simply receive less cash from the customer.

After the preceding entries are posted, all the accounts have up-to-date balances. Accounts Receivable has a $6,500 debit balance, as follows:

ACCOUNTS RECEIVABLE

July 7	Sale	7,200	July 12	Return	600
			15	Allowance	100
Bal.		6,500			

On July 17, the last day of the discount period, JVC collects $4,000 of this receivable. Assume JVC allows customers to take discounts on all amounts JVC receives within the discount period. JVC's cash receipt is $3,920 [$4,000 − ($4,000 × 0.02)], and the collection entry is

July 17	Cash	3,920	
	Sales Discounts ($4,000 × 0.02)	80	
	Accounts Receivable		4,000
	Cash collection within the discount period.		

● DAILY EXERCISE 5-8

● DAILY EXERCISE 5-9

● DAILY EXERCISE 5-10

Suppose that JVC collects the remainder, $2,500, on July 28. That date falls after the discount period, so there is no sales discount. To record this collection on account, JVC makes this entry:

July 28	Cash ($6,500 − $4,000)..............................	2,500	
	Accounts Receivable		2,500
	Cash collection within the discount period.		

Now, JVC's Accounts Receivable balance is zero, as follows:

ACCOUNTS RECEIVABLE

July 7	Sale	7,200	July 12	Return	600
			15	Allowance	100
			17	Collection	4,000
			28	Collection	2,500
Bal.		−0−			

SUMMARY PROBLEM

www.prenhall.com/horngren

Mid-Chapter Assessment

Brun Sales Company engaged in the following transactions during June of the current year:

June 3 Purchased inventory on credit terms of 1/10 net eom (end of month), $1,610.
   9 Returned 40% of the inventory purchased on June 3. It was defective.
   12 Sold goods for cash, $920 (cost, $550).
   15 Purchased goods of $5,000. Credit terms were 3/15 net 30.
   16 Paid a $260 freight bill on goods purchased.
   18 Sold inventory on credit terms of 2/10 n/30, $2,000 (cost, $1,180).
   22 Received damaged goods from the customer of the June 18 sale, $800 (cost, $480).
   24 Borrowed money from the bank to take advantage of the discount offered on the June 15 purchase. Signed a note payable to the bank for the net amount.
   24 Paid supplier for goods purchased on June 15, less the discount.
   28 Received cash in full settlement of the account from the customer who purchased inventory on June 18, less the return on June 22.
   29 Paid the amount owed on account from the purchase of June 3, less the June 9 return.

Required

1. Journalize the preceding transactions. Explanations are not required.
2. Set up T-accounts and post the journal entries to show the ending balances in the Inventory and the Cost of Goods Sold accounts.
3. Assume that the note payable signed on June 24 requires the payment of $95 interest expense. Was borrowing funds to take the cash discount a wise or unwise decision?

Solution

Requirement 1

June 3	Inventory		1,610	
	Accounts Payable			1,610
9	Accounts Payable ($1,610 × 0.40)		644	
	Inventory			644
12	Cash		920	
	Sales Revenue			920
12	Cost of Goods Sold		550	
	Inventory			550
15	Inventory		5,000	
	Accounts Payable			5,000
16	Inventory		260	
	Cash			260
18	Accounts Receivable		2,000	
	Sales Revenue			2,000
18	Cost of Goods Sold		1,180	
	Inventory			1,180
22	Sales Returns and Allowances		800	
	Accounts Receivable			800
22	Inventory		480	
	Cost of Goods Sold			480
24	Cash [$5,000 − 0.03($5,000)]		4,850	
	Note Payable			4,850
24	Accounts Payable		5,000	
	Inventory ($5,000 × 0.03)			150
	Cash ($5,000 × 0.97)			4,850
28	Cash [($2,000 − $800) × 0.98]		1,176	
	Sales Discounts [($2,000 − $800) × 0.02]		24	
	Accounts Receivable ($2,000 − $800)			1,200
29	Accounts Payable ($1,610 − $644)		966	
	Cash			966

Requirement 2

INVENTORY					COST OF GOODS SOLD			
June 3	1,610	June 9	644		June 12	550	June 22	480
15	5,000	12	550		18	1,180		
16	260	18	1,180		Bal.	1,250		
22	480	24	150					
Bal.	4,826							

Requirement 3

The decision to borrow funds was wise because the discount ($150) exceeded the interest paid ($95). Thus the entity was $55 better off as a result of its decision.

ADJUSTING AND CLOSING THE ACCOUNTS OF A MERCHANDISER

Objective 3
Adjust and close the accounts of a merchandising business

A merchandising business adjusts and closes the accounts the same way a service entity does. If a work sheet is used, the trial balance is entered, and the work sheet is completed to determine net income or net loss. The work sheet aids the adjusting and closing processes and helps the accountant prepare the financial statements.

Adjusting Inventory Based on a Physical Count

In theory, the Inventory account stays current at all times. However, the actual amount of inventory on hand may differ from what the books show. Theft losses and damage occur. Accounting errors can require adjustments. For this reason, virtually all businesses, like the bookstore chain **Barnes & Noble,** take a physical count of inventory at least once a year. The most common time for a business to count its inventory is at the end of the fiscal year, before the financial statements are prepared. The business then adjusts the Inventory account on the basis of the physical count.

Exhibit 5-5, **Austin Sound's** trial balance at December 31, 20X2, lists a $40,500 balance for inventory. With no shrinkage—due to theft or error—the business should have on hand inventory costing $40,500. But on December 31, when Charles Ernest, the owner of Austin Sound, counts the merchandise in the store, the total cost of the goods on hand comes to only $40,200. Austin Sound then records the $300 of inventory shrinkage with this adjusting entry:

Dec. 31	Cost of Goods Sold	300	
	Inventory ($40,500 − $40,200)		300

This entry brings Inventory and Cost of Goods Sold to their correct balances. Austin Sound's December 31, 20X2, adjustment data, including the correct inventory information [item (b)], are given at the bottom of Exhibit 5-5 on page 180.

The physical count can indicate that more inventory is present than the books show. Austin Sound may have made a purchase it did not record. This would be entered the standard way: Debit Inventory and credit Cash or Accounts Payable.

If the reason for the excess inventory cannot be identified, the business adjusts the accounts by debiting Inventory and crediting Cost of Goods Sold. To illustrate a merchandiser's adjusting and closing process, let's use Austin Sound's December 31, 20X2, trial balance in Exhibit 5-5. All the new accounts—Inventory, Cost of Goods Sold, and the contra accounts—are highlighted for emphasis.

Additional data at December 31, 20X2.
  a. Interest revenue earned but not yet collected, $400.
  b. Inventory on hand, $40,200.
  c. Supplies on hand, $100.
  d. Prepaid insurance expired during the year, $1,000.
  e. Depreciation, $600.
  f. Unearned sales revenue earned during the year, $1,300.
  g. Accrued wage expense, $400.
  h. Accrued interest expense, $200.

EXHIBIT 5-5   Trial Balance

AUSTIN SOUND CENTER
Trial Balance
December 31, 20X2

Cash	$ 2,850	
Accounts receivable	4,600	
Note receivable, current	8,000	
Interest receivable		
Inventory	40,500	
Supplies	650	
Prepaid insurance	1,200	
Furniture and fixtures	33,200	
Accumulated depreciation		$ 2,400
Accounts payable		47,000
Unearned sales revenue		2,000
Wages payable		
Interest payable		
Note payable, long-term		12,600
C. Ernest, capital		25,900
C. Ernest, withdrawals	54,100	
Sales revenue		168,000
Sales discounts	1,400	
Sales returns and allowances	2,000	
Interest revenue		600
Cost of goods sold	90,500	
Wage expense	9,800	
Rent expense	8,400	
Depreciation expense		
Insurance expense		
Supplies expense		
Interest expense	1,300	
Total	$258,500	$258,500

➡ This work sheet is slightly different from the one introduced in the Chapter 4 acetates following p. 130—it contains four pairs of columns, not five.

Preparing and Using the Work Sheet

The Exhibit 5-6 work sheet is similar to the work sheets we have seen so far, but there are a few differences. This work sheet does not include adjusted trial balance columns. ◄ In most accounting systems, a single operation combines trial balance amounts with the adjustments and extends the adjusted balances directly to the income statement and balance sheet columns. Therefore, to reduce clutter, the adjusted trial balance columns are omitted here.

ACCOUNT TITLE COLUMNS   The trial balance lists a number of accounts without balances. Ordinarily, these accounts are affected by the adjusting process. Examples include Interest Receivable, Wages Payable, and Depreciation Expense. The accounts are listed in the order they appear in the ledger. If additional accounts are needed, they can be entered at the bottom of the work sheet, above net income.

TRIAL BALANCE COLUMNS   Examine the Inventory account in the trial balance. Inventory has a balance of $40,500 before the physical count at the end of the year. Cost of Goods Sold's balance is $90,500 before any adjustment. Any difference between the Inventory amount on the trial balance ($40,500) and the correct amount based on the physical count ($40,200) is unexplained and should be debited or credited to Cost of Goods Sold.

EXHIBIT 5-6   Accounting Work Sheet

AUSTIN SOUND CENTER
Accounting Work Sheet
Year Ended December 31, 20X2

Account Title	Trial Balance Debit	Trial Balance Credit	Adjustments Debit		Adjustments Credit		Income Statement Debit	Income Statement Credit	Balance Sheet Debit	Balance Sheet Credit
Cash	2,850								2,850	
Accounts receivable	4,600								4,600	
Note receivable, current	8,000								8,000	
Interest receivable			(a)	400					400	
Inventory	**40,500**				(b)	**300**			40,200	
Supplies	650				(c)	550			100	
Prepaid insurance	1,200				(d)	1,000			200	
Furniture and fixtures	33,200								33,200	
Accumulated depreciation		2,400			(e)	600				3,000
Accounts payable		47,000								47,000
Unearned sales revenue		2,000	(f)	1,300						700
Wages payable					(g)	400				400
Interest payable					(h)	200				200
Note payable, long-term		12,600								12,600
C. Ernest, capital		25,900								25,900
C. Ernest, withdrawals	54,100								54,100	
Sales revenue		168,000			(f)	1,300		169,300		
Sales discounts	1,400						1,400			
Sales returns and allowances	2,000						2,000			
Interest revenue		600			(a)	400		1,000		
Cost of goods sold	**90,500**		(b)	**300**			90,800			
Wage expense	9,800		(g)	400			10,200			
Rent expense	8,400						8,400			
Depreciation expense			(e)	600			600			
Insurance expense			(d)	1,000			1,000			
Supplies expense			(c)	550			550			
Interest expense	1,300		(h)	200			1,500			
	258,500	258,500	4,750		4,750		116,450	170,300	143,650	89,800
Net income							53,850			53,850
							170,300	170,300	143,650	143,650

DAILY EXERCISE 5-11

ADJUSTMENTS COLUMNS   The adjustments are similar to those discussed in Chapters 3 and 4. The adjustments may be entered in any order desired. The debit amount of each entry should equal the credit amount, and total debits should equal total credits. You should review the adjusting data in Exhibit 5-5 to reassure yourself that the adjustments are correct.

INCOME STATEMENT COLUMNS   The income statement columns on the work sheet in Exhibit 5-6 contain adjusted amounts for the revenues and the expenses. Sales Revenue, for example, has an adjusted balance of $169,300.

The income statement column subtotals indicate whether the business had a net income or a net loss.

• Net income: Total credits > Total debits   • Net loss: Total debits > Total credits

Austin Sound's total credits of $170,300 exceed the total debits of $116,450, so the company earned a net income.

Insert the *net income* amount in the debit column to bring total debits into agreement with total credits. Insert a *net loss* amount in the credit column to equalize total debits and total credits. Net income or net loss is then extended to the opposite column of the balance sheet.

BALANCE-SHEET COLUMNS The only new item in the balance sheet columns is Inventory. The balance listed in Exhibit 5-6 is the ending amount of $40,200, as determined by the physical count of goods on hand at the end of the period.

PREPARING THE FINANCIAL STATEMENTS OF A MERCHANDISER

Objective 4
Prepare a merchandiser's financial statements

Exhibit 5-7 presents **Austin Sound's** financial statements.

EXHIBIT 5-7
Financial Statements of Austin Sound Center

⊙ DAILY EXERCISE 5-12

⊙ DAILY EXERCISE 5-13

⊙ DAILY EXERCISE 5-14

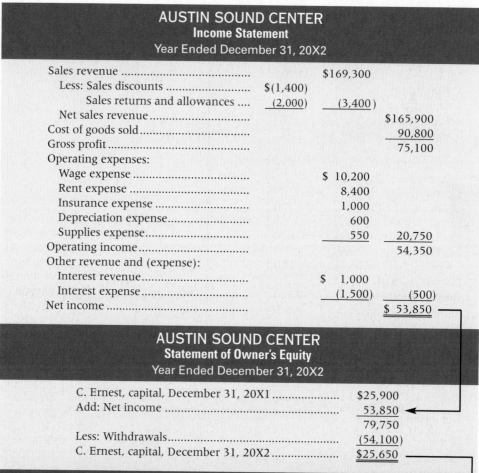

AUSTIN SOUND CENTER
Income Statement
Year Ended December 31, 20X2

Sales revenue		$169,300	
Less: Sales discounts	$(1,400)		
Sales returns and allowances	(2,000)	(3,400)	
Net sales revenue			$165,900
Cost of goods sold			90,800
Gross profit			75,100
Operating expenses:			
Wage expense		$ 10,200	
Rent expense		8,400	
Insurance expense		1,000	
Depreciation expense		600	
Supplies expense		550	20,750
Operating income			54,350
Other revenue and (expense):			
Interest revenue		$ 1,000	
Interest expense		(1,500)	(500)
Net income			$ 53,850

AUSTIN SOUND CENTER
Statement of Owner's Equity
Year Ended December 31, 20X2

C. Ernest, capital, December 31, 20X1	$25,900
Add: Net income	53,850
	79,750
Less: Withdrawals	(54,100)
C. Ernest, capital, December 31, 20X2	$25,650

AUSTIN SOUND CENTER
Balance Sheet
December 31, 20X2

Assets			**Liabilities**		
Current:			Current:		
Cash		$ 2,850	Accounts payable		$47,000
Accounts receivable		4,600	Unearned sales		
Note receivable		8,000	revenue		700
Interest receivable		400	Wages payable		400
Inventory		40,200	Interest payable		200
Prepaid insurance		200	Total current		
Supplies		100	liabilities		48,300
Total current assets		56,350	Long-term:		
Plant:			Note payable		12,600
Furniture and fixtures	$33,200		Total liabilities		60,900
Less: Accumulated					
depreciation	(3,000)	30,200	**Owner's Equity**		
			C. Ernest, capital		25,650
			Total liabilities and		
Total assets		$86,550	owner's equity		$86,550

To solidify your understanding of how the financial statements are prepared, you should trace the amounts in the work sheet (Exhibit 5-6) to the statements in Exhibit 5-7.

INCOME STATEMENT   The income statement reports **operating expenses,** which are those expenses other than cost of goods sold that are incurred in the entity's major line of business. Austin Sound's operating expenses include wage expense, rent, depreciation, insurance, and supplies expense.

OPERATING EXPENSES. Expenses, other than cost of goods sold, that are incurred in the entity's major line of business. Examples include rent, depreciation, salaries, wages, utilities, and supplies expense.

Many companies report their operating expenses in two categories:

- *Selling expenses* are expenses related to marketing the company's products—sales salaries; sales commissions; advertising; depreciation, rent, and utilities on store buildings; and delivery expense.
- *General expenses* include office expenses, such as the salaries of the company president and office employees; depreciation, rent, utilities, and property taxes on the home office building.

Target Corporation (Exhibit 5-1) groups selling, general, and administrative expenses together for reporting on the income statement.

Gross profit minus operating expenses plus any other operating revenues equals **operating income,** or **income from operations.** Many people view operating income as an important indicator of performance because it measures the results of the entity's major ongoing activities.

OPERATING INCOME. Gross profit minus operating expenses plus any other operating revenues. Also called **income from operations.**

The last section of Austin Sound's income statement is **other revenue and expense.** This category reports revenues and expenses that are outside the main operations of the business. Examples include gains and losses on the sale of plant assets (not inventory) and gains and losses on lawsuits. Accountants have traditionally viewed Interest Revenue and Interest Expense as "other" items because they arise from loaning and borrowing money. These financing activities are outside the operating scope of selling merchandise. Target (Exhibit 5-1) lists Interest expense among the operating expenses, also a common practice.

OTHER REVENUE. Revenue that is outside the main operations of a business, such as a gain on the sale of plant assets.

The bottom line of the income statement is net income:

OTHER EXPENSE. Expense that is outside the main operations of a business, such as a loss on the sale of plant assets.

Net income = Total revenues and gains − Total expenses and losses

We often hear the term *bottom line* used to refer to a final result. *Bottom line* originated from the position of net income on the income statement.

STATEMENT OF OWNER'S EQUITY   A merchandiser's statement of owner's equity looks exactly like that of a service business. In fact, you cannot determine whether the entity sells merchandise or services from looking at the statement of owner's equity.

BALANCE SHEET   If the business is a merchandiser, the balance sheet shows inventory as a major current asset. Service businesses usually have no inventory at all or minor amounts of inventory.

Journalizing the Adjusting and Closing Entries

Exhibit 5-8 presents Austin Sound's adjusting entries, which are similar to those you have seen previously, except for the inventory adjustment [entry (b)]. ➔ The closing entries in the exhibit also follow the pattern illustrated in Chapter 4.

The closing entries also close the Cost of Goods Sold expense account. See Chapter 4, pp. 135, 136.

The *first closing entry* debits the revenue accounts for their ending balances. The offsetting credit of $170,300 transfers the sum of total revenues to Income Summary. This amount comes directly from the credit column of the income statement on the work sheet (Exhibit 5-6).

The *second closing entry* includes credits to Cost of Goods Sold, to the contra revenue accounts (Sales Discounts and Sales Returns and Allowances), and to all the expense accounts. The offsetting $116,450 debit to Income Summary represents the amount of total expenses plus the contra revenues, which come from the debit column of the income statement on the work sheet.

The *last two closing entries* close net income from Income Summary to the Capital account and also close the owner Withdrawals into the Capital account.

EXHIBIT 5-8
Adjusting and Closing Entries for
a Merchandiser

DAILY EXERCISE 5-15

DAILY EXERCISE 5-16

Journal

Adjusting Entries

a.	Dec. 31	Interest Receivable..	400	
		Interest Revenue		400
b.	31	Cost of Goods Sold....................................	300	
		Inventory......................................		300
c.	31	Supplies Expense ($650 – $100).................	550	
		Supplies		550
d.	31	Insurance Expense......................................	1,000	
		Prepaid Insurance...........................		1,000
e.	31	Depreciation Expense	600	
		Accumulated Depreciation.................		600
f.	31	Unearned Sales Revenue	1,300	
		Sales Revenue		1,300
g.	31	Wage Expense	400	
		Wages Payable................................		400
h.	31	Interest Expense..	200	
		Interest Payable		200

Closing Entries

1.	Dec. 31	Sales Revenue...	169,300	
		Interest Revenue..	1,000	
		Income Summary..............................		170,300
2.	31	Income Summary	116,450	
		Sales Discounts..............................		1,400
		Sales Returns and Allowances............		2,000
		Cost of Goods Sold		90,800
		Wage Expense		10,200
		Rent Expense		8,400
		Depreciation Expense........................		600
		Insurance Expense...........................		1,000
		Supplies Expense.............................		550
		Interest Expense..............................		1,500
3.	31	Income Summary ($170,300 – $116,450)....	53,850	
		C. Ernest, Capital..............................		53,850
4.	31	C. Ernest, Capital	54,100	
		C. Ernest, Withdrawals........................		54,100

Study Exhibits 5-6, 5-7, and 5-8 carefully because they illustrate the entire end-of-period process that leads to the financial statements.

Here is an easy way to remember the closing process. First, look at the work sheet. Then:

1. Debit all income statement accounts with a credit balance. Credit Income Summary for the total.
2. Credit all income statement accounts with a debit balance. Debit Income Summary for the total.
3. Take the balance in the Income Summary account. A debit balance indicates a net loss; credit Income Summary for that amount, and debit Capital. If Income Summary has a credit balance, there is a net income; debit Income Summary for that amount, and credit Capital.
4. Withdrawals has a debit balance. Credit Withdrawals to close its balance, and debit Capital for the same amount.

Income Statement Formats: Multi-Step and Single-Step

We have seen that the balance sheet appears in two formats:

- the report format (assets on top, . . . , owner's equity at bottom)
- the account format (assets at left, liabilities and owner's equity at right)

→ There are also two basic formats for the income statement:

- the multi-step format
- the single-step format

The multi-step format is by far the more popular.

← For a review of balance sheet formats, see Chapter 4, p. 141.

Multi-Step Income Statement

The **multi-step format** shows subtotals to highlight significant relationships. In addition to net income, it also presents gross profit and income from operations. This format communicates a merchandiser's results of operations especially well because gross profit and income from operations are important to investors. Exhibit 5-1 shows the multi-step format. The income statements presented thus far in this chapter have also been multi-step. Austin Sound's multi-step income statement for the year ended December 31, 20X2, appears in Exhibit 5-7.

MULTI-STEP INCOME STATEMENT. Format that contains subtotals to highlight significant relationships. In addition to net income, it presents gross profit and operating income.

Single-Step Income Statement

The **single-step format** groups all revenues together and then lists and deducts all expenses together without drawing any subtotals. **IBM** and **Wal-Mart** use this format. The single-step format clearly distinguishes revenues from expenses as Exhibit 5-9 shows. This format works well for service entities because they have no gross profit to report.

SINGLE-STEP INCOME STATEMENT. Format that groups all revenues together and then lists and deducts all expenses together without drawing any subtotals.

EXHIBIT 5-9
Single-Step Income Statement

AUSTIN SOUND CENTER	
Income Statement	
Year Ended December 31, 20X2	
Revenues:	
Net sales (net of sales discounts, $1,400, and returns and allowances, $2,000)	$165,900
Interest revenue	1,000
Total revenues	166,900
Expenses:	
Cost of goods sold	90,800
Wage expense	10,200
Rent expense	8,400
Interest expense	1,500
Insurance expense	1,000
Depreciation expense	600
Supplies expense	550
Total expenses	113,050
Net Income	$ 53,850

Most published financial statements are highly condensed. Appendix A at the end of the book gives the income statement of Target Corporation. Of course, condensed statements can be supplemented with desired details.

TWO KEY RATIOS FOR DECISION MAKING

Merchandise inventory is the most important asset for a merchandising business. To manage the firm, owners and managers focus on the best way to sell the inventory. They use several ratios to evaluate operations, among them gross profit percentage and rate of inventory turnover.

Objective 5
Use the gross profit percentage and the inventory turnover ratio to evaluate a business

The Gross Profit Percentage

A key decision-making tool for a merchandiser is related to gross profit, which is net sales minus cost of goods sold. Merchandisers strive to increase the **gross profit percentage,** which is computed as follows:

GROSS PROFIT PERCENTAGE. Gross profit divided by net sales revenue. A measure of profitability. Also called **gross margin percentage.**

$$\text{Gross profit percentage} = \frac{\text{Gross profit}}{\text{Net sales revenue}} = \frac{\$75,100}{\$165,900} = 0.453 = 45.3\%$$

The gross profit percentage (also called the *gross margin percentage*) is one of the most carefully watched measures of profitability. A 45% gross margin means that each dollar of sales generates 45 cents of gross profit. On average, the goods cost the seller 55 cents. For most firms, the gross profit percentage changes little from year to year. A small increase may signal an important rise in income, and vice versa for a decrease.

Exhibit 5-10 compares **Austin Sound's** gross margin to that of both **Target** and **Wal-Mart.**

EXHIBIT 5-10
Gross Profit on $1 of Sales for Three Merchandisers

The Rate of Inventory Turnover

INVENTORY TURNOVER. Ratio of cost of goods sold to average inventory. Measures the number of times a company sells its average level of inventory during a year.

Owners and managers strive to sell inventory as quickly as possible because it generates no profit until it is sold. The faster the sales occur, the higher the income. The slower the sales, the lower the income. Ideally, a business could operate with zero inventory. Most businesses, however, including retailers such as Target and Austin Sound, must keep goods on hand. **Inventory turnover,** the ratio of cost of goods sold to average inventory, indicates how rapidly inventory is sold. It is computed as follows:

$$\frac{\text{Inventory}}{\text{turnover}} = \frac{\text{Cost of goods sold}}{\text{Average inventory}} = \frac{\text{Cost of goods sold}}{(\text{Beginning inventory} + \text{Ending inventory})/2}$$

$$= \frac{\$90,800}{(\$38,600^* + \$40,200)/2} = \frac{\text{2.3 times per year}}{(\text{every 159 days})}$$

*Taken from balance sheet at the end of the preceding period.

○ DAILY EXERCISE 5-17

○ DAILY EXERCISE 5-18

Inventory turnover is usually computed for an annual period, and the relevant cost-of-goods sold figure is the amount for the entire year. Average inventory is computed from the beginning and ending balances. Austin Sound's beginning inventory would be taken from the business's balance sheet at the end of the preceding year. A high turnover rate is preferable, and an increase in the turnover rate usually means higher profits.

Inventory turnover varies from industry to industry. Grocery stores, for example, turn their goods over much faster than automobile dealers do. Drug stores have a higher turnover rate than furniture stores. Retailers of electronic products, such as Austin Sound, have an average turnover of 3.6 times per year. A turnover rate of 2.3 times per year suggests that Austin Sound is not very successful. Exhibit 5-11 compares the inventory turnover rate of Austin Sound, Target, and Wal-Mart Stores.

Varsitybooks.com: A Textbook Case on the Fulfillment Cost Conundrum

Order the fifth edition of *Accounting* from **Varsitybooks.com** and the company arranges for **Baker & Taylor**—book distributors—to ship it to you immediately. Varsitybooks doesn't have a warehouse or any inventory, but it does have to pay Baker & Taylor for this convenient arrangement. How does the fledgling dot.com account for these costs?

As you know from personal experience, e-commerce has revolutionized business. It has bent certain accounting rules in the process. One such rule is that the cost of goods sold to customers is usually considered the "cost of goods sold." Yet, on-line powerhouses like Amazon.com and eToys, Inc. count some of this cost as "sales and marketing expenses because they never own the inventory." By listing these "fulfillment costs" as marketing expense, new-age companies don't have to subtract the costs from their gross profit. This seemed like a good idea to Varsitybooks, and its managers announced to their auditor, **KPMG**, that they wanted to do the same.

After all, Varsitybooks argued, mail-order companies have always done this. And the practice would allow the new agers to keep from reporting razor-thin profit margins. For instance, if the SEC tightens the rules and makes Amazon.com account for fulfillment cost as "cost of sales," gross profit margins for the last quarter of 1999 would go from 15% to −3%.

Small wonder that this approach is controversial! Varsitybooks.com fired KPMG when the auditors objected to it. They hired **PricewaterhouseCoopers** instead, but in the end Varsitybooks had to follow the traditional accounting procedures anyway. The auditors knew best after all.

Source: Based on Shannon Henry, "An E-Tail Identity Crisis," *The Washington Post,* May 4, 2000, p. E01. Anonymous, "Web Retailers' "Gross Profit" Questioned; E-commerce; The SEC may make some firms account for distribution costs, possibly turning their profits into losses," *The Los Angeles Times,* February 19, 2000, p. 2.

Exhibits 5-10 and 5-11 tell an interesting story. Wal-Mart sells a lot of inventory at a low gross profit percentage. Wal-Mart earns its profits by turning its inventory over rapidly—7.0 times during the year. Target sells slightly more upscale merchandise and therefore turns its inventory over only 6.3 times per year.

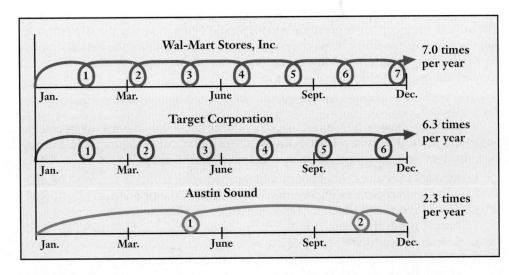

EXHIBIT 5-11
Rate of Inventory Turnover for Three Merchandisers

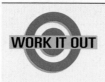

WORK IT OUT

Calculate the rate of inventory turnover for **Safeway, Inc.,** the large grocery chain (amounts in millions).

Beginning inventory..............	$ 1,856
Ending inventory...................	2,445
Cost of goods sold.................	20,349

Answer

$$\text{Inventory turnover} = \frac{\text{Cost of goods sold}}{(\text{Beginning inventory} + \text{Ending inventory})/2}$$

$$= \frac{\$20,349}{(\$1,856 + \$2,445)/2} = \textbf{9.5 times per year}$$

THE PERIODIC SYSTEM: MEASURING COST OF GOODS SOLD AND INVENTORY PURCHASES

Objective 6
Compute cost of goods sold

The perpetual inventory accounting system we have illustrated provides up-to-date records of inventory and cost of goods sold. That system aids both day-to-day decisions and the preparation of the financial statements. However, managers have other information needs that the perpetual system does not meet. For example, buyers for **Target** and **Austin Sound** must know how much inventory to purchase in order to reach their sales goals.

Computation of cost of goods sold from the periodic inventory system helps managers determine how much inventory to purchase. This alternative computation is used so often in accounting that your education would be incomplete without it. (The appendix at the end of the chapter covers the periodic inventory system in more detail.)

EXHIBIT 5-12
Measuring Austin Sound's Cost of Goods Sold in the Periodic Inventory System

Beginning inventory....................................	$ 38,600
+ **Net purchases**...	87,200*
+ Freight in	5,200
= Cost of goods available for sale..................	131,000
− Ending inventory.......................................	(40,200)
= Cost of goods sold	$ 90,800
*Computation of **Net purchases**:	
Purchases...	$ 91,400
− Purchase discounts	(3,000)
− Purchase returns and allowances	(1,200)
= Net purchases	$ 87,200

DAILY EXERCISE 5-19

DAILY EXERCISE 5-20

DAILY EXERCISE 5-21

NET PURCHASES. Purchases less purchase discounts and purchase returns and allowances.

Exhibit 5–12 gives the alternative computation of Austin Sound's cost of goods sold for 20X2. Austin Sound began the year with inventory of $38,600. During the year, it purchased more goods, also paying freight charges. Note that **net purchases** equals purchases minus purchase discounts and purchase returns and allowances. The sum of these amounts make up Austin Sound's cost of goods available for sale. Subtract ending inventory, and the result is cost of goods sold for the period. Exhibit 5–13 diagrams the alternative computation of cost of goods sold, with Austin Sound Center's amounts used for the illustration.

The Decision Guidelines feature summarizes some key decisions of a merchandising business.

One such decision is how much inventory the business should purchase in order to achieve its goals. Here is how Charles Ernest, the owner of Austin Sound, would decide how much inventory to buy (all numbers are taken from Exhibit 5-12):

1.	Managers predict Cost of goods sold for the period......................	$ 90,800
2.	Managers predict Ending inventory at the end of the period........	40,200
3.	Cost of goods available for sale = Sum of Ending inventory + Cost of goods sold	131,000
4.	Subtract the period's beginning inventory	(38,200)
5.	The difference is the amount of inventory to purchase (including Freight in) during the coming year	$ 92,000

Exhibit 5-13 Relationship Between the Inventory Account and Cost of Goods Sold in the Periodic Inventory System (Amounts for Austin Sound)

INVENTORY			
Beginning balance	38,600		
Net purchases	87,200		
Freight in	5,200	Cost of goods sold	90,800
Ending balance	40,200		

This T-account shows that the *perpetual* and the *periodic* inventory systems compute the same amounts for ending inventory and for cost of goods sold:

- The *perpetual* system accumulates the balances of Inventory and Cost of Goods Sold throughout the period.
- The *periodic* system determines the correct amounts for Inventory and Cost of Goods Sold only at the end of the period.

Source: The authors thank Betsy Willis for suggesting this exhibit.

DECISION GUIDELINES

Merchandising Operations and the Accounting Cycle

DECISION	GUIDELINES
How do merchandising operations differ from service operations?	• Merchandisers buy and sell *merchandise inventory* • Service entities perform a *service*.
How do a merchandiser's financial statements differ from the financial statements of a service business?	**Balance sheet:** • Merchandiser has *inventory,* an asset. • Service business has no inventory.

Income Statement:

Merchandiser		*Service Business*	
Sales revenue	$ XXX	Service revenue......................	$XX
− Cost of goods sold................	(X)	− Operating expenses	(X)
= Gross profit	XX	= Net income.........................	$ X
− Operating expenses..............	(X)		
= Net income	$ X		

Statements of Owner's Equity:	No difference
Which type of inventory system to use?	• *Perpetual system* shows the amount of *inventory* on hand (the asset) and the cost of goods sold (the expense) at all times. • *Periodic system* shows the correct balances of inventory and cost of goods sold only after a physical count of the inventory, which occurs at least once each year.
How do the adjusting and closing processes of merchandisers and service entities differ?	Very little. The merchandiser may have to *adjust* the Inventory account for spoilage and theft. The merchandiser must *close* the Cost of Goods Sold account. Service entities have no inventory to adjust or cost of goods sold to close.

DECISION GUIDELINES (CONT.)

How to format the merchandiser's income statement?

Multi-step Format

Sales revenue	$ XXX
− Cost of goods sold...............	(X)
= Gross profit	$ XX
− Operating expenses..............	(X)
+ Other revenues.....................	X
= Net income	$ XX

Single-step Format

Revenues:	
Sales revenue	$ XXX
Other revenues.....................	X
Total revenues	XXXX
Expenses:	
Cost of goods sold...............	(X)
Operating expenses	(X)
Total expenses......................	XX
Net income	$ XX

How to evaluate inventory operations?

Two key ratios:

$$\text{Gross profit percentage}^* = \frac{\text{Gross profit}}{\text{Net sales revenue}}$$

$$\text{Inventory turnover}^* = \frac{\text{Cost of goods sold}}{\text{Average inventory}}$$

*In most cases—the higher, the better

How to determine the amount of cost of goods sold?

Can use the *cost of goods sold* model (assumed amounts):

Beginning inventory............................	$100
+ Net purchases and freight in	800
= Cost of goods available	900
− Ending inventory	(200)
= Cost of goods sold	$700

REVIEW MERCHANDISING OPERATIONS

SUMMARY PROBLEM

www.prenhall.com/horngren

End-of-Chapter Assessment

The following trial balance and additional data are related to Jan King Distributing Company.

JAN KING DISTRIBUTING COMPANY
Trial Balance
December 31, 20X3

Cash	$ 5,670	
Accounts receivable	37,100	
Inventory..	60,500	
Supplies	3,930	
Prepaid rent	6,000	
Furniture and fixtures	26,500	
Accumulated depreciation...................		$ 21,200
Accounts payable.................................		46,340
Salary payable......................................		
Interest payable		
Unearned sales revenue.......................		3,500
Note payable, long-term		35,000
Jan King, capital		23,680
Jan King, withdrawals	48,000	
Sales revenue.......................................		346,700
Sales discounts	10,300	
Sales returns and allowances..............	8,200	
Cost of goods sold	171,770	
Salary expense.....................................	82,750	
Rent expense	7,000	
Depreciation expense...........................		
Utilities expense..................................	5,800	
Supplies expense		
Interest expense..................................	2,900	
Total...	$476,420	$476,420

Additional data at December 31, 20X3:

a. Supplies used during the year, $2,580.
b. Prepaid rent in force, $1,000.
c. Unearned sales revenue still not earned, $2,400.
d. Depreciation. The furniture and fixtures' estimated useful life is 10 years, and they are expected to be worthless when they are retired from service.
e. Accrued salaries, $1,300.
f. Accrued interest expense, $600.
g. Inventory on hand, $65,800.

Required

1. Enter the trial balance on a work sheet and complete the work sheet.
2. Journalize the adjusting and closing entries at December 31. Post to the Income Summary account as an accuracy check on the entries affecting that account. The credit balance closed out of Income Summary should equal net income computed on the work sheet.
3. Prepare the company's multi-step income statement, statement of owner's equity, and balance sheet in account format. Draw arrows linking the statements.
4. Compute the inventory turnover for 20X3. Inventory at December 31, 20X2, was $61,000. Turnover for 20X2 was 2.1 times. Would you expect Jan King Distributing Company to be more profitable or less profitable in 20X3 than in 20X2? Give your reason.

Solution

Requirement 1

JAN KING DISTRIBUTING COMPANY
Accounting Work Sheet (Perpetual Inventory System)
Year Ended December 31, 20X3

Account Title	Trial Balance Debit	Trial Balance Credit	Adjustments Debit		Adjustments Credit		Income Statement Debit	Income Statement Credit	Balance Sheet Debit	Balance Sheet Credit
Cash..............................	5,670								5,670	
Accounts receivable	37,100								37,100	
Inventory	60,500		(g)	5,300					65,800	
Supplies.......................	3,930				(a)	2,580			1,350	
Prepaid rent.................	6,000				(b)	5,000			1,000	
Furniture and fixtures.....................	26,500								26,500	
Accumulated depreciation.............		21,200			(d)	2,650				23,850
Accounts payable		46,340								46,340
Salary payable					(e)	1,300				1,300
Interest payable...........					(f)	600				600
Unearned sales revenue.....................		3,500	(c)	1,100						2,400
Note payable, long-term.................		35,000								35,000
Jan King, capital..........		23,680								23,680
Jan King, withdrawals	48,000								48,000	
Sales revenue		346,700			(c)	1,100		347,800		
Sales discounts	10,300						10,300			
Sales returns and allowances	8,200						8,200			
Cost of goods sold........	171,770				(g)	5,300	166,470			
Salary expense	82,750		(e)	1,300			84,050			
Rent expense...............	7,000		(b)	5,000			12,000			
Depreciation expense....................			(d)	2,650			2,650			
Utilities expense	5,800						5,800			
Supplies expense.........			(a)	2,580			2,580			
Interest expense	2,900		(f)	600			3,500			
	476,420	476,420		18,530		18,530	295,550	347,800	185,420	133,170
Net income..................							52,250			52,250
							347,800	347,800	185,420	185,420

Requirement 2

Adjusting Entries

20X3

Dec. 31	Supplies Expense		2,580	
	Supplies			2,580
31	Rent Expense		5,000	
	Prepaid Rent			5,000
31	Unearned Sales Revenue ($3,500 − $2,400)		1,100	
	Sales Revenue			1,100
31	Depreciation Expense ($26,500/10)		2,650	
	Accumulated Depreciation			2,650
31	Salary Expense		1,300	
	Salary Payable			1,300
31	Interest Expense		600	
	Interest Payable			600
31	Inventory ($65,800 − $60,500)		5,300*	
	Cost of Goods Sold			5,300

*Excess of inventory on hand over the balance in the Inventory account. This adjustment brings Inventory to its correct balance.

Closing Entries

20X3

Dec. 31	Sales Revenue		347,800	
	Income Summary			347,800
31	Income Summary		295,550	
	Sales Discounts			10,300
	Sales Returns and Allowances			8,200
	Cost of Goods Sold			166,470
	Salary Expense			84,050
	Rent Expense			12,000
	Depreciation Expense			2,650
	Utilities Expense			5,800
	Supplies Expense			2,580
	Interest Expense			3,500
31	Income Summary ($347,800 − $295,550)		52,250	
	Jan King, Capital			52,250
31	Jan King, Capital		48,000	
	Jan King, Withdrawals			48,000

INCOME SUMMARY			
Clo.	295,550	Clo.	347,800
Clo.	52,250	Bal.	52,250

Requirement 3

JAN KING DISTRIBUTING COMPANY
Income Statement
Year Ended December 31, 20X3

Sales revenue		$347,800
Less: Sales discounts	$(10,300)	
Sales returns and allowances	(8,200)	(18,500)
Net sales revenue		329,300
Cost of goods sold		166,470
Gross profit		162,830
Operating expenses:		
Salary expense	$ 84,050	
Rent expense	12,000	
Utilities expense	5,800	
Depreciation expense	2,650	
Supplies expense	2,580	107,080
Income from operations		55,750
Other expense:		
Interest expense		3,500
Net income		$ 52,250

JAN KING DISTRIBUTING COMPANY
Statement of Owner's Equity
Year Ended December 31, 20X3

Jan King, capital, December 31, 20X2	$23,680
Add: Net income	52,250
	75,930
Less: Withdrawals	(48,000)
Jan King, capital, December 31, 20X3	$27,930

JAN KING DISTRIBUTING COMPANY
Balance Sheet
December 31, 20X3

Assets			Liabilities		
Current:			Current:		
Cash		$ 5,670	Accounts payable		$ 46,340
Accounts receivable		37,100	Salary payable		1,300
Inventory		65,800	Interest payable		600
Supplies		1,350	Unearned sales revenue		2,400
Prepaid rent		1,000	Total current liabilities		50,640
Total current assets		110,920	Long-term:		
Plant:			Note payable		35,000
Furniture and					
fixtures	$26,500		Total liabilities		85,640
Less:					
Accumulated					
depreciation	(23,850)	2,650	**Owner's Equity**		
			Jan King, capital		27,930
			Total liabilities and owner's		
Total assets		$113,570	equity		$113,570

Requirement 4

$$\text{Inventory turnover} = \frac{\text{Cost of goods sold}}{\text{Average inventory}} = \frac{\$166,470}{(\$61,000 + \$65,800)/2} = 2.6 \text{ times}$$

The increase in the rate of inventory turnover from 2.1 to 2.6 suggests higher profits in 20X3 than in 20X2.

193

LESSONS LEARNED

1. **Use sales and gross profit to evaluate a company.** The major revenue of a merchandising business is *sales revenue,* or *sales*. The major expense is *cost of goods sold*. Net sales minus cost of goods sold is *gross profit,* or *gross margin*. This amount measures the business's success or failure in selling its products at a higher price than it paid for them.

2. **Account for the purchase and sale of inventory.** The merchandiser's major asset is inventory. In a merchandising entity, the accounting cycle is from cash to inventory as the inventory is purchased for resale, and back to cash as the inventory is sold. The *invoice* is the business document generated by a purchase or sale transaction. Most merchandising entities allow customers to *return* unsuitable merchandise and also offer *discounts* for early payment. They grant *allowances* for damaged goods that the buyer chooses to keep. Returns and Allowances and Discounts are contra accounts to Sales Revenue.

3. **Adjust and close the accounts of a merchandising business.** The end-of-period adjusting and closing process of a merchandising business is similar to that of a service business. In addition, a merchandiser adjusts inventory for theft losses, damage, and accounting errors.

4. **Prepare a merchandiser's financial statements.** The income statement may appear in *single-step format* or *multi-step format*. A single-step income statement has only two sections—one for revenues and the other for expenses—and a single income amount for net income. A multi-step income statement has subtotals for gross profit and income from operations. Both formats are widely used.

5. **Use the gross profit percentage and the inventory turnover ratio to evaluate a business:** Two key decision aids for a merchandiser are the *gross profit percentage* (gross profit/net sales revenue) and the *rate of inventory turnover* (cost of goods sold/average inventory). Increases in these measures usually signal an increase in profits.

6. **Compute cost of goods sold.** *Cost of goods sold* is the cost of the inventory that the business has sold. It is the largest single expense of most merchandising businesses. Cost of goods sold is the sum of the cost of goods sold amounts recorded during the period. In a periodic inventory system, Cost of goods sold = Beginning inventory + Purchases + Freight in − Ending inventory.

ACCOUNTING VOCABULARY

cost of goods sold   (p 168)
cost of sales   (p. 168)
gross margin   (p. 169)
gross margin percentage   (p. 185)
gross profit   (p. 169)
gross profit percentage   (p. 185)
income from operations   (p. 183)
inventory   (p. 167)
inventory turnover   (p. 186)
invoice   (p. 171)

multi-step income statement   (p. 185)
net purchases   (p. 188)
net sales   (p. 168)
operating expenses   (p. 183)
operating income   (p. 183)
other expense   (p. 183)
other revenue   (p. 183)
periodic inventory system   (p. 169)

perpetual inventory system   (p. 170)
sales   (p. 168)
sales discount   (p. 176)
sales returns and allowances   (p. 176)
sales revenue   (p. 168)
single-step income statement   (p. 185)

QUESTIONS

1. Gross profit is often mentioned in the business press as an important measure of success. What does gross profit measure, and why is it important?

2. Describe the operating cycle for (a) the purchase and cash sale of inventory, and (b) the purchase and sale of inventory on account.

3. Identify ten items of information on an invoice.

4. Indicate which accounts are debited and credited for (a) a credit purchase of inventory and the subsequent cash payment, and (b) a credit sale of inventory and the subsequent cash collection. Assume no discounts, returns, allowances, or freight.

5. Inventory costing $1,000 is purchased and invoiced on July 28 under terms of 3/10 n/30. Compute the payment amount on August 6. How much would the payment be on August 9? What explains the difference? What is the latest acceptable payment date under the terms of sale?

6. Name the new contra accounts introduced in this chapter.

7. Why is the title Cost of Goods Sold especially descriptive? What type of account is Cost of Goods Sold?

8. Beginning inventory is $5,000, net purchases total $30,000, and freight in is $1,000. If ending inventory is $8,000, what is the cost of goods sold?

9. You are beginning the adjusting and closing process at the end of your company's fiscal year. Does the trial balance carry the final ending amount of inventory? Why or why not?

10. Give the adjusting entry for inventory if shrinkage is $9,100.

11. Name and describe two formats for the income statement, and identify the type of business to which each format best applies.

12. Which financial statement reports sales discounts and sales returns and allowances? Show how they are reported, using any reasonable amounts in your illustration.

13. Does a merchandiser prefer a high or a low rate of inventory turnover? Explain.

14. In general, what does a decreasing gross profit percentage, coupled with an increasing rate of inventory turnover, suggest about a business's pricing strategy?

ASSESS YOUR PROGRESS

DAILY EXERCISES

DE5-1 Refer to Exhibit 5-1, page 168, **Target Corporation's** income statement. Identify the title and the amount of Target's

Using sales, gross profit, and net income to evaluate a company (Obj. 1)

a. Revenue before subtracting any expenses
b. Excess of sales revenue over cost of goods sold
c. Bottom-line operating performance

DE5-2 Compare the income statements of two merchandisers:

Using sales, cost of goods sold, gross profit, and net income (Obj. 1)

- **Target Corporation** (Exhibit 5-1, page 168)
- **Austin Sound Center** (Exhibit 5-7, page 182)

For every item on the Target income statement, give the title and the amount of the same item on Austin Sound's income statement. You can ignore Target's four individual *expenses* and the related total of $9,039 million.

DE5-3 Refer to Target's income statement in Exhibit 5-1. Give some alternative titles for the following items:

Using merchandising terminology (Obj. 1)

- Net sales revenue
- Gross profit
- Cost of goods sold
- Net earnings

DE5-4 You may have shopped at a **Gap** store. Suppose Gap purchases 2,000 pairs of slacks on account for $45,000. Credit terms are 2/10 n/30. As part of this shipment, the supplier, Miralu Products of Hong Kong, shipped $8,000 worth of defective merchandise, which Gap rejected and sent back. Gap then paid the balance within the discount period. Journalize the following transactions for Gap:

Recording purchase, purchase return, and cash payment transactions (Obj. 2)

a. Purchase of inventory.
b. Return of defective goods.
c. Payment within the discount period.

DE5-5 Toys "Я" Us purchases inventory from a variety of suppliers, including **Mattel, Hasbro,** and **Tonka.** Suppose Toys "Я" Us buys $150,000 worth of **Lego** toys on credit terms of 3/15 n/45. Unfortunately, the goods are damaged in shipment, so Toys "Я" Us returns $20,000 (original amount, before any discounts) of the merchandise to Lego.

Accounting for the purchase of inventory—quantity discount (Obj. 2)

How much must Toys "Я" Us pay Lego

a. After the discount period?
b. Within the discount period?

DE5-6 Refer to the Toys "Я" Us situation in Daily Exercise 5-5 and journalize the following transactions on the books of Toys "Я"Us. Explanations are not required.

Recording purchase, purchase return, and cash payment transactions (Obj. 2)

a. Original purchase of the goods on May 6, 20X1.
b. Return of the damaged goods on May 13.
c. Payment on May 15. Before journalizing this transaction, it is helpful to post the first two transactions to the Accounts Payable T-account.

DE5-7 Suppose a **Lord & Taylor** store purchases $140,000 of women's sportswear on account from **Liz Claiborne, Inc.** Credit terms are 2/10 net 30. Lord & Taylor pays electronically, and Liz Claiborne receives the money on the tenth day.

Recording purchase transactions (Obj. 2)

Journalize Lord & Taylor's (a) purchase and (b) payment transactions. What was Lord & Taylor's net cost of this inventory?

Note: Daily Exercise 5-8 covers this same situation for the seller.

DE5-8 **Liz Claiborne, Inc.,** sells $140,000 of women's sportswear to a **Lord & Taylor** store under credit terms of 2/10 net 30. Liz Claiborne's cost of the goods is $82,000, and Claiborne receives the appropriate amount of cash from Lord & Taylor on the tenth day.

Recording sales, cost of goods sold, and cash collections (Obj. 2)

Journalize Liz Claiborne's (a) sale, (b) cost of goods sold, and (c) cash receipt. How much gross profit did Liz Claiborne earn on this sale?

Note: Daily Exercise 5-7 covers the same situation for the buyer.

DE5-9 Refer to the **Gap/Miralu Products** situation in Daily Exercise 5-4. Record the three transactions on the books of the seller, Miralu Products. Assume Miralu keeps its records in U.S. dollars and that the goods cost Miralu $22,500. Miralu's transactions are

Recording sale, sales return, and cash collection entries
(Obj. 2)

a. Sale of inventory and the related cost of goods sold.
b. The $8,000 sales return and the related receipt of defective goods (cost, $4,000) from the purchaser.
c. Collection of cash within the discount period.

Computing net sales and gross profit
(Obj. 2)

DE5-10 **Intel Corporation,** famous for the Pentium© processor that powers many personal computers, offers sales discounts to the computer companies to which Intel sells its products. Intel also allows its customers to return defective processors. Suppose that during a recent period, Intel made sales of $600,000 on credit terms of 2/10 net 30. Assume that Intel received sales returns of $12,000. Later, Intel collected cash within the discount period. Cost of goods sold for the period was $255,000 after all sales returns.

For this particular period, compute Intel's

a. Net sales revenue   **b.** Gross profit

Adjusting the accounts of a merchandiser
(Obj. 3)

DE5-11 Examine the work sheet of **Austin Sound Center** in Exhibit 5-6, page 181. Focus on adjusting entries (a) and (b). Which entry is exactly the same as for a service company? Which entry relates to a merchandiser only? Explain the reason for the merchandiser's adjusting entry.

Using a merchandiser's financial statements
(Obj. 4)

DE5-12 Examine the financial statements of **Austin Sound Center** in Exhibit 5-7, page 182. Identify every item, including subtotals and totals, that relates exclusively to a merchandiser and will not appear in the financial statements of a service entity.

Note: An early-payment discount, similar to a sales discount, can relate to a service entity because a service business can allow its customers to take a discount for early payment.

Preparing a merchandiser's income statement
(Obj. 4)

DE5-13 **Dell Computer Corporation** reported these figures in its January 31, 2000, financial statements (adapted, and in millions):

Cash	$ 3,809	Other assets (long-term)	$ 3,025
Total operating expenses	3,552	Other current liabilities	1,654
Accounts payable	3,538	Property and equipment, net	765
Owners' equity	5,308	Net sales revenue	25,265
Long-term liabilities	971	Other current assets	873
Inventory	391	Accounts receivable	2,608
Cost of goods sold	20,047		

Prepare Dell's multi-step income statement for the year ended January 31, 2000.

Preparing a merchandiser's balance sheet
(Obj. 4)

DE5-14 Use the data in Daily Exercise 5-13 to prepare **Dell Computer's** classified balance sheet at January 31, 2000. Use the report format with all headings, and list accounts in proper order.

Making closing entries
(Obj. 3)

DE5-15 Refer to the work sheet of **Austin Sound Center** in Exhibit 5-6, page 181. Based solely on the Income Statement columns of the work sheet, make two closing entries, as follows:

- Journalize the closing entry for the *first account* listed that must be closed at the end of the period.
- Journalize the closing entry for the *last account* listed on the work sheet (not net income, which is not an account).

All closing entries for revenues and expenses follow the pattern of the closing entries you just made. Now make the final two closing entries of Austin Sound Center:

- Journalize the closing entry for the Owner's Withdrawals account.
- Journalize the closing entry for net income.

Set up a T-account for the Owner's Capital account, and insert the balance from the work sheet. Then post your closing entries to the Capital account. Its ending balance should be the same as the amount reported on Austin Sound's balance sheet in Exhibit 5-7 on page 182. Is it?

DE5-16 Refer to the income statement of **Target Corporation** in Exhibit 5-1, page 168.

*Closing the accounts
(Obj. 3)*

1. Identify every account on Target's income statement that the company will close out at the end of the year. Make two closing entries for these accounts at January 31, 2000:

   • Close the revenue   • Close the expenses

2. Target's balance sheet reports the following selected accounts:

   • Inventory   • Long-term debt
   • Accounts payable   • Other assets
   • Land   • Owners' equity

Which of these accounts does Target close, if any? Give your reason.

DE5-17 Refer to the **Dell Computer** situation in Daily Exercise 5-13. Compute Dell's gross profit percentage and rate of inventory turnover for 2000. One year earlier, at January 31, 1999, Dell's inventory balance was $320 million.

Computing the gross profit percentage and the rate of inventory turnover   (Obj. 5)

DE5-18 **Lands' End,** the catalog merchant, reported the following for the year ended January 31, 2000 (as adapted, with amounts in millions):

*Contrasting accounting income and cash flows
(Obj. 4)*

Cash collections from		Cash payments to suppliers	$ 682
customers	$1,323	Net sales revenue	1,320
Selling, general, and		Cost of sales	727
administrative expenses	529		

As an investor, you wonder which was greater, Lands' End's (a) gross profit, or (b) the company's excess of cash collections from customers over cash payments to suppliers? Compute both amounts to answer this question.

DE5-19 At January 31, 1999, **Target Corporation** had merchandise inventory of $3,475 million. During the following year, Target purchased inventory costing $23,352 million, including freight in. At January 31, 2000, Target's inventory stood at $3,798 million.

*Computing cost of goods sold in a periodic inventory system
(Obj. 6)*

1. Compute Target's cost of goods sold as in the periodic inventory system.
2. Compare your cost-of-goods-sold figure to Exhibit 5-1, page 000. The two amounts should be equal. Are they?

DE5-20 Les Fleurs, a boutique in Paris, France, had the following accounts in its accounting records at December 31, 20X2 (amounts in French francs, denoted as "F"):

*Computing net sales, cost of goods sold and gross profit in a periodic inventory system
(Obj. 6)*

Purchases	F250,000	Freight in................................	F 8,000
Sales discounts......................	4,000	Purchase returns	7,000
Inventory:..............................		Sales	400,000
December 31, 20X1...........	20,000	Purchase discounts...............	3,000
December 31, 20X2...........	30,000	Sales returns.........................	8,000

Compute the following for Les Fleurs during 20X2:

1. Net sales revenue   2. Cost of goods sold   3. Gross profit

DE5-21 **Gap Inc.,** reported Cost of Goods Sold totaling $6,775 million. Ending inventory was $1,462 million, and beginning inventory was $1,056 million. How much inventory did Gap purchase during the year?

*Computing inventory purchases
(Obj. 6)*

Evaluating a company's revenues, gross profit, operating income, and net income
(Obj. 1)

E5-1 Toys "Я" Us reported the following:

	TOYS "Я" US, INC. Statements of Earnings (adapted)	

	Fiscal Years Ended	
(In millions)	January 31, 2000	January 31, 1999
Net sales..	$11,862	$11,170
Costs and expenses:		
Cost of sales	8,321	8,191
Other expenses...	3,262	3,111
Net earnings (net loss)......................................	$ 279	$ (132)

	TOYS "Я" US, INC. Balance Sheets (partial, adapted)	

Assets (In millions)	January 31, 2000	January 31, 1999
Current Assets:		
Cash and cash equivalents..................................	$ 584	$ 410
Accounts and other receivables	182	204
Merchandise inventories	2,027	1,902
Prepaid expenses and other current assets..........	80	81
Total Current Assets...	$2,873	$2,597

Required

1. Is Toys "Я" Us a merchandising entity, a service business, or both? How can you tell? List the items in the Toys "Я" Us financial statements that influence your answer.
2. Compute Toys "Я" Us's gross profit for fiscal years 2000 and 1999. Did the gross profit increase or decrease in 2000? Is this a good sign or a bad sign about the company?
3. Write a brief memo to investors advising them of Toys "Я" Us's trend of sales, gross profit, and net income. Indicate whether the outlook for Toys "Я" Us is favorable or unfavorable, based on this trend. Use the following memo format:

Date: _____
To: Investors
From: Student Name
Subject: Trend of sales, gross profit and net income for Toys " Я " Us

Journalizing purchase and sales transactions
(Obj. 2)

E5-2 Journalize, without explanations, the following transactions of Lane's Fine Gifts during the month of September:

Sept. 3 Purchased $1,900 of inventory on account under terms of 2/10 n/eom (end of month) and FOB shipping point.

7 Returned $300 of defective merchandise purchased on September 3.

9 Paid freight bill of $30 on September 3 purchase.

10 Sold inventory on account for $3,100. Payment terms on the remainder were 2/15 n/30. These goods cost Lane's Fine Gifts $1,700.

12 Paid amount owed on credit purchase of September 3, less the discount and the return.

16 Granted a sales allowance of $800 on the September 10 sale.

23 Received cash from September 10 customer in full settlement of her debt, less the allowance and the discount.

Journalizing transactions from a purchase invoice *(Obj. 2)*

E5-3 As the proprietor of Stevens Goodyear Tire Co., you receive the following invoice from a supplier:

BELTLINE TIRE WHOLESALE DISTRIBUTORS, INC.
2600 Commonwealth Avenue
Boston, Massachusetts 02215

Invoice date: May 14, 20X3

Payment terms: 2/10 n/30

Sold to: Stevens Goodyear Tire Co.
4219 Crestwood Parkway
Lexington, Mass. 02173

Quantity Ordered	Description	Quantity Shipped	Price	Amount
4	P135–X4 Radials	4	$37.14	$ 148.56
8	L912 Belted-bias	8	41.32	330.56
14	R39 Truck tires	10	50.02	500.20
	Total			$979.32

Due date:	Amount:
May 24, 20X3	$959.73
May 25 through June 13, 20X3	$979.32

Paid:

Required

1. Stevens received the invoice on May 15. Record the May 15 purchase on account. Carry to the nearest cent throughout.
2. The R39 truck tires were ordered by mistake and were therefore returned to Beltline. Journalize the return on May 19.
3. Record the May 22 payment of the amount owed.

E5-4 On April 30, De Boulle Jewelers purchased inventory of $8,000 on account from Intergem Jewels, a jewelry importer. Terms were 3/15 net 45. On receiving the goods, De Boulle checked the order and found $800 of unsuitable merchandise. De Boulle returned $800 of the merchandise to Intergem on May 4.

Journalizing purchase transactions (Obj. 2)

To pay the remaining amount owed, De Boulle borrowed the net amount of the invoice from the bank. On May 14, De Boulle signed a short-term note payable to the bank and immediately paid the borrowed funds to Intergem. On June 14, De Boulle paid the bank the net amount of the invoice, which De Boulle had borrowed plus 1% monthly interest (round to the nearest dollar).

Required

Record the indicated transactions in the journal of De Boulle Jewelers. Explanations are not required.

E5-5 Refer to the business situation in Exercise 5-4. Journalize the transactions of Intergem Jewels. Intergem's gross profit is 40%, so cost of goods sold is 60% of sales. Explanations are not required.

Journalizing sales transactions (Obj. 2)

E5-6 **The Home Depot** is one of the largest retailers in the United States. For a recent year, The Home Depot's accounting records carried the following accounts (adapted, with amounts in millions) at January 31, 2000:

Making closing entries (Obj. 3)

Receivables	$ 587	Selling expense	$ 6,832
Interest revenue	37	Sales revenue	38,434
Accounts payable	1,993	Interest expense	28
Cost of goods sold	27,023	Merchandise inventories	5,489
Other expense	1,597	General and administrative	
Owner withdrawals	255	expense	671

Required

1. Journalize all of The Home Depot's closing entries at January 31, 2000. Use an Owner Capital account.

2. Set up T-accounts for the Income Summary account and the Owner Capital account. Post to these accounts and take their ending balances. One year earlier, at January 31, 1999, the Owner Capital balance was $8,740 million.

Using work sheet data to make the closing entries (Obj. 3)

E5-7 The trial balance and adjustments columns of the work sheet of Northstar Auto Supply at March 31, 20X2 follow.

Account Title	Trial Balance		Adjustments	
	Debit	Credit	Debit	Credit
Cash...	2,000			
Accounts receivable............................	8,500		(a) 6,100	
Inventory...	36,100			(b) 4,290
Supplies	13,000			(c) 8,600
Equipment...	42,470			
Accumulated depreciation...................		11,250		(d) 2,250
Accounts payable................................		9,300		
Salary payable				(e) 1,200
Note payable, long-term.....................		7,500		
Jack Potter, capital.............................		33,920		
Jack Potter, withdrawals.....................	45,000			
Sales revenue......................................		233,000		(a) 6,100
Sales discounts....................................	2,000			
Cost of goods sold	111,600		(b) 4,290	
Selling expense	21,050		(c) 5,200	
			(e) 1,200	
General expense	10,500		(c) 3,400	
			(d) 2,250	
Interest expense..................................	2,750			
Total...	294,970	294,970	22,440	22,440

Compute the adjusted balance for each account that must be closed. Then journalize Northstar's closing entries at March 31, 20X2. How much was Northstar's net income or net loss?

Preparing a multi-step income statement   (Obj. 4)

E5-8 Use the data in Exercise 5-7 to prepare the multi-step income statement of Northstar Auto Supply for the year ended March 31, 20X2.

Using the gross profit percentage and the rate of inventory turnover to evaluate profitability (Obj. 5)

E5-9 Refer to Exercise 5-8. After completing Northstar's income statement for the year ended March 31, 20X2, compute these ratios to evaluate Northstar's performance:

• Gross profit percentage
• Inventory turnover (Ending inventory one year earlier, at March 31, 20X1, was $30,500.)

Compare your figures with the 20X1 gross profit percentage of 48% and the inventory turnover rate of 3.16 for 20X1. Does the two-year trend suggest that Northstar's profits are increasing or decreasing?

Preparing a merchandiser's multi-step income statement to evaluate the business (Obj. 4, 5)

E5-10 Selected amounts from the accounting records of Barringer Boats, Ltd., are listed in alphabetical order.

Accounts payable	$16,200	Owner's equity,	
Accumulated depreciation	18,700	December 31, 20X0	$126,070
Cost of goods sold	99,300	Sales discounts.................	9,000
General expenses	23,500	Sales returns.....................	4,600
Interest revenue...........................	1,500	Sales revenue	204,000
Inventory, December 31, 19X9	21,000	Selling expenses	37,800
Inventory, December 31, 20X0	19,400	Unearned sales revenue....	6,500

Required

1. Prepare the business's multi-step income statement for the year ended December 31, 20X0.
2. Compute the rate of inventory turnover for the year. Last year the turnover rate was 3.8 times. Does this two-year trend suggest improvement or deterioration in inventory turnover?

Preparing a single-step income statement to evaluate the business
(Obj. 4, 5)

E5-11 Prepare Barringer Boats, Ltd.'s single-step income statement for 20X0, using the data from Exercise 5-10. Compute the gross profit percentage, and compare it with last year's gross profit percentage of 50%. Does this two-year trend in the gross profit percentage suggest better or worse profitability during the current year?

Comparing gross profit and cash flows
(Obj. 4)

E5-12 General Motors (GM) is a business empire, with both automotive operations and financial services. During 1999, GM's automotive operations made sales of $153 billion and had cost of goods sold totaling $127 billion. GM's automotive assets totaled $126 billion at December 31, 1999. Total automotive liabilities were $115 billion. During 1999, GM's automotive operations paid $123 billion for inventory and collected $152 billion from customers.

Required

As an investor, you wonder which was greater, (a) GM's gross profit on automotive sales or (b) GM's excess of cash collections from customers over cash payments to suppliers. Compute both amounts to answer this question.

Computing cost of goods sold in a periodic inventory system
(Obj. 6)

E5-13 The periodic inventory records of Barringer Boats, Ltd. include these accounts at December 31, 20X0:

Purchases of inventory	$98,600
Purchase discounts	3,000
Purchase returns and allowances	2,000
Freight in	4,100
Inventory	19,400

One year ago, at December 31, 19X9, Barringer's inventory balance stood at $21,000.

Required

Compute Barringer's cost of goods sold for 20X0 as in the periodic inventory system.

Computing inventory and cost of goods sold amounts in a periodic inventory system . *(Obj. 6)*

E5-14 Supply the missing income statement amounts in each of the following situations:

Sales	Sales Discounts	Net Sales	Beginning Inventory	Net Purchases	Ending Inventory	Cost of Goods Sold	Gross Profit
$98,300	(a)	$92,800	$32,500	$66,700	$39,400	(b)	$33,000
62,400	$2,100	(c)	27,450	43,000	(d)	$44,100	(e)
91,500	1,800	89,700	(f)	44,900	22,900	59,400	(g)
(h)	3,000	(i)	40,700	(j)	48,230	72,500 ·	39,600

Computing an actual company's net purchases
(Obj. 6

E5-15 For the year ended December 31, 20X1, Lighthouse Designs, a retailer of home-related products, reported net sales of $338 million and cost of goods sold of $154 million. The company's balance sheet at December 31, 20X0 and 20X1, reported inventories of $103 million and $129 million, respectively. How much were Lighthouse Designs' net purchases during 20X1?

Continuing Exercise. *This exercise completes the Amos Faraday, Consultant, situation from Exercise 2-15 of Chapter 2, Exercise 3-14 of Chapter 3, and Exercise 4-11 of Chapter 4.*

Accounting for both mechandis-
ing and service operations
(Obj. 2, 3, 4)

E5-16 Amos Faraday's consulting practice includes a great deal of systems consulting business. Faraday has begun selling accounting software. During January, the business completed these transactions:

Jan. 2   Completed a consulting engagement and received cash of $7,200.
     2   Prepaid three months' office rent, $1,500.
     7   Purchased accounting software inventory on account, $4,000.
   16   Paid employee salary, $1,400.
   18   Sold accounting software on account, $1,100 (cost $700).
   19   Consulted with a client for a fee of $900 on account.
   21   Paid on account, $2,000.
   24   Paid utilities, $300.
   28   Sold accounting software for cash, $600 (cost $400).
   31   Recorded these adjusting entries:
         Accrued salary expense, $1,400.
         Accounted for expiration of prepaid rent.
         Depreciation of office furniture, $200.

Required

1. Open the following selected T-accounts in the ledger: Cash; Accounts Receivable; Accounting Software Inventory; Prepaid Rent; Accumulated Depreciation; Accounts Payable; Salary Payable; Amos Faraday, Capital; Income Summary; Service Revenue; Sales Revenue; Cost of Goods Sold; Salary Expense; Rent Expense; Utilities Expense; and Depreciation Expense.
2. Journalize and post the January transactions. Key all items by date. Compute each account balance, and denote the balance as *Bal.* Journalize and post the closing entries. Denote each closing amount as Clo. After posting all closing entries, prove the equality of debits and credits in the ledger.
3. Prepare the January income statement of Amos Faraday, Consultant. Use the single-step format.

(Group A) PROBLEMS

P5-1A **Wal-Mart Stores, Inc.,** is the largest retailer in the world, with almost 4,000 stores. A key Wal-Mart advantage is its sophisticated perpetual inventory accounting system.

Required

You are the manager of a Wal-Mart store in Nashville, Tennessee. Write a one-paragraph business memo to a new employee explaining how the company accounts for the purchase and sale of merchandise inventory. Use the following heading for your memo:

Date:	_____
To:	New Employee
From:	Store Manager
Subject:	Wal-Mart's accounting system for inventories

Accounting for the purchase
and sale of inventory
(Obj. 2)

P5-2A Assume the following transactions occurred between **Johnson & Johnson (J&J)**, the healthcare products company, and **CVS Drugstores,** during February of the current year:

Feb. 6   Johnson & Johnson sold $8,000 worth of merchandise to CVS on terms of 2/10 n/30, FOB shipping point. J&J prepaid freight charges of $500 and included this amount in the invoice total. (J&J's entry to record the freight payment debits Accounts Receivable and credits Cash.) These goods cost J&J $6,100.
   10   CVS returned $900 of the merchandise purchased on February 6. J&J accounted for the $900 sales return and placed the goods back in inventory (cost, $590).
   15   CVS paid $3,000 of the invoice amount owed to J&J for the February 6 purchase, less the discount. This payment included none of the freight charge.
   27   CVS paid the remaining amount owed to J&J for the February 6 purchase.

Required

Journalize these transactions, first on the books of CVS and second on the books of Johnson & Johnson.

Required

1. Inventory on hand one year ago, at November 30, 20X3, was $32,650. Without entering the preceding data on a formal work sheet, prepare the company's multi-step income statement for the year ended November 30, 20X4.
2. Compute the gross profit percentage and the rate of inventory turnover for 20X4. For 20X3, Purcell's gross profit percentage was 55%, and inventory turnover was 1.91 times during the year. Does the two-year trend in these ratios suggest improvement or deterioration in profitability?

(Computing cost of goods sold and gross profit in a periodic inventory system; evaluating the business (Obj. 5, 6)

P5-9A The accounting records of Copeland Appliance list the following at November 30, 20X1:

Purchases of inventory	$132,000	Inventory: November 30, 20X0	$41,700
Selling expenses	8,800	November 30, 20X1	41,500
Furniture	37,200	Cash	3,700
Purchase returns and allowances	900	Freight in	1,600
Salary payable	300	Accumulated depreciation	
Jim Copeland, capital	52,800	—furniture	13,600
Sales revenue	199,600	Purchase discounts	600
Sales returns and allowances	3,200	Sales discounts	2,100
Accounts payable	9,500	General expenses	19,300

Required

1. Show the computation of Copeland's net sales, cost of goods sold, and gross profit for the year ended November 30, 20X1. Compute cost of goods sold as in the periodic inventory system.
2. Jim Copeland, owner of the company, strives to earn a gross profit percentage of 30%. Did he achieve this goal?
3. Did the rate of inventory turnover reach the industry average of 3.5 times per year?

PROBLEMS

(Group B)

P5-1B **Optic Nerve** is a regional chain of optical shops in the southwestern United States. The company offers a large selection of eyeglass frames, and Optic Nerve stores provide while-you-wait service. The company has launched a vigorous advertising campaign to promote two-for-the-price-of-one frame sales.

Explaining the perpetual inventory system (Obj. 2)

Required

Optic Nerve expects to grow rapidly and to increase its level of inventory. As the chief accountant of this company, you wish to install a perpetual inventory system. Write a one-paragraph business memo to the company president to explain how that system would work. Use the following heading for your memo:

Date:	_____
To:	Company President
From:	Chief Accountant
Subject:	How a perpetual inventory system works

P5-2B Assume the following transactions occurred between **Eckerd Drug Stores** and **Johnson & Johnson (J&J)**, the healthcare products company, during June of the current year:

Accounting for the purchase and sale of inventory (Obj. 2)

June 8   Johnson & Johnson sold $6,000 worth of merchandise to Eckerd Drug Stores on terms of 2/10 n/30, FOB shipping point. J&J prepaid freight charges of $200 and included this amount in the invoice total. (J&J's entry to record the freight payment debits Accounts Receivable and credits Cash.) These goods cost J&J $2,100.

11   Eckerd returned $600 of the merchandise purchased on June 8. J&J accounted for the $600 sales return and placed the goods back in inventory (J&J's cost, $250).

17   Eckerd paid $2,000 of the invoice amount owed to J&J for the June 8 purchase, less the discount. This payment included none of the freight charge.

26   Eckerd paid the remaining amount owed to J&J for the June 8 purchase.

Required

Journalize these transactions, first on the books of Eckerd Drug Stores and second on the books of Johnson & Johnson.

P5-3B Larkspur Lighting Company engaged in the following transactions during July:

July 2 Purchased inventory for cash, $800.
  5 Purchased store supplies on credit terms of net eom, $450.
  8 Purchased inventory of $3,000, plus freight charges of $230. Credit terms are 3/15 n/30.
  9 Sold goods for cash, $1,200. Larkspur's cost of these goods was $700.
  11 Returned $200 of the inventory purchased on July 8. It was damaged.
  12 Purchased inventory on credit terms of 3/10 n/30, $3,330.
  14 Sold inventory on credit terms of 2/10 n/30, $9,600 (cost $5,000).
  16 Paid utilities expense, $275.
  20 Received returned inventory from the July 14 sale, $400. Larkspur shipped the wrong goods by mistake. Larkspur's cost of the inventory received was $250.
  21 Borrowed the amount owed on the July 8 purchase. Signed a note payable to the bank for $2,946, which takes into account the return of inventory on July 11.
  21 Paid supplier for goods purchased on July 8 less the discount and the return.
  23 Received $6,860 cash in partial settlement of his account from the customer who purchased inventory on July 14. Granted the customer a 2% discount and credited his account receivable for $7,000.
  30 Paid for the store supplies purchased on July 5.

Required

1. Journalize the preceding transactions on the books of Larkspur Lighting Company.
2. Compute the amount of the receivable at July 31 from the customer to whom Larkspur sold inventory on July 14. What amount of cash discount applies to this receivable at July 31?

P5-4B Fresh Market Grocery's trial balance pertains to December 31, 20X1.

FRESH MARKET GROCERY Trial Balance December 31, 20X1		
Cash	$ 2,910	
Accounts receivable	6,560	
Inventory	101,760	
Store supplies	1,990	
Prepaid insurance	3,200	
Store fixtures	63,900	
Accumulated depreciation		$ 37,640
Accounts payable		29,770
Salary payable		
Interest payable		
Note payable, long-term		37,200
Elaine Lorens, capital		63,120
Elaine Lorens, withdrawals	36,300	
Sales revenue		286,370
Cost of goods sold	161,090	
Salary expense	46,580	
Rent expense	14,630	
Utilities expense	6,780	
Depreciation expense		
Insurance expense	5,300	
Store supplies expense		
Interest expense	3,100	
Total	$454,100	$454,100

Additional data at December 31, 20X1:

a. Insurance expense for the year, $6,090.
b. Store fixtures have an estimated useful life of ten years and are expected to be worthless when they are retired from service.
c. Accrued salaries at December 31, $1,260.
d. Accrued interest expense at December 31, $870.
e. Store supplies on hand at December 31, $760.
f. Inventory on hand at December 31, $94,780.

Required

Complete Fresh Market's accounting work sheet for the year ended December 31, 20X1. Key adjusting entries by letter.

P5-5B Refer to the data in Problem 5-4B at the bottom of the facing page.

Journalizing the adjusting and closing entries of a merchandising business (Obj. 3)

Required

1. Journalize the adjusting and closing entries of Fresh Market Grocery.
2. Determine the December 31 balance of Elaine Lorens, Capital.

P5-6B ◄ *Link Back to Chapter 4 (Classified Balance Sheet).* Selected accounts of Genesis Electronics are listed along with their balances before closing at July 31, 20X2.

Preparing a multi-step income statement and a classified balance sheet (Obj. 3, 4)

Accounts payable	$127,300	Interest payable	$ 3,000
Accounts receivable	46,200	Inventory: July 31	187,300
Accumulated depreciation—		Note payable, long-term	160,000
store equipment	16,400	Salary payable	6,100
A. L. Genesis, capital,		Sales discounts	8,300
June 30	69,100	Sales returns and allowances	17,900
A. L. Genesis, withdrawals	11,000	Sales revenue	556,600
Cash	24,300	Selling expense	84,600
Cost of goods sold	360,900	Store equipment	126,000
General expense	75,800	Supplies	4,300
Interest expense	1,200	Unearned sales revenue	9,300

(handwritten margin notes: —current / =plant / =less Accumulated / liabilities / current=~ / long term = O / capital owner's equity)

Required

1. Prepare the entity's *multi-step* income statement for the month ended July 31, 20X2.
2. Prepare Genesis's classified balance sheet in *report format* at July 31, 20X2. Show your computation of the July 31 balance of A.L. Genesis, Capital.

P5-7B ◄ *Link Back to Chapter 4 (Classified Balance Sheet).*

Preparing a single-step income statement and a classified balance sheet (Obj. 4)

Required

1. Use the data of Problem 5-6B to prepare Genesis Electronics' *single-step* income statement for July 31, 20X2.
2. Prepare Genesis's classified balance sheet in *report format* at July 31, 20X2. Show your computation of the July 31 balance of A. L. Genesis, Capital.

P5-8B The trial balance and adjustments columns of the work sheet of **Carolina Crystal Company** follow.

Using work sheet data to prepare financial statements and evaluate the business; multi-step income statement (Obj. 4, 5)

	Trial Balance		Adjustments	
Account Title	**Debit**	**Credit**	**Debit**	**Credit**
Cash	7,300			
Accounts receivable	4,360		(a) 1,400	
Inventory	9,630		(b) 2,100	
Supplies	10,700			(c) 7,940
Equipment	99,450			
Accumulated depreciation		29,800		(d) 9,900
Accounts payable		13,800		
Salary payable				(f) 200
Unearned sales revenue		3,780	(e) 2,600	
Note payable, long-term		10,000		
Claire Burke, capital		58,360		
Claire Burke, drawing	35,000			
Sales revenue		212,000		(a) 1,400
				(e) 2,600
Sales returns	3,100			
Cost of goods sold	95,600			(b) 2,100
Selling expense	40,600		(c) 7,940	
			(f) 200	
General expense	21,000		(d) 9,900	
Interest expense	1,000			
Total	327,740	327,740	24,140	24,140

Required

1. Inventory on hand at September 30, 20X2, was $9,250. Without completing a formal accounting work sheet, prepare the company's multi-step income statement for the year ended September 30, 20X3.
2. Compute the gross profit percentage and the inventory turnover for 20X3. For 20X2, Carolina's gross profit percentage was 50% and the inventory turnover rate was 7.8 times. Does the two-year trend in these ratios suggest improvement or deterioration in profitability?

Computing cost of goods sold and gross profit in a periodic inventory system; evaluating the business
(Obj. 5, 6)

P5-9B The accounting records of Vanguard Security Systems at June 30, 20X2 list the following:

Cash	$ 13,600	Inventory: June 30, 20X1		$23,800
Purchases of inventory	98,100	June 30, 20X2		28,500
Freight in	4,300	Equipment		44,700
Sales revenue	199,100	Purchase discounts		1,300
Purchase returns		Accumulated depreciation—		
and allowances	1,400	equipment		6,900
Salary payable	1,800	Sales discounts		3,400
Luke Stover, capital	36,000	General expenses		16,300
Sales returns and allowances	12,100	Accounts payable		23,800
Selling expenses	29,800			

Required

1. Show the computation of Vanguard Security Systems' net sales, cost of goods sold, and gross profit for the year ended June 30, 20X2. Compute cost of goods sold as in the periodic inventory system.
2. Luke Stover, owner of the business, strives to earn a gross profit percentage of 44%. Did he achieve this goal?
3. Did the rate of inventory turnover reach the industry average of 4.0 times per year?

APPLY YOUR KNOWLEDGE

DECISION CASES

Using the financial statements to decide on a business expansion
(Obj. 4, 5)

Case 1. ↞ *Link Back to Chapter 4 (Classified Balance Sheet, Current Ratio, Debt Ratio).* David Wheelis owns Heights Pharmacy, which has prospered during its second year of operation. In deciding whether to open another pharmacy in the area, Wheelis has prepared the current financial statements of the business (on page 209). Wheelis read in an industry trade journal that a successful pharmacy meets all of these criteria:

a. Gross profit percentage is at least 60%.
b. Current ratio is at least 2.0.
c. Debt ratio is no higher than 0.50.
d. Inventory turnover rate is at least 3.40. (Heights Pharmacy's inventory one year ago, at December 31, 20X0, was $19,200.)

Basing his opinion on the entity's financial statement data, Wheelis believes the business meets all four criteria. He intends to go ahead with the expansion plan and asks your advice on preparing the pharmacy's financial statements in accordance with generally accepted accounting principles. When you point out that the statements are not properly prepared, he assures you that all amounts are correct. However, he admits that some items may be listed in the wrong place.

Required

1. Compute the four ratios based on the Heights Pharmacy financial statements prepared by Wheelis. Does the business appear to be ready for expansion?
2. Prepare a correct multi-step income statement, a correct statement of owner's equity, and a correct classified balance sheet in report format.
3. On the basis of the corrected financial statements, compute correct measures of the four ratios listed in the trade journal.
4. Make a recommendation about whether Wheelis should undertake the expansion.

HEIGHTS PHARMACY
Income Statement
Year Ended December 31, 20X1

Sales revenue		$195,000
Gain on sale of land		24,600
Total revenue		219,600
Cost of goods sold		85,200
Gross profit		134,400
Operating expenses:		
Salary expense	$18,690	
Rent expense	12,000	
Interest expense	6,000	
Depreciation expense	4,900	
Utilities expense	2,330	
Supplies expense	1,400	
Total operating expense		45,320
Income from operations		89,080
Other expense:		
Sales discounts ($3,600)		
and returns ($7,100)		10,700
Net income		$78,380

HEIGHTS PHARMACY
Statement of Owner's Equity
Year Ended December 31, 20X1

D. Wheelis, capital, December 31, 20X0	$ 30,000
Add increases in owner's equity:	
Net income	78,380
D. Wheelis, capital, December 31, 20X1	$108,380

HEIGHTS PHARMACY
Balance Sheet
December 31, 20X1

Assets

Current:		
Cash		$ 5,320
Accounts receivable		9,710
Inventory		30,100
Supplies		2,760
Store fixtures		63,000
Total current assets		110,890
Other:		
Withdrawals		65,000
Total assets		$175,890

Liabilities

Current:		
Accumulated depreciation—store fixtures		$ 6,300
Accounts payable		10,310
Salary payable		900
Total current liabilities		17,510
Other:		
Note payable due in 90 days		50,000
Total liabilities		67,510

Owner's Equity

D. Wheelis, capital		108,380
Total liabilities and owner's equity		$175,890

Case 2. The employees of Ewald Systems made an error when they performed the inventory count at year end, October 31, 20X8. Part of one warehouse was not counted, and therefore its inventory was not included in the company's total ending inventory.

Required

1. Indicate the effect of the inventory error on ending inventory, cost of goods sold, gross profit, and net income for the year ended October 31, 20X8.
2. Will the error affect cost of goods sold, gross profit, and net income in 20X9? If so, what will the effects be?

ETHICAL ISSUE

Greg Ogden Belting Company makes all sales of industrial conveyor belts under terms of FOB shipping point. The company usually receives orders for sales approximately one week before shipping inventory to customers. For orders received late in December, Greg Ogden, the owner, decides when to ship the goods. If profits are already at an acceptable level, Ogden delays shipment until January. If profits for the current year are lagging behind expectations, Ogden ships the goods during December.

Required

1. Under Ogden's FOB policy, when should the company record a sale?
2. Do you approve or disapprove of Ogden's manner of deciding when to ship goods to customers and record the sales revenue? If you approve, give your reason. If you disapprove, identify a better way to decide when to ship goods. (There is no accounting rule against Ogden's practice.)

FINANCIAL STATEMENT CASE

This case uses both the income statement (statement of income) and the balance sheet of **Target Corporation,** in Appendix A. It will help you understand the closing process of a business with inventories.

Required

1. Journalize Target's closing entries for fiscal year 1999. You may be unfamiliar with certain revenues and expenses, but treat them as either revenues or expenses. *Net credit revenue* is interest revenue. *Provision for income taxes* is another name for income tax expense and the *extraordinary charge* is like an expense. Close the Income Summary account to the Retained Earnings account. For this purpose, Retained Earnings is similar to the Owner's Capital account.
2. What amount was closed to Retained Earnings? How is this amount labeled on the income statement?
3. Compute Target's gross profit percentage and inventory turnover rate for fiscal year 1999.

TEAM PROJECT

With a small team of classmates, visit one or more actual merchandising businesses in your area. Interview a responsible official of the company to learn about its inventory policies and accounting system. Obtain answers to the following questions, write a report, and be prepared to make a presentation to the class if your instructor so directs:

Required

1. What merchandise inventory does the business sell?
2. From whom does the business buy its inventory? Is the relationship with the supplier new or longstanding?
3. What are the FOB terms on inventory purchases? Who pays the freight, the buyer or the seller? Is freight a significant amount or is freight cost low? What percentage of total inventory cost is the freight?
4. What are the credit terms on inventory purchases—2/10 n/30, or other? Does the business pay early to get purchase discounts? If so, why? If not, why not?
5. How does the business actually pay its suppliers? Does it mail a check or pay electronically? What is the actual payment procedure?
6. Which type of inventory accounting system does the business use—perpetual or periodic? Is this system computerized?
7. How often does the business take a physical count of its inventory? When during the year is the count taken? Describe the count procedures followed by the company.
8. Does the owner or manager use the gross profit percentage and the rate of inventory turnover to evaluate the business? If not, show the manager how to use these ratios in decision making.
9. Ask any other questions your group considers appropriate.

INTERNET EXERCISE

You can now compare prices for consumer electronics, personal computers, and entertainment software online by visiting the **Best Buy** and **Circuit City** Web sites. You can also compare their financial information online. Let's see how these companies compare.

Required

1. Go to **http://www.hoovers.com** and then use the "Search" scroll bar to select *Company*. In the next box type *BBY,* the stock symbol for Best Buy, and click on *Go*. For Best Buy Co., Inc., click on *capsule* and read the written description of the company. In what parts of the country are Best Buy stores located?
2. Go to the top of the page and click on the *Financials* tab. Under "Free Financial Information," click on *Annual Financials*.
   a. For the two most recent fiscal years, list the amounts reported for "Revenue," "Cost of Goods Sold," "Gross Profit Margin" percentage, "Total Net Income," and "Inventories."
   b. For the most recent year, calculate the rate of inventory turnover. Explain what this ratio indicates for Best Buy.
3. In the "Search for" box at the top of page, type *CC,* the stock symbol for Circuit City, and click on *Go*. For Circuit City Stores, Inc., click on *capsule* and read the written description of the company. What is Circuit City's rank among major appliance and electronics chains? Which company is the leader?
4. Gather the same information requested in (2a) and (2b) above for Circuit City.
5. Which company is more profitable? Why?

Best Buy and Circuit City

Go to the "Alternative Income Statement Formats and Extraordinary Items" episode on the *Mastering Accounting* CD-ROM for an interactive, video-enhanced exercise on CanGo managers' need to consider the different income statement formats and their effect on investors.

APPENDIX TO CHAPTER 5

ACCOUNTING FOR MERCHANDISE IN A PERIODIC INVENTORY SYSTEM

After studying this appendix to Chapter 5, you should be able to:

A2. Account for purchase and sale of inventory
A3. Compute cost of goods sold
A4. Adjust and close the accounts of a merchandising business
A5. Prepare a merchandiser's financial statement

PURCHASING MERCHANDISE

Some businesses find it uneconomical to invest in a computerized (perpetual) inventory system. These types of business use a periodic system.

Recording Purchases of Inventory

All inventory systems use the Inventory account. But in a periodic system, purchases, purchase discounts, purchase returns and allowances, and transportation costs are recorded in separate accounts. Let's account for **Austin Sound Center's** purchase of the **JVC** goods in Exhibit 5A-1. The following entries record the purchase and payment on account within the discount period:

Objective A2
Account for the purchase and sale of inventory

May 27	Purchases	707.00	
	Accounts Payable		707.00
	Purchased inventory on account.		
June 10	Accounts Payable	707.00	
	Cash ($707.00 × 0.97)		685.79
	Purchase Discounts ($707.00 × 0.03)		21.21
	Paid on account.		

Recording Purchase Returns and Allowances

Suppose that, prior to payment, **Austin Sound** returned to **JVC** goods costing $70 and also received from JVC a purchase allowance of $10. Austin Sound would record these transactions as follows:

June 3	Accounts Payable	70.00	
	Purchase Returns and Allowances		70.00
	Returned inventory to seller.		

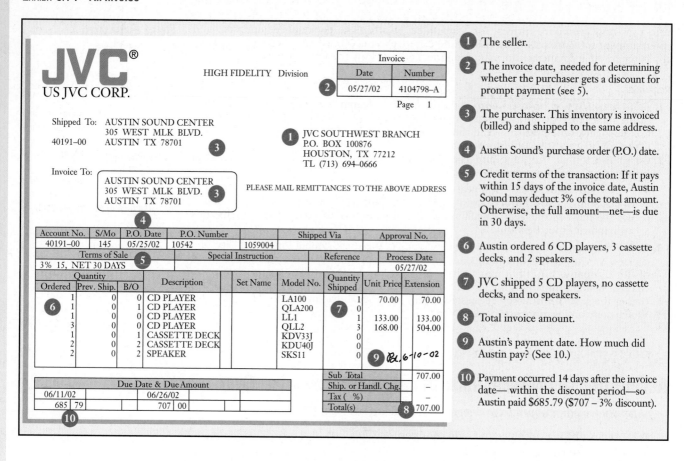

Exhibit 5A-1 An Invoice

1 The seller.

2 The invoice date, needed for determining whether the purchaser gets a discount for prompt payment (see 5).

3 The purchaser. This inventory is invoiced (billed) and shipped to the same address.

4 Austin Sound's purchase order (P.O.) date.

5 Credit terms of the transaction: If it pays within 15 days of the invoice date, Austin Sound may deduct 3% of the total amount. Otherwise, the full amount—net—is due in 30 days.

6 Austin ordered 6 CD players, 3 cassette decks, and 2 speakers.

7 JVC shipped 5 CD players, no cassette decks, and no speakers.

8 Total invoice amount.

9 Austin's payment date. How much did Austin pay? (See 10.)

10 Payment occurred 14 days after the invoice date— within the discount period—so Austin paid $685.79 ($707 – 3% discount).

June 4	Accounts Payable	10.00	
	Purchase Returns and Allowances..............		10.00
	Received a purchase allowance.		

During the period, the business records the cost of all inventory bought in the Purchases account. The balance of Purchases is a *gross* amount because it does not include subtractions for discounts, returns, or allowances. **Net purchases** is the remainder computed by subtracting the contra accounts from Purchases:

> **NET PURCHASES.** Purchases less purchase discounts and purchase returns and allowances.

      Purchases (*debit* **balance account)**
−   **Purchase Discounts** (*credit* **balance account)**
−   **Purchase Returns and Allowances** (*credit* **balance account)**
=   **Net purchases** (a *debit* **subtotal, not a separate account)**

Recording Transportation Costs

Under the periodic system, costs to transport purchased inventory from seller to buyer are debited to the freight in account, as shown for a $60 freight bill:

June 1	Freight In...	60.00	
	Cash		60.00
	Paid a freight bill.		

RECORDING THE SALE OF INVENTORY

Recording sales is streamlined in the periodic system. With no running record of inventory to maintain, we can record a $3,000 sale as follows:

June 5	Accounts Receivable...	3,000	
	Sales Revenue..		3,000
	Sale on account.		

No accompanying entry to Inventory and Cost of Goods Sold is required. Also, discounts and returns and allowances are recorded as shown for the perpetual system on pages 176–177, but with no entry to Inventory and Cost of Goods Sold.

Cost of goods sold (also called **cost of sales**) is the largest single expense of most businesses that sell merchandise, such as **Gap Inc.**, and **Austin Sound**. It is the cost of the inventory the business has sold to customers. In a periodic system, cost of goods sold must be computed as in Exhibit 5A-2.

Objective A3
Compute cost of goods sold

Exhibit 5A-2
Measuring Cost of Goods Sold in the Periodic Inventory System

PANEL A:
Beginning inventory
+ Net purchases
+ Freight in
= Cost of goods available for sale
– Ending inventory
= Cost of goods sold

PURCHASES OF INVENTORY
– Purchase discounts
– Purchase returns and allowances
= Net purchases

PANEL B:

Exhibit 5A-3
Partial Income Statement

AUSTIN SOUND CENTER
Income Statement
Year Ended December 31, 20X2

PANEL A—Detailed Gross Profit Section

Sales revenue			$169,300
Less: Sales discounts		$ (1,400)	
Sales returns and allowances		(2,000)	(3,400)
Net sales			$165,900
Cost of goods sold:			
Beginning inventory			$38,600
Purchases		$91,400	
Less: Purchase discounts	$(3,000)		
Purchase returns and allowances	(1,200)	(4,200)	
Net purchases			87,200
Freight in			5,200
Cost of goods available for sale			131,000
Less: Ending inventory			(40,200)
Cost of goods sold			90,800
Gross profit			$ 75,100

**PANEL B—Gross Profit Section
(Streamlined in Annual Reports to Outsiders)**

Net sales	$165,900
Cost of goods sold	90,800
Gross profit	$ 75,100

Exhibit 5A-3 on page 213 summarizes the first half of this appendix by showing Austin Sound's net sales revenue, cost of goods sold—including net purchases and freight in—and gross profit on the income statement for the periodic system. (All amounts are assumed.)

Objective A4
Adjust and close the accounts of a merchandising business

ADJUSTING AND CLOSING THE ACCOUNTS

A merchandising business adjusts and closes the accounts much as a service entity does. The steps of this end-of-period process are the same: If a work sheet is used, the trial balance is entered and the work sheet completed to determine net income or net loss. The work sheet provides the data for journalizing the adjusting and closing entries and preparing the financial statements.

At the end of the period, before any adjusting or closing entries, the Inventory account still holds the cost of the ending inventory from the preceding period. It is necessary to remove this beginning balance and replace it with the cost of the inventory on hand at the end of the current period. Various techniques may be used to bring the inventory records up to date.

To illustrate a merchandiser's adjusting and closing process under the periodic inventory system, let's use **Austin Sound's** December 31, 20X2, trial balance in Exhibit 5A-4. All the new accounts—Inventory, Freight In, and the contra accounts—are highlighted for emphasis. Additional data item (h) gives the ending inventory figure, $40,200.

EXHIBIT 5A-4
Trial Balance

AUSTIN SOUND CENTER		
Trial Balance		
December 31, 20X2		
Cash	$ 2,850	
Accounts receivable	4,600	
Note receivable, current............................	8,000	
Interest receivable....................................		
Inventory..	38,600	
Supplies..	650	
Prepaid insurance	1,200	
Furniture and fixtures...............................	33,200	
Accumulated depreciation........................		$ 2,400
Accounts payable		47,000
Unearned sales revenue...........................		2,000
Wages payable..		
Interest payable..		
Note payable, long-term		12,600
C. Ernest, capital		25,900
C. Ernest, withdrawals..............................	54,100	
Sales revenue...		168,000
Sales discounts...	1,400	
Sales returns and allowances....................	2,000	
Interest revenue..		600
Purchases...	91,400	
Purchase discounts....................................		3,000
Purchase returns and allowances..............		1,200
Freight in	5,200	
Wage expense	9,800	
Rent expense	8,400	
Depreciation expense................................		
Insurance expense		
Supplies expense......................................		
Interest expense.......................................	1,300	
Total	$262,700	$262,700

Additional data at December 31, 20X2

a. Interest revenue earned but not yet collected, $400.
b. Supplies on hand, $100.
c. Prepaid insurance expired during the year, $1,000.
d. Depreciation, $600.
e. Unearned sales revenue earned during the year, $1,300.
f. Accrued wage expense, $400.
g. Accrued interest expense, $200.
h. Inventory on hand, $40,200.

Preparing and Using the Work Sheet in a Periodic System

The Exhibit 5A-5 work sheet is similar to the work sheets we have seen so far, with a few differences. ➤➤ In most accounting systems, a single operation combines trial balance amounts with the adjustments and extends the adjusted balances directly to the income statement and balance sheet columns. Therefore, to reduce clutter, the adjusted trial balance columns are omitted.

◄◄ This work sheet is slightly different from the one introduced in the Chapter 4 acetates following page 128—it contains four pairs of columns, not five.

Exhibit **5A-5** Accounting Work Sheet

	AUSTIN SOUND CENTER Accounting Work Sheet (Periodic Inventory System) Year Ended December 31, 20X2							
	Trial Balance		**Adjustments**		**Income Statement**		**Balance Sheet**	
Account Title	Debit	Credit	Debit	Credit	Debit	Credit	Debit	Credit
Cash..................................	2,850						2,850	
Accounts receivable...........	4,600						4,600	
Note receivable, current....	8,000						8,000	
Interest receivable			(a) 400				400	
Inventory............................	38,600				38,600	40,200	40,200	
Supplies	650			(b) 550			100	
Prepaid insurance	1,200			(c) 1,000			200	
Furniture and fixtures........	33,200						33,200	
Accumulated depreciation		2,400		(d) 600				3,000
Accounts payable		47,000						47,000
Unearned sales revenue		2,000	(e) 1,300					700
Wages payable				(f) 400				400
Interest payable				(g) 200				200
Note payable, long-term....		12,600						12,600
C. Ernest, capital		25,900						25,900
C. Ernest, withdrawals	54,100						54,100	
Sales revenue		168,000		(e) 1,300		169,300		
Sales discounts	1,400				1,400			
Sales returns and allowances	2,000				2,000			
Interest revenue		600		(a) 400		1,000		
Purchases...........................	91,400				91,400			
Purchase discounts		3,000				3,000		
Purchase returns and allowances		1,200				1,200		
Freight in...........................	5,200				5,200			
Wage expense....................	9,800		(f) 400		10,200			
Rent expense.....................	8,400				8,400			
Depreciation expense			(d) 600		600			
Insurance expense.............			(c) 1,000		1,000			
Supplies expense			(b) 550		550			
Interest expense	1,300		(g) 200		1,500			
	262,700	262,700	4,450	4,450	160,850	214,700	143,650	89,800
Net income					53,850			53,850
					214,700	214,700	143,650	143,650

ACCOUNT TITLE COLUMNS The trial balance lists a number of accounts without balances. Ordinarily, these accounts are affected by the adjusting process. Examples include Interest Receivable, Interest Payable, and Depreciation Expense. The accounts are listed in the order they appear in the ledger. If additional accounts are needed, they are written in at the bottom, above net income.

TRIAL BALANCE COLUMNS Examine the Inventory account, $38,600 in the trial balance. This $38,600 is the cost of the beginning inventory. The work sheet is designed to replace this outdated amount with the new ending balance, which in our example is $40,200 [additional data item (h) in Exhibit 5A-4].

ADJUSTMENTS COLUMNS The adjustments are similar to those discussed in Chapters 3 and 4. They may be entered in any order desired. The debit amount of each entry should equal the credit amount, and total debits should equal total credits. You should review the adjusting data in Exhibit 5A-5 to reassure yourself that the adjustments are correct.

INCOME STATEMENT COLUMNS The income statement columns contain adjusted amounts for the revenues and the expenses. Sales Revenue, for example, is $169,300, which includes the $1,300 adjustment.

You may be wondering why the two inventory amounts appear in the income statement columns. The reason is that both beginning inventory and ending inventory enter the computation of cost of goods sold. *Placement of beginning inventory ($38,600) in the work sheet's income statement Debit column has the effect of adding beginning inventory in computing cost of goods sold. Placing ending inventory ($40,200) in the Credit column decreases cost of goods sold.*

Purchases and Freight In appear in the Debit column because they are added in computing cost of goods sold. Purchase Discounts and Purchase Returns and Allowances appear as Credits because they are subtracted in computing cost of good sold—$90,800 on the income statement in Exhibit 5A-6.

The income statement column subtotals on the work sheet indicate whether the business earned net income or incurred a net loss. If total credits are greater, the result is net income, as shown in Exhibit 5A-5. If total debits are greater, a net loss has occurred.

BALANCE SHEET COLUMNS The only new item on the balance sheet is inventory. The balance listed is the ending amount of $40,200, which is determined by a physical count of inventory on hand at the end of the period.

Objective A5
Prepare a merchandiser's financial statements

Preparing the Financial Statements of a Merchandiser

Exhibit 5A-6 presents Austin Sound's financial statements. The *income statement* through gross profit repeats Exhibit 5A-3. This information is followed by the **operating expenses,** expenses other than cost of goods sold that are incurred in the entity's major line of business. Wage expense is Austin Sound's cost of employing workers. Rent is the cost of obtaining store space. Insurance helps to protect the inventory. Store furniture and fixtures wear out; the expense is depreciation. Supplies expense is the cost of stationery, mailing, and the like, used in operations. Many companies report their operating expenses in two categories.

- *Selling expenses* are those expenses related to marketing the company's products—sales salaries, sales commissions, advertising, depreciation, rent, and utilities, delivery expense, and so on.
- *General expenses* include office expenses, such as the salaries of office employees, and depreciation, rent, utilities, and property taxes on the home office building.

Gross profit minus operating expenses and plus any other operating revenues equals **operating income,** or **income from operations.** Many businesspeople view operating income as the most reliable indicator of a business's success because it measures the results of the entity's major ongoing activities.

The last section of Austin Sound's income statement is **other revenue and expenses,** which is handled the same way in both inventory systems. This category reports revenues and expenses that are outside the company's main line of business.

AUSTIN SOUND CENTER
Income Statement
Year Ended December 31, 20X2

Sales revenue		$169,300	
Less: Sales discounts	$ (1,400)		
Sales returns and allowances	(2,000)	(3,400)	
Net sales revenue			$165,900
Cost of goods sold:			
Beginning inventory		$ 38,600	
Purchases	$91,400		
Less: Purchases discounts	$(3,000)		
Purchase returns and allowances	(1,200)	(4,200)	
Net purchases		87,200	
Freight in		5,200	
Cost of goods available for sale		131,000	
Less: Ending inventory		(40,200)	
Cost of goods sold			90,800
Gross profit			75,100
Operating expenses:			
Wage expense		10,200	
Rent expense		8,400	
Insurance expense		1,000	
Depreciation expense		600	
Supplies expense		550	20,750
Income from operations			54,350
Other revenue and (expense):			
Interest revenue		1,000	
Interest expense		(3,400)	(500)
Net income			$53,850

AUSTIN SOUND CENTER
Statement of Owner's Equity
Year Ended December 31, 20X2

C. Ernest, capital, December 31, 20X1	$25,900
Add: Net income	53,850
	79,750
Less: Withdrawals	(54,100)
C. Ernest, capital, December 31, 20X2	$25,650

AUSTIN SOUND CENTER
Balance Sheet
December 31, 20X2

Assets			Liabilities	
Current:			**Current:**	
Cash		$ 2,850	Accounts payable	$47,000
Accounts receivable		4,600	Unearned sales revenue	700
Note receivable		8,000	Wages payable	400
Interest receivable		400	Interest payable	200
Inventory		40,200	Total current liabilities	48,300
Prepaid insurance		200	**Long-term:**	
Supplies		100	Note payable	12,600
Total current assets		56,350	Total liabilities	60,900
Plant:				
Furniture and fixtures	$33,200		**Owner's Equity**	
Less: Accumulated			C. Ernest, capital	25,650
depreciation	(3,000)	30,200	Total liabilities and	
Total assets		$86,550	owner's equity	$86,550

Journalizing Adjusting and Closing Entries

Exhibit 5A-7 presents Austin Sound's adjusting entries. These entries follow the same pattern illustrated in Chapter 4 for a service entity.

Exhibit 5A-7
Adjusting and Closing Entries

Journal

Adjusting Entries

a.	Dec. 31	Interest Receivable		400	
		Interest Revenue			400
b.	31	Supplies Expense ($650 – $100)		550	
		Supplies			550
c.	31	Insurance Expense		1,000	
		Prepaid Insurance			1,000
d.	31	Depreciation Expense		600	
		Accumulated Depreciation			600
e.	31	Unearned Sales Revenue		1,300	
		Sales Revenue			1,300
f.	31	Wage Expense		400	
		Wages Payable			400
g.	31	Interest Expense		200	
		Interest Payable			200

Closing Entries

1.	Dec. 31	Sales Revenue		169,300	
		Interest Revenue		1,000	
		Income Summary			170,300
2.	31	Cost of Goods Sold		135,200	
		Inventory (beginning balance)			38,600
		Purchases			91,400
		Freight In			5,200
3.	31	Inventory (ending balance)		40,200	
		Purchase Discounts		3,000	
		Purchase Returns and Allowances		1,200	
		Cost of Goods Sold			44,400
4.	31	Income Summary		116,450	
		Sales Discounts			1,400
		Sales Returns and Allowances			2,000
		Cost of Goods Sold ($135,200 – $44,400)			90,800
		Wage Expense			10,200
		Rent Expense			8,400
		Depreciation Expense			600
		Insurance Expense			1,000
		Supplies Expense			550
		Interest Expense			1,500
5.	31	Income Summary ($170,300 – $116,450)		53,850	
		C. Ernest, Capital			53,850
6.	31	C. Ernest, Capital		54,100	
		C. Ernest, Withdrawals			54,100

The exhibit also gives Austin Sound's closing entries. The first closing entry closes the revenue accounts. Closing entries 2 and 3 are new. Entry 2 closes the beginning balance of the Inventory account ($38,600), along with Purchases and Freight In, into the Cost of Goods Sold account. Entry 3 sets up the ending balance of Inventory ($40,200) with a debit and also closes the Purchases contra accounts to Cost of Goods Sold.[1] Now Inventory and Cost of Goods Sold have their correct ending balances as follows:

INVENTORY					
Jan. 1 Bal.	38,600	Dec. 31	Clo.	38,600	
Dec. 31 Clo.	40,200				

COST OF GOODS SOLD			
Beg. Inventory	38,600	Pur. discounts	3,000
Purchases	91,400	Pur. returns and	
Freight in	5,200	allowances	1,200
		End. inventory	40,200

[1]Some accountants make the inventory entries as adjustments rather than as part of the closing process. The adjusting-entry approach adds these adjustments (shifted out of the closing entries):

The entries to the Inventory account deserve additional explanation. Recall that before the closing process, Inventory still had the period's beginning balance. At the end of the period, this balance is one year old and must be replaced with the ending balance in order to prepare the financial statements at December 31, 20X2. Closing entries 2 and 3 give Inventory its correct ending balance of $40,200.

Closing entry 4 then closes the Sales contra accounts and Cost of Goods Sold along with the other expense accounts into Income Summary. Closing entries 5 and 6 complete the closing process. All data for the closing entries are taken from the income statement columns of the work sheet.

Study Exhibits 5A-5, 5A-6, and 5A-7 carefully because they illustrate the entire end-of-period process that leads to the financial statements. As you progress through this book, you may want to refer to these exhibits to refresh your understanding of the adjusting and closing process for a merchandising business.

Net sales, cost of goods sold, operating income, and net income are unaffected by the choice of inventory system. You can prove this by comparing Austin Sound's financial statements given in Exhibit 5A-6 with the corresponding statements in Exhibit 5-7. The only differences appear in the cost-of-goods-sold section of the income statement, and those differences are unimportant. In fact, virtually all companies report cost of goods sold in streamlined fashion, as shown for **Target Corporation** in Exhibit 5-1 and for **Austin Sound** in Exhibit 5-7.

REVIEW PERIODIC INVENTORY SYSTEM

APPENDIX SUMMARY PROBLEM

The following trial balance pertains to Jan King Distributing Company:

JAN KING DISTRIBUTING COMPANY
Trial Balance (Periodic Inventory System)
December 31, 20X3

Cash	$ 5,670	
Accounts receivable	37,100	
Inventory	60,500	
Supplies	3,930	
Prepaid rent	6,000	
Furniture and fixtures	26,500	
Accumulated depreciation		$ 21,200
Accounts payable		46,340
Salary payable		
Interest payable		
Unearned sales revenue		3,500
Note payable, long-term		35,000
Jan King, capital		23,680
Jan King, withdrawals	48,000	
Sales revenue		346,700
Sales discounts	10,300	
Sales returns and allowances	8,200	
Purchases	175,900	
Purchase discounts		6,000
Purchase returns and allowances		7,430
Freight in	9,300	
Salary expense	82,750	
Rent expense	7,000	
Depreciation expense		
Utilities expense	5,800	
Supplies expense		
Interest expense	2,900	
Total	$489,850	$489,850

Additional data at December 31, 20X3:
  a. Supplies used during the year, $2,580.
  b. Prepaid rent in force, $1,000.
  c. Unearned sales revenue still not earned, $2,400. The company expects to earn this amount during the next few months.
  d. Depreciation. The furniture and fixtures' estimated useful life is ten years, and they are expected to be worthless when they are retired from service.
  e. Accrued salaries, $1,300.
  f. Accrued interest expense, $600.
  g. Inventory on hand, $65,800.

Required

1. Enter the trial balance on an accounting work sheet and complete the work sheet.
2. Journalize the adjusting and closing entries at December 31. Post to the Income Summary account as an accuracy check on the entries affecting that account. The credit balance closed out of Income Summary should equal net income computed on the work sheet.
3. Prepare the company's multi-step income statement, statement of owner's equity, and balance sheet in account format. Draw arrows linking the statements.

Solution

Requirement 1

JAN KING DISTRIBUTING COMPANY
Accounting Work Sheet (Periodic Inventory System)
Year Ended December 31, 20X3

Account Title	Trial Balance Debit	Trial Balance Credit	Adjustments Debit	Adjustments Credit	Income Statement Debit	Income Statement Credit	Balance Sheet Debit	Balance Sheet Credit
Cash	5,670						5,670	
Accounts receivable	37,100						37,100	
Inventory	60,500				60,500	65,800	65,800	
Supplies	3,930			(a) 2,580			1,350	
Prepaid rent	6,000			(b) 5,000			1,000	
Furniture and fixtures	26,500						26,500	
Accumulated depreciation		21,200		(d) 2,650				23,850
Accounts payable		46,340						46,340
Salary payable				(e) 1,300				1,300
Interest payable				(f) 600				600
Unearned sales revenue		3,500	(c) 1,100					2,400
Note payable, long-term		35,000						35,000
Jan King, capital		23,680						23,680
Jan King, withdrawals	48,000						48,000	
Sales revenue		346,700		(c) 1,100		347,800		
Sales discounts	10,300				10,300			
Sales returns and allowances	8,200				8,200			
Purchases	175,900				175,900			
Purchase discounts		6,000				6,000		
Purchase returns and allowances		7,430				7,430		
Freight in	9,300				9,300			
Salary expense	82,750		(e) 1,300		84,050			
Rent expense	7,000		(b) 5,000		12,000			
Depreciation expense			(d) 2,650		2,650			
Utilities expense	5,800				5,800			
Supplies expense			(a) 2,580		2,580			
Interest expense	2,900		(f) 600		3,500			
	489,850	489,850	13,230	13,230	374,780	427,030	185,420	133,170
Net income					52,250			52,250
					427,030	427,030	185,420	185,420

Adjusting Entries

20X3

Dec. 31	Supplies Expense	2,580	
	Supplies		2,580
31	Rent Expense	5,000	
	Prepaid Rent		5,000
31	Unearned Sales Revenue ($3,500 − $2,400)	1,100	
	Sales Revenue		1,100
31	Depreciation Expense ($26,500/10)	2,650	
	Accumulated Depreciation		2,650
31	Salary Expense	1,300	
	Salary Payable		1,300
31	Interest Expense	600	
	Interest Payable		600

Closing Entries

20X3

Dec. 31	Sales Revenue	347,800	
	Income Summary		347,800
31	Cost of Goods Sold	245,700	
	Inventory (beginning balance)		60,500
	Purchases		175,900
	Freight In		9,300
31	Inventory	65,800	
	Purchase Discounts	6,000	
	Purchase Returns and Allowances	7,430	
	Cost of Goods Sold		79,230
31	Income Summary	295,550	
	Sales Discounts		10,300
	Sales Returns and Allowances		8,200
	Cost of Goods Sold ($245,700 − $79,230)		166,470
	Salary Expense		84,050
	Rent Expense		12,000
	Depreciation Expense		2,650
	Utilities Expense		5,800
	Supplies Expense		2,580
	Interest Expense		3,500
31	Income Summary ($347,800 − $295,550)	52,250	
	Jan King, Capital		52,250
31	Jan King, Capital	48,000	
	Jan King, Withdrawals		48,000

INCOME SUMMARY			
Clo.	295,550	Clo.	347,800
Clo.	52,250	Bal.	52,250

Requirement 3

JAN KING DISTRIBUTING COMPANY
Income Statement
Year Ended December 31, 20X3

Sales revenue			$347,800
Less: Sales discounts	$(10,300)		
Sales returns and allowances	(8,230)	(18,500)	
Net sales revenue			$329,300
Cost of goods sold:			
Beginning inventory		$ 60,500	
Purchases	$175,900		
Less: Purchase discounts	$(6,000)		
Purchase returns and allowances	(7,430)	(13,430)	
Net purchases		162,470	
Freight in		9,300	
Cost of goods available for sale		232,270	
Less: Ending inventory		(65,800)	
Cost of goods sold			166,470
Gross profit			162,830
Operating expenses:			
Salary expense		84,050	
Rent expense		12,000	
Utilities expense		5,800	
Depreciation expense		2,650	
Supplies expense		2,580	107,080
Income from operations			55,750
Other expense:			
Interest expense			3,500
Net income			$ 52,250

JAN KING DISTRIBUTING COMPANY
Statement of Owner's Equity
Year Ended December 31, 20X3

Jan King, capital, December 31, 20X2	$23,680
Add: Net income	52,250
	75,930
Less: Withdrawals	(48,000)
Jan King, capital, December 31, 20X3	$27,930

JAN KING DISTRIBUTING COMPANY
Balance Sheet
December 31, 20X3

Assets			Liabilities		
Current:			Current:		
Cash		$ 5,670	Accounts payable		$ 46,340
Accounts receivable		37,100	Salary payable		1,300
Inventory		65,800	Interest payable		600
Supplies		1,350	Unearned sales revenue		2,400
Prepaid rent		1,000	Total current liabilities		50,640
Total current assets		110,920	Long-term:		
Plant:			Note payable		35,000
Furniture and fixtures	$26,500				
Less:			Total liabilities		85,640
Accumulated depreciation	(23,850)	2,650	**Owner's Equity**		
			Jan King, capital		27,930
			Total liabilities and owner's		
Total assets		$113,570	equity		$113,570

APPENDIX EXERCISES

E5A-1 Journalize, without explanations, the following transactions of Lane's Fine Gifts during June:

Journalizing purchase and sale transactions (Obj. A2)

June 3 Purchased $700 of inventory under terms of 2/10 n/eom (end of month) and FOB shipping point.
    7 Returned $300 of defective merchandise purchased on June 3.
    9 Paid freight bill of $30 on June 3 purchase.
  10 Sold inventory for $3,200. Payment terms were 2/15 n/30.
  12 Paid amount owed on credit purchase of June 3, less the discount and the return.
  16 Granted a sales allowance of $800 on the June 10 sale.
  23 Received cash from June 10 customer in full settlement of her debt, less the allowance and the discount.

E5A-2 As the proprietor of Stevens Goodyear Tire Company you receive the following invoice from a supplier:

Journalizing transactions from a purchase invoice (Obj. A2)

BELTLINE TIRE WHOLESALE DISTRIBUTORS, INC.
2600 Commonwealth Avenue
Boston, Massachusetts 02215

Invoice date: May 14, 20X3   **Payment terms:** 2/10 n/30

Sold to: Stevens Goodyear Tire Co.
4219 Crestwood Parkway
Lexington, Mass. 02173

Quantity Ordered	Description	Quantity Shipped	Price	Amount
4	P135–X4 Radials	4	$37.14	$ 148.56
8	L912 Belted-bias	8	41.32	330.56
14	R39 Truck tires	10	50.02	500.20
	Total			$979.32

Due date:	Amount:
May 24, 20X3	$959.73
May 25 through June 13, 20X3	$979.32

Paid:

Required

1. Stevens received the invoice on May 15. Record the May 15 purchase on account. Carry to the nearest cent throughout.
2. The R39 truck tires were ordered by mistake and were therefore returned to Beltline. Journalize the return on May 19.
3. Record the May 22 payment of the amount owed.

E5A-3 On April 30, De Boulle Jewelers purchased inventory of $8,000 on account from Intergem Jewels, a jewelry importer. Terms were 3/15 net 45. On receiving the goods, De Boulle checked the order and found $800 of unsuitable merchandise. Therefore, De Boulle returned $800 of merchandise to Intergem on May 4.

Journalizing purchase transactions (Obj. A2)

To pay the remaining amount owed, De Boulle borrowed the net amount of the invoice from the bank. On May 14, De Boulle signed a short-term note payable to the bank and immediately paid the borrowed funds to Intergem. On June 14, De Boulle paid the bank the net amount of the invoice, which De Boulle had borrowed, plus 1% monthly interest (round to the nearest dollar).

Required

Record the indicated transactions in the journal of De Boulle Jewelers. Explanations are not required.

E5A-4 Refer to the business situation in Exercise 5A-3. Journalize the transactions of Intergem Jewels. Explanations are not required.

Note: Exercises 5-13 (page 201), 5-14 (page 201), and 5-15 (page 201) also pertain to the periodic inventory system.

APPENDIX PROBLEMS

P5A-1 The following transactions occurred between Abba Medical Supply and a Hillcrest Drug store during November of the current year:

Nov. 6   Abba Medical Supply sold $6,200 worth of merchandise to Hillcrest on terms of 2/10 n/30, FOB shipping point. Abba prepaid freight charges of $300 and included this amount in the invoice total. (Abba's entry to record the freight payment debits Accounts Receivable and credits Cash.)

    10   Hillcrest returned $900 of the merchandise purchased on November 6. Abba issued a credit memo for this amount.

    15   Hillcrest paid $3,000 of the invoice amount owed to Abba for the November 6 purchase, less the discount. This payment included none of the freight charge.

    27   Hillcrest paid the remaining amount owed to Abba for the November 6 purchase.

Required

Journalize these transactions, first on the books of the Hillcrest Drug store and second on the books of Abba Medical Supply.

P5A-2 Preakness Wholesale Grocery engaged in the following transactions during May of the current year:

May 3   Purchased office supplies for cash, $300.

    7   Purchased inventory on credit terms of 3/10 net eom, $2,000.

    8   Returned half the inventory purchased on May 7. It was not the inventory ordered.

    10   Sold goods for cash, $450.

    13   Sold inventory on credit terms of 2/15 n/45, $3,900.

    16   Paid the amount owed on account from the purchase of May 7, less the discount and the return.

    17   Received defective inventory returned from May 13 sale, $900.

    18   Purchased inventory of $4,000 on account. Payment terms were 2/10 net 30.

    26   Borrowed $3,920 from the bank to take advantage of the discount offered on May 18 purchase. Signed a note payable to the bank for this amount.

    26   Paid supplier for goods purchased on May 18, less the discount.

    28   Received cash in full settlement of the account from the customer who purchased inventory on May 13, less the discount and the return.

    29   Purchased inventory for cash, $2,000, plus freight charges of $160.

Required

1. Journalize the preceding transactions. Explanations are not required.
2. The note payable signed on May 26 requires the payment of $30 interest expense. Was the decision to borrow funds in order to take advantage of the cash discount wise or unwise? Support your answer by comparing the discount to the interest paid.

P5A-3 Larkspur Lighting Company engaged in the following transactions during July of the current year:

July 2   Purchased inventory for cash, $800.

    5   Purchased store supplies on credit terms of net eom, $450.

    8   Purchased inventory of $3,000, plus freight charges of $230. Credit terms are 3/15 n/30.

    9   Sold goods for cash, $1,200.

    11   Returned $200 of the inventory purchased on July 8. It was damaged.

    12   Purchased inventory on credit terms of 3/10 n/30, $3,330.

    14   Sold inventory on credit terms of 2/10 n/30, $9,600.

    16   Paid utilities expense, $275

    20   Received a sales return from July 14 sale, $400. Larkspur shipped the wrong goods by mistake.

    21   Borrowed the amount owed on the July 8 purchase. Signed a note payable to the bank for $2,946, which takes into account the return of inventory on July 11.

       purchased inventory on July 14. Granted the customer a 2% discount and credited this account receivable for $7,000.

    30   Paid for the store supplies purchased on July 5.

Required

1. Journalize the preceding transactions. Explanations are not required.
2. Compute the amount of the receivable at July 31 from the customer to whom Larkspur sold inventory on July 14. What amount of cash discount applies to this receivable at July 31?

P5A-4 The year-end trial balance of Latham Sales Company pertains to March 31, 20X4.

Preparing a merchandiser's accounting work sheet, financial statements, and adjusting and closing entries
(Obj. A3, A4, A5)

LATHAM SALES COMPANY
Trial Balance
March 31, 20X4

Cash	$ 7,880	
Note receivable, current	12,400	
Interest receivable		
Inventory	130,050	
Prepaid insurance	3,600	
Notes receivable, long-term	62,000	
Furniture	6,000	
Accumulated depreciation		$ 4,000
Accounts payable		12,220
Sales commission payable		
Sales payable		
Unearned sales revenue		9,610
Ben Latham, capital		172,780
Ben Latham, withdrawals	66,040	
Sales revenue		440,000
Sales discounts	4,800	
Sales returns and allowances	11,300	
Interest revenue		8,600
Purchases	233,000	
Purchase discounts		3,100
Purchase returns and allowances		7,600
Freight in	10,000	
Sales commission expense	78,300	
Salary expense	24,700	
Rent expense	6,000	
Utilities expense	1,840	
Depreciation expense		
Insurance expense		
Total	$657,910	$657,910

Additional data at March 31, 20X4:

a. Accrued interest revenue, $1,030.
b. Insurance expense for the year, $3,000.
c. Furniture has an estimated useful life of six years. Its value is expected to be zero when it is retired from service.
d. Unearned sales revenue still unearned, $7,400.
e. Accrued salaries, $1,200.
f. Accrued sales commission expense, $1,700.
g. Inventory on hand, $133,200.

Required

1. Enter the trial balance on an accounting work sheet, and complete the work sheet for the year ended March 31, 20X4.
2. Prepare the company's multi-step income statement and statement of owner's equity for the year ended March 31, 20X4. Also prepare its classified balance sheet at that date. Long-term notes receivable should be reported on the balance sheet between current assets and plant assets in a separate section labeled Investments.
3. Journalize the adjusting and closing entries at March 31, 20X4.
4. Post to the Ben Latham, Capital account and to the Income Summary account as an accuracy check on the adjusting and closing process.

Note: Problems 5-9A (page 205) and 5-9B (page 208) also pertain to the periodic inventory system.

Accounting Information Systems

Price & Associates - Certified Public Accountants - Microsoft Internet Explorer

File Edit View Go Favorites Help

Back Forward Stop Refresh Home Search Favorites History Channels Fullscreen Mail Print Edit

Address http://www.price-assoc.com/

Price & Associates, PLLC
Certified Public Accountants

2711 LBJ Freeway, Suite 150
Dallas, TX 75234
Phone: (972) 888-0950
Fax: (972) 888-0956
brian@price-assoc.com

Do you want an accounting firm that can really make a difference in you bottom line results?

Letting Price & Associates work as a true partner in your business will pay dividends you can't imagine.

800x600x16M

Start

2:54 PM

LEARNING OBJECTIVES

After studying this chapter, you should be able to

1. Describe the features of an effective accounting information system

2. Understand how both computerized and manual accounting systems work

3. Understand how spreadsheets are used in accounting

4. Use the sales journal, the cash receipts journal, and the accounts receivable subsidiary ledger

5. Use the purchases journal, the cash payments journal, and the accounts payable subsidiary ledger

With QuickBooks and Peachtree taking over, you'd think accountants would be worried about the future. After all, why does a business need an accountant when there's a virtual one on a disk? But the reverse is true. The new developments in software and Web applications are creating lots of new career opportunities in accounting.

Many entrepreneurs don't know how to do more than boot up their software, and they don't have time to learn how to use it. Many won't pay a full-time accountant to do their books. Enter the Accounting Software Consultant. Brian Price of **Price and Associates** has built a $400,000 business by consulting on small business accounting software. Price's clients range from mom-and-pop businesses that bring in $100,000–$200,000 a year to a $2 million services firm. The typical engagement for his firm brings in $1,100 of revenue. For a flat fee, Price installs QuickBooks or other software and provides five hours of training. Of course, five hours is never enough, so clients end up buying additional training time for $65 to $100 an hour.

The best part for Price is that clients then can do the bookkeeping. This frees Price to do the more creative work: analyzing financial information and helping clients make decisions based on the information.

Source: Adapted from Jeff Stimpson, "The new consultant," *The Practical Accountant,* September 1999, pp. 325–42.

very organization needs an accounting system. An **accounting information system** is the combination of personnel, records, and procedures that a business uses to provide financial data. We have already been using an accounting information system in this text. It consists of two basic components: a general journal and a general ledger.

ACCOUNTING INFORMATION SYSTEM. The combination of personnel, records, and procedures that a business uses to provide financial data.

Every accounting system has these components, but this simple system can efficiently handle only a few transactions per period. Businesses cope with heavy transaction loads in two ways: computerization and specialization. We *computerize* to do the accounting faster and more reliably. *Specialization* comes when we group similar transactions to speed the process. We explore special journals in the second half of this chapter.

EFFECTIVE ACCOUNTING INFORMATION SYSTEMS

Objective 1
Describe the features of an effective accounting information system

Good personnel are critical to the success of any operation. Employees must be both competent and honest. And several design features can make the accounting system run more efficiently. A good system—whether computerized or manual—includes control, compatibility, flexibility, and a favorable cost/benefit relationship.

Features of Effective Systems

Managers need *control* over operations. *Internal controls* are the methods and procedures used to authorize transactions and safeguard assets. For example, in companies such as **Coca-Cola, America Online,** and **Kinko's,** managers control cash disbursements to avoid theft through unauthorized payments. **VISA, MasterCard,** and **Discover** keep records of their accounts receivable to ensure that they receive collections on time.

A *compatible* system is one that works smoothly with the business's operations, personnel, and organizational structure. An example is **Bank of America,** which is organized as a network of branch offices. Bank of America's top managers want to know revenues in each region where the bank does business. They also want to analyze loans in different geographic regions. If revenues in California are lagging, managers can concentrate their efforts in that state. They may relocate some branch offices or hire new personnel.

Organizations evolve. They develop new products, sell off unprofitable operations and acquire new ones, and adjust employee pay scales. Changes in the business often call for changes in the accounting system. A well-designed system is *flexible* if it accommodates changes without a complete overhaul. Consider **Monsanto Company's** acquisition of the pharmaceuticals firm **Searle** including Searle's Nutrasweet division. Monsanto's accounting system was flexible enough to fold Searle/Nutrasweet financial statements into those of Monsanto.

Achieving control, compatibility, and flexibility costs money. Managers strive for a system that offers maximum benefits at a minimum cost—that is, a favorable *cost/benefit relationship.* Most small companies use off-the-shelf computerized accounting packages, and the very smallest businesses might not computerize at all. But large companies, such as the brokerage firm **Edward Jones,** have specialized needs for information. For them, custom programming is a must. The benefits—in terms of information tailored to the company's needs—far outweigh the costs. The result? Better decisions.

Components of a Computerized System

Three components form the heart of a computerized accounting system: hardware, software, and company personnel. Each component is critical to the system's success.

Hardware is the electronic equipment: It includes computers, disk drives, monitors, printers, and the network that connects them. Most modern accounting systems require a **network,** the system of electronic linkages that allows different computers to share the same information. In a networked system, many computers can be connected to the main computer, or **server,** which stores the program and the data. With the right network, a **PricewaterhouseCoopers** auditor in London can access the data of a client located in Sydney, Australia. The result is a speedier audit for the client.

Software is the set of programs that drive the computer to perform the work desired. Accounting software accepts, edits (alters), and stores transaction data and generates the reports managers use to run the business. Many software packages operate independently from the other computing activities of the system. For example, a company that is only partly computerized may use software programs to account for employee payrolls and sales and accounts receivable. Other parts of the accounting system may not be automated.

For large enterprises, like **Hershey Foods** and **Caterpillar Tractor,** the accounting software is integrated within the overall company **database,** or computerized storehouse of information. Many business databases include accounting and nonaccounting data. In negotiating a union contract, the **Union Pacific Railroad** often needs to examine the relationship between the employment history and salary levels of company employees. Union Pacific's database provides the data managers need to negotiate effectively. During negotiations, both parties carry laptop computers to analyze the effects of decisions on the spot.

How Computerized and Manual Accounting Systems Work

Computerized accounting systems have replaced manual systems in many organizations—even in small businesses such as your neighborhood pharmacy. As we discuss the stages of data processing, observe the differences between a computerized system and a manual system. The three stages of data processing (inputs, processing, outputs) are shown in Exhibit 6-1.

⊙ Daily Exercise 6-1

Hardware. Electronic equipment that includes computers, disk drives, monitors, printers, and the network that connects them.

Network. The system of electronic linkages that allows different computers to share the same information.

Server. The main computer in a network, where the program and data are stored.

◉ Daily Exercise 6-2

◉ Daily Exercise 6-3

Software. Set of programs or instructions that drive the computer to perform the work desired.

Database. A computerized storehouse of information.

| Objective 2
Understand how both computerized and manual accounting systems work

Exhibit 6-1
The Three Stages of Data
Processing

Inputs represent data from source documents, such as sales receipts, bank deposit slips, fax orders, and other telecommunications. Inputs are usually grouped by type. For example, a firm would enter cash-sale transactions separately from credit sales and purchase transactions.

In a manual system, *processing* includes journalizing transactions, posting to the accounts, and preparing the financial statements. A computerized system also processes, but without the intermediate steps (journal, ledger, and trial balance).

Outputs are the reports used for decision making, including the financial statements (income statement, balance sheet). Business owners are making better decisions—and prospering—because of the reports produced by their accounting system. Exhibit 6-2 is an overview of a computerized system. Start with data inputs in the lower left corner.

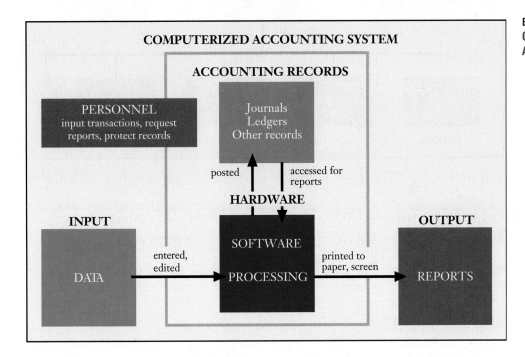

EXHIBIT 6-2
Overview of a Computerized Accounting System

Designing a System: The Chart of Accounts

Design of the accounting system begins with the chart of accounts. ➤ In the accounting system of a large, complex company such as **Eastman Kodak,** account numbers take on added importance. It is efficient to represent a complex account title, such as Accumulated Depreciation—Photographic Equipment, with a concise account number (for example, 12570).

◀ Recall from Chapter 2 that the chart of accounts lists all the accounts and their account numbers.

Recall that asset accounts generally begin with the digit 1, liabilities with the digit 2, owner's equity accounts with the digit 3, revenues with 4, and expenses with 5. Exhibit 6-3 diagrams one structure for computerized accounts. Assets are divided into current assets, fixed assets (property, plant, and equipment), and other assets. Among the current assets, we illustrate only three general ledger accounts: Cash in Bank (Account No. 111), Accounts Receivable (No. 112), and Prepaid Insurance (No. 115).

The account numbers in Exhibit 6-3 get longer and more detailed as you move from top to bottom. For example, Customer A's account number is 1120001: 112 represents Accounts Receivable, and 0001 refers to Customer A.

Computerized accounting systems rely on account *number ranges* to translate accounts and their balances into properly organized financial statements and other reports. For example, accounts numbered 101–399 (assets, liabilities, and owner's equity) are sorted to the balance sheet, while accounts numbered 401–599 (revenues and expenses) go to the income statement.

 DAILY EXERCISE 6-4

EXHIBIT 6-3
Structure for Computerized Accounts

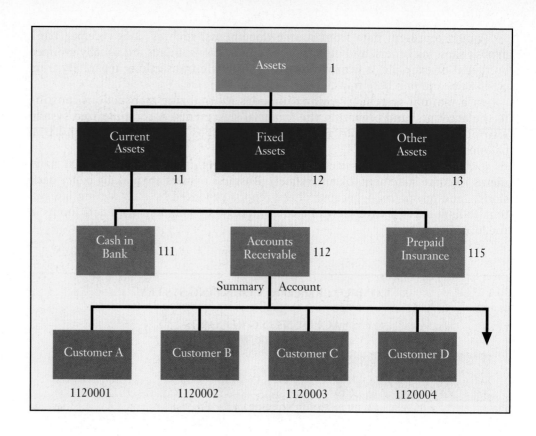

Processing Transactions: Manual and Menu-Driven Systems

Recording transactions in an actual accounting system requires an additional step that we have skipped thus far. A business of any size classifies transactions by type for efficient handling. In a manual system, credit sales, purchases on account, cash receipts, and cash payments are treated as four separate categories, with each entered into its own special journal. (We discuss these journals in detail later in this chapter.) For example:

- Credit sales are recorded in a special journal called a *sales journal.*
- Cash receipts are entered into a *cash receipts journal.*
- Credit purchases of inventory and other assets are recorded in a *purchases journal.*
- Cash payments are entered in a *cash payments journal.*
- Transactions that do not fit any of the special journals, such as the adjusting entries at the end of the period, are recorded in the *general journal,* which serves as the "journal of last resort."

 MENU. A list of options for choosing computer functions.

ON-LINE PROCESSING. Computerized processing of related functions, such as the recording and posting of transactions, on a continuous basis.

BATCH PROCESSING. Computerized accounting for similar transactions in a group or batch.

Computerized systems are organized by function, or task. Access to functions is arranged in terms of menus. A **menu** is a list of options for choosing computer functions. In a *menu-driven* system, you first access the most general group of functions, called the *main menu.* You then choose from one or more submenus until you finally reach the function you want.

Exhibit 6-4 illustrates one type of menu structure. The row at the top of the exhibit shows the main menu. The computer operator (or accountant) has chosen the General option (short for General Ledger), highlighted by the cursor. This action opened a submenu of four items—Transactions, Posting, Account Maintenance, and Closing. The Transactions option was then chosen (highlighted).

Posting in a computerized system can be performed continuously as transactions are being recorded (**on-line processing**) or later for a group or batch of similar transactions (**batch processing**). In either case, posting is automatic. Batch processing of accounting data allows accountants to check the entries for accuracy before posting them. In effect, data are "parked" in the computer to await posting, which simply updates the account balances.

Accounting Pioneers on the Virtual Frontier

As you saw in the chapter-opening story, computer and Internet technology are remaking the bookkeeping and tax aspects of accounting. There are "virtual" software consultants, and now there are "virtual" or "on-line" accountants. Slogans like "Real Accounting in a Virtual World" and "Outsourced Accounting Services for a Wired World" are advertising

- basic bookkeeping
- full-service outsourcing
- real-time accounting
- 24-hour access to accounting data

TADOnline, founded by Lance and Deanna Gildea in San Diego, is one such service. TAD starts clients out scanning their invoices, bank statements, and other documents into the computer. Scanned documents are transmitted to TAD, and within minutes, TAD updates the client's accounts. Customers then use a Web browser to sign in to a home page prepared by TAD, where they can view, print, and download reports, checks, and other information. Soon clients will be able to get real-time access to their accounting data through a new Web-based service.

For clients—typically small- to mid-sized businesses—the key benefits of TADOnline are price and reliability. In some cases, TAD's monthly fees are half what it would cost to hire a bookkeeper—and TAD doesn't call in sick or take vacations. A big plus for the "virtual accountants" is being able to live wherever they please, regardless of where clients are located. For TAD's Lance and Deanna Gildea, that means San Diego half the year and scenic Vashon Island, Washington, for the other half.

Source: Adapted from Antoinette Alexander, "Pioneers on the virtual frontier," *Accounting Technology,* Jan./Feb. 2000, pp. 18–24.

EXHIBIT **6-4** **Main Menu of a Computerized Accounting System**

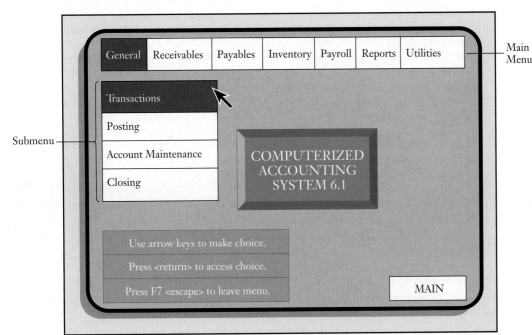

Outputs—accounting reports—are the final stage of data processing. In a computerized system, financial statements can be printed automatically. For example, the Reports option in the main menu gives the operator various report choices, which are expanded in the Reports submenu of Exhibit 6-5. In the exhibit, the operator is working with the financial statements, and specifically the balance sheet, as shown by the highlighting.

EXHIBIT 6-5
Reports Submenu of a Computerized Accounting System

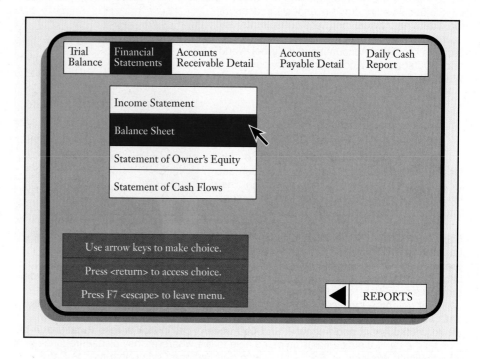

Exhibit 6-6 summarizes the accounting cycle in a computerized system and in a manual system. Compare and contrast the two types of systems.

EXHIBIT 6-6
Comparison of the Accounting Cycle in a Computerized and a Manual System

Computerized System	Manual System
1. Start with the account balances in the ledger at the beginning of the period.	1. Same.
2. Classify transactions by type. Access appropriate menus for data entry.	2. Analyze and journalize transactions as they occur.
3. Automatic posting of transactions as a batch or when entered on-line.	3. Post journal entries to the ledger accounts.
4. Unadjusted balances available immediately after each posting.	4. Compute the unadjusted balance in each account at the end of the period.
5. The trial balance, if needed, can be accessed as a report.	5. Enter the trial balance on the work sheet, and complete the work sheet.
6. Enter and post the adjusting entries. Print the financial statements. Run automatic closing procedure after backing up the period's accounting records.	6. Prepare the financial statements. Journalize and post the adjusting entries. Journalize and post the closing entries.
7. The next period's opening balances are created automatically as a result of closing.	7. Prepare the postclosing trial balance. This trial balance becomes step 1 for the next period.

MODULE. Separate compatible units of an accounting package that are integrated to function together.

Integrated Accounting Software: Spreadsheets

Computerized accounting packages are organized by **modules,** separate but integrated units that are compatible and that function together. Changes affecting one module will affect others. For example, entering and posting a credit-sale transaction will update two modules: Accounts Receivable/Sales and Inventory/Cost of Goods Sold. Accounting packages, such as QuickBooks and Peachtree, come as an integrated system.

You may be preparing your homework assignments manually. Imagine preparing a work sheet for **General Motors** (GM). Each adjustment changes the company's financial statement totals. Consider computing GM's revenue amounts by hand. The task would be overwhelming. For even a small business with only a few departments, the computations are tedious, time-consuming, and therefore expensive. Also, errors are likely.

Spreadsheets are computer programs that link data by means of formulas and functions. These electronic work sheets were invented to update budgets. Spreadsheets are organized as a rectangular grid composed of *cells,* each defined by a row number and a column number. A cell can contain words (called labels), numbers, or formulas (relationships among cells). The *cursor,* or electronic highlighter, indicates which cell is active. When the cursor is placed over any cell, information can be entered there for processing.

Exhibit 6-7 shows a simple income statement on a spreadsheet screen. The labels were entered in cells A1 through A4. The dollar amount of revenues was entered in cell B2 and expenses in cell B3. A formula was placed in cell B4 as follows: =B2−B3. This formula subtracts expenses from revenues to compute net income in cell B4. If revenues in cell B2 increase to $170,000, net income in B4 automatically increases to $80,000. No other cells will change.

Objective 3
Understand how spreadsheets are used in accounting

SPREADSHEET. A computer program that links data by means of formulas and functions; an electronic work sheet.

EXHIBIT 6-7
A Spreadsheet Screen

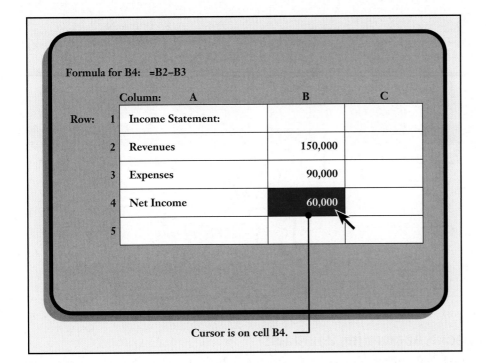

Formula for B4:   =B2−B3

Row:	Column: A	B	C
1	Income Statement:		
2	Revenues	150,000	
3	Expenses	90,000	
4	Net Income	60,000	
5			

Cursor is on cell B4.

Spreadsheets are ideally suited to preparing a budget, which summarizes the financial goals of a business. Consider **Procter & Gamble,** whose Health-Care Sector has an annual advertising budget of several hundred million dollars. Suppose Procter & Gamble allocates $50 million for its Crest Complete toothbrush. Procter & Gamble's advertising expenses will increase. The company will also forecast an increase in sales revenue, cost of goods sold, and other expenses. A spreadsheet computes all these changes in response to the advertising. It lets Procter & Gamble's managers track the profitability of each product. Armed with current data, the managers can make informed decisions. The result is higher profits.

We can add or delete whole rows and columns of data and move blocks of numbers and words on a spreadsheet. The power of a spreadsheet is apparent when enormous amounts of data must be analyzed. Change only one number, and you save hours of manual recalculation. Exhibit 6-8 shows the basic arithmetic operations in popular spreadsheet programs such as Excel.

EXHIBIT 6-8
Basic Arithmetic Operations in Excel Spreadsheets

Operation	Symbol
Addition	+
Subtraction...	−
Multiplication...	*
Division	/
Addition of a range of cells	=SUM(beginning cell:ending cell)
Examples:	
Add the contents of cells A2 through A9	=SUM(A2:A9)
Divide the contents of cell C2 by the	
contents of cell D1	=C2/D1

DAILY EXERCISE 6-5

www.prenhall.com/horngren
Mid-Chapter Assessment

SPECIAL JOURNALS

Exhibit 6-9 diagrams a typical accounting system for a merchandising business. The remainder of this chapter describes some of the more important aspects of that system.

EXHIBIT 6-9   **Overview of an Accounting System with Special Journals for a Merchandising Business**

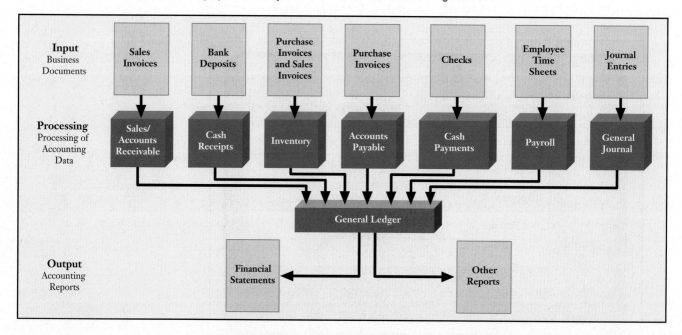

Special Accounting Journals

GENERAL JOURNAL. Journal used to record all transactions that do not fit one of the special journals.

SPECIAL JOURNAL. An accounting journal designed to record one specific type of transaction.

The journal entries illustrated so far in this book have been made in the **general journal.** This journal is used to record all transactions that do not fit one of the special journals. In practice, it is not efficient to record all transactions in the general journal, so we use special journals. A **special journal** is an accounting journal designed to record one specific type of transaction.

Both manual and computerized systems organize transaction entries by type using special journals and accounting modules. In a computerized system, accountants input data through various modules, such as the Accounts Receivable module for credit sales. In a manual system, they enter transaction data in special journals. But the underlying accounting principles are the same in both manual and computerized systems.

In all likelihood, you will be working with a computerized system. We would rather you *not* view the process as a black box. To help you understand the basic accounting, over the next several pages we take you through the steps in a manual system.

Most of a business's transactions fall into one of five categories, so accountants use five different journals to record these transactions. This system reduces the time and cost otherwise spent journalizing. The five categories of transactions, the related journal, and the posting abbreviations are as follows:

Transaction	Special Journal	Posting Abbreviation
1. Sale on account	Sales journal	S
2. Cash receipt	Cash receipts journal	CR
3. Purchase on account	Purchases journal	P
4. Cash payment	Cash payments journal	CP
5. All others	General journal	J

◉ DAILY EXERCISE 6-6

Adjusting and closing entries are entered in the general journal. Transactions are recorded in either the general journal or a special journal, but not in both.

Objective 4
Use the sales journal, the cash receipts journal, and the accounts receivable subsidiary ledger

Using the Sales Journal

Most merchandisers sell at least some of their inventory on account. These credit sales are entered in the **sales journal.** Credit sales of assets other than inventory—for example, buildings—occur infrequently and are recorded in the general journal.

SALES JOURNAL. Special journal used to record credit sales.

Exhibit 6-10 illustrates a sales journal (Panel A) and the related posting to the ledgers (Panel B) of **Austin Sound Center,** introduced in Chapter 5. Each entry in the Accounts Receivable/Sales Revenue column of the sales journal in Exhibit 6-10 is a debit (Dr.) to Accounts Receivable and a credit (Cr.) to Sales Revenue, as the heading above this column indicates. For each transaction, the accountant enters the date, invoice number, customer account, and transaction amount. This streamlined way of recording sales on account saves a vast amount of time that, in a manual system, would be spent entering account titles and dollar amounts in the general journal.

In recording credit sales in previous chapters, we did not keep a record of the names of credit-sale customers. In practice, the business must know the amount receivable from each customer. How else can the company keep track of who owes it money, when collection is due, and how much?

Consider the first transaction in Panel A. On November 2, Austin Sound sold stereo equipment on account to Maria Galvez for $935. The invoice number is 422. All this information appears on a single line in the sales journal. No explanation is necessary. The transaction's presence in the sales journal means it is a credit sale, debited to Accounts Receivable—Maria Galvez and credited to Sales Revenue. To gain additional information about the transaction, we would look up the actual invoice.

◉ DAILY EXERCISE 6-7

◉ DAILY EXERCISE 6-8

Recall from Chapter 5 that Austin Sound uses a *perpetual* inventory system. At the time of recording the sale, Austin Sound also records the cost of the goods sold and the decrease in inventory. Many computerized accounting systems are programmed to read both the sales amount (from the bar code on the package of the item sold) and the cost of goods sold. A separate column of the sales journal holds the cost of goods sold and inventory amount—$505 for the sale to Maria Galvez. If Austin Sound used a *periodic* inventory system, it would not record cost of goods sold and the decrease in inventory at the time of sale. The sales journal would need only one column to debit Accounts Receivable and to credit Sales Revenue for the amount of the sale.

POSTING TO THE GENERAL LEDGER   The ledger we have used so far is the **general ledger,** which holds the accounts reported in the financial statements. We will soon introduce other ledgers.

GENERAL LEDGER. Ledger of accounts that are reported in the financial statements.

Posting from the sales journal to the general ledger can be done only once each month. In Exhibit 6-10 (Panel A), November's credit sales total $4,319. This column has two headings, Accounts Receivable and Sales Revenue. When the $4,319 is posted to these accounts in the general ledger, their account numbers are written beneath the total in the sales journal. In Panel B of Exhibit 6-10, the account number for Accounts Receivable is 112 and the account number for Sales Revenue is

Exhibit 6-10 Sales Journal (Panel A) and Posting to the Ledgers (Panel B)

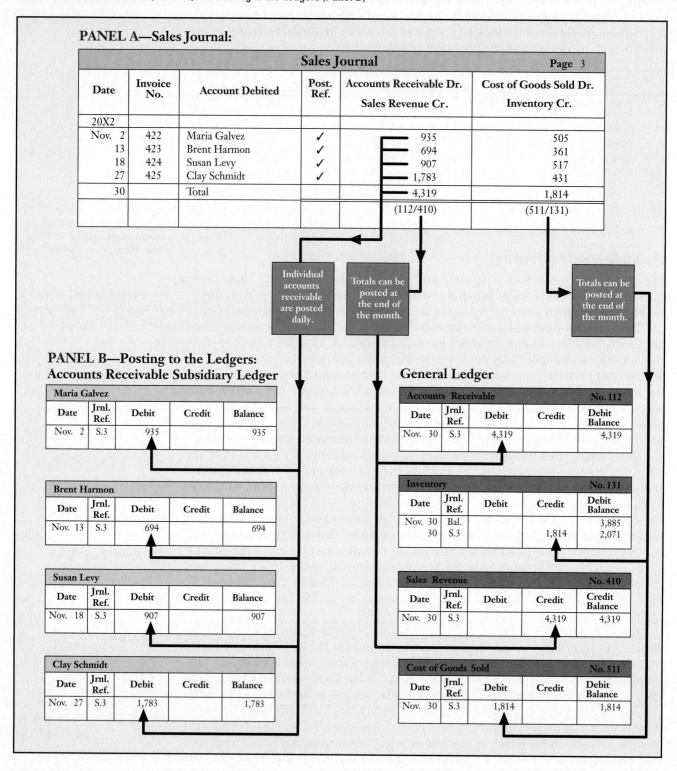

410. Printing these account numbers beneath the credit-sales total in the sales journal signifies that the $4,319 has been posted to the two accounts.

The debit to Cost of Goods Sold and the credit to Inventory for the monthly total of $1,814 can also be posted at the end of the month. After posting, these accounts' numbers are entered beneath the total to show that Cost of Goods Sold and Inventory have been updated.

POSTING TO THE ACCOUNTS RECEIVABLE SUBSIDIARY LEDGER The $4,319 sum of the November debits to Accounts Receivable does not identify the amount receivable from any specific customer. A business may have thousands of customers. For example, the **Consumers Digest Company,** a Chicago-based firm that publishes the bimonthly magazine *Consumers Digest,* has 1.2 million customer accounts—one for each subscriber.

To streamline operations, businesses place the accounts of their individual credit customers in a subsidiary ledger, called the Accounts Receivable ledger. A **subsidiary ledger** is a record of accounts that provides supporting details on individual balances, the total of which appears in a general ledger account. The customer accounts are arranged in alphabetical order.

Amounts in the sales journal are posted to the subsidiary ledger *daily* to keep a current record of the amount receivable from each customer. Daily posting allows the business to answer customer inquiries promptly. Suppose Maria Galvez telephones Austin Sound on November 3 to ask how much money she owes. The subsidiary ledger readily provides that information, $935 in Exhibit 6-10, Panel B.

When each transaction amount is posted to the subsidiary ledger, a check mark or some other notation is entered in the posting reference column of the sales journal (see Exhibit 6-10, Panel A).

SUBSIDIARY LEDGER. Record of accounts that provides supporting details on individual balances, the total of which appears in a general ledger account.

JOURNAL REFERENCES IN THE LEDGERS When amounts are posted to the ledgers, the journal page number is printed in the account to identify the source of the data. All transaction data in Exhibit 6-10 originated on page 3 of the sales journal, so all journal references in the ledger accounts are S.3. The "S." indicates sales journal.

Trace all the postings in Exhibit 6-10. The most effective way to learn about accounting systems and special journals is to study the flow of data. The arrows indicate the direction of the information. The arrows also show the links between the individual customer accounts in the subsidiary ledger and the Accounts Receivable account. The Accounts Receivable debit balance in the general ledger should equal the sum of the individual customer balances in the subsidiary ledger, as follows:

General Ledger	
Accounts Receivable debit balance..............	$4,319

Subsidiary Ledger: Customer Accounts Receivable	
Customer	**Balance**
Maria Galvez	$ 935
Brent Harmon	694
Susan Levy	907
Clay Schmidt	1,783
Total accounts receivable.............................	$4,319

Accounts Receivable in the general ledger is a **control account.** Its balance equals the sum of the balances of a group of related accounts in a subsidiary ledger. The individual customer accounts are subsidiary accounts. They are said to be "controlled" by the Accounts Receivable account in the general ledger.

Additional data can be recorded in the sales journal. For example, a company may add a column to record sales terms, such as 2/10 n/30. The design of the journal depends on managers' needs for information.

CONTROL ACCOUNT. An account whose balance equals the sum of the balances in a group of related accounts in a subsidiary ledger.

 THINK IT OVER Suppose Austin Sound had 400 credit sales for the month. How many postings to the general ledger would be made from the sales journal? (Ignore Cost of Goods Sold and Inventory.) How many would there be if all sales transactions were routed through the general journal?

Answer: There are only two postings from the sales journal to the general ledger: one to Accounts Receivable and one to Sales Revenue. There would be 800 postings from the general journal: 400 to Accounts Receivable and 400 to Sales Revenue. This difference clearly shows the benefit of using a sales journal.

Using Documents as Journals

Many small businesses streamline their accounting systems by using their business documents as the journals. This practice avoids the need for special journals and saves money. For example, Austin Sound could keep sales invoices in a loose-leaf binder and let the invoices serve as the sales journal. At the end of the period, the accountant simply totals the sales on account and posts the total as a debit to Accounts Receivable and a credit to Sales Revenue. The accountant can also post directly from the invoices to customer accounts in the accounts receivable ledger.

Using the Cash Receipts Journal

CASH RECEIPTS JOURNAL. Special journal used to record cash receipts.

Cash transactions are common in most businesses. To record repetitive cash receipt transactions, accountants use the **cash receipts journal.**

Exhibit 6-11, Panel A, illustrates the cash receipts journal. The related posting to ledgers is shown in Panel B. The exhibit illustrates November transactions for Austin Sound Center.

Every transaction recorded in this journal is a cash receipt, so the second column (after the date) is for debits to the Cash account. The next column is for debits to Sales Discounts on collections from customers. In a typical merchandising business, the main sources of cash are collections on account and cash sales.

The cash receipts journal has credit columns for Accounts Receivable and Sales Revenue. The journal also has a credit column for Other Accounts, which lists sources of cash other than cash sales and collections on account. This Other Accounts column is also used to record the names of customers from whom cash is received on account.

In Exhibit 6-11, cash sales occurred on November 6, 19, and 28. Observe the debits to Cash and the credits to Sales Revenue ($517, $853, and $1,802). Each sale entry is accompanied by a separate entry that debits Cost of Goods Sold and credits Inventory for the cost of the merchandise sold. The column for this entry is at the far right side of the cash receipts journal.

On November 11, Austin Sound borrowed $1,000 from First Bank. Cash is debited, and Note Payable to First Bank is credited in the Other Accounts column because no specific credit column is set up to account for borrowings. For this transaction, we print the account title, Note Payable to First Bank, in the Other Accounts/Account Title column. This entry records the source of cash.

On November 25, Austin Sound collected $762 of interest revenue. The account credited, Interest Revenue, is printed in the Other Accounts column. The November 11 and 25 transactions illustrate a key fact about business. Different entities have different types of transactions; they design their special journals to meet their particular needs for information. In this case, the Other Accounts credit column is the catchall used to record all nonroutine cash receipt transactions.

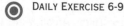

DAILY EXERCISE 6-9

On November 14, Austin Sound collected $900 from Maria Galvez. Referring to Exhibit 6-10, we see that on November 2, Austin Sound sold merchandise for $935 to Galvez. The terms of sale allowed a $35 discount for prompt payment, and she paid within the discount period. Austin's cash receipt is recorded by debiting Cash for $900 and Sales Discounts for $35, and by crediting Accounts Receivable for $935. The customer's name appears in the Other Accounts/Account Title column.

Total debits should equal total credits in the cash receipts journal. This equality holds for each transaction and for the monthly totals. For the month, total debits ($6,134 + $35 = $6,169) equal total credits ($1,235 + $3,172 + $1,762 = $6,169). The debit to Cost of Goods Sold and the credit to Inventory are separate.

POSTING TO THE GENERAL LEDGER Column totals can be posted monthly. To indicate their posting, the account number is written below the column total in the cash receipts journal. Note the account number for Cash (101) below the column total $6,134, and trace the posting to Cash in the general ledger. Likewise, the other column totals also are posted to the general ledger.

The column total for *Other Accounts* is *not* posted. Instead, these credits are posted individually. In Exhibit 6-11, the November 11 transaction reads "Note Payable to

PANEL A—Cash Receipts Journal:

Cash Receipts Journal
Page 5

| Date | Debits | | Credits | | | | | Cost of Goods Sold Dr. |
| | Cash | Sales Discounts | Accounts Receivable | Sales Revenue | Other Accounts | | | Inventory Cr. |
					Account Title	Post. Ref.	Amount	
20X2								
Nov. 6	517			517				290
11	1,000				Note Payable to First Bank	221	1,000	
14	900	35	935		Maria Galvez	✓		
19	853			853				426
22	300		300		Brent Harmon	✓		
25	762				Interest Revenue	460	762	
28	1,802			1,802				991
30	6,134	35	1,235	3,172	Totals		1,762	1,707
	(101)	(420)	(112)	(410)			(×)	(511/131)

PANEL B—Posting to the Ledgers: Accounts Receivable Subsidiary Ledger

Totals can be posted at the end of the month.

Individual accounts receivable are posted daily.

Individual amounts can be posted at the end of the month.

Total is not posted.

Totals can be posted at the end of the month.

Maria Galvez

Date	Jrnl. Ref.	Debit	Credit	Balance
Nov. 2	S.3	935		935
14	CR.5		935	-0-

Brent Harmon

Date	Jrnl. Ref.	Debit	Credit	Balance
Nov. 13	S.3	694		694
22	CR.5		300	394

Susan Levy

Date	Jrnl. Ref.	Debit	Credit	Balance
Nov. 18	S.3	907		907

Clay Schmidt

Date	Jrnl. Ref.	Debit	Credit	Balance
Nov. 27	S.3	1,783		1,783

General Ledger

Cash — No. 101

Date	Jrnl. Ref.	Debit	Credit	Debit Balance
Nov. 30	CR.5	6,134		

Accounts Receivable — No. 112

Date	Jrnl. Ref.	Debit	Credit	Debit Balance
Nov. 30	S.3	4,319		4,319
30	CR.5		1,235	3,084

Inventory — No. 131

Date	Jrnl. Ref.	Debit	Credit	Debit Balance
Nov. 30	Bal.			3,885
30	S.3		1,814	2,071
30	CR.5		1,707	364

Note Payable to First Bank — No. 221

Date	Jrnl. Ref.	Debit	Credit	Credit Balance
Nov. 11	CR.5		1,000	1,000

Sales Revenue — No. 410

Date	Jrnl. Ref.	Debit	Credit	Credit Balance
Nov. 30	S.3		4,319	4,319
30	CR.5		3,172	7,491

Sales Discounts — No. 420

Date	Jrnl. Ref.	Debit	Credit	Debit Balance
Nov. 30	CR.5	35		35

Interest Revenue — No. 460

Date	Jrnl. Ref.	Debit	Credit	Credit Balance
Nov. 25	CR.5		762	762

Cost of Goods Sold — No. 511

Date	Jrnl. Ref.	Debit	Credit	Debit Balance
Nov. 30	S.3	1,814		1,814
30	CR.5	1,707		3,521

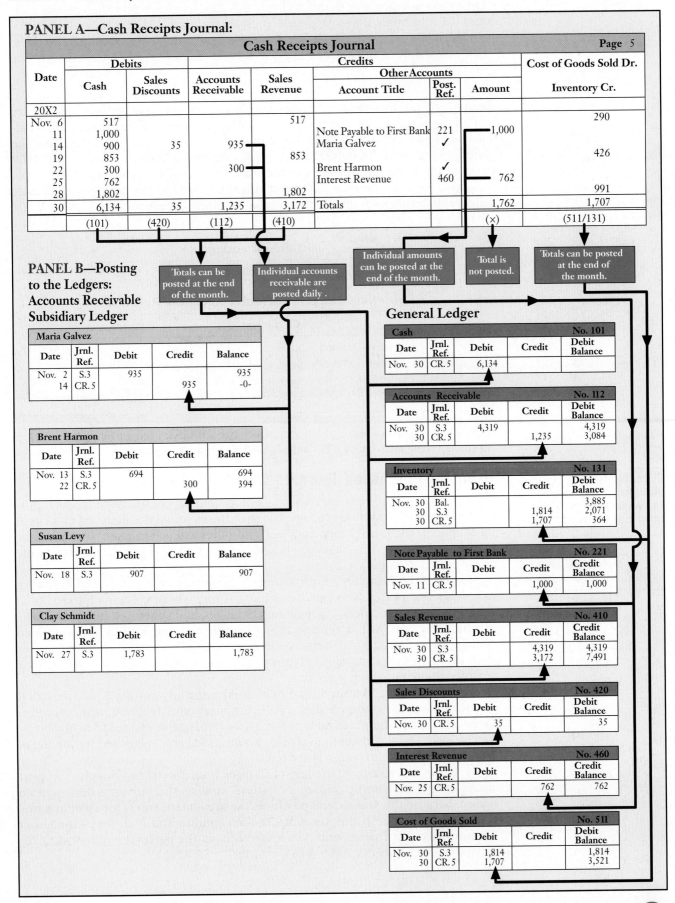

First Bank." This account's number (221) in the Post. Ref. column indicates that the transaction amount was posted individually. The letter x below the column indicates the column total was *not* posted. Individual amounts can be posted to the general ledger at the end of the month. But their date in the ledger accounts should be their actual date in the journal, to make it easier to trace each amount back to the journal.

POSTING TO THE SUBSIDIARY LEDGER   Amounts from the cash receipts journal are posted to the subsidiary accounts receivable ledger daily to keep the individual balances up to date. The postings to the accounts receivable ledger are credits. Trace the $935 posting to Maria Galvez's account. It reduces her balance to zero. The $300 receipt from Brent Harmon reduces his accounts receivable balance to $394.

After posting, the sum of the individual balances in the accounts receivable ledger equals the general ledger balance in Accounts Receivable.

General Ledger	
Accounts Receivable debit balance..............	$3,084

Subsidiary Ledger: Customer Accounts Receivable	
Customer	Balance
Brent Harmon	$ 394
Susan Levy	907
Clay Schmidt	1,783
Total accounts receivable............................	$3,084

Austin Sound's list of account balances from the subsidiary ledger helps it follow up on slow-paying customers. This helps a business manage cash.

Using the Purchases Journal

A merchandising business purchases inventory and supplies frequently. Such purchases are usually made on account. The **purchases journal** is designed to account for all purchases of inventory, supplies, and other assets *on account.* It can also be used to record expenses incurred on account. Cash purchases are recorded in the cash payments journal.

Exhibit 6-12 illustrates Austin Sound's purchases journal (Panel A) and posting to ledgers (Panel B).[1] This purchases journal has special columns for credits to Accounts Payable and debits to Inventory, Supplies, and Other Accounts. A periodic inventory system would replace the Inventory column with a column titled "Purchases." The Other Accounts columns accommodate purchases of items other than inventory and supplies. Accounts Payable is credited for all transactions recorded in the purchases journal.

On November 2, Austin Sound purchased inventory costing $700 from **JVC Corporation.** The creditor's name (JVC Corporation) is entered in the Account Credited column. The purchase terms of 3/15 n/30 are also entered to help identify the due date and the discount available. Accounts Payable is credited for the transaction amount, and Inventory is debited.

Note the November 9 purchase of fixtures from City Office Supply. The purchases journal contains no column for fixtures, so the Other Accounts debit column is used. Because this was a credit purchase, the accountant enters the creditor name (City Office Supply) in the Account Credited column and Fixtures in the Other Accounts/Account Title column. The total credits in the purchases journal ($2,876) equal the total debits ($1,706 + $103 + $1,067 = $2,876).

Objective 5
Use the purchases journal, the cash payments journal, and the accounts payable subsidiary ledger

PURCHASES JOURNAL. Special journal used to record all purchases of inventory, supplies, and other assets on account.

---

[1]This is the only special journal that we illustrate with the credit column placed to the left and the debit columns to the right. This arrangement of columns focuses on Accounts Payable (which is credited for each entry to this journal).

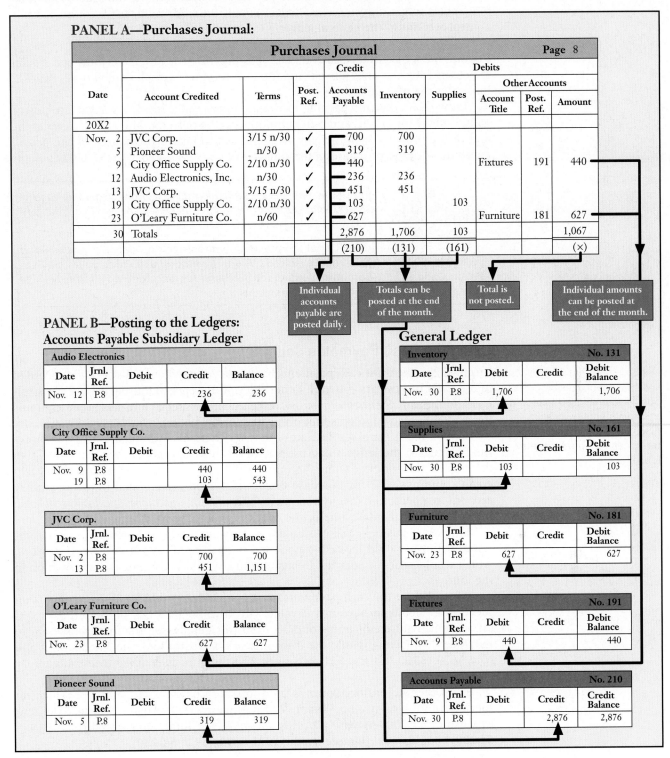

PANEL A—Purchases Journal:

ACCOUNTS PAYABLE SUBSIDIARY LEDGER To pay debts efficiently, a company must know how much it owes particular creditors. The Accounts Payable account in the general ledger shows only a single total for the amount owed on account. It does not indicate the amount owed to each creditor. Companies keep an accounts payable subsidiary ledger that is similar to the accounts receivable subsidiary ledger used in conjunction with credit sales.

The accounts payable subsidiary ledger lists the creditors in alphabetical order, along with the amounts owed to them. Exhibit 6-12, Panel B, shows Austin Sound's accounts payable subsidiary ledger, which includes accounts for Audio Electronics,

City Office Supply, and others. After the daily posting is done, the total of the individual balances in the subsidiary ledger equals the balance in the Accounts Payable control account in the general ledger.

POSTING FROM THE PURCHASES JOURNAL   Posting from the purchases journal is similar to posting from the sales journal and the cash receipts journal. Exhibit 6-12, Panel B, illustrates the posting process.

Individual accounts payable in the *accounts payable subsidiary ledger* are posted daily, and column totals and other amounts can be posted to the *general ledger* at the end of the month. In the ledger accounts, P.8 indicates the source of the posted amounts—that is, purchases journal page 8.

THINK IT OVER

Contrast the number of *general ledger* postings from the purchases journal in Exhibit 6-12 with the number that would be required if the general journal were used to record the same seven transactions.

Answer: Use of the purchases journal requires only five *general ledger* postings—$2,876 to Accounts Payable, $1,706 to Inventory, $103 to Supplies, $440 to Fixtures, and $627 to Furniture. Without the purchases journal, there would have been 14 postings, two for each of the seven transactions.

Using the Cash Payments Journal

CASH PAYMENTS JOURNAL.
Special journal used to record cash payments by check. Also called the **check register** or **cash disbursements journal.**

Businesses make most cash payments by check. All payments by check are recorded in the **cash payments journal.** Other titles of this special journal are the *check register* and the *cash disbursements journal.* Like the other special journals, it has columns for recording cash payments that occur frequently.

Exhibit 6-13, Panel A, illustrates the cash payments journal, and Panel B shows the postings to the ledgers of Austin Sound. This cash payments journal has two debit columns—one for Other Accounts and one for Accounts Payable. It has two credit columns—one for purchase discounts, which are credited to the Inventory account in a perpetual inventory system, and one for Cash. This special journal also has columns for the date and for the check number of each cash payment.

Suppose a business makes numerous cash purchases of inventory. What additional column would its cash payments journal need? A column for Inventory, which would appear under the Debits heading, would streamline the information in the journal.

All entries in the cash payments journal include a credit to Cash. Payments on account are debits to Accounts Payable. On November 15, Austin Sound paid JVC on account, with credit terms of 3/15 n/30 (for details, see the first transaction in Exhibit 6-12). Paying within the discount period, Austin took the 3% discount and paid $679 ($700 less the $21 discount). The discount is credited to the Inventory account.

The Other Accounts column is used to record debits to accounts for which no special column exists. For example, on November 3, Austin Sound paid rent expense of $1,200. As with all other journals, the total debits ($3,461 + $819 = $4,280) should equal the total credits ($21 + $4,259 = $4,280).

DAILY EXERCISE 6-10

DAILY EXERCISE 6-11

DAILY EXERCISE 6-12

POSTING FROM THE CASH PAYMENTS JOURNAL   Posting from the cash payments journal is similar to posting from the cash receipts journal. Individual creditor amounts are posted daily, and column totals and Other Accounts can be posted at the end of the month. Exhibit 6-13, Panel B, illustrates the posting process.

Observe the effect of posting to the Accounts Payable account in the general ledger. The first posted amount in the Accounts Payable account (credit $2,876) originated in the purchases journal, page 8 (P.8). The second posted amount (debit $819) came from the cash payments journal, page 6 (CP.6). The resulting credit balance in Accounts Payable is $2,057. Also, see the Cash account; after posting, its debit balance is $1,875.

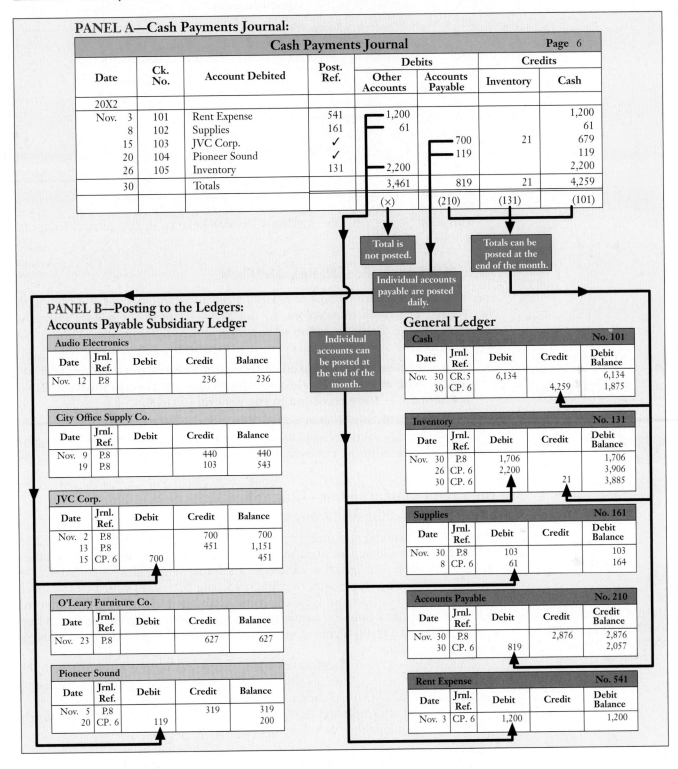

Amounts in the Other Accounts column are posted individually (for example, Rent Expense—debit $1,200). When each amount in the Other Accounts column is posted to the general ledger, the account number is entered in the Post. Ref. column of the journal. The letter x below the column signifies that the total is *not* posted.

To review their accounts payable, companies list the individual creditor balances in the accounts payable subsidiary ledger, as follows:

General Ledger

Accounts Receivable credit balance.............. $2,057

Subsidiary Ledger: Customer Accounts Receivable

Creditor	Balance
Audio Electronics	$ 326
City Office Supply	543
JVC Corp	451
O'Leary Furniture	627
Pioneer Sound..	200
Total accounts payable	$2,057

This total agrees with the Accounts Payable balance in the general ledger in Exhibit 6-13.

THE ROLE OF THE GENERAL JOURNAL

Special journals save much time in recording repetitive transactions and posting to the ledgers. But some transactions do not fit into any of the special journals. Examples include the depreciation of buildings and equipment, the expiration of prepaid insurance, and the accrual of salary payable at the end of the period.

Even the most sophisticated accounting system needs a general journal. The adjusting entries and the closing entries we illustrated in Chapters 3–5 are recorded in the general journal.

Accountants also record other transactions in the general journal. Many companies record their sales returns and allowances and their purchase returns in the general journal. Let's examine the *credit memorandum*, the document for sales returns and allowances.

The Credit Memorandum—Recording Sales Returns and Allowances

As we saw in Chapter 5, customers sometimes return merchandise to the seller, and sellers grant sales allowances to customers because of product defects and for other reasons. The effect of sales returns and sales allowances is the same—both decrease net sales in the same way a sales discount does. The document issued by the seller for a sales return or allowance is called a **credit memorandum,** or **credit memo,** because the company gives the customer credit for the returned merchandise. When a company issues a credit memo, it debits Sales Returns and Allowances and credits Accounts Receivable.

On November 27, Austin Sound sold four stereo speakers for $1,783 on account to Clay Schmidt. Later, Schmidt discovered a defect and returned the speakers. Austin Sound then issued to Schmidt a credit memo like the one in Exhibit 6-14.

To record the *sale return* and receipt of the defective speakers from the customer, Austin Sound would make the following entries in the general journal:

CREDIT MEMORANDUM OR CREDIT MEMO. A document issued by a seller to credit a customer account for returned merchandise.

	General Journal			Page 9
Date	Accounts	Post Ref.	Debit	Credit
Dec. 1	Sales Returns and Allowances	430	1,783	
	Accounts Receivable—Clay Schmidt............	112/✓		1,783
	Credit memo no. 27.			
Dec. 1	Inventory	131	431	
	Cost of Goods Sold	511		431
	Received defective goods from customer.			

Exhibit 6-14
Credit Memorandum Issued by
Austin Sound Center

| Credit Memorandum | No. 27 |

Austin Sound Center
305 West Martin Luther King Blvd.
Austin, Texas 78701

Date   December 1, 20X2

Customer Name   Clay Schmidt

538 Rio Grande, Apt.236

Austin, Texas 78703

Reason for Credit   Defective merchandise returned

Description	Amount
4 Trailblazer JU170456 Speakers	$1,783

Focus on the first entry. The debit side of the entry is posted to Sales Returns and Allowances. Its account number (430) is written in the posting reference column. The credit side of the entry requires two $1,783 postings, one to Accounts Receivable, the control account in the general ledger (account number 112), and the other to Clay Schmidt's account in the accounts receivable subsidiary ledger. These credit postings explain why the document is called a *credit memo*. The account number (112) denotes the posting to Accounts Receivable in the general ledger. The check mark (✓) denotes the posting to Schmidt's account in the subsidiary ledger. A business with a high volume of sales returns, such as a department store chain, may use a special journal for sales returns and allowances.

The second entry records Austin Sound's receipt of the defective inventory from the customer. The speakers cost Austin Sound $431, and Austin Sound, like all other merchandisers, records its inventory at cost. Now let's see how Austin Sound records the return of the defective speakers to JVC, from which Austin Sound purchased them.

The Debit Memorandum—Recording Purchase Returns and Allowances

Purchase returns occur when a business returns goods to the seller. The procedures for handling purchase returns are similar to those for handling sales returns. The purchaser gives the merchandise back to the seller and receives either a cash refund or replacement goods.

When a business returns merchandise to the seller, it may also send a business document known as a **debit memorandum,** or **debit memo.** This document states that the buyer no longer owes the seller for the goods. The buyer debits Accounts Payable and credits Inventory for the cost of the goods returned to the seller.

Many businesses record their purchase returns in the general journal. Austin Sound would record its return of defective speakers to JVC as follows:

DEBIT MEMORANDUM OR DEBIT MEMO. A document issued by a buyer when returning merchandise. The memo informs the seller that the buyer no longer owes the seller for the amount of the returned purchases.

	General Journal			Page 9
Date	Accounts	Post Ref.	Debit	Credit
Dec. 2	Accounts Payable—JVC Corp.	210/✓	431	
	Inventory	131		431
	Debit memo no. 16.			

Balancing the Ledgers

At the end of the period, after all postings, equality should exist between

1. *General ledger:*

> **Total debits = Total credits of all account balances**

2. *General ledger and Accounts receivable subsidiary ledger:*

> **Balance Accounts Receivable control account = Sum of individual customer account balances in the Accounts receivable subsidiary ledger**

3. *General ledger and Accounts payable subsidiary ledger:*

> **Balance of Accounts Payable control account = Sum of individual creditor account balances in the Accounts payable subsidiary ledger**

The process of ensuring that these equalities exist is called *balancing the ledgers*, or *proving the ledgers*. It is an important control procedure because it helps ensure the accuracy of the accounting records.

Blending Computers and Special Journals in an Accounting Information System

Computerizing special journals requires no drastic change in system design. Systems designers create a special screen for each accounting application (module)—credit sales, cash receipts, credit purchases, and cash payments. The special screen for credit sales would ask the computer operator to enter the following information: date, customer number, customer name, invoice number, and the dollar amount of the sale. These data can generate debits to the subsidiary accounts receivable and files from which the monthly customer statements that show account activity and ending balance are generated. For purchases on account, additional computer files keep the subsidiary ledger information on individual vendors.

The Decision Guidelines feature provides guidelines for some of the major decisions accountants must make as they use an information system.

DECISION GUIDELINES

Using Special Journals and Control Accounts

DECISION	GUIDELINES

What are the main components of an accounting system?	**Journals**
	• General journal
	• Special journals
	
	Ledgers
	• General ledger
	• Subsidiary ledgers
	   Accounts receivable
	   Accounts payable

Where to record • Sales on account? • Cash receipts? • Purchases on account? • Cash payments? • All other transactions?	**Journals** • Sales journal • Cash receipts journal • Purchases journal • Cash payments journal • General journal

How does the general ledger relate to the subsidiary ledgers?

GENERAL LEDGER

ACCOUNTS RECEIVABLE	ACCOUNTS PAYABLE
X,XXX		XX

SUBSIDIARY LEDGERS

ACCOUNTS RECEIVABLE FROM:

ARNOLD	BARNES
XX		XX	

ACCOUNTS PAYABLE TO:

AGNEW	BLACK
	X		X

Using Special Journals and Control Accounts

DECISION	GUIDELINES
When to post from the journals to • General ledger? • Subsidiary ledgers? How to achieve control over • Accounts receivable? • Accounts payable?	—Monthly (or more often, if needed) —Daily Balance the ledgers, as follows:

General Ledger		Subsidiary Ledger
Accounts receivable	=	Sum of individual *customer* account balances
Accounts payable	=	Sum of individual *creditor* account balances

REVIEW ACCOUNTING INFORMATION SYSTEMS

SUMMARY PROBLEM

Riggs Company completed the following selected transactions during March:

Mar. 4   Received $500 from a cash sale to a customer (cost, $319).

   6   Received $60 on account from Brady Lee. The full invoice amount was $65, but Lee paid within the discount period to gain the $5 discount.

   9   Received $1,080 on a note receivable from Beverly Mann. This amount includes the $1,000 note receivable plus interest revenue.

   15   Received $800 from a cash sale to a customer (cost, $522).

   24   Borrowed $2,200 by signing a note payable to Interstate Bank.

   27   Received $1,200 on account from Lance Albert. Collection was received after the discount period lapsed.

www.prenhall.com/horngren

End-of-Chapter Assessment

Required

The general ledger showed the following balances at February 28: Cash, $1,117; Accounts Receivable, $2,790; Note Receivable—Beverly Mann, $1,000; and Inventory, $1,819. The accounts receivable subsidiary ledger at February 28 contained debit balances as follows: Lance Albert, $1,840; Melinda Fultz, $885; Brady Lee, $65.

1. Record the transactions in the cash receipts journal, page 7.
2. Compute column totals at March 31. Show that total debits equal total credits in the cash receipts journal.
3. Post to the general ledger and the accounts receivable subsidiary ledger. Use complete posting references, including the following account numbers: Cash, 11; Accounts Receivable, 12; Note Receivable—Beverly Mann, 13; Inventory, 14; Note Payable—Interstate Bank, 22; Sales Revenue, 41; Sales Discounts, 42; Interest Revenue, 46; and Cost of Goods Sold, 51. Insert a check mark (✓) in the posting reference column for each February 28 account balance.
4. Show that the total of the customer balances in the subsidiary ledger equals the general ledger balance in Accounts Receivable.

Solution

Requirements 1 and 2

Cash Receipts Journal

	Debits		Credits					
					Other Accounts			
Date	Cash	Sales Discounts	Accounts Receivable	Sales Revenue	Account Title	Post. Ref.	Amount	Cost of Goods Sold Debit Inventory Credit
Mar. 4	500			500				319
6	60	5	65		Brady Lee	✓		
9	1,080				Note Receivable— Beverly Mann	13	1,000	
					Interest Revenue	46	80	
15	800			800				522
24	2,200				Note Payable— Interstate Bank	22	2,200	
27	1,200		1,200		Lance Albert	✓		
31	5,840	5	1,265	1,300	Total		3,280	841
	(11)	(42)	(12)	(41)			(✓)	(51/14)

Total Dr. = 5,845   Total Cr. = 5,845

Requirement 3

Accounts Receivable Ledger

Lance Albert

Date	Jrnl. Ref.	Debit	Credit	Balance
Feb. 28	✓			1,840
Mar. 27	CR.7		1,200	640

Melinda Fultz

Date	Jrnl. Ref.	Debit	Credit	Balance
Feb. 28	✓			885

Brady Lee

Date	Jrnl. Ref.	Debit	Credit	Balance
Feb. 28	✓			65
Mar. 6	CR.7		65	—

General Ledger

Cash   No. 11

Date	Jrnl. Ref.	Debit	Credit	Balance
Feb. 28	✓			1,117
Mar. 31	CR.7	5,840		6,957

Sales Revenue   No. 41

Date	Jrnl. Ref.	Debit	Credit	Balance
Mar. 31	CR.7		1,300	1,300

Accounts Receivable   No. 12

Date	Jrnl. Ref.	Debit	Credit	Balance
Feb. 28	✓			2,790
Mar. 31	CR.7		1,265	1,525

Sales Discounts   No. 42

Date	Jrnl. Ref.	Debit	Credit	Balance
Mar. 31	CR.7	5		5

Note Receivable—Beverly Mann   No. 13

Date	Jrnl. Ref.	Debit	Credit	Balance
Feb. 28	✓			1,000
Mar. 9	CR.7		1,000	—

Interest Revenue   No. 46

Date	Jrnl. Ref.	Debit	Credit	Balance
Mar. 9	CR.7		80	80

Inventory   No. 14

Date	Jrnl. Ref.	Debit	Credit	Balance
Feb. 28	✓			1,819
Mar. 31	CR.7		841	978

Cost of Goods Sold   No. 51

Date	Jrnl. Ref.	Debit	Credit	Balance
Mar. 31	CR.7	841		841

Note Payable—Interstate Bank   No. 22

Date	Jrnl. Ref.	Debit	Credit	Balance
Mar. 24	CR.7		2,200	2,200

Requirement 4

General Ledger

Accounts Receivable debit balance .... $1,525 ◄

Accounts Receivable Subsidiary Ledger: Customer Accounts Receivable

Customer	Balance
Lance Albert..	$ 640
Melinda Fultz..	885
Total accounts receivable	$1,525 ◄

LESSONS LEARNED

1. **Describe the features of an effective accounting information system.** An effective *accounting information system* has (1) control over operations; (2) compatibility with the particular features of the business; (3) flexibility in response to changes in the business; and (4) a favorable cost/benefit relationship.

2. **Understand how both computerized and manual accounting systems work.** Computerized accounting systems process inputs faster than manual systems. The key components of a system are *hardware, software,* and company personnel. Both computerized and manual accounting systems require transactions to be classified by type.

   Computerized accounting systems use a *menu* structure to organize accounting functions. Computerized systems are integrated so that the different modules are updated together. Manual systems use special journals for sales, cash receipts, purchases, and cash payments.

3. **Understand how spreadsheets are used in accounting.** *Spreadsheets* are electronic work sheets whose grid points, or cells, are linked by formulas. Numerical relationships remain whenever changes are made to the spreadsheet. Spreadsheets aid in detailed computations, such as budgeting.

4. **Use the sales journal, the cash receipts journal, and the accounts receivable subsidiary ledger.** Many accounting systems use special journals to record transactions by category. Credit sales are recorded in a *sales journal,* and cash receipts in a *cash receipts journal.* The accounts receivable *subsidiary ledger* lists each customer and the amount receivable from that customer. It is the main device for ensuring that the company collects from customers.

5. **Use the purchases journal, the cash payments journal, and the accounts payable subsidiary ledger.** Credit purchases in a manual system are recorded in a *purchases journal,* and cash payments in a *cash payments journal.* The accounts payable subsidiary ledger helps the company stay current in its payments to suppliers.

ACCOUNTING VOCABULARY

accounting information system (p. 227)
batch processing (p. 230)
cash disbursements journal (p. 242)
cash payments journal (p. 242)
cash receipts journal (p. 238)
check register (p. 242)
control account (p. 237)

credit memorandum or credit memo (p. 244)
database (p. 228)
debit memorandum or debit memo (p. 245)
general journal (p. 234)
general ledger (p. 235)
hardware (p. 228)
menu (p. 230)
module (p. 232)

network (p. 228)
on-line processing (p. 230)
purchases journal (p. 240)
sales journal (p. 235)
server (p. 228)
software (p. 228)
special journal (p. 234)
spreadsheet (p. 233)
subsidiary ledger (p. 237)

QUESTIONS

1. Describe the four criteria for an effective accounting system.
2. Distinguish batch computer processing from on-line computer processing.
3. What accounting categories correspond to the account numbers 1, 2, 3, 4, and 5 in a typical computerized accounting system?
4. Why might the number 112 be assigned to Accounts Receivable and the number 1120708 to Bill Thomas, a customer?
5. Describe the function of menus in a computerized accounting system.
6. How do formulas in spreadsheets speed the process of budget preparation and revision?
7. Name four special journals used in accounting systems. For what type of transaction is each designed?
8. Describe the two advantages that special journals have over recording all transactions in the general journal.
9. What is a control account, and how is it related to a subsidiary ledger? Name two common control accounts.
10. DeLay Company's sales journal has one amount column headed Accounts Receivable Dr. and Sales Revenue Cr. In this journal, 86 transactions are recorded. How many posting references appear in the journal? What does each posting reference represent?
11. The accountant for T-Questa Company posted all amounts correctly from the cash receipts journal to the general ledger. However, he failed to post three credits to customer accounts in the accounts receivable subsidiary ledger. How would this error be detected?
12. At what two times is posting done from a special journal? What items are posted at each time?
13. What is the purpose of balancing the ledgers?
14. Posting from the journals of Lexite Sales is complete. But the total of the individual balances in the accounts payable subsidiary ledger does not equal the balance in the Accounts Payable control account in the general ledger. Does this discrepancy necessarily indicate that the trial balance is out of balance? Explain.

Assess Your Progress

Daily Exercises

DE6-1 Suppose you have just invested your life savings in a **Baskin Robbins** franchise. The business is growing fast, and you need a better accounting information system. Consider the features of an effective system, as discussed on pages 227–228. Which do you regard as most important? Why? Which feature must you consider if your financial resources are limited?

Features of an effective information system (Obj. 1)

DE6-2 Match each component of a computerized accounting system with its meaning.

Components of a computerized accounting system (Obj. 1)

Component		Meaning
A. Server	_D_	Electronic linkages that allow different computers to share the same information
B. Hardware	_B_	Electronic equipment
C. Software	_C_	Programs that drive a computer
D. Network	_A_	Main computer in a networked system

DE6-3 Complete the crossword puzzle that follows.

Accounting system vocabulary (Obj. 1)

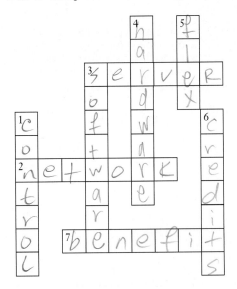

Down:

1. Managers need _____ over operations in order to authorize transactions and safeguard assets
3. Programs that drive a computer
4. Electronic computer equipment
5. A _____ible information system accommodates changes as the organization evolves
6. The opposite of debits

Across:

2. Electronic linkage that allows different computers to share the same information
3. Main computer in a networked system
7. Cost-_____ relationship must be favorable

DE6-4 Use account numbers 11–16, 21, 22, 31, 32, 41, 51, and 52 to correspond to the following selected accounts from the general ledger of Entreé Home Furnishings. List the accounts and their account numbers in proper order, starting with the most liquid current asset.

Setting up a chart of accounts (Obj. 2)

Depreciation expense	Madeline Jacobs, capital	Accounts receivable
Cash	Cost of goods sold	Note payable, long-term
Madeline Jacobs, withdrawals	Accounts payable	Store fixtures
Prepaid insurance	Inventory	
Accumulated depreciation	Sales revenue	

DE6-5 Refer to the spreadsheet screen in Exhibit 6-7, page 233. Suppose cells B1 through B4 are your business's actual income statement for the current year. You wish to develop your financial plan for the coming year. Assume that you expect revenues to increase by 15% and expenses to increase by 10%. Write the formulas in cells C2 through C4 to compute the amounts of expected revenues, expenses, and net income for the coming year.

Using a spreadsheet (Obj. 3)

DE6-6 Use the following abbreviations to indicate the journal in which you would record transactions a–n.

Using the journals (Obj. 4, 5)

J = General journal   P = Purchases journal
S = Sales journal   CP = Cash payments journal
CR = Cash receipts journal

Transactions:

CP a. Cash purchase of inventory.
CR b. Collection of dividend revenue earned on an investment.
CP c. Prepayment of insurance.
CR d. Borrowing money on a long-term note payable.
P e. Purchase of equipment on account.
S f. Cost of goods sold along with a credit sale.

CR g. Cash sale of inventory.
CP h. Payment of rent.
J i. Depreciation of computer equipment.
P j. Purchases of inventory on account.
CR k. Collection of accounts receivable.
J l. Expiration of prepaid insurance.
S m. Sale on account.
CP n. Payment on account.

Using the sales journal and the related ledgers (Obj. 4)

DE6-7 ← *Link Back to Chapter 5 (Gross Profit).* Use the sales journal and the related ledger accounts in Exhibit 6-10, page 236, to answer these questions about **Austin Sound Center.**

1. How much gross profit did Austin Sound earn on credit sales during November? For this answer, ignore sales discounts and sales returns and allowances.
2. What amount did Austin Sound post to the Sales Revenue account? When did Austin Sound post to the Sales Revenue account? Assume a manual accounting system.
3. After these transactions, how much does Susan Levy owe Austin Sound? Where do you obtain this information? Be specific.
4. If there were no discounts, how much would Austin Sound hope to collect from all its customers? Where is this amount stored in a single figure?

Using accounts receivable records (Obj. 4)

DE6-8

1. Where does the total amount receivable from all the customers appear? Be specific.
2. A key control feature of **Austin Sound Center's** accounting system lies in the agreement between the detailed customer receivable records and the summary total in the general ledger. Use the data in Exhibit 6-10, page 236, to prove that Austin Sound's accounts receivable records are accurate.
3. A business that sells on account must have good accounts receivable records to ensure collection from customers. What is the name of the detailed record of amounts collectible from individual customers?

Using cash receipts data (Obj. 4)

DE6-9 The cash receipts journal of **Austin Sound Center** appears in Exhibit 6-11, page 239, along with the company's various ledger accounts. Use the data in Exhibit 6-11 to answer the following questions that Charles Ernest, owner of the business, might face.

1. How much were cash sales during November?
2. How much did Austin Sound borrow during November? Where else could you look to determine whether Austin Sound has paid off part of the loan?
3. How much were total cash receipts during November?
4. How much cash did Austin Sound collect on account from customers? How much in total discounts did customers earn by paying quickly? How much did Austin Sound's accounts receivable decrease because of collections from customers during November?

Using the purchases journal and the cash payments journal (Obj. 5)

DE6-10 Refer to **Austin Sound Center's** purchases journal (Exhibit 6-12, page 241) and cash payments journal (Exhibit 6-13, page 243). Charles Ernest, the owner, has raised the following questions about the business.

1. At November 30, after all purchases and all cash payments, how much does Austin Sound owe **JVC Corporation?** How much in total does Austin Sound owe on account?
2. How much did total credit purchases of inventory, supplies, fixtures, and furniture increase Austin Sound's accounts payable during November?
3. How much of the accounts payable did Austin Sound pay off during November? What amount of cash did Austin Sound pay on account? Explain the difference.

Using the purchases journal and the cash payments journal (Obj. 5)

DE6-11 ← *Link Back to Chapters 1 and 2 (Recording transactions).* Use **Austin Sound's** purchases journal (Exhibit 6-12, page 241) and cash payments journal (Exhibit 6-13, page 243) to address these real-world questions faced by Charles Ernest, owner of the business.

1. Why did Austin Sound debit Rent Expense for the rent payment on November 3?
2. How much were Austin Sound's total purchases of inventory during November? How much were net purchases of inventory? What explains the difference between total purchases and net purchases? Which account holds these amounts?
3. Suppose it is December 1 and Ernest wishes to pay the full amount that Austin Sound owes on account. Examine the purchases journal (page 241) to determine whether Ernest can take any purchase discounts, and also consider the cash payments journal. Then make a general journal entry to record payment of the correct amount on December 1. Include an explanation.

DE6-12 Answer the following questions about the November transactions of Austin Sound Center. You will need to refer to Exhibits 6-10 through 6-13, which begin on page 236.

Using all the journals
(Obj. 4, 5)

1. How did Austin Sound purchase furniture—for cash or on account? Indicate the basis for your answer.
2. From whom did Austin Sound purchase supplies on account? How much in total does Austin Sound owe this company on November 30? Can Austin Sound take a discount when Austin Sound pays? Why or why not?
3. How much cash does Austin Sound have on hand at November 30? How much inventory does Austin Sound have after all transactions are recorded, including the cash receipts journal (Exhibit 6-11, page 239)? Indicate which exhibit provides each answer.
4. Determine Austin Sound's gross sales revenue and net sales revenue for November. Indicate which ledger provides the data for your answer.
5. Did Austin Sound's interest revenue for November result from a cash receipt or from an accrual of interest? How can you tell?

EXERCISES

E6-1 Assign account numbers (from the list that follows) to the accounts of AudioBasket. Identify the headings, which are *not* accounts and would not be assigned an account number.

Assigning account numbers
(Obj. 2)

Assets	Mark Lancaster, Capital
Current Assets	Mark Lancaster, Withdrawals
Accounts Receivable	Revenues
Note Payable, Long-Term	Depreciation Expense

Numbers from which to choose:

100	111	281
200	121	311
300	161	321
400	171	331
500	211	531

E6-2 The following accounts of Kim Fisher Company show some of the company's adjusted balances before closing:

Using a trial balance
(Obj. 2)

Total assets	$?	Long-term liabilities	$?
Current assets	31,600	Kim Fisher, capital	8,600
Plant assets	63,400	Kim Fisher, withdrawals	2,000
Total liabilities	?	Total revenues	28,000
Current liabilities	41,100	Total expenses	21,000

Compute the missing amounts. You must also compute ending owner's equity.

E6-3 Equipment listed on a spreadsheet has a cost of $400,000; this amount is located in cell B9. The number of years of the asset's useful life is found in cell C3. Write the spreadsheet formula to express annual depreciation expense for the equipment.

Using a spreadsheet to compute depreciation
(Obj. 3)

E6-4 The values of the following items are stored in the cells of a Kovar Associates spreadsheet:

Computing financial statement amounts with a spreadsheet
(Obj. 3)

Item	Cell
Total assets	B14
Current assets	B6
Fixed assets	B9
Total liabilities	C13
Current liabilities	C8
Long-term liabilities	C10

Write the spreadsheet formula to calculate the company's

a. Current ratio   **b.** Total owner's equity   **c.** Debt ratio

E6-5 The sales and cash receipts journals of Keester.com include the following entries:

Sales Journal

Date	Account Debited	Post. Ref.	Accounts Receivable Dr. Sales Revenue Cr.	Cost of Goods Sold Dr. Inventory Cr.
May 7	L. Ewald	✓	930	550
10	T. Ross	✓	4,100	1,970
10	E. Lovell	✓	690	410
12	B. Goebel	✓	5,470	3,340
31	Total		11,190	6,270

Cash Receipts Journal

	Debits				Credits			
						Other Accounts		Cost of Goods Sold Dr.
Date	Cash	Sales Discounts	Accounts Receivable	Sales Revenue	Account Title	Post. Ref.	Amount	Inventory Cr.
May 16					L. Ewald	✓		
19					E. Lovell	✓		
24	300			300				190
30					T. Ross	✓		

Keester.com makes all credit sales on terms of 2/10 n/30. Complete the cash receipts journal for those transactions indicated. Also, total the journal and show that total debits equal total credits. Each cash receipt was for the appropriate amount of the receivable.

E6-6 The cash receipts journal of EnvisioNet follows.

Cash Receipts Journal   Page 7

	Debits				Credits		
						Other Accounts	
Date	Cash	Sales Discounts	Accounts Receivable	Sales Revenue	Account Title	Post. Ref.	Amount
Jan. 2	794	16	810		Annan Corp.	(e)	
9	491		491		Kamm, Inc.	(f)	
19	4,480				Note Receivable	(g)	4,000
					Interest Revenue	(h)	480
30	314	7	321		J. T. Franz	(i)	
31	4,235			4,235			
31	10,314	23	1,622	4,235	Totals		4,480
	(a)	(b)	(c)	(d)			(j)

EnvisioNet's general ledger includes the following selected accounts, along with their account numbers:

Number	Account	Number	Account
111	Cash	511	Sales revenue
112	Accounts receivable	512	Sales discounts
113	Note receivable	513	Sales returns
119	Land	521	Interest revenue

Indicate whether each posting reference (a) through (j) should be a

- Check mark (✓) for a posting to a customer account in the accounts receivable subsidiary ledger.
- Account number for a posting to an account in the general ledger. If so, give the account number.
- Letter (x) for an amount not posted.

E6-7 A customer account in the accounts receivable ledger of Vitria Paint Company follows.

Identifying transactions from postings to the accounts receivable subsidiary ledger (Obj. 4)

Jo Mei Chang

Date		Jrnl. Ref.	Dr.	Cr.	Balance Dr.	Balance Cr.
Nov. 3	....				403	
6	....	S.5	1,180		1,583	
14	....	J.8		191	1,392	
27	....	CR.9		703	689	

Required

Describe the three posted transactions.

E6-8 During April, Nike/Time completed the following *credit purchase* transactions:

April	5	Purchased supplies, $1,106, from Disch Corporation
	11	Purchased inventory, $3,600, from Conn Corp. Nike/Time uses a perpetual inventory system.
	19	Purchased equipment, $14,300, from Saturn Co.
	22	Purchased inventory, $2,210, from Milan, Inc.

Recording purchase transactions in the general journal and in the purchases journal (Obj. 5)

Record these transactions first in the general journal—with explanations—and then in the purchases journal. Omit credit terms and posting references. Which procedure for recording transactions is quicker? Why?

Posting from the purchases journal; balancing the ledgers (Obj. 5)

E6-9 The purchases journal of Hans Bauman Company follows.

					Purchases Journal					Page 7

								Other Accounts Dr.		
Date	Account Credited	Terms	Post. Ref.	Account Payable Cr.	Inventory Dr.	Supplies Dr.	Acct. Title	Post. Ref.	Amt. Dr.
Sep. 2	Lancer Technologies	n/30		800	800				
5	Saturn Office Supply	n/30		175		175			
13	Lancer Technologies	2/10 n/30		1,151	1,151				
26	Faver Equipment Company	n/30		916			Equipment		916
30	Totals			3,042	1,951	175			916

Required

1. Open ledger accounts for Inventory, Supplies, Equipment, and Accounts Payable. Post to these accounts from the purchases journal. Use dates and posting references in the accounts.
2. Open accounts in the accounts payable subsidiary ledger for Faver Equipment Company, Lancer Technologies, and Saturn Office Supply. Post from the purchases journal. Use dates and journal references in the ledger accounts.
3. Balance the Accounts Payable control account in the general ledger with the total of the balances in the accounts payable subsidiary ledger.

E6-10 During August, Silicon Valley Sporting Goods had the following transactions:

Aug. 1 Paid $490 on account to Rabin Associates, net of a $10 discount for an earlier purchase of inventory.
5 Purchased inventory for cash, $4,300.
9 Paid $375 for supplies.
15 Purchased inventory on credit from Monroe Corporation, $774.
16 Paid $4,062 on account to LaGrange Company; there was no discount.
21 Purchased furniture for cash, $960.
26 Paid $3,910 on account to VisioNet Software for an earlier purchase of inventory. The discount was $90.
30 Made a semiannual interest payment of $800 on a long-term note payable. The entire payment was for interest.

Required

1. Prepare a cash payments journal similar to the one illustrated in this chapter. Omit the check number (Ck. No.) and posting reference (Post. Ref.) columns.
2. Record the transactions in the journal. Which transaction should not be recorded in the cash payments journal? In what journal does it belong?
3. Total the amount columns of the journal. Determine that total debits equal total credits.

E6-11 ◄ *Link Back to Chapter 5 (Recording Purchases, Sales, and Returns)*. The following documents describe two business transactions.

Invoice		
Date:	May 14, 20X0	
Sold to:	BiWheel Bicycle Shop	
Sold by:	Schwinn Company	
Terms:	2/10 n/30	

Items Purchased	Bicycles	
Quantity	**Price**	**Total**
8	$95	$760
1	70	70
5	60	300
Total		$1,130

Debit Memo		
Date:	May 20, 20X0	
Issued to:	Schwinn Company	
Issued by:	BiWheel Bicycle Shop	

Items Returned	Bicycles	
Quantity	**Price**	**Total**
1	$95	$ 95
1	70	70
Total		$165
Reason:	Damaged in shipment	

Required

Use the general journal to record these transactions and BiWheel's cash payment on May 21. Record the transactions first on the books of BiWheel Bicycle Shop and, second, on the books of **Schwinn Company,** which makes and sells bicycles. Both BiWheel and Schwinn use a perpetual inventory system as illustrated in Chapter 5. Schwinn's cost of the bicycles sold to BiWheel was $690. Schwinn's cost of the returned merchandise was $80. Round to the nearest dollar. Explanations are not required. Set up your answer in the following format:

Date	BiWheel Journal Entries	Schwinn Journal Entries

Challenge Exercise

E6-12 ◄ *Link Back to Chapter 5 (Cost of Goods Sold, Gross Profit)*.

1. **Austin Sound Center's** special journals in Exhibits 6-10 through 6-13 (pages 236–243) provide the owner with much of the data needed for preparation of the financial statements. Austin Sound uses the *perpetual* inventory system, so the amount of cost of goods sold is simply the ending balance in that account. Charles Ernest, the owner, needs to know the business's gross profit for November. Compute the gross profit.
2. Suppose Austin Sound uses the *periodic* inventory system. In that case, the business must compute cost of goods sold by the following formula:

Cost of goods sold:

Beginning inventory	$	X*
+ Net purchases		XXX
= Cost of goods available for sale		X,XXX
− Ending inventory		(XX)
= Cost of goods sold...............................	$	XX

*$0 for Austin Sound at November 1.

Perform this calculation of cost of goods sold for Austin Sound. Does this computation of cost of goods sold agree with your answer to requirement 1?

PROBLEMS

(Group A)

P6-1A The following spreadsheet shows the income statement of Tradex Technologies:

Using a spreadsheet to prepare an income statement and evaluate operations
(Obj. 3)

Row Number	Column	
	A	**B**
7	Revenues:	
8	Service revenue ⟶	
9	Rent revenue ⟶	
10		___
11	Total revenue ⟶	
12		
13	Expenses:	
14	Salary expense ⟶	
15	Supplies expense ⟶	
16	Rent expense ⟶	
17	Depreciation expense ⟶	
18		___
19	Total expenses ⟶	
20		___
21	Net income ⟶	
22		===

Required

1. Write the word *number* in the cells (indicated by arrows) where numbers will be entered.
2. Write the appropriate formula in each cell that will need a formula. Choose from these symbols.

+	add	*	multiply
−	subtract	/	divide
= SUM(beginning cell:ending cell)			

3. Last year, Tradex used this spreadsheet to prepare the company's budgeted income statement—which shows the company's net income goal—for the current year. It is now one year later, and Tradex has prepared its actual income statement for the year. State how the owner of the company can use this income statement in decision making.

P6-2A The general ledger of Ariba Genetics includes the following selected accounts:

Using the sales, cash receipts, and general journals
(Obj. 4)

Cash	11	Sales Revenue..................................	41
Accounts Receivable	12	Sales Discounts	42
Inventory	13	Sales Returns and Allowances.........	43
Notes Receivable	15	Interest Revenue	47
Supplies..	16	Cost of Goods Sold..........................	51
Land..	18		

All credit sales are on the company's standard terms of 2/10 n/30. Transactions in July that affected sales and cash receipts were as follows:

July 2   Sold inventory on credit to Intelysis, Inc., $2,400. Ariba's cost of these goods was $1,400.

3   As an accommodation to a competitor, sold supplies at cost, $85, receiving cash.

7   Cash sales for the week totaled $1,890 (cost, $1,640).

9   Sold merchandise on account to A. L. Prince, $7,320 (cost, $5,110).

10   Sold land that cost $10,000 for cash of $10,000.

11   Sold goods on account to Sloan Electric, $5,104 (cost, $3,520).

12   Received cash from Intelysis in full settlement of its account receivable from July 2.

14   Cash sales for the week were $2,106 (cost, $1,530).

15   Sold inventory on credit to the partnership of Wilkie & Blinn, $3,650 (cost, $2,260).

18   Received inventory sold on July 9 to A. L. Prince for $600. The goods shipped were unsatisfactory. These goods cost Ariba $440.

20   Sold merchandise on account to Sloan Electric, $629 (cost, $450).

21   Cash sales for the week were $990 (cost, $690).

22   Received $4,000 cash from A. L. Prince in partial settlement of his account receivable.

25   Received cash from Wilkie & Blinn for its account receivable from July 15.

25   Sold goods on account to Olsen Co., $1,520 (cost, $1,050).

27   Collected $5,125 on a note receivable, of which $125 was interest.

28   Cash sales for the week totaled $3,774 (cost, $2,460).

29   Sold inventory on account to R. O. Bankston, $242 (cost, $170).

30   Received goods sold on July 25 to Olsen Co. for $40. The inventory was damaged in shipment. The salvage value of these goods was $10. Record the inventory at its salvage value.

31   Received $2,720 cash on account from A. L. Prince.

Required

1. Ariba records sales returns and allowances in the general journal. Use the appropriate journal to record the preceding transactions in a sales journal (omit the Invoice No. column), a cash receipts journal, and a general journal.
2. Total each column of the cash receipts journal. Show that total debits equal total credits.
3. Show how postings would be made from the journals by writing the account numbers and check marks in the appropriate places in the journals.

Correcting errors in the cash receipts journal (Obj. 4)

P6-3A The following cash receipts journal of Trilogy Buying Cooperative contains five entries. All five entries are for legitimate cash receipt transactions, but the journal contains some errors in recording the transactions. In fact, only one entry is correct, and each of the other four entries contains one error.

Cash Receipts Journal   Page 22

| | Debits | | | Credits | | | | | Cost of Goods |
| | | | | | | Other Accounts | | | |
Date	Cash	Sales Discounts	Accounts Receivable	Sales Revenue	Account Title	Post. Ref.	Amount	Sold Debit Inventory Credit
2/6		7,200		7,200				2,900
7	429	22			Paul Dalton	✓	451	
14	8,200				Note Receivable	15	7,700	
					Interest Revenue	45	500	
18				330				150
24	1,100		770					
28	9,729	7,222	770	7,530	Totals		8,651	3,050
	(11)	(42)	(12)	(41)			(x)	(51/13)

Total Dr. = $16,951   Total Cr. = $16,951

Required

1. Identify the correct entry.
2. Identify the error in each of the other four entries.
3. Using the following format, prepare a corrected cash receipts journal.

Cash Receipts Journal

Date	Cash	Sales Discounts	Accounts Receivable	Sales Revenue	Account Title	Post. Ref.	Amount	Cost of Goods Sold Debit Inventory Credit
	Debits		**Credits**					
					Other Accounts			
2/6								
7					Paul Dalton	✓		
14					Note Receivable	15		
					Interest Revenue	45		
18								
24								
28	16,929	22	1,221	7,530	Totals		8,200	3,050
	(11)	(42)	(12)	(41)			(x)	(51/13)

Total Dr. = $16,951   Total Cr. = $16,951

P6-4A The general ledger of Sun Network.com includes the following accounts:

Using the purchases, cash payments, and general journals (Obj. 5)

Cash	111	Furniture	187
Inventory	131	Accounts Payable	211
Prepaid Insurance	161	Rent Expense	564
Supplies	171	Utilities Expense	583

Transactions in December that affected purchases and cash payments were as follows:

Dec. 2 Purchased inventory on credit from **Microsoft**, $4,000. Terms were 2/10 n/30.
  3 Paid monthly rent, debiting Rent Expense for $2,000.
  5 Purchased supplies on credit terms of 2/10 n/30 from Ross Supply, $450.
  8 Paid electricity utility bill, $588.
  9 Purchased furniture on account from A-1 Office Supply, $4,100. Payment terms were net 30.
  10 Returned the furniture to A-1 Office Supply. It was the wrong color.
  11 Paid Microsoft the amount owed on the purchase of December 2.
  12 Purchased inventory on account from Wynne, Inc., $4,400. Terms were 3/10 n/30.
  13 Purchased inventory for cash, $655.
  14 Paid a semiannual insurance premium, debiting Prepaid Insurance, $1,200.
  16 Paid our account payable to Ross Supply, from December 5.
  18 Paid gas and water utility bills, $196.
  21 Purchased inventory on credit terms of 1/10 n/45 from Software, Inc., $5,200.
  21 Paid account payable to Wynne, Inc., from December 12.
  22 Purchased supplies on account from Office Sales, Inc., $274. Terms were net 30.
  26 Returned to Software, Inc., $1,200 of the inventory purchased on December 21.
  31 Paid Software, Inc., the net amount owed from December 21 less the return on December 26.

Required

1. Sun Network.com records purchase returns in the general journal. Use the appropriate journal to record the preceding transactions in a purchases journal, a cash payments journal (omit the Check No. column), and a general journal.
2. Total each column of the special journals. Show that total debits equal total credits in each special journal.
3. Show how postings would be made from the journals by writing the account numbers and check marks in the appropriate places in the journals.

P6-5A Fairchild Fidelity Co., which uses the perpetual inventory system and makes all credit sales on terms of 2/10 n/30, completed the following transactions during May:

Using all the journals, posting, and balancing the ledgers (Obj. 4, 5)

May 2 Issued invoice no. 913 for sale on account to K. D. Forbes, $2,000. Fairchild's cost of this inventory was $900.
  3 Purchased inventory on credit terms of 3/10 n/60 from Chicosky Co., $2,467.
  5 Sold inventory for cash, $1,077 (cost, $480).
  5 Issued check no. 532 to purchase furniture for cash, $2,185.

May 8 Collected interest revenue of $1,775.
 9 Issued invoice no. 914 for sale on account to Bell Co., $5,550 (cost, $2,310).
 10 Purchased inventory for cash, $1,143, issuing check no. 533.
 12 Received cash from K. D. Forbes in full settlement of her account receivable from the sale on May 2.
 13 Issued check no. 534 to pay Chicosky Co. the net amount owed from May 3. Round to the nearest dollar.
 13 Purchased supplies on account from Manley, Inc., $441. Terms were net end-of-month.
 15 Sold inventory on account to M. O. Brown, issuing invoice no. 915 for $665 (cost, $240).
 17 Issued credit memo to M. O. Brown for $665 for defective merchandise returned to us by Brown. Also accounted for receipt of the inventory.
 18 Issued invoice no. 916 for credit sale to K. D. Forbes, $357 (cost, $127).
 19 Received $5,439 from Bell Co. in full settlement of its account receivable from May 9. Bell earned a discount by paying early.
 20 Purchased inventory on credit terms of net 30 from Sims Distributing, $2,047.
 22 Purchased furniture on credit terms of 3/10 n/60 from Chicosky Co., $645.
 22 Issued check no. 535 to pay for insurance coverage, debiting Prepaid Insurance for $1,000.
 24 Sold supplies to an employee for cash of $54, which was Fairchild's cost.
 25 Issued check no. 536 to pay utilities, $453.
 28 Purchased inventory on credit terms of 2/10 n/30 from Manley, Inc., $675.
 29 Returned damaged inventory to Manley, Inc., issuing a debit memo for $675.
 29 Sold goods on account to Bell Co., issuing invoice no. 917 for $496 (cost, $220).
 30 Issued check no. 537 to pay Manley, Inc., in full on account from May 13.
 31 Received cash in full on account from K. D. Forbes on credit sale of May 18. There was no discount.
 31 Issued check no. 538 to pay monthly salaries of $2,347.

Required

1. For Fairchild Fidelity, open the following general ledger accounts using the account numbers given:

Cash	111	Sales Revenue	411
Accounts Receivable	112	Sales Discounts	412
Supplies	116	Sales Returns and Allowances	413
Prepaid Insurance	117	Interest Revenue	419
Inventory	118	Cost of Goods Sold	511
Furniture	151	Salary Expense	531
Accounts Payable	211	Utilities Expense	541

2. Open these accounts in the subsidiary ledgers: Accounts receivable subsidiary ledger—Bell Co., M. O. Brown, and K. D. Forbes; accounts payable subsidiary ledger—Chicosky Co., Manley, Inc., and Sims Distributing.
3. Enter the transactions in a sales journal (page 7), a cash receipts journal (page 5), a purchases journal (page 10), a cash payments journal (page 8), and a general journal (page 6), as appropriate.
4. Post daily to the accounts receivable subsidiary ledger and to the accounts payable subsidiary ledger. On May 31, post to the general ledger.
5. Total each column of the special journals. Show that total debits equal total credits in each special journal.
6. Balance the total of the customer account balances in the accounts receivable subsidiary ledger against Accounts Receivable in the general ledger. Do the same for the accounts payable subsidiary ledger and Accounts Payable in the general ledger.

(Group B) PROBLEMS

Using a spreadsheet to prepare a partial balance sheet and evaluate financial positions (Obj. 3)

P6-1B The following spreadsheet on page 261 shows the assets of the Clarus Consulting balance sheet:

Required

1. Write the word *number* in the cells (indicated by arrows) where numbers will be entered.
2. Write the appropriate formula in each cell that will need a formula. Choose from these symbols:

Row Number	Column	
	A	B
2	Assets:	
3	Current assets:	
4	Cash ——————————→	
5	Receivables ——————→	
6	Inventory ————————→	_____
7		
8	Total current assets ———→	
9		
10	Equipment ———————→	
11	Accumulated depreciation ——→	
12		_____
13	Equipment, net ————→	
14		_____
15	Total assets ——————→	
16		════════

3. Last year Clarus used this spreadsheet to prepare the company's budgeted balance sheet for the current year. The budgeted balance sheet shows the company's goal for total current assets at the end of the year. It is now one year later, and Clarus has prepared its actual year-end balance sheet. State how the owner of the company can use this balance sheet in decision making.

P6-2B The general ledger of Remedy Corporation includes the following selected accounts:

Using the sales, cash receipts, and general journals
(Obj. 4)

Cash	111	Sales Revenue	411
Accounts Receivable	112	Sales Discounts	412
Notes Receivable	115	Sales Returns and Allowances	413
Inventory	131	Interest Revenue	417
Equipment	141	Gain on Sale of Land	418
Land	142	Cost of Goods Sold	511

All credit sales are on the company's standard terms of 2/10 n/30. Transactions in November that affected sales and cash receipts were as follows:

Nov. 2 Sold inventory on credit to Grant Thornton $800. Remedy's cost of these goods was $314.

6 As an accommodation to another company, sold new equipment for its cost of $770, receiving cash in this amount.

7 Cash sales for the week totaled $2,107 (cost, $1,362).

8 Sold merchandise on account to McNair Co., $2,830 (cost, $1,789).

9 Sold land that cost $22,000 for cash of $40,000. The difference is a gain.

11 Sold goods on account to Nickerson Builders, $6,099 (cost, $3,853).

11 Received cash from Grant Thornton in full settlement of his account receivable from November 2.

13 Cash sales for the week were $1,995 (cost, $1,286).

15 Sold inventory on credit to Montez and Montez, a partnership, $800 (cost, $517).

18 Received inventory sold on November 8 to McNair Co. for $120. The goods we shipped were unsatisfactory. These goods cost Remedy $73.

19 Sold merchandise on account to Nickerson Builders, $3,900 (cost, $2,618).

20 Cash sales for the week were $2,330 (cost, $1,574).

21 Received $1,200 cash from McNair Co. in partial settlement of its account receivable. There was no discount.

22 Received cash from Montez and Montez for its account receivable from November 15.

22 Sold goods on account to Diamond Co., $2,022 (cost, $1,325).

25 Collected $4,200 on a note receivable, of which $200 was interest.

Nov. 27 Cash sales for the week totaled $2,970 (cost, $1,936).
27 Sold inventory on account to Littleton Corporation, $2,290 (cost, $1,434).
28 Received goods sold on November 22 to Diamond Co. for $680. The goods were damaged in shipment. The salvage value of these goods was $96. Record the inventory at its salvage value.
30 Received $1,510 cash on account from McNair Co. There was no discount.

Required

1. Use the appropriate journal to record the preceding transactions in a sales journal (omit the Invoice No. column), a cash receipts journal, and a general journal. Remedy Corporation records sales returns and allowances in the general journal.
2. Total each column of the cash receipts journal. Determine that total debits equal total credits.
3. Show how postings would be made from the journals by writing the account numbers and check marks in the appropriate places in the journals.

Correcting errors in the cash receipts journal
(Obj. 4)

P6-3B The following cash receipts journal contains five entries. All five entries are for legitimate cash receipt transactions, but the journal contains some errors in recording the transactions. In fact, only one entry is correct, and each of the other four entries contains one error.

Cash Receipts Journal — Page 16

| | Debits | | | Credits | | | | | Cost of Goods Sold Debit |
| | | | | | | Other Accounts | | | |
Date	Cash	Sales Discounts	Accounts Receivable	Sales Revenue	Account Title	Post. Ref.	Amount	Inventory Credit
7/3	582	18	600		Alliance Chemicals	✓		
9			346	346	Carl Ryther	✓		
10	22,000			22,000	Land	19		
19	73							44
30	1,060			1,133				631
31	23,715	18	946	23,479	Totals			675
	(11)	(42)	(12)	(41)			(x)	(51/13)

Total Dr. = $23,733   Total Cr. = $24,425

Required

1. Identify the correct entry.
2. Identify the error in each of the other four entries.
3. Using the following format, prepare a corrected cash receipts journal.

Cash Receipts Journal — Page 16

| | Debits | | | Credits | | | | | Cost of Goods Sold Debit |
| | | | | | | Other Accounts | | | |
Date	Cash	Sales Discounts	Accounts Receivable	Sales Revenue	Account Title	Post. Ref.	Amount	Inventory Credit
7/3					Alliance Chemicals	✓		
9					Carl Ryther	✓		
10					Land	19		
19								
30								
31	24,061	18	946	1,133	Totals		22,000	675
	(11)	(42)	(12)	(41)			(x)	(51/13)

Total Dr. = $24,079   Total Cr. = $24,079

P6-4B The general ledger of Commerce One includes the following accounts:

Cash	111	Equipment	189
Inventory	131	Accounts Payable	211
Prepaid Insurance	161	Rent Expense	562
Supplies	171	Utilities Expense	565

Transactions in January that affected purchases and cash payments were as follows:

Jan.	4	Paid monthly rent, debiting Rent Expense for $1,350.
	5	Purchased inventory on credit from Sylvania Co., $5,000. Terms were 2/15 n/45.
	6	Purchased supplies on credit terms of 2/10 n/30 from Harmon Sales, $800.
	7	Paid gas and water utility bills, $406.
	10	Purchased equipment on account from Lancer Co., $1,050. Payment terms were 2/10 n/30.
	11	Returned the equipment to Lancer Co. It was defective.
	12	Paid Sylvania Co. the amount owed on the purchase of January 5.
	12	Purchased inventory on account from Lancer Co., $1,100. Terms were 2/10 n/30.
	14	Purchased inventory for cash, $1,585.
	15	Paid an insurance premium, debiting Prepaid Insurance, $2,416.
	17	Paid electricity utility bill, $165.
	19	Paid our account payable to Harmon Sales, from January 6.
	20	Paid account payable to Lancer Co., from January 12.
	21	Purchased supplies on account from Master Supply, $754. Terms were net 30.
	22	Purchased inventory on credit terms of 1/10 n/30 from Linz Brothers, $3,400.
	26	Returned inventory purchased for $500 on January 22, to Linz Brothers.
	31	Paid Linz Brothers the net amount owed from January 22, less the return on January 26.

Required

1. Use the appropriate journal to record the preceding transactions in a purchases journal, a cash payments journal (omit the Check No. column), and a general journal. Commerce One records purchase returns in the general journal.
2. Total each column of the special journals. Show that total debits equal total credits in each special journal.
3. Show how postings would be made from the journals by writing the account numbers and check marks in the appropriate places in the journals.

P6-5B Contour Publishing, which uses the perpetual inventory system and makes all credit sales of 2/10 n/30, had these transactions during March:

Mar.	2	Issued invoice no. 191 for sale on account to L. E. Wooten, $2,350. Contour's cost of this inventory was $1,390.
	3	Purchased inventory on credit terms of 3/10 n/60 from Delwood Plaza, $5,900.
	4	Sold inventory for cash, $1,413 (cost, $820).
	5	Issued check no. 473 to purchase furniture for cash, $1,087.
	8	Collected interest revenue of $2,440.
	9	Issued invoice no. 192 for sale on account to Cortez Co., $6,250 (cost, $3,300).
	10	Purchased inventory for cash, $776, issuing check no. 474.
	12	Received $2,303 cash from L. E. Wooten in full settlement of her account receivable, net of the discount, from the sale of March 2.
	13	Issued check no. 475 to pay Delwood Plaza net amount owed from March 3.
	13	Purchased supplies on account from Havrilla Corp., $689. Terms were net end-of-month.
	15	Sold inventory on account to J. R. Wakeland, issuing invoice no. 193 for $743 (cost, $410).
	17	Issued credit memo to J. R. Wakeland for $743 for defective merchandise returned to us by Wakeland. Also accounted for receipt of the inventory.
	18	Issued invoice no. 194 for credit sale to L. E. Wooten, $1,825 (cost, $970).
	19	Received $6,125 from Cortez Co. in full settlement of its account receivable from March 9.
	20	Purchased inventory on credit terms of net 30 from Jasper Sales, $2,150.
	22	Purchased furniture on credit terms of 3/10 n/60 from Delwood Plaza, $775.
	22	Issued check no. 476 to pay for insurance coverage, debiting Prepaid Insurance for $1,345.
	24	Sold supplies to an employee for cash of $86, which was Contour's cost.
	25	Issued check no. 477 to pay utilities, $388.
	28	Purchased inventory on credit terms of 2/10 n/30 from Havrilla Corp., $421.
	29	Returned damaged inventory to Havrilla Corp., issuing a debit memo for $421.
	29	Sold goods on account to Cortez Co., issuing invoice no. 195 for $567 (cost, $314).
	30	Issued check no. 478 to pay Havrilla Corp. on account from March 13.

Mar. 31 Received cash in full on account from L. E. Wooten on credit sale of March 18. There was no discount.

31 Issued check no. 479 to pay monthly salaries of $2,600.

Required

1. For Contour Publishing, open the following general ledger accounts using the account numbers given:

Cash	111	Sales Revenue	411
Accounts Receivable	112	Sales Discounts	412
Supplies.......................................	116	Sales Returns and Allowances	413
Prepaid Insurance	117	Interest Revenue...........................	419
Inventory	118	Cost of Goods Sold........................	511
Furniture......................................	151	Salary Expense.............................	531
Accounts Payable	211	Utilities Expense	541

2. Open these accounts in the subsidiary ledgers. Accounts receivable subsidiary ledger: Cortez Co., J. R. Wakeland, and L. E. Wooten. Accounts payable subsidiary ledger: Delwood Plaza, Havrilla Corp., and Jasper Sales.
3. Enter the transactions in a sales journal (page 8), a cash receipts journal (page 3), a purchases journal (page 6), a cash payments journal (page 9), and a general journal (page 4), as appropriate.
4. Post daily to the accounts receivable subsidiary ledger and to the accounts payable subsidiary ledger. On March 31, post to the general ledger.
5. Total each column of the special journals. Show that total debits equal total credits in each special journal.
6. Balance the total of the customer account balances in the accounts receivable subsidiary ledger against Accounts Receivable in the general ledger. Do the same for the accounts payable subsidiary ledger and Accounts Payable in the general ledger.

APPLY YOUR KNOWLEDGE

DECISION CASES

Designing a special journal (Obj. 4, 5)

Case 1. AccuTrac Software creates and sells cutting-edge networking software. AccuTrac's quality control officer estimates that 20% of the company's sales and purchases of inventory are returned for additional debugging. AccuTrac needs special journals for

- Sales returns and allowances
- Purchase returns and allowances

Required

1. Design the two special journals. For each journal, include a column for the appropriate business document.
2. Enter one transaction in each journal, using the **Austin Sound** transaction data illustrated on pages 236–243. Show all posting references, including those for column totals.

Reconstructing transactions from amounts posted to the accounts receivable subsidiary ledger (Obj. 4)

Case 2. A fire destroyed certain accounting records of DuPont Science Corp. The owner, François DuPont, asks for your help in reconstructing the records. *He needs to know the beginning and ending balances of Accounts Receivable and the credit sales and cash receipts on account from customers during March.* All of DuPont's sales are on credit, with payment terms of 2/10 n/30. All cash receipts on account reached DuPont within the 10-day discount period, except as noted. Round all amounts to the nearest dollar. The only accounting record preserved from the fire is the accounts receivable subsidiary ledger, which appears on page 265.

ETHICAL ISSUE

On a recent trip to Ireland, Ian O'Shea, sales manager of Elán, Inc., took his wife along at company expense. Martha Gibney, vice president of sales and O'Shea's boss, thought his travel and entertainment expenses seemed excessive. Gibney approved the reimbursement, however, because she owed O'Shea a favor. Gibney, well aware that the company president reviews all expenses recorded in the cash payments journal, had the accountant record O'Shea's wife's expenses in the *general* journal as follows:

Sales Promotion Expense	3,500	
Cash		3,500

Garcia Sales

Date	Item	Jrnl. Ref.	Debit	Credit	Balance
Apr. 1	Balance				440
3		CR.8		440	-0-
25		S.6	3,655		3,655
29		S.6	1,123		4,778

Leewright, Inc.

Date	Item	Jrnl. Ref.	Debit	Credit	Balance
Apr. 1	Balance				2,378
15		S.6	2,635		5,518
29		CR.8		2,883*	2,635

*Cash receipt did not occur within the discount period.

Sally Jones

Date	Item	Jrnl. Ref.	Debit	Credit	Balance
Apr. 1	Balance				1,096
5		CR.8		1,096	-0-
11		S.6	396		396
21		CR.8		396	-0-
24		S.6			5,108

Jacques LeHavre

Date	Item	Jrnl. Ref.	Debit	Credit	Balance
Apr. 8	Balance	S.6	2,378		2,378
16		S.6	903		3,281
18		CR.8		2,378	903
19		J.5		221	682
27		CR.8		682	-0-

Ethical Issue (continued)

Required

1. Does recording the transaction in the *general* journal rather than in the cash payments journal affect the amounts of cash and total expenses reported in the financial statements?
2. Why did O'Shea want this transaction recorded in the *general* journal?
3. What is the ethical issue in this situation? What role does accounting play in this issue?

TEAM PROJECTS

Project 1: Preparing a Business Plan for a Merchandising Entity. As you work through Part 2 of this book (Chapters 7–12), you will be examining in detail the current assets, current liabilities, and plant assets of a business. Most of the organizations that form the context for business activity in the remainder of the book are merchandising entities. Therefore, in a group or individually—as directed by your instructor—develop a plan for beginning and operating an audio/video store or other type of business. Develop your plan in as much detail as you can. Remember that the business manager who attends to the most details delivers the best product at the lowest price for customers!

Project 2: Preparing a Business Plan for a Service Entity. List what you have learned thus far in the course. On the basis of what you have learned, refine your plan for promoting a rock concert (from Team Project 2 in Chapter 1) to include everything you believe you must do to succeed in this business venture.

INTERNET EXERCISE

The Internet has opened new consulting opportunities for the accounting profession. The government has regulations and forms available on-line. Individual accountants have Web sites explaining the services they offer. Accounting organizations provide information to members at low cost through the Internet.

AICPA

1. Go to **http://www.AICPA.org** and read the information displayed. (Note: Make certain the URL uses the .org suffix for organizations rather than the .com suffix for companies.) What is the AICPA? How many accountants belong to this organization? What do the initials AICPA stand for?
2. In the left-hand column are links to a variety of accounting information. Click on *Students* and then *becoming a CPA*. List two characteristics of what earnings the CPA certification indicates.
3. In the left-hand column, click on *Pubs* and then the *current issue* of the "Journal of Accountancy." Scan one of the articles. List the title and author of the article and comment on one item of interest.
4. In the left-hand column, click on *CPA Links*.

   a. Click on *Accounting Associations*. Many of these associations offer scholarships and student memberships. What is Beta Alpha Psi?
   b. Go back to the CPA Links menu and click on *State Boards of Accountancy*. This board grants certificates and licenses to practice public accounting in that state. Click on the link to your state board of accountancy and comment on one item of interest.

7

Internal Control, Managing Cash, and Making Ethical Judgments

LEARNING OBJECTIVES

After studying this chapter, you should be able to

1. Define internal control

2. Identify the characteristics of an effective system of internal control

3. Prepare a bank reconciliation and the related journal entries

4. Apply internal controls to cash receipts

5. Apply internal controls to cash payments

6. Use a budget to manage cash

7. Make ethical judgments in business

Darlyne Lopez was a cashier at the Waco, Texas, office of the brokerage firm **Merrill Lynch.** Only after Lopez had an auto accident that landed her in the hospital did the Merrill Lynch office manager receive complaints from customers who had not received credit for their deposits. The result: Merrill Lynch uncovered a five-year-old embezzlement scheme.

The court found that Lopez stole over $600,000 in a "rob-Peter-to-pay-Paul" scheme. She transferred customer deposits into her own account and then concealed the missing amounts with deposits from other customers. Thus, customer accounts appeared to be in balance as long as Lopez manipulated the computerized records. But her replacement was unable to explain the missing deposits. All the evidence pointed in the direction of the absent employee. Lopez was sentenced to jail, and the Merrill Lynch office manager belatedly understood why his dedicated cashier never took a vacation.

What went wrong at **Merrill Lynch?** Darlyne Lopez controlled not only the cash received from customers, but also part of her company's computerized accounting records. By manipulating the records, she hid her theft for several years. Evidently, no one checked her work. Several procedures we discuss in this chapter will explain how Merrill Lynch could have prevented the embezzlement.

To protect people's money and avoid situations like the one at Merrill Lynch, the Foreign Corrupt Practices Act requires companies under SEC jurisdiction to maintain a system of internal control, whether or not they have foreign operations. This chapter discusses *internal control*—the organizational plan managers use to protect company assets. The chapter applies control techniques mainly to cash (the most liquid asset) and provides a framework for making ethical judgments in business. Later chapters discuss how managers control other assets.

INTERNAL CONTROL

A key responsibility of managers is to control operations. Owners and top managers set a company's goals, managers lead the way, and employees carry out the plan. **Internal control** is the organizational plan and all the related measures that an entity adopts to

1. Safeguard the assets the business uses in its operations,
2. Encourage adherence to company policies,
3. Promote operational efficiency (obtain the best outcome at the lowest cost), and
4. Ensure accurate and reliable accounting records.

Internal controls are most effective when employees at all levels adopt the organization's goals and ethical standards. Top managers need to communicate these goals and standards to workers. Lee Iacocca, former president of **Chrysler Corporation,** instilled goals in Chrysler employees by spending time with assembly-line workers. (Japanese firms pioneered this style of participative management.) The result? Defects decreased, and Chrysler products became more competitive.

Exhibit 7-1 presents an excerpt from **Target Corporation's** Report of Management. The company's top managers take responsibility for the financial statements and for the related system of internal control. Let's examine in more detail how companies create an effective system of internal control.

An Effective Internal Control System

Whether the business is **First Fidelity, Target Corporation,** or a local department store, an effective system of internal controls has the following characteristics.

Objective 1
Define internal control

INTERNAL CONTROL. Organizational plan and all the related measures adopted by an entity to safeguard assets, encourage adherence to company policies, promote operational efficiency, and ensure accurate and reliable accounting records.

 DAILY EXERCISE 7-1

Objective 2
Identify the characteristics of an effective system of internal control

Report of Management

Management is responsible for the consistency, integrity and presentation of the information in the Annual Report.

To fulfill our responsibility, we maintain comprehensive systems of internal control designed to provide reasonable assurance that assets are safeguarded and transactions are executed in accordance with established procedures.

Robert J. Ulrich
Chairman of the Board and
Chief Executive Officer
February 28, 2000

Douglas A. Scovanner
Executive Vice President and
Chief Financial Officer

COMPETENT, RELIABLE, AND ETHICAL PERSONNEL   Employees should be *competent, reliable,* and *ethical.* Paying top salaries to attract top-quality employees, training them to do their job well, and supervising their work all help a company build a competent staff.

ASSIGNMENT OF RESPONSIBILITIES   In a business with a good internal control system, no important duty is overlooked. Each employee is assigned certain responsibilities. A model of this *assignment of responsibilities* appears in the corporate organizational chart in Exhibit 7-2. Notice that the company has a vice president of finance and accounting. Two other officers, the treasurer and the controller, report to that vice president. The treasurer is responsible for cash management. The **controller** is the chief accounting officer.

Within this organization, the controller may be responsible for approving invoices (bills) for payment, and the treasurer may actually sign the checks. Working under the controller, one accountant may be responsible for payroll,

CONTROLLER. The chief accounting officer of a company.

EXHIBIT 7-2   **A Corporate Organization Chart**

The Barings Bank Debacle: What Your Internal Auditor Tells You Might Save Your Company

On February 26, 1995, one fresh-faced 28-year-old trader brought a venerable 233-year-old British bank to its knees. Nick Leeson, a trader for **Barings Bank,** had bought $27

billion worth of securities on Japan's Nikkei stock market. When the Nikkei plunged, Barings lost $27 billion and collapsed. All fingers pointed to Leeson. How could a conservative bank allow this to happen? It soon became clear that nobody was supervising Leeson's trades.

Leeson worked in Barings' Singapore office from 1992 to the time of the collapse. Barings fell because it lacked internal controls. Leeson was allowed to execute *cross trades,* transactions in which he acted as both buyer and seller. Leeson's transactions were not at "arms' length," where the seller tries to get the highest price, and the buyer tries to pay the lowest price. Without arms' length trading, the amount of the transaction could be anything Leeson entered into the system. Amazingly, the bank did not require Leeson to give up his job as head of selling when he became head of buying.

From the start, Leeson lost money in Singapore, but he hid the losses—$296 million in 1994 alone. What did Leeson's bosses think of his performance that year? They thought he made a $46 million profit for the bank, and proposed paying him a bonus of $720,000.

Months before the collapse, Barings knew of Leeson's dual role. Internal auditors warned of "significant general risk" because Leeson controlled both the buying and the selling sides of transactions. But Barings' higher-ups viewed Leeson as a golden boy, and they ignored the audit report—with disastrous consequences.

Source: Based on Lillian Chew, "Not just one man," *http://www.risk.ifci.ch/137560.htm.* Robert D. Allen, "Managing internal audit conflicts," *Internal Auditor,* August 1996, p. 58. Anonymous, "The collapse of Barings: A fallen star," *Economist,* March 4, 1995, p. 19.

another accountant for depreciation. All duties should be clearly defined and assigned to individuals who bear responsibility for carrying them out.

 DAILY EXERCISE 7-2

PROPER AUTHORIZATION   An organization generally has written rules to outline its procedures. Any deviation from policy requires *proper authorization.* For example, an assistant manager of a retail store must approve customer checks for amounts above a certain limit. Likewise, a dean or department chair of a college and university must authorize a junior to enroll in courses restricted to seniors.

SEPARATION OF DUTIES   Smart management divides responsibility for transactions between two or more people or departments. *Separation of duties* limits the chances for fraud and promotes the accuracy of the accounting records. This crucial component of the internal control system can be divided into four parts:

1. *Separation of operations from accounting.* Accounting should be completely separate from the operating departments, such as manufacturing and sales. This

allows reliable records to be kept. What would happen if the sales personnel controlled the company's revenue records? Sales figures would probably be inflated, and top managers wouldn't know how much the company actually sold. Notice how accounting and marketing (sales) are separate in Exhibit 7-2.

2. *Separation of the custody of assets from accounting.* Temptation and fraud are reduced if accountants do not handle cash and if cashiers do not have access to the accounting records. If one employee has both cash-handling and accounting duties, that person can steal cash and conceal the theft by making a bogus entry on the books. We see this component of internal control in Exhibit 7-2. The treasurer has custody of the cash, and the controller accounts for the cash. Neither person has both responsibilities. Darlyne Lopez was able to apply one customer's cash deposit to another customer's account at **Merrill Lynch.** Apparently, Lopez, a cashier, controlled some data that went into the accounting system.

3. *Separation of authorization of transactions from custody of related assets.* Persons who authorize transactions should not handle the related asset. For example, the same person should not authorize a payment and also sign the check to pay the bill. Otherwise the person can authorize payments to him- or herself and then sign the checks. When these duties are separated, only legitimate bills get paid.

4. *Separation of duties within the accounting function.* Different people should perform the various accounting duties to minimize errors and the opportunities for fraud. For example, different accountants should be responsible for recording cash receipts and cash payments. The employee who processes cash payments should have nothing to do with the approval process.

◎ DAILY EXERCISE 7-3

◎ DAILY EXERCISE 7-6

THINK IT OVER

Ralph works at the Galaxy Theater. Occasionally, he must both sell tickets and take them as customers enter the theater. Standard procedure requires that Ralph tear the tickets, give half to the customer, and keep the other half. To control cash receipts, the theater manager compares each night's cash receipts with the number of ticket stubs on hand.

1. How could Ralph steal cash receipts and hide the theft? What additional steps should the manager take to strengthen the control over cash receipts?
2. What is the internal control weakness in this situation? Explain the weakness.

Answers

1. Ralph could
   • Issue no ticket and keep the customer's cash.

   • Destroy some tickets and keep the customers' cash.

   Management could
   • Physically count the number of people watching a movie and compare that number to the number of ticket stubs retained.
   • Account for all ticket stubs by serial number. Missing serial numbers raise questions.

2. The internal control weakness is the lack of separation of duties. Ralph receives cash and also controls the tickets.

AUDIT. An examination of a company's financial statements and the accounting system.

INTERNAL AND EXTERNAL AUDITS To guarantee the accuracy of their accounting records, most companies undergo periodic audits. An **audit** is an examination of the company's financial statements and the accounting system.

It is not economically feasible for auditors to examine all transactions, so they must rely on the accounting system to produce accurate records. To evaluate the company's accounting system, auditors examine its system of internal controls. Auditors often spot weaknesses in the system because they are objective in their outlook. The company's managers, on the other hand, are immersed in day-to-day operations and may overlook their own weaknesses.

Audits can be internal or external. Exhibit 7-2 shows *internal auditors* as employees of the business. Throughout the year, the internal auditors examine various segments of the organization to ensure that employees are following company policies and that operations are running efficiently.

● DAILY EXERCISE 7-4

● DAILY EXERCISE 7-5

External auditors are entirely independent of the business. They are hired to determine that the company's financial statements are prepared in accordance with generally accepted accounting principles. Both internal and external auditors are independent of the operations they examine, and both suggest improvements that help the business run efficiently.

DOCUMENTS AND RECORDS Business *documents and records* vary from invoices and purchase orders to special journals and subsidiary ledgers. Documents should be prenumbered. A gap in the numbered sequence draws attention.

Prenumbering sale receipts discourages theft by cashiers because the copies retained by the cashiers list the amount of the sale. These figures can be checked against the actual amount of cash received. If the receipts are not prenumbered, a cashier can destroy the sale receipt and pocket the cash received.

In a bowling alley a key document is the score sheet. The manager can compare the number of games scored with the amount of cash received. By multiplying the number of games by the price per game and comparing the result with each day's cash receipts, the manager can see whether the business is collecting all the revenue.

ELECTRONIC DEVICES AND COMPUTER CONTROLS Accounting systems are relying less and less on documents and more and more on digital storage devices. Computers shift the internal controls to the people who write the programs. Programmers then become the focus of internal controls because they can write programs that transfer company assets to themselves.

Businesses use electronic devices to protect assets and control operations. Retailers such as **Target Stores, Macy's,** and **Dillard's** control inventory by attaching an electronic sensor to merchandise. The cashier removes the sensor when a sale is made. If a customer tries to remove an item from the store with the sensor attached, an alarm is activated. According to **Checkpoint Systems,** which manufactures the sensors, these devices reduce theft by as much as 50%.

OTHER CONTROLS Businesses keep cash and important business documents (such as contracts and titles to property) in *fireproof vaults. Burglar alarms* protect buildings and other property.

Retailers receive most of their cash from customers on the spot. To safeguard cash, they use *point-of-sale terminals* that serve as a cash register and also record each transaction entered into the machine. Several times each day, a supervisor removes the cash for deposit in the bank.

Employees who handle cash are in an especially tempting position. Many businesses purchase *fidelity bonds* on cashiers. The bond is an insurance policy that reimburses the company for any losses due to employee theft. Before issuing a fidelity bond, the insurance company investigates the employee's past record.

Mandatory vacations and *job rotation* require that employees be trained to do a variety of jobs. **General Electric, Eastman Kodak,** and other large companies move employees from job to job—often at six-month intervals. This improves morale by giving employees a broad view of the business and helps them decide where they want to specialize. Knowing that someone else will be doing their job next month also keeps employees honest. Had Merrill Lynch moved Darlyne Lopez from job to job and required her to take a vacation, her embezzlement would probably have been detected much earlier.

Internal Controls for e-Commerce

e-Commerce creates some new risks. Buying and selling over the Internet can give hackers access to confidential information unavailable in face-to-face transactions. Confidentiality is a significant challenge for dotcoms. Pitfalls include

1. Stolen credit-card numbers
2. Computer viruses and Trojan horses
3. Impersonation of companies

To convince people to buy on-line, companies must ensure security of data.

Stolen credit-card numbers. Suppose you buy several CDs from **EMusic.com.** To make the purchase, your credit-card number must travel through cyberspace. Amateur hacker Carlos Salgado, Jr., used his home computer to steal 100,000 credit-card numbers with a combined limit exceeding $1 billion from an Internet service provider. Salgado was caught when he tried to sell the credit-card numbers to an undercover FBI agent.

COMPUTER VIRUS. A malicious program that (a) reproduces itself, (b) gets included in program code without consent, and (c) performs actions that can be destructive.

Computer viruses and Trojan horses. A **computer virus** is a malicious program that (a) reproduces itself, (b) gets included into program code without consent, and (c) performs actions that can be destructive. A **Trojan horse** works like a virus, but it does not reproduce. Viruses can destroy or alter data, make bogus calculations, and infect word-processing and spreadsheet files. The International Computer Security Association reports that 99.3% of firms it surveyed found a virus somewhere in their system.

TROJAN HORSE. A malicious program that works like a virus but does not reproduce.

Suppose the U.S. Department of Defense solicits bids for the design of a missile defense system. **Raytheon, Lockheed-Martin,** and **General Dynamics** bid on the contract. A hacker infects Raytheon's system and alters two small details of Raytheon's design. In evaluating the three bids, Pentagon engineers label the Raytheon design as flawed even though Raytheon has designed the best system for the lowest price. The American public winds up paying too much—all because of a trickster's prank.

Impersonation. Hackers sometimes create bogus Web sites, such as AOL4Free.com. The neat-sounding Web site attracts lots of visitors, and the hackers are able to solicit confidential data from unsuspecting people. The hackers then use the data for a variety of illicit purposes.

FIREWALLS AND ENCRYPTION Information traveling the Internet is secure, but the server holding the information may be insecure. A server is a computer that performs a particular function (for example, data storage or printing) in a network. Two standard techniques companies use to secure e-commerce data are encryption and firewalls.

ENCRYPTION. Rearranging plain-text messages by a mathematical process; the primary method of achieving confidentiality in e-commerce.

Encryption is the primary method of achieving confidentiality in e-commerce. Plain-text messages are rearranged by some mathematical process. The encrypted message cannot be read by anyone who does not know the process. A simple accounting example is the use of check-sum digits for customer account numbers. Each account number is set up so that the last digit is the sum of the previous digits, for example Customer Number 2237, where $2 + 2 + 3 = 7$. Any account number that fails this test triggers an error message.

FIREWALLS. Devices that enable members of a local network to access the Internet but keep nonmembers out of the network.

Firewalls limit access to a local network. The intent is to keep intruders out. Often firewalls work between two networks, such as between a local network and the Internet. Firewalls enable members of the local network to access the Internet but keep nonmembers out of the network. Usually several firewalls are built into the local network so that hackers must work their way around more than one. Think of a fortress with multiple walls protecting the king's chamber in the center. At the point of entry, passwords, PINs (personal identification numbers), fingerprints, and signatures are used. More sophisticated firewalls are used deeper in the network.

The Limitations of Internal Control

Unfortunately, most internal control measures can be overcome. Two or more employees working as a team—*colluding*—can beat an internal control system and defraud the firm. Consider Galaxy Theater. Ralph and another employee could put together a scheme in which the ticket seller pockets the cash from ten customers and the ticket taker admits ten customers without tickets. To prevent this situation, the manager must take additional control measures, such as matching the number of people in the theater against the number of ticket stubs retained. But that would take time away from other duties. The stricter the internal control system, the more expensive and time-consuming it becomes.

A system of internal control that is too complex can strangle the business with red tape. How tight should controls be? Managers must make sensible judgments. Investments in internal control must be judged in light of the costs and benefits.

THE BANK ACCOUNT AS A CONTROL DEVICE

Cash is the most liquid asset because it is the medium of exchange. Cash often consists of electronic impulses in a bank's accounting system with no accompanying paper checks or deposit slips. Cash is easy to conceal, easy to move, and relatively easy to steal. As a result, most businesses create specific controls to safeguard cash.

Keeping cash in a *bank account* is important because banks have established practices for safeguarding cash. Banks also provide depositors with detailed records of their transactions. To take full advantage of these control features, the business should deposit all cash receipts in the bank account and make all cash payments through it (except petty cash transactions, which we examine later in this chapter).

The documents used to control a bank account include the

- signature card
- deposit ticket
- check
- bank statement
- bank reconciliation

SIGNATURE CARD Banks require each person authorized to transact business through an account to sign a *signature card.* The bank compares the signatures on documents against the signature card to protect against forgery.

DEPOSIT TICKET Banks supply standard forms such as *deposit tickets.* The customer fills in the dollar amount and the date of deposit. As proof of the transaction, the customer retains either (1) a duplicate copy of the deposit ticket, or (2) a deposit receipt, depending on the bank's practice.

CHECK To draw money from an account, the depositor writes a **check,** which is a document instructing the bank to pay the designated person or business a specified amount of money. There are three parties to a check: the *maker,* who signs the check; the *payee,* to whom the check is paid; and the *bank* on which the check is drawn. Most checks are serially numbered and preprinted with the name of the maker and the bank.

Exhibit 7-3 shows a check drawn on the bank account of Business Research, Inc. The check has two parts, the check itself and the *remittance advice,* an optional attachment that tells the payee the reason for the payment. The maker (Business Research) retains a duplicate copy of the check for its cash payments journal.

> **CHECK.** Document that instructs a bank to pay the designated person or business a specified amount of money.

EXHIBIT 7-3　**Check with Remittance Advice**

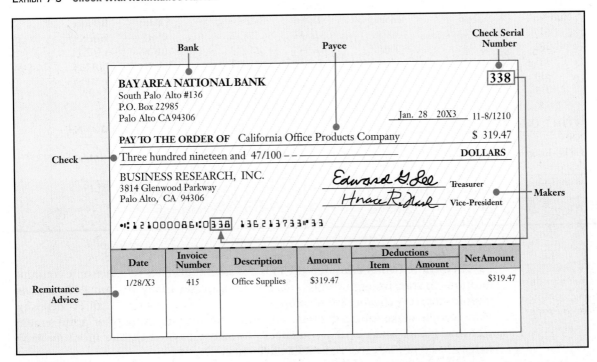

BANK STATEMENT. Document the bank uses to report what it did with the depositor's cash. Shows the bank account's beginning and ending balances and lists the month's cash transactions conducted through the bank.

BANK STATEMENT Banks send monthly bank statements to depositors. A **bank statement** is the document the bank uses to report what it did with the depositor's cash. The statement shows the bank account's beginning and ending cash balances for the period and lists the month's cash transactions conducted through the bank. Included with the statement are the maker's *canceled checks,* those checks the bank has paid on behalf of the depositor. The bank statement also lists any deposits and other changes in the account. Deposits appear in chronological order and checks in a logical order (usually by check serial number), along with the date each check cleared the bank. Exhibit 7-4 is the bank statement of Business Research, Inc., for the month ended January 31, 20X3.

EXHIBIT **7-4** Bank Statement

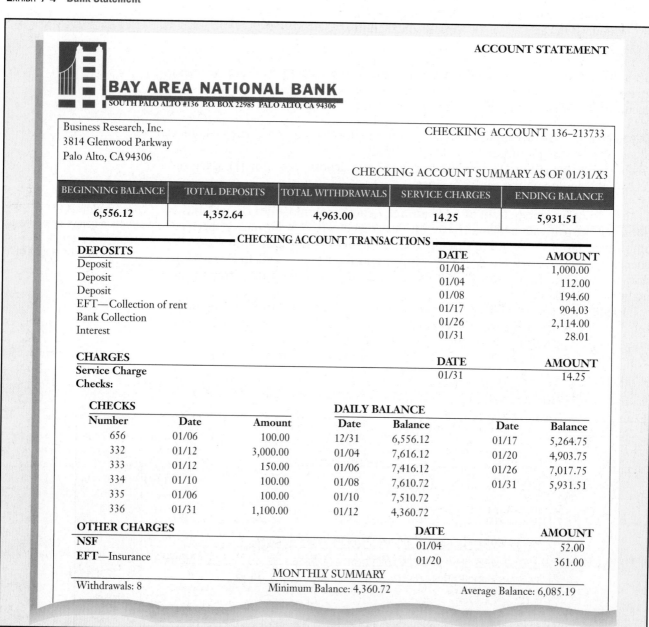

BAY AREA NATIONAL BANK
SOUTH PALO ALTO #136 P.O. BOX 22985 PALO ALTO, CA 94306

ACCOUNT STATEMENT

Business Research, Inc.
3814 Glenwood Parkway
Palo Alto, CA 94306

CHECKING ACCOUNT 136–213733

CHECKING ACCOUNT SUMMARY AS OF 01/31/X3

BEGINNING BALANCE	TOTAL DEPOSITS	TOTAL WITHDRAWALS	SERVICE CHARGES	ENDING BALANCE
6,556.12	4,352.64	4,963.00	14.25	5,931.51

———— CHECKING ACCOUNT TRANSACTIONS ————

DEPOSITS	DATE	AMOUNT
Deposit	01/04	1,000.00
Deposit	01/04	112.00
Deposit	01/08	194.60
EFT—Collection of rent	01/17	904.03
Bank Collection	01/26	2,114.00
Interest	01/31	28.01

CHARGES	DATE	AMOUNT
Service Charge	01/31	14.25

Checks:

CHECKS			DAILY BALANCE			
Number	Date	Amount	Date	Balance	Date	Balance
656	01/06	100.00	12/31	6,556.12	01/17	5,264.75
332	01/12	3,000.00	01/04	7,616.12	01/20	4,903.75
333	01/12	150.00	01/06	7,416.12	01/26	7,017.75
334	01/10	100.00	01/08	7,610.72	01/31	5,931.51
335	01/06	100.00	01/10	7,510.72		
336	01/31	1,100.00	01/12	4,360.72		

OTHER CHARGES	DATE	AMOUNT
NSF	01/04	52.00
EFT—Insurance	01/20	361.00

MONTHLY SUMMARY

Withdrawals: 8	Minimum Balance: 4,360.72	Average Balance: 6,085.19

ELECTRONIC FUNDS TRANSFER (EFT). System that transfers cash by electronic communication rather than by paper documents.

Electronic funds transfer (EFT) is a system that relies on electronic communications to transfer cash. More and more businesses today rely on EFT for cash transactions. It is cheaper for a company to pay employees by EFT (direct deposit). Many people make mortgage, rent, and insurance payments by prior arrangement with their bank and never write checks for those payments. The monthly bank statement lists EFT deposits and EFT payments.

The Bank Reconciliation

There are two records of a business's cash: (1) its Cash account in its own general ledger (Exhibit 7-5), and (2) the bank statement, which shows the actual amount of cash the business has in the bank.

EXHIBIT 7-5
Cash Records of Business Research, Inc.

DAILY EXERCISE 7-9

General Ledger:

ACCOUNT   Cash   No. 111

Date	Item	Jrnl. Ref.	Debit	Credit	Balance
20X3					
Jan. 1	Balance	✓			6,556.12
2	Cash receipt	CR. 9	1,112.00		7,668.12
7	Cash receipt	CR. 9	194.60		7,862.72
31	Cash payments	CP. 17		6,160.14	1,702.58
31	Cash receipt	CR. 10	1,591.63		3,294.21

Cash Payments:

Check No.	Amount	Check No.	Amount
332	$3,000.00	338	$ 319.47
333	510.00	339	83.00
334	100.00	340	203.14
335	100.00	341	458.53
336	1,100.00		
337	286.00	Total	$6,160.14

The books and the bank statement can show different amounts, yet both be correct. The difference arises because of a time lag in recording certain transactions. When a firm writes a check, it immediately credits its Cash account. The bank, however, does not subtract the amount of the check from the business's balance until the bank receives the check and pays it. This step may take days, even weeks, if the payee waits to cash the check. Likewise, the business immediately debits Cash for all cash receipts, but it may take a day or so for the bank to add these amounts to the business's bank balance.

To ensure accuracy of the financial records, the firm's accountant must explain all differences between the firm's own cash records and the bank statement figures on a certain date. The result of this process is a document called the **bank reconciliation,** which is prepared by the company (not by the bank). Properly done, the bank reconciliation ensures that all cash transactions have been accounted for and that the bank and book records of cash are correct. Knowing where cash comes from, how it is spent, and the balance of cash available is vital to success in business.

Here are some common items that cause differences between the bank balance and the book balance:

1. Items recorded by the company but not yet recorded by the bank
   a. **Deposits in transit** (outstanding deposits). The company has recorded these deposits, but the bank has not.
   b. **Outstanding checks.** The company has issued these checks and recorded them on its books, but the bank has not yet paid them.
2. Items recorded by the bank but not yet recorded by the company
   a. **Bank collections.** Banks sometimes collect money for their depositors. Many businesses have customers pay directly to the company bank account. This practice, called a *lock-box system,* reduces theft and places the business's cash in circulation faster than if the cash is collected and deposited by company personnel. An example is a bank's collecting cash and interest on a note receivable for the depositor.
   b. *Electronic funds transfers*. The bank may receive or pay cash on behalf of the depositor. The bank statement will list the EFTs.

BANK RECONCILIATION. Document explaining the reasons for the difference between a depositor's cash records and the depositor's cash balance in its bank account.

DEPOSIT IN TRANSIT. A deposit recorded by the company but not yet by its bank.

OUTSTANDING CHECK. A check issued by the company and recorded on its books but not yet paid by its bank.

BANK COLLECTION. Collection of money by the bank on behalf of a depositor.

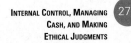

NONSUFFICIENT FUNDS (NSF) CHECK. A "hot" check, one for which the maker's bank account has insufficient money to pay the check.

c. *Service charge.* This is the bank's fee for processing the depositor's transactions. Banks base the service charge on the account balance or on the number of transactions. The depositor learns the amount of the service charge from the bank statement.

d. *Interest revenue on checking account.* Depositors earn interest if they keep enough cash in their account. The bank notifies depositors of this interest on the bank statement.

e. **Nonsufficient funds (NSF) checks** are worthless checks received from customers. To understand how NSF checks (sometimes called *hot checks*) are handled, consider the route a check takes. Exhibit 7-6 diagrams the paths that two checks take in the bank clearing process. The first diagram tracks the path of a good check. The second diagram shows what happens to an NSF (hot) check.

NSF checks are cash *receipts* that turn out to be worthless. The payee may learn of NSF checks through the bank statement, which lists the NSF check as a charge (subtraction). See the $52 item near the bottom of Exhibit 7-4. Because an NSF check is worthless, the customer still owes Business Research $52 in Exhibit 7-4. As a result, Business Research has a receivable from the customer who wrote the NSF check.

EXHIBIT 7-6 The Paths That Two Checks Take

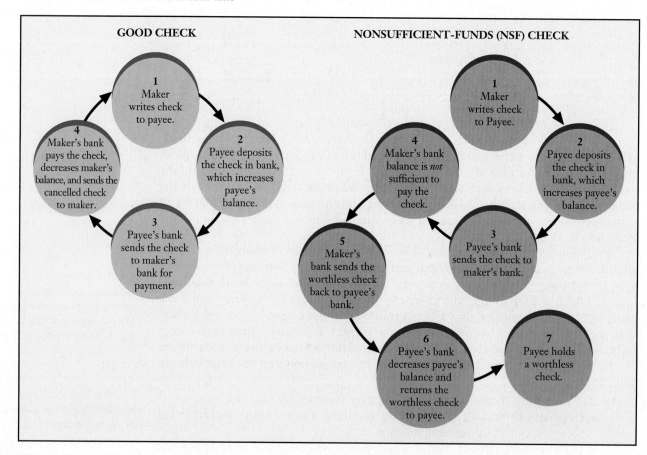

f. *Checks collected, deposited, and returned to payee by the bank for reasons other than NSF.* Banks return checks to the payee if (1) the maker's account has closed, (2) the date is "stale" (some checks state "void after 30 days"), (3) the signature is not authorized, (4) the check has been altered, or (5) the check form is improper (for example, a counterfeit). Accounting for all returned checks is the same as for NSF checks.

g. *The cost of printed checks.* This charge is handled like a service charge.

3. Errors by the company or the bank. For example, a bank may improperly charge (decrease) the bank balance of Business Research, Inc., for a check

drawn by another company, perhaps Business Research Associates. Or a company may miscompute its bank balance on its own books. Error correction will be part of the bank reconciliation.

PREPARING THE BANK RECONCILIATION   The steps in preparing the bank reconciliation are as follows:

Objective 3
Prepare a bank reconciliation and the related journal entries

1. Start with two figures, the balance shown on the bank statement (*balance per bank*) and the balance in the company's Cash account (*balance per books*). These two amounts will probably disagree because of the differences discussed earlier.
2. Add to, or subtract from, the *bank* balance those items that appear on the books but not on the bank statement:
    a. Add *deposits in transit* to the bank balance. Deposits in transit show up as cash receipts on the books but not as deposits on the bank statement.
    b. Subtract *outstanding checks* from the bank balance. Outstanding checks show up as cash payments on the books but not as paid checks on the bank statement. Outstanding checks are usually the most numerous items on a bank reconciliation.
3. Add to, or subtract from, the *book* balance those items that appear on the bank statement but not on the company books:
    a. Add to the book balance (1) *bank collections*, (2) *EFT cash receipts*, and (3) *interest revenue* earned on money in the bank. These items show up as cash receipts on the bank statement but not on the books.
    b. Subtract from the book balance (1) *EFT cash payments*, (2) *service charges*, (3) *cost of printed checks*, and (4) *NSF checks received, and other bank charges* (for example, stale-date checks). These items show up as subtractions on the bank statement but not as cash payments on the books.
4. Compute the *adjusted bank balance* and the *adjusted book balance*. The two adjusted balances should be equal.
5. Journalize each item in step 3—those items listed on the *Book* portion of the bank reconciliation. These transactions must be recorded on the company books because they affect cash.
6. Correct all book errors and notify the bank of any errors it has made.

BANK RECONCILIATION ILLUSTRATED   The bank statement in Exhibit 7-4 indicates that the January 31 bank balance of Business Research, Inc., is $5,931.51. However, the company's Cash account has a balance of $3,294.21, as shown in Exhibit 7-5. The following reconciling items explain why the bank balance and the book balance differ:

1. The January 31 deposit of $1,591.63 (deposit in transit) does not appear on the bank statement. See the last item in the Company's Cash Account (Exhibit 7-5).
2. The bank erroneously charged to the Business Research, Inc., account a $100 check—number 656—written by Business Research Associates (a bank error).
3. Five company checks issued late in January and recorded in the cash payments journal have not been paid by the bank. The following checks are outstanding:

Check No.	Date	Amount
337	Jan. 17	$286.00
338	26	319.47
339	27	83.00
340	28	203.14
341	30	458.53

These checks are listed under cash payments in Exhibit 7-5.

4. The bank received $904.03 by EFT on behalf of Business Research, Inc. (an EFT receipt).
5. The bank collected on behalf of the company a note receivable, $2,114 (including interest revenue of $214). Business Research has not recorded this cash receipt (a bank collection).

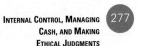

6. The bank statement shows interest revenue of $28.01, which the company has earned on its cash balance (interest revenue).

7. Check number 333 for $150 paid to Brown Company on account was recorded as a cash payment of $510, creating a $360 understatement of the Cash balance in the books (a book error).

◉ DAILY EXERCISE 7-7

8. The bank service charge for the month was $14.25 (service charge).

9. The bank statement shows an NSF check for $52, which was received from customer L. Ross (NSF check).

◉ DAILY EXERCISE 7-10

10. Business Research pays insurance expense monthly by EFT. The company has not yet recorded this $361 payment (an EFT payment).

Exhibit 7-7 is the bank reconciliation based on the preceding data. Panel A lists the reconciling items, which are keyed by number to the reconciliation in Panel B.

EXHIBIT 7-7 Bank Reconciliation

PANEL A—Reconciling Items

1. Deposit in transit, $1,591.63.
2. Bank error, add $100 to bank balance.
3. Outstanding checks; no. 337, $286; no. 338, $319.47; no. 339, $83; no. 340, $203.14; no. 341, $458.53.
4. EFT receipt of rent revenue, $904.03.
5. Bank collection, $2,114, including interest revenue of $214.

6. Interest earned on bank balance, $28.01.
7. Book error, add $360 to book balance.
8. Bank service charge, $14.25.
9. NSF check from L. Ross, $52.
10. EFT payment of insurance expense, $361.

PANEL B—Bank Reconciliation

BUSINESS RESEARCH, INC.
Bank Reconciliation
January 31, 20X3

Bank			Books		
Balance, January 31		$5,931.51	Balance, January 31		$3,294.21
Add:			Add:		
1. Deposit of January 31 in transit		1,591.63	4. EFT receipt of rent revenue		904.03
2. Correction of bank error— Business Research Associates check 656 erroneously charged against company account		100.00	5. Bank collection of note receivable, including interest revenue of $214		2,114.00
		7,623.14	6. Interest revenue earned on bank balance		28.01
			7. Correction of book error— overstated amount of check no. 333		360.00
					6,700.25
Less:					
3. Outstanding checks					
No. 337	$286.00		Less:		
No. 338	319.47		8. Service charge	$ 14.25	
No. 339	83.00		9. NSF check	52.00	
No. 340	203.14		10. EFT payment of insurance expense	361.00	(427.25)
No. 341	458.53	(1,350.14)			
Adjusted bank balance		$6,273.00	Adjusted book balance		$6,273.00

↑ Amounts agree. ↑

Each reconciling item is treated in the same way in every situation. Here is a summary of how to treat the various reconciling items:

BANK BALANCE—ALWAYS
- *Add* deposits in transit.
- *Subtract* outstanding checks.
- *Add* or *subtract* corrections of bank errors.

BOOK BALANCE—ALWAYS
- *Add* bank collections, interest revenue, and EFT receipts.
- *Subtract* service charges, NSF checks, and EFT payments.
- *Add* or *subtract* corrections of book errors.

JOURNALIZING TRANSACTIONS FROM THE RECONCILIATION The bank reconciliation does not place entries in the journals or the ledgers. The reconciliation is an accountant's tool, separate from the company's books.

The bank reconciliation acts as a control device. It signals the company to record transactions for all the reconciling items listed in the Books section of the reconciliation. The company has not yet recorded these items. For example, the bank collected the note receivable for the company, but the company has not yet recorded this cash receipt. In fact, the company learned of the cash receipt only when it received the bank statement.

THINK IT OVER

Why doesn't the company need to record the reconciling items on the Bank side of the reconciliation?

Answer: Those items have already been recorded on the company books.

On the basis of the reconciliation in Exhibit 7-7, Business Research, Inc., makes the following journal entries. They are dated January 31 to bring the Cash account to the correct balance on that date. Numbers in parentheses correspond to the reconciling items listed in Exhibit 7-7, Panel A.

DAILY EXERCISE 7-8

(4) Jan. 31	Cash	904.03		
	Rent Revenue.........		904.03	
	Receipt of monthly rent.			
(5) 31	Cash	2,114.00		
	Notes Receivable.....		1,900.00	
	Interest Revenue		214.00	
	Note receivable collected by bank.			
(6) 31	Cash	28.01		
	Interest Revenue		28.01	
	Interest earned on bank balance.			
(7) 31	Cash	360.00		
	Accounts Payable —Brown Co.........		360.00	
	Correction of check no. 333.			

(8) 31	Miscellaneous Expense[1]	14.25		
	Cash..............................		14.25	
	Bank service charge.			
(9) 31	Accounts Receivable —L. Ross.........................	52.00		
	Cash..............................		52.00	
	NSF check returned by bank.			
(10) 31	Insurance Expense...........	361.00		
	Cash..............................		361.00	
	Payment of monthly insurance.			

These entries bring the company's books up to date.

The entry for the NSF check (entry 9) needs explanation. Upon learning that L. Ross's $52 check was not good, Business Research credits Cash to bring the Cash account up to date. Business Research still has a receivable from Ross, so the company debits Accounts Receivable—L. Ross and pursues collection from him.

DAILY EXERCISE 7-11

WORK IT OUT

The bank statement balance is $4,500 and shows a service charge of $15, interest earned of $5, and an NSF check for $300. Deposits in transit total $1,200; outstanding checks are $575. The bookkeeper recorded as $152 a check of $125 in payment of an account payable.

1. What is the adjusted bank balance?

2. Prepare the journal entries needed to update the company's (not the bank's) books.

Answers

1. $5,125 ($4,500 + $1,200 − $575)

2. Journal entries on the books:

Miscellaneous Expense	15		Accounts Receivable	300	
Cash		15	Cash		300
Cash	5		Cash ($152 − $125)............	27	
Interest Revenue...............		5	Accounts Payable...........		27

---
[1]Note: Miscellaneous Expense is debited for the bank service charge because the service charge pertains to no particular expense category.

How Owners and Managers Use the Bank Reconciliation

The bank reconciliation is a powerful control device in the hands of a business owner or manager, as the following example illustrates.

Randy Vaughn is a CPA in Houston, Texas. He owns several apartment complexes that his aunt manages. His accounting practice leaves little time to devote to his apartments. Vaughn's aunt signs up tenants, collects the monthly rent, arranges custodial work, hires and fires employees, writes the checks, and performs the bank reconciliation. In short, she does it all. This concentration of duties in one person is terrible from an internal control standpoint. Vaughn's aunt could be stealing from him, and as a CPA he is aware of this possibility.

Vaughn trusts his aunt because she is a member of the family. Nevertheless, he exercises some loose controls over her management of his apartments. Vaughn periodically drops by his properties to see whether the custodial staff is keeping them in good condition.

To control cash, Vaughn uses the bank statement and the bank reconciliation. On an irregular basis, he examines the bank reconciliations. He matches every paid check to the journal entry on the books. Vaughn would know immediately if his aunt is writing checks to herself. Vaughn sometimes prepares his own bank reconciliation to see whether he agrees with his aunt's work. To keep his aunt on her toes, Vaughn lets her know that he periodically audits her work.

Vaughn has a simple method for controlling cash receipts. He knows the occupancy level of his apartments. He also knows the monthly rent he charges. He multiplies the number of apartments—say 20—by the monthly rent (which averages $500 per unit) to arrive at expected monthly rent revenue of $10,000. By tracing the $10,000 revenue to the bank statement, Vaughn can tell that his rent money went into his bank account.

Control activities such as these are critical in small businesses. With only a few employees, a separation of duties may not be feasible. The owner must oversee the operations of the business, or the assets will slip away, as they did for Merrill Lynch in the chapter opening story.

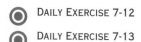 DAILY EXERCISE 7-12

DAILY EXERCISE 7-13

 MID-CHAPTER

SUMMARY PROBLEM

www.prenhall.com/horngren
Mid-Chapter Assessment

The Cash account of Zuboff Associates at February 28, 20X3, is as follows:

	CASH			
Feb. 1	Bal. 3,995	Feb. 3	400
6	800	12	3,100
15	1,800	19	1,100
23	1,100	25	500
28	2,400	27	900
Feb. 28	Bal. 4,095		

Zuboff Associates received the bank statement—shown on facing page—on February 28, 20X3 (as always, negative amounts are in parentheses):

Bank Statement for February 20X3

Beginning balance		$3,995
Deposits:		
Feb. 7	$ 800	
15	1,800	
24	1,100	3,700
Checks (total per day):		
Feb. 8	$ 400	
16	3,100	
23	1,100	(4,600)
Other items:		
Service charge		(10)
NSF check from M. E. Crown		(700)
Bank collection of note receivable for the company		1,000*
EFT—monthly rent expense		(330)
Interest on account balance		15
Ending balance		$3,070

*Includes interest of $119.

Additional data: Zuboff deposits all cash receipts in the bank and makes all payments by check.

Required

1. Prepare the bank reconciliation of Zuboff Associates at February 28, 20X3.
2. Record the entries based on the bank reconciliation.

Solution

Requirement 1

ZUBOFF ASSOCIATES
Bank Reconciliation
February 28, 20X3

Bank:		
Balance, February 28, 20X3		$3,070
Add: Deposit of February 28 in transit		2,400
		5,470
Less: Outstanding checks issued on Feb. 25 ($500)		
and Feb. 27 ($900)		(1,400)
Adjusted bank balance, February 28, 20X3		$4,070
Books:		
Balance, February 28, 20X3		$4,095
Add: Bank collection of note receivable, including		
interest of $119		1,000
Interest earned on bank balance		15
		5,110
Less: Service charge	$ 10	
NSF check	700	
EFT—Rent expense	330	(1,040)
Adjusted book balance, February 28, 20X3		$4,070

Requirement 2

Date	Account	Debit	Credit
Feb. 28	Cash	1,000	
	Note Receivable ($1,000 − $119) ...		881
	Interest Revenue		119
	Note receivable collected by bank.		
28	Cash	15	
	Interest Revenue		15
	Interest earned on bank balance.		
28	Miscellaneous Expense	10	
	Cash		10
	Bank service charge.		

Date	Account	Debit	Credit
Feb. 28	Accounts Receivable—M. E. Crown	700	
	Cash		700
	NSF check returned by bank.		
28	Rent Expense	330	
	Cash		330
	Monthly rent expense.		

INTERNAL CONTROL OVER CASH RECEIPTS

Internal control over cash receipts ensures that all cash receipts are deposited in the bank and that the company's accounting record is correct. Many businesses receive cash over the counter and through the mail. Each source of cash receipts calls for its own security measures.

Objective 4
Apply internal controls to cash receipts

CASH RECEIPTS OVER THE COUNTER The point-of-sale terminal (cash register) offers management control over the cash received in a store. Consider a **Macy's** store. First, the terminal should be positioned so that customers can see the amounts the cashier enters into the computer. Company policy should require issuance of a receipt to make sure each sale is recorded by the cash register.

Second, the cash drawer opens only when the sales clerk enters an amount on the keypad, and the machine records each sale and cash transaction. At the end of the day, a manager proves the cash by comparing the total amount in the cash drawer against the machine's record of the day's sales. This step helps prevent outright theft by the clerk.

⊙ DAILY EXERCISE 7-14

⊙ DAILY EXERCISE 7-15

Third, pricing merchandise at "uneven" amounts—say, $3.95 instead of $4.00—means that the clerk generally must make change, which in turn means having to get into the cash drawer. This requires entering the amount of the sale on the keypad and so onto the register tape—another way to prevent fraud.

At the end of the day, the cashier or other employee with cash-handling duties deposits the cash in the bank. The tape then goes to the accounting department as the basis for an entry in the accounting records. These security measures, coupled with periodic on-site inspection by a manager, discourage theft.

CASH RECEIPTS BY MAIL All incoming mail should be opened by a mailroom employee. This person should compare the amount of the check received with the attached remittance advice (the slip of paper that lists the amount of the check). If no advice was sent, the mailroom employee should prepare one and enter the amount of each receipt on a control tape. At the end of the day, this control tape is given to a responsible official, such as the controller, for verification. Cash receipts should be given to the cashier, who combines them with any cash received over the counter and prepares the bank deposit.

Having a mailroom employee handle postal cash receipts is another application of a good separation of duties. If the accountants were to open postal cash receipts, they could easily hide a theft.

The mailroom employee forwards the remittance advices to the accounting department. These provide the data for entries in the cash books and postings to customers' accounts in the accounts receivable ledger. As a final step, the controller compares the three records of the day's cash receipts:

1. The control tape total from the mailroom
2. The bank deposit amount from the cashier
3. The debit to Cash from the accounting department

⊙ DAILY EXERCISE 7-16

Many companies use a lock-box system to separate cash duties and establish control over cash receipts. Customers send their checks directly to an address that is essentially a bank account. Internal control over the cash is enhanced because company personnel do not handle incoming cash. The lock-box system improves efficiency because the cash goes to work for the company immediately.

THINK IT OVER

The bookkeeper in your company has stolen cash received from customers. The bookkeeper prepared fake documents that indicate the customers returned the merchandise. What internal control feature could have prevented this theft?

Answer: The bookkeeper should not have access to cash.

CASH SHORT AND OVER Differences sometimes exist between actual cash receipts and the day's record of cash received. Usually, these differences are small and result from honest errors. When the recorded cash balance exceeds cash on hand, a *cash short* situation exists. When actual cash exceeds the recorded cash balance, there is a *cash over* situation. Suppose the cash register tapes of Macy's indicated sales revenue of $25,000, but the cash received was $24,980. To record the day's sales, the store would make this entry:

Cash	24,980	
Cash Short and Over.............	20	
Sales Revenue		25,000
Daily cash sales.		

As the entry shows, Cash Short and Over is debited when cash receipts are less than sales revenue. This account is credited when cash receipts exceed sales. A debit balance in Cash Short and Over appears on the income statement as Miscellaneous Expense, a credit balance as Other Revenue.

Exhibit 7-8 summarizes the controls over cash receipts.

EXHIBIT 7-8   Internal Controls over Cash Receipts

Elements of Internal Control	Internal Controls over Cash Receipts
Competent, reliable, ethical personnel	Companies carefully screen employees for undesirable traits. They commit time and effort to training programs.
Assignment of responsibilities	Specific employees are designated as cashiers, supervisors, or accountants.
Proper authorization	Only designated employees, such as department managers, can approve check receipts above a certain amount.
Separation of duties	Cashiers and mailroom employees who handle cash do not have access to the accounting records. Accountants have no opportunity to handle cash.
Internal and external audits	Internal auditors examine company transactions for agreement with management policies. External auditors examine the internal controls to determine whether the accounting system produces accurate amounts for revenues and receivables.
Documents and records	Customers receive receipts as transaction records. Bank statements list cash receipts for deposits.
Electronic devices and computer controls	Cash registers serve as transaction records. Each day's receipts are matched with customer remittance advices and with the day's deposit ticket from the bank.
Other controls	Cashiers are bonded. Cash is stored in vaults and banks. Employees are rotated among jobs and are required to take vacations.

INTERNAL CONTROL OVER CASH PAYMENTS (DISBURSEMENTS)

Objective 5
Apply internal controls to cash payments

Exercising control over cash payments is as important as controlling cash receipts.

Controls over Payment by Check

Payment by check is an important control over cash payments. First, the check provides a record of the payment. Second, to be valid, the check must be signed by an authorized official. Before signing the check, the manager should study the evidence supporting the payment. To illustrate the internal control over cash payments, let's suppose the business is buying merchandise inventory.

CONTROLS OVER PURCHASING   The purchasing process—outlined in Exhibit 7-9— starts when the sales department prepares a *purchase request* (or *requisition*). A separate purchasing department locates the goods and mails a *purchase order* to the supplier. When the supplier ships the merchandise, the supplier also mails the *invoice*, or bill. ➡ The goods arrive, and the receiving department checks the goods for damage and lists the merchandise received on a document called the *receiving report*. The accounting department combines all the foregoing documents and forwards this *payment packet* to officers for payment. The packet includes the purchase request, purchase order, invoice, and receiving report, as shown in Exhibit 7-10.

➡ We introduced purchase orders and invoices in Chapter 5.

EXHIBIT 7-9
Purchasing Process

Business Document	Prepared by	Send to
Purchase request (requisition)	Sales department	Purchasing department
Purchase order	Purchasing department	Outside company that sells the needed merchandise (supplier or vendor)
Invoice (bill)	Outside company that sells the needed merchandise (supplier or vendor)	Accounting department
Receiving report	Receiving department	Accounting department
Payment packet	Accounting department	Officer who signs the check

EXHIBIT 7-10
Payment Packet

CONTROLS OVER APPROVAL OF PAYMENTS   Before approving the payment, the controller or the treasurer should examine the packet to ascertain that the accounting department has performed the following control steps:

1. The invoice is compared with a copy of the purchase order and purchase request to ensure that the business pays only for the goods that it ordered.
2. The invoice is compared with the receiving report to ensure that cash is paid only for the goods actually received.
3. The mathematical accuracy of the invoice is proved.

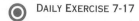

DAILY EXERCISE 7-17

To avoid document alteration, some firms use machines that stamp the amount on the check in indelible ink. After payment, the check signer punches a hole through the payment packet. This hole makes it hard to run the documents through for a duplicate payment.

Technology is streamlining cash payment procedures. Evaluated Receipts Settlement (ERS) compresses the approval process into a single step: compare the receiving report to the purchase order. If the two documents match, that proves **Kinko's** received the paper it ordered, and then Kinko's pays **Hammermill Paper,** the supplier. ERS requires fewer employees and saves on accounting expense.

An even more streamlined process bypasses people and documents altogether. In Electronic Data Interchange (EDI), **Wal-Mart's** computers communicate directly with the computers of suppliers like **Goodyear Tire, Rubbermaid,** and **Procter & Gamble.** When Wal-Mart's inventory of auto tires reaches a low level, the computer sends a purchase order to Goodyear. Goodyear ships the tires and invoices Wal-Mart electronically. Then an electronic fund transfer (EFT) sends the cash from Wal-Mart to Goodyear.

These streamlined procedures depend on the mutual trust of the companies involved. They know each other well and operate ethically. They cannot afford to do otherwise. Exhibit 7-11 summarizes the internal controls over cash payments.

Exhibit 7-11   Internal Controls over Cash Payments

Element of Internal Control	Internal Controls over Cash Payments
Competent, reliable, ethical personnel	Cash payments are entrusted to high-level employees.
Assignment of responsibilities	Specific employees approve purchase documents for payment. Executives examine approvals, then sign checks.
Proper authorization	Large expenditures must be authorized by the company owner or board of directors.
Separation of duties	Computer operators and other employees who handle checks have no access to the accounting records. Accountants have no opportunity to handle cash.
Internal and external audits	Internal auditors examine company transactions for agreement with management policies. External auditors examine the internal controls over cash payments and the accounting records.
Documents and records	Suppliers issue invoices. Bank statements list cash payments. Checks are renumbered in sequence to account for payments.
Electronic devices, computer controls, and other controls	Blank checks are stored in a vault and controlled by a responsible official. Machines stamp the amount on a check in indelible ink. Paid invoices are punched to avoid duplicate payment.

THINK IT OVER

Talon Computer Concepts processes payroll checks for small businesses. Clients give their employee time cards to Talon, and Talon programmers write the software to meet the clients' payrolls. Talon computer operators deliver the checks to clients for distribution to employees. Identify two employee functions of Talon's cash payment system that should be separated. Give your reason.

Answer: The *programmers* should not also be computer *operators*. Persons who both program and operate computers can write the program to process checks to themselves and then pocket the printed checks.

Controlling Petty Cash Payments

It is uneconomical for a business to write a separate check for an executive's taxi fare, floppy disks needed right away, or the delivery of a package across town. To meet these needs, companies keep a small amount of cash on hand to pay for such minor amounts. This fund is called **petty cash.**

Even though amounts paid through the petty cash fund are small, the business needs to set up controls such as the following:

1. Designate an employee to administer the fund as its custodian.
2. Keep a specific amount of cash on hand.
3. Support all fund payments with a petty cash ticket.
4. Replenish the fund through normal cash payment procedures.

The petty cash fund is opened when a payment is approved for a predetermined amount and a check for that amount is issued to Petty Cash. Assume that on February 28, the business decides to establish a petty cash fund of $200. The custodian cashes the check and places the currency and coin in the fund, which may be a cash box, safe, or other device. The petty cash custodian is responsible for controlling the fund. Starting the fund is recorded as follows:

Feb. 28	Petty Cash...	200	
	Cash in Bank		200
	To open the petty cash fund.		

PETTY CASH. Fund containing a small amount of cash that is used to pay for minor expenditures.

For each petty cash payment, the custodian prepares a *petty cash ticket* like the one illustrated in Exhibit 7-12.

EXHIBIT 7-12
Petty Cash Ticket

```
                    PETTY CASH TICKET

Date   Mar. 25, 20X6                          No.  47
Amount   $23.00
For    Box of floppy diskettes
Debit  Office Supplies, Acct. No. 145
Received by  Lewis Wright    Fund Custodian  MAR
```

Observe that signatures (or initials) identify the recipient of petty cash and the fund custodian. Requiring both signatures reduces unauthorized payments. The custodian keeps all the petty cash tickets in the fund. The sum of the cash plus the total of the ticket amounts should equal the opening balance at all times—in this case, $200. Also, the Petty Cash account keeps its prescribed $200 balance at all times. Maintaining the Petty Cash account at this balance, supported by the fund (cash plus tickets totaling the same amount), is a characteristic of an **imprest system.** In an imprest system, the amount of cash for which the custodian is responsible is clearly identified. This is the system's main internal control feature.

Payments reduce the amount of cash in the fund, so periodically the fund must be replenished. Suppose that on March 31, the fund has $118 in cash and $82 in tickets. A check for $82 is issued, made payable to Petty Cash. The fund custodian cashes this check and puts the money in the fund to return its actual cash to $200. The petty cash tickets identify the accounts to be debited, as shown in the entry to record replenishment of the fund:

> **IMPREST SYSTEM.** A way to account for petty cash by maintaining a constant balance in the petty cash account, supported by the fund (cash plus payment tickets) totaling the same amount.

Mar. 31	Office Supplies	23	
	Delivery Expense	17	
	Miscellaneous Selling Expense	42	
	Cash in Bank		82
	To replenish the petty cash fund.		

If this cash payment exceeds the sum of the tickets—that is, if the fund comes up short, Cash Short and Over is debited for the missing amount. If the sum of the tickets exceeds the payment, Cash Short and Over is credited. Replenishing the fund does *not* affect the Petty Cash account. Petty Cash keeps its $200 balance at all times.

Petty Cash is debited only when the fund is started (see the February 28 entry) or when its amount is changed. Suppose the business decides to raise the fund amount from $200 to $250. This step would require a $50 debit to Petty Cash.

> **DAILY EXERCISE 7-18**

USING A BUDGET TO MANAGE CASH

> **Objective 6**
> Use a budget to manage cash

Owners and managers control their organizations with the help of budgets. A **budget** is a quantitative expression of a plan that helps managers coordinate the entity's activities. Cash receives the most attention in the budgeting process because all transactions ultimately affect cash.

> **BUDGET.** A quantitative expression of a plan that helps managers coordinate the entity's activities.

How does **MCI WorldCom** decide when to invest in new telecommunications equipment? How will the company decide how much to spend? Similarly, by what process do you decide how much to spend on your education? On an automobile? All these decisions depend to some degree on the information that a cash budget provides. A cash budget helps a business manage its cash by expressing the plan for the receipt and payment of cash during a future period.

To prepare for the future, a company must determine how much cash it will need and then figure out how to obtain the needed cash. Preparation of a cash budget includes four steps:

1. Start with the entity's cash balance at the beginning of the period. This is the amount of cash left over from the preceding period.
2. Add the budgeted cash receipts and subtract the budgeted cash payments, including

a. Revenue and expense transactions

b. Asset acquisition and sale transactions

c. Liability and stockholders' equity transactions

3. The beginning balance plus the expected receipts minus the expected payments equals the expected cash balance at the end of the period.

4. Compare the expected cash balance to the desired, or *budgeted,* cash balance at the end of the period. Owners and managers know the minimum amount of cash they need (the budgeted balance) to keep the entity running. If there is excess cash, they can invest more than originally planned. If the expected cash balance falls below the budgeted amount, the company must raise more money to reach the desired cash balance.

Exhibit 7-13 shows a hypothetical cash budget for **Gap Inc.,** for the year ended January 31, 20X2. Study it carefully, because at some point in your career or personal affairs you will use a cash budget.

EXHIBIT 7-13
Cash Budget (Hypothetical)

 DAILY EXERCISE 7-19

GAP INC.
Cash Budget (Hypothetical)
Year Ended January 31, 20X2

		(In millions)	
(1)	Cash balance, February 1, 20X1		$ 203
	Estimated cash receipts:		
(2)	Collections from customers...	$ 2,858	
(3)	Interest and dividends on investments	6	
(4)	Sale of store fixtures..	5	2,869
			3,072
	Estimated cash payments:		
(5)	Purchases of inventory..	$(1,906)	
(6)	Operating expenses	(561)	
(7)	Expansions of existing stores..	(206)	
(8)	Opening of new stores	(349)	
(9)	Payment of long-term debt	(145)	
(10)	Payment to owners of the business.............................	(219)	(3,386)
(11)	Cash available (needed) before new financing...............		(314)
(12)	Budgeted cash balance, January 31, 20X2		(200)
(13)	Cash available for additional investments, or (New financing needed)...		$ (514)

The cash budget has sections for cash receipts and cash payments. The budget is prepared *before* the period's transactions and can take any form that helps people make decisions. The cash budget is an internal document, so it is not bound by generally accepted accounting principles.

Gap Inc.'s hypothetical cash budget in Exhibit 7-13 begins with the company's actual cash balance at the beginning of the period. At February 1, 20X1, Gap had cash of $203 million (line 1). The budgeted cash receipts and payments are expected to create a need for additional financing during the year (line 13).

Assume that managers of Gap wish to maintain a cash balance of at least $200 million (line 12). Because the year's activity is expected to leave the company with a *negative* cash balance of $314 million (line 11), Gap's managers must arrange $514 million of financing (line 13). *Add* lines 11 and 12 to arrive at the amount of new financing needed.

 DAILY EXERCISE 7-20

WORK IT OUT

Suppose line 11 of Exhibit 7-13 showed cash available of $250 million. What would Gap Inc. do, borrow additional money, or have an excess to invest?

Answer: Gap would have an additional $50 million to invest ($250 million available − $200 million needed = excess of $50 million).

International transactions add to the complexity of managing cash. When a U.S. company buys goods internationally, it may pay cash in a foreign currency, such as Canadian dollars or Mexican pesos. Foreign currencies change in value from day to day. In settling up, a company may have a gain or a loss on the foreign currency. We show how to account for foreign currency transactions in Chapter 16.

REPORTING CASH ON THE BALANCE SHEET

Cash is the first current asset listed on the balance sheet. Businesses often have many bank accounts and petty cash funds, but they usually combine all cash amounts into a single total called "Cash and Cash Equivalents."

Cash equivalents include liquid assets such as time deposits and certificates of deposit, which are interest-bearing accounts that can be withdrawn with no penalty. Although they are slightly less liquid than cash, these assets are sufficiently similar to be reported along with cash. The balance sheet of **Intel Corporation** recently reported the following:

INTEL CORPORATION Balance Sheet (Adapted) December 31, 1999	
	(In millions)
Assets	
Current assets:	
Cash and cash equivalents	$ 3,695
Short-term investments	8,093
Accounts receivable........................	3,700
Inventories	1,478
Other current assets	853
Total current assets............................	$17,819

Source: Intel Corporation. *Annual Report 1999*, p. 19.

Intel's cash balance means that $3,695 million is available for use as needed. Cash that is restricted should not be reported as a current asset. For example, banks require customers to keep a *compensating balance* on deposit in order to borrow from the bank. The compensating balance is restricted and therefore is not included in the cash amount on the balance sheet.

ETHICS AND ACCOUNTING

A *Wall Street Journal* article described a Russian entrepreneur who claimed he was getting ahead in business by breaking laws. "Older people have an ethics problem," he said. "By that I mean they *have* ethics." Conversely, Roger Smith, former chairman of **General Motors,** said, "Ethical practice is, quite simply, good business." Smith has been around long enough to see the danger in unethical behavior. Sooner or later unethical conduct comes to light. Moreover, ethical behavior wins out in the end because it is the right thing to do.

Corporate and Professional Codes of Ethics

Most large companies have a code of ethics to encourage employees to behave ethically and responsibly. But codes of ethics are not enough by themselves. Senior management must set a high ethical tone. They must make it clear that the company will not tolerate unethical conduct by employees.

As professionals, accountants are expected to maintain higher standards than society in general. Their ability to do business depends entirely on their reputation. Most independent accountants are members of the American Institute of Certified Public Accountants and must abide by the *AICPA Code of Professional Conduct.* Accountants who are members of the Institute of Management Accountants are bound by the *Standards of Ethical Conduct for Management Accountants.*

See Chapter 19, p. 776.

Ethical Issues in Accounting

Objective 7
Make ethical judgments in business

In many situations, the ethical choice is easy. For example, stealing cash is both unethical and illegal. In our chapter opening story, the cashier's actions landed her in jail. In other cases, the choices are more difficult. But in every instance, ethical judgments boil down to a personal decision: What should I do in a given situation? Let's consider three ethical issues in accounting. The first two are easy to resolve. The third is more difficult.

SITUATION 1   Sonja Kleberg is preparing the income tax return of a client who has had a particularly good year—higher income than expected. On January 2, the client pays for newspaper advertising and asks Sonja to backdate the expense to the preceding year. The tax deduction would help the client more in the year just ended than in the current year. Backdating would decrease taxable income of the earlier year and lower the client's tax payments. After all, there is a difference of only two days between January 2 and December 31. This client is important to Kleberg. What should she do?

She should refuse the request because the transaction took place in January of the new year.

What control device could prove that Kleberg behaved unethically if she backdated the transaction in the accounting records? An IRS audit and documents and records—the date of the cash payment could prove that the expense occurred in January rather than in December.

SITUATION 2   Jack Mellichamp's software company owes $40,000 to Bank of America. The loan agreement requires Mellichamp's company to maintain a current ratio (current assets divided by current liabilities) of 1.50 or higher. ➤ It is late in the year, and the bank will review Mellichamp's situation early next year. At present, the company's current ratio is 1.40. At this level, Mellichamp is in violation of his loan agreement. He can increase the current ratio to 1.53 by paying off some current liabilities right before year end. Is it ethical to do so?

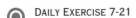
◄ For a review of the current ratio, see Chapter 4.

Yes, because the action is a real business transaction.

However, paying off the liabilities is only a delaying tactic. It will hold off the creditors for now, but the business still must improve its underlying operations.

SITUATION 3   Emilia Gomez, an accountant for the Democratic Party, discovers that her supervisor, Myles Packer, made several errors last year. Campaign contributions received from foreign citizens, which are illegal, were recorded as normal. It is not clear whether the errors were deliberate or accidental. Gomez knows that Packer evaluates her job performance. What should Gomez do? She is uncertain.

⊙ DAILY EXERCISE 7-21

   To make her decision, Gomez could follow the framework outlined in the Decision Guidelines feature on the next page.

DECISION GUIDELINES

Framework for Making Ethical Judgments

Weighing tough ethical judgments requires a decision framework. Answering these six questions will guide you through tough decisions. Apply them to Emilia Gomez's situation.

QUESTION	DECISION GUIDELINE
1. What are the facts?	**1.** *Determine the facts.* They are given on page 289.
2. What is the ethical issue, if any?	**2.** *Identify the ethical issues.* The root work of ethical is *ethics,* which Webster's dictionary defines as the "the discipline dealing with what is good and bad and with moral duty and obligation." Gomez's ethical dilemma is to decide what she should do with the information she has uncovered.
3. What are the options?	**3.** *Specify the alternatives.* For Emilia Gomez, three reasonable alternatives include (a) reporting the errors to Packer, (b) reporting the errors to Packer's boss, and (c) doing nothing.
4. Who is involved in the situation?	**4.** *Identify the people involved.* Individuals who could be affected include Gomez, Packer, the Democratic Party, and Gomez's co-workers who observe her behavior.
5. What are the possible consequences?	**5.** *Assess the possible outcomes.*
	a. If Gomez reports the errors to Packer, he may penalize her, or he may reward her for careful work. Reporting the errors preserves her integrity and will probably lead to returning the money to the donors. But the Democratic Party could suffer embarrassment if this situation is made public.
	b. If Gomez reports to Packer's boss, her integrity is preserved. Her relationship with Packer will be strained. If Packer's boss has colluded with Packer in recording the campaign contribution, Gomez could be penalized. If the error is corrected and outsiders notified, the Democratic Party will be embarrassed. Others observing this situation would be affected by the outcome.
	c. If Gomez does nothing, she avoids a confrontation with Packer or his boss. They may or may not discover the error. If they discover it, they may or may not correct it. They may criticize Gomez for not bringing the error to their attention. Colleagues might learn of the situation.
6. What shall I do?	**6.** *Make the decision.* The choice is difficult. Gomez must balance the likely effects on the various people against the dictates of her own conscience. Gomez should report the errors. Ordinarily, Packer should be the first person contacted. If Packer fails to act in an honest way, then Gomez should inform Packer's boss. Senior management should always protect the messenger of accurate news, whether good or bad.

Ethics and External Controls

There is another dimension to most ethical issues: *external controls,* the discipline placed on business conduct by outsiders who interact with the company.

- In situation 1, for example, Sonja Kleberg could give in to the client's request to backdate the advertising expense. But this action would be both dishonest and illegal. These external controls arise from the business's interaction with the taxing authorities. An IRS audit of Kleberg's client could uncover her action.

- In situation 2, the external controls arise from Jack Mellichamp's relationship with the bank that lent money to his software company. As long as the loan agreement is in effect, the company must maintain a current ratio of 1.50 or higher. Paying off current liabilities to improve the current ratio would be a short-term solution to Mellichamp's problem. Over the long run, his business must generate more current assets through operations.

- The primary external control in situation 3 results from U.S. laws and their enforcement through the legal system. Campaign contributions are public information, and sooner or later the public will learn that the Democratic Party received illegal campaign contributions. It would be in the party's best interest to admit its mistake and correct the errors as quickly as possible—by returning the illegal contributions to the donors.

REVIEW INTERNAL CONTROL AND CASH

SUMMARY PROBLEM

Grudnitski Company established a $300 petty cash fund. James C. Brown is the fund custodian. At the end of the first week, the petty cash fund contains the following:

a. Cash: $171   **b.** Petty cash tickets:

No.	Amount	Issued to	Signed by	Account Debited
44	$14	B. Jarvis	B. Jarvis and JCB	Office Supplies
45	9	S. Bell	S. Bell	Miscellaneous Expense
47	43	R. Tate	R. Tate and JCB	—
48	33	L. Blair	L. Blair and JCB	Travel Expense

www.prenhall.com/horngren

End-of-Chapter Assessment

Required

1. Identify the four internal control weaknesses revealed in the given data.
2. Prepare the general journal entries to record:
   a. Establishment of the petty cash fund.
   b. Replenishment of the fund. Assume that petty cash ticket no. 47 was issued for the purchase of office supplies.
3. What is the balance in the Petty Cash account immediately before replenishment? Immediately after replenishment?

Solution

Requirement 1

The four internal control weaknesses are

a. Petty cash ticket no. 46 is missing. Coupled with weakness (b), this omission raises questions about the administration of the petty cash fund and about how the petty cash funds were used.

b. The $171 cash balance means that $129 has been disbursed ($300 − $171 = $129). However, the total amount of the petty cash tickets is only $99 ($14 + $9 + $43 + $33). The fund, then, is $30 short of cash ($129 − $99 = $30). Was petty cash ticket no. 46 issued for $30? The data in the problem offer no hint that helps answer this question. In practice, management would investigate the problem.

c. The petty cash custodian (JCB) did not sign petty cash ticket no. 45. This omission may have been an oversight on his part. However, it raises the question of whether he authorized the payment. Both the fund custodian and the recipient of cash should sign the ticket.

d. Petty cash ticket no. 47 does not indicate which account to debit. What did Tate do with the money, and what account should be debited? With no better choice available, debit Miscellaneous Expense.

Requirement 2

Petty cash journal entries:
a. Entry to establish the petty cash fund: **b.** Entry to replenish the fund:

Petty Cash............................	300	
Cash in Bank............		300

Office Supplies ($14 + $43)............	57	
Miscellaneous Expense	9	
Travel Expense	33	
Cash Short and Over.......................	30	
Cash in Bank		129

Requirement 3

The balance in Petty Cash is *always* its specified balance, in this case $300.

LESSONS LEARNED

1. **Define internal control.** *Internal control* is the organizational plan and all the related measures an entity uses to safeguard assets, encourage adherence to company policies, promote operational efficiency, and ensure accurate and reliable accounting records.

2. **Identify the characteristics of an effective system of internal control.** An effective internal control system includes these features: competent, reliable, and ethical personnel; clear-cut assignment of responsibilities; proper authorization; separation of duties; internal and external audits; documents and records; and electronic devices and computer controls.

3. **Prepare a bank reconciliation and the related journal entries.** The *bank account* helps control and safeguard cash. Businesses use the *bank statement* and the *bank reconciliation* to account for banking transactions.

4. **Apply internal controls to cash receipts.** To control cash receipts over the counter, companies use point-of-sale terminals that customers can see, and require that cashiers provide customers with receipts. The machine records each sale and cash transaction.

   To control cash receipts by mail, a mailroom employee should be charged with opening the mail, comparing the enclosed amount with the remittance advice, and preparing a control tape. This is an essential separation of duties—the accounting department should not open the mail. At the end of the day, the controller compares the three records of the day's cash receipts: the control tape total from the mailroom, the bank deposit amount from the cashier, and the debit to Cash from the accounting department.

5. **Apply internal controls to cash payments.** To control payments by check, checks should be issued and signed only when a *payment packet* including the purchase request, purchase order, invoice (bill), and receiving report (with all appropriate signatures) has been prepared. To control petty cash payments, the custodian of the fund should require a completed petty cash ticket for all disbursements.

6. **Use a budget to manage cash.** A budget is a quantitative expression of a plan to help managers coordinate the entity's activities. First, a company must determine how much cash it will need. Then it budgets cash receipts and payments for the upcoming period. By comparing the ending budgeted cash balance to the amount needed, managers can determine whether they need to borrow or will have extra cash to invest.

7. **Make ethical judgments in business.** To make ethical decisions, people should follow six steps: (1) Determine the facts. (2) Identify the ethical issues. (3) Specify the alternatives. (4) Identify the people involved. (5) Assess the possible outcomes. (6) Make the decision.

ACCOUNTING VOCABULARY

audit (p. 270)
bank collection (p. 275)
bank reconciliation (p. 275)
bank statement (p. 274)
budget (p. 286)
check (p. 273)
computer virus (p. 272)

controller (p. 268)
deposit in transit (p. 275)
electronic funds transfer (EFT) (p. 274)
encryption (p. 272)
firewalls (p. 272)
imprest system (p. 286)

internal control (p. 267)
nonsufficient funds (NSF) check (p. 276)
outstanding check (p. 275)
petty cash (p. 285)
Trojan horse (p. 272)

QUESTIONS

1. Which feature of effective internal control is the most fundamental? Why?
2. Identify seven features of an effective system of internal control.
3. Separation of duties may be divided into four parts. What are they?
4. Are internal control systems designed to be foolproof and perfect? What is a fundamental constraint in planning and maintaining systems?
5. Briefly state how each of the following serves as an internal control measure over cash: bank account, signature card, deposit ticket, and bank statement.
6. Each of the following items affects the bank reconciliation. Next to each item, enter the appropriate letter from the following possible treatments: (a) bank side of reconciliation—add the item; (b) bank side of reconciliation—subtract the item; (c) book side of reconciliation—add the item; (d) book side of reconciliation—subtract the item.
   ____ Deposit in transit
   ____ Bank collection
   ____ Customer check returned because of un-authorized signature
   ____ Book error that increased balance of Cash account
   ____ Outstanding check
   ____ NSF check
   ____ Bank service charge
   ____ Cost of printed checks
   ____ Bank error that decreased bank balance
7. What purpose does a bank reconciliation serve?
8. A company has six bank accounts, two petty cash funds, and three certificates of deposit that can be withdrawn on demand. How many cash amounts would this company likely report on its balance sheet?
9. What role does a cash register play in an internal control system?
10. Describe internal control procedures for cash received by mail.
11. What documents make up the payment packet? Describe three procedures that use the payment packet to ensure that each payment is appropriate.
12. What balance does the Petty Cash account have at all times? Does this balance always equal the amount of cash in the fund? When are the two amounts equal? When are they unequal?
13. Describe how a budget helps a company manage its cash.
14. Why should accountants adhere to a higher standard of ethical conduct than many other members of society?

ASSESS YOUR PROGRESS

DAILY EXERCISES

DE7-1 Give the title of the chief finance officer and the title of the chief accounting officer in an organization. What are the responsibilities of each person? How does separating their duties provide good internal control?

Aspects of internal control (Obj. 1)

DE7-2 Internal controls are designed to safeguard assets, encourage employees to follow company policies, promote operational efficiency, and ensure accurate records. Which goal is most important? Which goal must the internal controls accomplish for the business to survive? Give your reason.

Definition of internal control (Obj. 1)

DE7-3 Explain in your own words why separation of duties is often described as the cornerstone of internal control for safeguarding assets. Describe what can happen if the same person has custody of an asset and also accounts for the asset.

Characteristics of an effective system of internal control (Obj. 2)

DE7-4 Examine the organization chart in Exhibit 7-2, page 268. What is the main duty of the internal auditors? To whom do the internal auditors report? Why don't the internal auditors report directly to the treasurer?

Characteristics of an effective system of internal control (Obj. 2)

DE7-5 How do external auditors differ from internal auditors? How does an external audit differ from an internal audit? How are the two types of audits similar?

Characteristics of an effective system of internal control (Obj. 2)

DE7-6 Review the characteristics of an effective system of internal control that begin on page 267. Then identify two things that **Merrill Lynch** in the chapter-opening story could have done to make it harder for Darlyne Lopez, the cashier, to steal from the company and hide the theft. Explain how each new measure taken by Merrill Lynch would have accomplished its goal.

Characteristics of an effective system of internal control (Obj. 2)

DE7-7 Make a simple diagram with three boxes and two arrows to show the relationships among (a) the bank statement, (b) the bank reconciliation, and (c) the accounting records. Use the arrows to show the flow of data.

Bank reconciliation (Obj. 3)

DE7-8 Answer the following questions about the bank reconciliation:

1. What is the difference between a bank statement and a bank reconciliation?
2. Is the bank reconciliation a journal, a ledger, an account, or a financial statement? If none of these, what is it?
3. Which side of the bank reconciliation generates data for new journal entries in the company's accounting records?

Aspects of a bank reconciliation (Obj. 3)

DE7-9 Compare Business Research, Inc.'s Cash account in Exhibit 7-5, page 275, with the bank statement that the company received in Exhibit 7-4, page 274.

1. Trace each cash receipt from the Cash account (Exhibit 7-5) to a deposit on the bank statement (Exhibit 7-4). Which deposit is in transit on January 31? Give its date and dollar amount.
2. Trace each Business Research check from the cash payments record in Exhibit 7-5 to the bank statement in Exhibit 7-4. List all outstanding checks by check number and dollar amount.
3. On which side of the bank reconciliation do deposits in transit and outstanding checks appear—the bank side or the book side? Are they added or subtracted on the bank reconciliation?

Identifying reconciling items from bank documents (Obj. 3)

DE7-10 The Cash account of Theraband Equipment reported a balance of $2,280 at May 31. Included were outstanding checks totaling $900 and a May 31 deposit of $200 that did not appear on the bank statement. The bank statement, which came from Park Cities Bank, listed a May 31 balance of $3,270. Included in the bank balance was a May 30 collection of $300 on account from Kelly Brooks, a Theraband customer who pays the bank directly. The bank statement also shows a $20 service charge and $10 of interest revenue that Theraband earned on its bank balance. *Prepare Theraband's bank reconciliation at May 31.*

Preparing a bank reconciliation (Obj. 3)

DE7-11 After preparing Theraband Equipment's bank reconciliation in Daily Exercise 7-10, make Theraband's general journal entries for transactions that arise from the bank reconciliation. Include an explanation with each entry.

Recording transactions from a bank reconciliation (Obj. 3)

DE7-12 Who in an organization should prepare the bank reconciliation? Should it be someone with cash-handling duties, someone with accounting duties, or someone with both duties? Does it matter? Give your reason.

Internal controls and the bank reconciliation (Obj. 2, 3)

DE7-13 Barry Cruise owns Cruise Vacation Planners. He fears that a trusted employee has been stealing from the company. This employee receives cash from customers and also prepares the monthly bank reconciliation. To check up on the employee, Cruise prepares his own bank reconciliation, as follows:

CRUISE VACATION PLANNERS
Bank Reconciliation
August 31, 20X7

Bank		**Books**	
Balance, August 31	$3,000	Balance, August 31	$2,500
Add: Deposit in transit..............	400	Add: Bank collection	800
		Interest revenue	10
Less: Outstanding checks..........	(1,100)	Less: Service charge.................	(30)
Adjusted bank balance	$2,300	Adjusted book balance	$3,280

Does it appear that the employee has stolen from the company? If so, how much? Explain your answer. Which side of the bank reconciliation shows the company's true cash balance?

DE7-14 Consider the men's sportswear department of a **Macy's** department store. What could a dishonest salesperson do if he had access to the record of transactions conducted through his cash register? How does Macy's keep employees from behaving in this manner?

DE7-15 Ted Carter sells furniture at Dupree Home & Garden in Huntsville, Alabama. Company procedure requires Carter to write a customer receipt for all sales. The receipt forms are prenumbered. Carter is having personal financial problems and takes $500 that he received from a customer. To hide his theft, Carter simply destroys the company copy of the sales receipt he gave the customer. What will alert Gerald Dupree, the owner, that something is wrong? What will this knowledge lead Dupree to do?

DE7-16 Review the internal controls over cash receipts by mail, discussed on page 282. Briefly describe how the final step in the process, performed by the controller, establishes that **(1)** the cash receipts went into the bank; and **(2)** the business's customers received credit for their payments.

How does a lock-box system protect cash from theft?

DE7-17 Answer the following questions about internal control over cash payments.

1. Payment of cash payments by check carries two basic controls over cash. What are they?
2. Suppose a purchasing agent receives the goods that he purchases and also approves payment for the goods. How could a dishonest purchasing agent cheat his company? How do companies avoid this internal control weakness?

DE7-18

1. Describe how an *imprest* petty cash system works. What is the main control feature of an imprest system?
2. Atlantic Press Publishers maintains an imprest $400 petty cash fund, which is under the control of Brenda Chavez. At November 30, the fund holds $220 cash and petty cash tickets for travel expense, $80; office supplies, $60; and delivery expense, $40.

   Journalize (a) establishment of the petty cash fund on November 1, and (b) replenishment of the fund on November 30.
3. Draw a T-account for Petty Cash, and post to the account. What is Petty Cash's account balance at all times?

DE7-19

1. Return to **Gap Inc.'s** hypothetical cash budget in Exhibit 7-13, page 287. Suppose Gap postpones the opening of new stores until 20X3. In that case, how much additional financing will Gap need for the year ended January 31, 20X2?
2. Now suppose Gap postpones both existing-store expansions and new-store openings until 20X3. How much new financing will Gap need, or how much cash would Gap have available for additional investment during the year ended January 31, 20X2?

DE7-20 Florida Progreso Growers is a major food cooperative. The company begins 2002 with cash of $6 million. Florida Progreso estimates cash receipts during 2002 will total $147 million. Planned disbursements for the year will require cash of $158 million. To meet daily cash needs, Florida Progreso must maintain a cash balance of at least $5 million.

Prepare Florida Progreso's cash budget for 2002.

DE7-21 Peter Larson, an accountant for BSI Consulting, discovers that his supervisor, Rose Kwan, made several errors last year. Overall, the errors overstated BSI's net income by 20%. It is not clear whether the errors were deliberate or accidental. What should Larson do?

Making an ethical judgment (Obj. 7)

EXERCISES

E7-1 Consider this adaptation of a *Wall Street Journal* article:

Correcting an internal control weakness (Obj. 2)

TOKYO—Toshima Corp., a Japanese trading company, said unauthorized trades by its former head of copper trading caused losses that may total $1.8 billion. Toshima learned of the damage when Yuji Takeda confessed to making unauthorized trades that led to losses over a 10-year period. Mr. Takeda concealed the losses by falsifying Toshima's books and records.

What internal control weakness at Toshima allowed this loss to grow so large? How could the company have avoided and/or limited the size of the loss?

E7-2 The following situations describe two cash receipts situations and two equipment purchase situations. In each pair, one situation's internal controls are significantly better than the other's. Evaluate the internal controls in each situation as strong or weak, and give the reason for your answers.

Identifying internal control strengths and weaknesses (Obj. 1)

Cash Receipts:

a. Cash received by mail goes straight to the accountant, who debits Cash and credits Accounts Receivable to record collections from customers. The accountant then deposits the cash in the bank.
b. Cash received by mail goes to the mail room, where a mail clerk opens envelopes and totals the cash receipts for the day. The mail clerk forwards customer checks to the cashier for deposit in the bank and forwards the remittance slips to the accounting department for posting credits to customer accounts.

Equipment Purchases:

a. Centennial Homes policy calls for construction supervisors to request the equipment needed for construction jobs. The home office then purchases the equipment and has it shipped to the construction site.
b. Wayside Construction Company policy calls for project supervisors to purchase the equipment needed for construction jobs. The supervisors then submit the paid receipts to the home office for reimbursement. This policy enables supervisors to get the equipment they need quickly and keep construction jobs moving along.

E7-3 The following situations suggest a strength or a weakness in internal control. Identify each as *strength* or *weakness,* and give the reason for your answer.

Identifying internal control strengths and weaknesses. (Obj. 2)

a. Cash received over the counter is controlled by the sales clerk, who rings up the sale and places the cash in the register. The sales clerk matches the total recorded on the control tape stored in the register to each day's cash sales.
b. The vice president who signs checks does not examine the payment packet because the accounting department has matched the invoice with other supporting documents.
c. Top managers delegate all internal control measures to the accounting department.
d. The accounting department orders merchandise and approves invoices for payment.
e. The operator of a computer has no other accounting or cash-handling duties.

E7-4 Identify the missing internal control characteristic in the following situations:

Identifying internal controls (Obj. 2)

a. When business is brisk, Stop-n-Go and many other retail stores deposit cash in the bank several times during the day. The manager at one store wants to reduce the time employees spend delivering cash to the bank, so he starts a new policy. Cash will build up over Saturdays and Sundays, and the total two-day amount will be deposited on Sunday evening.
b. While reviewing the records of Discount Pharmacy, you find that the same employee orders merchandise and approves invoices for payment.
c. Business is slow at Fun City Amusement Park on Tuesday, Wednesday, and Thursday nights. To reduce expenses, the owner decides not to use a ticket taker on those nights. The ticket seller (cashier) is told to keep the tickets as a record of the number sold.
d. The manager of a discount store wants to speed the flow of customers through check-out. She decides to reduce the time cashiers spend making change, so she prices merchandise at round dollar amounts—such as $8.00 and $15.00—instead of the customary amounts—$7.95 and $14.95.
e. Grocery stores such as **Safeway** and **Meier's** purchase large quantities of merchandise from a few suppliers. At another grocery store, the manager decides to reduce paperwork. He eliminates the requirement that a receiving department employee prepare a receiving report, which lists the quantities of items actually received from the supplier.

E7-5 The following questions pertain to internal control. Consider each situation separately.

a. Many managers think that safeguarding assets is the most important objective of internal control systems, while auditors emphasize internal control's role in ensuring reliable accounting data. Explain why managers are more concerned about safeguarding assets and auditors are more concerned about the quality of the accounting records.

b. Separation of duties is an important consideration if a system of internal control is to be effective. Why is this so?

c. Cash can be a relatively small item on the financial statements. Nevertheless, internal control over cash is very important. Why is this true?

d. Ling Ltd. requires that all documents supporting a check be canceled (stamped Paid) by the person who signs the check. Why do you think this practice is required? What might happen if it were not?

E7-6 The following items could appear on a bank reconciliation:

a. Book error: We debited Cash for $200. The correct debit was $2,000.
b. Outstanding checks.
c. Bank error: The bank charged our account for a check written by another customer.
d. Service charge.
e. Deposits in transit.
f. NSF check.
g. Bank collection of a note receivable on our behalf.

Required

Classify each item as (1) an addition to the book balance, (2) a subtraction from the book balance, (3) an addition to the bank balance, or (4) a subtraction from the bank balance.

E7-7 Bill Westphal's checkbook lists the following:

Date	Check No.	Item	Check	Deposit	Balance
9/1					$ 525
4	622	JD's Art Café	$ 19		506
9		Dividends received		$ 116	622
13	623	General Tire Co.	43		579
14	624	Exxon Oil Co.	58		521
18	625	Cash	50		471
26	626	Redeemer Presbyterian Church	75		396
28	627	Bent Tree Apartments	275		121
30		Paycheck		1,800	1,921

Westphal's September bank statement shows the following:

Balance			$525
Add: Deposits			116
Debit checks:	No.	Amount	
	622	$19	
	623	43	
	624	68*	
	625	50	(180)
Other charges:			
Printed checks		$ 8	
Service charge		12	(20)
Balance			$441

*This is the correct amount for check number 624.

Required

Prepare Westphal's bank reconciliation at September 30.

E7-8 Mario Bocelli operates four Quik Pak convenience stores. He has just received the monthly bank statement at October 31 from City National Bank, and the statement shows an ending balance of $2,750. Listed on the statement are an EFT rent collection of $400, a service charge of $12, two NSF checks totaling $74, and a $9 charge for printed checks. In reviewing his cash records, Bocelli identifies outstanding checks totaling $467 and an October 31 deposit in transit of $1,788. During October, he recorded a $290 check for the salary of a part-time employee by debiting Salary Expense and crediting Cash for $29. Bocelli's Cash account shows an October 31 cash balance of $4,027. *Prepare the bank reconciliation at October 31.*

Preparing a bank reconciliation (Obj. 3)

E7-9 Using the data from Exercise 7-8, make the journal entries Bocelli should record on October 31. Include an explanation for each entry.

Making journal entries from a bank reconciliation (Obj. 3)

E7-10 A grand jury indicted the manager of a Hickory Stick restaurant for stealing cash from the company. Over a 3-year period, the manager allegedly took almost $100,000 and attempted to cover the theft by manipulating the bank reconciliation.

What is the most likely way that a person would manipulate a bank reconciliation to cover a theft? Be specific. What internal control arrangement could have avoided this theft?

Applying internal controls to the bank reconciliation (Obj. 2, 3)

E7-11 At the check-out of **Best Buy** stores, cash registers display the amount of each sale, the cash received from the customer, and any change returned to the customer. The registers also produce a customer receipt but keep no internal record of transactions. At the end of the day, clerks count the cash in the register and give it to the cashier for deposit in the company bank account.

Write a memo to convince the store manager that there is an internal control weakness over cash receipts. Identify the weakness that gives an employee the best opportunity to steal cash, and state how to prevent such a theft.

Evaluating internal control over cash receipts (Obj. 4)

E7-12 Record the following selected transactions of Rosetree Florist in general journal format (explanations are not required):

Petty cash, cash short and over (Obj. 5)

April 1 Established a petty cash fund with a $300 balance.
2 Journalized the day's cash sales. Cash register tapes show a $2,869 total, but the cash in the register is $2,873.
10 The petty cash fund has $119 in cash and $161 in petty cash tickets that were issued to pay for Office Supplies ($111), Delivery Expense ($13), and Entertainment Expense ($37). Replenished the fund and recorded the expenses.

E7-13 Operation Recycle in Seattle created a $500 imprest petty cash fund. During the first month of use, the fund custodian authorized and signed petty cash tickets as follows:

Accounting for petty cash (Obj. 5)

Petty Cash Ticket No.	Item	Account Debited	Amount
1	Delivery of pledge cards to donors	Delivery Expense	$22.19
2	Mail package	Postage Expense	52.80
3	Newsletter	Supplies Expense	34.14
4	Key to closet	Miscellaneous Expense	2.85
5	Wastebasket	Miscellaneous Expense	13.78
6	Computer diskettes	Supplies Expense	85.37

Required

1. Make the general journal entries that **(a)** first create the petty cash fund and **(b)** show its replenishment. Include explanations.
2. Describe the items in the fund immediately before replenishment.
3. Describe the items in the fund immediately after replenishment.

E7-14 Suppose **Sprint Corporation,** the long-distance telephone company, is preparing its cash budget for 20X4. The company ended 20X3 with $135 million, and top management foresees the need for a cash balance of at least $137 million to pay all bills as they come due in 20X4.

Preparing a cash budget (Obj. 6)

Collections from customers are expected to total $11,813 million during 20X4, and payments for the cost of services and products should reach $6,166 million. Operating expense payments are budgeted at $2,744 million.

During 20X4, Sprint expects to invest $1,826 million in new equipment, $275 million in the company's cellular division, and to sell older assets for $116 million. Debt payments scheduled for 20X4 will total $597 million. The company forecasts net income of $890 million for 20X4 and plans to pay $338 million to its owners.

Required

Prepare Sprint's cash budget for 20X4. Will the budgeted level of cash receipts leave Sprint with the desired ending cash balance of $137 million, or will the company need additional financing?

E7-15 Approximately 300 current and former members of the U.S. House of Representatives—on a regular basis—wrote a quarter million dollars of checks on the House bank without having the cash in their accounts. In effect, the delinquent check writers were borrowing money from each other on an interest-free, no-service-charge basis. The House closed its bank after the events became public.

Required

Suppose you are a new congressional representative from your state. Apply the ethical judgment framework outlined in the Decision Guidelines feature on page 290 to decide whether you would write NSF checks on a regular basis through the House bank.

Challenge Exercise.

E7-16 ◄ *Link Back to Chapter 4 (Current Ratio and Debt Ratio).* Among its many products, Continental Paper Company makes paper for shopping bags, canned-food labels, and magazines. Ruth Majer, the Chief Budget Officer, is responsible for Continental's cash budget for 20X5. The budget helps Majer determine the amount of long-term borrowing needed to end the year with a cash balance of $300 million. Majer has assembled budget data for 20X5. Not all of the following items are used in preparing the cash budget. Receipts are positive amounts; payments are in parentheses.

	(In millions)
Acquisition of other companies	$ (1,168)
Actual cash balance, December 31, 20X4	340
Borrowing	?
Budgeted total assets before borrowing	23,977
Budgeted total current assets before borrowing	5,873
Budgeted total current liabilities before borrowing	4,863
Budgeted total liabilities before borrowing	16,180
Budgeted total stockholder's equity before borrowing	7,797
Collections from customers	19,467
Payments to owners	(237)
Investments by owners	516
Net income	1,153
Other cash receipts	111
Payment of long-term and short-term debt	(950)
Payment of operating expenses	(2,349)
Purchases of inventory	(14,345)
Purchase of property and equipment	(1,518)

Required

1. Prepare the cash budget to determine the amount of borrowing Continental Paper needs during 20X5.
2. Compute Continental Paper's expected current ratio and debt ratio at December 31, 20X5, both before and after borrowing on long-term debt. Assume you are the chief loan officer at a bank. Based on these figures, and on the budgeted levels of assets and liabilities, would you lend the requested amount to Continental Paper? Give the reason for your decision.

(Group A) PROBLEMS

P7-1A An employee of Suntech Oil Company recently stole thousands of dollars of the company's cash. The company has installed a new system of internal controls. As a consultant for Suntech Oil Company, write a memo to the president explaining how a separation of duties helps to safeguard assets.

P7-2A The following situations have an internal control weakness.

a. Roberson Computer Programs is a software company that specializes in programs with accounting applications. The company's most popular program prepares the journal, accounts receivable subsidiary ledger, and general ledger. In the company's early days, the owner and eight employees wrote the computer programs, sold the products to stores such as ComputerWorld, and performed general management and accounting. As the company has grown, the number of employees has increased dramatically. Recently, the development of a new software program stopped while the programmers redesigned Roberson's accounting system. Roberson's accountants could have performed this task.

b. Emma Blue, a widow with no known sources of outside income, has been a trusted employee of Stone Products Company for 15 years. She performs all cash-handling and accounting duties, including opening the mail, preparing the bank deposit, accounting for all aspects of cash and accounts receivable, and preparing the bank reconciliation. She has just purchased a new Mercedes and a new home in an expensive suburb. Juan Perez, owner of the company, wonders how she can afford these luxuries.

c. Harriet Laman employs three professional interior designers in her design studio. She is located in an area with a lot of new construction, and her business is booming. Ordinarily, Laman does all the purchasing of draperies, fabrics, and labor needed to complete jobs. During the summer she takes a long vacation, and in her absence she allows each designer to purchase materials and labor. On her return, Laman observes that expenses are much higher and net income much lower than in the past.

d. Discount stores such as **Target** and **Sam's** receive a large portion of their sales revenue in cash, with the remainder in credit-card sales. To reduce expenses, one store manager ceases purchasing fidelity bonds on the cashiers.

e. The office supply company from which Champs Sporting Goods purchases cash receipt forms recently notified Champs that the last shipped receipts were not prenumbered. Alex Champ, the owner, replied that he never uses the receipt numbers.

Required

1. Identify the missing internal control characteristics in each situation.
2. Identify the business's possible problem.
3. Propose a solution to the internal control problem.

P7-3A The cash receipts and the payments of Veralux Interiors for March 20X5 follow:

Using the bank reconciliation as a control device
(Obj. 3)

Cash Receipts (Posting reference is CR)		Cash Payments (Posting reference is CP)	
Date	**Cash Debit**	**Check No.**	**Cash Credit**
Mar. 4	$2,716	1413	$1,465
9	544	1414	1,004
11	1,655	1415	450
14	896	1416	8
17	367	1417	775
25	890	1418	88
31	2,038	1419	4,126
Total	$9,106	1420	970
		1421	200
		1422	2,267
		Total	$11,353

The Cash account of Veralux Interiors shows the following on March 31, 20X5:

Cash					
Date	**Item**	**Jrnl. Ref.**	**Debit**	**Credit**	**Balance**
Mar. 1	Balance				12,188
31		CR. 10	9,106		21,294
31		CP. 16		11,353	9,941

On March 31, 20X5, Veralux Interiors received the bank statement at the top of the next page.

Additional data for the bank reconciliation:

a. The EFT deposit was a receipt of rent. The EFT debit was payment of insurance.

b. The NSF check was received late in February from Mark Anthony.

c. The $1,000 bank collection of a note receivable on March 31 included $122 interest revenue.

d. The correct amount of check number 1419, a payment on account, is $4,216. (The Veralux Interiors accountant mistakenly recorded the check for $4,126.)

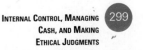

Bank Statement for March 20X5

Beginning balance $12,188

Deposits and other Credits:

Mar. 1	$ 625 EFT	
5	2,716	
10	544	
11	1,655	
15	896	
18	367	
25	890	
31	1,000 BC	8,693

Checks and other Debits:

Mar. 8	$ 441 NSF	
9	1,465	
13	1,004	
14	450	
15	8	
19	340 EFT	
22	775	
29	88	
31	4,216	
31	25 SC	(8,812)

Ending balance $12,069

Explanations: BC—bank collection, EFT—electronic funds transfer, NSF—nonsufficient funds check, SC—service charge.

Required

1. Prepare the bank reconciliation of Veralux Interiors at March 31, 20X5.
2. Describe how a bank account and the bank reconciliation help Veralux managers control the business's cash.

Preparing a bank reconciliation and the related journal entries (Obj. 3)

P7-4A The May 31 bank statement of Payne Stationers has just arrived from First State Bank. To prepare the Payne bank reconciliation, you gather the following data.

a. The May 31 bank balance is $21,110.82.

b. The bank statement includes two charges for returned checks from customers. One is an NSF check in the amount of $67.50 received from Sarah Batten, a student, recorded on the books by a debit to Cash, and deposited on May 19. The other is a $195.03 check received from Lena Masters and deposited on May 21. It was returned by Masters' bank with the imprint "Unauthorized Signature."

c. The following Payne checks are outstanding at May 31:

Check No.	Amount
616	$403.00
802	74.25
806	36.60
809	161.38
810	229.05
811	48.91

d. Payne Stationers collects from a few customers by EFT. The May bank statement lists a $200 deposit for a collection on account from customer Jack Oates.

e. The bank statement includes two special deposits: $899.14, which is the amount of dividend revenue the bank collected from General Electric Company on behalf of Payne, and $16.86, the interest revenue Payne earned on its bank balance during May.

f. The bank statement lists a $6.25 subtraction for the bank service charge.

g. On May 31, the Payne treasurer deposited $381.14, but this deposit does not appear on the bank statement.

h. The bank statement includes a $410.00 deduction for a check drawn by Marimont Freight Company. Payne promptly notified the bank of its error.

i. Payne's Cash account shows a balance of $20,101.55 on May 31.

Required

1. Prepare the bank reconciliation for Payne Stationers at May 31.
2. Record the entries necessary to bring the book balance of Cash into agreement with the adjusted book balance on the reconciliation. Include an explanation for each entry.

P7-5A East Coast Heating makes all sales on credit. Cash receipts arrive by mail. Kenneth Sartain opens envelopes and separates the checks from the accompanying remittance advices. Sartain forwards the checks to another employee, who makes the daily bank deposit but has no access to the accounting records. Sartain sends the remittance advices, which show cash received, to the accounting department for entry in the accounts. Sartain's only other duty is to grant sales allowances to customers. (Recall that a *sales allowance* decreases the amount receivable.) When Sartain receives a customer check for less than the full amount of the invoice, he records the sales allowance and forwards the document to the accounting department.

Identifying internal control weakness in cash receipts
(Obj. 4)

Required

You are a new employee of East Coast Heating. Write a memo to the company president identifying the internal control weakness in this situation. State how to correct the weakness.

P7-6A On April 1, Sealy Electronics creates a petty cash fund with an imprest balance of $400. During April, Elise Nelson, the fund custodian, signs the petty cash tickets:

Accounting for petty cash transactions
(Obj. 5)

Petty Cash Ticket Number	Item	Amount
101	Office supplies	$86.89
102	Cab fare for executive	25.00
103	Delivery of package across town	37.75
104	Dinner money for sales manager entertaining a customer	80.00
105	Inventory	85.70
106	Decorations for office party	19.22
107	Six boxes of floppy disks	44.37

On April 30, prior to replenishment, the fund contains these tickets plus $17.36. The accounts affected by petty cash payments are Office Supplies Expense, Travel Expense, Delivery Expense, Entertainment Expense, and Freight In.

Required

1. Explain the characteristics and the internal control features of an imprest fund.
2. Make the general journal entries to (a) create the fund and (b) replenish it. Include explanations. Also, briefly describe what the custodian does on April 1 and April 30.
3. Make the May 1 entry to increase the fund balance to $500. Include an explanation, and briefly describe what the custodian does.

P7-7A Suppose you are preparing your personal cash budget for the year 20X2. During 20X2, assume you expect to earn $3,600 from your summer job and $1,500 for work in the college cafeteria. Also, your family always gives you gifts totaling around $800 during the year. A scholarship from your home church adds $1,000 each year while you are in college.

Preparing a personal cash budget
(Obj. 6)

Your family pays your college costs except for room and board. Planned expenditures for 20X2 include apartment rent of $150 per month for 12 months and annual food costs of $4,800. Gas and other auto expenses usually run about $50 per month. You need to have a little fun, so entertainment will eat up $100 per month.

You need to keep a little cash in reserve for auto repairs and other emergencies, so you maintain a cash reserve of $300 at all times. To start 20X2, you have this cash reserve plus $200.

Will you need a loan during 20X2? To answer this question, prepare your personal cash budget for the year based on the data given.

P7-8A Lesa Krause, Chief Financial Officer of Datek Enterprises, is responsible for the company's budgeting process. Suppose Krause's staff is preparing the Datek cash budget for 20X9. A key input to the budgeting process is last year's statement of cash flows, which provides the data at the top of the next page for 20X8 (in millions). Cash receipts appear as positive amounts; cash payments are negative amounts, denoted within parentheses.

Preparing a cash budget
(Obj. 6)

DATEK ENTERPRISES			
Cash-Flow Data for 20X8			
Cash and Cash Equivalents			
Beginning of year 20X8	$ 764	Purchases of plant assets	$ (614)
End of year 20X8	792	Borrowings	160
Collections from customers	8,089	Long-term debt repayments	(1)
Interest revenue collected	24	Cash received for	
Purchases of inventory	(5,597)	investments by owners	30
Operating expenses paid	(1,859)	Payments to owners	(183)

Required

1. Prepare the Datek cash budget for 20X9. Date the budget "20X9" and denote the beginning and ending cash balances as "beginning" and "ending." Round to the nearest million dollars. Assume the company expects 20X9 to be similar to 20X8, but with the following changes:
   a. In 20X9, the company expects a 7% increase in collections from customers and a 5% increase in purchases of inventory.
   b. Krause plans for Datek to end the year with a cash balance of $400 million.
2. Based on the cash budget you prepared, how much additional cash does it appear that Datek will have available for other investments during 20X9?

Making an ethical judgment
(Obj. 7)

P7-9A Tri State Bank in Cairo, Illinois, has a loan receivable from Cortez Manufacturing Company. Cortez is six months late in making payments to the bank, and Milton Reed, a Tri State vice president, is helping Cortez restructure its debt. Reed learns that Cortez is depending on landing a manufacturing contract from Peters & Sons, another Tri State client. Reed also serves as Peters' loan officer at the bank. In this capacity, he is aware that Peters is considering declaring bankruptcy. No one outside Peters & Sons knows this. Reed has been a great help to Cortez Manufacturing, and Cortez's owner is counting on him to carry the company through this difficult restructuring. To help the bank collect on this large loan, Reed has a strong motivation to help Cortez survive.

Apply the ethical judgment framework from the chapter to help Reed plan his next action.

(Group B) PROBLEMS

Identifying the characteristics of an effective internal control system
(Obj. 1, 2)

P7-1B Caldwell-Bailey Development Company prospered during the lengthy economic expansion of the 1990s. Business was so good that the company used very few internal controls. A recent decline in the local real estate market caused Caldwell-Bailey to experience a shortage of cash. Dave Matthews, the company owner, is looking for ways to save money.

As a consultant for the company, write a memo to convince Matthews of the company's need for a system of internal control. Be specific in explaining how an internal control system could save the company money. Include the definition of internal control, and briefly discuss each characteristic of an effective internal control system, beginning with competent, reliable, and ethical personnel.

Correcting internal control weaknesses
(Obj. 2, 4, 5)

P7-2B Each of the following situations has an internal control weakness.

a. Aimee Atkins has been an employee of Mary V's Bridal Salon for many years. Because the business is relatively small, Atkins performs all accounting duties, including opening the mail, preparing the bank deposit, and preparing the bank reconciliation.
b. Most large companies have internal audit staffs that continuously evaluate the business's internal control. Part of the auditor's job is to evaluate how efficiently the company is running. For example, does the company purchase inventory from the least expensive wholesaler? After a particularly bad year, Design Company eliminates its internal audit department to reduce expenses.
c. CPA firms, law firms, and other professional organizations use paraprofessional employees to perform routine tasks. For example, an accounting paraprofessional might examine documents to assist a CPA in conducting an audit. In the CPA firm of Lee & Dunham, Joseph Lee, the senior partner, turns over a significant portion of his own audit work to his paraprofessional staff.
d. In evaluating the internal control over cash payments, an auditor learns that the purchasing agent is responsible for purchasing diamonds for use in the company's manufacturing process, approving the invoices for payment, and signing the checks.
e. Blake Lemmon owns an engineering firm. His staff consists of 12 engineers, and he manages the office. Often, his work requires him to travel. He notes that when he returns from business trips, the engineering jobs in the office have not pro-

gressed much. When he is away, his senior employees take over office management and neglect their engineering duties. One employee could manage the office.

Required

1. Identify the missing internal control characteristic in each situation.
2. Identify the business's possible problem.
3. Propose a solution to the internal control problem.

P7-3B The cash receipts and the cash payments of Good Eats Café for April 20X4 are as follows:

Using the bank reconciliation as a control device
(Obj. 3)

Cash Receipts (Posting reference is CR)		Cash Payments (Posting reference is CP)	
Date	Cash Debit	Check No.	Cash Credit
Apr. 2	$ 4,174	3113	$ 891
8	407	3114	147
10	559	3115	1,930
16	2,187	3116	664
22	1,854	3117	1,472
29	1,060	3118	1,000
30	337	3119	632
Total	$10,578	3120	1,675
		3121	100
		3122	2,413
		Total	$10,924

The Cash account of Good Eats Café shows the following at April 30, 20X4:

Cash					
Date	Item	Jrnl. Ref.	Debit	Credit	Balance
Apr. 1	Balance				5,911
30		CR. 6	10,578		16,489
30		CP. 11		10,924	5,565

On April 30, 20X4, Good Eats received the bank statement shown on the top of page 304. Additional data for the bank reconciliation:

a. The EFT deposit was a receipt of rent. The EFT debit was an insurance payment.
b. The unauthorized-signature check was received from S. M. Holt.
c. The $1,368 bank collection of a note receivable included $185 interest revenue.
d. The correct amount of check number 3115, a payment on account, is $1,390. (Good Eats' accountant mistakenly recorded the check for $1,930.)

Required

1. Prepare the Good Eats Café bank reconciliation at April 30, 20X4.
2. Describe how a bank account and the bank reconciliation help Good Eats managers control the business's cash. See the bank statement at the top of page 304.

P7-4B The August 31 bank statement of Beeson Nursery has just arrived from United Bank. To prepare the Beeson bank reconciliation, you gather the following data:

Preparing a bank reconciliation and the related journal entries
(Obj. 3)

a. Beeson's Cash account shows a balance of $3,998.14 on August 31.
b. The bank statement includes two charges for returned checks from customers. One is a $395.00 check received from Lakeland Express and deposited on August 20, returned by Lakeland's bank with the imprint "Unauthorized Signature." The other is an NSF check for $146.67 received from Veracruz, Inc. This check was deposited on August 17.
c. Beeson pays rent expense ($750) and insurance expense ($290) each month by EFT.

(continued near the middle of page 304)

Bank Statement for April 20X4		
Beginning balance.............................		$ 5,911
Deposits and other Credits:		
Apr. 1...	$ 326 EFT	
4...	4,174	
9...	407	
12...	559	
17...	2,187	
22...	1,368 BC	
23...	1,854	10,875
Checks and other Debits:		
Apr. 7...	$ 891	
13...	1,390	
14...	903 US	
15...	147	
18...	664	
21...	219 EFT	
26...	1,472	
30...	1,000	
30...	20 SC	(6,706)
Ending balance.............................		$10,080

Explanations: EFT—electronic funds transfer, BC—bank collection, US—unauthorized signature, SC—service charge.

d. The Beeson checks below are outstanding at August 31.

Check No.	Amount
237	$ 46.10
288	141.00
291	578.05
293	11.87
294	609.51
295	8.88
296	101.63

e. The bank statement includes a deposit of $1,191.17, collected by the bank on behalf of Beeson Nursery. Of the total, $1,011.81 is collection of a note receivable, and the remainder is interest revenue.
f. The bank statement shows that Beeson earned $38.19 of interest on its bank balance during August. This amount was added to Beeson's account by the bank.
g. The bank statement lists a $10.50 subtraction for the bank service charge.
h. On August 31, the Beeson treasurer deposited $316.15, but this deposit does not appear on the bank statement.
i. The bank statement includes a $300.00 deposit that Beeson did not make. The bank erroneously credited the Beeson account for another bank customer's deposit.
j. The August 31 bank balance is $5,116.22.

Required

1. Prepare the bank reconciliation for Beeson Nursery at August 31.
2. Record the journal entries necessary to bring the book balance of Cash into agreement with the adjusted book balance on the reconciliation. Include an explanation for each entry.

Identifying internal control weakness in cash receipts
(Obj. 4)

P7-5B SpreadMax, Inc., makes all sales of its spreadsheet software on credit. Cash receipts arrive by mail. Nick Vaughn opens envelopes and separates the checks from the accompanying remittance advices. Vaughn forwards the checks to another employee, who makes the daily bank deposit but has no access to the accounting records. Vaughn sends the remittance advices, which show the cash received, to the accounting department for entry in the accounts. Vaughn's only other duty is to grant sales allowances to customers. (Recall that a *sales allowance* decreases the amount receivable.) When he receives a customer check for less than the full amount of the invoice, he records the sales allowance and forwards the document to the accounting department.

Required

Required

You are a new employee of SpreadMax, Inc. Write a memo to the company president identifying the internal control weakness in this situation. State how to correct the weakness.

P7-6B Suppose that on June 1, Alpha Audio-Video opens a district office in Omaha and creates a petty cash fund with an imprest balance of $350. During June, Carol McColgin, fund custodian, signs the following petty cash tickets:

Accounting for petty cash transactions
(Obj. 5)

Petty Cash Ticket Number	Item	Amount
1	Postage for package received	$ 18.40
2	Decorations and refreshments for office party	13.19
3	Two boxes of floppy disks	20.82
4	Printer cartridges	27.13
5	Dinner money for sales manager entertaining a customer	50.00
6	Plane ticket for executive business trip to Memphis	169.00
7	Delivery of package across town	6.30

On June 30, prior to replenishment, the fund contains these tickets plus cash of $42.37. The accounts affected by petty cash payments are Office Supplies Expense, Travel Expense, Delivery Expense, Entertainment Expense, and Postage Expense.

Required

1. Explain the characteristics and the internal control features of an imprest fund.
2. Make the general journal entries to (a) create the fund and (b) replenish it. Include explanations. Also, briefly describe what the custodian does on these dates.
3. Make the entry on July 1 to increase the fund balance to $500. Include an explanation, and briefly describe what the custodian does.

P7-7B Suppose you are preparing your personal cash budget for 20X2. During 20X2, assume that you can expect to earn $3,000 from your summer job and $2,000 for work in the college cafeteria. Also, your family always gives you gifts totaling around $300 during the year. A scholarship from your home church adds $500 each year while you are in college.

Preparing a personal cash budget
(Obj. 6)

Assume your family pays your college costs except for room and board. Planned expenditures for 20X2 include apartment rent of $175 per month for 12 months and annual food costs of $5,000. Gas and other auto expenses usually run about $50 per month. You need to have a little fun, so entertainment will eat up $125 per month.

You need some cash in reserve for auto repairs and other emergencies, so you maintain a cash reserve of $500 at all times. To start 20X2, you have this cash reserve plus $100.

Will you need a loan during 20X2? To answer this question, prepare your personal cash budget for the year based on the data given.

P7-8B Len Filer, Chief Financial Officer of Toys.com, is responsible for the company's budgeting process. Filer's staff is preparing the company's cash budget for 20X1. A key input to the budgeting process is last year's statement of cash flows, which provides the data in the table (in millions) for 20X0. Cash receipts appear as positive amounts; cash payments are negative amounts, denoted within parentheses.

Preparing a cash budget
(Obj. 6)

TOYS.COM
Cash-Flow Data for 20X0

Cash and Cash Equivalents			
Beginning of year 20X0	$ 370	Purchases of plant assets	$(535)
End of year 20X0	203	Borrowings	292
Collections from customers	9,414	Long-term debt repayments	(9)
Interest revenue collected	17	Cash received for	
Purchases of inventory	(6,750)	investments by owners	16
Operating expenses paid	(2,431)	Payments to owners	(200)

Required

1. Prepare the Toys.com cash budget for 20X1. Date the budget "20X1" and denote the beginning and ending cash balances as "beginning" and "ending." Round to the nearest million dollars. Assume the company expects 20X1 to be the same as 20X0, but with the following changes:
   a. In 20X1, the company expects a 9% increase in collections from customers and an 8% increase in purchases of inventory.
   b. Filer plans for the company to end the year with a cash balance of $400 million.

2. Based on the cash budget you prepared, how much additional financing will Toys.com need beyond the borrowings already scheduled for 20X1?

Making an ethical judgment
(Obj. 7)

P7-9B Beth Youngdale is vice president of Stateline Loan Associates in Yellowstone, Wyoming. Active in community affairs, Youngdale serves on the board of directors of Baker Publishing Company. Baker is expanding and relocating its plant. At a recent meeting, board members decided to buy 15 acres of land on the edge of town. The owner of the property, Jack Fletcher, is a customer of Stateline Loan. Fletcher is completing a divorce, and Youngdale knows that Fletcher is eager to sell his property. In view of Fletcher's difficult situation, Youngdale believes he would accept almost any offer for the land. Realtors have appraised the property at $5 million.

Apply the ethical judgment framework from the Decision Guidelines feature (page 290) to help Youngdale decide what her role should be in Baker's attempt to buy the land from Fletcher.

APPLY YOUR KNOWLEDGE

DECISION CASES

Using the bank reconciliation to detect a theft
(Obj. 3)

Case 1. Flexall Plastics Company has poor internal control over its cash transactions. Genevieve Gilbreath, the owner, suspects Sam Knicks, the cashier, of stealing. Here are some details of the business's cash position at September 30.

a. The Cash account shows a balance of $17,502. This amount includes a September 30 deposit of $3,794 that does not appear on the September 30 bank statement.

b. The September 30 bank statement shows a balance of $14,124. The bank statement lists a $200 credit for a bank collection, an $8 debit for the service charge, and a $36 debit for an NSF check. The Flexall accountant has not recorded any of these items on the books.

c. At September 30, the following checks are outstanding:

Check No.	Amount
154	$116
256	150
278	353
291	190
292	206
293	145

d. The cashier handles all incoming cash and makes bank deposits. He also reconciles the monthly bank statement. Here is his September 30 reconciliation:

Balance per books, September 30.............			$17,502
Add: Outstanding checks........................			260
Bank collection			200
			17,962
Less: Deposits in transit		$3,794	
Service charge		8	
NSF check		36	3,838
Balance per bank, September 30..............			$14,124

Gilbreath asks you to determine whether the cashier has stolen cash from the business and, if so, how much. She also asks how the cashier concealed the theft. Perform your own bank reconciliation using the format illustrated in the chapter. There are no bank or book errors. Gilbreath also wants your input on changes that will improve Flexall's internal controls.

Correcting an internal control weakness
(Obj. 1, 5)

Case 2. This case is based on an actual situation. A-1 Construction Company, headquartered in Terre Haute, Indiana, built a Rest Easy Motel 35 miles east of Terre Haute. The construction foreman, whose name was Monty, hired the 40 workers needed to complete the project. Monty had the construction workers fill out the necessary tax forms, and sent the employment documents to the home office, which opened a payroll file for each employee.

Work on the motel began on April 1 and ended September 1. Each week, Monty filled out a time card of the hours worked by each employee during the week. Monty faxed the time sheets to the home office, which prepared the payroll checks on Friday morning. Monty drove to the home office after lunch on Friday, picked up the payroll checks, and returned to the construction site. At 5 P.M. on Friday, Monty distributed the payroll checks to the workers.

a. Describe in detail the main internal control weakness in this situation. Specify what negative result(s) could occur because of the internal control weakness.

b. Describe what you would do to correct the internal control weakness.

ETHICAL ISSUE

Internal control over cash payments; ethical considerations (Obj. 5, 7)

Jill Hudson owns apartment buildings in Oklahoma. Each property has a manager who collects rent, arranges for repairs, and runs advertisements in the local newspaper. The property managers transfer cash to Hudson monthly and prepare their own bank reconciliations. The manager in Tulsa has been stealing large sums of money. To cover the theft, he understates the amount of the outstanding checks on the monthly bank reconciliation. As a result, each monthly bank reconciliation appears to balance. However, the balance sheet reports more cash than Hudson actually has in the bank. In negotiating the sale of the Tulsa property, Hudson is showing the balance sheet to prospective investors.

Required

1. Identify two parties other than Hudson who can be harmed by this theft. In what ways can they be harmed?

2. Discuss the role accounting plays in this situation.

FINANCIAL STATEMENT CASE

Internal controls and cash (Obj. 1, 3)

Study the responsibility statement (labeled Report of Management) and the audit opinion (labeled Report of Independent Auditors) of **Target Corporation,** financial statements given at the end of Appendix A. Answer the following questions about the company's internal controls and cash position.

Required

1. What is the name of Target's outside auditing firm (independent auditors)? What office of this firm signed the audit report? How long after the Target year end did the auditors issue their opinion?

2. Who bears primary responsibility for the financial statements? How can you tell?

3. Does it appear that the Target internal controls are adequate? How can you tell?

4. What standard of auditing did the outside auditors use in examining the Target financial statements? By what accounting standards were the statements evaluated?

5. By how much did Target's cash balance (including cash equivalent) change during the year ended January 29, 2000? What were the beginning and ending cash balances?

TEAM PROJECT

You are promoting a rock concert in your area. Each member of your team will invest $10,000 of their hard-earned money in this venture. It is April 1, and the concert is on June 30. Your promotional activities begin immediately, and ticket sales start on May 1. You expect to sell all the business's assets, pay all the liabilities, and distribute all remaining cash to the group members by July 31.

Required

Write an internal control manual that will help safeguard the assets of the business. The starting point of the manual is to assign responsibilities among the group members. Authorize individuals, including group members and any outsiders that you need to hire, to perform specific jobs. Separate duties among the group and any employees.

INTERNET EXERCISE

Telemate.Net Software, Inc.

Corporate managers face internal control and ethical challenges with Internet access at the fingertips of many employees. Is it okay for an employee to log on to make a quick personal stock trade? What about sending personal e-mail, checking sports team scores, playing games, visiting chat rooms, or shopping online? These dilemmas face corporate America every day.

1. Discuss several internal control issues that may concern management regarding personal use of the Internet by employees during working hours.
2. Do any special issues arise for company e-mail?
3. Many web sites can trace and identify the company making visits. Do any special issues arise as to which Web sites are accessed by company employees?
4. Expanded Internet use has created a new industry to monitor Web site visits and the duration of employee time online. Go to **http://www.telemate.net/** and read the information displayed. What services does this company provide?
5. Go to **http://www.Forbes.com.** Under "Stocks" type *TMNT*, the stock symbol for **Telemate.Net Software, Inc.,** and then click on *Go.* In the left-hand column, click on *Financials.* Use the latest financial information to answer the following questions:
   a. Is the demand for the services and products of Telemate.Net Software, Inc., increasing? How can you tell?
   b. For the most recent year was Telemate.Net Software, Inc., profitable?
   c. How much did Cash/Equivalents increase (decrease) during the current year? Compute Telemate's current ratio at the most recent financial statement date.

APPENDIX TO CHAPTER 7

THE VOUCHER SYSTEM

The voucher system for recording cash payments improves internal control over cash payments by formalizing the process of approving and recording invoices for payment. The voucher system uses (1) vouchers, (2) a voucher register (similar to a purchases journal), (3) an unpaid voucher file, (4) a check register (similar to a cash payments journal), and (5) a paid voucher file. The improvement in internal control comes from recording all payments through the voucher register. In a voucher system, all expenditures must be approved before payment can be made. This approval takes the form of a voucher. The larger the business, the more likely it is to need strict control over payments. The voucher system helps supply this control.

VOUCHER. Instrument authorizing a cash payment.

A **voucher** is a document authorizing a cash payment. The accounting department prepares vouchers. Exhibit 7A-1 illustrates the voucher of Bliss Wholesale Company. In addition to places for writing in the *payee, due date, terms, description,* and *invoice amount,* the voucher includes a section for designated officers to sign their approval for payment. The back of the voucher has places for recording the *account debited, date paid,* and *check number.* You should locate these eight items in Exhibit 7A-1.

EXHIBIT 7A-1   Voucher

		Voucher No. 326
BLISS WHOLESALE COMPANY		

Payee Address: Van Heusen, Inc., 4619 Shotwell Avenue, Brooklyn, NY 10564

Due Date: March 7
Terms: 2/10, n/30

Date	Invoice No.	Description	Amount
Mar. 1	6380	144 men's shirts stock no. X14	$1,764

Approved _Jane Trent_ Controller   Approved _Bob Kraft_ Treasurer

Front of Voucher

Voucher No. 326
Payee   Van Heusen, Inc.

Invoice Amount	$1,800
Discount	36
Net Amount	$1,764

Due Date   Mar. 7
Date Paid   Mar. 6
Check No.   694

Account Distribution		
Account Debited	**Acct. No.**	**Amount**
Inventory	105	1,800
Store Supplies	145	
Salary Expense	538	
Advertising Expense	542	
Utilities Expense	548	
Delivery Expense	544	
Total		$1,800

Back of Voucher

Exhibit 7A-2 lists the various business documents used to ensure that the company receives the goods it ordered and pays only for the goods it receives. Exhibit 7A-3 shows how a voucher added to the other documents can provide the evidence for a cash payment. The amounts on all these documents should agree.

Business Document	Prepared by	Sent to
Purchase request	Sales department	Purchasing department
Purchase order	Purchasing department	Outside company that sells the needed merchandise (supplier or vendor)
Invoice	Outside company that sells the needed merchandise (supplier or vendor)	Accounting department
Receiving report	Receiving department	Accounting department
Voucher	Accounting department	Officer who signs the check

Purchase Request
Purchase Order
Invoice
Receiving Report
Voucher

Voucher Packet

8

Accounts and Notes Receivable

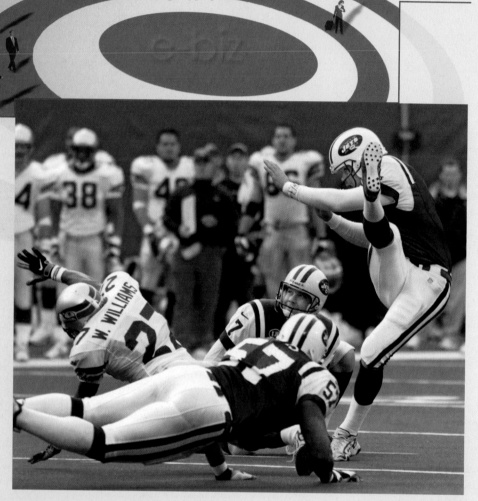

LEARNING OBJECTIVES

*After studying this chapter,
you should be able to*

1. Design internal controls for receivables

2. Use the allowance method to account for uncollectibles by the percent-of-sales and aging-of-accounts methods

3. Use the direct write-off method to account for uncollectibles

4. Account for notes receivable

5. Report receivables on the balance sheet

6. Use the acid-test ratio and days' sales in receivables to evaluate a company's financial position

In the **New York Jets** locker room, pregame reviews have taken on a whole new look. Gone are the old-style playbooks with *X-and-O* diagrams of opponents' alignments. In their place is an exciting world of multimedia.

Desktop computers turn football formations into live animation. With help from **Oracle Corporation,** Carl Banks, the Jets' director of player development, has turned passive training into an interactive success. Using Developer/2000 and multimedia software, Banks has developed a state-of-the-art teaching model that gives the Jets a competitive edge. Banks states: "By the time [the players] hit the practice field, [they] lose the ability to visualize *X's* and *O's* as actual plays. Oracle [helps] create a learning environment that increases [players'] retention by as much as 250%."

Oracle is the word's second largest software company. With annual revenues exceeding $8.0 billion, the company offers its products and services in more than 145 countries around the world.

Source: Adapted from Oracle Corporation's Web site.

W ith exciting new products and services like Developer/2000, **Oracle** is growing rapidly. Revenues are increasing, and so are the company's receivables. Accounts receivable (also called trade receivables) are the company's largest asset. Receivables present an accounting challenge: How much of its receivables will the company be able to collect in cash? This chapter shows how to answer this and other questions about receivables. It also covers notes receivable, a more formal type of receivable supported by a written promise.

Like most other assets, accounts receivable can represent good news or bad news: Good news because receivables represent a claim to the customer's cash; bad news when the business fails to collect the cash.

A *receivable* arises when a business (or person) sells goods or services to a second business (or person) on credit. The receivable is the seller's claim against the buyer for the amount of the transaction. Each credit transaction involves at least two parties:

- The **creditor** sells goods or a service and obtains a receivable, which is an asset.
- The **debtor** makes the purchase and has a payable, which is a liability.

This chapter focuses on accounting for receivables by the seller (the creditor).

CREDITOR. The party to a credit transaction who sells goods or a service and obtains a receivable.

DEBTOR. The party to a credit transaction who makes a purchase and has a payable.

RECEIVABLES: AN INTRODUCTION

The Types of Receivables

Receivables are monetary claims against businesses and individuals. The two major types of receivables are accounts receivable and notes receivable. A business's *accounts receivable* are the amounts to be collected from customers. Accounts receivable, which are *current assets,* are also called *trade receivables.*

The Accounts Receivable account in the general ledger serves as a *control account.* It summarizes the total amounts receivable from all customers. Companies also keep a *subsidiary ledger* of accounts receivable with a separate account for each customer, illustrated at the top of the next page. *Notes receivable* are more formal than accounts receivable. The debtor for a note receivable promises in writing to pay the creditor a definite sum at a future date—the *maturity date.* A written document known as a *promissory note* serves as evidence of the receivable. The note may require the debtor to pledge *security* for the loan: This means the borrower promises that the lender can claim certain assets if the borrower fails to pay the amount due at maturity.

Notes receivable due within one year or less are current assets. Notes due beyond one year are *long-term receivables.* Some notes receivable are collected in periodic installments. The portion due within one year is a current asset, and the

RECEIVABLES. Monetary claims against a business or individual.

○ DAILY EXERCISE 8-1

remaining amount is a long-term asset. **General Motors** may hold a $6,000 note receivable from you, but only the $2,000 you owe this year is a current asset to GM. The remaining $4,000 is a long-term receivable.

Other receivables is a miscellaneous category that includes loans to employees and subsidiary companies. Usually, these are long-term receivables, but they are current assets if due within one year or less. Long-term notes receivable and other receivables are often reported on the balance sheet, as illustrated in Exhibit 8-1. Receivables are highlighted for emphasis.

EXHIBIT 8-1 Balance Sheet with Receivables Highlighted for Emphasis

EXAMPLE COMPANY
Balance Sheet
Date

Assets			Liabilities		
Current:			Current:		
Cash...		$X,XXX	Accounts payable		$X,XXX
Accounts receivable.............................	$X,XXX		Notes payable, short-term...................		X,XXX
Less: Allowance for			Accrued current liabilities		X,XXX
uncollectible accounts	(XXX)	X,XXX	Total current liabilities........................		X,XXX
Notes receivable, short-term		X,XXX			
Inventories		X,XXX			
Prepaid expenses		X,XXX			
Total..		X,XXX	Long-term:		
Investments and long-term receivables:			Notes payable, long-term		X,XXX
Investments in other companies		X,XXX	Total liabilities		X,XXX
Notes receivable, long-term		X,XXX			
Other receivables..............................		X,XXX			
Total..		X,XXX	**Owner Equity**		
Plant assets:					
Property, plant, and equipment		X,XXX	Capital..		X,XXX
Total assets		$X,XXX	Total liabilities and owner equity............		$X,XXX

Objective 1
Design internal controls for receivables

Establishing Internal Control over Collection of Receivables

Businesses that sell on credit receive most cash receipts by mail. Internal control over collections of cash on account is an important part of the overall internal control system (see Chapter 7). A critical element of internal control is the separation of cash-handling and cash-accounting duties. Consider the following case.

> **Butler Supply Co. is a family-owned office supply business that takes pride in the loyalty of its workers. Most company employees have been with the Butlers for years. The company makes 90% of its sales on account.**
>
> **The office staff consists of a bookkeeper and a supervisor. The bookkeeper maintains the accounts receivable subsidiary ledger. He also makes the daily bank deposit. The supervisor prepares monthly financial statements and special reports.**

Can you identify the internal control weakness here? The bookkeeper has access to the accounts receivable subsidiary ledger, and also has custody of the cash. The bookkeeper could steal a customer check and write off the customer's account as uncollectible.[1] Unless the supervisor or some other manager reviews the bookkeeper's work, the theft may go undetected. In a small business like Butler Supply Co., such a review may never be performed.

How can this control weakness be corrected? The supervisor could open incoming mail and make the daily bank deposit. *The bookkeeper should not be allowed to handle cash.* Only the remittance advices would go to the bookkeeper to indicate which customer accounts to credit. By removing cash-handling duties from the bookkeeper, the company strengthens internal control.

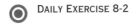

DAILY EXERCISE 8-2

Using a bank lock box achieves the same result. Customers send payments directly to Butler Supply's bank, which deposits the cash into the company's bank account. ➤➤

◄ We examined the lock-box system in detail in Chapter 7, p. 275.

Managing the Collection of Receivables: The Credit Department

Most companies have a department to evaluate customers who apply for credit. The extension of credit requires a balancing act. The company doesn't want to lose sales to good customers who need time to pay. It also wants to avoid selling to deadbeats.

For good internal control over the collections of receivables, it is critical that the credit department have no access to cash. For example, if a credit employee handles cash, he can pocket money received from a customer. He can then label the customer's account as uncollectible, and the accounting department will write off the account receivable, as discussed in the next section. The company stops billing the customer, and the credit employee has covered up the embezzlement. For this reason, a sharp separation of duties is important indeed.

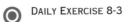

DAILY EXERCISE 8-3

The Decision Guidelines feature identifies the main issues in controlling, managing, and accounting for receivables. These guidelines serve as a framework for the remainder of the chapter.

DECISION GUIDELINES

Controlling, Managing, and Accounting for Receivables

The main issues in *controlling* and *managing* the collection of receivables, plus a plan of action, are as follows:

ISSUE	ACTION
Extend credit only to customers most likely to pay.	Run a credit check on prospective customers.
Separate cash-handling, credit, and accounting duties to keep employees from stealing the cash collected from customers.	Design the internal control system to separate duties.
Pursue collection from customers to maximize cash flow.	Keep a close eye on collections from customers.

The main issues in *accounting* for receivables, and the related plan of action, are as follows:

ISSUE	ACTION
Measure and report receivables on the balance sheet at their *net realizable value*, the amount we expect to collect. This is necessary to report assets accurately.	Estimate the amount of uncollectible receivables.
Measure and report the expense associated with failure to collect receivables, which we call *uncollectible-account expense*, on the income statement. This helps to report net income at a reasonable amount.	Report receivables at their net realizable value (accounts receivable minus the allowance for uncollectibles).
	Measure the expense of failing to collect from customers.

[1] The bookkeeper would need to forge the endorsements on the checks and deposit them in a bank account he controls.

ACCOUNTING FOR UNCOLLECTIBLE ACCOUNTS (BAD DEBTS)

Selling on credit creates both a benefit and a cost.

- *The benefit:* The business increases revenues and profits by making sales to good customers who cannot pay cash immediately.
- *The cost:* The company will be unable to collect from some customers, and that creates an expense, which is called **uncollectible-account expense, doubtful-account expense,** or **bad-debt expense.**

Uncollectible-account expense varies from company to company. In certain businesses, a six-month-old receivable of $1 is worth only 67 cents, and a five-year-old receivable of $1 is worth only 4 cents. The older the receivable, the less valuable it is because of the increasing likehood that the customer will not pay. For **Oracle Corporation,** featured in the chapter opening story, each $1 of accounts receivable is worth 91 cents.

For a firm that sells on credit, uncollectible-account expense is as much a part of doing business as salary expense and utilities expense. Uncollectible-Account Expense—an operating expense—must be measured, recorded, and reported. To do so, accountants use the allowance method or, in certain limited cases, the direct write-off method (which we discuss on page 318).

The Allowance Method

Accountants in firms with large credit sales use the **allowance method** to measure bad debts. This method does not wait to see which customers the business will not collect from. Instead, it records collection losses on the basis of estimates. In this sense, the allowance method can be viewed as an *indirect* approach.

Rather than try to guess which accounts will go bad, managers estimate the total bad-debt expense for the period on the basis of the company's experience. The business records Uncollectible-Account Expense for the estimated amount and sets up **Allowance for Uncollectible Accounts** (or **Allowance for Doubtful Accounts**), a contra account to Accounts Receivable. This allowance account shows the amount of receivables the business expects *not* to collect.

Subtracting the uncollectible allowance amount from Accounts Receivable yields the net amount the company does expect to collect, as shown here (using Oracle Corporation's actual figures, in millions):

Balance sheet (partial):

Accounts receivable	$2,455
Less: Allowance for uncollectible accounts..............	(217)
Accounts receivable, net	$2,238

Customers owe Oracle $2,455 million, of which Oracle expects to collect $2,238 million. Oracle estimates it will not collect $217 million of these accounts receivable.

Another way to report receivables follows the pattern actually used by Oracle and other companies, as adapted from the Oracle balance sheet (in millions):

Accounts receivable, net of allowance for uncollectible accounts of $217........	$2,238

The income statement can report Uncollectible-Account Expense (Doubtful-Account Expense) among the operating expenses, as follows (assumed figures):

Income statement (partial):

Expenses:	
Uncollectible-account expense	$4,000

UNCOLLECTIBLE-ACCOUNT EXPENSE. Cost to the seller of extending credit. Arises from the failure to collect from credit customers. Also called **doubtful-account expense,** or **bad-debt expense.**

ALLOWANCE METHOD. A method of recording collection losses on the basis of estimates, instead of waiting to see which customers the company will not collect from.

ALLOWANCE FOR UNCOLLECTIBLE ACCOUNTS. A contra account, related to accounts receivable, that holds the estimated amount of collection losses. Also called **Allowance for Doubtful Accounts.**

DAILY EXERCISE 8-4

Estimating Uncollectibles

The more accurate the estimate of uncollectibles, the more reliable the financial statements. How are bad-debt estimates made? Companies examine their past records. There are two basic ways to estimate uncollectibles:

- Percentage-of-sales method
- Aging-of-accounts method

Both approaches work with the allowance method.

Objective 2

Use the allowance method to account for uncollectibles by the percent-of-sales and aging methods

PERCENT-OF-SALES METHOD The **percent-of-sales method** computes uncollectible-account expense as a percentage of net credit sales. This method is also called the **income statement approach** because it focuses on the amount of expense to be reported on the income statement. Uncollectible-account expense is recorded as an adjusting entry at the end of the period. Assume it is December 31, 20X3, and the accounts have these balances *before the year-end adjustments:*

PERCENT-OF-SALES METHOD. A method of estimating uncollectible receivables that calculates uncollectible-account expense. Also called the **income statement approach.**

ACCOUNTS RECEIVABLE		ALLOWANCE FOR UNCOLLECTIBLE ACCOUNTS	
120,000			500

Customers owe the business $120,000, and the Allowance for Uncollectible Accounts is only $500. The $500 balance is left over from the preceding period. Prior to any adjustments, the net receivable amount is $119,500 ($120,000 − $500), which is more than the business expects to collect from customers.

Based on prior experience, the credit department estimates that uncollectible-account expense is 1.5% of net credit sales, which were $500,000 for 20X3. The adjusting entry to record uncollectible-account expense for the year and to update the allowance is

20X3
Dec. 31   Uncollectible-Account Expense
             ($500,000 × 0.015) 7,500
                    Allowance for Uncollectible Accounts   7,500
             Recorded expense for the year.

The accounting equation shows that the transaction to record the expense decreases the business's assets by the amount of the expense:

ASSETS	=	LIABILITIES	+	OWNER'S EQUITY	−	EXPENSES
−7,500	=	0			−	7,500

Now the accounts are ready for reporting in the 20X3 financial statements.

ACCOUNTS RECEIVABLE		ALLOWANCE FOR UNCOLLECTIBLE ACCOUNTS	
120,000			500
			7,500
			8,000

● DAILY EXERCISE 8-5

Customers still owe the business $120,000, but now the allowance for uncollectible accounts is realistic. The balance sheet will report accounts receivable at the net amount of $112,000 ($120,000 − $8,000). The income statement will report the period's uncollectible-account expense of $7,500, along with the other operating expenses for the period.

AGING-OF-ACCOUNTS The second popular approach for estimating uncollectibles is the **aging-of-accounts method.** This method is also called the **balance sheet approach** because it focuses on accounts receivable. Individual accounts receivable from specific customers are analyzed according to the length of time they have been receivable from the customer.

Computerized accounting packages now routinely age the accounts receivable. The computer sorts customer accounts by number and date of invoice. For example,

AGING-OF-ACCOUNTS METHOD. A way to estimate bad debts by analyzing individual accounts receivable according to the length of time they have been receivable from the customer. Also called the **balance-sheet approach.**

EXHIBIT 8-2 Aging the Accounts Receivable of Schmidt Builders Supply

| | Age of Account | | | | |
Customer Name	1–30 Days	31–60 Days	61–90 Days	Over 90 Days	Total Balance
T-Bar-M Co.	$20,000				$ 20,000
Chicago Pneumatic Parts.............................	10,000				10,000
Sarasota Pipe Corp.		$13,000	$10,000		23,000
Oneida, Inc.			3,000	$1,000	4,000
Other accounts*	39,000	12,000	2,000	2,000	55,000
Totals..	$69,000	$25,000	$15,000	$3,000	112,000
Estimated percent uncollectible	× 0.1%	× 1%	× 5%	× 90%	
Allowance for Uncollectible Accounts balance	$ 69 +	$ 250 +	$ 750 +	$2,700 +	$ 3,769

*Each of the "Other accounts" would appear individually.

the credit department of Schmidt Builders Supply groups its accounts receivable into 30-day periods, as Exhibit 8-2 shows.

Schmidt's accounts receivable total $112,000. Of this amount, the aging schedule estimates that Schmidt will *not* collect $3,769. The allowance for uncollectible accounts is not up-to-date *before the year-end adjustment,* as follows (note the $1,100 balance in the allowance):

ACCOUNTS RECEIVABLE	ALLOWANCE FOR UNCOLLECTIBLE ACCOUNTS
112,000	1,100

The aging method is designed to bring the balance of the allowance account to the needed amount as determined by the aging schedule in Exhibit 8-2 (see the lower-right corner for the final result—a needed credit balance of $3,769.)

To update the allowance, Schmidt makes this adjusting entry:

20X3			
Dec. 31	Uncollectible-Account Expense..............................	2,669	
	Allowance for Uncollectible Accounts		
	($3,769 − $1,100)...		2,669
	Recorded expense for the year.		

Again, the recording of the expense decreases the business's assets by the amount of the expenses. The accounting equation for the expense transaction is

ASSETS	=	LIABILITIES	+	OWNER'S EQUITY	−	EXPENSES
−2,669	=	0			−	2,669

Now the balance sheet can report receivables at the amount that Schmidt expects to collect from customers, $108,231 ($112,000 − $3,769), as follows:

ACCOUNTS RECEIVABLE	ALLOWANCE FOR UNCOLLECTIBLE ACCOUNTS	
112,000		1,100
	Adj.	2,669
	End. bal.	3,769

Net accounts receivable, 108,231

The *net* amount of accounts receivable—$108,231 in this case—is called *net realizable value* because it is the amount Schmidt expects to realize (collect in cash) from the receivables.

USING THE PERCENT-OF-SALES AND AGING METHODS TOGETHER In practice, companies use the percent-of-sales and the aging-of-accounts methods together.

- For *interim statements* (monthly or quarterly), companies use the percent-of-sales method because it is easier. This method focuses on the amount of uncollectible-account *expense*. But that is not enough.
- At the end of the year, these companies use the aging method to ensure that Accounts Receivable is reported at *expected realizable value*. The aging method focuses on the amount of the receivables—the *asset*—that is uncollectible.
- Using the two methods together provides good measures of both the expense and the asset. Exhibit 8-3 summarizes and compares the two methods.

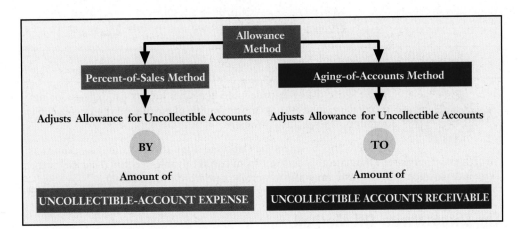

EXHIBIT 8-3
Comparing the Percent-of-Sales and Aging Methods

⊙ DAILY EXERCISE 8-6

⊙ DAILY EXERCISE 8-7

Writing Off Uncollectible Accounts

Early in 20X4, Schmidt Builders Supply collects on most of its $112,000 accounts receivable and records the cash receipts as follows:

```
20X4
Jan.–Mar.    Cash............................................................  92,000
                  Accounts Receivable ............................               92,000
             Collected on account.
```

Cash increases, and Accounts Receivable decrease by the same amount. Total assets are unchanged.

	ASSETS	=	LIABILITIES	+	OWNER'S EQUITY
	+92,000				
	−92,000	=	0	+	0

Suppose that, after repeated attempts to collect from customers, Schmidt's credit department determines that Schmidt cannot collect a total of $1,200 from customers Abbott ($900) and Smith ($300). Schmidt's accountant then writes off Schmidt's receivables from the two delinquent customers with this entry:

```
20X4
Mar. 31    Allowance for Uncollectible Accounts............  1,200
                  Accounts Receivable—Abbott..............         900
                  Accounts Receivable—Smith...............         300
           Wrote off uncollectible accounts.
```

The accounting equation shows that the write-off of the uncollectible receivables has no impact on total assets or liabilities or equity.

	ASSETS	=	LIABILITIES	+	OWNER'S EQUITY
	+1,200				
	−1,200	=	0	+	0

Study the write-off entry carefully. It affects no expense account, so it *does not affect net income.* The write-off has no effect on net receivables either, as shown for Schmidt Builders Supply in Exhibit 8-4.

EXHIBIT 8-4 Net Receivables Are the Same Before and After the Write-Off of Uncollectible Accounts

	Before Write-Off		After Write-Off	
Accounts Receivable ($112,000 − $92,000)..	$20,000		($20,000 − $1,200)	$18,800
Less: Allowance for uncollectible accounts ...	(3,769)		(3,769 − $1,200)	(2,569)
Accounts receivable, net	$16,231	←	same →	$16,231

THINK IT OVER

If the write off of uncollectible accounts affects no expense or net receivables, then why go to the trouble of writing off the uncollectible accounts of a specific customer?

Answer: The business has decided that the customer's account is worthless. Therefore, eliminate this account from the receivable records. That alerts the credit department not to waste time pursuing collection from this customer.

DIRECT WRITE-OFF METHOD. A method of accounting for uncollectible receivables, in which the company waits until the credit department decides that a customer's account receivable is uncollectible, and then debits Uncollectible-Account Expense and credits the customer's Account Receivable.

The Direct Write-Off Method

There is another way to account for uncollectible receivables. Under the **direct write-off method,** the company waits until it decides that it will never collect from the customer. Then the accountant writes off the customer's account receivable by debiting Uncollectible-Account Expense and crediting the customer's Account Receivable, as follows (using assumed data):

20X7			
Jan. 2	Uncollectible-Account Expense	2,000	
	Accounts Receivable—Jones		2,000
	Wrote off a bad account.		

This method is defective for two reasons:

1. It does not set up an allowance for uncollectibles. As a result, it always reports the receivables at their full amount, which is more than the business expects to collect. Assets are therefore overstated on the balance sheet.
2. It may not match the uncollectible-account expense of each period against the revenue of the period. In this example, the company made the sale to Jones in 20X6 and should have recorded the uncollectible-account expense during 20X6 to measure net income properly. By recording the expense in 20X7, the company overstates net income in 20X6 and understates net income in 20X7.

Don't confuse the direct write-off method with the allowance method. The two methods of accounting for uncollectible receivables are totally different, and a company adopts one method or the other. The direct write-off method is acceptable only when the amount of uncollectible receivables is very low. It works well for retailers such as **Wal-Mart, Lands' End,** and **Gap,** which carry almost no receivables.

Recovery of Accounts Previously Written Off

When an account receivable is written off as uncollectible, the receivable does not die: The customer still has an obligation to pay. However, the company stops pursuing collection and writes off the account as uncollectible.

Some companies turn delinquent receivables over to an attorney and recover some of the cash. This is called the recovery of a bad account. Let's see how to record the recovery of an account that we wrote off earlier. Recall that on March 31, 20X4, Schmidt Builders Supply wrote off the $900 receivable from customer Lou Abbott (see page 317). It is now January 4, 20X5, and Schmidt unexpectedly receives $900 from Abbott. To account for this recovery. Schmidt makes two journal entries to (1) reverse the earlier write-off and (2) record the cash collection, as follows:

(1)	Accounts Receivable—Abbott	900	
	Allowance for Uncollectible Accounts		900
	Reinstated Abbott's account receivable.		
(2)	Cash	900	
	Accounts Receivable—Abbott		900
	Collected on account.		

CREDIT-CARD, BANKCARD, AND DEBIT-CARD SALES

Credit-Card Sales

Credit-card sales are common in retailing. Customers present credit cards like **American Express** and **Discover** to pay for purchases. The credit-card company then pays the seller the transaction amount and bills the customer, who then pays the credit-card company.

Credit cards offer customers the convenience of buying without having to pay cash immediately. An American Express customer receives a monthly statement from American Express, detailing each of his or her transactions. The customer can write one check to cover the entire month's credit-card purchases.

Retailers also benefit from credit-card sales. They do not have to check a customer's credit rating. The company that issued the card has already done so. Retailers do not have to keep accounts receivable records, and they do not have to collect cash from customers.

These benefits do not come free. The seller receives less than 100% of the face value of the sale. The credit-card company takes a fee of 1–5% on the sale. Suppose you have lunch at the Russian Tea Room, and pay the bill—$100—with a Discover card. The Russian Tea Room's entry to record the $100 sale, subject to the credit-card company's 3% discount, is

Accounts Receivable—Discover	97	
Credit-Card Discount Expense	3	
Sales Revenue		100
Recorded credit-card sales.		

On collection of the discounted value, the Russian Tea Room records the following:

Cash	97	
Accounts Receivable—Discover		97
Collected from Discover.		

Bankcard Sales

Most banks issue their own cards, known as *bankcards,* which operate much like credit cards. **VISA** and **MasterCard** are the two main bankcards. When an **Exxon** station makes a sale and takes a VISA card, the station receives cash at the point of the sale. The cash received is less than the full amount of the sale because the bank deducts its fee. Suppose the Exxon station sells $150 of fuel to a family vacationing in its motor home. The station takes a VISA card, and the bank that issued the card charges a 2% fee. The Exxon station records the bankcard sale as follows:

Cash	147	
Bankcard Discount Expense ($150 × 0.02)	3	
Sales Revenue		150
Recorded a bankcard sale.		

⊙ DAILY EXERCISE 8-12

Debit-Card Sales

Debit cards are fundamentally different from credit cards and bankcards. Using a debit card to buy groceries is like paying with cash, except that the customer doesn't have to carry cash or write a check.

At **Safeway** (or **Kroger** or **Wal-Mart**), the buyer "swipes" the card through a special terminal, and the buyer's bank balance is automatically decreased. Safeway's Cash account is increased immediately—without having to deposit a check and wonder if it will clear the bank. With a debit card there is no third party, such as VISA or MasterCard, so there is no Credit-Card Discount Expense.

Merchant Beware: Credit Cards Boom with Online Sales . . . But So Does Fraud

The TV ad blends e-commerce and credit cards: A cloistered nun is shown with all the comforts of the outside world, compliments of **Amazon.com** and **VISA.** Currently 97% of all Web payments are made via credit cards. At the end of every month, e-tailers send up to 2.5% of their revenues to credit-card companies. **VISA, MasterCard, American Express,** and their cousins earn millions in transaction fees.

Who takes the hit when customers deny credit-card charges they actually made (chargebacks) or when criminals commit "identity theft" and make purchases with stolen card numbers? It's the online merchants.

Lack of face-to-face transactions has led to an increase in chargebacks for online sales. The online merchant never touches the card, and the online consumer never signs a ticket. The result: There is no paper trail to prove that the cardholder actually okayed the charge. Anonymity also paves the way for identity theft. Online travel company **Expedia, Inc.,** was recently victimized by criminals who used stolen credit-card numbers to buy airplane tickets. The Bellevue, Washington, company lost $6 million on the fraud.

Source: Based on Marcia Savage, "Online fraud: New twist on old issue," *Computer Reseller News,* March 27, 2000, p. 28. Leslie Beyer, "The Internet revolution," *Credit Card Management,* November 1999, Mercedes M. Cardona, "Visa teams up with e-tailers to acquire online dominance," *Advertising Age,* December 6, 1999, p. 4. Patricia A. Murphy, "The murky world of 'Net chargebacks," *Credit Card Management,* February 2000, pp. 54–60.

MID-CHAPTER

www.prenhall.com/horngren

Mid-Chapter Assessment

SUMMARY PROBLEM

CPC International, Inc., produces Skippy peanut butter, Hellmann's mayonnaise, and Mazola corn oil. Suppose CPC's balance sheet at December 31, 20X2, reported the following:

	Millions
Notes and accounts receivable [total]..............	$549.9
Allowance for uncollectible accounts..............	(12.5)

Required

1. How much of the December 31, 20X2, balance of the receivable did CPC expect to collect? Stated differently, what was the expected realizable value of these receivables?

2. Journalize, without explanations, 20X3 entries for CPC International, assuming
   a. Total estimated Uncollectible-Account Expense was $19.2 million for the first three quarters of the year, based on the percent-of-sales method.
   b. Write-offs of accounts receivable totaled $23.6 million.
   c. December 31, 20X3, aging of receivables, which indicates that $15.3 million of the total receivables of $582.7 million is uncollectible. Post all three entries to Allowance for Uncollectible Accounts.
3. Show how CPC International's receivables and related allowance will appear on the December 31, 20X3, balance sheet.
   What is the expected realizable value of receivables at December 31, 20X3? How much is uncollectible-account expense for 20X3?

Solution

Requirement 1

	(In millions)
Expected realizable value of receivables ($549.9 − $12.5)	$537.4

Requirement 2

	(In millions)	
(a) Uncollectible-Account Expense..	19.2	
Allowance for Uncollectible Accounts.......................		19.2
(b) Allowance for Uncollectible Accounts	23.6	
Accounts Receivable...		23.6
(c) Uncollectible-Account Expense ($15.3 − $8.1)	7.2	
Allowance for Uncollectible Accounts.......................		7.2

ALLOWANCE FOR UNCOLLECTIBLE ACCOUNTS

20X3 Write-offs	23.6	Dec. 31, 20X2 Bal.	12.5
		20X3 Expense	19.2
		Bal. before adj.	8.1
		Dec. 31, 20X3 Adj.	7.2
		Dec. 31, 20X3 Bal.	15.3

Requirement 3

	(In millions)
Notes and accounts receivable..	$582.7
Less: Allowance for uncollectible accounts	(15.3)
Notes and accounts receivable, net...	$567.4
Uncollectible-account expense for 20X3 ($19.2 + $7.2).......	$26.4

NOTES RECEIVABLE: AN OVERVIEW

As we pointed out earlier in this chapter, notes receivable are more formal arrangements than accounts receivable. The debtor signs a promissory note, which serves as evidence of the debt. Before launching into the accounting for notes receivable, let's define the special terms used for them.

- **Promissory note:** A written promise to pay a specified amount of money at a particular future date.
- **Maker of the note (debtor):** The person or business that signs the note and promises to pay the amount required by the note agreement; the maker of the note is the *debtor*.

- **Payee of the note (creditor):** The person or business to whom the maker promises future payment; the payee of the note is the *creditor.*
- **Principal amount,** or **principal:** The amount loaned out by the payee and borrowed by the maker of the note.
- **Interest:** The revenue to the payee for loaning money, and the expense of borrowing for the maker.
- **Interest period:** The period of time during which interest is to be computed. It extends from the original date of the note to the maturity date. Also called the **note period, note term,** or simply **time.**
- **Interest rate:** The percentage rate that is multiplied by the principal amount to compute the amount of interest on the note. Interest rates are almost always stated for a period of one year. A 9% note means that the amount of interest for *one year* is 9% of the principal amount of the note.
- **Maturity date:** The date when final payment of the note is due. Also called the **due date.**
- **Maturity value:** The sum of the principal plus interest due at the maturity date.

Exhibit 8-5 illustrates a promissory note. Study it carefully.

EXHIBIT 8-5 **A Promissory Note**

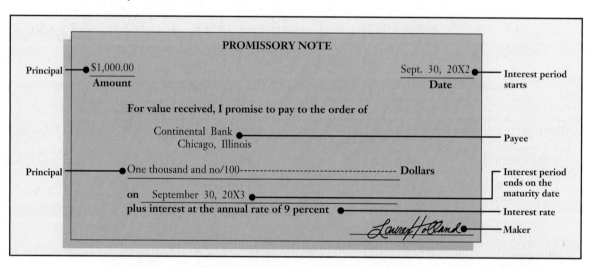

Identifying a Note's Maturity Date

Some notes specify the maturity date, as shown in Exhibit 8-5. Other notes state the period of the note in days or months. When the period is given in months, the note's maturity date falls on the same day of the month as the date the note was issued. For example, a six-month note dated February 16 matures on August 16.

When the period is given in days, the maturity date is determined by counting the days from the date of issue. A 120-day note dated September 14, 20X2, matures on January 12, 20X3, as shown here:

Month	Number of Days	Cumulative Total
Sep. 20X2	30 − 14 = 16	16
Oct. 20X2	31	47
Nov. 20X2	30	77
Dec. 20X2	31	108
Jan. 20X3	12	120

In counting the days remaining for a note, remember to count the maturity date and to omit the date the note was issued.

Computing Interest on a Note

The formula for computing the dollar amount of interest on a note is

Principal ×	Interest rate	× Time =	Amount of interest

⊙ DAILY EXERCISE 8-13

Using the data in Exhibit 8-5, Continental Bank computes its interest revenue for one year on its note receivable as

		Interest			Amount of
Principal	×	rate	× Time	=	interest
$1,000		0.09	1 yr.		$90

The maturity value of the note is $1,090 ($1,000 principal + $90 interest). The time element is 1 because interest is computed over a one-year period.

When the interest period of a note is stated in months, we compute the interest based on the 12-month year. Interest on a $2,000 note at 15% for three months is computed as

		Interest			Amount of
Principal	×	rate	× Time	=	interest
$2,000		0.15	3/12		$75

When the interest period is stated in days, we sometimes compute interest based on a 360-day year rather than on a 365-day year.[2] The interest on a $5,000 note at 12% for 60 days can be computed as

		Interest			Amount of
Principal	×	rate	× Time	=	interest
$5,000		0.12	60/360		$100

$$32{,}000 \times .09 \times \frac{3}{12} =$$

Keep in mind that interest rates are stated as an annual rate. Therefore, the time in the formula for computing interest should also be expressed in terms of a year.

WORK IT OUT

Practice calculating interest on
1. A $30,000, 12 1/2%, 180-day note
2. An $8,000, 9%, 6-month note

Answers

1. ($30,000 × 0.125 × 180/360) = $1,875   2. ($8,000 × 0.09 × 6/12) = $360

ACCOUNTING FOR NOTES RECEIVABLE
Recording Notes Receivable

Objective 4
Account for notes receivable

Consider the loan agreement shown in Exhibit 8-5. After Lauren Holland signs the note, Continental Bank gives her $1,000 cash. At maturity, Holland pays the bank $1,090 ($1,000 principal plus $90 interest). The bank's entries are

⊙ DAILY EXERCISE 8-14

Sep. 30, 20X2	Note Receivable—L. Holland.................................	1,000	
	Cash...		1,000
	Loaned out money.		
Sep. 30, 20X3	Cash	1,090	
	Note Receivable—L. Holland.........................		1,000
	Interest Revenue ($1,000 × 0.09 × 1)..........		90
	Collected note receivable.		

---

[2]A 360-day year eliminates some rounding, which is consistent with our use of whole-dollar amounts throughout this book.

Some companies sell merchandise in exchange for notes receivable. Suppose that on October 20, 20X3, **General Electric** sells household appliances for $15,000 to Dorman Builders. Dorman signs a 90-day promissory note at 10% annual interest. General Electric's entries to record the sale and collection from Dorman are

Oct. 20, 20X3	Note Receivable—Dorman Builders 15,000	
	Sales Revenue	15,000
	Made a sale.	
Jan. 18, 20X4	Cash 15,375	
	Note Receivable—Dorman Builders..................	15,000
	Interest Revenue ($15,000 × 0.10 × 90/360)	375
	Collected note receivable.	

⊙ DAILY EXERCISE 8-15

MAKER OF A NOTE. The person or business that signs the note and promises to pay the amount required by the note agreement; the debtor.

PAYEE OF A NOTE. The person or business to whom the maker of a note promises future payment; the creditor.

A company may accept a note receivable from a trade customer who fails to pay an account receivable within the customary 30–60 days. The customer signs a promissory note—that is, becomes the **maker of the note**—and gives it to the creditor, who becomes the **payee.** Suppose Interlogic, Inc., cannot pay Hoffman Supply. Hoffman may accept a one-year, $2,400 note receivable, with 9% interest, from Interlogic on October 1, 20X1. Hoffman's entry is

Oct. 1, 20X1	Note Receivable—Interlogic, Inc................................. 2,400	
	Accounts Receivable—Interlogic, Inc................	2,400
	Received a note on account.	

Accruing Interest Revenue

➤ We saw in Chapter 3 on p. 94 that accrued revenue creates an asset because the revenue has been earned but not received.

Notes receivable may be outstanding at the end of an accounting period. The interest revenue earned on the note during the year is part of that year's earnings. Recall that interest revenue is earned over time, not just when cash is received. ◄

Let's continue with the Hoffman Supply note receivable from Interlogic, Inc. Hoffman Supply's accounting period ends December 31. How much of the total interest revenue does Hoffman earn in 20X1? How much does it earn in 20X2?

Hoffman will earn three months' interest in 20X1—for October, November, and December. In 20X2, Hoffman will earn nine months' interest—for January through September. At December 31, 20X1, Hoffman Supply will make the following adjusting entry to accrue interest revenue:

Dec. 31, 20X1	Interest Receivable ($2,400 × 0.09 × 3/12)................. 54	
	Interest Revenue...	54
	Accrued interest revenue.	

Then, on the maturity date, Hoffman Supply records collection of principal and interest as follows:

Sep. 30, 20X2	Cash [$2,400 + ($2,400 × 0.09)]................................. 2,616	
	Note Receivable—Interlogic, Inc........................	2,400
	Interest Receivable ($2,400 × 0.09 × 3/12)	54
	Interest Revenue ($2,400 × 0.09 × 9/12)	162
	Collected note receivable on which interest has been accrued previously.	

⊙ DAILY EXERCISE 8-16

⊙ DAILY EXERCISE 8-17

The entries for interest earned in 20X1 and for collection in 20X2 assign the correct amount of interest to each year. This follows the revenue principle.

A company holding a note receivable may need the cash before the note matures. There is a procedure for selling the note, called discounting a note receivable. The chapter appendix covers this topic.

Dishonored Notes Receivable

DISHONOR OF A NOTE. Failure of a note's maker to pay a note receivable at maturity. Also called **default on a note.**

If the maker of a note does not pay at maturity, the maker is said to **dishonor,** or **default on,** the note. Because the term of the note has expired, the note agreement is no longer in force. However, the payee still has a claim against the debtor and usually transfers the note receivable amount to Accounts Receivable. The payee records

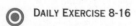

the amount of interest revenue the payee has earned on the note and debits Accounts Receivable for the maturity value of the note.

Rubinstein Jewelers has a six-month, 10% note receivable for $1,200 from Mario Adair, and on the February 3 maturity date, Adair defaulted. Rubinstein Jewelers will record the default as follows:

Feb. 3	Accounts Receivable—M. Adair		
	[$1,200 + ($1,200 × 0.10 × 6/12)]	1,260	
	Note Receivable—M. Adair		1,200
	Interest Revenue ($1,200 × 0.10 × 6/12)		60
	Recorded a dishonored note receivable.		

Rubinstein will pursue collection from Adair as an account receivable. If the account receivable later proves uncollectible, Rubinstein will then write off the account as previously discussed. Note that all notes receivable bear interest until they are proved dead.

Reporting Receivables on the Balance Sheet

Objective 5
Report receivables on the balance sheet

Let's look at how some well-known companies report their receivables and related allowances for uncollectibles on the balance sheet. All receivables and the related allowance accounts appear on the balance sheet, but terminology may vary. **Intel Corporation,** maker of the Pentium® processor, reports accounts receivable under Current Assets (in millions):

Accounts receivable, net of allowance for doubtful accounts of $67....	$3,700

The net realizable value of Intel's accounts receivable is $3,700 million. To compute Intel's total amount receivable, add the allowance to the net receivable: $67 + $3,700 = $3,767. Customers actually owe Intel $3,767 million, of which the company expects to collect $3,700 million.

General Electric Company reports a single amount—net realizable value—for receivables in the balance sheet and uses a note to give the details (adapted with amounts in millions):

Current receivables (note 10)	$8,743
Note 10: Current Receivables:	
Aircraft Engines	$1,541
Appliances	285
Power Systems................................	3,350
Other	3,887
	9,063
Less: Allowance for losses..............	(320)
	$8,743

WORK IT OUT

1. How much did customers owe General Electric (GE)?
2. How much did GE expect to collect?
3. How much did GE expect *not* to collect?

Answers

1. $9,063 million   **2.** $8,743 million   **3.** $320 million

◉ DAILY EXERCISE 8-18

◉ DAILY EXERCISE 8-19

Computers and Accounts Receivable

Accounting for receivables by a large company like **M&M Mars** requires tens of thousands of postings to customer accounts each month for credit sales and cash collections. Manual accounting methods cannot keep up.

As we saw in Chapter 6, Accounts Receivable can be set up on a computerized system. The order entry and shipping systems interface with the billing system, which credits Sales Revenue and debits Accounts Receivable. The computer then creates a sale invoice for each customer. At the same time, the computer prints out the sales for the period. Finally, computerized posting to the general ledger and accounts receivable subsidiary ledger occurs.

USING ACCOUNTING INFORMATION FOR DECISION MAKING

Objective 6
Use the acid-test ratio and days' sales in receivables to evaluate a company's financial position

The balance sheet lists assets in order of liquidity (closeness to cash):

- Cash comes first because it is the medium of exchange.
- Short-term investments (covered in a later chapter) come next because they can be sold for cash whenever the owner wishes.
- Current receivables are less liquid than short-term investments because the receivables must be collected.
- Merchandise inventory is less liquid than receivables because the goods must be sold.

The balance sheet of **Oracle Corporation,** as adapted, provides an example in Exhibit 8-6. Focus on the current assets at May 31, 1999. Oracle reports no inventory because the company earns revenue by providing services, not by selling products.

EXHIBIT 8-6
Oracle Corporation
Balance Sheet

Oracle Corporation Balance Sheet (partial, adapted) May 31, 1999 and May 31, 1998	(In millions)	
	May 31,	
Assets	1999	1998
Current assets:		
Cash and cash equivalents	$1,786	$1,274
Short-term investments	777	645
Trade receivables net of allowance for doubtful accounts of $217 in 1999 and $196 in 1998	2,238	1,857
Prepaid expenses	405	339
Other current assets	241	208
Total current assets	$5,447	$4,323
Liabilities		
Current liabilities:		
Total current liabilities	$3,046	$2,484

Acid-Test (or Quick) Ratio

Owners and managers use ratios for decision making. In Chapter 4, we discussed the current ratio, which measures the ability to pay current liabilities with current assets. A more stringent measure of ability to pay current liabilities is the **acid-test (or quick) ratio.** The acid-test ratio reveals whether the entity can pay all its current liabilities if they come due immediately:

ACID-TEST RATIO. Ratio of the sum of cash plus short-term investments plus net current receivables, to total current liabilities. Tells whether the entity could pay all its current liabilities if they came due immediately. Also called the quick ratio.

For Oracle Corporation (Exhibit 8-6)
(Dollar amounts in millions)

$$\text{Acid-test ratio} = \frac{\text{Cash} + \text{Short-term investments} + \text{Net current receivables}}{\text{Total current liabilities}} \quad \frac{\$1,786 + \$777 + \$2,238}{\$3,046} = 1.58$$

The higher the acid-test ratio, the more able the business is to pay its current liabilities. Oracle's acid-test ratio of 1.58 means that Oracle has $1.58 of quick assets to pay each $1 of current liabilities—an extremely strong position.

What is an acceptable acid-test ratio? The answer depends on the industry. **Wal-Mart** operates smoothly with an acid-test ratio of 0.18. Several things make this possible: Wal-Mart has almost no current receivables. The acid-test ratios for most department stores cluster about 0.80, while travel agencies average 1.10. In general, an acid-test ratio of 1.00 is considered safe.

WORK IT OUT

Use the data in Exhibit 8-6 to compute Oracle Corporation's current ratio at May 31, 1999. Then compare Oracle's current ratio and acid-test ratio. Why is the current ratio higher?

Answer:

$$\text{Current ratio} = \frac{\text{Total current assets}}{\text{Total current liabilities}} = \frac{\$5,447}{\$3,046} = 1.79$$

$$\text{Acid-test ratio} = \qquad\qquad 1.58$$

The current ratio is higher because it includes all current assets and not just cash, short-term investments, and receivables.

Days' Sales in Receivables

After making a credit sale, the next step is to collect the receivable. **Days' sales in receivables,** also called the **collection period,** indicates how many days it takes to collect the average level of receivables. The shorter the collection period, the more quickly the organization can use cash for operations. The longer the collection period, the less cash is available to pay bills and expand. Days' sales in receivables can be computed in two steps, as follows:[3]

DAYS' SALES IN RECEIVABLES. Ratio of average net accounts receivable to one day's sales. Tells how many days' sales it takes to collect the average level of receivables. Also called the **collection period.**

For Oracle Corporation (Exhibit 8-6)
(Dollar amounts in millions)

1.
$$\text{One day's sales} = \frac{\text{Net sales (or Total revenues)}}{365\text{ days}} = \qquad \frac{\$8,827*}{365} = \$24.2 \text{ per day}$$

2.
$$\text{Days' sales in average accounts receivable} = \frac{\text{Average net accounts receivable}}{\text{One day's sales}} = \frac{\left(\text{Beginning net receivables} + \text{Ending net receivables}\right) \div 2}{\text{One day's sales}}$$

$$= \frac{(\$1,857 + \$2,238)/2}{\$24.2} = 85 \text{ days}$$

*Taken from Oracle Corporation's 1999 income statement, which is not reproduced here.

The length of the collection period depends on the credit terms of the company's revenues. For example, sales on net 30 terms should be collected within approximately 30 days. When there is a discount, such as 2/10 net 30, the collection period may be shorter. Terms of net 45 or net 60 result in longer collection periods. ➤

Investors and creditors do not evaluate a company on the basis of one or two ratios. Instead, they perform a thorough analysis of all the information available. Then they stand back from the data and ask, "What is our overall impression of this company?"

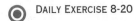
◀ We discussed sales discounts in Chapter 5, p. 172.

◉ DAILY EXERCISE 8-20

◉ DAILY EXERCISE 8-21

THINK IT OVER

AMR Corporation, the parent company of American Airlines, had a collection period of only 24 days during 1999. Why was it so short?

Answer: Generally, people pay for airline tickets before they travel. This causes the airlines' days' sales in receivables to be very low.

The **Decision Guidelines** feature summarizes some key decisions people must make in order to manage and evaluate receivables.

---

[3]Days' sales in average receivables can also be computed in this one step:

$$\frac{\text{Days' sales in average receivables}}{} = \frac{\text{Average net receivables}}{\text{Net sales}} \times 365$$

DECISION GUIDELINES

Accounting for Receivables Transactions

DECISION	GUIDELINES
Accounts Receivable	
How much of our receivables will we collect?	Less than the full amount of the receivables because we will be unable to collect from some customers.
How to report receivables at their net realizable value?	1. Use the *allowance method* to account for uncollectible receivables. Set up the allowance for Uncollectible Accounts.
	2. Estimate uncollectibles by the
	a. *Percent-of-sales method* (income statement approach)
	b. *Aging-of-accounts method* (balance sheet approach)
	3. Write off uncollectible receivables as they are deemed uncollectible.
	4. $\dfrac{\text{Net accounts}}{\text{receivable}} = \dfrac{\text{Accounts}}{\text{Receivable}} - \dfrac{\text{Allowance for}}{\text{Uncollectible Accounts}}$
Is there another way to account for uncollectible receivables?	The *direct write-off method* uses no Allowance for Uncollectibles Accounts. It simply debits Uncollectible-Account Expense and credits a customer's Account Receivable to write it off when uncollectible. This method is acceptable only when uncollectibles are insignificant.
Notes Receivable	
What two other accounts are related to notes receivable?	Notes receivable are related as follows:
	• Notes receivable earn *Interest Revenue*.
	• Interest revenue that has not been collected is debited to *Interest Receivable*.
How to compute the interest on a note receivable?	Amount of interest = Principal × Interest rate × Time
Receivables in General	
What two key decision aids use receivables to evaluate a company's financial position?	• Acid-test ratio $= \dfrac{\overset{\text{Short-term}}{\text{Cash}} + \text{investments} + \overset{\text{Net current}}{\text{receivables}}}{\text{Total current liabilities}}$
	• $\dfrac{\text{Day's sales in}}{\text{average receivables}} = \dfrac{\overset{\text{Average net}}{\text{accounts receivable}}}{\text{One day's sales}}$
How to report receivables on the balance sheet?	Accounts (or Notes) Receivable .... $XXX
	Less: Allowance for uncollectible accounts....... (X)
	Accounts (or notes) receivable, net..................... $ XX

REVIEW ACCOUNTS AND NOTES RECEIVABLE

SUMMARY PROBLEM

www.prenhall.com/horngren

End-of-Chapter Assessment

Suppose First Fidelity, Inc., engaged in the following transactions:

> 20X4
>
> Apr. 1   Loaned $8,000 to Bland Co. Received a six-month, 10% note.
> Oct.   1   Collected the Bland note at maturity.
> Dec. 1   Loaned $6,000 to Flores, Inc., on a 180-day, 12% note.
> Dec. 31   Accrued interest revenue on the Flores note.
>
> 20X5
>
> May 30   Collected the Flores note at maturity.

First Fidelity's accounting period ends on December 31.

Required

Explanations are not needed.
1. Record the 20X4 transactions on April 1 through December 1 on First Fidelity's books.
2. Make the adjusting entry needed on December 31, 20X4.
3. Record the May 30, 20X5, collection of the Flores note.

Solution

Requirement 1

20X4

Apr. 1	Note Receivable—Bland Co.	8,000	
	Cash...		8,000
Oct. 1	Cash ($8,000 + $400)	8,400	
	Note Receivable—Bland Co.		8,000
	Interest Revenue ($8,000 × 0.10 × 6/12)		400

Requirement 2

20X4

Dec. 1	Note Receivable—Flores, Inc.	6,000	
	Cash...		6,000
31	Interest Receivable	60	
	Interest Revenue ($6,000 × 0.12 × 30/360)		60

Requirement 3

20X5

May 30	Cash ($6,000 + $360)	6,360	
	Note Receivable—Flores, Inc.		6,000
	Interest Receivable		60
	Interest Revenue ($6,000 × 0.12 × 150/360)		300

LESSONS LEARNED

1. **Design internal controls for receivables.** Companies that sell on credit receive most customer collections in the mail. Good *internal control* over mailed-in cash receipts means separating cash-handling duties from cash-accounting duties.

2. **Use the allowance method to account for uncollectibles by the percent-of-sales and aging-of-accounts methods.** Uncollectible receivables are accounted for by the allowance method or the direct write-off method. The *allowance method* matches expenses against revenue and also results in a more realistic measure of net accounts receivable. The *percent-of-sales method* and the *aging-of-accounts method* are the two main approaches to estimating bad debts under the allowance method.

3. **Use the direct write-off method to account for uncollectibles.** The *direct write-off method* is easy to apply, but it fails to match bad debt expense to the corresponding revenue. Also, Accounts Receivable are reported at their full amount, which is misleading because it suggests that the company expects to collect all its accounts receivable.

4. **Account for notes receivable.** *Notes receivable* are formal credit agreements. Interest earned by the creditor is computed by multiplying the note's principal amount by the interest rate times the length of the interest period.

5. **Report receivables on the balance sheet.** All accounts receivable, notes receivable, and allowance accounts appear in the balance sheet. Companies use various formats to report these assets at net realizable value.

6. **Use the acid-test ratio and days' sales in receivables to evaluate a company's financial position.** The *acid-test ratio* measures the company's ability to pay current liabilities from the most liquid current assets. *Days' sales in receivables* indicates how long it takes to collect the average level of receivables.

ACCOUNTING VOCABULARY

acid-test ratio   (p. 326)
aging-of-accounts method
   (p. 315)
Allowance for Doubtful Accounts
   (p. 314)
Allowance for Uncollectible
   Accounts   (p. 314)
allowance method   (p. 314)
bad-debt expense   (p. 314)
balance sheet approach   (p. 315)
collection period   (p. 327)

contingent liability   (p. 344)
creditor   (p. 311)
days' sales in receivables   (p. 327)
debtor   (p. 311)
default on a note   (p. 324)
direct write-off method   (p. 318)
discounting a note receivable
   (p. 343)
dishonor of a note   (p. 324)
doubtful-account expense
   (p. 314)

due date   (p. 322)
income statement approach
   (p. 315)
interest   (p. 322)
interest period   (p. 322)
interest rate   (p. 322)
maker of a note   (p. 324)
maturity date   (p. 322)
maturity value   (p. 322)
note period   (p. 322)
note term   (p. 322)

payee of a note (p. 324)
percent-of-sales method (p. 315)
principal (p. 322)
principal amount (p. 322)

promissory note (p. 321)
quick ratio (p. 326)
receivables (p. 311)
time (p. 322)

uncollectible-account expense
(p. 314)

QUESTIONS

1. Name the two parties to a receivable/payable transaction. Which party has the receivable? Which has the payable? Which has the asset? The liability?
2. List the two main categories of receivables. State how receivables are classified for reporting on the balance sheet.
3. Name the two methods of accounting for uncollectible receivables. Which method is easier to apply? Which method is consistent with generally accepted accounting principles?
4. Identify the accounts debited and credited to account for uncollectibles under (a) the allowance method, and (b) the direct write-off method.
5. What is another term for Allowance for Uncollectible Accounts? What are two other terms for Uncollectible-Account Expense?
6. Identify and briefly describe the two ways to estimate bad-debt expense and uncollectible accounts, using the allowance method.

7. Use the terms *maker, payee, principal amount, maturity date, promissory note,* and *interest* in an appropriate sentence or two describing a note receivable.
8. Name three situations in which a company might receive a note receivable. For each situation, show the account debited and the account credited to record receipt of the note.
9. When the maker of a note dishonors the note at maturity, what accounts does the payee debit and credit?
10. Why does the payee of a note receivable usually need to make adjusting entries for interest at the end of the accounting period?
11. Show three ways to report Accounts Receivable of $100,000 and Allowance for Uncollectible Accounts of $2,800 on the balance sheet or in the related notes.
12. Why is the acid-test ratio a more stringent measure of the ability to pay current liabilities than the current ratio?
13. Which measure of days' sales in receivables is preferable, 30 or 40? Give your reason.

ASSESS YOUR PROGRESS

DAILY EXERCISES

Accounts receivable records (Obj. 1)

DE8-1 Examine the Accounts Receivable T-accounts on page 312, and answer these questions:

1. Which account (and which amount) will appear on the company's balance sheet? Suppose the company has cash of $2,000. Show how the balance sheet will report cash and the other item on page 312.
2. Who are Acker, Dell, and Taft? What do their accounts indicate that these three persons are obligated to do?

Internal control over the collection of receivables (Obj. 1)

DE8-2 Return to the Accounts Receivable T-accounts on page 312. Suppose Nathan Forester is the accountant responsible for these records. What duty will a good internal control system withhold from Forester? Why?

Internal control over the credit department (Obj. 1)

DE8-3 What duty must be withheld from a company's credit department in order to safeguard its cash? If this duty is granted to the credit department, what can a dishonest credit department employee do to hurt the company?

Applying the allowance method to account for uncollectibles (Obj. 2)

DE8-4 The allowance method of accounting for uncollectible receivables uses two accounts in addition to Accounts Receivable. Identify the two accounts and indicate which financial statement reports each account. Which of these is a contra account? Make up reasonable amounts to show how to report the contra account under its companion account on the balance sheet.

Applying the allowance method (percent-of-sales) to account for uncollectibles (Obj. 2)

DE8-5 During its first year of operations, SBC Communications had net sales of $600,000, all on account. Industry experience suggests that SBC's bad debts will amount to 2% of net sales. At December 31, 20X3, SBC's accounts receivable total $90,000. The company uses the allowance method to account for uncollectibles.

1. Journalize SBC's uncollectible-account expense using the percent-of-sales method.
2. Show how SBC should report accounts receivable on its balance sheet at December 31, 20X3. Follow the reporting format illustrated in the middle of page 314.

Applying the allowance method (percent-of-sales) to account for uncollectibles (Obj. 2)

DE8-6 ← *Link Back to Chapter 5 (Recording Sales Transactions).* This exercise continues the situation of Daily Exercise 8-5, in which SBC Communications ended the year 20X3 with accounts receivable of $90,000 and an allowance for uncollectible accounts of $12,000.

During 20X4, SBC Communications completed the following transactions:

1. Net credit sales, $800,000 (ignore cost of goods sold).
2. Collections on account, $690,000.
3. Write-offs of uncollectibles, $15,000.
4. Uncollectible-account expense, 1.8% of net credit sales.

Journalize the foregoing 20X4 transactions for SBC Communications.

DE8-7 Use the solution to Daily Exercise 8-6 to answer these questions about SBC Communications.

Applying the allowance method (percent-of-sales) to account for uncollectibles
(Obj. 2)

1. Start with Accounts Receivable's beginning balance ($90,000), and then post to the Accounts Receivable T-account. How much do SBC's customers owe the company at December 31, 20X4?
2. Start with the Allowance account's beginning balance ($12,000), and then post to the Allowance for Uncollectible Accounts T-account. How much of the receivables at December 31, 20X4, does SBC expect *not* to collect?
3. At December 31, 20X4, how much cash does SBC expect to collect on its accounts receivable?

DE8-8 ← *Link Back to Chapter 5 (Recording Sales Transactions).* Guardian Medical Group started 20X0 with accounts receivable of $120,000 and an allowance for uncollectible accounts of $6,000. The 20X0 credit sales were $800,000, and cash collections on account totaled $720,000. During 20X0, Guardian wrote off uncollectible accounts receivable of $12,000. At December 31, 20X0, the aging of accounts receivable indicated that Guardian will *not* collect $4,000 of its accounts receivable.

Applying the allowance method (aging-of-accounts) to account for uncollectibles
(Obj. 2)

Journalize Guardian's (a) credit sales (ignore cost of goods sold), (b) cash collections on account, (c) write-offs of uncollectible receivables, and (d) uncollectible-account expense for the year. Prepare a T-account for Allowance for Uncollectible Accounts to show your computation of uncollectible-account expense for the year.

DE8-9 Hot Button.com accounts include the following balances at December 31, 20X1, before the year-end adjustments:

Applying the allowance method (aging-of-accounts) to account for uncollectibles
(Obj. 2)

ACCOUNTS RECEIVABLE		ALLOWANCE FOR UNCOLLECTIBLE ACCOUNTS	
104,000			1,300

The aging of accounts receivable yields these data:

	Age of Accounts Receivable				
	0–30 Days	31–60 Days	61–90 Days	Over 90 Days	Total Receivables
Amount receivable	$70,000	$20,000	$10,000	$4,000	$104,000
Percent uncollectible..................	× 1%	× 2%	× 5%	× 50%	

Journalize Hot Button's entry to adjust the allowance account to its correct balance at December 31, 20X1.

DE8-10 Buchwald, Inc.'s experience indicates that Buchwald will fail to collect 3% of net credit sales, which totaled $100,000 during the three-month period January through March of 20X3. During this period Buchwald wrote off $4,000 of accounts receivable as uncollectible. Record Buchwald's uncollectible-account expense for January through March under

Contrasting the allowance method and the direct write-off method of accounting for uncollectibles
(Obj. 2, 3)

   a. The allowance method.
   b. The direct write-off method. You need not identify individual customer accounts.

Which method of accounting for uncollectibles is preferred? What makes this method better?

DE 8-11 Masahiro Oguchi is an attorney in San Francisco. Oguchi uses the direct write-off method to account for his uncollectible receivables.

Applying the direct write-off method to account for uncollectibles
(Obj. 3)

   At May 31, Oguchi's accounts receivable were $8,000. During June, he earned service revenue of $60,000 and collected $62,000 from clients on account. He also wrote off uncollectible receivables of $500. What is Oguchi's balance of Accounts Receivable at June 30? Does he expect to collect all of this amount? Why or why not?

DE 8-12 Gas stations do a large volume of business by customer credit cards and bankcards. Suppose the **Shell** station near Lenox Square in Atlanta, Georgia, had these transactions on a busy Saturday in July:

Recording credit-card sales
(Obj. 3)

American Express credit-card sales	$6,000
VISA bankcard sales	8,000

Suppose **American Express** charges merchants 4% and **VISA** charges 2%. Record these sale transactions for the Shell station.

DE 8-13 Examine the promissory note in Exhibit 8-5, page 322. Answer these questions:

1. When does interest on the note start running? When does the interest stop running?
2. Who is the debtor? Who is the creditor?
3. Which party to the note has a note receivable? Which party has a note payable? Which party has interest revenue? Which party has interest expense?
4. When must Lauren Holland pay off the note?
5. How much interest must Holland pay on the maturity date of the note? How much cash must Holland pay in total at maturity?

DE 8-14 For each of the following notes receivable, compute the amount of interest revenue earned during 20X5. Use a 360-day year.

	Principal	Interest Rate	Interest Period	Maturity Date
Note 1	$ 10,000	9%	60 days	11/30/20X5
Note 2	50,000	10%	3 months	9/30/20X5
Note 3	100,000	8%	$1\frac{1}{2}$ years	12/31/20X6
Note 4	15,000	12%	90 days	1/15/20X6

DE 8-15 Deutsche Bank lent $400,000 to Jean Nowlin on a 90-day, 8% note. Record the following transactions for Deutsche Bank (explanations are not required):

a. Lending the money on June 12.
b. Collecting the principal and interest at maturity. Specify the date. For the computation of interest, use a 360-day year.

DE 8-16 Return to the promissory note in Exhibit 8-5, page 322. The accounting year of Continental Bank ends on December 31, 20X2. Journalize Continental Bank's (a) lending money on the note receivable at September 30, 20X2, (b) accrual of interest at December 31, 20X2, and (c) collection of principal and interest at September 30, 20X3, the maturity date of the note. Carry amounts to the nearest cent.

DE 8-17 Using your answers to Daily Exercise 8–16 for Continental Bank, and carrying amounts to the nearest cent, show how the bank will report

a. Note receivable and interest receivable on the bank's classified balance sheet at December 31, 20X2.
b. Whatever needs to be reported on the bank's income statement for the year ended December 31, 20X2.
c. Whatever needs to be reported for the note and related interest on the bank's classified balance sheet at December 31, 20X3. You may ignore Cash.
d. Whatever needs to be reported on the bank's income statement for the year ended December 31, 20X3.

DE 8-18 Examine the receivables for **Intel, General Electric,** and **Oracle** shown on page 325 and in Exhibit 8-6, page 326. Complete the table below to show the amounts (in millions of dollars) that each company will report on its balance sheet:

Company	Total Current Receivables	−	Allowance for Uncollectibles =	Net Realizable Value
Intel Corporation......................	$		$( )	$
General Electric........................				
Oracle Corporation(1999 only).				

At May 31, 1999, how much does Oracle expect to collect from its customers?

DE 8-19 ◄ *Link Back to Chapters 1–3 (Debit/Credit Balances; Income Statement).* **Sprint Corporation,** the telecommunications company, included the following items in its financial statements (adapted, in millions):

Unearned revenues...................	$ 200	Service revenue	$14,045
Allowance for doubtful		Other assets............................	355
accounts.............................	117	Cost of services sold and	
Cash	1,151	other expenses	12,861
Accounts receivable	2,581	Notes payable.........................	3,281
Accounts payable	1,027		

1. How much net income did Sprint earn for the year?
2. Show how Sprint reported receivables on its classified balance sheet. Follow the reporting format shown in the middle of page 314.

DE 8-20 Vision Maker, a cable TV company, reported the following items at February 28, 20X0 (amounts in millions, with last-year's 19X9 amounts also given as needed):

Using the acid-test ratio and days' sales in receivables to evaluate an actual company (Obj. 6)

Accounts payable.............	$369	Accounts receivable:	
Cash............................	215	February 28, 20X0	$ 235
Allowance for uncollectible		February 29, 19X9	160
accounts:		Cost of goods sold..............	575
February 28, 20X0	15	Short-term investments...........	165
February 29, 19X9	7	Other current assets..............	93
Inventories:		Other current liabilities..........	145
February 28, 20X0	198	Net sales revenue................	1,406
February 29, 19X9	161	Long-term assets................	416
Long-term liabilities.............	11		

Compute Vision Maker's (a) acid-test ratio and (b) days' sales in average receivables for 20X0. Evaluate each ratio value as strong or weak. Assume Vision Maker sells on terms of net 45.

DE 8-21 ◄ *Link Back to Chapter 4 (Current Ratio and Debt Ratio) and Chapter 5 (Gross Profit Percentage and Inventory Turnover).* Using the data in Daily Exercise 8-20, compute for Vision Maker the following ratios for 20X0:

Computing key ratios for an actual company (Obj. 6)

a. Current ratio   c. Gross profit percentage
b. Debt ratio   d. Rate of inventory turnove

EXERCISES

E8-1 As a recent college graduate, you land your first job in the customer collections department of Sun Systems. Karla Bates, one of the owners, has asked you to propose a system to ensure that cash received by mail from customers is handled properly. Draft a short memorandum identifying the essential element in your plan, and state why it is important.

Controlling cash receipts from customers (Obj. 1)

Refer to Chapter 7 if necessary. Use this format for your memo:

Date: _____	
To:	Karla Bates
From:	Your Name
RE:	Essential element of internal control over customer collections

E8-2 ◄ *Link Back to Chapter 7 (Internal Control Over Cash Receipts).* Suppose **Carnation**, the instant breakfast company, is opening an office in Chicago. Timothy Mayborne, the office manager, is designing the internal control system. Mayborne proposes the following procedures for credit checks on new customers, sales on account, cash collections, and write-offs of uncollectible receivables:

Identifying and correcting an internal control weakness (Obj. 1)

- The credit department will run a credit check on all customers who apply for credit.
- Sales on account are the responsibility of the Carnation salespersons. Credit sales above a reasonable limit require the approval of the credit manager.
- Cash receipts come into the credit department, which separates the cash received from the customer remittance slips. The credit department lists all cash receipts by customer name and amount of cash received. The cash goes to the treasurer for deposit in the bank. The remittance slips go to the accounting department for posting to customer accounts. Each day's listing of cash receipts goes to the controller for comparison with the daily deposit slip and the day's listing of the total dollar amount posted to customer accounts. The three amounts must agree.

Identify the internal control weakness in this situation, and propose a way to correct it.

E8-3 On September 30, Ageless Technology had a $28,000 debit balance in Accounts Receivable. During October, the company had sales of $187,000, which included $120,000 in credit sales. October collections were $91,000. Other data include

Using the allowance method for bad debts (Obj. 2, 5)

- September 30 credit balance in Allowance for Uncollectible Accounts, $1,600.
- Uncollectible-account expense, estimated as 2% of credit sales.
- Write-offs of uncollectible receivables totaled $1,070.

Required

1. Prepare journal entries to record sales, collections, uncollectible-account expense by the allowance method (percent-of-sales method), and write-offs of uncollectibles during October.
2. Show the ending balances in Accounts Receivable, Allowance for Uncollectible Accounts, and *net* accounts receivable at October 31. How much does Ageless expect to collect?
3. Show how Ageless will report Accounts Receivable on its October 31 balance sheet. Use the format illustrated for Intel on page 325.

Using the direct write-off method for bad debts
(Obj. 3)

E8-4 Refer to Exercise 8-3.

Required

1. Record uncollectible-account expense for October using the direct write-off method.
2. What amount of accounts receivable would Ageless report on its October 31 balance sheet under the direct write-off method? Does Ageless expect to collect the full amount?

Using the aging method to estimate bad debts
(Obj. 2, 5)

E8-5 At December 31, 20X4, the accounts receivable balance of Quest Corp. is $300,000. The Allowance for Doubtful Accounts has a $3,910 credit balance. Accountants for Quest prepare the following aging schedule for its accounts receivable:

		Age of Accounts		
Total Balance	1–30 Days	31–60 Days	61–90 Days	Over 90 Days
$300,000............................	$140,000	$78,000	$69,000	$13,000
Estimated percent uncollectible..................	0.3%	1.2%	6.0%	50%

Required

1. Journalize the adjusting entry for doubtful accounts on the basis of the aging schedule. Show the T-account for the Allowance.
2. Show how Quest Corp. will report Accounts Receivable on its December 31 balance sheet.

Reporting bad debts by the allowance method
(Obj. 2, 5)

E8-6 At December 31, 20X2, Circuit Software has an accounts receivable balance of $137,000. Sales revenue for 20X2 is $950,000, including credit sales of $450,000. For each of the following situations, prepare the year-end adjusting entry to record uncollectible-account expense. Show how the accounts receivable and the allowance for uncollectible accounts are reported on the balance sheet. Use the reporting format illustrated for Intel on page 325.

a. Allowance for Uncollectible Accounts has a credit balance of $1,600 before adjustment. Circuit estimates that uncollectible-account expense for the year is 1/2 of 1% of credit sales.
b. Allowance for Uncollectible Accounts has a debit balance of $1,700 before adjustment. Circuit estimates that $2,600 of the accounts receivable will prove uncollectible.

Computing notes receivable amounts
(Obj. 4)

E8-7 On April 30, 20X7, First National Bank of Kansas City lent $1,000,000 to Marjorie Redwine on a two-year, 9% note.

Required

1. Compute the interest during 20X7, 20X8, and 20X9 for the Redwine note receivable.
2. Which party has a
   a. Note receivable?   c. Interest revenue?
   b. Note payable?   d. Interest expense?
3. How much in total would Redwine pay First National Bank if she paid off the note early—say, on November 30, 20X7?

Recording notes receivable and accruing interest revenue
(Obj. 4)

E8-8 Record the following transactions in the journal of Glacial Enterprises, Inc.:

Nov. 1 Loaned $50,000 cash to Victor Rashad on a one-year, 8% note.
Dec. 3 Sold goods to Lendox Corp., receiving a 90-day, 11% note for $3,750.
  16 Received a $4,000, six-month, 12% note on account from CFO Co.
  31 Accrued interest revenue on all notes receivable. Use a 360-day year for interest computations.

Recording bankcard sales and a note receivable, and accruing interest revenue
(Obj. 4)

E8-9 Record the following transactions in Wachovia Company's journal:

20X3
Feb. 12 Recorded VISA bankcard sales of $55,000, less a 2% discount.
Apr. 1 Loaned $8,000 to Peter Liu on a one-year, 12% note.
Dec. 31 Accrued interest revenue on the Liu note.

20X4
Apr. 1 Collected the maturity value of the note from Liu.

E8-10 Horizon Energy Corp. sells on account. When a customer account becomes two months old, Horizon converts the account to a note receivable. During 20X2, Horizon completed these transactions:

Recording notes receivable transactions
(Obj. 4)

Aug. 29 Sold goods on account to M. Tallus, $5,400.
Nov. 1 Received a $5,400, 60-day, 10% note from M. Tallus in satisfaction of his past-due account receivable.
Dec. 31 Collected the Tallus note at maturity.

Required

Record the transactions in Horizon Energy's journal.

E8-11 Bernstein Bros., a clothing store, reported the following amounts in its 20X3 financial statements. The 20X2 figures are given for comparison.

Evaluating ratio data
(Obj. 6)

	20X3		20X2	
Current assets:				
Cash		$ 3,000		$ 10,000
Short-term investments		23,000		11,000
Accounts receivable	$80,000		$74,000	
Less: Allowance for uncollectibles	(7,000)	73,000	(6,000)	68,000
Inventory		192,000		189,000
Prepaid insurance		2,000		2,000
Total current assets		293,000		280,000
Total current liabilities		$124,000		$127,000
Net sales		$703,000		$732,000

Required

1. Determine whether Bernstein's acid-test ratio improved or deteriorated from 20X2 to 20X3. How does Bernstein's acid-test ratio compare with the industry average of 0.80?
2. Compare the days' sales in receivables for 20X3 with Bernstein's credit terms of net 30.

E8-12 **Wal-Mart Stores, Inc.,** is the largest retailer in the United States. Recently, Wal-Mart reported these figures (in billions of dollars):

Analyzing a company's financial statements
(Obj. 6)

	1999	1998
Net sales	$165	$138
Receivables at end of year	1	1

The Wal-Mart financial statements include no uncollectible-account expense or allowance.

Required

1. Compute Wal-Mart's average collection period on receivables during 1999.
2. Why are Wal-Mart's receivables so low? How can Wal-Mart have $1 billion of receivables at January 31, 1999, and no significant allowance for uncollectibles?

Challenge Exercise

E8-13 Slazenger Sporting Equipment sells on store credit and manages its own receivables. Average experience each year for the past three years has been as follows:

Evaluating credit-card sales for profitability
(Obj. 2)

	Total
Sales	$350,000
Cost of goods sold	210,000
Uncollectible-account expense	4,000
Other expenses	61,000

Bruce Slazenger, the owner, is considering whether to accept bankcards (**VISA, MasterCard**). Typically, accepting bankcards increases total sales and cost of goods sold by 12%. But VISA and MasterCard charge approximately 2% of bankcard sales. If Slazenger switches to bankcards, he can save $2,000 on accounting and other expenses. After the switchover to bankcards, Slazenger expects cash sales of $200,000.

Required

Should Slazenger start accepting bankcards? Show the computations of net income under the present plan and under the bankcard plan.

(Group A) PROBLEMS

Controlling cash receipts from customers
(Obj. 1)

P8-1A Newcastle Sporting Goods distributes merchandise to sporting goods stores. All sales are on credit, so virtually all cash receipts arrive in the mail. William Borrows, the company president, has just returned from a meeting with new ideas for the business. Among other things, Borrows plans to institute stronger internal controls over cash receipts from customers.

Required

Assume you are William Borrows. Write a memo to employees outlining a set of procedures to ensure that all cash receipts are deposited in the bank and that the total amounts of each day's cash receipts are posted as credits to customer accounts receivable. Use the memorandum format given in Exercise 8-1, page 333.

Accounting for uncollectibles by the direct write-off and allowance methods
(Obj. 2, 3, 5)

P8-2A On February 28, Signa, Inc., had a $75,000 debit balance in Accounts Receivable. During March, Signa made sales of $445,000, all on credit. Other data for March include

- Collections on account, $422,600.
- Write-offs of uncollectible receivables, $3,500.

Required

1. Record sales and collections on account. Then record uncollectible-account expense for March using the *direct write-off* method. Post to Accounts Receivable and Uncollectible-Account Expense and show their balances at March 31.
2. Record sales and collections on account. Then record uncollectible-account expense and write-offs of customer accounts for March using the *allowance* method. Show all March activity in Accounts Receivable, Allowance for Uncollectible Accounts, and Uncollectible-Account Expense (post to these T-accounts). The February 28 unadjusted balance in Allowance for Uncollectible Accounts was $800 (debit). Uncollectible-account expense was estimated at 2% of credit sales.
3. What amount of uncollectible-account expense would Signa, Inc., report on its March income statement under the two methods? Which amount better matches expense with revenue? Give your reason.
4. What amount of *net* accounts receivable would Signa, Inc., report on its March 31 balance sheet under the two methods? Which amount is more realistic? Give your reason.

Using the percent-of-sales and aging methods for uncollectibles
(Obj. 2, 5)

P8-3A The June 30, 20X4, balance sheet of Delforce Associates, Inc., reports the following:

Accounts Receivable	$265,000
Allowance for Uncollectible Accounts (credit balance)	7,100

At the end of each quarter, Delforce estimates uncollectible-account expense to be 2% of credit sales. At the end of the year, the company ages its accounts receivable and adjusts the balance in Allowance for Uncollectible Accounts to correspond to the aging schedule. During the second half of 20X4, Delforce completed the following transactions:

July 14   Made a compound entry to write off the following uncollectible accounts: T. J. Dooley, $766; Design Works, Inc., $2,413; and S. DeWitt, $134.
Sep. 30   Recorded uncollectible-account expense equal to 2% of credit sales of $141,400.
Nov. 22   Wrote off the following accounts receivable as uncollectible: Transnet Corp., $1,345; Webvan, Inc., $2,109; and The Avenue Group, $755.
Dec. 31   Recorded uncollectible-account expense based on the aging of accounts receivable.

		Age of Accounts		
Total Balance	1–30 Days	31–60 Days	61–90 Days	Over 90 Days
$256,600	$121,500	$86,000	$34,000	$15,100
Estimated percent uncollectible	0.2%	0.5%	4.0%	50.0%

Required

1. Record the transactions in the journal.
2. Open the Allowance for Uncollectible Accounts, and post entries affecting that account. Keep a running balance.
3. Most companies report two-year comparative financial statements. If Delforce's Accounts Receivable balance was $271,400 and the Allowance for Uncollectible Accounts stood at

$8,240 at December 31, 20X3, show how the company will report its accounts receivable in a comparative balance sheet for 20X4 and 20X3.

P8-4A ← *Link Back to Chapter 4 (Closing Entries).* Minnetonk Enterprises completed the following selected transactions during 20X1 and 20X2:

Using the percent-of-sales method for uncollectibles (Obj. 2, 5)

20X1

Dec. 31	Estimated that uncollectible-account expense for the year was 2/3 of 1% on credit sales of $450,000, and recorded that amount as expense.
31	Made the closing entry for uncollectible-account expense.

20X2

Feb. 4	Sold inventory to Sam Vesper, $1,521, on credit terms of 2/10 n/30. Ignore cost of goods sold.
July 1	Wrote off Sam Vesper's account as uncollectible after repeated efforts to collect from him.
Oct. 19	Received $521 from Sam Vesper, along with a letter stating his intention to pay his debt in full within 30 days. Reinstated his account in full.
Nov. 15	Received the balance due from Sam Vesper.
Dec. 31	Made a compound entry to write off the following accounts as uncollectible: Kaycee Britt, $899; Tim Sands, $530; and Anna Chin, $1,272.
31	Estimated that uncollectible-account expense for the year was 2/3 of 1% on credit sales of $585,000 and recorded the expense.
31	Made the closing entry for uncollectible-account expense.

Required

1. Open general ledger accounts for Allowance for Uncollectible Accounts and Uncollectible-Account Expense. Keep running balances.
2. Record the transactions in the general journal, and post to the two ledger accounts.
3. The December 31, 20X2, balance of Accounts Receivable is $164,500. Show how Accounts Receivable would be reported on the balance sheet at that date.

P8-5A Windows Company received the following notes during 20X3.

Accounting for notes receivable, including accruing interest revenue (Obj. 4)

Note	Date	Principal Amount	Interest Rate	Term
(1)	Oct. 31	$11,000	12%	3 months
(2)	Nov. 19	15,000	10%	60 days
(3)	Dec. 1	12,000	9%	1 year

Required

Identify each note by number, compute interest using a 360-day year for those notes with terms specified in days or years, round all interest amounts to the nearest dollar, and present entries in general journal form. Explanations are not required.

1. Determine the due date and maturity value of each note.
2. Journalize a single adjusting entry at December 31, 20X3, to record accrued interest revenue on all three notes.
3. Journalize the collection of principal and interest on note (1).

P8-6A ← *Link Back to Chapter 4 (Closing Entries).* Record the following selected transactions in the general journal of Recognition Systems. Explanations are not required.

Accounting for notes receivable, dishonored notes, and accrued interest revenue (Obj. 4)

20X2

Dec. 21	Received a $2,800, 30-day, 10% note on account from Lindsey Fitzhugh.
31	Made an adjusting entry to accrue interest on the Fitzhugh note.
31	Made a closing entry for interest revenue.

20X3

Jan. 20	Collected the maturity value of the Fitzhugh note.
Sept. 14	Loaned $4,000 cash to Bullseye Investors, receiving a three-month, 13% note.
30	Received a $1,675, 60-day, 16% note from Chuck Powers on his past-due account receivable.
Nov. 29	Chuck Powers dishonored his note at maturity; wrote off the note as uncollectible, debiting Allowance for Uncollectible Accounts.
Dec. 14	Collected the maturity value of the Bullseye Investors note.

Journalizing uncollectibles, notes receivable, and accrued interest revenue (Obj. 4)

P8-7A Assume that **Sherwin Williams,** the paint manufacturer, completed the following selected transactions:

20X1

Dec.   1   Sold goods to Kelly Paint Supply, receiving a $13,500, three-month, 10% note. Ignore cost of goods sold.

      31   Made an adjusting entry to accrue interest on the Kelly note. Round the interest amount to the nearest dollar.

      31   Made an adjusting entry to record uncollectible-account expense based on an aging of accounts receivable. The aging analysis indicates that $355,800 of accounts receivable will not be collected. Prior to this adjustment, the credit balance in Allowance for Uncollectible Accounts is $346,100.

20X2

Mar.   1   Collected the maturity value of the Kelly Paint Supply note.

July   21   Sold merchandise to Mellon Co., receiving a 60-day, 9% note for $4,000. Ignore cost of goods sold.

Sep.   19   Mellon Co. dishonored its note (failed to pay) at maturity; we converted the maturity value of the note to an account receivable.

Nov.   11   Loaned $40,000 cash to Thermo Control, Inc., receiving a 90-day, 9% note.

Dec.   2   Collected in full from Mellon Co.

      31   Accrued the interest on the Thermo Control note.

Required

Record the transactions in the journal of Sherwin Williams. Explanations are not required.

Using ratio data to evaluate a company's financial position (Obj. 6)

P8-8A ⇐ *Link Back to Chapter 4 (Current Ratio).* The comparative financial statements of Grapevine Securities for 20X3, 20X2, and 20X1 include the data shown here:

	(In millions)		
	20X3	**20X2**	**20X1**
Balance sheet			
Current assets:			
Cash	$ 27	$ 26	$ 22
Short-term investments	93	101	69
Receivables, net of allowance for doubtful			
accounts of $7, $6, and $4, respectively	146	154	127
Inventories	454	383	341
Prepaid expenses	32	31	25
Total current assets	752	695	584
Total current liabilities	$ 440	$ 446	$ 388
Income statement			
Sales revenue	$2,671	$2,505	$1,944
Cost of sales	1,380	1,360	963

Required

1. Compute these ratios for 20X3 and 20X2:
     a. Current ratio   **b.** Acid-test ratio   **c.** Days' sales in receivables
2. Write a memo explaining to top management which ratios improved from 20X2 to 20X3 and which ratios deteriorated. Which item in the financial statements caused some ratios to improve and others to deteriorate? Discuss whether this factor conveys a favorable or an unfavorable sign about the company.

(Group B) PROBLEMS

Controlling cash receipts from customers (Obj. 1)

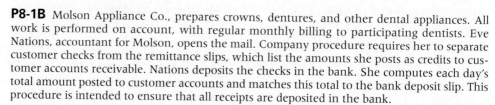

P8-1B Molson Appliance Co., prepares crowns, dentures, and other dental appliances. All work is performed on account, with regular monthly billing to participating dentists. Eve Nations, accountant for Molson, opens the mail. Company procedure requires her to separate customer checks from the remittance slips, which list the amounts she posts as credits to customer accounts receivable. Nations deposits the checks in the bank. She computes each day's total amount posted to customer accounts and matches this total to the bank deposit slip. This procedure is intended to ensure that all receipts are deposited in the bank.

Required

As a consultant hired by Molson Appliance Co., write a memo to management evaluating the company's internal controls over cash receipts from customers. If the system is effective, identify its strong features. If the system has flaws, propose a way to strengthen the controls. Use the memorandum format given in Exercise 8-1, page 333.

P8-2B On May 31, Nortell Networks, had a $210,000 debit balance in Accounts Receivable. During June, Nortell made sales of $640,000, all on credit. Other data for June include

Accounting for uncollectibles by the direct write-off and allowance methods
(Obj. 2, 3, 5)

- Collections on account, $567,400.
- Write-offs of uncollectible receivables, $8,900.

Required

1. Record sales and collections on account. Then record uncollectible-account expense for June using the *direct write-off* method. Post to Accounts Receivable and Uncollectible-Account Expense and show their balances at June 30.
2. Record sales and collections on account. Then record uncollectible-account expense and write-offs of customer accounts for June using the *allowance* method. Show all June activity in Accounts Receivable, Allowance for Uncollectible Accounts, and Uncollectible-Account Expense (post to these T-accounts). The May 31 unadjusted balance in Allowance for Uncollectible Accounts was $2,800 (credit). Uncollectible-account expense was estimated at 2% of credit sales.
3. What amount of uncollectible-account expense would Nortell report on its June income statement under the two methods? Which amount better matches expense with revenue? Give your reason.
4. What amount of *net* accounts receivable would Nortell report on its June 30 balance sheet under the two methods? Which amount is more realistic? Give your reason.

P8-3B The June 30, 20X1, balance sheet of Clarus Consultants, Inc., reports the following:

Using the percent-of-sales and aging methods for uncollectibles
(Obj. 2, 5)

Accounts Receivable..	$143,000
Allowance for Uncollectible Accounts (credit balance)..............	3,200

At the end of each quarter, Clarus estimates uncollectible-account expense to be 1 1/2% of credit sales. At the end of the year, the company ages its accounts receivable and adjusts the balance in Allowance for Uncollectible Accounts to correspond to the aging schedule. During the second half of 20X1, Clarus completed the following selected transactions:

Aug. 9   Made a compound entry to write off the following uncollectible accounts: Aguilar, Inc., $235; Seaton Co., $188; and T. Taylor, $706.

Sep. 30   Recorded uncollectible-account expense equal to $1\frac{1}{2}$% of credit sales of $140,000.

Oct. 18   Wrote off as uncollectible the $767 account receivable from Lintz Co. and the $430 account receivable from Navisor Corp.

Dec. 31   Recorded uncollectible-account expense based on the aging of accounts receivable.

	Age of Accounts			
Total Balance	1–30 Days	31–60 Days	61–90 Days	Over 90 Days
$136,500	$81,700	$31,100	$14,000	$9,700
Estimated percent uncollectible	0.1%	0.4%	5.0%	30.0%

Required

1. Record the transactions in the journal. Round all amounts to the nearest dollar.
2. Open the Allowance for Uncollectible Accounts, and post entries affecting that account. Keep a running balance.
3. Most companies report two-year comparative financial statements. If Clarus's Accounts Receivable balance was $118,000 and the Allowance for Uncollectible Accounts stood at $2,700 at December 31, 20X0 show how the company will report its accounts receivable on a comparative balance sheet for 20X1 and 20X0.

P8-4B ◄ *Link Back to Chapter 4 (Closing Entries).* Interbiz Interactive completed the following transactions during 20X1 and 20X2:

Using the percent-of-sales method for uncollectibles
(Obj. 2, 5)

20X1
Dec. 31   Estimated that uncollectible-account expense for the year was 3/4 of 1% on credit sales of $290,000, and recorded that amount as expense.

     31   Made the closing entry for uncollectible-account expense.

20X2

Jan. 17   Sold inventory to Mitch Vanez, $652, on credit terms of 2/10 n/30. Ignore cost of goods sold.

June 29   Wrote off the Mitch Vanez account as uncollectible after repeated efforts to collect from him.

Aug. 6   Received $250 from Mitch Vanez, along with a letter stating his intention to pay his debt in full within 30 days. Reinstated his account in full.

Sept. 4   Received the balance due from Mitch Vanez.

Dec. 31   Made a compound entry to write off the following accounts as uncollectible: Bernard Klaus, $737; Marie Monet, $348; and Terry Fuhrman, $622.

     31   Estimated that uncollectible-account expense for the year was 2/3 of 1% on credit sales of $400,000, and recorded that amount as expense. Round to the nearest dollar.

     31   Made the closing entry for uncollectible-account expense.

Required

1. Open general ledger accounts for Allowance for Uncollectible Accounts and Uncollectible-Account Expense. Keep running balances.
2. Record the transactions in the general journal, and post to the two ledger accounts.
3. The December 31, 20X2, balance of Accounts Receivable is $139,000. Show how Accounts Receivable would be reported on the balance sheet at that date.

Accounting for notes receivable, including accruing interest revenue (Obj. 4)

P8-5B   Mindgames Company received the following notes during 20X3.

Note	Date	Principal Amount	Interest Rate	Term
(1)	Nov. 30	$12,000	12%	6 months
(2)	Dec. 7	9,000	10%	30 days
(3)	Dec. 23	13,000	9%	1 year

Required

Identify each note by number, compute interest using a 360-day year for those notes with terms specified in days or years, round all interest amounts to the nearest dollar, and present entries in general journal form. Explanations are not required.

1. Determine the due date and maturity value of each note.
2. Journalize a single adjusting entry at December 31, 20X3, to record accrued interest revenue on all three notes.
3. Journalize the collection of principal and interest on note (2).

Accounting for notes receivable, dishonored notes, and accrued interest revenue (Obj. 4)

P8-6B   ← *Link Back to Chapter 4 (Closing Entries).* Record the following selected transactions in the general journal of SAS Services. Explanations are not required.

20X4

Dec. 19   Received a $3,000, 60-day, 12% note on account from Arnold Cohen.

     31   Made an adjusting entry to accrue interest on the Cohen note.

     31   Made a closing entry for interest revenue.

20X5

Feb. 17   Collected the maturity value of the Cohen note.

June 1   Loaned $8,000 cash to Blues Brothers, receiving a 6-month, 11% note.

Oct. 31   Received a $1,500, 60-day, 12% note from Juan Juarez on his past-due account receivable.

Dec. 1   Collected the maturity value of the Blues Brothers note.

     30   Juan Juarez dishonored his note at maturity; wrote off the note receivable as uncollectible, debiting Allowance for Uncollectible Accounts.

Journalizing uncollectibles, notes receivable, and accrued interest revenue (Obj. 4)

P8-7B   Assume that **Del Monte Foods,** famous for fruits and vegetables, completed the following selected transactions:

20X1

Nov. 1   Sold goods to **Kroger,** receiving a $20,000, three-month, 8% note. Ignore cost of goods sold.

Dec. 31   Made an adjusting entry to accrue interest on the Kroger note. Round to the nearest dollar.

     31   Made an adjusting entry to record uncollectible-account expense based on an aging of accounts receivable. The aging analysis indicates that $197,400 of accounts receivable will not be collected. Prior to this adjustment, the credit balance in Allowance for Uncollectible Accounts is $189,900.

20X2

Feb. 1 Collected the maturity value of the Kroger note.

June 23 Sold merchandise to Artesian Corp., receiving a 60-day, 10% note for $9,000. Ignore cost of goods sold.

Aug. 22 Artesian Corp. dishonored (failed to pay) its note at maturity; we converted the maturity value of the note to an account receivable.

Nov. 16 Loaned $6,800 cash to Crane, Inc., receiving a 90-day, 12% note.

Dec. 5 Collected in full from Artesian Corp.

31 Accrued the interest on the Crane, Inc., note.

Required

Record the transactions in the journal of Del Monte Foods. Explanations are not required.

P8-8B ⟵ *Link Back to Chapter 4 (Current Ratio).* The comparative financial statements of American Dataset, for 20X3, 20X2, and 20X1 include the following selected data:

Using ratio data to evaluate a company's financial position (Obj. 6)

	(In millions)		
	20X3	**20X2**	**20X1**
Balance sheet			
Current assets:			
Cash	$ 82	$ 80	$ 60
Short-term investments	140	174	122
Receivables, net of allowance for doubtful accounts of $6, $6, and $5, respectively	257	265	218
Inventories	429	341	302
Prepaid expenses	21	27	46
Total current assets	929	887	748
Total current liabilities	$ 503	$ 528	$ 413
Income statement			
Sales revenue	$5,189	$4,995	$4,206
Cost of sales	2,734	2,636	2,418

Required

1. Compute these ratios for 20X3 and 20X2:
   a. Current ratio   **b.** Acid-test ratio   **c.** Days' sales in receivables
2. Write a memo explaining to top management which ratios improved from 20X2 to 20X3 and which ratios deteriorated. Which item in the financial statements caused some ratios to improve and others to deteriorate? Discuss whether this factor conveys a favorable or an unfavorable impression about American Dataset.

APPLY YOUR KNOWLEDGE

DECISION CASES

Case 1. Deutschetek Corporation performs service either for cash or on notes receivable. The business uses the direct write-off method to account for bad debts. Hilda Lyth, the owner, has prepared the company's financial statements. The most recent comparative income statements, for 20X3 and 20X2, are as follows:

Uncollectible accounts and evaluating a business (Obj. 2, 3)

	20X3	**20X2**
Total revenue	$220,000	$195,000
Total expenses	107,000	103,000
Net income	$113,000	$ 92,000

On the basis of the increase in net income, Lyth wants to expand operations. She asks you to invest $50,000 in the business. You and Lyth have several meetings, at which you learn that notes receivable from customers were $200,000 at the end of 20X1 and $400,000 at the end of 20X2. Also, total revenues for 20X3 and 20X2 include interest at 13% on the year's beginning notes receivable balance. Total expenses include uncollectible-account expense of $2,000 each year, based on the direct write-off method. Lyth estimates that uncollectible-account expense would be 5% of sales revenue if the allowance method were used.

Required

1. Prepare for Deutschetek a comparative single-step income statement that identifies service revenue, interest revenue, uncollectible-account expense, and other expenses, all computed in accordance with generally accepted accounting principles.
2. Is Deutschetek's future as promising as Lyth's income statement makes it appear? Give the reason for your answer.

Computing receivables amounts to report on the balance sheet (Obj. 5)

Case 2. This case takes the statement of cash flows a step beyond the chapter's coverage of this topic. However, you should be able to apply the principles learned thus far to solve it. Treasure Point Jewelry's statement of cash flows reported the following for the year ended June 30, 20X1.

TREASURE POINT JEWELRY	
Statement of Cash Flows	
Year Ended June 30, 20X1	
Cash flows from operating activities:	
Collections from customers on account	$260,000
Cash flows from investing activities:	
Loaned out money on notes receivable	$ (45,000)
Collected on notes receivable	60,000

Treasure Point's balance sheet one year earlier—at June 30, 20X0—reported Accounts Receivable of $40,000 and Notes Receivable of $20,000. Credit sales for the year ended June 30, 20X1, totaled $310,000, and the company collects all of its accounts receivable because uncollectibles rarely occur.

Treasure Point Jewelry needs a loan and the owner is preparing Treasure Point's balance sheet at June 30, 20X1. To complete the balance sheet, the owner needs to know the balances of Accounts Receivable and Notes Receivable at June 30, 20X1. Supply the needed information; T-accounts are helpful.

ETHICAL ISSUE

QuiKash Finance Company is in the consumer loan business. It borrows from banks and loans out the money at higher interest rates. QuiKash's bank requires QuiKash to submit quarterly financial statements in order to keep its line of credit. QuiKash's main asset is Notes Receivable. Therefore, Uncollectible-Account Expense and Allowance for Uncollectible Accounts are important accounts.

Cameron Karr, the company's owner, wants net income to increase in a smooth pattern, rather than increase in some periods and decrease in others. To report smoothly increasing net income, Karr underestimates Uncollectible-Account Expense in some periods. In other periods, Karr overestimates the expense. He reasons that over time the income overstatements roughly offset the income understatements.

Required

Is QuiKash's practice of smoothing income ethical? Why or why not?

FINANCIAL STATEMENT CASE

Analyzing accounts receivable and uncollectibles (Obj. 2, 6)

Use the balance sheet and income statement of **Target Corporation,** in Appendix A.

1. How much did customers owe Target at January 29, 2000? Of this amount, how much did Target expect to collect? How much did Target expect *not* to collect? To answer these questions, refer to (a) Target's balance sheet (statement of financial position) and (b) the note entitled "Allowance for Doubtful Accounts" on page 22 of the Target Annual Report. *Retained securitized receivables* is Target's name for its accounts receivable.

2. During the year ended January 29, 2000, Target recorded doubtful-account expense of $147 million. The company also wrote off uncollectible receivables of $147 million. Prepare a T-account for Allowance for Doubtful Accounts. Insert the current year's beginning and ending balances as reported in the note. Then post the doubtful-account expense for the year and the write-offs for the year into the T-account. After your postings, the Allowance account should show all of Target's bad-debt activity for the current year.

3. Compute Target's acid-test ratio at January 29, 2000. If all the current liabilities came due immediately, could Target pay them?

342 CHAPTER 8

Bob Opper and Denise Shapp worked for several years as sales representatives for **Xerox Corporation.** During this time, they became close friends as they acquired expertise with the company's full range of copier equipment. Now they see an opportunity to put their experience to work and fulfill lifelong desires to establish their own business. Lakeside College, located in their city, is expanding, and there is no copy center within five miles of the campus. Business in the area is booming—office buildings and apartments are springing up, and the population in this section of the city is growing.

Opper and Shapp want to open a copy center, similar to a **Kinko's,** near the campus. A small shopping center across the street from the college has a vacancy that would fit their needs. Opper and Shapp each have $20,000 to invest in the business, and they forecast the need for $30,000 to renovate the store. **Xerox Corporation** will lease two large copiers to them at a total monthly rental of $4,000. With enough cash to see them through the first six months of operation, they are confident they can make the business succeed. The two work very well together, and both have excellent credit ratings. Opper and Shapp must borrow $80,000 to start the business, advertise its opening, and keep it running for its first six months.

Assume the roles of Opper and Shapp, the partners who will own Lakeside Copy Center.

1. As a group, visit a copy center to familiarize yourselves with its operations. If possible, interview the manager or another employee. Then write a loan request that Opper and Shapp will submit to a bank with the intent of borrowing $80,000 to be paid back over three years. The loan will be a personal loan to the partnership of Opper and Shapp, not to Lakeside Copy Center. The request should specify all the details of Opper's and Shapp's plan that will motivate the bank to grant the loan. Include a budgeted income statement for the first six months of the copy center's operation.

2. As a group, interview a loan officer in a bank. Have the loan officer evaluate your loan request. Write a report, or make a presentation to your class—as directed by your instructor—to reveal the loan officer's decision.

INTERNET EXERCISE

Pfizer Inc.

As the baby boomers age, the demand for pharmaceuticals has increased. Over the past several years **Pfizer Inc.** helped introduce three record-breaking products: Lipitor, Viagra, and Celebrex. As a result, in 1999 Pfizer became the world's number one pharmaceutical company in prescription sales.

1. Go to **http://www.Pfizer.com.** Click on *Investing in Pfizer* and select the *most recent annual report.* Use the pull-down menu to select *Our Global Presence.* In how many countries does Pfizer sell its products?

2. Use the pull-down menu to select the *Consolidated Balance Sheet.*
   a. To account for the uncollectible receivables, does Pfizer use the allowance method or the direct write-off method? How can you tell?
   b. For the most recent year, how much do customers owe Pfizer? How much does Pfizer expect to collect? How much does Pfizer expect not to collect?

3. Use the pull-down menu to select the *Consolidated Statement of Income.*
   a. Which expense listed includes the amount for uncollectible-account expense? How do you think Pfizer estimates its uncollectible-account expense? Do you think Pfizer wrote off any uncollectible accounts this past year?
   b. For the most recent year, research and development (R&D) expenses are what percentage of total revenues? R&D costs are a major expense for pharmaceutical companies. Explain why this is true.

4. For the two most recent years calculate the acid-test ratio. Show your work for the ratio calculations. For the most recent year comment on what the ratio indicates. Is the trend increasing or decreasing? Favorable or unfavorable? Explain why.

5. For the two most recent years calculate one day's sales using the amount reported for net sales in the numerator. For the two most recent years calculate days' sales in receivables. Please show your work for the ratio calculations. For the most recent year comment on what the days' sales in receivables ratio indicates. Is the trend increasing or decreasing? Favorable or unfavorable? Explain why.

APPENDIX TO CHAPTER 8

DISCOUNTING A NOTE RECEIVABLE

A payee of a note receivable may need the cash before the maturity date of the note. When this occurs, the payee may sell the note, a practice called **discounting a note receivable.** The price to be received for the note is determined by present-value

DISCOUNTING NOTE RECEIVABLE. Selling a note receivable before its maturity date.

➤ We discuss these concepts in Chapter 15.

concepts. ◄ But the transaction between the seller and the buyer of the note can take any form agreeable to the two parties. Here we illustrate one procedure used for discounting short-term notes receivable. To receive cash immediately, the seller accepts a lower price than the note's maturity value.

To illustrate discounting a note receivable, suppose **General Electric** loaned $15,000 to Dorman Builders on October 20, 20X3. GE took a note receivable from Dorman. The maturity date of the 90-day 10% Dorman note is January 18, 20X4. Suppose GE discounts the Dorman note at First City Bank on December 9, 20X3, when the note is 50 days old. The bank applies a 12% annual interest rate to determine the discounted value of the note. The bank will use a discount rate that is higher than the note's interest rate in order to earn some interest on the transaction. The discounted value, called the *proceeds*, is the amount GE receives from the bank. The proceeds can be computed in five steps, as shown in Exhibit 8A-1. GE's entry to record discounting (selling) the note on December 9, 20X3, is:

Dec. 9, 20X3	Cash...	15,170	
	Note Receivable—Dorman Builders		15,000
	Interest Revenue ($15,170 − $15,000)....		170
	Discounted a note receivable.		

EXHIBIT 8A-1
Discounting (Selling) a Note Receivable: GE Discounts the Dorman Builders Note

Step	Computation	
1. Compute the original amount of interest on the note receivable.	$15,000 × 0.10 × 90/360	= $375
2. Maturity value of the note = Principal + Interest	$15,000 + $375	= $15,375
3. Determine the period (number of days, months, or years) the *bank* will hold the note (the discount period).	Dec. 9, 19X3 to Jan. 18, 19X4	= 40 days
4. Compute the bank's discount on the note. This is the bank's interest revenue from holding the note.	$15,375 × 0.12 × 40/360	= $205
5. Seller's proceeds from discounting the note receivable = Maturity value of the note − Bank's discount on the note.	$15,375 − $205	= $15,170

The authors thank Doug Hamilton for suggesting this exhibit.

⊙ DAILY EXERCISE 8-1A

When the proceeds from discounting a note receivable are less than the principal amount of the note, the payee records a debit to Interest Expense for the amount of the difference. For example, GE could discount the note receivable for cash proceeds of $14,980. The entry to record this discounting transaction is

Dec. 9, 20X3	Cash	14,980	
	Interest Expense	20	
	Note Receivable—Dorman Builders		15,000
	Discounted a note receivable.		

CONTINGENT LIABILITIES ON DISCOUNTED NOTES RECEIVABLE

CONTINGENT LIABILITY. A potential liability that will become an actual liability only if a particular event does occur.

A **contingent liability** is a potential liability that will become an actual liability only if a particular event occurs. Discounting a note receivable creates a contingent liability for the endorser. If the maker of the note (Dorman, in our example) fails to pay at maturity, then the original payee (GE) must pay the bank the amount due.[1] If Dorman pays the bank, then GE can forget the note.

DAILY EXERCISE

Discounting notes receivable (Obj. 4)

DE 8A-1 General Telecom installs telephone systems and receives its pay in the form of notes receivable. General Telecom installed a system for the city of Durango, Colorado, receiv-

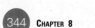

---

[1]The discounting agreement can be "without recourse." That means the seller of the note has no liability if the note is dishonored at maturity. In that case, there is no contingent liability.

ing a nine-month, 8%, $500,000 note receivable on May 31, 20X1. To obtain cash quickly, General Telecom discounted the note with Rocky Mountain Bank on June 30, 20X1. The bank charged a discount rate of 9%.

Compute General Telecom's cash proceeds from discounting the note. Follow the five-step procedure outlined in Exhibit 8A-1.

EXERCISES

E8A-1A ◄ *Link Back to Chapter 5 (Recording a Sale).* Use your answers to Daily Exercise 8A-1 to journalize General Telecom's transactions as follows:

Accounting for a discounted note receivable (Obj. 4)

May 31   Sold a telecommunications system, receiving a 9-month, 8%, $500,000 note from the city of Durango. General Telecom's cost of the system was $450,000.
June 30   Received cash for interest revenue for one month. Round to the nearest dollar.
     30   Discounted the note to Rocky Mountain Bank at a discount rate of 9%.

E8A-2A Rider Systems, Inc., sells on account. When a customer account becomes three months old, Rider converts the account to a note receivable and immediately discounts the note to a bank. During 20X4, Rider completed these transactions:

Recording notes receivable, discounting a note, and reporting the contingent liability in a note (Obj. 4)

Aug. 29   Sold goods on account to V. Moyer, $3,900.
Dec. 1   Received a $3,900, 60-day, 10% note from V. Moyer in satisfaction of his past-due account receivable.
      1   Sold the Moyer note by discounting it to a bank for $3,600.

Required

Record the transactions in Rider Systems' journal.

PROBLEMS

P8A-1 A company received the following notes during 20X3. Notes (1), (2), and (3) were discounted on the dates and at the rates indicated.

Discounting notes receivable (Obj. 4)

Note	Date	Principal Amount	Interest Rate	Term	Date Discounted	Discount Rate
(1)	July 12	$10,000	10%	3 months	Aug. 12	15%
(2)	Aug. 4	6,000	11%	90 days	Aug. 30	13%
(3)	Oct. 21	8,000	15%	60 days	Nov. 3	18%

Required

Identify each note by number, compute interest using a 360-day year for those notes with terms specified in days, round all interest amounts to the nearest dollar, and present entries in general journal form. Explanations are not required.

1. Determine the due date and maturity value of each note.
2. Determine the discount and proceeds from the sale (discounting) of each note.
3. Journalize the discounting of notes (1) and (2).

P8A-2 A company received the following notes during 20X5. Notes (1), (2), and (3) were discounted on the dates and at the rates indicated.

Discounting notes receivable (Obj. 4)

Note	Date	Principal Amount	Interest Rate	Term	Date Discounted	Discount Rate
(1)	July 15	$6,000	10%	6 months	Oct. 15	12%
(2)	Aug. 19	9,000	12%	90 days	Aug. 30	15%
(3)	Sept. 1	8,000	15%	120 days	Nov. 2	20%

Required

Identify each note by number, compute interest using a 360-day year for those notes with terms specified in days, round all interest amounts to the nearest dollar, and present entries in general journal form. Explanations are not required.

1. Determine the due date and maturity value of each note.
2. Determine the discount and proceeds from the sale (discounting) of each note.
3. Journalize the discounting of notes (1) and (2).

Merchandise Inventory

www.prenhall.com/horngren

LEARNING OBJECTIVES

*After studying this chapter,
you should be able to*

1. Account for inventory by the perpetual and periodic systems

2. Apply inventory costing methods: specific unit cost, weighted-average cost, FIFO, and LIFO

3. Identify the income effects and the tax effects of the inventory costing methods

4. Apply the lower-of-cost-or-market rule to inventory

5. Determine the effects of inventory errors on cost of goods sold and net income

6. Estimate ending inventory by the gross profit method

Readiness Assessment

Deckers Outdoor Corporation began when University of California at Santa Barbara student Doug Otto started making sandals. From a fledgling operation, Deckers has grown into an international company, with footwear brands Teva and Simple. The company also sells clothing lines Teva and Picante. (Teva is a play off the Hebrew word *Teh-vah* for *nature*.) Teva sandals were initially designed by a Grand Canyon river guide for river rafting. Their quality and stability touched off a small revolution in footwear.

Deckers Outdoor had sales of almost $110 million in 1999, and the company's assets totaled $73 million. As the company has grown, Doug Otto and Deckers have faced a number of accounting decisions. Which method should Deckers use to account for its inventory of sandals and clothing? How much inventory should the company purchase from suppliers? This chapter discusses how to account for and manage inventory—the asset that defines a merchandising business.

Deckers Outdoor is a **merchandising company.** This means that Deckers sells a product rather than a service. To a merchandiser, inventory is the lifeblood of the organization. Deckers' balance sheet in Exhibit 9-1 lists inventory of $18.1 million among its current assets.

A merchandiser's major expense is *cost of goods sold,* also called *cost of sales.* This is Deckers' cost of the sandals and clothing it sold. For Deckers and other merchandisers, cost of goods sold is greater than the sum of all the other expenses combined. Exhibit 9-1 shows that Deckers had cost of sales of $64.5 million during 1999.

MERCHANDISING COMPANY. A company that resells products bought from suppliers.

DECKERS OUTDOOR CORPORATION
Income Statement (partial, adapted)
Year Ended December 31, 1999

	Millions
Net sales	$109.6
Cost of goods sold	64.5
Gross profit	45.1
Total operating expenses (can be detailed)	42.2
Net income	$ 2.9

EXHIBIT 9-1
Financial Statements of Deckers Outdoor Corporation, Maker of Teva Sandals

---

DECKERS OUTDOOR CORPORATION
Balance Sheet (Current assets only)
December 31, 1999

Assets	Millions
Current assets:	
Cash	$ 1.6
Trade accounts receivable, Less Allowance of $1.8	24.4
Inventories	18.1
Prepaid expenses	4.9
Total current assets	$49.0

We begin this chapter with the basic concept of accounting for inventories. Then we examine different inventory systems (perpetual and periodic), the different inventory methods (FIFO, LIFO, and average), and several related topics.

Accounting for Inventory and Inventory Systems

Basic Concepts

The basic concept of accounting for inventory is straightforward. Suppose **Deckers Outdoor Corporation** buys three pairs of sandals for $30 each, marks them up by $20, and sells two of the pairs for $50 each. Deckers' balance sheet reports the inventory that the company still holds, and the income statement reports cost of goods sold for the units sold, as follows (focus on the highlights):

Balance Sheet (partial)		Income Statement (partial)	
Current assets:	$XXX	Sales revenue	
Cash	XXX	(2 pairs @ $50)	$100
Accounts receivable	XXX	Cost of goods sold	
Inventory (1 pair @ $30)	30	(2 pairs @ $30)	60
Prepaid expenses	XXX	Gross profit	$ 40

GROSS PROFIT OR GROSS MARGIN.
Excess of sales revenue over cost of goods sold.

 DAILY EXERCISE 9-1

Objective 1
Account for inventory by the perpetual and periodic systems

➡ We described these methods in Chapter 5.

PERIODIC INVENTORY SYSTEM. An inventory accounting system in which the business does not keep a continuous record of the inventory on hand. Instead, at the end of the period, the business counts the inventory on hand and uses this information to prepare the financial statements.

PERPETUAL INVENTORY SYSTEM. An inventory accounting system in which the business keeps a running record to show the inventory on hand at all times.

As we saw in Chapter 5, **gross profit,** also called **gross margin,** is the excess of sales revenue over cost of goods sold. It is called *gross* profit because operating expenses have not yet been subtracted. Gross profit minus all the operating expenses then equals *net* income. In practice, accounting for inventory is more complex than our simple example.

There are two main types of inventory accounting systems: the periodic system and the perpetual system. ← The **periodic inventory system** is used by businesses that sell relatively inexpensive goods. Many small businesses use the periodic system. Stores without optical-scanning cash registers do not keep a running record of every loaf of bread and every six-pack of drinks they sell. Instead, these stores count their inventory periodically—at least once a year—to determine the quantities on hand and prepare the financial statements.

Under the **perpetual inventory system,** the business maintains a running record of inventory on hand, usually on computer. This system achieves control over goods such as automobiles, jewelry, and furniture. The loss of one item would be significant and this justifies the cost of a perpetual system. Because computers are costing less and less, many small businesses now use perpetual inventory systems.

Under both systems, the business still counts its inventory annually. The physical count establishes the amount of ending inventory and serves as a check on the records. The following chart compares the periodic and perpetual systems:

Periodic Inventory System	Perpetual Inventory System
• Does not keep a running record of inventory	• Keeps a running record of all goods
• Used for inexpensive goods	• Used for all types of goods
• Inventory counted at least once a year	• Inventory counted at least once a year

Perpetual Inventory System

Perpetual inventory records can be a computer printout like the Deckers' record shown for a line of Teva sandals in Exhibit 9-2. The quantities of goods on hand are updated daily, as inventory transactions occur. Many companies keep their perpetual records in terms of quantities only, as shown in the exhibit. When a customer orders 10 pairs of sandals, Deckers can refer to its perpetual inventory record.

In the perpetual system, the business records purchases of inventory by debiting the Inventory account. When the business makes a sale, two entries are needed: one to record the sale and the other to record the decrease in inventory on hand.

Exhibit 9-3 illustrates the accounting in a perpetual system for a single line of Teva sandals at Deckers Outdoor. Panel A gives the journal entries and the

Computation of Budgeted Purchases

Cost of goods sold (budgeted for the next period)	$600,000
+ Ending inventory (budgeted for the next period)	150,000
= Cost of goods available for sale, as budgeted	750,000
− Beginning inventory (actual amount left over from the prior period)....	(120,000)
= Purchases (the inventory you need to buy to reach your goal)	$630,000

Business owners and managers use this formula to determine how much to spend on inventory, regardless of the inventory system used. The power of the cost-of-goods-sold model lies in the information it captures: beginning and ending inventory levels, purchases, and cost of goods sold.

Computing the Cost of Inventory

The Deckers Outdoor inventory record in Exhibit 9-2 follows the common practice of recording quantities only. The company multiplies the 20 pairs of Teva Sandals on hand by the cost of each pair to compute the ending inventory for the balance sheet, as follows:

Cost of inventory on hand	=	Quantity on hand	×	Unit cost
$600	=	20 pairs	×	$30

DETERMINING THE QUANTITY OF INVENTORY   Many businesses count their inventory on the last day of the fiscal year. If you have worked at a retail business, you will recall the process of "taking inventory." Some entities shut the business down to get a good inventory count.

A complication in counting inventory arises from consigned goods. In a **consignment** arrangement, the owner of the inventory (the *consignor*) transfers the goods to another business (the *consignee*). Then the consignee sells the inventory for the owner. The consignee does *not* own the consigned goods and therefore should not include them in its own inventory. Consignments are common in retailing. Suppose Deckers Outdoor is the consignee for a line of backpacks. Should Deckers include this consigned merchandise in its inventory? No, because Deckers does not own the goods. Instead, the backpack manufacturer—the consignor—includes the consigned goods in its inventory. *Include in inventory only what the business owns.*

> **CONSIGNMENT.** Transfer of goods by the owner (consignor) to another business (consignee) that sells the inventory on the owner's behalf. The consignee does not take title to the consigned goods.

DETERMINING THE UNIT COST OF INVENTORY   As we've seen, *inventory cost* is the price the business pays to purchase the goods—not the selling price. Suppose Deckers Outdoor purchases a T-shirt for $10 and sells it for $15. Deckers would report the inventory at its cost of $10 per unit, not at its selling price of $15.

Inventory cost includes invoice price, less any purchase discount, plus sales tax, tariffs, transportation charges, insurance while in transit, and all other costs incurred to make the goods ready for sale. *Net purchases* means the net cost of inventory acquired for resale, after subtracting any purchase discounts and purchase returns and allowances. As we stated earlier, we use the terms *purchases* and *net purchases* interchangeably.

Periodic Inventory System

In the periodic inventory system, the business does not keep a running record of the inventory on hand. Instead, at the end of the period, the business counts the goods on hand and computes the cost of ending inventory. This inventory figure appears on the balance sheet and is used to compute cost of goods sold. The periodic system is also called the *physical system* because it relies on the actual physical count of inventory.

It's a Bird . . . It's a Plane . . . It's a Warehouse!
DHL Worldwide Express

Say "inventory" and you probably conjure up a warehouse filled with auto tires awaiting shipment. In the new world economy, however, inventory is likely to be zipping overhead via overnight air express. At 3:00 A.M. in Brussels, Belgium, you get a snapshot of just what lean inventory means: Workers at the **DHL Air Express** hub use forklifts to hoist **Dell Computers, Nokia** cell phones and **Ford** car parts onto planes bound for Finland, South Africa, and Argentina. And all these products just came off other planes: nothing sits in a warehouse.

The pressure to keep inventory levels low has fueled the profits of the air express industry. "You can't have any dead space in your supply chain," says Lynnette McIntire of **UPS.** McIntire says her customers no longer stock a month of inventory. Instead, they depend on today's deliveries for tomorrow's manufacturing.

DHL may play second fiddle to **FedEx** and **UPS** in the United States, but it rules the world of overseas business-to-business transactions. In fact, DHL invented the industry. International air shipments are growing at 18% a year, twice the rate of domestic. With over 40% of the international market, DHL Worldwide Express was named the "World's Most Global Company" by *Global Finance* magazine.

Source: Based on Andrew Tanzer, "Warehouses that fly," *Forbes,* October 18, 1999, pp. 120–124. Vanessa Drucker, "B2B boom," *Global Finance,* April 2000, pp. 46–48. Anonymous, "New offerings: DHL considers an IPO after buyback of stake, "Daily Investing Report, *Atlanta Constitution,* December 14, 1999, p. F6. http://www.dhl-usa.com/press_display/press release dated 9/29/99.

In the periodic system (Exhibit 9-4, Panel A), the business uses a Purchases account to record the purchase of inventory. Purchases is an expense account. Throughout the period, the Inventory account carries the beginning balance left over from the end of the preceding period. Then at the end of the current period, the Inventory account is updated for the financial statements. The end-of-period entries can be made during the closing process. Exhibit 9-4 illustrates the accounting for inventory in the periodic system. Your professor may have you compare the perpetual and periodic inventory systems. The appendix to this chapter provides a side-by-side comparison.

INVENTORY COSTING METHODS

Measuring the cost of inventory is easy when $50 cost per unit remains constant. But the unit cost often changes. For example, during inflation, prices rise. A pair of Teva sandals that cost **Deckers Outdoor** $50 in January may cost $52 in June and $55 in October. Suppose Deckers sells 10,000 pairs of Tevas in December. How many of the pairs cost $50? How many cost $52 or $55? To compute the cost of goods sold and ending inventory, the accountant must assign a cost to each item sold. The four costing methods GAAP allows are

1. Specific unit cost
2. Weighted-average cost
3. First-in, first-out (FIFO) cost
4. Last-in, first-out (LIFO) cost

PANEL A—Recording in the Journal and Posting to the T-accounts—Periodic System			INVENTORY AND COST OF GOODS SOLD ACCOUNTS	

1. Credit purchases of $560,000:

Purchases	560,000	
Accounts Payable..............		560,000

2. Credit sales of $900,000:

Accounts Receivable	900,000	
Sales Revenue...................		900,000

3. End-of-period entries to update Inventory and record Cost of Goods Sold:

 a. Transfer the cost of beginning inventory ($100,000) to Cost of Goods Sold:

Cost of Goods Sold...........	100,000	
Inventory (beginning balance)........................		100,000

 b. Record the cost of ending inventory ($120,000) based on a count:

Inventory (ending balance)	120,000	
Cost of Goods Sold		120,000

 c. Transfer the cost of purchases to Cost of Goods Sold:

Cost of Goods Sold...........	560,000	
Purchases		560,000

INVENTORY

100,000*	100,000
120,000	

COST OF GOODS SOLD

100,000	120,000
560,000	
540,000	

* Beginning inventory was $100,000.

PANEL B—Reporting in the Financial Statements

Income Statement (partial)

Sales revenue............................		$900,000
Cost of goods sold:		
Beginning inventory	$100,000	
Purchases	560,000	
Cost of goods available	660,000	
Less: Ending inventory..........	(120,000)	
Cost of goods sold		540,000
Gross profit		$360,000

Balance Sheet (partial)

Current assets:		
Cash..	$	XXX
Short-term investments..............................		XXX
Accounts receivable.....................................		XXX
Inventories...		120,000
Prepaid expenses..		XXX

 DAILY EXERCISE 9-4

A company can use any of these methods. The computation of inventory cost is essentially the same under both the perpetual and the periodic systems.[1]

Specific Unit Cost

Some businesses deal in inventory items that differ from unit to unit, such as automobiles, jewels, and real estate. These businesses usually cost their inventory at the specific unit cost of the particular unit. For instance, a Chevrolet dealer may have two vehicles in the showroom—a "stripped-down" model that cost $14,000 and a "loaded" model that cost $17,000. If the dealer sells the loaded model for $19,700, cost of goods sold is $17,000, the cost of the specific unit. The gross margin on this sale is $2,700 ($19,700 − $17,000). If the stripped-down auto is the only unit left in inventory at the end of the period, ending inventory is $14,000, the dealer's cost of the specific unit on hand.

Objective 2

Apply the inventory costing methods: specific unit cost, weighted-average cost, FIFO, and LIFO

---

[1]Theoretically, there can be a difference between the last-in, first-out (LIFO) costs under the perpetual and the periodic systems. In actual practice, however, this difference does not exist. Complications with LIFO cause companies to wait until year end to compute ending inventory and cost of goods sold. Their computations for perpetual LIFO then parallel those for periodic LIFO. This topic is covered in later accounting courses.

SPECIFIC-UNIT-COST METHOD.
Inventory cost method based on the specific cost of particular units of inventory. Also called the **specific identification method.**

The **specific-unit-cost method** is also called the **specific identification method.** This method is not practical for inventory items that have common characteristics, such as bushels of wheat, gallons of paint, or boxes of laundry detergent.

The weighted-average cost, FIFO (first-in, first-out) cost, and LIFO (last-in, first-out) cost methods are fundamentally different from the specific-unit-cost method. These methods do not assign to inventory the specific cost of particular units. Instead, they assume different flows of costs into and out of inventory, as illustrated in Exhibit 9-5. Panel A gives the illustrative data for all three inventory cost methods.

EXHIBIT 9-5

Inventory and Cost of Goods Sold Under Three Costing Methods: *Weighted-Average (Panel B), FIFO (Panel C), LIFO (Panel D)*

 DAILY EXERCISE 9-5

 DAILY EXERCISE 9-6

 DAILY EXERCISE 9-7

PANEL A—Illustrative Data

Beginning inventory (10 units @ $10 per unit)		$ 100
Purchases:		
No. 1 (25 units @ $14 per unit)	$ 350	
No. 2 (25 units @ $18 per unit)	450	
Total purchases...		800
Cost of goods available for sale (60 units)		900
Ending inventory (20 units @ $? per unit)		(?)
Cost of goods sold (40 units @ $? per unit)		$?

PANEL B—Ending Inventory and Cost of Goods Sold (Weighted-Average Cost Method)

Cost of goods available for sale—see Panel A (60 units @ average cost of $15* per unit)	$ 900
Ending inventory (20 units @ $15 per unit)...............................	(300)
Cost of goods sold (40 units @ $15 per unit)	$ 600

$$\frac{\text{Cost of goods available for sale, \$900}}{\text{Number of units available for sale, 60}} = \text{Average cost per unit, \$15}$$

PANEL C—Ending Inventory and Cost of Goods Sold (FIFO Cost Method)

Cost of goods available for sale (60 units—see Panel A)		$ 900
Ending inventory (cost of the *last* 20 units available):		
20 units @ $18 per unit (from purchase No. 2)............................		(360)
Cost of goods sold (cost of the *first* 40 units available):		
10 units @ $10 per unit (all of beginning inventory).................	$ 100	
25 units @ $14 per unit (all of purchase No. 1)	350	
5 units @ $18 per unit (from purchase No. 2)	90	
Cost of goods sold..	$ 540	$ 540

PANEL D—Ending Inventory and Cost of Goods Sold (LIFO Cost Method)

Cost of goods available for sale (60 units—see Panel A)		$ 900
Ending inventory (cost of the *first* 20 units available):		
10 units @ $10 per unit (all of beginning inventory).................	$(100)	
10 units @ $14 per unit (from purchase No. 1)............................	(140)	
Ending inventory		(240)
Cost of goods sold (cost of the *last* 40 units available):		
25 units @ $18 per unit (all of purchase No. 2)	$ 450	
15 units @ $14 per unit (from purchase No. 1)..........................	210	
Cost of goods sold..	$ 660	$ 660

WEIGHTED-AVERAGE COST METHOD. Inventory costing method based on the weighted-average cost of inventory during the period. Weighted-average cost is determined by dividing the cost of goods available for sale by the number of units available. Also called the **average-cost method.**

Weighted-Average Cost

The **weighted-average cost method,** often called the *average-cost method,* is based on the weighted-average cost of inventory during the period. Weighted-average cost is determined as follows:

- Determine the weighted-average cost by dividing the cost of goods available for sale (beginning inventory plus purchases) by the number of units available (beginning inventory plus purchases).
- Compute the ending inventory and cost of goods sold by multiplying the number of units by the weighted-average cost per unit.

To illustrate the costing methods, suppose the business has 60 units of inventory available for sale during the period.

- Ending inventory consists of 20 units.
- Cost of goods sold is based on 40 units.

Panel A of Exhibit 9-5 gives the data for computing ending inventory and cost of goods sold, and Panel B shows the weighted-average cost computations.

First-In, First-Out (FIFO) Cost

Under the **first-in, first-out (FIFO) method,** the company must keep a record of the cost of each inventory unit purchased. The unit costs for ending inventory may differ from the unit costs used to compute the cost of goods sold. Under FIFO,

- The first costs into inventory are the first costs out to cost of goods sold—hence the name *first-in, first-out.*
- Ending inventory is based on the costs of the most recent purchases.

In Exhibit 9-5, the FIFO cost of ending inventory is $360. Cost of goods sold is $540. Panel A gives the data, and Panel C shows the computations.

Last-In, First-Out (LIFO) Cost

The **last-in, first-out (LIFO) method** also depends on the costs of particular inventory purchases. LIFO is the opposite of FIFO. Under LIFO,

- The last costs into inventory are the first costs out to cost of goods sold.
- Ending inventory is based on the oldest costs—those of beginning inventory and plus the earliest purchases of the period.

Exhibit 9-5 shows that the LIFO cost of ending inventory is $240. Cost of goods sold is $660. Again, Panel A gives the data, and Panel D shows the computations.

Remember that the terms *FIFO* and *LIFO* do not describe which goods are left in ending inventory, but rather which goods are sold. FIFO assumes that goods purchased first are sold first; therefore, the last goods purchased are left in ending inventory. LIFO assumes that the last goods in are sold first; therefore, the first goods purchased are left in ending inventory.

The Income Effects of FIFO, LIFO, and Weighted-Average Cost

In our example, the cost of inventory rose during the accounting period from $10 per unit to $14 and finally to $18 (Exhibit 9-5, Panel A). When inventory unit costs change, the different costing methods produce different cost of goods sold and ending inventory figures, as Exhibit 9-5 shows (Panels B, C, and D).

When inventory unit costs are *increasing,*

- FIFO ending inventory is *highest* because it is priced at the most recent (highest) costs.
- LIFO ending inventory is *lowest* because it is priced at the oldest (lowest) costs.

When inventory unit costs are *decreasing,*

- FIFO ending inventory is lowest.
- LIFO ending inventory is highest.

Exhibit 9-6 on page 356 summarizes the income effects of the three inventory methods, using the data from Exhibit 9-5. Study the exhibit carefully, focusing on ending inventory, cost of goods sold, and gross profit.

FIRST-IN, FIRST-OUT (FIFO) INVENTORY COSTING METHOD. Inventory costing method by which the first costs into inventory are the first costs out to cost of goods sold. Ending inventory is based on the costs of the most recent purchases.

LAST-IN, FIRST-OUT (LIFO) INVENTORY COSTING METHOD. Inventory costing method by which the last costs into inventory are the first costs out to cost of goods sold. This method leaves the oldest costs—those of beginning inventory and the earliest purchases of the period—in ending inventory.

	FIFO	LIFO	Weighted-Average
Sales revenue (assumed)........	$1,000	$1,000	$1,000
Cost of goods sold:			
Goods available for sale (from Exhibit 9-5)...........	$900	$900	$900
Ending inventory...............	(360)	(240)	(300)
Cost of goods sold	540	660	600
Gross profit.............................	$ 460	$ 340	$ 400

Summary of Income Effects—When inventory unit costs are *increasing*

FIFO:	Highest ending inventory	LIFO:	Lowest ending inventory	Weighted-average:	Results fall between
	Lowest cost of goods sold		Highest cost of goods sold		the extremes of FIFO
	Highest gross profit		Lowest gross profit		and LIFO

Summary of Income Effects—When inventory unit costs are *decreasing*

FIFO:	Lowest ending inventory	LIFO:	Highest ending inventory	Weighted-average:	Results fall between
	Highest cost of goods sold		Lowest cost of goods sold		the extremes of FIFO
	Lowest gross profit		Highest gross profit		and LIFO

 DAILY EXERCISE 9-8

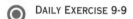 DAILY EXERCISE 9-9

Objective 3
Identify the income effects and the tax effects of the inventory costing methods

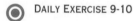 DAILY EXERCISE 9-10

The Income Tax Advantage of LIFO

When prices are rising, the LIFO method results in the *lowest taxable income* and thus the *lowest income taxes*. Using the gross profit data of Exhibit 9-6, we have the following (using assumed data):

	FIFO	LIFO	Weighted-Average
Gross profit..	$460	$340	$400
Operating expenses (assumed)	260	260	260
Income before income tax....................	200	80	140
Income tax expense (40%)	$ 80	$ 32	$ 56

Income tax expense is lowest under LIFO ($32) and highest under FIFO ($80). The most attractive feature of LIFO is reduced income tax payments, which is why **Lands' End, PepsiCo,** and **Wal-Mart** use the LIFO method. These companies are willing to report lower profits in order to save on taxes.

Some periods are marked by high inflation, and companies change to LIFO for its tax advantage. Exhibit 9-7, based on an American Institute of Certified Public Accountants (AICPA) survey of 600 companies, indicates that FIFO and LIFO are the most popular inventory costing methods.

EXHIBIT 9-7
Use of the various Inventory Costing Methods

GAAP and Practical Considerations: A Comparison of Inventory Methods

To judge the three major inventory costing methods, ask three questions:

1. How well does each method measure net income on the income statement?
2. Which method reports the most up-to-date inventory amount on the balance sheet?
3. What effects do the methods have on income taxes?

MEASURING NET INCOME ON THE INCOME STATEMENT   LIFO best matches the current value of cost of goods sold with current revenue by assigning to this expense the most recent inventory costs. Therefore, LIFO produces the cost-of-goods-sold figure that is closest to what it would cost the company to replace the goods that were sold. In this sense, LIFO produces the best measure of net income. In contrast, FIFO matches the oldest inventory costs against the period's revenue—a poor match of current expense with current revenue.

CURRENT INVENTORY COST ON THE BALANCE SHEET   FIFO reports the most current inventory costs on the balance sheet. LIFO can result in misleading inventory costs on the balance sheet because the oldest prices are left in ending inventory.

INCOME TAX   LIFO results in the lowest income tax payments when prices are rising. Tax payments are highest under FIFO. When inventory prices are falling, tax payments are highest under LIFO and lowest under FIFO. The weighted-average cost method produces amounts between the extremes of LIFO and FIFO.

LIFO ALLOWS OWNERS TO MANAGE REPORTED INCOME—UP OR DOWN   LIFO is often criticized because it allows managers to manipulate net income. When inventory prices are rising rapidly and a company wants to show less income for the year (in order to pay less taxes), managers can buy a large amount of inventory before the end of the year. Under LIFO, these high inventory costs immediately become expense—as cost of goods sold. As a result, the income statement reports a lower net income.

Conversely, if the business is having a bad year, the owner may wish to increase reported income. To do so, he or she can delay a large purchase of high-cost inventory until the next period. This high-cost inventory is not expensed as cost of goods sold in the current year. This avoids decreasing the current year's reported income. In the process, the company draws down inventory quantities below the level of the previous period, a practice known as **LIFO liquidation.**

LIFO LIQUIDATION. Situation when the LIFO inventory method is used and inventory quantities fall below the level of the previous period.

HIGHER INCOME OR LOWER TAXES?   A company may want to report the highest income, and FIFO meets this need when prices are rising. But FIFO leads to the highest income taxes. When prices are falling, LIFO reports the highest income.

Which inventory method is better—LIFO or FIFO? There is no single answer to this question. Different companies have different motives for the inventory method they choose. **The Gap** uses FIFO, **Lands' End** uses LIFO, and **Pier 1 Imports** uses weighted-average cost. Still other companies use more than one method. **The Quaker Oats Company** uses all three methods.

INTERNATIONAL PERSPECTIVE   Many companies manufacture their inventory in foreign countries. Companies that value inventory by the LIFO method often use another accounting method for inventories in foreign countries. Why? LIFO is allowed in the United States, but other countries are not bound by U.S. accounting practices. Australia and the United Kingdom, for example, do not permit the use of LIFO. Exhibit 9-8 lists a sampling of countries and whether or not they permit LIFO.

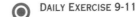
DAILY EXERCISE 9-11

EXHIBIT 9-8
LIFO Use by Country

Country	LIFO Permitted?	Country	LIFO Permitted?
Australia	No	Netherlands	Yes
Canada	Yes	Singapore	No
France	Yes	Switzerland	No
Germany	Yes	United Kingdom	No
Japan	Yes	United States	Yes

MID-CHAPTER

SUMMARY PROBLEM

Suppose a division of **IBM Corporation** that handles computer components has these inventory records for January 20X6:

www.prenhall.com/horngren
Mid-Chapter Assessment

Date	Item	Quantity	Unit Cost	Sale Price
Jan. 1	Beginning inventory.........	100 units	$ 8	
6	Purchase............................	60 units	9	
13	Sale	70 units		$20
21	Purchase............................	150 units	9	
24	Sale	210 units		22
27	Purchase...........................	90 units	10	
30	Sale	30 units		25

Company accounting records reveal that operating expense for January was $1,900.

Required

1. Prepare the January income statement, showing amounts for FIFO, LIFO, and weighted-average cost. Label the bottom line "Operating income." (Round the weighted-average cost per unit to three decimal places and all other figures to whole-dollar amounts.) Show your computations, and use the periodic inventory model in Exhibit 9-6 to compute cost of goods sold.
2. Suppose you are the financial vice president of IBM. Which inventory method will you use if your motive is to (state the reason for each answer)
   a. Minimize income taxes?
   b. Report the highest operating income?
   c. Report operating income between the extremes of FIFO and LIFO?
   d. Report inventory on the balance sheet at the most current cost?
   e. Attain the best measure of net income for the income statement?

Solution

Requirement 1

IBM CORPORATION
Income Statement for Component
Month Ended January 31, 20X6

		FIFO	LIFO	Weighted-Average
Sales revenue..............................		$6,770	$6,770	$6,770
Cost of goods sold:				
Beginning inventory	$ 800		$ 800	$ 800
Net purchases..........................	2,790		2,790	2,790
Cost of goods				
available for sale	3,590		3,590	3,590
Ending inventory	(900)		(720)	(808)
Cost of goods sold...................		2,690	2,870	2,782
Gross profit		4,080	3,900	3,988
Operating expenses.....................		1,900	1,900	1,900
Operating income		$2,180	$2,000	$2,088

Computations

Sales revenue:	$(70 \times \$20) + (210 \times \$22) + (30 \times \$25)$	= $6,770
Beginning inventory:	$100 \times \$8$	= $800
Purchases:	$(60 \times \$9) + (150 \times \$9) + (90 \times \$10)$	= $2,790
Ending inventory		
FIFO	$90^* \times \$10$	= $900
LIFO	$90 \times \$8$	= $720
Weighted-average:	$90 \times \$8.975^{**}$	= $808 (rounded from $807.75)

 * Number of units in ending inventory = $100 + 60 - 70 + 150 - 210 + 90 - 30 = 90$
** $\$3,590/400$ units† = $8.975 per unit
 † Number of units available = $100 + 60 + 150 + 90 = 400$

Requirement 2

a. Use LIFO to minimize income taxes because operating income is lowest when inventory costs are rising, as in this situation.

b. Use FIFO to report the highest operating income. Income under FIFO is highest when inventory unit costs are increasing, as in this situation.

c. Use weighted-average cost to report an operating income amount between the FIFO and LIFO extremes. This is true both in this situation and in others when inventory unit costs are increasing or decreasing.

d. Use FIFO to report inventory on the balance sheet at the most current cost. This is always true.

e. Use LIFO to best measure net income. LIFO always produces the best matching of current expense with current revenue.

THE PERPETUAL SYSTEM AND INVENTORY COSTING METHODS

Many companies keep their perpetual inventory records in quantities only, as illustrated in Exhibit 9-2. Other companies keep perpetual records in both quantities and dollar costs. Here we show how the inventory costing methods are applied in a *perpetual* inventory system.

FIFO

Deckers Outdoor uses the FIFO inventory method. Exhibit 9-9 shows Deckers' perpetual inventory record for a particular style of Teva sandals in both quantities and dollar costs for the month of November.

EXHIBIT 9-9 Perpetual Inventory Record—FIFO Cost for Deckers Outdoor Corporation

Item: Teva Sandals

Date	Received Qty.	Received Unit Cost	Received Total	Sold Qty.	Sold Unit Cost	Sold Total	Balance on Hand Qty.	Balance on Hand Unit Cost	Balance on Hand Total
Nov. 1							10	$30	$300
5				6	$30	$ 180	4	30	120
7	25	$31	$ 775				4	30	120
							25	31	775
12				4	30	120			
				9	31	279	16	31	496
26	25	32	800				16	31	496
							25	32	800
30				16	31	496			
				5	32	160	20	32	640
Totals	50		$1,575	40		$1,235	20	$32	$640

To prepare financial statements at November 30, Deckers can take the ending inventory cost ($640) straight to the balance sheet. Cost of goods sold for the November income statement is $1,235. Here is Deckers' cost of goods sold for the sandals during November (data taken from Exhibit 9-9):

Cost of Goods Sold (Teva sandals)—November	
Beginning inventory	$ 300
+ Purchases	1,575
= Cost of goods available for sale	1,875
– Ending inventory	(640)
= Cost of goods sold	$1,235

 DAILY EXERCISE 9-12

LIFO

Few companies keep perpetual inventory records at LIFO cost. The record-keeping is expensive, and LIFO liquidations can occur during the year. To avoid these problems, LIFO companies follow different strategies than FIFO and average-cost companies. LIFO companies can keep perpetual inventory records in terms of quantities only, as illustrated in Exhibit 9-2. For financial statements, they apply LIFO costs at the end of the period. Other LIFO companies maintain perpetual inventory records at FIFO cost and then convert the FIFO amounts to LIFO costs for the financial statements. These procedures arrive at ending inventory and cost-of-goods-sold figures that parallel those from the periodic inventory system.

Weighted-Average Cost

Perpetual inventory records can be kept at weighted-average cost. Most companies using this method compute the weighted-average cost for the entire period. They apply this cost to both ending inventory and cost of goods sold. These procedures parallel those used in the periodic inventory system (Exhibit 9-5).

WORK IT OUT

Examine Exhibit 9-9. What was Deckers' weighted-average unit cost during November? How much were ending inventory and cost of goods sold at weighted-average cost?

Answer

$$\text{Weighted-average unit cost} = \frac{\text{Cost of goods available for sale}}{\text{Units available for sale}}$$

$$= \frac{\text{Cost of beginning inventory} + \text{Cost of purchases}}{\text{Units of beginning inventory} + \text{Units purchased}}$$

$$= \frac{\$300 + \$1,575}{10 \text{ units} + 50 \text{ units}} = \frac{\$1,875}{60 \text{ units}} = \$31.25$$

Ending Inventory = 20 units × \$31.25 = \$ 625
Cost of goods sold = 40 units × \$31.25 = \$1,250

ACCOUNTING PRINCIPLES AND INVENTORIES

Several accounting principles have special relevance to inventories. Among them are consistency, disclosure, materiality, and accounting conservatism.

Consistency Principle

CONSISTENCY PRINCIPLE. A business should use the same accounting methods and procedures from period to period.

The **consistency principle** states that businesses should use the same accounting methods and procedures from period to period. Consistency helps investors compare a company's financial statements from one period to the next.

Suppose you are analyzing a company's net income pattern over a two-year period. The company switched from LIFO to FIFO during that time. Its net income increased dramatically but only as a result of the change in inventory method. If you did not know of the change, you might believe that the company's income increased because of improved operations.

The consistency principle does not require that all companies within an industry use the same accounting method. Nor does it mean that a company may *never* change its methods. However, a company making an accounting change must disclose the effect of the change on net income. **Sun Company, Inc.,** an oil company, disclosed the following in a note to its annual report:

EXCERPT FROM NOTE 6 OF SUN COMPANY STATEMENTS
. . . Sun changed its method of accounting for the cost of crude oil and refined product inventories . . . from . . . FIFO . . . to . . . LIFO . . . . Sun believes that the . . . LIFO method better matches current costs with current revenues . . . . The change decreased the 20X1 net loss . . . by \$3 million. . . .

Disclosure Principle

The **disclosure principle** holds that a company's financial statements should report enough information for outsiders to make knowledgeable decisions about the company. In short, the company should report *relevant, reliable,* and *comparable* information about its economic affairs. With respect to inventories, the disclosure principle means disclosing the method being used to value inventories. Suppose a banker is comparing two companies—one using LIFO and the other FIFO. The FIFO company reports higher net income, but only because it uses the FIFO inventory method. Without knowledge of the accounting methods the companies are using, the banker could loan money to the wrong business.

DISCLOSURE PRINCIPLE. A business's financial statements must report enough information for outsiders to make knowledgeable decisions about the company.

Materiality Concept

The **materiality concept** states that a company must perform strictly proper accounting *only* for items that are significant for the business's financial statements. Information is significant—or, in accounting terminology, *material*—when its presentation in the financial statements would cause someone to change a decision because of that information. Immaterial items justify less-than-perfect accounting. Their inclusion and proper presentation would not affect a statement user's decision. The materiality concept frees accountants from having to report every last item in strict accordance with GAAP.

MATERIALITY CONCEPT. A company must perform strictly proper accounting only for items that are significant to the business's financial statements.

How does a business decide where to draw the line between the material and the immaterial? This decision depends on how large the business is. **Lucent Technologies,** the maker of cordless phones, for example, has over $38 billion in assets. Management would likely treat as immaterial a $1,000 loss of inventory due to spoilage. A loss of this amount may be immaterial to Lucent's total assets and net income, so company accountants may not report the loss separately. Will this accounting treatment affect banker's or investor's decision about Lucent? Probably not. So it doesn't matter whether the loss is reported separately or simply embedded in cost of goods sold.

Accounting Conservatism

Conservatism in accounting means reporting items in the financial statements at amounts that lead to the most cautious immediate results. What advantage does conservatism give a business? Managers must be optimistic to be good leaders. This optimism sometimes causes them to look on the bright side of operations, and they may overstate a company's income and asset values. Many accountants regard conservatism as a counterbalance to managers' optimistic tendencies. The goal is for financial statements to present realistic figures.

CONSERVATISM. Reporting the least favorable figures in the financial statements.

Conservatism appears in accounting guidelines such as

- "Anticipate no gains, but provide for all probable losses."
- "If in doubt, record an asset at the lowest reasonable amount and a liability at the highest reasonable amount."
- When there's a question, record an expense rather than an asset."

Conservatism directs accountants to decrease the accounting value of an asset if it appears unrealistically high. Assume that a company paid $35,000 for inventory that has become obsolete and whose current value is only $12,000. Conservatism dictates that the inventory be *written down* (that is, decreased) to $12,000.

Objective 4
Apply the lower-of-cost-or-market rule to inventory

Lower-of-Cost-or-Market Rule

The **lower-of-cost-or-market rule** (abbreviated as **LCM**) shows accounting conservatism in action. LCM requires that inventory be reported in the financial statements at whichever is lower—the inventory's historical cost or its market value. For inventories, *market value* generally means *current replacement cost* (that is, the cost to replace the inventory on hand). If the replacement cost of inventory falls below its historical cost, the business must write down the value of its goods. The business reports ending inventory at its LCM value on the balance sheet.

LOWER-OF-COST-OR-MARKET (LCM) RULE. Rule that an asset should be reported in the financial statements at whichever is lower—its historical cost or its market value.

Suppose a business paid $3,000 for inventory on September 26. By December 31, its value has fallen. The inventory can now be replaced for $2,200 and the decline in value appears permanent. Market value is below cost, and the December 31 balance sheet reports this inventory at its LCM value of $2,200.

Exhibit 9-10 shows the effects of LCM on the income statement and the balance sheet. The exhibit shows that the lower of (a) cost or (b) market value is the relevant amount for valuing inventory on the balance sheet. Now examine the income statement in Exhibit 9-10. What expense absorbs the impact of the $800 inventory write-down? The entry to write down the inventory to LCM debits Cost of Goods Sold:

Cost of Goods Sold (cost, $3,000 − market, $2,200)	800	
Inventory		800

EXHIBIT 9-10
Lower-of-Cost-or-Market (LCM)
Effects

DAILY EXERCISE 9-13

Balance Sheet

Current assets:	
Inventories, at market	
(which is lower than $3,000 cost)	$ 2,200

Income Statement

Sales revenue		$20,000
Cost of goods sold:		
Beginning inventory (LCM = Cost)	$ 2,800	
Net purchases	11,000	
Cost of goods available for sale	13,800	
Ending inventory—		
Cost = $3,000		
Replacement cost (market value) = $2,200		
LCM = Market	(2,200)	
Cost of goods sold		11,600
Gross profit		$ 8,400

Companies often disclose LCM in notes to their financial statements, as shown here for **Cisco Systems,** the worldwide leader in networking for the Internet.

NOTE 2: STATEMENT OF SIGNIFICANT ACCOUNTING POLICIES
Inventories. Inventories are stated at the *lower of cost or market.* [Emphasis added.]

Objective 5
Determine the effects of inventory errors on cost of goods sold and net income

Effects of Inventory Errors

Businesses count their inventories at the end of the period. As the period 1 segment of Exhibit 9-11 shows, an error in the ending inventory creates errors in cost of goods sold and gross profit. Compare period 1, when ending inventory is overstated and cost of goods sold is understated, each by $5,000, with period 3, which is correct. Period 1 should look exactly like period 3.

DAILY EXERCISE 9-14

Recall that one period's ending inventory is the next period's beginning inventory. Thus, the error in ending inventory carries over into the next period; note the amounts highlighted in Exhibit 9-11.

Because ending inventory is *subtracted* in computing cost of goods sold in one period and the same amount is *added* as beginning inventory to compute next period's cost of goods sold, the error's effect cancels out at the end of the second period. The overstatement of cost of goods sold in period 2 counterbalances the understatement for period 1. Thus, the total gross profit for the two periods is correct. As a result, owner's equity at the end of period 2 is correct. These effects are summarized in Exhibit 9-12.

DAILY EXERCISE 9-15

Inventory errors cannot be ignored simply because they counterbalance, however. Suppose you are analyzing trends in the business's operations. Exhibit 9-11 shows a drop in gross margin from period 1 to period 2, followed by an increase in period 3. But that picture of operations is untrue because of the accounting error.

EXHIBIT 9-11   Inventory Errors: An Example

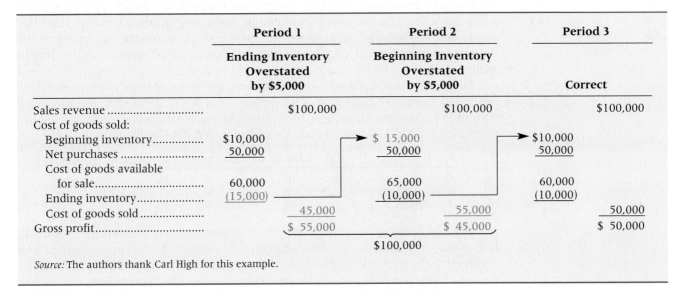

	Period 1 Ending Inventory Overstated by $5,000		Period 2 Beginning Inventory Overstated by $5,000		Period 3 Correct	
Sales revenue		$100,000		$100,000		$100,000
Cost of goods sold:						
Beginning inventory...............	$10,000		$ 15,000		$10,000	
Net purchases	50,000		50,000		50,000	
Cost of goods available						
for sale.................................	60,000		65,000		60,000	
Ending inventory....................	(15,000)		(10,000)		(10,000)	
Cost of goods sold...................		45,000		55,000		50,000
Gross profit...............................		$ 55,000		$ 45,000		$ 50,000

$100,000

Source: The authors thank Carl High for this example.

EXHIBIT 9-12   Effects of Inventory Errors

	Period 1			Period 2		
Inventory Error	Cost of Goods Sold	Gross Profit and Net Income	Ending Owner's Equity	Cost of Goods Sold	Gross Profit and Net Income	Ending Owner's Equity
Period 1 Ending inventory *overstated*	Understated	Overstated	Overstated	Overstated	Understated	Correct
Period 1 Ending inventory *understated*	Overstated	Understated	Understated	Understated	Overstated	Correct

The correct gross profit is $50,000 for each period. Providing accurate information for decision making requires that all inventory errors be corrected.

OTHER INVENTORY ISSUES

Ethical Issues

No area of accounting has a deeper ethical dimension than inventory. Owners and managers of companies whose profits are lagging are sometimes tempted to "cook the books" to increase reported income. The increase in income may lead investors and creditors to think the business is more successful than it really is.

There are two main schemes for cooking the books. The easiest, and the most obvious, is simply to overstate ending inventory. In Exhibit 9-12, we saw how an error in ending inventory affects net income. A company can intentionally overstate its ending inventory. Such an error understates cost of goods sold and overstates net income and owner's equity, as shown in the accounting equation. The upward-pointing arrows indicate an overstatement—reporting more assets and equity than are actually present:

ASSETS	=	LIABILITIES	+	OWNERS' EQUITY
↑	=	0	+	↑

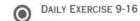
DAILY EXERCISE 9-16

The second way of using inventory to cook the books involves sales. Sales schemes are more complex than simple inventory overstatements. **Datapoint Corporation** and **MiniScribe,** both computer-related concerns, were charged with creating fictitious sales to boost reported profits.

Datapoint is alleged to have hired drivers to transport its inventory around San Antonio so that the goods could *not* be physically counted. Datapoint's logic seemed to be that excluding the goods from ending inventory would imply that they had been sold. The scheme broke down when the trucks returned the goods to the warehouse. What would you think of a company with $10 million in sales and $4 million of sales returns?

MiniScribe is alleged to have cooked its books by shipping boxes of bricks labeled as computer parts to its distributors right before year end. The following accounting equations show how the scheme affected MiniScribe's reported figures (assuming sales of $10 million and cost of goods sold of $6 million):

	ASSETS	=	LIABILITIES	+	OWNERS' EQUITY
Sales..........................	10	=	0	+	10
Cost of goods sold......	−6	=	0	−	6
Net effect	4	=	0	+	4

The bogus transactions increased the company's assets and equity by $4 million—but only temporarily. The distributors refused to accept the goods and returned them to MiniScribe—but in the next accounting period. In the earlier period, MiniScribe recorded sales revenue and temporarily reported millions of dollars of sales and income that did not exist. The scheme boomeranged in the next period when MiniScribe had to record the sales returns. In virtually every area, accounting imposes a discipline that works to keep every business honest in its financial reporting.

Estimating Inventory

Objective 6
Estimate ending inventory by the gross profit method

Often a business must *estimate* the value of its inventory. Because of cost and inconvenience, few companies physically count inventories at the end of each month, yet they may need monthly financial statements. Suppose the company does not use the perpetual inventory system and thus cannot determine ending inventory by looking at the Inventory account. Fortunately, there is a way to estimate ending inventory for monthly or quarterly financial statements. Also, a fire may destroy inventory, and to file an insurance claim, the business must estimate the value of its loss.

Gross Profit Method. A way to estimate inventory on the basis of the cost-of-goods-sold model: Beginning inventory + Net purchases = Cost of goods available for sale. Cost of goods available for sale − Cost of goods sold = Ending inventory. Also called the **gross margin method.**

The **gross profit method,** also known as the *gross margin method,* is a way of estimating inventory on the basis of the familiar cost-of-goods-sold model (amounts assumed for illustration):

Beginning inventory	**$10**
+ Purchases	**50**
= Cost of goods available for sale	**60**
− Ending inventory	**(20)**
= Cost of goods sold	**$40**

Rearranging *ending inventory* and *cost of goods sold* makes the model useful for estimating ending inventory and is illustrated in the following equation and in Exhibit 9-13 (amounts assumed for illustration):

Beginning inventory	**$10**
+ Purchases	**50**
= Cost of goods available for sale	**60**
− Cost of goods sold	**(40)**
= Ending inventory	**$20**

Daily Exercise 9-17

Suppose a fire destroys your inventory. To collect insurance, you must estimate the cost of the ending inventory. Using your normal *gross profit percent* (that is, gross profit divided by net sales revenue), you can estimate cost of goods sold. Then subtract cost of goods sold from goods available to estimate ending inventory. Exhibit 9-13 illustrates the gross profit method.

Beginning inventory		$14,000
Purchases		66,000
Cost of goods available for sale		80,000
Estimated cost of goods sold:		
Sales revenue	$100,000	
Less: Estimated gross profit of 40%	(40,000)	
Estimated cost of goods sold		(60,000)
Estimated cost of *ending inventory*		$20,000

WORK IT OUT

Beginning inventory is $70,000, net purchases total $298,000, and net sales are $480,000. With a normal gross profit rate of 40% of sales, how much is ending inventory?

Answer

Beginning inventory		$ 70,000
Net purchases		298,000
Cost of goods available for sale		368,000
Estimated cost of goods sold:		
Net sales revenue	$480,000	
Less: Estimated gross profit of 40%	(192,000)	
Estimated cost of goods sold		(288,000)
Estimated cost of ending inventory		$ 80,000

Internal Control

Internal control over inventory is important because inventory is such an important asset. Successful companies take great care to protect their inventory. Elements of good internal control include

1. Physically counting inventory at least once each year
2. Storing inventory to protect it against theft, damage, and decay
3. Giving access only to personnel who have *no* access to the accounting records
4. Not stockpiling too much inventory; this avoids tying up money in unneeded items

Computerized inventory systems allow companies to minimize the amount of inventory on hand (item 4). In a competitive environment, companies cannot afford to tie up cash in too much inventory. Many manufacturing companies use *just-in-time (JIT) inventory systems,* which require suppliers to deliver materials just in time to be used in the production process.

This chapter has discussed various aspects of controlling and accounting for inventory. The Decision Guidelines feature on page 366 summarizes some basic decision guidelines that are helpful in managing a business's inventory operations.

DECISION GUIDELINES

Guidelines for Inventory Management

DECISION	GUIDELINES	SYSTEM OR METHOD
Which inventory system to use?	• Expensive merchandise • Cannot control inventory by visual inspection	→ Perpetual system
	• Can control inventory by visual inspection	→ Periodic system
Which costing method to use?	• Unique inventory items	→ Specific unit cost
	• Most current cost of ending inventory • Maximizes reported income when costs are rising	→ FIFO
	• Most current measure of cost of goods sold and net income • Minimizes income tax when costs are rising	→ LIFO
	• Middle-of-the-road approach for income tax and reported income	→ Weighted-average
How to estimate the cost of ending inventory?	• The cost-of-goods-sold model provides the framework	→ Gross profit (gross margin) method

EXCEL APPLICATION PROBLEM

Goal: Create an Excel spreadsheet that compares gross profit, ending inventory, and cost of goods sold under the LIFO, FIFO, and weighted-average methods of inventory valuation.

Scenario: John Kalinich, Chief Operations Officer at Teva Sport Sandals in Flagstaff, Arizona, has a decision to make. He's in charge of Teva's on-line store, and is responsible for the inventory sold through the Web. John must decide which inventory method to use for the business.

Your task is to create a spreadsheet and embedded graph that compares gross profit, ending inventory, and cost of goods sold under three methods: weighted-average, FIFO, and LIFO. John has provided the following data from the most recent month of operations for your use in creating the spreadsheet:

July	1	Beginning inventory	2,000 units @ $30.00 cost per unit
	6	Purchase	600 units @ $31.25 cost per unit
	17	Purchase	400 units @ $33.50 cost per unit
	28	Purchase	200 units @ $34.75 cost per unit

Sales for July: 1,800 pairs of sandals sold @ $69.00 each

After you have prepared your spreadsheet, answer these questions:

1. Which method produces the lowest cost of goods sold? Why?
2. Which method produces the lowest ending inventory? Why?
3. If John Kalinich wants to maximize gross profit for Teva, which method should he choose? Does this method do a good job of matching inventory expense (cost of goods sold) to sales revenue?

Step-by-step:

1. Open a new Excel spreadsheet.
2. Create a heading for your spreadsheet that contains the following:
   a. Chapter 9 Decision Guidelines
   b. Inventory Management
   c. Teva Sport Sandals
   d. Today's date
3. At the top of your spreadsheet, create a "Data Section" for the July data provided by John Kalinich. Set up columns for Date, Activity (Beginning Inventory, Purchases, Goods Available for Sale, Sales, and Ending Inventory), Units, Unit Cost, and Total Cost. Compute goods available for sale and ending inventory.
4. Include the calculation for "average unit cost" on a separate row in this section.
5. Next, create a section titled "Inventory Method Comparison" in bold print and underlined. Include one column for each method (weighted-average, FIFO, and LIFO). Include rows for Ending Inventory, Cost of Goods Sold, and Gross Profit. Format as necessary. Be sure your calculations are based on the Data Section figures. Do not "hard-code" any amounts in this section.
6. When done, create an embedded bar chart underneath the Inventory Method Comparison section that compares Gross Profit, Ending Inventory, and Cost of Goods Sold for all three methods. (*Hint:* Use the Chart Wizard button on the Standard Excel toolbar.)
7. Save your spreadsheet, and print a copy for your files.

REVIEW MERCHANDISE INVENTORY

SUMMARY PROBLEM

Mesa Hardware Company began 20X4 with 60,000 units of inventory that cost $36,000. During 19X8, Mesa purchased merchandise on account for $352,500 as follows:

Purchase 1 (100,000 units costing)................ $ 65,000
Purchase 2 (270,000 units costing)................ 175,500
Purchase 3 (160,000 units costing)................ 112,000

www.prenhall.com/horngren
End-of-Chapter Assessment

Cash payments on account for inventory totaled $326,000 during the year.

Mesa's sales during 20X4 consisted of 520,000 units of inventory for $660,000, all on account. The company uses the FIFO inventory method.

Cash collections from customers were $630,000. Operating expenses totaled $240,500, of which Mesa paid $211,000 in cash. Mesa credited Accrued Liabilities for the remainder.

Required

1. Make summary journal entries to record Mesa Hardware's transactions for the year, assuming the company uses a perpetual inventory system.
2. Determine the FIFO cost of Mesa's ending inventory at December 31, 20X4, two ways:
   a. Use a T-account.
   b. Multiply the number of units by the unit cost.
3. Use the cost-of-goods-sold model to show how Mesa would compute cost of goods sold for 20X4 under the periodic inventory system.
4. Prepare Mesa Hardware's income statement for 20X4. Show totals for the gross profit and net income.

Solution

Requirement 1

Inventory ($65,000 + $175,500 + $112,000)..........	352,500	
Accounts Payable................................		352,500
Accounts Payable.....................................	326,000	
Cash..		326,000
Accounts Receivable	660,000	
Sales Revenue......................................		660,000
Cost of Goods Sold.................................	339,500	
Inventory..		339,500
[$36,000 + $65,000 + $175,500 + $63,000;		
(90,000 units × $0.70)]($112,000 ÷ 160,000		
units = $0.70 per unit)		
Cash	630,000	
Accounts Receivable		630,000
Operating Expenses	240,500	
Cash..		211,000
Accrued Liabilities		29,500

Requirement 2

a.

INVENTORY	
36,000	339,500
352,500	
49,000	

b. Number of units in ending inventory

(60,000 + 100,000 +
270,000 + 160,000 − 520,000)..................... 70,000

Unit cost of ending inventory at FIFO
($112,000 ÷ 160,000) .... × $0.70

FIFO cost of ending inventory........................... $49,000

Requirement 3

Cost of goods sold (periodic inventory system):	
Beginning inventory	$ 36,000
Purchases	352,500
Cost of goods available for sale	388,500
Less: Ending inventory	(49,000)
Cost of goods sold	$339,500

Requirement 4

MESA HARDWARE COMPANY
Income Statement
Year Ended December 31, 20X4

Sales revenue	$660,000
Cost of goods sold	339,500
Gross profit	320,500
Operating expenses	240,500
Net income	$ 80,000

LESSONS LEARNED

1. **Account for inventory by the perpetual and periodic systems.** Inventory is the heart of a merchandiser's business. *Cost of goods sold* is usually the largest expense on the income statement.

   Merchandisers can choose between two inventory systems. *A periodic system* does not keep a running record of the inventory on hand. Instead, at the end of the period, the business counts the inventory and then updates its records. In a *perpetual inventory system*, the business keeps a running record to show inventory on hand at all times. A physical count of inventory is needed in both systems.

2. **Apply the inventory costing methods: specific-unit-cost, weighted-average cost, FIFO, and LIFO.** Businesses multiply inventory quantity by unit cost to determine the cost of this asset. The four inventory costing methods are *specific-unit-cost; weighted-average cost; first-in, first-out (FIFO) cost; and last-in, first-out (LIFO) cost*. Businesses that sell unique items use the specific-unit-cost method. Most other companies use the other methods. FIFO reports ending inventory at the most current cost. LIFO reports cost of goods sold at the most current cost. Weighted-average cost falls in the middle.

3. **Identify the income effects and the tax effects of the inventory costing methods.** When prices are rising, LIFO produces the highest cost of goods sold and the lowest income, thus minimizing income taxes. FIFO results in the highest income. The weighted-average cost method falls between the extremes of FIFO and LIFO.

4. **Apply the lower-of-cost-or-market rule to inventory.** The *lower-of-cost-or-market (LCM) rule*—an example of accounting *conservatism*—requires that businesses report inventory on the balance sheet at the lower of its cost or current replacement value. Companies can disclose LCM in notes to their financial statements.

5. **Determine the effects of inventory errors on cost of goods sold and net income.** Inventory overstatements in one period are counterbalanced by understatements in the next period, and understatements are counterbalanced by overstatements.

6. **Estimate ending inventory by the gross profit method.** The *gross profit method* estimates the cost of inventory. It comes in handy for preparing interim financial statements and for estimating the cost of inventory destroyed by fire or other disasters.

ACCOUNTING VOCABULARY

average-cost method (p. 354)
conservatism (p. 361)
consignment (p. 351)
consistency principle (p. 360)
cost of goods available for sale (p. 350)
disclosure principle (p. 361)
first-in, first-out (FIFO) inventory costing method (p. 355)
gross margin (p. 347)

gross margin method (p. 364)
gross profit (p. 347)
gross profit method (p. 364)
last-in, first-out (LIFO) inventory costing method (p. 355)
LIFO liquidation (p. 357)
lower-of-cost-or-market (LCM) rule (p. 361)
materiality concept (p. 361)
merchandising company (p. 347)

periodic inventory system (p. 347)
perpetual inventory system (p. 348)
specific identification method (p. 354)
specific-unit-cost method (p. 354)
weighted-average cost method (p. 354)

QUESTIONS

1. Suppose your company deals in expensive jewelry. Which inventory system should you use to achieve good internal control over the inventory? If your business is a hardware store that sells low-cost goods, which inventory system would you be likely to use? Why would you choose this system?
2. Identify the accounts debited and credited in the standard purchase and sale entries under (a) the perpetual inventory system, and (b) the periodic inventory system.
3. If beginning inventory is $10,000, purchases total $85,000, and ending inventory is $12,700, how much is cost of goods sold?
4. If beginning inventory is $32,000, purchases total $119,000, and cost of goods sold is $127,000, how much is ending inventory?
5. Briefly describe the four generally accepted inventory cost methods. During a period of rising prices, which method produces the highest reported income? Which produces the lowest reported income?
6. Which inventory costing method produces the ending inventory valued at the most current cost? Which method produces the cost-of-goods-sold amount valued at the most current cost?
7. What is the most attractive feature of LIFO? Does LIFO have this advantage during periods of increasing prices or during periods of decreasing prices?
8. Identify the chief criticism of LIFO.
9. Briefly describe the influence that the concept of conservatism has on accounting for inventory.
10. Manley Company's inventory has a cost of $48,000 at the end of the year, and the current replacement cost of the inventory is $51,000. At which amount should the company report the inventory on its balance sheet? Suppose the current replacement cost of the inventory is $45,000 instead of $51,000. At which amount should Manley report the inventory? What rule governs your answers to these questions?
11. Gabriel Company accidentally overstated its ending inventory by $10,000 at the end of period 1. Is gross margin of period 1 overstated or understated? Is gross margin of period 2 overstated, understated, or unaffected by the period-1 error? Is total gross margin for the two periods overstated, understated, or correct? Give the reason for your answers.
12. Identify an important method of estimating inventory amounts. What familiar model underlies this estimation method?
13. True or false? A company that sells inventory of low unit cost needs no internal controls over the goods. Any inventory loss would probably be small.

ASSESS YOUR PROGRESS

DAILY EXERCISES

DE9-1 Beakman Ventures purchased 2,000 units of inventory for $60 each and marked up the goods by $40 per unit. It then sold 1,600 units. For these transactions, show what Beakman would report on its balance sheet at December 31, 20X0 and on its income statement for the year ended December 31, 20X0. Include a complete heading for each statement.

Basic concept of accounting for inventory (Obj. 1)

DE9-2 Study Exhibit 9-3, page 349, and answer these questions:

1. What was the cost of **Deckers'** inventory purchases during the year?
2. How much were Deckers' sales for the year? How much were cost of goods sold and the gross profit? What was the cost of ending inventory?
3. Study the journal entries in Panel A of the exhibit. How can you tell from the journal entries that Deckers is using the perpetual inventory system?

Using the inventory records (Obj. 1)

DE9-3 Rugged River Outfitters purchased inventory costing $85,000 and sold half the goods for $103,000, with all transactions on account.

Journalize these two transactions under the perpetual inventory system. How much gross profit did Rugged River earn on these sales? Which statement reports the gross profit?

Accounting for inventory in the perpetual system (Obj. 1)

DE9-4 Use the data in Daily Exercise 9-3 to record Rugged River Outfitters' purchase and sale transactions under the periodic inventory system. Why can't you measure Rugged River's gross profit under the periodic system? What additional information is needed to compute cost of goods sold and the gross profit?

Accounting for inventory in the periodic system (Obj. 1)

DE9-5 Study Exhibit 9-5, page 354, and answer these questions.

1. In Panel A, are the company's inventory costs stable, increasing, or decreasing during the period? Cite specific figures to support your answer.
2. Which inventory method results in the *lowest* amount for ending inventory (give this figure)? Explain why this method produces the lowest amount for ending inventory.
3. Does this method result in the highest, or the lowest, cost of goods sold? Explain.
4. Does this method result in the highest, or the lowest, gross profit? Explain your answer.

Applying the FIFO, LIFO, and weighted-average methods (Obj. 2)

DE9-6 Study Exhibit 9-5, page 354, and answer these questions.

1. In Panel A, are the company's inventory costs stable, increasing, or decreasing during the period? Cite specific figures to support your answer.
2. Which inventory method results in the *highest* amount for ending inventory (give this figure)? Explain why this method produces the highest amount for ending inventory.
3. Does this method result in the highest, or the lowest, cost of goods sold? Explain.
4. Does this method result in the highest, or the lowest, gross profit? Explain your answer.

DE9-7 Return to Exhibit 9-5, page 354, and assume that the business sold 50 units of inventory during the period (instead of 40 units as in the exhibit). Compute ending inventory and cost of goods sold for each of the following costing methods:

a. Weighted-average   **b.** FIFO   **c.** LIFO

Follow the computational format illustrated in the exhibit.

DE9-8 Jetlink Data Systems markets ink used in inkjet printers. Jetlink started the year with 100 containers of ink (weighted-average cost of $9.14 each; FIFO cost of $9 each, LIFO cost of $8 each). During the year, Jetlink purchased 800 containers of ink at $14 and sold 700 units for $22 each, with all transactions on account.

    Journalize Jetlink's purchases, sales, and cost of goods sold transactions using the following format. Jetlink uses the perpetual inventory method to account for inkjet-printer ink.

Accounts	Debit/Credit Amounts		
	Weighted-Average*	FIFO	LIFO

* Round weighted-average unit cost to the nearest cent.

DE9-9 This exercise uses the data from Daily Exercise 9-8. It can follow Daily Exercise 9-8, or it can be solved independently. Operating expenses totaled $4,000.

    Prepare Jetlink Data Systems' income statement for the current year ended December 31 under the weighted-average, FIFO, and LIFO inventory costing methods. Include a complete statement heading, and use a format similar to that illustrated for Daily Exercise 9-8 for the three inventory methods.

DE9-10 This exercise should be used in conjunction with Daily Exercise 9-9.

    Assume Jetlink Data Systems in Daily Exercise 9-9 is a corporation subject to a 40% income tax. Compute Jetlink's income tax expense under the weighted-average, FIFO, and LIFO inventory costing methods. Which method would you select to (a) maximize reported income, or (b) minimize income tax expense? Format your answer as shown on page 356.

DE9-11 **Lands' End,** the mail-order merchant, uses the LIFO method to account for inventory. Suppose Lands' End is having an unusually good year, with net income far above expectations. Assume Lands' End's inventory costs are rising rapidly. What can Lands' End managers do immediately before the end of the year to decrease reported profits and thereby save on income taxes? Explain how this action decreases reported income.

DE9-12 Examine the perpetual inventory record in Exhibit 9-9, page 359. Answer these questions about **Deckers Outdoor's** inventory of Teva sandals.

1. Which costing method does Deckers use? Prove your answer by citing cost data from the exhibit. Focus on the November 12 sale.
2. Deckers sold all the sandals in the exhibit for $50 each. How much did Deckers report for November sales revenue, cost of goods sold, and gross profit? On which financial statement did Deckers report these figures?

DE9-13 **Deckers Outdoor** uses the perpetual inventory record for Teva sandals in Exhibit 9-9, page 359. At December 31, 1999, Scott Ash, chief financial officer of the company, applied the lower-of-cost-or-market rule to Deckers' inventories. Suppose Ash determined that the current replacement cost (current market value) of the sandals was $550. Show how Decker would report this inventory on the balance sheet and cost of goods sold on the income statement.

DE9-14 Examine **Deckers Outdoor's** financial statements in Exhibit 9-1, on page 347. Suppose Deckers' reported cost of inventory at December 31 is overstated by $3 million. What are Deckers' correct amounts for (a) inventory, (b) cost of goods sold, (c) gross profit and (d) net income (net loss)? Ignore income tax.

DE9-15 Barbara Warren, staff accountant of Shimeido Fragrance Co., learned that Shimeido's $4 million cost of inventory at the end of last year was understated by $2 million. She notified the company president of the need to alert Shimeido's lenders that last year's reported net income was incorrect. Akiro Luhara, president of Shimeido, explained to Warren that there is no need to report the error to lenders because the error will counterbalance this year. This year's error will affect this year's net income in the opposite direction of last year's error. Even with no correction, Luhara reasons that net income for both years combined will be the same whether or not Shimeido corrects its error.

Measuring the effect of an inventory error on two years' statements
(Obj. 5)

1. Was last year's reported net income of $6.3 million overstated, understated, or correct? What was the correct amount of net income last year?
2. Is this year's net income of $7 million overstated, understated, or correct? What is the correct amount of net income for the current year?
3. Whose perspective is better, Warren's or Luhara's? Give your reason. Consider the trend of reported net income both without the correction and with the correction.

DE9-16 Determine whether each of the following actions in buying, selling, and accounting for inventories is ethical or unethical. Give your reason for each answer.

Ethical implications of inventory actions
(Obj. 3, 4, 5)

1. Lake Fork Motors consciously overstated purchases to produce a high figure for cost of goods sold (low amount of net income). The real reason was to decrease the company's income tax payments to the government.
2. In applying the lower-of-cost-or-market rule to inventories, Old World Restoration Co. recorded an excessively low market value for ending inventory. This allowed the company to keep from paying income tax for the year.
3. Lamplight Fixtures Ltd. purchased lots of inventory shortly before year end to increase the LIFO cost of goods sold and decrease reported income for the year.
4. T & M Beauty Products delayed the purchase of inventory until after December 31, 20X2, in order to keep 20X2's cost of goods sold from growing too large. The delay in purchasing inventory helped net income of 20X2 to reach the level of profit demanded by the company's investors.
5. Calais Ferry Supply deliberately overstated ending inventory in order to report higher profits (net income).

DE9-17 Answer the following questions.

Estimating ending inventory by the gross profit method
(Obj. 6)

1. Asamax Insulation Company began the year with inventory of $350,000. Inventory purchases for the year totaled $1,600,000. Asamax managers estimate that cost of goods sold for the year will be $1,800,000. How much is Asamax's estimated cost of ending inventory? Use the gross profit method.
2. Cyrus Roofing, a related company, began the year with inventory of $350,000 and purchased $1,600,000 of goods during the year (the same as in requirement 1). Sales for the year are $3,000,000, and Cyrus's gross profit percentage is 40% of sales. Compute Cyrus's estimated cost of ending inventory by the gross profit method. Compare this answer to your answer in requirement 1; they should be the same. Focus on the computation of estimated cost of goods sold to explain why the two answers are the same.

E X E R C I S E S

E9-1 Accounting records for Durall Luggage yield the following data for the year ended December 31, 20X5 (amounts in thousands):

Accounting for inventory in the perpetual system
(Obj. 1)

Inventory, December 31, 20X4..	$ 370
Purchases of inventory (on account)	3,105
Sales of inventory—80% on account; 20% for cash (cost $2,821)........	4,395
Inventory, December 31, 20X5...	?

Required

1. Journalize Durall's inventory transactions in the perpetual system. Show all amounts in thousands. Use Exhibit 9-3 on page 349 as a guide.
2. Report ending inventory, sales, cost of goods sold, and gross profit on the appropriate financial statement (amounts in thousands).
3. Show the computation of cost of goods sold in the periodic system.

E9-2 Use the data in Exercise 9-1.

Accounting for inventory in the periodic system   (Obj. 1)

Required

1. Journalize Durall's inventory transactions in the periodic system. Show all amounts in thousands, and use Exhibit 9-4, page 353, as a guide.

2. Report inventory, sales, cost of goods sold, and gross profit on the appropriate financial statement (amounts in thousands).

Budgeting inventory purchases
(Obj. 1)

E9-3 **Toys "Я" Us** is budgeting for the fiscal year ended January 31, 2000. During the preceding year ended January 31, 1999, cost of goods sold was $8,191 million. Inventory stood at $1,902 million at January 31, 1999.

During the upcoming 2000 year, suppose Toys "Я" Us expects sales and cost of goods sold to increase by 6%. The company budgets next year's ending inventory at $2,020 million.

Required

How much inventory should Toys "Я" Us purchase during the upcoming year in order to reach its budgeted figures? Round to the nearest $1 million.

Determining ending inventory
and cost of goods sold by four
methods
(Obj. 2)

E9-4 The inventory records of Flexon Prosthetics indicate the following at October 31:

Oct.	1	Beginning inventory......................	9 units @ $160
	8	Purchase...	4 units @ 160
	15	Purchase...	12 units @ 170
	26	Purchase...	3 units @ 176

The physical count of inventory at October 31 indicates that eight units are on hand, and there are no consignment goods.

Required

Compute ending inventory and cost of goods sold, using each of the following methods. Follow the approach illustrated in Exhibit 9-5.

1. Specific unit cost, assuming four $170 units and four $160 units are on hand
2. Weighted-average cost (round weighted-average unit cost to three decimal places)
3. First-in, first-out   4. Last-in, first-out

Recording inventory
transactions—perpetual
system
(Obj. 1, 2)

E9-5 Use the data in Exercise 9-4 to journalize the following for the perpetual inventory system.

a. Total October purchases in one summary entry. All purchases were on credit.
b. Total October sales in a summary entry. The selling price was $300 per unit and all sales were on credit. Flexon Prosthetics uses FIFO.

Recording inventory
transactions—periodic
system
(Obj. 1, 2)

E9-6 Use the data in Exercise 9-4 to journalize the following for the periodic system:

a. Total October purchases in one summary entry. All purchases were on credit.
b. Total October sales in a summary entry. The selling price was $300 per unit and all sales were on credit. Flexon Prosthetics uses LIFO.
c. October 31 end-of-period entries for inventory in the periodic system. Flexon Prosthetics uses LIFO. Post to the Cost of Goods Sold T-account. Label each item in the account. What is the balance of cost of goods sold?

Computing the tax advantage
of LIFO over FIFO   (Obj. 3)

E9-7 Use the data in Exercise 9-4 to illustrate income tax advantage of LIFO over FIFO for Flexon Prosthetics. Sales revenue is $8,000, operating expenses are $1,100, and the income tax rate is 30%. How much in taxes would Flexon Prosthetics save by using the LIFO method?

Determining amounts for the
income statement: periodic
system   (Obj. 1)

E9-8 Supply the missing income statement amounts for each of the following companies:

Company	Net Sales	Beginning Inventory	Net Purchases	Ending Inventory	Cost of Goods Sold	Gross Profit
Maple	$101,800	$12,500	$62,700	$19,400	(a)	$37,000
Walnut	(b)	25,450	93,000	(c)	$94,100	43,200
Pine	94,700	(d)	54,900	22,600	62,500	(e)
Magnolia	84,300	10,700	(f)	8,200	(g)	47,100

Prepare the income statement for Magnolia Company, which uses the periodic inventory system. Include a complete heading. Magnolia's operating expenses for the year were $31,600.

E9-9 ← *Link Back to Chapter 5 (Gross Profit Percentage and Inventory Turnover).* Refer to the data in Exercise 9-8. Suppose you are a financial analyst, and a client has asked you to recommend an investment in one of these companies. Which company is likely to be the most profitable, based on its gross profit percentage and rate of inventory turnover? Write a memo outlining which company you recommend, and explain your reasoning. Use the following format for your memo:

Measuring profitability (Obj. 3)

Date: _____	
To:	Investor
From: _____	
RE:	Investment recommendation

E9-10 Picker's Paradise carries a large inventory of guitars and other musical instruments. Because each item is expensive, Picker's uses a perpetual inventory system. Company records indicate the following for a particular line of Honeydew guitars:

Determining ending inventory and cost of goods sold in a perpetual system (Obj. 1, 2)

Date	Item	Quantity	Unit Cost
May 1	Balance.....................	5	$95
6	Sale...........................	3	
8	Purchase...................	11	83
17	Sale...........................	4	
30	Sale...........................	1	

Required

Determine the amounts that Picker's should report for ending inventory and cost of goods sold by the FIFO method. Prepare the perpetual inventory record for the guitars, using Exhibit 9-9 as a guide.

E9-11 Homestake Industries is considering a change from the LIFO inventory method to the FIFO method. Managers are concerned about the effect of this change on income tax expense and reported net income. If the change is made, it will become effective on March 1. Inventory on hand at February 28 is $63,000. During March, Homestake managers expect sales of $295,000, net purchases between $159,000 and $182,000, and operating expenses of $83,000. Inventories at March 31 are budgeted as follows: FIFO, $85,000; LIFO, $78,000.

Change from LIFO to FIFO (Obj. 3)

Required

Create a spreadsheet to compute estimated net income four ways: Net purchases may be $159,000 or $182,000 for March under both FIFO and LIFO. Format your answer as follows:

	A	B	C	D	E
1		**HOMESTAKE INDUSTRIES**			
2		**Estimated Income under FIFO and LIFO**			
3		**March 20XX**			
4					
5		**FIFO**	**LIFO**	**FIFO**	**LIFO**
6					
7	Sales	$295,000	$295,000	$295,000	$295,000
8					
9	Cost of goods sold				
10	Beginning inventory	63,000	63,000	63,000	63,000
11	Net purchases	159,000	159,000	182,000	182,000
12					
13	Cost of goods available				
14	Ending inventory	85,000	78,000	85,000	78,000
15					
16	Cost of goods sold				
17					
18	Gross profit				
19	Operating expenses	83,000	83,000	83,000	83,000
20					
21	Net income	$	$	$	$

E9-12 Willitz Paper Supply is nearing the end of its best year ever. With three weeks until year end, it appears that net income for the year will have increased by 70% over last year. Bruce Willitz, the principal stockholder and president, is pleased with the year's success but unhappy about the huge increase in income taxes that the business will have to pay.

He asks you, the financial vice president, to come up with a way to decrease the business's income tax. Inventory quantities are a little lower than normal because sales have been especially strong during the last few months. Willitz Paper Supply uses the LIFO inventory method, and inventory costs have risen dramatically late in the year.

Required

Write a memorandum to Bruce Willitz to explain how Willitz Paper Supply can decrease its income taxes for the current year. Willitz is a man of integrity, so your plan must be completely honest. Adapt the memo format given for Exercise 9-9.

E9-13 This exercise tests your understanding of the four inventory methods. In the space provided, write the name of the inventory method that best fits the description. Assume that the cost of inventory is rising.

_____ a. Generally associated with saving income taxes.

_____ b. Results in a cost of ending inventory that is close to the current cost of replacing the inventory.

_____ c. Used to account for automobiles, jewelry, and art objects.

_____ d. Provides a middle-ground measure of ending inventory and cost of goods sold.

_____ e. Maximizes reported income.

_____ f. Enables a company to buy high-cost inventory at year end and thereby decrease reported income.

_____ g. Reported income and income taxes rise when the company liquidates older, low-cost, layers of inventory.

_____ h. Matches the most current cost of goods sold against sales revenue.

_____ i. Results in an old measure of the cost of ending inventory.

E9-14 Alcoa Enterprises, which uses a perpetual inventory system, has these account balances at December 31, 20X1, prior to releasing the financial statements for the year:

INVENTORY	COST OF GOODS SOLD	SALES REVENUE
Beg. bal. 12,489		
End bal. 18,028	Bal. 113,245	Bal. 225,000

A year ago, when Alcoa prepared its 20X0 financial statements, the replacement cost of ending inventory was $13,051. Alcoa has determined that the replacement cost (current market value) of the December 31, 20X1, ending inventory is $16,840.

Required

Prepare Alcoa Enterprises 20X1 income statement through gross profit to show how Alcoa would apply the lower-of-cost-or-market rule to its inventories. Include a complete heading for the statement.

E9-15 Nash-Robin Food Wholesalers uses a periodic inventory system and reports inventory at the lower of FIFO cost or market. Prior to releasing its March 20X4 financial statements, Nash-Robin's preliminary income statement appears as follows:

NASH-ROBIN FOOD WHOLESALERS
Income Statement (partial)

Sales revenue		$112,000
Cost of goods sold:		
Beginning inventory	$17,200	
Net purchases	51,700	
Cost of goods available for sale	68,900	
Ending inventory	(23,800)	
Cost of goods sold		45,100
Gross profit		$ 66,900

Nash-Robin has determined that the current replacement cost of ending inventory is $19,800.

Required

Adjust the preceding income statement to apply the lower-of-cost-or market rule to Nash-Robin's inventory. Also show the relevant portion of Nash-Robin's balance sheet. The replacement cost of Nash-Robin's beginning inventory was $18,600.

E9-16 Lazlo Power Tools reported the following comparative income statement for the years ended September 30, 20X2 and 20X1.

Correcting an inventory error—two years
(Obj. 5)

LAZLO POWER TOOLS Income Statements Years Ended September 30, 20X2 and 20X1				
	20X2		**20X1**	
Sales revenue........................		$137,300		$121,700
Cost of goods sold:				
Beginning inventory........	$14,000		$12,800	
Net purchases...................	72,000		66,000	
Cost of goods available.....	86,000		78,800	
Ending inventory.............	(16,600)		(14,000)	
Cost of goods sold		69,400		64,800
Gross profit		67,900		56,900
Operating expenses		30,300		26,100
Net income		$ 37,600		$ 30,800

During 20X2, accountants for the company discovered that ending 20X1 inventory was overstated by $3,500. Prepare the corrected comparative income statement for the two-year period, complete with a heading for the statement. What was the effect of the error on net income for the two years combined? Explain your answer.

E9-17 Lakely Marineland began January with inventory of $47,500. The business made net purchases of $37,600 and had net sales of $60,000 before a fire destroyed the company's inventory. For the past several years, Lakely's gross profit on sales has been 40%. Use the gross profit method to estimate the cost of the inventory destroyed by the fire. Identify another purpose for which managers use the gross profit method to estimate inventory cost.

Estimating ending inventory by the gross profit method
(Obj. 6)

Challenge Exercises

E9-18 For each of the following situations, identify the inventory method that you would use, or, given the use of a particular method, state the strategy that you would follow to accomplish your goal.

Inventory policy decisions
(Obj. 2, 3)

  a. Suppliers of your inventory are threatening a labor strike, and it may be difficult for your company to obtain inventory. This situation could increase your income taxes.

  b. Inventory costs are decreasing, and your company's board of directors wants to minimize income taxes.

  c. Inventory costs are increasing. Your company uses LIFO and is having a very good year. It is near year end, and you need to keep net income from increasing too much.

  d. Inventory costs have been stable for several years, and you expect costs to remain stable for the indefinite future. (Give the reason for your choice of method.)

  e. Company management, like those of **Polaroid** and **Hewlett-Packard,** prefers a middle-of-the-road inventory policy that avoids extremes.

  f. Inventory costs are increasing, and the company prefers to report high income.

E9-19 ↤ *Link Back to Chapter 5 (Income Statement and Balance Sheet).* **Campbell Soup Company** uses a perpetual inventory system and the LIFO method to determine the cost of its inventory. During the year ended July 31, 19X9, Campbell Soup reported the following items (adapted) in its financial statements (amounts in millions)

Reporting inventory transactions on the income statement and balance sheet
(Obj. 1)

Cost of goods sold............	$3,050	Revenues, total	$6,424
Other expenses................	2,650	Total assets	5,522
Owners' equity................	?	Total liabilities	5,287

1. Prepare Campbell Soup Company's summary income statement for the year ended July 31, 19X9, complete with a heading.
2. Prepare Campbell Soup Company's summary balance sheet at July 31, 19X9, complete with a heading.

(Group A) PROBLEMS

Accounting for inventory in a perpetual system
(Obj. 1, 2)

P9-1A Pier 1 Imports operates more than 800 stores. Assume you are dealing with one department in a Pier 1 store in Dallas. The company's fiscal year ends each February 28. Also assume the department began fiscal year 20X0 with an inventory of 50 units that cost $2,135. During the year, the department purchased merchandise on account as follows:

March (60 units @ $32)	$1,920
August (40 units @ $34)	1,360
October (180 units @ $35)	6,300
Total purchases	$9,580

Cash payments on account during the year totaled $9,110.

During fiscal year 20X0, the department sold 300 units of merchandise for $13,400, of which $4,700 was for cash and the balance was on account. Pier 1 uses the weighted-average cost method for inventories.

Operating expenses for the year were $2,430. The department paid two-thirds in cash and accrued the rest.

Required

1. Make summary journal entries to record the department's transactions for the year ended February 28, 20X0. The company uses a perpetual inventory system.
2. Determine the weighted-average cost of the department's ending inventory at February 28, 20X0. Follow the computational approach illustrated in Exhibit 9-5.
3. Prepare the department's income statement for the year ended February 28, 20X0. Show totals for gross profit and net income.

Using the cost-of-goods-sold model to budget operations
(Obj. 1)

P9-2A Condensed versions of a **Shell** convenience store's most recent income statement and balance sheet reported the following. The business is organized as a proprietorship, so it pays no income tax. It uses a periodic inventory system.

SHELL CONVENIENCE STORE
Income Statement
Year Ended December 31, 20X1

(Thousands)	
Sales	$900
Cost of sales	720
Gross profit	180
Operating expenses	90
Net income	$ 90

SHELL CONVENIENCE STORE
Balance Sheet
December 31, 20X1

(Thousands) Assets		Liabilities and Capital	
Cash	$ 40	Accounts payable	$ 30
Inventories	70	Note payable	190
Land and buildings, net	270	Total liabilities	220
		Owner, capital	160
Total assets	$380	Total liabilities and capital	$380

The owner is budgeting for 20X2. He expects sales and cost of sales to increase by 9%. To meet customer demand for the increase in sales, ending inventory will need to be $80 thousand at December 31, 20X2. The owner can lower operating expenses by doing some of the work himself. He hopes to earn a net income of $110 thousand next year.

Required

1. A key variable the owner can control is the amount of inventory he purchases. Show how to determine the amount of purchases the owner should make in 20X2.
2. Prepare the store's budgeted income statement for 20X2 to reach the target net income of $110 thousand.

Using the perpetual and periodic inventory systems
(Obj. 1, 2)

P9-3A Rambler Lawn Supply began March with 50 units of inventory that cost $17 each. The sale price of each unit was $36. During March, Rambler completed these inventory transactions:

	Units	Unit Cost	Unit Sale Price
March 2 Purchase	12	$20	$37
8 Sale.......................	27	17	36
13 Sale.......................	23	17	36
	1	20	37
17 Purchase...............	24	20	37
22 Sale.......................	31	20	37
29 Purchase...............	24	21	39

Required

1. The preceding data are taken from Rambler's perpetual inventory records. Which cost method does Rambler use?
2. Determine Rambler's cost of goods sold for March under the

   a. Perpetual inventory system   b. Periodic inventory system

3. Compute gross profit for March.

P9-4A A Best Yet Electronic Center began December with 140 units of inventory that cost $75 each. During December, the store made the following purchases:

Computing inventory by three methods (Obj. 2, 3)

Dec. 3	217 @ $79
12	95 @ 82
18	210 @ 83
24	248 @ 87

The store uses the periodic inventory system, and the physical count at December 31 indicates that ending inventory consists of 229 units.

Required

1. Determine the ending inventory and cost-of-goods-sold amounts for the December financial statements under the weighted-average, FIFO, and LIFO cost methods. Round weighted-average cost per unit to the nearest cent and all other amounts to the nearest dollar.
2. How much income tax would Best Yet save during December for this one store by using LIFO versus FIFO? The income tax rate is 40%.

P9-5A Assume the records of **Drug Emporium** include the following accounts for one of its products at December 31 of the current year:

Preparing an income statement directly from the accounts (Obj. 2, 3)

INVENTORY

Jan. 1 Balance	300 units @ $3.00	1,215
	100 units @ 3.15	

PURCHASES

Feb. 6	800 units @ $3.15	2,520
May 19	600 units @ 3.35	2,010
Aug. 12	460 units @ 3.50	1,610
Oct. 4	800 units @ 3.95	3,160
Dec. 31—Balance		9,300

SALES REVENUE

Dec. 31	2,600 units	11,200

Required

1. Prepare a partial income statement through gross profit under the weighted-average, FIFO, and LIFO cost methods. Round weighted-average cost to the nearest cent and all other amounts to the nearest dollar. Assume **Drug Emporium** uses a periodic inventory system.
2. Which inventory method would you use to report the highest net income?

Applying the lower-of-cost-or-market rule to inventories
(Obj. 4)

P9-6A **Revco Drug** has been plagued with lackluster sales, and some of the company's merchandise is gathering dust. It is now December 31, 20X1. Assume the current replacement cost of a Revco store's ending inventory is $700,000 below what Revco paid for the goods, which was $3,900,000. Before any adjustments at the end of the period, assume the store's Cost of Goods Sold account has a balance of $22,400,000.

What action should Revco take in this situation, if any? Give any journal entry required. At what amount should Revco report Inventory on the balance sheet? At what amount should the company report Cost of Goods Sold on the income statement? Discuss the accounting principle or concept that is most relevant to this situation.

Correcting inventory errors over a three-year period
(Obj. 5)

P9-7A The accounting records of Treviño's Mexican Restaurant show these data (in thousands):

	20X3	20X2	20X1
Net sales revenue......................	$210	$165	$170
Cost of goods sold:			
Beginning inventory	$ 15	$ 25	$ 40
Net purchases........................	135	100	90
Cost of goods available..........	150	125	130
Less: Ending inventory.......	(30)	(15)	(25)
Cost of goods sold.................	120	110	105
Gross profit	90	55	65
Operating expenses..................	74	38	46
Net income..............................	$ 16	$ 17	$ 19

In early 20X4, internal auditors discovered that the ending inventory for 20X1 had been understated by $8 thousand and that the ending inventory for 20X3 had been overstated by $5 thousand. The ending inventory at December 31, 20X2, was correct.

Required

1. Show corrected income statements for the three years.
2. State whether each year's net income as reported here and the related owner's equity amounts are understated or overstated. Ignore income tax because Treviño's is organized as a proprietorship. For each incorrect figure, indicate the amount of the understatement or overstatement.

Estimating ending inventory by the gross profit method; preparing the income statement
(Obj. 6)

P9-8A Padgitt Camera Store estimates its inventory by the gross profit method when preparing monthly financial statements. For the past two years, gross profit has averaged 32% of net sales. Assume further that the company's inventory records for stores in the northwestern region reveal the following data (amounts in thousands):

Inventory, March 1	$ 292
Transactions during March:	
Purchases	6,585
Purchase discounts...........................	149
Purchase returns	8
Sales	8,657
Sales returns.....................................	17

Required

1. Estimate the March 31 inventory using the gross profit method.
2. Prepare the March income statement through gross profit for the Padgitt Camera Store stores in the northwestern region.

Reporting inventory items on the income statement and balance sheet
(Obj. 1)

P9-9A ↞ *Link Back to Chapter 5 (Merchandiser's Income Statement and Balance Sheet).* **Gap Inc.,** uses a perpetual inventory system and the FIFO method to determine the cost of its inventory. During a recent year, Gap reported the following items (as adapted) in its financial statements (amounts in millions):

Cost of goods sold....................	$ 6,775	Owners' equity	$?
Long-term liabilities................	1,203	Property, plant, and	
Net sales revenue	11,635	equipment, net......................	2,715
Other assets.............................	276	Total current assets	2,198
Other expenses........................	3,733	Total current liabilities.............	1,753

Required

1. Prepare Gap's single-step income statement for the year ended January 29, 20X0, complete with a heading.
2. Prepare Gap's balance sheet at January 29, 20X0, complete with a heading.

PROBLEMS

P9-1B **Toys "Я" Us** purchases inventory in crates of merchandise, so each unit of inventory is a crate of toys. Assume you are dealing with a single department in the Toys "Я" Us store in Santa Barbara, California. The fiscal year of Toys "Я" Us ends each January 31.

Accounting for inventory using the perpetual system (Obj. 1, 2)

Assume the department began fiscal year 20X5 with an inventory of 20 units that cost a total of $1,200. During the year, the department purchased merchandise on accounts as follows:

April (30 units @ $65)	$ 1,950
August (50 units @ $65)	3,250
November (110 units @ $70)...............	7,700
Total purchases	$12,900

Cash payments on account during the year totaled $11,390.

During fiscal year 20X5, the department sold 180 units of merchandise for $16,400, of which $5,300 was for cash and the balance was on account. Toys "Я" Us uses the LIFO method for inventories. Department operating expenses for the year were $3,630. The department paid two-thirds in cash and accrued the rest.

Required

1. Make summary journal entries to record the department's transactions for the year ended January 31, 20X5. Toys "Я" Us uses a perpetual inventory system.
2. Determine the LIFO cost of the store's ending inventory at January 31, 20X5. Use a T-account.
3. Prepare the department's income statement for the year ended January 31, 20X5. Include a complete heading, and show totals for gross profit and net income.

P9-2B Condensed versions of a **Chevron** convenience store's most recent income statement and balance sheet reported the following figures. The business uses a periodic inventory system.

Using the cost-of-goods-sold model to budget operations (Obj. 1)

CHEVRON CONVENIENCE STORE Balance Sheet December 31, 20X4			
(Thousands)	**Assets**	**Liabilities and Capital**	
Cash.................................	$ 70	Accounts payable.............	$ 35
Inventories	35	Note payable.....................	280
Land and buildings, net...	360	Total liabilities.................	315
		Owner, capital..................	150
Total assets......................	$465	Total liabilities and capital	$465

CHEVRON CONVENIENCE STORE Income Statement Year Ended December 31, 20X4	
	(Thousands)
Sales...	$800
Cost of sales...............................	660
Gross profit.................................	140
Operating expenses	80
Net income	$ 60

The owner is budgeting for 20X5. He expects sales and cost of sales to increase by 8%. To meet customer demand for the increase in sales, ending inventory will need to be $40 thousand at December 31, 20X5. The owner can lower operating expenses by doing some of the work himself. He hopes to earn a net income of $75 thousand next year.

Required

1. A key variable the owner can control is the amount of inventory he purchases. Show how to determine the amount of purchases he should make in 20X5 (amounts in thousands).
2. Prepare the store's budgeted income statement for 20X5 to reach the target net income of $75 thousand.

P9-3B A **Samsonite** outlet store began August 20X1 with 50 units of inventory that cost $40 each. The sale price of these units was $70. During August, the store completed these inventory transactions:

Using the perpetual and periodic inventory systems (Obj. 1, 2)

		Units	Unit Cost	Unit Sale Price
Aug. 3	Sale..........................	16	$40	$70
8	Purchase.................	80	41	72
11	Sale..........................	34	40	70
19	Sale..........................	9	41	72
24	Sale..........................	35	41	72
30	Purchase.................	18	42	73
31	Sale..........................	11	41	72

Required

1. The preceding data are taken from the store's perpetual inventory records. Which cost method does the store use?
2. Determine the store's cost of goods sold for August under the

    a. Perpetual inventory system   **b.** Periodic inventory system

3. Compute gross profit for August.

Computing inventory by three methods
(Obj. 2, 3)

P9-4B Lafferty Framing Co. began March with 73 units of inventory that cost $23 each. During the month, Lafferty made the following purchases:

March 4................................	113 @ $26
12................................	81 @ 30
19................................	167 @ 32
25................................	44 @ 35

The company uses the periodic inventory system, and the physical count at March 31 includes 51 units.

Required

1. Determine the ending inventory and cost-of-goods-sold amounts for the March financial statements under (a) weighted-average cost, (b) FIFO cost, and (c) LIFO cost. Round weighted-average cost per unit to the nearest cent and all other amounts to the nearest dollar.
2. How much income tax would Lafferty Framing save during the month by using LIFO versus FIFO? The income tax rate is 35%.

Preparing an income statement directly from the accounts
(Obj. 2, 3)

P9-5B The records of Heavenly Confection Co. include the following accounts at December 31 of the current year:

INVENTORY

Jan. 1	Balance (700 units @ $6.45)	4,515

PURCHASES

Jan. 6	300 units @ $7.05	2,115
Mar. 19	1,100 units @ 7.35	8,085
June 22	8,400 units @ 7.50	63,000
Oct. 4	500 units @ 8.50	4,250
Dec. 31	Balance	77,450

SALES REVENUE

Dec. 31	10,100 units	138,070

Required

1. Prepare a partial income statement through gross profit under the weighted-average, FIFO, and LIFO methods. Round weighted-average cost to the nearest cent and all other amounts to the nearest dollar. Heavenly Confection uses a periodic inventory system.
2. Which inventory method would you use to minimize income tax?

P9-6B **The Army/Navy Surplus Store** has experienced lackluster sales, and some of the company's merchandise is gathering dust. It is now December 31, 20X2, and the current replacement cost of the ending inventory is $650,000 below what Army/Navy actually paid for the goods, which was $4,900,000. Before any adjustments at the end of the period, the company's Cost of Goods Sold account has a balance of $29,600,000.

Applying the lower-of-cost-or-market rule to inventories (Obj. 4)

What action should The Army/Navy Surplus Store take in this situation, if any? Give any journal entry required. At what amount should Army/Navy report Inventory on the balance sheet? At what amount should the company report Cost of Goods Sold on the income statement? Discuss the accounting principle or concept that is most relevant to this situation.

P9-7B The Lamarque Copper Company books show the data (in thousands) on page 435. In early 20X3, internal auditors found that the ending inventory for 20X0 had been overstated by $8 thousand and that the ending inventory for 20X2 had been understated by $4 thousand. The ending inventory at December 31, 20X1, was correct.

Correcting inventory errors over a three-year period (Obj. 5)

(Thousands)	20X2		20X1		20X0	
Net sales revenue		$360		$285		$244
Cost of goods sold:						
Beginning inventory...........	$ 65		$ 55		$ 70	
Net purchases......................	195		135		130	
Cost of goods available	260		190		200	
Less: Ending inventory.....	(70)		(65)		(55)	
Cost of goods sold		190		125		145
Gross profit.............................		170		160		99
Operating expenses		113		109		76
Net income		$ 57		$ 51		$ 23

Required

1. Show corrected income statements for the three years.
2. State whether each year's net income and owner's equity amounts are understated or overstated. Ignore income tax because Lamarque is a proprietorship. For each incorrect figure, indicate the amount of the understatement or overstatement.

P9-8B Beaucock Publishing estimates its inventory by the gross profit method when preparing monthly financial statements. The gross profit has averaged 43% of net sales. The company's inventory records reveal the following data (amounts in thousands):

Estimating ending inventory by the gross profit method; preparing the income statement (Obj. 6)

Inventory, July 1............................	$ 367
Transactions during July:	
Purchases	3,789
Purchase discounts....................	26
Purchase returns	12
Sales	6,430
Sales returns.............................	25

Required

1. Estimate the July 31 inventory, using the gross profit method.
2. Prepare the July income statement through gross profit for Beaucock Publishing.

P9-9B ← *Link Back to Chapter 5 (Merchandiser's Income Statement and Balance Sheet).* **Lands' End, Inc.,** uses a perpetual inventory system and the LIFO method to determine the cost of its inventory. During a recent year, Lands' End reported the following items (adapted) in its financial statements (amounts in millions):

Reporting inventory items on the income statement and balance sheet (Obj. 1)

Cost of goods sold......................	$ 727	Interest revenue	$ 1
Long-term liabilities	9	Owners' equity............................	?
Net sales revenue	1,320	Property, plant, & equipment, net	166
Other assets..............................	1	Total current assets.......................	289
Other expenses..........................	546	Total current liabilities.................	151

Required

1. Prepare a single-step income statement for Lands' End for the year ended January 28, 2000, complete with a heading.
2. Prepare the Lands' End balance sheet at January 28, 2000, complete with a heading.

APPLY YOUR KNOWLEDGE

DECISION CASES

Measuring the impact of a year-end purchase of inventory (Obj. 2, 3)

Case 1. Lena's Shoes is nearing the end of its first year of operations. The company made inventory purchases of $745,000 during the year, as follows:

January...................	1,000 units @ $100.00	=	$100,000
July.......................	4,000	121.25	485,000
November.............	1,000	160.00	160,000
Totals....................	6,000		$745,000

Sales for the year will be 5,000 units for $1,200,000 revenue. Expenses other than cost of goods sold and income taxes will be $200,000. The president of the company is undecided about whether to adopt the FIFO method or the LIFO method for inventories.

The company has storage capacity for 5,000 additional units of inventory. Inventory prices are expected to stay at $160 per unit for the next few months. The president is considering purchasing 1,000 additional units of inventory at $160 each before the end of the year. He wishes to know how the purchase would affect net income under both FIFO and LIFO. The income tax rate is 42%.

Required

1. To aid the decision, prepare income statements under FIFO and under LIFO, both without and with the year-end purchase of 1,000 units of inventory at $160 per unit.
2. Compare net income under FIFO without and with the year-end purchase. Make the same comparison under LIFO. Under which method does the year-end purchase affect net income?

Assessing the impact of the inventory costing methods on the financial statements (Obj. 2, 3, 4)

Case 2. The inventory costing method a company chooses can affect the financial statements and thus the decisions of the people who use those statements.

Required

1. A leading accounting researcher stated that one inventory costing method reports the most recent costs in the income statement, while another reports the most recent costs in the balance sheet. What did the researcher mean? Name the methods.
2. Conservatism is an accepted accounting concept. Would you want the management of your company to be conservative in accounting for inventory? Give your reason.
3. TriArc Co. follows conservative accounting and writes the value of its inventory of bicycles down to market, which has declined below cost. The following year, an unexpected cycling craze results in a demand for bicycles that far exceeds supply, and the market price increases above the previous cost. What effect will conservatism have on the income of TriArc during each year?

ETHICAL ISSUE

During 20X2, Darden Furniture Company changed to the LIFO method of accounting for inventory. Suppose that during 20X3, Darden changes back to the FIFO method and the following year switches back to LIFO again.

Required

1. What would you think of a company's ethics if it changes accounting methods every year?

2. What accounting principle would changing methods every year violate?
3. Who can be harmed when a company changes its accounting methods too often? How?

FINANCIAL STATEMENT CASE

The notes are an important part of a company's financial statements, giving valuable details that would clutter the tabular data presented in the statements. This case will help you learn to use a company's inventory notes. Refer to the **Target** financial statements and related notes in Appendix A and answer the following questions:

Analyzing inventories
(Obj. 2)

Required

1. How much was the Target merchandise inventory at January 29, 2000? At January 30, 1999?
2. How does Target value its inventories? Which cost methods does the company use? Ignore the *retail method* that Target refers to.
3. By rearranging the cost-of-goods-sold formula, you can determine purchases, which are not disclosed in the Target statements. How much were the company's inventory purchases during the year ended January 29, 2000?

TEAM PROJECT

◂◂ *Link Back to Chapter 5 (Gross Profit Percentage and Inventory Turnover).* Obtain the annual reports of as many companies as you have team members—one company per team member. Most companies post their financial statements on their Web sites.

Required

1. Identify the inventory method used by each company.
2. Compute each company's gross profit percentage and rate of inventory turnover for the most recent two years.
3. For the industries of the companies you are analyzing, obtain the industry averages for gross profit percentage and inventory turnover from Robert Morris Associates, *Annual Statement Studies;* Dun and Bradstreet, *Industry Norms and Key Business Ratios;* or Leo Troy, *Almanac of Business and Industrial Financial Ratios.*
4. How well does each of your companies compare to the average for its industry? What insight about your companies can you glean from these ratios?

INTERNET EXERCISE

General Motors (GM) remains the world's Number 1 maker of cars and trucks, including the Buick, Cadillac, Chevrolet, GMC, Oldsmobile, Pontiac, and Saturn brands.

1. In the past, General Motors has also been ranked Number 1 in the Fortune 500 listing. Go to **http://www.Fortune.com** and under "Lists" click on *Fortune 500.* What is GM's Fortune 500 ranking this year?
2. Click on *General Motors* and then click on the URL for GM, **www.gm.com,** and go to GM's Web site. Click on *The Company* followed by *Investor Information.* Select the *most recent annual report* and watch the video show. Use the information in the annual report to answer the following questions.
   a. Read the "Letter to Stockholders." Did GM have a good year? Give the basis for your evaluation.
   b. Refer to the "Consolidated Statements of Income for General Motors Corporation and Subsidiaries." For the two most recent years, list the amounts reported for "Total net sales and revenues" and "Cost of sales and other operating expenses." For each year, calculate gross profit. Comment on the trend of gross profit, what the trend indicates, and whether the trend is favorable or unfavorable.
   c. Refer to the "Consolidated Balance Sheets for General Motors Corporation and Subsidiaries." For the two most recent years, list the amounts reported for "Inventories." For the most recent year, calculate the rate of inventory turnover. On average, how many days does GM hold inventory before selling it?

General Motors

[MASTERING
m
B
BUSINESS
accounting]

Go to the "Depreciation Methods and Inventory Cost Flow Assumptions" episode on the *Mastering Accounting* CD-Rom for an interactive, video-enhanced exercise focused on the different methods for depreciation and inventory. CanGo staff must prepare reports that present potential investors with the best possible financial outlook for the company.

COMPARING THE PERPETUAL AND PERIODIC INVENTORY SYSTEMS

○ DAILY EXERCISE 9-4

Exhibit 9A-1 provides a side-by-side comparison of the two inventory accounting systems. It combines the material from Exhibits 9-3 and 9-4. Both systems report the same amounts for inventory, cost of goods sold, and everything else.

Answer the following questions about various features of the perpetual inventory system and the periodic inventory system.

1. Do the perpetual and periodic inventory systems result in the same or different dollar amounts for Inventory and Cost of Goods Sold? Explain.

2. a. Which inventory system records the cost of inventory purchased as an asset and the cost of inventory sold as expense?

   b. Which inventory system records the cost of inventory purchased as an expense (name the expense account) and then sets up the cost of ending inventory as an asset?

3. Suppose your company produces microchips for use in making computer circuit boards. Technology is advancing rapidly, and you need monthly financial statements to remain competitive. Which inventory system should you use?

PANEL A — Recording in the Journal and Posting to the T-accounts

Perpetual System	Periodic System

1. Credit purchases of $560,000:
Inventory................................... 560,000
    Accounts Payable.............   560,000
	1. Credit purchases of $560,000:
	Purchases.................................... 560,000
	    Accounts Payable.............. 560,000

2. Credit sales of $900,000 (cost $540,000):
Accounts Receivable................... 900,000
    Sales Revenue.........................   900,000
 	
Cost of Goods Sold 540,000
    Inventory..........................   540,000
	2. Credit sales of $900,000:
	Accounts Receivable................... 900,000
	    Sales Revenue................... 900,000

3. End-of-period entries:
 	
No entries required. Both Inventory and Cost of Goods Sold are up-to-date.
	3. End-of-period entries to update Inventory and record Cost of Goods Sold:
	a. Transfer the cost of beginning inventory ($100,000) to Cost of Goods Sold:
	Cost of Goods Sold 100,000
	    Inventory (beginning balance) 100,000
	
	b. Record the cost of ending inventory ($120,000) based on a physical count:
	Inventory (ending balance)........ 120,000
	    Cost of Goods Sold............ 120,000
	
	c. Transfer the cost of purchases to Cost of Goods Sold:
	Cost of Goods Sold 560,000
	    Purchases.......................... 560,000

Perpetual System

INVENTORY AND COST OF GOODS SOLD ACCOUNTS

INVENTORY		COST OF GOODS SOLD	
100,000*	540,000	540,000	
560,000			
120,000			

*Beginning inventory was $100,000

Periodic System

INVENTORY AND COST OF GOODS SOLD ACCOUNTS

INVENTORY		COST OF GOODS SOLD	
100,000**	100,000	100,000	120,000
120,000		560,000	
		540,000	

**Beginning inventory was $100,000

PANEL B — Reporting in the Financial Statements

Perpetual System	Periodic System
Income Statement (partial)	
Sales revenue $900,000	Sales revenue $900,000
Cost of goods sold .... 540,000 ←	Cost of goods sold:
Gross profit............................. $360,000	Beginning inventory...................... $100,000
	Purchases...................................... 560,000
	Cost of goods available for sale...... 660,000
	Less: Ending inventory .... (120,000)
	Cost of goods sold 540,000
	Gross profit.. $360,000
Balance Sheet (partial)	
Current assets:	Current assets:
Cash .... $ XXX	Cash... $ XXX
Accounts receivable XXX	Accounts receivable...................... XXX
Inventories.......................... 120,000 ←→	Inventories 120,000

10

Plant Assets and Intangible Assets

LEARNING OBJECTIVES

*After studying this chapter,
you should be able to*

1. Measure the cost of a plant asset

2. Account for depreciation

3. Select the best depreciation method for income tax purposes

4. Account for the disposal of a plant asset

5. Account for natural resource assets and depletion

6. Account for intangible assets and amortization

The Home Depot is the world's largest home improvement dealer and ranks among the largest retailers in the United States. The company has experienced major growth, and it plans to keep expanding. The Home Depot's business strategy is twofold: (1) offer high-quality merchandise at "Day-In, Day-Out" warehouse prices and (2) provide exceptional customer service.

Fiscal 1999 (the year ended January 30, 2000) marked the 13th straight year of record profits. Assets topped $17 billion. Over $10 billion of these assets are property, plant, and equipment, the subject of this chapter.

Source: The Home Depot® *1999 Annual Report.*

ow did **The Home Depot** grow so rapidly? By opening new stores at a fast pace. The Home Depot's balance sheet (Exhibit 10-2) shows the effect of the company's growth. During the most recent year, total assets grew to $17.1 billion (line 13). Much of the growth shows up in Property and equipment (lines 2–10), collectively labeled *plant assets,* which we examine in this chapter. ➤➤

◄═ We introduced plant assets in Chapter 3, page 90.

This chapter also covers *intangibles,* those assets without physical form, such as Cost in excess of the fair value of net assets acquired—better known as *goodwill.* This is the next-to-last asset reported on Home Depot's balance sheet (line 11). Finally, we discuss natural resources (such as oil, gas, timber, and gravel). The expenses that relate to plant assets, natural resources, and intangible assets are *depreciation, depletion,* and *amortization.*

Chapter 10 concludes our coverage of assets, except for investments (Chapter 16). After completing this chapter, you should understand the various assets of a business and how to account for them.

MEASURING THE COST OF PLANT ASSETS

Plant assets, or **fixed assets,** are long-lived tangible assets—for instance, land, buildings, and equipment—used to operate a business and not held for sale. Their physical form provides their usefulness. The expense associated with plant assets is called *depreciation.* ➤➤ Of the plant assets, land is unique. Its cost is *not* depreciated—expensed over time—because its usefulness does not decrease. Most companies report plant assets under the heading Property, plant, and equipment on the balance sheet.

PLANT ASSETS. Long-lived tangible assets, such as land, buildings, and equipment, used to operate a business. Also called **fixed assets.**

◄═ We introduced the concept of depreciation in Chapter 3, page 90.

Intangible assets do not have a physical form. We cannot see or touch them. They are useful only because of the special rights they carry. Patents, copyrights, and trademarks are intangible assets, and their accounting is similar to that for plant assets. Accounting for intangibles has its own terminology. Exhibit 10-1 shows that we refer to the using up of intangibles as *amortization,* which is the same concept as depreciation.

INTANGIBLE ASSETS. Assets with no physical form. Valuable because of the special rights they carry. Examples are patents and copyrights.

To begin our study, let's take a tour of **The Home Depot** balance sheet in Exhibit 10-2. The company holds land, buildings, and other plant assets (lines 2–8). Total cost is $11.9 billion (line 8). Home Depot has used up (depreciated) $1.7 billion of its plant assets (line 9). This is what accumulated depreciation on the balance sheet means—the used-up portion of the plant asset. The book value of these assets (cost less accumulated depreciation) is $10.2 billion (line 10). Home Depot's goodwill has a book value of $311 million (line 11).

The *cost principle* directs a business to carry an asset on the balance sheet at its cost—the amount paid for the asset. The general rule for measuring cost (repeated from Chapter 9, page 350) is

Objective 1
Measure the cost of a plant asset

$$\text{The cost of an asset} = \begin{array}{c}\textbf{The sum of all the costs incurred to bring the asset}\\ \textbf{to its intended purpose, net of all discounts}\end{array}$$

The *cost of a plant asset* is its purchase price plus applicable taxes, purchase commissions, and all other amounts paid to acquire the asset and make it ready for its intended use. In Chapter 9, we applied this principle to inventory. The types of costs differ for the various plant assets, so we discuss each asset individually.

Asset Account on the Balance Sheet	Related Expense Account on the Income Statement
Plant Assets	
Land..	None
Buildings, Machinery, and Equipment, Furniture and Fixtures, and Land Improvements	Depreciation
Natural Resources	Depletion
Intangibles..	Amortization

EXHIBIT 10-2
The Home Depot Balance Sheet
(partial, adapted)

THE HOME DEPOT, INC.
Balance Sheet (Adapted, Assets Only)
Amounts in Millions
January 30, 2000

Assets

	Current Assets:	
1	Total Current Assets	$6,390
	Property and Equipment, at cost:	
2	Land	3,248
3	Buildings	4,834
4	Furniture, fixtures, and equipment	2,279
5	Leasehold improvements	493
6	Construction in progress	791
7	Capital leases	245
8	Total cost of plant assets	11,890
9	Less Accumulated depreciation	(1,663)
10	Net property and equipment	10,227
11	Cost in excess of the fair value of net assets acquired, net of accumulated amortization of $33	311
12	Other assets	153
13	Total Assets	$17,081

Plant assets: rows 2–7

Intangibles: rows 11–12

DAILY EXERCISE 10-1

Land and Land Improvements

The cost of land includes its purchase price, brokerage commission, survey and legal fees, and any back property taxes that the purchaser pays. Land cost also includes the cost of clearing the land and removing any unwanted buildings. The cost of land is not depreciated.

The cost of land does *not* include fencing, paving, sprinkler systems, and lighting. These separate plant assets—called *land improvements*—are subject to depreciation.

Suppose The Home Depot signs a $500,000 note payable to purchase land for a store site. Home Depot also pays $40,000 in back property tax, $8,000 in transfer taxes, $5,000 to remove an old building, a $1,000 survey fee, and $260,000 to pave the parking lot, all in cash. What is the cost of this land? The cost of paving the lot, $260,000, is *not* included in the Land account. The pavement is a land improvement.

Purchase price of land..............		$500,000
Add related costs:		
Back property taxes...............	$40,000	
Transfer taxes	8,000	
Removal of building..............	5,000	
Survey fee	1,000	
Total related costs..................		54,000
Total cost of land......................		$554,000

Home Depot's entries to record purchase of the land and pavement of the parking lot are as follows:

Land	554,000	
Note Payable		500,000
Cash		54,000

We would say that The Home Depot *capitalized* the cost of the land at $554,000. This means that the company debited an asset account (Land) for $554,000.

Land Improvements	260,000	
Cash		260,000

Land and Land Improvements are two entirely separate asset accounts. Land improvements include lighting, signs, fences, paving, sprinkler systems, and landscaping. These costs are debited to the Land Improvements account and then depreciated over their useful life.

Buildings

 DAILY EXERCISE 10-2

The cost of constructing a building includes architectural fees, building permits, contractors' charges, and payments for material, labor, and overhead. The time to complete a building can be months, even years. If the company constructs its own assets, the cost of the building may include the cost of interest on borrowed money. (We discuss this topic in the next section of the chapter.) When an existing building is purchased, its cost includes all the usual items, plus the cost to repair and renovate the building.

Machinery and Equipment

The cost of machinery and equipment includes its purchase price (less any discounts), plus transportation charges, insurance while in transit, sales and other taxes, purchase commission, installation costs, and the cost of testing the asset before it is used. After the asset is up and running, we cease capitalizing these costs to the Equipment account. Thereafter, insurance, taxes, and maintenance costs are recorded as expenses.

Leasehold Improvements

Leasehold improvements are similar to land improvements. Leasehold improvements are alterations to assets the company is leasing. For example, The Home Depot leases store buildings, warehouses, and vehicles. The company customizes leased assets by painting its logo on trucks and buildings.

These improvements are assets of The Home Depot even though the company does not own the truck or building. Leasehold improvements appear on the company's balance sheet (see line 5 of Home Depot's balance sheet on page 388). Leasehold improvements should be amortized (depreciated) over the term of the lease.

Construction in Progress and Capital Leases

The Home Depot's balance sheet includes two additional categories of plant assets: Construction in progress (line 6) and Capital leases (line 7).

CONSTRUCTION IN PROGRESS *Construction in progress* is an asset, such as a warehouse, that the company is constructing for its own use. The construction is incomplete and the warehouse is not ready for use. However, the construction costs are assets because the warehouse, when completed, will render future benefits for the company.

CAPITAL LEASES A *capital lease* is a lease arrangement similar to the installment purchase of an asset. Companies report assets leased through capital leases as assets even though they do not own them. After all, their lease payments secure the use of the asset over the term of the lease. For example, The Home Depot has long-term capital leases on some of its store buildings. The Home Depot reports the cost of these plant assets under Capital leases on the balance sheet.

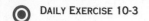 **DAILY EXERCISE 10-3**

A capital lease is different from an *operating lease,* which is an ordinary rental agreement, such as your dorm room or apartment lease or the rental of a **Hertz** automobile. The renter records rent expense for each payment under an operating lease.

Capitalizing the Cost of Interest

CAPITALIZE A COST. To record a cost as part of an asset's cost, rather than as an expense.

The Home Depot constructs some of its plant assets and finances the construction with borrowed money. The Home Depot pays interest that it includes as part of the cost of a self-constructed asset. Including interest in the asset's total cost is called *capitalizing interest.* To **capitalize a cost** means to debit an asset (versus an expense) account.

Suppose on July 2, 20X2, The Home Depot borrows $1,000,000 on a two-year, 10% note payable to build a warehouse. The interest cost for 20X2 on this note payable is $50,000 ($1,000,000 × .10 × 6/12). Assume all of this interest cost should be capitalized as part of the cost of the building. The Home Depot's entry for the construction cost is

20X2
July–Dec.   Building..   1,000,000
                 Cash   1,000,000
                 Incurred construction cost.

The Home Depot's entry to capitalize the interest paid at year end is as follows:

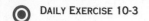 **DAILY EXERCISE 10-4**

20X2
Dec. 31   Building...   50,000
                 Cash   50,000
                 Paid interest on construction loan.

A Lump-Sum (Basket) Purchase of Assets

Businesses often purchase several assets as a group, or in a "basket," for a single amount. For example, a company may pay one price for land and an office building. For accounting purposes the company must identify the cost of each asset. The total cost is divided among the assets according to their relative sales (or market) values. This allocation technique is called the *relative-sales-value method.*

Suppose **Xerox Corporation** purchases land and a building in Kansas City for a midwestern sales office. The combined purchase price of land and building is $2,800,000. An appraisal indicates that the land's market (sales) value is $300,000 and that the building's market (sales) value is $2,700,000.

First, figure the ratio of each asset's market value to the total market value of both assets combined. Suppose the total appraised value is $2,700,000 + $300,000 = $3,000,000. Thus, the land, valued at $300,000, is 10% of the total market value. The building's appraised value is 90% of the total. The cost of each asset is determined as follows:

Asset	Market (Sales) Value	Percentage of Total Value			Total Purchase Price	Cost of Each Asset
Land	$ 300,000	$300,000/$3,000,000	= 10% ×	$2,800,000	=	$ 280,000
Building	2,700,000	$2,700,000/$3,000,000	= 90% ×	2,800,000	=	2,520,000
Total	$3,000,000		100%			$2,800,000

If Xerox pays cash, the entry to record the purchase of the land and building is

Land..   280,000
Building...   2,520,000
      Cash   2,800,000

WORK IT OUT

How would a business divide a $120,000 lump-sum purchase price for land, building, and equipment with estimated market values of $40,000, $95,000, and $15,000, respectively? Round decimals to three places.

Answer

Asset	Market (Sales) Value	Percentage of Total Value				Total Purchase Price		Cost of Each Asset
Land.............	$ 40,000	$40,000/$150,000	=	26.7%	×	$120,000	=	$ 32,040
Building.......	95,000	$95,000/$150,000	=	63.3%	×	120,000	=	75,960
Equipment...	15,000	$15,000/$150,000	=	10.0%	×	120,000	=	12,000
Total.............	$150,000			100.0%				$120,000

 DAILY EXERCISE 10-5

Capital Expenditures

When a company makes a plant asset expenditure, it must decide whether to debit an asset account or an expense account. In this context, *expenditure* refers to a cash or a credit purchase of goods or services related to the asset. Examples of such expenditures range from **General Motors'** purchase of robots for an assembly plant to a motorist's replacing the windshield on a Chevrolet.

Expenditures that increase the asset's capacity or efficiency or extend its useful life are called **capital expenditures.** For example, the cost of a major overhaul that extends a taxi's useful life is a capital expenditure. Repair work that generates a capital expenditure is called a **major repair,** or an **extraordinary repair.** The amount of the capital expenditure, said to be capitalized, is debited to an asset account. For an extraordinary repair on a taxi, we would debit the asset account Automobiles.

Other expenditures that do not extend the asset's capacity, which merely maintain the asset or restore it to working order, are called *expenses*. These costs are matched against revenue. Examples include the costs of repainting a taxi, repairing a dented fender, and replacing tires. These costs are debited to an expense account. For the **ordinary repairs** on the taxi, we would debit Repair Expense.

The distinction between capital and maintenance expenditures is often a matter of opinion. Does the cost extend the life of the asset (a capital expenditure), or does it only maintain the asset in good order (an expense)? When in doubt, companies tend to debit an expense, for two reasons. First, many expenditures are minor and most companies have a policy of debiting expense for all expenditures below a specific minimum, such as $1,000. Second, the income tax motive favors debiting all borderline expenditures to expense in order to create an immediate tax deduction. Exhibit 10-3 illustrates the distinction between capital expenditures and expenses for several delivery-truck expenditures.

CAPITAL EXPENDITURE. Expenditure that increases the capacity or efficiency of an asset or extends its useful life. Capital expenditures are debited to an asset account.

MAJOR REPAIR OR EXTRAORDINARY REPAIR. Repair work that generates a capital expenditure.

ORDINARY REPAIR. Repair work that is debited to an expense account.

DEBIT AN ASSET ACCOUNT FOR CAPITAL EXPENDITURES	DEBIT REPAIR AND MAINTENANCE EXPENSE FOR AN EXPENSE
Extraordinary repairs:	*Ordinary repairs:*
Major engine overhaul	Repair of transmission or engine
Modification of truck body for new use	Oil change, lubrication, and so on
Addition to storage capacity of truck	Replacement tires or windshield
	Paint job

EXHIBIT 10-3
Delivery-Truck Expenditures—Capital Expenditure or Expense

Treating a capital expenditure as an expense, or vice versa, creates errors in the financial statements. Suppose a company makes a capital expenditure and erroneously expenses this cost. A capital expenditure should have been debited to an asset account. This accounting error overstates expenses and understates net income on the income statement. On the balance sheet, the Equipment account is understated, and so is owner's equity, as follows:

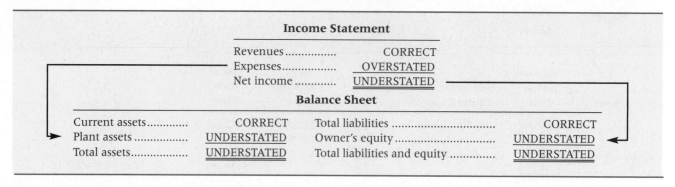

Income Statement

Revenues................	CORRECT
Expenses................	OVERSTATED
Net income	UNDERSTATED

Balance Sheet

Current assets.............	CORRECT	Total liabilities	CORRECT
Plant assets	UNDERSTATED	Owner's equity	UNDERSTATED
Total assets.................	UNDERSTATED	Total liabilities and equity	UNDERSTATED

◉ **DAILY EXERCISE 10-6**

Capitalizing the cost of an ordinary repair creates the opposite error. Expenses are then understated, and net income is overstated. The balance sheet overstates assets and owner's equity.

MEASURING PLANT ASSET DEPRECIATION

➡ See Chapter 3, page 86, for a discussion of the matching principle.

The allocation of a plant asset's cost to expense over the asset's useful life is called *depreciation*. Depreciation accounting matches the asset's cost (expense) against the revenue earned by the asset, as the matching principle directs. ◄ Exhibit 10-4 shows depreciation for the purchase of a Boeing 737 jet by **United Airlines.**

EXHIBIT 10-4
Depreciation and the Matching of Expense with Revenue

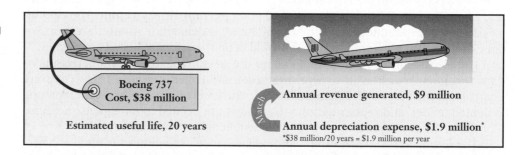

Boeing 737
Cost, $38 million

Estimated useful life, 20 years

Annual revenue generated, $9 million

Annual depreciation expense, $1.9 million*
*$38 million/20 years = $1.9 million per year

Suppose **The Home Depot** buys a computer for use in its accounting system. Home Depot believes it will get four years of service from the computer, and it will then be worthless. Using the straight-line depreciation method, The Home Depot expenses one-quarter of the asset's cost in each of its four years of use.

Let's contrast what depreciation accounting is with what it is *not*.

1. *Depreciation is not a process of valuation.* Businesses do not record depreciation based on the market (sales) value of their plant assets at the end of each year. Instead, businesses allocate an asset's cost to expense during the period of its use.

2. *Depreciation does not mean that the business sets aside cash to replace an asset when it is used up.* Establishing a cash fund is entirely separate from depreciation, and depreciation does not represent cash.

Causes of Depreciation

All assets but land wear out. For some plant assets, physical *wear and tear* and the elements cause depreciation. For example, physical deterioration wears out the trucks that move Home Depot merchandise from warehouses to company stores. The store fixtures used to display merchandise are also subject to physical wear and tear.

Assets such as computers, software, and airplanes may be *obsolete* before they deteriorate. An asset is obsolete when another asset can do the job better or more efficiently. Thus, an asset's useful life may be much shorter than its physical life.

Accountants usually depreciate computers over a short period—perhaps two to four years—even though the computers will continue working much longer. Whether wear and tear or obsolescence causes depreciation, the asset's cost is depreciated over its expected useful life.

Measuring Depreciation

Depreciation of a plant asset is based upon the asset's

  1. Cost   **2.** Estimated useful life   **3.** Estimated residual value

Cost is a known amount. The other two factors must be estimated.

    Estimated useful life is the length of the service period expected from the asset. Useful life may be expressed in years, units of output, miles, or another measure. For example, the useful life of a building is stated in years. The useful life of a bookbinding machine is the number of books the machine can bind—that is, its expected units of output. A delivery truck's useful life can be measured in miles. Companies make such estimates from past experience, industry information, and government publications.

    Estimated residual value—also called **scrap value** or **salvage value**—is the expected cash value of an asset at the end of its useful life. For example, a machine's useful life may be seven years. After seven years, the company expects to sell the machine as scrap metal. The cash the business thinks it can sell the machine for is its estimated residual value. Estimated residual value is *not* depreciated because the business expects to receive this amount from disposing of the asset. If there's no residual value, then it depreciates the full cost of the asset. Cost minus residual value is called the **depreciable cost** of the asset.

> **ESTIMATED USEFUL LIFE.** Length of the service period expected from an asset. May be expressed in years, units of output, miles, or another measure.

> **ESTIMATED RESIDUAL VALUE.** Expected cash value of an asset at the end of its useful life. Also called **scrap value,** or **salvage value.**

> **DEPRECIABLE COST.** The cost of a plant asset minus its estimated residual value.

Depreciation Methods

Three major methods exist for computing depreciation:

- straight-line   • units-of-production   • declining-balance

These methods allocate different amounts of depreciation to each period. However, they all result in the same total amount of depreciation over the life of the asset. Exhibit 10-5 gives the data we will use to illustrate the depreciation computations for a Home Depot truck. We cover the three most widely used methods. We omit the sum-of-years'-digits method because only around 1% of all companies use it.

> **Objective 2**
> Account for depreciation

Data Item	Amount
Cost of truck	$41,000
Less: Estimated residual value	(1,000)
Depreciable cost....................................	$40,000
Estimated useful life:	
Years......................................	5 years
Units of production..........................	100,000 units [miles]

EXHIBIT 10-5
Data for Depreciation Computations for a Home Depot Truck

STRAIGHT-LINE METHOD   In the **straight-line (SL) method,** an equal amount of depreciation is assigned to each year of asset use. Depreciable cost is divided by useful life in years to determine the annual amount of depreciation. The equation for SL depreciation, applied to the Home Depot truck data from Exhibit 10-5, is

> **STRAIGHT-LINE (SL) DEPRECIATION METHOD.** Depreciation method in which an equal amount of depreciation expense is assigned to each year of asset use.

$$\text{Straight-line depreciation per year} = \frac{\text{Cost} - \text{Residual value}}{\text{Useful life, in years}}$$

$$= \frac{\$41,000 - \$1,000}{5}$$

$$= \$8,000$$

The entry to record one year's depreciation is

$$\text{Depreciation Expense} \dots\dots\dots\dots\dots\dots\dots \quad 8,000$$
$$\text{Accumulated Depreciation} \dots\dots\dots\dots \quad\quad\quad\quad 8,000$$

This truck was purchased on January 1, 20X1, and let's assume The Home Depot's fiscal year ends on December 31. A *straight-line depreciation schedule* is given in Exhibit 10-6. The final column in the exhibit shows the asset's *book value,* which is its cost less accumulated depreciation. Book value is also called *carrying amount* or *carrying value.*

➡ We introduced book value in Chapter 3, page 91.

As an asset is used, accumulated depreciation increases, and the book value decreases. Compare the Accumulated Depreciation and the Book Value columns of Exhibit 10-6. An asset's final book value is its *residual value* ($1,000 in Exhibit 10-6). At the end of its useful life, the asset is said to be *fully depreciated.*

EXHIBIT 10-6
Straight-Line Depreciation Schedule for a Home Depot Truck

Date	Asset Cost	Depreciation for the Year				Accumulated Depreciation	Asset Book Value
		Depreciation Rate		Depreciable Cost	Depreciation Expense		
1-1-20X1	$41,000						$41,000
12-31-20X1		0.20*	×	$40,000	= $8,000	$ 8,000	33,000
12-31-20X2		0.20	×	40,000	= 8,000	16,000	25,000
12-31-20X3		0.20	×	40,000	= 8,000	24,000	17,000
12-31-20X4		0.20	×	40,000	= 8,000	32,000	9,000
12-31-20X5		0.20	×	40,000	= 8,000	40,000	1,000

*1/5 year = 0.20 per year

An asset with cost of $10,000, useful life of five years, and residual value of $2,000 was purchased on January 1. What is the SL depreciation for the first year? For the second year? For the fifth year?

Answer:
$$\frac{\text{SL depreciation}}{\text{per year}} = \frac{\text{Cost} - \text{Residual value}}{\text{Useful life, in years}}$$
$$= \frac{\$10,000 - \$2,000}{5} = \frac{\$1,600 \text{ per year}}{\textit{every year}}$$

UNITS-OF-PRODUCTION (UOP) METHOD In the **units-of-production (UOP) method,** a fixed amount of depreciation goes with each *unit of output* produced by the asset. Depreciable cost is divided by useful life, in units of production. This per-unit expense is then multiplied by the number of units produced each period to compute depreciation for that period. The UOP depreciation equation for the Home Depot truck data in Exhibit 10-5 is

UNITS-OF-PRODUCTION (UOP) DEPRECIATION METHOD. Depreciation method by which a fixed amount of depreciation is assigned to each unit of output produced by an asset.

$$\frac{\text{Units-of-production depreciation}}{\text{per unit of output}} = \frac{\text{Cost} - \text{Residual value}}{\text{Useful life, in units of production}}$$
$$= \frac{\$41,000 - \$1,000}{100,000 \text{ miles}}$$
$$= \$0.40 \text{ per mile}$$

This the truck is expected to be driven 20,000 miles during the first year, 30,000 during the second, 25,000 during the third, 15,000 during the fourth, and 10,000 during the fifth. The amount of UOP depreciation each period varies with the number of units the asset produces. The UOP schedule for this asset is shown in Exhibit 10-7.

| | | Depreciation for the Year | | | | |
Date	Asset Cost	Depreciation Per Unit	Number of Units	Depreciation Expense	Accumulated Depreciation	Asset Book Value
1-1-20X1	$41,000					$41,000
12-31-20X1		$0.40	× 20,000	= $ 8,000	$ 8,000	33,000
12-31-20X2		0.40	× 30,000	= 12,000	20,000	21,000
12-31-20X3		0.40	× 25,000	= 10,000	30,000	11,000
12-31-20X4		0.40	× 15,000	= 6,000	36,000	5,000
12-31-20X5		0.40	× 10,000	= 4,000	40,000	1,000

WORK IT OUT

The asset in the preceding Work It Out produced 3,000 units in the first year, 4,000 in the second, 4,500 in the third, 2,500 in the fourth, and 2,000 units in the last year. Its total estimated useful life is 16,000 miles. What is UOP depreciation for each year?

Answer

$$\frac{\text{Depreciation}}{\text{per unit}} = \frac{\text{Cost} - \text{Residual value}}{\text{Useful life, in units of production}} = \frac{\$10,000 - \$2,000}{16,000 \text{ miles}} = \$0.50 \text{ per mile}$$

Yr. 1: $1,500 (3,000 × $0.50)   Yr. 4: $1,250 (2,500 × $0.50)
Yr. 2: $2,000 (4,000 × $0.50)   Yr. 5: $1,000 (2,000 × $0.50)
Yr. 3: $2,250 (4,500 × $0.50)

DOUBLE-DECLINING BALANCE METHOD An **accelerated depreciation method** writes off more of the asset's cost near the start of its useful life than the straight-line method does. The main accelerated depreciation method, **double-declining-balance (DDB)**, multiplies the asset's decreasing book value by a constant percentage that is 2 times the straight-line depreciation rate. DDB amounts can be computed in four steps:

1. Compute the straight-line depreciation rate per year. A five-year truck has a straight-line depreciation rate of 1/5, or 20% per year. A ten-year asset has a straight-line rate of 1/10, or 10% per year, and so on.
2. Compute the DDB rate: Multiply the straight-line rate by 2. The DDB rate for a ten-year asset is 20% per year (10% × 2 = 20%). For a five-year asset, such as the Home Depot truck, the DDB rate is 40% (20% × 2 = 40%).
3. Compute DDB depreciation for each year. Multiply the asset's book value (cost less accumulated depreciation) at the beginning of each year by the DDB rate. You should ignore the asset's residual value in computing depreciation, except for the last year. The first-year depreciation for the truck in Exhibit 10-5 is

DDB depreciation for the first year	=	Asset book value at the begining of the year	× DDB rate
$16,400	=	$41,000	× 0.40

The same approach is used to compute DDB depreciation for all later years, except for the final year, as follows.

4. Determine the final year's depreciation, the amount needed to reduce the asset's carrying amount to its residual value. In the DDB depreciation schedule in Exhibit 10-8 (on page 396), the last year's depreciation is $4,314 — book value of $5,314 less the $1,000 residual value.

ACCELERATED DEPRECIATION METHOD. A depreciation method that writes off more of the asset's cost near the start of its useful life than the straight-line method does.

DOUBLE-DECLINING-BALANCE (DDB) DEPRECIATION METHOD. An accelerated depreciation method that computes annual depreciation by multiplying the asset's decreasing book value by a constant percent that is 2 times the straight-line rate.

Date	Asset Cost	Depreciation for the Year			Accumulated Depreciation	Asset Book Value
		DDB Rate	Asset Book Value	Depreciation Expense		
1-1-20X1	$41,000					$41,000
12-31-20X1		0.40 ×	$41,000 =	$16,400	$16,400	24,600
12-31-20X2		0.40 ×	24,600 =	9,840	26,240	14,760
12-31-20X3		0.40 ×	14,760 =	5,904	32,144	8,856
12-31-20X4		0.40 ×	8,856 =	3,542	35,686	5,314
12-31-20X5				4,314*	40,000	1,000

*Last-year depreciation is the amount needed to reduce asset book value to the residual value ($5,314 − $1,000 = $4,314).

The DDB method differs from the other methods in two ways:

- The asset's residual value is ignored at the start. In the first year, depreciation is computed on the asset's full cost.
- The final year's depreciation is the amount needed to bring the asset's carrying amount to residual value. The final-year depreciation amount is like a "plug" figure.

Many companies change to the straight-line method during the next-to-last year of the asset's life. Under this plan, annual depreciation for 20X4 and 20X5 is $3,928. Look at Exhibit 10-8. Depreciable cost at the end of 20X3 is $7,856 (book value of $8,856 less residual value of $1,000). Depreciable cost can be spread evenly over the last two years of the asset's life ($7,856 ÷ 2 remaining years = $3,928 per year).

What is DDB depreciation for each year for the asset in the Work It Out on page 394?

Answer: DDB rate = 1/5 × 2 = 40%

Yr. 1: $4,000 ($10,000 × 40%)
Yr. 2: $2,400 [($10,000 − $4,000 = $6,000) × 40%]
Yr. 3: $1,440 [($6,000 − $2,400 = $3,600) × 40%]
Yr. 4: $160 ($3,600 − $1,440 − $2,000*)

*An asset's cost is not depreciated below its residual value.

Comparing Depreciation Methods

Let's compare the depreciation methods we've just discussed. Annual depreciation varies by method, but the total is the same for all methods—$40,000.

DAILY EXERCISE 10-7

DAILY EXERCISE 10-8

	Amount of Depreciation Per Year		
			Accelerated Method
Year	Straight-Line	Units-of-Production	Double-Declining-Balance
1	$ 8,000	$ 8,000	$16,400
2	8,000	12,000	9,840
3	8,000	10,000	5,904
4	8,000	6,000	3,542
5	8,000	4,000	4,314
Total	$40,000	$40,000	$40,000

STRAIGHT-LINE A business should match an asset's expense against the revenue that asset produces. For an asset that generates revenue evenly over time, the straight-line method follows the matching principle. Each period the asset is used, an equal amount of depreciation is recorded.

UNITS-OF-PRODUCTION The units-of-production method best fits an asset that wears out because of physical use rather than obsolescence. Depreciation is expensed only when the asset is used, and more asset use causes greater depreciation.

DOUBLE-DECLINING-BALANCE The accelerated method (DDB) works best for assets that produce more revenue in their early years. The greater expense in the earlier periods is matched against those periods' greater revenue. This is the mark of an accelerated depreciation method.

COMPARISONS Exhibit 10-9 graphs annual depreciation for the three methods.

- The graph of *straight-line* depreciation is flat because annual depreciation is the same in all periods.
- Units-of-production depreciation follows no pattern because annual depreciation varies depending on the use of the asset. The greater the use, the greater the amount of depreciation.
- Accelerated depreciation is greatest in the asset's first year and less in the later years.

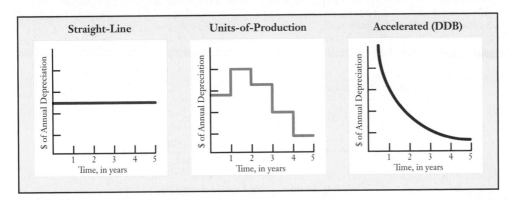

EXHIBIT 10-9
Depreciation Patterns Through Time

A recent survey of 600 companies, conducted by the American Institute of CPAs, indicated that the straight-line method is most popular. Exhibit 10-10 shows the percentages of companies that use each depreciation method.

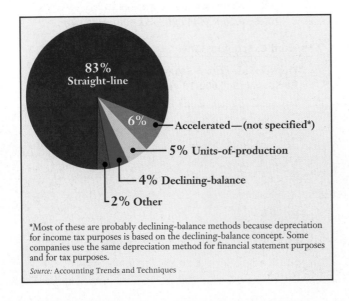

EXHIBIT 10-10
Use of Depreciation Methods

*Most of these are probably declining-balance methods because depreciation for income tax purposes is based on the declining-balance concept. Some companies use the same depreciation method for financial statement purposes and for tax purposes.
Source: Accounting Trends and Techniques

www.prenhall.com/horngren
Mid-Chapter Assessment

SUMMARY PROBLEM

Not Just Copies purchased equipment on January 1, 20X5, for $44,000. Its expected useful life is ten years or 100,000 units of production, and its residual value is $4,000. Under three depreciation methods, the annual depreciation and the balance of accumulated depreciation at the end of 20X5 and 20X6 are as follows:

	Method A		Method B		Method C	
Year	Annual Depreciation Expense	Accumulated Depreciation	Annual Depreciation Expense	Accumulated Depreciation	Annual Depreciation Expense	Accumulated Depreciation
20X5	$1,200	$1,200	$8,800	$ 8,800	$4,000	$4,000
20X6	5,600	6,800	7,040	15,840	4,000	8,000

Required

1. Identify the depreciation method used in each instance, and show the equation and computation for each. (Round amounts to the nearest dollar.)
2. Assume continued use of the same method through year 20X7. Determine the annual depreciation expense, accumulated depreciation, and book value of the equipment for 20X5 through 20X7 under each method, assuming 12,000 units of production in 20X7.

Solution

Requirement 1

Method A: Units-of-Production

$$\text{Depreciation per unit} = \frac{\$44,000 - \$4,000}{100,000 \text{ units}} = \$0.40$$

20X5: $0.40 × 3,000 units = $1,200
20X6: $0.40 × 14,000 units = $5,600

Method B: Double-Declining-Balance

$$\text{Rate} = \frac{1}{10 \text{ years}} \times 2 = 10\% \times 2 = 20\%$$

20X5: 0.20 × $44,000 = $8,800
20X6: 0.20 × ($44,000 − $8,800) = $7,040

Method C: Straight-Line

Depreciable cost = $44,000 − $4,000 = $40,000
Each year: $40,000/10 years = $4,000

Requirement 2

Method A: Units-of-Production

Year	Annual Depreciation Expense	Accumulated Depreciation	Book Value
Start			$44,000
20X5	$1,200	$ 1,200	42,800
20X6	5,600	6,800	37,200
20X7	4,800	11,600	32,400

Method B: Double-Declining-Balance

Year	Annual Depreciation Expense	Accumulated Depreciation	Book Value
Start			$44,000
20X5	$8,800	$ 8,800	35,200
20X6	7,040	15,840	28,160
20X7	5,632	21,472	22,528

Method C: Straight-Line

Year	Annual Depreciation Expense	Accumulated Depreciation	Book Value
Start			$44,000
20X5	$4,000	$ 4,000	40,000
20X6	4,000	8,000	36,000
20X7	4,000	12,000	32,000

Computations for 20X7:

Units-of-production	$0.40 × 12,000 units = $4,800
Double-declining-balance	0.20 × $28,160 = $5,632
Straight-line	$40,000/10 years = $4,000

OTHER ISSUES IN ACCOUNTING FOR PLANT ASSETS

Plant assets are complex because of their long lives. Depreciation affects income taxes, and companies may have gains or losses when they sell their plant assets. This section covers these topics.

Depreciation and Income Taxes

Most companies use the straight-line depreciation method for their financial statements. But they keep separate depreciation records for income taxes. For tax purposes, most companies use an accelerated method.

Suppose you manage a **Home Depot** store. The IRS allows the DDB depreciation method, and most managers prefer that to straight-line depreciation. Why? Because it provides the most depreciation expense as quickly as possible. The accelerated depreciation method decreases immediate tax payments. You can then invest the cash you save to earn more income. This is a common strategy.

To understand the relationships between cash flow (cash provided by operations), depreciation, and income tax, recall our earlier depreciation of the Home Depot truck: First-year depreciation is $8,000 under straight-line and $16,400 under double-declining-balance. Now let's assume that DDB is permitted for income tax reporting, and let's apply DDB to the Home Depot truck as before. This store has $400,000 in cash sales and $300,000 in cash operating expenses during the truck's first year and an income tax rate of 30%. The cash-flow analysis appears in Exhibit 10-11 on page 400.

Objective 3
Select the best depreciation method for income tax purposes

DAILY EXERCISE 10-9

		Income Tax Rate (30%)	
		SL	Accelerated
(1)	Cash revenues	$400,000	$400,000
(2)	*Cash* operating expenses	300,000	300,000
(3)	Cash provided by operations before income tax	100,000	100,000
(4)	Depreciation expense (a noncash expense)	8,000	16,400
(5)	Income before income tax.....................................	92,000	83,600
(6)	Income tax expense (30%)	27,600	25,080
(7)	Net income	$ 64,400	$ 58,520
	Cash-flow analysis:		
(8)	Cash provided by operations before income tax.....	$100,000	$100,000
(9)	Income tax expense	27,600	25,080
(10)	Cash provided by operations	$ 72,400	$ 74,920
(11)	Extra cash available for investment if DDB is used ($74,920 − $72,400)		$ 2,520

Exhibit 10-11 reveals some important relationships. Compare the amount of cash provided by operations before income tax (line 3). Both columns show $100,000. If there were no income taxes, the cash provided by operations would be the same for all depreciation methods. Depreciation is a noncash expense (it requires no outlay of cash) and thus does not affect cash from operations.

But depreciation is a tax-deductible expense. The higher the depreciation (line 4), the lower the income and the lower the tax payment. Therefore, accelerated depreciation helps conserve cash for use in the business. Exhibit 10-11 indicates that the business will have $2,520 more cash to invest at the end of the first year if it uses accelerated depreciation (line 11). The additional investment will earn a return and increase the company's net income.

A special depreciation method called the *modified accelerated cost recovery system (MACRS)* is used only for income tax purpose. Under MACRS, assets are segmented into classes by asset life, as shown in Exhibit 10-12. Depreciation for the first three classes is computed by the double-declining-balance method. Depreciation for 20-year assets is computed by the 150%-declining-balance method. Under 150% DB, the annual depreciation rate is computed by multiplying the straight-line rate by 1.50 (rather than by 2, as for DDB). For a 20-year asset, the straight-line rate is 0.05 $\times$ (1/20 = 0.05), so the annual MACRS depreciation rate is 0.075 (0.05 $\times$ 1.50 = 0.075). Finally, as the exhibit shows, most real estate is depreciated by the straight-line method.

Class Identified by Asset Life (years)	Representative Assets	Depreciation Method
3	Race horses	DDB
5	Automobiles, light trucks	DDB
10	Equipment	DDB
20	Certain real estate	150% DB
27 1/2	Residential rental property	SL
39	Nonresidential rental property	SL

Depreciation for Partial Years

Companies purchase plant assets whenever they need them. They don't wait until the beginning of a period. Therefore, companies must develop policies to compute depreciation for partial years. Suppose **Towels 'n Things** in St. Louis purchases a building on April 1 for $500,000. The building's estimated life is 20 years, and its estimated residual value is $80,000. How does Towels 'n Things compute depreciation for the year ended December 31?

Many companies compute partial-year depreciation by first computing a full year's depreciation. They then multiply the full-year amount by the fraction of the year that they held the asset. Assuming the straight-line method, the year's depreciation for the Towels 'n Things building is $15,750, computed as follows:

Full year depreciation: $$\frac{\$500,000 - \$80,000}{20 \text{ years}} = \$21,000$$

Partial-year depreciation: $\$21,000 \times 9/12 = \$15,750$

What if the company bought the asset on April 18? One widely used policy is to record no depreciation on assets purchased after the 15th of the month and to record a full month's depreciation on an asset bought on or before the 15th. In that case, the year's depreciation would be $14,000 for eight months ($21,000 × 8/12 = $14,000).

How is partial-year depreciation computed under the other depreciation methods? Suppose Towels 'n Things acquired the building on October 4 and uses the double-declining-balance method. For a 20-year asset, the DDB rate is 10% (1/20 = 5%; 5% × 2 = 10%). The annual depreciation computations for 20X1, 20X2, and 20X3 are shown in Exhibit 10-13.

EXHIBIT 10-13 Annual DDB Depreciation for Partial Years

| | | | Depreciation for the Year | | | | |
Date	Asset Cost	DDB Rate	Asset Book Value, Beginning	Fraction of the Year	Depreciation Expense	Accumulated Depreciation	Asset Book Value, Ending
10- 4-20X1	$500,000						$500,000
12-31-20X1		1/20 × 2 = 0.10 ×	$500,000 ×	3/12 =	$12,500	$ 12,500	487,500
12-31-20X2		0.10 ×	487,500 ×	12/12 =	48,750	61,250	438,750
12-31-20X3		0.10 ×	438,750 ×	12/12 =	43,875	105,125	394,875

Most companies use computerized systems to account for fixed assets. The system will automatically calculate the depreciation expense for each period.

⊙ DAILY EXERCISE 10-10

Changing the Useful Life of a Depreciable Asset

Estimating the useful life of each plant asset poses an accounting challenge. As the asset is being used, the business may refine its estimate on the basis of experience and new information. The **Walt Disney Company** made such a change, called a *change in accounting estimate*. Disney refigured depreciation for the revised useful lives of several theme-park assets. The following note in Disney's financial statements reports this change in accounting estimate:

Note 5
. . . [T]he Company extended the estimated useful lives of certain theme park . . . assets based upon . . . engineering studies. The effect of this change was to decrease depreciation by approximately $8 million (an increase in net income of approximately $4.2 million. . .).

Accounting changes like these are common because no one has perfect foresight. Generally accepted accounting principles require the business to report the nature, reason, and effect of the accounting change on net income, as the Disney example shows. For a change in accounting estimate, the remaining book value of the asset is spread over its remaining useful life. The new useful life may be longer or shorter than the original useful life.

Assume that a Disney World hot dog stand cost $40,000 and that the company originally believed the asset had an eight-year life with no residual value. Using the straight-line method, the company would record depreciation of $5,000 each year ($40,000/8 years = $5,000).

Suppose Disney used the asset for two years. Accumulated depreciation reached $10,000, leaving a remaining depreciable book value (cost *less* accumulated depreciation *less* residual value) of $30,000 ($40,000 − $10,000). Suppose Disney management believes the hot dog stand will remain useful for an additional ten years. The company would revise the annual depreciation amount as follows:

Asset's remaining depreciable book value	÷	(New) Estimated useful life remaining	=	(New) Annual depreciation
$30,000	÷	10 years	=	$3,000

The yearly depreciation entry based on the new useful life is

DAILY EXERCISE 10-11

| Depreciation Expense—Hot Dog Stand.............................. | 3,000 | |
| Accumulated Depreciation—Hot Dog Stand .... | | 3,000 |

The equation for revised straight-line depreciation is

$$\text{Revised SL depreciation} = \frac{\text{Cost} - \text{Accumulated depreciation} - \text{New residual value}}{\text{Estimated remaining useful life in years}}$$

Using Fully Depreciated Assets

A *fully depreciated asset* is an asset that has reached the end of its *estimated* useful life. No more depreciation is recorded for the asset. If the asset is no longer suitable for its purpose, it is disposed of. However, the company may be unable to replace the asset. Or the asset may remain useful. In any event, companies sometimes continue using fully depreciated assets. The asset account and its accumulated depreciation remain on the books, even though no additional depreciation is recorded.

THINK IT OVER

A fully depreciated asset has a cost of $80,000 and zero residual value. What is the asset's accumulated depreciation?

Answer: $80,000 (same as the asset's cost).

Now suppose the asset's residual value is $10,000. How much is accumulated depreciation?

Answer: $70,000 ($80,000 − $10,000).

Disposing of Plant Assets

Objective 4
Account for the disposal of a plant asset

Eventually, an asset ceases to serve its purpose. The asset may have become worn out or obsolete. In general, a company disposes of a plant asset by selling it or exchanging it. If the asset cannot be sold or exchanged, then it is junked. Whatever the method of disposal, the business should bring depreciation up-to-date to measure the asset's final book value properly.

To record the disposal, credit the asset account and debit its accumulated depreciation to remove these accounts from the books. Suppose the final year's depreciation expense has just been recorded for a machine that cost $6,000 with no residual value. The machine's accumulated depreciation thus totals $6,000. This asset cannot be sold or exchanged, so it is junked. The entry to record its disposal is

Accumulated Depreciation—Machinery	6,000	
Machinery...		6,000
To dispose of fully depreciated machine.		

MACHINERY	
6,000	**6,000**

ACCUMULATED DEPRECIATION—MACHINERY	
6,000	**6,000**

Now both accounts have a zero balance, as shown in the T-accounts at the right.

If assets are junked before being fully depreciated, the company records a loss equal to the asset's book value. Suppose Home Depot fixtures that cost $4,000 are junked at a loss. Accumulated depreciation is $3,000, and book value is therefore $1,000. Disposal of these store fixtures generates a loss equal to the book value of the asset, as follows:

```
Accumulated Depreciation—Store Fixtures ..................... 3,000
Loss on Disposal of Store Fixtures....................................... 1,000
        Store Fixtures ........................................................            4,000
    To dispose of store fixtures.
```

All losses, including this Loss on Disposal of Store Fixtures, decrease net income. Along with expenses, losses are reported on the income statement.

SELLING A PLANT ASSET   Suppose Clarkson Eyecare sells furniture (a plant asset) on September 30, 20X4, for $5,000 cash. The furniture cost $10,000 when purchased on January 1, 20X1, and has been depreciated on a straight-line basis. Clarkson estimated a ten-year useful life and no residual value. Prior to recording the sale of the furniture, accountants must update its depreciation. Because Clarkson uses the calendar year as its accounting period, partial-year depreciation must be recorded for the asset's expense from January 1, 20X4, to the sale date on September 30. The straight-line depreciation entry at September 30, 20X4, is

```
Sep. 30   Depreciation Expense ($10,000/10 years × 9/12).............     750
                Accumulated Depreciation—Furniture ...................            750
              To update depreciation.
```

After this entry is posted, the Furniture account and the Accumulated Depreciation—Furniture account appear as follows. The furniture book value is $6,250 ($10,000 − $3,750).

FURNITURE		ACCUMULATED DEPRECIATION—FURNITURE	
Jan. 1, 20X1 10,000		Dec. 31, 20X1 1,000	
		Dec. 31, 20X2 1,000	
		Dec. 31, 20X3 1,000	
		Sep. 30, 20X4 750	
		Balance 3,750	

Book Value = $6,250

Suppose Clarkson sells the furniture for $5,000 cash. The loss on the sale is $1,250, determined as follows:

Cash received from sale of the asset		$5,000
Book value of asset sold:		
Cost..	$10,000	
Less: Accumulated depreciation up to date of sale..............	(3,750)	6,250
Gain (loss) on sale of the asset...		($1,250)

Clarkson's entry to record sale of the furniture for $5,000 cash is

```
Sep. 30   Cash ................................................................................  5,000
          Accumulated Depreciation—Furniture .............................  3,750
          Loss on Sale of Furniture .................................................  1,250
              Furniture ..................................................................        10,000
              To sell furniture.
```

When recording the sale of a plant asset, the business must remove the balances in the asset account (Furniture, in this case) and its accumulated depreciation account and also record a gain or a loss if the amount of cash received differs from the asset's book value. In our example, cash of $5,000 is less than the book value of the furniture, $6,250. The result is a loss of $1,250.

If the sale price had been $7,000, Clarkson Eyecare would have had a gain of $750 (Cash, $7,000—asset book value, $6,250). The entry to record this transaction would be

Sep. 30	Cash	7,000	
	Accumulated Depreciation—Furniture	3,750	
	Furniture		10,000
	Gain on Sale of Furniture		750
	To sell furniture.		

 DAILY EXERCISE 10-12

A gain is recorded when an asset is sold for a price (sale proceeds) greater than the asset's book value. A loss is recorded when the sale price is less than book value.

> • **Gain = Sale proceeds > Book value**
> • **Loss = Sale proceeds < Book value**

Gains increase net income, and losses decrease net income. All gains and losses are reported on the income statement.

EXCHANGING PLANT ASSETS Businesses often exchange (trade in) their old plant assets for newer, more efficient assets. For example, **Domino's Pizza** may trade in a five-year-old delivery car for a newer model. To record the exchange, Domino's must remove from the books the balances for the old asset and its accumulated depreciation exactly as we did for the disposal of furniture in the preceding section.

In many cases, the business simply carries forward the book value of the old asset plus any cash payment as the cost of the new asset. For example, assume Domino's old delivery car cost $9,000 and has accumulated depreciation of $8,000. The car's book value is $1,000. Domino's trades in the old auto and pays cash of $10,000. Domino's should first record depreciation on its old auto up to the date of the exchange. This updates the asset's book value. Then the business records the exchange transaction with this journal entry:

Delivery Auto (new)	11,000	
Accumulated Depreciation (old)	8,000	
Delivery Auto (old)		9,000
Cash		10,000
Traded in old delivery car for new auto.		

Domino's cost of the new car is $11,000 (cash paid $10,000, plus the book value of the old auto, $1,000).

ACCOUNTING FOR NATURAL RESOURCES

Objective 5
Account for natural resource assets and depletion

DEPLETION EXPENSE. The portion of a natural resource's cost used up in a particular period. Depletion expense is computed in the same way as units-of-production depreciation.

Natural resources such as iron ore, petroleum (oil), natural gas, and timber are plant assets of a special type. Natural resources are like inventories in the ground (oil) or on top of the ground (timber). Natural resource assets are expensed through *depletion*. **Depletion expense** is that portion of the cost of natural resources used up in a particular period. Depletion expense is computed in the same way as units-of-production depreciation:

$$\frac{\text{Depletion}}{\text{per unit}} = \frac{\text{Cost} - \text{Residual value}}{\text{Estimated total units of natural resource}}$$

An oil well may cost $100,000 and contain an estimated 10,000 barrels of oil. The well has no residual value. The depletion rate would thus be $10 per barrel ($100,000/10,000 barrels). If 3,000 barrels are extracted during the year, depletion expense is $30,000 (3,000 barrels × $10 per barrel). The depletion entry for the year is

| Depletion Expense (3,000 barrels × $10) | 30,000 | |
| Accumulated Depletion—Oil | | 30,000 |

If 4,500 barrels are removed the next year, that period's depletion is $45,000 (4,500 barrels × $10 per barrel). Accumulated Depletion is a contra account similar to Accumulated Depreciation.

Natural resource assets can be reported on the balance sheet as follows:

Property, Plant, and Equipment:		
Land		$120,000
Buildings	$800,000	
Equipment	160,000	
	960,000	
Less: Accumulated depreciation	(410,000)	550,000
Oil..	$380,000	
Less: Accumulated depletion	(80,000)	300,000
Property, plant, and equipment, net		$970,000

 DAILY EXERCISE 10-13

WORK IT OUT

Ladue Paper Products pays $500,000 for land that contains an estimated 500,000 board feet of lumber. The land can be sold for $100,000 after the timber has been cut. If Ladue Paper harvests 200,000 board feet in the year of purchase, how much depletion should be recorded?

Answer: **(Cost − Residual) ÷ Total = Depletion rate × Production = Depletion**
($500,000 − $100,00) ÷ 500,000 = $0.80 per foot × 200,000 = $160,000

ACCOUNTING FOR INTANGIBLE ASSETS

Objective 6
Account for intangible assets and amortization

As we saw earlier in the chapter, *intangible assets* are long-lived and have no physical form. Instead, these assets are special rights from patents, copyrights, trademarks, and so on.

In today's technology-driven economy, intangibles are surpassing tangible assets in value. The electronic economy rewards brand and customer loyalty. Consider online auction pioneer **eBay.** The company has no physical products or equipment, but it helps people buy and sell everything from Batman toys to bathroom tiles. In 1999, eBay served 10 million customers and earned $225 billion in revenues with fewer than 150 employees.

Alas, accountants typically deal with historical costs rather than future value. A company's intellectual capital is difficult to measure. But when one company buys another, we get a glimpse of the value of the acquired company's intellectual capital. For example, **America Online** announced it would acquire **Time Warner.** AOL said it would exchange $146 billion worth of stock and agree to pay $38 billion of future liabilities for Time Warner's net tangible assets of only $9 billion. Why? Because Time Warner's intangible assets were worth $190 billion. Intangibles can account for as much as 85% of a company's perceived value, so companies must find ways to account for intangibles just as they do for their inventory and equipment.

The acquisition cost of a patent is debited to Patents, an asset account. The intangible is expensed through **amortization,** the systematic reduction of the asset's carrying value on the books. Amortization applies to intangible assets exactly as depreciation applies to plant assets and depletion applies to natural resources. Depreciation, depletion, and amortization are conceptually the same.

Amortization is generally computed on a straight-line basis over the asset's estimated useful life—up to a maximum of 40 years, according to generally accepted accounting principles. But obsolescence often shortens an intangible's useful life. Amortization expense for an intangible asset can be written off directly against the asset account rather than held in an accumulated amortization account. The residual value of most intangible assets is zero.

Assume that **Sealy Mattress Company** purchases a patent on a special manufacturing process. Legally, the patent may run for 20 years. Sealy realizes, however, that new technologies will limit the process's life to 4 years. If the patent cost $80,000, each year's amortization expense is $20,000 ($80,000/4). Sealy's balance sheet reports the patent at its acquisition cost less accumulated amortization to date. After 1 year, the patent has a $60,000 balance ($80,000 − $20,000), after 2 years a $40,000 balance ($80,000 − $40,000), and so on.

AMORTIZATION. The systematic reduction of the asset's carrying value on the books. Expense that applies to intangibles in the same way depreciation applies to plant assets and depletion applies to natural resources.

Specific Intangibles

PATENT. A federal government grant giving the holder the exclusive right to produce and sell an invention for 20 years.

PATENTS **Patents** are federal government grants giving the holder the exclusive 20-year right to produce and sell an invention. The invention may be a product or a process—for example, **Sony** compact disc players and the **Dolby** noise-reduction process. Like any other asset, a patent may be purchased. Suppose **General Electric Company (GE)** pays $170,000 to acquire a patent on January 1, and GE believes its expected useful life is only five years. Amortization expense is $34,000 per year ($170,000/5 years). Acquisition and amortization entries for this patent are

Jan. 1	Patents	170,000	
	Cash		170,000
	To acquire a patent.		
Dec. 31	Amortization Expense—Patents ($170,000/5)	34,000	
	Patents...		34,000
	To amortize the cost of a patent.		

COPYRIGHT. Exclusive right to reproduce and sell a book, musical composition, film, other work of art, or computer program. Issued by the federal government, copyrights extend 50 years beyond the author's life.

COPYRIGHTS **Copyrights** are exclusive rights to reproduce and sell a book, musical composition, film, or other work of art. Copyrights also protect computer software programs, such as **Microsoft** Windows® and the Excel spreadsheet. Issued by the federal government, copyrights extend 50 years beyond the author's (composer's, artist's, or programmer's) life.

The cost of obtaining a copyright from the government is low, but a company may pay a large sum to purchase an existing copyright. For example, **Simon & Schuster,** the publisher, may pay the author of a popular novel $1 million for the book's copyright. The useful life of a copyright is usually no longer than two or three years, so most copyrights have short lives.

TRADEMARKS, TRADE NAMES, OR BRAND NAMES. Assets that represent distinctive identifications of a product or service.

TRADEMARKS, BRAND NAMES **Trademarks** and **trade names** (or **brand names**) are assets that represent distinctive identifications of products or services. The "eye" symbol is the trademark of the **CBS** television network. You are probably also familiar with **NBC's** peacock. Seven-Up, Pepsi, and Egg McMuffin are everyday trade names. Advertising slogans that are legally protected include **United Airlines'** "Fly the friendly skies" and **Avis Rent A Car's** "We try harder."

The cost of a trademark or trade name is amortized over its useful life, not to exceed 40 years. The cost of advertising and promotion is not a part of the asset's cost, but rather an advertising expense.

FRANCHISES, LICENSES. Privileges granted by a private business or a government to sell a product or service under specified conditions.

FRANCHISES, LICENSES **Franchises** and **licenses** are privileges granted by a private business or a government to sell a product or service under specified conditions. The **Green Bay Packers** football organization is a franchise granted by the National Football League. **McDonald's** restaurants and **Holiday Inns** are popular business franchises. The acquisition costs of a franchise or license is amortized over its useful life, subject to the 40-year maximum.

GOODWILL. Excess of the cost of an acquired company over the sum of the market values of its net assets (assets minus liabilities).

GOODWILL The term *goodwill* in accounting has a very different meaning from the everyday term, "goodwill among men." In accounting, **goodwill** is the excess of the cost to purchase another company over the market value of the other company's net assets (assets minus liabilities). **Wal-Mart** has now expanded into Mexico. Suppose Wal-Mart acquired Mexana Company at a cost of $10 million. The sum of the market values of Mexana's assets was $9 million and its liabilities totaled $1 million, so Mexana's net assets totaled $8 million. In this case, Wal-Mart paid $2 million for goodwill, computed as follows:

Purchase price paid for Mexana Company		$10 million
The market value of Mexana Company's assets.................	$9 million	
Less: Mexana Company's liabilities	(1 million)	
Market value of Mexana Company's net assets		8 million
Excess is called *goodwill*		$ 2 million

Wal-Mart's entry to record the purchase of Mexana Company, including the goodwill that Wal-Mart purchases would be

Assets (Cash, Receivables, Inventories, Plant Assets, all at market value)	9,000,000	
Goodwill	2,000,000	
Liabilities		1,000,000
Cash		10,000,000
Purchased Mexana Company.		

Note that Wal-Mart acquired all of Mexana's assets *and* all of Mexana's liabilities. Goodwill has some special features:

1. Goodwill is recorded only when it is purchased in the acquisition of another company. A company's favorable location, superior product, or outstanding reputation may create goodwill for a company, but that entity never records goodwill for its own business. Instead, goodwill is recorded *only* by the acquiring entity when it buys another company.

2. According to generally accepted accounting principles (GAAP), goodwill is amortized over a period not to exceed 40 years. In reality, the goodwill of many entities actually increases in value. Nevertheless, GAAP requires that the cost of all intangible assets be amortized as expense.

 DAILY EXERCISE 10-14

DAILY EXERCISE 10-15

 e-Accounting

Singapore International Airlines: Ratcheting Up the Value of Tangibles and Intangibles

During the Asian recession of 1997–1998, **Singapore International Airlines (SIA)** was able to keep its profitability high. The secret to the airline's success has always been the impeccable quality of its assets, tangible and intangible: its fleet of 90 planes and its service. It recently spent $300 million for first-class seats that recline 180% and personal TV screens in all seats.

An airline's ground service is as important as its planes. You might be surprised to know that **American Airlines'** reservation system—Sabre—was valued at 60% of the company's assets, far more than American's fleet of planes. And **Singapore Airlines Terminal Services Group (SATS)** is so profitable that the company is taking it public. The company credits SATS for its success in reducing the adverse effects of the Asian economic downturn. "Ongoing investment in staff training continues to be a decisive, motivating factor in our success," says CEO Karmit Singh. The company's YES! campaign trains everyone—from baggage handlers to security personnel—to act like frontline staff. No wonder business travelers have chosen Singapore International Airlines as the "best airline" for eleven years running.

Source: Based on Leonard Hill, "Two for the money," *Air Transport World*, May 2000, pp. 59–63. Perry Flint, "SIA's global tilt," *Air Transport World*, May 2000, pp. 50–55. Anonymous, "Business travelers select Singapore Airlines No. 1," *Houston Chronicle*, January 23, 2000, p. 5. Ben Dolven, "Profitable romance," *Far Eastern Economic Review*, December 30, 1999–January 6, 2000, pp. 78–79. Staff Reports, Companies may be unwittingly ignoring the bulk of their asset value," *Investor Relations Business*, December 13, 1999, p. 4.

Special Issues

INTERNATIONAL ACCOUNTING FOR GOODWILL Companies in The Netherlands (such as **Royal Dutch Shell** and **Phillips**), in Great Britain (such as **British Petroleum** and **British Airways**), and in other European nations do not have to record goodwill when they purchase another business. Instead, they may record the cost of goodwill as a decrease in owner's equity. These companies never have to amortize the cost of goodwill, so their net income is higher than a U.S. company's net income would be. As a result, U.S. companies often cry "foul" when bidding against a European firm to acquire another business. Americans claim the Europeans can pay higher prices because their income never takes a hit for amortization expense.

> **THINK IT OVER**
>
> How could companies around the world be placed on the same accounting basis?
>
> *Answer:* If all companies worldwide followed the same accounting rules, they would be reporting income and other amounts computed similarly. But this is not the case. A company must follow the accounting rules of its own nation, and there are differences, as the goodwill situation illustrates.

RESEARCH AND DEVELOPMENT COSTS Accounting for research and development (R&D) costs is one of the toughest issues the accounting profession has faced. R&D is the lifeblood of companies such as **Procter & Gamble**, **General Electric**, **Intel**, and **Boeing** because it is vital to the development of new products and processes. The cost of R&D activities is one of these companies' most valuable (intangible) assets. But, in general, they do not report R&D assets on their balance sheets.

GAAP requires companies to expense R&D costs as they incur those costs. Only in certain circumstances may the company capitalize an R&D asset. Consider a company that incurs R&D costs under a contract guaranteeing it will recover the costs from the customer. In this case, the company records R&D cost as an asset. But this is the exception. Otherwise, the Financial Accounting Standards Board (FASB) requires that R&D cost be expensed as incurred.

ETHICAL ISSUES: PLANT ASSETS AND INTANGIBLES

The main ethical issue in accounting for plant assets and intangibles is whether to capitalize or to expense a particular cost. In this area, companies have split personalities. On the one hand, they all want to save on taxes. This motivates them to expense all costs in order to decrease their taxable income. On the other hand, most companies also want their financial statements to look as good as possible, with high net income and high reported amounts for assets.

In most cases, a cost that is capitalized or expensed for tax purposes must be treated the same way for reporting to stockholders and creditors in the financial statements. What, then, is the ethical path? Accountants should follow the general guidelines for capitalizing a cost: Capitalize all costs that provide a future benefit for the business, and expense all other costs, as outlined in the Decision Guidelines box that follows.

➡ We discussed accounting conservatism in Chapter 9, page 361.

Many companies have gotten into trouble by capitalizing costs they should have expensed. They made their financial statements look better than the facts warranted. But there are very few cases of companies getting into trouble by following the general guidelines, or even by erring on the side of expensing questionable costs. This is another example of accounting conservatism in action. It works. ◄

DECISION GUIDELINES

Accounting for Plant Assets and Related Expenses

DECISION	GUIDELINES
Capitalize or expense a cost?	General rule: Capitalize all costs that provide *future benefit* for the business. Expense all costs that provide *no future benefit*.
Capitalize or expense: • Cost associated with a new asset? • Cost associated with an existing asset? • Interest cost incurred to finance the asset's acquisition?	Capitalize all costs that bring the asset to its intended use. Capitalize only those costs that add to the asset's usefulness or its useful life. Expense all other costs as maintenance or repairs. Capitalize interest cost only on assets constructed by the business for its own use. Expense all other interest cost.
Which depreciation method to use: • For financial reporting? • For income tax?	Use the method that best matches depreciation expense against the revenues produced by the asset. Use the method that produces the fastest tax deductions (MACRS). A company can use different depreciation methods for financial reporting and for income tax purposes. In the United States, this practice is considered both legal and ethical.

REVIEW PLANT ASSETS

SUMMARY PROBLEM

The following figures appear in the Answers to the Mid-Chapter Summary Problem, requirement 2, on page 339.

	Method B: Double-Declining-Balance			Method C: Straight-Line		
Year	Annual Depreciation Expense	Accumulated Depreciation	Book Value	Annual Depreciation Expense	Accumulated Depreciation	Book Value
Start			$44,000			$44,000
20X5	$8,800	$ 8,800	35,200	$4,000	$ 4,000	40,000
20X6	7,040	15,840	28,160	4,000	8,000	36,000
20X7	5,632	21,472	22,528	4,000	12,000	32,000

Not Just Copies purchased equipment on January 1, 20X5. Management has depreciated the equipment by using the double-declining-balance method. On July 1, 20X7, the company sold the equipment for $27,000 cash.

Required

1. Suppose the income tax authorities permit a choice between the two depreciation methods shown. Which method would you select for income tax purposes? Why?
2. Record Not Just Copies' depreciation for 20X7 and the sale of the equipment on July 1, 20X7.

www.prenhall.com/horngren

End-of-Chapter Assessment

Solution

Requirement 1

For tax purposes, most companies select the accelerated method because it results in the most depreciation in the earliest years of the equipment's life. Accelerated depreciation minimizes taxable income and income tax payments in the early years of the asset's life, thereby maximizing the business's cash at the earliest possible time.

Requirement 2

To record depreciation to date of sale and sale of Not Just Copies' equipment:

20X7			
July 1	Depreciation Expense—Equipment ($5,632 × 1/2 year)	2,816	
	Accumulated Depreciation—Equipment		2,816
	To update depreciation.		
July 1	Cash	27,000	
	Accumulated Depreciation—Equipment ($15,840 + $2,816)	18,656	
	Equipment		44,000
	Gain on Sale of Equipment		1,656
	To record sale of equipment.		

LESSONS LEARNED

1. **Measure the cost of a plant asset.** Plant assets are long-lived tangible assets, such as land, buildings, and equipment, used in the operation of a business. The cost of a plant asset is the purchase price plus all taxes, purchase commissions, and all other amounts paid to acquire the asset and to prepare it for its intended use.

2. **Account for depreciation.** Businesses may account for depreciation (the allocation of a plant asset's cost to expense over its useful life) by four methods: *straight-line, units-of-production, double-declining-balance,* or *sum-of-the-years'-digits*. The SYD method is not used much.

3. **Select the best depreciation method for income tax purposes.** Most companies use an accelerated depreciation method for income tax purposes. Accelerated depreciation results in higher expenses, lower taxable income, and lower tax payments early in the asset's life.

4. **Account for the disposal of a plant asset.** Before disposing of a plant asset, the company must update the asset's depreciation. Disposal is then recorded by removing the book balances from both the asset and its accumulated depreciation account. Sales often result in a gain or loss, which is reported on the income statement.

5. **Account for natural resource assets and depletion.** The cost of natural resources, a special category of long-lived assets, is expensed through *depletion*. Depletion is computed on a units-of-production basis.

6. **Account for intangible assets and amortization.** *Intangible assets* have no physical form. They give their owners special rights. The major types of intangible assets are patents, copyrights, trademarks, franchises and licenses, leaseholds, and goodwill. The cost of intangibles is expensed through *amortization*, which is the same as depreciation.

ACCOUNTING VOCABULARY

accelerated depreciation method (p. 395)
amortization (p. 405)
brand names (p. 407)
capital expenditure (p. 391)
capitalize a cost (p. 390)
copyright (p. 406)
depletion expense (p. 404)
depreciable cost (p. 393)
double-declining-balance (DDB) depreciation method (p. 395)

estimated residual value (p. 393)
estimated useful life (p. 393)
extraordinary repair (p. 391)
fixed assets (p. 387)
franchises (p. 407)
goodwill (p. 407)
intangible asset (p. 387)
licenses (p. 407)
major repair (p. 391)
ordinary repair (p. 391)
patent (p. 406)

plant assets (p. 387)
salvage value (p. 393)
scrap value (p. 393)
straight-line (SL) depreciation method (p. 393)
trademark (p. 407)
trade name (p. 407)
units-of-production (UOP) depreciation method (p. 394)

QUESTIONS

1. To what types of long-lived assets do the following expenses apply: depreciation, depletion, and amortization?
2. Describe how to measure the cost of a plant asset. Would an ordinary cost of repairing the asset after it is placed in service be included in the asset's cost?
3. When assets are purchased as a group for a single price and no individual asset cost is given, how is each asset's cost determined?
4. Distinguish a capital expenditure from an expense.
5. Define depreciation. Present the common misconceptions about depreciation.
6. Explain the concept of accelerated depreciation. Which of the depreciation methods results in the most depreciation in the first year of the asset's life?

7. The level of business activity fluctuates widely for Harwood Delivery Service, reaching its peak around Christmas each year. At other times, business is slow. Which depreciation method is most appropriate for Harwood's fleet of minivans? Explain your answer.
8. Which type of depreciation method is best from an income tax standpoint? Why?
9. Describe how to compute depreciation for less than a full year and how to account for depreciation for less than a full month.
10. Describe how to determine whether a company experiences a gain or a loss when it sells an old plant asset.
11. What expense applies to natural resources? By which depreciation method is this expense computed?

12. How do intangible assets differ from most other assets? Why are they assets at all? What expense applies to intangible assets?

13. Your company has just purchased another company for $400,000. The market value of the other company's net assets is $325,000. What is the $75,000 excess called? What type of asset is it? What is the maximum period over which its cost is amortized under generally accepted accounting principles?

14. Oracle Corporation is a world leader in the development of software. The company's past success has created vast amounts of business goodwill. Would you expect to see this goodwill reported on Oracle's financial statements? Why or why not?

ASSESS YOUR PROGRESS

DAILY EXERCISES

DE10-1 Examine the balance sheet of **The Home Depot** in Exhibit 10-2 at the beginning of this chapter. Answer these questions about the company:

Cost and book value of a company's plant assets
(Obj. 1)

1. When does The Home Depot's fiscal year end? Why does the company's fiscal year end on this date?
2. What is The Home Depot's largest category of assets—current assets, property and equipment, or other category?
3. What was The Home Depot's cost of property and equipment at January 30, 2000? What was the book value of property and equipment on this date?

DE10-2 Page 388 of this chapter lists the costs included for the acquisition of land. First is the purchase price of the land, which is obviously included in the cost of the land. The reasons for including the related costs are not so obvious. For example, the removal of a building looks more like an expense. State why the costs listed are included as part of the cost of the land. After the land is ready for use, will these costs be capitalized or expensed?

Measuring the cost of a plant asset
(Obj. 1)

DE10-3 A lessee (who is renting an asset such as a building) makes periodic lease payments to the lessor (who owns the building). The lessee does not have a legal title to the building. Nevertheless, under certain conditions the lessee may account for the building as though the lessee owned an asset. How can a capital lease be fundamentally like an asset to the lessee?

Understanding leases
(Obj. 1)

DE10-4 Suppose Florida Power, the utility company, is constructing power-generating equipment for use in its operations. To finance construction, Florida Power borrows $800,000 on notes payable on January 2, 20X3. During 20X3, Florida Power incurs interest cost equal to 9% of its construction loan. All of the company's interest cost should be capitalized to the Equipment account.

Capitalizing interest cost
(Obj. 1)

1. Make the journal entry to pay Florida Power's interest cost at December 31, 20X3.
2. At December 31, 20X3, what is the balance in the Equipment account? Prepare a T-account for Equipment to answer this question.

DE10-5 Return to the Work It Out feature on page 391. Suppose at the time of your acquisition, the land has a current market value of $80,000, the building's market value is $60,000, and the equipment's market value is $20,000. Journalize the lump-sum purchase of the three assets for a total cost of $100,000. You sign a note payable for this amount.

Lump-sum purchase of assets
(Obj. 1)

DE10-6 Vantas Airways repaired one of its Boeing 767 aircraft at a cost of $750,000, which Vantas paid in cash. Vantas erroneously capitalized this cost as part of the cost of the plane.

Capitalizing versus expensing plant asset costs
(Obj. 1)

1. Journalize both the incorrect entry the accountant made to record this transaction and the correct entry that the accountant should have made.
2. Show the effects of the accounting error on Vantas Airways' income statement and balance sheet, using the format illustrated on page 392.

DE10-7 At the beginning of the year, Vantas Airways purchased a used Boeing MD-11 aircraft at a cost of $36,000,000. Vantas expects the plane to remain useful for five years (5 million miles) and to have a residual value of $6,000,000. Vantas expects the plane to be flown 750,000 miles the first year and 1,250,000 miles the last year.

Computing depreciation by three methods—first year only
(Obj. 2)

1. Compute Vantas' first-year depreciation on the plane using the following methods:
   a. Straight-line   b. Units-of-production   c. Double-declining-balance
2. Show the airplane's book value at the end of the first year under each depreciation method.

DE10-8 At the beginning of 20X1, Vantas Airways purchased a used Boeing MD-11 aircraft at a cost of $36,000,000. Vantas expects the plane to remain useful for five years (5 million miles) and to have a residual value of $6,000,000. Vantas expects the plane to be flown 750,000 miles the first year and 1,250,000 miles the fifth year. Compute Vantas's fifth-year depreciation on the plane using the following methods:

Computing depreciation by three methods—final year only
(Obj. 2)

a. Straight-line
b. Units-of-production
c. Double-declining-balance (you must compute depreciation for all five years)

DE10-9 This exercise uses the Vantas Airways' data from Daily Exercise 10-7. Assume Vantas Airways is trying to decide which depreciation method to use for income tax purposes.

1. Which depreciation method offers the tax advantage for the first year? Describe the nature of the tax advantage.
2. How much income tax will Vantas save for the first year of the airplane's use as compared to using the straight-line depreciation method? Vantas' income tax rate is 40%.

DE10-10 On March 31, 20X2, Vantas Airways purchased a used Boeing MD-11 aircraft at a cost of $36,000,000. Vantas expects the plane to remain useful for five years (5,000,000 miles) and to have a residual value of $6,000,000. Vantas expects the plane to be flown 800,000 miles during the remainder of the first year ended December 31, 20X2. Compute Vantas' depreciation on the plane for the year ended December 31, 20X2, using the following methods:

a. Straight-line b. Units-of-production c. Double-declining-balance

DE10-11 Return to the example of the **Disney World** hot dog stand on pages 401–402. Suppose that after using the hot dog stand for four years, the company determines that the asset will remain useful for only two more years. Record Disney's depreciation on the hot dog stand for year 5 by the straight-line method.

DE10-12 Return to the **Home Depot** delivery-truck depreciation example in Exhibits 10-6 and 10-8. Suppose The Home Depot sold the truck on December 31, 20X2, for $23,000 cash, after using the truck for two full years. Depreciation for 20X2 has already been recorded.

1. Make a separate journal entry to record The Home Depot's sale of the truck under
   a. Straight-line depreciation (Exhibit 10-6)
   b. Double-declining-balance depreciation (Exhibit 10-8)
2. Why is there such a big difference between the gain or loss on disposal under the two depreciation methods?

DE10-13 **Chevron,** the giant oil company, holds huge reserves of oil and gas assets. At the end of 20X0, Chevron's cost of mineral assets totaled approximately $18 billion, representing 2.4 billion barrels of oil and gas reserves in the ground.

1. Which depreciation method do Chevron and other oil companies use to compute their annual depletion expense for the minerals removed from the ground?
2. Suppose Chevron removed 0.6 billion barrels of oil during 20X1. Record Chevron's depletion expense for 20X1.
3. At December 31, 20X0, Chevron's Accumulated Depletion account stood at $11.5 billion. If Chevron did not add any new oil and gas reserves during 20X1, what would be the book value of the company's oil and gas reserves after recording depletion at December 31, 20X1?

DE10-14 Media-related companies have little in the way of tangible plant assets. Instead, their main asset is goodwill. When one media company buys another, goodwill is often the most costly asset acquired. Flannahan Newsprint paid $700,000 to acquire *The Thrifty Nickel*, an advertising paper headquartered in Texas. At the time of Flannahan's acquisition, *The Thrifty Nickel's* balance sheet reported total assets of $1,150,000 and liabilities of $600,000. The fair market value of *The Thrifty Nickel's* assets was $990,000.

1. How much goodwill did Flannahan purchase as part of the acquisition of *The Thrifty Nickel?*
2. Make Flannahan's summary journal entry to record the acquisition of *The Thrifty Nickel*.
3. What is the maximum useful life of the goodwill under GAAP? If Flannahan amortizes the goodwill over the maximum useful life, how much amortization expense will Flannahan record each year?

DE10-15 Examine the balance sheet of **The Home Depot** in Exhibit 10-2 at the beginning of this chapter. Answer these questions about the company:

1. What account title does The Home Depot use for goodwill?
2. What was the book value of The Home Depot's goodwill at January 30, 2000? What was the amount of accumulated amortization on the goodwill? What was The Home Depot's cost of its goodwill on this date?
3. One year earlier, on January 30, 1999, The Home Depot had Goodwill at a cost of $329 million, less Accumulated Amortization of $21 million, for a book value of $308 million. During the year ended January 30, 2000, The Home Depot sold no companies and thus sold none of its goodwill. Use your answer to requirement 2 to compute the cost of the goodwill The Home Depot purchased during the year ended January 30, 2000.

DE10-16 This exercise summarizes the accounting for patents, which like copyrights and trademarks, provide the owner with a special right. It also covers research and development.

Questor Applications paid $875,000 to research and develop a new software program. Questor also paid $300,000 to acquire a patent on the new software. After readying the software for production, Questor's sales revenue for the first year totaled $1,500,000. Cost of goods sold was $200,000 and selling expenses were $400,000. All these transactions occurred during 20X3. Questor expects the patent to have a useful life of three years.

1. Prepare Questor Applications' income statement for the year ended December 31, 20X3, complete with a heading.
2. Considering the makeup of Questor's expenses, what should the company's outlook for future profits be on the new software program?

EXERCISES

E10-1 Delmar Mining Company purchased land, paying $77,000 cash as a down payment and signing a $120,000 note payable for the balance. In addition, Delmar paid delinquent property tax of $2,000, title insurance costing $2,500, and a $5,400 charge for leveling the land and removing an unwanted building. The company constructed an office building on the land at a cost of $799,000. It also paid $51,000 for a fence around the boundary of the property, $10,400 for the company sign near the entrance to the property, and $6,000 for special lighting of the grounds. Determine the cost of the company's land, land improvements, and building. Which of the assets will Delmar depreciate?

Determining the cost of plant assets
(Obj. 1)

E10-2 Weidman Belts, Inc. manufactures conveyor belts in St. Louis, Missouri. Early in January 20X3, Weidman constructed its own factory building with borrowed money. The 9% loan was for $600,000. During the year, Weidman spent the loan amount on construction of the building. At year end, Weidman paid the interest for one year.

Measuring the cost of an asset; capitalizing interest
(Obj. 1)

Required

1. How much should Weidman record as the cost of the building in 20X3?
2. Record all of Weidman's transactions during 20X3.

E10-3 The Williamsburg Equestrian Center bought three valuable saddles in a $10,000 lump-sum purchase. An independent appraiser valued the saddles as follows:

Allocating cost to assets acquired in a lump-sum purchase
(Obj. 1)

Saddle	Appraised Value
1	$3,350
2	5,400
3	4,250

Williamsburg paid half in cash and signed a note payable for the remainder. Record the purchase in the journal, identifying each saddle's individual cost in a separate Saddle account. Round decimals to three places.

E10-4 Classify each of the following expenditures as a capital expenditure or an expense related to machinery: (a) major overhaul to extend useful life by three years; (b) ordinary recurring repairs to keep the machinery in good working order; (c) lubrication of the machinery before it is placed in service; (d) periodic lubrication after the machinery is placed in service; (e) purchase price; (f) sales tax paid on the purchase price; (g) transportation and insurance while machinery is in transit from seller to buyer; (h) installation; (i) training of personnel for initial operation of the machinery; (j) special reinforcement to the machinery platform; and (k) income tax paid on income earned from the sale of products manufactured by the machinery.

Distinguishing capital expenditures from expenses
(Obj. 1)

E10-5 Leslie Peres has just slept through the class in which Professor Dobbins explained the concept of depreciation. Because the next test is scheduled for Wednesday, Peres telephones Kim Barnes to get her notes from the lecture. Barnes's notes are concise: "Depreciation— Sounds like Greek to me." Peres next tries Tim Lake, who says he thinks depreciation is what happens when an asset wears out. Lee McPherson is confident that depreciation is the process of building up a cash fund to replace an asset at the end of its useful life. Explain the concept of depreciation for Peres. Evaluate the explanations of Lake and McPherson. Be specific.

Explaining the concept of depreciation
(Obj. 2)

E10-6 De Plain International bought a delivery truck on January 2, 20X1, for $15,000. The truck was expected to remain in service four years and to last 100,000 miles. At the end of its useful life, De Plain officials estimated that the truck's residual value would be $3,000. The truck traveled 34,000 miles the first year, 28,000 the second year, 18,000 the third year, and 20,000 the fourth year. Prepare a schedule of *depreciation expense* per year for the truck under the three depreciation methods. After two years under the double-declining-balance method, the company switched to the straight-line method. Show your computations.

Which method tracks the wear and tear on the truck most closely? Which method would De Plain prefer to use for income tax purposes? Explain in detail why De Plain prefers this method.

Determining depreciation amounts by three methods
(Obj. 2, 3)

PLANT ASSETS AND INTANGIBLE ASSETS   413

Selecting the best depreciation
method for income tax purposes
(Obj. 3)

E10-7 Taylor Marshall Co. paid $165,000 for equipment that is expected to have a seven-year life. The residual value of equipment is approximately 10% of the asset's cost.

Select the appropriate MACRS depreciation method for income tax purposes. Then determine the extra amount of cash that Marshall Co. can invest by using MACRS depreciation, versus straight-line, during the first two years of the equipment's life. Ignore any interest Marshall can earn by investing the extra cash.

Changing a plant asset's
useful life
(Obj. 2)

E10-8 Relax-the-Back Mattress Store purchased a building for $775,000 and depreciated it on a straight-line basis over a 40-year period. The estimated residual value was $100,000. After using the building for 15 years, Relax-the-Back realized that wear and tear on the building would force the company to replace it before 40 years. Starting with the 16th year, Relax-the-Back began depreciating the building over a revised total life of 30 years and increased the estimated residual value to $200,000. Record depreciation expense on the building for years 15 and 16.

Analyzing the effect of a sale of a
plant asset; DDB depreciation
(Obj. 4)

E10-9 On January 2, 20X3, Kloss Furniture Warehouse purchased showroom fixtures for $9,500 cash, expecting the fixtures to remain in service five years. Kloss has depreciated the fixtures on a double-declining-balance basis, with a $1,000 estimated residual value. On September 30, 20X4, Kloss sold the fixtures for $4,950 cash. Record both the depreciation expense on the fixtures for 20X4 and the sale of the fixtures on September 30, 20X4.

Measuring a plant asset's cost,
using UOP depreciation, and
trading in a used asset
(Obj. 1, 2, 4)

E10-10 Lasseter Transportation, based in Natchez, Mississippi, is a large trucking company that operates throughout the southern United States. Lasseter uses the units-of-production (UOP) method to depreciate its trucks because UOP depreciation best measures wear and tear. Lasseter trades in used trucks often to keep driver morale high and to maximize fuel efficiency. Consider these facts about one Mack truck in the company's fleet.

When acquired in 20X1, the tractor/trailer rig cost $385,000 and was expected to remain in service for ten years or 1,000,000 miles. Estimated residual value was $100,000. The truck was driven 75,000 miles in 20X1, 120,000 miles in 20X2, and 210,000 miles in 20X3. After 40,000 miles in 20X4, the company traded in the Mack truck for a less-expensive Freightliner. Lasseter paid cash of $80,000. Determine Lasseter's cost of the new truck. Journal entries are not required.

Recording natural resource
assets and depletion
(Obj. 5)

E10-11 El Dorado Drilling paid $298,500 for the right to extract ore from a 200,000-ton mineral deposit. In addition to the purchase price, El Dorado also paid a $500 filing fee, a $1,000 license fee to the state of Wyoming, and $60,000 for a geological survey of the property. Because the company purchased the rights to the minerals only, the company expected the asset to have zero residual value when fully depleted. During the first year, El Dorado removed 42,000 tons of ore. Make journal entries to record (a) purchase of the minerals (debit Mineral Asset), (b) payment of fees and other costs, and (c) depletion for the first year.

Recording intangibles, amortization, and a change in the asset's
useful life
(Obj. 6)

E10-12 *Part 1.* Westmark Printing Co., which manufactures high-speed printers, has recently paid $1.37 million for a patent on a new laser printer. Although it gives legal protection for 20 years, the patent is expected to provide Westmark with a competitive advantage for only 8 years. Assuming the straight-line method of amortization, make journal entries to record (a) the purchase of the patent, and (b) amortization for year 1.

Part 2. After using the patent for 4 years, Westmark learns at an industry trade show that another company is designing a more efficient printer. On the basis of this new information, Westmark decides, starting with year 5, to amortize the remaining cost of the patent over 2 remaining years, giving the patent a total useful life of 6 years. Record amortization for year 5.

Measuring goodwill
(Obj. 6)

E10-13 **Campbell Soup Company's** 19X9 statement of cash flows includes the following (adapted):

	Millions
	19X9
Cash Flows from Investing Activities:	
Payments to acquire other businesses..............	$105

Campbell's Note 16 to the balance sheet includes the following for Intangible Assets:

	Millions	
	19X9	**19X8**
Purchase price in excess of net assets of businesses acquired......................................	$1,697	$1,655
Less: Accumulated amortization	(219)	(179)

Required

1. What title does Campbell Soup Company use to describe its goodwill? How well does Campbell's title agree with the text definition of goodwill?
2. How much did Campbell Soup Company pay to acquire other businesses during 19X9? How much of the purchase price was for goodwill? How much did Campbell pay for the other assets of the businesses it acquired, such as receivables, inventory, property, and equipment?

E10-14 PepsiCo, Inc., has aggressively acquired other companies, such as **Frito-Lay,** famous for its snack foods. Assume that PepsiCo purchased Adelaide Bakeries for $12 million cash. The market value of Adelaide's assets is $15 million, and it has liabilities of $10 million.

Measuring and recording goodwill (Obj. 6)

Required

1. Compute the cost of the goodwill purchased by PepsiCo.
2. Record the purchase of Adelaide Bakeries by PepsiCo.
3. Record PepsiCo's amortization of goodwill for year 1, assuming the straight-line method and a useful life of ten years.

CHALLENGE EXERCISES

E10-15 Papillon Knits is a catalog merchant in France similar to **L. L. Bean** and **Lands' End** in the United States. The company's assets consist mainly of inventory, a warehouse, and automated shipping equipment. Assume that early in year 1, Papillon purchased equipment at a cost of $4.5 million francs (F4.5 million). Management expects the equipment to remain in service five years. Because the equipment is so specialized, estimated residual value is negligible. Papillon uses the straight-line depreciation method. Through an accounting error, Papillon accidentally expensed the entire cost of the equipment at the time of purchase. The company is family-owned and operated as a partnership, so it pays no income tax.

Capitalizing versus expensing; measuring the effect of an error (Obj. 1)

Required

Prepare a schedule to show the overstatement or understatement in the following items at the end of each year over the five-year life of the equipment.

1. Total current assets   2. Equipment, net   3. Net income

E10-16 General Motors Corporation's comparative balance sheet reported these amounts (in millions of dollars):

Reconstructing transactions from the financial statements (Obj. 2, 4)

| | December 31, | |
	19X9	19X8
Property:		
Land, plant, and equipment	$ 59,777	$ 59,565
Less accumulated depreciation...................	(34,363)	(34,641)
Net land, plant, and equipment..............	25,414	24,924
Unamortized special tools..........................	7,365	7,298
Net property...	$ 32,779	$ 32,222

GM's income statement for 19X9 reported the following expenses (in millions):

Depreciation	$4,155
Amortization of special tools	2,492

Unamortized special tools refers to the remaining asset balance after amortization expense has been subtracted. GM does not use an accumulated amortization account for special tools.

Required

1. There were no disposals of special tools during 19X9. Compute the cost of new acquisitions of special tools. Use a T-account for Special Tools.
2. Assume that during 19X9, GM sold land, plant, and equipment for $215 million and that this transaction produced a gain of $15 million. What was the book value of the assets sold?

PROBLEMS

(Group A)

P10-1A Metropolitan Glass Company incurred the following costs in acquiring land and a garage, making land improvements, and constructing and furnishing an office building:

Identifying the elements of a plant asset's cost (Obj. 1, 2)

a. Purchase price of 3 1/2 acres of land, including a building that will
be used as a garage for company vehicles (land market value is
$700,000; building market value is $100,000).. $640,000
b. Delinquent real estate taxes on the land to be paid by Metropolitan 3,700
c. Landscaping (additional dirt and earth moving) 5,175
d. Title insurance on the land acquisition 1,000
e. Fence around the boundary of the land.. 44,100
f. Building permit for the office building... 200
g. Architect's fee for the design of the office building 32,000
h. Company signs near the approaches to the company property 20,950
i. Renovation of the garage 27,500
j. Concrete, wood, and materials used to construct the office building 814,000
k. Masonry, carpentry, roofing, and other labor to construct the office
building... 734,000
l. Interest cost on construction loan for the office building........................... 3,400
m. Parking lots and concrete walks on the property 17,450
n. Lights for the parking lot, walkways, and company signs.......................... 8,900
o. Salary of construction supervisor (90% to office building; 6% to fencing,
parking lot, and concrete walks; and 4% to garage renovation) 55,000
p. Furniture for the office building... 123,500
q. Transportation of furniture from seller to the office building 1,100
r. Landscaping (trees and shrubs) 9,100

Metropolitan Glass depreciates buildings over 40 years, land improvements over 20 years, and
furniture over 8 years, all on a straight-line basis with zero residual value.

Required

1. Set up columns for Land, Land Improvements, Office Building, Garage, and Furniture.
Show how to account for each of Metropolitan's costs by listing the cost under the correct
account. Determine the total cost of each asset.
2. All construction was complete and the assets were placed in service on March 29. Record
depreciation for the year ended December 31. Round to the nearest dollar.

Recording plant asset transactions, exchange, and disposal (Obj, 1, 2, 4)

P10-2A Lee & Smythe surveys American television-viewing trends. The company's balance
sheet reports the following assets under Property and Equipment: Land, Buildings, Office
Equipment, Communication Equipment, and Televideo Equipment, with a separate
accumulated depreciation account for each depreciable asset. During 20X2, Lee & Smythe
completed the following transactions:

May 3   Purchased communication and televideo equipment from the Gallup polling organization. Total cost was $80,000 paid in cash. An independent appraisal valued
the communication equipment at $90,000 and the televideo equipment at
$10,000.

July 30   Traded in old office equipment with book value of $11,000 (cost of $96,000) for
new equipment with a cash cost of $88,000. The seller gave Lee & Smythe a trade-
in allowance of $20,000 on the old equipment, and Lee & Smythe paid the remain-
der in cash.

Sep. 1   Sold a building that had cost $475,000 (accumulated depreciation of $353,500
through December 31 of the preceding year. Depreciation is computed on a
straight-line basis. The building has a 30-year useful life and a residual value of
$47,500. Lee & Smythe received $150,000 cash and a $450,000 note receivable.

Dec. 31   Recorded depreciation as follows:
Communication equipment and televideo equipment are depreciated by the
double-declining-balance method over a five-year life with zero residual value.
Office equipment is depreciated straight-line over seven years with $9,000 residual
value. Record depreciation on the equipment acquired on May 3 and on July 30
separately.

Required

Record the transactions in the journal of Lee & Smythe.

Explaining the concept of depreciation (Obj. 2)

P10-3A The board of directors of Ameritech Satellite Technology is having its regular
quarterly meeting. Accounting policies are on the agenda, and depreciation is being discussed.
A new board member, an attorney, has some strong opinions about two aspects of
depreciation policy. Clay Fitzhugh argues that depreciation must be coupled with a fund to
replace company assets. Otherwise, there is no substance to depreciation, he argues. Fitzhugh
also challenges the three-year depreciable life of company computers. He states that the
computers will last much longer and should be depreciated over at least five years.

Required

Write a memo to explain the concept of depreciation to Fitzhugh and to answer his
arguments. Format your memo as follows:

450,000

30,000

```
MEMO
To:      _____
From:    _____
Subject: _____
```

P10-4A On January 2, 20X1, Machinery Unlimited purchased a used trailer at a cost of $63,000. Before placing the trailer in service, the company spent $2,200 painting it, $800 replacing tires, and $4,000 overhauling the chassis. Machinery Unlimited management estimates that the trailer will remain in service for six years and have a residual value of $14,200. The trailer's annual mileage is expected to be 18,000 miles in each of the first four years and 14,000 miles in each of the next two years. In deciding which depreciation method to use, Brett Vivecek, the general manager, requests a depreciation schedule for each of the depreciation methods (straight-line, units-of-production, and double-declining-balance).

Computing depreciation by three methods and the cash-flow advantage of accelerated depreciation for tax purposes (Obj. 2, 3)

Required

1. Prepare a depreciation schedule for each depreciation method, showing asset cost, depreciation expense, accumulated depreciation, and asset book value. For the units-of-production method, round depreciation per mile to three decimal places.
2. Machinery Unlimited reports to creditors in the financial statements using the depreciation method that maximizes reported income in the early years of asset use. For income tax purposes, however, the company uses the depreciation method that minimizes income tax payments in those early years. Consider the first year that Machinery Unlimited uses the trailer. Identify the depreciation methods that meet the general manager's objectives, assuming the income tax authorities permit the use of any of the methods.
3. Cash provided by operations before income tax is $150,000 for the trailer's first year. The combined federal and state income tax rate is 40%. For the two depreciation methods identified in requirement 2, compare the net income and cash provided by operations (cash flow). Show which method gives the net-income advantage and which method gives the cash-flow advantage.

P10-5A *Note:* This problem uses the statement of cash flows, but all items are self-explanatory. **Curtiss-Wright Corporation** is a medium-sized manufacturer of high-tech parts used in commercial and military aircraft. The following excerpts come from Curtiss-Wright's 19X9 financial statements:

Analyzing plant asset transactions from a company's financial statements (Obj. 2, 4)

CURTISS-WRIGHT CORPORATION
Balance Sheet (Adapted)

(In thousands) Assets	December 31, 19X9	19X8
Current assets:		
Cash and cash equivalents	$ 9,547	$ 5,809
Short-term investments	25,560	66,444
Receivables, net..	70,729	60,912
Inventories	60,584	54,048
Other current assets	13,950	11,360
Total current assets......................................	180,370	198,573
Property, plant, and equipment, at cost.............	242,000	237,215
Less: Accumulated depreciation.......................	(147,422)	(162,704)
Property, plant, and equipment, net..................	94,578	74,511
Other assets...	112,178	79,656
Total assets	$387,126	$352,740

CURTISS-WRIGHT CORPORATION
Statements of Cash Flows (Excerpts, Adapted)

(In thousands) Cash Flows from Investing Activities	For the Years Ended December 31, 19X9	19X8
Cash receipts from sales of plant assets	$ 2,586	$ 950
Payments for property, plant, and equipment...............	(19,883)	(10,642)

Required

Answer these questions about Curtiss-Wright's plant assets.

1. At December 31, 19X9, what was Curtiss-Wright's cost of its plant assets? What was the amount of accumulated depreciation? What was the book value of the plant assets? Does book value measure how much Curtiss-Wright could sell the assets for? Explain.
2. Curtiss-Wright's depreciation expense for 19X9 was $12,864 thousand. Why is the amount of depreciation expense so different from accumulated depreciation at December 31, 19X9?
3. How much did Curtiss-Wright pay to purchase plant assets during 19X9? Prepare a T-account showing the 19X8 and 19X9 balances of Property, Plant, and Equipment cost. Post to the T-account the cost of plant assets purchased during 19X9. Then compute the cost of plant assets *sold* during 19X9. Finally, determine whether Curtiss-Wright bought or sold more plant assets during the year.

*Accounting for intangibles, natural resources, and the related expenses
(Obj. 5, 6)*

P10-6A *Part 1.*   **United Telecommunications, Inc.** (United Telecom) provides communication services in Florida, North Carolina, New Jersey, Texas, and other states. The company's balance sheet reports the asset Cost of Acquisitions in Excess of the Fair Market Value of the Net Assets of Subsidiaries. Assume that United Telecom purchased this asset as part of the acquisition of another company, which had these figures:

Book value of assets	$575,000
Market value of assets	906,000
Liabilities	405,000

Required

1. What is another title for the asset Cost of Acquisitions in Excess of the Fair Market Value of the Net Assets of Subsidiaries?
2. Make the journal entry recording United Telecom's purchase of the other company for $1,650,000 cash. Use the account titled Goodwill.
3. Assume United Telecom amortizes Cost of Acquisitions in Excess of the Fair Market Value of the Net Assets of Subsidiaries over 20 years. Record straight-line amortization for one year. Use the account titled Goodwill.

Part 2. **Continental Pipeline Company** operates a pipeline that provides natural gas to Atlanta, Washington, D.C., Philadelphia, and New York City. The company's balance sheet includes the asset Oil and Gas Properties.

Suppose Continental paid $7 million cash for oil and gas reserves with an estimated 500,000 barrels of oil. Assume the company paid $350,000 for additional geological tests of the property and $110,000 to prepare the surface for drilling. Prior to production, the company signed a $65,000 note payable to have a building constructed on the property. The building will be abandoned when the oil is depleted, so its cost is debited to the Oil Properties account and included in depletion charges. During the first year of production, Continental removed 77,000 barrels of oil, which it sold on credit for $19 per barrel. Operating expenses related to this project totaled $185,000 for the first year, all paid in cash.

Required

1. Record all of Continental's transactions, including depletion, for the year.
2. Prepare the company's income statement for this oil and gas project for the first year. Evaluate the profitability of the project.

*Reporting plant asset transactions in the financial statements—a review
(Obj. 1, 2, 4)*

P10-7A At the end of 1998, **Sprint Corporation,** the telecommunications company, had total assets of $33.3 billion and total liabilities of $20.9 billion. Included among the assets were property, plant, and equipment with a cost of $32.1 billion and accumulated depreciation of $13.1 billion.

Assume that Sprint completed the following selected transactions during 1999: The company earned total revenues of $19.9 billion and incurred total expenses of $20.8 billion, which included depreciation of $3.7 billion. During the year, Sprint paid $6.1 billion for new property, plant, and equipment, and sold old plant assets for $0.2 billion. The cost of the assets sold was $1.1 billion, and their accumulated depreciation was also $1.1 billion.

Required

1. Show how Sprint Corporation would report property, plant, and equipment on the balance sheet at December 31, 1999.
2. How much of the plant assets that Sprint sold during 1999 had been depreciated? Did Sprint have a gain or a loss on the sale of plant assets? What was the amount of the gain or loss?
3. How much was Sprint's owner's equity at December 31, 1998?
4. Did Sprint report net income or net loss on its 1999 income statement? Compute the amount.

PROBLEMS

P10-1B Bobby Jones Golf Company incurred the following costs in acquiring land, making land improvements, and constructing and furnishing its own sales building.

a.	Purchase price of four acres of land, including a building that will be used for a garage (land market value is $280,000; building market value is $40,000)	$300,000
b.	Landscaping (additional dirt and earth moving)	8,100
c.	Fence around the boundary of the land	17,650
d.	Attorney fee for title search on the land	770
e.	Delinquent real estate taxes on the land to be paid by Bobby Jones	5,900
f.	Company signs at front of the company property	4,475
g.	Building permit for the sales building	350
h.	Architect's fee for the design of the sales building	22,500
i.	Masonry, carpentry, roofing, and labor to construct the sales building	709,000
j.	Concrete, wood, and other materials used to construct the sales building	214,000
k.	Renovation of the garage building	36,900
l.	Interest cost on construction loan for sales building	9,000
m.	Landscaping (trees and shrubs)	6,400
n.	Parking lot and concrete walks on the property	29,750
o.	Lights for the parking lot, walkways, and company signs	7,300
p.	Salary of construction supervisor (85% to sales building; 9% to fencing, parking lot, and concrete walks; and 6% to garage building)	40,000
q.	Furniture for the sales building	107,100
r.	Transportation and installation of furniture	2,270

Bobby Jones depreciates buildings over 40 years, land improvements over 20 years, and furniture over 8 years, all on a straight-line basis with zero residual value.

Required

1. Set up columns for Land, Land Improvements, Sales Building, Garage Building, and Furniture. Show how to account for each of Bobby Jones's costs by listing the cost under the correct account. Determine the total cost of each asset.
2. All construction was complete and the assets were placed in service on May 2. Record depreciation for the year ended December 31. Round to the nearest dollar.

P10-2B Westway Freight Co. provides local freight service in Lincoln, Nebraska. The company's balance sheet includes the following assets under Property, Plant, and Equipment: Land, Buildings, and Motor-Carrier Equipment. Westway has a separate accumulated depreciation account for each of these assets except land. Assume that Westway Freight Co. completed the following transactions:

Jan. 2 Traded in motor-carrier equipment with book value of $47,000 (cost of $130,000) for similar new equipment with a cash cost of $176,000. Westway received a trade-in allowance of $70,000 on the old equipment and paid the remainder in cash.

July 1 Sold a building that cost $550,000 and that had accumulated depreciation of $247,500 through December 31 of the preceding year. Depreciation is computed on a straight-line basis. The building has a 30-year useful life and a residual value of $55,000. Westway received $100,000 cash and a $600,000 note receivable.

Oct. 26 Purchased land and a building for a single price of $300,000. An independent appraisal valued the land at $115,000 and the building at $230,000.

Dec. 31 Recorded depreciation as follows:
Motor-carrier equipment has an expected useful life of six years and an estimated residual value of 5% of cost. Depreciation is double-declining-balance.
Depreciation on buildings is straight-line. The new building has a 40-year useful life and a residual value equal to 12% of its cost.

Required

Record the transactions in Westway Freight's journal.

P10-3B The board of directors of Wentzville Corporation is reviewing the 20X1 annual report. A new board member—a professor—questions the company accountant about the depreciation amounts. The professor wonders why depreciation expense has decreased from $200,000 in 19X9 to $184,000 in 20X0 to $172,000 in 20X1. He states that he could understand the decreasing annual amounts if the company had been selling properties each year, but that has not occurred. Further, growth in the city is increasing the values of property. Why is the company recording depreciation when property values are increasing?

Required

Write a paragraph or two to explain the concept of depreciation and answer the professor's questions. Which depreciation method does Wentzville appear to be using?

Computing depreciation by three
methods and the cash-flow
advantage of accelerated depreciation for tax purposes
(Obj. 2, 3)

P10-4B On January 3, 20X1, Dobb Automotive Company paid $224,000 for equipment used in manufacturing automotive supplies. In addition to the basic purchase price, the company paid $700 transportation charges, $100 insurance for the equipment while in transit, $12,100 sales tax, and $3,100 for a special platform on which to place the equipment in the plant. Dobb management estimates that the equipment will remain in service five years and have a residual value of $17,000. The equipment will produce 50,000 units the first year, with annual production decreasing by 5,000 units during each of the next four years (that is, 45,000 units in year 2; 40,000 units in year 3; and so on). In trying to decide which depreciation method to use, Jacqueline Dobb has requested a depreciation schedule for each of three depreciation methods (straight-line, units-of-production, and double-declining-balance).

Required

1. For each depreciation method, prepare a depreciation schedule showing asset cost, depreciation expense, accumulated depreciation, and asset book value. For the units-of-production method, round depreciation per unit to three decimal places.
2. Dobb reports to stockholders and creditors in the financial statements using the depreciation method that maximizes reported income in the early years of asset use. For income tax purposes, the company uses the depreciation method that minimizes income tax payments in those early years. Consider the first year Dobb uses the equipment. Identify the depreciation methods that meet Dobb's objectives, assuming the income tax authorities permit the use of any of the methods.
3. Assume that cash provided by operations before income tax is $180,000 for the equipment's first year. The combined federal and state income tax rate is 40%. For the two depreciation methods identified in requirement 2, compare the net income and cash provided by operations (cash flow). Show which method gives the net-income advantage and which method gives the cash-flow advantage.

Analyzing plant asset transactions
from a company's financial
statements
(Obj. 2, 4)

P10-5B *Note:* This problem uses the statement of cash flows, but all items are self-explanatory. **IBM** is the world's largest computer company. After a few lean years, Big Blue, as the company is called, has rebounded strongly with some new products and improving profits. The following excerpts come from IBM's 19X9 financial statements:

INTERNATIONAL BUSINESS MACHINES CORPORATION
Balance Sheet (Adapted)

(Dollars in Millions) At December 31:	19X9	19X8
Assets		
Current assets:		
Cash and cash equivalents	$ 5,043	$ 5,375
Marketable securities	788	393
Notes and accounts receivable—trade, net of allowances	20,039	18,958
Sales-type leases receivable	6,220	6,510
Other accounts receivable	1,359	1,313
Inventories	4,868	5,200
Prepaid expenses and other current assets	4,838	4,611
Total current assets	43,155	42,360
Plant, machines, and other property, at cost	39,616	44,870
Less: Accumulated depreciation	(22,026)	(25,239)
Plant, machines, and other property—net	17,590	19,631
Software	663	599
Investments and sundry assets	26,087	23,510
Total assets	$87,495	$86,100

INTERNATIONAL BUSINESS MACHINES CORPORATION
Statement of Cash Flows (Excerpts)

(Dollars in Millions) For the year ended December 31:	19X9	19X8
Cash flows from investing activities:		
Payments for plant, machines, and other property	$(5,959)	$(6,520)
Cash received from the sale of plant, rental machines, and other property	1,207	905

Required

1. At December 31, 19X9, what was IBM's cost of its plant assets? What was the amount of accumulated depreciation? What percent of the cost has been used up?
2. IBM's depreciation expense for 19X9 was $6,159 million. Why is the amount of depreciation expense so different from accumulated depreciation at December 31, 19X9?
3. How much did IBM pay to purchase plant assets during 19X9? Prepare a T-account showing the 19X8 and 19X9 balances of total Plant Assets at cost. Post the cost of plant asset purchases during 19X9. Then compute the cost of plant assets *sold* during 19X9. Finally, determine whether IBM bought or sold more plant assets during the year.
4. IBM's balance sheet reports Software. What category of asset is software?

P10-6B *Part 1.* **Collins Foods International Inc.** is the majority owner of Sizzler Restaurants. The company's balance sheet reports the asset Cost in Excess of Net Assets of Purchased Businesses. Assume that Collins purchased this asset as part of the acquisition of another company, which carried these figures:

Accounting for intangibles, natural resources, and the related expenses (Obj. 5, 6)

Book value of assets	$2.4 million
Market value of assets	2.8 million
Liabilities	2.2 million

Required

1. What is another title for the asset Cost in Excess of Net Assets of Purchased Businesses?
2. Make the journal entry to record Collins's purchase of the other company for $2.7 million cash. Use the account titled Goodwill.
3. Assume Collins amortizes Cost in Excess of Net Assets of Purchased Businesses over 20 years. Record the straight-line amortization for one year. Use the account titled Goodwill.

Part 2. **Georgia-Pacific Corporation** is one of the world's largest forest products companies. The company's balance sheet includes the assets Natural Gas, Oil, and Coal.

Suppose Georgia-Pacific paid $2.8 million cash for the right to work a mine with an estimated 100,000 tons of coal. Assume the company paid $60,000 to remove unwanted buildings from the land and $45,000 to prepare the surface for mining. Further, assume that Georgia-Pacific signed a $30,000 note payable to a company that will return the land surface to its original condition after the lease ends. During the first year, Georgia-Pacific removed 35,000 tons of coal, which it sold on account for $37 per ton. Operating expenses for the first year totaled $252,000, all paid in cash.

Required

1. Record all of Georgia-Pacific's transactions, including depletion, for the year.
2. Prepare the company's income statement for its coal operations for the first year. Evaluate the profitability of the coal operations.

P10-7B At the end of 19X8, **The Coca-Cola Company** had total assets of $19.1 billion and total liabilities of $10.7 billion. Included among the assets were property, plant, and equipment with a cost of $5.7 billion and accumulated depreciation of $2.0 billion.

Coca-Cola completed the following selected transactions during 19X9: The company earned total revenues of $19.8 billion and incurred total expenses of $17.3 billion, which included depreciation of $0.8 billion. During the year, Coca-Cola paid $1.1 billion for new property, plant, and equipment and sold old plant assets, receiving cash of $0.2 billion. The cost of the assets sold was $0.1 billion; their accumulated depreciation was also $0.1 billion.

Reporting plant asset transactions in the financial statements—a review (Obj. 1, 2, 4)

Required

1. Show how Coca-Cola would report property, plant, and equipment on the balance sheet at December 31, 19X9. What was the book value of property, plant, and equipment on that date?
2. How much of the assets that Coca-Cola sold during 19X9 had been depreciated? Did Coca-Cola have a gain or loss on the sale of plant assets during 19X9? What was the amount of the gain or loss?
3. How much was Coca-Cola's owners' equity at December 31, 19X8?
4. Did Coca-Cola report net income or net loss on its 19X9 income statement? Compute the amount.

DECISION CASES

Case 1. ← *Link Back to Chapter 9 (Inventory Methods).* Suppose you are considering investing in two businesses, Astoria Enterprises and Hilton Systems. The two companies are virtually identical, and both began operations at the beginning of the current year. During the year, each company purchased inventory as follows:

Jan.	4	10,000 units at $4 =	$ 40,000
Apr.	6	5,000 units at 5 =	25,000
Aug.	9	7,000 units at 6 =	42,000
Nov.	27	10,000 units at 7 =	70,000
Totals		32,000	$177,000

During the first year, both companies sold 25,000 units of inventory.

In early January, both companies purchased equipment costing $143,000 (ten-year estimated useful life and a $20,000 residual value). Astoria uses the inventory and depreciation methods that maximize reported income (FIFO and straight-line). By contrast, Hilton uses the inventory and depreciation methods that minimize income tax payments (LIFO and double-declining-balance). Both companies' trial balances at December 31 included the following:

Sales revenue............................	$370,000
Operating expenses	80,000

Required

1. Prepare both companies' income statements.
2. Write an investment newsletter to address the following questions for your clients: Which company appears to be more profitable? Which company has more cash to invest in promising projects? If prices continue rising in both companies' industries over the long-term, which company would you prefer to invest in? Why?

Case 2. The following questions are unrelated except that they all apply to fixed assets and intangible assets:

a. The manager of Clarkson Corporation regularly debits the cost of repairs and maintenance of plant assets to Plant and Equipment. Why would she do that, since she knows she is violating generally accepted accounting principles (GAAP)?
b. It has been suggested that, because many intangible assets have no value except to the company that owns them, they should be valued at $1.00 or zero on the balance sheet. Many accountants disagree with this view. Which view do you support? Why?
c. The manager of Ladue Company regularly buys plant assets and debits the cost to Repairs and Maintenance Expense. Why would he do that, since this action violates GAAP?

ETHICAL ISSUE

Reflection Cove Apartments purchased land and a building for the lump sum of $4.1 million. To get the maximum tax deduction, Reflection Cove managers allocated 90% of the purchase price to the building and only 10% to the land. A more realistic allocation would have been 70% to the building and 30% to the land.

Required

1. Explain the tax advantage of allocating too much to the building and too little to the land.
2. Was Reflection Cove's allocation ethical? If so, state why. If not, why not? Identify who was harmed.

FINANCIAL STATEMENT CASE

Refer to the **Target Corporation** financial statements in Appendix A, and answer the following questions.

Required

1. Which depreciation method does Target use for reporting in the financial statements? What type of depreciation method does the company probably use for income tax purposes? Why is this method preferable for tax purposes?
2. Depreciation and amortization expense is embedded in the selling, general, and administrative expense amounts listed on the income statement. The statement of cash flows gives the amount of depreciation and amortization expense. What was the amount of depreciation and amortization for fiscal year 1999? Record Target's depreciation and amortization expense for 1999.
3. The statement of cash flows reports the purchases of plant assets and the proceeds (sale prices) received on disposal of plant assets. How much were Target's plant asset acquisitions during 1999? Journalize the company's acquisition of plant assets.
4. How much cash did Target receive on the sale of plant assets during 1999? Assume the plant assets that were sold had a cost of $988 million and accumulated depreciation of $697 million. Record the sale of these plant assets. How much was the gain or loss on the sale of plant assets during the year?

TEAM PROJECT

Required

Visit a local business.

1. List all its plant assets.
2. If possible, interview the manager. Gain as much information as you can about the business's plant assets. For example, try to determine the assets' costs, the depreciation method the company is using, and the estimated useful life of each asset category. If an interview is impossible, then develop your own estimates of the assets' costs, useful lives, and book values, assuming an appropriate depreciation method.
3. Determine whether the business has any intangible assets. If so, list them and gain as much information as possible about their nature, cost, and estimated useful lives.
4. Write a detailed report of your findings and be prepared to present it to the class.

INTERNET EXERCISE

On Saturday, July 8, 2000, **FedEx** teamed up with **Amazon.com** to deliver 250,000 copies of the book *Harry Potter and the Goblet of Fire*. To deliver this unprecedented number of books, 100 regularly scheduled FedEx flights, 9,000 FedEx delivery personnel, and vehicles from 700 stations were mobilized from Amazon.com distribution centers to distribute approximately 675,000 pounds (more than 300 tons) of the book.

1. Go to **http://www.fedex.com** and in the left-hand column click on *Investor Relations*. Select the *on-line* version of the most recent annual report. Within the Annual Report menu, click on *Financial Information*. (Note: There are two links titled *Financial Information*. Use the link classified under Annual Report.) Use this information to answer the following questions.
   a. At the most recent year-end, examine *Property and Equipment, at cost*. List the four types of property and equipment reported by FedEx Corporation. What is the total cost of these assets? What is the book value? What amount of cost has already been expensed through depreciation? What is the expensed portion called?
   b. Which financial statement reports depreciation expense? For the most recent year identify the amount reported for *Depreciation and amortization expense*.
2. Refer to Note 2: Summary of Significant Accounting Policies to answer the following.
   a. Which method of depreciation does FedEx use for financial reporting purposes? For tax reporting purposes? Explain why a company uses different depreciation methods for tax reporting and for financial statement purposes. Is this ethical? Is it legal? Does this comply with the Consistency Principle?
   b. What is the range of useful lives FedEx uses for flight equipment? For computer and electronic equipment? Do these useful lives make sense?
   c. What amount of residual value does FedEx use for aircraft frames and engines? For all other property and equipment?

FedEx Corporation

Go to the "Depreciation Methods and Inventory Cost Flow Assumptions" episode on the *Mastering Accounting* CD-ROM for an interactive, video-enhanced exercise that shows how CanGo staff must choose when and how to depreciate fixed assets, such as a new warehouse the company needs.

11

Current Liabilities and Payroll

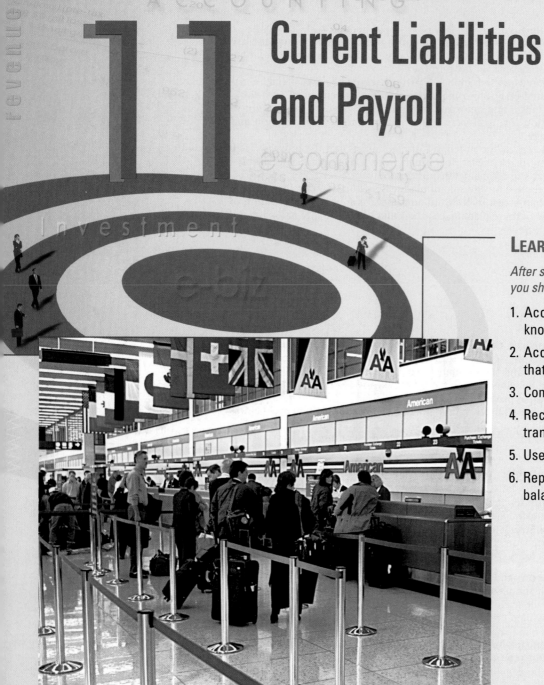

LEARNING OBJECTIVES

*After studying this chapter,
you should be able to*

1. Account for current liabilities of known amount

2. Account for current liabilities that must be estimated

3. Compute payroll amounts

4. Record basic payroll transactions

5. Use a payroll system

6. Report current liabilities on the balance sheet

Advantage®, Mileage Plus®, and SkyMiles®—these are the frequent-flier plans of **American Airlines, United,** and **Delta.** American was the first to capitalize on this mode of creating loyal customers. Boy, does it work!

When Ron and Lisa Schmidt fly on American Airlines, they get a mile of frequent-flier credit for every mile they fly. They also get mileage credit when they pay their VISA bill, whether it's for gas at the pump or carpet in their home. Had Ron and Lisa been able to fly American on a recent trip to Florida, they would have gotten VIP treatment. But flying on Delta landed them back in ordinary no-frills coach. Of course, it works both ways. Delta's frequent fliers don't automatically get kid-glove treatment when they fly American or United.

The mileage credit granted to frequent fliers adds up to quite an accounting challenge for the airlines. It's both promotion expense and a major liability. For each mile of credit granted to the Schmidts, American Airlines books a liability for their free travel in the future. How do the airlines estimate this payable—called Air Traffic Liability? The answer is "Very carefully, because they must report this liability on their balance sheets."

In this chapter, we explain how to account for all types of current liabilities. The first half of the chapter concentrates on current liabilities, and the second half on payrolls, which generate some specific current liabilities. Exhibit 11-1 shows how **AMR Corporation,** the parent company of American Airlines, reported its current liabilities at March 31, 2000. Recall that *current liabilities* are obligations due within one year or within the company's normal operating cycle if it is longer than one year. Obligations due beyond that period are classified as *long-term liabilities.* ➤

◄ We discussed current liabilities and long-term liabilities in Chapter 4, p. 139.

CURRENT LIABILITIES OF KNOWN AMOUNT

Current liabilities fall into two categories: liabilities of a known amount and liabilities that must be estimated. We look first at current liabilities of known amount.

Objective 1
Account for current liabilities of known amount

Accounts Payable

Amounts owed to suppliers for products or services purchased on open account are *accounts payable.* We have seen many accounts payable illustrations in preceding chapters. For example, most businesses purchase inventory and office supplies on account. **AMR Corporation** reported Accounts payable of $1,231 million at March 31, 2000 (see line 1 of Exhibit 11-1).

Let's see how AMR's accounts payable get onto the company's balance sheet. One of AMR's common transactions is the credit purchase of its inventory of food to be served on flights. AMR's accounts payable and inventory systems are integrated. When the food inventory dips below a certain level, the computer automatically prepares a purchase request for more food. The order is placed and the goods are received. AMR makes the following journal entry to buy the inventory of account (amount assumed):

Inventory	600	
Accounts Payable		600
Purchase on account.		

The computer thus increases Inventory and Accounts Payable. Then for payments, the computer debits Accounts Payable and credits Cash, as follows:

Accounts Payable	400	
Cash		400
Paid on account.		

EXHIBIT 11-1
How AMR Reports Its Current
Liabilities

AMR CORPORATION (PARENT COMPANY OF AMERICAN AIRLINES)
Balance Sheet (partial; adapted)
March 31, 2000

	Liabilities	(In Millions)
	Current Liabilities	
1	Accounts payable	$1,231
2	Accrued liabilities payable	1,818
3	Air traffic liability	2,758
4	Current maturities of long-term debt	241
5	Current obligations under capital leases	231
6	Total current liabilities	$6,279

After AMR Corporation buys inventory and pays the account payable in the two preceding transactions, how much does AMR owe the other company? Stated differently, how much is AMR's account payable to the supplier?

Answer: $200 ($600 − $400)

AMR Corporation completes thousands of transactions such as these. AMR's $1,231 million balance of Accounts Payable (Exhibit 11-1) is the sum of all the amounts AMR still owes on account.

Short-Term Notes Payable

SHORT-TERM NOTE PAYABLE. Promissory note payable due within one year, a common form of financing.

Short-term notes payable are a common form of financing. They are promissory notes that must be paid within one year. Companies often issue short-term notes payable to borrow cash or to purchase inventory. The following entries are typical for a short-term note payable:

```
20X1
Sep. 30   Inventory.............................................. 8,000
                 Note Payable, Short-Term........................... 8,000
          Purchased inventory on a one-year, 10% note.

20X1
Dec. 31   Interest Expense ($8,000 × 0.10 × 3/12) .............. 200
                 Interest Payable........................................ 200
          Accrued interest expense at year end.
```

The balance sheet at December 31, 20X1, will report the Note Payable of $8,000 and Interest Payable of $200 as current liabilities. The 20X1 income statement will report interest expense of $200, as illustrated.

Balance Sheet December 31, 20X1		Income Statement Year Ended December 31, 20X1	
Liabilities		**Expenses**	
Current liabilities:....................		Interest expense...........................	$200
Note payable, short-term	$8,000		
Interest payable...................	200		

The following entry records payment of the note at maturity:

20X2			
Sep. 30	Note Payable, Short-Term	8,000	
	Interest Payable	200	
	Interest Expense ($8,000 × 0.10 × 9/12).............	600	
	Cash [$8,000 + ($8,000 × 0.10)]		8,800
	Paid a note and interest at maturity.		

● DAILY EXERCISE 11-1

● DAILY EXERCISE 11-2

● DAILY EXERCISE 11-3

The cash payment entry must separate the total interest on the note ($800) between

- the interest expense of 20X1 ($200), and
- the interest expense of 20X2 ($600).

This way, each year's financial statements report the correct amounts for *that* year.

Short-Term Notes Payable Issued at a Discount

There is another way to set up a borrowing arrangement. It is called **discounting a note payable.** The lender subtracts the interest amount from the note's face value, and the borrower receives the net amount. At maturity, the borrower pays back the full face value, which includes all the interest.

Suppose **Procter & Gamble** discounts a $100,000, 60-day note payable to its bank at 12%. P&G will receive $98,000—that is, the $100,000 face value less interest of $2,000 ($100,000 × 0.12 × 60/360). Assume that this transaction occurs on November 25, 20X1. Procter & Gamble's entry to record discounting the note follows.[1]

DISCOUNTING A NOTE PAYABLE. A borrowing arrangement in which the bank subtracts the interest amount from a note's face value. The borrower receives the net amount.

20X1			
Nov. 25	Cash ($100,000 − $2,000*)	98,000	
	Note Payable, Short-Term.............................		98,000
	Discounted a $100,000, 60-day, 12% note payable.		
	*Discount = $100,000 × 0.12 × 60/360 = $2,000.		

THINK IT OVER How much did Procter & Gamble actually borrow from the bank—$98,000 or $100,000? How much will P&G pay back? How much interest expense will P&G record for the borrowing arrangement?

Answers: Procter & Gamble borrowed $98,000, the amount of cash the company received. P&G will pay back $100,000 at maturity. P&G's interest expense will be $2,000 ($100,000 paid back − $98,000 borrowed).

Procter & Gamble must record accrued interest at year end as it would for any note payable. P&G's adjusting entry at December 31 records interest for 36 days, as follows:

20X1			
Dec. 31	Interest Expense ($100,000 × 0.12 × 36/360)......	1,200	
	Note Payable		1,200
	Accrued interest expense at year end.		

After the year-end adjustment, the Note Payable account carries its current balance of $99,200.

NOTE PAYABLE		
	Nov. 25	98,000
	Dec. 31	1,200
	Bal.	**99,200**

[1]Another set of journal entries can be used to record the discounting of a note payable. The alternate method uses a separate Discount on Note Payable account and obscures the true nature of the borrowing arrangement.

At maturity, the business records the final amount of interest expense on the note:

20X2

Jan. 24   Interest Expense ($100,000 × 0.12 × 24/360)   800
                 Note Payable   800
             To record interest expense.

On the note's maturity date, the Note Payable account holds the maturity value of $100,000.

NOTE PAYABLE	
Nov. 25, 20X1	98,000
Dec. 31, 20X1	1,200
Jan. 24, 20X2	800
Bal.	100,000

DAILY EXERCISE 11-4

The final entry pays off the note at maturity.

20X2

Jan. 24   Note Payable, Short-Term   100,000
                 Cash...   100,000
             To pay note at maturity.

Sales Tax Payable

Most states levy a sales tax on retail sales. Only Delaware, Montana, New Hampshire, and Oregon do not have a sales tax. Retailers collect the sales tax in addition to the price of the item sold. The retailers owe the state the sales tax, so, the account Sales Tax Payable is a current liability. For example, **ShowBiz Pizza Time, Inc.** (operator of family restaurants and entertainment centers, such as Chuck E. Cheese), reported sales tax payable of $737,712 as a current liability.

Suppose one Saturday's sales at a ShowBiz Pizza Time totaled $10,000. The business collected an additional 5% in sales tax, which would equal $500 ($10,000 × 0.05). The business would record that day's sales as follows:

Cash ($10,000 × 1.05)   10,500
        Sales Revenue...   10,000
        Sales Tax Payable ($10,000 × 0.05)   500
To record cash sales and the related sales tax.

CASH		SALES TAX PAYABLE		SALES REVENUE	
10,500			500		10,000

Companies forward the collected sales tax to the taxing authority at regular intervals. Then they debit Sales Tax Payable and credit Cash.

Many companies do not credit Sales Tax Payable for each sale. Instead, they record sales revenue and sales tax together. Then, prior to paying the tax, they make an adjusting entry to bring Sales Revenue and Sales Tax Payable to their correct balances.

Suppose a **Kinko** store earned service revenue of $100,000 during July, subject to sales tax of 6%. Kinko's summary entry to record the month's revenue could be as follows:

July 31   Cash ($100,000 × 1.06)   106,000
                 Service Revenue...   106,000
             Revenue for the month.

The entry to adjust Service Revenue and Sales Tax Payable to their correct balances would then be

July 31   Service Revenue [$106,000 − ($106,000 ÷ 1.06)].....   6,000
                 Sales Tax Payable   6,000
             To record sales tax.

Now both accounts are ready for the financial statements:

SERVICE REVENUE			SALES TAX PAYABLE	
6,000	106,000			6,000
	100,000			

A Taxing Dilemma: Sales Tax Liability and the Internet

e-Commerce offers two big pluses: shopping from home in your pajamas and no sales tax. Say you live in New York City and purchase a CD from a music store. You pay the retail price of $15.99, plus sales tax of 8.25%. The sales tax is a current liability, payable to the State of New York. A purchase of the same CD from **Amazon.com** will be $1.32 cheaper. Fortunately for on-line (and mail-order) consumers, the Supreme Court ruled that only the U.S. Congress can require retailers who don't have a physical location in the state to charge sales taxes.

We consumers are always happy to pay less for a product, but we may be wise to consider the long-term effects of the e-commerce sales tax loophole. By 2003 state and local governments may lose $20 billion in tax revenues if Internet sales are exempted. The sales tax you pay builds roads and pays your governor, the mayor, and other state and local employees, such as firefighters and teachers. In addition, if e-commerce takes over, there may be no downtowns left in San Antonio or Tacoma—just boarded up businesses and empty strip malls.

If you are civic-minded, you can voluntarily pay your "use tax," which is imposed in the state in which you use the goods that you purchase. Most consumers don't pay this tax, but states may start collecting it if Congress continues to exempt dot.coms from sales tax. Expect to hear more on this issue. And if you're starting your own dot.com, see **EcommerceTax.com** for up-to-the-minute news. How sales tax is treated may influence how you set up your business.

Source: Based on Peter Schrag, "loophole.com," *The Nation,* May 15, 2000, pp. 6–7. Anonymous, "United States: Offline," *The Economist,* March 25, 2000, p. 35. http://www.ecommercetax.com/doc/043000.htm.

Current Portion of Long-Term Debt

Some long-term notes payable and bonds payable are paid in installments. The **current portion of long-term debt,** or **current maturity,** is the amount of the principal payable within one year. At the end of each year, a company reclassifies (from long-term debt to a current liability) the amount that must be paid during the upcoming year.

AMR's balance sheet (Exhibit 11-1) reports Current maturities of long-term debt, the next-to-last current liability (line 4). On its full balance sheet, AMR reports Long-term debt immediately after total current liabilities. *Long-term debt* refers to notes payable that are payable later than one year beyond the balance sheet date.

The liability for the current portion of long-term debt (line 4) does *not* include any accrued interest payable. The account, Current Maturities of Long-Term Debt, represents only the *principal amount owed.* Interest Payable is a separate account for a

CURRENT PORTION OF LONG-TERM DEBT. Amount of the principal that is payable within one year. Also called **current maturity.**

different liability. AMR includes interest payable under the current liability caption Accrued liabilities payable (line 2).

AMR Corporation reports Current obligations under capital leases as its last current liability (line 5). This liability is similar to current maturities of long-term debt because it is next year's lease payment on leases that AMR has capitalized as an asset.

 WORK IT OUT Suppose AMR Corporation owes $600 million on long-term notes payable at December 31, 20X5. The borrowing agreement requires AMR to pay $241 million of this debt on September 30, 20X6. Show how AMR will report both current and long-term liabilities on its balance sheet at December 31, 20X5.

Answer

	(Millions)
Current liabilities:	
Current maturities of long-term debt	$241
Long-term liabilities:	
Long-term debt ($600 − $241)........................	359

Accrued Expenses (Accrued Liabilities)

ACCRUED EXPENSE. An expense that the business has not yet paid. Also called **accrued liability.**

An **accrued expense** is an expense that the business has not yet paid. Therefore, an accrued expense is also a liability. This explains why accrued expenses are also called **accrued liabilities.** Accrued expenses typically occur with the passage of time, such as interest payable on long-term debt. By contrast, an account payable results from the purchase of a good or a service. ◄

➡ We introduced accrued expenses in Chapter 3, p. 92.

Like most other companies, AMR Corporation reports accrued liabilities on its balance sheet (line 2 in Exhibit 11-1). The total of $1,818 million includes salaries and wages payable. This caption also includes other payroll-related liabilities, such as taxes withheld from employee paychecks, plus current liabilities for interest payable and income tax payable. AMR Corporation's Air traffic liability, discussed in the chapter opening story, is another example of an accrued liability. See line 3 of Exhibit 11-1.

We illustrate accounting for interest payable under the heading Short-Term Notes Payable on page 426. The next section, plus the second half of this chapter, covers accounting for accrued salaries, wages, and other payroll liabilities.

Payroll Liabilities

PAYROLL. A major expense. Also called **employee compensation.**

Payroll, also called **employee compensation,** is a major expense. For service organizations—such as CPA firms, physicians, and travel agents—payroll is *the* major expense. Service organizations sell their personnel's services, so employee compensation is their primary cost of doing business, just as cost of goods sold is the largest expense for a merchandising company.

Employee compensation takes different forms:

- *Salary* is pay expressed in a yearly, monthly, or weekly rate.
- *Wages* are employee pay amounts stated at an hourly figure.
- *Commissions* are compensation computed as a percentage of the sales the employee made.
- *Bonus* is an amount over and above regular compensation.

Journalizing all these forms of compensation follows the same pattern, as illustrated in Exhibit 11-2 (using assumed figures).

EXHIBIT 11-2
**Accounting for Payroll
Expenses and Liabilities**

Salary Expense (or Wage Expense or Commission Expense)..............	10,000	
Employee Income Tax Payable...		1,200
FICA Tax Payable..		800
Employee Union Dues Payable		140
Salary Payable to Employees [take-home pay]..........................		7,860
To record salary expense.		

Salary (or other payroll) expense represents employees' *gross pay* (pay before subtractions for taxes and other deductions). Salary expense creates several liabilities.

- Salary payable to employees is their net (take-home) pay.
- *Employee Income Tax Payable* is income tax that has been withheld from employee paychecks.
- *FICA Tax Payable* is the employees' Social Security tax, which also is withheld from paychecks. (FICA stands for the Federal Insurance Contributions Act, which created the Social Security tax.) The company owes these liabilities to the U.S. government.
- In Exhibit 11-2, employees authorize the company to withhold union dues. These amounts are payable to the union.

In addition to salaries and wages, companies also pay some payroll taxes and other expenses for employee fringe benefits. Accounting for these expenses is similar to the illustration in Exhibit 11-2 and is covered in more detail in the second half of this chapter.

Unearned Revenues

Unearned revenues are also called *deferred revenues, revenues collected in advance,* and *customer prepayments.* ➡ All these account titles indicate that the business has received cash from its customers before earning the revenue. For unearned revenue, the company has an obligation to provide goods or services to the customer. Let's consider an example.

◄◄ As we saw in Chapter 3, p. 94, an unearned revenue is a liability because it represents an obligation to provide a good or service.

The **Dun & Bradstreet (D&B) Corporation** provides credit reports for subscribers. Finance companies pay D&B in advance to have D&B investigate the credit histories of potential customers. By receiving cash before earning the revenue, D&B incurs a liability for future service. The liability account is called Unearned Subscription Revenue (or Unearned Subscription *Income*).

Assume that D&B charges $600 for a three-year subscription. D&B's cash-receipt entry would be

20X1			
Jan. 1	Cash	600	
	Unearned Subscription Revenue..............		600
	Received cash in advance.		

After receiving the cash on January 1, 20X1, D&B owes its professional service to customers over three years. D&B's liability is

UNEARNED SUBSCRIPTION REVENUE

	600

During 20X1, D&B performs one-third of the total service and earns $200 ($600 × 1/3) of the revenue. At December 31, 20X1, D&B makes the following adjusting entry to decrease Unearned Subscription Revenue, the liability account, and to increase Subscription Revenue:

20X1			
Dec. 31	Unearned Subscription Revenue	200	
	Subscription Revenue ($600 × 1/3)		200
	Earned revenue that was collected in advance.		

After posting, the two accounts are

UNEARNED SUBSCRIPTION REVENUE			
Dec. 31	200	Jan. 1	600
		Bal.	400

SUBSCRIPTION REVENUE	
Dec. 31	200

At December 31, 20X1, D&B has earned $200 of the revenue. D&B still owes its customer $400 in total liabilities:

- $200 for the service D&B will perform during 20X2. This is a current liability.
- $200 for the service D&B will perform during 20X3. This is a long-term liability.

D&B's financial statements would report the following at the end of the first year:

DAILY EXERCISE 11-5

Balance Sheet at December 31, 20X1		Income Statement for the Year Ended December 31, 20X1	
Current liabilities:		Revenues:	
Unearned subscription revenue	$200	Subscription revenue	$200
Long-term liabilities:			
Unearned subscription revenue	$200		

CURRENT LIABILITIES THAT MUST BE ESTIMATED

Objective 2
Account for current liabilities that must be estimated

A business may know that a liability exists but not know the exact amount. It cannot simply ignore the liability. The unknown amount must be estimated, recorded in the accounts, and reported on the balance sheet.

Estimated current liabilities vary among companies. As a first example, let's look at Estimated Warranty Payable, a common liability for merchandisers.

Estimated Warranty Payable

Many companies guarantee their products against defects under *warranty* agreements. Ninety-day warranties and one-year warranties are common. The automobile companies—**Toyota, Ford,** and **BMW,** for example—accrue liabilities for their five-year, 50,000-mile warranties.

➤ For a review of the matching principle, see Chapter 3, p. 86.

The matching principle demands that the company record the *warranty expense* in the same period that the business recognizes sales revenue, regardless of when the company pays warranty claims. ◄ Offering the warranty—and incurring warranty expense—is a cost of making sales. At the time of the sale, the company does not know the exact amount of warranty expense. But the business must estimate its warranty expense and the related liability.

Assume that **Whirlpool Corporation,** which manufactures appliances for **Sears** and other companies, made sales of $200,000, subject to product warranties. Assume that in the past between 2% and 4% of the products proved defective. Whirlpool management could estimate that 3% of the products it sells this year will require warranty payments. The company would record the sales of $200,000 and the warranty expense of $6,000 ($200,000 × 0.03) in the same period as follows:

Accounts Receivable.....................................	200,000	
Sales Revenue....................................		200,000
Sales on account.		
Warranty Expense	6,000	
Estimated Warranty Payable..............		6,000
To accrue warranty expense.		

Assume that Whirlpool's warranty payments total $5,800. If Whirlpool repairs the defective appliances, Whirlpool makes this journal entry:

| Estimated Warranty Payable | 5,800 | |
| Cash | | 5,800 |

To *repair* defective products sold under warranty.

If Whirlpool gives customers replacement appliances for their warranty claims, Whirlpool would instead make this entry:

| Estimated Warranty Payable | 5,800 | |
| Inventory | | 5,800 |

To *replace* defective products sold under warranty.

Whirlpool's expense on the income statement is $6,000 in all cases. The amount of the cash payment or the cost of the replacement inventory has no bearing on the amount of warranty expense for the period. After paying these warranty claims, Whirlpool's Estimated Warranty Payable account appears as follows:

ESTIMATED WARRANTY PAYABLE

| 5,800 | 6,000 |
| | Bal. 200 |

The balance sheet reports a current liability for Estimated Warranty Payable of $200.

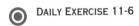

DAILY EXERCISE 11-6

DAILY EXERCISE 11-7

WORK IT OUT

Maxim Company made sales of $400,000 and estimated warranty repairs at 5% of the sales. Maxim's actual warranty outlays were $19,000. Record the sales (ignore cost of goods sold), the warranty expense, and the warranty payments. The beginning balance of Estimated Warranty Payable was zero. How much is Maxim's estimated warranty payable at the end of the period?

Answer

Accounts Receivable	400,000	
Sales Revenue		400,000
Warranty Expense ($400,000 × 0.05)	20,000	
Estimated Warranty Payable		20,000
Estimated Warranty Payable	19,000	
Cash		19,000

ESTIMATED WARRANTY PAYABLE

| 19,000 | 20,000 |
| | Bal. 1,000 |

Estimated Vacation Pay Liability

Most companies grant paid vacations to their employees. The employees receive this benefit when they take their vacation, but they earn the benefit by working the remainder of the year. Two-week vacations are common. To match expense with revenue, the company accrues the vacation pay expense and liability over the course of the year. Then, the company records payment during the two-week vacation period. Companies must estimate their vacation pay liability.

Suppose a company's January payroll is $100,000 and vacation pay adds 4%, or $4,000. Experience indicates that only 90% of the available vacations will be taken, so the January vacation pay estimate is $3,600 ($4,000 × 0.90). In January, the company records vacation pay as follows:

| Jan. 31 | Vacation Pay Expense | 3,600 | |
| | Estimated Vacation Pay Liability | | 3,600 |

Each month thereafter, the company makes a similar entry.

If an employee takes a two-week vacation during August, his or her $2,000 salary is recorded as follows:

| Aug. 31 | Estimated Vacation Pay Liability.............. | 2,000 | |
| | Cash... | | 2,000 |

Income Tax Payable (for a Corporation)

Corporations pay income tax in the same way that individuals do. Corporations file their tax returns after the end of the year, so they must estimate their income tax payable for the balance sheet. During the year, corporations make quarterly tax payments to the government. A corporation would record the payment of $100,000 of income tax expense for the third quarter as follows:

Sept. 30	Income Tax Expense	100,000	
	Cash...		100,000
	To pay quarterly income tax.		

The corporation's entry to accrue $40,000 of income tax expense and payable at year end is

Dec. 31	Income Tax Expense	40,000	
	Income Tax Payable.......................		40,000
	To accrue income tax at year end.		

The corporation will pay off this tax liability early in the next year, so Income Tax Payable is a current liability.

Contingent Liabilities

➤ We introduced contingent liabilities in the Appendix to Chapter 8, p. 344.

A *contingent liability* is not an actual liability. Instead, it is a potential liability that depends on a *future* event. ◄ For example, suppose **AMR Corporation,** the parent company of **American Airlines,** faces a possible loss if its pilots walk off the job in a threatened labor strike. The future event is the negotiation between the airline and the pilots' labor union. The airline thus faces a contingent liability, which may or may not become an actual liability.

It would be unethical for the airline to withhold knowledge of the labor negotiations from anyone considering investing in the business. Another contingent liability arises when one company *cosigns a note payable* for another company. Suppose Company A guarantees that Company B will pay a note payable owed to another party. This practice obligates Company A to pay the note and interest if Company B fails to pay. Thus, Company A has a contingent liability until the note becomes due. If Company B pays off the note, the contingent liability ceases to exist. If not, Company A's liability becomes actual.

The most important source of contingent liabilities is a lawsuit in which the company is being sued. Until the case is settled, the defendant has a contingent liability. One of the most famous lawsuits occurred when **Microsoft Corporation** was sued for matters related to the Java programming language technology. Until the court reached its decision, Microsoft reported the contingency in the notes to its financial statements. In its 1999 annual report, Microsoft included the following (excerpt):

> **Sun Microsystems, Inc. brought suit against Microsoft in the U.S. District Court for [. . .] California. Sun's complaint alleges several claims against Microsoft, all related to the [. . .] Java programming language technology.**

SHORT PRESENTATION. A way to report contingent liabilities in the body of the balance sheet, after total liabilities but with no amount given. An explanatory note accompanies the presentation.

Contingent liabilities may be reported in two ways. In what is called a **short presentation,** the contingent liability appears in the body of the balance sheet, after total liabilities, but with no amounts given. In general, an explanatory note accompanies a short presentation. The Microsoft note is typical for a contingent liability arising from a lawsuit.

◉ DAILY EXERCISE 11-8

ETHICAL ISSUES IN REPORTING LIABILITIES

Accounting for current liabilities poses ethical and legal challenges. Business owners and managers want their company to look as successful as possible. They like to report high levels of net income on the income statement. High net income makes the company look profitable and helps the company raise money from investors. And high net income leads to large bonuses for managers. Owners want their balance sheet to report high asset values and low liability amounts, which make the company look safe to lenders and help the company borrow money at low interest rates.

- Low expenses $\longrightarrow$ High net income
- Low liabilities $\longrightarrow$ High owner's equity

Owners and managers may be tempted to overlook some accrued expenses at the end of the accounting period. For example, a company can fail to accrue warranty expense. This failure will cause total expenses to be understated and net income to be overstated on the income statement.

Contingent liabilities also pose an ethical challenge. Because contingencies are not real liabilities, they are easy to overlook. But a contingent liability can be very important. The **Microsoft** contingency is an example. Ethical business owners and managers do not play games with their accounting. Falsifying financial statements can ruin one's reputation. It can also land a person in a federal or state prison.

At this half-way point in the chapter, review what you have learned by studying the following Decision Guidelines.

DECISION GUIDELINES

Accounting for Current and Contingent Liabilities, Including Payroll

DECISION	GUIDELINES
What are the two main issues in accounting for current liabilities?	• *Recording* the liability and the asset acquired or the expense incurred • *Reporting* the liability on the balance sheet

What are the two basic categories of current liabilities?	• Current liabilities of *known amount:*
	  Accounts payable Accrued expenses
	  Short-term notes payable (accrued liabilities)
	  Sales tax payable Payroll liabilities
	  Current portion of long- Salary, wages, commission,
	    term debt and bonus payable
	  Unearned revenues
	• Current liabilities that *must be estimated:*
	  Estimated warranty payable
	  Estimated vacation pay liability
	  Income tax payable (for a corporation)

How to account for contingent (potential) liabilities?	Report contingent liabilities either • *Short* (with no dollar amount) on the balance sheet, along with an explanatory note, or • With *only* the explanatory note
What is the ethical and legal challenge in accounting for current and contingent liabilities?	To ensure that the balance sheet (and the related notes) reports the *full amount of all* the business's current and contingent liabilities

www.prenhall.com/horngren
Mid-Chapter Assessment

SUMMARY PROBLEM

This problem consists of three independent parts.

Required

1. A **Wendy's** hamburger restaurant made cash sales of $4,000 subject to a 5% sales tax. Record the sales and the related sales tax. Also record Wendy's payment of the tax to the state government.

2. Assume that at April 30, 20X2, **H. J. Heinz Company** reported its 6% long-term debt as follows:

Current Liabilities (in part)

Portion of long-term debt due within one year	$ 14,000,000
Interest payable ($200,000,000 × 0.06 × 5/12)	5,000,000

Long-Term Debt and Other Liabilities (in part)

Long-term debt..	$186,000,000

The company pays interest on its long-term debt on November 30 each year.

Show how Heinz Company would report its liabilities on the year-end balance sheet one year later—April 30, 20X3. Assume that the current maturity of its long-term debt is $16 million.

3. What distinguishes a contingent liability from an actual liability?

Solution

1.

Cash ($4,000 × 1.05)	4,200		
Sales Revenue		4,000	
Sales Tax Payable ($4,000 × 0.05)		200	
To record cash sales and related sales tax.			
Sales Tax Payable..	200		
Cash		200	
To pay sales tax to the state government.			

2. H. J. Heinz Company balance sheet at April 30, 20X3:

Current Liabilities (in part)

Portion of long-term debt due within one year	$ 16,000,000
Interest payable ($186,000,000 × 0.06 × 5/12)	4,650,000

Long-Term Debt and Other Liabilities (in part)

Long-term debt..	$170,000,000

---

3. A contingent liability is a *potential* liability, which may or may not become an actual liability.

Objective 3
Compute payroll amounts

ACCOUNTING FOR PAYROLL

Payroll costs are so important to most businesses that they adopt special systems to account for their labor costs. This section covers the basics of accounting for payroll.

Businesses often pay employees at a base rate for a set number of hours—called *straight time.* For working any additional hours—called *overtime*—the employee receives a higher rate.

Lucy Childres is an accountant for Bobby Jones Golf Company. Lucy earns $600 per week straight time. The company work week runs 40 hours, so Lucy's hourly straight-time pay is $15 ($600/40). Her company pays her *time and a half* for overtime. That rate is 150% (1.5 times) the straight-time rate. Thus, Lucy earns $22.50 for each hour of overtime she works ($15.00 × 1.5 = $22.50). For working 42 hours during a week, she earns $645, computed as follows:

Straight-time pay for 40 hours..	$600
Overtime pay for 2 overtime hours: 2 × $22.50..............	45
Total pay...	$645

Gross Pay and Net Pay

Before withholding taxes were introduced in 1943, employees brought home all they earned. Back in 1940, Lucy Childres would have taken home the full $645 that she made. Those days are long past.

The federal government, most state governments, and even some city governments require employers to act as collection agents for employee taxes. Employers then deduct the taxes from employee checks. Insurance companies, labor unions, and other organizations may also receive pieces of employees' pay. Amounts withheld from an employee's check are called *deductions*.

Gross pay is the total amount of salary, wages, commissions, or any other employee compensation before taxes and other deductions. **Net pay**—or "take-home pay"—equals gross pay minus all deductions. As Exhibit 11-3 shows, net pay is the amount the employee actually takes home.

GROSS PAY. Total amount of salary, wages, commissions, or any other employee compensation before taxes and other deductions.

NET PAY. Gross pay minus all deductions. The amount of compensation that the employee actually takes home.

Gross Pay   −   (Taxes + Other Deductions)   =   Net Pay

**EXHIBIT 11-3
Gross Pay and Net Pay**

Many companies also pay employee *benefits,* another form of employee compensation. Examples include health and life insurance. Other examples include retirement pay and health insurance during the retirement years. Payroll accounting has become quite complex.

Payroll Deductions

Payroll deductions withheld from employees' pay fall into two categories: (1) *required deductions,* such as employee income tax and social security tax; and (2) *optional deductions* for union dues, insurance premiums, charitable contributions, and other amounts withheld at the employee's request. After their withholding, payroll deductions become the liability of the employer, who then must pay the outside party. For example, the employer pays the government the employee income tax withheld and pays the union the union dues withheld.

 DAILY EXERCISE 11-9

REQUIRED PAYROLL DEDUCTIONS: EMPLOYEE INCOME TAX   In the United States, the law requires most employers to withhold income tax from employees' pay. Income tax is the largest sources of national tax revenues. Employee income tax generates approximately 36% of tax receipts in the United States, 38% in Sweden, and 41% in Canada.

The amount of income tax deducted from gross pay is called **withheld income tax.** The amount withheld depends on the employee's gross pay and on the number of *withholding allowances* the employee claims.

All employees file a Form W-4 with their employer to indicate the number of allowances claimed for withholding purposes. Each allowance lowers the tax

WITHHELD INCOME TAX. Income tax deducted from employees' gross pay.

withheld from the employee's paycheck. An unmarried taxpayer can claim only one allowance; a childless married couple, up to two allowances; a married couple with one child, up to three allowances; and so on. Exhibit 11-4 shows a W-4 for R. C. Dean, who claims four allowances (line 5).

EXHIBIT 11-4 Form W-4

Form **W-4** Department of the Treasury Internal Revenue Service	**Employee's Withholding Allowance Certificate** ▶ For Privacy Act and Paperwork Reduction Act Notice, see page 2.	OMB No. 1545-0010 **2000**

| 1 Type or print your first name and middle initial R. C. | Last name Dean | 2 Your social security number 344 ꞉ 86 ꞉ 4529 |

Home address (number and street or rural route)
4376 Palm Drive

3 ☐ Single ☒ Married ☐ Married, but withhold at higher Single rate.
Note: If married, but legally separated, or spouse is a nonresident alien, check the Single box.

City or town, state, and ZIP code
Fort Lauderdale, FL 33317

4 If your last name differs from that on your social security card, check here. **You must call 1-800-772-1213 for a new card** . . ▶ ☐

5 Total number of allowances you are claiming (from line **H** above **OR** from the applicable worksheet on page 2) | **5** | 4
6 Additional amount, if any, you want withheld from each paycheck . . . . | **6** | $
7 I claim exemption from withholding for 2000, and I certify that I meet **BOTH** of the following conditions for exemption:
● Last year I had a right to a refund of **ALL** Federal income tax withheld because I had **NO** tax liability **AND**
● This year I expect a refund of **ALL** Federal income tax withheld because I expect to have **NO** tax liability.
If you meet both conditions, write "EXEMPT" here . . . . ▶ | **7** |

Under penalties of perjury, I certify that I am entitled to the number of withholding allowances claimed on this certificate, or I am entitled to claim exempt status.
Employee's signature
(Form is not valid unless you sign it) ▶ *R. C. Dean*   Date ▶ 7-22,1997

8 Employer's name and address (Employer: Complete lines 8 and 10 only if sending to the IRS.)
Blumenthal's
Crescent Square Shopping Center
Fort Lauderdale, FL 33310 | 9 Office code (optional) 14 | 10 Employer identification number 83 ꞉ 19475

Cat. No. 10220Q

REQUIRED PAYROLL DEDUCTIONS: EMPLOYEE SOCIAL SECURITY (FICA) TAX   The *Federal Insurance Contributions Act (FICA)*, also known as the Social Security Act, created the Social Security Tax. The Social Security program provides retirement, disability, and medical benefits. The law requires employers to withhold **Social Security (FICA) tax** from employees' pay. The FICA tax has two components:

SOCIAL SECURITY TAX. Federal Insurance Contributions Act (FICA) tax, which is withheld from employees' pay. Also called **FICA tax**.

1. Old age, survivors', and disability insurance (OASDI)
2. Health insurance (Medicare)

The amount of tax withheld from employees' pay varies from year to year. As of 2000, the OASDI portion of the tax applies to the first $76,200 of employee earnings in a year. The taxable amount of earnings is adjusted annually depending on the rate of inflation. The OASDI tax rate is 6.2%. Therefore, the maximum OASDI tax that an employee paid in 2000 was $4,724 ($76,200 × 0.062).

The Medicare portion of the FICA tax applies to all employee earnings. This tax rate is 1.45%. An employee thus pays a combined FICA tax rate of 7.65% (6.2% + 1.45%) of the first $76,200 of annual earnings, plus 1.45% of earnings above $76,200.

To ease the computational burden and focus on the concepts, we assume that the FICA tax is 8% of the first $75,000 of employee earnings each year. (Use these numbers when you complete this chapter's assignment material, unless instructed otherwise.) For each employee who earns $75,000 or more, the employer withholds $6,000 ($75,000 × 0.08) and sends that amount to the federal government. The employer records this employee tax in the account FICA Tax Payable.

Assume that Rex Jennings, an employee, earned $73,500 prior to December. Jennings' salary for December is $7,000. How much FICA tax will be withheld from his December paycheck? The computation is as follows:

Employee earnings subject to the tax in one year	$75,000
Employee earnings prior to the current pay period	−73,500
Current pay subject to FICA tax..	$ 1,500
FICA tax rate	×0.08
FICA tax to be withheld from current pay...........................	$ 120

OPTIONAL PAYROLL DEDUCTIONS   As a convenience to employees, many companies make payroll deductions and disburse cash according to employee instructions. Union dues, insurance payments, payroll savings plans, and gifts to charities such as **United Way** and **Habitat for Humanity** are examples.

Many employers offer *cafeteria plans* that allow workers to select from a menu of insurance coverage. Suppose **Ford Motor Company** provides each employee with $450 of insurance coverage each month. One employee may use the monthly allowance to purchase only life insurance. Another employee may select only disability coverage. A third worker may choose a combination of life insurance and disability coverage.

Employer Payroll Taxes

Employers must bear the expense of at least three payroll taxes:

1. Employer Social Security (FICA) tax
2. State **unemployment compensation tax**
3. Federal **unemployment compensation tax.**

UNEMPLOYMENT COMPENSATION TAX. Payroll tax paid by employers to the government, which uses the money to pay unemployment benefits to people who are out of work.

EMPLOYER FICA TAX In addition to collecting the employee's Social Security tax, the employer also must pay into the program. The employer's Social Security tax is the same as the amount withheld from employee pay. Thus, the Social Security system is funded by equal contributions from employees and employers. Using our 8% and $75,000 annual pay figures, the maximum annual employer tax on each employee is $6,000 ($75,000 × 0.08). The employer records this payroll tax in the same FICA Tax Payable account that is used for the withholding from employee paychecks.

STATE AND FEDERAL UNEMPLOYMENT COMPENSATION TAXES State and federal unemployment taxes are products of the Federal Unemployment Tax Act (FUTA). These taxes finance workmen's compensation for people who have been laid off from work. *In recent years, employers have paid a combined tax of 6.2% on the first $7,000 of each employee's annual earnings.* The proportion paid to the state is 5.4%, and 0.8% is paid to the federal government. The employer uses the accounts Federal Unemployment Tax Payable and State Unemployment Tax Payable. Exhibit 11-5 shows a typical disbursement of payroll costs by an employer company.

◉ DAILY EXERCISE 11-10

◉ DAILY EXERCISE 11-11

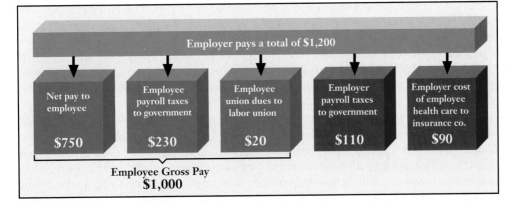

EXHIBIT 11-5
Typical Breakdown of Payroll Costs for One Employee

Payroll Entries

Exhibit 11-6 summarizes an employer's entries to record a monthly payroll of $10,000. All amounts are assumed for illustration only.

Entry A in Exhibit 11-6 records the employer's *salary expense.* The *gross salary* of all employees, $10,000, is their monthly pay before any deductions. The federal government imposes the income tax and the FICA tax. Most states and some cities also levy income taxes, which are accounted for in the same way. The union dues are optional. Employees' take-home (net) pay is $7,860. One important point about this payroll transaction is that the employees pay their own income and FICA taxes and union dues. The employer serves merely as collecting agent and sends these amounts to the government and the union.

Entry B records the employer's *payroll tax expense.* In addition to the employee's FICA tax ($800 in entry A), the employer also pays the $800 FICA tax

Objective 4
Record basic payroll transactions

◉ DAILY EXERCISE 11-12

EXHIBIT 11-6 **Payroll Accounting by the Employer**

A. Salary Expense

Salary Expense (or Wage Expense or Commission Expense)	10,000	
Employee Income Tax Payable		1,200
FICA Tax Payable ($10,000 × 0.08)		800
Employee Union Dues Payable...		140
Salary Payable to Employees [take-home pay]		7,860

To record *salary expense.*

B. Payroll Tax Expense

Payroll Tax Expense	1,420	
FICA Tax Payable ($10,000 × 0.08)		800
State Unemployment Tax Payable ($10,000 × 0.054).................		540
Federal Unemployment Tax Payable ($10,000 × 0.008).............		80

To record employer's *payroll taxes.*

C. Benefits Expense

Health Insurance Expense for Employees..	800	
Life Insurance Expense for Employees	200	
Pension Expense	500	
Employee Benefits Payable...		1,500

To record employee benefits payable by employer.

Total Payroll Expense ($12,920) = Salary Expense ($10,000) + Payroll Tax Expense ($1,420) + Benefits Expense ($1,500)

in entry B. The other two employer payroll taxes are for state and federal unemployment. Employees do not pay the unemployment taxes. Only the employer pays them.

Entry C records employee *benefits* paid by the employer. The company pays for health and life insurance on its employees, a common practice. Also, the employer funds pensions (that is, pays cash into a pension plan) for the benefit of employees when they retire. In the exhibit, the employer's pension expense for the month is $500, and the total employer expense for benefits is $1,500. *The total payroll expense of the employer in Exhibit 11-6 is $12,920 (salary expense of $10,000 + payroll tax expense of $1,420 + benefits expense of $1,500).*

A company's payments to people who are not employees—outsiders called independent contractors—are *not* company payroll expenses. Consider two CPAs, Lyon and Franco. Lyon is a corporation's chief financial officer. Franco is the corporation's outside auditor. Lyon is an employee of the corporation, and his compensation is recorded with a debit to Salary Expense. Franco, on the other hand, performs consulting services for many clients, and the corporation debits Consulting Expense when it pays her. *Any payment for services performed by a person outside the company is a debit to an expense account other than payroll.*

 DAILY EXERCISE 11-13

 DAILY EXERCISE 11-14

 WORK IT OUT

Record the payroll and payroll taxes for the following information:

Gross salary (subject to all taxes)	$190,000
Employees' federal income tax withheld	35,800
Life insurance withheld from employees..............	2,000
FICA tax rate	8%
State unemployment tax rate................................	5.4%
Federal unemployment tax rate	0.8%

Answer

Payroll Entry:

Salary Expense..	190,000	
FICA Tax Payable ($190,000 × 0.08)		15,200
Life Insurance Premium Payable..............................		2,000
Employee Income Tax Payable.................................		35,800
Salary Payable		137,000

Payroll Tax Entry:

Payroll Tax Expense..	26,980	
FICA Tax Payable...		15,200
State Unemployment Tax Payable ($190,000 × 0.054)		10,260
Federal Unemployment Tax Payable ($190,000 × 0.008)		1,520

THE PAYROLL SYSTEM

Good business means paying employees accurately and on time. Companies must handle both employees' and their own payroll taxes, as we have seen. Thus, companies process lots of payroll data. For accurate and timely payrolls, accountants have developed the *payroll system.*

Objective 5
Use a payroll system

The components of the payroll system are

- A payroll record
- A special payroll bank account
- Payroll checks
- An earnings record for each employee

Payroll Record

Each pay period the company organizes the payroll data in a special journal called the *payroll record* or *payroll journal.* This record lists each employee and the figures the business needs to record payroll amounts. The payroll record, which resembles the cash payments journal, also serves as a check register by providing a place to record each payroll check. ➤

A payroll record similar to that for **Blumenthal's** in Exhibit 11-7 is used by companies such as **Marriott Corp.,** the hotel chain. The *Gross Pay* section has columns for straight-time pay, overtime pay, and total gross pay for each employee. The *Deductions* columns vary from company to company, but every employer must deduct federal income tax and FICA tax. (State income tax is left out for convenience.) Additional column headings depend on the optional deductions the business handles. In Exhibit 11-7, the employer deducts employee payroll taxes, union dues, and gifts to **United Way,** and then sends the amounts to the proper parties. The *Net Pay* section lists each employee's net (take-home) pay and the number of the check issued to him or her. The last two columns indicate the *Account Debited* for the employee's gross pay. (The company has both office workers and salespeople.)

The payroll record in Exhibit 11-7 gives the employer the information needed to record salary expense for the pay period. Using the total amounts for columns (d) through (l), the employer records total salary expense as follows:

◄ We introduced the cash payments journal in Chapter 6, p. 242.

Dec. 31	Office Salary Expense	4,464.00	
	Sales Salary Expense	9,190.00	
	Employee Income Tax Payable...............		3,167.76
	FICA Tax Payable		861.94
	Employee Union Dues Payable		85.00
	Employee United Way Payable		155.00
	Salary Payable to Employees..................		9,384.30

 DAILY EXERCISE 11-15

Payroll Bank Account

After journalizing the payroll, the company books show a credit balance in Salary Payable to Employees for net pay of $9,384.30. (See column (i) in Exhibit 11-7.) How the business pays this liability depends on its payroll system. Many companies

Week ended December 31, 2000

Employee Name	Hours	a Straight-Time	b Overtime	c Total	d Federal Income Tax	e FICA Tax	f Union Dues	g United Way Charities	b Total	i (c − h) Amount	j Check No.	k Office Salary Expense	l Sales Salary Expense
		Gross Pay			**Deductions**					**Net Pay**		**Account Debited**	
Chen, W. L.*	40	500.00		500.00	71.05	40.00	5.00	2.50	118.55	381.45	1621	500.00	
Dean, R. C.	46	400.00	90.00	490.00	59.94	39.20		2.00	101.14	388.86	1622		490.00
Ellis, M.	41	560.00	21.00	581.00	86.14	46.48	5.00		137.62	443.38	1623	581.00	
Trimble, E. A.†	40	1,360.00		1,360.00	463.22			15.00	478.22	881.78	1641		1,360.00
Total		12,940.00	714.00	13,654.00	3,167.76	861.94	85.00	155.00	4,269.70	9,384.30		4,464.00	9,190.00

*W. L. Chen earned gross pay of $500. His net pay was $381.45, paid with check number 1621. Chen is an office worker, so his salary is debited to Office Salary Expense.

†The business deducted no FICA tax from E. A. Trimble. She has already earned more than $75,000. Any employee whose earnings exceed this annual maximum pays no additional FICA tax during that year.

Note: For simplicity we ignore the additional tax for Medicare benefits.

ЕХНІВІТ 11-7 **Blumenthal's Payroll Record**

pay employees from a special *payroll bank account*. The employer transfers the net pay ($9,384.30 in our illustration) from its regular bank account into the special payroll bank account. Then the company writes paychecks to employees from the payroll account. When the paychecks clear the bank, the payroll account has a zero balance. Writing paychecks from a separate bank account isolates payroll amounts for analysis and control, as we discuss later in the chapter.

Payroll Checks

Most companies pay employees by check or by electronic fund transfer (EFT). A *paycheck* is like any other check except that its attachment details the employee's payroll amounts. These figures come from the payroll record in Exhibit 11-7. Exhibit 11-8 shows payroll check number 1622, issued to R. C. Dean for net pay of $388.86 earned during the week ended December 31, 2000. To enhance your ability to use payroll data, trace all amounts on the check attachment to the payroll record in Exhibit 11-7.

EXHIBIT 11-8   Payroll Check

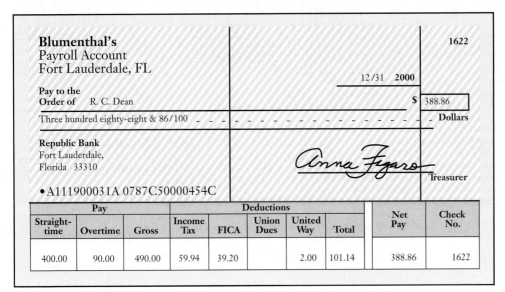

Increasingly, companies are paying employees by electronic funds transfer. The employee can authorize the company to make all deposits directly to his or her bank. With no check to deliver to the employee, the company saves time and money. As evidence of the deposit, most companies, including **American Airlines,** issue a voided check to employees. The employee doesn't have to receive, endorse, and deposit the paycheck.

Earnings Record

The employer must file payroll tax returns with the federal and state governments. Exhibit 11-9 (on page 444) is the Form 941 that Blumenthal's filed with the Internal Revenue Service for the quarter ended December 31, 2000. These forms must be filed no later than one month after the end of a quarter.

Line 13 of the exhibit shows that Blumenthal's payroll taxes for the quarter totaled $35,200. Line 14 indicates that during the quarter Blumenthal's paid the full tax bill, so the balance due on line 15 was zero. (There are heavy penalties for paying these taxes late.)

The employer must also provide the employee with a wage and tax statement, Form W-2, at the end of the year. Therefore, employers maintain an *earnings record* for each employee. Exhibit 11-10 (on page 445) is a five-week excerpt from the earnings record of employee R. C. Dean.

The employee earnings record is not a journal or a ledger, and it is not required by law. It is an accounting tool—like the work sheet—that the employer uses to prepare payroll tax reports to the Internal Revenue Service.

Exhibit 11-11 (on page 445) is the Wage and Tax Statement, Form W-2, for employee R. C. Dean. The employer prepares this statement and gives copies to the employee and to the Internal Revenue Service (IRS). Dean uses the W-2 to prepare

EXHIBIT 11-9 Payroll Tax Return

Form **941** (Rev. January 2000) Department of the Treasury Internal Revenue Service	**Employer's Quarterly Federal Tax Return** ▶ See separate instructions for information on completing this return. Please type or print.		OMB No. 1545-0029

Enter state code for state in which deposits were made ONLY if different from state in address to the right ▶ F:L (see page 2 of instructions).

Name (as distinguished from trade name) — Date quarter ended

Trade name, if any — Employer identification number
Blumenthal's

Address (number and street) — City, state, and ZIP code
Crescent Square Shopping Center
Fort Lauderdale, FL 33310-1234

	T
	FF
	FD
	FP
	I
	T

If address is different from prior return, check here ▶ ☐

IRS Use

1 1 1 1 1 1 1 1 1 1   2   3 3 3 3 3 3 3   4 4 4   5 5 5
6   7   8 8 8 8 8 8 8   9 9 9 9   10 10 10 10 10 10 10 10 10 10

If you do not have to file returns in the future, check here ▶ ☐   and enter date final wages paid ▶

If you are a seasonal employer, see **Seasonal employers** on page 1 of the instructions and check here ▶ ☐

1	Number of employees in the pay period that includes March 12th ▶	1	19
2	Total wages and tips, plus other compensation	2	113,654
3	Total income tax withheld from wages, tips, and sick pay	3	18,168
4	Adjustment of withheld income tax for preceding quarters of calendar year	4	—
5	Adjusted total of income tax withheld (line 3 as adjusted by line 4—see instructions) . .	5	18,168

6	Taxable social security wages	6a	110,774	× 12.4% (.124) =	6b	13,736
	Taxable social security tips	6c		× 12.4% (.124) =	6d	
7	Taxable Medicare wages and tips . . .	7a	113,654	× 2.9% (.029) =	7b	3,296

8	Total social security and Medicare taxes (add lines 6b, 6d, and 7b). Check here if wages are not subject to social security and/or Medicare tax . . . . ▶ ☐	8	17,032
9	Adjustment of social security and Medicare taxes (see instructions for required explanation) Sick Pay $ _____ ± Fractions of Cents $ _____ ± Other $ _____ =	9	—
10	Adjusted total of social security and Medicare taxes (line 8 as adjusted by line 9—see instructions)	10	17,032
11	**Total taxes** (add lines 5 and 10)	11	35,200
12	Advance earned income credit (EIC) payments made to employees	12	—
13	Net taxes (subtract line 12 from line 11). **If $1,000 or more, this must equal line 17, column (d) below (or line D of Schedule B (Form 941))**	13	35,200
14	Total deposits for quarter, including overpayment applied from a prior quarter	14	35,200
15	**Balance due** (subtract line 14 from line 13). See instructions	15	–0–

16 **Overpayment.** If line 14 is more than line 13, enter excess here ▶ $ _____
and check if to be: ☐ Applied to next return   **OR**   ☐ Refunded.

● **All filers:** If line 13 is less than $1,000, you need not complete line 17 or Schedule B (Form 941).
● **Semiweekly schedule depositors:** Complete Schedule B (Form 941) and check here . . . . ▶ ☐
● **Monthly schedule depositors:** Complete line 17, columns (a) through (d), and check here. . . . . ▶ ☐

17   Monthly Summary of Federal Tax Liability. Do not complete if you were a semiweekly schedule depositor.

(a) First month liability	(b) Second month liability	(c) Third month liability	(d) Total liability for quarter
35,017	35,336	34,967	35,200

Sign Here — Under penalties of perjury, I declare that I have examined this return, including accompanying schedules and statements, and to the best of my knowledge and belief, it is true, correct, and complete.

Signature ▶ *Anna Figaro*   Print Your Name and Title ▶ Anna Figaro, Treasurer   Date ▶ 1/30/00

For Privacy Act and Paperwork Reduction Act Notice, see back of Payment Voucher.   Cat. No. 17001Z   Form **941** (Rev. 1-2000)

his income tax return. To ensure that Dean is paying income tax on all his income from that job, the IRS matches Dean's income as reported on his tax return with his earnings as reported on the W-2.

Paying the Payroll

Up to this point, we have talked about the recording of payroll expenses. We now turn to the *payment* of these liabilities. Most employers must record at least three cash payments for payrolls:

- net pay to employees
- payroll taxes to the government and other payroll deductions
- employee benefits

EXHIBIT 11-10 Employee Earnings Record for 2000

EMPLOYEE NAME AND ADDRESS:

DEAN, R. C.
4376 PALM DRIVE
FORT LAUDERDALE, FL 33317

SOCIAL SECURITY NO.: 344-86-4529
MARITAL STATUS: MARRIED
WITHHOLDING EXEMPTIONS: 4
PAY RATE: $400 PER WEEK
JOB TITLE: SALESPERSON

| Week Ended | Hrs. | Gross Pay | | | | Deductions | | | | | Net Pay | |
		Straight-Time	Over-time	Total	To Date	Federal Income Tax	FICA Tax	Union Dues	United Way Charity	Total	Amount	Check No.
Dec. 3	40	400.00		400.00	21,340.00	42.19	32.00		2.00	76.19	323.81	1525
Dec. 10	40	400.00		400.00	21,740.00	42.19	32.00		2.00	76.19	323.81	1548
Dec. 17	44	400.00	60.00	460.00	22,200.00	54.76	36.80		2.00	93.56	366.44	1574
Dec. 24	48	400.00	120.00	520.00	22,720.00	66.75	41.60		2.00	110.35	409.65	1598
Dec. 31	46	400.00	90.00	490.00	23,210.00	59.94	39.20		2.00	101.14	388.86	1622
Total		20,800.00	2,410.00	23,210.00		1,946.72	1,856.80		104.00	3,907.52	19,302.48	

EXHIBIT 11-11
Employee Wage and Tax Statement, Form W-2

a Control number	22222	Void □	For Official Use Only ► OMB No. 1545-0008		
b Employer identification number 83-19475				1 Wages, tips, other compensation 23,210.00	2 Federal income tax withheld 1,946.72
c Employer's name, address, and ZIP code Blumenthal's Crescent Square Shopping Center Fort Lauderdale, FL 33310-1234				3 Social security wages 23,210.00	4 Social security tax withheld 1,439.02
				5 Medicare wages and tips 23,210.00	6 Medicare tax withheld 417.78
				7 Social security tips	8 Allocated tips
d Employee's social security number 344-86-4529				9 Advance EIC payment	10 Dependent care benefits
e Employee's name (first, middle initial, last) R. C. Dean				11 Nonqualified plans	12 Benefits included in box 1
4376 Palm Drive Fort Lauderdale, FL 33317				13 See instrs. for box 13	14 Other
				15 Statutory employee □ Deceased □ Pension plan □ Legal rep. □ Deferred compensation □	
f Employee's address and ZIP code					
16 State Employer's state I.D. no.	17 State wages, tips, etc.		18 State income tax	19 Locality name 20 Local wages, tips, etc.	21 Local income tax

Form **W-2** Wage and Tax Statement **2000**

Copy A For Social Security Administration—Send this entire page with Form W-3 to the Social Security Administration; photocopies are **not** acceptable.

Cat. No. 10134D

Department of the Treasury—Internal Revenue Service
For Privacy Act and Paperwork Reduction Act Notice, see separate instructions.

NET PAY TO EMPLOYEES   When the company pays employees, it debits Salary Payable to Employees and credits Cash. Using the data in Exhibit 11-7, the company would make the following entry to record the cash payment (column (i)) for the December 31 weekly payroll:

Dec. 31   Salary Payable to Employees 9,384.30
                 Cash 9,384.30

PAYROLL TAXES TO THE GOVERNMENT AND OTHER PAYROLL DEDUCTIONS   The employer must send the government two sets of payroll taxes: those withheld from employees' pay and those paid by the employer. In Exhibit 11-7, columns (d) through (g), the business would record a series of cash payment entries that can be summarized as follows (the unemployment tax amounts are assumed):

Dec. 31	Employee Income Tax Payable	3,167.76	
	FICA Tax Payable ($861.94 × 2)	1,723.88	
	Employee Union Dues Payable	85.00	
	Employee United Way Payable	155.00	
	State Unemployment Tax Payable	104.62	
	Federal Unemployment Tax Payable	15.50	
	Cash		5,251.76

DAILY EXERCISE 11-16

BENEFITS The employer might pay for employees' insurance coverage and their pension plan. If the total cash payment for these benefits is $1,927.14, the entry is

| Dec. 31 | Employee Benefits Payable | 1,927.14 | |
| | Cash | | 1,927.14 |

Many companies provide *postretirement benefits* such as medical insurance for retired workers. The companies accrue this liability during the employees' working years and then pay it off during their retirement.

Internal Control over Payroll

The internal controls over cash payments discussed in Chapter 7 apply to payroll. The large number of transactions and the complex arrangements increase the risk of a control failure. There are two main types of special controls for payroll: controls for efficiency and controls for safeguarding payroll disbursements.

CONTROLS FOR EFFICIENCY Reconciling the bank account can be time-consuming because of the large number of paychecks. For example, a March 30 paycheck would probably clear the bank before a March 31 bank statement. This check and others would be outstanding. A large number of outstanding checks for the bank reconciliation increases accounting expense. To limit the number of outstanding paychecks, many companies use two payroll bank accounts. They pay the payroll from one bank account one month and from the other payroll account the next month. This way they can reconcile each account every other month. In this system, a March 30 paycheck has until April 30 to clear the bank before the account is reconciled. Outstanding checks are almost eliminated, the bank reconciliation is streamlined, and accounting expense decreases.

Payroll transactions are ideal for computer processing. Employee payroll data are stored in a file. Each pay period, keyboarders enter the number of hours worked by each employee. The computer makes all calculations, prints the payroll record and the paychecks, and updates employee earnings records. The program also computes payroll taxes and prepares the quarterly tax reports.

CONTROLS FOR SAFEGUARDING PAYROLL DISBURSEMENTS Owners and managers of small businesses can monitor their payrolls by personal contact with employees. Large corporations cannot. These businesses must establish controls to ensure that paychecks go only to legitimate employees and for the correct amounts. A particular danger is that a paycheck may be written to a fictitious employee and cashed by a dishonest employee. To guard against this and other crimes, large businesses adopt strict internal control policies.

The duties of hiring and firing employees should be separated from the duties of payroll accounting and passing out paychecks. Requiring a photo ID also helps internal control. Issuing paychecks only to employees with badges ensures that only actual employees receive pay.

A formal timekeeping system helps ensure that employees actually worked the number of hours claimed. Having employees punch time cards at the start and end of the workday proves their attendance.

DAILY EXERCISE 11-17

As we saw in Chapter 7, the key to good internal control is separation of duties. The responsibilities of the personnel department, the payroll department, the accounting department, time-card management, and paycheck distribution should be separate.

THINK IT OVER

Centurion Homes of Omaha, Nebraska, builds houses with four construction crews. The foremen hire—and fire—workers and keep their hourly records. Each Friday morning, the foremen telephone their workers' hours to the home office, where accountants prepare the weekly paychecks. Around noon, the foremen pick up the paychecks. They return to the construction site and pay the workers at day's end. What is the internal control weakness in this situation? Propose a way to improve the internal controls.

Answer: Construction workers often have limited contact with the home office. The foremen control most of the payroll information, so they can forge the payroll records of fictitious employees and pocket their pay. To improve internal control, Centurion could hire and fire all workers through the home office. This practice would establish the identity of all workers listed in the payroll records. Another way to improve the internal controls would be to have a home-office employee distribute paychecks on a surprise basis. Any unclaimed checks would arouse suspicion. This system would probably prevent foremen from cheating the company.

REPORTING PAYROLL EXPENSE AND LIABILITIES

On the balance sheet, **IBM** and other companies report the amount of *payroll liability* owed to all parties—employees, governments, unions, and so on. Payroll liability is *not* the payroll expense for the year. The liability at year end is the amount of the expense that is still unpaid. Payroll expense appears on the income statement payroll liability on the balance sheet. On a recent balance sheet, IBM reported compensation and benefits payable of $3,840 million as a current liability as shown in Exhibit 11-12. The exhibit also presents the other current liabilities we have discussed.

Current Liabilities	Millions
Taxes payable	$ 4,792
Short-term debt	14,230
Accounts payable	6,400
Compensation and benefits payable	3,840
Unearned revenue	4,529
Other accrued expenses and liabilities	5,787
Total current liabilities	**$39,578**

Objective 6
Report current liabilities on the balance sheet

EXHIBIT 11-12
IBM Balance Sheet (partial, adapted) December 31, 1999

 DAILY EXERCISE 11-18

 DAILY EXERCISE 11-19

The following Decision Guidelines feature summarizes some of the more important payroll decisions that a business must consider.

DECISION GUIDELINES

Accounting for Payroll

DECISION	GUIDELINES
What are the key elements of a payroll accounting system?	• Employee's Withholding Allowance Certificate, Form W-4 • Payroll register • Payroll bank account and payroll checks • Employer's quarterly tax returns, such as Form 941 • Employee earnings record • Employee wage and tax statement, Form W-2
What are the key terms in the payroll area?	Gross pay (Total amount earned by the employee) − *Payroll deductions* **a.** Withheld income tax **b.** FICA (Social Security) tax—equal amount also payable by employer **c.** Optional deductions (insurance, savings, charitable contributions, union dues) = *Net (take-home) pay*
What is the employer's total payroll expense?	Gross pay + *Employer's payroll taxes* **a.** FICA (Social Security) tax—equal amount also payable by employee **b.** State and federal unemployment taxes + *Benefits for employees* **a.** Insurance (health, life, and disability) **b.** Pension (and other retirement) benefits **c.** Club memberships and other = *Employer's total payroll costs*
Where to report payroll costs?	• Payroll expenses on the income statement • Payroll liabilities on the balance sheet

REVIEW CURRENT LIABILITIES

SUMMARY PROBLEM

www.prenhall.com/horngren
End-of-Chapter Assessment

Beth Denius, Limited, a clothing store, employs one salesperson, Alan Kingsley. His straight-time salary is $360 per week. He earns time and a half for hours worked in excess of 40 per week. The owner, Beth Denius, withholds income tax (11.0%) and FICA tax (8.0%) from Kingsley's pay. She pays the following employer payroll taxes: FICA (8.0%) and state and federal unemployment (5.4% and 0.8%, respectively). In addition, Denius contributes to a pension plan an amount equal to 10% of Kingsley's gross pay.

During the week ended December 26, 20X4, Kingsley worked 48 hours. Prior to this week, Kingsley had earned $5,470.

Required

1. Compute Kingsley's gross pay and net pay for the week.
2. Record the following payroll entries that Denius would make:
   - **a.** Expense for Kingsley's salary, including overtime pay
   - **b.** Employer payroll taxes
   - **c.** Expense for employee benefits
   - **d.** Payment of cash to Kingsley
   - **e.** Payment of all payroll taxes
   - **f.** Payment for employee benefits
3. How much total payroll expense did Denius incur for the week? How much cash did the business spend on its payroll?

Solutions

Requirement 1

Gross pay:	Straight-time pay for 40 hours		$360.00
	Overtime pay:		
	Rate per hour ($360/40 × 1.5)	$13.50	
	Hours (48 − 40)	8	108.00
	Total gross pay		$468.00
Net pay:	Gross pay		$468.00
	Less: Withheld income tax ($468 × 0.11)	$51.48	
	Withheld FICA tax ($468 × 0.08)	37.44	88.92
	Net pay..		$379.08

Requirement 2

a.	Sales Salary Expense	468.00	
	Employee Income Tax Payable		51.48
	FICA Tax Payable...		37.44
	Salary Payable to Employee		379.08
b.	Payroll Tax Expense	66.45	
	FICA Tax Payable ($468 × 0.08)		37.44
	State Unemployment Tax Payable ($468 × 0.054)		25.27
	Federal Unemployment Tax Payable (468 × 0.008)		3.74
c.	Pension Expense ($468 × 0.10)	46.80	
	Employee Benefits Payable...................................		46.80
d.	Salary Payable to Employee	379.08	
	Cash		379.08
e.	Employee Income Tax Payable.....................................	51.48	
	FICA Tax Payable ($37.44 × 2)	74.88	
	State Unemployment Tax Payable	25.27	
	Federal Unemployment Tax Payable............................	3.74	
	Cash		155.37
f.	Employee Benefits Payable	46.80	
	Cash		46.80

Requirement 3

- Denius incurred *total payroll expense* of $581.25 (gross salary of $468.00 + payroll taxes of $66.45 + benefits of $46.80). See entries (a) through (c).
- Denius *paid cash* of $581.25 on payroll (Kingsley's net pay of $379.08 + payroll taxes of $155.37 + benefits of $46.80). See entries (d) through (f).

LESSONS LEARNED

1. **Account for current liabilities of known amount.** Trade accounts payable, short-term notes payable, interest payable, sales tax payable, payrolls, and unearned revenues are current liabilities of known amount.

2. **Account for current liabilities that must be estimated.** Current liabilities that must be estimated include warranties payable, vacation pay, and corporations' income tax payable. *Contingent liabilities* are potential liabilities that may arise in the future.

3. **Compute payroll amounts.** *Payroll* accounting handles the expenses and liabilities arising from compensating employees. Employers must withhold income and FICA taxes from employees' pay and send these tax amounts to the government. In addition, many employers allow employees to pay for insurance and union dues and to make gifts to charities through payroll deductions. An employee's net pay is the gross pay less all payroll taxes and optional deductions.

4. **Record basic payroll transactions.** An *employer's* payroll expenses include FICA and unemployment taxes, which are separate from the payroll taxes borne by the employees. Also, most employers provide employees with benefits such as insurance coverage and pensions.

5. **Use a payroll system.** A *payroll system* consists of a payroll record, a payroll bank account, payroll checks, and an earnings record for each employee. Good *internal controls* over payrolls help the business to achieve efficiency and to safeguard the company's cash.

6. **Report current liabilities on the balance sheet.** The company reports on the balance sheet all current liabilities that it owes: current liabilities of known amount, including payroll liabilities, and current liabilities that must be estimated.

ACCOUNTING VOCABULARY

accrued expense (p. 430)	**employee compensation** (p. 430)	**Social Security tax** (p. 438)
accrued liability (p. 430)	**FICA tax** (p. 438)	**unemployment compensation tax**
current portion of long-term debt	**gross pay** (p. 437)	(p. 439)
(p. 429)	**net pay** (p. 437)	**withheld income tax** (p. 437)
current maturity (p. 429)	**payroll** (p. 430)	
discounting a note payable	**short presentation** (p. 434)	
(p. 427)	**short-term note payable** (p. 426)	

QUESTIONS

1. What distinguishes a current liability from a long-term liability? What distinguishes a contingent liability from an actual liability?
2. A company purchases a machine by signing a $21,000, one-year, 10% note payable on July 31. Interest is to be paid at maturity. What two current liabilities related to this purchase does the company report on its December 31 balance sheet? What is the amount of each current liability?
3. Explain why sales tax that is paid by consumers is a liability of the store that sold the merchandise.
4. What is meant by the term *current portion of long-term debt*, and how is this item reported in the financial statements?
5. At the beginning of the school term, what type of account is the tuition that your college or university collects from students? What type of account is the tuition at the end of the school term?
6. Patton Company warrants its products against defects for three years from date of sale. During the current year, the company made sales of $300,000. Store management estimated that warranty costs on those sales would total 6% of sales over the three-year warranty period. Ultimately, the company paid $22,000 cash on warranties. What was the company's warranty expense for the year? What accounting principle governs this answer?

7. Why is payroll expense more important to a service business such as a CPA firm than it is to a merchandising company such as **Target?**
8. Two persons are studying Allen Company's manufacturing process. One person is Allen's factory supervisor, and the other is an outside consultant who is an expert in the industry. Which person's salary is the payroll expense of Allen Company? Identify the expense account that Allen would debit to record the pay of each person.
9. What are two elements of an employer's payroll expense in addition to salaries, wages, commissions, and overtime pay?
10. What are FICA taxes? Who pays them? What are the funds used for?
11. Identify two required deductions and four optional deductions from employee paychecks.
12. Who pays state and federal unemployment taxes? What are these funds used for?
13. How much Social Security tax is withheld from the pay of an employee who earns $70,000 during the current year? How much Social Security tax is withheld if the employee earns $77,000?
14. Identify three internal controls designed to safeguard payroll cash.

ASSESS YOUR PROGRESS

DAILY EXERCISES

Accounts payable and notes payable (Obj. 1)

DE11-1 Describe the similarities and the differences between an account payable and a short-term note payable. If necessary, review notes receivable in Chapter 8.

Accounting for a note payable (Obj. 1)

DE11-2 Return to the $8,000 purchase of inventory on a short-term note payable that begins on page 426. Assume that the purchase of inventory occurred on June 30, 20X1, instead of September 30, 20X1. Journalize the company's (a) purchase of inventory, (b) accrual of interest expense on December 31, 20X1, and (c) payment of the note plus interest on June 30, 20X2.

Reporting a short-term note payable and the related interest in the financial statements (Obj. 1)

DE11-3 This exercise should be done in conjunction with Daily Exercise 11-2.

1. Refer to the data in Daily Exercise 11-2. Show what the company would report for the note payable on its balance sheet at December 31, 20X1, and on its income statement for the year ended on that date.
2. What one item will the financial statements for the year ended December 31, 20X2, report? Identify the financial statement, the item, and its amount.

Accounting for a discounted note payable (Obj. 1)

DE11-4 Accounting for a discounted note payable is illustrated for a $100,000 note at the top of page 427.

1. Why did **Procter & Gamble (P&G)** sign the note payable? What did P&G receive?
2. Suppose P&G signed the note payable on November 16, 20X1, instead of November 25, 20X1. Make P&G's adjusting entry to accrue interest expense at December 31, 20X1.
3. Show how P&G would report the note payable on its balance sheet at December 31, 20X1.
4. Journalize P&G's interest expense and payment of the note payable at maturity. Give the date.

DE11-5 The chapter opening story describes the airlines' frequent-flier programs. Suppose passengers fly 1,000,000 miles on **American Airlines** and the AAdvantage® frequent-flier program costs American $.0015 per mile. During the next six months, AAdvantage® customers use 200,000 of the miles for free trips on American Airlines.

Accounting for unearned revenue
(Obj. 1)

1. Using American Airlines' actual account titles (see Exhibit 11-1), journalize American's (a) accrual of Promotion Expense and Air Traffic Liability and (b) the provision of free transportation for the AAdvantage® customers (credit Cash). Explanations are not required.
2. Post to the Air Traffic Liability T-account. How much does American Airlines owe the AAdvantage® customers after the preceding transactions?

DE11-6 **Ford,** the automaker, guarantees its automobiles for three years or 36,000 miles, whichever comes first. Suppose Ford's experience indicates that the company can expect warranty costs during the three-year period to add up to 5% of sales.

*Accounting for warranty expense
and estimated warranty payable*
(Obj. 2)

Assume that Five Points Ford in Cincinnati made sales of Ford Escorts totaling $600,000 during 20X7, its first year of operations. The company received cash for 30% of the sales and notes receivable for the remainder. Payments to satisfy customer warranty claims totaled $22,000 during 20X7.

1. Record the sales, warranty expense, and warranty payments for Five Points Ford.
2. Post to the Estimated Warranty Payable T-account. At the end of 20X7, how much in estimated warranty payable does Five Points Ford owe its customers? Why must the warranty payable amount be estimated?

DE11-7 Refer to the data given in Daily Exercise 11-6.

*Applying GAAP; reporting
warranties in the financial
statements*
(Obj. 2)

What amount of warranty expense will Five Points Ford report during 20X7? Which accounting principle addresses this situation? Does the warranty expense for the year equal the year's cash payments for warranties? Explain how the accounting principle works for measuring warranty expense.

DE11-8 **Harley-Davidson, Inc.,** the motorcycle manufacturer, included the following note (adapted) in its annual report:

*Interpreting a company's
contingent liabilities*
(Obj. 2)

NOTES TO CONSOLIDATED FINANCIAL STATEMENTS

7 (In Part): Commitments and Contingencies

The Company self-insures its product liability losses in the United States up to $3 million (catastrophic coverage is maintained for individual claims in excess of $3 million up to $25 million). Outside the United States, the Company is insured for product liability up to $25 million per individual claim and in the aggregate.

---

1. Why are these *contingent* (versus real) liabilities?
2. In the United States, how can the contingent liability become a real liability for Harley-Davidson? What are the limits to the company's product liabilities in the United States? Explain how these limits work.
3. How can a contingency outside the United States become a real liability for the company? How does Harley-Davidson's potential liability differ for claims outside the United States?

DE11-9 Consider the operations of a **Wendy's** restaurant, **Toyota Motor Corporation,** and a large accounting firm. Rank these businesses in terms of the percentage of labor cost to the company's total expenses—from most important to least important. Give the reason for your ranking.

*Assessing the importance of
payroll expenses*
(Obj. 3)

Daily Exercise 11-10 begins a sequence of exercises that ends with Daily Exercise 11-12.

DE11-10 Examine the payroll situation of Lucy Childres on page 437.

*Computing an employee's
total pay*
(Obj. 3)

1. Compute Childres's total pay for working 50 hours during the first week of February.
2. Childres is single, and her income tax withholding is 9% of total pay. Her only payroll deductions are payroll taxes. Compute Childres's net pay for the week. (Use an 8% FICA tax rate.)

DE11-11 Return to the Lucy Childres payroll situation in Daily Exercise 11-10. Childres's employer, Bobby Jones Golf Company, pays all the standard payroll taxes plus benefits for employee pensions (6% of total pay), health insurance ($60 per employee per month), and disability insurance ($8 per employee per month).

*Computing total payroll expense
of an employer*
(Obj. 3)

Compute Bobby Jones's total expense of employing Lucy Childres for the 50 hours that she worked during the first week of February. Carry amounts to the nearest cent.

DE11-12 After solving Daily Exercises 11-10 and 11-11, journalize for Bobby Jones Golf Company the following expenses related to the employment of Lucy Childres:

Making payroll entries
(Obj. 4)

a. Salary expense   **b.** Employer payroll taxes   **c.** Benefits

Use Exhibit 11-6 (p. 440) to format your journal entries. Carry all amounts to the nearest cent.

DE11-13 Suppose you have worked for an accounting firm all year and you earn a monthly salary of $8,000. Your withheld income taxes consume 15% of your gross pay. In addition to payroll taxes, which are required, you elect to contribute 5% monthly to your pension plan. Your employer also deducts $200 monthly for your co-pay of the health insurance premium.

Compute your net pay for October. Use an 8% FICA tax rate on the first $75,000 of income.

DE11-14 Exhibit 11-5, page 439, shows the breakdown of an employer's total payroll cost of $1,180 for one employee. Journalize the employer's (a) salary expense (use a single Payroll Tax Payable account), (b) payroll taxes (use a single Payroll Tax Payable account), and (c) cost of health insurance. Follow the pattern of the entries in Exhibit 11-6, page 440.

DE11-15 Refer to the payroll record in Exhibit 11-7, page 442.

1. How much cash did the employees take home for their work this week?
2. How much was the company's total salary expense for the week? What accounts were debited? How much was debited to each account?
3. How much did *employees* pay this week for
   a. Withheld federal income tax?
   b. Withheld FICA tax?
4. How much expense did the *employer* have this week for
   a. Employee federal income tax?
   b. FICA tax?
5. Which employees earned less than $75,000, and which employees earned more than $75,000 this year? How can you tell?

DE11-16 Study the Employee Earnings Record for R. C. Dean in Exhibit 11-10, page 445. In addition to the amounts shown in the exhibit, the employer also paid all payroll taxes plus (a) an amount equal to 7% of gross pay into Dean's pension retirement account, and (b) health insurance for Dean at a cost of $140 per month.

Compute the employer's total payroll expense for employee R. C. Dean during 2000. Carry all amounts to the nearest cent.

DE11-17 ◀ *Link Back to Chapter 7 (Internal Controls)*

1. What are some of the important elements of good internal control to safeguard payroll disbursements?
2. Explain how the use of two payroll bank accounts (one account the first month, the other account the next month) makes accounting for the payroll of a large company more efficient. Identify another control for efficiency in the payroll area.

DE11-18 Study the payroll record of **Blumenthal's** in Exhibit 11-7, page 442. Assume Blumenthal's will pay this payroll on January 2, 2001. In addition to the payroll liabilities shown in the exhibit, Blumenthal's has the following liabilities at December 31, 2000:

Accounts payable...................	$44,140	Current portion of	
Employer FICA tax payable....	862	long-term debt	$20,000
Long-term debt......................	80,000	Interest payable	1,116
Unearned revenue.................	4,430	Contingent liabilities..............	—

Prepare the current liabilities section of Blumenthal's balance sheet at December 31, 2000. List current liabilities in descending order starting with the largest first. Also list each of the payroll liabilities from Exhibit 11-7, rounded to the nearest dollar. Show the total of current liabilities.

DE11-19 Refer to **IBM Corporation's** current liabilities in Exhibit 11-12, page 447.

1. Explain in your own words each of the company's current liabilities.
2. When will IBM pay these liabilities? When is the latest date that IBM will pay the liabilities? How can you tell?

EXERCISES

E11-1 Make general journal entries to record the following transactions of Club Lanai Vacation Co. for a two-month period. Explanations are not required.

March 31 Recorded cash sales of $200,000 for the month, plus sales tax of 5% collected on behalf of the state of Arizona. Recorded sales tax in a separate account.
April 6 Sent March sales tax to the state.

Required

Journalize these transactions a second time. Record the sales tax initially in the Sales Revenue account.

E11-2 **Pier 1 Imports, Inc.,** reported the following current liabilities (adapted, all amounts in thousands):

Analyzing current liabilities (Obj. 1)

	February 28,	
	20X2	**20X1**
Accrued payroll liabilities.................	$27,194	$25,068
Gift certificates outstanding	11,276	8,242

Required

1. The purpose of this requirement is to show how Pier 1's ending balance of accrued payroll liabilities arose from the company's transactions during the year ended February 28, 20X2. Create a T-account for accrued Payroll Liabilities. Insert the balance at February 28, 20X1 as the beginning balance. Assume that during the year ended February 28, 20X2, Pier 1 accrued payroll expense of $265,000 and paid $262,874 of this total. Post both amounts directly into the Accrued Payroll Liabilities T-account and compute its ending balance. Compare your result to Pier 1's actual ending balance. The two amounts should be the same.
2. Explain the nature of Pier 1's Gift certificates outstanding. What is another name for this account?

E11-3 Assume **The Dallas Morning News** publishing company completed the following transactions during 20X1:

Recording and reporting current liabilities (Obj. 1)

Nov. 1   Sold a six-month subscription, collecting cash of $120, plus sales tax of 5%.
Dec. 15   Remitted (paid) the sales tax to the state of Texas.
     31   Made the necessary adjustment at year end to record the amount of subscription revenue earned during the year.

Required

Journalize these transactions (explanations are not required). Then report the liability on the company's balance sheet at December 31, 20X1.

E11-4 The accounting records of Blaze Electronics included the following balances at the end of the period:

Accounting for warranty expense and the related liability (Obj. 2)

ESTIMATES WARRANTY PAYABLE	SALES REVENUE	WARRANTY EXPENSE
Beg. bal. 3,100	161,000	

In the past, Blaze's warranty expense has been 7% of sales. During the current period, the business paid $10,400 to satisfy the warranty claims of customers.

Required

1. Journalize Blaze's warranty expense for the period and the company's cash payments during the period to satisfy warranty claims. Explanations are not required.
2. What ending balance of Estimated Warranty Payable will Blaze report on its balance sheet?

E11-5 Record the following note payable transactions of Carnegie Publishing, Inc., in the company's general journal. Explanations are not required.

Recording note payable transactions (Obj. 1)

20X2
Apr. 1   Purchased equipment costing $15,000 by issuing a one-year, 8% note payable.
Dec. 31   Accrued interest on the note payable.

20X3
Apr. 1   Paid the note payable at maturity.

E11-6 On September 1, 20X4, Tic-Toc Watch Repair discounted a six-month, $12,000 note payable to the bank at 8%.

Discounting a note payable (Obj. 1)

Required

1. Prepare general journal entries to record (a) issuance of the note, (b) accrual of interest at December 31, and (c) payment of the note at maturity in 20X5. Explanations are not required.
2. Show how Tic-Toc would report the note on the December 31, 20X4, balance sheet.

E11-7 Vanguard Security Systems is a defendant in lawsuits brought against the marketing and distribution of its products. Damages of $9.1 million are claimed against Vanguard, but the company denies the charges and is vigorously defending itself. In a recent press conference, the president of the company said management does not believe that any

Reporting a contingent liability (Obj. 3)

actual liabilities resulting from the lawsuits will significantly affect the company's financial position.

Required

Write Note X to describe the contingency.

Reporting current liabilities (Obj. 6)

E11-8 ← *Link Back to Chapter 4 (Current Ratio).* The owner of Ciliotta Pharmacy examines the company accounting records at December 29, immediately before the end of the year:

Total current assets...................	$ 490,000
Noncurrent assets.....................	730,000
	$1,220,000
Total current liabilities..............	$ 260,000
Noncurrent liabilities................	300,000
Owner's equity........................	660,000
	$1,220,000

Ciliotta's borrowing agreements with creditors require the company to keep a current ratio of 2.0 or better. How much in current liabilities should Ciliotta pay off within the next two days in order to comply with its borrowing agreements?

Computing net pay (Obj. 3)

E11-9 Ken Shermac is manager of the men's department of Parisian Department Store in Birmingham. He earns a base monthly salary of $750 plus a 10% commission on his personal sales. Through payroll deductions, Shermac donates $25 per month to a charitable organization, and he authorizes Parisian to deduct $22.50 monthly for his family's health insurance. Tax rates on Shermac's earnings are 10% for income tax and 8% of the first $75,000 for FICA. During the first 11 months of the year, he earned $72,140.

Required

Compute Shermac's gross pay and net pay for December, assuming his sales for the month are $80,000.

Computing and recording gross pay and net pay (Obj. 3, 4)

E11-10 Ruby Degrate works for a Steak 'n Shake diner for straight-time earnings of $6 per hour, with time-and-a-half compensation for hours in excess of 40 per week. Degrate's payroll deductions include withheld income tax of 7% of total earnings, FICA tax of 8% of total earnings, and a weekly deduction of $5 for a charitable contribution to United Fund.

Required

Assuming she worked 50 hours during the week, (a) compute her gross pay and net pay for the week, and (b) make a general journal entry to record the store's wage expense for Degrate's work, including her payroll deductions. Explanations are not required. Round all amounts to the nearest cent.

Recording a payroll (Obj. 3, 4)

E11-11 Clarkson Eyecare incurred salary expense of $92,000 for December. The store's payroll expense includes employer FICA tax of 8% in addition to state unemployment tax of 5.4% and federal unemployment tax of 0.8%. Of the total salaries, $88,400 is subject to FICA tax, and $9,100 is subject to unemployment tax. Also, the store provides the following benefits for employees: health insurance (cost to the store, $2,062.15), life insurance (cost to the store, $351.07), and pension benefits (cost to the store, 8% of salary expense).

Required

Record Clarkson's payroll taxes and its expenses for employee benefits. Explanations are not required.

Reporting payroll expense and liabilities (Obj. 6)

E11-12 Norwest Bank has annual salary expense of $900,000. In addition, the bank incurs payroll tax expense equal to 9% of the total payroll. At December 31, the end of the bank's accounting year, Norwest owes salaries of $4,000 and FICA and other payroll tax of $1,000. The bank will pay these amounts early next year.

Required

Show what Norwest Bank will report for these facts on its income statement and year-end balance sheet.

Reporting current and long-term liabilities (Obj. 6)

E11-13 Suppose Unity Medical Group borrowed $5,000,000 on January 2, 20X1, by issuing 9% long-term debt that must be paid in five equal annual installments plus interest each January 2.

Required

Insert the appropriate amounts to show how Unity Medical Group would report its long-term debt.

	December 31,				
	20X1	20X2	20X3	20X4	20X5
Current liabilities:					
Current portion of long-term debt	$___	$___	$___	$___	$___
Interest payable	___	___	___	___	___
Long-term liabilities:					
Long-term debt.....................................	___	___	___	___	___

E11-14 Assume that **Wilson Sporting Goods** completed these selected transactions during December 20X1:

Reporting current and long-term liabilities (Obj. 6)

a. Sales of $1,000,000 are subject to estimated warranty cost of 3.4%.
b. On December 1, Wilson signed a $200,000 note payable that requires annual payments of $20,000 plus 9% interest on the unpaid balance each December 1.
c. Champs, a chain of sporting goods stores, ordered $9,000 of tennis and golf equipment. With its order, Champs sent a check for $9,000 in advance. Wilson will ship the goods on January 3, 20X2.
d. The December payroll of $195,000 is subject to employee withheld income tax of 9%, FICA tax of 8% (employee and employer), state unemployment tax of 5.4%, and federal unemployment tax of 0.8%. On December 31, Wilson pays employees but accrues all tax amounts.

Required

Classify each liability as current or long-term, and report the amount that would appear for each item on Wilson's balance sheet at December 31, 20X1. Show total current liabilities.

Challenge Exercises

E11-15 ← *Link Back to Chapter 4 (Current Ratio).* The balance sheets of **PepsiCo, Inc.,** for two years reported these figures:

Analyzing current liabilities (Obj. 1, 6)

	Billions	
	20X2	20X1
Total current assets....................	$ 4.6	$ 4.1
Noncurrent assets......................	14.2	13.0
	$18.8	$17.1
Total current liabilities	$ 3.7	$ 4.8
Noncurrent liabilities	9.5	7.4
Stockholders' equity	5.6	4.9
	$18.8	$17.1

Assume that during 20X2, PepsiCo reclassified $2.1 billion of current liabilities as long-term.

Required

1. Compute PepsiCo's current ratio as reported at the end of each year. Describe the trend you observe.
2. Assume that PepsiCo had not reclassified $2.1 billion of current liabilities as long-term during 20X2. Recompute the current ratio at the end of 20X2. Why do you think PepsiCo reclassified the liabilities as long-term?

E11-16 **PepsiCo, Inc.,** reported short-term debt payable and salary payable (adapted, in millions), as follows:

Analyzing current liabilities (Obj. 1, 6)

	December 31,	
	20X2	20X1
Current liabilities (partial):		
Short-term debt payable..............	$707	$228
Salary payable............................	327	334

Assume that during 20X2, PepsiCo borrowed $1,106 million on short-term debt. Also assume that PepsiCo paid $3,200 million for salaries during 20X2.

Required

1. Compute PepsiCo's payment of short-term debt during 20X2.
2. Compute PepsiCo's salary expense during 20X2.

(Group A) PROBLEMS

Journalizing liability-related transactions
(Obj. 1, 2)

P11-1A The following transactions of Leland Communications occurred during 20X4 and 20X5:

20X4

Jan. 9 Purchased equipment at a cost of $20,000, signing a six-month, 8% note payable for that amount.

29 Recorded the week's sales of $40,200, three-fourths on credit, and one-fourth for cash. Sales amounts are subject to an additional 6% state sales tax.

Feb. 5 Sent the last week's sales tax to the state.

28 Borrowed $200,000 on a four-year, 9% note payable that calls for annual installment payments of $50,000 principal plus interest.

July 9 Paid the six-month, 8% note at maturity.

Oct. 22 Discounted a $10,000, 90-day, 8% note payable to the bank, receiving cash for the net amount after interest was deducted from the note's maturity value.

Nov. 30 Purchased inventory for $3,100, signing a six-month, 10% note payable.

Dec. 31 Accrued warranty expense, which is estimated at 3% of sales of $650,000.

31 Accrued interest on all outstanding notes payable. Made a separate interest accrual entry for each note payable.

20X5

Jan. 20 Paid off the 8% discounted note payable. Made a separate entry for the interest.

Feb. 28 Paid the first installment and interest for one year on the long-term note payable.

May 31 Paid off the 10% note plus interest on maturity.

Required

Record the transactions in the company's general journal. Explanations are not required.

Identifying contingent liabilities
(Obj. 2)

P11-2A Rountree Acura is one of the largest **Acura** dealers in the Midwest. The dealership sells new and used cars and operates a body shop and a service department. Mitch McGee, the general manager, is considering changing insurance companies because of a disagreement with Hank Callendar, agent for the **Travelers Insurance Company.** Travelers is doubling Rountree's liability insurance cost for the next year. In discussing insurance coverage with you, a trusted business associate, McGee brings up the subject of contingent liabilities.

Required

Write a memorandum to inform Rountree Acura of specific contingent liabilities arising from the business. In your discussion, define a contingent liability.

Computing and recording payroll amounts
(Obj. 3, 4)

P11-3A The partial monthly records of Allstar Cycle Co. show the following figures:

Employee Earnings	
(a) Straight-time earnings	$16,431
(b) Overtime pay	?
(c) Total employee earnings	?

Deductions and Net Pay	
(d) Withheld income tax	$ 2,403
(e) FICA tax	?
(f) Charitable contributions	340
(g) Medical insurance	668
(h) Total deductions	5,409
(i) Net pay	18,540

Accounts Debited	
(j) Salary Expense	$?
(k) Wage Expense	8,573
(l) Sales Commission Expense	2,077

Required

1. Determine the missing amounts on lines (b), (c), (e), and (j).
2. Prepare the general journal entry to record Allstar's payroll for the month. Credit Payrolls Payable for net pay. No explanation is required.

Computing and recording payroll amounts

(Obj. 3, 4)

P11-4A Virginia Nadair is a vice president of Palm City Bank's leasing operations in Pensacola, Florida. During 20X2, she worked for the company all year at a $5,625 monthly salary. She also earned a year-end bonus equal to 12% of her salary.

Nadair's federal income tax withheld during 20X2 was $737 per month. Also, there was a one-time federal withholding tax of $1,007 on her bonus check. State income tax withheld came to $43 per month, and there was a one-time state withholding tax of $27 on the bonus. The FICA tax withheld was 8.0% of the first $75,000 in annual earnings. Nadair authorized the following payroll deductions: United Fund contribution of 1% of total earnings and life insurance of $19 per month.

Palm City Bank incurred payroll tax expense on Nadair for FICA tax of 8% of the first $75,000 in annual earnings. The bank also paid state unemployment tax of 5.4% and federal unemployment tax of 0.8% on the first $7,000 in annual earnings. In addition, the bank provides Nadair with health insurance at a cost of $35 per month and pension benefits. During 20X2, Palm City Bank paid $7,178 into Nadair's pension program.

Required

1. Compute Nadair's gross pay, payroll deductions, and net pay for the full year 20X2. Round all amounts to the nearest dollar.
2. Compute Palm City Bank's total 20X2 payroll cost for Nadair.
3. Prepare Palm City Bank's summary general journal entries to record its expense for the following:
   a. Nadair's total earnings for the year, her payroll deductions, and her net pay. Debit Salary Expense and Executive Bonus Compensation as appropriate. Credit liability accounts for the payroll deductions and Cash for net pay.
   b. Employer payroll taxes on Nadair. Credit liability accounts.
   c. Benefits provided to Nadair. Credit a liability account. Explanations are not required.

Journalizing, posting, and reporting liabilities

(Obj. 1, 2, 3, 4, 5, 6)

P11-5A The general ledger of Red Mountain Investments at June 30, 20X3, the end of the company's fiscal year, includes the following account balances before adjusting entries.

Accounts Payable	$105,520
Current Portion of Long-Term Debt	_____
Interest Payable	_____
Salary Payable	_____
Employee Payroll Taxes Payable	_____
Employer Payroll Taxes Payable	_____
Estimated Vacation Pay Liability	7,620
Unearned Rent Revenue	6,000
Long-Term Debt	200,000

The additional data needed to develop the adjusting entries at June 30 are as follows:

a. The long-term debt is payable in annual installments of $40,000 with the next installment due on July 31. On that date, Red Mountain will also pay one year's interest at 9%. Interest was last paid on July 31 of the preceding year. (Make the adjusting entry to shift the current installment of the long-term debt to a current liability.)
b. Gross salaries for the last payroll of the fiscal year were $5,044. Of this amount, employee payroll taxes payable were $1,088, and salary payable was $3,956.
c. Employer payroll taxes payable were $876.
d. Red Mountain estimates that vacation pay expense is 5% of gross salaries.
e. On February 1, the company collected one year's rent of $6,000 in advance.
f. At June 30, Red Mountain is the defendant in a $300,000 lawsuit, which the company expects to win. However, the outcome is uncertain. Write the note to report this contingent liability in the financial statements.

Required

1. Open the listed accounts, inserting their unadjusted June 30 balances.
2. Journalize and post the June 30 adjusting entries to the accounts opened. Key adjusting entries by letter.
3. Prepare the liability section of the balance sheet at June 30.

P11-6A Assume that the payroll records of a district sales office of **Spalding Sporting Goods** provided the following information for the weekly pay period ended December 21, 20X3.

Using a payroll record; recording a payroll

(Obj. 5)

Employee	Hours Worked	Hourly Earnings Rate	Federal Income Tax	Union Dues	United Way Contributions	Earnings Through Previous Week
Larry Fisher...............	42	$28	$278	$6	$35	$77,474
Felicia Jones..............	47	8	87	4	4	23,154
Sara Opper	40	11	64	—	4	4,880
Brian Tate	41	22	188	6	8	74,600

Fisher and Tate are salesmen. Jones and Opper work in the office. All employees are paid time and a half for hours worked in excess of 40 per week. Round all amounts to the nearest dollar. Show your computations. Explanations are not required for journal entries.

Required

1. Enter the appropriate information in a payroll record similar to Exhibit 11-7, page 442. In addition to the deductions listed, the employer also takes out FICA tax: 8% of the first $75,000 of each employee's annual earnings.
2. Record the payroll information in the general journal.
3. Assume that the first payroll check is number 319, paid to Larry Fisher. Record the check numbers in the payroll record. Also, prepare the general journal entry to record payment of net pay to the employees
4. The employer's payroll taxes include FICA tax of 8% of the first $75,000 of each employee's earnings. The employer also pays unemployment taxes of 6.2% (5.4% for the state and 0.8% for the federal government on the first $7,000 of each employee's annual earnings). Record the employer's payroll taxes in the general journal.

Reporting current liabilities
(Obj. 6)

P11-7A Following are pertinent facts about events during the current year at Innovech, Inc.:

a. On November 30, Innovech received rent of $6,600 in advance for a lease on a building. This rent will be earned evenly over three months.
b. December sales totaled $113,000, and Innovech collected an additional state sales tax of 7%. This amount will be sent to the State of Tennessee early in January.
c. Innovech owes $100,000 on a long-term note payable. At December 31, 6% interest since July 31 and $20,000 of this principal are payable within one year.
d. Sales of $430,000 were covered by Innovech's product warranty. At January 1, estimated warranty payable was $8,100. During the year, Innovech recorded warranty expense of $22,300 and paid warranty claims of $24,900.
e. On September 30, Innovech signed a six-month, 9% note payable to purchase equipment costing $30,000. The note requires payment of principal and interest at maturity.

Required

For each item, indicate the account and the related amount to be reported as a current liability on Innovech's December 31 balance sheet.

(Group B) PROBLEMS

Journalizing liability-related transactions
(Obj. 1, 2)

P11-1B The following transactions of **Bethlehem Steel** occurred during 20X2 and 20X3.

20X2
Feb. 3 Purchased equipment for $10,200, signing a six-month, 9% note payable.
 28 Recorded the week's sales of $51,000, one-third for cash, and two-thirds on credit. All sales amounts are subject to a 5% state sales tax.
Mar. 7 Sent the last week's sales tax to the state.
Apr. 30 Borrowed $100,000 on a four-year, 9% note payable that calls for annual installment payments of $25,000 principal plus interest.
Aug. 3 Paid the six-month, 9% note at maturity.
Sep. 14 Discounted a $6,000, 60-day, 7% note payable to the bank, receiving cash for the net amount after interest was deducted from the note's maturity value.
Nov. 13 Recorded interest on the 7% discounted note and paid off the note at maturity.
 30 Purchased inventory at a cost of $7,200, signing a three-month, 9% note payable for that amount.
Dec. 31 Accrued warranty expense, which is estimated at 3% of sales of $260,000.
 31 Accrued interest on all outstanding notes payable. Made a separate interest accrual entry for each note payable.

20X3
Feb. 28 Paid off the 9% inventory note, plus interest, at maturity.
Apr. 30 Paid the first installment and interest for one year on the long-term note payable.

Required

Record the transactions in the company's general journal. Explanations are not required.

P11-2B Briarwood Stables provides riding lessons for girls ages 8–15. Most students are beginners, and none of the girls owns her own horse. Sally Arnold, the owner of the stable, uses horses stabled at her farm and owned by the O'Malleys. Most of the horses are for sale, but the economy has been bad for several years and sales have been slow. The O'Malleys are happy that Arnold uses their horses in exchange for boarding them. Because of a recent financial setback, Arnold cannot afford liability insurance. She seeks your advice about her business's exposure to liabilities.

Identifying contingent liabilities
(Obj. 2)

Required

Write a memorandum to inform Arnold of specific contingent liabilities arising from the business. It will be necessary to define a contingent liability because she is a professional horse trainer, not a businessperson. Propose a way for Arnold to limit her risk due to these liabilities.

P11-3B The partial monthly records of Aramark Food Service show the following figures:

Computing and recording payroll amounts
(Obj. 3, 4)

Employee Earnings

(a)	Straight-time earnings	$?
(b)	Overtime pay	5,109
(c)	Total employee earnings	?

Deductions and Net Pay

(d)	Withheld income tax	$ 9,293
(e)	FICA tax	6,052
(f)	Charitable contributions	?
(g)	Medical insurance	1,373
(h)	Total deductions	18,880
(i)	Net pay	64,813

Accounts Debited

(j)	Salary Expense	$31,278
(k)	Wage Expense	?
(l)	Sales Commission Expense	27,931

Required

1. Determine the missing amounts on lines (a), (c), (f), and (k).
2. Prepare the general journal entry to record Aramark's payroll for the month. Credit Payrolls Payable for net pay. No explanation is required.

P11-4B Jan Summers is a commercial lender at Harbor State Bank in Boston. During 20X2, she worked for the bank all year at a $5,195 monthly salary. She also earned a year-end bonus equal to 10% of her annual salary.

Computing and recording payroll amounts
(Obj. 3, 4)

Summers' federal income tax withheld during 20X2 was $822 per month. Also, there was a one-time withholding of $2,487 on her bonus check. State income tax withheld came to $61 per month, and the city of Boston withheld income tax of $21 per month. In addition, Summers paid one-time withholdings of $64 (state) and $19 (city) on the bonus. The FICA tax withheld was 8% of the first $75,000 in annual earnings. Summers authorized the following payroll deductions: United Fund contribution of 1% of total earnings and life insurance of $17 per month.

Harbor State Bank incurred payroll tax expense on Summers for FICA tax of 8% of the first $75,000 in total annual earnings. The bank also paid state unemployment tax of 5.4% and federal unemployment tax of 0.8% on the first $7,000 in annual earnings. The bank provided Summers with the following benefits: health insurance at a cost of $48 per month, and pension benefits to be paid to Summers during her retirement. During 20X2, the bank's cost of Summers' pension program was $4,083.

Required

1. Compute Summers' gross pay, payroll deductions, and net pay during 20X2. Round all amounts to the nearest dollar.
2. Compute Harbor State Bank's total 20X2 payroll cost for Summers.
3. Prepare the bank's summary general journal entries to record its expense for the following:
   a. Summers' total earnings for the year, her payroll deductions, and her net pay. Debit Salary Expense and Executive Bonus Compensation as appropriate. Credit liability accounts for the payroll deductions and Cash for net pay.
   b. Employer payroll taxes for Summers. Credit liability accounts.
   c. Benefits provided to Summers. Credit a liability account.

Explanations are not required.

P11-5B The St. Charles Consulting general ledger at September 30, 20X2, the end of the company's fiscal year, includes the following account balances before adjusting entries. Parentheses indicate a debit balance.

Accounts Payable...	$ 88,240
Current Portion of Long-Term Debt	_____
Interest Payable	_____
Salary Payable..	_____
Employee Payroll Taxes Payable....................	_____
Employer Payroll Taxes Payable	_____
Estimated Vacation Pay Liability....................	2,105
Unearned Rent Revenue	3,900
Long-Term Debt..	100,000

The additional data needed to develop the adjusting entries at September 30 are as follows:

a. The long-term debt is payable in annual installments of $50,000, with the next installment due on January 31, 20X3. On that date, St. Charles Consulting will also pay one year's interest at 6.6%. Interest was last paid on January 31. (Make the adjusting entry to shift the current installment of the long-term debt to a current liability.)

b. Gross salaries for the last payroll of the fiscal year were $4,319. Of this amount, employee payroll taxes payable were $958, and salary payable was $3,361.

c. Employer payroll taxes payable were $890.

d. St. Charles estimates that vacation pay is 4% of gross salaries.

e. On August 1, the company collected six months' rent of $3,900 in advance.

f. At September 30, St. Charles is the defendant in a $500,000 lawsuit, which the company expects to win. However, the outcome is uncertain. Write the note to report this contingent liability in the financial statements.

Required

1. Open the listed accounts, inserting their unadjusted September 30 balances.
2. Journalize and post the September 30 adjusting entries to the accounts opened. Key adjusting entries by letter.
3. Prepare the liability section of St. Charles Consulting's balance sheet at September 30. Show total current liabilities.

P11-6B Assume that payroll records of a district sales office of Audi Motor Systems provided the following information for the weekly pay period ended December 26, 20X3:

Employee	Hours Worked	Weekly Earnings Rate	Federal Income Tax	Health Insurance	United Way Contributions	Earnings Through Previous Week
Clay Cooper	43	$ 400	$ 74	$ 9	$ 7	$17,060
Tim LeMann..............	46	480	90	5	5	22,365
Lena Marx.................	47	1,200	319	16	30	74,247
Karen York	40	240	32	4	2	3,413

Cooper and York work in the office, and LeMann and Marx work in sales. All employees are paid time and a half for hours worked in excess of 40 per week.

Required

For convenience, round all amounts to the nearest dollar. Show your computations. Explanations are not required for journal entries.

1. Enter the appropriate information in a payroll record similar to Exhibit 11-7. In addition to the deductions listed, the employer also takes out FICA tax: 8% of the first $75,000 of each employee's annual earnings.
2. Record the payroll information in the general journal.
3. Assume that the first payroll check is number 178, paid to Cooper. Record the check numbers in the payroll record. Also, prepare the general journal entry to record payment of net pay to the employees.
4. The employer's payroll taxes include FICA of 8% of the first $75,000 of each employee's annual earnings. The employer also pays unemployment taxes of 6.2% (5.4% for the state and 0.8% for the federal government) on the first $7,000 of each employee's annual earnings. Record the employer's payroll taxes in the general journal.

P11-7B Following are pertinent facts about events during the current year at Nevis Marine Company:

Reporting current liabilities (Obj. 6)

a. December sales totaled $404,000 and Nevis collected sales tax of 9%. The sales tax will be sent to the state of Washington early in January.

b. Nevis owes $75,000 on a long-term note payable. At December 31, 6% interest for the year plus $25,000 of this principal are payable within one year.

c. On August 31, Nevis signed a six-month, 6% note payable to purchase a machine costing $80,000. The note requires payment of principal and interest at maturity.

d. Sales of $909,000 were covered by Nevis' product warranty. At January 1, estimated warranty payable was $11,300. During the year, Nevis recorded warranty expense of $27,900 and paid warranty claims of $30,100.

e. On October 31, Nevis received rent of $2,400 in advance for a lease on a building. This rent will be earned evenly over four months.

Required

For each item, indicate the account and the related amount to be reported as a current liability on Nevis's December 31 balance sheet.

APPLY YOUR KNOWLEDGE

DECISION CASES

Case 1. SureBuilt Homes is a construction company in Fond du Lac, Wisconsin. The owner and manager, Art Waverly, oversees all company operations. He employs 15 work crews, each made up of six to ten members. Construction supervisors, who report directly to Waverly, lead the crews. Most supervisors are longtime employees, so Waverly trusts them. Waverly's office staff consists of an accountant and an office manager.

Identifying internal control weaknesses and their solution (Obj. 5)

Because employee turnover is high in the construction industry, supervisors hire and fire their own crew members. Supervisors notify the office of all personnel changes. Also, supervisors forward to the office the employee W-4 forms, which the crew members fill out. Each Thursday, the supervisors submit weekly time sheets for their crews, and the accountant prepares the payroll. At noon on Friday, the supervisors come to the office to get paychecks for distribution to the workers at 5 p.m.

SureBuilt's accountant prepares the payroll, including the payroll checks, which are written on a single payroll bank account. Waverly signs all payroll checks after matching the employee name to the time sheets submitted by the foremen. Often the workers wait several days to cash their paychecks. To verify that each construction worker is a bona fide employee, the accountant matches the employee's endorsement signature on the back of the canceled payroll check with the signature on that employee's W-4 form.

Required

1. Identify one *efficiency* weakness in SureBuilt's payroll accounting system. How can the business correct this weakness?
2. Identify one way that a supervisor can defraud SureBuilt Homes under the present system.
3. Discuss a control feature that SureBuilt Homes can use to *safeguard* against the frauds you identified in requirement 2.

Case 2. The Boeing Company, manufacturer of jet aircraft, is the defendant in numerous lawsuits claiming unfair trade practices. Boeing has strong incentives not to disclose these contingent liabilities. However, GAAP requires that companies report their contingent liabilities.

Unearned revenues, warranties, and contingent liabilities (Obj. 1, 2)

Required

1. Why would a company prefer *not* to disclose its contingent liabilities.
2. Describe how a bank could be harmed if a company seeking a loan did not disclose its contingent liabilities.
3. What ethical tightrope must companies walk when they report contingent liabilities?

ETHICAL ISSUE

LTV, manufacturer of aircraft and aircraft-related electronic devices, has at times borrowed heavily to finance operations. Often LTV is able to earn operating income much higher than its interest expense and is therefore quite profitable. However, when the business cycle turns down, LTV's debt burden has pushed the company to the brink of bankruptcy. Operating income is sometimes less than interest expense.

Required

Is it unethical for managers to saddle a company with a high level of debt? Or is it just risky? Who can get hurt when a company takes on too much debt? Discuss.

FINANCIAL STATEMENT CASE

Details about a company's current and contingent liabilities appear in a number of places in the annual report. Use **Target's** financial statements to answer the following questions.

Required

1. Give the breakdown of Target's current liabilities at January 29, 2000. Give the February 2000 entry to record the payment of accounts payable that Target owed at January 29, 2000.
2. How much was Target's long-term debt at January 29, 2000? Of this amount, how much was due within one year? How much was payable beyond one year in the future?
3. The balance sheet lists a $318 million liability for "Income Taxes Payable." Was income tax expense for the year, as reported on the income statement, equal to, less than, or greater than this amount? Why is one amount greater than the other?
4. Locate Target's report of its contingent liabilities. What event caused Target's contingent liabilities?

TEAM PROJECTS

Project 1. In recent years, the airline industry has dominated headlines. Consumers are shopping **Priceline.com** and other Internet sites for the lowest rates. The airlines have also lured customers with frequent-flyer programs, which award free flights to passengers who accumulate specified miles of travel. Unredeemed frequent-flyer mileage represents a liability that airlines must report on their balance sheets, usually as Air Traffic Liability.

Southwest Airlines, a profitable, no-frills carrier based in Dallas, has been rated near the top of the industry. Southwest controls costs by flying to smaller, less expensive airports; using only one model of aircraft; serving no meals; increasing staff efficiency; and having a shorter turnaround time on the ground between flights. The fact that most of the cities served by Southwest have predictable weather maximizes its on-time arrival record.

Required

With a partner or group, lead your class in a discussion of the following questions, or write a report as directed by your instructor.

1. Frequent-flyer programs have grown into significant obligations for airlines. Why should a liability be recorded for those programs? Discuss how you might calculate the amount of this liability. Can you think of other industries that offer similar incentives that create a liability?
2. One of Southwest Airlines' strategies for success is shortening stops at airport gates between flights. The company's chairman has stated, "What [you] produce is lower fares for the customers because you generate more revenue from the same fixed cost in that airplane." Look up *fixed cost* in the index of this book. What are some of the "fixed costs" of an airline? How can better utilization of assets improve a company's profits?

Project 2. Consider three different businesses:

a. A bank   **b.** A magazine publisher   **c.** A department store

Required

For each business, list all of its liabilities—both current and long-term. If necessary, study Chapter 15 on long-term liabilities. Then compare your lists to identify what liabilities the three businesses have in common. Also identify the liabilities that are unique to each type of business.

INTERNET EXERCISE

In 1995, **Amazon.com** opened its virtual doors and now serves over 17 million customers in over 150 different countries.

1. Go to **http://www.hoovers.com** and use the "Search" scroll bar to select *Company,* in the next box type <u>AMZN,</u> and then click on *Go.* For Amazon.com, Inc., click on *Capsule.* Scan the paragraph description of the company. What products does Amazon.com offer online?
2. Go to the top of the page and click on the *Financials* tab. Under "Free Financial Information" click on *Annual Financials.*

a. For the two most recent years, list the amounts reported for "Total Current Assets" and "Total Current Liabilities." Calculate the current ratio. Does Amazon.com have the ability to pay its current liabilities? Which year reports a stronger ratio?

b. For the two most recent years, list the amounts reported for "Total Liabilities" and "Total Assets." Calculate the debt ratio. How is Amazon.com financing its asset growth? Founder Jeff Bezos and family own about 34% of the company. Why do you think Mr. Bezos has chosen this method to finance asset growth?

c. Of approximately 100 Internet stocks, most showed staggering increases in revenue but only five showed net income in 1999. Is Amazon.com a typical Internet stock? Why or why not?

12

Partnerships

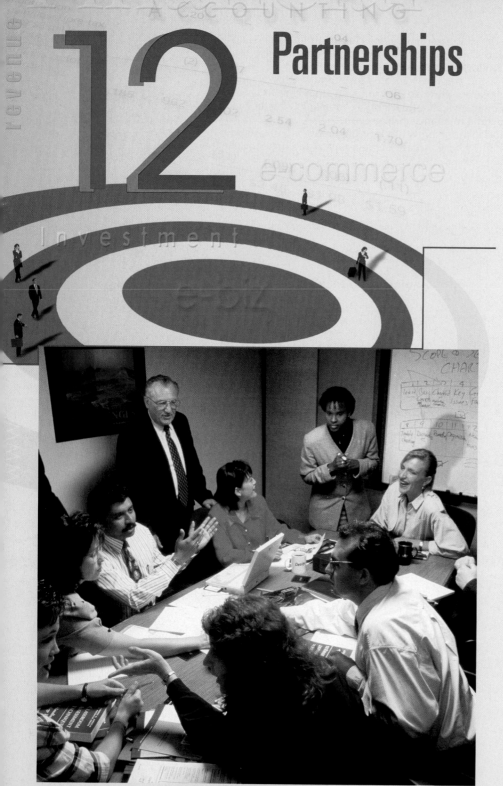

LEARNING OBJECTIVES

After studying this chapter, you should be able to

1. Identify the characteristics of a partnership

2. Account for the partners' investments in a partnership

3. Allocate profits and losses to the partners

4. Account for the admission of a partner to the business

5. Account for a partner's withdrawal from the firm

6. Account for the liquidation of a partnership

7. Prepare partnership financial statements

www.prenhall.com/horngren

Readiness Assessment

Once upon a time **Arthur Andersen LLP** was a stodgy accounting firm. No longer. Arthur Andersen—or "Arthur" as insiders call it—has shed its old image. For starters, the firm now earns much of its income from consulting, not accounting.

The firm is a profit-making machine, and it doesn't have to share its income with millions of stockholders the way corporations do. Arthur Andersen LLP is a partnership. That means the people who own the firm, around 2,000 of them—are all partners. Each partner's profit from the firm averages well over a half million dollars a year.

The most interesting thing about Arthur Andersen is the divorce the partners worked out. The consulting partners formed **Andersen Consulting,** a different firm. But they wanted to continue using the Andersen name, and that's where the rub came. The partners of Arthur Andersen, the original firm, demanded billions from Andersen Consulting because the consulting firm was launched from contacts with the firm's audit clients. As a compromise, the consulting firm took the name of !**Accenture.**

Is all this confusing? You bet it is. That's why the Andersen divorce was so difficult. It is a classic case for showing the fragile nature of a partnership. So, if you ever consider going into business with anyone besides your mother, choose your partners carefully. And don't forget to get the partnership agreement in writing.

The partnership form of business introduces some complexities that a proprietorship avoids. How much cash should a new partner contribute to the business? How should the partners divide profits and losses? This seems to be the most difficult issue for the partners. How should a partner who leaves the firm be compensated for his or her share of the business? This issue seems paramount to the partners of **Arthur Andersen LLP.**

A **partnership** is an association of two or more persons who co-own a business for profit. This definition comes from the Uniform Partnership Act, which nearly every state in the United States has adopted to regulate partnership practice.

Forming a partnership is easy. It requires no permission from the government and no legal procedures. When two persons decide to go into business together, a partnership is automatically formed.

A partnership brings together the assets and the experience of the partners. Business opportunities closed to an individual may open up to a partnership. Perhaps none of the Arthur Andersen partners has enough money individually to operate a large firm. But they are able to afford it together in a partnership. They pool their talents and know-how. Their partnership thus offers clients a fuller range of services than any one person can offer alone.

Partnerships come in all sizes. Many partnerships have fewer than ten partners. Some medical and law firms have 20 or more partners. The largest accounting/consulting firms have over 2,000 partners. Exhibit 12-1 lists the eight largest accounting/consulting firms in the United States, the number of partners in each firm, and their revenues in 1999.

CHARACTERISTICS OF A PARTNERSHIP

Starting a partnership is voluntary. A person cannot be forced to join a partnership, and partners cannot be forced to accept another person as a partner. Although the partnership agreement may be oral, a written agreement between the partners reduces the chance of a misunderstanding. The following characteristics distinguish partnerships from sole proprietorships and corporations.

The Written Agreement

A business partnership is like a marriage. To be successful, the partners must cooperate. But business partners do not vow to remain together for life. To make certain that each partner fully understands how the partnership operates and to lower the chances that any partner might misunderstand how the business is run, partners may draw up a **partnership agreement,** also called the **articles of**

PARTNERSHIP. An association of two or more persons who co-own a business for profit.

Objective 1
Identify the characteristics of a partnership

PARTNERSHIP AGREEMENT. The contract between partners that specifies such items as the name, location, and nature of the business; the name, capital investment, and duties of each partner; and the method of sharing profits and losses among the partners. Also called **articles of partnership.**

Revenue Rank (1999)	Firm Location	Partners	Revenue Per Partner (in millions)
1	Arthur Andersen, New York	2,117	$3.7
2	PricewaterhouseCoopers, New York	2,938	$2.3
3	Ernst & Young, New York	2,546	$2.5
4	Deloitte & Touche, Wilton, Connecticut	1,913	$2.8
5	KPMG, New York	1,800	$2.6
6	RSM McGladrey, Bloomington, Minnesota	369	$1.1
7	Grant Thornton, Chicago	274	$1.5
8	BDO Seidman, Chicago	335	$0.9

Source: Adapted from *Accounting Today* (March 13–April 2, 2000), Special Supplement, and the *Wall Street Journal,* August 8, 2000, page A3.

partnership. This agreement is a contract between the partners, so transactions involving the agreement are governed by contract law. The articles of partnership should make the following points clear:

1. Name, location, and nature of the business
2. Name, capital investment, and duties of each partner
3. Method of sharing profits and losses among the partners
4. Withdrawals of assets allowed to the partners
5. Procedures for settling disputes between the partners
6. Procedures for admitting new partners
7. Procedures for settling up with a partner who withdraws from the business
8. Procedures for liquidating the partnership—selling the assets, paying the liabilities, and disbursing any remaining cash to the partners

Limited Life

DISSOLUTION. Ending of a partnership.

A partnership has a life limited by the length of time that all partners continue to own the business. If one or more **Arthur Andersen** partners withdraws from the business, the old partnership will cease to exist. A new partnership may emerge to continue the same business, but the old partnership will have been dissolved. **Dissolution** is the ending of a partnership. The addition of a new partner dissolves the old partnership and creates a new partnership. Large partnerships such as Arthur Andersen retain the firm name even after partners resign from the firm.

Mutual Agency

MUTUAL AGENCY. Every partner can bind the business to a contract within the scope of the partnership's regular business operations.

Mutual agency in a partnership means that every partner can bind the business to a contract within the scope of the partnership's regular business operations. If Jana Jones, a partner in the firm of Willis and Jones, enters into a contract with a business to provide accounting service, then the firm of Willis & Jones—not just Jones—is bound to provide that service. If Jones signs a contract to purchase lawn services for her home, however, the partnership will not be bound to pay because the lawn service is a personal matter for Jones. It is not a regular business operation of the partnership.

Unlimited Liability

UNLIMITED PERSONAL LIABILITY. When a partnership (or a proprietorship) cannot pay its debts with business assets, the partners (or the proprietor) must use personal assets to meet the debt.

Each partner has an **unlimited personal liability** for the debts of the partnership. When a partnership cannot pay its debts with business assets, the partners must use their personal assets to meet the debt. Proprietors also have unlimited personal liability for the debts of their business.

Suppose the Willis & Jones firm has had an unsuccessful year and the partnership's liabilities exceed its assets by $20,000. Willis and Jones must pay this amount with their personal assets. Because each partner has unlimited liability, if a partner is unable to pay his or her part of the debt, the other partner (or partners) must pay. If Jones can pay only $5,000 of the liability, Willis must pay $15,000.

Unlimited liability and mutual agency are closely related. A dishonest partner or a partner with poor judgment may commit the partnership to a contract under which the business loses money. In turn, creditors may force *all* the partners to pay the debt from personal assets.

Partners can avoid unlimited personal liability for partnership obligations by forming a *limited partnership*. **Arthur Andersen LLP** is a limited liability partnership, as are the other large accounting and consulting firms in Exhibit 12-1. In this form of business organization, the partners have limited liability similar to the limited liability enjoyed by the stockholders of a corporation.

Co-Ownership of Property

Any asset—cash, inventory, machinery, and so on—that a partner invests in the partnership becomes the joint property of all the partners. Also, each partner has a claim to his or her share of the business's profits.

No Partnership Income Taxes

A partnership pays no income tax on its business income. Instead, the net income of the partnership is divided and becomes the taxable income of the partners. Suppose Willis & Jones, Certified Public Accountants, earned net income of $200,000, shared equally by the partners. The firm would pay no income tax *as a business entity.* Willis and Jones, however, would each pay income tax as individuals on their $100,000 shares of partnership income.

Partners' Owner's Equity Accounts

⊙ DAILY EXERCISE 12-1

Accounting for a partnership is much like accounting for a proprietorship. We record buying and selling goods and services and collecting and paying cash for a partnership just as we do for a proprietorship. But because a partnership has more than one owner, the partnership must have more than one owner's equity account.

Every partner in the business—whether the firm has 2 or 2,000 partners—has an individual owner's equity account. Often these accounts carry the name of the particular partner and the word *capital*. For example, the owner's equity account for Blake Willis would read "Willis, Capital." Similarly, each partner has a withdrawal account. If the number of partners is large, the general ledger may contain the single account Partners' Capital, or Owners' Equity. A subsidiary ledger can be used for individual partner accounts.

⊙ DAILY EXERCISE 12-2

Exhibit 12-2 lists the advantages and disadvantages of partnerships (compared with proprietorships and corporations). A partnership is really a "multiple proprietorship." Most features of a proprietorship also apply to a partnership—in particular, limited life and unlimited liability.

Partnership Advantages	Partnership Disadvantages
Versus Proprietorships:	1. Partnership agreement may be difficult to formulate. Each time a new partner is admitted or a partner withdraws, the business needs a new partnership agreement.
1. Can raise more capital.	
2. Brings together the expertise of more than one person.	
3. 1 + 1 > 2 in a good partnership. If the partners work well together, they can add more value than by working alone.	2. Relationships among partners may be fragile.
Versus Corporations:	3. Mutual agency and unlimited personal liability create personal obligations for each partner.
4. Less expensive to organize than a corporation, which requires a charter from the state.	
5. No taxation of business income, which is taxed to the partners as individuals.	

EXHIBIT 12-2
Advantages and Disadvantages of Partnerships

TYPES OF PARTNERSHIPS

There are two basic types of partnerships: general and limited.

General Partnerships

GENERAL PARTNERSHIP. A form of partnership in which each partner is an owner of the business, with all the privileges and risks of ownership.

A **general partnership** is the basic form of partnership organization. Each partner is an owner of the business with all the privileges and risks of ownership. The general partners share the profits, losses, and the risks of the business. The partnership *reports* its income to governmental tax authorities (the Internal Revenue Service in the United States), but the partnership itself pays *no* income tax. The profits and losses of the partnership pass through the business to the partners, who then pay personal income tax on their income.

Limited Partnerships

LIMITED PARTNERSHIP. A partnership with at least two classes of partners: a general partner and limited partners.

A **limited partnership** has at least two classes of partners. There must be at least one *general partner,* who takes primary responsibility for the management of the business. The general partner also takes the bulk of the risk of failure in the event the partnership goes bankrupt (liabilities exceed assets). In real-estate limited partnerships, the general partner often invests little cash in the business. Instead, the general partner's contribution is his or her skill in managing the organization. Usually, the general partner is the last owner to receive a share of partnership profits and losses. But the general partner may earn all excess profits after satisfying the limited partners' demands for income.

The *limited partners* are so named because their personal obligation for the partnership's liabilities is limited to the amount they have invested in the business. Usually, the limited partners have invested the bulk of the partnership's assets and capital. They therefore usually have first claim to partnership profits and losses, but only up to a specified limit. In exchange for their limited liability, their potential for profits usually has a limit as well.

LIMITED LIABILITY PARTNERSHIP. A form of partnership in which each partner's personal liability for the business's debts is limited to a certain amount. Also called **LLPs.**

Most of the large accounting firms are organized as **limited liability partnerships,** or **LLPs,** which means that each partner's personal liability for the business's debts is limited to a certain amount. The LLP must carry a large insurance policy to protect the public in case the partnership is found guilty of malpractice. Medical, legal, and other firms of professionals can also be organized as LLPs.

S Corporations

S CORPORATION. A corporation taxed in the same way as a partnership.

An **S Corporation** is a corporation that is taxed in the same way that a partnership is taxed. Therefore, S corporations are often discussed in conjunction with partnerships. This form of business organization derives its name from Subchapter S of the U.S. Internal Revenue Code.

An S corporation offers its owners the benefits of a corporation—no personal liability for business debts—and of a partnership—no double taxation. An ordinary (Subchapter C) corporation is subject to double taxation. First, the corporation pays corporate income tax on its income. Then, when the corporation pays dividends to the stockholders, they pay personal income tax on their dividend income. An S corporation pays no corporate income tax. Instead, the corporation's income flows through directly to the stockholders (the owners), who pay personal income tax on their share of the S corporation's income. The one-time taxation of an S corporation's income is an important advantage over an ordinary corporation. From a tax standpoint, an S corporation operates like a partnership.

To qualify as an S corporation, a company can have no more than 75 stockholders, all of whom must be citizens or residents of the United States. Accounting for an S corporation resembles that of accounting for a partnership because the allocation of corporate income follows the same procedure used by partnerships.

The popularity of S corporations rises and falls with the passage of new legislation. When individual income tax rates exceed corporate tax rates, S corporations increase in number. When corporate tax rates fall, there is less incentive to form an S corporation. Also, new entities called limited-liability companies have formed. **Arthur Andersen Limited Liability Partnership (LLP)** is an example. An LLP offers its owners the same limited liability as a corporation, and an LLP avoids some of the restrictions that S corporations face. Currently, LLPs are more popular than S corporations.

THE PARTNERSHIP START-UP

Let's examine the start-up of a partnership. We will see how to account for the owner's equity accounts of the partners. We will also learn how they appear on the balance sheet.

Objective 2

Account for the partners' investments in a partnership

Partners in a new partnership may invest assets and liabilities in the business. These contributions are entered in the books in the same way that a proprietor's

The Limited but Lively Life of a Dot.Com Partnership

Founding partners say that starting up a business is *the life*. Sleep is scant and cash is low, but hopes and energy run high. Some Internet businesses have started with nothing more than enthusiastic partners and a winning idea.

- The story of **Yahoo!** founders Jerry Yang and David Filo is now legend. In 1994, the two Stanford graduate students came up with a way to categorize Web sites. Their guide, named Yahoo!, was the first place for Web browsers to find sites easily. Now Yahoo! is a global Internet communications, commerce, and media company with over 2,000 employees. Yahoo! has a global Web network of 21 properties and offices in Europe, Asia, Latin America, Canada, and the United States.
- Founded in 1999 by 19-year-old Shawn Fanning and 20-year-old Sean Parker, **Napster** created software that lets people trade music files on the Internet for free. In almost no time, the company was turning the music industry upside down. Twenty million users downloaded the free software in just seven months, and *Fortune* magazine commended the company for pioneering one of the hottest business concepts of our time: peer-to-peer information sharing. Napster is so successful at stealing copyrighted music that the music industry threatens to put the organization out of business.
- In 1994, Todd Krizelman and Stephan Paternot, both 25 and at Cornell, came up with an on-line community where participants go to find news, discussion forums, and products—**TheGlobe.com.** Krizelman and Paternot recruited employees in the student lounge, paid them with Domino pizza, drained their own bank accounts, and lived off credit cards. Four years later, TheGlobe.com brought in $27 million in an initial public offering, and the former dorm buddies are now joint CEOs.

Sources: Based on [Yahoo!] Information from http://join.yahoo.com/chief.html and http://join.yahoo.com/overview.html. [Napster] Chuck Philips, "Company town; THE BIZ Q & A; Humming a hopeful tune at napster," *The Los Angeles Times*, July 19, 2000, p. 1. Amy Kover, "Napster: The hot idea of the year," *Fortune*, June 26, 2000, pp. 128–136. [TheGlobe.com] Stephanie Armour, "Tech grads loving life: Pizza, jeans, happy hour," June 21, 1999, *USA Today*, p. 01B assets and liabilities are recorded. Subtraction of each partner's liabilities from his or her assets yields the amount to be credited to that partner's capital account. Often, the partners hire an independent firm to appraise their assets and liabilities at current market value at the time a partnership is formed. This outside evaluation assures an objective accounting for what each partner brings into the business.

Assume that Dave Benz and Joan Hanna form a partnership to manufacture and sell computer software. The partners agree on the following values based on an independent appraisal:

Benz's Contributions

- Cash, $10,000; inventory, $70,000; and accounts payable, $85,000 (The appraiser believes that the current market values for these items equal Benz's values.)
- Accounts receivable, $30,000, less allowance for doubtful accounts of $5,000
- Computer equipment—cost, $800,000; accumulated depreciation, $200,000; current market value, $450,000

Hanna's Contributions

- Cash, $5,000
- Computer software: cost, $18,000; market value, $100,000

The partnership records receipt of the partners' initial investments at the current market values of the assets and liabilities because, in effect, the partnership is buying the assets and assuming the liabilities at their current market values. The partnership entries are as follows:

Benz's Investment

June 1	Cash..		10,000	
	Accounts Receivable..		30,000	
	Inventory..		70,000	
	Computer Equipment...		450,000	
	Allowance for Doubtful Accounts.........................			5,000
	Accounts Payable			85,000
	Benz, Capital ($560,000 − $90,000)			470,000
	To record Benz's investment in the partnership.			

Hanna's Investment

June 1	Cash..			5,000
	Computer Software		100,000	
	Hanna, Capital			105,000
	To record Hanna's investment in the partnership.			

 DAILY EXERCISE 12-3

 DAILY EXERCISE 12-4

The initial partnership balance sheet reports the amounts shown in Exhibit 12-3. Note that the asset and liability sections on the balance sheet are the same for a proprietorship and a partnership.

SHARING PROFITS AND LOSSES, AND DRAWINGS

Objective 3
Allocate profits and losses to the partners

Allocating profits and losses among partners is one of the most challenging aspects of managing a partnership. If the partners have not drawn up an agreement or if the agreement does not state how the partners will divide profits and losses, then by law, the partners must share profits and losses equally. If the agreement specifies a method for sharing profits but not losses, then losses are shared in the same proportion as profits. For example, a partner who was allocated 75% of the profits would likewise absorb 75% of any losses. Partners may agree to any profit-and-loss-sharing method they desire.

EXHIBIT 12-3
Partnership Balance Sheet

BENZ AND HANNA
Balance Sheet
June 1, 20X5

Assets			Liabilities	
Cash.............................		$ 15,000	Accounts payable	$ 85,000
Accounts receivable......	$30,000			
Less Allowance				
for doubtful				
accounts	(5,000)	25,000	**Capital**	
Inventory......................		70,000	Benz, capital..............	470,000
Computer equipment...		450,000	Hanna, capital	105,000
Computer software.......		100,000	Total liabilities	
Total assets..................		$660,000	and capital	$660,000

In some cases, an equal division is not fair. One partner may perform more work for the business than the other partner, or one partner may make a larger capital contribution. In the preceding example, Joan Hanna might agree to work longer hours for the partnership than Dave Benz to earn a greater share of profits. Benz could argue that he should share in more of the profits because he contributed more net assets ($470,000) than Hanna did ($105,000). Hanna might contend that her computer software program is the partnership's most important asset and that her share of the profits should be greater than Benz's share. Agreeing on a fair sharing of profits and losses in a partnership may be difficult.

Sharing Based on a Stated Fraction

Partners may state a particular fraction of the total profits and losses each individual partner will share. Suppose the partnership agreement of Lou Cagle and Justin Dean allocates two-thirds of the business profits and losses to Cagle and one-third to Dean. If net income for the year is $90,000 and all revenue and expense accounts have been closed, the Income Summary account has a credit balance of $90,000:

INCOME SUMMARY	
	Bal. 90,000

● DAILY EXERCISE 12-5

The entry to close this account and allocate the profit to the partners' capital accounts is

Dec. 31	Income Summary	90,000	
	Cagle, Capital ($90,000 × 2/3)...........		60,000
	Dean, Capital ($90,000 × 1/3)		30,000
	To allocate net income to partners.		

Consider the effect of this entry. Does Cagle get cash of $60,000 and Dean cash of $30,000? No. The increase in the partners' capital accounts cannot be linked to any particular asset, including cash. Instead, the entry indicates that Cagle's ownership in *all* the assets of the business increased by $60,000 and Dean's by $30,000.

If the year's operations resulted in a net loss of $66,000, the Income Summary account would have a debit balance of $66,000. In that case, the closing entry to allocate the loss to the partners' capital accounts would be

Dec. 31	Cagle, Capital ($66,000 × 2/3).....................	44,000	
	Dean, Capital ($66,000 × 1/3)	22,000	
	Income Summary		66,000
	To allocate net loss to partners.		

● DAILY EXERCISE 12-6

Just as a profit of $90,000 did not mean that the partners received cash of $60,000 and $30,000, so the loss of $66,000 does not mean that the partners must contribute cash of $44,000 and $22,000. A profit or loss will increase or decrease each partner's capital account, but cash may not change hands.

Sharing Based on Capital Contributions

Profits and losses are often allocated in proportion to capital contributions in the business. Suppose that Jenny Aycock, Erika Barber, and Sue Cordoba are partners in ABC Company. Their capital accounts have the following balances at the end of the year, before the closing entries:

Aycock, Capital.......................	$ 40,000
Barber, Capital.......................	60,000
Cordoba, Capital....................	50,000
Total capital balances..............	$150,000

Assume that the partnership earned a profit of $120,000 for the year. To allocate this amount on the basis of capital contributions, compute each partner's percentage share of the partnership's total capital balance by dividing each partner's contribution by the total capital amount. These figures, multiplied by the $120,000 profit amount, yield each partner's share of the year's profits:

Aycock:	($40,000/$150,000) × $120,000 =	$ 32,000
Barber:	($60,000/$150,000) × $120,000 =	48,000
Cordoba:	($50,000/$150,000) × $120,000 =	40,000
	Net income allocated to partners =	$120,000

The closing entry to allocate the profit to the partners' capital accounts is

Dec. 31	Income Summary	120,000	
	Aycock, Capital....................................		32,000
	Barber, Capital.....................................		48,000
	Cordoba, Capital..................................		40,000
	To allocate net income to partners.		

After this closing entry, the partners' capital balances are

Aycock, Capital ($40,000 + $32,000).....................................	$ 72,000
Barber, Capital ($60,000 + $48,000).....................................	108,000
Cordoba, Capital ($50,000 + $40,000)..................................	90,000
Total capital balances after allocation of net income	$270,000

Sharing Based on Capital Contributions and on Service

One partner, regardless of capital contribution, may put more work into the business than the other partners do. Even among partners who log equal service time, one person's superior experience and knowledge may command a greater share of income. To reward the harder-working or more valuable person, the profit-and-loss-sharing method may be based on a combination of contributed capital *and* service to the business. The Chicago-based law firm **Baker & McKenzie,** for example, which has nearly 500 partners, takes seniority into account in determining partner compensation.

Assume that Debbie Randolph and Nancy Scott formed a partnership in which Randolph invested $60,000 and Scott invested $40,000, a total of $100,000. Scott devotes more time to the partnership and earns the larger salary. Accordingly, the two partners have agreed to share profits as follows:

1. The first $50,000 of partnership profits is to be allocated on the basis of partners' capital contributions to the business.
2. The next $60,000 of profits is to be allocated on the basis of service, with Randolph receiving $24,000 and Scott receiving $36,000.
3. Any remaining amount is to be allocated equally.

If net income for the first year is $125,000, the partners' shares of this profit are computed as follows:

	Randolph	Scott	Total
Total net income			$125,000
Sharing of first $50,000 of net income, based on capital contributions:			
Randolph ($60,000/$100,000 × $50,000) ..	$30,000		
Scott ($40,000/$100,000 × $50,000)		$20,000	
Total...			50,000
Net income remaining for allocation...............			75,000
Sharing of next $60,000, based on service:			
Randolph	24,000		
Scott		36,000	
Total...			60,000
Net income remaining for allocation...............			15,000
Remainder shared equally:			
Randolph ($15,000 × 1/2)	7,500		
Scott ($15,000 × 1/2)		7,500	
Total...			15,000
Net income remaining for allocation...............			$ 0
Net income allocated to the partners................	$61,500	$63,500	$125,000

On the basis of this allocation, the closing entry is

Dec. 31	Income Summary..	125,000	
	Randolph, Capital...............................		61,500
	Scott, Capital		63,500
	To allocate net income to partners.		

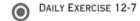
DAILY EXERCISE 12-7

Sharing Based on Salaries and on Interest

Partners may be rewarded for service and capital contributions in other ways. In one sharing plan, the partners are allocated salaries plus interest on their capital balances. Assume that Randy Lewis and Gerald Clark form an oil-exploration partnership. At the beginning of the year, their capital balances are $80,000 and $100,000, respectively. The partnership agreement allocates annual salaries of $43,000 to Lewis and $35,000 to Clark. After salaries are allocated, each partner earns 8% interest on his beginning capital balance. Any remaining net income is divided equally. Partnership profit of $96,000 will be allocated as follows:

	Lewis	Clark	Total
Total net income			$96,000
First, salaries:			
Lewis	$43,000		
Clark...		$35,000	
Total			78,000
Net income remaining for allocation			18,000
Second, interest on beginning capital balances:			
Lewis ($80,000 × 0.08).......................................	6,400		
Clark ($100,000 × 0.08)		8,000	
Total			14,400
Net income remaining for allocation			3,600
Third, remainder shared equally:			
Lewis ($3,600 × 1/2)	1,800		
Cleark ($3,600 × 1/2)		1,800	
Total			3,600
Net income remaining for allocation			$ 0
Net income allocated to the partners....................	$51,200	$44,800	$96,000

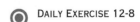
DAILY EXERCISE 12-8

In the preceding illustration, net income exceeded the sum of salary and interest. If the partnership profit is less than the allocated sum of salary and interest, a negative remainder will occur at some stage in the allocation process. Even so, the partners use the same method for allocation purposes. For example, assume that Lewis and Clark Partnership earned only $82,000:

	Lewis	Clark	Total
Total net income			$82,000
First, salaries:			
Lewis	$43,000		
Clark...		$35,000	
Total			78,000
Net income remaining for allocation			4,000
Second, interest on beginning capital balances:			
Lewis ($80,000 × 0.08).....................................	6,400		
Clark ($100,000 × 0.08)		8,000	
Total			14,400
Net income remaining for allocation			10,400
Third, remainder shared equally:			
Lewis ($10,400 × 1/2)	(5,200)		
Clark ($10,400 × 1/2).......................................		(5,200)	
Total			(10,400)
Net income remaining for allocation			$ 0
Net income allocated to the partners..................	$44,200	$37,800	$82,000

A net loss would be allocated to Lewis and Clark in the same manner outlined for net income. The sharing procedure would begin with the net loss and then allocate salary, interest, and any other specified amounts to the partners.

THINK IT OVER

Are these salaries and interest amounts business expenses in the usual sense? Explain your answer.

Answer: No, partners do not work for their own business to earn a salary, as an employee does. They do not loan money to their own business to earn interest. Their goal is for the partnership to earn a profit. Therefore, salaries and interest in partnership agreements are simply ways of expressing the allocation of profits and losses to the partners. For example, the salary component of partner income rewards service to the partnership. The interest component rewards a partner's investment of cash or other assets in the business. But the partners' salary and interest amounts are *not* salary expense and interest expense in the partnership's accounting or tax records.

Partner Drawings of Cash and Other Assets

Like anyone else, partners need cash for personal living expenses. Partnership agreements usually allow partners to withdraw cash or other assets from the business. Drawings from a partnership are recorded exactly as for a proprietorship. Assume that both Randy Lewis and Gerald Clark are allowed a monthly withdrawal of $3,500. The partnership records the March withdrawals with this entry:

Mar. 31	Lewis, Drawing	3,500	
	Clark, Drawing...	3,500	
	Cash...		7,000
	Monthly partner withdrawals of cash.		

During the year, each partner's drawing account accumulates 12 such amounts, a total of $42,000 ($3,500 × 12) per partner. At the end of the period, the general ledger shows the following account balances immediately after net income has been closed to the partners' capital accounts. Assume these beginning balances for Lewis and Clark at the start of the year and that $82,000 of profit has been allocated on the basis of the preceding illustration.

LEWIS, CAPITAL			CLARK, CAPITAL		
	Jan. 1 Bal.	80,000		Jan. 1 Bal.	100,000
	Dec. 31 Net. inc.	44,200		Dec. 31 Net. inc.	37,800

LEWIS, DRAWING			CLARK, DRAWING		
Dec. 31 Bal.	42,000		Dec. 31 Bal.	42,000	

The drawing accounts must be closed at the end of the period, exactly as for a proprietorship: The closing entry credits each partner's drawing account and debits each capital account. ➤➤

◄ We covered this closing entry in Chapter 4, page 137.

ADMISSION OF A PARTNER

The addition of a new member or the withdrawal of an existing member dissolves the partnership. We turn now to a discussion of how partnerships dissolve—and how new partnerships arise.

Objective 4
Account for the admission of a new partner to the business

Often, a new partnership is formed to carry on the former partnership's business. In fact, the new partnership may retain the dissolved partnership's name. **PricewaterhouseCoopers LLP,** for example, is an accounting/consulting firm that retires and hires partners during the year. Thus, the former partnership dissolves and a new partnership begins many times. But the business retains its name and continues operations. Other partnerships may dissolve and then re-form under a new name. Let's look at the ways a new member may gain admission into an existing partnership.

Admission by Purchasing a Partner's Interest

A person may become a member of a partnership by gaining the approval of the other partner (or partners) for entrance into the firm *and* by purchasing a present partner's interest in the business. Let's assume that Roberta Fisher and Benitez Garcia have a partnership that carries these figures:

Cash	$ 40,000	Total liabilities	$120,000	
Other assets	360,000	Fisher, capital	110,000	
		Garcia, capital	170,000	
Total assets	$400,000	Total liabilities and capital	$400,000	

Business is going so well that Fisher receives an offer from Barry Dynak, an outside party, to buy her $110,000 interest in the business for $150,000. Fisher agrees to sell out to Dynak, and Garcia approves Dynak as a new partner. The firm records the transfer of capital interest in the business with this entry:

Apr. 16	Fisher, Capital	110,000	
	Dynak, Capital		110,000
	To transfer Fisher's equity in the business to Dynak.		

The debit side of the entry closes Fisher's capital account because she is no longer a partner in the firm. The credit side opens Dynak's capital account because Fisher's equity has been transferred to Dynak. The entry amount is Fisher's capital balance ($110,000) and not the $150,000 Dynak paid Fisher to buy into the business. The full $150,000 goes to Fisher, including the $40,000 difference between her capital balance and the price received from Dynak. In this example, the partnership receives no cash because the transaction was between Dynak and Fisher, not between Dynak and the partnership. Suppose Dynak pays Fisher less than Fisher's capital balance. The entry on the partnership books is not affected. Fisher's equity is transferred to Dynak at book value ($110,000).

The old partnership has dissolved. Garcia and Dynak draw up a new partnership agreement with a new profit-and-loss-sharing ratio and continue business operations. If Garcia does not accept Dynak as a partner, Dynak gets no voice in management of the firm. However, under the Uniform Partnership Act, the purchaser shares in the profits and losses of the firm and in its assets at liquidation.

Admission by Investing in the Partnership

A person may be admitted as a partner by investing directly in the partnership rather than by purchasing an existing partner's interest. The new partner contributes assets—for example, cash, inventory, or equipment—to the business. Assume that the partnership of Robin Ingel and Michael Jay has the following assets, liabilities, and capital:

Cash	$ 20,000	Total liabilities	$ 60,000
Other assets	200,000	Ingel, capital	70,000
		Jay, capital	90,000
Total assets	$220,000	Total liabilities and capital	$220,000

Laura Kahn offers to invest equipment and land (Other Assets) with a market value of $80,000 to persuade the existing partners to take her into the business. Ingel and Jay agree to dissolve the existing partnership and to start up a new business, giving Kahn one-third interest—[$80,000/($70,000 + $90,000 + $80,000) = 1/3]—in exchange for the contributed assets. Notice that Kahn is buying into the partnership at book value because her one-third investment ($80,000) equals one-third of the new partnership's total capital ($240,000). The entry to record Kahn's investment is

July 18	Other Assets	80,000	
	Kahn, Capital		80,000
	To admit L. Kahn as a partner with a one-third interest in the business.		

After this entry, the partnership books show

Cash	$ 20,000	Total liabilities	$ 60,000
Other assets		Ingel, capital	70,000
($200,000 + $80,000)	280,000	Jay, capital	90,000
		Kahn, capital	80,000
Total assets	$300,000	Total liabilities and capital	$300,000

DAILY EXERCISE 12-9

DAILY EXERCISE 12-10

Kahn's one-third interest in the partnership does not necessarily entitle her to one-third of the profits. The sharing of profits and losses is a separate element in the partnership agreement.

ADMISSION BY INVESTING IN THE PARTNERSHIP—BONUS TO THE OLD PARTNERS The more successful a partnership, the higher the payment the partners may demand from a person entering the business. Partners in a business that is doing quite well might require an incoming person to pay them a bonus. The bonus increases the current partners' capital accounts.

Suppose that Hiro Nagasawa and Ralph Osburn's partnership has earned above-average profits for ten years. The two partners share profits and losses equally. The partnership balance sheet carries these figures:

Cash	$ 40,000	Total liabilities	$100,000
Other assets	210,000	Nagasawa, capital	70,000
		Osburn, capital	80,000
Total assets	$250,000	Total liabilities and capital	$250,000

The partners agree to admit Glen Parker to a one-fourth interest with his cash investment of $90,000. Parker's capital balance on the partnership books is only $60,000, computed as follows:

Partnership capital before Parker is admitted ($70,000 + $80,000)	$150,000
Parker's investment in the partnership..	90,000
Partnership capital after Parker is admitted..	$240,000
Parker's capital in the partnership ($240,000 × 1/4)	$ 60,000
Bonus to the old partners ($90,000 − $60,000)	$ 30,000

◉ DAILY EXERCISE 12-11

In effect, Parker had to buy into the partnership at a price ($90,000) above the book value of his one-fourth interest ($60,000). Parker's investment of an extra $30,000 creates a *bonus* for the existing partners. The entry on the partnership books to record Parker's investment is

Mar. 1	Cash	90,000	
	Parker, Capital		60,000
	Nagasawa, Capital ($30,000 × 1/2)............................		15,000
	Osburn, Capital ($30,000 × 1/2)................................		15,000
	To admit G. Parker as a partner with a one-fourth interest in the business.		

Parker's capital account is credited for his one-fourth interest in the partnership. The *bonus* is allocated to the partners on the basis of their profit-and-loss ratio.

The new partnership's balance sheet reports these amounts:

Cash ($40,000 + $90,000)...	$130,000	Total liabilities........................	$100,000
Other assets..........................	210,000	Nagasawa, capital	
		($70,000 + $15,000)	85,000
		Osburn, capital	
		($80,000 + $15,000)	95,000
		Parker, capital......................	60,000
Total assets	$340,000	Total liabilities and capital	$340,000

◉ DAILY EXERCISE 12-12

Mia and Susan are partners with capital balances of $25,000 and $75,000, respectively. They share profits and losses in a 30:70 ratio. Mia and Susan admit Tab to a 10% interest in a new partnership when Tab invests $20,000 in the business.

1. Journalize the partnership's receipt of cash from Tab.
2. What is each partner's capital in the new partnership?

Answers

1.	Cash	20,000	
	Tab, Capital		12,000
	Mia, Capital ($8,000 × 0.30)		2,400
	Susan, Capital ($8,000 × 0.70).................................		5,600
	To admit Tab with a 10% interest in the business.		

Partnership capital before Tab is admitted ($25,000 + $75,000).............	$100,000
Tab's investment in the partnership..	20,000
Partnership capital after Tab is admitted	$120,000
Tab's capital in the partnership ($120,000 × 1/10)	$ 12,000
Bonus to the old partners ($20,000 − $12,000).....................................	$ 8,000

2. Partners' capital balances:

Mia, capital ($25,000 + $2,400).................	$ 27,400
Susan, capital ($75,000 + $5,600)	80,600
Tab, capital	12,000
Total partnership capital..............................	$120,000

ADMISSION BY INVESTING IN THE PARTNERSHIP—BONUS TO THE NEW PARTNER A potential new partner may be so important that the existing partners offer him or her a partnership share that includes a bonus. A law firm may strongly desire a former governor or other official as a partner because of the person's reputation and connections. A restaurant owner may want to go into partnership with a famous sports personality, movie star, or model. The popular chain **Planet Hollywood,** for example, opened its first restaurant in New York City with the help of celebrity partners Sylvester Stallone, Arnold Schwarzenegger, Bruce Willis, and Don Johnson.

Suppose that Allan Page and Olivia Franco have a law partnership. The firm's balance sheet appears as follows:

DAILY EXERCISE 12-13

Cash	$140,000	Total liabilities.......................	$120,000
Other assets..........................	360,000	Page, capital............................	230,000
		Franco, capital	150,000
Total assets	$500,000	Total liabilities and capital	$500,000

Page and Franco admit Martin Schiller, a former attorney general, as a partner with a one-third interest in exchange for his cash investment of $100,000. At the time of Schiller's admission, the firm's capital is $380,000 (Page, $230,000, plus Franco, $150,000). Page and Franco share profits and losses in the ratio of two-thirds to Page and one-third to Franco. The computation of Schiller's equity in the partnership is

Partnership capital before Schiller is admitted ($230,000 + $150,000)	$380,000
Schiller's investment in the partnership	100,000
Partnership capital after Schiller is admitted	$480,000
Schiller's capital in the partnership ($480,000 × 1/3).................................	$160,000
Bonus to the new partner ($160,000 − $100,000)	$ 60,000

In this case, Schiller bought into the partnership at a price ($100,000) below the book value of his interest ($160,000). The bonus of $60,000 went to Schiller from the other partners. The capital accounts of Page and Franco are debited for the $60,000 difference between the new partner's equity ($160,000) and his investment ($100,000). The existing partners share this decrease in capital as though it were a loss, on the basis of their profit-and-loss ratio. The entry to record Schiller's investment is

Aug. 24	Cash	100,000	
	Page, Capital ($60,000 × 2/3).............................	40,000	
	Franco, Capital ($60,000 × 1/3)	20,000	
	Schiller, Capital..		160,000
	To admit M. Schiller as a partner with a		
	one-third interest in the business.		

The new partnership's balance sheet reports these amounts:

Cash		Total liabilities.......................	$120,000
($140,000 + $100,000)....	$240,000	Page, capital	
Other assets..........................	360,000	($230,000 − $40,000)	190,000
		Franco, capital	
		($150,000 − $20,000)	130,000
		Schiller, capital	160,000
Total assets	$600,000	Total liabilities and capital	$600,000

WORK IT OUT

John and Ron are partners with capital balances of $30,000 and $40,000, respectively. They share profits and losses in a 25:75 ratio. John and Ron admit Lou to a 20% interest in a new partnership when Lou invests $10,000 in the business.

1. Journalize the partnership's receipt of cash from Lou.
2. What is each partner's capital in the new partnership?

Answers

1.

Cash	10,000	
John, Capital ($6,000 × 0.25)	1,500	
Ron, Capital ($6,000 × 0.75)...	4,500	
Lou, Capital		16,000
To admit Lou with a 20% interest in the business.		

Partnership capital before Lou is admitted ($30,000 + $40,000)	$70,000
Lou's investment in the partnership..	10,000
Partnership capital after Lou is admitted	$80,000
Lou's capital in the partnership ($80,000 × 0.20)	$16,000
Bonus to the new partner ($16,000 − $10,000)	$ 6,000

2. Partners' capital balances:

John, capital ($30,000 − $1,500)	$28,500
Ron, capital ($40,000 − $4,500)...............	35,500
Lou, capital...	16,000
Total partnership capital............................	$80,000

WITHDRAWAL (RESIGNATION OR DEATH) OF A PARTNER

Objective 5
Account for a partner's withdrawal (resignation) from the firm

A partner may withdraw from the business for many reasons, including retirement or a dispute with the other partners. The resignation of a partner dissolves the old partnership. The partnership agreement should contain a provision to govern how to settle with a withdrawing partner. In the simplest case, illustrated on page 476, a partner may resign and sell his or her interest to another partner in a personal transaction.

The only entry needed to record this transfer of equity debits the withdrawing partner's capital account and credits the purchaser's capital account. The dollar amount of the entry is the capital balance of the withdrawing partner, regardless of the price paid by the purchaser. The accounting when one current partner buys a second partner's interest is the same as when an outside party buys a current partner's interest.

If the partner resigns in the middle of an accounting period, the partnership books should be updated to determine each partner's capital balance. The business must measure net income or net loss for the fraction of the year up to the resignation date and allocate profit or loss according to the existing ratio. After the books have been closed, the business accounts for the change in partnership capital.

The withdrawing partner may receive his or her share of the business in partnership assets other than cash. Then the question is what value to assign the partnership assets—book value or current market value? The settlement procedure may specify an independent appraisal to determine current market value. If market values have changed, the appraisal will result in revaluing the partnership assets. The partners share in any market value changes that their efforts caused.

Suppose that Keith Isaac is retiring in midyear from the partnership of Green, Henry, and Isaac. After the books have been adjusted for partial-period income but before the asset appraisal, revaluation, and closing entries, the balance sheet reports the following:

Cash.........................		$ 39,000	Total liabilities..........		$ 80,000
Inventory..................		44,000	Green, capital...........		54,000
Land		55,000	Henry, capital...........		43,000
Building...................	$95,000		Isaac, capital.............		21,000
Less Accum. depr. ...	(35,000)	60,000	Total liabilities and		
Total assets...............		$198,000	capital		$198,000

An independent appraiser revalues the inventory at $38,000 (down from $44,000) and the land at $101,000 (up from $55,000). The partners share the differences between these assets' market values and their prior book values on the basis of their profit-and-loss ratio.

The partnership agreement has allocated one-fourth of the profits to Susan Green, one-half to Charles Henry, and one-fourth to Keith Isaac. (This ratio may be written 1:2:1 for one part to Green, two parts to Henry, and one part to Isaac.) For each share that Green or Isaac has, Henry has two. The entries to record the revaluation of the inventory and land are

July 31	Green, Capital ($6,000 × 1/4)	1,500	
	Henry, Capital ($6,000 × 1/2)	3,000	
	Isaac, Capital ($6,000 × 1/4)	1,500	
	Inventory ($44,000 − $38,000)...........................		6,000
	To revalue the inventory and allocate the loss to the partners.		
31	Land ($101,000 − $55,000)	46,000	
	Green, Capital ($46,000 × 1/4)		11,500
	Henry, Capital ($46,000 × 1/2)		23,000
	Isaac, Capital ($46,000 × 1/4)		11,500
	To revalue the land and allocate the gain to the partners.		

After the revaluations, the partnership balance sheet reports the following:

Cash		$ 39,000	Total liabilities...		$80,000
Inventory		38,000	Green, capital ($54,000 − $1,500 + $11,500).........		64,000
Land..............................		101,000	Henry, capital ($43,000 − $3,000 + $23,000)		63,000
Building	$95,000		Isaac, capital ($21,000 − $1,500 + $11,500)............		31,000
Less Accum. depr.	(35,000)	60,000			
Total assets		$238,000	Total liabilities and capital		$238,000

The books now carry the assets at current market value, which becomes the new book value, and the capital accounts have been adjusted accordingly. As the balance sheet shows, Isaac has a claim to $31,000 in partnership assets. How is his withdrawal from the business accounted for?

Withdrawal at Book Value

If Keith Isaac withdraws by receiving cash equal to the book value of his owner's equity, the entry will be

July 31	Isaac, Capital...	31,000	
	Cash...		31,000
	To record withdrawal of K. Isaac from the business.		

 DAILY EXERCISE 12-14

This entry records the payment of partnership cash to Isaac and the closing of his capital account upon his withdrawal from the business.

Withdrawal at Less than Book Value

The withdrawing partner may be so eager to leave the business that he or she is willing to take less than his or her equity. Assume that Keith Isaac withdraws from the business and agrees to receive partnership cash of $10,000 and the new partnership's note for $15,000. This $25,000 settlement is $6,000 less than Isaac's $31,000 equity in the business. The remaining partners share this $6,000 difference—which is a bonus to them—according to their profit-and-loss ratio.

Because Isaac has withdrawn from the partnership, a new agreement—and a new profit-and-loss ratio—must be drawn up. In forming a new partnership, Henry and Green may decide on any ratio that they see fit. Let's assume they agree that Henry will earn two-thirds of partnership profits and losses and Green one-third. The entry to record Isaac's withdrawal at less than book value is

July 31	Isaac, Capital	31,000	
	Cash		10,000
	Note Payable to K. Isaac		15,000
	Green, Capital ($6,000 × 1/3)		2,000
	Henry, Capital ($6,000 × 2/3)		4,000
	To record withdrawal of K. Isaac from the business.		

Isaac's account is closed, and Henry and Green may or may not continue the business as a new partnership.

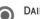 **DAILY EXERCISE 12-15**

Withdrawal at More than Book Value

The settlement with a withdrawing partner may allow him or her to take assets of greater value than the book value of that partner's capital. Also, the remaining partners may be so eager for the withdrawing partner to leave the firm that they pay him or her a bonus to withdraw from the business. In either case, the partner's withdrawal causes a decrease in the book equity of the remaining partners. This decrease is allocated to the partners on the basis of their profit-and-loss ratio.

The accounting for this situation follows the pattern illustrated for withdrawal at less than book value—with one exception. The remaining partners' capital accounts are debited because the withdrawing partner receives more than his or her book equity.

 DAILY EXERCISE 12-16

WORK IT OUT

Matt is withdrawing from the partnership of Matt, Lee, and Karla. The partners share profits and losses in a 1:2:3 ratio for Matt, Lee, and Karla, respectively. After the revaluation of assets, Matt's capital balance is $50,000, and the other partners agree to pay her $60,000. Journalize the payment to Matt and his withdrawal from the partnership.

Answer

Matt, Capital	50,000	
Lee, Capital [($60,000 − $50,000) × 2/5]	4,000	
Karla, Capital [($60,000 − $50,000) × 3/5]	6,000	
Cash		60,000
To record withdrawal of Matt from the business.		

Death of a Partner

Like any other form of partnership withdrawal, the death of a partner dissolves a partnership. The partnership accounts are adjusted to measure net income or loss for the fraction of the year up to the date of death, then closed to determine the partners' capital balances on that date. Settlement with the deceased partner's estate is based on the partnership agreement. The estate commonly receives partnership assets equal to the partner's capital balance. The partnership closes the deceased partner's capital account with a debit. This entry credits a payable to the estate.

Suppose Susan Green (of the partnership on page 480) dies after all accounts have been adjusted to current market value. Green's capital balance is $64,000. Green's estate may request cash for her final share of the partnership's assets. At this time the business has only $39,000 of cash, so it must borrow. Let's assume the partnership borrows $50,000 and then pays Green's estate for her capital balance. The partnership's journal entries are

Objective 6
Account for the liquidation of a partnership

Aug. 1	Cash	50,000	
	Note Payable		50,000
	To borrow money		
Aug. 1	Green, Capital	64,000	
	Cash		64,000
	To record withdrawal of Green from the business.		

Alternatively, a remaining partner may purchase the deceased partner's equity. The deceased partner's equity is debited, and the purchaser's equity is credited. The journal entry to record this transaction follows the pattern given on page 475 for the transfer of Fisher's equity over to Dynak. The amount of this entry is the ending credit balance in the deceased partner's capital account.

LIQUIDATION OF A PARTNERSHIP

LIQUIDATION. The process of going out of business by selling the entity's assets and paying its liabilities. The final step in liquidation is the distribution of any remaining cash to the owner(s).

Admission of a new partner or withdrawal or death of an existing partner dissolves the partnership. However, the business may continue operating with no apparent change to outsiders such as customers and creditors. In contrast, business **liquidation** is the process of going out of business by selling the entity's assets and paying its liabilities. The final step in liquidation is the *distribution of the remaining cash to the owners.* Before the business is liquidated, its books should be adjusted and closed. After closing, only asset, liability, and partners' capital accounts remain open.

Liquidation of a partnership includes three basic steps:

1. Sell the assets. Allocate the gain or loss to the partners' capital accounts on the basis of the profit-and-loss ratio.
2. Pay the partnership liabilities.
3. Disburse the remaining cash to the partners on the basis of their capital balances.

In practice, the liquidation of a business can stretch over weeks or months. Selling every asset and paying every liability of the entity takes time. After the partners of **Shea & Gould,** one of New York's best-known law firms, voted to dissolve their partnership, the firm remained open for an extra year to collect bills and pay off liabilities.

To avoid excessive detail in our illustrations, we include only two asset categories—Cash and Noncash Assets—and a single liability category—Liabilities. Our examples assume that the business sells the noncash assets in a single transaction and pays the liabilities in a single transaction.

Assume that Jane Avignon, Elaine Bloch, and Mark Crane have shared profits and losses in the ratio of 3:1:1. (This ratio is equal to 3/5, 1/5, 1/5, or a 60%, 20%, 20% sharing ratio.) They decide to liquidate their partnership. After the books are adjusted and closed, the general ledger contains the following balances:

Cash	$ 10,000	Liabilities	$ 30,000
Noncash assets	90,000	Avignon, capital...................	40,000
		Bloch, capital........................	20,000
		Crane, capital	10,000
Total assets	$100,000	Total liabilities and capital	$100,000

Sale of Noncash Assets at a Gain

Assume that the Avignon, Bloch, and Crane partnership sells its noncash assets (shown on the balance sheet as $90,000) for cash of $150,000. The partnership realizes a gain of $60,000, which is allocated to the partners on the basis of their profit-and-loss-sharing ratio. The entry to record this sale and allocation of the gain is

Oct. 31	Cash	150,000	
	Noncash Assets...		90,000
	Avignon, Capital ($60,000 × 0.60)		36,000
	Bloch, Capital ($60,000 × 0.20)		12,000
	Crane, Capital ($60,000 × 0.20)....................		12,000
	To sell noncash assets at a gain.		

The partnership must next pay off its liabilities:

Oct. 31	Liabilities...	30,000	
	Cash		30,000
	To pay liabilities.		

In the final liquidation transaction, the remaining cash is disbursed to the partners. *The partners share in the cash according to their capital balances.* (*Gains and losses* on the sale of assets are shared by the partners on the basis of their profit-and-loss-sharing ratio.) The amount of cash left in the partnership is $130,000—the $10,000 beginning balance plus the $150,000 cash sale of assets minus the $30,000 cash payment of liabilities. The partners divide the remaining cash according to their capital balances:

Oct. 31	Avignon, Capital ($40,000 + $36,000)...............	76,000	
	Bloch, Capital ($20,000 + $12,000)	32,000	
	Crane, Capital ($10,000 + $12,000)..................	22,000	
	Cash		130,000
	To pay cash in liquidation.		

A convenient way to summarize the transactions in a partnership liquidation is given in Exhibit 12-4. Remember: Upon liquidation, gains on the sale of assets are divided according to the *profit-and-loss ratio*. The final cash payment to the partners is based on *capital balances*.

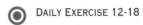

DAILY EXERCISE 12-17

DAILY EXERCISE 12-18

EXHIBIT 12-4 **Partnership Liquidation—Sale of Assets at a Gain**

						Capital	
	Cash	+	Noncash Assets	= Liabilities	+	Avignon (60%) +	Bloch (20%) +	Crane (20%)
Balance before sale of assets	$ 10,000		$90,000	$30,000		$40,000	$20,000	$10,000
Sale of assets and sharing of gain ...	150,000		(90,000)			36,000	12,000	12,000
Balances.......................................	160,000		0	30,000		76,000	32,000	22,000
Payment of liabilities......................	(30,000)			(30,000)				
Balances.......................................	130,000		0	0		76,000	32,000	22,000
Payment of cash to partners	(130,000)					(76,000)	(32,000)	(22,000)
Balances.......................................	$ 0		$ 0	$ 0		$ 0	$ 0	$ 0

After the payment of cash to the partners, the business has no assets, liabilities, or owners' equity. All the balances are zero. By the accounting equation, partnership assets *must* equal partnership liabilities plus partnership capital.

Sale of Noncash Assets at a Loss

Liquidation of a business often includes the sale of noncash assets at a loss. When this occurs, the partners' capital accounts are debited as they share the loss in their profit-and-loss-sharing ratio. Otherwise, the accounting follows the pattern illustrated for the sale of noncash assets at a gain.

THINK IT OVER

The liquidation of the Dirk & Cross partnership included the sale of assets at a $150,000 loss. Lorraine Dirk's capital balance of $45,000 was less than her $60,000 share of the loss. Allocation of losses to the partners created a $15,000 deficit (debit balance) in Dirk's capital account. Identify ways that the partnership could deal with the negative balance (a capital deficiency) in Dirk's capital account.

Answer: Two possibilities are

1. Dirk could contribute assets to the partnership in an amount equal to her capital deficiency.
2. Joseph Cross could absorb Dirk's capital deficiency by decreasing his own capital balance.

PARTNERSHIP FINANCIAL STATEMENTS

EXHIBIT 12-5 Financial Statements of a Partnership and a Proprietorship

Partnership financial statements are much like those of a proprietorship. However, a partnership income statement includes a section showing the division of net income to the partners. For example, the partnership of Leslie Gray and Wayne Hayward might report its statements for the year ended December 31, 20X3, as shown in Panel A of Exhibit 12-5. A proprietorship's statements are presented in Panel B for comparison.

PANEL A—Partnership

GRAY & HAYWARD CONSULTING
Income Statement
Year Ended December 31, 20X3

		Thousands
Revenues		$460
Expenses		(270)
Net income		$190
Allocation of net income:		
To Gray	$114	
To Hayward	76	$190

GRAY & HAYWARD CONSULTING
Statement of Owners' Equity
Year Ended December 31, 20X3

	Thousands	
	Gray	Hayward
Capital, December 31, 20X2	$ 50	$ 40
Additional investments	10	—
Net income	114	76
Subtotal	174	116
Drawings	(72)	(48)
Capital, December 31, 20X3	$102	$ 68

GRAY & HAYWARD CONSULTING
Balance Sheet
December 31, 20X3

Assets	Thousands
Cash and other assets	$170
Owners' Equity	
Gray, capital	$102
Hayward, capital	68
Total capital	$170

PANEL B—Proprietorship

GRAY CONSULTING
Income Statement
Year Ended December 31, 20X3

	Thousands
Revenues	$460
Expenses	(270)
Net income	$190

GRAY CONSULTING
Statement of Owners' Equity
Year Ended December 31, 20X3

	Thousands
Capital, December 31, 20X2	$ 90
Additional investment	10
Net income	190
Subtotal	290
Drawings	(120)
Capital, December 31, 20X3	$170

GRAY CONSULTING
Balance Sheet
December 31, 20X3

Assets	Thousands
Cash and other assets	$170
Owner's Equity	
Gray, capital	$170

EXHIBIT 12-6 Reporting Net Income for a Large Partnership

DAILY EXERCISE 12-19

DAILY EXERCISE 12-20

MAIN PRICE & ANDERS
Statements of Earnings
Year Ended August 31, 20X4

	Thousands
Fees for professional services	$2,507,690
Earnings for the year	$ 832,340
Allocation of Earnings:	
To partners active during the year—	
Resigned, retired, and deceased partners	$ 109,901
Partners active at year end	627,730
To retired and deceased partners—retirement and death benefits	18,310
Not allocated to partners—retained for specific partnership purposes	76,399
	$ 832,340
Average earnings per partner active at year end (1,340 partners)	$ 621

Large partnerships may not find it feasible to report the net income of every partner. Instead, the firm may report the allocation of net income to active and retired partners and average earnings per partner. Exhibit 12-6 shows how the accounting/consulting firm Main Price & Anders reported its earnings.

The following Decision Guidelines feature summarizes the main points of accounting for partnerships.

DECISION GUIDELINES

Accounting for Partnerships

DECISION	GUIDELINES
How to organize the business?	A partnership offers both advantages and disadvantages in comparison with proprietorships and corporations. (See Exhibit 12-2).
On what matters should the partners agree?	See the list on page 466, under the heading "The Written Partnership Agreement."
At what value does the partnership record assets and liabilities?	Current market value on the date of acquisition, because, in effect, the partnership is buying its assets at their current market value.

How are partnership profits and losses shared among the partners?	• Equally if there is no profit-and-loss-sharing agreement.
	 • As provided in the partnership agreement. Can be based on the partners'
	   a. Stated fractions
	   b. Capital contributions
	   c. Service to the partnership
	   d. Salaries and interest on their capital contributions

What happens when a partner withdraws from the partnership?	The old partnership ceases to exist. The remaining partners may or may not form a new partnership.
How are new partners admitted to the partnership?	• *Purchase a partner's interest.* The old partnership is dissolved. The remaining partners may admit the new partner to the partnership. If not, the new partner gets no voice in the management of the firm but shares in the profits and losses. Close the withdrawing partner's Capital account, and open a Capital account for the new partner. Carry over the old partner's Capital balance to the Capital account of the new partner. • *Invest in the partnership.* Buying in at book value creates no bonus to any partner. Buying in at a price above book value creates a bonus to the old partners. Buying in at a price below book value creates a bonus for the new partner.

How to account for the withdrawal of a partner from the business?	• First, adjust and close the books up to the date of the partner's withdrawal from the business.
	 • Second, appraise the assets and the liabilities at their current market value.
	 • Third, account for the partner's withdrawal
	   a. At book value (no change in remaining partners' Capital balances)
	   b. At less than book value (increase the remaining partners' Capital balances)
	   c. At more than book value (decrease the remaining partners' Capital balances)

What happens if the partnership goes out of business?	Liquidate the partnership, as follows:
	   a. Adjust and close the partnership books up to the date of liquidation.
	   b. Sell the partnership's assets. Allocate gain or loss to the partner's Capital accounts based on their profit-and-loss ratio.
	   c. Pay the partnership liabilities.
	   d. Pay any remaining cash to the partners based on their Capital balances.

How do partnership financial statements differ from those of a proprietorship?	• The partnership income statement reports the allocation of net income or net loss to the partners. • The partnership balance sheet (or a separate schedule) reports the Capital balance of each partner. • The statement of cash flows is the same for a partnership as for a proprietorship.

485

www.prenhall.com/horngren

End-of-Chapter Assessment

SUMMARY PROBLEM

The partnership of Taylor & Uvalde is considering admitting Steven Vaughn as a partner on January 1, 20X5. The partnership general ledger includes the following balances on that date:

Cash....................................	$ 9,000		Total liabilities	$ 50,000
Other assets	110,000		Taylor, capital	45,000
			Uvalde, capital.........................	24,000
Total assets...........................	$119,000		Total liabilities and capital.......	$119,000

Ross Taylor's share of profits and losses is 60%, and Thomas Uvalde's share is 40%.

Required (Items 1 and 2 Are Independent)

1. Suppose that Vaughn pays Uvalde $31,000 to acquire Uvalde's interest in the business. Taylor approves Vaughn as a partner.
   a. Record the transfer of owner's equity on the partnership books.
   b. Prepare the partnership balance sheet immediately after Vaughn is admitted as a partner.
2. Suppose that Vaughn becomes a partner by investing $31,000 cash to acquire a one-fourth interest in the business.
   a. Compute Vaughn's capital balance, and record his investment in the business.
   b. Prepare the partnership balance sheet immediately after Vaughn is admitted as a partner. Include the heading.
3. Which way of admitting Vaughn to the partnership increases its total assets? Give your reason.

Solution

Requirement 1

a. Jan. 1   Uvalde, Capital..   24,000
               Vaughn, Capital.................................   24,000
            To transfer Uvalde's equity in the partnership to Vaughn.

b. The balance sheet for the partnership of Taylor and Vaughn is identical to the balance sheet given for Taylor and Uvalde in the problem, except that Vaughn's name replaces Uvalde's name in the title and in the listing of Capital accounts.

Requirement 2

a. Computations of Vaughn's capital balance:

Partnership capital before Vaughn is admitted ($45,000 + $24,000)...	$ 69,000
Vaughn's investment in the partnership....................................	31,000
Partnership capital after Vaughn is admitted............................	$100,000
Vaughn's capital in the partnership ($100,000 × 1/4)	$ 25,000

Jan. 1   Cash   31,000
                 Vaughn, Capital   25,000
                 Taylor, Capital [($31,000 − $25,000) × 0.60]........   3,600
                 Uvalde, Capital [($31,000 − $25,000) × 0.40]   2,400
            To admit Vaughn as a partner with a one-fourth interest in the business.

b.

TAYLOR, UVALDE, & VAUGHN
Balance Sheet
January 1, 20X5

Cash ($9,000 + $31,000)	$ 40,000		Total liabilities	$ 50,000
Other assets	110,000		Taylor, capital ($45,000 + $3,600)	48,600
			Uvalde, capital ($24,000 + $2,400)	26,400
			Vaughn, capital	25,000
Total assets..............................	$150,000		Total liabilities and capital......	$150,000

> **Requirement 3**
>
> Vaughn's investment in the partnership increases its total assets by the amount of his contribution. Total assets of the business are $150,000 after his investment, compared with $119,000 before. In contrast, Vaughn's purchase of Uvalde's interest in the business is a personal transaction between the two individuals. It does not affect the assets of the partnership regardless of the amount Vaughn pays Uvalde.

LESSONS LEARNED

1. **Identify the characteristics of a partnership.** A *partnership* is a business co-owned by two or more persons for profit. The characteristics of this form of business organization are its *ease of formation, limited life, mutual agency, unlimited liability,* and *no partnership income taxes.* A written *partnership agreement* establishes procedures for admission of a new partner, withdrawal of a partner, and the sharing of profits and losses among the partners.

2. **Account for the partners' investments in a partnership.** Accounting for a partnership is similar to accounting for a proprietorship. Each partner has an individual capital account and a withdrawal account.

3. **Allocate profits and losses to the partners.** Partners share net income or loss in any manner they choose. Common sharing agreements base the *profit-and-loss ratio* on a stated fraction, partners' capital contributions, and/or their service to the partnership.

4. **Account for the admission of a partner to the business.** An outside person may become a partner by purchasing a current partner's interest or by investing in the partnership. The new partner may pay the current partners a bonus to join. Or the new partner may receive a bonus to join.

5. **Account for a partner's withdrawal (resignation) from the firm.** When a partner withdraws, partnership assets may be reappraised. Partners share any gain or loss on the asset revaluation on the basis of their profit-and-loss ratio. The withdrawing partner may receive payment equal to, greater than, or less than his or her capital book value, depending on the agreement with the other partners.

6. **Account for the liquidation of a partnership.** In *liquidation,* a partnership goes out of business by selling the assets, paying the liabilities, and disbursing any remaining cash to the partners.

7. **Prepare partnership financial statements.** Partnership *financial statements* are similar to those of a proprietorship. The partnership income statement commonly allocates net income to the partners, and the balance sheet has a Capital account for each partner.

ACCOUNTING VOCABULARY

articles of partnership (p. 465)
dissolution (p. 466)
general partnership (p. 468)
limited liability partnership (p. 468)

limited partnership (p. 468)
liquidation (p. 482)
LLPs (p. 468)
mutual agency (p. 466)
partnership (p. 465)

partnership agreement (p. 465)
S Corporation (p. 468)
unlimited personal liability (p. 466)

QUESTIONS

1. What is another name for a partnership agreement? List eight items that the agreement should specify.
2. Ron Montgomery, who is a partner in M&N Associates, commits the firm to a contract for a job within the scope of its regular business operations. What term describes Montgomery's ability to obligate the partnership?
3. If a partnership cannot pay a debt, who must make the payment? What term describes this obligation of the partners?
4. How is the income of a partnership taxed?
5. Identify the advantages and disadvantages of the partnership form of business organization.
6. Rex Randall and Ken Smith's partnership agreement states that Randall gets 60% of profits and Smith gets 40%. If the agreement does not discuss the treatment of losses, how are losses shared? How do the partners share profits and losses if the agreement specifies no profit-and-loss-sharing ratio?

7. Do partner withdrawals of cash for personal use affect the sharing of profits and losses by the partner? If so, explain how. If not, explain why not.
8. Name two events that can cause the dissolution of a partnership.
9. When a partner resigns from the partnership and receives assets greater than his or her capital balance, how is the excess shared by the other partners?
10. Name the three steps in liquidating a partnership.
11. The partnership of Cope and Hope is in the process of liquidation. How do the partners share (a) gains and losses on the sale of noncash assets, and (b) the final cash distribution?
12. Summarize the situations in which partnership allocations are based on (a) the profit-and-loss-sharing ratio, and (b) the partners' capital balances.

DAILY EXERCISES

Partnership characteristics
(Obj. 1)

DE12-1 After studying the characteristics of a partnership, write two short paragraphs, as follows:

1. Explain the *advantages* of a partnership over a proprietorship and a corporation.
2. Explain the *disadvantages* of a partnership over a proprietorship and a corporation.

Partnership characteristics
(Obj. 1)

DE12-2 Timothy Lane and Sam Medford are forming a business to imprint T-shirts. Lane suggests that they organize as a partnership in order to avoid the unlimited personal liability of a proprietorship. According to Lane, partnerships are not very risky.

Lane explains to Medford that if the business does not succeed, each partner can withdraw from the business, taking the same assets that he or she invested at its beginning. Lane states that the main disadvantage of the partnership form of organization is double taxation: First, the partnership pays a business income tax; second, each partner also pays personal income tax on his or her share of the business's profits.

Correct the errors in Lane's explanation.

A partner's investment in a
partnership
(Obj. 2)

DE12-3 Dean Hahn invests a building in a partnership with Margo Klem. Hahn purchased the building in 20X1 for $300,000. Accumulated depreciation to the date of forming the partnership is $80,000. A real estate appraiser states that the building is now worth $285,000. Hahn wants $400,000 capital in the new partnership, but Klem objects. Klem believes that capital contribution into the partnership should be measured by the book value of his building.

Klem and Hahn seek your advice. Which value of the building is appropriate for measuring Hahn's capital, book value or current market value? State the reason for your answer. Give the partnership's journal entry to record Hahn's investment in the business.

Investments by partners
(Obj. 2)

DE12-4 Seth Green and Nate Smith are forming the partnership Sun Florida Development to develop a theme park near Panama City. Green contributes cash of $4 million and land valued at $17 million. When Green purchased the land in 20X1, its cost was $8 million. The partnership will assume Green's $3 million note payable on the land. Smith invests cash of $10 million and construction equipment that he purchased for $7 million (accumulated depreciation to date, $3 million). The equipment's market value is equal to its book value.

1. Before recording any journal entries, compute the partnership's total assets, total liabilities, and total owners' equity immediately after organizing.
2. Journalize the partnership's receipt of assets and liabilities from Green and from Smith. Record each asset at its current market value with no entry to accumulated depreciation.
3. Use your journal entries to prove the correctness of total owners' equity from requirement 1.

Partners' profits, losses, and
capital balances
(Obj. 3)

DE12-5 Examine the Benz and Hanna balance sheet in Exhibit 12-3, page 471. Note that Benz invested far more in the partnership than Hanna. Suppose the two partners fail to agree upon a profit-and-loss-sharing ratio. For the first month (June 20X5), the partnership lost $15,000.

1. How much of this loss goes to Benz? How much goes to Hanna?
2. Assume the partners withdrew no cash or other assets during June. What is each partner's capital balance at June 30? Prepare a T-account for each partner's capital to answer this question.

Partners' profits, drawings, and
capital balances; closing entries
(Obj. 3)

DE12-6 ← *Link Back to Chapter 4 (Closing Entries).* Return to the Benz and Hanna balance sheet in Exhibit 12-3, page 471. The partnership earned $115,000 during the year ended May 31, 20X6, its first year of operation. The partners share profits and losses based on their capital balances at the beginning of the year. During the first year, Benz withdrew $70,000 cash from the business and Hanna's drawings totaled $50,000.

1. Journalize the entries for (a) partner withdrawals of cash, (b) closing the business's profits into the partner's capital accounts at May 31, 20X6, and (c) closing the partners' drawing accounts.
2. Post to the partners' capital accounts after inserting their beginning amounts. What is the amount of total partnership capital at May 31, 20X6?

Allocating partnership profits
based on capital contributions
and service
(Obj. 3)

DE12-7 Lawson, Martinez, and Edwards have capital balances of $20,000, $30,000, and $50,000, respectively. The partners share profits and losses as follows:

a. The first $40,000 is divided based on the partners' capital balances.
b. The next $40,000 is based on service, equally shared by Lawson and Edwards.
c. The remainder is divided equally.

Compute each partner's share of the business's $140,000 net income for the year.

DE12-8 Lucy Fung and Ako Kiawa have capital balances of $30,000 and $40,000, respectively. The partners share profits and losses as follows:

Allocating partnership profits based on salaries and interest (Obj. 3)

a. Fung receives a salary of $15,000 and Kiawa a salary of $10,000.
b. The partners earn 7% interest on their capital balances.
c. The remainder is shared equally.

Compute each partner's share of the year's net income of $50,000.

DE12-9 Study the Ingel and Jay partnership balance sheet near the top of page 476. Claire Reynoldo pays $110,000 to purchase Michael Jay's interest in the partnership.

Admitting a partner who purchases an existing partner's interest (Obj. 4)

1. Journalize the partnership's transaction to admit Reynoldo to the partnership. What happens to the $20,000 difference between Reynoldo's payment and Jay's capital balance?
2. Must Robin Ingel accept Claire Reynoldo as a full partner? What right does Reynoldo have after purchasing Jay's interest in the partnership?

DE12-10 Return to the partnership balance sheet of Ingel and Jay near the top of page 476. Larry Welsh invests cash of $80,000 to acquire a one-third interest in the partnership.

Admitting a partner who invests in the business (Obj. 4)

1. Does Welsh's investment provide a bonus to the partners? Show calculations to support your answer.
2. Journalize the partnership's receipt of the $80,000 from Welsh.

Admitting a new partner; bonus to the existing partners (Obj. 4)

DE12-11 Study the partnership balance sheet of Nagasawa and Osburn on page 476. Suppose Christine Kliptel invests $50,000 to purchase a one-fifth interest in the new partnership of Nagasawa, Osburn, and Kliptel (NOK Partners).
Journalize the partnership's receipt of cash from Kliptel.

Preparing a partnership balance sheet (Obj. 7)

DE12-12 This exercise uses the data given in Daily Exercise 12-11. After recording the partnership's receipt of cash from Kliptel in Daily Exercise 12-11, prepare the balance sheet of the new partnership of NOK Partners at June 30, 20X2. Include a complete heading.

Admitting a new partner; bonus to the new partner (Obj. 4)

DE12-13 Refer to the partnership balance sheet of Page and Franco near the top of page 478 and the paragraph immediately following the balance sheet. Assume Everett invests $140,000 to acquire a 30% interest in the new partnership of Page, Franco, and Everett.
Journalize the partnership's receipt of cash from Everett.

DE12-14 Examine the Green, Henry, and Isaac balance sheet at the top of page 480.

Withdrawal of a partner (Obj. 5)

1. The partners share profits and losses as follows: 25% to Green, 50% to Henry, and 25% to Isaac. Suppose Susan Green is withdrawing from the business, and the partners agree that no appraisal of assets is needed. How much in assets can Green take from the partnership? Give the reason for your answer, including an explanation of why the profit-and-loss-sharing ratio is not used for this determination.
2. Henry and Isaac plan to form a new partnership to continue the business. If Green demands cash for her full settlement upon withdrawing from the business, how can Henry and Isaac come up with the cash to pay Green? Identify two ways.

Withdrawal of a partner at more than book value; asset revaluation (Obj. 5)

DE12-15 Return to the Green, Henry, and Isaac partnership balance sheet near the middle of page 480. Suppose Henry is retiring from the business and the partners agree to revalue the assets at their current market value. A real-estate appraiser issues his professional opinion that the current market value of the land is $150,000. The book values of all other assets approximate their current market value.
Journalize (a) the revaluation of the land, (b) borrowing $90,500 on a note payable in order to pay Henry, and (c) payment of $90,500 to Henry upon his retirement from the business on July 31.

Withdrawal of a partner at less than book value (Obj. 5)

DE12-16 This exercise uses the data given in Daily Exercise 12-15 with one modification. Assume Henry is retiring from the partnership and agrees to take cash of $60,500.
Journalize the payment of $60,500 to Henry upon his withdrawal from the partnership.

Liquidation of a partnership at a loss (Obj. 6)

DE12-17 Use the data in Exhibit 12-4, page 483. Suppose the partnership of Avignon, Bloch, and Crane liquidates by selling all noncash assets for $75,000.
Complete the liquidation schedule as shown in Exhibit 12-4.

Liquidation of a partnership (Obj. 6)

DE12-18 This exercise builds on the solution to Daily Exercise 12-17. After completing the liquidation schedule in Daily Exercise 12-17, journalize the partnership's (a) sale of noncash assets for $75,000 (use a single account for Noncash Assets), (b) payment of liabilities, and (c) payment of cash to the partners. Include an explanation with each entry.

Partnership balance sheet (Obj. 7)

DE12-19 This exercise uses the Green, Henry, and Isaac balance sheet, after revaluation of inventory and land, given in the middle of page 480. Furthermore, assume Isaac has withdrawn from the partnership at less than his book value, as recorded at the top of page 481.
Prepare the balance sheet of the new partnership of Green and Henry on July 31.

Partnership income statement
(Obj. 7)

DE12-20 The partnership of Frost and Martin had these balances at September 30, 20X4:

Cash	$20,000	Service revenue	$140,000
Liabilities	40,000	Frost, capital	30,000
Martin, capital	10,000	Total expenses	35,000
Other assets	60,000		

Frost gets two-thirds of profits and losses, and Martin one-third.

Prepare the partnership's income statement for the year ended September 30, 20X4.

EXERCISES

Organizing a partnership
(Obj. 1)

E12-1 Suzanne Drake, a friend from college, approaches you about forming a partnership to export software. Since graduating, Drake has worked for the International Trade Bank, developing important contacts among government officials and business leaders in Eastern Europe. Drake believes she is in a unique position to capitalize on the growing market in Eastern Europe for American computers. With expertise in finance, you would have responsibility for accounting and finance in the partnership.

Required

Discuss the advantages and disadvantages of organizing the export business as a partnership rather than a proprietorship. Comment on how partnership income is taxed and how your taxes would change if you organized as an S corporation.

Recording a partner's investment
(Obj. 2)

E12-2 Mason Flute has been operating an apartment-locater service as a proprietorship. He and Barrett Schraeder have decided to reorganize the business as a partnership. Flute's investment in the partnership consists of cash, $16,300; accounts receivable, $10,600, less allowance for uncollectibles, $800; office furniture, $2,700, less accumulated depreciation, $1,100; a small building, $55,000, less accumulated depreciation, $27,500; accounts payable, $3,300; and a note payable to the bank, $10,000.

To determine Flute's equity in the partnership, he and Schraeder hire an independent appraiser. This outside party provides the following market values of the assets and liabilities that Flute is contributing to the business: cash, accounts receivable, office furniture, accounts payable, and note payable—the same as Flute's book value; allowance for uncollectible accounts, $2,900; building, $71,000; and accrued expenses payable (including interest on the note payable), $1,200.

Required

Make the entry on the partnership books to record Flute's investment.

Computing partners' shares of
net income and net loss
(Obj. 3)

E12-3 Adam Meppen and Bailey Quaid form a partnership, investing $40,000 and $70,000, respectively. Determine their shares of net income or net loss for each of the following situations:

a. Net loss is $52,000 and the partners have no written partnership agreement.
b. Net income is $77,000, and the partnership agreement states that the partners share profits and losses on the basis of their capital contributions.
c. Net loss is $33,000, and the partnership agreement states that the partners share profits on the basis of their capital contributions.
d. Net income is $98,000. The first $60,000 is shared on the basis of partner capital contributions. The next $30,000 is based on partner service, with Meppen receiving 30% and Quaid receiving 70%. The remainder is shared equally.

Computing partners' capital
balances
(Obj. 3)

E12-4 Adam Meppen withdrew cash of $47,000 for personal use, and Bailey Quaid withdrew cash of $53,000 during the year. Using the data from situation (d) in Exercise 12-3, journalize the entries to close (a) the income summary account, and (b) the partners' drawing accounts. Explanations are not required. What was the overall effect on partnership capital?

Admitting a new partner
(Obj. 4)

E12-5 Trey Falco is admitted to a partnership. Prior to his admission, the partnership books show Sean Graham's capital balance at $100,000 and Kelly Ott's capital balance at $50,000. Compute each partner's equity on the books of the new partnership under the following plans:

a. Falco pays $92,000 for Ott's equity. Falco's payment is not an investment in the partnership, but instead goes directly to Ott.
b. Falco invests $75,000 to acquire a one-third interest in the partnership.
c. Falco invests $60,000 to acquire a one-fourth interest in the partnership.

E12-6 Make the partnership journal entry to record the admission of Falco under plans (a), (b), and (c) in Exercise 12-5. Explanations are not required.

Admitting a new partner **(Obj. 4)**

E12-7 After the books are closed, Echols & Schaeffer's partnership balance sheet reports capital of $60,000 for Echols and $80,000 for Schaeffer. Echols is withdrawing from the firm. The partners agree to write down partnership assets by $45,000. They have shared profits and losses in the ratio of one-third to Echols and two-thirds to Schaeffer. The partnership agreement states that a withdrawing partner will receive assets equal to the book value of his owner's equity.

Withdrawal of a partner **(Obj. 5)**

1. How much will Echols receive? Schaeffer will continue to operate the business as a proprietorship.
2. What is Schaeffer's beginning capital on the proprietorship books?

E12-8 Eve Bermuda is retiring from the partnership of Bermuda, Rye, and Augustine on May 31. The partner capital balances are Bermuda, $36,000; Rye, $51,000; and Augustine, $22,000. The partners agree to have the partnership assets revalued to current market values. The independent appraiser reports that the book value of the inventory should be decreased by $12,000, and the book value of the land should be increased by $32,000. The partners agree to these revaluations. The profit-and-loss ratio has been 5 : 3 : 2 for Bermuda, Rye, and Augustine, respectively. In retiring from the firm, Bermuda receives $25,000 cash and a $25,000 note from the partnership.

Withdrawal of a partner **(Obj. 5)**

Required

Journalize (a) the asset revaluations, and (b) Bermuda's withdrawal from the firm.

E12-9 Barry, McCall, and Flaten are liquidating their partnership. Before selling the noncash assets and paying the liabilities, the capital balances are Barry, $23,000; McCall, $20,000; and Flaten, $11,000. The partnership agreement divides profits and losses equally.

Liquidation of a partnership **(Obj. 6)**

Required

1. After selling the noncash assets and paying the liabilities, the partnership has cash of $54,000. How much cash will each partner receive in final liquidation?
2. After selling the noncash assets and paying the liabilities, the partnership has cash of $45,000. How much cash will each partner receive in final liquidation?

E12-10 Prior to liquidation, the accounting records of Deluth, Liu, and Bush included the following balances and profit-and-loss-sharing percentages:

Liquidation of a partnership **(Obj. 6)**

					Capital		
	Cash	+	Noncash Assets	= Liabilities +	Deluth (40%) +	Liu (30%) +	Bush (30%)
Balances before sale of assets.............	$ 8,000		$57,000	$19,000	$20,000	$15,000	$11,000

The partnership sold the noncash assets for $69,000, paid the liabilities, and disbursed the remaining cash to the partners. Complete the summary of transactions in the liquidation of the partnership. Use the format illustrated in Exhibit 12-4.

E12-11 The partnership of Valahu, Leman, and Sucre is dissolving. Business assets, liabilities, and partners' capital balances prior to dissolution follow. The partners share profits and losses as follows: Marie Valahu, 25%; Pierre Leman, 45%; and Anna Sucre, 30%.

Liquidation of a partnership **(Obj. 6)**

Required

Create a spreadsheet or solve manually (see the top of page 492)—as directed by your instructor—to show the ending balances in all accounts after the noncash assets are sold for $136,000 and for $90,000. Determine the unknown amounts. Identify two ways the partners can deal with the negative ending balance in Sucre's capital account.

Challenge Exercise

E12-12 On October 31, 20X2, Steve Klatt and Russell Stover agree to combine their proprietorships as a partnership. Their balance sheets on October 31 are shown on page 492.

Partnership balance sheet **(Obj. 7)**

Required

Prepare the partnership balance sheet at October 31, 20X2.

	A	B	C	D	E	F
1			**VALAHU, LEMAN, AND SUCRE**			
2			**Sale of Noncash Assets**			
3			**(For $136,000)**			
4						
5		Noncash		Valahu	Leman	Sucre
6	**Cash**	**Assets**	**Liabilities**	**Capital**	**Capital**	**Capital**
7	$ 6,000	$126,000	$77,000	$12,000	$37,000	$6,000
8	136,000	(126,000)		?	?	?
9						
10	$142,000	$ 0	$77,000	$?	$?	$?
11						
12				($A8–$B7) ∗ .25		
13						
14						
15			**(For $90,000)**			
16		Noncash		Valahu	Leman	Sucre
17	**Cash**	**Assets**	**Liabilities**	**Capital**	**Capital**	**Capital**
18	$ 6,000	$126,000	$77,000	$12,000	$37,000	$6,000
19	90,000	(126,000)		?	?	?
20						
21	$96,000	$ 0	$77,000	$?	$?	$?
22						
23				($A19–$B18) ∗ .25		
24						

EXERCISE 12-12
Klatt and Stover

	Klatt's Business		Stover's Business	
	Book Value	**Current Market Value**	**Book Value**	**Current Market Value**
Assets				
Cash	$ 3,700	$ 3,700	$ 4,000	$ 4,000
Accounts receivable (net)	22,000	20,200	8,000	6,300
Inventory	51,000	46,000	34,000	35,100
Plant assets (net)	121,800	103,500	53,500	57,400
Total assets	$198,500	$173,400	$99,500	$102,800
Liabilities and Capital				
Accounts payable	$ 25,500	$ 25,500	$ 8,300	$ 8,300
Accrued expenses payable	2,200	2,200	1,400	1,400
Notes payable	55,000	55,000		
Klatt, capital	115,800	?		
Stover, capital			89,800	?
Total liabilities and capital	$198,500	$173,400	$99,500	$102,800

(Group A) PROBLEMS

Writing a partnership agreement
(Obj. 1)

P12-1A Levita Nuñez and Rosa Lupe Gaitan are discussing the formation of a partnership to import dresses from Guatemala. Nuñez is especially artistic, so she will travel to Central America to buy merchandise. Gaitan is a super salesperson and has already lined up several large stores to which she can sell the dresses.

Required

Write a partnership agreement to cover all elements essential for the business to operate smoothly. Make up names, amounts, profit-and-loss-sharing percentages, and so on as needed.

Investments by partners
(Obj. 2, 7)

P12-2A Beth Saran and Jake Gentry formed a partnership on March 15. The partners agreed to invest equal amounts of capital. Gentry invested his proprietorship's assets and liabilities (credit balances in parentheses). See the table at the top of the next page.

	Gentry's Book Value	Current Market Value
Accounts receivable............................	$12,000	$12,000
Allowance for doubtful accounts......	(740)	(1,360)
Inventory...	43,850	31,220
Prepaid expenses	3,700	3,700
Store equipment.................................	36,700	26,600
Accumulated depreciation................	(9,200)	(–0–)
Accounts payable...............................	(22,300)	(22,300)

On March 15, Saran invested cash in an amount equal to the current market value of Gentry's partnership capital. The partners decided that Gentry would earn 70% of partnership profits because he would manage the business. Saran agreed to accept 30% of profits. During the period ended December 31, the partnership earned net income of $70,000. Saran's drawings were $27,000, and Gentry's drawings were $41,000.

Required

1. Journalize the partners' initial investments.
2. Prepare the partnership balance sheet immediately after its formation on March 15.
3. Journalize the December 31 entries to close the Income Summary account and the partners' drawing accounts.

P12-3A Lost Pines Escape is a partnership, and its owners are considering admitting Victor Lampe as a new partner. On July 31 of the current year, the capital accounts of the three existing partners and their shares of profits and losses are as follows:

Admitting a new partner (Obj. 4)

	Capital	Profit-and-Loss Ratio
Eric Runyan................	$48,000	1/6
Sara Braden................	64,000	1/3
Ken Maness................	88,000	1/2

Required

Journalize the admission of Lampe as a partner on July 31 for each of the following independent situations:

1. Lampe pays Maness $114,000 cash to purchase Maness's interest.
2. Lampe invests $50,000 in the partnership, acquiring a one-fifth interest in the business.
3. Lampe invests $50,000 in the partnership, acquiring a one-eighth interest in the business.
4. Lampe invests $30,000 in the partnership, acquiring an 18% interest in the business.

P12-4A Rudy Trump, Monica Rivers, and Courtney Jetta have formed a partnership. Trump invested $20,000; Rivers, $40,000; and Jetta, $60,000. Trump will manage the store, Rivers will work in the store three-quarters of the time, and Jetta will not work.

Computing partners' shares of net income and net loss (Obj. 3, 7)

Required

1. Compute the partners' shares of profits and losses under each of the following plans:
   a. Net income is $87,000, and the articles of partnership do not specify how profits and losses are shared.
   b. Net loss is $47,000, and the partnership agreement allocates 45% of profits to Trump, 35% to Rivers, and 20% to Jetta. The agreement does not discuss the sharing of losses.
   c. Net income is $104,000. The first $50,000 is allocated on the basis of salaries of $34,000 for Trump and $16,000 for Rivers. The remainder is allocated on the basis of partner capital contributions.
   d. Net income for the year ended September 30, 20X4, is $86,000. The first $30,000 is allocated on the basis of partner capital contributions. The next $30,000 is based on service, with $20,000 going to Trump and $10,000 going to Rivers. Any remainder is shared equally.
2. Revenues for the year ended September 30, 20X4, were $572,000, and expenses were $486,000. Under plan (d), prepare the partnership income statement for the year.

P12-5A Custom Homes is a partnership owned by three individuals. The partners share profits and losses in the ratio of 30% to Pam Tracy, 40% to Bill Mertz, and 30% to Cameron Brucks. At December 31, 20X3, the firm has the balance sheet shown at the top of page 494. Tracy withdraws from the partnership on this date.

Withdrawal of a partner (Obj. 4, 5)

Required

Record Tracy's withdrawal from the partnership under the following plans:

Cash		$ 25,000	Total liabilities		$103,000
Accounts receivable	$ 16,000				
Less allowance for					
uncollectibles	(1,000)	15,000			
Inventory		92,000	Tracy, capital		38,000
Equipment	130,000		Mertz, capital		49,000
Less accumulated			Brucks, capital		42,000
depreciation	(30,000)	100,000	Total liabilities and		
Total assets		$232,000	capital		$232,000

1. Tracy gives her interest in the business to Sally Schuster, her cousin.
2. In personal transactions, Tracy sells her equity in the partnership to Walt Fair and Beverly Holtz, who each pay Tracy $35,000 for half her interest. Mertz and Brucks agree to accept Fair and Holtz as partners.
3. The partnership pays Tracy cash of $9,000 and gives her a note payable for the remainder of her book equity in settlement of her partnership interest.
4. Tracy receives cash of $6,000 and a note payable for $34,000 from the partnership.
5. The partners agree that the equipment is worth $160,000 and that accumulated depreciation should remain at $30,000. After the revaluation, the partnership settles with Tracy by giving her cash of $15,000 and inventory for the remainder of her book equity.

Liquidation of a partnership
(Obj. 6)

P12-6A The partnership of Jackson, Pierce, & Fenner has experienced operating losses for three consecutive years. The partners—who have shared profits and losses in the ratio of Leigh Jackson, 15%; Trent Pierce, 60%; and Bruce Fenner, 25%—are considering the liquidation of the business. They ask you to analyze the effects of liquidation under various possibilities regarding the sale of the noncash assets. They present the following condensed partnership balance sheet at December 31, end of the current year:

Cash	$ 7,000	Liabilities	$ 63,000
Noncash assets	163,000	Jackson, capital	24,000
		Pierce, capital	66,000
		Fenner, capital	17,000
		Total liabilities and	
Total assets	$170,000	capital	$170,000

Required

1. Prepare a summary of liquidation transactions (as illustrated in Exhibit 12-4) for each of the following situations:
   a. The noncash assets are sold for $183,000.
   b. The noncash assets are sold for $141,000.
2. Make the journal entries to record the liquidation transactions in requirement 1(b).

Liquidation of a partnership
(Obj. 6)

P12-7A ◄ *Link Back to Chapter 4 (Closing Entries).* ABS & Company is a partnership owned by Alberts, Beech, and Sumner, who share profits and losses in the ratio of 1:3:4. The adjusted trial balance of the partnership (in condensed form) at June 30, end of the current fiscal year, follows.

ABS & COMPANY
Adjusted Trial Balance
June 30, 20XX

Cash	$ 24,000	
Noncash assets	116,000	
Liabilities		$100,000
Alberts, capital		22,000
Beech, capital		41,000
Sumner, capital		62,000
Alberts, drawing	14,000	
Beech, drawing	35,000	
Sumner, drawing	54,000	
Revenues		108,000
Expenses	90,000	
Totals	$333,000	$333,000

Required

1. Prepare the June 30 entries to close the revenue, expense, income summary, and drawing accounts.
2. Insert the opening capital balances in the partners' capital accounts, post the closing entries to the capital accounts, and determine each partner's ending capital balance.
3. The partnership liquidates on June 30 by selling the noncash assets for $105,000. Using the ending balances of the partners' capital accounts computed in requirement 2, prepare a summary of liquidation transactions (as illustrated in Exhibit 12-4).

Problems

(Group B)

P12-1B Anne Avonlee and Gus Teamley are discussing the formation of a partnership to install payroll accounting systems. Avonlee is skilled in systems design, and she is convinced that her designs will draw large sales volumes. Teamley is a super salesperson and has already lined up several clients.

Writing a partnership agreement (Obj. 1)

Required

Write a partnership agreement to cover all elements essential for the business to operate smoothly. Make up names, amounts, profit-and-loss-sharing percentages, and so on as needed.

P12-2B On June 30, Lou Busby and Marshall Box formed a partnership. The partners agreed to invest equal amounts of capital. Busby invested his proprietorship's assets and liabilities (credit balances in parentheses).

Investments by partners (Obj. 2, 7)

	Busby Book Value	Current Market Value
Accounts receivable	$ 7,200	$ 7,200
Allowance for doubtful accounts..........	(–0–)	(1,050)
Inventory..	22,340	24,100
Prepaid expenses	1,700	1,700
Office equipment	45,900	27,600
Accumulated depreciation....................	(15,300)	–0–
Accounts payable...................................	(19,100)	(19,100)

On June 30, Box invested cash in an amount equal to the current market value of Busby's partnership capital. The partners decided that Busby would earn two-thirds of partnership profits because he would manage the business. Box agreed to accept one-third of the profits. During the remainder of the year, the partnership earned net income of $75,000. Busby's drawings were $39,100, and Box's drawings were $31,000.

Required

1. Journalize the partners' initial investments.
2. Prepare the partnership balance sheet immediately after its formation on June 30.
3. Journalize the December 31 entries to close the Income Summary account and the partners' drawing accounts.

P12-3B Cedarlake Solutions is a partnership, and its owners are considering admitting Emily Conyers as a new partner. On March 31 of the current year, the capital accounts of the three existing partners and their shares of profits and losses are as follows:

Admitting a new partner (Obj. 4)

	Capital	Profit-and-Loss Share
Nick Nelson...............	$ 40,000	15%
Luke Bright	100,000	30
Lela Clapton..............	160,000	55

Required

Journalize the admission of Conyers as a partner on March 31 for each of the following independent situations:

1. Conyers pays Clapton $219,000 cash to purchase Clapton's interest in the partnership.
2. Conyers invests $60,000 in the partnership, acquiring a one-sixth interest in the business.
3. Conyers invests $80,000 in the partnership, acquiring a one-fourth interest in the business.
4. Conyers invests $50,000 in the partnership, acquiring a 12% interest in the business.

Computing partners' shares of
net income and net loss
(Obj. 3, 7)

P12-4B Charles Lake, Liz Wood, and Hal Parks have formed a partnership. Lake invested $15,000, Wood $18,000, and Parks $27,000. Lake will manage the store, Wood will work in the store half-time, and Parks will not work in the business.

Required

1. Compute the partners' shares of profits and losses under each of the following plans:
   a. Net loss is $42,900, and the articles of partnership do not specify how profits and losses are shared.
   b. Net loss is $60,000, and the partnership agreement allocates 40% of profits to Lake, 25% to Wood, and 35% to Parks. The agreement does not discuss the sharing of losses.
   c. Net income is $92,000. The first $40,000 is allocated on the basis of salaries, with Lake receiving $28,000 and Wood receiving $12,000. The remainder is allocated on the basis of partner capital contributions.
   d. Net income for the year ended January 31, 20X4, is $210,000. The first $75,000 is allocated on the basis of partner capital contributions, and the next $36,000 is based on service, with Lake receiving $28,000 and Wood receiving $8,000. Any remainder is shared equally.

2. Revenues for the year ended January 31, 20X4, were $870,000, and expenses were $660,000. Under plan (d), prepare the partnership income statement for the year.

P12-5B Priority Accounting Firm is a partnership owned by three individuals. The partners share profits and losses in the ratio of 28% to Cary Blesh, 38% to Dick McNut, and 34% to Jen Tate. At December 31, 20X2, the firm has the following balance sheet:

Cash		$ 12,000	Total liabilities	$ 75,000
Accounts receivable	$ 22,000			
Less allowance for uncollectibles	(4,000)	18,000		
Building	$310,000		Blesh, capital..............	83,000
Less accumulated			McNut, capital............	50,000
depreciation	(70,000)	240,000	Tate, capital	62,000
			Total liabilities and	
Total assets		$270,000	capital	$270,000

McNut withdraws from the partnership on December 31, 20X2, to establish his own consulting practice.

Required

Record McNut's withdrawal from the partnership under the following plans:

1. McNut gives his interest in the business to Rich Blynn, his nephew.
2. In personal transactions, McNut sells his equity in the partnership to Ashley Napper and Jim Lucks, who each pay McNut $40,000 for half his interest. Blesh and Tate agree to accept Napper and Lucks as partners.
3. The partnership pays McNut cash of $15,000 and gives him a note payable for the remainder of his book equity in settlement of his partnership interest.
4. McNut receives cash of $10,000 and a note for $70,000 from the partnership.
5. The partners agree that the building is worth only $250,000 and that its accumulated depreciation should remain at $70,000. After the revaluation, the partnership settles with McNut by giving him cash of $14,100 and a note payable for the remainder of his book equity.

P12-6B The partnership of Parr, Johnston, & Rake has experienced operating losses for three consecutive years. The partners—who have shared profits and losses in the ratio of Sharon Parr 10%; Alicia Johnston, 30%; and Chet Rake, 60%—are considering the liquidation of the business. They ask you to analyze the effects of liquidation under various possibilities regarding the sale of the noncash assets. They present the following condensed partnership balance sheet at December 31, end of the current year:

Cash	$ 27,000	Liabilities	$131,000
Noncash assets....................	202,000	Parr, capital..........................	21,000
		Johnston, capital	39,000
		Rake, capital	38,000
Total assets........................	$229,000	Total liabilities and capital ...	$229,000

Required

1. Prepare a summary of liquidation transactions (as illustrated in Exhibit 12-4) for each of the following situations:
   a. The noncash assets are sold for $208,000.
   b. The noncash assets are sold for $189,000.
2. Make the journal entries to record the liquidation transactions in requirement 1(b).

Liquidation of a partnership (Obj. 6)

P12-7B ◄ *Link Back to Chapter 4 (Closing Entries).* VT&P is a partnership owned by Vela, Thomas, and Prago, who share profits and losses in the ratio of 5:3:2. The adjusted trial balance of the partnership (in condensed form) at September 30, end of the current fiscal year, follows.

VT&P Adjusted Trial Balance September 30, 20XX		
Cash	$ 10,000	
Noncash assets	177,000	
Liabilities		$135,000
Vela, capital		57,000
Thomas, capital		44,000
Prago, capital		21,000
Vela, drawing	45,000	
Thomas, drawing	37,000	
Prago, drawing	18,000	
Revenues		211,000
Expenses	181,000	
Totals	$468,000	$468,000

Required

1. Prepare the September 30 entries to close the revenue, expense, income summary, and drawing accounts.
2. Insert the opening capital balances in the partner capital accounts, post the closing entries to the capital accounts, and determine each partner's ending capital balance.
3. The partnership liquidates on September 30 by selling the noncash assets for $147,000. Using the ending balances of the partner capital accounts computed in requirement 2, prepare a summary of liquidation transactions (as illustrated in Exhibit 12-4).

APPLY YOUR KNOWLEDGE

DECISION CASES

Settling disagreements among partners (Obj. 3)

Case 1. Kimberly Gardner invested $20,000 and Leah Johanssen invested $10,000 in a public relations firm that has operated for ten years. Neither partner has made an additional investment. Gardner and Johanssen have shared profits and losses in the ratio of 2:1, which is the ratio of their investments in the business. Gardner manages the office, supervises the 16 employees, and does the accounting. Johanssen, the moderator of a television talk show, is responsible for marketing. Her high profile generates important revenue for the business. During the year ended December 20X4, the partnership earned net income of $87,000, shared in the 2:1 ratio. On December 31, 20X4, Gardner's capital balance was $150,000, and Johanssen's capital balance was $100,000.

Required

Respond to each of the following situations.

1. What explains the difference between the ratio of partner capital balances at December 31, 20X4, and the 2:1 ratio of partner investments and profit sharing?
2. Johanssen believes that the profit-and-loss-sharing ratio is unfair. She proposes a change, but Gardner insists on keeping the 2:1 ratio. What two factors may underlie Johanssen's unhappiness?
3. During January 20X5, Gardner learned that revenues of $18,000 were omitted from the reported 20X4 income. She brings this omission to Johanssen's attention, pointing out that Gardner's share of this added income is two-thirds, or $12,000, and Johanssen's share is one-third, or $6,000. Johanssen believes that they should share this added income on the basis of their capital balances—60%, or $10,800, to Gardner and 40%, or $7,200, to herself. Which partner is correct? Why?

4. Assume that the 20X4 $18,000 omission was an account payable for an operating expense. On what basis would the partners share this amount?

Case 2. The following questions relate to issues faced by partnerships.

1. The text suggests that a written partnership agreement should be drawn up between the partners in a partnership. One benefit of an agreement is that it provides a mechanism for resolving disputes between the partners. List five areas of dispute that might be resolved by a partnership agreement.
2. The statement has been made that "if you must take on a partner, make sure the partner is richer than you are." Why is this statement valid?
3. Corwin & Corwin is a law partnership. Natalie Corwin is planning to retire from the partnership and move to Israel. What options are available to Corwin to enable her to convert her share of the partnership assets to cash?

ETHICAL ISSUE

Tracy Wynn and Lee Spitz operate New England Engraving in Portsmouth, New Hampshire. The partners split profits and losses equally, and each takes an annual salary of $80,000. To even out the workload, Spitz does the buying and Wynn serves as the accountant. From time to time, they use small amounts of store merchandise for personal use. In preparing for her daughter's wedding, Wynn took engraved invitations and other goods that cost $2,700. She recorded the transaction as follows:

Cost of Goods Sold	2,700	
Inventory		2,700

1. How should Wynn have recorded this transaction?
2. Discuss the ethical dimensions of Wynn's action.

FINANCIAL STATEMENT CASE

KPMG is an international accounting firm. Summary data from the partnership's *19X7 Annual Report* follow:

(Dollars in millions except where indicated)	Years Ended June 30				
	19X7	19X6	19X5	19X4	19X3
Revenues					
Assurance	$1,234	$1,122	$1,064	$1,093	$1,070
Consulting	1,007	775	658	473	349
Tax	743	628	567	515	557
Total Revenues	$2,984	$2,525	$2,289	$2,081	$1,976
Operating Summary					
Revenues	$2,984	$2,525	$2,289	$2,081	$1,976
Personnel Costs	1,215	1,004	887	805	726
Other Costs	1,212	1,030	967	898	829
Income to Partners	$ 557	$ 491	$ 435	$ 378	$ 421
Statistical Data					
Average Number of Partners	1,494	1,428	1,413	1,449	1,453

Required

1. What percentages of total revenues did KPMG earn by performing assurance services (similar to audit), consulting services, and tax services during 19X3? What were the percentages in 19X7? Which type of services grew the most from 19X3 to 19X7?
2. Compute the average revenue per partner in 19X7.
3. How much net income did each KPMG partner earn, on average, in 19X7?

TEAM PROJECT

Visit a business partnership in your area, and interview one or more of the partners. Obtain answers to the following questions and ask your instructor for directions. As directed by your instructor, either (a) prepare a written report of your findings, or (b) make a presentation to your class.

Required

1. Why did you organize the business as a partnership? What advantages does the partnership form of organization offer the business? What are the disadvantages of the partnership form of organization?
2. Is the business a general partnership, or is it a limited partnership?
3. Do the partners have a written partnership agreement? What does the agreement cover? Obtain a copy if possible.
4. Who manages the business? Do all partners participate in day-to-day management, or is management the responsibility of only certain partners?
5. If there is no written agreement, what is the mechanism for making key decisions?
6. Have you ever admitted a new partner? If so, when? What are the partnership's procedures for admitting a new partner?
7. Has a partner ever withdrawn from the business? If so, when? What are the partnership's procedures for settling up with a withdrawing partner?
8. If possible, learn how the partnership divides profits and losses among the partners.
9. Ask for any additional insights the partner you interview can provide about the business.

INTERNET EXERCISE

Arthur Andersen LLP

Arthur Andersen LLP is a limited liability partnership and one of the most respected accounting/consulting firms in the world. Since 1913, Arthur Andersen has offered accounting and business solutions and helped companies view change as an opportunity to learn, think, see, and leap ahead.

1. Go to **http://www.arthurandersen.com** and watch the video. Click on *About Us*. What does Arthur Andersen LLP do to stay ahead of its competitors?
2. Under "Our Scorecard" click on *facts*. For the most recent years, Arthur Andersen LLP reported how much in revenue? Information is available on the revenues of the company, but the entire set of financial statements is not publicly available. Why not? Does Arthur Andersen LLP pay income tax? Are the partners of a limited liability partnership personally liable for the debts of the partnership?
3. Click on *Careers*. Arthur Andersen LLP provides services in how many different countries?
4. Arthur Andersen, the founder of the company, was a university professor and recruited the brightest students into his classes. He helped his students understand how to improve financial performance. Click on "start your career *here*." What characteristics is Arthur Andersen LLP currently looking for in an employee?
5. Click on *Words of Wisdom*. What words of wisdom does Arthur Andersen LLP offer?

13 Corporations: Paid-in Capital and the Balance Sheet

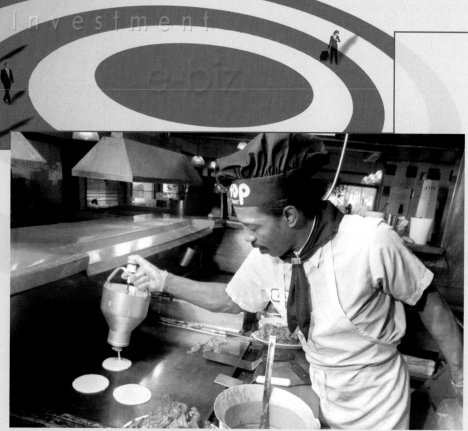

LEARNING OBJECTIVES

After studying this chapter, you should be able to

1. Identify the characteristics of a corporation

2. Record the issuance of stock

3. Prepare the stockholders' equity section of a corporation's balance sheet

4. Account for cash dividends

5. Use different stock values in decision making

6. Evaluate a company's return on assets and return on stockholders' equity

7. Account for the income tax of a corporation

Initial public offerings of stock, or IPOs as they are called, reached new highs during the late 1990s. Consider what happened to this well-known company.

IHOP Corporation operates International House of Pancakes restaurants throughout the United States and in several foreign countries. IHOP serves pancakes, sandwiches, and other casual food along the interstate highway system. The restaurant chain caters to college students and families, with late hours and reasonable prices.

IHOP began as a small company in Glendale, California. To spur growth, IHOP *went public*. This means that IHOP offered its stock to anyone who would buy it. The initial public offering of IHOP's stock was fairly successful. The company offered to sell 6.2 million shares of its stock for $10 per share. As it turned out, investors bought only 3.2 million shares. IHOP thus received $32 million (3.2 million $\times$ $10), which the company then invested to open new restaurants and upgrade old ones.

This chapter covers the issuance of stock by large corporations such as IHOP. Any company—large or small—can sell (issue) its stock to investors. All companies issue their stock for the same reasons: to raise money (cash), to obtain assets such as land and buildings, or to pay off debt. Now let's explore how corporations differ from the proprietorships and partnerships we have been studying.

CORPORATIONS: AN OVERVIEW

Objective 1
Identify the characteristics of a corporation

The corporation is the dominant form of business organization in the United States. **IHOP** is one example. Proprietorships and partnerships are more numerous, but corporations transact more business and are larger in terms of total assets and sales revenue. Most well-known companies, such as **Target** and **Intel,** are corporations. Their full names include *Corporation* or *Incorporated* (abbreviated *Corp.* and *Inc.*) to show that they are corporations—for example, Target Corporation and **Nike, Inc.**

Characteristics of a Corporation

What makes the corporate form of organization so attractive? We now examine how corporations differ from proprietorships and partnerships and the advantages and disadvantages of corporations.

SEPARATE LEGAL ENTITY   A corporation is a business entity formed under state law. The state grants a **charter,** a document that gives a business the state's permission to form a corporation. Neither a proprietorship nor a partnership requires a charter, because in the eyes of the law the business is the same as the owner(s).

From a legal perspective, a corporation is a totally separate entity from its owners, who are called **stockholders** or **shareholders.** The corporation has many of the rights that a person has. For example, a corporation may buy, own, and sell property. The assets and liabilities of IHOP belong to the corporation rather than to its owners. The corporation may enter into contracts, sue, and be sued. If IHOP accidentally serves contaminated food and customers get sick, they may sue IHOP.

CONTINUOUS LIFE AND TRANSFERABILITY OF OWNERSHIP   The owners' equity of a corporation is divided into shares of **stock.** Most corporations have *continuous lives* regardless of changes in the ownership of their stock. The stockholders of IHOP or any corporation may sell or trade the stock to another person, give it away, or bequeath it in a will. The transfer of the stock does not affect the continuity of the corporation. In contrast, proprietorships and partnerships terminate when their ownership changes.

NO MUTUAL AGENCY   *Mutual agency* means that all owners act as agents of the business. A contract signed by one owner is binding for the whole company.

CHARTER. Document that gives the state's permission to form a corporation.

STOCKHOLDER. A person who owns the stock of a corporation. Also called **shareholder.**

STOCK. Shares into which the owners' equity of a corporation is divided.

⇒ We introduced the idea of mutual agency for partnerships in Chapter 12, page 466.

Mutual agency operates in partnerships but *not* in corporations. ⇐ A stockholder of IHOP Corp. cannot commit the corporation to a contract (unless he or she is also an officer in the business).

LIMITED LIABILITY. No personal obligation of a stockholder for corporation debts. A stockholder can lose no more on an investment in a corporation's stock than the cost of the investment.

LIMITED STOCKHOLDER LIABILITY   Stockholders have **limited liability** for corporation debts. That means they have no personal obligation for corporation liabilities. The most that a stockholder can lose on an investment in a corporation is the amount invested. In contrast, proprietors and partners are personally liable for all the debts of their businesses.

The combination of limited liability and no mutual agency means that persons can invest in a corporation without fear of losing all their personal wealth if the business fails. This feature enables a corporation to raise more money from a wider group of investors than proprietorships and partnerships can.

SEPARATION OF OWNERSHIP AND MANAGEMENT   Stockholders own the business, but a *board of directors*—elected by the stockholders—appoints the officers to manage the business. Stockholders may invest $1,000 or $1 million in the corporation without having to manage the business or disrupt their personal affairs.

Management's goal is to maximize the firm's value for the benefit of the stockholders. However, the separation between the owners—stockholders—and management can create problems. Corporate officers may decide to run the business for their own benefit and not for the stockholders. The distance between the stockholders and management may make it difficult for stockholders to protest bad management. How else can stockholders protest? They can sell their stock in that corporation.

CORPORATE TAXATION   Corporations are separate taxable entities. They pay several taxes not borne by proprietorships or partnerships, including an annual franchise tax levied by the state. The franchise tax keeps the corporate charter in force and enables the corporation to continue in business. Corporations also pay federal and state income taxes just as individuals do.

DOUBLE TAXATION. Corporations pay their own income taxes on corporate income. Then, the stockholders pay personal income tax on the cash dividends they receive from corporations.

Corporate earnings are subject to **double taxation.** First, corporations pay income taxes on corporate income. Then, stockholders pay personal income tax on the cash dividends they receive from corporations. Proprietorships and partnerships pay no business income tax. Instead, the tax falls solely on the owners.

GOVERNMENT REGULATION   As we have seen, stockholders have only limited liability for corporation debts. Outsiders can look no further than the corporation for any claims that may arise against the business. To protect persons who do business with the corporation, both federal agencies and the states monitor corporations. This *government regulation* consists mainly of ensuring that corporations disclose adequate information for investors and creditors.

Exhibit 13-1 summarizes the advantages and disadvantages of the corporate form of business organization.

⊙ DAILY EXERCISE 13-1

EXHIBIT 13-1
Advantages and Disadvantages of a Corporation

Advantages	Disadvantages
1. Can raise more money than a proprietorship or partnership	1. Separation of ownership and management
2. Continuous life	2. Corporate taxation
3. Easy transfer of ownership	3. Government regulation
4. No mutual agency of the stockholders	
5. Limited liability of the stockholders	

Organizing a Corporation

AUTHORIZATION OF STOCK. Provision in a corporate charter that gives the state's permission for the corporation to issue—that is, to sell—a certain number of shares of stock.

The process of creating a corporation begins when its organizers, called the *incorporators,* obtain a charter from the state. The charter includes the **authorization** for the corporation to issue a certain number of shares of stock for the ownership in the corporation. The incorporators pay fees, sign the charter, and file documents with the state. The corporation then becomes a legal entity. The stockholders agree to a set of **bylaws,** which act as the constitution for the corporation.

Ultimate control of the corporation rests with the stockholders. The stockholders elect the **board of directors,** which sets policy and appoints the officers. The board elects a **chairperson,** who is the most powerful person in the corporation. The board also designates the **president,** who is in charge of day-to-day operations. Most corporations also have vice presidents of sales, manufacturing, accounting and finance, and other key areas. The president and one or more vice presidents are usually elected to the board of directors. Exhibit 13-2 shows the authority structure in a corporation.

BYLAWS. Constitution for governing a corporation.

BOARD OF DIRECTORS. Group elected by the stockholders to set policy and to appoint the officers.

CHAIRPERSON. Elected by a corporation's board of directors, the most powerful person in the corporation.

EXHIBIT 13-2 **Authority Structure in a Corporation**

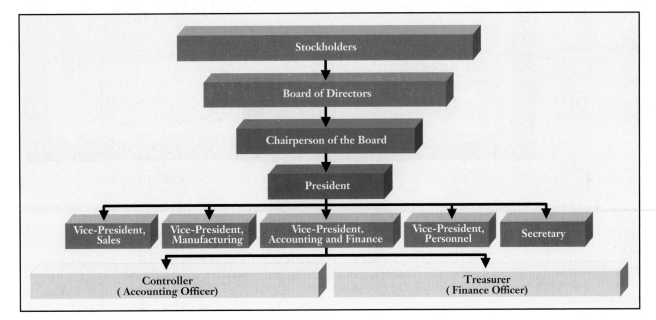

Capital Stock

A corporation issues *stock certificates* to its owners when they invest in the business. The stock represents the corporation's capital, so it is called *capital stock*. The basic unit of stock is a *share*. A corporation may issue a stock certificate for any number of shares—1, 100, or any other number—but the total number of *authorized* shares is limited by charter. Exhibit 13-3, at the top of the next page, depicts an actual stock certificate for 288 shares of **Central Jersey Bancorp** common stock. The certificate shows the company's name, the stockholder's name, the number of shares, and the par value of the stock (discussed later in this chapter).

Stock that is held by a stockholder is said to be **outstanding.** The total shares of stock outstanding represent 100% ownership of the corporation.

STOCKHOLDERS' EQUITY: THE BASICS

The balance sheet of a corporation reports assets and liabilities in the same way as a proprietorship or a partnership. However, the owners' equity of a corporation—called **stockholders' equity**—is reported differently. State laws require corporations to report the sources of their capital. The two basic sources of capital are

- **Paid-in capital** (also called **contributed capital**) represents stockholder investments in the corporation.
- **Retained earnings** is capital that the corporation has earned through profitable operations.

PRESIDENT. Chief operating officer in charge of managing the day-to-day operations of a corporation.

 DAILY EXERCISE 13-2

OUTSTANDING STOCK. Stock in the hands of of stockholders.

STOCKHOLDERS' EQUITY. Owners' equity of a corporation.

PAID-IN CAPITAL. A corporation's capital from investments by the stockholders. Also called **contributed capital.**

RETAINED EARNINGS. A corporation's capital that is earned through profitable operation of the business.

EXHIBIT 13-3 Stock Certificate

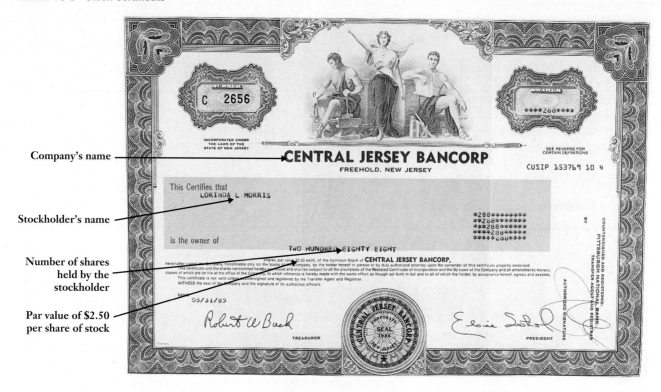

Company's name

Stockholder's name

Number of shares held by the stockholder

Par value of $2.50 per share of stock

Exhibit 13-4 outlines a summarized version of the balance sheet of **Target Corporation** to show how to report these categories of stockholders' equity.

EXHIBIT 13-4
Summarized Balance
Sheet of Target Corporation
(Amounts in Millions)

 DAILY EXERCISE 13-3

Assets	$17,143	Liabilities................................	$11,281
		Stockholders' Equity	
		Paid-in capital:	
		Common stock...............	806
		Retained earnings..............	5,056
		Total stockholders' equity...	5,862
		Total liabilities and	
Total assets	$17,143	stockholders' equity	$17,143

Paid-in Capital Is Received from the Stockholders

COMMON STOCK. The basic form of capital stock. In a corporation, the common stockholders are the owners of the business.

Common stock is paid-in capital because it comes from the stockholders. Target's entry to record the receipt of $20,000 cash and the issuance of Target stock is

Oct. 20	Cash	20,000	
	Common Stock..............		20,000
	Issued stock.		

This entry illustrates the fact that the issuance of stock increases both the assets and the stockholders' equity of the corporation.

Retained Earnings Are Earned from the Customers

Profitable operations generate income for the corporation, and income increases stockholders' equity through a separate account called Retained Earnings. At the end of the year, the balance of the Income Summary account (a net income or a net loss) is closed to Retained Earnings. For example, if Target's net income is $1,200 million, Income Summary will have a $1,200 million credit balance (see the T-account on p. 505). Target's closing entry will debit Income Summary to close that account. The credit side of the closing entry transfers net income to Retained

Earnings as follows (in millions of dollars):

Jan. 31 Income Summary 1,200
            Retained Earnings...   1,200
            To close *net income* to Retained Earnings.

INCOME SUMMARY			RETAINED EARNINGS		
Closing	**1,200**	Net income 1,200		**Closing**	**1,200**
		Balance -0-			

The T-accounts show that net income winds up in the Retained Earnings account.

If operations produce a net *loss* rather than net income, the Income Summary account will have a debit balance. To close a $60,000 loss, the closing entry credits Income Summary and debits Retained Earnings as follows:

Dec. 31 Retained Earnings... 60,000
            Income Summary...................................   60,000
            To close *net loss* to Retained Earnings.

Prepare a T-account for Income Summary to show its debit balance of $60,000. Also prepare a T-account for Retained Earnings (no balance yet). Then post the $60,000 closing entry and take the balance for Income Summary and Retained Earnings. Where does the net loss of $60,000 end up?

Answer:

INCOME SUMMARY				RETAINED EARNINGS		
Net loss	**60,000**	**Closing**	**60,000**	**Closing**	**60,000**	
Balance	**-0-**					

A large loss may cause a debit balance in the Retained Earnings account. This condition—called a Retained Earnings **deficit**—is reported on the balance sheet as a negative amount in stockholders' equity. **HAL, Inc.**, which owns Hawaiian Airlines, Inc., reported this deficit:

DEFICIT. Debit balance in the Retained Earnings account.

Stockholders' Equity	(In Millions)
Paid-in capital: Common stock..............	$ 50
Deficit..	(193)
Total stockholders' equity......................	$(143)

HAL's deficit was so large that it produced a negative amount of stockholders' equity. This situation is unusual for a going concern.

Corporations May Pay Dividends to the Stockholders

If the corporation has been profitable and has sufficient cash, it may distribute cash to the stockholders. Such distributions—called **dividends**—are similar to a proprietor's withdrawal of cash from a business or by a partner from a partnership. Dividends decrease both the assets and the retained earnings of the business. Most states prohibit using paid-in capital for dividends. Accountants use the term **legal capital** to refer to the portion of stockholders' equity that *cannot* be used for dividends.

DIVIDENDS. Distributions by a corporation to its stockholders.

LEGAL CAPITAL. The portion of stockholders' equity that cannot be used for dividends.

Some people think of Retained Earnings as a fund of cash. It is not, because Retained Earnings is an element of stockholders' equity. *Remember that cash dividends are paid out of assets, not out of retained earnings.*

Stockholders' Rights

The ownership of stock entitles stockholders to four basic rights, unless specific rights are withheld by agreement with the stockholders:

1. *Vote.* Stockholders participate in management by voting on matters that come before them. This is a stockholder's sole right to manage the corporation. Each share of stock carries one vote.
2. *Dividends.* Stockholders receive a proportionate part of any dividend. Each share of stock receives an equal dividend with every other share of the same class.
3. *Liquidation.* Stockholders receive their proportionate share of any assets remaining after the corporation pays its liabilities in liquidation (goes out of business).
4. *Preemption.* Stockholders can maintain their proportionate ownership in the corporation. Suppose you own 5% of a corporation's stock. If the corporation issues 100,000 new shares of stock, it must offer you the opportunity to buy 5% (5,000) of the new shares. This right, called the *preemptive right,* is usually withheld from the stockholders.

Classes of Stock

Corporations issue different types of stock. The stock of a corporation may be either common or preferred and either par or no-par.

PREFERRED STOCK. Stock that gives its owners certain advantages over common stockholders, such as the right to receive dividends before the common stockholders and the right to receive assets before the common stockholders if the corporation liquidates.

COMMON AND PREFERRED STOCK   Every corporation issues *common stock,* the basic form of capital stock. Unless designated otherwise, the word *stock* is understood to mean "common stock." Common stockholders have the four basic rights of stock ownership, unless a right is specifically withheld. For example, some companies issue Class A common stock, which carries the right to vote. They may also issue Class B common stock, which may be nonvoting. (Classes of common stock may also be designated Series A, Series B, and so on.) There is a separate account for each class of stock.

Investors who buy common stock take the ultimate risk with a corporation. The corporation makes no promises to pay them. If the corporation succeeds, it will pay dividends to its stockholders, but if net income and cash are too low, stockholders may receive no dividends. The stock of successful corporations increases in value, and investors may sell the stock at a gain. But stock prices can decrease, leaving the investors holding worthless stock. Because common stockholders take a risk, they demand increases in stock prices, high dividends, or both. If the corporation does not deliver, the stockholders sell the stock.

Preferred stock gives its owners certain advantages over common stockholders. These benefits include the right to receive dividends before the common stockholders and the right to receive assets before the common stockholders if the corporation liquidates. Corporations pay a fixed amount of dividends on preferred stock. Investors usually buy preferred stock to earn those fixed dividends.

Owners of preferred stock also have the four basic stockholder rights, unless a right is specifically denied. The right to vote may be withheld from preferred stockholders. Companies may issue different classes of preferred stock (Class A and Class B or Series A and Series B, for example). Each class of stock is recorded in a separate account. Preferred stock is rarer than you might think. A recent survey of 600 corporations revealed that only 99 of them (16.5%) had some preferred stock outstanding (Exhibit 13-5).

All corporations have common stock. Exhibit 13-6 summarizes the similarities and differences among common stock, preferred stock, and long-term debt.

EXHIBIT 13-5
Preferred Stock

EXHIBIT 13-6
Comparison of Common Stock, Preferred Stock, and Long-Term Debt

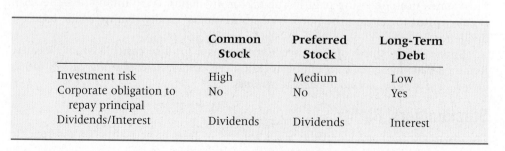

	Common Stock	Preferred Stock	Long-Term Debt
Investment risk	High	Medium	Low
Corporate obligation to repay principal	No	No	Yes
Dividends/Interest	Dividends	Dividends	Interest

PAR VALUE, STATED VALUE, AND NO-PAR STOCK   Stock may be par-value stock or no-par stock. **Par value** is an arbitrary amount assigned by a company to a share of its stock. Most companies set the par value of their common stock quite low to avoid legal difficulties from issuing their stock below par. Most states require companies to maintain a minimum amount of stockholders' equity for the protection of creditors, and this minimum represents the corporation's legal capital. For corporations with par-value stock, *legal capital* is usually the par value of the shares issued.

The common stock par value of **Oracle Corporation,** the software giant, is $0.01 (1 cent) per share. **Pier 1 Imports'** common carries a par value of $1 per share. Par value of preferred stock is often higher; some preferred stocks have par values of $25 and $100. Par value is used to compute dividends on preferred stock, as we shall see.

No-par stock does not have par value. **Kimberly Clark** has 20 million shares of preferred stock authorized with no par value. But some no-par stock has a **stated value,** which makes it similar to par-value stock. The stated value is an arbitrary amount that accountants treat as though it were par value.

PAR VALUE. Arbitrary amount assigned to a share of stock.

 DAILY EXERCISE 13-4

STATED VALUE. An arbitrary amount that accountants treat as though it were par value.

ISSUING STOCK

Objective 2
Record the issuance of stock

Large corporations such as **Hewlett-Packard, Coca-Cola,** and **British Petroleum Amoco** need huge quantities of money to operate. They cannot finance all their operations through borrowing. They need capital that they raise by issuing stock. Corporations may sell the stock directly to stockholders or use the services of an *underwriter,* such as the brokerage firms **Merrill Lynch** and **Morgan Stanley, Dean Witter.** An underwriter agrees to buy all the stock it cannot sell to its clients.

The price that the corporation receives from issuance of its stock is called the *issue price.* Often, the issue price far exceeds the stock's par value because the par value is intentionally set quite low. The company's profits, financial position, and future prospects determine the issue price. Investors will pay no more than market value for the stock. In the following sections, we show how to account for the issuance of stock.

Issuing Common Stock

Companies advertise their stock to attract investors. The *Wall Street Journal* is the most popular medium for the advertisements. They are called *tombstones.* Exhibit 13-7 at the top of page 508 is a reproduction of IHOP's tombstone, which appeared in the *Wall Street Journal.*

The lead underwriter of **IHOP's** public offering was **The First Boston Corporation.** Other brokerage firms and investment bankers also sold IHOP's stock to their clients. IHOP's tombstone shows that IHOP hoped to raise approximately $62 million of capital. But in the final analysis, IHOP issued only 3.2 million of the shares and received cash of approximately $32 million.

COMMON STOCK AT PAR   Suppose IHOP's common stock carried a par value of $10 per share. The stock issuance entry of 3.2 million shares would be

Jan. 31	Cash (3,200,000 × $10)	32,000,000
	Common Stock........................	32,000,000
	Issued common stock at par.	

COMMON STOCK AT A PREMIUM   Most corporations set par value low and issue common stock for a price above par value. The amount above par is called a *premium.* IHOP's common stock has an actual par value of $0.01 (1 cent) per share. The $9.99 difference between issue price ($10) and par value ($0.01) is a premium. This sale of stock increases the corporation's paid-in capital by the full $10, the total issue price of the stock.

A premium on the sale of stock is not gain, income, or profit to the corporation, because the entity is dealing with its own stockholders. This situation illustrates one of the fundamentals of accounting: *A company neither earns a profit nor incurs a loss when it sells its stock to, or buys its stock from, its own stockholders.*

EXHIBIT 13-7   Announcement of Public Offering of IHOP Stock (Partial)

Number of shares offered to the public

Company issuing the stock

Class of stock

Par value per share

Issue price—the amount per share that IHOP received for the stock

Lead U.S. underwriter

Lead foreign underwriter

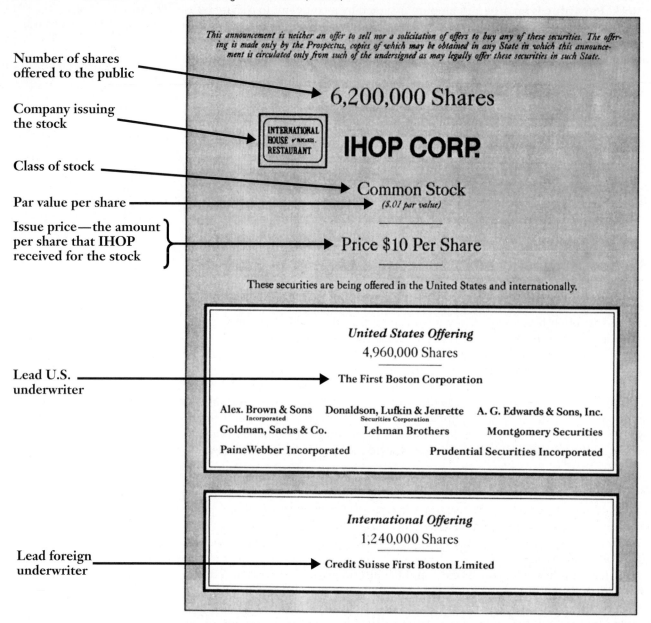

This announcement is neither an offer to sell nor a solicitation of offers to buy any of these securities. The offering is made only by the Prospectus, copies of which may be obtained in any State in which this announcement is circulated only from such of the undersigned as may legally offer these securities in such State.

6,200,000 Shares

IHOP CORP.

Common Stock
($.01 par value)

Price $10 Per Share

These securities are being offered in the United States and internationally.

United States Offering
4,960,000 Shares

The First Boston Corporation

Alex. Brown & Sons
Incorporated

Donaldson, Lufkin & Jenrette
Securities Corporation

A. G. Edwards & Sons, Inc.

Goldman, Sachs & Co.

Lehman Brothers

Montgomery Securities

PaineWebber Incorporated

Prudential Securities Incorporated

International Offering
1,240,000 Shares

Credit Suisse First Boston Limited

WORK IT OUT

Prepare IHOP's classified balance sheet immediately after this issuance of stock. Assume zero balances prior to the transaction.

Answer

IHOP CORPORATION
Balance Sheet
January 31, 20XX

Assets		Liabilities	
Current:			
Cash..............................	$32,000,000	No liabilities..................	0
		Stockholders' Equity	
		Common stock..............	$32,000,000
		Total liabilities and	
Total assets..................	$32,000,000	stockholders' equity..	$32,000,000

With a par value of $0.01, IHOP's entry to record the issuance of the stock is

July 31	Cash (3,200,000 × $10)..	32,000,000	
	Common Stock (3,200,000 × $0.01)		32,000
	Paid-in Capital in Excess of Par—		
	Common (3,200,000 × $9.99)		31,968,000
	Issued common stock at a premium.		

 DAILY EXERCISE 13-5

Account titles that could be used in place of Paid-in Capital in Excess of Par—Common are *Additional Paid-in Capital—Common* and *Premium on Common Stock*. Since both par value and premium amounts increase the corporation's capital, they appear in the stockholders' equity section of the balance sheet.

At the end of the year, IHOP Corp. would report stockholders' equity on its balance sheet as follows, assuming that the corporate charter authorizes 40,000,000 shares of common stock and the balance of retained earnings is $26,000,000.

Stockholders' Equity	
Paid-in capital:	
Common stock, $0.01 par, 40 million shares	
authorized, 3.2 million shares issued	$ 32,000
Paid-in capital in excess of par	31,968,000
Total paid-in capital	32,000,000
Retained earnings	26,000,000
Total stockholders' equity	$58,000,000

DAILY EXERCISE 13-6

DAILY EXERCISE 13-7

We determine the dollar amount reported for common stock by multiplying the total number of shares *issued* (3.2 million) by the par value per share ($0.01). The *authorization* reports the maximum number of shares of stock the company may issue under its charter.

All transactions recorded in this section include a receipt of cash by the corporation as it issues new stock to stockholders. These transactions are different from

e-Accounting

UPS Delivers the Dough at Record-Breaking IPO

If you want stock in a company that operates in the global electronic marketplace, what comes to mind? Pioneering dot.coms like **Amazon.com** or **eBay**? Think again. There's a 97-year-old business whose workers drive old-fashioned brown trucks and run parcels up to your door. **United Parcel Service (UPS)** is a business as traditional as apple pie. UPS raised a record-breaking $5.5 billion at its IPO (initial public offering) when it went public. All this money came from investors who saw UPS as a sign of the new economy.

Why would UPS sell its stock to the public? To build a cross-border, USA/European infrastructure, UPS figured it would need to acquire and merge with foreign firms. That required a lot of money. During the first hours of trading in UPS stock, the company's share price soared 40%. By the end of a week, the UPS workforce included 10,000 new millionaires.

Source: Based on Avital Louria Hahn, "Men in brown: A growth story—UPS recasts itself for IPO," *The Investment Dealers' Digest: IDD*, December 13, 1999, p. 35. Elise Ackerman, "UPS delivers as IPO investors give the world's no. 1 package-delivery company full dot-com treatment," *U.S. News & World Report*, November 22, 1999, p. 53. Jenny Anderson, "Up, UPS and away," *Institutional Investor*, January 2000, pp. 96–98.

the vast majority of stock transactions reported each day in the financial press. In those transactions, one stockholder sells his or her stock to another investor, and the corporation makes no formal journal entry because its paid-in capital is unchanged.

NO-PAR COMMON STOCK   When a company issues stock that has no par value, there can be no premium. A recent survey of 600 companies revealed 59 issues of no-par stock.

When a company issues no-par stock, it debits the asset received and credits the stock account. Glenwood Corporation, which manufactures ski equipment, issues 4,000 shares of no-par common stock for $20 per share. The stock issuance entry is

Aug. 14	Cash (4,000 × $20)	80,000	
	Common Stock		80,000
	Issued no-par common stock.		

Regardless of the stock's price, Cash is debited and Common Stock is credited for the cash received. There is no Paid-in Capital in Excess of Par for no-par stock.

Glenwood Corporation's charter authorizes Glenwood to issue 10,000 shares of no-par stock, and the company has $151,000 in retained earnings. The corporation reports stockholders' equity on the balance sheet as follows:

Stockholders' Equity	
Paid-in capital:	
Common stock, no par, 10,000 shares authorized, 4,000 shares issued	$ 80,000
Retained earnings	151,000
Total stockholders' equity	$231,000

DAILY EXERCISE 13-8

NO-PAR COMMON STOCK WITH A STATED VALUE   Accounting for no-par stock with a stated value is identical to accounting for par-value stock. The premium account for no-par common stock with a stated value is Paid-in Capital in Excess of *Stated Value*—Common.

COMMON STOCK FOR ASSETS OTHER THAN CASH   When a corporation issues stock and receives assets other than cash, it records the assets received at their current market value and credits the capital accounts accordingly. The assets' prior book value is irrelevant because the stockholder will demand stock equal to the market value of the asset given. Kahn Corporation issued 15,000 shares of its $1 par common stock for equipment worth $4,000 and a building worth $120,000. Kahn's entry is

Nov. 30	Equipment	4,000	
	Building	120,000	
	Common Stock (15,000 × $1)		15,000
	Paid-in Capital in Excess of Par—		
	Common ($124,000 − $15,000)		109,000
	Issued common stock in exchange for equipment and a building.		

WORK IT OUT   Prepare the stockholders' equity section of Kahn's balance sheet immediately after this transaction. Before this issuance of stock, Kahn already had outstanding 10,000 shares of common stock that the company had issued for $8 per share. Kahn's corporate charter authorizes the issuance of 100,000 shares of common stock. Retained earnings is $519,000 and liabilities total $622,000.

Answer

Stockholders' Equity

Paid-in capital:
Common stock, $1 par, 100,000 shares authorized,
    25,000 (10,000 + 15,000) shares issued .... $ 25,000
Paid-in capital in excess of par ($70,000* + $109,000) 179,000
    Total paid-in capital 204,000
Retained earnings 519,000
Total stockholders' equity $723,000

*10,000 shares $\times$ ($8 − $1 par) = $70,000

Issuing Preferred Stock

Accounting for preferred stock follows the pattern illustrated for common stock. **Chiquita Brands International, Inc.,** famous for its bananas, has some preferred stock outstanding. Assume Chiquita issued 110,887 shares of preferred stock at par value of $1 per share. The issuance entry is

July 31	Cash	110,887	
	Preferred Stock (110,887 shares $\times$ $1)		110,887
	Issued preferred stock at par.		

If Chiquita had issued the preferred stock at a premium, the entry would have credited Paid-in Capital in Excess of Par—Preferred for the excess over par value. A corporation lists separate accounts for Paid-in Capital in Excess of Par on Preferred Stock and on Common Stock to differentiate the two classes of equity. The balance sheet then lists preferred stock, common stock, and retained earnings, in that order.

Ethical Considerations in Accounting for the Issuance of Stock

Issuance of stock for *cash* poses no ethical challenge. The company receives cash and issues stock, giving the stockholders certificates as evidence of their ownership.

Issuing stock for assets other than cash can pose an ethical challenge. The company issuing the stock often wishes to record a large amount for the asset received (such as land or a building) and for the stock being issued. Why? Because large asset and equity amounts make the business look prosperous and creditworthy. The motivation to look good can inject a subtle bias into the amount recorded for the assets received and the stock issued.

A company is supposed to record an asset received at its current market value. But one person's evaluation of a building can differ from another person's valuation. One person may appraise the building at a market value of $4 million. Another may honestly believe it is worth only $3 million. A company receiving the building in exchange for its stock must decide whether to record the building received and the stock issued at $3 million, $4 million, or some other amount.

The ethical course of action is to record the asset at its current fair market value, as determined by a good-faith estimate of market value from independent appraisers. It is rare for a public corporation to be found guilty of *understating* the asset values on its balance sheet, but companies have been embarrassed by *overstating* their asset values. Investors who rely on the financial statements may be able to prove that an overstatement of asset values caused them to pay too much for the company's stock. In that case, a court of law may render a judgment against the company. So companies tend to value assets conservatively (that is, on the low side) in order to avoid an overstatement of their book value.

Review of Accounting for Paid-in Capital

Let's review the first half of this chapter by showing the stockholders' equity section of MedTech.com Corporation's balance sheet in Exhibit 13-8 on page 512.

| Objective 3
Prepare the stockholders' equity section of a corporation's balance sheet

511

EXHIBIT 13-8

Part of MedTech.com
Corporation's Balance Sheet

DAILY EXERCISE 13-10

DAILY EXERCISE 13-11

DAILY EXERCISE 13-12

Stockholders' Equity

Paid-in capital:		
Preferred stock, 5%, $100 par, 5,000 shares		
authorized, 400 shares issued		$ 40,000
Paid-in capital in excess of par—preferred................		14,000
Common stock, $10 par, 20,000 shares		
authorized, 4,500 shares issued		45,000
Paid-in capital in excess of par—common		72,000
Total paid-in capital...		171,000
Retained earnings...		85,000
Total stockholders' equity..		$256,000

Note the two sections of stockholders' equity: paid-in capital and retained earnings. Also observe the order of the equity accounts:

- Preferred stock at par value
- Paid-in capital in excess of par—preferred
- Common stock at par value
- Paid-in capital in excess of par—common
- Retained earnings (after the paid-in capital accounts)

ADDITIONAL PAID-IN CAPITAL. The paid-in capital in excess of par—common plus other accounts combined for reporting on the balance sheet.

Many companies combine several accounts, including Paid-in Capital in Excess of Par—Common, and report the sum as **Additional Paid-in Capital** on the balance sheet. However, they are careful not to include Paid-in Capital in Excess of Par—Preferred because that paid-in capital belongs to the preferred stockholders.

THINK IT OVER

Examine MedTech.com Corporation's stockholders' equity in Exhibit 13-8, and answer these questions.

1. How much did MedTech.com's preferred stockholders pay into the corporation?
2. How much did the common stockholders pay into MedTech.com?
3. What did the stockholders get for their payments into the company?

Answers

1. $54,000 ($40,000 + $14,000)
2. $117,000 ($45,000 + $72,000)
3. The stockholders received stock, which represents their ownership in the assets of the corporation.

Now review the Decision Guidelines feature to solidify your understanding of stockholders' equity as it is reported on the balance sheet.

DECISION GUIDELINES

Reporting Stockholders' Equity on the Balance Sheet

DECISION	GUIDELINES
What are the two main segments of stockholders' equity?	• Paid-in capital • Retained earnings
Which is more permanent, paid-in capital or retained earnings?	Paid-in capital is more permanent because corporations use their retained earnings for declaring dividends.
How are paid-in capital and retained earnings	
• Similar?	• Both represent the stockholders' equity (ownership) in the assets of the corporation.
• Different?	• Paid-in capital and retained earnings come from different sources: **a.** *Paid-in capital* comes from the corporation's stockholders, who invested in the company. **b.** *Retained earnings* comes from the corporation's customers. It was earned by profitable operations.
What are the main categories of paid-in capital?	• Preferred stock, plus paid-in-capital in excess of par • Common stock, plus paid-in-capital in excess of par

SUMMARY PROBLEM

1. Test your understanding of the first half of this chapter: Is each of the following statements true or false?
   a. Issuance of 1,000 shares of $5 par-value stock at $12 increases contributed capital by $7,000.
   b. The issuance of no-par stock with a stated value is fundamentally different from issuing par-value stock.
   c. A corporation issues its preferred stock in exchange for land and a building with a combined market value of $200,000. This transaction increases the corporation's owners' equity by $200,000 regardless of the assets' prior book value.
   d. A stockholder may bind the corporation to a contract.
   e. The policy-making body in a corporation is called the board of directors.
   f. The owner of 100 shares of preferred stock has greater voting rights than the owner of 100 shares of common stock.
   g. Par-value stock is worth more than no-par stock.

2. The brewery **Adolph Coors Company** has two classes of common stock. Only the Class A common stockholders are entitled to vote. The company's balance sheet included the following presentation:

Stockholders' Equity

Capital stock	
Class A common stock, voting, $1 par value,	
authorized and issued 1,260,000 shares	$ 1,260,000
Class B common stock, nonvoting, no par value,	
authorized and issued 46,200,000 shares	11,000,000
	12,260,000
Additional paid-in capital	2,011,000
Retained earnings	872,403,000
	$886,674,000

Required

1. Record the issuance of the Class A common stock. The additional paid-in capital is related to the Class A common stock. Use the Coors account titles.
2. Record the issuance of the Class B common stock. Use the Coors account titles.
3. Rearrange the Coors stockholders' equity section to correspond to the following format:

Stockholders' Equity

Paid-in capital:	
Class A common stock..	$
Paid-in capital in excess of par—Class A common stock...............	
Class B common stock..	
Total paid-in capital...	_____
Retained earnings	
Total stockholders' equity	$

4. What is the total paid-in capital of the company?
5. How did Coors withhold the voting privilege from the Class B common stockholders?

Solutions

1. Answers to true/false statements:
   a. False   **c.** True   **e.** True   **g.** False
   b. False   **d.** False   **f.** False

```
(1)  Cash ..................................................................    3,271,000
          Class A Common Stock .......................................                    1,260,000
          Additional Paid-in Capital ..................................                    2,011,000
          To record issuance of Class A common stock at a premium.

(2)  Cash ..................................................................   11,000,000
          Class B Common Stock .......................................                   11,000,000
          To record issuance of Class B common stock.

(3)  Shareholders' Equity
     Paid-in capital:
          Class A common stock, voting, $1 par value,
              authorized and issued 1,260,000 shares .....................   $   1,260,000
          Paid-in capital in excess of par—Class A common stock ...........       2,011,000
          Class B common stock, nonvoting, no par value,
              authorized and issued 46,200,000 shares .....................      11,000,000
          Total paid-in capital .......................................          14,271,000
          Retained earnings ...........................................         872,403,000
          Total shareholders' equity ..................................        $886,674,000

(4)  Total paid-in capital is $14,271,000.

(5)  The voting privilege was withheld by specific agreement with the stockholders.
```

ACCOUNTING FOR CASH DIVIDENDS

Corporations share the company's wealth with their stockholders through dividends. Corporations declare dividends from retained earnings and pay the dividends with cash. The corporation must have enough *retained earnings* to declare the dividend and enough *cash* to pay the dividend.

Dividend Dates

A corporation must declare a dividend before paying it. The board of directors alone has the authority to declare a dividend. The corporation has no obligation to pay a dividend until the board declares one, but once declared, the dividend becomes a legal liability of the corporation. Three relevant dates for dividends are

1. *Declaration date.* On the declaration date, the board of directors announces the intention to pay the dividend. The declaration creates a liability for the corporation. Declaration is recorded by debiting Retained Earnings and crediting Dividends Payable.

2. *Date of record.* At declaration, the corporation also announces the record date, which follows the declaration date by a few weeks. Those stockholders who own the stock on the date of record will receive the dividend when it is paid. The corporation makes no journal entry on the date of record because no transaction occurs. But much work takes place behind the scenes to identify stockholders of record on this date.

3. *Payment date.* Payment of the dividend usually follows the record date by two to three weeks. Payment is recorded by debiting Dividends Payable and crediting Cash.

Objective 4
Account for cash dividends

Dividends on Preferred and Common Stock

Declaration of a cash dividend is recorded by debiting Retained Earnings and crediting Dividends Payable as follows:[1]

```
June 19   Retained Earnings ........................   XXX
                Dividends Payable ...............               XXX
          Declared a cash dividend.
```

[1]In Chapters 1–4, we debited the Dividends account, which is closed to Retained Earnings. Many businesses debit Retained Earnings directly, as shown here.

Payment of the dividend, which usually follows declaration by a few weeks, is recorded by debiting Dividends Payable and crediting Cash:

July 2	Dividends Payable.........................	XXX	
	Cash......................................		XXX
	Paid the cash dividend.		

◉ DAILY EXERCISE 13-13

Dividends Payable is a current liability. When a company has issued both preferred stock and common stock, the preferred stockholders receive their dividends first. The common stockholders receive dividends only if the total declared dividend is large enough to pay the preferred stockholders first.

In addition to its common stock, Pine Industries, Inc., has 9,000 shares of preferred stock outstanding. Preferred dividends are paid at the annual rate of $1.75 per share. Exhibit 13-9 shows the division between preferred and common for three amounts of the total annual dividend declared by Pine Industries.

Case A: Total dividend of $150,000
Preferred dividend (9,000 shares × $1.75 per share)	$ 15,750
Common dividend ($150,000 − $15,750)	134,250
Total dividend..	$150,000

Case B: Total dividend of $20,000
Preferred dividend (9,000 shares × $1.75 per share)	$ 15,750
Common dividend ($20,000 − $15,750)	4,250
Total dividend..	$ 20,000

Case C: Total dividend of $8,000
Preferred dividend (the full $8,000 goes to preferred because the annual preferred dividend is $15,750)	$ 8,000
Common dividend (none because the total dividend did not cover the preferred dividend for the year).............	0
Total dividend	$ 8,000

EXHIBIT 13-9
Division of a Dividend Between Preferred Stock and Common Stock

If Pine Industries' annual dividend is large enough to cover the preferred dividend for the year (Cases A and B), the preferred stockholders receive their regular dividend, and the common stockholders receive the remainder. But if the year's dividend falls below the amount of the annual preferred dividend (Case C), the preferred stockholders receive the entire dividend, and the common stockholders receive nothing that year.

This example illustrates an important relationship between preferred stock and common stock. To an investor, the preferred stock is safer because it receives dividends first. However, the earnings potential from an investment in common stock is much greater. Preferred stockholders usually receive only the specified dividend, but there is no upper limit on the amount of common dividends.

When a company has more than one class of preferred stock or common stock, the division of dividends among the various classes of stock follows this same pattern: The most senior preferred stock gets the first dividends, and so on.

We noted that preferred stockholders enjoy the advantage of priority over common stockholders in receiving dividends. The dividend preference is stated as a percentage rate or a dollar amount. For example, preferred stock may be "6% preferred," which means that owners of the preferred stock receive an annual dividend of 6% of the par value of the stock. If par value is $100 per share, preferred stockholders receive an annual cash dividend of $6 per share (6% of $100). The preferred stock may be "$3 preferred," which means that stockholders receive an annual dividend of $3 per share regardless of the preferred stock's par value. The dividend rate on no-par preferred stock is stated in a dollar amount per share.

◉ DAILY EXERCISE 13-14

Dividends on Cumulative and Noncumulative Preferred Stock

The allocation of dividends may be complex if the preferred stock is *cumulative*. Corporations sometimes fail to pay a dividend to their preferred stockholders. This is called *passing the dividend,* and the passed dividends are said to be *in arrears.* The owners

CUMULATIVE PREFERRED STOCK.
Preferred stock whose owners must receive all dividends in arrears before the corporation pays dividends to the common stockholders.

of **cumulative preferred stock** must receive all dividends in arrears plus the current year's dividend before the corporation pays dividends to the common stockholders.

The preferred stock of Pine Industries is cumulative. Suppose the company passed the 20X4 preferred dividend of $15,750. Before paying dividends to its common stockholders in 20X5, the company must first pay preferred dividends of $15,750 for both 20X4 and 20X5, a total of $31,500. *Preferred stock is cumulative in the eyes of the law unless it is labeled as noncumulative.* Most preferred stock is cumulative.

Assume that Pine Industries passes its 20X4 preferred dividend. In 20X5, the company declares a $50,000 dividend. The entry to record the declaration of this dividend is

Sep. 6	Retained Earnings	50,000	
	Dividends Payable, Preferred ($15,750 × 2)............		31,500
	Dividends Payable, Common		
	($50,000 − $31,500)		18,500
	Declared a cash dividend.		

If the preferred stock is *noncumulative*, the corporation is not obligated to pay dividends in arrears. Suppose the Pine Industries preferred stock was noncumulative and the company passed the 20X4 preferred dividend of $15,750. The preferred stockholders would lose the 20X4 dividend forever. Of course, the common stockholders would not receive a 20X4 dividend either. Before paying any common dividends in 20X5, the company would have to pay the 20X5 preferred dividend of $15,750.

Having dividends in arrears on cumulative preferred stock is *not* a liability for the corporation. (A liability for dividends arises only after the board of directors declares the dividend.) Nevertheless, a corporation must report cumulative preferred dividends in arrears. This information alerts common stockholders as to how much in preferred dividends must be paid before the common stockholders will receive any dividends.

Dividends in arrears are often disclosed in notes, as follows (all dates and amounts assumed). Observe the two references to Note 3 in this section of the balance sheet. The "6%" after "Preferred stock" is the annual dividend rate.

Preferred stock, 6%, $50 par, 2,000 shares issued (Note 3)	$100,000
Retained earnings (Note 3)	414,000

Note 3—Cumulative preferred dividends in arrears. At December 31, 20X2, dividends on the preferred stock were in arrears for 20X1 and 20X2, in the amount of $12,000 (6% × $100,000 × 2 years).

Objective 5
Use different stock values in decision making

DIFFERENT VALUES OF STOCK

There are several different *stock values* in addition to par value. Market value, liquidation value, and book value are used for various investor decisions.

Market Value

MARKET VALUE. Price for which a person could buy or sell a share of stock.

A stock's **market value,** or *market price,* is the price for which a person could buy or sell a share of the stock. The issuing corporation's net income, financial position, and future prospects and general economic conditions determine market value. The Internet and most newspapers report the market price of many stocks. Log onto any company's Web site to track its stock price. *In almost all cases, stockholders are more concerned about the market value of a stock than about any other value.* In the chapter-opening story, **IHOP's** stock had a market price of $10 when it was issued. Shortly thereafter, the stock shot up to a market price of $36, which means that the stock could be sold for, or bought for, $36 per share. The purchase of 100 shares of IHOP stock at $36 would cost $3,600 ($36 × 100), plus a commission. If you were selling 100 shares of IHOP stock, you would receive cash of $3,600 less a commission. The commission is the fee an investor pays to a stockbroker for buying or selling the stock. The price of a share of IHOP stock has fluctuated from $10 at issuance to a recent high of $25.

If you buy IHOP stock from another investor, IHOP gets no cash. The transaction is a sale between you and the other investor. IHOP records only the change in stockholder name.

Liquidation Value

Some preferred stocks have a liquidation value. The *liquidation value* is the amount the corporation agrees to pay the preferred stockholder per share if the company liquidates. Dividends in arrears are added to liquidation value in determining the payment to the preferred stockholders if the company liquidates.

Some companies report their preferred stock at its liquidation value on the balance sheet. Consider **BF Goodrich Company,** which makes chemicals and aerospace components and sells tires under the Michelin label. BF Goodrich has 2.2 million shares of convertible preferred stock that is stated at "a liquidation value of $50 per share." The balance in BF Goodrich's preferred stock account is thus $110 million (2.2 million shares × $50).

 DAILY EXERCISE 13-15

Book Value

The **book value** of a stock is the amount of owners' equity on the company's books for each share of its stock. Corporations often report this amount in their annual reports. If the company has only common stock outstanding, its book value is computed by dividing total stockholders' equity by the number of shares *outstanding*. A company with stockholders' equity of $180,000 and 5,000 shares of common stock outstanding has a book value of $36 per share ($180,000/5,000 shares).

BOOK VALUE. Amount of owners' equity on the company's books for each share of its stock.

If the company has both preferred stock and common stock outstanding, the preferred stockholders have the first claim to owners' equity. Ordinarily, preferred stock has a specified liquidation value. The book value of preferred stock is its liquidation value plus any cumulative dividends in arrears on the stock. Its book value *per share* equals the sum of liquidation value and any cumulative dividends in arrears divided by the number of preferred shares *outstanding*. After the corporation figures the book value of the preferred shares, it computes the book value per share of the common. The corporation divides the common equity (total stockholders' equity minus preferred equity) by the number of common shares outstanding.

Lille Corporation's balance sheet reports the following amounts:

Stockholders' Equity	
Paid-in capital:	
Preferred stock, 6%, $10 par, 5,000 shares authorized,	
5,000 shares issued (liquidation value $13 per share)	$ 50,000
Paid-in capital in excess of par—preferred..................................	14,000
Common stock, $1 par, 20,000 shares authorized,	
15,000 shares issued...	15,000
Paid-in capital in excess of par—common	172,000
Total paid-in capital	251,000
Retained earnings	422,000
Total stockholders' equity	$673,000

Suppose that four years' (including the current year) cumulative preferred dividends are in arrears. The book-value-per-share computations are as follows:

Preferred	
Liquidation value (5,000 shares × $13).......................................	$ 65,000
Cumulative dividends ($50,000 × 0.06 × 4)	12,000
Stockholders' equity allocated to preferred.................................	$ 77,000
Book value per share ($77,000/5,000 shares)	$ 15.40
Common	
Total stockholders' equity...	$673,000
Less stockholders' equity allocated to preferred.........................	(77,000)
Stockholders' equity allocated to common	$596,000
Book value per share ($596,000/15,000 shares)	$39.73

 DAILY EXERCISE 13-16

If the preferred stock has no specified liquidation value, then we would use the sum of par value plus paid-in capital in excess of par-preferred, $64,000, plus cumulative dividends to compute the book value of the preferred stock.

BOOK VALUE AND DECISION MAKING   How is book value used in decision making? Book value may figure into the negotiated purchase price of a corporation whose stock is not publicly traded. Also, a corporation may buy out a retiring executive or other stockholder by agreeing to pay the book value of the person's stock in the company.

Some investors have traditionally compared the book value of a share of a company's stock with the stock's market value. The idea was that a stock selling below its book value was underpriced and thus a good buy. The relationship between book value and market value is far from clear. Some investors believe that a company whose stock sells at a price below book value must be experiencing financial difficulty. Exhibit 13-10 contrasts the book values and ranges of market values for the common stocks of three well-known companies. For all three companies, the market value of the stock exceeds its book value—a mark of success. The market price of **Dell Computer's** stock far exceeds its book value per share.

⊙ DAILY EXERCISE 13-17

EXHIBIT 13-10
Book Value and Market Value for Three Well-Known Companies

	Book Value Per Share	July 6, 2000 Stock Price
IHOP Corp.*	$11.28	$17.13
MCI WORLDCOM*	18.02	$46.44
Dell Computer**	2.06	$47.75

  * December 31, 1999.
** January 28, 2000.

Objective 6
Evaluate a company's return on assets and return on stockholders' equity

EVALUATING OPERATIONS

Investors and creditors are constantly evaluating companies' profits. Investors search for companies whose stocks are likely to increase in value. The decision often requires a comparison of companies. But **IHOP's** net income may not be comparable with the net income of a new company. IHOP's profits may run into the millions of dollars, which far exceed a new company's net income. To compare companies of different size, investors use standard profitability measures. Two of the most widely used are the rate of return on total assets and rate of return on stockholders' equity.

Rate of Return on Total Assets

RATE OF RETURN ON TOTAL ASSETS. The sum of net income plus interest expense divided by average total assets. This ratio measures the success a company has in using its assets to earn income for the persons who finance the business. Also called **return on assets.**

The **rate of return on total assets,** or simply **return on assets,** measures a company's success in using its assets to earn income for those who are financing the business.

- Creditors have loaned money to the corporation and thus earn interest.
- Stockholders have invested in the corporation's stock and therefore own the company's net income.

The sum of interest expense and net income is the return to the two groups that have financed the corporation's assets, and this is the numerator of the return-on-assets ratio. The denominator is average total assets. Return on assets is computed as follows, using data from the 1999 annual report of IHOP Corp. (dollar amounts in thousands):

$$\text{Rate of return on total assets} = \frac{\text{Net income} + \text{Interest expense}}{\text{Average total assets}}$$

$$= \frac{\$32,125 + \$19,391}{(\$443,032 + \$520,402)/2} = \frac{\$51,516}{\$481,717} = 0.107$$

Net income and interest expense are taken from the income statement. Average total assets is computed from the beginning and ending balance sheets.

What is a good rate of return on total assets? There is no single answer to this question because rates of return vary widely by industry. For example, high technology companies such as **Intel** and **Hewlett-Packard** earn higher returns than utility companies and manufacturers of consumer goods such as toothpaste. In most industries a return on assets of 10% is considered good.

Rate of Return on Common Stockholders' Equity

Rate of return on common stockholders' equity, often called **return on equity,** shows the relationship between net income and average common stockholders' equity. The numerator is net income minus preferred dividends. Preferred dividends are subtracted because the preferred stockholders have the first claim to dividends from the company's net income. The denominator is average *common stockholders' equity*—total stockholders' equity minus preferred equity. IHOP's rate of return on common stockholders' equity for 1999 is computed as follows (dollar amounts in thousands):

RATE OF RETURN ON COMMON STOCKHOLDERS' EQUITY. Net income minus preferred dividends, divided by average common stockholders' equity. A measure of profitability. Also called **return on equity.**

◉ DAILY EXERCISE 13-18

◉ DAILY EXERCISE 13-19

$$\begin{array}{l} \text{Rate of return} \\ \text{on common} \\ \text{stockholders'} \\ \text{equity} \end{array} = \frac{\text{Net income} - \text{Preferred dividends}}{\text{Average common stockholders' equity}}$$

$$= \frac{\$32,125 - \$0}{(\$187,868 + \$226,480)/2} = \frac{\$32,125}{\$207,174} = 0.155$$

IHOP Corp. has no preferred stock, so preferred dividends are zero. With no preferred stock outstanding, average *common* stockholders' equity is the same as average *total* equity—the average of the beginning and ending amounts.

IHOP's return on equity (15.5%) is higher than its return on assets (10.7%). This indicates a financially healthy company because IHOP is earning more for its stockholders than it is paying for interest expense. Companies such as IHOP borrow at one rate (say, 7%) and invest the funds to earn a higher rate (almost 16%). Borrowing at a lower rate than the return on investments is called *using leverage.*

If return on assets is higher than return on equity, the company is in trouble because its interest expense is greater than its return on equity. Interest expense should always be lower than the amount the company earns on its investments. Investors and creditors use return on common stockholders' equity in much the same way they use return on total assets—to compare companies. The higher the rate of return, the more successful the company. IHOP's 15.5% return on common stockholders' equity would be considered good in most industries.

ACCOUNTING FOR INCOME TAXES BY CORPORATIONS

Objective 7
Account for the income tax of a corporation

Corporations pay income tax just as individuals do, but not at the same rates. At this writing, the federal tax rate on most corporate income is 35%. Most states also levy a corporate income tax, so most corporations have a combined federal and state income tax rate of approximately 40%.

To account for income tax, the corporation measures

- Income tax expense, an expense on the income statement
- Income tax payable, a liability on the balance sheet

Accounting for income tax by a corporation follows the general principles that govern accounting for all other transactions. Let's return to **IHOP Corp.** In 20X0, suppose IHOP reported income before tax (also called pretax accounting income) of approximately $50 million on its income statement. IHOP's combined income tax rate is 40%. Assume IHOP's income tax expense and income tax payable are the same. Then IHOP would record income tax for the year as follows (amounts in millions):

20X0			
Dec. 31	Income Tax Expense ($50 × 0.40)..............	20	
	Income Tax Payable		20
	Recorded income tax for the year.		

IHOP's 20X0 financial statements would report these figures (adapted, in millions):

Income Statement		Balance Sheet	
Income before income tax	$ 50	Current liabilities:	
Income tax expense	(20)	Income tax payable	$20
Net income	$ 30		

Early in 20X1, IHOP would pay its income tax payable when the company files its 20X0 income tax return with the Internal Revenue Service. Now, let's move to 20X1 with a more realistic income tax example. In general, income tax expense and income tax payable can be computed as follows:[2]

Income tax *expense*	=	Income before income tax (from the income statement)	×	Income tax rate

Income tax *payable*	=	Taxable income (from the income tax return filed with the IRS)	×	Income tax rate

For most companies, income tax expense and income tax payable differ. The most important difference between income tax expense and income tax payable occurs when a corporation uses the straight-line depreciation method for the financial statements and an accelerated depreciation method for the tax return. The tax depreciation method is called the *modified accelerated cost recovery system,* abbreviated as MACRS. ← For any one year, MACRS depreciation may differ from accounting depreciation on the income statement.

→ We learned in Chapter 10, page 400, that the MACRS depreciation method is similar to the double-declining-balance method.

Continuing with the IHOP illustration, suppose for 20X1 that IHOP Corp. has

- Income before income tax of $60 million on the income statement
- Taxable income of $55 million on the company's income tax return

IHOP will record income tax for 20X1 as follows (dollar amounts in millions and an income tax rate of 40%):

20X1			
Dec. 31	Income Tax Expense ($60 × 0.40)	24	
	Income Tax Payable ($55 × 0.40)............		22
	Deferred Tax Liability		2
	Recorded income tax for the year.		

IHOP will pay the $22 million of Income Tax Payable, a current liability, within a few months. The Deferred Tax Liability account is long-term, so IHOP will pay this debt over a number of years. IHOP's 20X1 financial statements would report these figures (adapted, in millions):

DAILY EXERCISE 13-20

Income Statement		Balance Sheet	
Income before income tax............	$60	Current liabilities:	
Income tax expense.....................	(24)	Income tax payable	$22
Net income	$36	Long-term liabilities:	
		Deferred tax liability................	2*

*Assumes the beginning balance of Deferred tax liability was zero.

The Decision Guidelines feature provides an overview of the second half of the chapter.

---

[2] The authors thank Jean Marie Hudson for suggesting this presentation.

DECISION GUIDELINES

Dividends, Stock Values, Evaluating Operations, & Accounting for Income Tax

DECISION	GUIDELINES
Dividends	
Whether to declare a cash dividend?	• Must have enough retained earnings to declare the dividend.
	• Must have enough cash to pay the dividend.
What happens with a dividend?	• The corporation's board of directors declares the dividend. Then the dividend becomes a liability of the corporation.
	• The date of record fixes who will receive the dividend.
	• Payment of the dividend occurs later.
Who receives the dividend?	• Preferred stockholders first receive their dividends at a specified rate.
	• Common stockholders receive the remainder.
Stock Values	
How much to pay for a stock?	Its market value.
What unique value applies to preferred stock?	• Liquidation value—the amount the corporation agrees to pay if the company liquidates
What is book value's role in decision making?	Sometimes used to help determine the market value of a stock that is not traded on a stock exchange.
Evaluating Operations	
How to evaluate the operations of a corporation?	Two measures that relate earnings to the amount stockholders have invested include
	• Rate of return on assets
	• Rate of return on common stockholders' equity
	For a healthy company, return on stockholders' equity should exceed return on assets.
Accounting for Income Tax	
What are the three main accounts?	• Income tax expense
	• Income tax payable, a current liability
	• Deferred tax liability, usually a long-term liability
How to measure	
• Income tax expense?	Income before income tax × Income tax rate (from the income statement)
• Income tax payable?	Taxable income × Income tax rate (from the income tax return filed with the Internal Revenue Service)
• Deferred tax liability?	Difference between income tax expense and income tax payable for any one year

EXCEL APPLICATION PROBLEM

Goal: Create an Excel spreadsheet that compares financial performance of several publicly traded stocks.

Scenario: Your task is to create an Excel spreadsheet that compares the historical performance of **The Gap** and **Abercrombie & Fitch** on three key financial measures. Embedded graphs of each financial dimension also must be created. All data used in your spreadsheet will come from Morningstar's Web site.

When done, answer these questions:

1. Which company has earned a consistently higher return on equity?
2. Which company has earned a consistently higher return on assets?
3. Increasing cash flow from operations is a good sign for investing. Which company has experienced increasing cash flows over the past five years?
4. Based on these very limited data, would you invest in either of these companies? Why or why not?

EXCEL APPLICATION PROBLEM (CONT.)

Step-by-step:

1. Locate **www.morningstar.com** on the Web.
2. Under the "Quotes & Reports" section, enter the ticker symbol for each company. Then, look under "Company Performance" and "Historical Overview." You should see a five-year summary of fiscal-year-end financial performance. Print out the Historical Overview for each company.
3. Open a new Excel spreadsheet.
4. Create a boldfaced heading for your spreadsheet that contains the following:
   a. Chapter 13 Decision Guidelines
   b. Investing in Stock
   c. Stock Performance Analysis
   d. Today's date
5. Under the heading, create a boldfaced, underlined section titled "Return on Equity %." Move down one row.

Create one column each for the last five years (for example, "1999," "1998," and so on). Create one row each for The Gap and Abercrombie & Fitch.

6. Enter the return on equity data for the past five years found on the Morningstar Historical Overview for each company.
7. Repeat steps 5 and 6 for "Return on Assets %" and "Operating Cash Flow (in millions)."
8. Using the Excel Chart Wizard, create separate graphs for Return on Equity %, Return on Assets %, and Operating Cash Flow. Resize and position each graph to the right of the data so that everything appears on one page when you print.
9. Save your work, and print your spreadsheet in landscape mode (with graphs) for your files.

REVIEW CORPORATIONS: PAID-IN CAPITAL AND THE BALANCE SHEET

SUMMARY PROBLEM

www.prenhall.com/horngren

End-of-Chapter Assessment

1. Use the following accounts and related balances to prepare the classified balance sheet of Whitehall, Inc., at September 30, 20X4. Use the account format of the balance sheet.

Common stock, $1 par, 50,000 shares authorized, 20,000 shares issued	$ 20,000	Long-term note payable	$ 73,000
		Inventory	85,000
Dividends payable	4,000	Property, plant, and equipment, net	225,000
Cash	9,000	Accounts receivable, net	23,000
Accounts payable	28,000	Preferred stock, $3.75, no-par, 10,000 shares authorized, 2,000 shares issued	24,000
Retained earnings	75,000		
Paid-in capital in excess of par—common	115,000	Accrued liabilities	3,000

2. The balance sheet of Trendline Corporation reported the following at March 31, 20X6, the end of its fiscal year. Note that Trendline reports paid-in capital in excess of par or stated value after the stock accounts.

Stockholders' Equity

Preferred stock, 4%, $10 par, 10,000 shares authorized (liquidation value $110,000)	$100,000
Common stock, no-par, $5 stated value, 100,000 shares authorized	250,000
Paid-in capital in excess of par:	
Common stock	231,500
Retained earnings	395,000
Total stockholders' equity	$976,500

Required

1. Is the preferred stock cumulative or noncumulative? How can you tell?
2. What is the total amount of the annual preferred dividend?
3. How many shares of preferred and common stock has the company issued?

4. Compute the book value per share of the preferred and the common stock. No prior year pre-ferred dividends are in arrears, but Trendline has not declared the current-year dividend.

Solution

WHITEHALL, INC.
Balance Sheet
September 30, 20X4

Assets			Liabilities		
Current:			**Current:**		
Cash	$ 9,000		Accounts payable..................		$ 28,000
Accounts receivable, net	23,000		Dividends payable..................		4,000
Inventory	85,000		Accrued liabilities		3,000
Total current assets.....................................	117,000		Total current liabilities.........		35,000
Property, plant and equipment, net..............	225,000		Long-term note payable		73,000
			Total liabilities..........................		108,000
			Stockholders' Equity		
			Paid-in capital:		
			Preferred stock, $3.75, no-par,		
			10,000 shares authorized,		
			2,000 shares issued	$ 24,000	
			Common stock, $1 par, 50,000		
			shares authorized, 20,000		
			shares issued	20,000	
			Paid-in capital in excess of		
			par—common	115,000	
			Total paid-in capital	159,000	
			Retained earnings......................	75,000	
			Total stockholders' equity.......		234,000
			Total liabilities and		
Total assets...	$342,000		stockholders' equity...............		$342,000

Required

1. The preferred stock is cumulative because it is not specifically labeled otherwise.
2. Total annual preferred dividend: $4,000 ($100,000 × 0.04).
3. Preferred stock issued: 10,000 shares ($100,000/$10 par value).
   Common stock issued: 50,000 shares ($250,000/$5 stated value).
4. Book values per share of preferred and common stock:

Preferred:	
Liquidation value	$110,000
Cumulative dividend for current year ($100,000 × 0.04)	4,000
Stockholders' equity allocated to preferred...........................	$114,000
Book value per share ($114,000/10,000 shares)	$11.40
Common:	
Total stockholders' equity...	$976,500
Less stockholders' equity allocated to preferred....................	(114,000)
Stockholders' equity allocated to common	$862,500
Book value per share ($862,500/50,000 shares)	$17.25

LESSONS LEARNED

1. *Identify the characteristics of a corporation.* A corporation is a separate legal and business entity. *Continuous life,* the *ease of raising large amounts of capital and transferring ownership,* and *limited liability* are among the advantages of the corporate form of organization. An important disadvantage is *double taxation.* Corporations pay *income taxes,* and stockholders pay tax on dividends. *Stockholders* are the owners of the corpora-tions. They elect a *board of directors,* which elects a chairper-son and appoints the officers to manage the business.

2. *Record the issuance of stock.* Corporations may issue dif-ferent classes of stock: *par value, no-par value, common,* and *preferred.* Stock is usually issued at a *premium*—an amount above par value.

3. *Prepare the stockholders' equity section of a corporation's balance sheet.* The balance sheet carries the capital raised through stock issuance under the heading Paid-in Capital or Contributed Capital in the stockholders' equity section.

4. Account for cash dividends. Only when the board of directors declares a *dividend* does the corporation incur the liability to pay dividends. Preferred stock has priority over common stock as to dividends, which may be stated as a percent of par value or as a dollar amount per share. In addition, preferred stock has a claim to dividends in arrears if it is *cumulative*.

5. Use different stock values in decision making. A stock's *market value* is the price for which a share may be bought or sold. *Liquidation value* and *book value*—the amount of owners' equity per share of company stock—are other values that may apply to stock.

6. Evaluate a company's return on assets and return on stockholders' equity. *Return on assets* and *return on stockholders' equity* are two standard measures of profitability. A healthy company's return on equity will exceed its return on assets.

7. Account for the income tax of a corporation. Corporations pay income tax and must account for the income tax expense and income tax payable. A difference between the expense and the payable creates another account, Deferred Tax Liability.

ACCOUNTING VOCABULARY

additional paid-in capital (p. 512)
authorization of stock (p. 502)
board of directors (p. 503)
book value (p. 517)
bylaws (p. 503)
chairperson (p. 503)
charter (p. 501)
common stock (p. 504)
contributed capital (p. 503)
cumulative preferred stock (p. 516)
deficit (p. 505)

dividends (p. 505)
double taxation (p. 502)
legal capital (p. 505)
limited liability (p. 502)
market value (p. 516)
outstanding stock (p. 503)
paid-in capital (p. 503)
par value (p. 507)
preferred stock (p. 506)
president (p. 503)
rate of return on common stockholders' equity (p. 519)

rate of return on total assets (p. 518)
retained earnings (p. 503)
return on assets (p. 518)
return on equity (p. 519)
shareholder (p. 501)
stated value (p. 507)
stock (p. 501)
stockholder (p. 501)
stockholders' equity (p. 503)

QUESTIONS

1. Identify the characteristics of a corporation.
2. Explain why corporations face a tax disadvantage.
3. How are the structures of a partnership and a corporation similar, and how are they different?
4. Dividends on preferred stock may be stated as a percent or a dollar amount. What is the annual dividend on these preferred stocks: 4%, $100 par; $3.50, $20 par; and 6%, no-par with $50 stated value?
5. Which event increases the assets of the corporation: authorization of stock or issuance of stock? Explain.
6. Suppose H. J. Heinz Company issued 1,000 shares of its 3.65%, $100 par preferred stock for $120. How much would this transaction increase the company's paid-in capital? How much would it increase Heinz's retained earnings? How much would it increase Heinz's annual cash dividend payments?
7. Give two alternative account titles for Paid-in Capital in Excess of Par—Common Stock.
8. How does issuance of 1,000 shares of no-par stock for

land and a building, together worth $150,000, affect paid-in capital? Total stockholders' equity?
9. Rank the following accounts in the order they would appear on the balance sheet: Common Stock, Preferred Stock, Retained Earnings, Dividends Payable. Also, give each account's balance sheet classification.
10. As a preferred stockholder, would you rather own cumulative or noncumulative preferred? If all other factors are the same, would the corporation rather the preferred stock be cumulative or noncumulative? Give your reason.
11. Distinguish between the market value of stock and the book value of stock. Which is more important to investors?
12. How is book value per share of common stock computed when the company has both preferred stock and common stock outstanding?
13. Why should a healthy company's rate of return on stockholders' equity exceed its rate of return on total assets?
14. Explain the difference between the income tax expense and the income tax payable of a corporation.

ASSESS YOUR PROGRESS

DAILY EXERCISES

Characteristics of a corporation
(Obj. 1)

DE13-1 Suppose you are forming Spuds, Inc., which will feature 20 different toppings for baked potatoes. You need some outside money from other investors, and you have decided to organize the business as a corporation that will issue stock to raise the needed funds. Briefly discuss your most important reason for organizing Spuds as a corporation rather than as a partnership. If you had organized as a partnership, what would be your most important reason for not organizing as a corporation?

Authority structure in a corporation
(Obj. 1)

DE13-2 Consider the authority structure in a corporation, as diagrammed in Exhibit 13-2.

1. Who is in charge of day-to-day operations?
2. Who manages the accounting?

3. Who has primary responsibility for the corporation's cash?

4. What group holds the ultimate power in a corporation?

5. Who is the most powerful person in the corporation?

Similarities and differences between the balance sheets of a corporation and a proprietorship (Obj. 1)

DE13-3 Examine the summarized balance sheet of **Target Corporation** in Exhibit 13-4 page 504. Suppose Target were a proprietorship owned by Lee Target. How would the Target proprietorship balance sheet differ from the one given in Exhibit 13-4? How would the proprietorship balance sheet be similar to the one given in Exhibit 13-4?

Characteristics of preferred and common stock (Obj. 1)

DE13-4 Answer the following questions about the characteristics of a corporation's stock.

1. What privileges do preferred stockholders enjoy that common stockholders do not have?

2. Which class of stockholders would expect to reap greater benefits from a highly profitable corporation? Why?

3. Which stockholders are the real owners of a corporation?

4. Which right clearly distinguishes a stockholder from a creditor (who has lent money to the corporation)?

Effect of a stock issuance on net income (Obj. 2)

DE13-5 Study **IHOP's** July 31 stock issuance entry given on page 507, and answer these questions about the nature of the IHOP transaction.

1. IHOP received $32,000,000 for the issuance of its stock. The par value of the IHOP stock was only $32,000. Was the excess amount of $31,968,000 a profit to IHOP? If not, what was it?

2. Suppose the par value of the IHOP stock had been $1 per share, $5 per share, or $10 per share. Would a change in the par value of the company's stock affect IHOP's net income? Give the reason for your answer.

Issuing stock and interpreting stockholders' equity (Obj. 2)

DE13-6 **The Coca-Cola Company** reported the following on its balance sheet at December 31, 1999 (adapted, amounts in millions, except for par value):

Common stock, $0.25 par value	
Authorized: 5,600 shares	
Issued: 3,466 shares	$ 867
Paid-in capital in excess of par	2,584
Retained earnings	20,773

1. Assume Coca-Cola issued all of its stock during 1999. Journalize the company's issuance of the stock for cash.

2. Was Coca-Cola's main source of stockholders' equity paid-in capital or profitable operations? How can you tell?

Issuing stock and analyzing retained earnings (Obj. 2)

DE13-7 At December 31, 1999, **The Coca-Cola Company** reported the following on its comparative balance sheet, which included 1998 amounts for comparison (adapted, with all amounts except par value in millions):

	December 31,	
	1999	**1998**
Common stock $0.25 par value		
Authorized: 5,600 shares		
Issued: 3,466 shares in 1999	$ 867	
3,460 shares in 1998		$ 865
Paid-in capital in excess of par	2,584	2,158
Retained earnings	20,773	19,922

1. How much did Coca-Cola's total paid-in capital increase during 1999? What caused total paid-in capital to increase? How can you tell?

2. Journalize Coca-Cola's issuance of stock for cash during 1999.

3. Did Coca-Cola have a profit or a loss for 1999? How can you tell?

Issuing stock (Obj. 2)

DE13-8 Brunnheimer Corporation has three classes of stock: Common, $1 par; Preferred Class A, $10 par; and Preferred Class B, no-par.

Journalize Brunnheimer's issuance of

a. 1,000 shares of common stock for $30 per share

b. 1,000 shares of Class A preferred stock for a total of $32,000

c. 1,000 shares of Class B preferred stock for $14 per share

Explanations are not required.

Issuing stock to finance the
purchase of assets
(Obj. 2)

DE13-9 This exercise shows the similarity and the difference between two ways to acquire plant assets.

Case A—Issue stock and buy the assets in separate transactions:

> Avisa Machines, Inc., issued 10,000 shares of its $10 par common stock for cash of $700,000. In a separate transaction, Avisa Machines purchased a warehouse building for $480,000 and equipment for $220,000. Journalize the two transactions.

Case B—Issue stock to acquire the assets:

> Avisa Machines issued 10,000 shares of its $10 par common stock to acquire a warehouse building valued at $480,000 and equipment worth $220,000. Journalize this transaction.

Compare the balances in all accounts after making both sets of entries. Are the account balances similar or different?

Preparing the stockholders'
equity section of a balance sheet
(Obj. 3)

DE13-10 The financial statements of Arthur Binding, Inc., reported the following accounts (adapted, in millions except for par value):

Paid-in capital in excess of par	$ 17.3	Net sales	$1,081.5
Cost of goods sold	588.0	Accounts payable	62.4
Common stock $0.01 par,		Retained earnings	166.2
40.2 shares issued	0.4	Other current liabilities	52.3
Cash	24.0	Operating expenses	412.9
Long-term debt	7.6	Total assets	?

Prepare the stockholders' equity section of the Arthur Binding balance sheet. Net income has already been closed to Retained Earnings.

Using stockholders' equity data
(Obj. 3)

DE13-11 ◄ *Link Back to Chapter 1 (Accounting Equation, Income Statement).* Use the Arthur Binding data in Daily Exercise 13-10 to compute Arthur's

   a. Net income   **b.** Total liabilities   **c.** Total assets

Reporting stockholders' equity on
the balance sheet
(Obj. 3)

DE13-12 Varlux Corporation began operations in 20X3 with a charter that authorized the company to issue 10,000 shares of 5%, $8 par preferred stock and 100,000 shares of no-par common stock. During 20X3 through 20X8, Varlux issued 3,000 shares of the preferred stock for $25 per share and 50,000 shares of its common stock for $5 per share. At December 31, 20X8, Varlux had retained earnings of $110,000. During 20X9, Varlux earned net income of $70,000 and declared cash dividends of $15,000.

   Show how Varlux Corporation reported stockholders' equity on its balance sheet at December 31, 20X9.

Accounting for cash dividends
(Obj. 4)

DE13-13 Colombia Coffee Company earned net income of $85,000 during the year ended December 31, 20X3. On December 15, Colombia declared the annual cash dividend on its 6% preferred stock (10,000 shares with total par value of $100,000) and a $0.50 per share cash dividend on its common stock (50,000 shares with total par value of $250,000). Colombia then paid the dividends on January 4, 20X4.

   Journalize for Colombia Company
   a. Declaring the cash dividends on December 15
   b. Closing net income to Retained Earnings on December 31, 20X3
   c. Paying the cash dividends on January 4, 20X4

Did Retained Earnings increase or decrease during 20X3? By how much?

Dividing cash dividends between
preferred and common stock
(Obj. 4)

DE13-14 Refer to the stockholders' equity of MedTech.com Corporation in Exhibit 13-8, page 512. Answer these questions about MedTech.com's dividends.

   1. How much in dividends must MedTech.com declare each year before the common stockholders receive cash dividends for the year?
   2. Suppose MedTech.com declares cash dividends of $20,000 for 20X1. How much of the dividends goes to preferred? How much goes to common?
   3. Is MedTech.com's preferred stock cumulative or noncumulative? How can you tell?
   4. Suppose MedTech.com passed the preferred dividend in 20X2 and 20X3. In 20X4, the company declares cash dividends of $9,000. How much of the dividends goes to preferred? How much goes to common?

Similarities and differences
between preferred stock and
common stock
(Obj. 5)

DE13-15 Indicate whether each of the following characteristics applies to preferred stock, common stock, or both.

   a. Cumulative   **d.** Stated dividend
   b. Callable   **e.** Voting rights
   c. Liquidation value   **f.** Priority to receive assets in the event of liquidation

DE13-16 Refer to the stockholders' equity of MedTech.com Corporation in Exhibit 13-8, page 512. MedTech.com's preferred stock has a liquidation value of $125 per share, and MedTech.com has not declared preferred dividends for three years (including the current year). Compute the book value of MedTech.com's (a) preferred stock and (b) common stock.

Book value per share of preferred and common stock
(Obj. 5)

DE13-17 Answer the following questions about various stock values.

Explaining the use of different stock values for decision making
(Obj. 5)

1. Suppose you are an investor considering the purchase of **Intel** common stock as an investment. You have called your stockbroker to inquire about the stock. Which stock value are you most concerned about and why?
2. How is the book value of a stock used in decision making?
3. Suppose you are the general manager of a small company that is considering going public, as **IHOP Corp.** did in the chapter-opening story. Which stock value are you most concerned about and why?

DE13-18 Answer these questions about two rates of return.

Computing and explaining return on assets and return on equity
(Obj. 6)

1. Give the formula for computing (a) rate of return on common stockholders' equity and (b) rate of return on total assets.
2. Why are preferred dividends subtracted from net income to compute return on common stockholders' equity?
3. Why is interest expense added to net income to compute return on assets?

DE13-19 **The Coca-Cola Company** has earned solid rates of return on its assets and its stockholders' equity in recent years. Coca-Cola's 1999 financial statements reported the following items—with 1998 figures given for comparison (adapted, in millions):

Computing return on assets and return on equity for a leading company
(Obj. 6)

	1999	1998
Balance sheet		
Total current assets	$ 6,480	$ 6,380
Total long-term assets	15,143	12,765
Total assets	$21,623	$19,145
Total liabilities	$12,110	$10,742
Total stockholders' equity (all common)	9,513	8,403
Total liabilities and equity	$21,623	$19,145
Income statement		
Net sales	$19,805	
Cost of goods sold	6,009	
Gross profit	13,796	
Selling, administrative, and general expenses	9,814	
Interest expense	337	
All other expenses, net	1,214	
Net income	$ 2,431	

Compute Coca-Cola's rate of return on total assets and rate of return on common stockholders' equity for 1999. Do these rates of return look high or low?

DE13-20 Harry's Hot Dogs had income before income tax of $120,000 and taxable income of $90,000 for 20X1, the company's first year of operations. The income tax rate is 40%.

Accounting for a corporation's income tax
(Obj. 7)

1. Make the entry to record Harry's income taxes for 20X1.
2. Show what Harry's Hot Dogs will report on its 20X1 income statement starting with income before income tax. Also show what Harry will report for current and long-term liabilities on its December 31, 20X1, balance sheet.

EXERCISES

E13-1 Dena Kelly and Tiffany Lewis are opening a limousine service to be named D & T Limo. They need outside capital, so they plan to organize the business as a corporation. They come to you for advice. Write a memorandum informing them of the steps in forming a corporation. Identify specific documents used in this process, and name the different parties involved in the ownership and management of a corporation.

Organizing a corporation
(Obj. 1)

E13-2 New England Systems completed the following stock issuance transactions:

April 19   Issued 1,000 shares of $1.50 par common stock for cash of $10.50 per share.
May   3   Sold 300 shares of $4.50, no-par Class A preferred stock for $12,000 cash.
     11   Received inventory valued at $23,000 and equipment with market value of $11,000. Issued 3,300 shares of the $1.50 par common stock.
     15   Issued 1,000 shares of 5%, no-par Class B preferred stock with stated value of $50 per share. The issue price was cash of $62 per share.

Required

1. Journalize the transactions. Explanations are not required.
2. How much paid-in capital did these transactions generate for New England Systems?

Issuing stock and preparing the
stockholders' equity section of
the balance sheet
(Obj. 2, 3)

E13-3 The charter for Sartis Rugs, Inc., authorizes the company to issue 100,000 shares of $3, no-par preferred stock and 500,000 shares of common stock with $1 par value. During its start-up phase, Sartis completed the following transactions:

Aug.   6   Issued 500 shares of common stock to the promoters who organized the corporation, receiving cash of $15,000.
    12   Issued 300 shares of preferred stock for cash of $18,000.
    14   Issued 1,000 shares of common stock in exchange for land valued at $26,000.
    31   Earned a small profit for August and closed the $13,000 net income into Retained Earnings.

Required

1. Record the transactions in the general journal.
2. Prepare the stockholders' equity section of the Sartis balance sheet at August 31.

E13-4 The balance sheet of Levitz Corporation, as adapted, reported the following stockholders' equity. Levitz has two separate classes of preferred stock, labeled Series A and Series B.

Stockholders' Equity	$ Thousands
Preferred stock, $2 par, authorized 4,000,000 shares (Note 7)	
Series A	$ 100
Series B	740
Common stock, $0.10 par, authorized 20,000,000,	
issued 9,000,000 shares	900
Capital in excess of par (sum of preferred and common)	74,580

Note 7. Preferred Stock:

Shares Issued	
Series A	50,000
Series B	370,000

Required

The Series A preferred stock was issued for $5 cash per share, the Series B preferred was issued for $10 cash per share, and the common was issued for cash of $72,370 thousand. Make the summary journal entries to record issuance of all the Levitz stock. Explanations are not required. After you record these entries, what is the total balance of Capital in Excess of Par?

E13-5 Modern Furniture Co., located in Boston, Massachusetts, imports European furniture and Oriental rugs. The corporation issued 5,000 shares of no-par common stock for $8 per share. Record issuance of the stock if the stock (a) is true no-par stock and (b) has stated value of $2 per share.

E13-6 The charter of Laurelake Corporation authorizes the issuance of 5,000 shares of Class A preferred stock, 1,000 shares of Class B preferred stock, and 10,000 shares of common stock. During a two-month period, Laurelake completed these stock-issuance transactions:

Nov. 23	Issued 2,000 shares of $1 par common stock for cash of $12.50 per share.
Dec. 2	Sold 300 shares of $4.50, no-par Class A preferred stock for $20,000 cash.
12	Received inventory valued at $25,000 and equipment with market value of $16,000 for 3,300 shares of the $1 par common stock.
17	Issued 1,000 shares of 5%, no-par Class B preferred stock with stated value of $50 per share. The issue price was cash of $60 per share.

Required

Prepare the stockholders' equity section of the Laurelake balance sheet for the transactions given in this exercise. Retained Earnings has a balance of $46,000.

E13-7 ReadyTech Co. recently organized. The company issued common stock to an attorney in exchange for his patent with a market value of $40,000. In addition, ReadyTech received cash both for 2,000 shares of its $50 par preferred stock at $80 per share and for 26,000 shares of its no-par common stock at $11 per share. Retained Earnings at the end of the first year was $70,000. Without making journal entries, determine the total paid-in capital created by these transactions.

Paid-in capital for a corporation
(Obj. 2)

E13-8 Gene Shattler, Inc., has the following selected account balances at June 30, 20X2. Prepare the stockholders' equity section of the company's balance sheet.

Stockholders' equity section of a balance sheet
(Obj. 3)

Common stock, no par with $1 stated value, 100,000 shares authorized and issued	$100,000	Inventory	$112,000
		Machinery and equipment ...	109,000
		Preferred stock, 5%, $20 par, 20,000 shares authorized, 5,000 shares issued	100,000
Accumulated depreciation— machinery and equipment	62,000	Paid-in capital in excess of par—preferred stock	88,000
Retained earnings	119,000		
Cost of goods sold	81,000		

E13-9 Qualcomm Communications has the following stockholders' equity:

Dividing dividends between preferred and common stock
(Obj. 4)

Preferred stock, 8%, $10 par, 100,000 shares authorized, 20,000 shares issued	$ 200,000
Common stock, $0.50 par, 500,000 shares authorized, 300,000 shares issued	150,000
Paid-in capital in excess of par—common	600,000
Total paid-in capital	$ 950,000
Retained earnings	150,000
Total stockholders' equity	$1,100,000

First, determine whether preferred stock is cumulative or noncumulative. Then compute the amount of dividends to preferred and to common for 20X1 and 20X2 if total dividends are $10,000 in 20X1 and $60,000 in 20X2.

E13-10 The following elements of stockholders' equity are adapted from the balance sheet of Levitz Corporation.

Computing dividends on preferred and common stock
(Obj. 4)

Stockholders' Equity	$ Thousands
Preferred stock, cumulative, $2 par (Note 7)	
Series A, 50,000 shares issued	$100
Series B, 370,000 shares issued	740
Common stock, $0.10 par, 9,000,000 shares issued	900

Note 7. Preferred Stock:

	Designated Annual Cash Dividend per Share
Series A	$0.40
Series B	1.30

The Series A preferred has preference over the Series B preferred, and the company has paid all preferred dividends through 20X3.

Required

Compute the dividends to both series of preferred stock and to common for 20X4 and 20X5 if total dividends are $0 in 20X4 and $1,100,000 in 20X5.

E13-11 The balance sheet of Iota Corporation reported the following:

Preferred stock; 100 shares issued and outstanding, liquidation value $6,000	$ 4,800
Common stockholders' equity, 10,000 shares issued and outstanding	222,000
Total stockholders' equity	$226,800

Assume that Iota has paid preferred dividends for the current year and all prior years (no dividends in arrears). Compute the book value per share of the preferred stock and the common stock.

E13-12 Refer to Exercise 13-11. Compute the book value per share of the preferred stock and the common stock if three years' preferred dividends (including dividends for the current year) are in arrears. The preferred stock dividend rate is 6%. Round book value to the nearest cent.

E13-13 Weimeyer Furniture, Inc., reported these figures for 20X3 and 20X2:

	20X3	20X2
Income statement:		
Interest expense	$ 17,400,000	$ 7,100,000
Net income	12,000,000	18,700,000
Balance sheet:		
Total assets	326,000,000	317,000,000
Preferred stock, $1.30, no-par, 100,000 shares issued and outstanding	2,500,000	2,500,000
Common stockholders' equity	164,000,000	157,000,000
Total stockholders' equity	166,500,000	159,500,000

Compute rate of return on total assets and rate of return on common stockholders' equity for 20X3. Do these rates of return suggest strength or weakness? Give your reason.

E13-14 The income statement of **Pier 1 Imports, Inc.,** reported income before income tax of $130 million during a recent year. Assume Pier 1's taxable income for the year was $100 million. The company's income tax rate was 40%.

1. Journalize Pier 1's entry to record income tax for the year.
2. Show how Pier 1 would report income tax on its income statement and on its balance sheet. Complete the income statement, starting with income before tax. For the balance sheet, assume all beginning balances were zero.

Challenge Exercise

E13-15 **Wal-Mart Stores, Inc.,** reported these comparative stockholders' equity data (adapted, with amounts in millions except par value):

	January 31,	
	20X0	19X9
Common stock ($0.10 par value)	$ 446	$ 445
Capital in excess of par value	714	435
Retained earnings	25,129	20,741

Book value per share of preferred and common stock
(Obj. 5)

Book value per share of preferred and common stock; preferred dividends in arrears *(Obj. 5)*

Evaluating profitability
(Obj. 6)

Accounting for income tax by a corporation
(Obj. 7)

Accounting for stockholders' equity transactions
(Obj. 2, 4)

During 20X0, Wal-Mart completed these transactions:

a. Net income, $5,377
b. Cash dividends declared and paid, $989
c. Issuance of stock for cash, $280

Required

1. Journalize these 20X0 transactions.
2. For each stockholders' equity account, start with the January 31, 19X9, balance and work toward the balance at January 31, 20X0 to show how your journal entries accounted for the changes in the Wal-Mart accounts.

P ROBLEMS

P13-1A Joy Shields and Lin Liu are opening a **Cracker Barrel Restaurant** in Denver, Colorado. There are no competing family restaurants in the immediate vicinity. Their fundamental decision is how to organize the business, which will manage the restaurant and country store. Shields thinks the partnership form is best for their business. Liu favors the corporate form of organization. They seek your advice.

Organizing a corporation
(Obj. 1)

Required

Write a memo to Shields and Liu to make them aware of the advantages and the disadvantages of organizing the business as a corporation. Use the following format:

Date: _____	
To:	Joy Shields and Lin Liu
From:	Student Name
Subject:	Advantages and disadvantages of the corporate form of business organization

P13-2A The partnership of Duran & Nueces needed additional capital to expand into new markets, so the business incorporated as Ventura, Inc. The charter from the state of Arizona authorizes Ventura to issue 50,000 shares of 6%, $100-par preferred stock and 100,000 shares of no-par common stock. To start, Ventura completed the following transactions:

Journalizing corporation transactions and preparing the stockholders' equity section of the balance sheet
(Obj. 2, 3)

Dec. 2   Issued 9,000 shares of common stock to Duran and 12,000 shares to Nueces, both for cash of $5 per share.
     10   Issued 400 shares of preferred stock to acquire a patent with a market value of $50,000.
     27   Issued 12,000 shares of common stock to other investors for cash of $96,000.

Required

1. Record the transactions in the general journal.
2. Prepare the stockholders' equity section of the Ventura, Inc., balance sheet at December 31. The ending balance of Retained Earnings is $57,100.

P13-3A Hudson Corporation was organized in 20X1. At December 31, 20X1, Hudson's balance sheet reported the following stockholders' equity:

Issuing stock and preparing the stockholders' equity section of the balance sheet
(Obj. 2, 3)

Preferred stock, 6%, $50 par, 100,000 shares authorized, none issued	$ —
Common stock, $1 par, 500,000 shares authorized, 60,000 shares issued..	60,000
Paid-in capital in excess of par—common	40,000
Retained earnings	25,000
Total stockholders' equity..	$125,000

Required

Answer the following questions, making journal entries as needed.

1. What does the 6% mean for the preferred stock? After Hudson issues preferred stock, how much in annual cash dividends will Hudson expect to pay on 1,000 shares?
2. At what price per share did Hudson issue the common stock during 20X1?

3. Were first-year operations profitable? Give your reason.
4. During 20X2, the company completed the following selected transactions. Journalize each transaction. Explanations are not required.
   a. Issued for cash 1,000 shares of preferred stock at par value.
   b. Issued for cash 2,000 shares of common stock at a price of $3 per share.
   c. Issued 50,000 shares of common stock to acquire a building valued at $150,000.
   d. Net income for the year was $82,000, and the company declared no dividends. Make the closing entry for net income.
5. Prepare the stockholders' equity section of the Hudson Corporation balance sheet at December 31, 20X2.

Stockholders' equity section of the balance sheet
(Obj. 3)

P13-4A The following summaries for Yurman Jewelry, Inc., and Northern Lights Insurance Company provide the information needed to prepare the stockholders' equity section of each company's balance sheet. The two companies are independent.

- *Yurman Jewelry, Inc.* Yurman Jewelry is authorized to issue 40,000 shares of $1 par common stock. All the stock was issued at $12 per share. The company incurred net losses of $50,000 in 20X1 and $14,000 in 20X2. It earned net income of $23,000 in 20X3 and $71,000 in 20X4. The company declared no dividends during the four-year period.
- *Northern Lights Insurance Company.* Northern Lights Insurance Company's charter authorizes the company to issue 50,000 shares of 7%, $10 par preferred stock and 500,000 shares of no-par common stock. Northern Lights Insurance issued 1,000 shares of the preferred stock at $15 per share. It issued 100,000 shares of the common stock for $400,000. The company's retained earnings balance at the beginning of 20X4 was $120,000. Net income for 20X4 was $90,000, and the company declared the specified preferred dividend for 20X4. Preferred dividends for 20X3 were in arrears.

Required

For each company, prepare the stockholders' equity section of its balance sheet at December 31, 20X4. Show the computation of all amounts. Entries are not required.

Analyzing the stockholders' equity of an actual corporation
(Obj. 3, 4)

P13-5A **The Procter & Gamble Company** reported the following stockholders' equity, as adapted, on its balance sheet at June 30, 19X9:

Stockholders' Equity	$ Millions
Preferred stock, 6.125%—	
Authorized 600,000,000 shares; issued 1,781,000 shares	$ 1,781
Common stock—$1 stated value—	
Authorized 5,000,000,000 shares; issued 1,320,000,000	1,320
Additional paid-in capital, common..	1,337
Retained earnings...	10,778
Other	(3,158)
Total...	$12,058

Required

1. Identify the different issues of stock Procter & Gamble has outstanding.
2. Make two summary journal entries to record issuance of all the Procter & Gamble stock. Assume all the stock was issued for cash. Explanations are not required.
3. Assume preferred dividends are in arrears for fiscal year 19X9. Journalize the declaration of a $1,626 million dividend at June 30, 20X0. Use separate Dividends Payable accounts for Preferred and Common. Round to the nearest $1 million. An explanation is not required.

Preparing a corporation balance sheet; measuring profitability
(Obj. 3, 6)

P13-6A ◄ *Link Back to Chapter 1 (Accounting Equation).* The following accounts and related balances of Omaha Mutual, Inc., are arranged in no particular order.

Common stock, $5 par,			Retained earnings........................	$?
100,000 shares authorized,			Inventory.....................................	181,000
22,000 shares issued..............	$110,000		Property, plant, and	
Dividends payable	3,000		equipment, net	278,000
Total assets,			Prepaid expenses	13,000
November 30, 20X1...............	581,000		Goodwill, net................................	37,000
Net income	47,200		Accrued liabilities	17,000
Common stockholders' equity,			Long-term note payable	104,000
November 30, 20X1...............	383,000		Accounts receivable, net..............	102,000
Interest expense	12,800		Preferred stock, 4%, $10 par,	
Additional paid-in capital—			25,000 shares authorized,	
common..................................	140,000		3,700 shares issued	37,000
Accounts payable	31,000		Cash..	43,000

Required

1. Prepare the company's classified balance sheet in the account format at November 30, 20X2. Use the accounting equation to compute Retained Earnings.
2. Compute rate of return on total assets and rate of return on common stockholders' equity for the year ended November 30, 20X2.
3. Do these rates of return suggest strength or weakness? Give your reason.

P13-7A Eastern Seaboard Airline Corporation has 5,000 shares of 5%, $10 par value preferred stock and 100,000 shares of $1.50 par common stock outstanding. During a three-year period, Eastern Seaboard declared and paid cash dividends as follows: 20X1, $1,500; 20X2, $15,000; and 20X3, $23,000.

Computing dividends on preferred and common stock (Obj. 4)

Required

1. Compute the total dividends to preferred stock and to common stock for each of the three years if
   a. Preferred is noncumulative
   b. Preferred is cumulative
2. For case (1b), record the declaration of the 20X3 dividends on December 22, 20X3, and the payment of the dividends on January 14, 20X4. Use separate Dividends Payable accounts for Preferred and Common.

P13-8A The balance sheet of Hardwood Furniture, Inc., reported the following:

Analyzing the stockholders' equity of an actual corporation (Obj. 4, 5)

Stockholders' Investment [same as Stockholders' Equity]	($ Thousands)
Cumulative preferred stock..	$ 45
Common stock, $1 par, authorized 40,000,000 shares; issued 16,000,000 shares	16,000
Additional paid-in capital...	217,000
Retained earnings (Deficit)...	(77,165)
Total stockholders' investment..	$155,880

Notes to the financial statements indicate that 9,000 shares of $1.45 preferred stock with a stated value of $5 per share were issued and outstanding. The preferred stock has a liquidation value of $25 per share, and preferred dividends are in arrears for two years, including the current year. The additional paid-in capital belongs to common. On the balance sheet date, the market value of the Hardwood Furniture common stock was $9.50 per share.

Required

1. Is the preferred stock cumulative or noncumulative? How can you tell?
2. What is the amount of the annual preferred dividend?
3. What is the total paid-in capital of the company?
4. What was the total market value of the common stock?
5. Compute the book value per share of the preferred stock and the common stock.

P13-9A The accounting (not the income tax) records of Solarex Energy Corporation provide the income statement for 20X4.

Computing and recording a corporation's income tax (Obj. 7)

Total revenue.....................................	$930,000
Expenses:	
Cost of goods sold	$430,000
Operating expenses........................	270,000
Total expenses before tax..............	700,000
Income before income tax...............	$230,000

The operating expenses include depreciation of $50,000 computed on the straight-line method. In calculating taxable income on the tax return, Solarex uses the modified accelerated cost recovery system (MACRS). MACRS depreciation was $80,000 for 20X4. The corporate income tax rate is 35%.

Required

1. Compute taxable income for the year.
2. Journalize the corporation's income tax for 20X4.
3. Prepare the corporation's single-step income statement for 20X4.

(Group B) PROBLEMS

P13-1B Ted Andrews and Ron Durham are opening a **Pier 1 Imports** store in a shopping center in Taos, New Mexico. The area is growing, and no competitors are located nearby. Their basic decision is how to organize the business. Andrews thinks the partnership form is best. Durham favors the corporate form of organization. They seek your advice.

Required

Write a memo to Andrews and Durham to make them aware of the advantages and the disadvantages of organizing the business as a corporate. Use the following format for your memo:

Date:	_____
To:	Ted Andrews and Ron Durham
From:	Student Name
Subject:	Advantages and disadvantages of the corporate form of business organization

P13-2B The partners who own Craven & Thames wished to avoid the unlimited personal liability of the partnership form of business, so they incorporated the partnership as C & T Services, Inc. The charter from the state of Louisiana authorizes the corporation to issue 10,000 shares of 6%, $100 par preferred stock and 250,000 shares of no-par common stock. In its first month, C & T Services completed the following transactions:

Jan. 3 Issued 6,300 shares of common stock to Craven and 3,800 shares to Thames, both for cash of $10 per share.
  12 Issued 1,000 shares of preferred stock to acquire a patent with a market value of $110,000.
  22 Issued 1,500 shares of common stock to other investors for $15 cash per share.

Required

1. Record the transactions in the general journal.
2. Prepare the stockholders' equity section of the C & T Services, Inc., balance sheet at January 31. The ending balance of Retained Earnings is $40,300.

P13-3B Zaponata Corporation was organized in 20X1. At December 31, 20X1, Zaponata's balance sheet reported the following stockholders' equity:

Preferred stock, 5%, $10 par, 50,000 shares authorized, none issued	$ —
Common stock, $2 par, 100,000 shares authorized, 10,000 shares issued	20,000
Paid-in capital in excess of par—common............................	30,000
Retained earnings (Deficit)...	(5,000)
Total stockholders' equity...	$45,000

Required

Answer the following questions, making journal entries as needed.

1. What does the 5% mean for the preferred stock? After Zaponata issues preferred stock, how much in annual cash dividends will Zaponata expect to pay on 1,000 shares?
2. At what price per share did Zaponata issue the common stock during 20X1?
3. Were first-year operations profitable? Give your reason.
4. During 20X2, the company completed the following selected transactions. Journalize each transaction. Explanations are not required.
   a. Issued for cash 5,000 shares of preferred stock at par value.
   b. Issued for cash 1,000 shares of common stock at a price of $7 per share.
   c. Issued 20,000 shares of common stock to acquire a building valued at $120,000.
   d. Net income for the year was $50,000, and the company declared no dividends. Make the closing entry for net income.
5. Prepare the stockholders' equity section of the Zaponata Corporation balance sheet at December 31, 20X2.

P13-4B Stockholders' equity information for two independent companies, Granada Enterprises, Inc., and Traigon Corp. is as follows:

Stockholders' equity section of the balance sheet (Obj. 3)

- *Granada Enterprises, Inc.* Granada is authorized to issue 60,000 shares of $5 par common stock. All the stock was issued at $12 per share. The company incurred a net loss of $41,000 in 20X1. It earned net income of $60,000 in 20X2 and $90,000 in 20X3. The company declared no dividends during the three-year period.
- *Traigon Corp.* Traigon's charter authorizes the company to issue 10,000 shares of $2.50 preferred stock with par value of $50 and 120,000 shares of no-par common stock. Traigon issued 1,000 shares of the preferred stock at $54 per share. It issued 40,000 shares of the common stock for a total of $220,000. The company's Retained Earnings balance at the beginning of 20X3 was $64,000, and net income for the year was $90,000. During 20X3, the company declared the specified dividend on preferred and a $0.50 per share dividend on common. Preferred dividends for 20X2 were in arrears.

Required

For each company, prepare the stockholders' equity section of its balance sheet at December 31, 20X3. Show the computation of all amounts. Entries are not required.

P13-5B **Tandy Corporation,** which operates Radio Shack stores, included the following stockholders' equity on its year-end balance sheet at December 31, 19X8, with all dollar amounts, except par value per share, in millions:

Analyzing the stockholders' equity of an actual corporation (Obj. 3, 4)

Stockholders' Equity	($ Millions)
Preferred stock, 6% cumulative	$ 100
Common stock—par value $1 per share; 250,000,000 shares authorized, 139,000,000 shares issued	139
Paid-in capital in excess of par—common	110
Retained earnings	1,693
	$2,042

Required

1. Identify the different issues of stock Tandy has outstanding.
2. Give two summary entries to record issuance of all the Tandy stock. Assume that all the stock was issued for cash. Explanations are not required.
3. Assume that preferred dividends are in arrears for 19X7 and 19X8. Record the declaration of a $50 million cash dividend on December 30, 19X9. Use separate Dividends Payable accounts for Preferred and Common. An explanation is not required.

P13-6B ◄ *Link Back to Chapter 1 (Accounting Equation).* The following accounts and related balances of Witt, Inc., are arranged in no particular order:

Preparing a corporation balance sheet; measuring profitability (Obj. 3, 6)

Interest expense	$ 6,100	Accounts receivable, net	$ 46,000
Property, plant, and equipment, net	261,000	Paid-in capital in excess of par—common	19,000
Common stock, $1 par, 500,000 shares authorized, 236,000 shares issued	236,000	Accrued liabilities	26,000
		Long-term note payable	42,000
		Inventory	81,000
Dividends payable	9,000	Prepaid expenses	10,000
Retained earnings	?	Common stockholders' equity, June 30, 20X1	222,000
Accounts payable	31,000		
Trademark, net	9,000	Net income	51,000
Preferred stock, $0.10, no-par, 10,000 shares authorized and issued	25,000	Total assets, June 30, 20X1	404,000
		Cash	10,000

Required

1. Prepare the company's classified balance sheet in the account format at June 30, 20X2. Use the accounting equation to compute Retained Earnings.
2. Compute rate of return on total assets and rate of return on common stockholders' equity for the year ended June 30, 20X2.
3. Do these rates of return suggest strength or weakness? Give your reason.

Computing dividends on
preferred and common stock
(Obj. 4)

P13-7B OnPoint Consulting, Inc., has 10,000 shares of $4.50, no-par preferred stock and 50,000 shares of no-par common stock outstanding. OnPoint declared and paid the following dividends during a three-year period: 20X1, $20,000; 20X2, $100,000; and 20X3, $215,000.

Required

1. Compute the total dividends to preferred stock and to common stock for each of the three years if
   a. Preferred is noncumulative   **b.** Preferred is cumulative
2. For case (1b), record the declaration of the 20X3 dividends on December 28, 20X3, and the payment of the dividends on January 17, 20X4. Use separate Dividends Payable accounts for Preferred and Common.

Analyzing the stockholders'
equity of an actual corporation
(Obj. 4, 5)

P13-8B The balance sheet of The Gonzalez Group reported the following:

Stockholders' Investment [same as stockholders' equity]	
Nonvoting preferred stock, no-par (liquidation value, $358,000)	$320,000
Common stock, $1.50 par value, authorized 75,000 shares; issued 36,000 shares	54,000
[Additional] paid-in capital	231,000
Retained earnings	141,000
Total stockholders' investment	$746,000

Notes to the financial statements indicate that 8,000 shares of $3.40 preferred stock with a stated value of $40 per share were issued and outstanding. Preferred dividends are in arrears for three years, including the current year. The additional paid-in capital belongs to common. On the balance sheet date, the market value of the Gonzalez common stock was $10 per share.

Required

1. Is the preferred stock cumulative or noncumulative? How can you tell?
2. What is the amount of the annual preferred dividend?
3. Which class of stockholders controls the company? Give your reason.
4. What is the total paid-in capital of the company?
5. What was the total market value of the common stock?
6. Compute the book value per share of the preferred stock and the common stock.

Computing and recording a
corporation's income tax
(Obj. 7)

P13-9B The accounting (not the income tax) records of Fox Security Systems, Inc., provide the income statement for 20X3.

Total revenue	$680,000
Expenses:	
Cost of goods sold	$290,000
Operating expenses	180,000
Total expenses before tax	470,000
Income before income tax	$210,000

The operating expenses include depreciation of $40,000 computed under the straight-line method. In calculating taxable income on the tax return, Fox uses the modified accelerated cost recovery system (MACRS). MACRS depreciation was $50,000 for 20X3. The corporate income tax rate is 40%.

Required

1. Compute taxable income for the year.
2. Journalize the corporation's income tax for 20X3.
3. Prepare the corporation's single-step income statement for 20X3.

DECISION CASES

Case 1. Terry Caine and Nicole Jacks have written a spreadsheet program that they believe will rival Excel and Lotus. They need additional capital to market the product, and they plan to incorporate the business. They are considering alternative capital structures for the corporation. Their primary goal is to raise as much capital as possible without giving up control of the business. The partners plan to invest the software program and receive 110,000 shares of the corporation's common stock. The partners have been offered $110,000 for the rights to the software program.

Evaluating alternative ways to raise capital
(Obj. 2, 3)

The corporation's plans for a charter include an authorization to issue 5,000 shares of preferred stock and 500,000 shares of $1 par common stock. Caine and Jacks are uncertain about the most desirable features for the preferred stock. Prior to incorporating, the partners are discussing their plans with two investment groups. The corporation can obtain capital from outside investors under either of the following plans:

- *Plan 1.* Group 1 will invest $105,000 to acquire 1,000 shares of $5, no-par preferred stock and $70,000 to acquire 70,000 shares of common stock. Each preferred share receives 50 votes on matters that come before the stockholders.
- *Plan 2.* Group 2 will invest $160,000 to acquire 1,400 shares of 6%, $100 par nonvoting, noncumulative preferred stock.

Required

Assume that the corporation is chartered.

1. Journalize the issuance of common stock to Caine and Jacks. Explanations are not required.
2. Journalize the issuance of stock to the outsiders under both plans. Explanations are not required.
3. Assume that net income for the first year is $180,000 and total dividends are $30,000. Prepare the stockholders' equity section of the corporation's balance sheet under both plans.
4. Recommend one of the plans to Caine and Jacks. Give your reasons.

Case 2. Answering the following questions will enhance your understanding of the capital stock of corporations. Consider each question independently of the others.

Characteristics of corporations' capital stock
(Obj. 2, 5)

1. Why are capital stock and retained earnings shown separately in the shareholders' equity section?
2. Chiu Wang, major shareholder of C-W, Inc., proposes to sell some land she owns to the company for common shares in C-W. What problem does C-W, Inc., face in recording the transaction?
3. Preferred shares have advantages with respect to dividends and corporate liquidation. Why would investors buy common stock when preferred stock is available?
4. What does it mean if the liquidation value of a company's preferred stock is greater than its market value?
5. If you owned 100 shares of stock in **Dell Computer Corporation** and someone offered to buy the stock for its book value, would you accept the offer? Why or why not?

ETHICAL ISSUE

Note: This case is based on an actual situation.

Jeremy Copeland paid $50,000 for a franchise that entitled him to market Success Associates software programs in the countries of the European Common Market. Copeland intended to sell individual franchises for the major language groups of western Europe — German, French, English, Spanish, and Italian. Naturally, investors considering buying a franchise from Copeland asked to see the financial statements of his business.

Believing the value of the franchise to be greater than $50,000, Copeland sought to capitalize his own franchise at $500,000. The law firm of St. Charles & LaDue helped Copeland form a corporation chartered to issue 500,000 shares of common stock with par value of $1 per share. Attorneys suggested the following chain of transactions:

- **a.** A third party borrows $500,000 and purchases the franchise from Copeland.
- **b.** Copeland pays the corporation $500,000 to acquire all its stock.
- **c.** The corporation buys the franchise from the third party, who repays the loan.

In the final analysis, the third party is debt-free and out of the picture. Copeland owns all the corporation's stock, and the corporation owns the franchise. The corporation's balance sheet lists a franchise acquired at a cost of $500,000. This balance sheet is Copeland's most valuable marketing tool.

Required

1. What is unethical about this situation?
2. Who can be harmed? How can they be harmed? What role does accounting play?

FINANCIAL STATEMENT CASE

Analyzing stockholders' equity
(Obj. 2, 3)

The **Target Corporation** financial statements appear in Appendix A. Answer the following questions about Target's stock.

Required

1. How much of Target's preferred stock was outstanding at January 29, 2000? How can you tell? The statement of shareholders' investment (stockholders' equity) reports what happened to Target's preferred stock during the fiscal year ended January 29, 2000. What was it?
2. Examine Target's balance sheet. Which stockholders' equity account increased the most during the year ended January 29, 2000 (fiscal year 2000)? Did this increase occur because of new paid-in capital that Target received from stockholders during this year? If not, explain where the additional paid-in capital came from.
3. Give Target's journal entries during fiscal year 2000 to record (a) closing net income to Retained Earnings and (b) declaring cash dividends. The statement of shareholders' investment gives the details for these transactions.

TEAM PROJECT

Competitive pressures are the norm in business. **Lexus** automobiles (made in Japan) have cut into the sales of **Mercedes Benz** (a German company), **Jaguar Motors** (a British company), **General Motors'** Cadillac Division, and **Ford's** Lincoln Division (both U.S. companies). **Dell, Gateway,** and **Compaq** computers have siphoned business away from **IBM.** Foreign steelmakers have reduced the once-massive U.S. steel industry to a fraction of its former size.

Indeed, corporate downsizing has occurred on a massive scale. During the past few years, each company or industry mentioned here has pared down plant and equipment, laid off employees, or restructured operations.

Required

1. Identify all the stakeholders of a corporation and the stake each group has in the company. A *stakeholder* is a person or a group who has an interest (that is, a stake) in the success of the organization.
2. Identify several measures by which a corporation may be considered deficient and which may indicate the need for downsizing. How can downsizing help to solve this problem? Discuss how each measure can indicate the need for downsizing.
3. Debate the downsizing issue. One group of students takes the perspective of the company and its stockholders, and another group of students takes the perspective of other stakeholders of the company.

INTERNET EXERCISE

Yahoo! Inc.

Go to the "Dividends and Treasury Stock" episode on the *Mastering Accounting* CD-ROM for an interactive, video-enhanced exercise on how CanGo can boost investor confidence after poor quarterly performance reports. The episode focuses on the difference between cash and stock dividends.

1. Go to **http://finance.yahoo.com** and type in the stock symbol YHOO. Using the pull-down menu, select *Basic,* and then click on *Get Quotes.* In the chart under "Last Trade," identify how much investors were willing to pay for a share of stock on the last trade.
2. In the chart under "More Info" click on *Profile.*
   a. Review the "Business Summary." How many users does **Yahoo!** serve each month?
   b. Scroll down to review "Statistics at a Glance." What is Yahoo!'s book value per share? Compare the book value to the market value of the last trade. Which is greater?
   c. What is Yahoo!'s return on assets and return on equity? Explain what both of these ratios indicate for Yahoo! Which ratio is greater? What does this indicate?
   d. How much is Yahoo's annual dividend?
3. Go to **http://www.forbes.com** and under "Stocks" type YHOO, and then click on *Go.* In the left-hand column click on "Financials" to find the answers to the following questions.

a. As of the most recent balance sheet date, how much have shareholders paid in total for Yahoo! stock? During the most recent year, how much capital did Yahoo! raise through the issuance of stock? Yahoo! does not pay dividends. Why would shareholders be interested in purchasing stock in this company?

b. As of the most recent balance sheet date, what is Yahoo!'s reported retained earnings balance? Is this balance positive or negative? How does a company get a retained earnings deficit? Does Yahoo! have enough retained earnings to declare dividends?

c. What is the primary source of financing for Yahoo!'s assets?

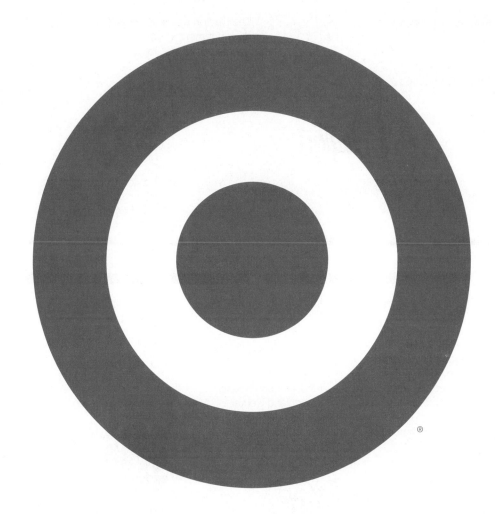

We are Target Corporation.

Annual Report 1999

The Dayton Company.

Dayton Dry Goods Company changes its name to The Dayton Company.

Dayton's

The Dayton Company adopts a new logo.

Target *is a new idea in discount stores*

The Dayton Company enters discount merchandising with the opening of its first Target stores.

Target becomes the corporation's top revenue producer.

Dayton Corporation has its first public offering of common stock.

1902   **1946**   **1954**   **1969**   **1978**

1910   **1953**   **1962**   **1967**   **1979**

The Dayton Company begins the tradition that keeps us strong today: 5% of profits go back to the communities we serve.

J.L. Hudson opens Northland Center in Detroit, the world's largest shopping center at that time.

The Dayton Hudson Corporation is formed through a merger of the Dayton Corporation and the J.L. Hudson Company.

Dayton Hudson Corporation acquires Mervyn's.

MERVYN'S

George Dayton opens Goodfellows in downtown Minneapolis, the same location as today's downtown store. In 1903, the corporate name is changed to the Dayton Dry Goods Company.

Dayton Hudson
Corporation acquires
Rivertown Trading
Company and
The Associated
Merchandising
Corporation.

Marshall Field's

Mervyn's changes
its name to
Mervyn's California.

Target launches
the industry's first
discount store credit
card, the Target
Guest Card.

First SuperTarget
stores open.

1984	1990		1999

1995	1998	2000

Dayton Hudson
Corporation acquires
Marshall Field's.

Dayton Hudson
Corporation launches its
e-commerce capability
with new store brand
web sites.

Dayton Hudson
Corporation
celebrates its
name change to
Target Corporation.

Dayton's and
Hudson's combine
to form Dayton
Hudson Department
Store Company.

TARGET CORPORATION

DAYTON'S
HUDSON'S

TARGET CORPORATION

Our mission is to be the retailer of choice in

the discount, middle market and department store

retail segments. By focusing on trend leadership, excellent

guest service, exciting team member opportunities, and

community outreach, we create long-term

shareholder value.

Revenues

(millions)

Pre-tax Segment Profit

(millions)

Net Earnings

(millions)

Diluted Earnings per Share

Operating Results ($ millions)	1999	1998	Change
Revenues	**$33,702**	$30,662	10%
Pre-tax segment profit	**$ 2,523**	$ 2,097	20%
Net earnings*	**$ 1,144**	$ 935	22%

Per Share Data			
Diluted earnings*	**$ 2.45**	$ 1.98	24%
Cash dividends declared	**$ .40**	$ .36	11%

At Year-End			
Common shares outstanding	**455,841,388**	441,809,806	
Retail square feet	**138,640,000**	130,172,000	
Number of stores	**1,243**	1,182	

*Includes unusual items, resulting in net after-tax charges of $44 million ($.09 per share) in 1999, $35 million ($.08 per share) in 1998, $24 million ($.05 per share) in 1997, and $92 million ($.20 per share) in 1996.

Acknowledging the strength of the Target brand and the future growth

opportunities of our largest retail division, we recently changed our name to Target Corporation. Our new name recognizes that the Target division, today, comprises more than 75 percent of the company's sales and profits, and that this contribution will continue to increase over time as we further expand our store base. Our new name also reflects our continuing commitment to leverage our resources for the benefit of the total corporation, and as a result, to improve our overall financial results and create substantial value for our shareholders.

Our performance in 1999 was driven by superior results at our Target division. Revenues for the segment increased 13 percent to $26 billion and pre-tax profit grew 28 percent to over $2 billion, establishing a new milestone in Target's history. In addition, Target's pre-tax profit as a percent of revenues equaled the reported profit margin at Wal*Mart's domestic discount/supercenter division for the year, eliminating a significant differential that existed in prior years. These outstanding results at Target in 1999, combined with record sales and profits at our Department Stores, produced our fourth consecutive year of earnings per share growth in excess of 20 percent.

We are very pleased with our performance in the past year and we are excited about the opportunities for profitable growth in 2000 and beyond. As we look forward, we remain confident that Target Corporation can continue to deliver average annual earnings per share growth of 15 percent or more over time.

New Store Growth With less than 1,000 stores in the U.S. today, Target's opportunities for domestic new store growth remain plentiful. During 1999, Target added a total of 74 new stores, increasing square footage by 9 percent. We continued to focus our efforts on markets in the Northeast and Mid-Atlantic, devoting nearly 40 percent of our new store openings to this region.

Importantly, by becoming more flexible in our site selection and store design without compromising the Target brand, we continue to have success in penetrating these markets despite difficult real estate challenges. In 1999, we entered two new markets, Boston and Pittsburgh, and in 2000, we will enter two new states, Connecticut and West Virginia, bringing the number of states in which we operate to 46.

Bob Ulrich,
Chairman and
Chief Executive Officer

Our store expansion in 2000 will also include a significant acceleration of SuperTarget store openings, reflecting our increased confidence in the sales and profit potential of this concept. We will essentially double our number of SuperTarget stores during the year, adding 15 new locations, primarily in the Midwest and South. About half of these stores will be relocations of existing discount stores, giving us the ability to capture greater market share in key metropolitan areas. With plans for at least 200 SuperTarget locations within the next ten years, we believe this strategy will generate profitable growth for many years to come.

Other Growth Opportunities At the core of Target's future growth and financial success is our differentiated merchandise strategy — with an emphasis on quality and original design, unique product, impactful presentation and value pricing. During the past year, we strengthened our merchandise assortment with the addition of new brands such as Calphalon, Stiffel, Discovery Channel toys and designs by Michael Graves and Robert Abbey. In 2000, we will continue to create excitement for our guests with new initiatives. Examples include an expanded offering of Michael Graves housewares and a new assortment of electronics; the introduction of Martex bed and bath collections; exclusive new lines of sporting goods equipment and accessories; and the expansion of our Archer Farms brand of premier food. Each of these efforts reinforces and enhances Target's brand image in the marketplace and contributes to our financial strength.

Credit is also an important contributor to our overall earnings growth. During the past five years, contribution from credit has increased at a compound annual rate of 17 percent, and both return on investment and EVA have risen sharply. While we continue to invest in credit programs at all three of our segments, the Target Guest Card is the primary driver of growth for this business. In 2000, we will continue to increase our card penetration, enhance our guest loyalty programs and leverage our credit operation to sustain our profitable growth.

In 1999, Target Corporation devoted greater resources to developing web-based strategies, reflecting our belief that the Internet and e-commerce are vital to our future. In our view, the Internet provides an important tool for communicating with our guests as well as a new distribution channel for our merchandise. Through our new business unit called target.direct, we are focused on leveraging our strengths as a well-known and trusted retailer to increase guest service and generate profitable sales. We believe our powerful marketing, our differentiated merchandise and more than 1,200 convenient store locations give us a competitive advantage in the on-line world. In 2000, we will continue to make the necessary investments in this business to attract experienced and talented team members, to improve our technology and fulfillment capability, and to provide our guests with appropriate services and merchandise selection.

Though our name has changed to reflect the growth and importance of Target, we remain committed to Dayton's, Marshall Field's, Hudson's and Mervyn's. During the past five years, Target Corporation has averaged a total return to shareholders on an annualized basis of 43 percent. During this same period, both Mervyn's and our Department Stores were key contributors to our overall strategy and financial performance. In 1999 alone, their combined net pre-tax cash flow again exceeded a half billion dollars. We believe that these two segments will continue to create value for Target Corporation in the years ahead.

We are excited about the future for Target Corporation and believe that we are well-positioned to build on our past performance. As we look forward, we remain confident that we will continue to deliver strong growth in sales and earnings and achieve our objective of generating at least 15 percent average annual earnings per share growth over time.

March 24, 2000

Bob Ulrich, Chairman and Chief Executive Officer

We are now

Target Corporation, a name that reflects

the powerful recognition of our largest retail brand.

Today, Target Stores makes up more than 75 percent of our

sales and profits, a percentage that will continue to grow as we

open new Target stores across the country. The Target name best

reflects our business and our company, today and in the future.

We remain a company that is committed to growth

and delivering superior returns to our

shareholders.

Target Corporation's goal is to deliver average annual earnings per share growth of 15 percent or more over time. To deliver on that pledge to shareholders we will continue to grow the Target store base; innovate to grow sales at existing stores; pursue new retail strategies; and enhance our credit programs. Our continued success depends on clearly defined brand strategies at each of our stores, great execution every day for our guests, a commitment to constant innovation and reinvention, and support of our communities.

New Store Growth Our primary growth comes from new store expansion. Target continues to open stores in new U.S. markets and increase store density in existing markets, growing retail square footage by 8 to 10 percent annually. In 2000, Target will open approximately 80 total new stores, including 15 new SuperTarget stores, essentially doubling the number of SuperTarget locations we operated at year end. Target will add locations in two new states—West Virginia and Connecticut—and expand our presence in key markets like Pittsburgh, Boston and Dallas/Fort Worth. As Target's brand becomes stronger, it allows us to add more stores in existing metropolitan markets. To provide guests with added value and convenience, all new Target stores and remodels will feature pharmacies, optical shops, one-hour photo labs and portrait studios. Our newest stores will feature an updated look with an arched entrance with more glass for a brighter, more inviting feel. We will also continue to invest in store remodels to ensure that all Target stores continue to represent the Target brand.

Our goal at SuperTarget is to bring "fashion to food."

Target entered the Boston market in July 1999 with five stores, under the advertising theme, "the store you've been waiting for." Northeast and Mid-Atlantic markets are key areas for Target's expansion.

Differentiated Merchandise and Presentation Target's core merchandising strategy centers on consistent delivery of differentiation and value. We know we have to deliver excitement and value in dramatic new ways every time our guests visit our stores. The primary way we do this is by offering well-designed, trend-right merchandise at great prices, with powerful presentations in attractive stores. We are adding more exclusive product to our stores, with a greater emphasis on design and a greater depth of trend-right product.

For example, in 1999 Target completely reinvented the toy area. While we still carry traditional toy categories, we increased our offering of toys characterized by quality, craftsmanship, exclusivity and value. We carry great brand names such as Playmobil and Sanrio — and toys from the Discovery Channel. We also completely redesigned our in-store presentation of toys with new, vibrant signing and displays.

The Target "Sign of the Times" advertising campaign leverages the acceptance of the Target bullseye logo. The campaign was launched in New York City with posters, images on New York metro water towers and postings on construction sites.

In addition, our home department is evolving to become a shopping destination similar to a specialty store. In the past year we have added brands like Calphalon and Stiffel, and designs by Michael Graves and Robert Abbey. Most recently, Target introduced exclusive bedding and bath products from Martex, featuring 250-thread-count cotton sheets, duvets and plush towels. These assortments enhance Target's powerful brand image among our guests and are the heart of our strategy to offer compelling, differentiated merchandise.

Target's new toy offerings and the toy area's new signing reflect the company's commitment to constant innovation and reinvention in all merchandise areas. Target continues to add more exclusive products to its stores, with offerings like Sonia Kashuk Professional Makeup.

Better Guest Service In addition to our merchandise, we are working to differentiate Target's service as well. We know that guests want ultra-fast service with a respectful tone. That means getting in and out of the store quickly, finding merchandise in-stock, and obtaining rapid and knowledgeable answers to questions. We want to inject speed in every service area that affects the guest. Guests at Target tell us service is more important to them than any other aspect of their store experience, and therefore service is our highest priority.

Target is investing in technology and training to deliver faster, more knowledgeable service for our guests.

In addition to speed of service, ensuring that merchandise is available and in-stock is essential to delivering great guest service. To improve Target's in-stocks we have made supply chain performance a top priority.

SuperTarget Expansion SuperTarget provides us with tremendous opportunities for future growth. SuperTarget combines general merchandise with high-quality grocery items to offer a convenient one-stop shopping experience for guests. Our SuperTarget strategy is exactly the same as our general merchandise strategy: "Expect More. Pay Less." Our goal is to leverage Target's brand heritage and differentiate ourselves from other supercenters. Expanding the Archer Farms brand for the grocery side of the business — including an extensive line of Archer Farms private label grocery products that are of higher quality than most national brands — is key to this differentiation.

Target is including pharmacies in all new and remodeled Target stores, adding more than 100 pharmacies in 2000 alone. Pharmacy was one of the top performing areas at Target in 1999, producing double-digit comparable-store sales results.

In 1999, SuperTarget improved its gross margin performance, the quality of its perishable foods offering and its expense structure. As a result of these merchandising and operational improvements, we are accelerating the growth of SuperTarget, adding 15 stores in 2000. In the next ten years, we expect to open at least 200 SuperTarget stores that will generate $15 billion or more in sales. Relocations of existing Target stores provide significant opportunity for SuperTarget growth, allowing us to update our store base as it ages, and replace older stores with our newest and biggest stores. This will help fuel many years of growth for Target.

E-Commerce In early 2000, Target formed a new business unit called target.direct, which is responsible for the company's electronic retailing and direct marketing efforts. The Internet and e-commerce are a vital part of Target Corporation; target.direct will help us leverage the power of all our store brands and catalogs.

We see the Internet not only as a channel for selling merchandise, but as an important communications tool to reach guests and drive increased guest service. In 1999, we devoted more resources to building the merchandising, marketing, fulfillment and technology processes required to support this new channel. Today we operate ten websites — eight of which are full-service selling sites. The largest is target.com, an exciting site that is consistent with the Target brand, offering thousands of unique and highly differentiated items that are also available in Target Stores. In addition to buying merchandise, guests can apply for a Target Guest Card, access information on programs like Take Charge of Education, find out what's new in our stores, get a map to a specific store location, or even apply for a job.

SuperTarget offers the best in high-quality groceries and general merchandise. We plan to open more than 200 SuperTarget locations in the next ten years.

Target.com will add bridal and baby gift registries in 2000 and significantly increase the number of items for sale on-line.

We are excited about the possibilities of this medium to drive profitable sales, increase guest service and enhance the brand equity of our stores. We believe our competitive advantage in the electronic world will come from leveraging our existing strengths as a retailer, including our trusted brand names, marketing power, store presence and differentiated merchandise. We will continue investing in this area in 2000, expanding our on-line merchandise assortments and guest services.

Multiple Retail Segments Target Corporation also competes in the middle-market and traditional department store segments of the retail marketplace through Mervyn's California and Dayton's, Marshall Field's and Hudson's. Mervyn's and the Department Stores are key contributors to our overall strategy.

At our Department Stores, we remain focused on our commitment to be "The Best Store in Town" in our core Midwest markets as we strive to deliver fashion leadership and superior guest service. In 2000, we are working to enhance the shopping experience at our stores in several ways: by building stronger relationships with our guests through more personalized selling and enhanced guest loyalty programs; through a stronger commitment to newness and fashion product in our assortments; and with the creation of a more captivating store environment, with visual drama and ease of shopping. One way we are reinventing the shopping experience is through events like the Paris Flea Market and our popular "Fash Bash" fashion shows. Marketing initiatives for our department stores will continue to reinforce the strong brand heritage of our stores.

At Dayton's, Marshall Field's and Hudson's, we are committed to being "The Best Store in Town."

At Mervyn's, we are working to differentiate ourselves in the middle-market with our national and owned brands. Over the last three years, Mervyn's has added more than 125 national and market brands to the sales floor. In 1999, we made a more concerted effort to let our guests know about our brands by reinforcing our "Big Brands. Small Prices." promise in all of our marketing vehicles. We also updated our in-store presentations with more national brand shops and stronger in-store brand identification. We have introduced into our assortment more exclusive merchandise designed by individuals with national

Mervyn's California offers a strong assortment of national brands and high-quality owned brands for the middle market.

or international reputations, like craft artist Debbie Mumm and Australian painter and designer Ken Done. We also continue to upgrade and improve the quality and fashion content of our core owned brands, like Hillard & Hanson. In addition to better merchandise content, in 2000 Mervyn's will focus on improving in-stocks, guest service and merchandise presentation.

Credit Programs We offer proprietary credit in each of our business segments. Our credit portfolio is the second largest among retailers that issue their own cards and currently includes more than 30 million cards held by our guests. The growth of the Target Guest Card continues to drive increases in profit contribution from credit. Guest loyalty programs at each of our stores help us build stronger relationships with our guests and increase patronage of our stores. At Target, more than 4 million guests are enrolled in our Take Charge of Education program, where 1 percent of purchases made on the Target Guest Card are donated to a K-12 school of the guest's choice. We plan to grow credit's contribution to our results in the future by opening new accounts, enhancing guest loyalty programs and managing the business with financial discipline.

Credit programs contribute to earnings growth by driving sales at our stores and through credit's contribution to profits. The Target Guest card is now carried by more than 15 million Americans.

A Community Partner Our commitment to be an active member of the communities where we operate is also essential to our success. In 1999, we gave more than $67 million to nonprofit organizations across the country. We support the United Way with a $3 million corporate contribution — and our team members donated another $9 million to their local United Ways. In 2000, our grantmaking will exceed $80 million.

One of our greatest and most heartfelt contributions is called Target House. Dedicated in May 1999, Target House is a home-away-from-home for patients and their families undergoing treatment at St. Jude Children's Research Hospital in Memphis. Our guests help support Target House and the families it serves whenever they make pharmacy, and health and beauty product purchases at Target. In March, Target announced its intention to build a Target House annex, with an additional 44 suites, to serve even more families.

At Target House, which opened in May 1999, children who are undergoing long-term treatment at St. Jude Children's Research Hospital have a home-away-from-home for themselves and their families.

Education is important to our guests and to our company. Target has donated more than $18 million to schools across the country since our Take Charge of Education program began in 1997. More than 100,000 schools across the country participate in the program.

The Target Foundation was created in early 2000, with a continued emphasis on funding arts and social action initiatives in Minnesota. A key focus area for giving is to support immediate community needs for food, clothing and shelter. To that end, the Foundation awarded a $1 million grant to Sharing & Caring Hands, the Minneapolis nonprofit organization that serves the needs of inner city residents.

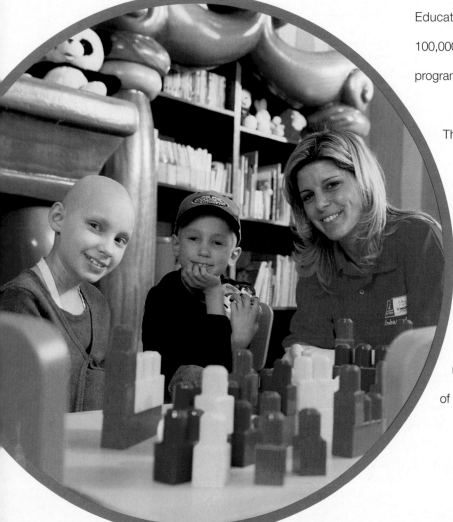

Mervyn's award-winning Community Closet program toured 15 cities in 10 states in 1999. In
partnership with 82 nonprofit agencies, the
Community Closet clothed 1,000 women
making the transition from welfare to work.
In addition, Mervyn's helped send
more than 15,000 economically
disadvantaged kids back to
school in new clothes in 1999
through our ChildSpree program.

**Target and artist
Peter Max launched a new line of gift
bags, greeting cards and wrapping
paper featuring the artist's vibrant
designs from the '60s to the '90s, an
example of our exclusive, trend-right
products.**

Dayton's, Marshall Field's and Hudson's have always placed a special emphasis on supporting arts and cultural
institutions. The Department Stores' "Project Imagine" showcases the arts in our communities, putting the promotional power of our stores behind arts organizations to help them achieve new levels of public awareness.
Project Imagine has made possible events ranging from "Free Tuesdays" at Chicago's Museum of Contemporary
Art to MacBeth at the Minnesota Opera. In recognition of the positive influence of the arts in young people's lives,
the Project Imagine Scholarship was launched, awarding two scholarships per store to high school seniors.

We continue to look for innovative ways to partner with nonprofit agencies to build stronger communities across
the country.

**Target now offers 12 new high-style chairs from a number of designers, including Philippe Starck.
Fresh design and differentiated merchandise are key to Target's merchandising strategy.**

	Revenues (percent of total)	Pre-tax Segment Profit (percent of total)	Retail Square Feet (percent of total)
Department Stores	9%	12%	10%
Mervyn's	12%	8%	16%
Target	78%	80%	74%
Other	1%		

Target

(dollars in millions)	1999	1998	1997
Revenues	$26,080	$23,014	$20,298
Pre-tax Segment Profit	$ 2,022	$ 1,578	$ 1,287
Stores	912	851	796
Retail Square Feet*	102,945	94,553	87,158

* In thousands, reflects total square feet less office, warehouse and vacant space.

Target (at year end) Employees: 214,000

=Store Occupied State
=Major Market

	Retail Sq. Ft. (in thousands)	No. of Stores		Retail Sq. Ft. (in thousands)	No. of Stores		Retail Sq. Ft. (in thousands)	No. of Stores		Retail Sq. Ft. (in thousands)	No. of Stores
Alabama	117	1	Kansas	1,290	10	New Hampshire	392	3	South Dakota	391	4
Arizona	2,982	27	Kentucky	1,274	12	New Jersey	1,625	13	Tennessee	2,001	19
Arkansas	229	2	Louisiana	203	2	New Mexico	870	8	Texas	9,297	85
California	16,355	145	Maryland	2,158	18	New York	2,288	18	Utah	1,178	7
Colorado	2,533	23	Massachusetts	522	4	North Carolina	2,668	24	Virginia	2,769	23
Delaware	146	1	Michigan	4,908	46	North Dakota	437	4	Washington	2,557	24
Florida	7,442	66	Minnesota	6,024	51	Ohio	3,571	31	Wisconsin	2,599	24
Georgia	3,445	30	Mississippi	239	2	Oklahoma	817	8	Wyoming	182	2
Idaho	406	4	Missouri	1,885	17	Oregon	1,194	11			
Illinois	6,050	52	Montana	423	4	Pennsylvania	1,600	13			
Indiana	2,876	30	Nebraska	1,074	9	Rhode Island	128	1			
Iowa	1,868	17	Nevada	1,267	11	South Carolina	665	6	**Total**	**102,945**	**912**

Major Markets	No. of Stores
Greater Los Angeles	71
Chicago	38
Minneapolis/St. Paul	34
San Francisco Bay Area	28
Dallas/Ft. Worth	24
Atlanta	24
Detroit	23
Houston	21
Greater Miami	20
Phoenix	18
Denver/Boulder	15
Greater New York City	15
San Diego	14
Washington DC	14
Seattle/Tacoma	13
St. Louis	13
Tampa/St. Petersburg	12
Greater Philadelphia	12
Greater Cleveland	11
Indianapolis	11
Orlando	10
Sacramento	10
Baltimore	10

Mervyn's

(dollars in millions)	1999	1998	1997
Revenues	$4,099	$4,150	$4,219
Pre-tax Segment Profit	$ 205	$ 240	$ 280
Stores	267	268	269
Retail Square Feet*	21,635	21,729	21,810

* In thousands, reflects total square feet less office, warehouse and vacant space.

Mervyn's (at year end) Employees: 32,000

=Store Occupied State
=Major Market

	Retail Sq. Ft. (in thousands)	No. of Stores		Retail Sq. Ft. (in thousands)	No. of Stores		Retail Sq. Ft. (in thousands)	No. of Stores		Retail Sq. Ft. (in thousands)	No. of Stores
Arizona	1,202	15	Louisiana	449	6	New Mexico	267	3	Utah	753	8
California	9,607	124	Michigan	1,162	15	Oklahoma	269	3	Washington	1,440	16
Colorado	853	11	Minnesota	1,157	9	Oregon	559	7			
Idaho	82	1	Nevada	491	7	Texas	3,344	42	**Total**	**21,635**	**267**

Major Markets	No. of Stores
Greater Los Angeles	48
San Francisco Bay Area	29
Dallas/Ft. Worth	12
San Diego	12
Phoenix	11
Detroit	9
Houston	9
Minneapolis/St. Paul	9
Seattle/Tacoma	9
Greater Salt Lake City	8
Denver/Boulder	6

Department Stores

(dollars in millions)	1999	1998	1997
Revenues	$3,074	$3,064	$2,970
Pre-tax Segment Profit	$ 296	$ 279	$ 240
Stores	64	63	65
Retail Square Feet*	14,060	13,890	14,090

* In thousands, reflects total square feet less office, warehouse and vacant space.

Department Stores (at year end) Employees: 34,000

=Store Occupied State
=Major Market

	Retail Sq. Ft. (in thousands)	No. of Stores		Retail Sq. Ft. (in thousands)	No. of Stores		Retail Sq. Ft. (in thousands)	No. of Stores
Dayton's			**Hudson's**			**Marshall Field's**		
Minnesota	3,040	12	Michigan	4,784	21	Illinois	4,173	17
North Dakota	297	3				Indiana	246	2
South Dakota	102	1				Ohio	618	3
Wisconsin	373	3				Wisconsin	427	2
						Total	**14,060**	**64**

Major Markets	No. of Stores
Chicago	16
Detroit	11
Minneapolis/St.Paul	10

Analysis of Operations

Our 1999 results mark the fourth consecutive year of earnings per share growth in excess of 20 percent. This exceptional growth in earnings per share was driven by substantial expansion in Target's gross margin rate.

Diluted Earnings per Share

● / ● as reported
● before unusual items

Earnings

Our net earnings were $1,144 million in 1999, compared with $935 million in 1998 and $751 million in 1997. Earnings per share were $2.45 in 1999, $1.98 in 1998 and $1.59 in 1997. References to earnings per share refer to diluted earnings per share. Earnings per share, dividends per share and common shares outstanding reflect our 1998 two-for-one share split and our 1996 three-for-one share split.

Management's discussion and analysis is based on our reclassified Consolidated Results of Operations as shown and discussed on page 24.

Revenues and Comparable-Store Sales

In 1999, our total revenues increased 9.9 percent and comparable-store sales increased 5.1 percent. Total revenues include retail sales and net credit revenues. Comparable-store sales are sales from stores open longer than one year. Revenue growth in 1999 and 1998 reflected Target's strong comparable-store sales growth and new store expansion. The impact of inflation was minimal and, as a result, the overall comparable-store sales increase closely approximated real growth.

Revenues
(millions)

Earnings Analysis
(millions, except per share data)

	Earnings			Diluted Earnings per Share		
	1999	1998	1997	**1999**	1998	1997
Net earnings before unusual items	**$1,188**	$970	$775	**$2.54**	$2.06	$1.64
Mainframe outsourcing (pre-tax 1999 $5 mil, 1998 $42 mil)	(3)	(26)	–	(.01)	(.06)	–
Favorable outcome of inventory shortage tax matter	–	20	–	–	.04	–
Securitization gain/(loss) (pre-tax 1998 $3 mil loss, 1997 $45 mil gain)	–	(2)	27	–	–	.06
Net earnings before extraordinary charges	1,185	962	802	2.54	2.04	1.70
Extraordinary charges — debt repurchase	(41)	(27)	(51)	(.09)	(.06)	(.11)
Net earnings	**$1,144**	$935	$751	**$2.45**	$1.98	$1.59

Management uses net earnings before unusual items, among other standards, to measure operating performance. It supplements, and is not intended to represent a measure of performance in accordance with, disclosures required by generally accepted accounting principles. Each per share amount is calculated independently.

Revenues and Comparable-Store Sales Growth

	1999		1998	
	Revenues	**Comparable-Store Sales**	Revenues	Comparable-Store Sales
Target	**13.3%**	**6.7%**	13.4%	6.1%
Mervyn's	**(1.2)**	**(0.7)**	(1.6)	0.9
Department Stores	**0.3**	**0.8**	3.2	4.5
Total	**9.9%**	**5.1%**	11.6%	5.2%

Revenues per Square Foot

	1999	1998	1997
Target	**$264**	$253	$243
Mervyn's	**189**	191	187
Department Stores	**220**	219	211

Thirteen-month average retail square feet.

Gross Margin Rate

The gross margin rate represents gross margin as a percent of sales. In 1999, our gross margin rate increased primarily due to rate expansion at Target and the Department Stores, resulting from improved markup and markdowns at Target and improved markup at the Department Stores. This increase was partially offset by the mix impact of strong growth at Target, our lowest gross margin rate division. In 1998, our overall gross margin rate increased modestly from the prior year, primarily due to lower markdowns at Target.

The LIFO provision, included in cost of sales, is calculated based on inventory levels, markup rates and internally generated retail price indices. In 1999, the LIFO provision was a $7 million credit ($.01 per share), compared with an $18 million credit ($.02 per share) in 1998 and a $6 million charge ($.01 per share) in 1997. The 1999 LIFO credit resulted primarily from higher markup. The 1998 LIFO credit resulted primarily from higher markup and higher inventory levels.

Operating Expense Rate

Operating expense rate represents selling, general and administrative expense (including buying and occupancy, advertising, start-up and other expense) as a percent of revenues. Our operating expense rate was essentially even with the prior year, benefiting from the overall growth of Target, our lowest expense rate division, and lower bad debt expense. These factors were offset by the lack of sales leverage in 1999 at Mervyn's and the Department Stores. The operating expense rate in 1998 was essentially even with 1997.

Pre-tax Segment Profit

Pre-tax segment profit increased 20 percent in 1999 to $2,523 million, compared with $2,097 million in 1998 and $1,807 million in 1997. Pre-tax segment profit is earnings before LIFO, securitization effects, interest, other expense and unusual items. Target provided substantially all of our pre-tax profit growth in 1999 with a 28 percent pre-tax profit increase. Target's full-year profit margin rate increased to 7.8 percent of revenues in 1999 from 6.9 percent in 1998.

Pre-tax Segment Profit
(millions)

'95 $1,030
'96 $1,471
'97 $1,807
'98 $2,097
'99 $2,523

Pre-tax Segment Profit and Percent Change from Prior Year

(millions)	1999		1998	
Target	$2,022	28%	$1,578	23%
Mervyn's	205	(14)	240	(14)
Department Stores	296	6	279	16
Total	$2,523	20%	$2,097	16%

Pre-tax Segment Profit as a Percent of Revenues

	1999	1998
Target	7.8%	6.9%
Mervyn's	5.0%	5.8%
Department Stores	9.6%	9.1%

EBITDA

EBITDA is pre-tax segment profit before depreciation and amortization.

EBITDA and Percent Change from Prior Year

(millions)	1999		1998	
Target	$2,589	25%	$2,074	20%
Mervyn's	343	(9)	378	(7)
Department Stores	429	4	414	12
Total	$3,361	17%	$2,866	15%

EBITDA as a Percent of Revenues

	1999	1998
Target	9.9%	9.0%
Mervyn's	8.4%	9.1%
Department Stores	14.0%	13.5%

Management uses pre-tax segment profit and EBITDA, among other standards, to measure operating performance. Pre-tax segment profit and EBITDA supplement, and are not intended to represent measures of performance in accordance with, disclosures required by generally accepted accounting principles.

Interest Expense

We consider payments to holders of our sold securitized receivables as "interest equivalent." In 1999, the total of interest expense and interest equivalent was $442 million, $4 million lower than 1998. The average portfolio interest rate in 1999 was 7.5 percent. In 1998, the total of interest expense and interest equivalent was $3 million lower than 1997. The average portfolio interest rate in 1998 was 7.8 percent. In both years, the reduction in interest expense and interest equivalent was due to a lower average portfolio interest rate, partially offset by higher average funded balances.

During 1999, we repurchased $381 million of debt for $444 million, resulting in an after-tax extraordinary charge of $41 million ($.09 per share). The debt repurchased had a weighted-average interest rate of 9.3 percent and an average remaining life of 18 years. The replacement of this debt with lower interest rate financing will have a favorable impact on interest expense going forward. In 1998 and 1997, we repurchased $127 million and $503 million of long-term debt, resulting in after-tax extraordinary charges of $27 million ($.06 per share) and $51 million ($.11 per share), respectively.

Income Tax Rate

The effective income tax rate was 38.8 percent in 1999, and 38.2 percent and 39.5 percent in 1998 and 1997, respectively. The 1998 effective tax rate reflected the beneficial effect of $20 million ($.04 per share), resulting from the favorable outcome of our inventory shortage tax matter.

Securitized Receivables

In 1998, Target Receivables Corporation (TRC), a special-purpose subsidiary, sold to the public $400 million of securitized receivables. This issue of asset-backed securities had an expected maturity of five years and a stated rate of 5.90 percent. Proceeds from the sale were used for general corporate purposes, including funding the growth of receivables. The 1998 sale transaction and the maturity of our 1995 securitization resulted in a net pre-tax loss of $3 million (less than $.01 per share), which reduced 1998 finance charge revenues and pre-tax earnings.

In 1997, TRC sold to the public $400 million of securitized receivables, with an expected maturity of five years and a stated rate of 6.25 percent. This transaction, combined with the impact of the application of SFAS No. 125 to our 1995 securitization, resulted in a $45 million ($.06 per share) increase in finance charge revenues and pre-tax earnings.

Our Consolidated Results of Operations also include reductions of finance charge revenues and bad debt expense related to sold securitized receivables. The amounts that represent payments to holders of our sold securitized receivables are included in our pre-tax earnings reconciliation on page 37 as interest equivalent. Interest equivalent was $49 million in 1999, $48 million in 1998 and $33 million in 1997.

Mainframe Outsourcing

In 1998, we announced our plan to outsource our mainframe computer data center functions and expensed $42 million ($.06 per share) of related charges. During 1999, we completed the transition and expensed an additional $5 million ($.01 per share) related to the outsourcing. These expenses are included in selling, general and administrative expense.

Year 2000 Readiness Disclosure

We began mitigating the risks associated with the year 2000 date conversion in 1993. In 1997, we established a corporate-wide, comprehensive plan of action designed to achieve an uninterrupted transition into the year 2000. This project included three major elements: 1) information technology (IT) systems, 2) non-IT, or embedded technology, systems and 3) relationships with our key business partners. The project was divided into five phases: awareness, assessment, renovation, validation and implementation. During 1999, we completed all phases for the three elements, using both internal and external resources to implement our plan.

For our IT systems, we assessed both existing and newly implemented hardware, application software and operating systems. We also assessed non-IT systems, or embedded technology/infrastructure, risks at our stores, distribution centers and headquarters facilities. We identified our key business partners and worked closely with them to assess their readiness and mitigate the risk to us if they were not prepared for the year 2000. We installed the year 2000 ready version of Electronic Data Interchange (EDI) software and tested the software with our key vendors.

To date, we have not experienced any significant issues associated with the date rollover. We have experienced no systems failures, no unusually high levels of returned merchandise, no interruptions of data transmission using EDI software and no major disruptions in the supply of product from our vendors. We continue to test and monitor our systems and applications for such issues in order to address them promptly, should any arise.

In 1999, we expensed $16 million related to year 2000 readiness. Prior to 1999, we expensed $32 million related to year 2000 readiness. In addition, this program accelerated the timing of $15 million of planned capital expenditures. All expenditures related to our year 2000 readiness initiative were within our estimates, were funded by cash flow from operations and did not materially impact our other operating or investment plans.

Fourth Quarter Results

Due to the seasonal nature of the retail industry, fourth quarter operating results typically represent a substantially larger share of total year revenues and earnings due to the inclusion of the holiday shopping season.

Fourth quarter 1999 net earnings were $494 million, compared with $423 million in 1998. Earnings per share were $1.06 for the quarter, compared with $.90 in 1998. Total revenues increased 8.7 percent and comparable-store sales increased 3.5 percent. Our pre-tax profit increased 16 percent to $1,000 million, driven by Target's strong results.

Fourth Quarter Pre-tax Segment Profit and Percent Change from Prior Year

(millions)	1999		1998	
Target	$ 811	26%	$646	26%
Mervyn's	69	(34)	104	–
Department Stores	120	5	115	12
Total	$1,000	16%	$865	20%

Analysis of Financial Condition

Our financial condition remains strong. Cash flow from operations was $2,252 million, driven by earnings growth, strong inventory control and accounts payable leveraging. Internally generated funds continue to be the most important component of our capital resources and, along with our ability to access a variety of financial markets, provide funding for our expansion plans. We continue to fund the growth in our business through a combination of internally generated funds, debt and sold securitized receivables.

During 1999, our average total receivables serviced (which includes both retained and sold securitized receivables)

Cash Flow from Operations

(millions)

increased 5 percent, or $124 million, due to growth of the Target Guest Card. Year-end total receivables serviced increased 7 percent from last year. In 1999, the number of Target Guest Card holders grew to over 15 million accounts at year end, compared with 12 million in 1998.

Inventory levels increased $323 million in 1999. This growth was more than fully funded by the $364 million increase in accounts payable over the same period.

Capital expenditures were $1,918 million in 1999, compared with $1,657 million in 1998. Investment in Target accounted for 87 percent of 1999 capital expenditures and included the purchase of real estate assets of a membership-based, general merchandise retailer for approximately $125 million. Net property and equipment increased $930 million. During 1999, Target opened 61 net new stores.

Capital Expenditures

(millions)

Approximately 69 percent of total expenditures was for new stores, expansions and remodels. Other capital investments were for information systems, distribution and other infrastructure to support store growth, primarily at Target. Over the past five years, Target's retail square footage has grown at a compound annual rate of approximately 10 percent.

Our financing strategy is to ensure liquidity and access to capital markets, to manage the amount of floating-rate debt and to maintain a balanced spectrum of debt maturities. Within these parameters, we seek to minimize our cost of borrowing.

In January 1999, our Board of Directors authorized the repurchase of $1 billion of our common stock. We repurchased 9.4 million shares of stock during 1999 at a total cost of $588 million ($62.58 per share), net of the premium from exercised and expired put options. In March 2000, our Board of Directors authorized the repurchase of an additional $1 billion of our common stock.

Repurchases are made primarily in open market transactions, subject to market conditions. Our program also includes the sale of put options that entitle the holder to sell shares of our common stock to us, at a specified price, if the holder exercises the option. During 2000, we expect to continue to repurchase shares at a pace similar to that of 1999.

A key to our access to liquidity and capital markets is maintaining strong investment-grade debt ratings. During the year, our debt ratings were upgraded by Duff & Phelps. Subsequent to year-end, as reflected in the table below, our debt ratings were also upgraded by Moody's. Further liquidity is provided by $1.6 billion of committed lines of credit obtained through a group of 31 banks.

Credit Ratings

	Moody's	Standard and Poor's	Duff & Phelps
Long-term debt	A2	A-	A
Commercial paper	P-1	A-2	D-1
Sold securitized receivables	Aaa	AAA	N/A

Performance Objectives

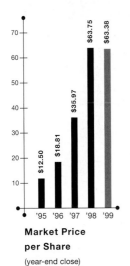

Market Price per Share
(year-end close)

Shareholder Return

Our primary objective is to maximize shareholder value over time through a combination of share price appreciation and dividend income while maintaining a prudent and flexible capital structure. Our total return to shareholders over the last five years averaged 43 percent annually, returning about $618 for each $100 invested in our stock at the beginning of this period.

Measuring Value Creation

We measure value creation internally using a form of Economic Value Added (EVA), which we define as after-tax segment profit less a capital charge for all investment employed. The capital charge is an estimate of our after-tax cost of capital adjusted for the age of our stores, recognizing that mature stores inherently have higher returns than newly opened stores. We estimate the after-tax cost of capital for our retail business is approximately 9 percent, while our credit operations' after-tax cost of capital is approximately 5 percent as a result of its ability to support higher debt levels. We expect to generate returns in excess of these costs of capital, thereby producing EVA.

EVA is used to evaluate our performance and to guide capital investment decisions. A significant portion of executive incentive compensation is tied to the achievement of targeted levels of annual EVA improvement.

Financial Objectives

We believe that managing our business with a focus on EVA helps achieve our objective of average annual earnings per share growth of 15 percent or more over time. Our financial strategy is to produce these results with strong interest coverage and prudent levels of debt, which will allow efficient capital market access to fund our growth. Earnings per share before unusual items has grown at a compound annual rate of 23 percent over the last five years.

Reflecting our strong cash flow, we ended 1999 with a retail debt ratio of 40 percent. In evaluating our debt level, we separate retail operations from credit operations due to their inherently different financial characteristics. We view the appropriate capitalization of our credit operations to be 88 percent debt and 12 percent equity, similar to ratios of comparable credit card businesses.

Debt Ratios and Interest Coverage

	1999	1998	1997
Retail	40%	41%	45%
Credit	88%	88%	88%
Total debt ratio	49%	50%	54%
Interest coverage	4.6x	4.0x	3.4x

Debt ratios and interest coverage include the impact of sold securitized receivables and off-balance sheet operating leases as if they were debt. Interest coverage represents the ratio of pre-tax earnings before unusual items and fixed charges to fixed charges (interest expense, interest equivalent and the interest portion of rent expense).

Retail Capitalization
(millions)
● debt ● total

Credit Capitalization
(millions)
● debt ● total

Credit Operations

We offer proprietary credit in each of our business segments. These credit programs strategically support our core retail operations and are an integral component of each business segment. The programs contribute to our earnings growth by driving sales at our stores and through growth in credit contribution. Therefore, credit contribution, shown below, is reflected in each business segment's pre-tax profit on a receivables serviced basis. Because we service both the retained and sold securitized receivables, we manage our portfolio on a serviced basis. In contrast, our consolidated financial statements reflect only our retained securitized receivables.

In 1999, pre-tax contribution from credit increased 16 percent over the prior year, compared with a 5 percent growth in average receivables serviced. The improved credit performance reflects continued growth of the Target Guest Card, improved delinquency experience and a decrease in write-offs as a percent of receivables. In 1998 and 1997, the bad debt provision exceeded net write-offs during the year. In 1999, the bad debt provision was equal to net write-offs.

Average Receivables Serviced

(millions)	1999	1998	1997
Target	$ 974	$ 803	$ 644
Mervyn's	718	764	812
Department Stores	719	720	707
Total average receivables serviced	$2,411	$2,287	$2,163
Total year-end receivables serviced	$2,681	$2,496	$2,424

Allowance for Doubtful Accounts

(millions)	1999	1998	1997
Allowance at beginning of year	$203	$168	$119
Bad debt provision	147	180	190
Net write-offs	(147)	(145)	(141)
Allowance at end of year	$203	$203	$168
As a percent of year-end receivables serviced	7.6%	8.1%	6.9%
As a multiple of current year net write-offs	1.4x	1.4x	1.2x

Credit Contribution

(millions)	1999	1998	1997
Revenues:			
Finance charges, late fees and other revenues	$609	$588	$510
Merchant fees	90	81	77
Total revenues	699	669	587
Expenses:			
Bad debt	147	180	190
Operations and marketing	182	169	125
Total expenses	329	349	315
Pre-tax credit contribution	**$370**	**$320**	**$272**

Merchant fees are intercompany fees charged to our retail operations on a basis similar to fees charged by third-party credit card issuers. These fees, which include deferred billing fees charged for carrying non-revenue-earning revolving balances, are eliminated in consolidation. Operations and marketing expenses include costs associated with the opening, retention and servicing of accounts.

Credit Contribution
(millions)

New Accounts Opened
(millions)

● Target ● Mervyn's
● Department Stores

Fiscal Year 2000

As we look forward into 2000, we believe that we will deliver another year of strong growth in revenues and earnings, driven primarily by increases in comparable-store sales and new store growth at Target. Our gross margin rate is expected to be essentially even with 1999. Our operating expense rate is expected to benefit modestly from the leveraging of fixed costs. Our credit operations are also expected to contribute to our growth in earnings as we continue to open new accounts, especially at Target, and leverage operating expenses.

In 2000, we expect to reinvest $2.5 to $3 billion in our business, through a combination of capital investment and repurchase of our shares. In the upcoming year, Target plans to open approximately 80 total new stores, including locations in two new states, West Virginia and Connecticut. Once again, our opening plans will focus on markets in the Mid-Atlantic and Northeast, and we will essentially double our number of SuperTarget locations from the 16 we operated at year-end. We expect Target's retail square footage to expand in the range of 8 to 10 percent annually for the foreseeable future. Our planned capital expenditures also include ongoing remodeling programs at all three operating segments and other capital support. Funding sources for the growth of our business include internally generated funds, debt and sold securitized receivables.

The total of interest expense and interest equivalent is expected to be moderately higher than 1999 due to higher average funded balances, partially offset by a lower average portfolio interest rate. Our $800 million of sold securitized receivables will result in approximately $50 million of interest equivalent for the year.

The effective income tax rate is expected to approximate 38.5 percent.

Forward-Looking Statements

This Annual Report, including the preceding management's discussion and analysis, contains forward-looking statements regarding our performance, liquidity and the adequacy of our capital resources. Those statements are based on our current assumptions and expectations and are subject to certain risks and uncertainties that could cause actual results to differ materially from those projected. We caution that the forward-looking statements are qualified by the risks and challenges posed by increased competition, shifting consumer demand, changing consumer credit markets, changing capital markets and general economic conditions, hiring and retaining effective team members, sourcing merchandise from domestic and international vendors, investing in new business strategies, achieving our growth objectives, and other risks and uncertainties. As a result, while we believe that there is a reasonable basis for the forward-looking statements, you should not place undue reliance on those statements. You are encouraged to review Exhibit (99)C attached to our Form 10-K Report for the year ended January 29, 2000, which contains additional important factors that may cause actual results to differ materially from those predicted in the forward-looking statements.

As we look forward into 2000, we believe that we will deliver another year of strong growth in revenues and earnings.

(millions, except per share data)	1999	1998	1997
Sales	$33,212	$30,203	$27,019
Net credit revenues	490	459	468
Total revenues	33,702	30,662	27,487
Cost of sales	23,029	21,085	18,944
Selling, general and administrative expense	7,490	6,843	6,108
Depreciation and amortization	854	780	693
Interest expense	393	398	416
Earnings before income taxes and extraordinary charges	1,936	1,556	1,326
Provision for income taxes	751	594	524
Net earnings before extraordinary charges	1,185	962	802
Extraordinary charges from purchase and redemption of debt, net of tax	41	27	51
Net earnings	$ 1,144	$ 935	$ 751
Earnings before extraordinary charges	$ 2.64	$ 2.14	$ 1.80
Extraordinary charges	(.09)	(.06)	(.12)
Basic earnings per share	$ 2.55	$ 2.08	$ 1.68
Earnings before extraordinary charges	$ 2.54	$ 2.04	$ 1.70
Extraordinary charges	(.09)	(.06)	(.11)
Diluted earnings per share	$ 2.45	$ 1.98	$ 1.59
Weighted average common shares outstanding:			
Basic	441.3	440.0	436.1
Diluted	465.7	467.3	463.7

See Notes to Consolidated Financial Statements throughout pages 24-37.

Summary of Accounting Policies

Organization Effective beginning of fiscal year 2000, Dayton Hudson Corporation changed its name to Target Corporation. We are a general merchandise retailer, comprised of three operating segments: Target; Mervyn's; and Dayton's, Marshall Field's, Hudson's (the Department Stores). Target, an upscale discount chain located in 44 states at year-end, contributed 78 percent of our 1999 total revenues. Mervyn's, a middle-market promotional department store located in 14 states in the West, South and Midwest, contributed 12 percent of total revenues. The Department Stores, traditional department stores located in eight states in the upper Midwest, contributed 9 percent of total revenues.

Consolidation The financial statements include the balances of the Corporation and its subsidiaries after elimination of material intercompany balances and transactions. All material subsidiaries are wholly owned.

Use of Estimates The preparation of our financial statements, in conformity with generally accepted accounting principles, requires management to make estimates and assumptions that affect the reported amounts in the financial statements and accompanying notes. Actual results may differ from those estimates.

Fiscal Year Our fiscal year ends on the Saturday nearest January 31. Unless otherwise stated, references to years in this report relate to fiscal years rather than to calendar years. Fiscal years 1999, 1998 and 1997 consisted of 52 weeks.

Reclassifications Within the Consolidated Results of Operations, certain reclassifications have been made to prior years' income and expense amounts to conform to the 1999 presentation. None of the reclassifications impacted our net earnings or earnings per share in any period. The reclassifications include the separate presentation of sales and net credit revenues; the application of the provisions of Staff Accounting Bulletin No. 101, "Revenue Recognition in Financial Statements"; the classification of buying and occupancy expenses in selling, general and administrative expense rather than cost of sales; and the classification of taxes other than income taxes in selling, general and administrative expense.

Revenues

Revenue from retail sales is recognized at the time of sale. Leased department sales, net of related cost of sales, are included within sales and were $31 million in 1999, $29 million in 1998, and $25 million in 1997. Net credit revenues include finance charges and late fees on internal credit sales, net of the effect of sold securitized receivables. Internal credit sales were $5.0 billion, $4.5 billion and $4.2 billion in 1999, 1998 and 1997, respectively.

Advertising Costs

Advertising costs, included in selling, general and administrative expense, are expensed as incurred and were $791 million, $745 million and $679 million for 1999, 1998 and 1997, respectively.

Impact of Year 2000

Year 2000 related costs, included in selling, general and administrative expense, were expensed as incurred. In 1999, we expensed $16 million related to year 2000 readiness. Prior to 1999, we expensed $32 million. In addition, we accelerated the timing of $15 million of planned capital expenditures, which are recorded in property and equipment at cost less accumulated depreciation.

Mainframe Outsourcing

In 1998, we announced our plan to outsource our mainframe computer data center functions and expensed $42 million ($.06 per share) of related charges. During 1999, we completed the transition and expensed an additional $5 million ($.01 per share) related to the outsourcing. These expenses are included in selling, general and administrative expense.

Start-up Expense

In first quarter 1999, we adopted SOP 98-5, "Reporting on the Costs of Start-Up Activities." The adoption did not impact total year start-up expense, which is included in selling, general and administrative expense.

Earnings per Share

Basic EPS is net earnings, less dividend requirements on the Employee Stock Ownership Plan (ESOP) preferred shares prior to their conversion to common shares, divided by the average number of common shares outstanding during the period. In January 2000, each outstanding ESOP preferred share was converted into 60 shares of our common stock. These shares are now included within weighted average common shares outstanding.

Diluted EPS assumed conversion of the ESOP preferred shares into common shares and replacement of the ESOP preferred dividends with common stock dividends, prior to the conversion of all preferred shares in January 2000. In addition, net earnings were adjusted for expense required to fund the ESOP debt service, prior to repayment of the loan in 1998. References herein to earnings per share refer to Diluted EPS.

All earnings per share, dividends per share and common shares outstanding reflect our 1998 two-for-one share split.

(millions, except per share data)	Basic EPS			Diluted EPS		
	1999	1998	1997	**1999**	1998	1997
Net earnings*	**$1,185**	$ 962	$ 802	**$1,185**	$ 962	$ 802
Less: ESOP net earnings adjustment	**(18)**	(20)	(20)	**(4)**	(8)	(13)
Adjusted net earnings*	**$1,167**	$ 942	$ 782	**$1,181**	$ 954	$ 789
Weighted average common shares outstanding	**441.3**	440.0	436.1	**441.3**	440.0	436.1
Performance shares	–	–	–	**.1**	.8	1.3
Stock options	–	–	–	**5.8**	5.5	3.9
Assumed conversion of ESOP preferred shares	–	–	–	**18.5**	21.0	22.4
Total common equivalent shares outstanding	**441.3**	440.0	436.1	**465.7**	467.3	463.7
Earnings per share*	**$ 2.64**	$2.14	$1.80	**$ 2.54**	$2.04	$1.70

*Before extraordinary charges

(millions)	January 29, 2000	January 30, 1999
Assets		
Cash and cash equivalents	$ 220	$ 255
Retained securitized receivables	1,837	1,656
Inventory	3,798	3,475
Other	628	619
Total current assets	6,483	6,005
Property and equipment		
Land	2,069	1,868
Buildings and improvements	7,807	7,217
Fixtures and equipment	3,422	3,274
Construction-in-progress	526	378
Accumulated depreciation	(3,925)	(3,768)
Property and equipment, net	9,899	8,969
Other	761	692
Total assets	$17,143	$15,666
Liabilities and shareholders' investment		
Accounts payable	$ 3,514	$ 3,150
Accrued liabilities	1,520	1,444
Income taxes payable	318	207
Current portion of long-term debt and notes payable	498	256
Total current liabilities	5,850	5,057
Long-term debt	4,521	4,452
Deferred income taxes and other	910	822
Convertible preferred stock, net	–	24
Shareholders' investment		
Convertible preferred stock	–	268
Common stock	76	74
Additional paid-in-capital	730	286
Retained earnings	5,056	4,683
Total shareholders' investment	5,862	5,311
Total liabilities and shareholders' investment	$17,143	$15,666

See Notes to Consolidated Financial Statements throughout pages 24-37.

Cash Equivalents

Cash equivalents represent short-term investments with a maturity of three months or less from the time of purchase.

Retained Securitized Receivables

Through our special purpose subsidiary, Target Receivables Corporation (TRC), we transfer, on an ongoing basis, substantially all of our receivables to a trust in return for certificates representing undivided interests in the trust's assets. TRC owns the undivided interest in the trust's assets, other than the sold securitized receivables and the 2 percent of trust assets held by Retailers National Bank (RNB), a wholly owned subsidiary of the Corporation that also services the receivables. Prior to June 1998, RNB held 5 percent of trust assets. The undivided interests held by TRC and RNB, as well as related income and expenses, are reflected in each operating segment's assets and operating results based on the origin of the credit sale giving rise to the receivable.

In 1998, TRC sold to the public $400 million of securitized receivables. This issue of asset-backed securities had an expected maturity of five years and a stated rate of 5.90 percent. Proceeds from the sale were used for general corporate purposes, including funding the growth of receivables. The 1998 sale transaction and the maturity of our 1995 securitization resulted in a net loss of $3 million (less than $.01 per share), which reduced 1998 finance charge revenues and pre-tax earnings.

In 1997, TRC sold to the public $400 million of securitized receivables, with an expected maturity of five years and a stated rate of 6.25 percent. This transaction, combined with the impact of the application of SFAS No. 125 to our 1995 securitization, resulted in a $45 million ($.06 per share) increase in finance charge revenues and pre-tax earnings.

At year-end 1999, $800 million of securitized receivables had been sold to investors and TRC had borrowed $100 million through the issuance of notes payable secured by receivables.

The fair value of the retained securitized receivables, classified as available for sale, was $1,837 million and $1,656 million at year-end 1999 and 1998, respectively. The fair value of the retained securitized receivables was lower than the aggregate receivables value by $157 million and $156 million at year-end 1999 and 1998, respectively, due to our estimates of ultimate collectibility. Write-downs have been included in selling, general and administrative expense.

Inventory

Inventory and the related cost of sales are accounted for by the retail inventory accounting method using the last-in, first-out (LIFO) basis and are stated at the lower of LIFO cost or market. The cumulative LIFO provision was $53 million and $60 million at year-end 1999 and 1998, respectively.

Property and Long-lived Assets

Property and long-lived assets are recorded at cost less accumulated depreciation or amortization. Depreciation and amortization are computed using the straight-line method over estimated useful lives. Accelerated depreciation methods are generally used for income tax purposes.

Estimated useful lives by major asset category are as follows:

Asset	Life (in years)
Buildings and improvements	8 – 50
Fixtures and equipment	5 – 8
Computer hardware and software	4
Intangible assets and goodwill	3 – 20

On an ongoing basis, we evaluate our long-lived assets for impairment using undiscounted cash flow analysis.

Accounts Payable

Outstanding drafts included in accounts payable were $599 million and $519 million at year-end 1999 and 1998, respectively.

(millions)	1999	1998	1997
Operating activities			
Net earnings before extraordinary charges	$ 1,185	$ 962	$ 802
Reconciliation to cash flow:			
Depreciation and amortization	854	780	693
Deferred tax provision	75	(11)	(63)
Other noncash items affecting earnings	163	70	43
Changes in operating accounts providing/(requiring) cash:			
Retained securitized receivables	(181)	(56)	(235)
Sold securitized receivables	–	400	400
Maturity of sold securitized receivables	–	(400)	–
Inventory	(323)	(198)	(220)
Other current assets	(57)	(46)	(35)
Other assets	(65)	(65)	(33)
Accounts payable	364	336	199
Accrued liabilities	100	75	182
Income taxes payable	137	15	62
Cash flow provided by operations	2,252	1,862	1,795
Investing activities			
Expenditures for property and equipment	(1,918)	(1,657)	(1,354)
Proceeds from disposals of property and equipment	126	107	123
Acquisition of subsidiaries, net of cash received	–	(100)	–
Other	(15)	(5)	–
Cash flow required for investing activities	(1,807)	(1,655)	(1,231)
Net financing sources	445	207	564
Financing activities			
Increase/(decrease) in notes payable, net	564	(305)	(127)
Additions to long-term debt	285	600	375
Reductions of long-term debt	(600)	(343)	(690)
Principal payments received on loan to ESOP	–	8	22
Dividends paid	(195)	(178)	(165)
Repurchase of stock	(581)	–	–
Other	47	55	31
Cash flow used for financing activities	(480)	(163)	(554)
Net (decrease)/increase in cash and cash equivalents	(35)	44	10
Cash and cash equivalents at beginning of year	255	211	201
Cash and cash equivalents at end of year	$ 220	$ 255	$ 211

Amounts presented herein are on a cash basis and therefore may differ from those shown in other sections of this Annual Report. Cash paid for income taxes was $575 million, $564 million and $454 million during 1999, 1998 and 1997, respectively. Cash paid for interest (including interest capitalized) was $405 million, $393 million and $485 million during 1999, 1998 and 1997, respectively.

See Notes to Consolidated Financial Statements throughout pages 24-37.

Lines of Credit

At January 29, 2000, two committed credit agreements totaling $1.6 billion were in place through a group of 31 banks at specified rates. There were no balances outstanding at any time during 1999 or 1998 under these agreements.

Long-term Debt and Notes Payable

At January 29, 2000, $664 million of notes payable were outstanding, $564 million of which were classified as long-term debt as they were supported by our $800 million committed credit agreement that expires in 2002. The remaining $100 million of notes payable is financing secured by the Target Credit Card Master Trust Series 1996-1 Class A variable funding certificate. This certificate is debt of TRC and is classified in the current portion of long-term debt and notes payable. The average amount of secured and unsecured notes payable outstanding during 1999 was $775 million at a weighted-average interest rate of 5.5 percent.

In 1999, we issued $285 million of floating-rate notes bearing interest at initial rates between 5.32 and 5.52 percent, maturing in July through September 2001. The proceeds were used for general corporate purposes. Also during 1999, we repurchased $381 million of long-term debt with an average remaining life of 18 years and a weighted-average interest rate of 9.3 percent, resulting in an after-tax extraordinary charge of $41 million ($.09 per share).

In 1998, we issued $200 million of long-term debt at 6.65 percent, maturing in 2028 and $200 million at 5.88 percent, maturing in 2008. We also issued $200 million of long-term debt maturing in 2010, which is puttable in 2000, and we sold to a third party the right to call and remarket these securities in 2000 to their final maturity. Also during 1998, we repurchased $127 million of long-term debt, resulting in an after-tax extraordinary charge of $27 million ($.06 per share).

At year end our debt portfolio was as follows:

Long-term Debt and Notes Payable

(millions)	January 29, 2000 Rate*	Balance	January 30, 1999 Rate*	Balance
Notes payable	5.8%	$ 664	5.2%	$ 100
Notes and debentures:				
Due 1999-2003	7.8	1,682	8.1	1,544
Due 2004-2008	7.5	699	7.6	701
Due 2009-2013	7.9	472	8.1	564
Due 2014-2018	9.5	34	9.6	70
Due 2019-2023	8.5	759	8.7	1,009
Due 2024-2028	6.6	474	6.6	475
Due 2029-2037	5.9	100	5.9	100
Total notes payable, notes and debentures**	7.5%	$4,884	7.9%	$4,563
Capital lease obligations		135		145
Less: current portion		(498)		(256)
Long-term debt and notes payable		$4,521		$4,452

*Reflects the weighted-average stated interest rate as of year end.
**The estimated fair value of total notes payable and notes and debentures, using a discounted cash flow analysis based on our incremental interest rates for similar types of financial instruments, was $4,893 million at January 29, 2000 and $5,123 million at January 30, 1999.

Required principal payments on long-term debt and notes payable over the next five years, excluding capital lease obligations, are $488 million in 2000, $638 million in 2001, $756 million in 2002, $464 million in 2003 and $105 million in 2004.

Subsequent to year-end 1999, we issued $500 million of additional long-term debt bearing interest at 7.50 percent, maturing in February 2005.

Derivatives

From time to time we use interest rate swaps to hedge our exposure to interest rate risk. The fair value of the swaps is not reflected in the financial statements and any gain or loss recognized upon early termination is amortized over the life of the related debt obligation. The fair value of existing swaps is immaterial.

In 1998, the Financial Accounting Standards Board issued SFAS No. 133, "Accounting for Derivative Instruments and Hedging Activities," which is required to be adopted for fiscal years beginning after June 15, 2000. We have analyzed the impact of SFAS No. 133 on our existing and currently anticipated activities and do not believe the adoption of this new statement will have a material effect on our earnings or financial position.

(millions, except share data)	Convertible Preferred Stock	Common Stock	Additional Paid-in Capital	Retained Earnings	Loan to ESOP	Total
February 1, 1997	$271	$72	$146	$3,348	$(47)	$3,790
Consolidated net earnings	–	–	–	751	–	751
Dividends declared	–	–	–	(169)	–	(169)
Tax benefit on unallocated preferred stock dividends and options	–	–	17	–	–	17
Conversion of preferred stock and other	9	–	18	–	–	27
Net reduction in loan to ESOP	–	–	–	–	28	28
Stock option activity	–	1	15	–	–	16
January 31, 1998	280	73	196	3,930	(19)	4,460
Consolidated net earnings	–	–	–	935	–	935
Dividends declared	–	–	–	(182)	–	(182)
Tax benefit on unallocated preferred stock dividends and options	–	–	25	–	–	25
Conversion of preferred stock and other	(12)	–	37	–	–	25
Net reduction in loan to ESOP	–	–	–	–	19	19
Stock option activity	–	1	28	–	–	29
January 30, 1999	268	74	286	4,683	–	5,311
Consolidated net earnings	–	–	–	1,144	–	1,144
Dividends declared	–	–	–	(191)	–	(191)
Repurchase of stock	–	(1)	–	(580)	–	(581)
Issuance of stock for ESOP	–	–	81	–	–	81
Tax benefit on unallocated preferred stock dividends and options	–	–	29	–	–	29
Conversion of preferred stock	(268)	3	289	–	–	24
Stock option activity	–	–	45	–	–	45
January 29, 2000	$ –	$76	$730	$5,056	$ –	$5,862

Common Stock Authorized 3,000,000,000 shares, $.1667 par value; 455,841,388 shares issued and outstanding at January 29, 2000; 441,809,806 shares issued and outstanding at January 30, 1999.

In January 1999, our Board of Directors authorized the repurchase of $1 billion of our common stock. We repurchased 9.4 million shares of stock during 1999 at a total cost of $588 million ($62.58 per share), net of the premium from exercised and expired put options. In March 2000, our Board of Directors authorized the repurchase of an additional $1 billion of our common stock. Repurchases are made primarily in open market transactions, subject to market conditions. Our program also includes the sale of put options that entitle the holder to sell shares of our common stock to us, at a specified price, if the holder exercises the option.

We sold put options on 4.7 million shares in 1999. Options on 1.4 million shares outstanding at the end of 1999 entitled their holders to sell shares of our common stock to us at prices ranging from $63 to $74 per share on specific dates during February through June 2000. Premiums received from the sale of put options during the year were recorded in retained earnings and totaled $23 million, $7 million of which represents premiums received on put options outstanding at year end.

Preferred Stock Authorized 5,000,000 shares; no shares of Series B ESOP Convertible Preferred Stock, $.01 par value, were issued and outstanding at January 29, 2000 and 338,492 shares were issued and outstanding at January 30, 1999. In January 2000, each share of Series B ESOP Convertible Preferred Stock was converted into 60 shares of our common stock. Prior to conversion, these shares had voting rights equal to the equivalent number of common shares and were entitled to cumulative annual dividends of $56.20.

Junior Preferred Stock Rights In 1996, we declared a distribution of shares of preferred share purchase rights. Terms of the plan provide for a distribution of one preferred share purchase right for each outstanding share of our common stock. Each right will entitle shareholders to buy one six-hundredth of a share of a new series of junior participating preferred stock at an exercise price of $50.00, subject to adjustment. The rights will be exercisable only if a person or group acquires ownership of 20 percent or more of our common stock or announces a tender offer to acquire 30 percent or more of our common stock.

See Notes to Consolidated Financial Statements throughout pages 24-37.

Stock Option Plan

We have a stock option plan for key employees. Options include incentive stock options, non-qualified stock options or a combination of the two. A majority of the options vest annually in equal amounts over a four-year period. These options are cumulatively exercisable and expire no later than ten years after the date of the grant. The non-employee members of our Board of Directors also participate in our stock option plan. Their options become exercisable after one year and have a ten-year term. The typical frequency of stock option grants is once each fiscal year.

We also have a performance share and restricted share plan for key employees. The last grant was made in 1995, and all shares relating to outstanding grants were issued in 1999 pursuant to the plan. Performance shares were issued to the extent certain financial goals were met over the four-year period from the date of grant. Restricted shares were issued four years from the date of grant. Once issued, performance shares and restricted shares generally vest only upon retirement.

Options, Performance Shares and Restricted Shares Outstanding

(shares in thousands)	Total Outstanding Number of Shares	Total Outstanding Weighted Average Exercise Price	Currently Exercisable Number of Shares	Currently Exercisable Weighted Average Exercise Price	Performance Shares	Restricted Shares
February 1, 1997	14,610	$13.48	4,782	$10.88	1,264	311
Granted	2,653	33.63				
Canceled	(346)	15.02				
Exercised	(2,450)	10.27				
January 31, 1998	14,467	$17.69	4,860	$13.15	794	212
Granted	3,309	48.16				
Canceled	(173)	23.77				
Exercised	(2,023)	12.27				
January 30, 1999	15,580	$24.79	5,685	$16.49	519*	123*
Granted	1,906	67.63				
Canceled	(176)	34.91				
Exercised	(1,279)	14.03				
January 29, 2000	**16,031**	**$30.63**	**7,858**	**$20.46**	–	–

*All shares were issued in 1999 pursuant to the plan.

Options Outstanding

(shares in thousands)	Shares Outstanding at January 29, 2000	Range of Exercise Price
	5,209	$ 9.97 - $15.00
	3,424	$15.00 - $25.00
	2,246	$25.00 - $35.00
	1,211	$35.00 - $45.00
	2,032	$45.00 - $55.00
	1,909	$55.00 - $68.69
Total	16,031	$ 9.97 - $68.69

As of January 29, 2000, outstanding options had a weighted-average remaining contractual life of 7.2 years. The number of unissued common shares reserved for future grants under the stock option plans was 24,489,897 at January 29, 2000, and 4,136,969 at January 30, 1999.

We apply APB No. 25, "Accounting for Stock Issued to Employees," to account for our stock option and performance share plans. Because the exercise price of our employee stock options equals the market price of the underlying stock on the grant date, no compensation expense related to options is recognized. Performance share compensation expense was recognized based on the fair value of the shares at the end of each reporting period. If we had elected to recognize compensation cost based on the fair value of the options and performance shares at grant date as prescribed by SFAS No. 123, "Accounting for Stock-Based Compensation," net earnings would have been the pro forma amounts shown below. EPS calculated under SFAS No. 123 would be $.03 lower than reported EPS in 1999 and unchanged from reported EPS in 1998 and 1997.

Pro Forma Earnings

(millions)	1999	1998	1997
Net earnings — as reported	**$1,144**	$935	$751
Net earnings — pro forma	**$1,132**	$934	$751

The Black-Scholes method was used to estimate the fair value of the options at grant date based on the following factors:

	1999	1998	1997
Dividend yield	**.6%**	.7%	1.0%
Volatility	**30%**	30%	25%
Risk free interest rate	**6.6%**	4.6%	5.4%
Expected life in years	**5.6**	5.6	5.6
Weighted average fair value at grant date	**$25.81**	$16.24	$10.52

Pension and Postretirement Health Care Benefits

We have defined benefit pension plans that cover all employees who meet certain age, length of service and hours worked per year requirements. Benefits are provided based upon years of service and the employee's compensation. Retired employees also become eligible for certain health care benefits if they meet minimum age and service requirements and agree to contribute a portion of the cost.

In 1999, we adopted a change in the measurement date of our pension and postretirement health care benefits plans from December 31 to October 31. Prior periods have not been restated, as the impact of the change is not material.

Change in Benefit Obligation

(millions)	Pension Benefits		Postretirement Health Care Benefits	
	1999	1998	**1999**	1998
Benefit obligation at beginning of measurement period	**$729**	$610	**$ 85**	$ 81
Service cost	**44**	35	**2**	1
Interest cost	**53**	45	**6**	6
Actuarial loss	**76**	65	**9**	5
Acquisitions	**–**	26	**–**	–
Benefits paid	**(40)**	(52)	**(8)**	(8)
Benefit obligation at end of measurement period	**$862**	$729	**$ 94**	$ 85

Change in Plan Assets

	Pension Benefits		Postretirement Health Care Benefits	
Fair value of plan assets at beginning of measurement period	**$859**	$718	**$ –**	$ –
Actual return on plan assets	**62**	106	**–**	–
Employer contribution	**100**	59	**8**	8
Acquisitions	**–**	25	**–**	–
Benefits paid	**(39)**	(49)	**(8)**	(8)
Fair value of plan assets at end of measurement period	**$982**	$859	**$ –**	$ –

Reconciliation of Prepaid/(Accrued) Cost

	Pension Benefits		Postretirement Health Care Benefits	
Funded status	**$120**	$130	**$(94)**	$ (85)
Unrecognized actuarial loss/(gain)	**51**	(16)	**(7)**	(18)
Unrecognized prior service cost	**8**	2	**2**	3
Net prepaid/(accrued) cost	**$179**	$116	**$(99)**	$(100)

The benefit obligation and fair value of plan assets, for the pension plans with benefit obligations in excess of plan assets, were $49 and $0 as of October 31, 1999, and $34 and $0 as of December 31, 1998.

Net Pension and Postretirement Health Care Benefits Expense

(millions)	Pension Benefits			Postretirement Health Care Benefits		
	1999	1998	1997	**1999**	1998	1997
Service cost benefits earned during the period	**$44**	$35	$27	**$2**	$1	$1
Interest cost on projected benefit obligation	**53**	45	39	**6**	6	6
Expected return on assets	**(72)**	(58)	(48)	**–**	–	–
Recognized gains and losses	**9**	3	–	**–**	(1)	(2)
Recognized prior service cost	**1**	–	1	**–**	–	1
Total	**$35**	$25	$19	**$8**	$6	$6

The amortization of any prior service cost is determined using a straight-line amortization of the cost over the average remaining service period of employees expected to receive benefits under the plan.

Actuarial Assumptions

	Pension Benefits			Postretirement Health Care Benefits		
	1999	1998	1997	**1999**	1998	1997
Discount rate	**7½%**	7%	7¼%	**7½%**	7%	7¼%
Expected long-term rate of return on plans' assets	**9**	9	9	**n/a**	n/a	n/a
Average assumed rate of compensation increase	**4½**	4	4¼	**n/a**	n/a	n/a

An increase in the cost of covered health care benefits of 6 percent is assumed for 2000. The rate is assumed to remain at 6 percent in the future. The health care cost trend rate assumption has a significant effect on the amounts reported. A 1 percent change in assumed health care cost trend rates would have the following effects:

	1% Increase	1% Decrease
Effect on total of service and interest cost components of net periodic postretirement health care benefit cost	$–	$ –
Effect on the health care component of the postretirement benefit obligation	$5	$(4)

Employee Stock Ownership Plan

We sponsor a defined contribution employee benefit plan. Employees who meet certain eligibility requirements can participate by investing up to 20 percent of their compensation. We match 100 percent of each employee's contribution up to 5 percent of respective total compensation. Our contribution to the plan is invested in the ESOP. Through December 1998, ESOP preferred shares (401(k) preferred shares) were allocated to participants. In January 1999, we began providing new common shares to the ESOP to fund the employer match.

In 1989, we loaned $379 million to the ESOP at a 9 percent interest rate. Proceeds from the loan were then used by the ESOP to purchase 438,353 shares of 401(k) preferred shares. The original issue value of the 401(k) preferred shares of $864.60 per share was guaranteed by the Corporation. The loan was paid off during 1998 using dividends paid on all 401(k) preferred shares held by the ESOP. In January 2000, each 401(k) preferred share was converted into 60 shares of common stock.

Prior to the conversion of all 401(k) preferred shares to common stock, we were required to exchange at fair value each 401(k) preferred share for 60 shares of common stock and cash, if any, upon a participant's termination. The 401(k) preferred shares were classified as shareholders' investment to the extent the preferred shares were permanent equity.

Dividends earned on 401(k) preferred shares held by the ESOP were $19 million in both 1999 and 1998 and $21 million in 1997. The dividends on allocated 401(k) preferred shares were paid to participants' accounts in additional 401(k) preferred shares until June 1998. Dividends are now paid to participants in cash. Benefits expense was $78 million in 1999, $29 million in 1998 and $17 million in 1997.

Leases

Assets held under capital leases are included in property and equipment and are charged to depreciation and interest over the life of the lease. Operating leases are not capitalized and lease rentals are expensed. Rent expense on buildings, classified in selling, general and administrative expense, includes percentage rents that are based on a percentage of retail sales over stated levels. Total rent expense was $168 million, $150 million and $143 million in 1999, 1998 and 1997, respectively. Most of the long-term leases include options to renew, with terms varying from five to 30 years. Certain leases also include options to purchase the property.

Future minimum lease payments required under non-cancelable lease agreements existing at January 29, 2000, were:

Future Minimum Lease Payments

(millions)	Operating Leases	Capital Leases
2000	$ 113	$ 22
2001	105	21
2002	96	21
2003	80	19
2004	70	18
After 2004	634	124
Total future minimum lease payments	$1,098	$225
Less: interest*	(302)	(90)
Present value of minimum lease payments	$ 796	$135**

*Calculated using the interest rate at inception for each lease (the weighted average interest rate was 8.8 percent).

**Includes current portion of $10 million.

Owned and Leased Store Locations

At year end, owned, leased and "combined" (combination owned/leased) store locations by operating segment were as follows:

	Owned	Leased	Combined	Total
Target	705	92	115	912
Mervyn's	160	68	39	267
Department Stores	51	12	1	64
Total	916	172	155	1,243

Income Taxes

Reconciliation of tax rates is as follows:

Percent of Earnings Before Income Taxes

	1999	1998	1997
Federal statutory rate	35.0%	35.0%	35.0%
State income taxes,			
net of federal tax benefit	3.9	4.5	4.5
Dividends on ESOP stock	(.4)	(.5)	(.5)
Work opportunity tax credits	(.2)	(.2)	(.1)
Inventory shortage tax matter	–	(1.3)	–
Other	.5	.7	.6
Effective tax rate	38.8%	38.2%	39.5%

The components of the provision for income taxes were:

Income Tax Provision: Expense/(Benefit)

(millions)	1999	1998	1997
Current:			
Federal	$570	$497	$488
State	106	110	99
	676	607	587
Deferred:			
Federal	63	(10)	(55)
State	12	(3)	(8)
	75	(13)	(63)
Total	$751	$594	$524

The components of the net deferred tax asset/(liability) were:

Net Deferred Tax Asset/(Liability)

(millions)	January 29, 2000	January 30, 1999
Gross deferred tax assets:		
Self-insured benefits	$ 146	$ 132
Deferred compensation	130	128
Inventory	84	72
Valuation allowance	63	64
Postretirement health care obligation	41	42
Other	106	132
	570	570
Gross deferred tax liabilities:		
Property and equipment	(408)	(374)
Other	(104)	(63)
	(512)	(437)
Total	$ 58	$ 133

Inventory Shortage Tax Matter

In 1998, we received a favorable ruling from the United States Court of Appeals on a 1983 case related to the deductibility of accrued inventory shortage expense. The beneficial effect resulting from the outcome of the case was $20 million ($.04 per share) and was reflected as a reduction in the 1998 effective income tax rate. This issue has been settled for all years.

Acquisitions

In 1998, we acquired The Associated Merchandising Corporation, an international sourcing company that provides services to our operating divisions and other retailers, and we also acquired Rivertown Trading Company, a direct marketing firm. Both subsidiaries are included in the consolidated financial statements. Their revenues and operating results are included in "other" in revenues and in our pre-tax earnings reconciliation on page 37 and were immaterial in 1999 and 1998.

Commitments and Contingencies

Commitments for the purchase, construction, lease or remodeling of real estate, facilities and equipment were approximately $534 million at year-end 1999. We are exposed to claims and litigation arising out of the ordinary course of business. Management, after consulting with legal counsel, believes the currently identified claims and litigation will not have a material adverse effect on our results of operations or our financial condition taken as a whole.

Quarterly Results (Unaudited)

The same accounting policies are followed in preparing quarterly financial data as are followed in preparing annual data. The table below summarizes results by quarter for 1999 and 1998:

(millions, except per share data)	First Quarter 1999	1998	Second Quarter 1999	1998	Third Quarter 1999	1998	Fourth Quarter 1999	1998	Total Year 1999	1998
Total revenues	$7,158	6,402	$7,687	6,987	$7,927	7,218	$10,930	10,055	$33,702	30,662
Gross margin (a)	$2,182	1,924	$2,376	2,097	$2,441	2,172	$ 3,184	2,925	$10,183	9,118
Net earnings before extraordinary charges (c) (d)	$ 194	160	$ 228	172	$ 241	183	$ 522	447	$ 1,185	962
Net earnings (b) (c) (d)	$ 194	158	$ 224	172	$ 232	182	$ 494	423	$ 1,144	935
Basic earnings per share (b) (c) (d) (e)	$ .43	.35	$ .50	.38	$ .52	.40	$ 1.11	.95	$ 2.55	2.08
Diluted earnings per share (b) (c) (d) (e)	$ .41	.33	$ .48	.36	$ .50	.39	$ 1.06	.90	$ 2.45	1.98
Dividends declared per share (e)	$ .10	.09	$ .10	.09	$ .10	.09	$ .10	.09	$ .40	.36
Common stock price (f) High	$75.75	44.81	$72.44	52.63	$69.50	48.25	$ 75.00	63.75	$ 75.75	63.75
Low	$58.75	36.25	$57.94	42.50	$55.25	33.75	$ 60.75	42.69	$ 55.25	33.75

(a) Gross margin is sales less cost of sales. The LIFO provision, included in gross margin, is analyzed each quarter for estimated changes in year-end inventory levels, markup rates and internally generated retail price indices. A final adjustment is recorded in the fourth quarter for the difference between the prior quarters' estimates and the actual total year LIFO provision.

(b) In 1999, second, third and fourth quarter net earnings include extraordinary charges, net of tax, related to the purchase and redemption of debt of $4 million, $9 million and $28 million ($.01, $.02 and $.06 per basic and diluted share), respectively. In 1998, first, third and fourth quarter net earnings include extraordinary charges, net of tax of $2 million, $1 million and $24 million ($.01, $.00 and $.05 per basic and diluted share), respectively.

(c) Third quarter and total year 1999 net earnings before extraordinary charges, net earnings and earnings per share include a mainframe outsourcing pre-tax charge of $5 million ($.01 per share). Fourth quarter and total year 1998 net earnings before extraordinary charges, net earnings and earnings per share include a mainframe outsourcing pre-tax charge of $42 million ($.06 per basic and diluted share) and the beneficial effect of $20 million ($.04 per basic and diluted share) of the favorable outcome of our inventory shortage tax matter.

(d) Third quarter 1998 net earnings include a $3 million securitization pre-tax net loss (less than $.01 per basic and diluted share).

(e) Per share amounts are computed independently for each of the quarters presented. The sum of the quarters may not equal the total year amount due to the impact of changes in average quarterly shares outstanding and/or rounding caused by the 1998 two-for-one common share split.

(f) Our common stock is listed on the New York Stock Exchange and Pacific Exchange. At March 17, 2000, there were 13,883 shareholders of record and the common stock price was $69.50 per share.

(dollars in millions, except per share data)	1999	1998	1997	1996	1995(a)	1994
Results of operations						
Total revenues	$33,702	30,662	27,487	25,092	23,234	21,093
Net earnings (c) (d) (e)	$ 1,144	935	751	463	311	434
Financial position data						
Total assets	$17,143	15,666	14,191	13,389	12,570	11,697
Long-term debt	$ 4,521	4,452	4,425	4,808	4,959	4,488
Per common share data (b)						
Diluted earnings per share (c) (d) (e)	$ 2.45	1.98	1.59	.97	.65	.92
Cash dividend declared	$ .40	.36	.33	.32	.30	.28
Other data						
Weighted average common shares outstanding (b)	441.3	440.0	436.1	433.3	431.0	429.6
Diluted average common shares outstanding (b)	465.7	467.3	463.7	460.9	458.3	457.4
Capital expenditures	$ 1,918	1,657	1,354	1,301	1,522	1,095
Number of stores: Target	912	851	796	736	670	611
Mervyn's	267	268	269	300	295	286
Department Stores	64	63	65	65	64	63
Total stores	1,243	1,182	1,130	1,101	1,029	960
Total retail square footage (thousands)	138,640	130,172	123,058	117,989	109,091	101,163
Number of employees	281,000	256,000	230,000	218,000	214,000	194,000

(a) Consisted of 53 weeks.

(b) Earnings per share, dividends per share and common shares outstanding reflect our 1998 two-for-one common share split and our 1996 three-for-one common share split.

(c) Extraordinary charges, net of tax, related to the purchase and redemption of debt were $41 million ($.09 per share) in 1999, $27 million ($.06 per share) in 1998, $51 million ($.11 per share) in 1997 and $11 million ($.02 per share) in 1996.

(d) 1999 includes a mainframe outsourcing pre-tax charge of $5 million ($.01 per share). 1998 included a mainframe outsourcing pre-tax charge of $42 million ($.06 per share) and the beneficial effect of $20 million ($.04 per share) of the favorable outcome of our inventory shortage tax matter. 1996 included a real estate repositioning pre-tax charge of $134 million ($.18 per share).

(e) 1998 included a $3 million pre-tax net loss (less than $.01 per share) related to securitization maturity and sale transactions. 1997 included a $45 million pre-tax gain ($.06 per share) related to securitization sale transactions.

The Summary Financial and Operating Data should be read in conjunction with the Notes to Consolidated Financial Statements throughout pages 24-37.

Business Segment Comparisons

(millions)	1999	1998	1997	1996	1995*	1994
Revenues						
Target	$26,080	$23,014	$20,298	$17,810	$15,752	$13,574
Mervyn's	4,099	4,150	4,219	4,350	4,491	4,565
Department Stores	3,074	3,064	2,970	2,932	2,991	2,954
Other	449	434	–	–	–	–
Total revenues	$33,702	$30,662	$27,487	$25,092	$23,234	$21,093
Pre-tax segment profit and earnings reconciliation						
Target	$ 2,022	$ 1,578	$ 1,287	$ 1,048	$ 721	$ 732
Mervyn's	205	240	280	272	117	198
Department Stores	296	279	240	151	192	259
Total pre-tax segment profit	$ 2,523	$ 2,097	$ 1,807	$ 1,471	$ 1,030	$ 1,189
LIFO provision credit/(expense)	7	18	(6)	(9)	(17)	19
Securitization adjustments:						
Gain/(loss)	–	(3)	45	–	–	–
Interest equivalent	(49)	(48)	(33)	(25)	(10)	–
Interest expense	(393)	(398)	(416)	(442)	(442)	(426)
Mainframe outsourcing	(5)	(42)	–	–	–	–
Real estate repositioning	–	–	–	(134)	–	–
Other	(147)	(68)	(71)	(78)	(60)	(68)
Earnings before income taxes and extraordinary charges	$ 1,936	$ 1,556	$ 1,326	$ 783	$ 501	$ 714
Assets						
Target	$12,048	$10,475	$ 9,487	$ 8,257	$ 7,330	$ 6,247
Mervyn's	2,248	2,339	2,281	2,658	2,776	2,917
Department Stores	2,149	2,123	2,188	2,296	2,309	2,392
Other	698	729	235	178	155	141
Total assets	$17,143	$15,666	$14,191	$13,389	$12,570	$11,697
Depreciation and amortization						
Target	$ 567	$ 496	$ 437	$ 377	$ 328	$ 294
Mervyn's	138	138	126	151	150	145
Department Stores	133	135	128	119	113	108
Other	16	11	2	3	3	1
Total depreciation and amortization	$ 854	$ 780	$ 693	$ 650	$ 594	$ 548
Capital expenditures						
Target	$ 1,665	$ 1,352	$ 1,155	$ 1,048	$ 1,067	$ 842
Mervyn's	108	169	72	79	273	146
Department Stores	124	127	124	173	161	96
Other	21	9	3	1	21	11
Total capital expenditures	$ 1,918	$ 1,657	$ 1,354	$ 1,301	$ 1,522	$ 1,095
Segment EBITDA						
Target	$ 2,589	$ 2,074	$ 1,724	$ 1,425	$ 1,049	$ 1,026
Mervyn's	343	378	406	423	267	343
Department Stores	429	414	368	270	305	367
Total segment EBITDA	$ 3,361	$ 2,866	$ 2,498	$ 2,118	$ 1,621	$ 1,736
Net assets**						
Target	$ 8,413	$ 7,302	$ 6,602	$ 5,711	$ 5,109	$ 4,269
Mervyn's	1,908	2,017	2,019	2,268	2,484	2,363
Department Stores	1,795	1,785	1,896	1,879	1,940	1,812
Other	428	514	169	53	96	72
Total net assets	$12,544	$11,618	$10,686	$ 9,911	$ 9,629	$ 8,516

Each operating segment's assets and operating results include the retained securitized receivables held by Target Receivables Corporation and Retailers National Bank, as well as related income and expense.

*Consisted of 53 weeks

** Net assets represent total assets (including sold securitized receivables) less non-interest bearing current liabilities.

Report of Independent Auditors

Board of Directors and Shareholders

Target Corporation

We have audited the accompanying consolidated statements of financial position of Target Corporation and subsidiaries as of January 29, 2000 and January 30, 1999 and the related consolidated results of operations, cash flows and shareholders' investment for each of the three years in the period ended January 29, 2000. These financial statements are the responsibility of the Corporation's management. Our responsibility is to express an opinion on these financial statements based on our audits.

We conducted our audits in accordance with auditing standards generally accepted in the United States. Those standards require that we plan and perform the audit to obtain reasonable assurance about whether the financial statements are free of material misstatement. An audit includes examining, on a test basis, evidence supporting the amounts and disclosures in the financial statements. An audit also includes assessing the accounting principles used and significant estimates made by management, as well as evaluating the overall financial statement presentation. We believe that our audits provide a reasonable basis for our opinion.

In our opinion, the financial statements referred to above present fairly, in all material respects, the consolidated financial position of Target Corporation and subsidiaries at January 29, 2000 and January 30, 1999 and the consolidated results of their operations and their cash flows for each of the three years in the period ended January 29, 2000 in conformity with accounting principles generally accepted in the United States.

Minneapolis, Minnesota
February 28, 2000

Ernst & Young LLP

Report of Management

Management is responsible for the consistency, integrity and presentation of the information in the Annual Report. The consolidated financial statements and other information presented in this Annual Report have been prepared in accordance with accounting principles generally accepted in the United States and include necessary judgments and estimates by management.

To fulfill our responsibility, we maintain comprehensive systems of internal control designed to provide reasonable assurance that assets are safeguarded and transactions are executed in accordance with established procedures. The concept of reasonable assurance is based upon a recognition that the cost of the controls should not exceed the benefit derived. We believe our systems of internal control provide this reasonable assurance.

The Board of Directors exercises its oversight role with respect to the Corporation's systems of internal control primarily through its Audit Committee, which is comprised of five independent directors. The Committee oversees the Corporation's systems of internal control, accounting practices, financial reporting and audits to assess whether their quality, integrity and objectivity are sufficient to protect shareholders' investments. The Committee's report appears on this page.

In addition, our consolidated financial statements have been audited by Ernst & Young LLP, independent auditors, whose report also appears on this page. As a part of its audit, Ernst & Young LLP develops and maintains an understanding of the Corporation's internal accounting controls and conducts such tests and employs such procedures as it considers necessary to render its opinion on the consolidated financial statements. Their report expresses an opinion as to the fair presentation, in all material respects, of the consolidated financial statements and is based on independent audits made in accordance with auditing standards generally accepted in the United States.

Robert J. Ulrich
Chairman of the Board and
Chief Executive Officer
February 28, 2000

Douglas A. Scovanner
Executive Vice President and
Chief Financial Officer

Report of Audit Committee

The Audit Committee met two times during fiscal 1999 to review the overall audit scope, plans for internal and independent audits, the Corporation's systems of internal control, emerging accounting issues, officer and director expenses, audit fees and retirement plans. The Committee also met individually with the independent auditors, without management present, to discuss the results of their audits. The Committee encourages the internal and independent auditors to communicate closely with the Committee.

Audit Committee results were reported to the full Board of Directors and the Corporation's annual financial statements were reviewed and approved by the Board of Directors before issuance. The Audit Committee also recommended to the Board of Directors that the independent auditors be reappointed for fiscal 2000, subject to the approval of the shareholders at the annual meeting.

February 28, 2000

Directors

LIVIO D. DESIMONE
Chairman and
Chief Executive Officer,
3M
(diversified manufacturer)
(1) (5) (6)

ROGER A. ENRICO
Chairman and
Chief Executive Officer,
PepsiCo, Inc.
(domestic and international
beverage and food company)
(1) (2) (3)

WILLIAM W. GEORGE
Chairman and
Chief Executive Officer,
Medtronic, Inc.
(therapeutic medical device
company) (1) (2) (4)

MICHELE J. HOOPER
President and
Chief Executive Officer,
Voyager Expanded Learning
(educational development
company) (1) (2) (6)

JAMES A. JOHNSON
Chairman and
Chief Executive Officer,
Johnson Capital Partners
(private investment
company) (1) (3) (4) (5)

RICHARD M. KOVACEVICH
President and
Chief Executive Officer,
Wells Fargo & Company
(banking and financial
services company) (1) (2) (6)

SUSAN A. MCLAUGHLIN
President, Consumer
Services, BellSouth
Telecommunications, Inc.
(communications services
company) (1) (2) (4)

ANNE M. MULCAHY
Executive Vice President and
President,
General Markets Operations,
Xerox Corporation
(document management
company) (1) (4) (5)

STEPHEN W. SANGER
Chairman and
Chief Executive Officer,
General Mills, Inc.
(consumer food products
company) (1) (3) (5) (6)

GEORGE W. TAMKE
Former Vice Chairman and
Co-Chief Executive Officer,
Emerson Electric Co.
(industrial manufacturer) (1)

SOLOMON D. TRUJILLO
Chairman, President and
Chief Executive Officer,
US WEST, Inc.
(telecommunications
company) (1) (3) (4) (5)

ROBERT J. ULRICH
Chairman and
Chief Executive Officer,
Target Corporation and
Target Stores (1)

(1) *Executive Committee*
(2) *Audit Committee*
(3) *Compensation Committee*
(4) *Corporate Responsibility
    Committee*
(5) *Finance Committee*
(6) *Nominating Committee*

Officers

ROBERT J. ULRICH*
Chairman and
Chief Executive Officer,
Target Corporation and
Target Stores

KENNETH B. WOODROW*
Vice Chairman,
Target Corporation

LINDA L. AHLERS*
President, Dayton's
Marshall Field's and Hudson's

BART BUTZER*
President, Mervyn's

GREGG W. STEINHAFEL*
President, Target Stores

GERALD L. STORCH*
President, Financial Services
and New Businesses,
Target Corporation

LARRY V. GILPIN*
Executive Vice President,
Team, Guest and
Community Relations,
Target Corporation and
Target Stores

JAMES T. HALE*
Executive Vice President,
General Counsel and
Corporate Secretary,
Target Corporation

JOHN E. PELLEGRENE*
Executive Vice President,
Marketing,
Target Corporation and
Target Stores

DOUGLAS A. SCOVANNER*
Executive Vice President,
Finance and
Chief Financial Officer,
Target Corporation and
Target Stores

ERTUGRUL TUZCU*
Executive Vice President,
Store Operations,
Dayton's Marshall Field's and
Hudson's

TODD V. BLACKWELL*
Senior Vice President, Stores,
Mervyn's

JOHN D. GRIFFITH*
Senior Vice President,
Property Development,
Target Corporation

MAUREEN W. KYER*
Senior Vice President,
Merchandising, Mervyn's

PAUL L. SINGER*
Senior Vice President,
Technology Services and
Chief Information Officer,
Target Corporation

GAIL J. DORN
Vice President,
Communications and
Community Relations,
Target Corporation

NATE K. GARVIS
Vice President,
Government Affairs,
Target Corporation

SUSAN D. KAHN
Vice President,
Investor Relations,
Target Corporation

STEPHEN C. KOWALKE
Vice President and Treasurer,
Target Corporation

JANE P. WINDMEIER
Vice President, Finance,
Target Corporation and
Target Stores

RICHARD J. KUZMICH
President and
Chief Executive Officer,
Associated Merchandising Corp.

DALE NITSCHKE
President, target.direct

ERICA C. STREET
President, Target Brands, Inc.

JACK N. REIF
Assistant Treasurer,
Target Corporation

SARA J. ROSS
Assistant Treasurer,
Target Corporation

*Executive Officer and Corporate
Operating Committee Member*

A-41

Annual Meeting

The Annual Meeting of Shareholders is scheduled for May 17, 2000, at 9:30 a.m. CDT at The Children's Theatre, 2400 Third Avenue South, Minneapolis, Minnesota.

Shareholder Information

Quarterly and annual shareholder information, including the Form 10-Q and Form 10-K Annual Report, which are filed with the Securities and Exchange Commission, is available at no charge to shareholders. To obtain copies of these materials, you may call 612-370-6736, send an email to InvestorRelations@target.com, or write to:

Vice President, Investor Relations
Target Corporation
777 Nicollet Mall
Minneapolis, MN 55402

Our quarterly earnings release conference calls are webcast on the Internet through our website www.targetcorp.com. For additional information call investor relations at 612-370-6736.

Other information about Target Corporation is available at the same website.

Sales Information

Comments regarding the company's sales results are provided periodically throughout the year on a recorded telephone message. You may access this message by calling 612-370-6500.

Direct Stock Purchase/Dividend Reinvestment Plan

First Chicago Trust Company of New York administers a direct service investment plan that allows interested investors to purchase Target Corporation stock directly, rather than through a broker, and become a registered shareholder of the Company. The program offers many features including dividend reinvestment. For detailed information regarding this program, call First Chicago Trust toll free at 888-268-0203, or write to:

The DirectSERVICE Investment Program
c/o First Chicago Trust Company
P.O. Box 2598
Jersey City, NJ 07303-2598

Transfer Agent, Registrar and Dividend Disbursing Agent

First Chicago Trust Company of New York, a division of Equiserve

Trustee, Employee Savings 401(k) and Pension Plans

State Street Bank and Trust Company

Stock Exchange Listings

Trading symbol TGT
New York Stock Exchange and Pacific Exchange

Shareholder Assistance

For assistance regarding individual stock records, lost certificates, name or address changes, dividend or tax questions, call First Chicago Trust at 800-317-4445, or write to:

First Chicago Trust Company of New York
P.O. Box 2500
Jersey City, NJ 07303-2500.

Target, The Bullseye Design, SuperTarget, Target Greatland, Dayton's, Marshall Field's, Hudson's, target.com, target.direct, Target House, Archer Farms, Expect More. Pay Less., Sign of the Times, Take Charge of Education, Target Guest Card and Project Imagine are trademarks of Target Brands, Inc. Mervyn's, Hillard & Hanson, Big Brands. Small Prices. and ChildSpree are trademarks of Mervyn's Brands, Inc. Calphalon is a trademark of Calphalon Corporation. Discovery Channel is a trademark of Discovery Communications, Inc. Fash Bash is a trademark of The Founders Society Detroit Institute of Arts. Martex is a trademark of Westpoint-Pepperell Enterprises, Inc. Playmobil is a trademark of Geobra-Brandstatter GMBH & Co. Sanrio is a trademark of Sanrio Company, Ltd. Stiffel is a trademark of The Stiffel Company.

Taking big steps, growing in size, moving forward.

APPENDIX B

Typical Charts of Accounts for Different Types of Businesses

(FOR BUSINESSES DISCUSSED IN CHAPTERS 1–12)

Service Proprietorship

Assets

Cash
Accounts Receivable
Allowance for Uncollectible Accounts
Notes Receivable, Short-Term
Interest Receivable
Supplies
Prepaid Rent
Prepaid Insurance
Notes Receivable, Long-Term
Land
Furniture
Accumulated Depreciation—Furniture
Equipment
Accumulated Depreciation—Equipment
Building
Accumulated Depreciation—Building

Liabilities

Accounts Payable
Notes Payable, Short-Term
Salary Payable
Wage Payable
Employee Income Tax Payable
FICA Tax Payable
State Unemployment Tax Payable
Federal Unemployment Tax Payable
Employee Benefits Payable
Interest Payable
Unearned Service Revenue
Notes Payable, Long-Term

Owner's Equity

Owner, Capital
Owner, Withdrawals

Revenues and Gains

Service Revenue
Interest Revenue
Gain on Sale of Land (or Furniture,
  Equipment, or Building)

Expenses and Losses

Salary Expense
Payroll Tax Expense
Insurance Expense for Employees
Rent Expense
Insurance Expense
Supplies Expense
Uncollectible Account Expense
Depreciation Expense—Furniture
Depreciation Expense—Equipment
Depreciation Expense—Building
Property Tax Expense
Interest Expense
Miscellaneous Expense
Loss on Sale (or Exchange) of Land
  (Furniture, Equipment, or Building)

Service Partnership

Same as Service Proprietorship, except for
Owners' Equity:

Owners' Equity

Partner 1, Capital
Partner 2, Capital
Partner N, Capital

Partner 1, Drawing
Partner 2, Drawing
Partner N, Drawing

Merchandising Corporation

Assets	Liabilities	Stockholders' Equity	

Assets

Cash
Short-Term Investments (Trading Securities)
Accounts Receivable
Allowance for Uncollectible Accounts
Notes Receivable, Short-Term
Interest Receivable
Inventory
Supplies
Prepaid Rent
Prepaid Insurance
Notes Receivable, Long-Term
Investments in Subsidiaries
Investments in Stock (Available-for-Sale Securities)
Investments in Bonds (Held-to-Maturity Securities)
Other Receivables, Long-Term
Land
Land Improvements
Furniture and Fixtures
Accumulated Depreciation—Furniture and Fixtures
Equipment
Accumulated Depreciation—Equipment
Buildings
Accumulated Depreciation—Buildings
Organization Cost
Franchises
Patents
Leaseholds
Goodwill

Liabilities

Accounts Payable
Notes Payable, Short-Term
Current Portion of Bonds Payable
Salary Payable
Wage Payable
Employee Income Tax Payable
FICA Tax Payable
State Unemployment Tax Payable
Federal Unemployment Tax Payable
Employee Benefits Payable
Interest Payable
Income Tax Payable
Unearned Sales Revenue
Notes Payable, Long-Term
Bonds Payable
Lease Liability
Minority Interest

Stockholders' Equity

Preferred Stock
Paid-in Capital in Excess of Par—Preferred
Common Stock
Paid-in Capital in Excess of Par—Common
Paid-in Capital from Treasury Stock Transactions
Paid-in Capital from Retirement of Stock
Retained Earnings
Foreign Currency Translation Adjustment
Treasury Stock

Revenues and Gains

Sales Revenue
Interest Revenue
Dividend Revenue
Equity-Method Investment Revenue
Unrealized Holding Gain on Trading Investments
Gain on Sale of Investments
Gain on Sale of Land (Furniture and Fixtures, Equipment, or Buildings)
Discontinued Operations—Gain
Extraordinary Gains

Expenses and Losses

Cost of Goods Sold
Salary Expense
Wage Expense
Commission Expense
Payroll Tax Expense
Insurance Expense for Employees
Rent Expense
Insurance Expense
Supplies Expense
Uncollectible Account Expense
Depreciation Expense—Land Improvements
Depreciation Expense—Furniture and Fixtures
Depreciation Expense—Equipment
Depreciation Expense—Buildings
Organization Expense
Amortization Expense—Franchises
Amortization Expense—Leaseholds
Amortization Expense—Goodwill
Income Tax Expense
Unrealized Holding Loss on Trading Investments
Loss on Sale of Investments
Loss on Sale (or Exchange) of Land (Furniture and Fixtures, Equipment, or Buildings)
Discontinued Operations—Loss
Extraordinary Losses

Manufacturing Corporation

Same as Merchandising Corporation, except for
Assets and Expenses:

Assets

Inventories:
  Materials Inventory
  Work in Process Inventory
  Finished Goods Inventory

Expenses (Contra Expenses If Credit Balance)

Direct Materials Price Variance
Direct Materials Efficiency Variance
Direct Labor Price Variance
Direct Labor Efficiency Variance
Manufacturing Overhead Flexible Budget Variance
Manufacturing Overhead Production Volume Variance

APPENDIX C

Present-Value Tables and Future-Value Tables

This appendix provides present value tables and future-value tables (more complete than those in the Chapter 15 appendix and in Chapter 26).

EXHIBIT C-1
Present Value of $1

Periods	1%	2%	3%	4%	Present Value 5%	6%	7%	8%	9%	10%	12%
1	0.990	0.980	0.971	0.962	0.952	0.943	0.935	0.926	0.917	0.909	0.893
2	0.980	0.961	0.943	0.925	0.907	0.890	0.873	0.857	0.842	0.826	0.797
3	0.971	0.942	0.915	0.889	0.864	0.840	0.816	0.794	0.772	0.751	0.712
4	0.961	0.924	0.888	0.855	0.823	0.792	0.763	0.735	0.708	0.683	0.636
5	0.951	0.906	0.883	0.822	0.784	0.747	0.713	0.681	0.650	0.621	0.567
6	0.942	0.888	0.837	0.790	0.746	0.705	0.666	0.630	0.596	0.564	0.507
7	0.933	0.871	0.813	0.760	0.711	0.665	0.623	0.583	0.547	0.513	0.452
8	0.923	0.853	0.789	0.731	0.677	0.627	0.582	0.540	0.502	0.467	0.404
9	0.914	0.837	0.766	0.703	0.645	0.592	0.544	0.500	0.460	0.424	0.361
10	0.905	0.820	0.744	0.676	0.614	0.558	0.508	0.463	0.422	0.386	0.322
11	0.896	0.804	0.722	0.650	0.585	0.527	0.475	0.429	0.388	0.350	0.287
12	0.887	0.788	0.701	0.625	0.557	0.497	0.444	0.397	0.356	0.319	0.257
13	0.879	0.773	0.681	0.601	0.530	0.469	0.415	0.368	0.326	0.290	0.229
14	0.870	0.758	0.661	0.577	0.505	0.442	0.388	0.340	0.299	0.263	0.205
15	0.861	0.743	0.642	0.555	0.481	0.417	0.362	0.315	0.275	0.239	0.183
16	0.853	0.728	0.623	0.534	0.458	0.394	0.339	0.292	0.252	0.218	0.163
17	0.844	0.714	0.605	0.513	0.436	0.371	0.317	0.270	0.231	0.198	0.146
18	0.836	0.700	0.587	0.494	0.416	0.350	0.296	0.250	0.212	0.180	0.130
19	0.828	0.686	0.570	0.475	0.396	0.331	0.277	0.232	0.194	0.164	0.116
20	0.820	0.673	0.554	0.456	0.377	0.312	0.258	0.215	0.178	0.149	0.104
21	0.811	0.660	0.538	0.439	0.359	0.294	0.242	0.199	0.164	0.135	0.093
22	0.803	0.647	0.522	0.422	0.342	0.278	0.226	0.184	0.150	0.123	0.083
23	0.795	0.634	0.507	0.406	0.326	0.262	0.211	0.170	0.138	0.112	0.074
24	0.788	0.622	0.492	0.390	0.310	0.247	0.197	0.158	0.126	0.102	0.066
25	0.780	0.610	0.478	0.375	0.295	0.233	0.184	0.146	0.116	0.092	0.059
26	0.772	0.598	0.464	0.361	0.281	0.220	0.172	0.135	0.106	0.084	0.053
27	0.764	0.586	0.450	0.347	0.268	0.207	0.161	0.125	0.098	0.076	0.047
28	0.757	0.574	0.437	0.333	0.255	0.196	0.150	0.116	0.090	0.069	0.042
29	0.749	0.563	0.424	0.321	0.243	0.185	0.141	0.107	0.082	0.063	0.037
30	0.742	0.552	0.412	0.308	0.231	0.174	0.131	0.099	0.075	0.057	0.033
40	0.672	0.453	0.307	0.208	0.142	0.097	0.067	0.046	0.032	0.022	0.011
50	0.608	0.372	0.228	0.141	0.087	0.054	0.034	0.021	0.013	0.009	0.003

EXHIBIT C-1

(cont'd)

Present Value

14%	15%	16%	18%	20%	25%	30%	35%	40%	45%	50%	Periods
0.877	0.870	0.862	0.847	0.833	0.800	0.769	0.741	0.714	0.690	0.667	1
0.769	0.756	0.743	0.718	0.694	0.640	0.592	0.549	0.510	0.476	0.444	2
0.675	0.658	0.641	0.609	0.579	0.512	0.455	0.406	0.364	0.328	0.296	3
0.592	0.572	0.552	0.516	0.482	0.410	0.350	0.301	0.260	0.226	0.198	4
0.519	0.497	0.476	0.437	0.402	0.328	0.269	0.223	0.186	0.156	0.132	5
0.456	0.432	0.410	0.370	0.335	0.262	0.207	0.165	0.133	0.108	0.088	6
0.400	0.376	0.354	0.314	0.279	0.210	0.159	0.122	0.095	0.074	0.059	7
0.351	0.327	0.305	0.266	0.233	0.168	0.123	0.091	0.068	0.051	0.039	8
0.308	0.284	0.263	0.225	0.194	0.134	0.094	0.067	0.048	0.035	0.026	9
0.270	0.247	0.227	0.191	0.162	0.107	0.073	0.050	0.035	0.024	0.017	10
0.237	0.215	0.195	0.162	0.135	0.086	0.056	0.037	0.025	0.017	0.012	11
0.208	0.187	0.168	0.137	0.112	0.069	0.043	0.027	0.018	0.012	0.008	12
0.182	0.163	0.145	0.116	0.093	0.055	0.033	0.020	0.013	0.008	0.005	13
0.160	0.141	0.125	0.099	0.078	0.044	0.025	0.015	0.009	0.006	0.003	14
0.140	0.123	0.108	0.084	0.065	0.035	0.020	0.011	0.006	0.004	0.002	15
0.123	0.107	0.093	0.071	0.054	0.028	0.015	0.008	0.005	0.003	0.002	16
0.108	0.093	0.080	0.060	0.045	0.023	0.012	0.006	0.003	0.002	0.001	17
0.095	0.081	0.069	0.051	0.038	0.018	0.009	0.005	0.002	0.001	0.001	18
0.083	0.070	0.060	0.043	0.031	0.014	0.007	0.003	0.002	0.001		19
0.073	0.061	0.051	0.037	0.026	0.012	0.005	0.002	0.001	0.001		20
0.064	0.053	0.044	0.031	0.022	0.009	0.004	0.002	0.001			21
0.056	0.046	0.038	0.026	0.018	0.007	0.003	0.001	0.001			22
0.049	0.040	0.033	0.022	0.015	0.006	0.002	0.001				23
0.043	0.035	0.028	0.019	0.013	0.005	0.002	0.001				24
0.038	0.030	0.024	0.016	0.010	0.004	0.001	0.001				25
0.033	0.026	0.021	0.014	0.009	0.003	0.001					26
0.029	0.023	0.018	0.011	0.007	0.002	0.001					27
0.026	0.020	0.016	0.010	0.006	0.002	0.001					28
0.022	0.017	0.014	0.008	0.005	0.002						29
0.020	0.015	0.012	0.007	0.004	0.001						30
0.005	0.004	0.003	0.001	0.001							40
0.001	0.001	0.001									50

EXHIBIT C-2
Present Value of Annuity of $1

Present Value

Periods	1%	2%	3%	4%	5%	6%	7%	8%	9%	10%	12%
1	0.990	0.980	0.971	0.962	0.952	0.943	0.935	0.926	0.917	0.909	0.893
2	1.970	1.942	1.913	1.886	1.859	1.833	1.808	1.783	1.759	1.736	1.690
3	2.941	2.884	2.829	2.775	2.723	2.673	2.624	2.577	2.531	2.487	2.402
4	3.902	3.808	3.717	3.630	3.546	3.465	3.387	3.312	3.240	3.170	3.037
5	4.853	4.713	4.580	4.452	4.329	4.212	4.100	3.993	3.890	3.791	3.605
6	5.795	5.601	5.417	5.242	5.076	4.917	4.767	4.623	4.486	4.355	4.111
7	6.728	6.472	6.230	6.002	5.786	5.582	5.389	5.206	5.033	4.868	4.564
8	7.652	7.325	7.020	6.733	6.463	6.210	5.971	5.747	5.535	5.335	4.968
9	8.566	8.162	7.786	7.435	7.108	6.802	6.515	6.247	5.995	5.759	5.328
10	9.471	8.983	8.530	8.111	7.722	7.360	7.024	6.710	6.418	6.145	5.650
11	10.368	9.787	9.253	8.760	8.306	7.887	7.499	7.139	6.805	6.495	5.938
12	11.255	10.575	9.954	9.385	8.863	8.384	7.943	7.536	7.161	6.814	6.194
13	12.134	11.348	10.635	9.986	9.394	8.853	8.358	7.904	7.487	7.103	6.424
14	13.004	12.106	11.296	10.563	9.899	9.295	8.745	8.244	7.786	7.367	6.628
15	13.865	12.849	11.938	11.118	10.380	9.712	9.108	8.559	8.061	7.606	6.811
16	14.718	13.578	12.561	11.652	10.838	10.106	9.447	8.851	8.313	7.824	6.974
17	15.562	14.292	13.166	12.166	11.274	10.477	9.763	9.122	8.544	8.022	7.120
18	16.398	14.992	13.754	12.659	11.690	10.828	10.059	9.372	8.756	8.201	7.250
19	17.226	15.678	14.324	13.134	12.085	11.158	10.336	9.604	8.950	8.365	7.366
20	18.046	16.351	14.878	13.590	12.462	11.470	10.594	9.818	9.129	8.514	7.469
21	18.857	17.011	15.415	14.029	12.821	11.764	10.836	10.017	9.292	8.649	7.562
22	19.660	17.658	15.937	14.451	13.163	12.042	11.061	10.201	9.442	8.772	7.645
23	20.456	18.292	16.444	14.857	13.489	12.303	11.272	10.371	9.580	8.883	7.718
24	21.243	18.914	16.936	15.247	13.799	12.550	11.469	10.529	9.707	8.985	7.784
25	22.023	19.523	17.413	15.622	14.094	12.783	11.654	10.675	9.823	9.077	7.843
26	22.795	20.121	17.877	15.983	14.375	13.003	11.826	10.810	9.929	9.161	7.896
27	23.560	20.707	18.327	16.330	14.643	13.211	11.987	10.935	10.027	9.237	7.943
28	24.316	21.281	18.764	16.663	14.898	13.406	12.137	11.051	10.116	9.307	7.984
29	25.066	21.844	19.189	16.984	15.141	13.591	12.278	11.158	10.198	9.370	8.022
30	25.808	22.396	19.600	17.292	15.373	13.765	12.409	11.258	10.274	9.427	8.055
40	32.835	27.355	23.115	19.793	17.159	15.046	13.332	11.925	10.757	9.779	8.244
50	39.196	31.424	25.730	21.482	18.256	15.762	13.801	12.234	10.962	9.915	8.305

EXHIBIT C-2
(cont'd)

Present Value

14%	15%	16%	18%	20%	25%	30%	35%	40%	45%	50%	Periods
0.877	0.870	0.862	0.847	0.833	0.800	0.769	0.741	0.714	0.690	0.667	1
1.647	1.626	1.605	1.566	1.528	1.440	1.361	1.289	1.224	1.165	1.111	2
2.322	2.283	2.246	2.174	2.106	1.952	1.816	1.696	1.589	1.493	1.407	3
2.914	2.855	2.798	2.690	2.589	2.362	2.166	1.997	1.849	1.720	1.605	4
3.433	3.352	3.274	3.127	2.991	2.689	2.436	2.220	2.035	1.876	1.737	5
3.889	3.784	3.685	3.498	3.326	2.951	2.643	2.385	2.168	1.983	1.824	6
4.288	4.160	4.039	3.812	3.605	3.161	2.802	2.508	2.263	2.057	1.883	7
4.639	4.487	4.344	4.078	3.837	3.329	2.925	2.598	2.331	2.109	1.922	8
4.946	4.772	4.607	4.303	4.031	3.463	3.019	2.665	2.379	2.144	1.948	9
5.216	5.019	4.833	4.494	4.192	3.571	3.092	2.715	2.414	2.168	1.965	10
5.553	5.234	5.029	4.656	4.327	3.656	3.147	2.752	2.438	2.185	1.977	11
5.660	5.421	5.197	4.793	4.439	3.725	3.190	2.779	2.456	2.197	1.985	12
5.842	5.583	5.342	4.910	4.533	3.780	3.223	2.799	2.469	2.204	1.990	13
6.002	5.724	5.468	5.008	4.611	3.824	3.249	2.814	2.478	2.210	1.993	14
6.142	5.847	5.575	5.092	4.675	3.859	3.268	2.825	2.484	2.214	1.995	15
6.265	5.954	5.669	5.162	4.730	3.887	3.283	2.834	2.489	2.216	1.997	16
6.373	6.047	5.749	5.222	4.775	3.910	3.295	2.840	2.492	2.218	1.998	17
6.467	6.128	5.818	5.273	4.812	3.928	3.304	2.844	2.494	2.219	1.999	18
6.550	6.198	5.877	5.316	4.844	3.942	3.311	2.848	2.496	2.220	1.999	19
6.623	6.259	5.929	5.353	4.870	3.954	3.316	2.850	2.497	2.221	1.999	20
6.687	6.312	5.973	5.384	4.891	3.963	3.320	2.852	2.498	2.221	2.000	21
6.743	6.359	6.011	5.410	4.909	3.970	3.323	2.853	2.498	2.222	2.000	22
6.792	6.399	6.044	5.432	4.925	3.976	3.325	2.854	2.499	2.222	2.000	23
6.835	6.434	6.073	5.451	4.937	3.981	3.327	2.855	2.499	2.222	2.000	24
6.873	6.464	6.097	5.467	4.948	3.985	3.329	2.856	2.499	2.222	2.000	25
6.906	6.491	6.118	5.480	4.956	3.988	3.330	2.856	2.500	2.222	2.000	26
6.935	6.514	6.136	5.492	4.964	3.990	3.331	2.856	2.500	2.222	2.000	27
6.961	6.534	6.152	5.502	4.970	3.992	3.331	2.857	2.500	2.222	2.000	28
6.983	6.551	6.166	5.510	4.975	3.994	3.332	2.857	2.500	2.222	2.000	29
7.003	6.566	6.177	5.517	4.979	3.995	3.332	2.857	2.500	2.222	2.000	30
7.105	6.642	6.234	5.548	4.997	3.999	3.333	2.857	2.500	2.222	2.000	40
7.133	6.661	6.246	5.554	4.999	4.000	3.333	2.857	2.500	2.222	2.000	50

EXHIBIT C-3

Future Value of $1

Future Value

Periods	1%	2%	3%	4%	5%	6%	7%	8%	9%	10%	12%	14%	15%
1	1.010	1.020	1.030	1.040	1.050	1.060	1.070	1.080	1.090	1.100	1.120	1.140	1.150
2	1.020	1.040	1.061	1.082	1.103	1.124	1.145	1.166	1.188	1.210	1.254	1.300	1.323
3	1.030	1.061	1.093	1.125	1.158	1.191	1.225	1.260	1.295	1.331	1.405	1.482	1.521
4	1.041	1.082	1.126	1.170	1.216	1.262	1.311	1.360	1.412	1.464	1.574	1.689	1.749
5	1.051	1.104	1.159	1.217	1.276	1.338	1.403	1.469	1.539	1.611	1.762	1.925	2.011
6	1.062	1.126	1.194	1.265	1.340	1.419	1.501	1.587	1.677	1.772	1.974	2.195	2.313
7	1.072	1.149	1.230	1.316	1.407	1.504	1.606	1.714	1.828	1.949	2.211	2.502	2.660
8	1.083	1.172	1.267	1.369	1.477	1.594	1.718	1.851	1.993	2.144	2.476	2.853	3.059
9	1.094	1.195	1.305	1.423	1.551	1.689	1.838	1.999	2.172	2.358	2.773	3.252	3.518
10	1.105	1.219	1.344	1.480	1.629	1.791	1.967	2.159	2.367	2.594	3.106	3.707	4.046
11	1.116	1.243	1.384	1.539	1.710	1.898	2.105	2.332	2.580	2.853	3.479	4.226	4.652
12	1.127	1.268	1.426	1.601	1.796	2.012	2.252	2.518	2.813	3.138	3.896	4.818	5.350
13	1.138	1.294	1.469	1.665	1.886	2.133	2.410	2.720	3.066	3.452	4.363	5.492	6.153
14	1.149	1.319	1.513	1.732	1.980	2.261	2.579	2.937	3.342	3.798	4.887	6.261	7.076
15	1.161	1.346	1.558	1.801	2.079	2.397	2.759	3.172	3.642	4.177	5.474	7.138	8.137
16	1.173	1.373	1.605	1.873	2.183	2.540	2.952	3.426	3.970	4.595	6.130	8.137	9.358
17	1.184	1.400	1.653	1.948	2.292	2.693	3.159	3.700	4.328	5.054	6.866	9.276	10.76
18	1.196	1.428	1.702	2.026	2.407	2.854	3.380	3.996	4.717	5.560	7.690	10.58	12.38
19	1.208	1.457	1.754	2.107	2.527	3.026	3.617	4.316	5.142	6.116	8.613	12.06	14.23
20	1.220	1.486	1.806	2.191	2.653	3.207	3.870	4.661	5.604	6.728	9.646	13.74	16.37
21	1.232	1.516	1.860	2.279	2.786	3.400	4.141	5.034	6.109	7.400	10.80	15.67	18.82
22	1.245	1.546	1.916	2.370	2.925	3.604	4.430	5.437	6.659	8.140	12.10	17.86	21.64
23	1.257	1.577	1.974	2.465	3.072	3.820	4.741	5.871	7.258	8.954	13.55	20.36	24.89
24	1.270	1.608	2.033	2.563	3.225	4.049	5.072	6.341	7.911	9.850	15.18	23.21	28.63
25	1.282	1.641	2.094	2.666	3.386	4.292	5.427	6.848	8.623	10.83	17.00	26.46	32.92
26	1.295	1.673	2.157	2.772	3.556	4.549	5.807	7.396	9.399	11.92	19.04	30.17	37.86
27	1.308	1.707	2.221	2.883	3.733	4.822	6.214	7.988	10.25	13.11	21.32	34.39	43.54
28	1.321	1.741	2.288	2.999	3.920	5.112	6.649	8.627	11.17	14.42	23.88	39.20	50.07
29	1.335	1.776	2.357	3.119	4.116	5.418	7.114	9.317	12.17	15.86	26.75	44.69	57.58
30	1.348	1.811	2.427	3.243	4.322	5.743	7.612	10.06	13.27	17.45	29.96	50.95	66.21
40	1.489	2.208	3.262	4.801	7.040	10.29	14.97	21.72	31.41	45.26	93.05	188.9	267.9
50	1.645	2.692	4.384	7.107	11.47	18.42	29.46	46.90	74.36	117.4	289.0	700.2	1,084

EXHIBIT C-4
Future Value of Annuity $1

Future Value

Periods	1%	2%	3%	4%	5%	6%	7%	8%	9%	10%	12%	14%	15%
1	1.000	1.000	1.000	1.000	1.000	1.000	1.000	1.000	1.000	1.000	1.000	1.000	1.000
2	2.010	2.020	2.030	2.040	2.050	2.060	2.070	2.080	2.090	2.100	2.120	2.140	2.150
3	3.030	3.060	3.091	3.122	3.153	3.184	3.215	3.246	3.278	3.310	3.374	3.440	3.473
4	4.060	4.122	4.184	4.246	4.310	4.375	4.440	4.506	4.573	4.641	4.779	4.921	4.993
5	5.101	5.204	5.309	5.416	5.526	5.637	5.751	5.867	5.985	6.105	6.353	6.610	6.742
6	6.152	6.308	6.468	6.633	6.802	6.975	7.153	7.336	7.523	7.716	8.115	8.536	8.754
7	7.214	7.434	7.662	7.898	8.142	8.394	8.654	8.923	9.200	9.487	10.09	10.73	11.07
8	8.286	8.583	8.892	9.214	9.549	9.897	10.26	10.64	11.03	11.44	12.30	13.23	13.73
9	9.369	9.755	10.16	10.58	11.03	11.49	11.98	12.49	13.02	13.58	14.78	16.09	16.79
10	10.46	10.95	11.46	12.01	12.58	13.18	13.82	14.49	15.19	15.94	17.55	19.34	20.30
11	11.57	12.17	12.81	13.49	14.21	14.97	15.78	16.65	17.56	18.53	20.65	23.04	24.35
12	12.68	13.41	14.19	15.03	15.92	16.87	17.89	18.98	20.14	21.38	24.13	27.27	29.00
13	13.81	14.68	15.62	16.63	17.71	18.88	20.14	21.50	22.95	24.52	28.03	32.09	34.35
14	14.95	15.97	17.09	18.29	19.60	21.02	22.55	24.21	26.02	27.98	32.39	37.58	40.50
15	16.10	17.29	18.60	20.02	21.58	23.28	25.13	27.15	29.36	31.77	37.28	43.84	47.58
16	17.26	18.64	20.16	21.82	23.66	25.67	27.89	30.32	33.00	35.95	42.75	50.98	55.72
17	18.43	20.01	21.76	23.70	25.84	28.21	30.84	33.75	36.97	40.54	48.88	59.12	65.08
18	19.61	21.41	23.41	25.65	28.13	30.91	34.00	37.45	41.30	45.60	55.75	68.39	75.84
19	20.81	22.84	25.12	27.67	30.54	33.76	37.38	41.45	46.02	51.16	63.44	78.97	88.21
20	22.02	24.30	26.87	29.78	33.07	36.79	41.00	45.76	51.16	57.28	72.05	91.02	102.4
21	23.24	25.78	28.68	31.97	35.72	39.99	44.87	50.42	56.76	64.00	81.70	104.8	118.8
22	24.47	27.30	30.54	34.25	38.51	43.39	49.01	55.46	62.87	71.40	92.50	120.4	137.6
23	25.72	28.85	32.45	36.62	41.43	47.00	53.44	60.89	69.53	79.54	104.6	138.3	159.3
24	26.97	30.42	34.43	39.08	44.50	50.82	58.18	66.76	76.79	88.50	118.2	158.7	184.2
25	28.24	32.03	36.46	41.65	47.73	54.86	63.25	73.11	84.70	98.35	133.3	181.9	212.8
26	29.53	33.67	38.55	44.31	51.11	59.16	68.68	79.95	93.32	109.2	150.3	208.3	245.7
27	30.82	35.34	40.71	47.08	54.67	63.71	74.48	87.35	102.7	121.1	169.4	238.5	283.6
28	32.13	37.05	42.93	49.97	58.40	68.53	80.70	95.34	113.0	134.2	190.7	272.9	327.1
29	33.45	38.79	45.22	52.97	62.32	73.64	87.35	104.0	124.1	148.6	214.6	312.1	377.2
30	34.78	40.57	47.58	56.08	66.44	79.06	94.46	113.3	136.3	164.5	241.3	356.8	434.7
40	48.89	60.40	75.40	95.03	120.8	154.8	199.6	259.1	337.9	442.6	767.1	1,342	1,779
50	64.46	84.58	112.8	152.7	209.3	290.3	406.5	573.8	815.1	1,164	2,400	4,995	7,218

A P P E N D I X D

Check Figures

Check Figures—Chapter 1

DE1-1	No check figure
DE1-2	No check figure
DE1-3	No check figure
DE1-4	Capital $2,000
DE1-5	Capital $10,000
DE1-6	No check figure
DE1-7	Capital $33,500
DE1-8	No check figure
DE1-9	Capital $30,000
DE1-10	Net inc. $5,400
	Capital $35,400
DE1-11	No check figure
DE1-12	No check figure
DE1-13	1. Net inc. $4,100
	2. Capital $32,000
DE1-14	No check figure
DE1-15	Net inc. $50,000
DE1-16	Capital, 12/31/X3 $27,000
DE1-17	Total assets $35,000
DE1-18	No check figure
E1-1	No check figure
E1-2	No check figure
E1-3	No check figure
E1-4	C: $1,900
E1-5	OE increased by $737 mil.
E1-6	1. Net inc. $18,000
	3. Net loss $12,000
E1-7	No check figure
E1-8	Total assets $94,800
E1-9	2. Net inc. $5,400
1-10	2. Capital $14,200
E1-11	1. Net inc. $76,200
	2. Capital $27,100
E1-12	1. Net loss for 19X9 $132 mil.
E1-13	Cash bal., end of year $21 mil.
E1-14	Circle $25,000
	Triangle $185,000
	Square $170,000
P1-1A	Total assets $90,000
P1-2A	Total assets $68,000
P1-3A	Total assets $160,000
P1-4A	No check figure
P1-5A	1. Net inc. $64,000
	3. Total assets $279,000
P1-6A	2. Net inc. $2,100
	4. Total assets $30,750
P1-1B	Total assets $105,100
P1-2B	Total assets $61,000
P1-3B	Total assets $95,000
P1-4B	No check figure
P1-5B	1. Net inc. $47,000
	3. Total assets $102,000
P1-6B	2. Net inc. $4,240
	4. Total assets $40,920
Case 1	No check figure
Case 2	No check figure
Financial Statement Case	3. Stockholders' equity $5,862 mil.
	4. Rev. increased by $3,040 mil.

Check Figures—Chapter 2

DE2-1	1. $3,000
DE2-2	No check figure
DE2-3	No check figure
DE2-4	No check figure
DE2-5	No check figure
DE2-6	No check figure
DE2-7	No check figure
DE2-8	No check figure
DE2-9	No check figure
DE2-10	3. $1,500
DE2-11	3. a. $5,000
	b. $5,000
DE2-12	Trial bal. total $40,000
DE2-13	Trial bal. total $66 bil.
DE2-14	Incorrect trial bal. total assets $24,200
DE2-15	No check figure
DE2-16	Total debits $145,000
E2-1	No check figure
E2-2	2. Net inc. $2 bil.
E2-3	No check figure
E2-4	Total debits $183,600
E2-5	No check figure
E2-6	Trial bal. total $59,700
E2-7	Trial bal. total $37,850
E2-8	No check figure
E2-9	Trial bal. total $69,400
E2-10	Trial bal. total $124,100
E2-11	Trial bal. total $76,100
E2-12	Cash bal. $1,700
E2-13	Trial bal. total $19,700
E2-14	Total debits $78,000
E2-15	4. Trial bal. total $20,400
E2-16	b. $66,000
	c. $74,000
	d. $2,500
E2-17	No check figure
P2-1A	No check figure
P2-2A	No check figure
P2-3A	3. Trial bal. total $50,300
P2-4A	3. Trial bal. total $41,600
P2-5A	1. Trial bal. total $70,500
	2. Net inc. $6,370
P2-6A	3. Trial bal. total $103,600
P2-7A	1. Net inc. $2,800
	3. Total assets $92,200
P2-1B	No check figure
P2-2B	No check figure
P2-3B	3. Trial bal. total $55,500
P2-4B	3. Trial bal. total $53,500
P2-5B	1. Trial bal. total $65,100
	2. Net inc. $10,140
P2-6B	3. Trial bal. total $66,200
P2-7B	1. Net inc. $400
	3. Total assets $59,900
Case 1	No check figure
Case 2	3. Trial bal. total $22,800
	4. Net inc. $5,550
Financial Statement Case	No check figure

Check Figures—Chapter 3

DE3-1	No check figure
DE3-2	No check figure
DE3-3	Revenue $750,000
DE3-4	Expense $280,000
DE3-5	1. $55 mil.
DE3-6	1. Salary Expense for 2000 $9 mil.
DE3-7	1. Prepaid Rent $2,750
	Rent Expense $250
DE3-8	3. $34,500
DE3-9	3. Interest Payable Nov. 30 $200
DE3-10	3. Interest Receivable Nov. 30 $200
DE3-11	No check figure
DE3-12	No check figure
DE3-13	No check figure
DE3-14	No check figure
DE3-15	1. Assets $47,250
	Liabilities $13,550
DE3-16	1. Net inc. $5,650
E3-1	No check figure
E3-2	No check figure
E3-3	No check figure
E3-4	A: Insur. Exp. $1,600
E3-5	No check figure
E3-6	Net income overstated by $4,300
E3-7	No check figure
E3-8	Service Rev. $5,550
E3-9	Adj. trial bal. total $55,090
E3-10	No check figure
E3-11	Net inc. $7,150
	Total assets $29,100
E3-12	Net inc. $74,500
E3-13	1. End. capital $191,000
E3-14	7. net inc. $1,690
	Total assets $18,790
E3-15	Revenue $8,500
E3-16	Cash collected $4,400
P3-1A	2. Net inc. $750
P3-2A	No check figure
P3-3A	c. Art Supplies Exp. $6,360
	f. Insurance Exp. $2,700
P3-4A	No check figure
P3-5A	3. Adj. trial bal. total $62,500
P3-6A	1. Net inc. $78,470
	Total assets $129,030
P3-7A	2. Net inc. $6,950
	Total assets $44,550
P3-1B	2. Net inc. $683
P3-2B	No check figure
P3-3B	a. Rent Exp. $2,400
	d. Supplies Exp. $6,710
P3-4B	No check figure
P3-5B	3. Adj. trial bal. total $50,080
P3-6B	1. Net inc. $42,030
	Total assets $58,810

Check Figures—Chapter 4 (continued)

P3-7B	2. Net inc. $7,500
	Total assets $46,200
Case 1	Your highest price $127,000
Case 2	No check figure
Financial Statement Case	No check figure
E3A-1	Supplies $860
E3A-2	Unearned Service Rev. $3,700
P3A-1	Prepaid Rent $2,250
	Unearned Service Rev. $2,400

Check Figures—Chapter 4

DE4-1	No check figure
DE4-2	No check figure
DE4-3	No check figure
DE4-4	No check figure
DE4-5	No check figure
DE4-6	1. d. Close $3,525
	3. a. $31,575
DE4-7	1. $31,575
DE4-8	No check figure
DE4-9	No check figure
DE4-10	Trial bal. total $7,260 mil.
DE4-11	No check figure
DE4-12	c. $5,266 mil.
	d. $13,378 mil.
	e. $6,882 mil.
DE4-13	1. $1.79
	2. 49%
	3. 51%
DE4-14	1. Current ratio 2.07
	Debt ratio 0.31
E4-1	Net inc. $2,330
E4-2	No check figure
E4-3	End. bal. Gail Pfeiffer, Capital $36,360
E4-4	Trial bal. total $42,340
E4-5	No check figure
E4-6	Liu Hyundai, Capital $50,900
E4-7	2. Felix Rohr, Capital $175,700
E4-8	Matthew Knowles, Capital Dec. 31, 20X2 $465,000
E4-9	2. Net inc. $12,400
E4-10	1. Total assets $52,700
E4-11	2. Total assets $18,790
	Amos Faraday, Capital $14,090
E4-12	Net inc. $53,100
P4-1A	Net inc. $16,300
P4-2A	2. Net inc. $87,630
	Total assets $240,680
P4-3A	2. Net inc. $90,000
	Total assets $131,000
P4-4A	Trial bal. total $153,000
P4-5A	3. Net inc. $26,000
	Total assets $104,320
	5. Trial bal. total $146,220
P4-6A	1. Total assets $114,600
	2. Debt ratio 0.41
P4-7A	c. Overall, net inc. understated by $1,060
P4-1B	Net inc. $15,000
P4-2B	2. Net inc. $30,000
	Total assets $175,860
P4-3B	2. Net inc. $87,000
	Total assets $134,000
P4-4B	2. Trial bal. total $151,000
P4-5B	3. Net inc. $12,090

	Total assets $101,080
	5. Trial bal. total $117,410
P4-6B	1. Total assets $108,200
	2. Debt ratio 0.40
P4-7B	c. Overall, net inc. understated by $2,520
Case 1	1. Net inc. $55,440
	2. Total assets $58,390
Case 2	No check figure
Financial Statement Case	3. Debt ratio at 2/29/00 0.66
	5. Cost of plant assets $13,824 mil.
Team Project	Net inc. $1,500
	Total assets $1,640
P4A-1	No check figure

Check Figures—Chapter 5

DE5-1	No check figure
DE5-2	No check figure
DE5-3	No check figure
DE5-4	No check figure
DE5-5	a. $130,000
	b. $126,100
DE5-6	c. Credit Cash for $126,100
DE5-7	Net cost $137,200
DE5-8	Gross profit $55,200
DE5-9	c. Debit Cash for $36,260
DE5-10	b. $321,240
DE5-11	No check figure
DE5-12	No check figure
DE5-13	Net inc. $1,666 mil.
DE5-14	Total assets $11,471 mil.
DE5-15	C. Ernest, Capital bal. $25,650
DE5-16	No check figure
DE5-17	Gross profit % 20.7%
	Invy. turnover 56.4 times
DE5-18	b. Excess of collections over payments $641 mil.
DE5-19	1. COGS $23,029 mil.
DE5-20	3. F150,000
DE5-21	Purchases $7,181 mil.
E5-1	2. Gross profit for 2000 $3,541 mil.
E5-2	Sept. 23 Debit Cash for $2,254
E5-3	May 22 Credit Cash for $469.54
E5-4	June 14 Credit Cash for $7,054
E5-5	May 14 Debit Cash for $6,984
E5-6	Owner Capital bal. at 12/31/00 $10,805
E5-7	Net inc. $74,860
E5-8	Net inc. $74,860
E5-9	20X2 Gross profit % 51%; Invy. turnover 3.72 times
E5-10	1. Net inc. $31,300
E5-11	Net inc. $31,300
E5-12	Excess of collections over payments $29 bil.
E5-13	COGS $99,300
E5-14	(e) $16,200 (f) $37,400 (i) $112,100
E5-15	$180 mil.
E5-16	3. Net inc. $4,900
P5-1A	No check figure
P5-2A	No check figure
P5-3A	No check figure
P5-4A	Net inc. $49,890
P5-5A	2. $66,260
P5-6A	1. Net inc. $55,600
	2. Total assets $200,100

P5-7A	1. Net inc. $55,600
	2. Total assets $200,100
P5-8A	1. Net inc. $58,710
	2. 20X4 Gross profit % 60%
	Invy. turnover 2.03 times
P5-9A	2. Gross profit % 32%
	3. Invy. turnover 3.2 times
P5-1B	No check figure
P5-2B	No check figure
P5-3B	No check figure
P5-4B	Net inc. $31,370
P5-5B	2. $58,190
P5-6B	1. Net inc. $7,900
	2. Total assets $371,700
P5-7B	1. Net inc. $7,900
	2. Total assets $371,700
P5-8B	1. Net inc. $38,760
	2. 2000 Gross profit % 56%
	Invy. turnover 8.9 times
P5-9B	2. Gross profit % 48%
	3. Invy. turnover 3.63 times
Case 1	2. Net inc. $78,380
	Total assets $104,590
Case 2	No check figure
Financial Statement Case	2. $1,144 mil. closed to R/E
	3. Gross profit % 30.7%
	Invy. turnover 6.3 times
E5A-1	June 23 Debit Cash for $2,352
E5A-2	May 22 Credit Cash for $469.54
E5A-3	June 14 Credit Cash for $7,054
E5A-4	May 14 Debit Cash for $6,984
P5A-1	Hillcrest: Nov. 27 Credit Cash for $2,600
P5A-2	No check figure
P5A-3	No check figure
P5A-4	1. Net inc. $88,850
	2. Total assets $218,110
	4. Ben Latham, Capital bal. $195,590

Check Figures—Chapter 6

DE6-1	No check figure
DE6-2	No check figure
DE6-3	No check figure
DE6-4	No check figure
DE6-5	No check figure
DE6-6	No check figure
DE6-7	No check figure
DE6-8	No check figure
DE6-9	4. Decrease in Accts. Rec. $1,235
DE6-10	2. $2,876
	3. Payments $798
DE6-11	2. Net Purchases $3,885
DE6-12	4. Net sales revenue $7,456
E6-1	No check figure
E6-2	No check figure
E6-3	No check figure
E6-4	No check figure
E6-5	Total Debit to Cash $5,987.60
E6-6	No check figure
E6-7	No check figure
E6-8	Purchases journal: Total credit to Accts. Pay. $21,216
E6-9	3. Total Accts.Pay. $3,042
E6-10	3. Total credit to Cash $14,897
E6-11	No check figure
E6-12	1. Gross profit $3,935
P6-1A	No check figure

P6-2A 1. Cash receipts journal:
Total debit to Cash $36,619

P6-3A No check figure

P6-4A 2. Cash pay. journal:
Total credit to Cash $17,237

P6-5A 6. Total Accts. Rec. $496
Total Accts. Pay. $2,692

P6-1B No check figure

P6-2B 1. Cash recpts. journal:
Total debit to Cash $58,650

P6-3B No check figure

P6-4B 2. Cash pay. journal:
Total credit to Cash $15,571

P6-5B 6. Total Accts. Rec. $567
Total Accts. Pay. $2,925

Case 1 No check figure

Case 2 Sales journal: Total $16,198
Cash recpts. journal:
Total debit to Cash $7,774

Check Figures—Chapter 7

DE7-1 No check figure
DE7-2 No check figure
DE7-3 No check figure
DE7-4 No check figure
DE7-5 No check figure
DE7-6 No check figure
DE7-7 No check figure
DE7-8 No check figure
DE7-9 No check figure
DE7-10 Adj. bal. $2,570
DE7-11 No check figure
DE7-12 No check figure
DE7-13 Employee stole $980
DE7-14 No check figure
DE7-15 No check figure
DE7-16 No check figure
DE7-17 No check figure
DE7-18 3. $400
DE7-19 1. New financing needed $165 mil.
DE7-20 New financing needed $10 mil.
DE7-21 No check figure
E7-1 No check figure
E7-2 No check figure
E7-3 No check figure
E7-4 No check figure
E7-5 No check figure
E7-6 No check figure
E7-7 Adj. bal. $1,891
E7-8 Adj. bal. $4,071
E7-9 No check figure
E7-10 No check figure
E7-11 No check figure
E7-12 Apr. 10 Credit Cash for $181
E7-13 1. Credit Cash for $211.13
E7-14 New financing needed $19 mil.
E7-15 No check figure
E7-16 1. New financing needed $433 mil.
2. Current ratio after borrowing 1.30
P7-1A No check figure
P7-2A No check figure
P7-3A 1. Adj bal. $10,670
P7-4A 1. Adj. bal. $20,948.77
P7-5A No check figure
P7-6A Apr. 30 Credit Cash in Bank for $382.64
P7-7A New financing needed $1,300

P7-8A 1. Cash available for additional investments $727 mil.
P7-9A No check figure
P7-1B No check figure
P7-2B No check figure
P7-3B 1. Adj. bal. $6,657
P7-4B 1. Adj. bal. $3,635.33
P7-5B No check figure
P7-6B June 30 Credit Cash in Bank for $307.63
P7-7B New financing needed $3,300
P7-8B 1. New financing needed $76 mil.
P7-9B No check figure
Case 1 Cashier stole $900
Case 2 No check figure
Financial Statement Case 5. Cash decreased by $35 mil.

Check Figures—Chapter 8

DE8-1 No check figure
DE8-2 No check figure
DE8-3 No check figure
DE8-4 No check figure
DE8-5 A/R, net $78,000
DE8-6 4. Uncollect. Acct. Exp. $14,400
DE8-7 3. A/R, net $173,600
DE8-8 Allowance for U/A end. bal. $4,000
DE8-9 Debit Uncollect. Acct. Exp. $4,900
DE8-10 No check figure
DE8-11 A/R bal., June 30 $5,500
DE8-12 Debit Cash $7,840
DE8-13 5. Pay at maturity $1,090
DE8-14 Note 1 $150
Note 4 $375
DE8-15 a. Credit Cash $400,000
b. Debit Cash $408,000
DE8-16 c. Debit Cash $1,090
DE8-17 a. Note rec. $1,000
Interest rec. $22.50
d. Interest rev. $67.50
DE8-18 Net realizable value:
Intel $3,700 mil.
Oracle $2,238 mil.
DE8-19 1. Net inc. $1,184 mil.
2. A/R, net $2,464 mil.
DE8-20 a. 1.17
b. 48 days
DE8-21 1. 1.73
c. 0.59
d. 3.20
E8-1 No check figure
E8-2 No check figure
E8-3 2 & 3. A/R, net $53,000
E8-4 2. A/R $55,930
E8-5 2. A/R, net $288,004
E8-6 Debit Uncollect. Acct.Exp.:
a. $2,250; b. $4,300
E8-7 1. Interest for:
20X7 $60,000
20X8 $90,000
20X9 $30,000
E8-8 Dec. 31 Debit Interest Rec. $719
E8-9 Apr. 1, 20X4 Debit Cash $8,960
E8-10 Dec. 31 Debit Cash $5,490
E8-11 1. 20X3 0.80
2. 37 days
E8-12 1. 2 days
E8-13 Net inc.: Without bankcards $75,000; With bankcards $93,960

P8-1A No check figure
P8-2A Uncollected. Acct. Exp.:
1. $3,500
2. $8,900
P8-3A 3. A/R, net:
20X4 $247,017
20X3 $263,160
P8-4A 3. A/R, net $160,301
P8-5A 1. Note 1 $11,330
Note 2 $15,250
Note 3 $13,080
P8-6A No check figure
P8-7A Dec. 31, 20X1 Uncollect. Acct. Exp. $9,700
P8-8A 1. Ratios for 20X3:
a. 1.71; b. 0.60; c. 20 days
P8-1B No check figure
P8-2B Uncollect. Acct. Exp.:
1. $8,900
2. $12,800
P8-3B 3. A/R, net:
20X1 $132,684
20X0 $115,300
P8-4B 3. A/R, net $135,865
P8-5B 1. Note 1 $12,720
Note 2 $9,075
Note 3 $14,170
P8-6B No check figure
P8-7B Dec. 31, 20X1 Uncollect. Acct. Exp. $7,500
P8-8B 1. Ratios for 20X3:
a. 1.85; b. 0.95; c. 18 days
Case 1 1. Net inc.:
20X3 $106,600
20X2 $85,550
Case 2 A/R bal. $90,000
Note Rec. bal. $5,000
Financial Statement Case 3. Acid test ratio 0.35
DE8A-1 Proceeds $498,200
E8A-1A June 30 Debit Cash $498,200
E8A-2A Dec. 1 Debit Interest Exp. $300
P8A-1 2. Note 1 $9,994; Note 2 $6,023; Note 3 $8,007
P8A-2 2. Note 1 $6,111; Note 2 $8,965; Note 3 $8,129

Check Figures—Chapter 9

DE9-1 Inventory $24,000
Gross profit $64,000
DE9-2 2. Gross profit $360,000
DE9-3 Gross profit $60,500
DE9-4 No check figure
DE9-5 No check figure
DE9-6 No check figure
DE9-7 COGS: wtd-avg. $750
LIFO $800
DE9-8 COGS: wtd-avg. $9,422
LIFO $9,800
DE9-9 Net inc.: wtd-avg. $1,978;
LIFO $1,600
DE9-10 Inc. tax Exp.: wtd-avg. $791;
LIFO $640
DE9-11 No check figure
DE9-12 2. Gross profit $765
DE9-13 Inventory $550
COGS $1,325

DE9-14	b. COGS $67.5 mil.
	d. Net loss $(0.1) mil.
DE9-15	3. Correct net inc.:
	Last yr. $8.3 mil.;
	This yr. $5 mil.
DE9-16	No check figure
DE9-17	1. & 2. End. invy. $150,000
E9-1	2. Gross profit $1,574 thou.
E9-2	2. Gross profit $1,574 thou.
E9-3	Purchase $8,800 mil.
E9-4	COGS: wtd-avg. $3,320
	LIFO $3,368
E9-5	b. COGS $3,270
E9-6	c. COGS $3,368
E9-7	LIFO tax saving $29
E9-8	a. $64,800; d. $30,200
	f. $34,700
E9-9	Magnolia gross profit % 55.9%;
	Invy. T/O 3.9 times
E9-10	COGS $724; End. invy. $664
E9-11	Net inc. for cell B21 $75,000;
	cell C21 $68,000
E9-12	No check figure
E9-13	No check figure
E9-14	Gross profit $110,567
E9-15	Gross profit $62,900
	Inventory $19,800
E9-16	Net inc.: 20X2 $41,100
	20X1 $27,300
E9-17	Est. cost of invy. destroyed
	$49,100
E9-18	No check figure
E9-19	1. Net inc. $724 mil.
	2. Total assets $5,522 mil.
P9-1A	3. Net inc. $320
P9-2A	2. Net inc. $110 thou.
P9-3A	3. Gross profit $1,494
P9-4A	1. COGS: wtd-avg. $55,707
	FIFO $54,516
	LIFO $56,908
P9-5A	1. Gross profit:
	wtd-avg. $2,267
	FIFO $2,502
	LIFO $2,089
P9-6A	No check figure
P9-7A	1. Correct net inc.:
	20X3 $11 thou.
	20X2 $9 thou.
	20X1 $27 thou.
P9-8A	1. Est. cost of end.
	invy. $845 thou.
P9-9A	1. Net inc. $1,127 mil.
	2. Total assets $5,189 mil.
P9-1B	3. Net inc. $520
P9-2B	2. Net inc. $75 thou.
P9-3B	3. Gross profit $3,205
P9-4B	1. COGS: wtd-avg. $12,445
	FIFO $12,167
	LIFO $12,758
P9-5B	1. Gross profit:
	wtd-avg. $62,810
	FIFO $63,355
	LIFO $62,030
P9-6B	No check figure
P9-7B	1. Correct net inc.:
	20X2 $61 thou.
	20X1 $59 thou.
	20X0 $15 thou.

P9-8B	1. Est. cost of end.
	invy. $467 thou.
P9-9B	1. Net inc. $48 mil.
	2. Total assets $456 mil.
Case 1	Net inc.: FIFO with and without
	purchase $240,700;
	LIFO without purchase
	$205,900; with purchase
	$183,425
Case 2	No check figure
Financial Statement Case	Purchases
	$23,352 mil.

Check Figures—Chapter 10

DE10-1	3. Book value $10,227 mil.
DE10-2	No check figure
DE10-3	No check figure
DE10-4	2. Bal. $872,000
DE10-5	Land $50,000; Building $37,500
	Equipment $12,500
DE10-6	No check figure
DE10-7	2. Book value—SL $30,000,000;
	DDB $21,600,000
DE10-8	b. Depr. $7,500,000
	c. Depr. $–0–
DE10-9	2. Tax saved $3,360,000
DE10-10	b. Depr. $4,800,000
	c. Depr. $10,800,000
DE10-11	Depr. $10,000
DE10-12	1. a. Loss on Sale $2,000
	b. Gain on Sale $8,240
DE10-13	2. Depletion $4.5 bil.
	3. Book value $2.0 bil.
DE10-14	1. Goodwill $310,000
	3. Amort. exp. $7,750
DE10-15	2. Book value $311 mil.
	3. Goodwill purchased $15 mil.
DE10-16	1. Net loss $75,000
E10-1	Land $206,900
	Land improve. $67,400
E10-2	1. Cost $654,000
E10-3	Saddle 1 $2,580
	Saddle 2 $4,150
	Saddle 3 $3,270
E10-4	No check figure
E10-5	No check figure
E10-6	20X4 Depr.: SL $3,000;
	UOP $2,400; DDB $375
E10-7	Extra cash to invest with DDB
	$38,388
E10-8	Depr. Yr. 16 $21,458
E10-9	Gain on Sale $960
E10-10	Cost of new truck $338,175
E10-11	Depletion $75,600
E10-12	Part 2. Amortiz. $342,500
E10-13	Payment for other assets $63 mil.
E10-14	3. Amortiz. of goodwill $700,000
E10-15	Yr. 5 Equip., net Correct;
	Net inc. 0.9 over
E10-16	1. Acquisitions $2,559 mil.
P10-1A	2. Depr.-Land improve. $3,893;
	Office bldg. $30,621; Garage
	$2,057; Furniture $11,681
P10-2A	Dec. 31 Depr.-Commun. Equip.
	$19,200; Televideo Equip.
	$2,133; Office Equip. $10,000
P10-3A	No check figure
P10-4A	3. Net inc. advantage of SL
	$8,420; Cash flow advantage of
	DDB $5,613

P10-5A	3. Cost of assets sold
	$15,098,000
P10-6A	Part 1. 3. Amortiz. of goodwill.
	$57,450;
	Part 2. 2. Net inc. $119,150
P10-7A	1. Book value $21.4 bil.
	2. Gain on sale $0.2 bil.
	3. Owners' equity $12.4 bil.
	4. Net loss $0.9 bil.
P10-1B	2. Depr.-Land improve. $2,306;
	Sales bldg. $16,481; Garage
	$1,280; Furniture $9,114
P10-2B	Dec. 31 Depr.—Motor-Carrier
	Equip. $51,000; Buildings
	$733
P10-3B	No check figure
P10-4B	3. Net inc. advantage of SL
	$30,840; Cash flow advantage of
	DDB $20,560
P10-5B	3. Cost of assets sold $11,213 mil.
P10-6B	Part 1. 3. Amortiz. of goodwill
	$105,000;
	Part 2. 2. Net inc. $15,750
P10-7B	1. Book value $4.0 bil.
	2. Gain on sale $0.2 bil.
	3. Owners' equity $8.4 bil.
	4. Net inc. $2.5 bil.
Case 1	1. Net inc.-Astoria $149,700;
	Hilton $112,400
Case 2	No check figure
Financial Statement Case	4. Loss on
	Sale $165 mil.

Check Figures—Chapter 11

DE11-1	No check figure
DE11-2	c. Credit Cash $8,800
DE11-3	2. Interest exp. $400
DE11-4	3. Note pay. $99,500
DE11-5	2. Air Traffic Liab. $1,200
DE11-6	2. Est. Warranty Pay. $8,000
DE11-7	No check figure
DE11-8	No check figure
DE11-9	No check figure
DE11-10	2. Net pay $684.75
DE11-11	Total exp. $1,008.65
DE11-12	No check figure
DE11-13	Net pay $5,960
DE11-14	No check figure
DE11-15	No check figure
DE11-16	Total payroll exp. $28,805.50
DE11-17	No check figure
DE11-18	Total current liab. $84,202
DE11-19	No check figure
E11-1	No check figure
E11-2	1. Accrued Payroll Liab. $27,194
E11-3	Unearned subscription rev. $80
E11-4	2. Est. Warranty Pay. $3,970
E11-5	Apr. 1, 20X3 Credit Cash $16,200
E11-6	2. Note pay, short-term $11,840
E11-7	No check figure
E11-8	Pay off $30,000
E11-9	Net pay $7,598.70
E11-10	a. Net pay $275.50
E11-11	Payroll Tax Exp. $7,636.20
E11-12	Salary exp. $900,000
	Salary pay. $4,000
E11-13	20X1: Current portion of LT debt
	$1,000,000; Interest pay.
	$450,000
E11-14	Total current liab. $125,340

E11-15	1. Current ratio 0.85
	2. Current ratio 0.79
E11-16	1. Payments $627 mil.
	2. Salary exp. $3,193 mil.
P11-1A	No check figure
P11-2A	No check figure
P11-3A	1. b. $7,518
	c. $23,949
	e. $1,998
	j. $13,299
P11-4A	1. Net pay $58,222
	2. Total cost $89,632
P11-5A	3. Total liab. $339,312
P11-6A	3. Credit Cash $2,178
	4. Debit Payroll Tax Exp. $127
P11-7A	No check figure
P11-1B	No check figure
P11-2B	No check figure
P11-3B	1. a. $78,584
	c. $83,693
	f. $2,162
	k. $24,484
P11-4B	1. Net pay $48,780
	2. Total cost $79,153
P11-5B	3. Total liab. $202,727
P11-6B	3. Credit Cash $2,033
	4. Debit Payroll Tax Exp. $177
P11-7B	No check figure
Case 1	No check figure
Case 2	No check figure
Financial Statement Case	No check figure

Check Figures—Chapter 12

DE12-1	No check figure
DE12-2	No check figure
DE12-3	Debit Building $285,000
DE12-4	3. Total equity $32 mil.
DE12-5	2. Benz, Cap. $462,500
	Hanna, Cap. $97,500
DE12-6	2. Benz, Cap. $494,000
	Hanna, Cap. $76,000
DE12-7	Lawson $48,000; Martinez $32,000; Edwards $60,000
DE12-8	Fung $27,150
	Kiawa $22,850
DE12-9	No check figure
DE12-10	No check figure
DE12-11	Credit Kliptel, Cap. $40,000; Nagasawa, Cap. $5,000; Osburn, Cap. $5,000
DE12-12	Nagasawa, Cap. $75,000 Osburn, Cap. $85,000 Kliptel, Cap. $40,000
DE12-13	Debit Page, Cap. $10,667; Franco, Cap. $5,333; Credit Everett, Cap. $156,000
DE12-14	No check figure
DE12-15	a. Credit Green, Cap. $23,750; Henry, Cap. $47,500; Isaac, Cap. $23,750
DE12-16	Debit Henry, Cap. $90,500; Credit Green, Cap. $15,000; Isaac, Cap. $15,000
DE12-17	Pay Avignon $31,000; Bloch $17,000; Crane $7,000
DE12-18	No check figure
DE12-19	Green, Cap. $66,000 Henry, Cap. $67,000
DE12-20	Net inc.: Frost $70,000; Martin $35,000

E12-1	No check figure
E12-2	Credit Flute, Cap. $82,100
E12-3	d. Net inc.: Meppen $34,818; Quaid $63,182
E12-4	Partnership capital decreased $2,000
E12-5	c. Falco, Cap. $52,500; Graham, Cap. $103,750 Ott, Cap. $53,750
E12-6	c. Credit Falco, Cap. $52,500; Graham, Cap. $3,750; Ott, Cap. $3,750
E12-7	1. Echols receives $45,000; 2. Schaeffer's equity $50,000
E12-8	b. Debit Bermuda, Cap. $46,000
E12-9	2. Barry gets $20,000; McCall gets $17,000; Flaten gets $8,000
E12-10	Pay Deluth $24,800; Liu $18,600; Bush $14,600
E12-11	Selling for $90,000—Valahu, Cap. $3,000; Leman, Cap. $20,800; Sucre, Cap. $(4,800)
E12-12	Total assets $276,200 Klatt, Cap. $90,700 Stover, Cap. $93,100
P12-1A	No check figure
P12-2A	2. Total assets $122,020 Saran, Cap. $49,860 Gentry, Cap. $49,860
P12-3A	Lampe's Cap.: 2. $50,000 3. $31,250 4. $41,400
P12-4A	1. d. Net inc. to: Trump $33,667 Rivers $28,667 Jetta $23,666
P12-5A	No check figure
P12-6A	1. b. Pay: Jackson $20,700; Pierce $52,800; Fenner $11,500
P12-7A	3. Pay: Alberts $8,875; Beech $8,625; Sumner $11,500
P12-8A	No check figure
P12-9A	2. Total assets $100,000 Busby, Cap. $40,450 Box, Cap. $40,450
P12-3B	Conyers' Cap.: 2. $60,000 3. $95,000 4. $42,000
P12-4B	1. d. Net inc. to: Lake $79,750 Wood $63,500 Parks $66,750
P12-5B	No check figure
P12-6B	1. b. Pay: Parr $19,700; Johnston $35,100; Rake $30,200
P12-7B	3. Pay: Vela $12,000; Thomas $7,000; Prago $3,000
Case 1	No check figure
Case 2	No check figure
Financial Statement Case	2. $1,997,323; 3. Avg. net inc. per partner $372,825

Check Figures—Chapter 13

DE13-1	No check figure
DE13-2	No check figure

DE13-3	No check figure
DE13-4	No check figure
DE13-5	No check figure
DE13-6	No check figure
DE13-7	1. Incr. in paid-in cap. $428 mil.
DE13-8	No check figure
DE13-9	Bldg. $480,000; Equip $220,000; Common Stock $100,000; PIC in Excess $600,000
DE13-10	Total S/E $183.9 mil.
DE13-11	a. Net inc. $80.6 mil. b. Total liab. $122.3 mil. c. Total assets $306.2 mil
DE13-12	Total S/E $490,000
DE13-13	R/E incr. $54,000
DE13-14	4. Pfd. gets $6,000 Com. gets $3,000
DE13-15	No check figure
DE13-16	a. Book value-Pfd.$140; b. Book value-Com. $44.44
DE13-17	No check figure
DE13-18	No check figure
DE13-19	ROA 13.6% ROE 27.1%
DE13-20	2. Net inc. $72,000 Inc. tax pay $36,000 Deferred tax liab. $12,000
E13-1	No check figure
E13-2	2. Total PIC $118,500
E13-3	2. Total S/E $72,000
E13-4	Cap. in Excess of Par $74,850
E13-5	No check figure
E13-6	Total S/E $192,000
E13-7	Total S/E $486,000
E13-8	Total S/E $407,000
E13-9	Pfd. gets $22,000; Com. gets $38,000
E13-10	Pfd. A gets $40,000; Pfd. B gets $962,000; Com. gets $98,000
E13-11	Book value-Pdf. $60; Com. $22.08
E13-12	Book value-Pfd. $68.64; Com. $21.99
E13-13	ROA .091 ROE .074
E13-14	2. Net inc. $78 mil. Inc. tax pay. $40 mil. Deferred tax liab. $12 mil.
E13-15	2. Bal. at Jan. 31, 20X0; Com. Stk. $446 mil.; Cap. in Excess $714 mil.; R/E $25, 129 mil.
P13-1A	No check figure
P13-2A	2. Total S/E $308,100
P13-3A	5. Total S/E $413,000
P13-4A	Total S/E: Yurman $510,000; No. Lights $623,600
P13-5A	3. Div. Pay., Pfd. $218 mil.; Div. Pay., Com. $1,408 mil.
P13-6A	1. Total assets $654,000; Total S/E $499,000
P13-7A	1. b. 20X2 Pfd. gets $3,500; Com. gets $11,500.
P13-8A	5. Book value-Pfd. $27.90; Com. $9.73
P13-9A	3. Net inc. $149,500
P13-1B	No check figure

P13-2B	2. Total S/E $273,800
P13-3B	5. Total S/E $272,000
P13-4B	Total S/E: Granada $829,000; Traigon $403,000
P13-5B	3. Div. Pay., Pfd. $18 mil.; Div. Pay., Com. $32 mil.

P13-6B	1. Total assets $417,000 Total S/E $309,000
P13-7B	1. b. 20X2 Pfd. gets $70,000; Com. gets $30,000
P13-8B	6. Book value-Pfd. $54.95; Com. $8.51

P13-9B	3. Net inc. $126,000
Case 1.	3. Total S/E: Plan 1 $435,000; Plan 2 $420,000
Case 2.	No check figure
Financial Statement Case	No check figure

Glossary

Absorption Costing. The costing method that assigns both variable and fixed manufacturing costs to products.

Accelerated Depreciation Method. A depreciation method that writes off more of the asset's cost near the start of its useful life than the straight-line method does.

Account. The detailed record of the changes that have occurred in a particular asset, liability, or owner's equity during a period. The basic summary device of accounting.

Account Payable. A liability backed by the general reputation and credit standing of the debtor.

Account Receivable. A promise to receive cash from customers to whom the business has sold goods or for whom the business has performed services.

Accounting. The information system that measures business activities, processes that information into reports, and communicates the results to decision makers.

Accounting Equation. The basic tool of accounting, presenting the resources of the business and the claims to those resources: Assets = Liabilities + Owner's Equity.

Accounting Information System. The combination of personnel, records, and procedures that a business uses to provide financial data.

Accrual-Basis Accounting. Accounting that records the impact of a business event as it occurs, regardless of whether the transaction affected cash.

Accrued Expense. An expense that the business has not yet paid. Also called accrued liability.

Accrued Revenue. A revenue that has been earned but not yet collected in cash.

Accumulated Depreciation. The cumulative sum of all depreciation expense recorded for an asset.

Additional Paid-in Capital. The paid-in capital in excess of par—common plus other accounts combined for reporting on the balance sheet.

Adjusted Trial Balance. A list of all the ledger accounts with their adjusted balances.

Adjusting Entry. Entry made at the end of the period to assign revenues to the period in which they are earned and expenses to the period in which they are incurred. Adjusting entries help measure the period's income and bring the related asset and liability accounts to correct balances for the financial statements.

Aging-of-Accounts Method. A way to estimate bad debts by analyzing individual accounts receivable according to the length of time they have been receivable from the customer. Also called the **balance-sheet approach**.

Allowance for Uncollectible Accounts. A contra account, related to accounts receivable, that holds the estimated amount of collection losses. Also called **Allowance for Doubtful Accounts**.

Allowance Method. A method of recording collection losses on the basis of estimates, instead of waiting to see which customers the company will not collect from.

Amortization. The systematic reduction of the asset's carrying value on the books. Expense that applies to intangibles in the same way depreciation applies to plant assets and depletion applies to natural resources.

Asset. An economic resource that is expected to be of benefit in the future.

Audit. An examination of a company's financial statements and the accounting system.

Authorization of Stock. Provision in a corporate charter that gives the state's permission for the corporation to issue—that is, to sell—a certain number of shares of stock.

Balance Sheet. List of an entity's assets, liabilities, and owner's equity as of a specific date. Also called the **statement of financial position**.

Bank Collection. Collection of money by the bank on behalf of a depositor.

Bank Reconciliation. Document explaining the reasons for the difference between a depositor's cash records and the depositor's cash balance in its bank account.

Bank Statement. Document the bank uses to report what it did with the depositor's cash. Shows the bank account's beginning and ending balances and lists the month's cash transactions conducted through the bank.

Batch Processing. Computerized accounting for similar transactions in a group or batch.

Board of Directors. Group elected by the stockholders to set policy and to appoint the officers.

Book Value. Amount of owners' equity on the company's books for each share of its stock.

Book Value (of a Plant Asset). The asset's cost minus accumulated depreciation.

Breakeven Point. The sales level at which operating income is zero: Total revenues equal total expenses.

Bylaws. Constitution for governing a corporation.

Callable Bonds. Bonds that the issuer may call or pay off at a specified price whenever the issuer wants.

Capital Expenditure. Expenditure that increases the capacity or efficiency of an asset or extends its useful life. Capital expendtures are debited to an asset account.

Capital Lease. Lease agreement that meets any one of four criteria: (1) The lease transfers title of the leased asset to the lessee. (2) The lease contains a bargain purchase option. (3) The lease term is 75% or more of the estimated useful life of the leased asset. (4) The present value of the lease payments is 90% or more of the market value of the leased asset.

Capitalize a Cost. To record a cost as part of an asset's cost, rather than as an expense.

Cash-Basis Accounting. Accounting that records transactions only when cash is received or paid.

Cash Payments Journal. Special journal used to record cash payments by check. Also called the **check register** or **cash disbursements journal**.

Cash Receipts Journal. Special journal used to record cash receipts.

Certified Management Accountant (CMA). A licensed accountant who works for a single company.

Certified Public Accountant (CPA). A licensed accountant who serves the general public rather than one particular company.

Chairperson. Elected by a corporation's board of directors, the most powerful person in the corporation.

Chart of Accounts. List of all the accounts and their account numbers in the ledger.

Charter. Document that gives the state's permission to form a corporation.

Check. Document that instructs a bank to pay the designated person or business a specified amount of money.

Closing Entries. Entries that transfer the revenue, expense, and owner withdrawal balances from these respective accounts to the capital account.

Closing the Accounts. Step in the accounting cycle at the end of the period. Closing the accounts consists of journalizing and posting the closing entries to set the balances of the revenue, expense, and withdrawal accounts to zero for the next period.

Common Stock. The basic form of capital stock. In a corporation, the common stockholders are the owners of the business.

Computer Virus. A malicious program that (a) reproduces itself, (b) gets included in program code without consent, and (c) performs actions that can be destructive.

Conservatism. Reporting the least favorable figures in the financial statements.

Consignment. Transfer of goods by the owner (consignor) to another business (consignee) that sells the inventory on the owner's behalf. The consignee does not take title to the consigned goods.

Consistency Principle. A business should use the same accounting methods and procedures from period to period.

Contingent Liability. A potential liability that will become an actual liability only if a particular event does occur.

Contra Account. An account that always has a companion account and whose normal balance is opposite that of the companion account.

Contract Interest Rate. Interest rate that determines the amount of cash interest the borrower pays and the investor receives each year. Also called the **stated interest rate**.

Contribution Margin per Unit. Excess of the sales revenue per unit (sale price) over the variable expense per unit.

Contribution Margin Ratio. The ratio of contribution margin to sales revenue.

Contribution Margin. Sales revenue minus all variable expenses. Also called **sales revenue per unit (sale price) minus variable expense per unit.**

Control Account. An account whose balance equals the sum of the balances in a group of related accounts in a subsidiary ledger.

Controller. The chief accounting officer of a company.

Convertible Bonds. Bonds (or notes payable) that may be converted into the common stock of the issuing company at the option of the investor.

Copyright. Exclusive right to reproduce and sell a book, musical composition, film, other work of art, or computer program. Issued by the federal government, copyrights extend 50 years beyond the author's life.

Corporation. A business owned by stockholders; it begins when the state approves its articles of incorporation. A corporation is a legal entity, an "artificial person," in the eyes of the law.

Cost of Goods Available for Sale Beginning inventory plus purchases.

Cost of Goods Sold. The cost of the inventory that the business has sold to customers. Also called **cost of sales.**

Credit. The right side of an account.

Credit Memorandum or Credit Memo. A document issued by a seller to credit a customer account for returned merchandise.

Creditor. The party to a credit transaction who sells goods or a service and obtains a receivable.

Cumulative Preferred Stock. Preferred stock whose owners must receive all dividends in arrears before the corporation pays dividends to the common stockholders.

Current Asset. An asset that is expected to be converted to cash, sold, or consumed during the next 12 months, or within the business's normal operating cycle.

Current Liability. A debt due to be paid with cash or with goods and services within one year or within the entity's operating cycle if the cycle is longer than a year.

Current Portion of Long-Term Debt. Amount of the principal that is payable within one year. Also called **current maturity.**

Database. A computerized storehouse of information.

Debit. The left side of an account.

Debit Memorandum or Debit Memo. A document issued by a buyer when returning merchandise. The memo informs the seller that the buyer no longer owes the seller for the amount of the returned purchases.

Debtor. The party to a credit transaction who makes a purchase and has a payable.

Deficit. Debit balance in the Retained Earnings account.

Depletion Expense. The portion of a natural resource's cost used up in a particular period. Depletion expense is computed in the same way as units-of-production depreciation.

Deposit in Transit. A deposit recorded by the company but not yet by its bank.

Depreciable Cost. The cost of a plant asset minus its estimated residual value.

Depreciation. The allocation of a plant asset's cost to expense over its useful life.

Direct Write-off Method. A method of accounting for uncollectible receivables, in which the company waits until the credit department decides that a customer's account receivable is uncollectible, and then debits Uncollectible-Account Expense and credits the customer's Account Receivable.

Disclosure Principle. A business's financial statements must report enough information for outsiders to make knowledgeable decisions about the company.

Discount (on a Bond). Excess of a bond's maturity (par value) over its issue price. Also called a **bond discount.**

Discounting a Note Payable. A borrowing arrangement in which the bank subtracts the interest amount from a note's face value. The borrower receives the net amount.

Discounting Note Receivable. Selling a note receivable before its maturity date.

Dishonor of a Note. Failure of a note's maker to pay a note receivable at maturity. Also called **default on a note.**

Dissolution. Ending of a partnership.

Dividends. Distributions by a corporation to its stockholders.

Double Taxation. Corporations pay their own income taxes on cor-porate income. Then, the stock-holders pay personal income tax on the cash dividends they receive from corporations.

Double-Declining-Balance (DDB) Depreciation Method. An accelerated depreciation method that computes annual depreciation by multiplying the asset's decreasing book value by a constant percent that is 2 times the straight-line rate.

Electronic Funds Transfer (EFT). System that transfers cash by electronic communication rather than by paper documents.

Encryption. Rearranging plain-text messages by a mathematical process; the primary method of achieving confidentiality in e-commerce.

Entity. An organization or a section of an organization that, for accounting purposes, stands apart from other organizations and individuals as a separate economic unit.

Estimated Residual Value. Expected cash value of an asset at the end of its useful life. Also called **scrap value,** or **salvage value.**

Estimated Useful Life. Length of the service period expected from an asset. May be expressed in years, units of output, miles, or another measure.

Expense. Decrease in owner's equity that occurs from using assets or increasing liabilities in the course of delivering goods or services to customers.

Financial Accounting. The branch of accounting that focuses on information for people outside the firm.

Financial Accounting Standards Board (FASB). The private organization that determines how accounting is practiced in the United States.

Financial Statements. Documents that report on a business in monetary amounts, providing information to help people make informed business decisions.

Firewalls. Devices that enable members of a local network to access the Internet but keep nonmembers out of the network.

First-In, First-Out (FIFO) Inventory Costing Method. Inventory costing method by which the first costs into inventory are the first costs out to cost of goods sold. Ending inventory is based on the costs of the most recent purchases.

Franchises, Licenses. Privileges granted by a private business or a government to sell a product or service under specified conditions.

General Journal. Journal used to record all transactions that do not fit one of the special journals.

General Ledger. Ledger of accounts that are reported in the financial statements.

General Partnership. A form of partnership in which each partner is an owner of the business, with all the privileges and risks of ownership.

Generally Accepted Accounting Principles (GAAP). Accounting guidelines, formulated by the Financial Accounting Standards Board, that govern how accountants measure, process, and communicate financial information.

Goodwill. Excess of the cost of an acquired company over the sum of the market values of its net assets (assets minus liabilities).

Gross Pay. Total amount of salary, wages, commissions, or any other employee compensation before taxes and other deductions.

Gross Profit. Excess of net sales revenue over cost of goods sold. Also called **gross margin.**

Gross Profit Method. A way to estimate inventory on the basis of the cost-of-goods-sold model: Beginning inventory + Net purchases = Cost of goods available for sale. Cost of goods available for sale − Cost of goods sold = Ending inventory. Also called the **gross margin method.**

Gross Profit or Gross Margin. Excess of sales revenue over cost of goods sold.

Gross Profit Percentage. Gross profit divided by net sales revenue. A measure of profitability. Also called **gross margin percentage.**

Hardware. Electronic equipment that includes computers, disk drives, monitors, printers, and the network that connects them.

Imprest System. A way to account for petty cash by maintaining a constant balance in the petty cash account, supported by the fund (cash plus payment tickets) totaling the same amount.

Income Statement. Summary of an entity's revenues, expenses, and net income or net loss for a specific period. Also called the **statement of earnings** or the **statement of operations.**

Income Summary. A temporary "holding tank" account into which revenues and expenses are transferred prior to their final transfer to the capital account.

Intangible Assets. Assets with no physical form. Valuable because of the special rights they carry. Examples are patents and copyrights.

Internal Control. Organizational plan and all the related measures adopted by an entity to safeguard assets, encourage adherence to company policies, promote operational efficiency, and ensure accurate and reliable accounting records.

Inventory Profit. Difference between gross profit figured on the FIFO basis and gross profit figured on the LIFO basis.

Inventory. All the goods that the company owns and expects to sell in the normal course of operations.

Invoice. A seller's request for cash from the purchaser.

Journal. The chronological accounting record of an entity's transactions.

Last-In, First-Out (LIFO) Inventory Costing Method. Inventory costing method by which the last costs into inventory are the first costs out to cost of goods sold. This method leaves the oldest costs—those of beginning inventory and the earliest purchases of the period—in ending inventory.

Lease. Rental agreement in which the tenant (lessee) agrees to make rent payments to the property owner (lessor) to obtain the use of the asset.

Ledger. The book of accounts.

Legal Capital. The portion of stockholders' equity that cannot be used for dividends.

Lessee. Tenant in a lease agreement.

Lessor. Property owner in a lease agreement.

Leverage. Earning more income on borrowed money than the related interest expense, thereby increasing the earnings for the owners of the business.

Liability. An economic obligation (a debt) payable to an individual or an organization outside the business.

LIFO Liquidation. Situation when the LIFO inventory method is used and inventory quantities fall below the level of the previous period.

Limited Liability. No personal obligation of a stockholder for corporation debts. A stockholder can lose no more on an investment in a corporation's stock than the cost of the investment.

Limited Liability Partnership. A form of partnership in which each partner's personal liability for the business's debts is limited to a certain amount. Also called **LLPs**.

Limited Partnership. A partnership with at least two classes of partners: a general partner and limited partners.

Liquidation. The process of going out of business by selling the entity's assets and paying its liabilities. The final step in liquidation is the distribution of any remaining cash to the owner(s).

Liquidity. Measure of how quickly an item can be converted to cash.

Long-Term Asset. An asset other than a current asset.

Long-Term Liability. A liability other than a current liability.

Lower-of-Cost-or-Market (LCM) Rule. Rule that an asset should be reported in the financial statements at whichever is lower—its historical cost or its market value.

Major Repair or Extraordinary Repair. Repair work that generates a capital expenditure.

Maker of a Note. The person or business that signs the note and promises to pay the amount required by the note agreement; the debtor.

Management Accounting. The branch of accounting that focuses on information for internal decision makers of a business.

Margin of Safety. Excess of expected sales over breakeven sales. Drop in sales a company can absorb before incurring an operating loss.

Market Interest Rate. Interest rate that investors demand in order to loan their money. Also called **effective interest rate**.

Market Value. Price for which a person could buy or sell a share of stock.

Matching Principle. The basis for recording expenses. Directs accountants to identify all expenses incurred during the period, to measure the expenses, and to match them against the revenues earned during that same span of time.

Materiality Concept. A company must perform strictly proper accounting only for items that are significant to the business's financial statements.

Menu. A list of options for choosing computer functions.

Module. Separate compatible units of an accounting package that are integrated to function together.

Mortgage. Borrower's promise to transfer the legal title to certain assets to the lender if the debt is not paid on schedule.

Multi-step Income Statement. Format that contains subtotals to highlight significant relationships. In addition to net income, it presents gross profit and operating income.

Mutual Agency. Every partner can bind the business to a contract within the scope of the partnership's regular business operations.

Net Income. Excess of total revenues over total expenses. Also called **net earnings** or **net profit**.

Net Loss. Excess of total expenses over total revenues.

Net Pay. Gross pay minus all deductions. The amount of compensation that the employee actually takes home.

Net Purchases. Purchases less purchase discounts and purchase returns and allowances.

Net Sales. Sales revenue less sales discounts and sales returns and allowances.

Network. The system of electronic linkages that allows different computers to share the same information.

Nonsufficient Funds (NSF) Check. A "hot" check, one for which the maker's bank account has insufficient money to pay the check.

Normal Balance. The account balance that appears on the side of the account—debit or credit—where we record increases.

Note Payable. A written promise of future payment.

Note Receivable. A written promise for future collection of cash.

On-line Processing. Computerized processing of related functions, such as the recording and posting of transactions, on a continuous basis.

Operating Cycle. Time span during which cash is paid for goods and services, which are then sold to customers from whom the business collects cash.

Operating Expenses. Expenses, other than cost of goods sold, that are incurred in the entity's major line of business. Examples include rent, depreciation, salaries, wages, utilities, and supplies expense.

Operating Income. Gross profit minus operating expenses plus any other operating revenues. Also called **income from operations**.

Operating Lease. Usually a short-term or cancelable rental agreement.

Ordinary Repair. Repair work that is debited to an expense account.

Other Expense. Expense that is outside the main operations of a business, such as a loss on the sale of plant assets.

Other Revenue. Revenue that is outside the main operations of a business, such as a gain on the sale of plant assets.

Outstanding Check. A check issued by the company and recorded on its books but not yet paid by its bank.

Outstanding Stock. Stock in the hands of stockholders.

Owner Withdrawals. Amounts removed from the business by an owner.

Owner's Equity. The claim of a business owner to the assets of the business. Also called **capital**.

Paid-in Capital. A corporation's capital from investments by the stockholders. Also called **contributed capital**.

Par Value. Arbitrary amount assigned to a share of stock.

Partnership Agreement. The contract between partners that specifies such items as the name, location, and nature of the business; the name, capital investment, and duties of each partner; and the method of sharing profits and losses among the partners. Also called **articles of partnership**.

Partnership. An association of two or more persons who co-own a business for profit.

Patent. A federal government grant giving the holder the exclusive right to produce and sell an invention for 20 years.

Payee of a Note. The person or business to whom the maker of a note promises future payment; the creditor.

Payroll. A major expense. Also called **employee compensation**.

Pension. Employee compensation that will be received during retirement.

Percent-of-Sales Method. A method of estimating uncollectible receivables that calculates uncollectible-account expense. Also called the **income statement approach**.

Periodic Inventory System. An inventory accounting system in which the business does not keep a continuous record of the inventory on hand. Instead, at the end of the period, the business counts the inventory on hand and uses this information to prepare the financial statements.

Permanent Accounts. Accounts that are not closed at the end of the period—asset, liability, and capital accounts. Also called **real accounts**.

Perpetual Inventory System. The accounting inventory system in which the business keeps a running record of inventory and cost of goods sold.

Petty Cash. Fund containing a small amount of cash that is used to pay for minor expenditures.

Plant Assets. Long-lived tangible assets, such as land, buildings, and equipment, used to operate a business. Also called **fixed assets**.

Plant or Fixed Asset. Another name for property, plant, and equipment.

Postclosing Trial Balance. List of the accounts and their balances at the end of the period after journalizing and posting the closing entries. The last step of the accounting cycle, the postclosing trial balance ensures that the ledger is in balance to start the next accounting period.

Posting. Copying amounts from the journal to the ledger.

Preferred Stock. Stock that gives its owners certain advantages over common stockholders, such as the right to receive dividends before the common stockholders and the right to receive assets before the common stockholders if the corporation liquidates.

Premium. Excess of a bond's issue price over its maturity (par) value. Also called **bond premium**.

Prepaid Expense. Advance payments of expenses. A category of current assets that typically expire or are used up in the near future. Examples include prepaid rent, prepaid insurance, and supplies.

Present Value. Amount a person would invest now to receive a greater amount at a future date.

President. Chief operating officer in charge of managing the day-to-day operations of a corporation.

Proprietorship. A business with a single owner.

Purchases Journal. Special journal used to record all purchases of inventory, supplies, and other assets on account.

Receivables. Monetary claims against a business or individual.

Retained Earnings. A corporation's capital that is earned through profitable operation of the business.

Revenue. Amounts earned by delivering goods or services to customers. Revenues increase owner's equity.

Revenue Principle. The basis for recording revenues; tells accountants when to record revenue and the amount of revenue to record.

Reversing Entry. An entry that switches the debit and the credit of a previous adjusting entry. The reversing entry is dated the first day of the period after the adjusting entry.

S Corporation. A corporation taxed in the same way as a partnership.

Sales Discount. Reduction in the amount receivable from a customer, offered by the seller as an incentive for the customer to pay promptly. A contra account to Sales Revenue.

Sales Journal. Special journal used to record credit sales.

Sales Mix. Combination of products that make up total sales.

Sales Returns and Allowances. Decreases in the seller's receivable from a customer's return of merchandise or from granting the customer an allowance from the amount owed to the seller. A contra account to Sales Revenue.

Sales Revenue. The amount that a merchandiser earns from selling its inventory. Also called **sales.**

Sensitivity Analysis. A "what if" technique that asks what a result will be if a predicted amount is not achieved or if an underlying assumption changes.

Server. The main computer in a network, where the program and data are stored.

Short Presentation. A way to report contingent liabilities in the body of the balance sheet, after total liabilities but with no amount given. An explanatory note accompanies the presentation.

Short-Term Note Payable. Promissory note payable due within one year, a common form of financing.

Single-Step Income Statement. Format that groups all revenues together and then lists and deducts all expenses together without drawing any subtotals.

Social Security Tax. Federal Insurance Contributions Act (FICA) tax, which is with-held from employees' pay. Also called FICA tax.

Software. Set of programs or instructions that drive the computer to perform the work desired.

Special Journal. An accounting journal designed to record one specific type of transaction.

Specific-Unit-Cost Method. Inventory cost method based on the specific cost of particular units of inventory. Also called the **specific identification method.**

Spreadsheet. A computer program that links data by means of formulas and functions; an electronic work sheet.

Standard Cost. A carefully predetermined cost that usually is expressed on a per-unit basis.

Stated Value. An arbitrary amount that accountants treat as though it were par value.

Statement of Owner's Equity. Summary of the changes in an entity's owner's equity during a specific period.

Stock. Shares into which the owners' equity of a corporation is divided.

Stockholder. A person who owns the stock of a corporation. Also called a **shareholder.**

Stockholders' Equity. Owners' equity of a corporation.

Straight-Line (SL) Depreciation Method. Depreciation method in which an equal amount of depreciation expense is assigned to each year of asset use.

Subsidiary Ledger. Record of ac-counts that provides supporting details on individual balances, the total of which appears in a general ledger account.

Temporary Accounts. The revenue and expense accounts that relate to a particular accounting period and are closed at the end of the period. For a proprietorship, the owner withdrawal account is also temporary. Also called **nominal accounts.**

Time-Period Concept. Ensures that accounting information is reported at regular intervals.

Trademarks, Trade Names, or Brand Names. Assets that represent distinctive identifications of a product or service.

Transaction. An event that affects the financial position of a particular entity and can be recorded reliably.

Trial Balance. A list of all the accounts with their balances.

Trojan Horse. A malicious program that works like a virus but does not reproduce.

Uncollectible-Account Expense. Cost to the seller of extending credit. Arises from the failure to collect from credit customers. Also called **doubtful-account expense,** or **bad-debt expense.**

Unearned Revenue. A liability created when a business collects cash from customers in advance of doing work. The obligation is to provide a product or a service in the future. Also called **deferred revenue.**

Unemployment Compensation Tax. Payroll tax paid by employers to the government, which uses the money to pay unemployment benefits to people who are out of work.

Units-of-Production (UOP) Depreciation Method. Depreciation method by which a fixed amount of depreciation is assigned to each unit of output produced by an asset.

Unlimited Personal Liability. When a partnership (or a proprietorship) cannot pay its debts with business assets, the partners (or the proprietor) must use personal assets to meet the debt.

Variable Costing. The costing method that assigns only variable manufacturing costs to products.

Voucher. Instrument authorizing a cash payment.

Weighted-Average Cost Method. Inventory costing method based on the weighted-average cost of inventory during the period. Weighted-average cost is determined by dividing the cost of goods available for sale by the number of units available. Also called the **average-cost method.**

Withheld Income Tax. Income tax deducted from employees' gross pay.

Work Sheet. A columnar document designed to help move data from the trial balance to the financial statements.

Company Index

Subject Index

Summary of Generally Accepted Accounting Principles (GAAP)

Every technical area has professional associations and regulatory bodies that govern the practice of the profession. Accounting is no exception. In the United States, generally accepted accounting principles (GAAP) are influenced most by the Financial Accounting Standards Board (FASB). The FASB has seven full-time members and a large staff. Its financial support comes from professional associations such as the American Institute of Certified Public Accountants (AICPA).

The FASB is an independent organization with no government or professional affiliation. The FASB's pronouncements, called *Statements of Financial Accounting Standards*, specify how to account for certain business transactions. Each new *Standard* becomes part of GAAP, the "accounting law of the land." In the same way that our laws draw authority from their acceptance by the people, GAAP depends on general acceptance by the business community. Throughout this book, we refer to GAAP as the proper way to do financial accounting.

The U.S. Congress has given the Securities and Exchange Commission (SEC), a government organization that regulates the trading of investments, ultimate responsibility for establishing accounting rules for companies that are owned by the general investing public. However, the SEC has delegated much of its rule-making power to the FASB.

Flow of Authority for Developing GAAP

| United States Congress | Securities and Exchange Commission | Financial Accounting Standards Board | Pronouncements that make up generally accepted accounting principles (GAAP) |

The Objective of Financial Reporting

The basic objective of financial reporting is to provide information that is useful in making investment and lending decisions. The FASB believes that accounting information can be useful in decision making only if it is *relevant*, *reliable*, *comparable*, and *consistent*.

Relevant information is useful in making predictions and for evaluating past performance—that is, the information has feedback value. For example, PepsiCo's disclosure of the profitability of each of its lines of business is relevant for investor evaluations of the company. To be relevant, information must be timely. *Reliable* information is free from significant error—that is, it has validity. Also, it is free from the bias of a particular viewpoint—that is, it is verifiable and neutral. *Comparable* and *consistent* information can be compared from period to period to help investors and creditors track the entity's progress through time. These characteristics combine to shape the concepts and principles that make up GAAP.

Summary of Important Accounting Concepts, Principles, and Financial Statements

Concepts, Principles, and Financial Statements	Quick Summary	Chapter Reference
Concepts		
Entity concept	Accounting draws a boundary around each organization to be accounted for.	Chapter 1
Going-concern concept	Accountants assume the business will continue operating for the foreseeable future.	Chapter 1
Stable-monetary-unit concept	Accounting information is expressed primarily in monetary terms.	Chapter 1
Time-period concept	Ensures that accounting information is reported at regular intervals.	Chapter 3
Conservatism concept	Accountants report items in the financial statements in a way that avoids overstating assets, owners' equity, and revenues and avoids understating liabilities and expenses.	Chapter 9
Materiality concept	Accountants perform strictly proper accounting only for items that are significant to the company's financial statements.	Chapter 9
Principles		
Reliability (objectivity) principle	Accounting records and statements are based on the most reliable data available.	Chapter 1
Cost principle	Assets and services, revenues and expenses are recorded at their actual historical cost.	Chapter 1
Revenue principle	Tells accountants when to record revenue (only after it has been earned) and the amount of revenue to record (the cash value of what has been received).	Chapter 3
Matching principle	Directs accountants to (1) identify all expenses incurred during the period, (2) measure the expenses, and (3) match the expenses against the revenues earned during the period. The goal is to measure net income.	Chapter 3
Consistency principle	Businesses should use the same accounting methods from period to period.	Chapter 9
Disclosure principle	A company's financial statements should report enough information for outsiders to make informed decisions about the company.	Chapter 9
Financial Statements		
Balance sheet	Assets = Liabilities + Owners' Equity at a point in time.	Chapters 1 and 13
Income statement	Revenues and gains – Expenses and losses ――――――――― = Net income or net loss for the period.	Chapters 1 and 14
Statement of cash flows	Cash receipts – Cash disbursements ――――――――― = Increase or decrease in cash during the period, grouped under operating, investing, and financing activities.	Chapter 1 and 17
Statement of retained earnings	Beginning retained earnings + Net income (or – Net loss) – Dividends ――――――――― = Ending retained earnings.	Chapter 1
Statement of stockholders' equity	Shows the reason for the change in each stockholders' equity account, including retained earnings.	Chapter 15